INTRODUCTION TO AVIATION LAW

TIMOTHY M. RAVICH
UNIVERSITY OF CENTRAL FLORIDA

WEST
ACADEMIC
PUBLISHING

© 2020 LEG, Inc. d/b/a West Academic
    444 Cedar Street, Suite 700
    St. Paul, MN 55101
    1-877-888-1330

West, West Academic Publishing, and West Academic are trademarks of West Publishing Corporation, used under license.

Printed in the United States of America

ISBN: 978-1-68328-678-3

For Sara and Rachel

Preface

In substance and form, this book was from its inception designed to fill the market between West Academic's Nutshell Series and a formal case book or treatise, which is to say between a legal overview and a deep-dive into the subject matter. It thus aims to present the topic of aviation law in an approachable way while also giving the reader an opportunity to directly read and consider primary source material.

Each chapter begins with background commentary intended to set the stage for the reader and to encourage the reader's understanding of court opinions, statutes, regulations, and treaties. The materials included in this book were selected because they convey foundational ideas in an interesting and comprehensive and sometimes even entertaining way. To make the reader's job easier, main ideas of each case are highlighted by guideposts and key words in the margins and with break-out quotes within the text. A set of questions and notes follow each case and are presented for the purpose of summarizing key points and/or identifying other interesting issues that go beyond the provided material. Also available and accompanying the book are PowerPoints featuring the chapter cases along with a comprehensive teacher's manual that contains a proposed syllabus for an aviation law course, a test bank, and teaching tips and comments from the author based on almost two decades of teaching aviation law at the graduate and undergraduate level.

Altogether, INTRODUCTION TO AVIATION LAW is organized in 13 chapters that feature aspects of public and private aviation law. Chapters 1 through 8 fall under the heading of public law in that they focus primarily on government action and policy, including the Right to Travel (Chapter 1), Airspace (Chapter 2), Aircraft (Chapter 3), Airmen (Chapter 4), Federalism and Preemption (Chapter 5), Airline Deregulation (Chapter 6), Airline Passenger Rights (Chapter 7), and Air Piracy and Crime (Chapter 8). Next, Chapters 9 through 13—relating to aircraft transactions, labor and employment, airports, accident litigation, and international accident litigation, respectively—focus on issues that arise in private party disputes. The distinction between public and private aviation law is imprecise sometimes, but the book's organization is designed in this way to give some definite structure to issues that sometimes overlap.

In all, this book is what the title says it is—an "introduction" to aviation law. As introductions go, it features all of the benefits and restrictions of a primer, *i.e.*, the presentation and discussion of seminal materials with the inevitable (but often intentional) omission or light treatment of issues warranting further and deeper analysis. But, if readers come away understanding and appreciating—and perhaps even wanting to study further—the major pieces of aviation law and the prevailing themes and policies informing global aviation regulations, including consumer protection, labor relations, aircraft transactions, deregulation, and national security, INTRODUCTION TO AVIATION LAW will be a successful addition to the corpus of aviation law. Comments and suggestions for future editions: Timothy M. Ravich, University of Central Florida, 500 W. Livingstone Street, DPAC 430I, Orlando, Florida 32801, timothy.ravich@ucf.edu.

Acknowledgements

Thanks to Brian Havel, Full Professor and Director of McGill's Institute of Air and Space Law, and S.V. (Steve) Dedmon, Professor of Aeronautical Science and Associate Chair of the Department of Aeronautical Science at Embry-Riddle Aeronautical University, for their peer review and unvarnished critical and constructive comments of earlier versions of this book.

Thanks, too, to Alisa Smith, Chair of the Department of Legal Studies at the University of Central Florida, and my colleagues and current and former students for their thoughts, feedback, and support in connection with this text. Thanks, too, to Katie Connolly for outstanding support.

Additionally, West Academic's editorial staff deserve recognition for their excellent work and care in producing this book.

Thanks also to the following authors and entities for permission to reprint their works: Delta Air Lines (Chapter 6, "Wolf in Sheep's Clothing") and Uber/PickardChilton (Chapter 11, Uber Elevate).

And, finally, I am so grateful for my wife, Sara, who actively encourages and makes better this and every project of mine while doing so much professionally and personally herself.

About the Author

Timothy M. Ravich, Assistant Professor at the University of Central Florida, is an internationally recognized authority in aviation law and one of only thirty-seven lawyers recognized as a Florida Bar Board Certified Aviation Lawyer. He earned his M.B.A. in Aviation Policy and Planning from Embry-Riddle Aeronautical University, and as a Martindale-Hubbell® AV-rated lawyer, served as the inaugural general counsel for a multinational precision-agriculture drone company during its successful efforts to obtain one of the first Federal Aviation Administration "333" authorizations for commercial drone activity in the United States. The principal of Ravich Law Firm, PLLC, he regularly consults and represents drone owners, operators, and manufacturers in the United States and abroad.

Professor Ravich has written extensively in connection with aviation issues, including airline deregulation and passenger rights, aviation security and terrorism, law and technology, and unmanned aerial systems ("UASs" or "drones").

He has published numerous articles in peer-reviewed journals and is widely cited and has appeared in publications such as the *Columbia Journal of Law and Social Problems*, *William and Mary Business Law Review*, *American Business Law Journal*, *Washington University Journal of Law and Policy*, *Georgetown Journal of International Law*, and *U.C. Davis Journal of International Law and Policy*.

In addition, national and international media outlets regularly feature Professor Ravich in television and radio programming, podcasts, and articles featuring aviation and aerospace issues, including BLOOMBERGNEWS, *Christian Science Monitor*, NBC Universal, MSNTravel, FOX, China Central Television, HUFFPost, Mercatus Center at George Mason University, National Public Radio, the *Atlantic*, *Daily Business Review*, NTV (Russia), *Asia Times*, and Scientific American. He blogs at *droninglawyer.com* and is followed on Twitter @ravichaviation.

Prior to joining the University of Central Florida, Professor Ravich practiced as a commercial trial lawyer with McDermott, Will & Emery and Hunton & Williams LLP. He also served as President and CEO of the Dade County Bar Association, the largest voluntary bar association in the State of Florida, and two-terms as a member of the ABA House of Delegates and as the Chair of the Florida Bar Aviation Law Committee. Professor Ravich has consistently been selected by his colleagues as a Florida "Super Lawyer."

Summary of Contents

Table of Contents

Table of Cases

The principal cases are in bold type.

INTRODUCTION TO AVIATION LAW

CHAPTER 1

The Right to Travel

Several airline passengers who were citizens and lawful permanent residents of the United States (including four veterans of the United States Armed Forces) were not allowed to board flights to or from the United States or over United States airspace.

They believe they were denied boarding because they are on the No-Fly List, a government terrorist watch list of individuals who are prohibited from boarding commercial flights that will pass through or over United States airspace. Federal and local government officials told some of the passengers that they are on the No-Fly List.

Each aggrieved passenger submitted applications for redress through the Department of Homeland Security Traveler Redress Inquiry Program ("DHS TRIP"). Despite their requests to officials and agencies for explanations as to why they were not permitted to board flights, explanations were not provided and the passengers do not know whether they will be permitted to fly in the future.

Latif v. Holder, 28 F. Supp. 3d 1134 (D. Ore. 2014)

A. OVERVIEW

More than 5,000 airplanes, millions of people, and tons of cargo fly over the United States at any given moment, shuttling between different cities for countless commercial, recreational, and government purposes. It is easy to take the excitement of air travel for granted in this context. But, air travel is an enduring and constantly emerging activity from a legal and socio-technological perspective.

At the outset of the jet age, Max Lerner, in his influential 1957 book *America as a Civilization: Life and Thought in the United States*, captured the American origins and fascination with aviation, writing that the Air Age had furthered the mobility of Americans and made the far-away vacation possible for "the boss's secretary as well as for the boss." Roger Bilstein, in an essay, *The Airplane and The American Experience* (2005), similarly celebrated the internationally democratizing impact of flight, writing that transoceanic leisure travel consumed many days of travel before World War II, when only the wealthy could afford the expense and time of air travel. But, postwar transatlantic flights "fit both the pocketbook and allocated vacation time for an astonishing cross-section of travelers." Equally important as these developments, and at the center of this chapter and this book, are the laws that facilitate the movement of people and things across the world.

Dating back perhaps to the Magna Carta, the freedom to travel is a fundamental liberty guaranteed by the U.S. Constitution. As U.S. Supreme Court Justice William Douglas wrote in *Kent v. Dulles*, 357 U.S. 116 (1958) (see, Part B, *supra*), the socio-political value of travel is central to the American experience, past and present:

> Foreign correspondents and lecturers on public affairs need first-hand information. Scientists and scholars gain greatly from consultations with colleagues in other countries. Students equip themselves for more fruitful careers in the United States by instruction in foreign universities. Then there are reasons close to the core of personal life—marriage, reuniting families, spending hours with old friends. Finally, travel abroad enables American citizens to understand that people like themselves live in Europe and helps them to be well-informed on public issues. An American who has crossed the ocean is not obliged to form his opinions about our foreign policy merely from what he is told by officials of our government or by a few correspondents of American newspapers. Moreover, his views on domestic questions are enriched by seeing how foreigners are trying to solve similar problems. In many different ways direct contact with other countries contributes to sounder decisions at home.

Given the broad importance of mobility, studying the laws and policies that govern the movement of people and things across boundaries is a sensible starting point for the study of aviation law. Consider that exercising many of the freedoms and rights in the U.S. Constitution, and the Bill of Rights particularly, depends strictly on free movement. For example, how else can citizens enjoy "the right of the people peaceably to assemble" as is guaranteed by the First Amendment, without a corresponding privilege to travel? Indeed, without travel rights, many of the most basic rights enjoyed under the U.S. Constitution are valueless.

Alternatively, travel rights are not—and should not be—unlimited. Governments have the authority to restrict the travel of people or things that threaten the health, safety, or welfare of others. The terrorism of September 11, 2001, for example, prompted global travel restrictions in the nature of protocols and scanning machines that are now fixtures at airports around the world. In 2017, President Donald J. Trump signed an executive order banning all entries to the United States from people from seven Muslim-majority countries—an action upheld by the U.S. Supreme Court. Opposition to these measures—including protests and lawsuits—played out at airports and on airplanes in the United States and abroad. But, the fact remains that the government has broad powers to restrict the movement of its citizens and enforce its borders to others.

How the government goes about restricting travel rights and whether the government does so consistent with the law is enormously important, of course. With this background in mind, this chapter will focus or the origin and application of the right to travel under the U.S. Constitution. In doing so, the materials in this chapter examines how executives, legislators, and judges expand or restrict travel rights in anticipation of or reaction to changes in the national and international political, security, and economic environments.

———————————

Table 1-1. Global Survey: Source and Scope of Freedom of Movement

Canada	"Mobility Rights" enshrined in Section 6 of the Canadian Charter of Rights and Freedoms: "Every citizen of Canada has the right to enter, remain in and leave Canada."
China	*Hukou* passport-type system "immobilize China's large rural population," limiting public services to the birthplace of the holder. *See* Andreas Fulda, *In China, There's No Freedom of Movement, Even Between Country and City*, CITYMETRIC, 2017.
Ireland	In 1992, the Republic of Ireland adopted by referendum the Thirteenth Amendment, specifying that a legal prohibition on abortion would not limit freedom to travel in and out of the state.
Israel	Basic Law: Human Dignity and Liberty—"all persons are free to leave Israel; every Israeli national has the right of entry into Israel from abroad."
Kuwait	Kuwaiti law prohibits domestic companies from conducting business with Israeli citizens. *See* Jad Mouawad, *Kuwait Airways Drops Flights to Avoid Israeli Passengers*, N.Y. TIMES, Jan. 15, 2016.
North Korea	Article 62 of the Criminal Code bans citizens from travelling to another country without permission.
Russia	Russian Constitution, Article 27: "Everyone who is lawfully in the territory of the Russian Federation has the right to freely move and choose a place of stay or living . . . Everyone may freely exit the territory of the Russian Federation. Citizens of the Russian Federation may return onto the territory of the Russian Federation without hindrance."

In studying aviation law, you will be reading primarily federal court decisions addressing the constitutionality of national regulations and international treaties with respect to travel rights. The judicial power to say whether a citizen (or non-citizen) can traverse borders is substantial, raising important questions about the limitations on lawmakers and courts, the role of sovereign governments in defining and enforcing travel rights, and the opportunity for the governed (or regulated) to petition authorities to safeguard their rights. This chapter proceeds in three sections:

- Part B presents *Saenz v. Roe* and *Kent v. Dulles*, cases that explore the government's justification for limiting the movement of citizens across state lines and the right to travel internationally, respectively.

- Part C examines specific due process and equal protection clause issues connected to international travel presented in *Lee v. China Airlines, Ltd.*, as well as airport security protocols such as the "selectee list" examined in *Beydoun v. Sessions*.

- Finally, Part D explores whether the Constitutional right to travel includes a right to the most convenient form of travel, which is often by commercial airline (*Gilmore v. Gonzales*), and how economic policies impact the right to travel domestically (*Houston v. Fed. Aviation Admin*).

Following each case in this chapter and throughout the book are review-type questions intended to sharpen your understanding of the main legal and policy underpinnings of the right to travel. This is intended to inform your understanding of the materials throughout this book relevant to aviation law. Additional commentary and insight are offered in notes following select cases.

At the conclusion of this chapter, the reader should understand the constitutional basis and limits of the right to travel and how courts have interpreted the right in the context of interstate and international air travel. Moreover, with this understanding, readers should be able to anticipate how lawmakers and courts will approach future issues implicating the right to travel. And, more broadly, readers should begin to appreciate how courts analyze legal problems and issues (*e.g.* interpreting text and effecting policy) and whether they do so independently of national and international political realities.

B. CONSTITUTIONAL MATTERS

SAENZ V. ROE

526 U.S. 489 (1999)

JUSTICE STEVENS delivered the opinion of the Court.

In 1992, California enacted a statute limiting the maximum welfare benefits available to newly arrived residents. The scheme limited the amount payable to a family that had resided in the State for less than 12 months to the amount payable by the State of the family's prior residence, i.e., a durational residency requirement. In order to make a relatively modest reduction in its vast welfare budget, the California Legislature enacted § 11450.03 of the state Welfare and Institutions Code. That section sought to change the California Aid to Families with Dependent Children program by limiting new residents, for the first year they live in California, to the benefits they would have received in the State of their prior residence. Because in 1992 a state program either had to conform to federal specifications or receive a waiver from the Secretary of Health and Human Services in order to qualify for federal reimbursement, § 11450.03 required approval by the Secretary to take effect. In October 1992, the Secretary issued a waiver purporting to grant such approval.

On December 21, 1992, three California residents who were eligible for AFDC benefits filed an action in the Eastern District of California challenging the constitutionality of the durational residency requirement in § 11450.03. Each plaintiff alleged that she had recently moved to California to live with relatives in order to escape abusive family circumstances. One returned to California after living in Louisiana for seven years, the second had been living in Oklahoma for six weeks and the third came from Colorado. Each alleged that her monthly AFDC grant for the ensuing 12 months would be substantially lower under § 11450.03 than if the statute were not in effect. Thus, the former residents of Louisiana and Oklahoma would receive $190 and $341 respectively for a family of three even though the full California grant was $641; the former resident of Colorado, who had just one child, was limited to $280 a month as opposed to the full California grant of $504 for a family of two.

One of the questions presented was whether the 1992 statute was constitutional when it was enacted.

The word "travel" is not found in the text of the Constitution. Yet the "constitutional right to travel from one State to another" is firmly embedded in our jurisprudence. Indeed, as Justice Stewart reminded us in *Shapiro v. Thompson*,

394 U.S. 618 (1969), the right is so important that it is "assertable against private interference as well as governmental action . . . a virtually unconditional personal right, guaranteed by the Constitution to us all."

In *Shapiro*, we reviewed the constitutionality of three statutory provisions that denied welfare assistance to residents of Connecticut, the District of Columbia, and Pennsylvania, who had resided within those respective jurisdictions less than one year immediately preceding their applications for assistance. Without pausing to identify the specific source of the right, we began by noting that the Court had long "recognized that the nature of our Federal Union and our constitutional concepts of personal liberty unite to require that all citizens be free to travel throughout the length and breadth of our land uninhibited by statutes, rules, or regulations which unreasonably burden or restrict this movement." We squarely held that it was "constitutionally impermissible" for a State to enact durational residency requirements for the purpose of inhibiting the migration by needy persons into the State. We further held that a classification that had the effect of imposing a penalty on the exercise of the right to travel violated the Equal Protection Clause "unless shown to be necessary to promote a compelling governmental interest," and that no such showing had been made.

The "right to travel" discussed in our cases embraces at least three different components. It protects the right of a citizen of one State to enter and to leave another State, the right to be treated as a welcome visitor rather than an unfriendly alien when temporarily present in the second State, and, for those travelers who elect to become permanent residents, the right to be treated like other citizens of that State.

Components of the Right to Travel

It was the right to go from one place to another, including the right to cross state borders while enroute, that was vindicated in *Edwards v. California*, 314 U.S. 160 (1941), which invalidated a state law that impeded the free interstate passage of the indigent. We reaffirmed that right in *United States v. Guest*, 383 U.S. 745 (1966), which afforded protection to the "right to travel freely to and from the State of Georgia and to use highway facilities and other instrumentalities of interstate commerce within the State of Georgia." The right of "free ingress and regress to and from" neighboring States, which was expressly mentioned in the Articles of Confederation, may simply have been "conceived from the beginning to be a necessary concomitant of the stronger Union the Constitution created."

The second component of the right to travel is, however, expressly protected by the text of the Constitution. The first sentence of Article IV, § 2, provides: "The Citizens of each State shall be entitled to all Privileges and Immunities of

Citizens in the several States." Thus, by virtue of a person's state citizenship, a citizen of one State who travels in other States, intending to return home at the end of his journey, is entitled to enjoy the "Privileges and Immunities of Citizens in the several States" that he visits. This provision removes "from the citizens of each State the disabilities of alienage in the other States." Those protections are not "absolute," but the Clause "does bar discrimination against citizens of other States where there is no substantial reason for the discrimination beyond the mere fact that they are citizens of other States."

At issue in this case is this third aspect of the right to travel—the right of the newly arrived citizen to the same privileges and immunities enjoyed by other citizens of the same State. That right is protected not only by the new arrival's status as a state citizen, but also by her status as a citizen of the United States. That additional source of protection is plainly identified in the opening words of the Fourteenth Amendment: "All persons born or naturalized in the United States, and subject to the jurisdiction thereof, are citizens of the United States and of the State wherein they reside. No State shall make or enforce any law which shall abridge the privileges or immunities of citizens of the United States." Despite fundamentally differing views concerning the coverage of the Privileges or Immunities Clause of the Fourteenth Amendment, most notably expressed in the *Slaughter-House Cases*, 83 U.S. 36 (1872), it has always been common ground that this Clause protects the third component of the right to travel.

Standard of Review

That newly arrived citizens "have two political capacities, one state and one federal," adds special force to their claim that they have the same rights as others who share their citizenship. Neither mere rationality nor some intermediate standard of review should be used to judge the constitutionality of a state rule that discriminates against some of its citizens because they have been domiciled in the State for less than a year. The appropriate standard may be more categorical than that articulated in *Shapiro*, but it is surely no less strict.

Because this case involves discrimination against citizens who have completed their interstate travel, the State's argument that its welfare scheme affects the right to travel only "incidentally" is beside the point. Were we concerned solely with actual deterrence to migration, we might be persuaded that a partial withholding of benefits constitutes a lesser incursion on the right to travel than an outright denial of all benefits. But since the right to travel embraces the citizen's right to be treated equally in her new State of residence, the discriminatory classification is itself a penalty.

CHIEF JUSTICE REHNQUIST, with JUSTICE THOMAS joining, dissenting.

The Court today breathes new life into the previously dormant Privileges or Immunities Clause of the Fourteenth Amendment—a Clause relied upon by this Court in only one other decision, *Colgate v. Harvey*, 296 U.S. 404 (1935), overruled five years later by *Madden v. Kentucky*, 309 U.S. 83 (1940). It uses this Clause to strike down what I believe is a reasonable measure falling under the head of a "good-faith residency requirement." Because I do not think any provision of the Constitution—and surely not a provision relied upon for only the second time since its enactment 130 years ago—requires this result, I dissent.

Much of the Court's opinion is unremarkable and sound. The right to travel clearly embraces the right to go from one place to another, and prohibits States from impeding the free interstate passage of citizens. The state law in *Edwards v. California*, 314 U.S. 160 (1941) which prohibited the transport of any indigent person into California, was a classic barrier to travel or migration and the Court rightly struck it down. Indeed, for most of this country's history, what the Court today calls the first "component" of the right to travel, was the entirety of this right.

But I cannot see how the right to become a citizen of another State is a necessary "component" of the right to travel, or why the Court tries to marry these separate and distinct rights. A person is no longer "traveling" in any sense of the word when he finishes his journey to a State which he plans to make his home. Indeed, under the Court's logic, the protections of the Privileges or Immunities Clause recognized in this case come into play only when an individual stops traveling with the intent to remain and become a citizen of a new State. The right to travel and the right to become a citizen are distinct, their relationship is not reciprocal, and one is not a "component" of the other.

EXERCISE 1-1. *SAENZ V. ROE*—COMPONENTS OF THE RIGHT TO TRAVEL

1. What are the elements of the right to travel as expressed in *Saenz v. Roe*, and which is at issue in the case?

2. How is the right to travel and the right to citizenship related under *Saenz v. Roe*?

3. In what provision of the Constitution are citizens guaranteed a right to travel according to the Court?

4. What does the *Saenz v. Roe* court establish as the standard of review?

5. Articulate the main point of the dissenting opinion.

KENT V. DULLES
357 U.S. 116 (1958)

JUSTICE DOUGLAS delivered the opinion of the Court.

This case concerns two applications for passports, denied by the Secretary of State. One was by Rockwell Kent who desired to visit England and attend a meeting of an organization known as the "World Council of Peace" in Helsinki, Finland. The Director of the Passport Office informed Kent that issuance of a passport was precluded by the Regulations promulgated by the Secretary of State on two grounds: (1) that he was a Communist and (2) that he had had "a consistent and prolonged adherence to the Communist Party line." Kent was told that, before a passport would be issued, he would need to submit an affidavit as to whether he was then or ever had been a Communist.

Kent took the position that the requirement of an affidavit concerning Communist Party membership "is unlawful and that for that reason and as a matter of conscience," he would not supply one. He did, however, have a hearing at which the principal evidence against him was from his book "It's Me O Lord," which Kent agreed was accurate.

Fifth Amendment

The right to travel is a part of the "liberty" of which the citizen cannot be deprived without the due process of law under the Fifth Amendment. So much is conceded by the Solicitor General. In Anglo-Saxon law that right was emerging at least as early as the Magna Carta. Freedom of movement across frontiers in either direction, and inside frontiers as well, was a part of our heritage.

> *The right to travel is a part of the "liberty" of which the citizen cannot be deprived without the due process of law under the Fifth Amendment . . . Freedom of movement across frontiers in either direction, and inside frontiers as well, was a part of our heritage.*

Travel abroad, like travel within the country, may be necessary for a livelihood. It may be as close to the heart of the individual as the choice of what he eats, or wears, or reads. Freedom of movement is basic in our scheme of values. "Our nation," wrote Chafee, "has thrived on the principle that, outside areas of plainly harmful conduct, every American is left to shape his own life as he thinks best, do what he pleases, go where he pleases." Freedom of movement also has large social values. As Chafee put it:

Foreign correspondents and lecturers on public affairs need first-hand information. Scientists and scholars gain greatly from consultations with colleagues in other countries. Students equip themselves for more fruitful careers in the United States by instruction in foreign universities. Then there are reasons close to the core of personal life—marriage, reuniting families, spending hours with old friends. Finally, travel abroad enables American citizens to understand that people like themselves live in Europe and helps them to be well-informed on public issues. An American who has crossed the ocean is not obliged to form his opinions about our foreign policy merely from what he is told by officials of our government or by a few correspondents of American newspapers. Moreover, his views on domestic questions are enriched by seeing how foreigners are trying to solve similar problems. In many different ways direct contact with other countries contributes to sounder decisions at home.

Freedom to travel is, indeed, an important aspect of the citizen's "liberty." We need not decide the extent to which it can be curtailed. We are first concerned with the extent, if any, to which Congress has authorized its curtailment. The difficulty is that while the power of the Secretary of State over the issuance of passports is expressed in broad terms, it was apparently long exercised quite narrowly.

So far as material here, the cases of refusal of passports generally fell into two categories. First, questions pertinent to the citizenship of the applicant and his allegiance to the United States had to be resolved by the Secretary, for the command of Congress was that "No passport shall be granted or issued to or verified for any other persons than those owing allegiance, whether citizens or not, to the United States." Second, was the question whether the applicant was participating in illegal conduct, trying to escape the toils of the law, promoting passport frauds, or otherwise engaging in conduct which would violate the laws of the United States. The grounds for refusal asserted here do not relate to citizenship or allegiance on the one hand or to criminal or unlawful conduct on the other. We, therefore, hesitate to impute to Congress, when in 1952 it made a passport necessary for foreign travel and left its issuance to the discretion of the Secretary of State, a purpose to give him unbridled discretion to grant or withhold a passport from a citizen for any substantive reason he may choose.

Matters of Allegiance and Legality

More restrictive regulations were applied in 1918 and in 1941 as war measures. In a case of comparable magnitude, *Korematsu v. United States*, 323 U.S. 214 (1944), we allowed the Government in time of war to exclude citizens from their homes and restrict their freedom of movement only on a showing of "the gravest imminent danger to the public safety." There the Congress and the Chief

War Measure

Executive moved in coordinated action; and, as we said, the Nation was then at war. No such condition presently exists. No such showing of extremity, no such showing of joint action by the Chief Executive and the Congress to curtail a constitutional right of the citizen has been made here.

Scope of Authority

Thus we do not reach the question of constitutionality. We only conclude that the law does not delegate to the Secretary the kind of authority exercised here. We deal with beliefs, with associations, with ideological matters. We must remember that we are dealing here with citizens who have neither been accused of crimes nor found guilty. They are being denied their freedom of movement solely because of their refusal to be subjected to inquiry into their beliefs and associations. They do not seek to escape the law nor to violate it. They may or may not be Communists. But assuming they are, the only law which Congress has passed expressly curtailing the movement of Communists across our borders has not yet become effective. It would therefore be strange to infer that pending the effectiveness of that law, the Secretary has been silently granted by Congress the larger, the more pervasive power to curtail in his discretion the free movement of citizens in order to satisfy himself about their beliefs or associations. We would be faced with important constitutional questions were we to hold that Congress had given the Secretary authority to withhold passports to citizens because of their beliefs or associations. Congress has made no such provision in explicit terms; and absent one, the Secretary may not employ that standard to restrict the citizens' right of free movement.

MR. JUSTICE CLARK, *with whom* MR. JUSTICE BURTON, MR. JUSTICE HARLAN, *and* MR. JUSTICE WHITTAKER *concur, dissenting.*

The Secretary's action clearly must be held authorized by Congress if the requested information is relevant to any ground upon which the Secretary might properly refuse to issue a passport. The Court purports today to preclude the existence of such a ground by holding that the Secretary has not been authorized to deny a passport to a Communist whose travel abroad would be inimical to our national security. In thus construing the authority of the Secretary, the Court recognizes that all during our history he has had discretion to grant or withhold passports. This discretionary authority, which we previously acknowledged in *Perkins v. Elg*, 307 U.S. 325 (1939), was exercised both in times of peace and in periods of war. During war and other periods of national emergency, however, the importance of the Secretary's passport power was tremendously magnified by a succession of "travel-control statutes" making possession of a passport a legal necessity to leaving or entering this country.

The first of these was enacted in 1815 just prior to the end of the War of 1812, when it was made illegal for any citizen to "cross the frontier" into enemy territory without a passport. After the same result was accomplished during the Civil War without congressional sanction, World War I prompted passage in 1918 of the second travel-control statute. The 1918 statute, directly antecedent to presently controlling legislation, provided that in time of war and upon public proclamation by the President that the public safety required additional travel restrictions, no citizen could depart from or enter into the country without a passport. Shortly thereafter, President Wilson made the required proclamation of public necessity, and provided that no citizen should be granted a passport unless it affirmatively appeared that his "departure or entry is not prejudicial to the interests of the United States."

Orders promulgated by the Passport Office periodically have required denial of passports to "political adventurers" and "revolutionary radicals," the latter phrase being defined to include "those who wish to go abroad to take part in the political or military affairs of foreign countries in ways which would be contrary to the policy or inimical to the welfare of the United States."

Were this a time of peace, there might very well be no problem for us to decide, since petitioners then would not need a passport to leave the country. Either war or national emergency is prerequisite to imposition of its restrictions. Indeed, rather than being irrelevant, the wartime practice may be the only relevant one, for the discretion with which we are concerned is a discretionary control over international travel. Yet only in times of war and national emergency has a passport been required to leave or enter this country, and hence only in such times has passport power necessarily meant power to control travel.

EXERCISE 1-2. *KENT V. DULLES*—LIMITATIONS ON THE RIGHT TO TRAVEL

1. Identify the parties and their respective claims and defenses.

2. Detail the different personal and social values the court associates with the "freedom of movement."

3. The court notes that cases involving the refusal of passports generally fell into two categories. Explain.

4. The court refers extensively to concepts of liberty and Due Process arising out of the Fifth Amendment of the Constitution. Yet, *Kent v. Dulles* is not about the

constitutionality of the right to travel. What is the issue, then? And, what is the holding of the case?

5.   What, according to the dissenting opinion, are "travel-control" statutes, and how would that justify denial of a passport in *Kent v. Dulles*?

NOTES ON *KENT V. DULLES*—TRAVEL IN CONTEXT

1.   *Who Is Dulles?*

The defendant in *Kent v. Dulles* is John Foster Dulles, not personally, but in his capacity as the U.S. Secretary of State. He is the namesake of Dulles International Airport in Northern Virginia. The airport is described in more detail in *Houston v. Fed. Aviation Admin.*, *supra*, as follows:

> Completed in 1962, situated 26 miles west of downtown in the rolling green hills of Loudoun and Fairfax Counties in Virginia, Dulles boasts one of the most spectacular terminals in the world. Designed by the architect Eero Saarinen, the terminal possesses a roof that defies both gravity and common sense, modern facilities, comfortable mobile lounges that carry passengers from the terminal building out to an awaiting plane and thus eliminate much of the walking endemic to airports, and, what is central here, three 10,000-foot runways that can accommodate any and all airplanes currently constructed. The first airport in the nation planned for jet aircraft, Dulles services the bulk of nonstop flights from Washington to the West Coast and abroad.

For further insight see John Kelly, *Why Name and Airport "Dulles"?*, WASH. POST, Dec. 1, 2012. And, for an interesting video history of the airport see *Dulles International Airport*, https://www.youtube.com/watch?v=6fYPDXaWty8.

2.   *Interstate Travel.*

Though sometimes read expansively as the case in which the Supreme Court announced or confirmed a right to travel, *Kent v. Dulles*, by its own terms, is narrower in scope—at most, a case or an opinion not about the Constitution, but merely about the fact that Congress had not authorized the Secretary of State to deny certain passports.

In any event, a right to *inter*state travel is well-established and its origins appear to reflect a concern over state discrimination against outsiders rather than concerns over the general ability to move about, *i.e.*, a right to movement. *See Saenz v. Roe*, 526 U.S. 489 (1999) (grounding at least one component of the right to interstate travel in the Privileges and Immunities Clause of the Fourteenth Amendment); *Shapiro v. Thompson*, 394 U.S. 618 (1969) (describing the right as deriving from general principles of federalism); *United States v. Guest*, 383 U.S. 745 (1966) (describing the right to interstate travel as originating in the Articles of Confederation and as being a "necessary concomitant of the stronger Union the Constitution created"); *Zobel v. Williams*, 457 U.S. 55 (1982) (O'Connor, J., concurring) (describing the right as originating in the Privileges and Immunities Clause of Art. IV); *Edwards v. California*, 314 U.S. 160 (1941) (describing the right as being grounded in the Commerce Clause).

3.   ***An International Right.***

Note that the international right to travel involved in *Kent v. Dulles* is distinct from a right to *interstate* travel. Courts have opined that *international* travel is no more than an aspect of liberty that is subject to reasonable government regulation within the bounds of due process, whereas *interstate* travel is a fundamental right subject to a more exacting standard. *See Haig v. Agee*, 453 U.S. 280 (1981) (upholding constitutionality of regulation authorizing the revocation of passport on the ground that the regulation authorized revocation only where the holder's activities in foreign countries are causing or are likely to cause serious damage to national security). As such, the right to travel is not an unlimited right, as the Supreme Court stated in *Zemel v. Rusk*, 381 U.S. 1 (1965):

> The right to travel within the United States is of course also constitutionally protected, but that freedom does not mean that areas ravaged by flood, fire or pestilence cannot be quarantined when it can be demonstrated that unlimited travel to the area would directly and materially interfere with the safety and welfare of the area or the Nation as a whole. So it is with international travel.

4.   ***Travel or Movement?***

Apart from a right to *travel*, federal law has recognized a generalized freedom or right of *movement*:

> Freedom of movement, at home and abroad, is important for job and business opportunities—for cultural, political, and social activities—for all the commingling which gregarious man enjoys. Those with the right of free movement use it at times for mischievous purposes. But that is true of many liberties we enjoy. We nevertheless place our faith in them, and against restraint, knowing that the risk of abusing liberty so as to give rise to punishable conduct is part of the price we pay for this free society.

Aptheker v. Sec. of State, 378 U.S. 500 (1964) (Douglas, J., concurring). *See also Kent v. Dulles*, 357 U.S. 116 (1958), *supra* ("Freedom of movement is basic in our scheme of values"); *United States v. Guest*, 383 U.S. 745 (1966) (proclaiming that citizens of the United States "must have the right to pass and repass through every part of [the country] without interruption, as freely as in [their] own states"); *Williams v. Fears*, 179

U.S. 270 (1900) (indicating that the "right of locomotion," like the "right to contract," is protected by substantive due process). *But see Memorial Hospital v. Maricopa County*, 415 U.S. 250 (1974) ("[e]ven a bona fide residence requirement would burden the right to travel if travel meant merely movement").

Modernly, the creation and activities of the Transportation Security Administration ("TSA") have brought attention to the issue of freedom of movement. The TSA was established by the Aviation and Transportation Security Act of 2001, by which the TSA's mission is to "protect the nation's transportation systems to ensure freedom of movement for people and commerce." As detailed in *Gilmore v. Gonzales*, 434 F.3d 1125 (9th Cir. 2006) *infra*, some TSA measures, including the "No Fly List" and "Selectee List" may impede movement without also infringing on the Constitution.

Moreover, the Air Transportation Security and Anti-Hijacking Acts of 1974 (P.L. 93–366), which relate to weapons-detecting screening of all passengers and carry-on property, requires or permits airlines to refuse to transport passengers and property in certain circumstances:

49 U.S.C. § 44902 ("Refusal to transport passengers and property")

(a) **Mandatory Refusal.** The Under Secretary of Transportation for Security shall prescribe regulations requiring an air carrier, intrastate air carrier, or foreign air carrier to refuse to transport—

(1) a passenger who does not consent to a search . . . establishing whether the passenger is carrying unlawfully a dangerous weapon, explosive, or other destructive substance; or

(2) property of a passenger who does not consent to a search of the property establishing whether the property unlawfully contains a dangerous weapon, explosive, or other destructive substance.

(b) **Permissive Refusal.** Subject to regulations of the Under Secretary, an air carrier, intrastate air carrier, or foreign air carrier may refuse to transport a passenger or property the carrier decides is, or might be, inimical to safety.

See also Chapter 7, *infra*, Part C.

5. *Travel as Speech.*

Under *Kent v. Dulles's* approach, the right to travel is an aspect of a citizen's liberty under the Fifth Amendment. But, is it more accurate to think of the right to travel as arising out of the First Amendment, which guarantees the right of assembly? Justice

William Douglas, in a dissenting opinion in *Zemel v. Rusk*, 381 U.S. 1 (1965), has answered in the negative:

> As I have said, the right to travel is at the periphery of the First Amendment, rather than at its core, largely because travel is, of course, more than speech: it is speech brigaded with conduct. "Conduct remains subject to regulation for the protection of society. * * * (But i)n every case the power to regulate must be so exercised as not, in attaining a permissible end, unduly to infringe the protected freedom." Restrictions on the right to travel in times of peace should be so particularized that a First Amendment right is not precluded unless some clear countervailing national interest stands in the way of its assertion.

6.   ***Passports Post September 11, 2001.***

With the advent of profiling, screening devices, and evermore intrusive security measures at airports, does Dr. Walter Briehl's argument in *Kent v. Dulles*, that "every American has the right to travel regardless of politics," ring true after September 11th? What does the presence of these machines say about the health of our democracy? Related, how would you describe the state of the "right to travel" or "freedom of movement" today? See Heather E. Reser, Comment, *Airline Terrorism: The Effect of Tightened Security on the Right to Travel*, 63 J. AIR L. & COM. 819 (1998).

What limits, if any, should be imposed upon government requirements of citizens to demonstrate nationality? For example, would a passport containing a citizen's biometric information synch with constitutionally protected civil liberties? See generally Arnold Henson, *Constitutional Law: Right to Travel: Authority of Secretary of State to Deny Passports*, 57 MICH. L. REV. 119 (1958). *See also* James D. Barnett, *Passport Administration and the Courts*, 32 ORE. L. REV. 193 (1953); Leonard B. Boudin, *The Constitutional Right to Travel*, 56 COLUM. L. REV. 47 (1956); Reginald Parker, *The Right to Go Abroad: To Have and to Hold a Passport*, 40 VA. L. REV. 853 (1954).

7.   ***Korematsu and War Measures.***

War measures are discussed in *Kent v. Dulles*, one of which was at the heart of one of the most discredited opinions ever rendered by the U.S. Supreme Court.

At the age of 23 Fred Korematsu, an American citizen of Japanese descent, was ordered to go to an internment camp west of the Rockies pursuant to Executive Order 2525, which President Franklin D. Roosevelt signed the day after the Japanese attack on Pearl Harbor in December 1941. The order authorized the federal government to apprehend and confine "alien enemies." The order resulted in the imprisonment of thousands of Americans, including Norman Mineta who would later serve as the Secretary of the Department of Transportation during the administrations of President Bill Clinton and George W. Bush. *See* Abigail Simon, *This Bush Cabinet*

Official Was Imprisoned in a Japanese Internment Camp. He Sees Troubling Parallels with Family Separations, TIME, June 21, 2018, https://time.com/5318725/family-separation-policy-japanese-internment-camp-norman-mineta/ ("After the attack on Pearl Harbor, Mineta was taken from his family by train, forced to say goodbye to his friends, his dog, and even his baseball bat when he was sent to an internment camp in Heart Mountain, Wyoming. He was only 10.")

In *Korematsu v. United States*, 323 U.S. 214 (1944), the court ruled 6–3 allowed Executive Order 2525 to stand as an exercise of the president's national security powers. After more than 70 years on the books, the U.S. Supreme Court officially rejected and overruled the *Korematsu v. United States* decision in *Trump v. Hawaii*, 138 S.Ct. 2392 (2018), a case in which the U.S. Supreme Court upheld President Donald Trump's ban on migration from certain mostly Muslim countries. *See generally* Philip Bump, *How a 1944 Decision on Japanese Internment Affected the Supreme Court's Travel Ban Case*, WASH. POST, June 26, 2018.

C. INTERNATIONAL APPLICATION

LEE V. CHINA AIRLINES, LTD.

669 F. Supp. 979 (C.D. Cal. 1987)

WILSON, DISTRICT JUDGE.

This case is one of several involving China Airlines Flight 006 (a Boeing 747) on February 19, 1985. The Lees were injured on that flight when the 747 made an unexpected and uncontrolled 31,000-foot descent off the coast of California.

The Lees are permanent residents of California. Mr. Lee is in the international garment manufacturing business, so he makes frequent trips to Asia. They purchased the tickets which allowed them to travel on Flight 006 in Hong Kong. These tickets were for round trip travel from Hong Kong to San Francisco. The date and flight number on the return portion of the ticket were left open.

International Transportation, Defined

Article 28 of the Warsaw Convention will not allow the Lees' case against China Airlines to be heard in the United States. The Lees argue that the Warsaw Convention does not apply in this case because their ill-fated flight did not depart from a country that is a party to the Convention. They are incorrect. The Convention applies to "international transportation." This term is defined in Article 1, Paragraph (2) of the Convention as:

[A]ny transportation in which, according to the contract made by the parties, the place of departure and the place of destination, whether or not there be a break in the transportation or a transshipment, are situated either in the territories of two High Contracting Parties, or within the territory of a single High Contracting Party, if there is an agreed stopping place in a territory subject to the sovereignty, suzerainty, mandate or authority of another power, even though that power is not a party to this Convention.

According to this language, the Convention will apply in two situations. First, it applies, if according to the contract of transportation (*e.g.*, a plane ticket), travel will be from one High Contracting Party to another. Second, if the contract of transportation provides for travel from a High Contracting Party, for stops abroad, and then for a return to that same High Contracting Party, then the Convention also applies. The ticket in this case provided for transportation from Hong Kong to Taipei to San Francisco to Hong Kong. Because the Convention only allows for one destination, the departure point and the destination of the Lees must officially be considered Hong Kong. Thus, the Convention will not apply here unless Hong Kong is a High Contracting Party. And, Hong Kong qualifies as a High Contracting Party to the Convention. The United Kingdom is a High Contracting party, and its adherence to the Convention covers Hong Kong.

The Lees argue that even if the court finds that Article 28 requires dismissal of China Airlines, the court should still not dismiss them because the Warsaw Convention is unconstitutional. The Lees make three different arguments on the constitutionality issue. First, they argue that the Convention constitutes a substantive due process violation because it impairs the allegedly fundamental right to international travel. Second, they argue that the Convention constitutes an equal protection violation because it treats passengers on the same airplane differently depending upon the content of their tickets. Finally, they argue, at the suggestion of the court, that the Convention is a procedural due process violation because it deprives them of the opportunity to have their tort claim heard in the United States. The court finds all three arguments to be without merit.

Warsaw Convention: Constitutional?

A.   Substantive Due Process

The Lees argue that the Convention violates the Fifth Amendment because it impairs a fundamental right. They assert that they have a fundamental right to travel internationally and that the liability limitation of the Convention infringes upon this right. If such a right is impaired, then the court must examine the Convention with strict scrutiny to see if the Convention furthers a compelling governmental interest. The strict scrutiny analysis need not be reached, however, because the court finds that while the right to travel interstate is fundamental, the right to international travel is not. Therefore, the court need only evaluate the Convention under a rational basis test, and under that test, the Convention passes muster.

International Travel as Fundamental Right?

In support of their argument that international travel is a fundamental right, the Lees cite *In re Aircrash in Bali, Indonesia*, 684 F.2d 1301 (9th Cir.1982) ("International travel, like interstate travel, is a fundamental right."). This case, however, does not appear in accordance with prior Supreme Court authority. *See Califano v. Aznavorian*, 439 U.S. 170 (1978) ("[L]egislation which is said to infringe the freedom to travel abroad is not to be judged by the same standard applied to laws that penalize the right of interstate travel, such as durational residency requirements imposed by the States."). The Court added:

> [T]his court has often pointed out the crucial difference between the freedom to travel internationally and the right of interstate travel. The constitutional right of interstate travel is virtually unqualified. . . . by contrast, the "right" of international travel has been considered to be no more than an aspect of the "liberty" protected by the Due Process Clause of the Fifth Amendment. As such, this "right" the Court has held, can be regulated within the bounds of due process.

Rational Basis Test for Limitations on International Travel

Aznavorian makes clear that limitations upon international travel are to be evaluated under a rational basis test. *Aznavorian* dealt with legislation that provided that a person could not receive SSI benefits during a month when that individual was out of the country. The Court upheld this legislation, saying that it only had an "incidental" effect on international travel. Given this incidental impact, the Court said that the limitation should be upheld unless it is "wholly irrational." This court turns, then, to an evaluation of the Lees' contention that the Convention impairs their right to travel and holds that the Convention has only an incidental impact on international travel and that this limitation is not wholly irrational.

The Convention was designed to establish uniformity in the law regarding international aviation. It recognizes that aviation links many countries with different languages, customs, and legal systems, and this goal is achieved somewhat through standard documentation, procedures for claims, and jurisdictional requirements. Because the Warsaw Convention helps to achieve the goal of uniformity in the law regarding international air travel, the court finds the treaty passes the rational basis test.

First, the court notes that the impact of the Convention upon international travel is *de minimus*. While the liability and jurisdictional limitations in the Convention may have a slight chilling effect upon some people considering a trip abroad, the Convention does not prevent anyone from taking such a journey. The court notes that the Convention does not prevent someone who is concerned about the liability limitation from obtaining additional insurance before embarking on a journey abroad. Whatever limitation there is, however, is justifiable. The Convention was designed to establish uniformity in the law regarding international aviation. It recognizes that aviation links many countries with different languages, customs, and legal systems, and this goal is achieved somewhat through standard documentation, procedures for claims, and jurisdictional requirements. Because the Warsaw Convention helps to achieve the goal of uniformity in the law regarding international air travel, the court finds the treaty passes the rational basis test.

B.   Equal Protection

The Lees also suggest that Article 28 violates the equal protection clause of the Fifth Amendment because it makes distinctions among passengers on the same plane depending upon their tickets. They note that while the journeys of some passengers on a particular plane may be governed by the Convention, other journeys may not be so covered. Furthermore, even when the Convention applies to two passengers on the same plane, the Convention may allow one passenger to sue in the United States, but prohibit the other passenger from doing so. This differentiation among passengers, however, does not amount to an equal protection violation because no fundamental right is impaired by the distinction, and the distinction has a rational basis.

Treating similarly situated people differently is not always unconstitutional. Usually, making such distinctions is acceptable if a rational basis exists for the distinction.

Treating similarly situated people differently is not always unconstitutional. *See, e.g., Williamson v. Lee Optical of Oklahoma*, 348 U.S. 483 (1955). Usually, making such distinctions is acceptable if a rational basis exists for the distinction. If, however, the classification created is suspect or impinges upon a fundamental right, then a court should apply strict scrutiny in reviewing the law creating the classification. *See, e.g., Korematsu v. United States*, 323 U.S. 214 (1944) (suspect class); *Shapiro v. Thompson*, 394 U.S. 618 (1969) (fundamental right). In this case, the court must apply a rational basis test. First, as set forth above, the Convention does not

Treating Similarly Situated People Differently: Constitutional?

impinge on any fundamental rights. Second, the classifications created are not suspect.

The court finds that the distinctions made between passengers on the same plane because of the provisions of the Convention are rational. The goal of the Convention is to bring uniformity to the law governing international air travel. This goal is fostered by the method set up by the Convention to determine whether it is applicable to a particular journey. The Convention dictates that applicability is determined by the place of departure and the place of destination as listed upon a passenger's ticket. This mechanism insures that the Convention will only apply to journeys with a clear nexus to High Contracting Parties, and it also ensures that passengers will have had some notice and an opportunity to choose whether they are willing to subject themselves to the dictates of the Convention. Thus, the Convention does create a rational system for bringing some uniformity to the law regarding international air travel in a world in which every nation has not agreed to abide by its terms. In light of this analysis, the court cannot say that distinctions created by the Convention among passengers on the same plane are irrational.

C.   Procedural Due Process

Two-Step Due Process Analysis

The Lees argue that the jurisdictional limitation violates due process because it prevents American residents who were injured in or near the United States from bringing a tort action here. This argument also fails. When engaging in due process analysis, the court must first examine if a governmental action is infringing upon a life, liberty, or property interest. If the court finds that such an interest is affected, then the next question is what process is due. To determine what process is due, the court must go through a three-part analysis:

> First, the private interest that will be affected by the official action; second, the risk of an erroneous deprivation of such interest through the procedures used, and the probable value, if any, of additional or substitute procedural safeguards; and finally, the Government's interest, including the function involved and the fiscal and administrative burdens that the additional or substitute procedural requirement would entail.

Matthews v. Eldridge, 424 U.S. 319 (1976). Assuming for the sake of argument, then, that the Lees have a property interest in their claim, the next question is what process is due.

Turning to the *Mathews v. Eldridge* test quoted above, the court finds that dismissal here would not be a due process violation. The Lees assert that if their claim against China Airlines is dismissed, they will not be able to receive an adequate hearing of their claims abroad in either Taiwan or Hong Kong. The Lees have not shown, however, that having their claims heard abroad will create a substantial risk of "erroneous deprivation." They have come forward with almost no evidence regarding the nature of judicial proceedings in either Hong Kong or Taiwan. The Lees' only contention regarding the unfairness of potential proceedings in either Taiwan or Hong Kong is that it would be unfair to subject them to the uncertainty regarding what law will apply to this case in those countries. At least in this case, however, some of the usual mystery regarding what law a foreign forum will apply disappears.

The court surmises that the Warsaw Convention will figure prominently in the decision-making process over there since both Hong Kong and Taiwan adhere to it. The Ninth Circuit recently noted that "the cardinal purpose of the [Convention] is to ensure the existence of a uniform and universal system of recovery for losses incurred in the course of international air transportation." Because the plaintiffs have not met their burden of showing the proceedings abroad are likely to be erroneous, the court cannot act further on the Lees' due process contentions. In conclusion, then, the court disagrees with the Lees' contention that the Warsaw Convention is unconstitutional and dismisses their claims in accordance with the Convention's mandate.

EXERCISE 1-3. *LEE V. CHINA AIRLINES, LTD.*—DUE PROCESS IN INTERNATIONAL AIR TRAVEL

1. What is the departure point for the Lees? What is their destination? Why is this important from a legal perspective?

2. The plaintiffs assert three different arguments about the constitutionality of the Warsaw Convention. Identify each.

3. Explain how the court treats interstate travel and international travel differently as a matter of law.

4. Do the liability and jurisdictional limitations in the Warsaw Convention impermissibly impede the right to travel? Explain.

5. Does the result reached in *Lee v. China Airlines, Ltd.* afford the plaintiffs with due process of the law? Why or why not?

NOTES ON *LEE V. CHINA AIRLINES, LTD.*—LEGAL CONSTRAINTS IN INTERNATIONAL TRAVEL

The dispute in *Lee v. China Airlines, Ltd.*, *supra*, underscores an important legal peril uniquely related to the nature of air travel—different laws at the origin and destination of a flight potentially mean different rights (including the absence of rights) for litigants. Just as the Lees argued that application of an international treaty might impact their constitutional rights, passengers frequently litigate choice of law issues where the rights and remedies available to a plaintiff may be more favorable in one state over another. (*See, e.g.*, *Piper Aircraft v. Reyno*, Chapter 12, *infra*.) Some examples of international limitations of the right to air travel—for understandable and controversial reasons—follow.

1. ***Travel Limitations Based on Nationality.***

A German court ruled in 2016 that Kuwait Airways had the right to refuse to carry an Israeli passenger due to his nationality. A Frankfurt state court opined that the airline was merely respecting the laws of Kuwait, which does not recognize the state of Israel, and that the German court lacked authority to rule on Kuwaiti law. *See German Court Rules Kuwait Airline in Allowed to Ban Israelis*, REUTERS, Nov. 16, 2017, https://www.reuters.com/article/germany-court-kuwait-airways/german-court-rules-kuwait-airline-is-allowed-to-ban-israelis-idUSL1N1NM1NJ.

2. ***Protection for Nationals.***

The U.S. Department of State provides safety and security information for international travelers, including specific guidance for journalists, faith-based travel, and travelers identifying as LGBTI, woman, disabled, or older. *See* U.S. Dep't of State, *International Travel*, https://travel.state.gov/content/travel/en/international-travel. html.

Additionally, the U.S. State Department provides information about every country of the world to assist passengers assess for themselves the risk of travel. Each country information page contains a Travel Advisory, Alerts, and other important details specific to that country that could affect travelers. The Department of State further advises travelers to pay close attention to the entry and exit requirements, local laws and customs, health conditions, and other details to decide whether traveling to that country is right for them. Also provided is the address and phone number of the nearest U.S. embassy or consulate. *See* U.S. Dep't of State, *Country Information*, https://travel.state.gov/content/travel/en/international-travel/International-Travel-Country-Information-Pages.html.

Illustration 1-1. U.S. Department of State Travel Advisory: Iran

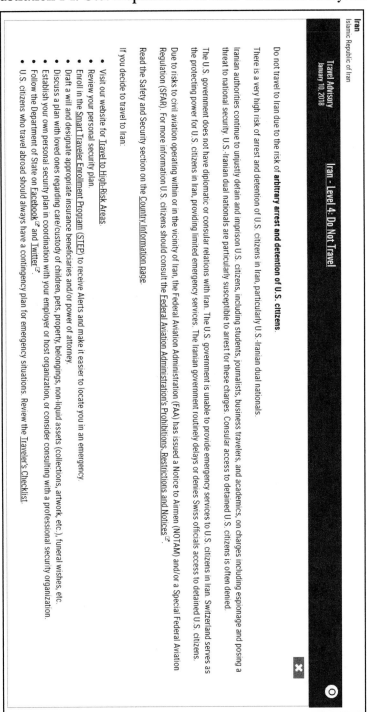

Source: https://travel.state.gov/content/travel/en/international-travel/International-Travel-Country-Information-Pages/Iran.html

3.   ***Brexit.***

"Brexit"—the portmanteau for the British referendum on June 23, 2016 to withdraw the United Kingdom from the European Union—presented an enormous and unprecedented challenge to the concept of freedom of movement within an economic bloc.

Free movement of people had been one of the "four freedoms" guaranteed by membership in the EU and exercised under Article 21 of the Treaty of the Functioning of the European Union. Difficulties in negotiations about the terms by which the United Kingdom would leave and prospectively deal with the EU prompted the Director General and CEO of the International Air Transport Association ("IATA") to release a statement:

> The UK government's papers on the air transport implications of a "no deal" departure from the EU clearly exposes the extreme seriousness of what is at stake and underscores the huge amount of work that would be required to maintain vital air links. It is not just permission for flights to take off and land. Everything from pilots' licenses to security arrangements need to be agreed. Much of this could be secured through mutual recognition of existing standards. But formalizing this cannot happen overnight. And even when that is done, there will still be an administrative burden for the airlines and governments involved that will take time and significant resources. While we still hope for a comprehensive EU-UK deal, an assumption that "it will be all right on the night" is far too risky to accept. Every contingency should be prepared for, and we call upon both the EU and the UK to be far more transparent with the state of the discussions.

See generally Angela Dewan, *It's Official—A No-Deal Brexit will Make Traveling a Pain*, CNN, Sept. 13, 2018 ("Traveling between the UK and European Union will get a whole lot more complicated—and expensive—should Brexit talks end without a deal.")

4.   ***Health and Public Welfare.***

"Planes provide the quickest way to get from one part of the world to another," an Associated Press article noted in 2005, adding, "for deadline contagious diseases as well as for people." In fact, in the spring of 2003, the respiratory virus SARS (also known as "bird flu") spread to five countries in 24 hours after first emerging in rural China. Airline and tourism industries lost billions of dollars "because people were afraid to travel and governments ordered flights canceled." *See Planes Could Spread Bird Flu Virus at Jet Speed*, NBC NEWS, Oct. 14, 2005, http://www.nbcnews.com/id/9687610/ns/health-infectious_diseases/t/planes-could-spread-bird-flu-virus-jet-speed/#.W4Qr6-hKg2w. Unsurprisingly, then, airlines routinely condition travel on passenger health. For example, Finnair requires medical clearance in specific circumstances:

Illustration 1-2. Finnair Guidance on Medical Conditions

MEDICAL CONDITIONS

Most people with existing medical conditions are able to fly without difficulty. However, certain precautions sometimes need to be taken and in some cases we request medical clearance.

MEDA FORMS

If you have one of the illnesses or conditions below, you must notify us when you book your ticket, or at least 72 hours before your travel date. This will enable us to take appropriate precautionary measures. Please fill this preliminary information form. After submitting the form, you will receive your personal case number, e.g. 1- 456789078. This will allow you to update the information and insert attachments to the case. Sign in with your case number.

- recent myocardial infarction
- recent cerebral circulatory disorders
- recent injuries
- recent surgeries
- symptomatic coronary disease
- chronic obstructive pulmonary disease
- a need for oxygen therapy
- psychoses
- an infectious disease (tuberculosis, diphtheria)
- anaemia (Hb less than 75 g/l)
- chickenpox in the vesicle phase
- severe allergy

Source: https://www.finnair.com/no/gb/information-services/before-the-flight/special-services-health/medical-conditions.

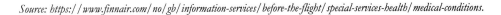

BEYDOUN V. SESSIONS

871 F.3d 459 (6th Cir. 2017)

CLAY, CIRCUIT JUDGE.

Plaintiffs Nasser Beydoun and Maan Bazzi each separately sued various federal government officials challenging their placement on the federal government's "Selectee List," which designates them for enhanced screening at the airport. Asserting that their Fifth Amendment right to due process was violated, Plaintiffs sought declaratory and injunctive relief, with the ultimate aim of having their names removed from the government's enhanced screening list.

Plaintiff Nasser Beydoun is a United States citizen and resident of Dearborn, Michigan. According to his complaint, every time Beydoun attempts to board an airplane, he is subjected to "excessive delays, secondary screening, being singled out at check points, and being singled out for additional screening at the gate." As a result, Beydoun "has missed countless flights." He also claims that he has been humiliated and that his business ventures have suffered because he is subjected to extra security measures.

Plaintiff Maan Bazzi, who is also a United States citizen, similarly claims that he is only allowed to board flights after undergoing additional screening and experiencing excessive delays. For example, when Bazzi was flying from Brazil to Texas, he "was subjected to extra screening for approximately 10 minutes after receiving a boarding pass and was told to wait as [he] was going to be the last person boarded on the flight." After arriving in Texas, Bazzi underwent an additional hour of questioning and had his bags searched for explosives. Bazzi also had his passport "confiscated" for an hour at the Las Vegas airport and was taken for additional screening that lasted thirty minutes. At least once, Bazzi canceled one of his planned trips in order to avoid the "the stress and embarrassment of extra screening."

Selectee List

Based on their experiences going through airport security and boarding airplanes, Beydoun and Bazzi believe that they are on the Selectee List, which designates individuals for enhanced security screening due to the threat they may pose to "civil aviation or national security." *See* U.S. Gov't Accountability Office, GAO–08–110, Terrorist Watchlist Screening: Opportunities Exist to Enhance Management Oversight, Reduce Vulnerabilities in Agency Screening Processes, and Expand Use of the List 35 (2007). For example, individuals on the Selectee List "are to receive additional security screening prior to being permitted to board an aircraft, which may involve a physical inspection of the person and a hand-search of the passenger's luggage."

The Selectee List is a subset of the government's Terrorist Screening Database ("TSDB"). The TSDB "is developed and maintained by the Terrorist Screening Center ('TSC'), a multi-agency center that was created in 2003 and is administered by the Federal Bureau of Investigation ('FBI'), which in turn is part of the Department of Justice." *Mokdad v. Lynch*, 804 F.3d 807 (6th Cir. 2015). Officials from multiple agencies staff the TSC, including individuals from the FBI, the Department of Homeland Security ("DHS"), the Department of State, Customs and Border Protection, and the Transportation Security Administration ("TSA"). "TSC personnel decide whether to accept or reject the 'nomination' of a person by the FBI or the National Counterterrorism Center (NCTC) to the

TSDB" or the Selectee List. "TSC also decides whether to remove a name from the TSDB after it receives a redress request that has been submitted through" DHS's Traveler Redress Inquiry Program ("DHS TRIP").

According to their complaints, Beydoun and Bazzi have both attempted to use the procedure established by DHS TRIP to challenge their inclusion on the Selectee List. However, each time, the government failed to remove them from the list and has only sent them generalized responses to their inquiries. In addition, in both cases, the government has neither confirmed nor denied that Plaintiffs are on the Selectee List.

Plaintiffs contend that the district court erred in determining that their alleged inclusion on the Selectee List does not implicate a liberty interest protected by the Fifth Amendment. We address each issue in turn.

The Supreme Court has recognized that "[f]reedom to travel throughout the United States has long been recognized as a basic right under the Constitution." *Dunn v. Blumstein*, 405 U.S. 330 (1972); see also *Kent v. Dulles*, 357 U.S. 116 (1958) ("The right to travel is a part of the 'liberty' of which the citizen cannot be deprived without the due process of law under the Fifth Amendment . . . Travel abroad, like travel within the country, may be necessary for a livelihood. It may be as close to the heart of the individual as the choice of what he eats, or wears, or reads. Freedom of movement is basic in our scheme of values." Indeed, "[t]he constitutional right of interstate travel is virtually unqualified." *Califano v. Aznavorian*, 439 U.S. 170 (1978). However, "the freedom to travel outside the United States must be distinguished from the right to travel within the United States." *Haig v. Agee*, 453 U.S. 280 (1981). Therefore, "the freedom to travel abroad . . . is subject to reasonable governmental regulation."

A fundamental right will only be implicated by government action that, at a minimum, "significantly interferes with the exercise of a fundamental right." Burdens that are incidental or negligible are "insufficient to implicate [the] denial of the right to travel.

A fundamental right will only be implicated by government action that, at a minimum, "significantly interferes with the exercise of a fundamental right." Burdens that are incidental or negligible are "insufficient to implicate [the] denial of the right to travel." *League of United Latin Am. Citizens v. Bredesen*, 500 F.3d 523 (6th Cir. 2007). At issue in these cases is whether Plaintiffs' alleged placement on the Selectee List has created more than an incidental burden on their right to travel. The district court found that the instances alleged by Plaintiffs do not rise to such a level as to implicate a constitutional right, and therefore that Plaintiffs have failed to state a claim.

On appeal, Plaintiffs argue that the district court erred in considering the burden placed on Plaintiffs by their inclusion on the Selectee List as negligible or incidental. Beydoun alleged that he has missed "countless flights" after being subjected to lengthy secondary screenings. According to Beydoun, these delays had the effect of deterring him from flying and taking away his right to travel. However, Beydoun has not attempted to provide any information about when those delays occurred, how long the delays were, what type of enhanced screening he was subjected to, or indeed any information beyond general allegations that he has been prevented from traveling.

Bazzi's complaint provides a few more details. For example, Bazzi mentions several instances when he has been delayed or subjected to additional screening, with delays ranging from ten minutes to one hour in duration. Bazzi also points to the fact that, in his complaint, he specifically alleged that he had been deterred from flying on one occasion.

Inconveniences Are Not Constitutional Violations

The district court correctly held that Plaintiffs did not allege that any protected interest was violated by them being on the Selectee List. While Plaintiffs may have been inconvenienced by the extra security hurdles they endured in order to board an airplane, these burdens do not amount to a constitutional violation. Importantly, Plaintiffs have not actually been prevented from flying altogether or from traveling by means other than an airplane. Therefore, Plaintiffs' cases are distinguishable from those in which the plaintiffs claimed they could not fly at all because they were on the No Fly List.

The burdens alleged by Plaintiffs, to the extent they provided specific details about those incidents, can only be described as incidental or negligible and therefore do not implicate the right to travel. Plaintiffs point to no authority supporting their claim that a delay of ten minutes, thirty minutes, or even an hour at the airport violates their fundamental right to travel, and we are aware of none. Indeed, the Second Circuit rejected a claim that plaintiffs were impeded from exercising their right to travel when they were delayed for an entire day. When Plaintiffs' only allegations amount to delays that many individuals are likely to experience at the airport, it is hard to conclude that the fundamental right to travel has been implicated.

Finally, we are not convinced by Plaintiffs' contention that, because they were deterred from traveling, they have a constitutional claim. In support of their argument, Plaintiffs cite to *Attorney Gen. of New York v. Soto-Lopez*, 476 U.S. 898

(1986), in which a plurality of the Supreme Court remarked that "[a] state law implicates the right to travel when it actually deters such travel, when impeding travel is its primary objective, or when it uses any classification which serves to penalize the exercise of that right." However, we have recognized that burdens that are incidental or negligible can "hardly be said to deter or penalize travel." *Pollack v. Duff*, 793 F.3d 34, 45 (D.C. Cir. 2015) (remarking that if a law's "effect upon [a plaintiff's] willingness to travel, i.e., to exercise her right to travel, is 'negligible[,]' [it] does not warrant scrutiny under the Constitution"); *Matsuo v. United States*, 586 F.3d 1180, 1183 (9th Cir. 2009) ("[N]ot everything that deters travel burdens the fundamental right to travel.").

Indeed, even if Plaintiffs were, in fact, deterred from flying after being delayed for an hour, we cannot conclude that this minor disturbance actually resulted in denying Plaintiffs the right to travel. *See Torraco v. Port Auth. of New York and New Jersey*, 615 F.3d 129, 141 (2d Cir. 2010) ("Assuming that the actions the defendants took did in fact deter these plaintiffs . . ., the most-inconvenienced plaintiff was delayed a little over one day. This was a minor restriction that did not result in a denial of the right to travel."). Therefore, the district court correctly concluded that Plaintiffs failed to state a claim that their right to travel was infringed upon by Defendants.

EXERCISE 1-4. *BEYDOUN V. SESSIONS*—THE "NO FLY LIST"

1. A number of important procedural issues present in *Beydoun v. Sessions*. To understand their application, define the following terms using a legal dictionary: (a) declaratory relief; and (b) injunctive relief.

2. What is the "No Fly List"?

3. What is the Terrorist Screening Database? How does it operate and by whom?

4. According to the court, what is the minimum type of government action necessary to implicate a fundamental right? Explain.

5. Are the plaintiffs' claims based on procedural or substantive due process, according to the court? What is the difference?

D. INTERSTATE AIR TRAVEL

GILMORE V. GONZALES

435 F.3d 1125 (9th Cir. 2006)

PAEZ, CIRCUIT JUDGE.

On July 4, 2002, John Gilmore ("Gilmore"), a California resident and United States citizen, attempted to fly from Oakland International Airport to Baltimore-Washington International Airport on a Southwest Airlines flight. Gilmore intended to travel to Washington, D.C. to "petition the government for redress of grievances and to associate with others for that purpose." He was not allowed to fly, however, because he refused to present identification to Southwest Airlines when asked to do so.

Identification Requirement

Gilmore approached the Southwest ticketing counter with paper tickets that he already had purchased. When a Southwest ticketing clerk asked to see his identification, Gilmore refused. Although the clerk informed Gilmore that identification was required, he refused again. Gilmore asked whether the requirement was a government or Southwest rule, and whether there was any way that he could board the plane without presenting his identification. The clerk was unsure, but posited that the rule was an "FAA security requirement." The clerk informed Gilmore that he could opt to be screened at the gate in lieu of presenting the requisite identification. The clerk then issued Gilmore a new boarding pass, which indicated that he was to be searched before boarding the airplane. At the gate, Gilmore again refused to show identification. In response to his question about the source of the identification rule, a Southwest employee stated that it was a government law. Gilmore then met with a Southwest customer service supervisor, who told him that the identification requirement was an airline policy. Gilmore left the airport, without being searched at the gate.

That same day, Gilmore went to San Francisco International Airport and attempted to buy a ticket for a United Airlines flight to Washington, D.C. While at the ticket counter, Gilmore saw a sign that read: "PASSENGERS MUST PRESENT IDENTIFICATION UPON INITIAL CHECK-IN." Gilmore again refused to present identification when asked by the ticketing agent. The agent told him that he had to show identification at the ticket counter, security checkpoint, and before boarding; and that there was no way to circumvent the identification policy.

A United Airlines Service Director told Gilmore that a United traveler without identification is subject to secondary screening, but did not disclose the source of the identification policy. United's Ground Security Chief reiterated the need for identification, but also did not cite the source of the policy. The Security Chief informed Gilmore that he could fly without presenting identification by undergoing a more intensive search, *i.e.* by being a "selectee." A "selectee" search includes walking through a magnetometer, being subjected to a handheld magnetometer scan, having a light body patdown, removing one's shoes, and having one's carry-on baggage searched by hand and a CAT-scan machine. Gilmore refused to allow his bag to be searched by hand and was therefore barred from flying.

Secondary Screening "Option"

The Security Chief told Gilmore that he did not know the law or government regulation that required airlines to enforce the identification policy. Another member of United's security force later told Gilmore that the policy was set out in government Security Directives, which he was not permitted to disclose. He also told Gilmore that the Security Directives were revised frequently, as often as weekly; were transmitted orally; and differed according to airport. The airline security personnel could not, according to the Government, disclose to Gilmore the Security Directive that imposed the identification policy because the Directive was classified as "sensitive security information" ("SSI"). Gilmore left the airport and has not flown since September 11, 2001 because he is unwilling to show identification or be subjected to the "selectee" screening process.

Gilmore filed a complaint against Southwest Airlines and the United State Attorney General, challenging the constitutionality of several security measures, which he collectively referred to as "the Scheme," including the identification policy, CAPPS and CAPPS II, and No-Fly and Selectee lists. Gilmore alleged that these government security policies and provisions violated his right to due process, right to travel, right to be free from unreasonable searches and seizures, right to freely associate, and right to petition the government for redress of grievances. Gilmore also alleged that "similar requirements have been placed on travelers who use government-regulated passenger trains, and that similar requirements are being instituted for interstate bus travel."

Gilmore also alleged that the identification policy violates his constitutional right to travel because he cannot travel by commercial airlines without presenting identification, which is an impermissible federal condition. We reject Gilmore's right to travel argument because the Constitution does not guarantee the right to travel by any particular form of transportation.

Identification Request

Gilmore alleges that both options under the identification policy—presenting identification or undergoing a more intrusive search—are subject to Fourth Amendment limitations and violated his right to be free from unreasonable searches and seizures. Gilmore argues that the request for identification implicates the Fourth Amendment because "the government imposes a severe penalty on citizens who do not comply." Gilmore highlights the fact that he was once arrested at an airport for refusing to show identification and argues that the request for identification "[i]mposes the severe penalty of arrest." Gilmore further argues that the request for identification violates the Fourth Amendment because it constitutes "a warrantless general search for identification" that is unrelated to the goals of detecting weapons or explosives.

The request for identification, however, does not implicate the Fourth Amendment. "[A] request for identification by the police does not, by itself, constitute a Fourth Amendment seizure." Rather, "[a]n individual is seized within the meaning of the Fourth Amendment only if, in view of all of the circumstances surrounding the incident, a reasonable person would have believed that he was not free to leave." Similarly, an airline personnel's request for Gilmore's identification was not a seizure within the meaning of the Fourth Amendment.

Gilmore's experiences at the Oakland and San Francisco airports provide the best rebuttal to his argument that the requests for identification imposed a risk of arrest and were therefore seizures. Gilmore twice tried to board a plane without presenting identification, and twice left the airport when he was unsuccessful. He was not threatened with arrest or some other form of punishment; rather he simply was told that unless he complied with the policy, he would not be permitted to board the plane. There was no penalty for noncompliance.

Request to Search

Gilmore argues that the selectee option is also unconstitutional because the degree of intrusion is unreasonable. We reject this argument because it is foreclosed by our decisions in *United States v. Davis*, 482 F.2d 893 (9th Cir. 1973) and *Torbet v. United Airlines, Inc.*, 298 F.3d 1087 (9th Cir. 2002). The identification policy's search option implicates the Fourth Amendment. *See Davis*, 482 F.2d at 895 (holding that the government's participation in airport search programs brings any search conducted pursuant to those programs within the reach of the Fourth Amendment). Airport screening searches, however, do not *per se* violate a traveler's Fourth Amendment rights, and therefore must be analyzed for reasonableness. As we explained in *Davis*:

To meet the test of reasonableness, an administrative screening search must be as limited in its intrusiveness as is consistent with satisfaction of the administrative need that justifies it. It follows that airport screening searches are valid only if they recognize the right of a person to avoid search by electing not to board the aircraft.

Gilmore was free to reject either option under the identification policy, and leave the airport. In fact, Gilmore did just that. United Airlines presented him with the "selectee" option, which included walking through a magnetometer screening device, being subjected to a handheld magnetometer scan, having a light body patdown, removing his shoes, and having his bags hand searched and put through a CAT-scan machine. Gilmore declined and instead left the airport.

Additionally, the search option "is no more extensive or intensive than necessary, in light of current technology, to detect weapons or explosives . . . [and] is confined in good faith to [prevent the carrying of weapons or explosives aboard aircrafts]; and . . . passengers may avoid the search by electing not to fly." Therefore, the search option was reasonable and did not violate Gilmore's Fourth Amendment rights.

> *Gilmore had a meaningful choice. He could have presented identification, submitted to a search, or left the airport. That he chose the latter does not detract from the fact that he could have boarded the airplane had he chosen one of the other two options.*

Gilmore also suggests that the identification policy did not present a meaningful choice, but rather a "Hobson's Choice," in violation of the unconstitutional conditions doctrine. We have held, as a matter of constitutional law, that an airline passenger has a choice regarding searches:

Meaningful Choice, Options?

> [H]e may submit to a search of his person and immediate possessions as a condition to boarding; or he may turn around and leave. If he chooses to proceed, that choice, whether viewed as a relinquishment of an option to leave or an election to submit to the search, is essentially a "consent," granting the government a license to do what it would otherwise be barred from doing by the Fourth Amendment.

Gilmore had a meaningful choice. He could have presented identification, submitted to a search, or left the airport. That he chose the latter does not detract from the fact that he could have boarded the airplane had he chosen one of the other two options. Thus, we reject Gilmore's Fourth Amendment arguments.

Right to Associate and Right to Petition the Government

Finally, Gilmore argues that because the identification policy violates his right to travel, it follows that it also violates his right to petition the government and freely associate. These claims, as Gilmore argued in his appellate brief, are based on the notion that "[f]reedom to physically travel and the free exercise of First Amendment rights are inextricably intertwined." Here, this logic works to Gilmore's detriment. That is, even accepting Gilmore's assertion that there is a connection between the right to travel and First Amendment freedoms, his argument fails because, as we explained, his right to travel was not unreasonably impaired.

Gilmore argues that the identification requirement impinges his First Amendment right to associate anonymously. In support of this argument he relies principally on *Thomas v. Collins*, 323 U.S. 516 (1945), in which the Supreme Court concluded that a registration requirement for public speeches is "generally incompatible with an exercise of the rights of free speech and free assembly." Unlike the regulation in *Thomas*, the identification policy is not a direct restriction on public association; rather it is an airline security measure.

Further, Gilmore did not allege that he was exercising his right to freely associate in the airport, but rather that he was attempting to fly to Washington, D.C. so that he could exercise his right to associate there. The enforcement of the identification policy did not prevent him from associating anonymously in Washington, D.C. because he could have abided by the policy, or taken a different mode of transport. Although the policy did inconvenience Gilmore, this inconvenience did not rise to the level of a constitutional violation. In the end, Gilmore's free association claim fails because there was no direct and substantial action impairing this right.

Gilmore's right to petition claim similarly fails. Although Gilmore did not fly to Washington, D.C., where he planned to petition the government for redress of grievances, the identification policy did not prevent him from doing so. The identification policy is not a direct regulation of any First Amendment expressive activity, nor does it impermissibly inhibit such activity. Gilmore's claims that Defendants violated his rights to associate anonymously and petition the government are without merit.

EXERCISE 1-5. *GILMORE V. GONZALES*—"SELECTEES" AND AIRPORT SECURITY

1. What was the stated purpose of Gilmore's trip?

2. What is a "selectee" and what does the search of a selectee entail?

3. Does a refusal to present identification upon initial check-in implicate the Fourth Amendment protection against unreasonable government searches and seizures? Why or why not?

4. According to the court, what choices, if any, does a passenger have when asked to submit to a search of his person and immediate possession as a condition to boarding? Do you agree with this rationale? Explain.

5. Did the identification policy in this case violate Gilmore's constitutional rights?

———————

HOUSTON V. FED. AVIATION ADMIN.

679 F.2d 1184 (5th Cir. 1982)

JOHN R. BROWN, CIRCUIT JUDGE.

This flight from Houston, Texas to our Nation's Capital takes us to both Dulles International and Washington National Airports. The Administrative Procedure Act ("APA"), 5 U.S.C. § 701 *et seq.*, will serve as our flight plan, and the Supreme Court as air traffic control. In the course of our flight, our passengers— the City of Houston, American Airlines and the Federal Aviation Administration—will be informed of our conclusion that Department of Transportation ("DOT") regulations imposing a "perimeter rule" upon flights to and from Washington National Airport are valid and thus, as we disembark, we shall deny the petitions for review.

Destination: Washington—A Capitol City

Our Nation's Capital, Washington, D. C., attracts millions of visitors each year, be it for pleasure or for business. Nestled in the green hills of the Mid-Atlantic region, snug and smug along the banks of the beautiful Potomac River, this celebrated town of "Northern charm and Southern efficiency" offers visitors a potpourri of museums, art galleries, monuments, historic sites, parks, Panda bears, politicians, and a climate that is charitably described as ghastly. And for one group of travelers, Washington offers something else: our federal government, with its milch cow departments and regulatory agencies. For the business traveler, Washington is Mecca.

One If By Land, Two If By Sea, and Three If By Air

Yet the road to Mecca is not an easy one. The metropolitan Washington area supports three airports: Washington National ("National"), Dulles International ("Dulles")—both owned by the FAA, an arm of the DOT and Baltimore-Washington International ("BWI"). For those citizens living within 1,000 miles of Washington, nonstop air service to close-in National allows them to earn their wings, every day. Served directly by Metro, Washington's vintage 2001 subway network, National lies across the Potomac River from downtown Washington, a few minutes' ride from the seat of government and from most of its appendages as well.

If Washington is the city of cherry blossoms, National is a faded bloom. Constructed in the early 1940's to handle propeller planes, it now handles jet aircraft which disgorge up to 3,500 passengers/hour in peak periods, for a total of 17 million passengers per year. Those figures represent 67% of the air traffic in the metropolitan Washington area. National's 6,870-foot runway can handle Boeing 727's and similar jet aircraft but cannot accommodate the "jumbo" widebody jets that serve the coast-to-coast and international markets. To the west of the airport is Arlington County, Virginia, and to the south, the city of Alexandria, Virginia—both densely populated areas whose residents with increasing vehemence have protested the noise and congestion that National engenders.

You Can't Get There from Here

For those travelers who live beyond 1,000 miles from Washington, only a flying carpet can assure them nonstop service to National, since the DOT regulations we confront prohibit such flights. They may select from two alternatives: a non-nonstop flight to National, stopping or changing planes in a city less than 1,000 miles distant, or a direct flight to Dulles or Baltimore-Washington Airport.

Dulles, the other federal airport, is National's younger and substantially more glamorous sister. Completed in 1962, situated 26 miles west of downtown in the rolling green hills of Loudoun and Fairfax Counties in Virginia, Dulles boasts one of the most spectacular terminals in the world. Designed by the architect Eero Saarinen, the terminal possesses a roof that defies both gravity and common sense, modern facilities, comfortable mobile lounges that carry passengers from the terminal building out to an awaiting plane and thus eliminate much of the walking endemic to airports, and, what is central here, three 10,000-foot runways that can accommodate any and all airplanes currently constructed. The first airport in the nation planned for jet aircraft, Dulles services the bulk of nonstop flights from Washington to the West Coast and abroad.

For all its attributes, however, Dulles suffers from one small problem: unpopularity. The 30-mile trip to Washington from Dulles doth a lengthy and expensive taxi ride make. Ground transportation to downtown by bus or limousine, while not as expensive, still takes approximately 45 minutes in light traffic. Rapid rail transport along the Dulles Access Road, a limited access parkway that services only the airport, is unlikely to begin in the near—or even distant— future. Thus travelers arriving in Washington generally prefer National, however crowded, however congested, however decrepit, to the spacious and graceful, but inconvenient, Dulles. Traffic figures confirm its loneliness. While Dulles can accommodate 1,800 passengers per hour, the total daily average passenger load is less than 7,000. And since the majority arrive or depart late in the afternoon, when the crowded West Coast flights are scheduled, the daily average figures are deceptive. As overcrowding plagues National, arousing the ire of its neighbors, during most of the day the younger sister pines away, unwanted.

The FAA, like any prudent entrepreneur, seeks to increase business and has resorted to the regulatory process to attempt to transfer "long-haul" flights to Dulles. The City of Houston and American complain. And on that note, we must fasten our seat belts, for our flight begins.

Pre-Flight Procedure

American and Houston seek review of DOT regulations imposing a "perimeter rule" that prohibits air carriers from operating nonstop flights between National and any airport more than 1000 statute miles away. 46 Fed. Reg. 36068 (1981), 14 C.F.R § 159.60. The procedural background to this rule could fill several Boeing 747's. Lest we deter the reader, we will throttle back on unnecessary details.

Perimeter Rule

Prior to the dawn of the jet age, the air carriers serving National agreed to a 650-mile perimeter rule on nonstop flights to and from National, with exceptions for seven cities between 650 and 1,000 miles away which enjoyed grandfathered nonstop service as of December 1, 1965. The agreement expired on January 1, 1967, but the carriers continued to adhere to its terms until May 1981, when three carriers—American, Pan American and Braniff—announced plans to fly nonstop to National from cities outside the perimeter.

The perimeter rule did not rest upon operational or safety considerations—all parties concede that the Boeing 727's that land at National have a range well beyond 1000 miles. Rather, the FAA viewed the rule as a means of controlling the increasing traffic at National. The rule did not placate area residents, who found the noise from jet aircraft equally disturbing whether the flight originated within 1000 miles or on the Moon. The neighboring states of Maryland and Virginia, the District of Columbia, local planning organizations, and area Senators and Congressmen all urged the FAA to "do something" about National. In 1970, a coalition of citizen groups and individuals brought suit against the DOT, FAA and eleven major airlines to abate noise and air pollution at the airport. The U.S. Court of Appeals for the Fourth Circuit ordered the FAA to prepare an Environmental Impact Statement ("EIS") concerning its operation of its two airports.

Responding to the Fourth Circuit's flight instructions, the FAA on March 23, 1978 issued a Notice of Proposed Policy for the Metropolitan Washington Airports and a draft EIS. In discussing a wide range of policy options, from no change to various restrictions on growth, the proposal declared as its purpose "to rationalize the role and use of the two airports (National and Dulles) from an overall transportation viewpoint." The FAA solicited and received comments from the public, members of Congress, federal agencies, state, municipal and local agencies, public organizations, private companies, and interested individuals.

The comments fell into two categories. Local governments and residents argued that the concentration of service at National imposed an unnecessary burden on the airport's neighbors. The airlines and distant cities, on the other hand, argued that National's convenience outweighed the objections.

The FAA, after further public comment, modified its 1978 proposal and issued a supplementary draft EIS and a Notice of Proposed Rulemaking in January 1980. For the first time, FAA mentioned a flat 1000-mile rule as an alternative to the existing policy. Still more comments followed. The House Committee on Public Works and Transportation got into the act and held oversight hearings.

In response, FAA further refined its policy proposal. The final EIS appeared in August 1980. It contained five policy alternatives, essentially variations on a theme. None suggested abandonment of the perimeter rule.

On August 15, 1980, then-Secretary of Transportation Goldschmidt unveiled an amended Metropolitan Washington Airport Policy. 45 Fed. Reg. 62398 (1980). The FAA issued several regulations to implement this policy, which abolished the

650-mile perimeter and its exceptions and replaced it with a flat 1,000-mile perimeter. In support of the new rule, FAA advanced three reasons:

(1) To assure the full utilization of Dulles;

(2) To preserve the short- and medium-haul nature of National; and

(3) To eliminate the inequity that the prior rule, with its exceptions for the grandfathered cities, created.

The new policy also set a ceiling of 17 million passengers per year at National, changed the distribution of slots between certificated air carriers and air taxis, imposed a strict curfew on departures and arrivals at night, removed the restriction on those widebody aircraft that can safely operate on National's short runway, called for a master plan governing physical redevelopment of National, and required Dulles to remain open 24 hours per day with unrestricted access.

We've Only Just Begun

These rules were to take effect on January 5, 1981. Just when it seemed that FAA had taken a giant step for traveling mankind, Congress stepped in and prohibited the FAA from reducing the number of air carrier slots until April 26, 1981. *See* Department of Transportation and Related Agencies Appropriations Act of 1981, Pub. L. 96–400, 94 Stat. 1681 (October 9, 1980). Since the rules formed a package, the FAA chose to defer the effective date of the remainder, including the perimeter rule, to the later date.

On February 27, 1981, the newly-appointed Secretary of Transportation, Drew Lewis, proposed to delay the effective date of the package until October 25, 1981, to enable him thoroughly to reconsider the matter. On July 8, 1981, he issued a new proposal and regulations which superseded the Goldschmidt policy and regulations. Although he made some changes, the Secretary approved the 1,000-mile perimeter restriction. The DOT promulgated new regulations on November 27, 1981, as part of a coherent operating policy for National and Dulles.

As if these rules were not enough, the Secretary, on May 8, 1981, ordered the FAA to promulgate a separate, interim perimeter regulation to maintain the existing 650-mile rule in the face of the decision of three airlines to inaugurate nonstop flights to National from Dallas and Houston, Texas. This interim rule, the Secretary declared, met the "emergency" situation created by the airlines' action. It took effect after only one week's comment period instead of the customary 45 or 60 days.

The Friendly Skies—Filled with Litigants

The City of Houston filed a petition for review (No. 80–2030) of the Goldschmidt perimeter rule on September 22, 1980. American sought review of both the perimeter and the Goldschmidt slot reallocation rules (No. 80–2251). The Air Transport Association of America and Eastern Airlines filed a petition for review of the slot redistribution rule in Unit B of this Court (now the U.S. Court of Appeals for the Eleventh Circuit). New York Air filed a petition for review of the slot reallocation rule in the D.C. Circuit (No. 81–4004).

The May 8, 1981 interim perimeter rule also spawned litigation. On May 20, 1981, Houston and American moved to enjoin issuance of the interim perimeter regulation. We denied their motions by order filed May 27, 1981. Houston then filed a petition for review of the interim perimeter rule (No. 81–4194), which we consolidated with the petitions seeking review of the final perimeter rule. Only the perimeter rules-interim and final-stand in the dock before us.

Scope of Review—

We're the Administrative Agency, Doing What We Do Best

Administrative Procedures Act and Agency Rulemaking

Before we reach cruising altitude, we need, as always, first to delineate the flight plan we must follow. Rulemaking by an administrative agency is governed by the Administrative Procedure Act, 5 U.S.C. § 706(2)(A), which prohibits agency action that is "arbitrary, capricious, an abuse of discretion, or otherwise not in accordance with law" and prescribes proper methods of administrative action. Reviewing courts have taken a radar fix on this amorphous standard on many occasions, but invariably have encountered turbulence during the flight. In general, we review the agency's procedures to ensure reasoned decision-making, but we defer to its expertise in the final analysis. *Citizens to Preserve Overton Park v. Volpe*, 401 U.S. 402, 415 (1971), obliges us "to engage in a substantial inquiry." The agency's decision "is entitled to a presumption of regularity. But that presumption is not to shield (the agency's) action from a thorough, probing, in-depth review.

Rulemaking by an administrative agency is governed by the Administrative Procedure Act, 5 U.S.C. § 706(2)(A), which prohibits agency action that is "arbitrary, capricious, an abuse of discretion, or otherwise not in accordance with law" and prescribes proper methods of administrative action.

We must consider "whether the decision was based on a consideration of the relevant factors and whether there has been a clear error of judgment . . . Although this inquiry into the facts is to be searching and careful, the ultimate standard of review is a narrow one. The court is not empowered to substitute its judgment for that of the agency." The record plays a pivotal role, for "the orderly functioning of the process of review requires that the grounds upon which the administrative agency acted be clearly disclosed and adequately sustained." Yet we "will uphold a decision of less than ideal clarity if the agency's path may reasonably be discerned." *Bowman Transportation v. Arkansas-Best Freight*, 419 U.S. 281, 286 (1974). As we recently concluded,

> (W)e must accord the agency considerable, but not too much deference; it is entitled to exercise its discretion, but only so far and no further; and its decision need not be ideal or even, perhaps, correct so long as not "arbitrary" or "capricious" and so long as the agency gave at least minimal consideration to the relevant facts as contained in the record.

American Petroleum Institute v. EPA, 661 F.2d 340, 349 (5th Cir. 1981).

You Deserve National Attention?

Houston and American label as arbitrary and capricious the FAA's decision administratively to impose a perimeter rule on flights to and from National. We disagree. While the Courts of Appeals have on numerous occasions taken an administrative agency to task for its failure to follow correct procedures or to proffer an acceptable reason for its actions, we find that the FAA and DOT have acted reasonably and in good faith to solve a difficult problem. The agency carefully considered all the factors and arrived at a reasonable judgment. In no way do the rules before us constitute arbitrary and capricious agency action. The enormous record in this case bolsters the decision, and the arguments of Houston and American, although sincere and not without merit, do not convince us to the contrary.

Houston and American contend that no rational basis connects the FAA's goals—to protect Dulles and to preserve the short-haul status of National—to the means it has adopted. This argument ignores reality and, in the process, misreads the factual record. Having traveled through these two airports, we may take judicial notice of their problems of under- and over-use. The FAA's actions, while not the only way of treating these problems, fall well within the APA's radar scope for agency action.

A perimeter rule, Houston and American allege, will not protect Dulles. Moreover, there is no showing that Dulles needs protection. They are wrong on both counts. As counsel for the FAA pointed out at oral argument, one could shoot off a cannon in the Dulles terminal at midday without a chance in the world of hitting anyone. Except for the hours from 4:00 to 8:00 p. m., when the complement of West Coast nonstop and international flights arrive and depart, Dulles is deserted. In those same hours, National is saturated with passengers. Dulles needs help, which the perimeter rule, by preventing the further concentration of flights at National, can provide.

We point out what Houston and American conveniently ignore, that Dulles since 1967 has depended upon a perimeter rule of some sort at National. Already empty for much of the day with a rule, Dulles might, if we invalidate the perimeter, cease to exist. Carriers would schedule nonstop flights from National to Denver, Dallas and Houston. The shift would leave Dulles with only the California and Seattle nonstops, which employ aircraft that cannot land on National's short runway, and the international trade. That small amount of traffic, contrary to petitioners' predictions, would not prove adequate to sustain the airport. Their zeal for overturning these regulations confirms the FAA's view that "as long as carriers are able to increase the number of passengers carried at National, they will continue to do so." 45 Fed. Reg. at 62399.

Houston and American suggest that since the FAA has imposed a ceiling on the number of flights per day at National, the lifting of the perimeter rule would allow the market to determine the level of service. Even if true, that redistribution would not necessarily serve the public interest. The airlines, having only so many slots at their disposal, would drop service to Podunk in place of the more profitable, longer-haul markets.

> As long as carriers are able to increase the number of passengers carried
> at National, they will continue to do so. It has been to their advantage
> to shift longer haul flights formerly scheduled at Dulles to National, at
> the expense of shorter haul markets traditionally served there.

Metropolitan Washington Airports Policy, *Final EIS*, August 1980, at 5. That course not only undercuts National's short-haul status, but it reduces the level and quality of service to smaller towns in our nation, which the FAA and CAB are sworn to uphold.

In the same breath, Houston and American retort that the FAA could always increase the number of slots to protect the commuter and short-haul flights. Yet that idea puts us back where we started. The FAA wants to decrease traffic at National, not increase it. For the same reasons that international traffic in New York centers at John F. Kennedy Airport, it makes sense to the FAA that one Washington airport handle the volume of nonstop traffic to the distant cities.

The Long and Short Haul of It

Next, Houston and American insist that National "has not been, is not and will not be" a short-haul airport. They correctly point out that National serves as many, if not more, of the long-haul cities as does Dulles, e.g., San Francisco, Los Angeles, Seattle, Portland, Las Vegas, Denver. See Official Airline Guide, North American Edition (June 1, 1982). Yet their argument ignores the very point at issue. Those flights must stop somewhere less than 1000 miles from National. No one has ever attempted completely to bar travelers from distant cities from flying to National Airport. Such an attempt might well give rise to a constitutional claim. Rather, the perimeter rule gives travelers a choice. Those who prefer nonstop service may use Dulles; those who do not mind a stopover in Chicago, Atlanta, St. Louis, Memphis, Pittsburgh, New Orleans, or Charlotte, may take a slightly lengthier trip and arrive at or depart from National. Whether they simply stop over or must change planes, the passengers who elect that alternative do leave from or arrive at National on a short-haul flight. The ultimate destination on the ticket cannot change that fact.

The rule comports with common sense. We propose the following example by way of illustration. A New Yorker with business in Washington will make the 53-minute flight in the morning, have a full day to transact his business, and still return home by evening. He carries with him nothing but a briefcase. By contrast, a business traveler from Houston who leaves at 7:00 a. m. does not arrive in the Washington area until 11:48 a.m. If he seeks to return home the same day, he has only the afternoon in which to complete his affairs. If, as seems more likely, he plans to stay overnight, he will carry baggage. Such luggage-laden travelers are precisely those who make National congested. They have less need of National's convenience to downtown than the one-day, arrive-and-return traveler whom we have described. The FAA's determination to reserve National for the short-haul passenger finds ample support in the practicalities of air travel.

A Modest Alternative

Houston generously proposes an alternative perimeter rule. Acting, apparently, on the theory that a perimeter rule is arbitrary, capricious, irrational, and unconstitutional if it excludes Houston but hunky-dory if not, Houston suggests that the FAA promulgate a 1,500-mile rule. That distance coincides with the approximate range of those jets currently serving National and, curiously enough, embraces Houston.

The FAA could have selected such a perimeter, just as it could have continued the status quo or closed National altogether, but it chose not to do so.

As it conceded, "The resultant policy is not likely to be acceptable to all factions, but it represents the (DOT's) views of the proper role and best use of these two airports in the public interest." Ours is not to reason why, ours is but to uphold the agency's decision if not arbitrary and capricious. Houston's suggestion finds even less support in logic or tradition than the FAA's rule. While the 1,000-mile rule at least possesses the virtue of continuity, the Houston proposal would bind National, a few years down the runway, to the traveling range of outdated aircraft. One might as well limit the perimeter to the range of the Wright Flyer.

The FAA has produced copious reasons for its choice. The various drafts of the EIS run several hundred pages, accompanied by exhibits and tables covering every possible alternative for National and Dulles. The EIS points to the problems that currently plague National-overcrowded parking lots and aircraft aprons, insufficient counterspace, traffic congestion, too little baggage claim area, harsh environmental effects on the airport's neighbors-and convincingly shows that, in the absence of a perimeter rule, National would absorb long-distance flights over and above its already overcrowded capacity, while Dulles would wither on the vine. The agency defends its choice of a 1,000-mile perimeter on the basis that it preserves the *status quo* but relieves the inequity that the 650-mile rule with its exceptions created.

As Justice Holmes once remarked,

> When a legal distinction is determined, as no one doubts that it may be, between night and day, childhood and maturity, or any other extremes, a point has to be fixed or a line has to be drawn, or gradually picked out by successive decisions, to mark where the change takes place. Looked at by itself, without regard to the necessity behind it, the line or point seems arbitrary. It might as well, or nearly as well, be a little more to one side or the other. But when it is seen that a line or point there must be, and that there is no mathematical or logical way of fixing it precisely, the decision of the legislature must be accepted unless we can say that it is very wide of any reasonable mark.

Louisville Gas & Electric Co. v. Coleman, 277 U.S. 32, 41, 48 (1928) (Holmes, J., dissenting). The FAA's line is not "very wide of any reasonable mark." Our "thorough, probing, in-depth review," obliges us to uphold the FAA's decision.

Who's In Charge Here?

Even if it did not act arbitrarily and capriciously, the FAA, say American and Houston, lacked the statutory authority to impose a perimeter restriction. That argument fails to make it off the ground. The Federal Aviation Act and the FAA's status as proprietor of National and Dulles provide independent support for its decision.

Curiously enough, the FAA has never grounded its decision on safety concerns. Rather, it asserts its rights as the proprietor of the two airports. Analogizing to the right of a store owner to run his business, FAA acted to manage, as best it could, the great and increasing volume of air traffic in the Washington area.

At the outset, we dispense with the claim that § 105 of the Federal Aviation Act, 49 U.S.C. § 1301 *et seq.*, bars the FAA from taking the actions it did. Section 105 of the Act, 49 U.S.C. § 1305, entitled Federal preemption, delineates the powers of airport proprietors. It reserves for the federal authorities control over "rates, routes or services of any (interstate) air carrier." Yet the statute also specifies that it deals with "the authority of any State or political subdivision thereof or any interstate agency or other political agency of two or more States as the owner or operator of an airport." The FAA does not fit within that definition. Nothing could be more certain than that the restrictions of § 1305 do not bind the FAA, an arm of the federal government which just happens to own two airports.

While it is true that Congress had reserved an extremely limited role for airport proprietors in our system of aviation management," the FAA is not the typical airport proprietor. To avoid interference with the preeminent authority of the federal government in the field of aviation, Congress, in § 1305, sought to prevent the proprietor of a rural airstrip from infringing upon the federal government's turf.

While it is true that "Congress had reserved (an) extremely limited role . . . for airport proprietors in our system of aviation management," *British Airways Board v. Port Authority of New York and New Jersey*, 564 F.2d 1002, 1010 (2nd Cir. 1977), the FAA is not the typical airport proprietor. Why did Congress specify such a limited role? To avoid interference with the preeminent authority of the federal government in the field of aviation, Congress, in § 1305, sought to prevent the proprietor of a rural airstrip from infringing upon the federal government's turf. FAA obviously plays a different role. Houston and American claim, in effect, that the FAA may not take certain actions for fear of interfering with itself. The argument reduces to tautological gibberish.

Houston and American call attention to the FAA's actions in seeking an injunction against the John Wayne Airport ("JWA") in Orange County, California. JWA imposed a perimeter on flights from more than 500 miles away. The FAA intervened, arguing that the airport exceeded its proprietary authority. The District Court agreed and granted the injunction. *Pacific Southwest Airlines v. County of Orange*, No. CV 81–3248 (C.D. Cal. Nov. 30, 1981).

The JWA affair does not undercut the FAA's actions. A local airport with no connection to nearby Los Angeles International or Ontario Airports, JWA could not blithely take such an action upon itself. Section 1305 removes control over routes, etc., from local airport proprietors. Petitioners again miss the key question, that is, whether the FAA is governed by the same rules as a local proprietor. The answer, obviously, is no.

Even if proprietary interest cannot legitimate its decision, the Federal Aviation Act grants the FAA the power to impose a perimeter. Section 1303 provides:

> In the exercise and performance of his powers and duties under this Act the (Secretary of Transportation) shall consider the following, among other things, as being in the public interest:
>
> (c)   The control of the use of the navigable airspace of the United States and the regulation of both civil and military operations in such airspace in the interest of the safety and efficiency of both.

Section 1348(a) of the Act states:

> The (Secretary) is authorized and directed to develop plans for and formulate policy with respect to the use of the navigable airspace; and assign by rule, regulation, or order the use of the navigable airspace under such terms, conditions, and limitations as he may deem necessary in order to insure the safety of aircraft and the efficient utilization of such airspace.

In a similar vein, § 1353(a) declares:

> The (Secretary) is directed to make long range plans for and formulate policy with respect to the orderly development and use of the navigable airspace, and the orderly development and location of landing areas. . . .

To top it off, § 1354(a) provides:

> The (Secretary) is empowered to perform such acts, to conduct such investigations, to issue and amend such general or special rules, regulations, and procedures, pursuant to and consistent with the provisions of this Act, as he shall deem necessary to carry out the

provisions of, and to exercise and perform his powers and duties under, this Act.

The terms of the Act clothe the FAA with authority to formulate policy for the efficient use of navigable airspace and landing areas. Without engaging in a word by word definition of those terms, we find these sections support the FAA's actions. Section 1354(a), finally, grants the Secretary the power to effectuate such policies.

We cannot, consistent with common sense, read these sections in any other way. The navigable airspace is of surprisingly little use if a plane cannot land or take off. To promote its "efficient utilization", the FAA must have the power to make rules and regulations governing not only the corridors of air traffic, but the use of airports as well. The perimeter rules help to accomplish that goal in the Washington area: by setting up an orderly plan for the development of National and Dulles, they aid in the efficient use of now-crowded airspace.

Houston and American refer us to provisions of the D.C. Code which govern such critical aspects of airport operation as the lost and found desk or water fountains. They cannot seriously contend that such powers, although important in their own way, constitute the outer limits of an airport proprietor's authority. The Federal Aviation Act is our handbook, and it ordains that the FAA may take whatever steps it considers necessary to carry out its statutory responsibilities.

Houston suggests that in the absence of statutory authority, the perimeter rule requires an "explicit grant of authority by Congress". We have already found that the Federal Aviation Act authorizes the rule. Even if the Act did not reach so far, however, Congress has stepped into the breach. In the Department of Transportation and Related Agencies Appropriations Act, *supra*, Congress froze the number of air carrier operations at National. The legislative record makes clear that Congress did not intend to hold up any of the other aspects of the Metropolitan Washington Airports Policy. Congressman Duncan, the Chairman of the House Committee, stated,

> In delaying the reduction of hourly slots, it was not our intention to disapprove or negate the overall Washington National Airport policy or to delay the balance of the plan. . . . It is not the intent of the conferees to interfere with whatever ultimate responsibility and authority the FAA may have for the orderly management of traffic at Washington National Airport. . . .

126 Cong. Rec. H 10049 (daily ed. Sept. 30, 1980) (statement of Rep. Duncan). The Senate Report on the bill confers that body's blessing as well. It states:

The Committee is pleased to see the FAA adopt a final metropolitan Washington airports policy regarding the operations of Washington National and Dulles International Airports. The Committee has raised no objections to the proposed changes in operating procedures at Washington National.... The Committee expects prompt implementation of this policy through the issuance of appropriate Federal regulations.

An obvious imbalance exists in the utilization of the three major airports serving the Baltimore-Washington metropolitan area. While on the one hand we have a gross underutilization of two large international airports, we find that on the other hand, National Airport absorbs approximately as much traffic as the other two combined. Although it is difficult to achieve a balance in addressing this problem, the Committee feels that the *FAA's recent announcement of a metropolitan Washington airports policy is a step in the right direction.*

S. Rep. No. 96–932, 96th Cong., 2d Sess. 27 (1980) (emphasis added).

Congress, whose members frequent the Washington area airports, knew of the FAA's actions in restricting service at National. These excerpts from the legislative record demonstrate that Congress in effect ratified that policy. "(A) consistent administrative interpretation of a statute, shown clearly to have been brought to the attention of Congress and not changed by it, is almost conclusive evidence that the interpretation has Congressional approval." *Kay v. FCC*, 443 F.2d 638, 646–47 (D.C. Cir. 1970). Thus, even if the FAA's action necessitated Congressional support, which it did not, Congress concurred in the agency's decision.

Authority, Authority, Who's Got the Authority?

In a last gasp objection, American and Houston protest that the CAB rather than the FAA bears the responsibility for economic regulation of aviation. Obviously they have not read the newspapers. For all intents and purposes, the CAB has folded its wings and gone into retirement. The Airline Deregulation Act of 1978 mandated a significant reduction in the governmental regulation of the airlines, and the CAB obediently has committed regulatory suicide. Surely someone must have the responsibility for National and Dulles airport. The CAB had it, but it has lost it. *See House Committee on Public Works & Transportation, Legislative History of the Airline Deregulation Act of 1978* (Comm. Print 1978). With the CAB off the radar scope, only the FAA-under the terms of the Federal Aviation Act-can assume such responsibility.

We find that the FAA, acting in its proprietary capacity as the owner/ operator of National and Dulles, had express authority under the Federal Aviation Act to promulgate reasonable regulations concerning the efficient use of the navigable airspace. The perimeter rule falls within its grasp as a means of promoting such efficiency. Since we have held, *supra*, that the rule does not violate the APA, it follows that we must deny the petitions for review.

We find that the FAA, acting in its proprietary capacity as the owner/operator of National and Dulles, had express authority under the Federal Aviation Act to promulgate reasonable regulations concerning the efficient use of the navigable airspace. The perimeter rule falls within its grasp as a means of promoting such efficiency.

Have Perimeter Rule, Will Travel

Houston and American finally make the unlikely contention that the perimeter rule violates passengers' constitutional right to travel. While one could search forever for a clause explicitly conferring such a right and never discover one, the Supreme Court, in *Shapiro v. Thompson*, 394 U.S. 618 (1969), did find such a guarantee. The Justices struck down a residency requirement for welfare recipients on the ground that it violated the constitutional right to travel freely from state to state.

> (T)he purpose of inhibiting migration by needy persons into the state is constitutionally impermissible. This Court long ago recognized that the nature of our Federal Union and our constitutional concepts of personal liberty unite to require that all citizens be free to travel throughout the length and breadth of our land uninhibited by statutes, rules or regulations which unreasonably burden or restrict this movement.

Justice Brennan's opinion rested on the right of poor persons to migrate to another state in search of a better life. Residency requirements that might hinder such movement could not survive constitutional challenge. We have here no such claim. Neither Houston nor American suggests, nor could they, that the perimeter rule operates as a residency requirement to deny persons their constitutional right to travel. At most, their argument reduces to the feeble claim that passengers have a constitutional right to the most convenient form of travel. That notion, as any experienced traveler can attest, finds no support whatsoever in *Shapiro* or in the airlines' own schedules.

Final Approach

As we line up for our final approach, we glance back over the route we have taken. The FAA's perimeter rule for National Airport, we hold, rests on an adequate factual and statutory basis and does not violate the terms of the APA. We uphold the agency's actions and deny the petitions for review.

EXERCISE 1-6. *HOUSTON V. FED. AVIATION ADMIN.*—AIRPORT FLIGHT RESTRICTIONS

1. The *Houston v. Fed. Aviation Admin.* court described the FAA as "like any prudent entrepreneur, seek[ing] to increase business." Is the promotion of aviation commerce—in addition to safety—a part of the FAA's agency mission? *See* https://www.faa.gov/about/mission/. Should it be? Or, would that pose a conflict of interest? Explain.

2. Describe the "perimeter rule" created by the Department of Transportation in 1981, including a summary of its development. Also, discuss what powers does the FAA have under the Federal Aviation Act with respect to airport operations?

3. Explain how the Administrative Procedures Act ("APA") constrains agency action in legal proceedings, focusing on these elements:

    a. What type of agency action is prohibited under the APA?

    b. What is the standard by which a court reviews agency procedures?

    c. What presumptions do courts make under the APA with respect to agency decision-making?

    d. How much deference are federal agencies such as the DOT owed by courts?

4. What are the main arguments of the City of Houston and American Airlines with respect to the administrative imposition of a perimeter rule? Is the court persuaded by these positions? Explain.

5. Did the perimeter rule violate the constitutional right of airline passengers to travel? What did the court say? Explain your agreement or disagreement.

NOTES ON *HOUSTON V. FED. AVIATION ADMIN.*—LEGISLATIVE RESTRICTIONS ON AIR TRAVEL

1. *Wright Amendment.*

The "perimeter rule" established in *Houston v. Fed. Aviation Admin.*—prohibiting airlines from operating nonstop flights between National Airport (now known as Reagan National Airport) in Washington, D.C.—is striking in that it impacted the right to travel not for operational or safety purposes but for traffic control. The Wright Amendment is another example of 1970s-era airport traffic diversion law, but for economic development purposes.

The 1979-law governed air traffic at Dallas Love Field. It restricted the number of non-stop flights airlines could fly from Love Field to destinations within Texas and neighboring states. It did so to encourage airlines flying in and out of Love Field to shift their operations to the then-new Dallas-Ft. Worth International Airport ("DFW"). Southwest Airlines refused to move to DFW or sign a related use agreement and litigation ensued to force Southwest from Love Field.

Southwest won. The Fifth Circuit Court of Appeals concluded that, "Southwest Airlines Co. has a federally declared right to the continued use of and access to Love Field, so long as Love Field remains open." *Southwest Airlines Co. v. Texas Int'l Airlines, Inc.*, 546 F.2d 84, 103 (5th Cir. 1977). *See also American Airlines v. Dep't of Transp.*, 202 F.3d 788 (5th Cir. 2000); *Legend Airlines, Inc. v. City of Fort Worth*, 23 S.W.3d 83 (Tx. Ct. App. 2000). The Wright Amendment was repealed in 2014, six years after an agreement among American Airlines, Southwest Airlines, and the Cities of Dallas and Ft. Worth to end the law.

Southwest Airlines founder (and lawyer) Herbert D. Kelleher—used the litigation to fuel the airline's narrative as the proverbial little guy in a veritable David-versus-Goliath battle for the right to fly. *See generally* KEVIN FREIBERG & JACKIE FRIEBERG, NUTS! SOUTHWEST AIRLINES' CRAZY RECIPE FOR BUSINESS AND PERSONAL SUCCESS 10 (Broadway Books 1996) ("The people of Southwest Airlines are crusaders with an egalitarian spirit who truly believe they are in the business of freedom."). That said, even Kelleher noted that, "[t]he Wright Amendment is a pain in the ass, but not every pain in the ass is a constitutional infringement." *See also* John Grantham, *A Free Bird Sings the Song of the Caged: Southwest Airlines' Fight to Repeal the Wright Amendment*, 72 J. AIR L. & COM. 429 (2007); Robert B. Gilbreath & Paul C. Watler, *Perimeter Rules, Proprietary Powers, and the Airline Deregulation Act: A Tale of Two Cities . . . and Two Airports*, 66 J. AIR L. & COM. 223 (2000).

2. ***Taxes and the Right to Travel.***

Taxes can be a significant burden on aviation interests and may potentially interfere with the fundamental right to travel to an unacceptable extent. For example, in *Evansville-Vanderburgh Airport Authority Dist. v. Delta Airlines, Inc.*, 405 U.S. 707 (1972), the Supreme Court of the United States held that the Commerce Clause does not prohibit states or municipalities from charging commercial airlines a "head tax" on passengers boarding flights at airports within their jurisdiction, to defray the costs of airport construction and maintenance: "At least so long as the toll is based on some fair approximation of use or privilege for use, . . . and is neither discriminatory against interstate commerce nor excessive in comparison with the governmental benefit conferred, it will pass constitutional muster, even though some other formula might reflect more exactly the relative use of the state facilities by individual users."

Congress enacted the Anti-Head Tax Act ("AHTA") to address a concern that the Evansville-Vanderburgh Airport Authority Dist. case would prompt a proliferation of local taxes burdensome to interstate air transportation. *See Aloha Airlines, Inc. v. Director of Taxation of Haw.*, 460 U.S. 1078 (1983) ("The head tax . . . cuts against the grain of the traditional American right to travel among the States."). *See also* S. Rep. No. 93–12, p. 4 (1973) (Congress intended AHTA to "ensure . . . that local 'head' taxes will not be permitted to inhibit the flow of interstate commerce."). *See, e.g., Northwest Airlines, Inc. v. County of Kent, Michigan*, 510 U.S. 355 (1994) (evaluating the claim of seven commercial airlines that certain airport user fees charged to them were unreasonable and discriminatory in violation of the AHTA and the Commerce Clause). For further discussion of the taxation of aviation commerce see generally *Wardair Canada Inc. v. Florida Dep't of Revenue*, 477 U.S. 1 (1986) and *Massachusetts v. United States*, 435 U.S. 444 (1978).

For further discussion of taxes of aviation operations see generally Anthony Ryan, *How Airline Security Fees in a Post September 11, 2001 Environment are Spiraling Out of Control*, 29 TRANSP. L.J. 253 (2002); Carolyn P. Meade, Note, *Aviation Taxes: Can We Leave FAA Funding on Auto-Pilot?*, 20 VA. TAX. REV. 191 (2000).

Suggested Further Reading

Lindsay Ray Altmeyer, *Freedom to Fly: An Analysis of the Constitutional Right to Air Travel*, 80 J. AIR L. & COM. 719 (2015)

Richard Sobel, *The Right to Travel and Privacy: Intersecting Fundamental Freedoms*, 30 J. INFO. TECH. & PRIVACY L. 639 (2014)

Kathryn E. Wilhelm, *Freedom of Movement at a Standstill? Toward the Establishment of a Fundamental Right to Intrastate Travel*, 90 B.U. L. Rev. 2461 (2010)

Gregory B. Hartch, *Wrong Turns: A Critique of the Supreme Court's Right to Travel Cases*, 21 WM. MITCHELL L. REV. 457 (1995)

Tracy Maclin, *The Decline of the Right of Locomotion: The Fourth Amendment on* the *Streets*, 75 CORNELL L. REV. 1258 (1990)

Note, *State Parochialism, and Right to Travel, and the Privileges and Immunities Clause of Article IV*, 41 STAN. L. REV. 1557 (1989)

CHAPTER 2

Airspace

NOTAM 4/3646

FLIGHT RESTRICTIONS IN THIS NOTAM COMPLY WITH STATUTORY MANDATES DETAILED IN SECTION 352 OF PUBLIC LAW 108–7 AS AMENDED BY SECTION 521 OF PUBLIC LAW 108–199. PURSUANT TO 49 USC 40103(B), THE FEDERAL AVIATION ADMINISTRATION (FAA) CLASSIFIES THE AIRSPACE DEFINED IN THIS NOTAM AS 'NATIONAL DEFENSE AIRSPACE'.

Notice to Airmen ("NOTAM"): Orlando, Florida

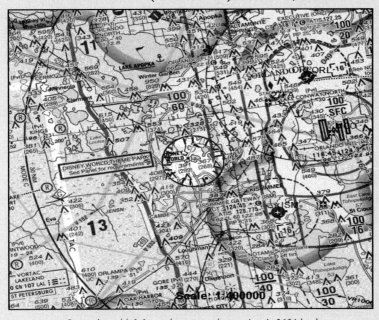

Source: https://tfr.faa.gov/save_pages/sect_print_4_3634.html

ANY PERSON WHO KNOWINGLY OR WILLFULLY VIOLATES THE RULES PERTAINING TO OPERATIONS IN THIS AIRSPACE MAY BE SUBJECT TO CERTAIN CRIMINAL PENALTIES UNDER 49 USC 46307. PILOTS WHO DO NOT ADHERE TO THE FOLLOWING PROCEDURES MAY BE INTERCEPTED, DETAINED AND INTERVIEWED BY LAW ENFORCEMENT/SECURITY PERSONNEL. PURSUANT TO 14 CFR SECTION 99.7, SPECIAL SECURITY INSTRUCTIONS; ALL AIRCRAFT FLIGHT OPERATIONS, INCLUDING UNMANNED AND REMOTE CONTROLLED AIRCRAFT, ARE PROHIBITED WITHIN A 3 NMR OF 282445N/0813420W OR THE ORL238014.8 UP TO AND INCLUDING 3000FT AGL. 1410271500-PERM THE RESTRICTIONS DO NOT APPLY TO THOSE AIRCRAFT AUTHORIZED BY AND IN CONTACT WITH ATC FOR OPERATIONAL OR SAFETY OF FLIGHT PURPOSES, DEPARTMENT OF DEFENSE, LAW ENFORCEMENT, AND AIR AMBULANCE FLIGHT OPERATIONS. FLIGHTS CONDUCTED FOR OPERATIONAL PURPOSES OF ANY DISNEY WORLD EVENT AND VENUE ARE AUTHORIZED WITH AN APPROVED WAIVER. AN FAA AIRSPACE WAIVER DOES NOT RELIEVE OPERATORS FROM OBTAINING ALL OTHER NECESSARY AUTHORIZATIONS AND COMPLYING WITH ALL APPLICABLE FEDERAL AVIATION REGULATIONS. ALL PREVIOUSLY ISSUED WAIVERS TO FDC NOTAM 4/4985 REMAIN VALID UNTIL THE SPECIFIED END DATE BUT NOT TO EXCEED 90 DAYS FOLLOWING THE EFFECTIVE DATE OF THIS NOTAM. INFORMATION ABOUT AIRSPACE WAIVER APPLICATIONS AND TSA SECURITY AUTHORIZATIONS CAN BE FOUND AT HTTP://WWW.TSA.GOV/ STAKEHOLDERS/AIRSPACE-WAIVERS-0 OR BY CALLING TSA AT 571-227-2071. SUBMIT REQUESTS FOR FAA AIRSPACE WAIVERS AT HTTPS://WAIVERS. FAA.GOV.

A. OVERVIEW

The illustration above is from a "sectional," an aeronautical chart or map intended for navigational purposes. It is accompanied by a NOTAM—Notice to Airman—alerting pilots and air traffic controllers that flight in the airspace over Walt Disney World in Orlando, Florida is prohibited. (See the center of the image.) Other similar types of prohibited airspace exist over the White House, government buildings, and so forth. Such prohibitions are permanent compared to "TFRs"—"Temporary Flight Restrictions," through which aviation regulators restrict the use of air space over temporary events like the Super Bowl or a presidential motorcade. *See* NBAA, *Temporary Flight Restrictions,* https://nbaa.org/aircraft-operations/airspace/alerts/notams-and-tfrs/temporary-flight-restrictions/. Altogether, these type of flight limitations reflect the fact that the local, state, and national airspace is not as free and open as it looks, but strictly delimited and controlled by regulatory authorities.

This is so internationally, too. Flying from Los Angeles to Tokyo, or Paris to London, is easy to take for granted given the extent of international travel today. But, the right to travel from one "state" to another is informed by serious political and national security considerations. The existential danger presented by modern intercontinental ballistic missiles (and even outer space weapons), and the wars of the Twentieth Century, make clear why nations worry about who can intercept their airspace. In fact, in the aftermath of World War II, delegates from around the world convened the Convention on International Civil Aviation, among other things, to discuss whether and how to permit the airplanes of one nation to fly over foreign states. Also known as the Chicago Convention, this Convention established the International Civil Aviation Organization ("ICAO"), a specialized arm of the United Nations charged with developing unified rules for airspace management. The modern representation of its work is embodied in *Annex 11 to the Convention on International Civil Aviation,* which makes possible global air travel today.

Thanks to the Chicago Convention, numerous air routes exist today between almost every nation on earth. But, significant airspace restrictions continue to exist. For example, Israel and Saudi Arabia do not have diplomatic relations and that reality has impacted air travel globally. As a result, flying between New Delhi, India and Tel Aviv, Israel took longer than necessary—as long as nine hours because planes were routed over the Arabian Sea, flying west over the Horn of Africa to avoid Saudi Arabia and north across the Red Sea to reach Israel. That changed in March 2018 when a commercial airliner flying to Tel Aviv crossed through the skies of Saudi Arabia for the first time, ending an era during which Arab states prevented a direct route because of political tensions with Israel. *See* Jonathan Ferziger, *An Israel-Bound Commercial Flight Passes Through Saudi Airspace for First Time*, SKIFT, Mar. 23, 2018. (Saudi Arabia's maintains its ban on Israeli planes flying over its territory and El Al Israel Airlines has appealed to ICAO, alleging that it suffers discriminatory treatment compared to Air India. *Id.*) Meanwhile, in 2017, Bahrain, Egypt, Saudi Arabia, and the United Arab Emirates closed their respective airspaces to Qatari-owned Qatar Airlines on the basis of alleged support by Qatar of terrorist groups in the region. *See generally The "Aeropolitics" of the Qatar Blockade Present New Challenges*, MIDDLE EAST MONITORS, March, 25, 2019, https://www.middleeastmonitor.com/20190325-the-aeropolitics-of-the-qatar-blockade-present-new-challenges/.

In the foregoing context, this chapter centers on the intersection of aviation and property law, where property law means not only ground-based rights, but the bundle of legal rights and privileges attendant to the ownership of and use of airspace. (*See also* Chapter 11, Airports.) It does so by focusing on cases within the United States, whose legislative, executive, and judicial formulation of airspace use and ownership influences and is influenced by international conceptions of airspace use and ownership internationally.

Whether considered from a domestic or international perspective, the issues are largely the same. Land, like the sky (and even some aspects of outer space), is a limited and finite resource, casting doubt on the phrase "the sky knows no limits." Consequently, tribunals are frequently called on to resolve conflicts between parties with respect to the ownership and use of land for aviation and non-aeronautical purposes, on the one hand, and between stakeholders on the ground and users of the national and international airspace, on the other hand. Consider:

- *NIMBY—"Not in My Back Yard."* The development of a federally-funded airport may benefit a community with new jobs or improved access to other cities around the nation and world, yet residents may oppose the project on the ground that airport operations generate noise or traffic. Should the project proceed? *See* Eli Dourado & Raymond Russell, *Airport Noise NIMBYism: An Empirical Investigation*, MERCATUS ON POLICY (2016).

- *NAMBY—"Not Above My Back Yard."* Imagine that an aviation enthusiast flies his hobby drone (equipped with a high definition camera) above his neighbor's property, potentially giving rise to state law claims for trespass or invasion of privacy. The law may recognize the claim if the drone was flying at or below 200 feet above the property, but not 500 feet or higher. Should the aggrieved homeowner be allowed to shoot the drone down with a shotgun? In any case, who controls the airspace in the "gray area" between 200 and 500 feet above ground level? *See, e.g., Boggs v. Merideth,* 2017 WL 1088093 (W.D. Ky. 2017). *See also* Annie Sneed, *So Your Neighbor Got a Drone for Christmas,* SCIENTIFIC AMERICAN, Dec. 22, 2015.

These scenarios illustrate the basic challenge before lawmakers and judges to balance ground-based rights and privileges against other ground-based rights and privileges, or alternatively, between ground-based rights and privileges against the rights and privileges corresponding to the ownership and use of airplanes in the sky. This chapter addresses both of these theoretical and existing tensions and broadly aims to show how the law has evolved to manage the impact aviation and aviation infrastructure have had (and continue to have) on traditional conceptions of property law.

It begins with the nineteenth century case of *Guille v. Swan,* 19 Johns. 381 (N.Y. Sup. Ct. 1822), which was one of the first cases requiring lawmakers to balance manned activities in the airspace with the rights of property owners below, for example. There, the operator of an air balloon crash-landed into a private garden in New York. "When the balloon descended [the balloonist called for assistance and] more than two hundred persons broke into [the] garden through the fences, and came onto the premises [to his rescue], beating down [the garden's] vegetables and flowers." The landowner sued for damages and won, convincing the court that the balloonist was liable because the damages caused by his trespass were foreseeable as a matter of law:

> Ascending in a balloon is not an unlawful act . . .; but, it is certain, that the aeronaut has no control over its motion horizontally; he is at the sport of the winds and is to descend when and how he can; his reaching the earth is a matter of hazard. He did descend on the premises of the plaintiff below, at a short distance from the place where he ascended. Now, if his descent, under such circumstances, would, ordinarily and naturally, draw a crowd of people about him, either from curiosity, or for the purpose of rescuing him from a perilous situation; all this he ought to have foreseen, and must be responsible for.

Guille reflected an early view of aviation as an "ultra-hazardous" activity for which balloon and airplane owners, operators, and manufacturers were strictly liable. (See Chapter 12, Accident Litigation, for further discussion of the liability standards historically and currently applicable to aviation operations.) *Guile* thus imposed legal responsibility and liability on aviators while relaxing the legal burden on landowners to prove fault. More than 100 years after *Guile*, however, courts moved in a different direction, promoting airplane operations in the national airspace and imposing a greater burden of proof on private landowners to obtain a legal remedy where aviation operations conflicted with the use and enjoyment of their land.

Indeed, historically landowners benefitted from the ancient doctrine *cujus est solum ejus usque ad coelom*—"whoever owns the soil, it is theirs up to Heaven." This doctrine was long a part of the American common law. But, in the 1940s lawmakers abandoned the idea that ownership of land extended to the periphery of the universe. Specifically, in *United States v. Causby*, 328 U.S. 256 (1948), the Supreme Court reasoned that this expansive view of property rights above the ground was incompatible with modern airplane travel. To hold otherwise, the court noted, would lead to an unworkable legal regime:

> It is ancient doctrine that at common law ownership of the land extended to the periphery of the universe—*Cujus est solum ejus est usque ad coelum*. But that doctrine has no place in the modern world. The air is a public highway, as Congress has declared. Were that not true, every transcontinental flight would subject the operator to countless trespass suits. Common sense revolts at the idea. To recognize such private claims to the airspace would clog these highways, seriously interfere with their control and development in the public interest, and transfer into private ownership that to which only the public has a just claim.

Supported by this and other precedent, regulators have segmented the national airspace system ("NAS") into different areas in which different types of operations are allowed or disallowed, in much the same manner as city or urban planners design space for pedestrian, bicycle, and/or and vehicular traffic on sidewalks, rural roads, and highways.

For example, FAA regulations define minimum safe operating altitudes for different kinds of aircraft that operate in the so-called highways in the sky. Other than for takeoff and landing, fixed-wing aircraft must fly at an altitude that allows its operators to conduct an emergency landing "without undue hazard to persons or property on the surface." 14 C.F.R. 91.119(a). Over congested areas, aircraft must operate at least "1,000 feet above the highest obstacle within a horizontal radius of 2,000 feet of the aircraft." 14 C.F.R. 91.119(b). Regulations further reduce this altitude to "500 feet above the surface" over non-congested areas. 14 C.F.R. § 91.119(c). In contrast to fixed-wing aircraft, a helicopter may be flown below the minimum safe altitudes prescribed for fixed-wing aircraft if operated "without hazard to person or property on the surface." 14 C.F.R. 91.119(d).

Innovations in *unmanned* aviation, including the exponential rise in ownership and use of "drones" and the potential of urban air transport (think Uber in the sky), are stretching these rules in new directions, pitting new technologies against long-standing legal principles. New technologies likely will require new thinking about whether airports are necessary and how airspace is designed. But, for the time being, airspace is divided into two categories: *regulatory* airspace (*i.e.*, Class A, B, C, D and E airspace areas, restricted and prohibited areas) and *non-regulatory* airspace (military operations areas ("MOAs"), warning areas, alert areas, and controlled firing areas). Within these two categories, there are four types of airspace or airspace areas: controlled, uncontrolled, special use, and other airspace, extending to outer space (flight level 60,000 feet ("FL 600")), illustrated as follows:

Illustration 2-1. FAA Airspace Classes

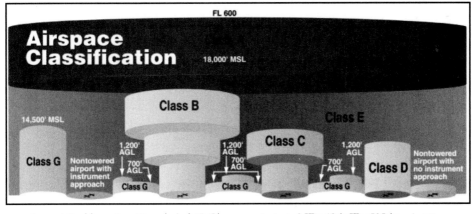

Source: https://www.faasafety.gov/gslac/ALC/course_content.aspx?cID=42&sID=505&preview=true.

In all, the cases in this chapter introduce the seminal legal authorities respecting the ownership and use of airspace. It proceeds chronologically, beginning with the 1820s, when airplane travel was still an exotic concept, to the present, when drones represent a major disruption of more settled principles involving airspace.

This chapter also features both domestic and international dimensions of airspace with a focus on air rights in the United States and abroad. Note 3 following the *United States v. Causby* case is particularly important in this context as it sets out the international understanding of airspace use internationally under the Chicago Convention of 1944.

In reading these materials, consider how advances in aviation—in the air and on the ground—altered and are reconfiguring property law. Today, a world without airports and airplanes is unimaginable. But over the next decade regulators and jurists must be able to imagine lasting answers to the question of where the newest airplanes like drones can fly or where ride-sharing services can occur. The precedents below are a useful starting point.

B. AIRSPACE

GUILLE V. SWAN

19 Johns. 381 (N.Y. Sup. Ct. 1822)

In error, *on certiorari*, to the Justices' Court in the city of New-York. Swan sued Guille in the Justices' Court, in an action of trespass, for entering his close, and treading down his roots and vegetables, &c. in a garden in the city of New-York. The facts were, that Guille ascended in a balloon in the vicinity of Swan's garden, and descended into his garden. When he descended, his body was hanging out of the car of the balloon in a very perilous situation, and he called to a person at work in Swan's field, to help him, in a voice audible to the pursuing crowd. After the balloon descended, it dragged along over potatoes and radishes, about thirty feet, when Guille was taken out. The balloon was carried to a barn at the farther end of the premises. When the balloon descended, more than two hundred persons broke into Swan's garden through the fences, and came on his premises, beating down his vegetables and flowers. The damage done by Guille, with his balloon, was about 15 dollars, but the crowd did much more. The plaintiff's damages, in all, amounted to 90 dollars. It was contended before the Justice, that Guille was answerable only for the damage done by himself, and not for the damage done by the crowd. The Justice was of the opinion, and so instructed the jury, that the defendant was answerable for all the damages done to the plaintiff. The jury, accordingly, found a verdict for him, for 90 dollars, on which the judgment was given, and for costs.

SPENCER, CH. J., delivered the opinion of the Court.

The counsel for the plaintiff in error supposes, that the injury committed by his client was involuntary, and that done by the crowd was voluntary, and that, therefore, there was no union of intent; and that upon the same principle which would render *Guille* answerable for the acts of the crowd, in treading down and destroying the vegetables and flowers of S., he would be responsible for a battery, or a murder committed on the owner of the premises.

The *intent* with which an act is done, is by no means the test of the liability of a party to an action of trespass. If the act cause the immediate injury, whether it was intentional, or unintentional, trespass is the proper action to redress the wrong. It was so decided, upon a review of all the cases, in *Percival v. Hickey*, 18 Johns. Rep. 257. Where an immediate act is done by the co-operation, or the joint act of several persons, they are all trespassers, and may be sued jointly or severally; and any one of them is liable for the injury done by all. To render one man liable in trespass for the acts of others, it must appear, either that they acted in concert, or that the act of the individual sought to be charged, ordinarily and naturally, produced the acts of the others.

Intent Irrelevant to Liability

The case of *Scott v. Shepard*, 2 Black. Rep. 892, is a strong instance of the responsibility of an individual who was the first, though not the immediate, agent in producing an injury. Shepard threw a lighted squib, composed of gunpowder, into a market house, where a large concourse of people were assembled; it fell on the standing of Y., and to prevent injury, it was thrown off his standing, across the market, when it fell on another standing; from thence, to save the goods of the owner, it was thrown to another part of the market house, and in so throwing it, it struck the plaintiff in the face, and, bursting, put out one of his eyes. It was decided, by the opinions of three Judges against one, that Shepard was answerable in an action of trespass, and assault and battery.

De Grey, Ch. J., held, that throwing the squib was an unlawful act, and that whatever mischief followed, the person throwing it was the author of the mischief. All that was done subsequent to the original throwing, was a continuation of the first force and first act. Any innocent person removing the danger from himself was justifiable; the blame lights upon the first thrower; the new direction and new force, flow out of the first force. He laid it down as a principle, that everyone who does an unlawful act, is considered as the doer of all that follows. A person breaking a horse in Lincolns-Inn-Fields, hurt a man, and it was held, that trespass would lie. In *Leame v. Bray*, 3 East Rep. 595, Lord Ellenborough said, if I put in motion a dangerous thing, as if I let loose a dangerous animal, and leave to hazard what may happen, and mischief en sue, I am answerable in trespass; and if one (he says) put an animal or carriage in motion, which causes an immediate injury to another, he is the actor, the *causa causans*.

I will not say that ascending in a balloon is an unlawful act, for it is not so; but, it is certain, that the *Æronaut* has no control over its motion horizontally; he is at the sport of the winds, and is to descend when and how he can; his reaching the earth is a matter of hazard. He did descend on the premises of the plaintiff below, at a short distance from the place where he ascended. Now, if his descent, under such circumstances, would, ordinarily and naturally, draw a crowd of people about him, either from curiosity, or for the purpose of rescuing him from a perilous situation; all this he ought to have foreseen, and must be responsible for. Whether the crowd heard him call for help or not, is immaterial; he had put himself in a situation to invite help, and they rushed forward, impelled, perhaps, by the double motive of rendering aid, and gratifying a curiosity which he had excited. Can it be doubted, that if the plaintiff in error had beckoned to the crowd to come to his assistance, that he would be liable for their trespass in entering the enclosure? I think not. In that case, they would have been co-trespassers, and we must consider the situation in which he placed himself, voluntarily and designedly, as equivalent to a direct request to the crowd to follow him. In the present case, he did call for help, and may have been heard by the crowd; he is, therefore, undoubtedly, liable for all the injury sustained. Judgment affirmed.

EXERCISE 2-1. *GUILLE V. SWAN*—AERIAL TRESPASS

The earliest aeronautical tort and insurance cases involved balloons, and the earliest recorded case was *Guille v. Swan, infra.*

1. What are the facts of the case?

2. What is the legal definition of trespass? Can a trespass occur unintentionally? Explain.

3. Explain the relationship between intent and liability, according to the court.

4. The court notes that, "[t]o render one man liable in trespass for the acts of others, it must appear, either that they acted in concert, or that the act of the individual sought to be charged, ordinarily and naturally, produced the acts of the others." Explain.

5. Did the trespass in *Guille v. Swan* occur on the land or the air? Why might the distinction be important?

UNITED STATES V. CAUSBY

328 U.S. 256 (1946)

MR. JUSTICE DOUGLAS delivered the opinion of the Court.

This is a case of first impression. The problem presented is whether respondents' property was taken within the meaning of the Fifth Amendment by frequent and regular flights of army and navy aircraft over respondents' land at low altitudes. The Court of Claims held that there was a taking and entered judgment for respondent, one judge dissenting. The case is here on a petition for a *writ of certiorari* which we granted because of the importance of the question presented.

Respondents own 2.8 acres near an airport outside of Greensboro, North Carolina. It has on it a dwelling house, and also various outbuildings which were mainly used for raising chickens. The end of the airport's northwest-southeast runway is 2,220 feet from respondents' barn and 2,275 feet from their house. The path of glide to this runway passes directly over the property, which is 100 feet wide and 1,200 feet long. The 30 to 1 safe glide angle approved by the Civil Aeronautics Authority passes over this property at 83 feet, which is 67 feet above the house, 63 feet above the barn and 18 feet above the highest tree. The use by the United States of this airport is pursuant to a lease executed in May, 1942, for a term commencing June 1, 1942 and ending June 30, 1942, with a provision for renewals until June 30, 1967, or six months after the end of the national emergency, whichever is the earlier.

Various aircraft of the United States use this airport—bombers, transports and fighters. The direction of the prevailing wind determines when a particular runway is used. The north-west-southeast runway in question is used about four per cent of the time in taking off and about seven per cent of the time in landing. Since the United States began operations in May, 1942, its four-motored heavy bombers, other planes of the heavier type, and its fighter planes have frequently passed over respondents' land buildings in considerable numbers and rather close together. They come close enough at times to appear barely to miss the tops of the trees and at times so close to the tops of the trees as to blow the old leaves off. The noise is startling. And at night the glare from the planes brightly lights up the place.

As a result of the noise, respondents had to give up their chicken business. As many as six to ten of their chickens were killed in one day by flying into the walls from fright. The total chickens lost in that manner was about 150. Production also fell off. The result was the destruction of the use of the property as a commercial chicken farm. Respondents are frequently deprived of their sleep and the family has become nervous and frightened. Although there have been no airplane accidents on respondents' property, there have been several accidents near the airport and close to respondents' place. These are the essential facts found by the Court of Claims. On the basis of these facts, it found that respondents' property had depreciated in value. It held that the United States had taken an easement over the property on June 1, 1942, and that the value of the property destroyed and the easement taken was $2,000. * * *

Air Commerce Act of 1926

The United States relies on the Air Commerce Act of 1926, as amended by the Civil Aeronautics Act of 1938. Under those statutes the United States has "complete and exclusive national sovereignty in the air space" over this country. They grant any citizen of the United States "a public right of freedom of transit in air commerce through the navigable air space of the United States." And "navigable air space" is defined as "airspace above the minimum safe altitudes of flight prescribed by the Civil Aeronautics Authority." And it is provided that "such navigable airspace shall be subject to a public right of freedom of interstate and foreign air navigation." It is, therefore, argued that since these flights were within the minimum safe altitudes of flight which had been prescribed, they were an exercise of the declared right of travel through the airspace.

The United States concludes that when flights are made within the navigable airspace without any physical invasion of the property of the landowners, there has been no taking of property. It says that at most there was merely incidental damage occurring as a consequence of authorized air navigation. It also argues that the landowner does not own superadjacent airspace which he has not subjected to possession by the erection of structures or other occupancy. Moreover, it is argued that even if the United States took airspace owned by respondents, no compensable damage was shown. Any damages are said to be merely consequential for which no compensation may be obtained under the Fifth Amendment.

It is ancient doctrine that at common law ownership of the land extended to the periphery of the universe. But that doctrine has no place in the modern world. The air is a public highway . . . Were that not true, every transcontinental flight would subject the operator to countless trespass suits. Common sense revolts at the idea. To recognize such private claims to the airspace would clog these highways, seriously interfere with their control and development in the public interest, and transfer into private ownership that to which only the public has a just claim.

It is ancient doctrine that at common law ownership of the land extended to the periphery of the universe—*Cujus est solum ejus est usque ad coelum*. But that doctrine has no place in the modern world. The air is a public highway, as Congress has declared. Were that not true, every transcontinental flight would subject the operator to countless trespass suits. Common sense revolts at the idea. To recognize such private claims to the airspace would clog these highways, seriously interfere with their control and development in the public interest, and transfer into private ownership that to which only the public has a just claim.

But that general principle does not control the present case. For the United States conceded on oral argument that if the flights over respondents' property rendered it uninhabitable, there would be a taking compensable under the Fifth Amendment. It is the owner's loss, not the taker's gain, which is the measure of the value of the property taken. Market value fairly determined is the normal measure of the recovery. And that value may reflect the use to which the land could readily be converted, as well as the existing use. If, by reason of the frequency and altitude of the flights, respondents could not use this land for any purpose, their loss would be complete. It would be as complete as if the United States had entered upon the surface of the land and taken exclusive possession of it.

Departure from Roman Law

We agree that in those circumstances there would be a taking. Though it would be only an easement of flight which was taken, that easement, if permanent and not merely temporary, normally would be the equivalent of a fee interest. It would be a definite exercise of complete dominion and control over the surface of the land. The fact that the planes never touched the surface would be as irrelevant as the absence in this day of the feudal livery of seisin on the transfer of real estate. The owner's right to possess and exploit the land—that is to say, his beneficial ownership of it—would be destroyed. It would not be a case of incidental damages arising from a legalized nuisance such as was involved in *Richards v. Washington Terminal Co.*, 233 U.S. 546 (1914). In that case property owners whose lands adjoined a railroad line were denied recovery for damages resulting from the noise, vibrations, smoke and the like, incidental to the operations of the trains. In the supposed case the line of flight is over the land. And the land is appropriated as directly and completely as if it were used for the runways themselves.

There is no material difference between the supposed case and the present one, except that here enjoyment and use of the land are not completely destroyed. But that does not seem to us to be controlling. The path of glide for airplanes might reduce a valuable factory site to grazing land, an orchard to a vegetable patch, a residential section to a wheat field. Some value would remain. But the use of the airspace immediately above the land would limit the utility of the land and cause a diminution in its value. That was the philosophy of *Portsmouth Harbor Land & Hotel Co. v. United States*, 260 U.S. 327 (1922). In that case the petition alleged that the United States erected a fort on nearby land, established a battery and a fire control station there, and fired guns over petitioner's land. The Court, speaking through Mr. Justice Holmes, reversed the Court of Claims which dismissed the petition on a demurrer, holding that "the specific facts set forth would warrant a finding that a servitude has been imposed."

The fact that the path of glide taken by the planes was that approved by the Civil Aeronautics Authority does not change the result. The navigable airspace which Congress has placed in the public domain is "airspace above the minimum safe altitudes of flight prescribed by the Civil Aeronautics Authority." 49 U.S.C. § 180. If that agency prescribed 83 feet as the minimum safe altitude, then we would have presented the question of the validity of the regulation. But nothing of the sort has been done. The path of glide governs the method of operating— of landing or taking off. The altitude required for that operation is not the minimum safe altitude of flight which is the downward reach of the navigable airspace. The minimum prescribed by the authority is 500 feet during the day and 1000 feet at night for air carriers (Civil Air Regulations, Pt. 61, §§ 61.7400, 61.7401) and from 300 to 1000 feet for other aircraft depending on the type of plane and the character of the terrain. *Id.*

Hence, the flights in question were not within the navigable airspace which Congress placed within the public domain. If any airspace needed for landing or taking off were included, flights which were so close to the land as to render it uninhabitable would be immune. But the United States concedes, as we have said, that in that event there would be a taking. Thus, it is apparent that the path of glide is not the minimum safe altitude of flight within the meaning of the statute. The Civil Aeronautics Authority has, of course, the power to prescribe air traffic rules. But Congress has defined navigable airspace only in terms of one of them— the minimum safe altitudes of flight.

We have said that the airspace is a public highway. Yet it is obvious that if the landowner is to have full enjoyment of the land, he must have exclusive control of the immediate reaches of the enveloping atmosphere. Otherwise buildings could not be erected, trees could not be planted, and even fences could not be run. The principle is recognized when the law gives a remedy in case overhanging structures are erected on adjoining land.

The landowner owns at least as much of the space above the ground as the can occupy or use in connection with the land. *See Hinman v. Pacific Air Transport*, 84 F.2d 755 (9th Cir. 1936). The fact that he does not occupy it in a physical sense—by the erection of buildings and the like—is not material. As we have said, the flight of airplanes, which skim the surface but do not touch it, is as much an appropriation of the use of the land as a more conventional entry upon it. We would not doubt that if the United States erected an elevated railway over respondents' land at the precise altitude where its planes now fly, there would be a partial taking, even though none of the supports of the structure rested on the land. The reason is that there would be an intrusion so immediate and direct as to subtract from the owner's full enjoyment of the property and to limit his exploitation of it. While the owner does not in any physical manner occupy that stratum of airspace or make use of it in the conventional sense, he does use it in somewhat the same sense that space left between buildings for the purpose of light and air is used. The superadjacent airspace at this low altitude is so close to the land that continuous invasions of it affect the use of the surface of the land itself. We think that the landowner, as an incident to his ownership, has a claim to it and that invasions of it are in the same category as invasions of the surface.

The flight of airplanes, which skim the surface but do not touch it, is as much an appropriation of the use of the land as a more conventional entry upon it. We would not doubt that if the United States erected an elevated railway over respondents' land at the precise altitude where its planes now fly, there would be a partial taking, even though none of the supports of the structure rested on the land. The reason is that there would be an intrusion so immediate and direct as to subtract from the owner's full enjoyment of the property and to limit his exploitation of it.

In this case, as in *Portsmouth Harbor Land & Hotel Co.*, the damages were not merely consequential. They were the product of a direct invasion of respondents' domain. As stated in *United States v. Cress*, 243 U.S. 316, 328 (1917), "* * * it is the character of the invasion, not the amount of damage resulting from it, so long as the damage is substantial, that determines the question whether it is a taking." We said in *United States v. Powelson*, 319 U.S. 266, 279 (1943), that while the meaning of "property" as used in the Fifth Amendment was a federal question, "it will normally obtain its content by reference to local law."

If we look to North Carolina law, we reach the same result. Sovereignty in the airspace rests in the State "except where granted to and assumed by the United States." Gen. Stats. 1943, § 63–11. The flight of aircraft is lawful "unless at such a low altitude as to interfere with the then existing use to which the land or water,

"Immediate Reaches Above the Land"

or the space over the land or water, is put by the owner, or unless so conducted as to be imminently dangerous to persons or property lawfully on the land or water beneath." *Id.* Subject to that right of flight, "ownership of the space above the lands and waters of this State is declared to be vested in the several owners of the surface beneath." *Id.* Our holding that there was an invasion of respondents' property is thus not inconsistent with the local law governing a landowner's claim to the immediate reaches of the superadjacent airspace.

> *The airplane is part of the modern environment of life, and the inconveniences which it causes are normally not compensable under the Fifth Amendment. The airspace, apart from the immediate reaches above the land, is part of the public domain . . . Flights over private land are not a taking, unless they are so low and so frequent as to be a direct and immediate interference with the enjoyment and use of the land.*

The airplane is part of the modern environment of life, and the inconveniences which it causes are normally not compensable under the Fifth Amendment. The airspace, apart from the immediate reaches above the land, is part of the public domain. We need not determine at this time what those precise limits are. Flights over private land are not a taking, unless they are so low and so frequent as to be a direct and immediate interference with the enjoyment and use of the land. We need not speculate on that phase of the present case. For the findings of the Court of Claims plainly establish that there was a diminution in value of the property and that the frequent, low-level flights were the direct and immediate cause. We agree with the Court of Claims that a servitude has been imposed upon the land.

* * *

The Court of Claims held, as we have noted, that an easement was taken. But the findings of fact contain no precise description as to its nature. It is not described in terms of frequency of flight, permissible altitude, or type of airplane. Nor is there a finding as to whether the easement taken was temporary or permanent. Yet an accurate description of the property taken is essential, since that interest vests in the United States. *Cress*, 243 U.S. at 329. Since on this record it is not clear whether the easement taken is a permanent or a temporary one, it would be premature for us to consider whether the amount of the award made by the Court of Claims was proper.

The judgment is reversed and the cause is remanded to the Court of Claims so that it may make the necessary findings in conformity with this opinion. Reversed.

MR. JUSTICE BLACK, dissenting.

The Fifth Amendment provides that "private property" shall not "be taken for public use, without just compensation." The Court holds today that the Government has "taken" respondents' property by repeatedly flying Army bombers directly above respondents' land at a height of eighty-three feet where the light and noise from these planes caused respondents to lose sleep and their chickens to be killed. Since the effect of the Court's decision is to limit, by the imposition of relatively absolute Constitutional barriers, possible future adjustments through legislation and regulation which might become necessary with the growth of air transportation, and since in my view the Constitution does not contain such barriers, I dissent.

The Court's opinion seems to indicate that the mere flying of planes through the column of air directly above respondents' land does not constitute a "taking." Consequently, it appears to be noise and glare, to the extent and under the circumstances shown here, which make the government a seizer of private property. But the allegation of noise and glare resulting in damages, constitutes at best an action in tort where there might be recovery if the noise and light constituted a nuisance, a violation of a statute, or were the result of negligence.

But the Government has not consented to be sued in the Court of Claims except in actions based on express or implied contract. And there is no implied contract here, unless by reason of the noise and glare caused by the bombers the Government can be said to have "taken" respondents' property in a Constitutional sense.

The concept of taking property as used in the Constitution has heretofore never been given so sweeping a meaning. The Court's opinion presents no case where a man who makes noise or shines light onto his neighbor's property has been ejected from that property for wrongfully taking possession of it. Nor would anyone take seriously a claim that noisy automobiles passing on a highway are taking wrongful possession of the homes located thereon, or that a city elevated train which greatly interferes with the sleep of those who live next to it wrongfully takes their property.

Even the one case in this Court which in considering the sufficiency of a complaint gave the most elastic meaning to the phrase "private property be taken" as used in the Fifth Amendment, did not go so far. *Portsmouth Harbor Land & Hotel Co.*, 260 U.S. at 327. I am not willing, nor do I think the Constitution and the decisions authorize me, to extend that phrase so as to guarantee an absolute Constitutional right to relief not subject to legislative change, which is based on averments that at best show mere torts committed by Government agents while flying over land. The future adjustment of the rights and remedies of property owners, which might be found necessary because of the flight of planes at safe altitudes, should, especially in view of the imminent expansion of air navigation, be left where I think the Constitution left it, with Congress.

> *It is inconceivable to me that the Constitution guarantees that the airspace of this Nation needed for air navigation, is owned by the particular persons who happen to own the land beneath to the same degree as they own the surface below. No rigid Constitutional rule, in my judgment, commands that the air must be considered as marked off into separate compartments by imaginary metes and bounds in order to synchronize air ownership with land ownership.*

Nor do I reach a different conclusion because of the fact that the particular circumstance which under the Court's opinion makes the tort here absolutely actionable, is the passing of planes through a column of air at an elevation of eighty-three feet directly over respondents' property. It is inconceivable to me that the Constitution guarantees that the airspace of this Nation needed for air navigation, is owned by the particular persons who happen to own the land beneath to the same degree as they own the surface below. No rigid Constitutional rule, in my judgment, commands that the air must be considered as marked off into separate compartments by imaginary metes and bounds in order to synchronize air ownership with land ownership.

Judicial Restraint; Deference to Agency

Congress has given the Civil Aeronautics Authority exclusive power to determine what is navigable airspace subject to its exclusive control. This power derives specifically from the Section which authorizes the Authority to prescribe "air traffic rules governing the flight of, and for the navigation, protection, and identification of, aircraft, including rules as to safe altitudes of flight and rules for the prevention of collisions between aircraft, and between aircraft and land or water vehicles." 49 U.S.C. § 551. Here there was no showing that the bombers flying over respondents' land violated any rule or regulation of the Civil Aeronautics Authority. Yet, unless we hold the Act unconstitutional, at least such a showing would be necessary before the courts could act without interfering with the exclusive authority which Congress gave to the administrative agency. Not even a showing that the Authority has not acted at all would be sufficient. For in that event, were the courts to have any authority to act in this case at all, they should stay their hand till the Authority has acted.

The broad provisions of the Congressional statute cannot properly be circumscribed by making a distinction as the Court's opinion does between rules of safe altitude of flight while on the level of cross-country flight and rules of safe altitude during landing and taking off. First, such a distinction cannot be maintained from the practical standpoint. It is unlikely that Congress intended that the Authority prescribe safe altitudes for planes making cross-country flights, while at the same time it left the more hazardous landing and take-off operations unregulated. The legislative history, moreover, clearly shows that the Authority's power to prescribe air traffic rules includes the power to make rules governing landing and take-off. Nor is the Court justified in ignoring that history by labeling rules of safe altitude while on the level of cross-country flight as rules prescribing the safe altitude proper and rules governing take-off and landing as rules of operation. For the Conference Report explicitly states that such distinctions were purposely eliminated from the original House Bill in order that the Section on air traffic rules "might be given the broadest construction by the * * * (Civil Aeronautics Authority) * * * and the courts." In construing the statute narrowly the Court thwarts the intent of Congress. A proper broad construction, such as Congress commanded, would not permit the Court to decide what it has today without declaring the Act of Congress unconstitutional. I think the Act given the broad construction intended is constitutional.

That the rules for landing and take-off are rules prescribing "minimum safe altitudes of flight" is shown by the following further statement in the House Report: "* * * the minimum safe altitudes of flight * * * would vary with the terrain and location of cities and would coincide with the surface of the land or water at airports."

> *The solution of the problems precipitated by these technological advances and new ways of living cannot come about through the application of rigid Constitutional restraints formulated and enforced by the courts.*

No greater confusion could be brought about in the coming age of air transportation than that which would result were courts by Constitutional interpretation to hamper Congress in its efforts to keep the air free. Old concepts of private ownership of land should not be introduced into the field of air regulation. I have no doubt that Congress will, if not handicapped by judicial interpretations of the Constitution, preserve the freedom of the air, and at the same time, satisfy the just claims of aggrieved persons. The noise of newer, larger, and more powerful planes may grow louder and louder and disturb people more and more. But the solution of the problems precipitated by these technological advances and new ways of living cannot come about through the application of rigid Constitutional restraints formulated and enforced by the courts.

What adjustments may have to be made, only the future can reveal. It seems certain, however, the courts do not possess the techniques or the personnel to consider and act upon the complex combinations of factors entering into the problems. The contribution of courts must be made through the awarding of damages for injuries suffered from the flying of planes, or by the granting of injunctions to prohibit their flying. When these two simple remedial devices are elevated to a Constitutional level under the Fifth Amendment, as the Court today seems to have done, they can stand as obstacles to better adapted techniques that might be offered by experienced experts and accepted by Congress. Today's opinion is, I fear, an opening wedge for an unwarranted judicial interference with the power of Congress to develop solutions for new and vital and national problems. In my opinion this case should be reversed on the ground that there has been no "taking" in the Constitutional sense.

EXERCISE 2-2. *UNITED STATES V. CAUSBY*—AVIGATIONAL EASEMENT

1. Prior to reading *United States v. Causby*, review the meaning of the following legal terms: (a) eminent domain; (b) inverse condemnation; and (c) avigational easement.

2. Is the defendant in *United States v. Causby* a private or public entity? What difference does it make—practically and legally?

3. Under whose authority is the national air space according to the Air Commerce Act of 1926, as amended by the Civil Aeronautics Act of 1938?

4. The court abandons the ancient and common law doctrine that ownership of land extended to the periphery of the universe, concluding instead that "[t]he airspace, apart from the immediate reaches above the land, is part of the public domain." After *United States v. Causby* was decided, at what altitude did the "immediate reaches above the land" extend to?

5. What is the principle objection raised by the dissent? Is it persuasive?

NOTES ON *UNITED STATES V. CAUSBY*—OPEN SKIES

1. *Open Skies.*

Microsoft Chief Executive Bill Gates articulated the freedom that flight has represented from its earliest stage: "The Wright brothers created the single greatest cultural force since the invention of writing. The airplane became the first world wide web, bringing people of different languages, ideas and values together." Gregory P. Sreenan, *Aviation Law*, JUN. FLA. B.J. 44, 47–48 (2003). While commercial jets regularly traverse state boundaries (*i.e.*, "transcontinental"), the notion of truly "Open Skies" is an emerging and challenging issue internationally.

For example, when Continental Airlines Flight 28 from New York arrived at London's Heathrow Terminal 4 on March 30, 2008, at 6:45 A.M., it was decades overdue in the minds of some airline executives. Until that time, several pacts between the United States and Great Britain controlled which foreign airlines could serve the that airport. Continental Airlines was excluded from one of the world's busiest aviation gateways. Only four airlines—British Airways, Virgin Atlantic, American Airlines, and United Airlines—operated between London's Heathrow Airport and the United States pursuant to the "Bermuda II" accord, a 1977 agreement between Great Britain and the United States that permitted only two airlines from each country to serve London Heathrow Airport, prohibited U.S. carriers from serving inter-European routes originating from the United Kingdom, and restricted British carriers from servicing points between U.S. cities. *See* Agreement Between the Government of the United States of America and the Government of the United Kingdom of Great Britain Relating to Air Services Between Their Respective Territories, Feb. 11, 1946. U.S.-U.K., 60 Stat. 1499 ["Bermuda I"], and 23 July 1977, 28 U.S.T. 5367, T.I.A.S. No. 8641 ["Bermuda II"].

This restriction eased on April 30, 2007, when the United States and European Union Member States completed the first phase of a new era of "Open Skies" agreement that would increase international flight routes and landing rights for transatlantic commercial airlines. *See* 2007 O.J. (L 134) 4–41, 46 I.L.M. 470 (2007). *See generally Open Skies Causes a Continental Shift*, TRAVEL TRADE GAZETTE (United Kingdom), Mar. 21, 2008, at 2008 WLNR 5741461 (quoting Continental Airlines Senior Director for the United Kingdom and Ireland: "The world's premier airport was permanently written out of our brief by the most anti-competitive air service agreement, which has protected the incumbents wonderfully."). *See also* Michelle Higgins, *Open-Skies Promises More Flights to Europe*, CHI. TRIB., Mar. 30, 2008, at 2.

For further discussion of Open Skies initiatives across European and Asian markets see Allan P. Dobson & Joseph A. McKinney, *Sovereignty, Politics, and U.S. International Airline Policy*, 74 J. AIR L. & COM. 527 (2009); Miron Mushkat & Roda

Mushkat, *The Political Economy of Hong Kong's "Open Skies" Legal Regime: An Empirical and Theoretical Exploration*, 10 SAN DIEGO INT'L L.J. 381 (2009); Robert M. Hardaway, *Of Cabbages and Cabotage: The Case for Opening Up the U.S. Airline Industry to International Competition*, 34 TRANSP. L.J. 1 (2007); Ruwantissa Abeyratne, *US/EU Open Skies Agreement—Some Issues*, 75 J. AIR L. & COM. 21 (2007); Bruce Stockfish, *Opening Closed Skies: The Prospects for Further Liberalization of Trade in International Air Transport Services*, 57 J. AIR L. & COM. 599 (1992). *See also* A.J. THOMAS, JR., ECONOMIC REGULATION OF SCHEDULED AIR TRANSPORT 174 (1955).

2.   *Chicago Convention.*

In terms of international aviation property law rights, airline operations are bound by legal boundaries and barriers intended to fortify national security, economic, and protectionist concerns. Dating back at least to the Paris Convention of 1919, the evolution of international aviation necessarily has been tied to the principle that nation states enjoy and should safeguard exclusive sovereignty over their airspace. In 1944, more than fifty nations gathered near the conclusion of World War II to create and implement a global civil aviation marketplace that respected national sovereignty without also hamstringing the development of international aviation. Convention on International Civil Aviation, *opened for signature*, Dec. 7, 1944, 61 Stat. 1180, T.I.A.S. No. 1951 ("Chicago Convention").

> At the "Chicago Convention," delegates announced their objectives:
>
> WHEREAS, the development of international civil aviation can greatly help to create and preserve friendship and understanding among the nations and peoples of the world, yet its abuse can become a threat to the general security; and
>
> WHEREAS, it is desirable to avoid friction and to promote that cooperation between nations and peoples which the peace of the world depends;
>
> THEREFORE, the undersigned governments have agreed on certain principles and arrangements in order that international civil aviation may be developed in a safe and orderly manner and that international air transport services may be established on the basis of equal opportunity and operating soundly and economically[.]

Int'l Civ. Aviation Org., International Civil Aviation Conference: Chicago, Ill., 1 Nov. to 7 Dec. 1994.

The Chicago Convention delegates formed the International Civil Aviation Organization ("ICAO"), a United Nations agency that has successfully created international technical standards for global aviation (*e.g.*, requiring communications with air traffic facilities worldwide in the English language and establishing international standards for aircraft airworthiness, flight crew certification, and radio aids to navigation). *See* www.icao.int/. Over 190 nations are signatories to the Chicago Convention and the success of ICAO in establishing international technical standards for aircraft (*e.g.*, a series of published Annexes known as International Standards and Recommended Practices ("SARPs")) is widely recognized.

The Chicago Convention delegates sought to develop principles and procedures for the economic regulation of rates, fares, frequency, and capacity in international commercial aviation and overcome restrictions on foreign competition in domestic airline markets. That objective is elusive.

3.   *Freedoms of the Air.*

Chicago Convention delegates were successful in affirming "that every State has complete and exclusive sovereignty over the air space above its territory" and defining "five freedoms of the air."

Those freedoms included:

(1)   the right to fly over the territory of another country without landing;

(2)   the right to land in another country for technical, non-traffic reasons such as refueling or maintenance;

(3)   the right to discharge traffic from the home country in a foreign country, for example, international airline travel between the United States and destinations in particular European nations;

(4)   the right to pick up traffic in a foreign country bound for the home country; and

(5)   "beyond rights" or the right to pick up traffic in a foreign country and convey them to a different foreign country, provided that the flight originated or terminated in the home country.

Only the first two freedoms were annexed to the Chicago Convention, leaving the remaining "freedoms"—including the right of "cabotage" (*i.e.*, the right of a foreign-flagged carrier to serve domestic passenger and cargo routes between points *within* a foreign nation)—to be negotiated individually between states as restrictive bilateral or multilateral agreements.

Illustration 2-2. Freedoms of the Air

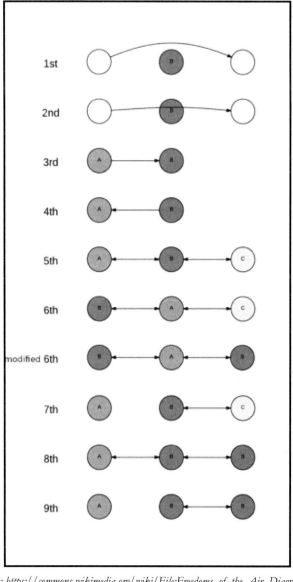

Source: https://commons.wikimedia.org/wiki/File:Freedoms_of_the_Air_Diagram.png

4.   ***Unmanned Aerial Systems—UASs or Drones.***

The Federal Aviation Administration has extensive and plenary authority concerning the use and management of the navigable airspace, air traffic control, and air navigation facilities. 49 U.S.C. §§ 40103(b), 44502, and 44721. How "unmanned aerial vehicles"—UAVs—will be incorporated into the national airspace, if at all, will present a significant practical and regulatory challenge for lawmakers in the decade ahead, however.

In the near term, the FAA has rolled out its UAS Data Exchange, a collaborative approach between government and private industry facilitating the sharing of airspace data between the two parties. Under the FAA UAS Data Exchange umbrella, the agency will support multiple partnerships, the first of which is the Low Altitude Authorization and Notification Capability ("LAANC"). According to the FAA, "LAANC automates the application and approval process for airspace authorizations. Through automated applications developed by an FAA Approved UAS Service Suppliers (USS) pilots apply for an airspace authorization. Requests are checked against airspace data in the FAA UAS Data Exchange such as temporary flight restrictions, NOTAMS and the UAS Facility Maps. If approved, pilots receive their authorization in near-real time. LAANC also provides FAA's Air Traffic visibility into where and when planned drone operations will take place ... By September 2018, LAANC will be available at nearly 300 air traffic facilities covering approximately 500 airports." *See* Fed. Aviation Admin., *FAA UAS Data Exchange*, https://www.faa.gov/uas/programs_partnerships/uas_data_exchange/.

Illustration 2-3. Future Classes of Airspace?

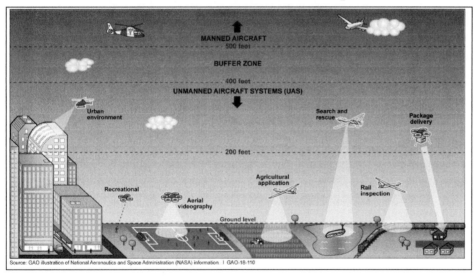

For further reading see Fed. Aviation Admin., AFS–400 UAS Policy 05–01, UNMANNED AIRCRAFT SYSTEMS OPERATIONS IN THE U.S. NATIONAL AIRSPACE SYSTEM—INTERIM OPERATIONAL APPROVAL GUIDANCE (2005). *See also* Timothy M. Ravich, *The Integration of Unmanned Aerial Vehicles into the National Airspace*, 85 N.D. L. Rev. 597 (2009); Douglas Marshall, *Unmanned Aerial Systems and International Civil Aviation Organization Regulations*, 85 N.D. L. Rev. 693 (2009); Mark E. Peterson, *The UAV and the Current and Future Regulatory Construct for Integration into the National Airspace System*, 71 J. Air L. & Com. 521 (2006).

GRIGGS V. COUNTY OF ALLEGHENY

369 U.S. 84 (1962)

MR. JUSTICE DOUGLAS *delivered the opinion of the Court.*

This case is here on a petition for a *writ of certiorari* to the Supreme Court of Pennsylvania which we granted because its decision seemed to be in conflict with *United States v. Causby*, 328 U.S. 256 (1946). The question is whether respondent has taken an air easement over petitioner's property for which it must pay just compensation as required by the Fourteenth Amendment.

National Airport Plan

Respondent owns and maintains the Greater Pittsburgh Airport on land which it purchased to provide airport and air-transport facilities. The airport was designed for public use in conformity with the rules and regulations of the Civil Aeronautics Administration within the scope of the National Airport Plan provided for in 49 U.S.C. § 1101 *et seq.*, 49 U.S.C.A. § 1101 *et seq.*

Respondent executed three agreements with the Administrator of Civil Aeronautics in which it agreed, among other things, to abide by and adhere to the Rules and Regulations of C.A.A. and to "maintain a master plan of the airport," including "approach areas." It was provided that the "airport approach standards to be followed in this connection shall be those established by the Administrator"; and it was also agreed that respondent "will acquire such easements or other interests in lands and air space as may be necessary to perform the covenants of this paragraph."

The "master plan" laid out and submitted by respondent included the required "approach areas" and the "master plan" was approved. One "approach area" was to the northeast runway. As designed and approved, it passed over petitioner's home which is 3,250 feet from the end of that runway. The elevation at the end of that runway is 1,150.50 feet above sea level; the door sill at petitioner's residence, 1,183.64 feet; the top of petitioner's chimney, 1,219.64 feet. The slope gradient of the approach leaves a clearance of 11.36 feet between the bottom of the glide angle and petitioner's chimney.

The airlines that use the airport are lessees of respondent; and the leases give them, among other things, the right "to land" and "take off." No flights were in violation of the regulations of C.A.A.; nor were any flights lower than necessary for a safe landing or take-off. The planes taking off from the northeast runway observed regular flight patterns ranging from 30 feet to 300 feet over petitioner's residence; and on let-down they were within 53 feet to 153 feet.

On take-off the noise of the planes is comparable "to the noise of a riveting machine or steam hammer." On the let-down the planes make a noise comparable "to that of a noisy factory." The Board of Viewers found that "[t]he low altitude flights over plaintiff's property caused the plaintiff and occupants of his property to become nervous and distraught, eventually causing their removal therefrom as undesirable and unbearable for their residential use." Judge Bell, dissenting below, accurately summarized the uncontroverted facts as follows:

> Regular and almost continuous daily flights, often several minutes apart, have been made by a number of airlines directly over and very, very close to plaintiff's residence. During these flights it was often impossible for people in the house to converse or to talk on the telephone. The plaintiff and the members of his household (depending on the flight which in turn sometimes depended on the wind) were frequently unable to sleep even with ear plugs and sleeping pills; they would frequently be awakened by the flight and the noise of the planes; the windows of their home would frequently rattle and at times plaster fell down from the walls and ceilings; their health was affected and impaired, and they sometimes were compelled to sleep elsewhere. Moreover, their house was so close to the runways or path of glide that as the spokesman for the members of the Airlines Pilot Association admitted, "If we had engine failure we would have no course but to plow into your house."

It is argued that though there was a "taking," someone other than respondent was the taker—the airlines or the C.A.A. acting as an authorized representative of the United States. We think, however, that respondent, which was the promoter, owner, and lessor of the airport, was in these circumstances the one who took the air easement in the constitutional sense.

Respondent decided, subject to the approval of the C.A.A., where the airport would be built, what runways it would need, their direction and length, and what land and navigation easements would be needed. The Federal Government takes nothing; it is the local authority which decides to build an airport *vel non*, and where it is to be located. We see no difference between its responsibility for the air easements necessary for operation of the airport and its responsibility for the land on which the runways were built. Nor did the Congress when it designed the legislation for a National Airport Plan. For, as we have already noted, Congress provided in 49 U.S.C. § 1109, 49 U.S.C.A. § 1109, for the payment to the owners of airports, whose plans were approved by the Administrator, of a share of "the allowable project costs" including the "costs of acquiring land or interests therein or easements through or other interests in air space."

Local—Not Federal— Matter

A county that designed and constructed a bridge would not have a usable facility unless it had at least an easement over the land necessary for the approaches to the bridge. Why should one who designs, constructs, and uses an airport be in a more favorable position so far as the Fourteenth Amendment is concerned? That the instant "taking" was "for public use" is not debatable. For respondent agreed with the C.A.A. that it would operate the airport "for the use and benefit of the public," that it would operate it 'on fair and reasonable terms and without unjust discrimination,' and that it would not allow any carrier to acquire 'any exclusive right' to its use.

The glide path for the northeast runway is as necessary for the operation of the airport as is a surface right of way for operation of a bridge, or as is the land for the operation of a dam. As stated by the Supreme Court of Washington in *Ackerman v. Port of Seattle*, 348 P.2d 664 (Wash. 1960) "* * * an adequate approach way is as necessary a part of an airport as is the ground on which the airstrip, itself, is constructed * * *." Without the "approach areas," an airport is indeed not operable. Respondent in designing it had to acquire some private property. Our conclusion is that by constitutional standards it did not acquire enough. Reversed.

MR. JUSTICE BLACK, with whom MR. JUSTICE FRANKFURTER concurs, dissenting.

In *United States v. Causby*, 328 U.S. 256 (1946), the Court held that by flying its military aircraft frequently on low landing and takeoff flights over Causby's chicken farm the United States had so disturbed the peace of the occupants and so frightened the chickens that it had "taken" a flight easement from Causby for which it was required to pay "just compensation" under the Fifth Amendment.

Today the Court holds that similar low landing and take-off flights, making petitioner Griggs' property "undesirable and unbearable for residential use," constitute a "taking" of airspace over Griggs' property—not, however, by the owner and operator of the planes as in *Causby*, but by Allegheny County, the owner and operator of the Greater Pittsburgh Airport to and from which the planes fly.

Although I dissented in *Causby* because I did not believe that the individual aircraft flights "took" property in the constitutional sense merely by going over it and because I believed that the complexities of adjusting atmospheric property rights to the air age could best be handled by Congress, I agree with the Court that the noise, vibrations and fear caused by constant and extremely low overflights in this case have so interfered with the use and enjoyment of petitioner's property as to amount to a "taking" of it under the *Causby* holding.

I cannot agree, however, that it was the County of Allegheny that did the "taking." I think that the United States, not the Greater Pittsburgh Airport, has "taken" the airspace over Griggs' property necessary for flight. While the County did design the plan for the airport, including the arrangement of its takeoff and approach areas, in order to comply with federal requirements, it did so under the supervision of and subject to the approval of the Civil Aeronautics Administrator of the United States.

Federal, Not Local, Taking?

Congress has over the years adopted a comprehensive plan for national and international air commerce, regulating in minute detail virtually every aspect of air transit—from construction and planning of ground facilities to safety and methods of flight operations. As part of this overall scheme of development, Congress in 1938 declared that the United States has "complete and exclusive national sovereignty in the air space above the United States" and that every citizen has "a public right of freedom of transit in air commerce through the navigable air space of the United States."

Although in *Causby* the Court held that under the then existing laws and regulations the airspace used in landing and take-off was not part of the "navigable airspace" as to which all have a right of free transit, Congress has since, in 1958, enacted a new law, as part of a regulatory scheme even more comprehensive than those before it, making it clear that the "airspace needed to insure safety in take-off and landing of aircraft" is "navigable airspace." Thus, Congress has not only appropriated the airspace necessary for planes to fly at high altitudes throughout the country but has also provided the low altitude airspace essential for those same planes to approach and take off from airports. These airspaces are so much under the control of the Federal Government that every take-off from and every landing at airports such as the Greater Pittsburgh Airport is made under the direct signal and supervisory control of some federal agent.

Merely because local communities might eventually be reimbursed for the acquisition of necessary easements does not mean that local communities must acquire easements that the United States has already acquired. And where Congress has already declared airspace free to all—a fact not denied by the Court—pretty clearly it need not again be acquired by an airport.

Duty on Local Community?

Having taken the airspace over Griggs' private property for a public use, it is the United States which owes just compensation. The construction of the Greater Pittsburgh Airport was financed in large part by funds supplied by the United States as part of its plan to induce localities like Allegheny County to assist in setting up a national and international air transportation system. The Court's imposition of liability on Allegheny County, however, goes a long way toward defeating that plan because of the greatly increased financial burdens (how great one can only guess) which will hereafter fall on all the cities and counties which til now have given or may hereafter give support to the national program. I do not believe that Congress ever intended any such frustration of its own purpose.

> *The construction of the Greater Pittsburgh Airport was financed in large part by funds supplied by the United States as part of its plan to induce localities like Allegheny County to assist in setting up a national and international air transportation system. The Court's imposition of liability on Allegheny County, however, goes a long way toward defeating that plan.*

Nor do I believe that Congress intended the wholly inequitable and unjust saddling of the entire financial burden of this part of the national program on the people of local communities like Allegheny County. The planes that take off and land at the Greater Pittsburgh Airport wind their rapid way through space not for the peculiar benefit of the citizens of Allegheny County but as part of a great, reliable transportation system of immense advantage to the whole Nation in time of peace and war.

Just as it would be unfair to require petitioner and others who suffer serious and peculiar injuries by reason of these transportation flights to bear an unfair proportion of the burdens of air commerce, so it would be unfair to make Allegheny County bear expenses wholly out of proportion to the advantages it can receive from the national transportation system. I can see no justification at all for throwing this monkey wrench into Congress' finely tuned national transit mechanism. I would affirm the state court's judgment holding that the County of Allegheny has not "taken" petitioner's property.

EXERCISE 2-3. *GRIGGS V. COUNTY OF ALLEGHENY*—TAKINGS AND JUST COMPENSATION

1. What is an "air easement"?

2. As between the owner and operator of the airplanes causing the noise at issue in *Griggs v. County of Allegheny*, and the owner and operator of the airport, which party was responsible for the "taking" of an air easement?

3. How does Justice Black address the issue of fairness, in his dissent?

4. As mentioned in Justice Black's dissenting opinion, Congress refined the term "navigable airspace" in 1958. How does it differ from the definition of the same

term in *United States v. Causby*, and what is the significance of that change for takings cases generally?

5. Explain the difference between Justice Black's dissenting opinion in *Griggs v. County* and his dissent in *United States v. Causby*?

NOTES ON *GRIGGS V. COUNTY OF ALLEGHENY*—NATIONAL PLAN OF INTEGRATED AIRPORT SYSTEMS ("NPIAS") AND THE AIRPORT IMPROVEMENT PROGRAM ("AIP")

1. *National Plan of Integrated Airport Systems ("NPIAS").*

Through its National Plan of Integrated Airport Systems ("NPIAS"), the FAA identifies nearly 3,400 existing and proposed airports that are significant to national air transportation and thus eligible to receive Federal grants under the Airport Improvement Program ("AIP"). The NPIAS, which contains all commercial service airports, all reliever airports, and selected general aviation airports, also includes estimates of the amount of AIP money needed to fund infrastructure development projects that will bring these airports up to current design standards and add capacity to congested airports. The FAA is required to provide Congress with a 5-year estimate of AIP eligible development every two years. *See* https://www.faa.gov/airports/planning_capacity/npias/.

2. *Airport Improvement Program ("AIP").*

The FAA's Airport Improvement Program ("AIP") provides grants to public agencies (and, in some cases, to private owners and entities) for the planning and development of public-use airports that are included in the National Plan of Integrated Airports Systems ("NPIAS").

> To promote the development of a system of airports to meet the nation's needs, the federal government embarked on a grants-in-aid program to units of state and local governments shortly after the end of World War II. The early program, the Federal-Aid Airport Program ("FAAP") was authorized by the Federal Airport Act of 1946 and drew its funding from the general fund of the U.S. Treasury.

> In 1970, a more comprehensive program was established with the passage of the Airport and Airway Development Act of 1970. This Act provided grants for airport planning under the Planning Grant Program ("PGP") and for airport development under the Airport Development Aid Program ("ADAP").

> These programs were funded from a newly established Airport and Airway Trust Fund, into which were deposited revenues from several aviation-user

taxes on such items as airline fares, air freight, and aviation fuel. The authority to issue grants under these two programs expired on September 30, 1981. During this 11-year period, 8,809 grants totaling $4.5 billion were approved.

The current program, known as the Airport Improvement Program ("AIP"), was established by the Airport and Airway Improvement Act of 1982 (Public Law 97–248). Since then, the AIP has been amended several times, most recently with the passage of the FAA Modernization and Reform Act of 2012. Funds obligated for the AIP are drawn from the Airport and Airway Trust fund, which is supported by user fees, fuel taxes, and other similar revenue sources.

See Fed. Aviation Admin., *Overview: What is AIP*, https://www.faa.gov/airports/aip/overview/.

According to the FAA, because the demand for AIP funds exceeds the availability, the FAA bases distribution of these funds on present national priorities and objectives. AIP funds are typically first apportioned into major entitlement categories such as primary, cargo, and general aviation.

Remaining funds are distributed to a discretionary fund. Set-aside projects (airport noise and the Military Airport Program) receive first attention from this discretionary distribution. The remaining funds are true discretionary funds that are distributed according to a national prioritization formula.

Table 2-1. Eligible vs. Ineligible Airport Improvement Program Projects

Examples of Eligible Versus Ineligible AIP Projects	
Eligible Projects	**Ineligible Projects**
Runway construction/rehabilitation	Maintenance equipment and vehicles
Taxiway construction/rehabilitation	Office and office equipment
Apron construction/rehabilitation	Fuel farms*
Airfield lighting	Landscaping
Airfield signage	Artworks
Airfield drainage	Aircraft hangars*
Land acquisition	Industrial park development
Weather observation stations (AWOS)	Marketing plans
NAVAIDs such as REILs and PAPIs	Training
Planning studies	Improvements for commercial enterprises
Environmental studies	Maintenance or repairs of buildings
Safety area improvements	
Airport layout plans (ALPs)	
Access roads only located on airport property	
Removing, lowering, moving, marking, and lighting hazards	
Glycol Recovery Trucks/Glycol Vacuum Trucks** (11/29/2007)	

Source: https://www.faa.gov/airports/aip/overview/.

3.   *Avigation Easement.*

One author defined "[a]n avigation easement [as] an easement of use of the airspace above property located within the direct flight path of an airport's runway." *See* David Casanova, *The Possibility and Consequences of the Recognition of Prescriptive Easements by State Courts*, 28 B.C. ENVTL. AFF. L. REV. 399 (2001). Unlike the takings at issue in *United States v. Causby* and *Griggs v. County of Allegheny, supra*, such rights may be voluntarily bargained by contract as illustrated in the following template by the Federal Aviation Administration:

Figure 2-1. Avigation Easement Agreement

 Airport Division
FAA Central Region   Validated 09/2012

Suggested Template for Avigation Easements
We have provided this sample Avigation Easement language to assist Sponsors with the preparation of an agreement for their specific location and situation. We recommend Sponsors furnish this sample language to their attorney tasked with preparing the actual Avigation Easement.

Limitations of Use
The FAA's provision of this sample language serves as a starting point for the Sponsor for preparing their customized avigation easement. Sponsors must not construe provision of this sample document as being complete and legally sufficient. Sponsors are solely responsible for verifying the legal status of all contractual matters, including establishment of avigation easements.

SURFACE AND OVERHEAD AVIGATION EASEMENT

WHEREAS, (Property Owner), hereinafter called the Grantors are the fee owners of the following specifically described parcel of land situated in (City, County & State):

(Metes & bounds description of easement parcel)

hereinafter called "Grantors' property" and outlined on an attached Exhibit A map.

NOW, THEREFORE, in consideration of the sum of $_____ and other good and valuable consideration, the receipt and sufficiency of which is hereby acknowledged, the Grantors, for themselves, their heirs, administrators, executors, successors and assigns do hereby grant the following appurtenant rights and benefits to the (Name of Airport) hereinafter called the "Grantee" for the use and benefit of the public.

The appurtenant rights and benefits include the uses, rights and restrictions described as follows:

The unobstructed use and passage of all types of aircraft in and through the airspace at any height or altitude above the surface of the land.

The right of said aircraft to cause noise, vibrations, fumes, deposits of dust, fuel particles (incidental to the normal operation of aircraft); fear, interference with sleep or communication, and any other effects associated with the normal operation of aircraft taking off, landing or operating in the vicinity of (Airport).

As used herein, the term "aircraft" shall mean any and all types of aircraft, whether now in existence or hereafter manufactured and developed, to include jet, propeller-driven, civil, military or commercial aircraft; helicopters, regardless of existing or future noise levels, for the purpose of transporting persons or property through the air, by whoever owned or operated.

Airport Division
FAA Central Region

Validated 09/2012

In granting this easement, the Grantors agree to make no modifications to the following "accepted" existing structures lying within the bounds of the easement area of the Grantors' property.

(Example: 20' x 25' utility shed, see attached Exhibit A map)

The Grantors agree that during the life of this easement, they will not construct, erect, suffer to permit or allow any structure or trees on the surface of the burdened property. The Grantors may not permit any places of public assembly or gatherings within the easement area. (Examples: churches, schools, day care facilities, hospitals, restaurants, stadiums, office buildings, etc.) The Grantors are permitted to continue to grow and harvest crops or graze livestock in the easement area

The Grantors agree to keep the easement area free of the following: structures (permanent or temporary) that might create glare or contain misleading lights; residences, fuel handling and storage facilities and smoke generating activities and creation of any means of electrical interference that could effect the movement of aircraft over the easement area.

Grantors agree to waive all damages and claims for damages caused or alleged to be caused by the Grantors violation of any aspect of this easement document. The (Airport) has a perpetual right of ingress/egress in the easement area and the right to remove any new structure or vegetation that is not specifically mentioned above as "accepted."

TO HAVE AND TO HOLD said easement and right of way, and all rights appertaining thereto unto the Grantee, its successors, and assigns, until said (Airport) shall be abandoned and shall cease to be used for public airport purposes. It is understood and agreed that all provisions herein shall run with the land and shall be binding upon the Grantors, their heirs, administrators, executors, successors and assigns until such time that the easement is extinguished.

IN WITNESS WHEREOF, the grantors have hereunto set their hands and seals this _____ day of _____, 20_____. (Local recordation and subordination practices must also be met. If subordination is necessary in which case the mortgagee must join in the agreement, a statement must be made to assure that the mortgage is subordinate to the Easement and the Easement recording superior and prior to lien in said mortgage without consideration of the date of the mortgage instrument)

_____
_____(SEAL)
Grantor(s)

Source: https://www.faa.gov/airports/central/airports_resources/media/RPZeasement.pdf.

4.   *Federal Airport Grants.*

As introduced in *Goodspeed Airport, LLC v. East Haddam Inland Wetlands and Watercourses Comm'n*, 681 F. Supp. 2d 182 (D. Conn. 2010), Chapter 11, *supra*, airports—their operations, land use, finances, and safety—are regulated extensively. Public or private agencies that control airports (*e.g.*, "sponsors") assume certain obligations in exchange for accepting airport development assistance from the federal government.

Such obligations are undertaken either by contract or by restrictive covenants in property deeds, to maintain and operate airport facilities safely and efficiently in accordance with specified conditions. Some grant programs include the Federal Aid to Airports Program ("FAAP"), the National Plan of Integrated Airport Systems ("NPIAS"), the Airport Development Aid Program ("ADAP"), and the Airport Improvement Program ("AIP") (49 U.S.C. § 47101 *et seq.*) *See* FED. AVIATION ADMIN., AIRPORT COMPLIANCE MANUAL, ORDER 5190.6B (Sept. 30, 2009) http://www.faa.gov/airports/resources/publications/orders/compliance_5190_6/.

When airport owners or sponsors, planning agencies, or other organizations accept funds from FAA-administered airport financial assistance programs, they must agree to certain obligations (or assurances). These obligations require the recipients to maintain and operate their facilities safely and efficiently and in accordance with specified conditions. The assurances may be attached to the application or the grant for Federal assistance and become part of the final grant offer or in restrictive covenants to property deeds. The duration of these obligations depends on the type of recipient, the useful life of the facility being developed, and other conditions stipulated in the assurances.

Sponsors are obligated to make "grant assurances" as part of their grant agreement with the government. That is, [w]hen airport owners or sponsors, planning agencies, or other organizations accept funds from FAA-administered airport financial assistance programs, they must agree to certain obligations (or assurances). These obligations require the recipients to maintain and operate their facilities safely and efficiently and in accordance with specified conditions. The assurances may be attached to the application or the grant for Federal assistance and become part of the final grant offer or in restrictive covenants to property deeds. The duration of these obligations depends on the type of recipient, the useful life of the facility being developed, and other conditions stipulated in the assurances." *See* https://www.faa.gov/airports/aip/grant_assurances/.

One of the most litigating assurances involves "economic nondiscrimination," *i.e.* the promise to make an airport available for public use to any entity for aeronautical use on reasonable terms and without unjust discrimination. *See Lange v. Fed. Aviation Admin.*, 208 F.3d 389 (2d Cir. 2000); *Penobscot Air Svcs. Ltd. v. Fed. Aviation Admin.*, 164 F.3d 714 (1st Cir. 1999). *See also* 49 U.S.C. § 47107 (2010).

SINGER V. CITY OF NEWTON

284 F. Supp. 3d 125 (D. Mass. 2017)

WILLIAM G. YOUNG, DISTRICT JUDGE.

The crux of this dispute is whether portions of a certain ordinance (the "Ordinance") passed by the City of Newton ("Newton") on December 19, 2016 are preempted. Michael S. Singer ("Singer") challenges portions of the Ordinance which require that all owners of pilotless aircraft (commonly referred to as "drones" or "UAS") register their pilotless aircraft with Newton, and also prohibit operation of pilotless aircraft out of the operator's line of sight or in certain areas without permit or express permission.

Newton is a municipality in the Commonwealth of Massachusetts and is organized under a charter pursuant to the Home Rule Amendment of the Massachusetts Constitution. Singer resides in Newton. He is a Federal Aviation Administration ("FAA")-certified small unmanned aircraft pilot and owns and operates multiple drones in Newton. Singer does not operate or register his drones as a hobbyist.

In August 2015, members of Newton's City Council proposed discussing the possibility of regulating drones for the principal purpose of protecting the privacy interests of Newton's residents. On March 23, 2016, an initial draft of the Ordinance was presented for discussion. Following further inquiry and amendment, but without FAA approval, Newton's City Council approved the final Ordinance on December 19, 2016. The Ordinance states in part:

Local Ordinance

> Purpose: The use of pilotless aircraft is an increasingly popular pastime as well as learning tool. It is important to allow beneficial uses of these devices while also protecting the privacy of residents throughout the City. In order to prevent nuisances and other disturbances of the enjoyment of both public and private space, regulation of pilotless aircraft is required. The following section is intended to promote the public safety and welfare of the City and its residents. In furtherance of its stated purpose, this section is intended to be read and interpreted in harmony with all relevant rules and regulations of the Federal Aviation Administration, and any other federal, state and local laws and regulations.

Newton Ordinances § 20–64, ECF No. 40–3. "Pilotless aircraft" is defined as "an unmanned, powered aerial vehicle, weighing less than 55 pounds, that is operated without direct human contact from within or on the aircraft." *Id.* § 20–64(a). In section (b), the Ordinance imposes certain registration requirements upon owners of all pilotless aircraft. *Id.* § 20–64(b). Section (c) sets forth operating prohibitions, including, *inter alia*, a ban on the use of a pilotless aircraft below an altitude of 400 feet over private property without the express permission of the owner of the private property, id. § 20–64(c)(1)(a), "beyond the visual line of sight of the Operator," id. § 20–64(c)(1)(b), "in a manner that interferes with any manned aircraft," *id.* § 20–64(c)(1)(c), over Newton city property without prior permission, *id.* § 20–64(c)(1)(e), or to conduct surveillance or invade any place where a person has a reasonable expectation of privacy, id. § 20–64(c)(1)(f)–(g). Violations of the Ordinance are punishable by a $50 fine following a one-time warning. *Id.* § 20–64(f).

RULINGS OF LAW

Specifically, Singer challenges four subsections of the Ordinance: the registration requirements of section (b) and the operation limits of subsections (c)(1)(a), (c)(1)(b), and (c)(1)(e). Singer argues that the Ordinance is preempted by federal law because it attempts to regulate an almost exclusively federal area of law in a way that conflicts with Congress's purpose, *id.* at 14–15. In turn, Newton posits that the Ordinance is not preempted by federal law because it falls within an area of law that the FAA expressly carved out for local governments to regulate, and thus can be read in harmony with federal aviation laws and regulations.

A.   Preemption Standards

The Supremacy Clause of the United States Constitution provides that federal laws are supreme, U.S. Const. art. VI, cl. 2, thus requiring that federal laws preempt any conflicting state or local regulations, *see Maryland v. Louisiana*, 451 U.S. 725, 746 (1981) (citing *McCulloch v. Maryland*, 4 Wheat. 316, 427 (1819)). Under our federalist system, however, a court must be wary of invalidating laws in areas traditionally left to the states unless the court is entirely convinced that Congress intended to override state regulation. *See, e.g., Gregory v. Ashcroft*, 501 U.S. 452, 460. In contrast, if a state government attempts to regulate an area traditionally occupied by the federal government, a court need not seek to avoid preemption. *See United States v. Locke*, 529 U.S. 89, 108 (2000). Neither of these circumstances requires that Congress explicitly have stated its purpose; "[t]he question, at bottom, is one of statutory intent." *Morales v. Trans World Airlines, Inc.*, 504 U.S. 374, 383 (1992).

If Congress has not expressly preempted an area of law, then a court must determine whether field or conflict preemption is evident. *See French v. Pan Am Express, Inc.*, 869 F.2d 1, 2 (1st Cir. 1989). Field preemption occurs where federal regulation is so pervasive and dominant that one can infer Congressional intent to occupy the field. *See Massachusetts Ass'n of Health Maint. Orgs. v. Ruthardt*, 194 F.3d 176, 179 (1st Cir. 1999) (citing *Rice v. Santa Fe Elevator Corp.*, 331 U.S. 218, 230 (1947)). Conflict preemption arises when compliance with both state and federal regulations is impossible or if state law obstructs the objectives of the federal regulation.

B.   The Federal Aviation Administration

Congress has stated that "[t]he United States Government has exclusive sovereignty of airspace of the United States." 49 U.S.C. § 40103(a)(1). This declaration does not preclude states or municipalities from passing any valid aviation regulations, *see Braniff Airways v. Nebraska State Bd. of Equalization & Assessment*, 347 U.S. 590, 595 (1954), but courts generally recognize that Congress extensively controls much of the field, *see, e.g., Chicago & S. Air Lines, Inc. v. Waterman Steamship Corp.*, 333 U.S. 103, 105, 107 (1948); *United Parcel Serv., Inc. v. Flores-Galarza*, 318 F.3d 323, 336 (1st Cir. 2003). Accordingly, where a state's exercise of police power infringes upon the federal government's regulation of aviation, state law is preempted. *See City of Burbank v. Lockheed Air Terminal Inc.*, 411 U.S. 624, 638–39 (1973).

In the FAA Modernization and Reform Act of 2012, Congress directed the FAA to "develop a comprehensive plan to safely accelerate the integration of civil unmanned aircraft systems into the national airspace system," FAA Modernization and Reform Act of 2012, Pub. L. No. 112–95 § 332, 126 Stat. 11, 73 (2012) (codified at 49 U.S.C. § 40101 note), while limiting the FAA from "promulgat[ing] any rule or regulation regarding a model aircraft," id. § 336(a). Under this directive, the FAA promulgated 14 C.F.R. part 107, which declares that it "applies to the registration, airman certification, and operation of civil small unmanned aircraft systems within the United States." 14 C.F.R. § 107.1(a). (The FAA defines "small unmanned aircraft" as "an unmanned aircraft weighing less than 55 pounds on takeoff, including everything that is on board or otherwise attached to the aircraft," and "small unmanned aircraft system" as "a small unmanned aircraft and its associated elements." 14 C.F.R. § 107.3.) The rule requires, *inter alia*, that anyone controlling a small unmanned aircraft system register with the FAA, *id.* §§ 91.203, 107.13; and keep the aircraft within the visual line of sight of the operator or a designated visual observer, *id.* §§ 107.3, 107.31, and below an altitude of 400 feet above ground level or within a 400-foot radius of a structure, *id.* § 107.51(b).

FAA Modernization and Reform Act of 2012 ("FMRA")

Visual Line of Sight ("VLOS")

C. Field Preemption

Singer argues that because the federal government regulates unmanned aircraft and local aircraft operations, there is federal intent to occupy the field. Newton does not challenge that aviation is a traditionally federal field, but counters that federal regulations explicitly grant local authorities the power to co-regulate unmanned aircraft.

The FAA has stated:

[C]ertain legal aspects concerning small UAS use may be best addressed at the State or local level. For example, State law and other legal protections for individual privacy may provide recourse for a person whose privacy may be affected through another person's use of a UAS.

. . . The Fact Sheet also summarizes the Federal responsibility for ensuring the safety of flight as well as the safety of people and property on the ground as a result of the operation of aircraft. Substantial air safety issues are implicated when State or local governments attempt to regulate the operation of aircraft in the national airspace. The Fact Sheet provides examples of State and local laws affecting UAS for which consultation with the FAA is recommended and those that are likely to fall within State and local government authority. For example, consultation with FAA is recommended when State or local governments enact operation UAS restrictions on flight altitude, flight paths; operational bans; or any regulation of the navigable airspace. The Fact Sheet also notes that laws traditionally related to State and local police power—including land use, zoning, privacy, trespass, and law enforcement operations—generally are not subject to Federal regulation.

81 Fed. Reg. 42063 § (III)(K)(6). Thus, the FAA explicitly contemplates state or local regulation of pilotless aircraft, defeating Singer's argument that the whole field is exclusive to the federal government. The FAA's guidance, however, does not go quite as far as Newton argues—rather than an express carve-out for state and localities to regulate, the guidance hints that whether parallel regulations are enforceable depends on the principles of conflict preemption. In fact, Newton has acknowledged that "[c]ommercial drone use is heavily regulated by the FAA [and] pre-empted from municipal regulations." Public Safety & Transportation Committee Report dated Mar. 23, 2016, 3.

D. Conflict Preemption

Singer argues that the challenged sections of the Ordinance obstruct federal objectives and directly conflict with federal regulations. Newton fails to respond specifically to these arguments, again asserting that the FAA has granted states and localities the power to co-regulate pilotless aircraft. The Court addresses each challenged subsection of the Ordinance in turn.

1. Section (b)

Singer argues that section (b) of the Ordinance infringes upon and impermissibly exceeds the FAA's exclusive registration requirements. Section (b) states: "Owners of all pilotless aircraft shall register their pilotless aircraft with the City Clerk's Office, either individually or as a member of a club. . . ." Newton Ordinances § 20–64(b). The Ordinance defines "pilotless aircraft" as "an unmanned, powered aerial vehicle, weighing less than 55 pounds, that is operated without direct human contact from within or on the aircraft." *Id.* § 20–64(a).

The FAA has also implemented mandatory registration of certain drones. *See* 14 C.F.R. §§ 48.1–48.205. Although such registration initially applied both to model and commercial drones, the FAA may not require registration of model aircraft, because doing so would directly conflict with the Congressional mandate in the FAA Modernization and Reform Act. *See Taylor v. Huerta*, 856 F.3d 1089, 1092, 1094 (D.C. Cir. 2017). Newton argues that this space creates a void in which the city may regulate drones. The FAA, however, explicitly has indicated its intent to be the exclusive regulatory authority for registration of pilotless aircraft: "Because Federal registration is the exclusive means for registering UAS for purposes of operating an aircraft in navigable airspace, no state or local government may impose an additional registration requirement on the operation of UAS in navigable airspace without first obtaining FAA approval." *State and Local Regulation of Unmanned Aircraft Systems (UAS) Fact Sheet* ("FAA UAS Fact Sheet"). Although the FAA UAS Fact Sheet is not a formal rule, it is the FAA's interpretation of its own rule, which this Court accords deference under *Bowles v. Seminole Rock & Sand Co.,* 325 U.S. 410, 413–14 (1945).

Newton did not obtain FAA approval before enacting the Ordinance. Further, regardless of whether there is some space that would allow Newton to require registration of model drones, here Newton seeks to register all drones without limit as to the at which altitude they operate, in clear derogation of the FAA's intended authority. Accordingly, the Ordinance's registration requirements are preempted.

Newton did not obtain FAA approval before enacting the Ordinance. Further, regardless of whether there is some space that would allow Newton to require registration of model drones, here Newton seeks to register all drones without limit as to the at which altitude they operate, in clear derogation of the FAA's intended authority. Accordingly, the Ordinance's registration requirements are preempted.

2.   Subsections (c)(1)(a) and (c)(1)(e)

Singer argues that subsections (c)(1)(a) and (c)(1)(e) conflict with FAA-permitted flight and restrict flight within the navigable airspace, *id.* at 12–14. Subsection (c)(1)(a) prohibits pilotless aircraft flight below an altitude of 400 feet over any private property without the express permission of the property owner. Newton Ordinances § 20–64(c)(1)(a). Subsection (c)(1)(e) prohibits pilotless aircraft flight over public property without prior permission from Newton. *Id.* § 20–64(c)(1)(e). Notably, subsection (c)(1)(e) does not limit its reach to any altitude. *See id.* This alone is a ground for preemption of the subsection because it certainly reaches into navigable airspace, see 49 U.S.C. § 40102(a)(32); 14 C.F.R. § 91.119. Subsections (c)(1)(a) and (c)(1)(e) work in tandem, however, to create an essential ban on drone use within the limits of Newton. Nowhere in the city may an individual operate a drone without first having permission from the owner of the land below, be that Newton or a private landowner.

The FAA mandated that drone operators keep drones below an altitude of 400 feet from the ground or a structure. 14 C.F.R. § 107.51(b). Newton's choice to restrict any drone use below this altitude thus works to eliminate any drone use in the confines of the city, absent prior permission. This thwarts not only the FAA's objectives, but also those of Congress for the FAA to integrate drones into the national airspace.

The FAA is charged with "prescrib[ing] air traffic regulations on the flight of aircraft . . . for—(A) navigating, protecting, and identifying aircraft; (B) protecting individuals and property on the ground; [and] (C) using the navigable airspace efficiently." 49 U.S.C. § 40103(b)(2). In 2012, Congress tasked the FAA with "develop[ing] a comprehensive plan to safely accelerate the integration of civil unmanned aircraft systems into the national airspace system." Pub. L. No. 112–95 § 332. In so doing, the FAA mandated that drone operators keep drones below an altitude of 400 feet from the ground or a structure. 14 C.F.R. § 107.51(b). Newton's choice to restrict any drone use below this altitude thus works to eliminate any drone use in the confines of the city, absent prior permission. This thwarts not only the FAA's objectives, but also those of Congress for the FAA to integrate drones into the national airspace. Although Congress and the FAA may have contemplated co-regulation of drones to a certain extent, see 81 Fed. Reg. 42063 § (III)(K)(6), this hardly permits an interpretation that essentially constitutes a wholesale ban on drone use in Newton. Accordingly, subsections (c)(1)(a) and (c)(1)(e) are preempted.

3.   Subsection (c)(1)(b)

Singer argues that subsection (c)(1)(b) conflicts with the FAA's visual observer rule and related waiver process, which only the FAA can modify. Subsection (c)(1)(b) states that no pilotless aircraft may be operated "at a distance beyond the visual line of sight of the Operator." Newton Ordinances § 20–64(c)(1)(b). The Ordinance neither defines the term "Operator," nor sets an altitude limit.

The FAA "requires a delicate balance between safety and efficiency, and the protection of persons on the ground. . . . The interdependence of these factors requires a uniform and exclusive system of federal regulation." *City of Burbank*, 411 U.S. at 638–39. The Ordinance seeks to regulate the method of operating of drones, necessarily implicating the safe operation of aircraft. Courts have recognized that aviation safety is an area of exclusive federal regulation. *See, e.g., Goodspeed Airport LLC v. East Haddam Inland Wetlands & Watercourses Comm'n*, 634 F.3d 206, 208 (2d Cir. 2011) ("Congress has established its intent to occupy the entire field of air safety, thereby preempting state regulation of that field."); *U.S. Airways, Inc. v. O'Donnell*, 627 F.3d 1318, 1326 (10th Cir. 2010) ("[F]ederal regulation occupies the field of aviation safety to the exclusion of state regulations."); *Montalvo v. Spirit Airlines*, 508 F.3d 464, 470 (9th Cir. 2007) ("Congress has indicated its intent to occupy the field of aviation safety."). The First Circuit, in fact, has ruled "that Congress intended to occupy the field of pilot regulation related to air safety." *French*, 869 F.2d at 4.

In *French*, the First Circuit took note of Congress's delegation of authority to the FAA to issue the certificate—and the terms for obtaining it—required for any person to pilot a commercial aircraft. Concluding that this grant of authority and the FAA's subsequent regulations expressed Congress's intent to preempt any state law in the area, the First Circuit struck down Rhode Island's statute requiring airline pilots to submit to drug testing.

The circumstances are not so different here. Congress has given the FAA the responsibility of regulating the use of airspace for aircraft navigation and to protect individuals and property on the ground, 49 U.S.C. § 40103(b)(2), and has specifically directed the FAA to integrate drones into the national airspace system,

Pub. L. No. 112–95 § 332. In furtherance of this duty, the FAA has designated specific rules regarding the visual line of sight for pilotless aircraft operation. See 14 C.F.R. §§ 107.31–35, 107.205. First, the FAA requires either that (1) a remote pilot both command and manipulate the flight controls or (2) a visual observer be able to see the drone throughout its flight. *Id.* § 107.31. The regulations define "visual observer" as "a person who is designated by the remote pilot in command to assist the remote pilot in command and the person manipulating the flight controls of the small UAS to see and avoid other air traffic or objects aloft or on the ground." *Id.* § 107.3. Second, the FAA allows waiver of the visual observer rule. *Id.* §§ 107.200, 205.

The Ordinance limits the methods of piloting a drone beyond that which the FAA has already designated, while also reaching into navigable space. *See* Newton Ordinances § 20–64(c)(1)(b). Intervening in the FAA's careful regulation of aircraft safety cannot stand; thus subsection (c)(1)(b) is preempted.

For the foregoing reasons, this Court holds that Ordinance sections (b), (c)(1)(a), (c)(1)(b), and (c)(1)(e) are preempted and judgment will enter so declaring. As it is unchallenged, the remainder of Newton's Ordinance stands. Of course, nothing prevents Newton from re-drafting the Ordinance to avoid conflict preemption.

EXERCISE 2-4. *SINGER V. CITY OF NEWTON*—LOCAL AIRSPACE REGULATION

1. Explain the purpose of Newton Ordinance § 20–64.

2. What does subsection (b) of Newton Ordinance § 20–64 require of the owners of unmanned aerial vehicles?

3. What does subsection (c) of Newton Ordinance § 20–64 require of the owners of pilotless aircraft?

4. What is Singer's argument as to why the Newton Ordinance is invalid?

5. In finding the local ordinance preempted, does the court's analysis fall under "field" or "conflict" preemption? Explain.

NOTES ON *SINGER V. CITY OF NEWTON*—FEDERAL PREEMPTION OF LOCAL AIRSPACE

Notwithstanding *Singer v. City of Newton*, an open question exists as to whether federal law preempts state law with respect to the private use of unmanned aerial systems—"drones."

Consider that the Idaho legislature enacted a statute that prohibits citizens from using "an unmanned aircraft system to intentionally conduct surveillance of, gather evidence or collect information about, or photographically or electronically record specifically targeted persons or specifically targeted private property." *See* IDAHO CODE ANN. § 21–213(2)(a) (2013). Similarly, Oregon prohibits the "operat[ion] of a drone that is flown at a height of less than 400 feet" over private property without the consent of the property owner. *See* OREGON LAWS CH. 686 § 15(1). Florida and Texas, in turn, prohibit citizens from using drones to capture the image of an individual or privately owned real property with the intent to conduct surveillance on the individual or property captured in the image. *See* TEX. GOV'T CODE ANN. § 423.003(a) (2013) and FLA. STAT. § 934.50 (2015). *See generally* Jol A. Silversmith, *You Can't Regulate This: State Regulation of the Private Use of Unmanned Aircraft*, 26 No. 3 AIR AND SPACE L. (2013).

As federal and state UAV authorities jockey for position, local authorities are beginning to regulate the operation of drones to the displeasure of state lawmakers. For example, in 2014, the town of Deer Trail, Colorado, attempted to authorize the issuance of licenses to allow residents to hunt and shoot down drones. In November 2015, Chicago became the first major American city to pass a drone ordinance because, "[n]otwithstanding those proposals being discussed in Washington, Chicago simply needs local laws in place to authorize the city to take action against those who operate drones recklessly and threaten public safety." *See* Fran Spielman, *Drone Regulations Fly with City Council*, CHICAGO SUNTIMES, Nov. 18, 2015. Alongside these initiatives, North Carolina gave units of local government explicit authority to adopt ordinances to regulate the use of the local government's property for the launch and recovery of UAS. N.C. Stat. § 15A–300.2(b).

But, some states have cut off the ability of cities, municipalities, and local governments to regulate UAVs altogether. For example, in December 2017, New Jersey lawmakers, in an effort to preempt local ordinances that may vary, advanced laws criminalizing the operation of a drone while drunk. A number of other states have exerted their authority over local UAV proposals and rules:

- Alaska state law preempts local law with respect to images captured by drone, stating, "[a] municipality may not adopt an ordinance that permits the release of images captured by an unmanned aircraft system in a manner inconsistent with Alaska Stat. 18.65.903, which governs the retention of images. Alaska Stat. § 29.35.146.

- Arizona state law provides that "[e]xcept as authorized by law, a city, town or county may not enact or adopt any ordinance, policy, or rule that relates to the ownership or operation of an unmanned aircraft system or otherwise engage in the regulation of the ownership or operation of an unmanned aircraft or unmanned aircraft system. Any ordinance that violates this subsection, whether enacted or adopted by the city, town or ordinance before or after the effective dates of this section, is void. Ariz. Rev. Stat. § 13–3729.

- Maryland codified a law that vests the state government with exclusive authority to regulate the testing or operation of unmanned aircraft systems, preempting the authority of counties and municipalities: "Only the State may enact a law or take any other action to prohibit, restrict, or regulate the testing or operation of unmanned aircraft systems in the State." As such, the law "preempts the authority of a county or municipality to prohibit, restrict, or regulate the testing or operation of unmanned aircraft systems; and supersedes any existing law or ordinance of a county or municipality that prohibits, restricts, or regulates the testing or operation of unmanned aircraft systems." Md. Code Com. Law § 14–301.

- In 2016, Rhode Island enacted its first drone law, giving the state and the Rhode Island Airport Cooperation exclusive authority to regulate "any object capable of flying, which is remotely controlled, and flies autonomously through software controlled flight plans embedded in the object's system by a global positioning system, commonly known as unpiloted aerial vehicles, remotely piloted aircraft, drones, or unmanned aircraft systems." But all of this may be for naught as the law concludes by stating that "if federal law preempts any provision of this chapter, that provision shall not apply." 2016 Rhode Island Law Ch. 16–256 (16–S 3099); 2016 Rhode Island Law Ch. 16–261 (16–H 7511B).

One scholar has resisted the suggestion that Congress should establish nationwide regulations to govern both law enforcement and civilian drone use, recommending instead "drone federalism: a state-based approach to privacy regulation that governs drone use by civilians, drawing on states' experience regulating other forms of civilian-on-civilian surveillance. *See generally* Margot E. Kaminski, *Drone Federalism: Civilian Drones and the Things They Carry*, 4 CAL. L. REV. Circuit 57, 73–74. (2013).

Suggested Further Reading

PROPERTY RIGHTS IN CONTEMPORARY GOVERNANCE (State University Press of New York 2019, Staci M. Zavattaro et al. eds.)

Who Makes the Rules for Outer Space?, NOVA, Nov. 30, 2015, https://www.pbs.org/wgbh/nova/article/space-law/

Caitlin Dewey, *The Curious Case of the Woman Suing eBay over Ownership of the Sun*, WASH. POST, June 4, 2015

UNMANNED AIRCRAFT IN THE NATIONAL AIRSPACE: CRITICAL ISSUES, TECHNOLOGY, AND THE LAW (AMERICAN BAR ASSOCIATION 2015, Donna Dulo ed.)

BRIAN HAVEL, BEYOND OPEN SKIES: A NEW REGIME FOR INTERNATIONAL AVIATION (WOLTERS KLUWER 2009)

Stuart Banner's *Who Owns the Sky: The Struggle to Control Airspace from the Wright Brothers On* (2008)

CHAPTER 3

Aircraft

In March 1977, Larry Gowan, a 32-year-old man, died an accidental death as a result of multiple fractures received in a fall while using a "hang kite," which was tethered to the ground. More specifically, he was using a "Muller Hang Kite," which could be used in "free" flight. Due to local circumstances, Gowan attempted to get himself into the air by tethering the kite to the ground with rope 160 feet in length, and in a strong wind, jumping up with it so the wind would catch it, and go aloft carrying him.

This it did, eventually taking him up to a height of some 50 feet. The cross bar of this kite, with a normal wingspread of 28 feet, buckled and broke while in the air, due to the strength of the wind, and came down sideways and fast, and the death ensued as a result. Gowan was insured in the amount of $32,000 at the time of the accident.

His insurance company refused to pay his wife, as beneficiary, however, on the basis that the applicable policy explicitly excluded coverage of a loss resulting "from or while making or attempting to make any aerial flight of any kind except solely as a passenger not a member of the aircraft crew nor having any duties in connection with such flight."

Was Gowan's "Muller Hang Kite" an "aircraft" such that his insurance company properly denied coverage?

See Gowan v. North American Life Assurance Co., [1980] 30 N.B.R.(2d) 304 [Canada]

A. OVERVIEW

This chapter is different from the other chapters of the book in that it focuses not on the legal environment relating to airplane operations or the people or things flying in aircraft, but on the law applicable to flying devices—aircraft themselves, including a new generation of unmanned aerial systems (*i.e.*, drones). In presenting the profits and perils attendant to aircraft operation and use, this chapter is segmented into two parts:

- Part B presents two cases, *Ickes v. Federal Aviation Admin.* and *Huerta v. Pirker*, that explore the legal definition of "airplane" and the importance of this definition from the point of view of operation and liability.

- Part C, through *Vreeland v. Ferrer*, examines the issue of aircraft leasing and lessor liability under the state law "dangerous instrumentality doctrine" and federal statutory law. (*See also Crosby v. Cox Aircraft Co. of Washington, infra,* Chapter 9.B.)

After reading the cases and materials in this chapter, the reader should appreciate the intricacies of the law respecting aircraft ownership, use, and liability.

But, before moving into these sections, consider these basic questions: What is an aircraft? Who is the "owner" of an aircraft? These seemingly straightforward questions can be complicated as a matter of law. That is the main point of the excerpt from the case of *Gowan v. North American Life Assurance Co.* at the outset of this chapter; there, whether a widow received insurance proceeds turned on the question of whether a "hang kite" was an "aircraft" as a matter of law. Indeed, as the materials in this chapter show, the rudimentary question of what is an aircraft is at the center of an important body of law that has produced nuanced answers.

For starters, the law recognizes three general type of "conveyances"—aircraft, vehicles, and vessels:

"Aircraft," as defined by the Federal Aviation Act of 1958, means "any contrivance invented, used, or designed to navigate, or fly in, the air." 49 U.S.C. § 40102(a)(6).

The word " 'vessel' includes every description of watercraft or other artificial contrivance used, or capable of being used, as a means of transportation *on water.*" 1 U.S.C. § 3.

The word " 'vehicle' includes every description of carriage or other artificial contrivance used, or capable of being used, as a means of transportation *on land.*" 1 U.S.C. § 4.

While these definitions appear distinctive, controversies arise when the legal rights of disputants turn on the operability of an "aircraft" "on water" or "on land."

Illustration 3-1. First Flight: December 17, 1903

Source: https://en.wikipedia.org/wiki/Airplane#/media/File:First_flight2.jpg

How lawyers and judges define types of conveyances is important, therefore, particularly as a new generation of aircraft on the horizon (*i.e.*, drones) may not fall neatly within one of these categories.

Vehicles

Courts first construed the word "aircraft" and "vehicle" in the last century. In *McBoyle v. United States*, 283 U.S. 25 (1931), the Supreme Court of the United States analyzed and compared the terms "vehicle" and "aircraft" to reverse the conviction of a man who transported a stolen airplane from Illinois to Oklahoma in violation of the National Motor Vehicle Theft Act ("NMVTA").

The NMVTA defined a "motor vehicle" as "an automobile, automobile truck, automobile wagon, motor cycle, or other self-propelled vehicle not designed for running on rails." Justice Oliver Wendell Holmes observed that "in everyday speech 'vehicle' calls up the picture of a thing moving on land," and that while airplanes were well known by the first quarter of the twentieth century, Congress had not apparently intended at that time to include motor vehicles that could leave the earth within the definition of "vehicle." Consequently, the statute prohibiting stealing any "self-propelled vehicle not designed for running on rails" neither extended to "aircraft" nor gave fair warning that interstate transport of stolen aircraft was prohibited. In other words, an "aircraft" was not a "vehicle" under the NMVTA and the prosecution failed for transport of a stolen airplane under the NMVTA failed.

More than seventy-years after *McBoyle*, the Supreme Court of the United States again evaluated the legal relationship between an "aircraft" and a "vehicle" in a criminal context. In *United States v. Reid*, 206 F. Supp. 2d 132 (D. Mass. 2002), Richard Reid—the foiled "shoe bomber" who tried to ignite and detonate the tongue of his sneaker aboard a Miami-Paris commercial jetliner on December 22, 2001—successfully moved to dismiss an indictment against him under the USA PATRIOT Act of 2001 on the basis that an airplane was not a "vehicle" engaged in "mass transportation." The district court agreed that the word "vehicle" in section 1993 of the USA PATRIOT Act did not include "aircraft."

An aircraft is not a vehicle?

While the USA PATRIOT Act prohibited terroristic acts against "mass transportation vehicles," Congress did not intend to provide additional punishment for the act of destroying or attempting to destroy aircraft, the *Reid* court found. Separate provisions of federal law already made such an act illegal. Section 32 of Title 18, for instance, authorized the punishment of any individual who "willfully sets fire to, damages, destroys, disables, or wrecks any aircraft in the special aircraft jurisdiction of the United States" and any individual who "attempts or conspires" to do the same. Thus, Congress intended to "fill the gaps" by enacting the USA PATRIOT Act, *e.g.*, to ensure that other modes of transportation vulnerable to terrorist attack but believed to be outside the reach of the federal criminal laws came within the reach of those laws. Consequently, Reid's attempted crime did not come within the scope of conduct prohibited by the USA PATRIOT Act because while the airplane he attempted to destroy was engaged in "mass transportation," it was not a "vehicle" as defined by Congress."

Vessels

The legal distinction between "aircraft" and "vehicle" discussed above has been sharper compared to the more nuanced and overlapping terms "aircraft" and "vessel." That "aircraft" are more akin to "vessels" than "vehicles" as a matter of law is not surprising considering that early aviation operations arose from and largely supplanted traditional maritime activities. Modern commercial aviation originated with amphibious-type airplanes. The first commercial flight occurred on January 1, 1914 when a Benoist XIV flying boat crossed Tampa Bay, Florida (a journey that would take two hours on a steam ship). That milestone ushered in the 1920s-era Pan American World Airways' "Clipper" class of large flying boats deployed out of Dinner Key in Miami, Florida bound for international destinations.

Lawmakers globally recognized the close relationship between aviation and admiralty operations when, in 1909, the International Juridical Committee on Aviation was organized at Paris, France for the purpose of outlining a legal code of the air. In doing so, delegates from around the world analogized rules applicable to water craft to aircraft, including rules as to the nationality and registration of aircraft, flag regulations, documentary requirements (*e.g.*, logbook), jurisdiction, and the aerial rules of the road. Courts, too, played a central role in distinguishing aircraft from vessels on an operational basis, though judges initially resisted overlaying aviation operations with admiralty law.

International Juridical Committee on Aviation

In *The Crawford Bros. No. 2*, 215 F. 269 (W.D. Wash. 1914), a federal district court considered a libel *in rem* action for repairs to an airplane that had fallen into navigable water of the Puget Sound, Washington. The court noticed the peculiar qualities of aircraft vis-à-vis vessels: "They are neither of the land nor sea, and, not being of the sea or restricted in their activities to navigable waters, they are not maritime." As such, the court declined to extend admiralty jurisdiction absent a legislative imperative to do so:

> In view of the novelty and complexity of the questions that must necessarily arise out of this new engine of transportation and commerce, it appears to the court that, in the absence of legislation conferring jurisdiction, none would obtain in this court, and that questions such as those raised by the libelant must be relegated to the common-law courts, courts of general jurisdiction.

A few years after *The Crawford Bros. No. 2*, then-Judge Benjamin Cardozo of the New York Court of Appeals offered a framework for determining whether an "aircraft" was a "vessel" under the law. In *Reinhardt v. Newport Flying Service Corporation*, 133 N.E. 371 (N.Y. 1921), an employee was responsible for the care and management of a hydro-aeroplane operating between New York and Florida. While moored in the navigable waters at Gravesend Bay, Brooklyn, the craft dragged anchor and drifted toward the beach where it was in danger of being wrecked. Reinhardt waded into the water to turn the plane about and was struck by one of the propellers. He sued and obtained benefits under applicable workers' compensation law. However, his employer and its insurer appealed on the basis that admiralty jurisdiction displaced the workers' compensation commission.

In approaching this dispute, Judge Cardozo captured the novelty of airplane travel and the legal regime evolving around manned flight, writing that "[t]he latest of man's devices for locomotion has invaded the navigable waters, the most ancient of his highways. Riding at anchor is a new craft which would have mystified the Lord High Admiral in the days when he was competing for jurisdiction with Coke and the courts of common law."

Judge Cardozo recognized that a hydroaeroplane, while in the air, was not subject to admiralty because it was not then in navigable waters. Alternatively, "a hydroaeroplane, while afloat upon waters capable of navigation, is subject to the admiralty, because location and function stamp it as a means of water transportation." Thus, the fact a hydroaeroplane was both a seaplane and an aeroplane was not dispositive, and the medium through which it traveled was analytically controlling.

Navigability Test

Ultimately, Judge Cardozo agreed with the employer and insurer, reasoning that a seaplane anchored on or afloat on navigable waters was subject to the laws of the sea, but it was not to be treated as a "vessel" within admiralty jurisdiction when it was navigating through the air on a regular passage between points over sea or land. (The issue of admiralty jurisdiction will again become important in the context of accident litigation. *See* Chapter 12, *Executive Jet, Inc. v. City of Cleveland, Ohio.*) Employing a navigability test, Judge Cardozo recognized that a hydroaeroplane, while in the air, was not subject to admiralty because it was not then in navigable waters. Alternatively, "a hydroaeroplane, while afloat upon waters capable of navigation, is subject to the admiralty, because location and function stamp it as a means of water transportation." Thus, the fact a hydroaeroplane was both a seaplane and an aeroplane was not dispositive, and the medium through which it traveled was analytically controlling:

> If a seaplane, incapable of flight, breaks its moorings and causes injury to man or ship, there will be a remedy against the offending *res*. If, moving upon the water, it becomes disabled, and is rescued on the high seas by a ship, it will be subject to a lien for salvage. We think the jurisdiction of the admiralty is not less where the structure found afloat is seaplane and aeroplane combined.

> The records of the Navy Department show that there have been times, in transatlantic flights, when planes, abandoning the air, moved for days upon the water. The cause might be lack of fuel or other disability. Even in the absence of such causes, there must always, for at least some space, be movement upon the water before there is ascent into the air. Jurisdiction cannot vary as the distance is short or longer. That would

require us to say that the plane, by keeping to the water, could transform itself into a vessel, but would leave us helpless to define the point at which transformation would be suffered.

From such embarrassments of definition there is but one avenue of escape. It is found in the conclusion that the plane is a vessel, and hence within the jurisdiction of the admiralty, when it is in the fulfillment of its function as a traveler through water, and has put aside its functions and capacities as a traveler through air.

The conclusion to which we are thus led is in accordance with the practice of the government, so far as practice has developed. The Treasury Department of the United States requires seaplanes or hydroplanes to be registered as vessels. The same department has held that in navigating the water they are subject to the rules of the road. It has also held them to be vessels within the meaning of the Tariff Law, Act Oct. 3, 1913. Rulings not dissimilar have been made by the Department of Commerce.

Five years after the *Reinhardt* decision, on May 20, 1926, Congress enacted the Civil Aeronautics Act. The law aimed to encourage and regulate the use of aircraft in commerce, but made certain that admiralty rules were inapplicable to the young aviation industry: "Section 7 (Sec. 177). Application of existing laws relating to foreign commerce. (a) The navigation and shipping laws of the United States, including any definition of 'vessel' or 'vehicle' found therein and including the rules for the prevention of collisions, shall not be construed to apply to seaplanes or other aircraft." 49 U.S.C. § 177.

Civil Aeronautics Act of 1926

In decades since, courts have considered various scenarios requiring additional analysis of the functionality of a "vessel" or "aircraft" as expressed in *Reinhardt* and aviation regulators have expanded the meaning of the term "aircraft" itself to reflect technological advances. For example, in *Dollins v. Pan American Grace Airways*, 27 F. Supp. 487 (S.D.N.Y. 1939), a federal court characterized an airship as follows: "While [an] airship must effect its ascent either from (and likewise its descent upon) water or land, its real purpose is to navigate through the air, although it may operate on the water in a smooth sea, but that is purely an auxiliary function. It does not seem conceivable that it can be seriously contended that the Congress ever had such craft in mind in granting a limitation of liability to the owner of a vessel, if such this be, within the definition [of a vessel]."

[For further discussion of admiralty jurisdiction see Chapter 12.C, *infra*.]

Aircraft

"Contrivance," Federal Aviation Act of 1958; "Device," Federal Aviation Regulations

The definition of "aircraft" can be found in two primary places. First, the Federal Aviation Act of 1958 defines an "aircraft" as "any contrivance invented, used, or designed to navigate, or fly in, the air." 49 U.S.C. § 40102(a)(6). The Federal Aviation Regulations ("FARs") define an "aircraft" slightly differently, but not inconsistently, *e.g.,* as "a device that is used or intended to be used for flight in the air." 14 C.F.R. § 1.1. Whether called a "contrivance," as expressed under the Federal Aviation Act of 1958, or a "device," as defined under the FARs, numerous different type of "aircraft" exist under the law. Categorized by their intended use or operating limitations, "aircraft" are characterized as transport, normal, utility, acrobatic, limited, restricted, and provisional. Aircraft are also categorized as large or small where aircraft with more than 12,500 pounds, maximum certificated takeoff weight are large aircraft and small aircraft are those of 12,500 pounds or less, maximum certificated takeoff weight.

> *Categorized by their intended use or operating limitations, "aircraft" are characterized as transport, normal, utility, acrobatic, limited, restricted, and provisional. Aircraft are also categorized as large or small where aircraft with more than 12,500 pounds, maximum certificated takeoff weight are large aircraft and small aircraft are those of 12,500 pounds or less, maximum certificated takeoff weight.*

The term "aircraft" broadly extends beyond traditional fixed-wing aircraft. For example, it includes "rockets," which are defined as "aircraft propelled by ejected expanding gases generated in the engine from self-contained propellants and not dependent on the intake of outside substances. It includes any part which becomes separated during the operation." 14 C.F.R. § 1.1.

The definition of "aircraft" also encompasses a "kite," which is a "framework, covered with paper, cloth, or other material, intended to be flown at the end of a rope or cable, and having as its only support the force of the wind moving past its surfaces." 14 C.F.R. § 1.1. Also included in the definition of "aircraft" is a "parachute," which is a "device used or intended to be sued to retard the fall of a body or object through the air." 14 C.F.R. § 1.1. A "powered parachute" is "[a] powered aircraft comprised of a flexible or semi-rigid wing connected to a fuselage so that the wing is not in position for flight until the aircraft is in motion. The fuselage of a powered parachute contains the aircraft engine, a seat for each occupant and is attached to the aircraft's landing gear." 14 C.F.R. § 1.1.

Aircraft are further differentiated by performance so that an "airplane" is a particular type of "aircraft." An "airplane" is an "engine-driven fixed-wing aircraft heavier than air, that is supported in flight by the dynamic reaction of the air against its wings." 14 C.F.R. § 1.1. Examples of heavier-than-air airplanes range from the Wright Brothers' "Flyer 1" flown at Kitty Hawk, North Carolina in 1903 to major general aviation airplanes flown by private pilots to modern jumbo-jetliners that transport commercial passengers around the world.

In contrast, a "glider" is not an engine-driven aircraft, but a "heavier-than-air aircraft, that is supported in flight by the dynamic reaction of the air against its lifting surfaces and whose free flight does not depend principally on an engine." 14 C.F.R. § 1.1. Lighter-than-air aircraft, meanwhile, are "aircraft that can rise and remain suspended by using contained gas weighing less than the air that is displaced by the gas." 14 C.F.R. § 1.1. This would include the famous Montgolfier brothers' "balloons" of 1780s pre-revolutionary France and blimps of the modern aviation era, including "airships," or "engine-driven lighter-than-air aircraft that can be steered." A "balloon" is "a lighter-than-air aircraft that is not engine drive, and that sustains flight through the use of either gas buoyancy or an airborne heater." 14 C.F.R. § 1.1.

Finally, there are "light-sport aircraft"—a unique type of aircraft, other than a helicopter or powered-lift that have operational properties, *e.g.*, a maximum takeoff weight of not more than 1,320 pounds and a maximum airspeed in level flight with maximum continuous power of not more than 120 knots calibrated air speed under standard atmospheric conditions at sea level. 14 C.F.R. § 1.1.

While all flying devices or contrivances are "aircraft," not all may qualify as an "airplane." A helicopter is an example. A helicopter is not an "aircraft," but a "rotorcraft" or "heavier-than-air aircraft that depends principally for its support in flight on the lift generated by one or more rotors." 14 C.F.R. § 1.1. The FARs define a "helicopter" specifically as a "rotorcraft that, for its horizontal motion, depends principally on its engine-driven motors." 14 C.F.R. § 1.1. Within this category are "gyrodyne" and "gyroplanes." A "gyrodyne" is "a rotorcraft whose rotors are normally engine-driven for take-off, hovering, and landing, and for forward flight through part of its speed range, and whose means of propulsion, consisting usually of conventional propellers, is independent of the rotor system." 14 C.F.R. § 1.1. "Gyroplane means a rotorcraft whose rotors are not engine-driven, except for initial starting, but are made to rotate by action of their when the rotorcraft is moving; and whose means of propulsion, consisting usually of conventional propellers, is independent of the rotor system." 14 C.F.R. § 1.1.

Finally, as further detailed in *Huerta v. Pirker*, NTSB Order No. EA–5730 (2014), *infra*, unmanned aerial vehicles—"UAVs" or "drones"—represent the most recent addition to the regulatory framework governing aircraft, though flying cars, taxis, and personal hover craft may not be too far off in the horizon.

B. AIRPLANE, DEFINED

ICKES V. FEDERAL AVIATION ADMIN.
299 F.3d 260 (3d Cir. 2002)

Per Curiam.

The petitioner, Don R. Ickes ("Ickes"), seeks review of an Emergency Cease and Desist Order (the "Emergency Order") issued by the respondent, the Federal Aviation Administration (the "FAA"). The FAA issued the Emergency Order to bring Ickes and his aircraft into compliance with federal regulations and to prevent the flight of aircraft during a weekend of fly-by demonstrations that Ickes planned to conduct on his property in Osterburg, Pennsylvania.

Ickes claims that the FAA abused its authority in issuing the Emergency Order because he flies only ultralight vehicles, which, unlike aircraft, are not subject to federal certification and registration requirements. He also contends that the circumstances surrounding his air show did not give rise to an emergency so as to justify the issuance of a cease and desist order with immediate effect. We hold that the FAA did not err in subjecting Ickes and his aircraft to regulation or in determining that his air show posed an exigent danger warranting an immediate response. We will, therefore, affirm the Emergency Order.

* * *

Ickes resides in Osterburg, where he owns a thirty-eight-acre tract of land that he refers to as both "Ickes Airport" and "Ickes Recreational Park." Ickes claims to be an experienced aviator, and he has operated an airfield on the Osterburg property since at least 1987. According to Ickes, he uses the airfield solely for the recreational purpose of flying ultralight vehicles.

Ultralight, Defined

An "ultralight vehicle" is defined in relevant part as one that "[i]s used or intended to be used for manned operation in the air by a single occupant; . . . and, "[i]f powered: (1) weighs less than 254 pounds empty weight . . .; (2) has a fuel capacity not exceeding 5 U.S. gallons; [and] (3) is not capable of more than 55 knots calibrated airspeed at full power in level flight. . . ." 14 C.F.R. § 103.1).

Unlike "aircraft," which can be operated only if registered under 49 U.S.C. § 44103 (1997), see 49 U.S.C. § 44101; 14 C.F.R. § 47.3, vehicles that meet the definition of an ultralight presently are not required to be registered or to bear markings of any type, are not required to meet airworthiness certification standards, and their operators are not required to meet any aeronautical knowledge, age, or experience requirements or to have airman or medical certificates. 14 C.F.R. § 103.7. Ickes' particular contention in this proceeding is that a two-seat "Challenger II" airplane that he has flown from his property for many years qualifies as an ultralight vehicle.

Unlike "aircraft," which can be operated only if registered under 49 U.S.C. § 44103 (1997), vehicles that meet the definition of an ultralight presently are not required to be registered or to bear markings of any type, are not required to meet airworthiness certification standards, and their operators are not required to meet any aeronautical knowledge, age, or experience requirements or to have airman or medical certificates.

The FAA, however, has repeatedly cited Ickes for his failure to register the Challenger II as an aircraft and for other regulatory infractions. Specifically, on February 25, 1992, the FAA's Eastern Regional Counsel assessed Ickes a civil penalty of $3,000 after finding that he piloted the Challenger II to and from Altoona-Blair County Airport (a short distance from Ickes' property) without an airworthiness certificate, registration, or pilot certificate. The FAA expressly found that the Challenger II must be registered as an aircraft. Notably, Ickes did not seek agency or judicial review of this order.

On May 6, 1999, the FAA's Eastern Regional Counsel then issued an emergency order to revoke Ickes' Student Pilot Certificate. Among other things, the FAA found that Ickes operated the Challenger II on numerous occasions in the latter half of 1998 in a manner that endangered life and property on the ground, including flying too low and without proper training for solo flight. The FAA concluded that Ickes lacked the "degree of care, judgment, and responsibility required of the holder of a Student Pilot Certificate." Ickes again did not seek review of the FAA order.

On January 25, 2001, the FAA's Eastern Regional Counsel assessed Ickes another civil penalty, this time for $28,000, after finding that he operated the Challenger II from October through November, 1998, without a registration, proper markings, or an airworthiness certificate. Once again, the FAA determined that Ickes' Challenger II—which it found was capable of more than 50 knots calibrated airspeed at full power in level flight, had an empty weight of 300 pounds, a 42-horsepower engine, and a fuel capacity in excess of 5 gallons—was an aircraft. Ickes did not seek further review.

Finally, between February and May, 2001, the FAA received reports, mainly from Ickes' neighbors, that Ickes continued to fly the Challenger II. The FAA then learned that Ickes posted an advertisement on an Internet website in which he invited the public to attend a gathering on his property from June 29, 2001 through July 1, 2001. Ickes billed the event as an "EAA Ultralight Chapter Gathering at the Ickes Recreational Park." He promised fly-by demonstrations as well as a "candy drop for children," "horseback riding," and "dirtbike trails and demonstrations."

Upon learning of Ickes' proposed air show, and noting Ickes' history of unlawful use of the Challenger II, the FAA issued the Emergency Order on June 28, 2001, to preempt Ickes' use of aircraft during the event. In particular, the FAA required in the Emergency Order that Ickes immediately cease and desist from operating the Challenger II or any other aircraft until such time as he obtains airman, airworthiness, medical, and registration certificates; affixes appropriate identification markings to his aircraft; and submits the aircraft to an authorized person for appropriate maintenance inspection and approval for service prior to operation.

Defenses

Ickes timely filed a petition for review of the Emergency Order in this Court. We have jurisdiction pursuant to 49 U.S.C. § 46110(a).

Ickes presents three main arguments for our review. First, he maintains that the Commerce Clause does not give Congress the power to regulate his Challenger II because it never flies across state lines. Second, he asserts that his Challenger II is an ultralight vehicle and that the FAA has improperly treated it as an aircraft. Third, he claims that no exigent circumstances existed to justify the FAA's issuance of a preemptive cease and desist order. We review his constitutional claim first.

Ickes argues that Congress lacked Commerce Clause authority to regulate his operation of the Challenger II, as he contends that his flights are purely an intrastate recreational activity and do not affect interstate air commerce or endanger air safety. The Supreme Court has identified three broad areas of activity subject to regulation under the Commerce Clause: (1) the use of the channels of interstate commerce; (2) protection of the instrumentalities of interstate commerce, or persons or things in interstate commerce, even though the threat may come only from intrastate activities; and (3) activities having a substantial relation to interstate commerce. It is beyond dispute that Congress's power over interstate commerce includes the power to regulate use of the nation's navigable airspace, which is a channel of interstate commerce. In addition, because airplanes constitute instrumentalities of interstate commerce, any threat to them, such as the one posed by Ickes' flights of his Challenger II, is properly subjected to regulation even if the threat comes from a purely intrastate activity. Ickes' constitutional challenge, therefore, is without merit.

Ickes next asserts that his Challenger II is an ultralight vehicle and that the FAA has improperly treated it as an aircraft. He also claims that no exigent circumstances existed to justify the FAA's issuance of a preemptive cease and desist order. We will address each of these arguments in turn.

Ickes insists that his Challenger II is an ultralight vehicle notwithstanding the FAA's repeated findings that it is eligible for registration as an aircraft. He claims that the vehicle qualifies as an "ultralight trainer" and that he is authorized to use it for instructional purposes. He contends that the plane was properly registered with Aero Sports Connection ("ASC"), a nonprofit organization that supports ultralight flying activities. The FAA granted ASC an exemption from regulation in 1995 so that it could train and then authorize individuals to give basic flight instruction using two-seat aircraft (like the Challenger II) that would otherwise exceed the weight and speed specifications for ultralights. Ickes received instructor certification under the ASC program, and the ASC issued him an exemption to operate a two-seat aircraft for instructional purposes. Thus, Ickes contends, the FAA improperly determined that his Challenger II is an aircraft.

Our review of this purely factual question is limited. We must accept the FAA's finding as conclusive "if it is supported by substantial evidence." 49 U.S.C. § 46110(c). "Substantial evidence is such relevant evidence as a reasonable mind might accept as adequate to support a conclusion . . . taking into account whatever in the record fairly detracts from its weight." *Van Dyke v. NTSB*, 286 F.3d 594 (D.C. Cir. 2002).

Evidentiary Standard on Appeal

It is undisputed that the Challenger II has two seats, and that fact alone removes it from the ultralight category because it is not "used or intended to be used for manned operation in the air by a single occupant." 14 C.F.R. § 103.1(a). Furthermore, Ickes does not dispute the FAA's finding (nor did he ever appeal or petition for review of the findings in the earlier FAA proceedings) that his plane has an empty weight of 300 pounds, a fuel capacity in excess of 5 gallons, and a potential cruise speed of approximately 56–69 knots. See 14 C.F.R. § 103.1(e). Thus, based on its physical characteristics, Ickes' Challenger II is not an ultralight.

As to the ASC exemption, the record reflects that Ickes' authorization to conduct ultralight training using his Challenger II expired on June 30, 2000, almost one year before the FAA issued the Emergency Order. Ickes has failed to show that he can claim a valid exemption extending through the time when the Emergency Order was issued. The only evidence Ickes cites from the relevant period in 2001 are two letters, dated January 14, 2001 and April 16, 2001, from Bob Enos, a basic flight instructor certified by the United States Ultralight Association. The Enos letters reflect that Ickes completed a written examination demonstrating aeronautical knowledge for flight in a "Challenger II Trainer." Enos also offered an endorsement of Ickes' ability to make safe solo flights in a Challenger II for a period of 90 days from issuance of the letters. Ickes seems to suggest that, because Enos authorized him to make solo flights in a "Challenger II Trainer," the vehicle qualified as an ultralight.

We find nothing in the Enos letters, however, that even arguably exempts the Challenger II from regulation as an aircraft. Although the letters referred to Ickes' plane as a "Challenger II Trainer," it is undisputed that the plane's physical and operational characteristics placed it outside the ultralight category. Moreover, Ickes has produced no evidence to show that he could claim the benefit of the ASC exemption, or any other exemption from regulation, during 2001. As such, the record fails to support his assertion that the Challenger II qualified as an ultralight trainer during that time.

In sum, while Ickes has shown that his Challenger II might have been properly deemed an ultralight trainer when his ASC exemption was in effect, we find substantial evidence to support the FAA's determination that the vehicle qualified as an aircraft when the FAA issued the Emergency Order on June 28, 2001.

* * *

Exigent Circumstances?

Ickes next contends that his air show presented no exigent circumstances, that the FAA's treatment of the situation as an emergency was an error in judgment, and that the FAA abused its authority by issuing a cease and desist order without providing him with notice and an opportunity to be heard. According to Ickes, "[t]he grievances feeding this controversy have been primarily non-safety in nature and had accumulated [over] a one or two-year period." Ickes thus contends that the FAA's treatment of the situation as an emergency was an error in judgment. We reject this contention.

Contrary to Ickes' suggestion that "[t]he grievances feeding this controversy have been primarily non-safety in nature," the FAA's concerns were almost exclusively safety-related. Ickes' decision to conduct a public air show at which he intended to fly his Challenger II—an aircraft that had not been properly registered or inspected in compliance with federal law—raised an indisputable safety concern for the people who would attend the show, for anyone or anything on the ground within the potential flight range of that aircraft, and for any aircraft that might pass through the airspace surrounding Ickes' property. The record reveals that a low-level federal airway, identified as V469, passes immediately north of Osterburg, and a number of additional airways are within several miles of Osterburg, as are Altoona-Blair County Airport and Johnstown-Cambria County Airport, both of which receive commercial air traffic.

Congress has conferred broad power upon the FAA Administrator to conduct investigations and to issue orders that the Administrator "considers necessary" to carry out the FAA's mandate. 49 U.S.C. § 40113(a). Moreover, the Administrator has the express power to act quickly and decisively in response to perceived air safety emergencies.

Moreover, Ickes had a history of endangering life and property on the ground, as evidenced by the FAA's finding in 1999 that he operated the Challenger II in a reckless manner on numerous occasions. Ickes never sought review of that agency finding, and in fact he never formally challenged any of the numerous infractions cited in the FAA's prior orders against him. Given this record, safety was undoubtedly the FAA's predominant concern in treating the situation here as an emergency.

FAA Emergency Powers

As to the FAA's authority to respond to an emergency, Congress has conferred broad power upon the FAA Administrator to conduct investigations and to issue orders that the Administrator "considers necessary" to carry out the FAA's mandate. 49 U.S.C. § 40113(a). Moreover, the Administrator has the express power to act quickly and decisively in response to perceived air safety emergencies.

In view of this broad discretion, our standard of review when assessing an FAA response to a perceived emergency is appropriately deferential: we ask only whether the finding of an emergency " 'was a "clear error of judgment" lacking any rational basis in fact.' " *Nevada Airlines, Inc. v. Bond*, 622 F.2d 1017 (9th Cir.1980). The present record reveals no clear error of judgment. The FAA duly noted the inherent public danger posed by those who operate aircraft unlawfully in this country. Ickes, moreover, had a verified history of unlawful operation of the Challenger II, the FAA had received reports in early 2001 that he continued making such flights, and Ickes' advertisement over the Internet invited the public to gather on his property for a weekend of fly-by demonstrations. It is undisputed that the demonstrations were to include the Challenger II, an aircraft that Ickes failed to have certified as airworthy or inspected by an authorized mechanic.

In view of this broad discretion, our standard of review when assessing an FAA response to a perceived emergency is appropriately deferential: we ask only whether the finding of an emergency " 'was a "clear error of judgment" lacking any rational basis in fact.' "

Ickes also did not hold a valid pilot certificate or airman medical certificate. The FAA thus had concrete information as to specific dates on which Ickes planned to conduct unlawful flights of an aircraft, and it had a limited time in which to stop those flights so as to protect the safety of the people and property that could be harmed by Ickes' malfeasance. We conclude that Ickes' air show posed an undeniable exigent danger. We see no clear error of judgment in the FAA's invocation of its broad powers under § 46105(c) in an attempt to stop his unlawful flights. Given that the FAA committed no error in deeming Ickes' air show an emergency that required an immediate response, the agency certainly did not err in foregoing prior notice pursuant to 14 C.F.R. § 13.20(b).

EXERCISE 3-1. *ICKES V. FEDERAL AVIATION ADMIN.*— ULTRALIGHT AIRCRAFT

1.   Define "ultralight vehicle." Is it an aircraft?

2.   Identify and list the regulatory requirements applicable to aircraft that are *not* applicable to ultralights.

3.   Explain what remedy the FAA sought by seeking an emergency order to preempt Ickes' use of an ultralight aircraft.

4.   The ultralight owner challenged the FAA's action in several ways. Discuss how the court resolved Ickes' argument under the Commerce Clause.

5.   Explain how the court characterized the FAA's authority to respond to emergencies and by what standard the agency's actions are reviewed as a matter of law.

HUERTA V. PIRKER

2014 WL 8095629, NTSB Order No. EA–5730 (2014)

The Administrator of the Federal Aviation Administration ("FAA") appeals the decisional order of Administrative Law Judge Patrick G. Geraghty, issued March 6, 2014, vacating the Administrator's order of assessment against respondent. The assessment ordered respondent to pay a civil penalty in the amount of $10,000.00 based on a violation of 14 C.F.R. § 91.13(a) for alleged careless or reckless operation of an unmanned aircraft. (Section 91.13(a) prohibits operation of "an aircraft in a careless or reckless manner so as to endanger the life or property of another.")

The law judge's order terminated the enforcement proceeding against respondent, and found § 91.13(a) did not apply to respondent's unmanned aircraft because the device was not an "aircraft" for purposes of the regulation. For the following reasons, we reverse the law judge's decisional order and remand for further proceedings.

14 C.F.R. § 91.13(a)

The Administrator issued an assessment order, which served as the complaint in the underlying proceeding, on June 27, 2013. The complaint alleged respondent remotely piloted an unmanned aircraft—a Ritewing Zephyr—in a series of maneuvers around the University of Virginia (UVA) campus in Charlottesville, Virginia, on October 17, 2011. The complaint alleged respondent operated the unmanned aircraft at altitudes ranging from the "extremely low"—10 feet above ground level (AGL)—up to 1,500 feet AGL. In the complaint, the Administrator also asserted respondent operated the aircraft, *inter alia*, "directly towards an individual standing on a . . . sidewalk causing the individual to take immediate evasive maneuvers so as to avoid being struck by [the] aircraft"; "through a . . . tunnel containing moving vehicles"; "under a crane"; "below tree top level over a tree lined walkway"; "under an elevated pedestrian walkway"; and "within approximately 100 feet of an active heliport." Respondent allegedly conducted these maneuvers as part of flights for compensation, as the aircraft was equipped with a camera and respondent was "being paid by [a third party] to supply aerial photographs and video of the UVA campus and medical center."

Respondent appealed the Administrator's order, and subsequently filed a motion to dismiss the complaint as a matter of law. The Administrator contested respondent's motion, and the law judge later permitted additional pleadings from the parties. The law judge's decisional order granted respondent's appeal.

Law Judge's Decisional Order

When respondent moved to dismiss the complaint, he argued the Federal Aviation Regulations ("FARs"), 14 C.F.R. § 1.1 *et seq.* which govern the operation of "aircraft," did not apply to respondent's Ritewing Zephyr. In this regard, respondent argued the aircraft was a "model aircraft" not subject to the regulatory provisions applicable to "aircraft." After considering the parties' written submissions on the motion, the law judge concluded in his decisional order the Zephyr was a "model aircraft" to which § 91.13(a) did not apply.

Accepting the Administrator's position that respondent's Zephyr was an "aircraft" for purposes of the FARs, the law judge reasoned, "would . . . result in the risible argument that a flight in the air of, e.g., a paper aircraft, or a toy balsa wood glider, could subject the 'operator' to the regulatory provisions of [14 C.F.R. part 91 and] Section 91.13(a)."

Citing the FAA's 1981 advisory circular setting forth "safety standards" for "model aircraft" operations (AC 91–57, June 9, 1981), as well as a 2007 policy notice, Fed. Aviation Admin., *Unmanned Aircraft Operation in the National Airspace System*, Notice 07–01, 72 Fed. Reg. 6689 (Feb. 13 2007) ("FAA Notice 07–01"), the law judge explained the "FAA has distinguished model aircraft as a class excluded from the regulatory and statutory definitions [of the term 'aircraft']." The law judge further stated, "[b]y affixing the word 'model' to 'aircraft' the reasonable inference is that [the Administrator] intended to distinguish and exclude model aircraft" from regulatory provisions applicable to "aircraft." Accepting the Administrator's position that respondent's Zephyr was an "aircraft" for purposes of the FARs, the law judge reasoned, "would . . . result in the risible argument that a flight in the air of, *e.g.*, a paper aircraft, or a toy balsa wood glider, could subject the 'operator' to the regulatory provisions of [14 C.F.R. part 91 and] Section 91.13(a)."

The Administrator appeals the law judge's order, and presents two main issues. The Administrator argues the law judge erred in determining respondent's Zephyr was not an "aircraft" under 49 U.S.C. § 40102(a)(6) and 14 C.F.R. § 1.1. The Administrator contends the law judge erred in determining respondent's aircraft was not subject to 14 C.F.R. § 91.13(a). We reverse and remand for further proceedings consistent with this Opinion and Order.

Decision

We review the law judge's order *de novo*. In addition, we apply rules of construction to interpret statutes and regulations. If the language of a provision is clear and unambiguous on its face, the language controls; if the language is ambiguous, we interpret the provision in reference to, among other factors, the context in which it appears.

Definition of "Aircraft"

This case has provoked interest from a diverse set of stakeholders in the Nation's aviation system, and numerous stakeholders have submitted *amici briefs* in this case on matters ranging from principles of rulemaking and due process to First Amendment issues. At this stage of the proceeding, however, we decline to address issues beyond the threshold question that produced the decisional order on appeal: Is respondent's unmanned aircraft system ("UAS") an "aircraft" for purposes of § 91.13(a), which prohibits any "person" from "operat[ing] an aircraft in a careless or reckless manner so as to endanger the life or property of another"? We answer that question in the affirmative.

Plain Language

The Administrator's authority to ensure aviation safety largely rests upon the Administrator's statutory responsibility to regulate the operation of "aircraft." Title 49 U.S.C. § 40103(b)(1), states: "The Administrator . . . shall . . . assign by regulation or order the use of the airspace necessary to ensure the safety of aircraft and the efficient use of airspace." and § 44701 states, "The Administrator of the Federal Aviation Administration shall promote safe flight of civil aircraft in air commerce by prescribing [safety regulations in various areas]."

Title 49 U.S.C. § 40102(a)(6) defines "aircraft" as "any contrivance invented, used, or designed to navigate, or fly in, the air." Similarly, 14 C.F.R. § 1.1 defines "aircraft" for purposes of the FARs, including § 91.13, as "a device that is used or intended to be used for flight in the air." The definitions are clear on their face. Even if we were to accept the law judge's characterization of respondent's aircraft, allegedly used at altitudes up to 1,500 feet AGL for commercial purposes, as a "model aircraft," the definitions on their face do not exclude even a "model aircraft" from the meaning of "aircraft." Furthermore, the definitions draw no distinction between whether a device is manned or unmanned. An aircraft is "any" "device" that is "used for flight." We acknowledge the definitions are as broad as they are clear, but they are clear nonetheless.

An aircraft is "any" "device" that is "used for flight." We acknowledge the definitions are as broad as they are clear, but they are clear nonetheless.

Respondent points out the statutory and regulatory definitions of "aircraft" are drafted in passive voice and reflect what respondent views as an implication that an individual flies or navigates in the air by "using" an aircraft to do so. Respondent argues the term "aircraft" means a device that sustains one or more individuals in flight, thus excluding unmanned aircraft from the definition.13 We disagree.

When Congress enacted the Federal Aviation Act of 1958 (which created the Federal Aviation Agency) and defined "aircraft" in the predecessor provision of 49 U.S.C. § 40102(a)(6), so-called "drones" were largely the currency of science fiction. Congress demonstrated prescience, however, in the early definition of "aircraft"; it expressly defined the term as any airborne contrivance "now known or *hereafter* invented, used, or designed for navigation of or flight in the air."

Legislative History and Intent

Respondent points to the legislative history of the Act—as well as a reference in the Act to policies in furtherance of "air transportation"—as evidence Congress intended the term "aircraft" to mean a manned aircraft. However, the Act did not contain such a distinction, and the definition's use of the passive voice in describing a device that is "used" for flight does not exclude unmanned aircraft. If the operator of an unmanned aircraft is not "using" the aircraft for flight and some derivative purpose—be it aerial photography or purely recreational pleasure—there would be little point in buying such a device. In summary, the plain language of the statutory and regulatory definitions is clear: an "aircraft" is any device used for flight in the air.

Furthermore, the statutory and regulatory definitions, as well as Advisory Circular 91–57, and FAA Notice 07–01, contain no express exclusion for unmanned or model aircraft. Neither these definitions nor the plain text of § 91.13(a) implies model aircraft are exempt from certain requirements. The Administrator may choose to exclude certain types of aircraft in a practical sense, by refraining from bringing a charge under the FARs against a model aircraft operator; Advisory Circular 91–57 implies such a practice, and the processes outlined in 14 C.F.R. §§ 11.81–11.103 provide a more formal means of seeking exemption. However, for the case *sub judice*, the plain language of § 91.13(a), as well as the definitions quoted above, does not exclude certain categories of aircraft. Therefore, we find the law judge erred in presuming the regulations categorically do not apply to model aircraft. The plain language of the definitions and regulation at issue simply does not support such a conclusion.

FAA Policies Regarding Unmanned Aircraft

In 1981, the FAA issued Advisory Circular 91–57, which "outlines, and encourages voluntary compliance with, safety standards for model aircraft operators." The advisory circular directs such operators, for example, not to "fly model aircraft higher than 400 feet above the surface" and to take measures to keep model aircraft clear of other aircraft, "populated areas," and "noise sensitive areas." The advisory circular does not on its face exclude "model aircraft" from the ambit of 14 C.F.R. Part 91. In addition, the advisory circular neither defines "model aircraft" nor excludes "model aircraft" from the definition of "aircraft" for purposes of the FARs.

AC 91–57

In 2007, some 26 years after issuing the advisory circular, amidst growing Congressional interest in rulemaking on unmanned aircraft and growing public interest in the subject of UASs generally, the FAA issued Notice 07–01. The notice clarified the FAA's requirements regarding unmanned aircraft operations. However, as explained below, the notice does not dispose of the issue in this case, which is whether § 91.13(a) applies to unmanned aircraft operations.

Applicability of § 91.13(a) to Respondent's Aircraft

Turning to the issue of the Administrator's interpretation that § 91.13(a) applies to unmanned aircraft, we find the interpretation is reasonable. The Supreme Court has stated an agency may articulate an interpretation of a regulation via the adjudicative process. Courts have deferred to such interpretations as long as the interpretation is grounded in a reasonable reading of the regulation's text and purpose. Furthermore, even when the interpretation is novel, courts will defer to it, as long as an agency "adequately explains the reasons for a reversal of policy."

Agency Deference

The Supreme Court has stated an agency may articulate an interpretation of a regulation via the adjudicative process. Courts have deferred to such interpretations as long as the interpretation is grounded in a reasonable reading of the regulation's text and purpose. Furthermore, even when the interpretation is novel, courts will defer to it, as long as an agency "adequately explains the reasons for a reversal of policy."

As stated above, in the case *sub judice*, the Administrator's application of § 91.13(a) to respondent's aircraft is reasonable. Section 91.13(a) states, "*Aircraft operations for the purpose of air navigation.* No person may operate an aircraft in a careless or reckless manner so as to endanger the life or property of another." As discussed above, neither the plain language of § 91.13(a) nor the definitions of "aircraft" applicable to regulations in 14 C.F.R. part 91 exclude unmanned aircraft.

The Administrator's interpretation of this text—that it applies to respondent's operation of his Zephyr to prohibit careless or reckless operations—is reasonable, given the broad language of the section. In addition, the Administrator's preamble text in its Notices of Proposed Rulemaking, published in the *Federal Register* under the Administrative Procedure Act for promulgation of § 91.13(a), do not contain any language indicating its application of § 91.13(a) to respondent's aircraft is an unreasonable reading of the regulation's text and purpose. The Board has affirmed the Administrator's application of § 91.13(a) as an alleged independent violation in other cases in which, presumably, no other regulation would have explicitly prohibited the alleged conduct.

Moreover, the Administrator's position that respondent's Zephyr is an "aircraft" is consistent with the Administrator's regulations at 14 C.F.R. part 101, promulgated in part on authority of some of the same statutory provisions underlying § 91.13(a), which imposes specific operating limitations with respect to unmanned free balloons, kites, rockets, and moored balloons that rise or travel above the surface of the earth. The language of 14 C.F.R. § 91.1(a) specifically excludes these aircraft, as well as ultralights, from the requirements of part 91. Instead, 14 C.F.R. parts 101 and 103 contain regulations governing those types of aircraft. Though they are subject to special operating rules, the unmanned devices covered under part 101 nonetheless are "aircraft." The regulations contain no text suggesting the Administrator considers those devices to be something other than "aircraft"; in fact, § 91.1(a), in excluding the devices from the ambit of part 91, specifically refers to the devices as a subset of the term "aircraft." The Administrator's position in this matter that respondent's unmanned aircraft is an "aircraft," to which § 91.13(a) applies, comports with the regulatory approach contained in part 101.

Respondent and some *amici* challenge the Administrator's position as based on a "new" interpretation of 14 C.F.R. §§ 1.1 and 91.13(a) that conflicts with prior agency practice and policy and thus, does not warrant deference. In particular, respondent cites a 2001 internal memorandum by a manager within the FAA's Air Traffic Organization advising the FARs do not apply to "[m]odel aircraft." In addition, respondent relies on a letter, which appears to be the FAA's position in response to the request that precipitated the aforementioned memorandum. The letter makes no mention of whether § 91.13(a) applies to unmanned aircraft. Respondent also cites a letter by the then director of the FAA's Flight Standards Division advising a Member of Congress: "a more stringent regulatory approach [than the advisory circular] was necessary" to address increasing unmanned aircraft operations. However, this document, like the others, does not state § 91.13(a) only applies to manned aircraft.

Nothing in Advisory Circular 91–57, on its face, reflects any intent on the part of the FAA to exempt operators of unmanned or "model aircraft" from the prohibition on careless or reckless operation in § 91.13(a). At most, we discern in the advisory circular a recognition on the Administrator's part that certain provisions of the FARs may not be logically applicable to model aircraft flown for recreational purposes. But nothing in the text of the document disclaims, implicitly or explicitly, the Administrator's interest in regulating operations of model aircraft that pose a safety hazard. More importantly, the advisory circular puts the reasonable reader on notice of the Administrator's intent to ensure the safe operation of model aircraft by appropriate means.

Conclusion

This case calls upon us to ascertain a clear, reasonable definition of "aircraft" for purposes of the prohibition on careless and reckless operation in 14 C.F.R. § 91.13(a). We must look no further than the clear, unambiguous plain language of 49 U.S.C. § 40102(a)(6) and 14 C.F.R. § 1.1: an "aircraft" is any "device" "used for flight in the air." This definition includes any aircraft, manned or unmanned, large or small. The prohibition on careless and reckless operation in § 91.13(a) applies with respect to the operation of any "aircraft" other than those subject to parts 101 and 103. We therefore remand to the law judge for a full factual hearing to determine whether respondent operated the aircraft "in a careless or reckless manner so as to endanger the life or property of another," contrary to § 91.13(a). Accordingly, it is ordered that: The Administrator's appeal is granted; the law judge's decisional order is reversed; and the case is remanded to the law judge for further proceedings consistent with this Opinion and Order.

EXERCISE 3-2. *HUERTA V. PIRKER*—UNMANNED AERIAL VEHICLES ("UAVs")—DRONES

1. What is an administrative law judge ("ALJ")? Who is "Huerta"?

2. Discuss the terms of the Administrative Law Judge's decisional order of March 2014.

3. Explain the argument distinguishing a "model aircraft" from an "aircraft." What did the ALJ conclude in this context?

4. To what type of aircraft does 14 C.F.R. Part 101 apply? Does this help or hinder the Pirker's position? Explain.

5.   Is *Huerta v. Pirker* a case primarily about jurisdiction or operator misconduct. Explain.

C. DANGEROUS INSTRUMENTALITY— OWNER LIABILITY

VREELAND V. FERRER
71 So. 3d 70 (Fla. 2011)

LEWIS, J.

Danny Ferrer entered into an agreement to lease an airplane from Aerolease of America, Inc. ("Aerolease") for a period of one year. On January 14, 2005, after taking off from an airport in Lakeland, Florida, the plane crashed. The pilot, Donald Palas, and his passenger, Jose Martinez, were killed in the crash.

John Vreeland, in his capacity as administrator *ad litem* and personal representative of the Martinez estate, filed a wrongful death action against Aerolease. In support of the action, Vreeland first contended that Aerolease, as owner of the aircraft, was liable and responsible for the negligence of Palas in the operation and inspection of the aircraft. Second, Vreeland asserted that prior to the transfer of the aircraft to Ferrer, Aerolease negligently performed inspections and maintenance on the aircraft such that it was in a defective condition, which directly contributed to the crash. Lastly, Vreeland claimed that Aerolease published false information concerning the condition of the aircraft, which Ferrer relied upon. According to Vreeland, the actual condition of the aircraft significantly contributed to the crash.

Aerolease moved for summary final judgment, contending that a provision of federal law, 49 U.S.C. § 44112 ("Limitation of Liability"), preempted Florida law. The trial court held a hearing entered a summary final judgment in favor of Aerolease. The trial court noted that under Florida's "dangerous instrumentality" doctrine, the owner or lessor of an aircraft is vicariously liable for the negligent conduct of a pilot. However, the court concluded that 49 U.S.C. § 44112 preempted Florida law and, because Aerolease was not in actual possession or control of the aircraft at the time of the crash, the company was not responsible under the provisions of the federal statute. Vreeland filed a motion for reconsideration, asserting that the trial court's decision on vicarious liability effectively overruled the 1970 decision of the Florida Supreme Court in *Orefice v. Albert*, 237 So.2d 142 (Fla. 1970). In *Orefice,* the Court held that an airplane was a dangerous instrumentality, and a wrongful death action could properly proceed against the co-owner of an airplane on the basis of vicarious liability.

Vreeland also asserted that Aerolease was in possession and control of the aircraft at the time of the alleged negligent maintenance and inspection and, therefore, federal law did not preempt this claim. The trial court denied reconsideration. On appeal, the Second District affirmed the decision of the trial court to the extent it held that the vicarious liability claim was preempted by federal law, but reversed the entry of the summary final judgment on the claim of negligent maintenance and inspection.

With regard to vicarious liability, the Second District examined the legislative history of the statutory predecessors to 49 U.S.C. § 44112, and concluded that the provision was enacted to shield an owner or lessor of a civil aircraft from vicarious liability under state law whenever the aircraft is not under his or her control. The Second District distinguished this Court's decision in *Orefice* on two bases.

First, the district court reasoned that the 1970 decision did not mention a predecessor statute to section 44112 that was in effect at the time that decision was issued. The absence of discussion concerning that predecessor statute, section 1404, in *Orefice* led the district court below to conclude that the parties failed to raise the issue of preemption before the Florida Supreme Court or the lower courts in *Orefice*. Second, the district court explained:

> The *Orefice* court's ruling that the dangerous instrumentality law imposed vicarious liability on owners of aircraft was based in part on its observation that Chapter 330, Florida Statutes (1970), reflected "a specific policy by the State of Florida to license and otherwise see after aircraft safety." The Florida statutes addressing aircraft safety have since been repealed.

With regard to the negligent inspection and maintenance claim, however, the Second District reversed the entry of the summary final judgment. The court below was of the opinion that the purpose of section 44112 was to shield an owner or lessor from the negligence of another when the aircraft is not in the possession or control of the owner or lessor. The statute was not intended to shield owners or lessors from negligence while in control or possession of the aircraft. The district court concluded that the claim that Aerolease was negligent with regard to maintenance and inspection while the aircraft was in its possession was not preempted by federal law and, therefore, the trial court erred when it entered summary final judgment on this claim. Vreeland filed a petition with this Court seeking review of the Second District's decision on the basis that it expressly and directly conflicts with the decision of this Court in *Orefice,* and we accepted review.

ANALYSIS

Florida Law—Dangerous Instrumentality Doctrine

The dangerous instrumentality doctrine has been a part of Florida common law for almost one hundred years. In 1920, the Florida Supreme Court considered whether a corporation could be held responsible for the negligence of an operator who injured another while driving an automobile owned by the corporation. *See Southern Cotton Oil Co. v. Anderson,* 86 So. 629 (1920). In its analysis, the Court articulated what is now known as the dangerous instrumentality doctrine and concluded that the doctrine is applicable to motor vehicles:

> The principles of the common law do not permit the owner of an instrumentality that is not dangerous *per se*, but is peculiarly dangerous in its operation, to authorize another to use such instrumentality on the public highways without imposing upon such owner liability for negligent use. The liability grows out of the obligation of the owner to have the vehicle properly operated when it is by his authority on the public highway.

> An automobile being a dangerous machine, its owner should be responsible for the manner in which it is used; and his liability should extend to its use by any one with his consent. He may not deliver it over to any one he pleases and not be responsible for the consequences.

In a subsequent decision, this Court held that an individual who rented vehicles as part of a business was responsible for the negligence of the driver who rented the vehicle. In *Susco Car Rental System of Florida v. Leonard,* 112 So. 2d 832 (Fla. 1959), this Court determined that a car rental agency was responsible under the dangerous instrumentality doctrine for the operation of a motor vehicle where the vehicle was driven by a person not named in the rental contract, *even though* the individual who rented the car had agreed in the contract to be the sole driver.

Dangerous Instrumentality Doctrine, Purpose

Recently, in *Burch v. Sun State Ford, Inc.,* 864 So.2 d 466 (Fla. 5th DCA 2004), the Fifth District Court of Appeal reiterated the concept and framework of the dangerous instrumentality doctrine and the purpose behind it:

> The doctrine imposes strict liability upon the owner of a motor vehicle by requiring that an owner who "gives authority to another to operate the owner's vehicle, by either express or implied consent, has a *nondelegable obligation to ensure that the vehicle is operated safely.*"

The doctrine is intended to foster greater financial responsibility to pay for injuries caused by motor vehicles because the owner is in the best position to ensure that there are adequate resources to pay for damages caused by its misuse. The doctrine deters vehicle owners from entrusting their vehicles to drivers who are not responsible by making the owners strictly liable for any resulting loss.

Liability of the owner is said to be "strict" because a plaintiff need not prove that an owner negligently entrusted the vehicle to its operator for liability to attach. However, the doctrine is distinguished from strict liability for ultra-hazardous activity, because the plaintiff must prove some fault, albeit on the part of the operator, which is then imputed to the owner under vicarious liability principles.

It was a federal court in 1951 that first applied Florida's dangerous instrumentality doctrine to aircraft. Specifically, in *Grain Dealers National Mutual Fire Insurance Co. v. Harrison*, 190 F.2d 726 (5th Cir. 1951), an airplane passenger filed an action against the company that owned the aircraft for injuries suffered due to the negligence of the pilot. The Fifth Circuit Court of Appeals noted that there was no state decisional law that applied the doctrine to aircraft. However, the federal appellate court reviewed state judicial decisions that applied the dangerous instrumentality doctrine to motor vehicles and ultimately concluded:

First Application of Florida Doctrine

> Our examination of these authorities and the reasoning underlying their pronouncements leave no room for doubt that, under Florida law, by which we are here governed, the airplane should be similarly classified with the automobile as "a dangerous agency when in operation."

> We can perceive no logical basis for any difference of classification which would authorize a holding that the rule of "dangerous agency" or "dangerous machine," which the Florida law applies to automobiles in operation, should be relaxed in the case of an airplane. This rule imposes liability upon the defendant for the acts and omissions of the pilot of its airplane which the jury was authorized to, and did, find constituted negligence.

Subsequently, this Court in *Orefice v. Albert* held that "an airplane, like an automobile, is a dangerous instrumentality when in operation." This Court concluded that the owner of an airplane who was not in control of the aircraft at the time of a crash that caused the death of a passenger could be held vicariously liable for the negligent conduct of the co-owner pilot. It is clear that the dangerous instrumentality doctrine applies to aircraft in Florida.

This Court in Orefice v. Albert *held that "an airplane, like an automobile, is a dangerous instrumentality when in operation." This Court concluded that the owner of an airplane who was not in control of the aircraft at the time of a crash that caused the death of a passenger could be held vicariously liable for the negligent conduct of the co-owner pilot. It is clear that the dangerous instrumentality doctrine applies to aircraft in Florida.*

Preemption? At issue in this case is whether the federal law currently codified at 49 U.S.C. § 44112 preempts Florida state law with regard to the liability of aircraft owners under the dangerous instrumentality doctrine and, if it does, how broadly the scope of that preemption covers.

49 U.S.C. § 44112 and its Legislative History

Title 49, section 44112, of the United States Code currently provides:

§ 44112. Limitation of liability

(a)   *Definitions.* In this section—

    (1)   "lessor" means a person leasing for at least 30 days a civil aircraft, aircraft engine, or propeller.

    (2)   "owner" means a person that owns a civil aircraft, aircraft engine, or propeller.

    (3)   "secured party" means a person having a security interest in, or security title to, a civil aircraft, aircraft engine, or propeller under a conditional sales contract, equipment trust contract, chattel or corporate mortgage, or similar instrument.

(b)   *Liability.* A lessor, owner, or secured party is liable for personal injury, death, or property loss or damage on land or water only when a civil aircraft, aircraft engine, or propeller is in the actual possession or control of the lessor, owner, or secured party, and the personal injury, death, or property loss or damage occurs because of—

    (1)   the aircraft, engine, or propeller; or

    (2)   the flight of, or an object falling from, the aircraft, engine, or propeller.

There is *no* express preemption language within this clause. Therefore, if Florida law with regard to aircraft owner/lessor liability is preempted by section 44112, that preemption can only be implied because there is *no* express preemption.

In 1948, Congress enacted section 504 of the Civil Aeronautics Act, the original federal provision limiting the liability of aircraft owners and lessors. The reasons for enacting section 504 were articulated in great detail in the House Report that accompanied the legislation. Due to the importance of the report in the determination of Congressional intent, we must analyze its full text, which provides:

> This bill proposes to insert after section 503 of the Civil Aeronautics Act of 1938 a new section 504, as follows:
>
> Sec. 504.
>
> No person having a security interest in, or security title to, any civil aircraft under a contract of conditional sale, equipment trust, chattel or corporate mortgage, or other instrument of similar nature, and no lessor of any such aircraft under a bona fide lease of thirty days or more, shall be liable by reason of such interest or title, or by reason of his interest as lessor or owner of the aircraft so leased, for any injury to or death of persons, or damage to or loss of property, *on the surface of the earth (whether on land or water)* caused by such aircraft, or by the ascent, descent, or flight of such aircraft or by the dropping or falling of an object therefrom, unless such aircraft is in the actual possession or control of such person at the time of such injury, death, damage, or loss.
>
> Provisions of present Federal and State law might be construed to impose upon persons who are owners of aircraft *for security purposes only,* or who are lessors of aircraft, liability for damages caused by the operation of such aircraft even though they have no control over the operation of the aircraft. This bill would remove this doubt by providing clearly that such persons have no liability under such circumstances. The relief thus provided from potential unjust and discriminatory liability is necessary to encourage such persons to participate in the financing of aircraft purchases.
>
> The provisions of present law above referred to are section 1(26) of the Civil Aeronautics Act of 1938 and section 5 of the Uniform Aeronautics Act. Section 1(26) of the Civil Aeronautics Act of 1938 reads as follows:
>
> > "operation of aircraft" or "operate aircraft" means the use of aircraft for the purpose of air navigation and includes the navigation of aircraft. Any person who causes or authorizes the operation of aircraft, whether with or without the right of legal control (in the capacity of owner, lessee, or otherwise) of the

*Civil
Aeronautics
Act of 1938,
Section 504*

aircraft, shall be deemed to be engaged in the operation of aircraft within the meaning of this Act.

Section 5 of the Uniform Aeronautics Act is in force in at least 10 States and Hawaii. That section reads, in part, as follows:

> The owner of every aircraft which is operated over the lands or the waters of this State is absolutely liable for injuries to persons or property on the land or water beneath, caused by the ascent, descent, or flight of the aircraft, or the dropping or falling of any object therefrom, whether such owner was negligent or not, unless the injury is caused in whole or in part by the negligence of the person injured, or of the owner or bailee of the property injured.
>
> If the aircraft is leased at the time of the injury to persons or property, both owner and lessee shall be liable, and they may be sued jointly or either or both of them may be sued separately.
>
> This provision thus imposes absolute liability on owners of aircraft for damage caused on the surface of the earth. It is susceptible of a construction which would impose liability upon any person registered as owner, even though he holds title only as security under a mortgage or similar security instrument or as lessor under an equipment trust. If such interpretation were adopted, the security title holder could become liable for extensive damages on the surface caused by the operation of the aircraft.
>
> An owner in possession or control of aircraft, either personally or through an agent, should be liable for damages caused. A security owner not in possession or control of the aircraft, however, should not be liable for such damages. This bill would make it clear that this generally accepted rule applies and assures the security owner or lessee, that he would not be liable when he is not in possession or control of the aircraft.
>
> The limitation with respect to leases of 30 days or more, in case of lessors of aircraft, was included for the purpose of confining the section to leases executed as a part of some arrangement for financing purchases of aircraft. Any lease in connection with any such arrangement would almost certainly be for a period in excess of 30 days.

The language clearly references airplane owner/lessor liability for damages to persons and property that are *on the surface of the earth*.

In 1958, section 504 was incorporated into the newly enacted Federal Aviation Act. It was codified in the United States Code as 49 U.S.C. § 1404. In 1959, section 1404 was amended to broaden the protections of the provision to include not only owners or lessors of aircraft, but also owners and lessors of aircraft engines and propellers. Section 1404 then remained unchanged until 1994 when, as part of a revision of Title 49 of the United States Code, which governs transportation, it was merely reworded and recodified without substantive change as section 44112(b).

The House Report that accompanied the 1994 recodification specifically stated that the purpose of the revision to Title 49 was "to revise, codify, and enact *without substantive change* certain general and permanent laws related to transportation . . . and to make other technical improvements in the Code." Given that the House Report expressly states that the revision of Title 49 was not intended to affect any substantive change, the Congressional intent behind the enactment of section 504 in 1948 still remains.

The Preemptive Scope of Section 44112

Every version of the owner/lessor liability federal statute since its enactment in 1948 has referenced injury, death, or property damage that has occurred *on land or water,* or *on the surface of the earth.* At no time has Congress removed this geographic requirement from the federal statute. With regard to statutory interpretation, the United States Supreme Court has stated that it is the duty of a court "to give effect, if possible, to every clause and word of a statute." To fulfill this directive, we must determine the Congressional intent embodied in this very specific geographic language.

The words "on land or water" or "on the surface of the earth" may be read to specify that the limitation on liability only applies to death, injury, or damage that is caused to people or property that are *physically* on the ground or in the water. Specifically, the limitation on liability would apply only to individuals and property that are underneath the aircraft during its flight, ascent, or descent.

The words "on land or water" or "on the surface of the earth" may be read to specify that the limitation on liability only applies to death, injury, or damage that is caused to people or property that are physically *on the ground or in the water. Specifically, the limitation on liability would apply only to individuals and property that are underneath the aircraft during its flight, ascent, or descent.*

Under this interpretation, Aerolease would not benefit from any limitation articulated by section 44112 because Martinez was not "on land or water" at the time of the crash—he was a passenger inside the aircraft.

To determine if such interpretation is consistent with Congressional intent, we return to the circumstances that led to the enactment of section 504 in 1948. The House Report that accompanied section 504 criticized a law in effect in multiple states that imposed "absolute liability on owners of aircraft for damage caused *on the surface of the earth*." As previously stated, section 5 of the Uniform Aeronautics Act ("UAA") allowed absolute liability for "*injuries to persons or property on the land or water beneath*." The specific language of the UAA that imposed absolute liability for injuries to people or property *beneath* the plane supports the more narrow interpretation of the phrase "on land or water" in current section 44112. Indeed, the title of section 5 of the UAA was "*Damage on Land*."

Although Aerolease contends that Congress intended for section 44112 to cover *any* injuries, death, or damages caused by a plane striking the surface of the earth, Vreeland is correct that the Uniform Aeronautics Act contained a separate section that addressed injuries to airmen or passengers who were in the plane at the time of the incident. In fact, as demonstrated below, the UAA viewed the tort rights of individuals who were aboard the aircraft quite differently from those of people on the ground beneath the aircraft:

§ 4. **Lawfulness of flight**.—Flight in aircraft over the lands and waters of this State is lawful . . . unless so conducted as to be imminently dangerous to *persons or property lawfully on the land or water beneath*.

§ 5. **Damage on land**.—The owner of *every aircraft which is operated over the lands or the waters of this State is absolutely liable for injuries to persons or property on the land or water beneath*, caused by the ascent, descent or flight of the aircraft, or the dropping or falling of any object therefrom, whether such owner was negligent or not, unless the injury is caused in whole or in part by the negligence of the person injured, or of the owner or bailee of the property injured.

If the aircraft is leased at the time of the injury to persons or property, both owner and lessee shall be liable, and they may be sued jointly or either or both of them may be sued separately. An aeronaut who is not the owner or lessee shall be liable only for the consequences of his own negligence. The injured person, or owner or bailee of the injured property, shall have a lien on the aircraft causing the injury to the extent of the damage caused by the aircraft or objects falling from it.

§ 6. **Collision of Aircraft**.—The liability of the owner of one aircraft to the owner of another aircraft, *or to aeronauts or passengers on either aircraft,* for damage caused by collision on land or in the air, shall be determined by the rules of law applicable to torts on land.

§ 7. **Jurisdiction Over Crimes and Torts**.—All crimes, torts, and other wrongs *committed by or against an aeronaut or passenger while in flight over this State* shall be governed by the laws of this State.

Unif. Aeronautics Act §§ 4–7, 11 U.L.A. 160–64 (1938). Thus, while the UAA imposed absolute liability for injury, death, or damage that occurred on the land or water beneath, the rights of airplane passengers and crew members were governed by the law of the state that adopted the UAA.

Congress was indisputably aware of the Uniform Aeronautics Act when it enacted section 504 in 1948. When Congress drafted language to limit the liability of airplane owners and lessors, it only addressed liability toward persons or property "on the surface of the earth." Section 504 did not expressly address airplane passengers or airmen, even though there were separate sections of the UAA that did so. Had Congress intended to preempt the provisions of the UAA that governed the tort rights of passengers and airmen, it could have easily modified the language of section 504 to not solely address injuries or damage that occur "on the surface of the earth (whether on land or water)." We conclude that by adopting a federal law that specifically referenced damages or injuries that occur *on the surface of the earth,* the 1948 Congress did not intend to preempt state law with regard to injuries to passengers or aircraft crew.

We conclude that by adopting a federal law that specifically referenced damages or injuries that occur on the surface of the earth, *the 1948 Congress did not intend to preempt state law with regard to injuries to passengers or aircraft crew.*

Further, section 1404/44112 is not the only federal aviation statute that references persons and property that are on the ground, *i.e.,* beneath the aircraft in the course of its ascent, descent, or flight. 49 U.S.C. § 40103 provides:

(b) *Use of airspace.*—(1) The Administrator of the Federal Aviation Administration shall develop plans and policy for the use of the navigable airspace and assign by regulation or order the use of the airspace necessary to ensure the safety of aircraft and the efficient use of airspace. The Administrator may modify or revoke an assignment when required in the public interest.

(2) The Administrator shall prescribe air traffic regulations on the flight of aircraft (including regulations on safe altitudes) for—(A) navigating, protecting, and identifying aircraft; (B) *protecting individuals and property on the ground;* (C) using the navigable airspace efficiently; and (D) preventing collision between aircraft, between aircraft and land or water vehicles, and between aircraft and airborne objects.

This provision was adapted from and enacted as part of the 1958 Federal Aviation Act. Thus, at a time when the airplane owner/lessor liability provision was incorporated into the FAA, Congress expressed an interest in protecting people and property on the ground. Hence, to not afford meaning to the words "on land or water" in current section 44112, this Court would not only be acting contrary to congressional intent, but would also be failing to give meaning to every word in section 44112. This would be completely contrary to the directive of the United States Supreme Court.

Decisional Law—Preemption

Decisions with regard to how section 44112/1404 should be interpreted are varied. Some cases narrowly hold that the enactment of the preemption provision in section 1404 did not demonstrate that Congress had preempted the entire field of aviation law. For example, in *Rogers v. Ray Gardner Flying Service, Inc.*, 435 F.2d 1389 (5th Cir. 1970), upon which Aerolease relies in support of its preemption claim, plaintiffs Mr. and Ms. Rogers filed a wrongful death action against Ray Gardner Flying Service for the death of their daughters in a plane crash. The plaintiffs conceded that no cause of action existed against the corporation for the alleged negligent conduct of the pilot under Oklahoma state law. However, the claimants asserted 49 U.S.C. § 1301(26) operated to *create a cause of action* for vicarious liability against the corporation under Oklahoma law. Section 1301(26) defined what constitutes the "operation of aircraft":

(26) "Operation of aircraft" or "operate aircraft" means the use of aircraft, for the purpose of air navigation and includes the navigation of aircraft. Any person who causes or authorizes the operation of aircraft, whether with or without the right of legal control (in the capacity of owner, lessee, or otherwise) of the aircraft, shall be deemed to be engaged in the operation of aircraft within the meaning of this chapter.

The plaintiffs relied upon a provision in section 1404 to support their contention that section 1301(26) preempted state law and created a cause of action not authorized under Oklahoma state law. They asserted that "Congress purposefully considered the question of pre-empting state laws on bailment of airplanes and concluded that only those persons exempted by Section 1404 should not be held liable as operators."

The Fifth Circuit Court of Appeals disagreed with this reverse limitation/ cause of action assertion. The court concluded that, had Congress intended to preempt state tort law of bailments to broaden liability with regard to the operation of aircraft, "it was *fully capable of making that intent clear directly* and not by indirection requiring the circuitous reasoning plaintiffs find themselves driven to employ." The Fifth Circuit expressed "*disbelief*, in the absence of clearer evidence, that Congress would undertake to alter the tort laws of numbers of states in such oblique fashion." The Fifth Circuit ultimately held that section 1301(26) did not preempt state tort law with regard to aircraft liability, and the plaintiffs' cause of action was governed strictly by Oklahoma state law.

Other courts have concluded that airplane owner/lessors are not responsible for *any* injuries if they are not in control or possession of the aircraft at the time of the incident. For example, in *Matei v. Cessna Aircraft Co.*, 35 F.3d 1142 (7th Cir. 1994), also relied upon by Aerolease, the Seventh Circuit Court of Appeals affirmed a trial court entry of a summary final judgment that held an aircraft owner who leased the aircraft to another company could not be held liable under either section 1404 or Illinois bailment law for the death of the pilot. However, in affirming the trial court decision, the Seventh Circuit provided a limited text of section 1404 as follows: "[N]o lessor of any [civil] aircraft . . . under a bona fide lease of thirty days or more, shall be liable by reason of . . . his interest as lessor or owner of the aircraft . . . so leased, for any injury to or death of persons . . . caused by such aircraft *unless such aircraft . . . is in the actual possession or control of such person at the time of such injury, death, damage or loss*." Thus, the Seventh Circuit in *Matei* relied upon an incomplete version of section 1404 that *omitted* any reference to the actual words of the statute, which stated injuries or damage that occur "on land or water," when it affirmed the determination of the district court that federal law exempted an owner/lessor from vicarious liability for the death of a pilot in a plane crash.

Finally, well-reasoned decisional law exists which expressly supports the limited preemption that we deem correct with regard to section 44112. In *Storie v. Southfield Leasing, Inc.*, 282 N.W.2d 417 (Mich. Ct. App. 1979), an aircraft owned by Southfield Leasing crashed and a passenger on the plane, Charles Storie, was killed. At the time of the crash, the aircraft was leased to Lebow Associates, for whom Storie worked. The administrator of Storie's estate filed a wrongful death action against Southfield. Southfield filed a motion for summary judgment contending that 49 U.S.C. § 1404 (1970) preempted Michigan state law with regard to a lessor's liability for airplane collisions.

The trial court entered summary final judgment on a different basis (the doctrine of *lex loci delecti*). The administrator appealed the summary judgment, and Southfield Leasing cross-appealed with regard to the failure of the trial court to grant summary judgment on the issue of preemption. The Michigan Appellate Court rejected Southfield Leasing's preemption argument and applied a reasoning which is consistent with our decision today:

> We do conclude that M.C.L. § 259.180a(1); M.S.A. § 10.280(1) does, in part, conflict with the provisions of 49 U.S.C. § 1404. The latter statute shields a lessor of an airplane from tort liability for any injury or loss suffered "on the surface of the earth." To the extent that M.C.L. § 259.180a(1); M.S.A. § 10.280(1) would impose liability for such an injury or loss upon the lessor of the airplane, the statute directly conflicts with Federal law and is preempted by it.

> A close reading of 49 U.S.C. § 1404 leads us to conclude, however, that the Federal statute is inapplicable to the situation presented under the circumstances of this case.

> *In the present case the injury occurred inside the aircraft and not upon the surface of the earth. We do not read 49 U.S.C. § 1404 as preventing the states from imposing liability upon the owners of airplanes in these circumstances.*

> Therefore, we conclude that M.C.L. § 259.180a(1); M.S.A. § 10.280(1) is not entirely preempted by the Federal legislation. As written, the Michigan statute imposes liability upon aircraft owners both for injuries incurred on the ground and those suffered inside the aircraft. Although liability for the former species of injury must yield to the Federal mandate, the liability imposed by the statute for the latter type of injury may be severed from the statute without doing injustice to the legislative intent.

The Michigan Supreme Court affirmed the lower court with little discussion directed to the holding of the Michigan appellate court with regard to federal preemption.

We conclude that the preemption analysis in *Storie* correctly tracks the legislative history of section 44112, and is also consistent with both the well-established presumption against federal preemption of state tort remedies and the savings clause that is now codified in section 40120(c) of the United States Code, which preserves "any other remedies provided by law." Therefore, we follow the reasoning of the Michigan Court of Appeals.

Florida's dangerous instrumentality doctrine imposes vicarious liability upon owners and lessors of aircraft, even where the aircraft is not within their immediate control or possession at the time of the loss. To the extent that the doctrine applies to injuries, damages, or deaths that occur on the surface of the earth, the doctrine conflicts with, and is therefore preempted by, section 44112.

Application to this Case

Florida's dangerous instrumentality doctrine imposes vicarious liability upon owners and lessors of aircraft, even where the aircraft is not within their immediate control or possession at the time of the loss. To the extent that the doctrine applies to injuries, damages, or deaths that occur on the surface of the earth, the doctrine conflicts with, and is therefore preempted by, section 44112. However, because the death of Martinez occurred while he was a passenger in a plane that crashed—not on the ground beneath the plane—the wrongful death action filed by Vreeland is not preempted by section 44112. Rather, Florida's dangerous instrumentality doctrine applies, and the Second District erroneously affirmed the summary final judgment entered by the trial court in favor of Aerolease on the basis of federal preemption.

The dissent contends that our holding today "defies reality." However, the dissent fails to provide any legal reasoning or precedent in support of this assertion other than the erroneous decision of the Second District below and completely disregards the fifty years of congressional history that surrounds this federal provision. Rather than presenting a basis for disagreement that is grounded in sound legal analysis and historical consideration, the dissent simply turns a blind eye to the well-documented creation and evolution of what is now section 44112 and the longstanding presumption against preemption of traditional state law remedies. It is certainly easy to proclaim that a legal analysis is absurd or nonsensical merely by pretending the extensive history in support of that analysis does not exist. If reality is defied in this case, the dissent is the culprit for willful blindness and a lack of cogent legal analysis.

POLSTON, J., dissenting.

I agree with the Second District that federal law preempts the application of Florida's dangerous instrumentality doctrine to Vreeland's claim that Aerolease, as the owner of the aircraft, is vicariously liable for the pilot's negligence.

The relevant portion of the Federal Aviation Act provides as follows:

> (b) Liability.—A lessor, owner, or secured party is liable for personal injury, death, or property loss or damage on land or water only when a civil aircraft, aircraft engine, or propeller is in the actual possession or control of the lessor, owner, or secured party, and the personal injury, death, or property loss or damage occurs because of—
>
> (1) the aircraft, engine, or propeller; or
>
> (2) the flight of, or an object falling from, the aircraft, engine, or propeller.

Based upon the plain meaning of this language, "the federal statute [shields] the owner or lessor of a civil aircraft from liability for the negligence of others committed when the aircraft was not in the owner's or lessor's possession or control." Therefore, like the Second District, I believe federal law preempts Florida's dangerous instrumentality doctrine here.

By narrowly construing the "on land or water" language of the statute, the majority holds that the federal statute only preempts Florida law when the loss of life occurs to someone on the ground beneath the aircraft. However, as the Second District noted, this reasoning does not "explain why an airplane crash does not cause an injury on the surface of the earth regardless of whether the injured person was in the airplane or standing on the ground."

The majority's assertion that the federal statute does not apply because "Martinez was not 'on land or water' at the time of the crash—he was a passenger inside the aircraft" defies reality. Even though Martinez was in the aircraft when it hit land, his death occurred "on land," not in the aircraft prior to contact with land. The majority's view is inconsistent with the plain meaning of the statute, specifically the plain meaning of "on land."

Therefore, I respectfully dissent.

————————————

EXERCISE 3-3. *VREELAND V. FERRER*—AIRCRAFT AS DANGEROUS INSTRUMENTALITY

1. Detail the facts of the case and identify each of the parties, taking care to understand the relationship of each to the other, *i.e.*, Danny Ferrer, Donald Palas, Jose Martinez, John Vreeland, Aerolease of America, Inc.

2. Define vicarious liability.

3. Explain the holding of *Orefice v. Albert*, as discussed in *Vreeland v. Ferrer*.

4. Describe Florida's dangerous instrumentality doctrine and Section (b) of 49 U.S.C. § 44112. Does the latter preempt the former? Explain why or why not.

5. Explain the central point expressed in the dissent. Is this convincing?

Suggested Further Reading

EUROPEAN UNION AVIATION SAFETY AGENCY, *Aircraft Certification*, https://www.easa.europa.eu/easa-and-you/aircraft-products/aircraft-certification

Andy Pasztor & Andrew Tangel, *U.S. Federal Investigators Probe Boeing 737 MAX Development Choices*, WALL ST. J., Mar. 19, 2019

David Grizzle, *The FAA's Move to Performance-Based Oversight: Developments, Challenges, and Shifting Legal Landscapes*, 29 No. 1 AIR & SPACE L. 1 (2016)

DAVID MCCULLOUGH, THE WRIGHT BROTHERS (SIMON AND SCHUSTER 2015)

THE AIRPLANE IN AMERICAN CULTURE (UNIVERSITY OF MICHIGAN PRESS 2003, DOMINICK A. PISANO, ED.)

G. Van Ingen, *Aeroplanes and Aeronautics*, 99 A.L.R. 173 (1935)

CHAPTER 4

Airmen

While we are early in the investigations, many appear to have already concluded that the FAA's processes are to blame. Should the various investigations reveal problems with the certification of the 737 MAX, Congress can and should act. But any actions Congress or regulators consider must be based on facts, not a panicked desire to "do something." The preliminary accident report prepared by the Ethiopian authorities concludes that the pilots followed proper procedures, but there are several facts that contradict that conclusion.

First, the aircraft accelerated throughout the flight; the pilots never pulled back the throttles after setting them at full thrust for takeoff. The aircraft actually accelerated to between 450 and 500 knots—far beyond the maximum certified speed of 340 knots. That fundamental error appears to have had a domino effect on all the events that followed. After an apparent faulty sensor caused the plane's MCAS to angle the plane's nose down, the pilots did follow the procedures by turning off the automated system and trying to manually trim the plane. However, they were simply going too fast to manually level the plane—imagine trying to open a car door at 100 mph.

Boeing is developing an MCAS software fix, but we can never eliminate every risk or anticipate all scenarios, no matter how much technology is in the cockpit. Failures will occur.

The most important safety feature in any cockpit is a well-trained pilot. Regardless of what the investigations conclude, airlines must ensure their pilots are sufficiently trained and experienced to handle the aircraft. Pilots can master the cockpit's technology, but they must be able to fall back on their training to fly the plane—not just fly a computer.

Opening Remarks (excerpted), as prepared, of Committee on Transportation and Infrastructure Ranking Member Sam Graves (R-Mo.) and Subcommittee on Aviation Ranking Member Garret Graves (R-La) from Congressional hearing entitled, "Status of the Boeing 737 MAX."

A. OVERVIEW

A patient faced with a life or death situation is likely to familiarize himself with the background of his doctor and to seek a second opinion. Flight presents existential perils too, yet most airline passengers never meet or seek to know the qualifications of the flight crew responsible for their wellbeing. To some degree this may be because modern airplane travel, particularly commercial aviation, is extraordinarily safe and passengers have come to take for granted the competence and professionalism of their flight crew and the airplanes in which they fly (but see Chapter 12, *infra*). Whether this trust and confidence is misplaced or not, the need for qualified and professional "airmen"—pilots, mechanics, and flight attendants—is unquestionably important.

Consider the events of March 2015 when a Germanwings copilot locked himself alone in the flight deck of a commercial jet, set the automated altimeter for the ground, and crashed the airplane into a French mountainside, killing all 150 people onboard. Three days after the incident, the European Aviation Safety Agency ("EASA") issued a temporary recommendation for airlines to ensure that at least two crew, including at least one qualified pilot, be in the flight crew compartment at all times and that "[a]irlines should re-assess the safety and security risks associated with a flight crew leaving the cockpit due to operational or physiological needs."

The Germanwings tragedy frames dramatically the internal and external pressures borne by airmen in providing safe air travel. To be sure, what happened aboard Germanwings Flight 9525 was unusual and unprecedented. (But also see Alex Horton & Nick Miroff, *Authorities Identify Man Who Stole Horizon Airplane from Seattle Airport and Crashed It into Island*, WASH. POST, Aug. 11, 2018) *See also* NTSB Aviation Accident Preliminary Report, Excerpt at Chapter 8, *infra*.) But, the event underscored the important role that regulators can and should play in ensuring that airmen are competent and accountable.

In fact, airmen are extensively regulated, though curiously, aviation regulations in the United States do not even define the term "airman." The FAA offers guidance, however. The *U.S. Civil Airmen Statistics*, an annual study that presents information obtained from the official airmen certification records maintained at the FAA's Aeronautical Center in Oklahoma City, Oklahoma, shows that airmen are men and women certified as pilots, mechanics or other aviation technicians. [The term air*man* includes women but is a relic of early aviation when women and minorities were often characterized as unfit to fly on account of their sex and race, respectively.]

An active airman, fundamentally, is one who holds both an airmen certificate and a valid medical certificate. *See* 14 C.F.R. Pts. 61, 65. Airmen who must have a valid medical to exercise the privileges of their certificate are all airplane pilots, rotorcraft pilots, flight navigators, and flight engineers (glider pilots are not required to have a medical examination). And, as of 2016, an entirely new breed of pilot—a "remote pilot" of unmanned aerial systems or drones—was codified under 14 C.F.R. Pt. 107. Regulators recognize various other types of airmen in addition to pilots, too, including mechanics, repairmen, flight attendants, and flight engineers. All told, there are more than 1.2 million certificated airmen—both pilots and non-pilots.

This chapter focuses on legal issues related to airmen in the United States, as follows:

- Part B explores key regulatory requirements with which airmen must comply and the legal consequences that stem from noncompliance, including the loss of the privilege to fly—which impacts the very livelihood of an airman. *Lindsay v. National Transportation Safety Bd.*, for example, analyzes Title 14 of the Code of Federal Regulations and the foundational rule of 14 C.F.R. § 91.13, which prohibits any person from operating "an aircraft in a careless or reckless manner so as to endanger the life or property of another." *Del Balzo v. Collier* presents and endorses the power of regulators to punish airmen for misconduct that is intentional or negligent. Finally, *Friedman v. Fed. Aviation Admin.* examines the (sometimes contested) way in which regulators establish and enforce airmen medical qualifications.

- Whereas Part B, focuses on the power of regulators to promote aviation safety by qualifying and disciplining airmen, Part C evaluates historical and current distinctions drawn by airmen-specific regulations along the lines of gender, age, race, and nationality. The cases in this section invite the reader to question the wisdom and objective of such regulations, particularly as such regulations differentiate airmen based on gender and age as in *Cooper v. Delta Air Lines, Inc.* and *Baker v. Fed. Aviation Admin.* in which regulators imposed marital status and age requirements, respectively, on airmen on debatable policy and "scientific" grounds. Alternatively, *Jifry v. Fed. Aviation Admin.* focuses on the constitutional and property rights airmen have vis-à-vis their qualifications and the circumstances in which administrative agencies and courts can restrict or eliminate such rights.

At the conclusion of this chapter, readers should be able to both identify and critique the central laws that govern airmen. Additionally, readers should understand how the regulatory environment associated with airmen promotes— and sometimes even inhibits and conflicts with—commercial aspects of aviation.

Ultimately, the reader should appreciate the centrality of airmen and the "human factor" in the operation of aircraft in the national airspace system. This chapter also invites the reader to consider the future of airmen as automated technologies and unmanned systems may be the future of aviation.

For example, should pilots be eliminated from the flight deck? In April 2018, a provision was inserted into the House version of the FAA Reauthorization Act of 2018 (H.R. 4) Section 744, which was designed to establish a research and development program in support of single-pilot cargo aircraft assisted by remote and computer piloting. In other words, the legislation proposed to eliminate the requirement of a two-person flight crew. Indeed, to the extent that machines already have the physical ability to fly and "knowledge" to manage aircraft systems and procedures, pilotless airplanes may become a reality before driverless cars.

See Jason Hansberger, *Left Seat Out*, AVIATION WK. & SPACE TECH., Aug. 20– Sept. 2, 2018, at 66. That sound, machines may lack the judgement and intuition airmen have and the role of men and women in aviation will likely endure. In an historical and current context, then, this chapter evaluates what happens when airmen fail to demonstrate good judgment and/or how the law also successfully and unsuccessfully influences the capabilities, regulatory knowledge, and professionalism of airmen.

Table 4-1. FAA Estimated Active Airmen Certifications (2017)

ESTIMATED ACTIVE AIRMEN CERTIFICATES HELD
as of DECEMBER 31, 2017

CATEGORY	2017	2016	2015	2014	2013	2012	2011	2010	2009	2008
Pilot–Total	609,306	584,362	590,039	593,499	599,086	610,576	617,128	627,588	594,285	613,746
Student 1/	149,121	128,501	122,729	120,546	120,285	119,946	118,657	119,119	72,280	80,989
Recreational (only)	153	175	190	220	238	218	227	212	234	252
Sport (only)	6,097	5,889	5,482	5,157	4,824	4,493	4,066	3,682	3,248	2,623
Airplane 2/										
Private	162,455	162,313	170,718	174,883	180,214	188,001	194,441	202,020	211,619	222,596
Commercial	98,161	96,081	101,164	104,322	108,206	116,400	120,865	123,705	125,738	124,746
Airline Transport	159,825	157,894	154,730	152,933	149,824	145,590	142,511	142,198	144,600	146,838
Rotorcraft (only) 3/	15,355	15,518	15,566	15,511	15,114	15,126	15,220	15,377	15,298	14,647
Glider (only) 4,5/	18,139	17,991	19,460	19,927	20,381	20,802	21,141	21,275	21,268	21,055
Flight Instructor Certificates 6/	106,692	104,382	102,628	100,993	98,842	98,328	97,409	96,473	94,863	93,202
Instrument Ratings 6,7/	306,652	302,572	304,329	304,066	307,120	311,952	314,122	318,001	323,495	325,247
Remote Pilots 9/	69,166	20,362	NA	NA	NA	NA	NA	NA	NA	NA
Non Pilot–Total 8/	671,222	652,943	728,329	717,399	707,155	701,291	695,515	686,717	682,315	678,181
Mechanic 8/	286,268	279,435	342,528	341,049	338,844	337,775	335,431	331,989	329,027	326,276
Repairmen 8/	35,040	34,411	39,363	39,566	39,952	40,444	40,802	41,267	41,389	41,056
Parachute Rigger 8/	6,192	5,851	8,846	8,702	8,491	8,474	8,491	8,407	8,362	8,248
Ground Instructor 8/	66,423	65,053	70,957	71,755	72,493	73,599	74,586	75,205	75,461	74,983
Dispatcher 8/	20,664	19,758	23,754	23,113	22,401	21,862	21,363	20,691	20,132	19,590
Flight Navigator	64	67	102	115	126	141	146	174	181	222
Flight Attendant	222,037	212,607	200,319	188,936	179,531	172,357	167,037	159,946	156,741	154,671
Flight Engineer	34,534	35,761	42,460	43,803	45,317	46,639	47,659	49,038	51,022	53,135

Note: The term airmen includes men and women certified as pilots, mechanics or other aviation technicians.

1/ In July 2010, the FAA issued a rule that increased the duration of validity for student pilot certificates for pilots under the age of 40 from 36 to 60 months. This resulted in the increase in active student pilots to 119,119 from 72,280 at the end of 2009. Starting with April 2016, there is no expiration date on the new student pilot certificate, which generates a cumulative increase in the numbers.

2/ Includes pilots with an airplane only certificate. Also includes those with an airplane and a helicopter and/or glider certificate. Prior to 1995, these pilots were categorized as private, commercial, or airline transport, based on their airplane certificate. In 1995 and after, they are categorized based on their highest certificate. For example, if a pilots holds a private airplane certificate and a commercial helicopter certificate, prior 1995, the pilot would be categorized as private; 1995 and after as commercial.

3/ See table 7 for the total number of pilots with a helicopter certificate.

4/ See table 8 for the total number of pilots with a glider certificate.

5/ Glider pilots are not required to have a medical examination. Beginning with 2002, glider pilots with another rating but no current medical are counted as "Glider (only)."

6/ Not included in total.

7/ Special ratings shown on pilot certificates, do not indicate additional certificates.

8/ Historically, numbers represented all certificates on record. No medical examination required. In 2016, Federal Regulation required that airmen without a plastic certificate no longer considered active. Therefore, starting with 2016, those airmen with a paper certificate only were excluded. Data for 1996 and 1997 are limited to certificates held by those under 70 years of age.

9/ Remote pilot certification started in August 2016. These numbers are not included in the pilot totals.

NA Not available.

Source: Fed. Aviation Admin., U.S. Civil Airmen Statistics, 2017 Active Civil Airmen Statistics, https://www.faa.gov/data_research/aviation_data_statistics/civil_airmen_statistics/.

B. LICENSING, CERTIFICATION, AND ENFORCEMENT

LINDSAY V. NATIONAL TRANSPORTATION SAFETY BOARD

47 F.3d 1209 (D.C. Cir. 1995)

RANDOLPH, CIRCUIT JUDGE.

The most remarkable thing about this case is that petitioner thinks he is fit to hold a pilot's certificate. The Administrator of the Federal Aviation Administration revoked his certificate, a decision the National Transportation Safety Board sustained. To reconstruct the events precipitating this agency action, and to understand this petition for review of the Board's decision, we must go to central Florida and the pre-dawn hours of Sunday, October 17, 1993.

Two men and two women are at the Shamrock Lounge in Leesburg, drinking heavily. Their common interest is skydiving. Both men are also pilots. Neither woman is. One of the men, Phillip Smith, owns an aging Cessna Model 182, a single engine four-seater aircraft. He keeps his plane at the Leesburg Municipal Airport. Smith is with his girlfriend, Debra Hall, a bartender at the Shamrock. The other man, petitioner Paul Lindsay, holds an FAA airline transportation pilot certificate and has logged 4,500 hours of flying time. Lindsay is with his girlfriend, Sandra Sprincis, a nurse who resides in a trailer in the nearby town of Umatilla. Lindsay lives with his mother some 10 miles away, but sometimes stays with Sprincis. They have driven to the bar together in Sprincis' car.

It is 1:30 A.M., and the Shamrock Lounge is about to close for the evening. "It's a nice night for a flight," the men observe. With that, their reckless, irresponsible plan is hatched. Lindsay wants to pilot Smith's plane. He has flown it before. Smith decides to fly it himself. That detail settled, the four men and women leave the bar and drive in Debra Hall's car to Leesburg Airport, 3 miles away. On the way, they stop to buy some beer.

Later, reports reach the Leesburg sheriff's office about a plane flying erratically over the town, a plane perhaps in trouble. Officers arriving at Leesburg Airport at 2:39 A.M. discover Hall's car and piles of clothing on the ground. No one is around. The runway is dark. While the officers wait, a Cessna 182 lands. Philip Smith is in the pilot's seat and very drunk. Hall is next to him. In the back are Lindsay and Sprincis, both naked.

The officers ask Smith to step out. He complies, promptly fails a sobriety test and is arrested for violating Florida law. A deputy sheriff escorts Smith to his cruiser and drives him to the county jail. Other officers stay behind interviewing Hall, Lindsay and Sprincis. Hall gets out of the plane. Lindsay refuses to budge. He is loud, obnoxious and, like Smith, very drunk. He brags about his flying skills. He refuses to tell the officers his address. His girlfriend Sprincis gives them her address in Umatilla and gives the same address for Lindsay.

Sprincis tries to persuade Lindsay to leave with her and Debra Hall. He refuses. He tells Sprincis to "go ahead with" Hall. Lindsay promises to "beat her home anyway." The officers radio the lieutenant to report Lindsay's recalcitrance. By this time, it is 4:00 A.M. The lieutenant radios back that Smith has given Lindsay permission to stay in his plane. Sprincis decides to remain with him. Hall departs in her car, apparently sufficiently recovered from the effects of alcohol. At 4:12 A.M., the officers drive out of the airport, leaving Lindsay and Sprincis there alone. Two of the officers park close by, hidden in the darkness, watching the airport entrance and runway, concerned that Lindsay might try to take off in Smith's plane. The officers maintain their lookout until 4:41 A.M. All is quiet, and they leave to respond to another call.

About 5:00 A.M., a lieutenant and his deputy, having left Smith in jail, return to the Leesburg Airport. It is not yet light. The Cessna is gone. So are Lindsay and Sprincis. Remembering the address Sprincis had given them, they drive 12 miles to Umatilla. There on the runway of the Umatilla Airport they find Smith's plane. Sprincis' trailer is a few hundred yards away, across the street. The door is locked, and when the lieutenant knocks, no one answers. Later that day the police impound the plane.

FAA regulations prohibited Lindsay from recklessly operating an aircraft, 14 C.F.R. § 91.13, and from acting as a crewmember of a civil aircraft "[w]ithin 8 hours after the consumption of any alcoholic beverage," 14 C.F.R. § 91.17(a)(1).

These largely undisputed facts were adduced during a two-day hearing before an administrative law judge on Lindsay's challenge to the FAA Administrator's emergency order revoking his pilot's certificate. FAA regulations prohibited Lindsay from recklessly operating an aircraft, 14 C.F.R. § 91.13, and from acting as a crewmember of a civil aircraft "[w]ithin 8 hours after the consumption of any alcoholic beverage," 14 C.F.R. § 91.17(a)(1). Attorneys for both sides stipulated that the only issue at the hearing would be whether Lindsay piloted Smith's plane on its October 17 flight from Leesburg to Umatilla. The ALJ, for reasons we will describe, found that the FAA Administrator had not proven his case. The National Transportation Safety Board reinstated the revocation on appeal.

14 C.F.R. Pt. 91, Reckless Operation

We have three issues. The first is whether the Board erred in reversing the ALJ's decision. The second is whether the Board's decision upholding the order of revocation is supported by substantial evidence. The third is whether, by presenting an affirmative defense, Lindsay waived any objection to the ALJ's refusal to rule in his favor at the close of the Administrator's case-in-chief.

The Board overturned the ALJ's decision because the ALJ had failed to apply the preponderance of evidence standard in assessing the Administrator's proof. In order to put the Board's reversal in perspective, we need to recount some of the additional evidence produced during the hearing.

The FAA's investigation revealed that when Debra Hall left Leesburg Airport shortly after 4:00 A.M. on October 17 she took Smith's keys with her. Unknown to Hall, however, Smith's plane could be operated without those keys. The pilot-side door did not lock and any sort of key inserted into the ignition switch would turn on the engine. An FAA investigator called Hall on October 18, the day after the flights, and asked her whether she knew who flew the plane to Umatilla. Hall said Lindsay flew it. Asked about the source of her knowledge, Hall stated—in language the investigator recorded in his notes—that because she could not figure out how the plane could have been flown to Umatilla without the keys, "I confronted [Lindsay] at the jail when I bailed Phillip out [about noon on October 17] and he told me he flew it to Umatillo [sic]."

At the hearing, Hall admitted having told the investigator that Lindsay piloted the plane to Umatilla. But she then denied having any knowledge to back up her assertion and said that when she had asked Lindsay at the jail, he told her he had not flown the plane. The investigator's contemporaneous notes show otherwise, of course, as does the investigator's testimony at the hearing. It is true, as Lindsay stresses, that at one point the transcript reports the investigator saying Hall told him Lindsay flew the plane to "Leesburg." But this appears to be either a slip of the tongue or a mistranscription. There is no other indication of any flight from Umatilla to Leesburg, and the ALJ understood the investigator to have been testifying about the flight from Leesburg to Umatilla.

When the Administrator rested, Lindsay moved for a judgment vacating the emergency revocation order on the ground that the FAA had failed to make out a *prima facie* case against him. The ALJ denied the motion, and Lindsay proceeded to put on his defense. There is no need to recite the defense in great detail. The ALJ found Lindsay's witnesses, including Lindsay himself, not credible. Lindsay testified that after the police left the airport, he and Sprincis got out of the plane, walked over to a phone booth and called Keith Jordan, a skydiver friend who lived in Leesburg. Jordan said he received the call about 4:00 A.M. With him in his apartment was Edward Carter, an aerial photographer who videotaped skydivers. Carter said he had travelled with Lindsay and Sprincis to Leesburg the evening before, and had been waiting for them to pick him up so that he could spend the night in Sprincis' trailer in Umatilla.

After Lindsay's call awakened him, Jordan dressed, and he and Carter drove in Jordan's car to the Leesburg Airport, about 10 minutes away. When they arrived, Carter got out of the car, spoke with Lindsay, walked over to the plane with him, and together they unsuccessfully tried to secure the pilot-side door. Lindsay came back to the car and told Jordan and Sprincis that Carter was going to fly the plane to Umatilla. Jordan, Lindsay and Sprincis then drove out of the airport and back to Jordan's apartment, where they spent the night. Carter testified that he flew Smith's plane to Umatilla, about a 10-minute flight. He talked briefly with the security guard, Raymond Cruitt, and then walked over to Sprincis' trailer and fell asleep. He heard the officers knocking on the door of the trailer later in the morning, but decided not to answer.

The holes in this story are large, and the ALJ did not believe it. We will put aside the fact that if Jordan and Carter had arrived at the Leesburg Airport when they said, the officers maintaining surveillance would have seen them, but did not. The most glaring defect in Lindsay's defense is elsewhere—in the utter implausibility of Carter's having flown Smith's plane to Umatilla.

Carter was a pilot, but he was not much of one. Since 1969 he had logged only 100 hours. When the FAA Administrator started inquiring about whether he still had a valid license to fly, Carter invoked his Fifth Amendment privilege against self-incrimination. Carter had never flown Smith's plane, and he did not have Smith's permission to fly it on October 17. He was unfamiliar with the Leesburg Airport. Yet according to him he decided to take off in the dead of night, without lights, on an unfamiliar runway that dropped off into a lake, in a plane he had never flown, without checking the oil level in the plane, and without even knowing how much, if any, fuel it had remaining.

What was the urgency that caused Carter to decide to risk his life to get to Umatilla, a mere 15-minute drive away? When the FAA investigator asked him this rather obvious question before the hearing, Carter said he had no particular reason. At the hearing he changed his story. He explained that he had to get back to open up "Skyworld," a skydiving school at the Umatilla Airport, at 7:30 A.M., and when he met Lindsay and Sprincis at the Leesburg Airport he did not know where Sprincis had left her car. This is, to put it mildly, lame. Sprincis surely knew where she had left her car—at the Shamrock Lounge, only 3 miles from the Leesburg Airport. All Carter had to do was ask her. Besides, Jordan was supposedly there with his car. There is no reasonable explanation why, if he were telling the truth, Carter did not even ask Jordan to give him a lift to Umatilla. Carter still had hours to go before he supposedly had to open up at Skyworld. And yet he says he borrowed—that is, stole—Smith's plane to make the 12-mile trip.

What of Raymond Cruitt, the self-described person responsible for keeping "things clean and neat and security" at the Umatilla Airport, the person to whom Carter allegedly spoke as he was walking from Smith's plane to the trailer? In rambling and disjointed testimony, Cruitt said that Carter had committed "perjury," that Carter had not flown Smith's plane because the actual pilot was one "Lawrence Eugene Kavel," a member of a group dealing in "hypnosis, mind control, disguises," a person Cruitt met some twenty years ago in Washington, D.C., but still recognized through the darkness despite his older appearance, a person Cruitt thought might be a government agent. Cruitt "yelled out to him, I said, well who are you screwing over tonight?" and "he says, you better go back and get in bed because the police are on their way." And so Cruitt went back to bed. Needless to say, the ALJ found Cruitt to be "unreliable" and attached no weight to his "bizarre" testimony.

As to the Administrator's witnesses, the ALJ viewed them as "entirely credible." The ALJ also found that Debra Hall had made the statements the FAA investigator attributed to her; her contrary testimony at the hearing was not "credible." As to Jordan and Sprincis, they had an obvious "bias," and there was "considerable doubt" about their version of the events at the Leesburg Airport. Carter was simply not "a credible witness."

Despite these findings, the ALJ thought Lindsay had introduced "an element of doubt" sufficient to preclude a finding that the Administrator had satisfied his burden of proof. Nonetheless, the ALJ said that he was unconvinced Lindsay "did not commit the alleged violations."

Evidentiary Standard

We sustain the Board's ruling that the ALJ misapplied the preponderance of evidence standard. The ALJ had two versions of the events before him. For the Administrator to prevail, the ALJ had to find only that it was, in the familiar formulation, "more likely true than not true" that Lindsay flew the plane to Umatilla. This standard called for the ALJ to make a comparative judgment about the evidence, rather than a statement about what actually occurred. Certainty was not necessary, nor was the absence of any reasonable doubt. As the Board correctly put it, the ALJ's own findings reveal his belief that it was more probable than not that Lindsay made the flight.

As to the Board's ruling that Lindsay violated the regulations, there is substantial evidence to support it. Someone flew Smith's plane to Umatilla. All the credible evidence points to that someone being Lindsay. He had already demonstrated no hesitation about flying while intoxicated. At the bar he offered to fly the plane on its first outing of the night. Drunk or not, he was the only one among the cast of possible pilots who had the experience and ability to fly out of Leesburg in the dark and land safely in Umatilla. He had flown Smith's plane before. It is fair to assume that while he was sitting in the plane waiting for the police to leave, he knew that he could start the engine without Smith's keys. He was the one who defiantly remained in the plane. He is the one who bragged that without any means of transportation other than the plane, he would beat Sprincis back to Umatilla if she drove there with Hall. And he is the one Hall identified as having admitted to being the pilot on that flight. Substantial evidence is "such relevant evidence as a reasonable mind might accept as adequate to support a conclusion," taking "into account whatever in the record fairly detracts from its weight." That standard has been satisfied.

EXERCISE 4-1. *LINDSAY V. NAT'L TRANSP. SAFETY BD.*—CARELESS AND RECKLESS OPERATION

1. What is the function of an administrative law judge ("ALJ")?

2. What does 14 C.F.R. § 91.13 regulate?

3. What does 14 C.F.R. § 91.17(a)(1) regulate?

4. Describe the relationship between the FAA and NTSB with respect to airmen enforcement action. *See* Fed. Aviation Admin., *Legal Enforcement Actions*, https://www.faa.gov/about/office_org/headquarters_offices/agc/practice_areas/enforcement/enforcement_actions/.

5. What must a party prove to satisfy the standard of "preponderance of the evidence"?

NOTES ON *LINDSAY V. NATIONAL TRANSPORTATION SAFETY BOARD*—SUBSTANCE USE AND ABUSE

1. *Hughes v. State—"8 Hours from Bottle to Throttle."*

Misuse of alcohol by airmen received extensive national attention when two inebriated pilots of America West Airlines operated a commercial aircraft with approximately 125 passengers aboard from Miami to Phoenix. The case—*Hughes v. State*, 943 So. 2d 176 (Fla. 3d DCA 2006)—represented a particularly public deviation from airmen regulations, specifically the "eight hours from bottle-to-throttle" rule under 14 C.F.R. § 91.17(a), which prohibits any person from acting or attempting to act as a crewmember of a civil aircraft within eight hours after the consumption of any alcoholic beverage.

2. *Driving Under the Influence as Violation of FARs.*

Aviation authorities consider controlled substance violations and alcohol offenses so serious that "airmen" under 14 C.F.R. § 61.15(e) must advise the Federal Aviation Administration within sixty days of any conviction for operating a motor vehicle while intoxicated.

3. *Over-the-Counter Medicines.*

Some airmen have unwittingly run afoul of applicable aviation regulations by consuming over-the-counter medicines that contain slight alcohol content within the relevant pre-flight time period. *See* Fed. Aviation Admin., FAA Compliance and Enforcement Program, Order 2150.3B (Oct. 1, 2007). *See also* Denise Urzendowski Scofield, *Knowing When to Say When: Federal Regulation of Alcohol Consumption by Air Pilots*, 57 J. Air L. & Com. 937 (1992).

FRIEDMAN V. FEDERAL AVIATION ADMIN.
890 F.3d 1092 (D.C. Cir. 2018)

Tatel, Circuit Judge.

For the second time, Eric Friedman, a type-one diabetic and aspiring commercial pilot, challenges the Federal Aviation Administration's refusal to grant him a medical certificate required for commercial flight. Because Friedman uses insulin to manage his blood sugar, the FAA required him to submit data from a relatively new method of blood-glucose testing known as continuous glucose monitoring ("CGM"), which Friedman declined to provide. In a prior decision, our court held that the FAA "ha[d] not borne its burden of justification" for requiring CGM data. *Friedman v. FAA (Friedman I)*, 841 F.3d 537, 544 (D.C. Cir.

2016). On remand, the FAA explained that it needed the data because CGM is able to detect hypoglycemic episodes often missed by more traditional monitoring, and it supported that explanation with medical studies in the administrative record. Because that explanation satisfies our remand order, we deny the petition for review.

The FAA requires pilots to hold medical certificates of one of three classes: pilots who fly commercial airliners must have first-class medical certificates, 14 C.F.R. § 61.23(a)(1), pilots who otherwise fly commercially must have second-class certificates, id. § 61.23(a)(2), and pilots who fly privately must have third-class certificates, id. § 61.23(a)(3).

Congress has directed the FAA to promulgate regulations that "promote safe flight of civil aircraft," 49 U.S.C. § 44701(a), and to discharge this obligation "in a way that best tends to reduce or eliminate . . . accidents in air transportation," *id.* § 44701(c). Specifically, Congress has instructed the FAA to ensure that pilots are "physically able to perform the duties related to[ ] [their] position." *Id.* § 44703(a). To implement this directive, the FAA requires pilots to hold medical certificates of one of three classes: pilots who fly commercial airliners must have first-class medical certificates, 14 C.F.R. § 61.23(a)(1), pilots who otherwise fly commercially must have second-class certificates, *id.* § 61.23(a)(2), and pilots who fly privately must have third-class certificates, *id.* § 61.23(a)(3). In keeping with Congress's instruction that the FAA consider "the duty of [a commercial] air carrier to provide service with the highest possible degree of safety in the public interest," 49 U.S.C. § 44701(d)(1), the Federal Air Surgeon, to whom the FAA Administrator has delegated his medical certification authority, 14 C.F.R. § 67.407, has adopted more rigorous medical standards for pilots who fly commercially (first- and second-class) than for those who fly privately (third-class), *see id.* §§ 61.23(a), 67.101–67.315.

Classes of Airmen Medical Certification

Under FAA regulations, some medical conditions, including diabetes treated with insulin, are presumptively disqualifying for any class of medical certificate. *Id.* §§ 67.113(a) (first-class), 67.213(a) (second-class), 67.313(a) (third-class). The primary danger of flying with insulin-treated diabetes, the FAA has explained, is the risk of hypoglycemia, a state of abnormally low blood-glucose levels, which is common among diabetics, especially those who use insulin, and which can impair a range of cognitive functions, including reaction time, memory, problem solving, and spatial reasoning. *Special Issuance of Third-Class Airman Medical Certificates to Insulin-Treated Diabetic Airman Applicants*, 61 Fed. Reg. 59,282, 59,282 (Nov. 21,

1996) (explaining that the FAA's disqualification policy was based in large part on concerns about hypoglycemia).

Notwithstanding this presumptive disqualification, FAA regulations provide that, "[a]t the discretion of the Federal Air Surgeon," the agency may grant a "Special Issuance" medical certificate to any applicant who shows an ability to safely perform all authorized duties "to the satisfaction of the . . . Air Surgeon." 14 C.F.R. § 67.401(a). Pursuant to this authority, the Air Surgeon has awarded special-issuance third-class medical certificates to some insulin-treated diabetics—a practice that has led to "no medically related accident, incident, or inflight incapacitation, from any cause." *Friedman I*, 841 F.3d at 540.

Although the Air Surgeon has never granted a special-issuance first- or second-class medical certificate to an insulin-treated diabetic, the FAA announced in 2013 that it "hope[d] that in the future [it] may be able to . . . safely certificate . . . a subset of [insulin-treated diabetics]" at the first- and second-class level, and asked the American Diabetes Association (ADA) to form an expert panel "to investigate the possibility of identifying" such diabetics. *Letter from Michael P. Huerta, Administrator, FAA, to Robert Ratner, Chief Scientific & Medical Officer*, ADA (July 15, 2013). In its report, the panel recommended a protocol for identifying low-risk insulin-treated diabetics and concluded that for such pilots "there is no incremental risk of permitting [them] to fly." ADA, *Expert Panel Recommendations for Pilots with Insulin-Treated Diabetes* 6 (2015).

The FAA declined to adopt the recommended protocol, explaining that it found the panel's recommendations lacking in "evidentiary support" and neither "operationally feasible" nor sensitive to commercial pilots' "real-world challenges." The FAA also believed that the panel's protocol was too lax, as it would have allowed certification of pilots with blood-glucose levels "outside the normal glycemic range at least 20 percent of the time." Despite declining to adopt this (or any) protocol for special issuance of first- or second-class medical certificates to insulin-treated diabetics, the FAA emphasized that it did not have a "blanket ban," stating it was open to issuing certificates on an ad hoc basis.

In April 2015, Petitioner, Eric Friedman, an insulin-treated diabetic who currently holds a special-issuance third-class medical certificate, applied to upgrade his certificate to first class. After receiving Friedman's application, the FAA requested blood-glucose testing results either from finger-stick testing, which involves pricking a finger and using a glucometer to test extracted blood, or "if applicable," from CGM, a newer and less commonly used method of blood-glucose testing that measures glucose levels continuously using a subcutaneously inserted sensor and a small, wearable device.

In response, Friedman provided only finger-stick data, explaining that he does not use CGM. Over the next several months, the FAA again suggested—and later demanded—that Friedman provide CGM data for a minimum of 90 days, eventually warning that failure to do so would result in denial of his application. Friedman reiterated that he does not use a CGM device "because neither of [his] treating physicians . . . has found . . . [the device] is clinically indicated or medically necessary." Friedman also pointed out that the ADA expert panel had recommended against CGM's use due to its tendency to "record transient postprandial spikes in glucose levels," which are "of no clinical significance." The panel itself wrote in support of Friedman's application, stating that although CGM is "useful in identifying trends" in blood-glucose levels, it is less accurate than fingerstick monitoring and thus neither necessary nor appropriate for medical certification decisions.

Unconvinced, the FAA informed Friedman that it was "unable to proceed with" his application "until [it] receive[d] the information previously requested." Friedman then filed a petition for review in this court, in which he claimed that the FAA's denial violated the Administrative Procedure Act ("APA"), 5 U.S.C. § 706(2)(A), and the Pilot's Bill of Rights, Pub. L. No. 112–153, 126 Stat. 1159 (2012) (codified at 49 U.S.C. § 44703 note).

Our court granted the petition, explaining that "[t]he FAA's letters communicating its demand for CGM data to Friedman . . . fail[ed] to articulate any rationale for consideration of the additional information." *Friedman I*, 841 F.3d at 544. Although, in its brief before the court, the FAA relied on the expert panel's acknowledgment of CGM's value, we found this argument unconvincing given the panel's unequivocal opposition to the use of CGM for medical-certification decisions. The agency, we emphasized, was unable to "identify any FAA statements that could be construed as explaining its denial of Friedman's application." Because the FAA had "not borne its burden of justification," we remanded for it to "offer reasons for its denial of Friedman's application."

Two months later, on January 27, 2017, the FAA sent Friedman a letter "in response to the D.C. Circuit's decision." The FAA began by explaining that although it "ha[s] not allowed special issuance first- or second-class medical certification for [insulin-treated diabetics]," its "goal" was to change that, and "[t]o that end," it was "working to develop an evidence-based framework." Turning to Friedman's application, the FAA acknowledged his "assertion, supported by [his] treating physicians, that [he] demonstrate[s] excellent glycemic management as evidenced by self-monitoring with a traditional 'finger-stick' recording glucometer." That said, the FAA went on to explain why it nonetheless demanded that Friedman submit CGM data in order to obtain a medical certificate. Because the adequacy of that explanation is central to this appeal, we quote it in full:

> Current studies of the safety and efficacy of CGM devices . . . show . . . that . . . hypoglycemia remains common and frequently goes unrecognized by traditional finger-stick testing. Thus, self-monitoring using finger-stick testing alone is not an adequate mitigation strategy for operations requiring a first- or second-class medical certificate.

> Because it is impossible to know the true extent of glycemic variability through self-monitoring with traditional "finger-stick" tests, we have determined that a fixed period (90 days) of CGM is necessary in order to consider your eligibility for an Authorization for special issuance of a first-class medical certificate. The CGM data that we have requested will be reviewed for evidence of glycemic control and stability, as well as to evaluate the potential use of CGM as risk mitigation during operations requiring a first- or second-class medical certificate.

Since Friedman had "not provided the requested CGM report and related data," the FAA concluded, it was "unable to consider [him] for a special issuance first-class medical certificate."

In this petition for review, Friedman argues that the FAA "still fails to articulate a defensible rationale for denying [his] application." Again arguing that the FAA has violated both the APA and the Pilot's Bill of Rights, Friedman urges us to "remand for the FAA to (finally) grant [him] a first-class medical certificate." The ADA has filed an amicus brief in support of Friedman.

* * *

At the outset, we emphasize the narrowness of the issue before us. Because the FAA sent its January 27 letter in response to this court's remand, the only question we must answer is whether it has "fill[ed] the analytical gap identified in [our] opinion." *Heartland Regional Medical Center v. Leavitt*, 415 F.3d 24, 29 (D.C. Cir. 2005). Here, that gap is the FAA's failure to "offer reasons for its denial of Friedman's application." *Friedman I*, 841 F.3d at 545.

In determining whether the FAA has satisfactorily provided such reasons, we are guided by well-settled principles of administrative law. We look to see whether the agency has "examine[d] the relevant data and articulate[d] a satisfactory explanation for its action," which may not neglect any "important aspect of the problem," "run[ ] counter to the evidence," or be "so implausible that it could not be ascribed to a difference in view or the product of agency expertise." *Motor Vehicle Manufacturers Ass'n of the United States, Inc. v. State Farm Mutual Automobile Insurance Co.*, 463 U.S. 29, 43 (1983). Although we will not, as in *Friedman I*, "supply a reasoned basis for the agency's action that the agency itself has not given," we may—central to this petition—" 'uphold a decision of less than ideal clarity if the agency's path may reasonably be discerned.' "

Examination of Data and a Satisfactory Explanation

Friedman insists that the explanation the FAA provided in its January 27 letter is "no better" than that considered in *Friedman I*. This is inaccurate.

In *Friedman I*, the FAA had simply demanded, without explanation, that Friedman submit CGM data. Not until its brief before this court did the FAA provide a reason, namely that the ADA panel had acknowledged CGM's value. But as we pointed out, the FAA "overstate[d] the usefulness of this concession," given the panel's conclusion that CGM was inappropriate for this purpose. The agency, in other words, "[did] not identify any FAA statements that could be construed as explaining its denial of Friedman's application."

By contrast, in its January 27 letter, the FAA provided its own, unequivocal medical explanation for requiring CGM data: that such data is needed to detect hypoglycemic episodes that could well be missed by traditional finger-stick monitoring. "Current studies of the safety and efficacy of CGM devices," the FAA explained, show that "hypoglycemia remains common and frequently goes unrecognized by traditional finger-stick testing." As a result, "self-monitoring using finger-stick testing alone is not an adequate mitigation strategy for operations requiring a first- or second-class medical certificate." The FAA thus concluded that "CGM is necessary in order to consider [Friedman's] eligibility for" a special-issuance first-class medical certificate.

This explanation, moreover, finds support in the administrative record. In contrast to *Friedman I*, where there was a "complete absence of a relevant administrative record to review," the administrative record now before us includes "[c]urrent studies" finding that because finger-stick monitoring involves only static measurements, it often fails to detect hypoglycemic episodes occurring between test.

In response to our remand, the FAA "offer[ed] reasons for its denial of Friedman's application." *Friedman I*, 841 F.3d at 545. Put another way, it can no longer be said that the agency has "not identif[ied] any FAA statements" explaining why it needs CGM data. Equally important, the FAA offered its explanation in accordance with APA standards: it "examine[d] the relevant data"—the medical studies and Friedman's medical record—"and articulate[d] a satisfactory explanation for its action"—that CGM data is necessary to detect hypoglycemic events that finger-stick monitoring misses. Friedman, moreover, has given us no basis for believing that the FAA either neglected an "important aspect of the problem," or that its position is "so implausible that it could not be ascribed to a difference in view or the product of agency expertise."

Pilot's Bill of Rights

We can easily dispose of Friedman's claims under the Pilot's Bill of Rights. That statute provides, in part, that the "[g]oals of the [FAA]'s medical certification process are . . . to give medical standards greater meaning by ensuring the information requested aligns with present-day medical judgment and practices" and "to ensure that . . . the application of such medical standards provides an appropriate and fair evaluation of an individual's qualifications." Pilot's Bill of Rights, Pub. L. No. 112–153, § 4(b), 126 Stat. 1159, 1163 (codified at 49 U.S.C. § 44703 note).

According to Friedman, this provision requires the FAA to "align[ ]" its requests with "present-day medical judgment" and "provide[ ] an appropriate and fair evaluation." That, of course, is precisely what the FAA—as required both by our remand and the APA—has now done, and we think it quite obvious that the Pilot's Bill of Rights' aspirational, goal-setting language creates no additional obligations. *Cf. Rothe Development, Inc. v. United States Dep't of Defense*, 836 F.3d 57, 65 (D.C. Cir. 2016) (describing a statute's "goal[s]" as "aspirational").

For the foregoing reasons, we deny the petition for review. In doing so, we have taken the FAA at its word: that it is "working to develop an evidence-based framework" to allow special issuance of first- and second-class medical certificates to certain insulin-treated diabetics, and that "should Mr. Friedman's CGM data corroborate his assertion" that he "does not pose a risk while he is in the cockpit," he will receive a certificate.

EXERCISE 4-2. *FRIEDMAN V. FEDERAL AVIATION ADMIN.*—AIRMEN MEDICAL CERTIFICATION

1. What information did the FAA require of Friedman? On what basis did the airmen refuse?

2. Detail the categories of FAA airman medical certification, including a "special issuance."

3. What, according to the FAA, is the primary danger of flying with insulin-treated diabetes?

4. To what principle of administrative law did the court look to in determining whether the FAA offered satisfactory justification for its demand? What action, if any, can the court take if it finds the agency's decision of "less than ideal clarity"?

5. Explain how the court decides the argument that the FAA has violated the Pilot's Bill of Rights.

DEL BALZO V. COLLIER

1993 WL 657778 (N.T.S.B. 1993)

POE, ADMINISTRATIVE LAW JUDGE.

This has been a proceeding under the provisions of Section 609 of the Federal Aviation Act and the provisions of the rules of practice in air safety proceedings of the National Transportation Safety Board. Larry J. Collier, the Respondent, has appealed an Order of Suspension dated March 22, 1993, in which the Administrator suspends any and all Airman Certificates held by the Respondent, including his Commercial Pilot Certificate Number 302388019.

The Administrator's Order of Suspension suspends any and all Airman's Certificates held by the Respondent, including his Commercial Pilot Certificate Number 302388019 for a period of 180 days because of alleged violations of the Federal Aviation Regulations.

The Administrator's Order of Suspension, which pursuant to Section 821.31(a) of the Board's Rules serves as the Complaint, alleges that:

Airman Order or Suspension

1. At all times material herein you were and are now the holder of Commercial Pilot Certificate 302388019;

2. On or about May 7, 1992, you operated N8321B, a Cessna 172, as Pilot-in-Command on a flight in the vicinity of the National Aeronautics and Space Administration's Space Shuttle Launch Facility, Port Canaveral, Florida;

3. During the aforementioned flight you operated your aircraft within Restricted Area R-2934 without permission of the using or

controlling agency once at approximately 2130 hours local time and again at approximately 2200 hours local time, notwithstanding that the R-2934 area was being used for the launch of the Space Shuttle and that a NOTAM had been issued for said launch;

4. After departing R-2934 you flew to and landed at the Melbourne Airport, Melbourne, Florida, where the FAA conducted a ramp inspection;

5. The FAA Inspectors found the following during the ramp inspection: (1) during the aforementioned flight you did not have in your possession a current Pilot Certificate or an appropriate Medical Certificate; (2) N8321B had a pair of vice-grip pliers in place of a door handle;

6. Additionally during the ramp inspection the FAA Inspectors found the following concerning the maintenance records for N8321B: (1) entry on July 18, 1987, signed by Mr. Collier stating, "generator rebuilt and overhauled and voltage regulator replaced"; (2) entry on January 27, 1988, signed by Mr. Collier stating, "directional gyro and vacuum gauge tube replaced"; and (3) entry on July 15, 1988, signed by Mr. Collier stating, "replaced ELT battery."

7. Notwithstanding that the FAA Inspectors told you not to fly the aircraft as a result of the above you took off from Melbourne Airport, Melbourne, Florida, at approximately 2230 hours;

8. As a result, you violated the following sections of the Federal Aviation Regulations:

   • Section 91.103(a) in that you as Pilot-in-Command began a flight without familiarizing yourself with the boundaries and confines of Restricted Area R-2934.

   • Section 91.133(a) in that you operated an aircraft within a restricted area contrary to the restrictions imposed when you did not have permission of the using or controlling agency.

   • Section 91.13 in that you operated an aircraft in a reckless or careless manner so as to endanger the lives or property of another.

   • Section 61.3(a) and 61.3(c) in that you acted as Pilot-in-Command of an aircraft when you did not have in your

possession a current Pilot Certificate or an appropriate
Medical Certificate.

- Section 91.7(a) in that you operated an unairworthy aircraft.

- Section 91.213(a) in that you took off in your aircraft with
  inoperative equipment.

- Section 91.405(a) in that between required inspections you
  failed to have discrepancies repaired in accordance with Part
  43 of the FAR.

- 91.407(a) in that you operated an aircraft that had undergone
  maintenance when the aircraft had not been properly returned
  to service.

- Section 43.3(a) and 91.403(b) in that you performed
  maintenance on an aircraft when you did not hold a certificate
  to perform said maintenance.

To prove his case with regard to the remainder of the Complaint the
Administrator called three witnesses. His first witness was Air Safety Inspector
Dawn Veatch who testified to her observations and actions on May 7, 1992, when
she was aboard an FAA aircraft providing aerial security in the vicinity of the
Space Center for a Shuttle launch where there are areas of restricted airspace
above and in the vicinity of the Space Center.

The inner zone, designated as R-2934, which goes from the ground to infinity
is prohibited to air traffic 24 hours a day, seven days a week. The outer zone from
11,000 feet to infinity is in effect during the times of launches and is announced
by NOTAMs. She stated that a NOTAM was in effect when she observed
Respondent's aircraft on May 7th, 1992.

Inspector Veatch and her partner, Inspector Hunt, were operating an
unmarked FAA aircraft at 12,000 feet when they received notice of a possible
intruder from Air Traffic Control at Patrick Air Force Base. Shortly after that, Air
Traffic Control notified them that there was an intruder at 12,000 feet and
vectored them to an interception. The interception took place at 12,000 feet in
the outer restricted zone and Inspector Veatch travelled with the intruder into the
inner restricted zone to a point about one mile west of the Shuttle landing strip.
She said that she circled the intruding aircraft, the Cessna 172, waggled her wings,
lowered her gear, tried to establish radio contact, and otherwise tried to get the
attention of the pilot, but was unsuccessful. The intruder turned and headed out
of the inner zone and Inspector Veatch discontinued surveillance and resumed

patrol. She said that the Shuttle launch was delayed because of the intruder and the countdown resumed after the intruder left the inner zone.

After the launch, Inspector Veatch was notified that the intruder was back and she observed him again penetrate the inner zone. This time she followed the intruder out of the restricted zones to the Melbourne Airport where the intruder landed and at her request was detained by Airport Security.

When she and her partner interviewed the pilot he identified himself as the Respondent but did not have a Pilot or Medical Certificate in his possession or on his aircraft. She saw that instead of a door handle on one of his aircraft's doors he was using a pair of vice-grip pliers, which is not provided for in the aircraft's Type certification. She also discovered in his log book that he had made a number of repairs to his aircraft himself, as described in Paragraphs 6(1), (2) and (3) of the Complaint. She advised him that he would be in violation if he operated the aircraft without a Pilot and Medical Certificate in his possession and while the plane was unairworthy because of unapproved repairs. She did not ground the aircraft. After she and her partner departed she learned from the Airport Authorities that the Respondent also took off in his aircraft. She conceded that while the original intercept was at 12,000 feet she may have descended to 11,000 feet while circling and following the Respondent, and as he exited the inner control zone Air Traffic Control told her that he was at 11,000 feet.

Inspector Veatch's testimony was corroborated in important details by the testimony of her partner, Inspector Hunt, and as to radar observation and tracking of the intruder by the deposition containing the testimony of Dina M. Tomczak, the Patrick Air Force Base Air Traffic Controller. Ms. Tomczak is out of the country pursuant to military orders and was unavailable as a witness. Her observation of her radar show the Respondent at 12,000 feet in the inner restricted zone and at 11,000 feet in the outer restricted zone, in violation of both restricted zones.

Defense:
Inadvertence

Respondent testified that his violation of the restricted zone was inadvertent. He stated that instead of setting his VOR for a 340 degree radial he mistakenly entered a 350 degree radial and that took him into the inner restricted zone without his knowledge. He was very rattled by being buzzed and circled by the unmarked aircraft and turned and left the inner zone at 10,500 feet, which was under the outer restrictive zone. He showed a videotape which he took showing the FAA plane above his aircraft.

He said that he subsequently discovered that he needed bifocal glasses and that vision problems had caused him to mis-set his VOR radial. He said that he did not violate the restricted airspace a second time, although he admitted that he turned back to videotape the launch when he heard the countdown reach nine minutes.

He admitted that he made the repairs noted in the log book and said that he did not know that was improper. There is no evidence here that the Respondent holds any kind of certificate authorizing him to make aircraft repairs. He said the vice-grips did not make the plane unairworthy, which he equated to being unsafe.

He admitted that he did not have his License or Medical Certificate with him and that he took off again that night from the Melbourne Airport even though Inspector Veatch had told him it would be a violation. He explained that it would have been too inconvenient to return to his home any other way.

Upon consideration of the entire record and having had the opportunity to observe the demeanor of the witnesses I make the following findings of fact in law. I conclude that Respondent is a credible witness; however, I also find that although he may not have intended to violate the restricted airspace zones around the Space Center on May 7, 1992, there is overwhelming evidence that he did so as described by the two Aviation Safety Inspectors who observed him visually and the Air Traffic Controller who observed the violations on radar.

Respondent admitted that on the first occasion he inadvertently strayed into the restricted zone through a mis-setting of instruments, but he said that he was flying at 10,500 feet when he turned back to videotape the launch, so that he did not enter the outer restricted zone whose bottom is at 11,000 feet.

In this regard, however, whatever the Respondent may generally think he had done the visual observations of the two Safety Inspectors and by the radar operator confirm the two separate violations, both of which penetrated both the outer and inner zones, the first of which disrupted the space Shuttle countdown and both of which would have endangered the Shuttle astronauts and the Shuttle had it had to attempt an emergency landing on the Shuttle landing strip.

Inadvertence in no defense to violation of restricted airspace. Respondent should not have been flying an aircraft if his vision did not allow him to accurately read and set his instruments. And as a pilot he is charged with the responsibility to familiarize himself with applicable charts and navigate his aircraft accurately. Clearly he did neither.

Inadvertence in no defense to violation of restricted airspace. Respondent should not have been flying an aircraft if his vision did not allow him to accurately read and set his instruments. And as a pilot he is charged with the responsibility to familiarize himself with applicable charts and navigate his aircraft accurately. Clearly he did neither.

In his testimony, Respondent virtually admitted all other of the alleged violations by admitting the underlying facts. That he may have thought that they were trivial or stale or inconvenient to observe is no defense.

Upon consideration of all the substantial, reliable and probative evidence of record I find that the Administrator has proven by a preponderance of the evidence that Respondent on or about May 7, 1992, violated Section 91.103(a), 91.133(a), 91.13, 61.3(a), 61.3(c), 91.7(a), 91.213(a), 91.405(a), 91.407(a), 43.3(a), and 91.403(b) of the Federal Aviation Regulations.

EXERCISE 4-3. *DEL BALZO V. COLLIER*—CERTIFICATE ACTION

1. What did the airmen do wrong that warranted a suspension, according to the FAA? Identify the Federal Aviation Regulations corresponding to each alleged wrong.

2. What does 14 C.F.R. § 91.13 prohibit?

3. What is a NOTAM? What NOTAM applied to R-2934 in this case?

4. What is "restricted airspace" and what is a TFR? Is inadvertence a defense to a violation of restricted airspace? Explain.

5. What is VOR?

NOTES ON PILOT RIGHTS AND RESPONSIBILITIES

1.   *Pilot's License and Flight Schools.*

Illustration 4-1. First Pilot's License

Source: https://commons.wikimedia.org/wiki/File:First_pilot%27s_license.JPG

Though commonly referred to as a "pilot's license," the right to fly is evidenced by an appropriate "certificate." Airmen complete stringent training requirements to obtain the appropriate operational certificate (*e.g.*, "student," "sport," "recreational," "private," "commercial," or "air transport" pilot) and rating certificate (*e.g.,* category, class, and type or equipment). *See* http://www.faa.gov/licenses_certificates/airmen_certification/.

Where to learn to fly is an important consideration. Some—but not all pilot training operators—are regulated by the FAA pursuant to 14 C.F.R. Part 141:

> Pilot training is available on-site at most airports, either through an FAA-certificated (approved) pilot school or through other training providers. An approved school may be able to provide a greater variety of training aids, dedicated facilities, and more flexibility in scheduling. A number of colleges and universities also provide pilot training as a part of their curricula.

> Enrollment in an FAA-approved pilot school usually ensures a high quality of training. Approved schools must meet prescribed standards with respect to equipment, facilities, personnel, and curricula. However, individual flight instructors and training companies that are not certificated by the FAA as "pilot schools" may also offer high quality training, but find it impractical to qualify for FAA certification.

> Another difference between training provided by FAA-approved pilot schools and other providers is that fewer flight hours are required to be

eligible for a pilot certificate when the training is received through an approved school. The flight hour requirement for a private pilot certificate is normally 40 hours, but may be reduced to 35 hours when training with an approved school. However, since most people require 60 to 75 hours of training, this difference may be insignificant.

See Fed. Aviation Admin., *Types of Pilot Schools & Choosing a Pilot School*, https://www. faa.gov/training_testing/training/pilot_schools/.

2.   ***Airmen Medical Requirements.***

Pursuant to 14 C.F.R Pt. 67, airmen must meet minimum medical standards for a First-, Second-, or Third-Class Medical Certificate. Each of the certificates requires a person to have 20/20 distant vision and near vision of 20/40 or better; to satisfy certain ear, nose, and throat equilibrium standards; to have no established medical history or clinical diagnosis of a personality disorder, a psychosis, a bipolar disorder, or substance dependence; to establish neurologic health and to rule-out epilepsy and other seizure disorders; to establish cardiovascular health; and to show a general medical condition that makes the person able to safely perform the duties or exercise the privileges of a particular airmen certificate (*e.g.*, no established medical history or clinical diagnosis of diabetes mellitus that requires insulin or any other hypoglycemic drug for control). *See, e.g.*, 14 C.F.R. §§ 67.101 to –.115; 14 C.F.R. §§ 67.201 to .215; and 14 C.F.R. §§ 67.301 to –.315.

In certain circumstances, medical officers of the Federal Aviation Administration ("FAA") (*e.g.*, the Federal Air Surgeon, Manager, Aerospace Medical Certification Division, or a Regional Flight Surgeon) recommend that an airman medical certificate be suspended or revoked, for example, when an airman does not meet the medical certification standards; there is a reasonable basis to question his or her qualifications; an airman fails to provide requested medical information, or provides intentionally false or incorrect information in support of medical certification. FAA Order 2150.3B, Compliance Enforcement Program, at 5-15 to 5-16. *See generally* Fed. Aviation Admin., *Medical Certification*, http://www.faa.gov/ licenses_certificates/medical_certification/.

Below is the FAA Application for Airmen Certificate and/or Rating for Flight Engineers, Flight Navigators, Aircraft Dispatchers, and Control Tower Operators:

Figure 4-1. FAA Application for Airmen Certificate and/or Rating for Flight Engineers, Flight Navigators, Aircraft Dispatchers, and Control Tower Operators

Form Approved
OMB NO. 2120-0007
09/30/2018

U.S. Department of Transportation
Federal Aviation Administration

Application for an Airman Certificate and/or Rating

A. ☐ Flight Engineer	B. ☐ Flight Navigator	D. ☐ Aircraft Dispatcher
A1. ☐ Reciprocating Engine Powered	C. ☐ Control Tower Operator	E. ☐ Reissuance of Certificate
A2. ☐ Turbo Propeller Powered	C1. ☐ VFR Tower Rating	F. ☐ Additional Rating
A3. ☐ Turbojet Powered	C2. ☐ Non-Radar Approach Control Tower Rating	

1. TYPE OF AIRCRAFT TO BE USED	2. TIME IN THIS AIRCRAFT	3. NAME OF EMPLOYER

4. APPLICANT IDENTIFICATION

A. Name (First, Middle, Last)	K. Permanent Mailing Address (include zip code)

B. Social Security Number	C. Date Of Birth	D. Height	E. Weight

F. Hair	G. Eyes	H. Sex	I. Nationality

J. Place Of Birth	L. Telephone Number.

5. CERTIFICATES HELD BY APPLICANT

A. ☐ Pilot	B. ☐ Flight Navigator	E. ☐ Ground Instructor
A1. ☐ Airline Transport A3. ☐ Flight Instructor	C. ☐ Control Tower Operator	F. ☐ Aircraft Dispatcher
A2. ☐ Commercial A4. ☐ Private	D. ☐ Flight Engineer	G. ☐ Mechanic

6. Controlled Substance Violation History: Have you ever been convicted for violation of any Federal or State statutes relating to narcotic drugs, marijuana, or depressant or stimulant drugs or substances? Do not include alcohol offenses involving motor vehicle mode of transportation as those offenses are covered on the FAA Form 8500-8, Airman Medical Application Form   ☐ Yes   ☐ No   Date of Final Conviction

7. APPLICANT'S CERTIFICATION: I certify that all statements and answers provided by me on this application form are complete and true to the best of my knowledge and I agree that they are to be considered as part of the basis for issuance of any FAA certificate to me. I have received the Pilot's Bill of Rights Written Notification of Investigation that accompanies this form. I have also read and understand the Privacy Act statement that accompanies this form.

Signature of Applicant   Date (mm/dd/yyyy)

8. INSTRUCTOR'S RECOMMENDATION: I consider the above applicant ready to take the test for which he/she is applying: A. ☐ Oral Test   C. ☐ Practical Test   B. ☐ Flight

D. Date	D1. Instructor's Signature	D2. Instructor's Certificate No. & Expiration Date	D3. Grade & Certificate No.
E. Date	E1. Instructor's Signature	E2. Instructor's Certificate No. & Expiration Date	E3. Grade & Certificate No.

9. EVALUATION RECORD

	Inspector	Examiner	Signature	Date
A. Oral	☐	☐		
B. Practical Test Aircraft Dispatcher	☐	☐		
C. Practical Test Control Tower Operator	☐	☐		
D. Simulator Check	☐	☐		
E. Aircraft Flight Check	☐	☐		

10. INSPECTOR'S RECORD

A. ☐ Temporary Airman Certificate	B. ☐ Notice of Disapproval of Application Issued	C. ☐ Examiner's Action Accepted

D. Date	E. Inspector's signature	F. FAA office

CP	REG	OFFICE	COM	ISS	ACT	EMP	TRN	M.T.	D.S	CLASS	SEX	RATING	STATE	COUNTY	
															☐ Aircraft Dispatcher ☐ IFO Mailing ☐ Special Mailing ☐ Correspondence ☐ Airmail

FAA Form 8400-3 (1-18) Supersedes Previous Edition   Electronic Version Only   1

<table>
<tr><td colspan="2" align="right">Form Approved
OMB NO. 2120-0007
09/30/2018</td></tr>
</table>

10. Practical Test Report

Grading Legend (All applicable items must be graded S or U)
    Explain in "Remarks" all items which are not graded.
    S-Satisfactory, U-Unsatisfactory

Item No.	A. Flight Engineer	Examiner	Inspector
1	Equipment Examination *(Oral)*		
2	Preflight Inspection		
3	Normal Operating Procedures		
4	Abnormal Operating Procedures		
5	Performance Data and Cruise Control		
6	Trouble Shooting		
7	Emergency Procedures		
8	Forms and Records		
9	Post Flight		
10	Crew Coordination		
11	Judgment		

Item No.	B. Flight Navigator	Examiner	Inspector
1	Equipment (Oral)		
2	Equipment Check		
3	Preflight Training		
4	Normal Navigation Procedures		
5	Knowledge of Navigation Methods		
6	Coordination of Navigational Methods		
7	Emergency Procedures		
8	Coordination of Duties		
9	Crew Coordination		
10	Judgment		

11. Route of Flight Check

From	To	Hours Day	Night

Airman's Identification (ID)

Form of ID

Number

Expiration Date

Item No.	C. Aircraft Dispatcher	Examiner	Inspector
1	Flight Planning/ Dispatch/Release		
2	Preflight Takeoff, Departure		
3	In-flight Procedures		
4	Arrival, Approach, Landing		
5	Post Flight		
6	Abnormal Emergency Procedures		
7	English Language Proficiency		

Item No.	D. Control Tower Operator	Examiner	Inspector
	VFR TOWER RATING		
1	The Control Tower		
2	The Airport		
3	The Control Zone		
4	Notice to Airmen		
5	Weather Facilities and Procedures		
6	A Demonstration of Ability to Control Air Traffic Under VFR		
	NON-RADAR APPROACH CONTROL TOWER RATING		
1	Air Traffic Control Facilities		
2	Air Navigation Facilities		
3	Use of Airman's Information Manual		
4	Holding Procedures		
5	Approach Procedures		
6	Missed Approach Facilities		
7	Alternate Airports		
8	Search and Rescue Procedures		
9	A Demonstration of Ability to Control Air Traffic Under IFR		
10	Airport Identification		

FAA Form 8400-3 (1-18) Supersedes Previous Edition   Electronic Version Only   2

Source: https://www.faa.gov/documentLibrary/media/Form/FAA_Form_8400-3.pdf

3. *FAA Enforcement Actions Against Airmen.*

An elaborate administrative scheme—featuring administrative judges, the Federal Aviation Administration, and National Transportation Safety Board—exists to oversee civil penalties and/or the denial, suspension, or revocation of medical and operational certificates through enforcement actions and related formal and informal proceedings involving airmen. *See* 14 C.F.R. Pts. 13, 61, 67, 91; 49 U.S.C. §§ 1101–

1155, 44701–44723, 46301; 49 C.F.R. Pt. 821. *See also* Jack Harrington, *The FAA Wants to Suspend Your Airman Certificate*, 10 AIR & SPACE L. 3 (1995); Alan Armstrong, *Pilot Certificate Actions and Civil Penalties*, 52 J. AIR L. & COM. 77 (1986); Colin S. Diver, *The Assessment and Mitigation of Civil Money Penalties by Federal Administrative Agencies*, 79 COLUM. L. REV. 1435 (1979); W. J. Dunn, *Revocation or Suspension of Airman's License or Certificate*, 78 A.L.R.2d 1150 (1968).

4.   ***FAA Enforcement Authority.***

Certificated airmen must adhere to extensive operational regulations in order to maintain their certificate(s). Mistakes and human error occur, of course, and the Federal Aviation Administration ("FAA") enforces the Federal Aviation Act of 1958 and Federal Aviation Regulations ("FARs") through administrative actions, reexaminations, certificate actions, civil penalties, and criminal investigations. *See* 49 U.S.C. §§ 46308, 46310–13. *See also* 14 C.F.R. § 13.23. There is "no right to demand that the FAA select a statutory enforcement action that encompasses a jury trial option." *E.g., Go Leasing, Inc. v. Nat'l Transp. Safety Bd.,* 800 F.2d 1514, 1519 (9th Cir. 1986).

Administrative actions against airmen are not legal or adjudicative proceedings in nature, therefore the opportunity for notice and hearing is not required. *See* Fed. Aviation Admin., FAA Compliance and Enforcement Program, Order 2150.3B (Oct. 1, 2007). Administrative action may be taken instead of legal enforcement when all of the following elements are present:

- Applicable law does not require legal enforcement action and administrative action would serve as an adequate deterrent to future violations;

- The nature of the violation does not indicate that the certificate holder lacks qualifications to hold a certificate;

- The violation was inadvertent and not deliberate and not the result of purposeful conduct (*see Ferguson v. Nat'l Transp. Safety Bd.* (9th Cir. 1982));

- The violation was not the result of a substantial disregard for safety or security and the circumstances of the violation are not aggravated;

- The alleged violator has a constructive attitude toward complying with regulations; and

- The alleged violator has not been involved previously in similar violations and the apparent violation does not indicate a trend of noncompliance.

In evaluating the fourth criterion, above, two different meanings and applications of the term "substantial disregard" exist. In the case of a certificate holder, "the act or failure to act must involve a substantial deviation from the degree of care, judgment, and responsibility normally expected of a person holding a certificate with that type, quality and level experience, knowledge and proficiency." In the case of a violator who is not a certificate holder, however, "substantial disregard" involves an act or failure to act that represents a substantial deviation from the degree of care and diligence expected of a "reasonable person in those circumstances."

FAA investigative personnel may take enforcement action once they determine that legal enforcement action is necessary. For example, through certificate actions, the FAA may amend, modify, suspend, or revoke a pilot's certificate if it determines "that safety in air commerce or air transportation and the public interest require that action." *See* 49 U.S.C. § 44709(b). *See also* 14 C.F.R. § 13.19(b). If an infraction is operational in nature, the FAA may seek to suspend a pilot's license. On the other hand, the FAA may seek to revoke the license of a pilot who shows a lack of qualification or an attitude that is at odds with compliance with air safety regulations.

In certain cases, the FAA Administrator may make certificate actions effective immediately where an emergency exists and safety in air commerce or air transportation require imminent action. An emergency certificate action immediately deprives the certificate holder of the right to exercise the privileges of that certificate. Order 2150.3B, at 5-16. In this circumstance, the certificate holder may not continue to exercise the privileges of that certificate while an appeal is pending unless the National Transportation Safety Board reverses the emergency nature of the order.

5.   *Pilot's Bill of Rights.*

On August 3, 2012, the Pilot's Bill of Rights became effective, requiring the FAA provide certain written notifications to individuals who are the subject of an investigation relating to a certificate suspension, revocation, or modification action or the approval or denial of a certificate. Applicable to all cases before the National Transportation Safety Board ("NTSB"), the law also requires that the FAA make accessible to such individuals air traffic data that would facilitate the individual's ability to productively participate in a proceeding relating to an investigation described in the Act. The "PBR" further requires written notification of the following as applicable:

- The nature of the investigation;

- That oral or written response to a Letter of Investigation ("LOI") from the Administrator is not required;

- That no action or adverse inference can be taken against the individual for declining to respond to a LOI from the Administrator;

- That any response to a LOI from the Administrator or to an inquiry made by a representative of the Administrator by the individual may be used as evidence against the individual;

- That the releasable portions of the Administrator's investigative report will be available to the individual at an appropriate time; and

- Where applicable, that the individual is entitled to access or otherwise obtain air traffic data.

The law establishes several exceptions to the notification requirement under the PBR, however. The Administrator may delay timely written notification required under the PBR if he determines that notification may threaten the integrity of the investigation. Notification must be provided once the threat to the integrity of the investigation has ceased. Examples of circumstances where the integrity of the investigation could be threatened by providing written notification to an airman include:

- **Destruction/Concealment**. Providing the required notification under the PBR presents a risk of destruction or concealment of evidence.

- **Death or Serious Bodily Harm**. Delay caused by giving the required notification under the PBR presents a risk of death or serious bodily injury, or destruction of property;

- **Time**. Circumstances where there is not enough time to give written notification under the PBR but oral notification can be provided. For example, the individual subject to investigation will be unavailable within required timeframes for processing an FAA certificate action.

Fed. Aviation Admin. *Requirements for Written Notification During Investigations of Airman Certificate Holders or Applicants*, N8900.195 (2012) (cancelled 2013), https://www.faa.gov/documentLibrary/media/Notice/N8900.195.pdf.

6. ***NASA Report—Aviation Safety Action Program.***

To avoid civil penalty actions, airmen may voluntarily disclose violations of federal aviation regulations. *See* Fed. Aviation Admin., FAA Compliance and Enforcement Program, Order 2150.3B, at 5-8 (Oct. 1, 2007). The voluntary disclosure reporting program applies to certificate-holding entities, production approval holders, and other entities subject to regulation under 14 C.F.R. Pts. 21, 119, 125, 129, 133, 135, 137, 141, 142, 145, and 147 and, for qualified fractional ownership programs operating under part 91, subpart K. *See also* Fed. Aviation Admin., Aviation Safety Reporting Program, Advisory Circular 00–46D (Feb. 26, 1997). According to the FAA:

The goal of the Aviation Safety Action Program (ASAP) is to enhance aviation safety through the prevention of accidents and incidents. Its focus is to encourage voluntary reporting of safety issues and events that come to the attention of employees of certain certificate holders.

To encourage an employee to voluntarily report safety issues even though they may involve an alleged violation of Title 14 of the Code of Federal Regulations (14 CFR), enforcement-related incentives have been designed into the program. An ASAP is based on a safety partnership that will include the Federal Aviation Administration (FAA) and the certificate holder, and may include any third party such as the employee's labor organization.

Fed. Aviation Admin., *Aviation Safety Action Program*, https://www.faa.gov/about/initiatives/asap/.

C. GENDER, AGE, RACE, AND NATIONALITY

COOPER V. DELTA AIR LINES, INC.

274 F. Supp. 781 (E.D. La. 1967)

COMISKEY, DISTRICT JUDGE.

Delta fired stewardess, Eulalie E. Cooper, plaintiff, on April 1, 1966 because she had gotten married on October 17, 1964. Delta's policy was to employ only single women as stewardesses and plaintiff got the job knowing this when she signed the following agreement:

Delta Air Lines, Inc.

Employment Termination in the Event of Marriage

(Stewardess)

As a further consideration for employment I hereby certify that I have never been married and that I shall terminate automatically and voluntarily my employment with Delta Air Lines prior to the event of my entry into a contract of marriage any time during the Stewardess Training Course, after successfully completing the stewardess training class and prior to the assignment of regular stewardess duties or after assignment to regular stewardess duties. I understand and further agree that my employment as a stewardess will not be continued beyond the end of the month during which my thirty-fifth (35th) birthday occurs.

Plaintiff charged Delta with discrimination in violation of 42 U.S.C. § 2000e *et seq.* before the Equal Employment Opportunity Commission ("EEOC"), which wrote plaintiff a statutory letter advising her to file this suit if she wanted. The letter from EEOC admitted it had not "made a determination" as to the legal validity of her case under the 1964 Civil Rights Law. The plaintiff's suit complains that Delta's policy of limiting her job to single women is an unlawful employment practice.

§ 2000e–2.   Unlawful employment practices—Employer practices

(a)   It shall be an unlawful employment practice for an employer—

    (1)   to fail or refuse to hire or to discharge any individual, or otherwise to discriminate against any individual with respect to his compensation, terms, conditions, or privileges of employment, because of such individual's race, color, religion, sex, or national origin; or

    (2)   to limit, segregate, or classify his employees in any way which would deprive or tend to deprive any individual of employment opportunities or otherwise adversely affect his status as an employee, because of such individual's race, color, religion, sex, or national origin.

Delta admits that it applies this "single woman rule" to only its stewardesses and not to any of its other employees, male or female. Delta urges, however, that its "single woman rule" is "reasonably necessary to the normal operation of its" business and comes within the legal exception of the Civil Rights Law, 42 U.S.C. § 2000e–2(e), known as a "bona fide occupational qualification"—

> it shall not be an unlawful employment practice for an employer to hire * * * employees, * * *, on the basis of his religion, sex, or national origin in those certain instances where religion, sex, or national origin is a bona fide occupational qualification reasonably necessary to the normal operation of that particular business

After numerous defense motions which were denied with reasons, this case was tried on the merits with plaintiff seeking reinstatement, back wages, and injunctive relief, all of which we deny and we dismiss the plaintiff's suit.

> *Delta's stewardesses must have 'good complexions,' must be 'neat,' must be 'attractive,' and their 'family background' and 'moral character' must be 'good.' Finally, Delta proved that it does not hire males to be stewards, only females, and finally Delta's experience shows that 'single women' are better stewardesses than 'married women' for various reasons viz: better passenger acceptance, change flight schedules easier, less likelihood of pregnancy.*

Congress branded as illegal almost every employment practice which discriminates against an individual because of her race, color, religion, sex, or national origin. But Congress did not outlaw Delta's discretion to hire only stewardesses who are single and young, 20 to 26 years of age, average height, 5'2' to 5'6', slim, not more than 135 pounds, educated, at least two years of college. These qualities, Delta's witness testified, are requirements before we employ a stewardess, or keep her afterwards, along with the requirements that Delta's stewardesses must have 'good complexions,' must be 'neat,' must be 'attractive,' and their 'family background' and 'moral character' must be 'good.' Finally, Delta proved that it does not hire males to be stewards, only females, and finally Delta's experience shows that 'single women' are better stewardesses than 'married women' for various reasons viz: better passenger acceptance, change flight schedules easier, less likelihood of pregnancy.

As far as we can see, this is the first case on this point and legislative history is silent on this point and many others. The addition of "sex" to the prohibition against discrimination based on race, religion or national origin just sort of found its way into the equal employment opportunities section of the Civil Rights Bill.

It is notably omitted from the public accommodations section. Congressional hearings on the sex amendment were never held and therefore any clear legislative history is absent. The only congressional debate that touched on the subject centered on the exception based on a bona fide employment qualification.

Actually, the U.S. Department of Labor went on record in a letter to Congressman Celler (D., N.Y.) "that to attempt (to add sex) would not be to the best advantage to women at this time." Judicial precedent in state jurisprudence is likewise barren since "only two states, Wisconsin and Hawaii, include sex discrimination as an unlawful practice in fair employment laws," 50 IOWA L. REV. 778, 791 (1965); Hawaii Rev. Laws Section 90A–1 (Supp.1963); Wis. Stat. Ann. § 111.31–.32(5), .36(3)–(4) (Supp.1964). New York recognizes as a civil right the opportunity to obtain employment without serious discrimination. New York Executive Law, McKinney's Consol. Laws, c. 18, Section 291.

But the absence of legislative intent or the shortage of judicial precedent among the states is no real problem in this case. By reading the act it is plain that Congress did not ban discrimination in employment due to one's marital status and that is the issue in this case. Delta has a right to employ single females and to refuse to employ married females, and this discretion is in no way limited by the Civil Rights Law from a plain reading of the above quoted sections.

The plaintiff argues that no such unmarried status is required of Delta's male employees and therefore this is discrimination against the plaintiff because she is female. But that reasoning is faulty. The discrimination lies in the fact that the plaintiff is married—and the law does not prevent discrimination against married people in favor of the single ones. Perhaps if this were a suit by a prospective male steward who was refused employment because he is a male, our answer might be different, but then the "bona fide occupational qualification" would have to be considered.

The only case cited by defendant is *Bowe v. Colgate-Palmolive Co.*, 272 F. Supp. 332 (S.D. Ind. 1967), but the case concerns itself exclusively with the refusal of Colgate to employ females in jobs which require lifting of heavy weights and the case goes off on the bona fide occupational qualification exception which is inapplicable in the instant case. Under the circumstances, the plaintiff's suit is dismissed at her costs and the Clerk will accordingly prepare a judgment.

NOTES ON *COOPER V. DELTA AIR LINES, INC.*—WOMEN IN AVIATION

1. *Stewardess or Flight Attendant?*

Suzanne L. Kolm, in an essay entitled *Who Says It's a Man's World?*, wrote about women's work and travel in the first decades of flight:

> Working women had a place in aviation thanks to the vision and courage of the first generation of stewardesses. The occupation was invented by a graduate nurse named Ellen Church who had been intrigued by aviation . . . In 1930, Church visited the San Francisco airport hoping to find a job piloting one of Boeing Air Transport's Small aircraft that carried mail and a few passengers between Chicago and western cities. When the traffic manager at the airport, Steve Stimpson refused to consider Church as a pilot, she suggested that her nursing training could be useful in the cabin. . .

> Stewardesses exercised their "home-making instincts" by greeting passengers and conversing with them, serving coffee and meals, as well as

helping with tickets and arranging for hotels or railroad tickets if a flight was canceled or ground by the storm.

. . . For a period in the late 1960s and early 1970s, airline companies tried to make air travel more exciting; their strategy was part of a tradition in aviation that associated flight with sex and thrill, and it also was part of the 1960s "sexual revolution." One fact of the sexual revolution was a utopian vision of equality and freedom for women and men, but another side was more libertine and commercial . . . Airline advertisements expressed this latter side . . . To accommodate the tired businessman, Braniff Airline introduced "The Air Strip" in 1965 that featured stewardesses removing pieces of their new, layered uniforms at intervals during the flight . . .

By the era of airline deregulation, beginning in 1978, stewardesses had succeeded in redefining themselves as safety professionals and their formal title was now "flight attendants." The reference to safety laid claim to being skilled workers, worthy of respect, and the emphasis on professionalism made clear that their friendliness was paid and impersonal. With this new designation, the women recaptured some of the dignity and control that cabin crews had enjoyed in the first three decades of air travel. But a few problems have remained. Their employers' advertisements punctured a hole in the protection they had once enjoyed as professionals, as it has been slow to mend. The many recent incidents of "air rage" directed at flight attendants, whatever the mitigating factors such as cramped space and overbooking, show that some passengers do not give the cabin crew the respect they received in the first decades of air travel.

Suzanne L. Kolm, *"Who Says It's a Man's World?" Women's Work and Travel in the First Decade of Flight in* THE AIRPLANE IN AMERICAN CULTURE (Pisano ed. 2006). *See also Marital Restrictions on Stewardesses: Is this Any Way to Run an Airline?*, 117 U. PA. L. REV. 616 (1969); Pamela L. Whitesides, *Flight Attendant Weight Policies: A Title VII Wrong Without a Remedy*, 64 S. CAL. L. REV. 175 (1990).

2.   *Women in Aviation International.*

Women have been involved in aviation since its earliest days, from E. Lillian Todd, who designed and built aircraft in 1906 to Helen Richey, who became the first woman pilot for a U.S. commercial airline in 1934, to astronaut Eileen Collins, the first female space shuttle commander.

Women in Aviation International ("WAI") is a nonprofit organization established in 1994 that is dedicated to the encouragement and advancement of women in all aviation career fields and interests. Its membership includes astronauts, corporate pilots, maintenance technicians, air traffic controllers, business owners, educators, journalists, flight attendants, high school and university students, air show performers, airport managers and many others. It also provides year-round resources to assist women in aviation and to encourage young women to consider aviation as a career. WAI also offers educational outreach programs to educators, aviation industry members, and young people nationally and internationally.

One of its most recent initiative is the Girls in Aviation Day program for girls ages 8 to 17. Today, WAI has more than 12,000 members worldwide, including aviation professionals, students and enthusiasts. Women and men from all segments of the industry, including general, corporate and commercial aviation, education, government and the military, are eligible for WAI membership. Due to a strong commitment in promoting women in the aviation industry, WAI has gained wide recognition. This recognition is evident from partnerships with NASA, the FAA and other organizations.

See Women in Aviation International, *Current Statistics of Women in Aviation Careers in U.S.*, https://www.wai.org/resources/waistats.

3.   ***By the Numbers.***

According to Women in Aviation, International, during the last two decades, the number of women involved in the aviation industry has steadily increased and women can be found in nearly every aviation occupation today. However, the numbers are small by comparison.

Women pilots, for example, represent only approximately seven percent of the total pilot population, but almost 80 percent of the flight attendant population. And, it was not until 2016 until a commercial jet was piloted by an all-woman cockpit. *See* Toi Staff, *El Al Makes History with Its First All-Woman Cockpit*, TIME OF ISRAEL, Jan 22, 2016, https://www.timesofisrael.com/el-al-makes-history-with-its-first-all-woman-cockpit/. *See also* Eric Egan, *1st African-American, All-Female Flight Crew Honored for Black History Month*, WKRN.com, Feb. 11, 2016, https://www.pridepublishinggroup.com/pride/2016/02/18/first-african-american-all-female-flight-crew-honored/.

Table 4-2. FAA Estimated Active Women Airmen Certifications Held (2017)

ESTIMATED ACTIVE WOMEN AIRMEN CERTIFICATES HELD
as of DECEMBER 31, 2017

CATEGORY	2017	2016	2015	2014	2013	2012	2011	2010	2009	2008
Pilot--Total	42,694	39,187	39,287	39,322	39,621	40,621	41,316	42,218	36,808	37,981
Student 1/	19,219	15,971	14,580	14,369	14,405	14,643	14,683	14,767	8,450	9,127
Recreational (only)	14	15	16	16	17	16	18	12	13	20
Sport	229	223	192	174	152	135	118	98	79	
Private 2/	9,971	10,009	11,339	11,652	11,909	12,456	12,927	13,566	14,322	15,015
Commercial 2/	6,267	6,081	6,587	6,685	6,911	7,536	7,956	8,175	8,289	8,083
Airline Transport 2/	6,994	6,888	6,554	6,408	6,205	5,818	5,597	5,580	5,636	5,657
Flight Instructor Certificates 4/	7,105	6,848	6,669	6,521	6,386	6,371	6,350	6,359	6,362	6,293
Remote Pilots 6/	3,462	793	NA	NA	NA	NA	NA	NA	NA	NA
Non Pilot--Total	195,993	187,914	183,259	174,000	166,294	160,452	155,918	150,019	147,052	144,968
Mechanic 5/	6,855	6,536	8,419	8,151	7,917	7,729	7,487	7,215	6,980	6,740
Repairmen 5/	1,847	1,822	2,289	2,278	2,288	2,307	2,278	2,312	2,335	2,284
Parachute Rigger 5/	597	540	811	763	712	697	683	655	633	615
Ground Instructor 5/	4,924	4,772	5,907	5,889	5,869	5,853	5,880	5,894	5,860	5,785
Dispatcher 5/	3,867	3,615	4,503	4,326	4,115	3,930	3,744	3,530	3,381	3,230
Flight Navigator	0	1	1	1	1	1	1	1	1	1
Flight Attendant	176,471	169,170	159,703	150,941	143,701	138,223	134,114	128,646	126,034	124,419
Flight Engineer	1,432	1,458	1,626	1,651	1,691	1,712	1,731	1,766	1,828	1,894

Note: The term airmen includes men and women certified as pilots, mechanics or other aviation technicians. This table (Table 2) represents data for females only.

Data in the Pilot Categories does not directly correspond to the same category in Table 1 as glider and/or helicopter and/or gyroplane certs are not broken out separately.

Data in the Non Pilot Categories as well as Flight Instructor Certificates does directly correspond to the same category in Table 1.

1/ In July 2010, the FAA issued a rule that increased the duration of validity for student pilot certificates for pilots under the age of 40 from 36 to 60 months. This resulted in the increase in active student pilots to 14,767 from 8,450 at the end of 2009. Starting with April 2016, there is no expiration date on the new student pilot certificates, which generates a cumulative increase in the numbers.

2/ Includes those with an airplane and/or a helicopter and/or glider and/or a gyroplane certificate.

3/ Glider and lighter-than-air pilots are not required to have a medical examination.

4/ Not included in total.

5/ Historically, numbers represented all certificates on record. No medical examination required. In 2016, Federal Regulation required that airmen without a plastic certificate no longer considered active. Therefore, starting with 2016, those airmen with a paper certificate only were excluded.

6/ Remote pilot certification started in August 2016. These numbers are not included in the pilot totals.

NA Not available.

Source: Fed. Aviation Admin., U.S. Civil Airmen Statistics, 2017 Active Civil Airmen Statistics,
https://www.faa.gov/data_research/aviation_data_statistics/civil_airmen_statistics/.

See also Centre for Aviation, *Women Airline Pilots: A Tiny Percentage, and Only Growing Slowly,* Aug, 7, 2018, https://centreforaviation.com/analysis/reports/women-airline-pilots-a-tiny-percentage-and-only-growing-slowly-432247; A. Pawlowski, *Why Aren't More Women Airline Pilots?*, CNN, Mar. 18, 2011, http://www.cnn.com/2011/ TRAVEL/03/18/female.airline.pilots/index.html.

———————

BAKER V. FED. AVIATION ADMIN.
917 F.2d 318 (7th Cir. 1990)

CUDAHY, CIRCUIT JUDGE.

In 1988, this court decided *Aman v. Fed. Aviation Admin.*, 856 F.2d 946 (7th Cir. 1988) ("*Aman I*"), in which current and former airline captains sought review under 49 U.S.C. § 1486(a) of a Federal Aviation Administration ("FAA") order denying a petition for exemptions from Federal Aviation Administration ("FAA") regulation § 121.383(c) ("age sixty rule").

FAA Age 60 Rule

The age sixty rule prohibits flights under Part 121 of FAA regulations, including commercial flights of aircraft seating more than thirty passengers, from taking off under the command of pilots age sixty or older. While the FAA is empowered to grant exemptions to this rule if it "finds that such action would be in the public interest," *see* 49 U.S.C. § 1421(c) (the public interest standard), no exemptions have ever been granted.

> *The age sixty rule prohibits flights under Part 121 of FAA regulations, including commercial flights of aircraft seating more than thirty passengers, from taking off under the command of pilots age sixty or older. While the FAA is empowered to grant exemptions to this rule if it "finds that such action would be in the public interest," see 49 U.S.C. § 1421(c) (the public interest standard), no exemptions have ever been granted.*

After recounting the age sixty rule's tortured thirty-year history and establishing the appropriate "substantial evidence" standard of review, this court in *Aman I* carefully demarcated petitioners' two claims. The first was that pilots, age sixty or older, meeting petitioners' proposed battery of physical and psychological tests (the protocol), were no more likely to cause accidents due to sudden incapacitation or undetected deterioration of piloting skills than other pilots. The FAA rejected this claim, finding that it was not in the public interest to grant exemptions when petitioners' protocol did not surely reduce all incremental risks associated with the aging process. Although this court noted that it might well have concluded otherwise as a matter of first impression, it held that substantial evidence supported the FAA's finding.

Petitioners' second claim was that the flying experience gained by allowing pilots age sixty and older to fly offset any increased risk of accident due to sudden incapacitation or skill deterioration, and that granting limited exemptions effectively produced a net increase or, at least, no net decline in safety. The FAA summarily rejected this claim. Unsatisfied with the agency's cursory treatment, this court vacated the FAA order and remanded the matter to the agency for further proceedings.

On remand, the FAA again refused to grant exemptions, and an order to that effect is presently before us for review. After considering the FAA's new order and both parties' somewhat flawed evidence, we cannot justify a conclusion that, on average, experience sufficiently offsets possible age-related impairment of health or skills to clearly guarantee a net constancy or increase in safety. Accordingly, we affirm.

* * *

*Exemption—
Burden of
Persuasion*

While substantial evidence must support the FAA's decision, petitioners have the burden of showing that circumstances justify exemptions from the age sixty rule, especially given the FAA's discretionary authority to act in this area. It is a heavy burden here involving obviously daunting problems of public safety. Age discrimination may form a dimension of the issue, but safety is the dominant and controlling consideration. The fact that it is apparently very difficult to demonstrate any clear conclusion with respect to the trade-off between experience and possible age-related impairment makes the task extremely onerous for the bearer of the burden of persuasion.

Petitioners have presented anecdotal evidence of superannuated pilots performing heroic deeds. Consider, for example, Captain David Cronin, who at age 59, on his second to last scheduled flight, heroically landed a Boeing 747 en route from Honolulu, Hawaii to Auckland, New Zealand after a forward cargo door blew open 17 minutes after take-off, opening a huge hole in the side of the plane. After two of the plane's four engines became disabled, Captain Cronin consulted emergency operating procedures which directed him to dive, reduce speed and drop the landing gear. However, 38 years of experience told him that, if that course were followed, the plane would lose too much altitude given its weight and multiple emergency situation. Captain Cronin instead operated many of the controls manually, constantly readjusting his speed and altitude calculations. With the exception of the nine passengers killed when the cargo door blew off, Cronin saved the lives of all passengers and crew aboard, safely landing the disabled plane at a much higher than normal speed.

In an appropriate context, we might give considerably more weight to the "anecdotal" evidence of pilots in their late fifties immediately before retirement performing amazing feats of airmanship than presumably would the FAA. As noted at oral argument, were the passengers of Flight 811 asked whether their Captain Cronin should be permitted to continue flying beyond the mandatory retirement age of sixty, few could doubt their answer. Nor are we in a position to say they would be incorrect. In the case before us, however, it is apparently not pilots who have performed aeronautical miracles who have sought exemptions, and we need not consider the arguable entitlement of such "special" pilots to exemptions from the age sixty rule.

Anecdotal Evidence

While petitioners have thus made some suggestive anecdotal showings and presented impressive expert opinion evidence, they have been unable to develop a persuasive statistical record comparing average risks for pilots in various relevant age categories. Petitioners, relying on figures from the National Transportation Safety Board, presented evidence that pilots age sixty and older had a lower accident rate per 1,000 pilots than pilots in other age groups.

This evidence, however, failed to account for exposure to risk in terms of hours of flight time. Thus, a pilot who had flown only a relatively few hours in a year and therefore incurred only a reduced risk of accident would carry the same weight as a pilot who flew many hundreds of hours with their greater attendant risks. Such a study is, of course, of questionable value. In addition, no analysis indicated whether the difference in accident experience by age group was statistically significant, a sort of failure specifically criticized in *Aman I*. Petitioners also presented evidence that allowing pilots, sixty or older, to fly would increase crew experience on the average, but failed to show with any rigor that there was a significant lack of pilot experience in need of correction.

This is not to say that the FAA's evidence was any more persuasive. The agency relied heavily on an accident experience report by age category referred to as the Flight Time Study. Like petitioners' studies this report has serious flaws. Perhaps the Flight Time Study's greatest failing is that the data for pilots under age sixty include millions of relatively safe air carrier miles flown, miles which because of the age sixty rule were unavailable to pilots over sixty. In calculating the accident rate for pilots sixty and older, the Flight Time Study divides the number of general aviation accidents by general aviation flight time, the only category open to this group. But for pilots under age sixty, the study divides the number of general aviation accidents by general aviation flight time and, in addition, air carrier operations flight time.

Flight Time Study

Because miles flown in air carrier operations are nearly accident free, and millions of these extra miles are included in the figures for younger pilots but not for older ones, the accident rate for all pilots under age sixty is significantly understated compared to the rate for older pilots, whose accident rate is overstated. Indeed, looking at the Flight Time Study's chart of accident risk for Class I (airline transport) and Class II (commercial) pilots with greater than 5,000 hours total flight time, the jump in accidents at age sixty to sixty-nine from age fifty to fifty-nine simply looks too large to be credible. Even without correcting the Flight Time Study for this disparity in types of current flight hours, the FAA's own study on its face may in some aspects be construed to support the petitioners' claims, the raw data supporting a number of different possible conclusions.

Consider, for example, the data showing accident rates as a function of both total and recent flight time for Class III pilots (general aviation and student). These data indicate that pilots age 60–69 (even 70 and over) with more than 1,000 hours total flight time and more than 50 hours recent flight time apparently have two of the lowest accident rates of any age groups of pilots in Class III having various indicated combinations of total and recent flight time. These comparisons apply, of course, even with respect to younger pilots in their thirties and forties, whose safety qualifications are generally unquestioned. More than 1000 hours total flight time and more than 50 hours recent flight time might be a telling statistic if the FAA could, for example, condition exemptions on total and recent flight time. Safety would be advanced, presumably, if the FAA required pilots to have at least a total of 1,000 flight hours and at least 50 recent flight hours as a condition for exemption.

Another arguable flaw in the Flight Time Study is that all pilots in a ten-year age cohort are combined into a single statistic. Thus, a single point represents pilots aged sixty to sixty-nine. Presumably, more exemptions from the age sixty rule would likely be granted to pilots under, say, sixty-five than pilots over that age. Therefore, the cumulation of accidents caused by pilots in their late sixties with accidents caused by pilots in their early sixties may as a practical matter tend to skew the Study.

The FAA also presented evidence of automobile traffic accidents and fatalities related to age. The connection between automobile drivers and pilots itself seems tenuous given the pilots' training, demonstrated proficiency, medical fitness, etc. Some of the FAA's evidence does not reflect "exposure" and some of it attempts to relate the nonparallel categories of automobile fatalities and aircraft accidents. Because elderly people seem more likely to die as a result of traffic accidents than younger people, the probative value of this latter showing is diminished.

Along with a directive for a more complete consideration of petitioners' second claim on remand, the FAA was also requested to explain how it could rationally grant exemptions to younger pilots who had suffered from alcohol abuse, heart conditions and the like but not grant exemptions to apparently healthy and proficient pilots over age sixty. The agency's justification was that, where particular and identifiable health problems are shown, specific medical tests may be conducted to indicate whether the pilot in question can continue to perform. On the other hand, "[a]ssessing the risks associated with determining which pilots may fly beyond age 60 concerns detrimental conditions which are unknown." Exactly how this distinction applies as a practical matter is not entirely clear to us, but neither have the petitioners been able to demonstrate its invalidity either theoretically or practically. Nor have petitioners apparently yet been able to present to the FAA a totally reliable test or group of tests which would reveal with certainty any general deterioration of piloting skills associated with advancing age. For present purposes, we will not require more of the FAA with respect to the consistency of restoring stricken younger pilots to duty while barring oldsters whose records are impeccable.

Admittedly, petitioners in this case face a Catch-22: from one perspective they cannot get exemptions until they show they can fly large passenger aircraft safely, and they cannot show they can fly such planes safely until they get exemptions. Thus, a valid statistical demonstration of comparative safety records by age seems difficult to obtain unless all age groups are engaged in the same kinds of flying. Since the age sixty and over group may not pilot large passenger transport aircraft, statistical comparisons are suspect.

Nevertheless, it was the petitioners' burden to present persuasive evidence that granting exemptions would not impair safety. While we have seen no compelling evidence that granting exemptions would increase the risk of accident, neither have we seen strong evidence that the experience of the 60-and-over pilot clearly overbears the danger of deterioration of piloting skills (or of sudden incapacitation) associated with the aging process. Where crucial issues of public safety are at stake, we would look for such a showing. Were the FAA to grant exemptions, it (and we) would no doubt be better able to resolve the question before us, but, absent the requisite compelling evidence, we must defer in these circumstances to the expert agency.

Burden to Make a Safety Case

We believe the agency's order is supported by substantial, albeit certainly not compelling, evidence. We reach this conclusion because of the obvious difficulty in attempting to balance on a statistical basis experience against reliable indicators of good health and ability to perform as age advances. Certainly the record abounds with testimonials by experts in both flying and medicine to the experience and judgment of the older aviator and the feasibility of assuring the good health and performance of this kind of pilot through frequent and sophisticated testing. We are certainly not in a position to say that the numerous supporters of the petitioners' case are wrong. And it is obvious that the FAA must continue and must enhance its efforts to accommodate their points of view. At this time, however, we are not prepared to overrule the agency in a matter of such immense sensitivity as this one. The FAA should not take this as a signal that the age sixty rule is sacrosanct and untouchable. Obviously, there is a great body of opinion that the time has come to move on. The agency must give serious attention to this opinion. Accordingly, the order of the Federal Aviation Administration is affirmed.

We believe the agency's order is supported by substantial, albeit certainly not compelling, evidence. We reach this conclusion because of the obvious difficulty in attempting to balance on a statistical basis experience against reliable indicators of good health and ability to perform as age advances.

WILL, SENIOR DISTRICT JUDGE, *dissenting.*

Initial Justification for the Age 60 Rule

This court, in *Aman I*, reviewed the age 60 rule's "tortured history," established the appropriate "substantial evidence" standard of review, noted that while the FAA is theoretically empowered to grant exemptions from the rule, none has ever been granted, vacated the FAA's order and remanded the case to the agency for further proceedings and the presentation of further evidence that no airline pilot older than age 59, regardless of physical condition and experience, is qualified to fly a plane seating more than thirty passengers.

When the FAA adopted its age 60 and out rule some thirty-one years ago, in 1959, it justified the rule by stating

that there is a progressive deterioration of certain important physiological and psychological functions with age, that significant medical defects attributable to the degenerative process occur at an increasing rate as age increases, and that sudden incapacity due to such medical defects becomes significantly more frequent in any group reaching age 60, and that such incapacity, due primarily to heart attacks and strokes, cannot be predicted accurately as to any specific individual on the basis of presently available scientific tests and criteria [so that] any attempt to be selective in predicting which individuals are likely to suffer an incapacitating attack would be futile under the circumstances and would not be medically sound.

24 Fed. Reg. 9767 (Dec. 5, 1959). At the same time, the FAA also found that:

Other factors, even less susceptible to precise measurement [also] must be considered. These relate to loss of ability to perform highly skilled tasks rapidly, to resist fatigue, to maintain physical stamina, to perform, effectively in a complex and stressful environment, to apply experience, judgment and reasoning rapidly to new, changing and emergency situations, and to learn new techniques, skills and procedures. The progressive loss of these abilities . . . even though they may be significant in themselves prior to age 60 . . . assume greater significance at the older ages when coupled with medical defects leading to increased risk of sudden incapacitation.

Since 1959, numerous pilots, approaching or having celebrated their sixtieth birthdays, have petitioned for individual exemptions from the FAA's rigid enforcement of its age 60 and out rule. The agency, however, has never granted an exemption—to anyone, regardless of his or her physical qualifications or experience. Pilots with tens of thousands of hours of flight time and flawless records, and who pass every physical test with flying colors, suddenly are grounded on their sixtieth birthdays, even though the day before they were flying, without restrictions, and were acknowledged to be qualified and, ironically, are still deemed qualified to pilot planes with thirty passengers or less.

The FAA actually admits to a policy of uniformly denying all petitions for exemptions from the age 60 rule. It's not that the FAA pretends that no person over the age of 59 could ever safely pilot a Part 121 flight. In fact, the agency concedes that some over-59 captains would do just fine. Then why not grant exemptions to those pilots? Why does the FAA persist in refusing ever to exempt any pilot, no matter how able, from its 60 and out rule? And why does it refuse to issue meaningful standards and criteria for granting at least some exemptions? Because, says the FAA, although many pilots 60 and over would make safe captains, there is simply no way to tell the safe ones from the dangerous ones in advance.

It's not that the FAA pretends that no person over the age of 59 could ever safely pilot a Part 121 flight. In fact, the agency concedes that some over-59 captains would do just fine. Then why not grant exemptions to those pilots? Why does the FAA persist in refusing ever to exempt any pilot, no matter how able, from its 60 and out rule? And why does it refuse to issue meaningful standards and criteria for granting at least some exemptions? Because, says the FAA, although many pilots 60 and over would make safe captains, there is simply no way to tell the safe ones from the dangerous ones in advance.

In support of this position, the FAA advances, today, in 1990, the same kinds of justifications it originally offered thirty-one years ago, in 1959. And in 1990, just as in 1959, these justifications are of two types. The first starts from the proposition that "some psychomotor, emotional, intellectual and physical attributes necessary for enhanced flight crew performance deteriorate with age," resulting in a "sharp decline in physical and cognitive performance after age 60"; adds that there is no reliable way of measuring (or even necessarily detecting) the extent of an aging pilot's deterioration; and concludes that it is not scientifically possible to screen out safe 60-year-old pilots from dangerous ones without actually putting them up in the skies and letting them fly.

The FAA's second longstanding justification begins with the observation that at age 60 skills are not only deteriorating but beginning to do so at an increasing and increasingly unpredictable rate; adds that the dangers of their deteriorating to the point of sudden incapacitation (in flight, presumably) is significantly greater at age 60 and beyond than it was before; and finishes, again, with the assertion that there is no reliable way to tell a safe 60-year-old pilot, who won't suddenly collapse in flight, from a dangerous one, who will. "The aging process is largely unpredictable, and generally is not measurable. [T]here are no generally applicable medical tests that can, at this time, adequately determine which individual pilots are subject to incapacitation secondary to either acute cardiovascular or neurological events or to more subtle conditions related to cognitive functioning."

* * *

Two years ago, in *Aman I*, the FAA, advancing both of its customary justifications, defended its original denial of many of the same petitions that are before us again on this appeal. At that time, this court partially upheld the logic of the FAA's customary justifications, finding what the FAA itself has repeatedly held in connection with every request for an exemption since 1959, *i.e.*, "substantial evidence [to] support[ ] . . . rejection of the contention that the petitioners' protocol, combined with existing methods of operational testing, would screen out all increased risks of incapacitation or undetected skill deterioration among pilots older than sixty." The *Aman I* panel, however, ultimately vacated the FAA's denial and remanded for further proceedings, concluding that the FAA had "failed to set forth a sufficient factual or legal basis for its rejection of the petitioners' claim that older pilots' edge in experience offsets any undetected physical losses."

It is unclear to me just what the panel in *Aman I* meant for the FAA to do on remand. Given the number and variety of tests that are available and commonly used to measure the physical and cognitive powers of pilots-flight simulator tests, vision and depth perception tests, hearing tests, stress tests, blood tests, psychological workups, X-rays, angiograms and EKGs—I find it difficult to believe that there are skills or physical or cognitive abilities which the FAA can identify as necessary for safe flying but for which it either cannot or does not reliably test all pilots, including 60-year-olds and regardless of whether they pilot flights with more than thirty passengers or other flights with fewer passengers.

> *If it is true, however, that physical deterioration can't be tested and measured accurately, as the panel in* Aman I *found "substantial evidence" to show, then it baffles me how the FAA, on remand, was supposed to reconsider the relationship between physical skills and abilities, on the one hand, and experience on the other.*

If it is true, however, that physical deterioration can't be tested and measured accurately, as the panel in *Aman I* found "substantial evidence" to show, then it baffles me how the FAA, on remand, was supposed to reconsider the relationship between physical skills and abilities, on the one hand, and experience on the other. For whether, if as a pilot grows older, experience lends an edge which offsets waning skills and abilities, necessarily depends on at least two things: (1) how much experience the pilot has and (2) how severely physical skills and abilities have "deteriorated." And if one of those things can't be reliably measured for risk, or even spotted—"[A] substantial body of medical opinion continues 'to doubt the feasibility' " of measuring the "incremental risk associated with . . . undetected deterioration of skills among pilots over sixty,"—then balancing an intangible like experience against undetectable or unmeasurable deterioration would be some trick. The same problem, of course, must have faced the FAA on remand in trying to weigh the benefits of experience against its asserted concern about the allegedly unpredictable risks of "sudden incapacitation."

The more serious difficulty, however, with the FAA's continuing reliance on "sudden incapacitation"—the specter of a pilot in the cockpit, of no matter what age, suddenly stricken by a heart attack or a stroke—hasn't much to do with whether the incapacitated pilot, suddenly stricken, could by dint of experience avert a crash. At that point, the safety net obviously is not experience but the presence of one or two other qualified pilots in the cockpit. Instead, the troubling problem with the FAA's "sudden incapacitation" justification is its premise. The panel in *Aman I* found substantial evidence to support the FAA's conclusion that current medical science cannot determine which pilots over 60 will be most vulnerable to sudden and incapacitating disability.

But that should have been a follow-up inquiry, not the first one. The first inquiry should be whether there is substantial evidence, current and valid in 1990, to support the proposition that all pilots, age 60 and older, are significantly more prone to sudden medical catastrophe than other pilots. For the age 60 and out rule makes sense only if it screens for risks that are significantly higher for all 60-year-olds than for 30, 40 or 50-year-olds. Otherwise, the rule is simply an arbitrary, overly broad and outmoded presumption, smelling of age discrimination, about infirmities which do not uniformly afflict all pilots over 60 and should not be assumed to.

The panel in *Aman I* also remanded with instructions to the FAA to "make sense" of its increasing willingness to issue "special certificates" to younger pilots with records of heart disease, drug abuse and alcoholism—which conditions, like aging, can be progressive—in the face of its stubborn refusal ever to grant exemptions from the age 60 rule. In response, the FAA has now explained that "present tests can predict the expected course of a known medical deficiency" such as heart disease or alcoholism "with sufficient accuracy to allow valid, individualized judgments" but that "the same accuracy is not possible when assessing the decrements associated with the aging process."

The FAA, however, has not offered any evidence to support this distinction between the special certificates it grants to younger pilots and its refusal even to promulgate meaningful regulations and criteria for age exemptions for older pilots, much less to grant an age exemption to an older pilot. And there is no citation, either in the FAA's brief or its latest order, for the proposition that the symptoms of alcoholism, drug abuse and heart disease can be monitored more closely and reliably than the "decrements" of aging. We defer to agency expertise, where expertise has been demonstrated, but "deference should not be equated with a license to issue inconsistent determinations." The pilots have plausibly alleged that the FAA's distinctions and exemption practices are inconsistent. The FAA has only answered with unsupported and unconvincing assertions.

> *We defer to agency expertise, where expertise has been demonstrated, but "deference should not be equated with a license to issue inconsistent determinations." The pilots have plausibly alleged that the FAA's distinctions and exemption practices are inconsistent. The FAA has only answered with unsupported and unconvincing assertions.*

The majority acknowledges that "exactly how [the FAA's asserted] distinction [between aging and other conditions] applies as a practical matter is not entirely clear to us," but concludes that for present purposes, it will not require more of the FAA with respect to the consistency of restoring stricken younger (59 and under) pilots (suffering from alcohol abuse, drug abuse, heart conditions) to duty while grounding other pilots, 60 and over, whose records and physical condition are, by contrast, impeccable.

* * *

The FAA's record here is more than just "disappointing." The agency has relied on a seriously flawed Flight Time study even though, as the majority points out, "various experts, even some from the FAA, state that the study should not be relied on as determinative-or even probative on the question of the continued validity of the age sixty rule." In addition, as the majority also recognizes, "the FAA's own study on its face may in some aspects be construed to support the petitioners' claims." The FAA has also relied on evidence of automobile traffic accidents involving fatalities as related to age. But again, as the majority points out, "The connection between automobile drivers and pilots itself seems tenuous given the pilots' training, demonstrated proficiency, medical fitness, etc." and "attempts to relate nonparallel categories of automobile fatalities with aircraft accidents" does not reflect "exposure."

The petitioners, as the majority also concedes, face a Catch-22, if the FAA and this court require them to prove, with statistics that reflect actual flight time in large passenger transport planes with more than thirty passengers, that they can fly those planes as safely as pilots who are not yet 60. For until at least one exemption has been granted, none of the petitioners are eligible to pilot such flights and consequently no such statistics can be compiled. It is possible that statistics might be available for petitioners' flight time in the same large passenger aircraft but carrying thirty passengers or less or cargo. If such statistics are available, they have not been referred to by the FAA or the pilots.

In lieu of statistics, petitioners have presented impressive evidence of pilots on the brink of age 60 performing heroic deeds and saving lives where less experienced pilots might have failed. They have also presented what the majority concedes is "impressive expert opinion evidence" that at least some experienced pilots over age 60 are qualified to fly large commercial aircraft and may be even better qualified than younger, less experienced pilots. And, relying on figures from the National Transportation Safety Board, they have presented evidence that licensed pilots age 60 and older show a lower accident rate per 1,000 pilots than pilots in other age groups, although those statistics do not reflect the number of hours flown by members of each age group and we do not know, therefore, whether pilots age 60 and over fly more or fewer hours per year than pilots in other age groups.

The majority concludes, on the basis of the foregoing, that the FAA has presented "substantial evidence" in support of an absolute 60 and out rule, although it admits that it has seen "no compelling evidence that granting exemptions would increase the risk of accident . . ." The majority also concludes that it has seen "no strong evidence that the experience of the 60-and-over pilot clearly overbears the danger of deterioration of piloting skills (or of sudden incapacitation) associated with the aging process."

Since the FAA has refused as a matter of policy to grant any exemptions, what the FAA and the majority are holding, in effect, is that every airline pilot, on his or her 60th birthday, and regardless of physical condition or experience, becomes a significantly greater safety hazard than before, even though, just one day before, he or she was FAA certified, qualified and safe. The evidence in this case does not warrant that conclusion. Nor does everyday, ordinary good old common sense.

Since the FAA has refused as a matter of policy to grant any exemptions, what the FAA and the majority are holding, in effect, is that every airline pilot, on his or her 60th birthday, and regardless of physical condition or experience, becomes a significantly greater safety hazard than before, even though, just one day before, he or she was FAA certified, qualified and safe. The evidence in this case does not warrant that conclusion. Nor does everyday, ordinary good old common sense.

* * *

Rather than again urging the FAA to recognize the need for keeping up with advanced technologies and accommodating other points of view, I would vacate the FAA's latest order and remand for action on three fronts.

I would remand, first, for consideration of the adoption of regulations establishing ascertainable and meaningful standards to govern the granting of at least some exemptions to the age 60 rule. The FAA's present regulations—which dangle the possibility of an exemption to a pilot who can show "why the exemption would not adversely affect safety" or why, at least, it "would provide a level of safety equal to that provided by the rule," 14 C.F.R. § 11.25(5)—do not sufficiently guide the agency in exercising its discretion and do not begin to provide adequate notice to pilots about the kind of showing that would justify an exemption. Moreover, in light of the agency's policy of never granting age 60 exemptions, its present regulations are a fraud.

Call for Standards

I would also remand for a showing, by current and substantial evidence, that all pilots age 60 and over are significantly more prone to "sudden incapacitation" than all pilots under 60. The agency should re-examine the relevant data and articulate a satisfactory explanation, rationally connected to the facts, for its ongoing reliance on "sudden incapacitation" and for drawing a line at age 60.

Finally, I would remand, yet again, for a reasoned and full explanation for treating requests for special medical certificates under 14 C.F.R. § 67.19 differently than petitions for exemptions from the age 60 and out rule. And in that connection, I would require the FAA to consider the possibility that obligating pilots 60 and older to undergo more frequent medical and skills examinations than other pilots—a technique the agency already uses to monitor the condition of pilots who have been granted "special issuances" under 14 C.F.R. § 67.19—might provide enough accurate and up-to-the-minute information about a pilot's health and skills to enable the agency to make individualized determinations about the risks of letting any particular captain, 60 or older, pilot a Part 121 flight, rather than arbitrarily and capriciously denying exemptions to all.

EXERCISE 4-4. *BAKER V. FED. AVIATION ADMIN.*—THE AGE 60 RULE

1. What is the "age sixty rule"? On what basis did the claimants in *Baker v. Fed. Aviation Admin.* seek an exemption from the age sixty rule?

2. Which party bore the burden to present persuasive evidence that an exemption to the age sixty would not impact safety?

3. In what two ways has the FAA justified the age sixty rule?

4. What anecdotal evidence did the petitioners present? How did this compare with any statistical evidence?

5. Discuss the critique presented in the dissenting opinion. Is it convincing? Are the dissenting opinion's regulatory and policy suggestions consistent with the role of a judge? Explain.

NOTES ON *BAKER V. FED. AVIATION ADMIN.*—AIRMEN AGE DISCRIMINATION

1. *Fair Treatment for Experienced Pilots Act of 2007.*

Baker v. Fed. Aviation Admin., supra, forecast the end of the "Age 60 Rule"—a regulation of dubious foundation that arguably forced accomplished and compliant pilots to retire prematurely. More recently, *Emory v. United Air Lines, Inc.,* 720 F.3d 915 (D.D.C. 2013) considered the Fair Treatment for Experienced Pilots Act of 2007 through which Congress repealed the Federal Aviation Administration's ("FAA") long-contested "Age 60 Rule" and extended the maximum age for piloting commercial flights by five years to 65. FTEPA marked a significant victory for opponents of the old regime. Under the Act's nonretroactivity provision pilots who had turned 60 prior to FTEPA's enactment date and did not qualify for either one of two narrowly drawn statutory exceptions would be denied the benefits of the Age 65 Rule and, as was often the case, terminated. The *Emory* court explained:

> First implemented in 1959, The Federal Aviation Administration's ("FAA") so-called Age 60 Rule barred any person 60 years of age or older from serving as a pilot in flights conducted under Part 121 of the Federal Aviation Regulations. *See* 14 C.F.R. § 121.383(c) (2007).
>
> Although the Rule survived nearly a half-century's worth of challenges in federal courts, institutional support for the age 60 ceiling dwindled. In 2006, the International Civil Aviation Organization ("ICAO") revised the maximum age from 60 to 65 for certain pilots in international operations. The FAA responded by establishing the Age 60 Aviation Rulemaking Committee ("ARC") to make recommendations regarding the adoption of the ICAO standard, but the "polarized" Commission, with its 17 members "representing pilot unions, airlines, the aeromedical community, and the FAA," agreed on just one thing: "Any change to the Age 60 Rule should be prospective."
>
> Undeterred by the false start, FAA soldiered on. In January 2007, the agency announced it would amend the Age 60 Rule. Congress, however, preempted this rulemaking with the passage of FTEPA in December 2007. Among other changes, FTEPA abrogated the Age 60 Rule as of the Act's December 13, 2007, enactment date and replaced it with a new ceiling colloquially referred to as the "Age 65 Rule." Crucially, Congress gave the

Age 65 Rule entirely prospective effect with just two exceptions. As codified in the Act's "Nonretroactivity" provision, an over-60 pilot that served as a "required flight deck crew member" ("RFDCM") on December 13, 2007, or was subsequently hired as a new pilot without seniority, could return to piloting Part 121 flights until age 65.

The "Age 60 Rule" was first scrutinized in *Air Line Pilots Ass'n Int'l v. Quesada*, 276 F.2d 892 (2d Cir. 1960). There, the Air Line Pilots Association ("ALPA") sued for an injunction preventing enforcement of the Age 60 Rule and for a judicial declaration that the rule was null and void. However, a federal appellate court deferred to and upheld the conclusions of Federal Aviation Administrator Elwood R. ("Pete") Quesada that "older pilots because of their seniority under collective bargaining agreements often fly the newest, largest, and fastest planes [and] that available medical studies show that sudden incapacitation due to heart attacks or strokes becomes more frequent as men approach age sixty and present medical knowledge is such that it is impossible to predict with accuracy those individuals most likely to suffer attacks." Accordingly, ALPA—which subsequently and until recently supported the Age 60 Rule for almost three decades—lost its case.

The Age 60 Rule may have been more a product of economics and politics than medicine and law. It arose out of a labor dispute at American Airlines in the 1950s. That era began the jet age as the Boeing 707 and DC-8 replaced piston-driven airplanes. To save training costs, American Airlines Chief Executive Officer C.R. Smith preferred employing young pilots, including Korean-War veterans with jet experience. American Airlines (like Western Airlines and TWA) unilaterally set 60 as the age at which pilots would be required to retire. *See, e.g. Criswell v. Western Air Lines, Inc.*, 709 F.2d 544 (9th Cir. 1985). In large measure, that decision led to a 21-day walkout at American Airlines. Ultimately, American Airlines acceded to an arbitrator's ruling that it allow its over-60 pilots to fly.

Not to be defeated, C.R. Smith turned to his friend, the war-time commander for President Dwight D. Eisenhower and the first FAA Administrator—Pete Quesada. By letter dated February 5, 1959, Smith asked Quesada to establish 60 as a federally-mandated retirement age for pilots. Without any Congressional or FAA hearing to debate the matter, the Age 60 Rule was codified. Later, in 1962, Quesada retired from the FAA and was elected to the Board of Directors of American Airlines.

Given this history, opponents of the Age 60 Rule contend that the regulation is arbitrary, promoting business not safety. After all, airline pilots must pass flight physicals administered by an FAA-licensed examiner to retain their commercial license. Pilots must also pass semiannual simulator training and flight checks. Critics of the Age 60 Rule therefore suggest that these battery of proficiency requirements show why a rigid mandatory retirement law is unnecessary and unsubstantiated.

For further discussion of the Age 65 Law—also known as the Fair Treatment of Experienced Pilots Act see https://www.faa.gov/other_visit/aviation_industry/airline_operators/airline_safety/info/all_infos/media/age65_qa.pdf.

2.   ***United 232.***

"Anecdotal evidence" relied upon in *Baker v. Fed. Aviation Admin.*, merits attention. A 747 captain who safely landed a jet whose cargo door blew open in mid-air (*In re Air Disaster near Honolulu, Hawaii on Feb. 24, 1989*, 792 F. Supp. 1541 (N.D. Cal. 1990) (N.D. Cal. 1990)) was probative of the advantage of pilot experience. Just five months later, on July 19, 1989, Captain Al Haynes, a 57 years old commercial pilot radioed trouble:

> Confirm we have no hydraulic fluid, which means we have no elevator control, almost none, and very little aileron control. I have serious doubts about making the airport. Have you got someplace near there, that we might be able to ditch? Unless we get control of this airplane, we're going to put it down wherever it happens to be.

Engine number two of United Airlines Flight 232, a DC-10 traveling from Denver to Chicago, exploded in-flight. A fatigued fan disk separated from the engine housing and pierced two of the aircraft's three hydraulic lines. Captain Haynes and his crew improvised for more than 40 minutes to maneuver their doomed airplane down for an emergency landing in Sioux City, Iowa. They did so by alternating power between the two remaining engines. Ultimately the 296 passengers aboard United Flight 232 cart wheeled wing-over-wing across airport asphalt and Iowa cornfields. That 185 passengers survived was miraculous. *See In re Air Crash Disaster at Sioux City, Iowa, on July 19, 1989*, 133 F.R.D. 515 (N.D. Ill. 1990). [The pilot in command of Flight 232, Al Haynes, died in August 2019. *See generally* Keerthi Vedantam, *Al Haynes, United Airlines Pilot Who Saved 184 Lives Durings 1989 Plane Crash, Dies at 87*, SEATTLE TIMES, Aug. 27, 2019, https://www.seattletimes.com/business/boeing-aerospace/al-haynes-united-airlines-pilot-who-saved-184-lives-during-1989-plane-crash-dies/.]

Later in 1989, two pilots made rookie mistakes aboard USAir Flight 5050. *See* David Fields, *Airlines, Agency to Study Link between Crews, Crashes*, WASH. TIMES, Jan. 1, 1990, at A8. The Boeing 737 overshot the end of a runway at LaGuardia Airport and skidded into New York's East River. The airplane was split in two and two passengers died. The pilot of Flight 5050, who had been trained on small commuter airplanes, had logged less than 150 hours of flying time as an aircraft commander.

These accidents all happened in 1989, a year in which more commercial airplane accidents occurred than in the preceding twenty years. That fact, combined with the record-setting pace of new pilot hires in that year, prompted federal and industry officials to investigate whether there was a link between an increase in commercial airplane disasters and the influx of pilots with limited experience. *See also* Bob Moos, *Don't Jettison Pilot Experience*, J. COMMERCE 8A (1989).

In fact, no study undertaken in connection with the Age 60 Rule between 1978 and 2005—including the National Academy of Science's Institute of Medicine Study (1978), the National Institute of Health Aging Report (1981), the Golaszewski Flight Time Study (1983), and the Civil Aeromedical Institute Hilton Systems Study (1984)—conclusively established that airline piloting becomes critical at any given age. While tentatively suggesting that 63 might be a good cut-off for mandatory pilot retirement, the Hilton Systems Study concluded *that* there was "no support for the hypothesis that pilots of scheduled air carriers had increased accident rates as they neared the age of 60." (*See, e.g.*, http://www.age60rule.com/docs/data_quality_ltr. html.) Courts themselves have noticed "serious flaws" in the data underlying the Age 60 Rule, including the Golaszewski Flight Time Study in which "the accident rate for all pilots under age sixty is significantly understated compared to the rate for older pilots, whose accident rate is overstated." *See Baker, supra.*

The Age 60 Rule may be as the President of the Southwest Airlines Pilots' Association once described it, "a solution in search of a problem." Its political and scientific legitimacy was questioned for nearly 50 years and its economic impact cut particularly deep as bankrupt and financially distressed airlines with expensive defined-benefit pensions need pilots to retire while older pilots need to work longer to make up lost retirement funds. Meanwhile, application of the Age 60 Rule to domestic pilots was inconsistent with the waivers the FAA grants for over-60 pilots of foreign airlines. *See, e.g., Avera v. United Air Lines, Inc.*, 2010 WL 419400 (N.D. Fla. 2010); *Brooks v. Air Line Pilots Ass'n, Int'l* (D.D.C. 2009); *Adams v. Fed. Aviation Admin.* (D.C. Cir. 2008). *See generally* Nicholas D. O'Conner, *Too Experienced for the Flight Deck? Why the Age 65 Rule is Not Enough*, 17 ELDER L.J. 375 (2010).

Table 4-3. FAA Average Age of Active Pilots by Category (2017)

AVERAGE AGE OF ACTIVE PILOTS BY CATEGORY
as of DECEMBER 31, 2017

| Calendar Year | Type of Pilot Certificates | | | | | | | Flight Instructor | Remote Pilot |
	Total 1/	Student 3/	Sport	Recre-ational	Private 2/	Commercial 2/	Airline Transport 2/	CFI	
2017	44.9	32.5	57.1	49.0	48.9	46.2	50.6	48.0	41.9
2016	44.9	31.7	56.4	44.0	48.4	46.0	50.2	48.0	42.7
2015	44.8	31.4	56.2	44.6	48.5	45.6	49.9	47.8	N/A
2014	44.8	31.5	55.8	43.1	48.5	45.5	49.8	47.7	N/A
2013	44.8	31.5	55.2	44.8	48.5	45.4	49.7	47.5	N/A
2012	44.7	31.5	54.7	47.8	48.3	44.8	49.9	47.2	N/A
2011	44.4	31.4	54.4	48.8	47.9	44.4	49.7	46.8	N/A
2010	44.2	31.4	53.8	50.8	47.6	44.2	49.4	46.4	N/A
2009	45.3	33.5	53.5	50.4	47.1	44.2	48.9	46.0	N/A
2008	45.1	33.6	53.2	50.1	46.9	44.8	48.5	45.8	N/A
2007	45.7	34.0	52.9	52.4	48.0	46.1	48.3	45.5	N/A
2006	45.6	34.4	52.9	51.5	47.7	46.1	48.1	45.2	N/A
2005	45.5	34.6	53.2	50.9	47.4	46.0	47.8	44.9	N/A
2004	45.1	34.2	N/A	51.3	47.0	45.9	47.5	44.6	N/A
2003	44.7	34.0	N/A	51.5	46.5	45.6	47.0	44.4	N/A
2002	44.4	33.7	N/A	51.0	46.2	45.5	46.6	44.2	N/A

1/ Includes helicopter (only) and glider (only).
2/ Includes pilots with an airplane and/or a helicopter and/or a glider and/or a gyroplane certificate. Pilots with multiple ratings will be reported under highest rating. For example a pilot with a private
 helicopter and commercial airplane certificates will be reported in the commercial category.
3/ In July 2010, the FAA issued a rule that increased the duration of validity for student pilot certificates for pilots under the age of 40 from 36 to 60 months.
N/A Not available. Sport certificate first issued in 2005. Remote pilot certificate first issued in 2016.

Source: Fed. Aviation Admin., U.S. Civil Airmen Statistics, 2017 Active Civil Airmen Statistics, https://www.faa.gov/data_research/aviation_data_statistics/civil_airmen_statistics/.

JIFRY V. FED. AVIATION ADMIN.

370 F.3d 1174 (D.C. Cir. 2004)

ROGERS, CIRCUIT JUDGE.

Petitions filed by two non-resident alien pilots challenge certain aviation regulations adopted in the wake of the September 11, 2001 terrorist attacks.

From the establishment of the Transportation Security Administration ("TSA") in November 2001 to the promulgation of the challenged regulations in January 2003, aviation security has undergone a fundamental transformation. The pilots contend that the new procedures resulting in the revocation of their airman certificates issued by the Federal Aviation Administration ("FAA") violated the Administrative Procedure Act ("APA") and the due process clause of the Fifth Amendment to the United States Constitution. Specifically, they contend that the

January 2003 regulations were unlawfully promulgated without notice and comment, that the revocations were not supported by substantial evidence in the record, and that they were denied meaningful notice of the evidence against them and a meaningful opportunity to be heard.

> *The FAA may "at any time" reexamine the issuance of an airman certificate and issue an order "modifying, suspending, or revoking" a certificate if the Administrator determines that such action is required for "safety in air commerce" and "the public interest."*

Congress has delegated broad discretion to the Federal Aviation Administration ("FAA") to prescribe regulations and standards for safety in air commerce and national security. The FAA may "at any time" reexamine the issuance of an airman certificate and issue an order "modifying, suspending, or revoking" a certificate if the Administrator determines that such action is required for "safety in air commerce" and "the public interest." With regard to issuing airman certificates to qualified individuals, Congress distinguished between citizens and aliens, conferring broad discretion to the FAA regarding alien pilots.

After the September 11, 2001 terrorist attacks, Congress established the Transportation Security Administration ("TSA") on November 19, 2001, and transferred much of the responsibility for civil aviation security from the FAA to the TSA.

Transfer of Security Authority

This case concerns alien pilots only. The two pilots, Jifry and Zarie, are citizens of Saudi Arabia who have used their FAA certificates to pilot flights abroad, but have not operated Saudi Arabian Airlines flights to the United States in the past nine and four years, respectively. On August 14, 2002, the TSA sent letters to the FAA requesting that Captain Jifry and Captain Zarie have their airman certificates revoked, stating that "[b]ased upon information available to us," they presented "a security risk to civil aviation or national security." The FAA notified Jifry and Zarie by letters of August 20, 2002, that their airman certificates would be revoked because the Acting Under Secretary of Transportation for Security, pursuant 49 U.S.C. §§ 44709(b)(1)(A) and 46105(c), had determined that they presented risks to aviation or national security. The FAA revoked the pilots' certificates and the pilots appealed the revocations to the National Transportation Safety Board ("NTSB").

In January 24, 2003, the FAA dismissed the revocation actions against Jifry and Zarie, and in conjunction with the TSA, published, without notice and comment, new regulations governing the suspension and revocation of airman certificates for security reasons. The new FAA regulation, 14 C.F.R. § 61.18, provides for automatic suspension by the FAA of airman certificates upon written notification from the TSA that the pilot poses a security threat and, therefore, is not eligible to hold an airman certificate. The TSA simultaneously promulgated 49 C.F.R. § 1540.117, which establishes the procedure by which the TSA initially and finally notifies non-resident aliens who hold or apply for FAA certificates that they pose a security threat, and requires the TSA to notify the FAA once the TSA has determined that a pilot is a security threat.

Process for Determining "Security Threat"

Upon finding that a pilot poses a "security threat" the TSA Assistant Administrator for Intelligence issues an Initial Notification of Threat Assessment ("Initial Notice") to the individual and serves that determination upon the FAA. The FAA then suspends the pilot's certificate. No later than 15 days after service, the pilot may make a written request for copies of releasable materials upon which the Initial Notice was based. The TSA must respond not later than 30 days after receiving the request, and the pilot may submit a written reply within 15 days of receiving the TSA's response. At that point, the TSA Deputy Administrator must review the entire record *de novo* to determine if the pilot poses a security risk. If the Deputy so determines, the TSA serves a Final Notification of Threat Assessment ("Final Notice") and the FAA revokes the certificate. The pilot may appeal the certificate revocation to the NTSB. Upon exhaustion of these administrative remedies, the pilot may seek review in the court of appeals, which may review the case on the merits.

On January 24, 2003, the TSA also served an Initial Notice of Threat Assessment designating Jifry and Zarie as security threats, and the FAA suspended their certificates. The pilots appealed the Initial Notice, and requested the materials upon which the Initial Notice had been issued. The TSA provided the releasable materials, but did not include the factual basis for TSA's determination, which was based on classified information.

The pilots then appealed the suspension of their certificates to the NTSB. The ALJ granted the TSA's motion for summary judgment, ruling that the only question was procedural—whether the pilots had been duly advised by the TSA, in writing, that they posed a security threat, and finding that they had. Upon the pilots' appeals, the NTSB affirmed the ALJ's order in favor of the TSA. Jifry and Zarie then filed replies to the TSA's Initial Notice, stating that the "lack of evidence and information about the basis for the determination contained in the TSA's response" made it impossible for them to specifically rebut the TSA's allegations, and denying that they were security threats.

On May 8, 2003, the TSA Deputy Administrator, upon *de novo* review of the administrative record, denied the pilots' challenge to the Initial Notice and issued a Final Notice based on finding that Jifry and Zarie posed security threats. *See* 49 C.F.R. § 1540.117(c). The FAA then revoked the pilots' airman certificates. On August 13, 2003, the NTSB denied the pilots' appeal of the revocation of their certificates for the same reasons it had denied their challenges to the suspensions, and affirmed the ALJ's grant of summary judgment to the TSA and the emergency orders of revocation.

* * *

The pilots make three challenges to the revocations of their FAA airman certificates: first, that the January 2003 regulations were unlawfully promulgated without notice and comment; second, that the revocations were not supported by substantial evidence in the record; and third, that the procedures provided by the January 2003 regulations violated their due process rights under the Fifth Amendment to the Constitution. We address each in turn.

Grounds for Appeal

Section 553 of the Administrative Procedure Act ("APA") requires an agency to publish a general notice of proposed rulemaking and to afford an opportunity for interested persons to participate in the rulemaking. *See* 5 U.S.C. § 553(b), (c). The "good cause" exception, however, provides that "when the agency for good cause finds . . . that notice and public procedure thereon are impracticable, unnecessary, or contrary to the public interest," the agency need not engage in notice and comment.

The pilots contend that the regulations of January 2003 are invalid because they were unlawfully promulgated without notice and comment, and there was no rational basis for eliminating the right to a meaningful appeal before the NTSB. They maintain that the "good cause" exception does not apply because notice and comment had not been "impracticable, unnecessary or contrary to the public interest" inasmuch as the FAA already had the authority to immediately suspend or revoke a certificate upon finding that "safety in air commerce or air transportation and the public interest" required such an action.

Generally, the "good cause" exception to notice and comment rulemaking, is to be "narrowly construed and only reluctantly countenanced." The exception excuses notice and comment in emergency situations or where delay could result in serious harm. The latter circumstance is applicable here in examining the TSA's determination that "[t]he use of notice and comment prior to issuance of th[e] [January 2003 regulations] could delay the ability of TSA and the FAA to take effective action to keep persons found by TSA to pose a security threat from holding an airman certificate," and was "necessary to prevent a possible imminent hazard to aircraft, persons, and property within the United States."

Good Cause Exception

The pilots contend that the "good cause" exception does not apply because the FAA already had unlimited power to revoke a certificate immediately if it believed an airman to be a security risk, and the TSA was already authorized to make security assessments under 49 U.S.C. § 114(f). While true, the pilots fail to acknowledge that at the time the challenged regulations were adopted, the FAA's power to suspend or revoke certificates was permissive only. Congress had not yet enacted 49 U.S.C. § 46111, which formalized the requirement that the FAA shall suspend, modify, or revoke a certificate if notified by the TSA that an individual posed a security risk.

As the respondents explain, the January 2003 regulations mandated a "streamlined process" by which an individual's pilot certificate would be automatically suspended or revoked by the FAA upon notification by the TSA that a pilot posed a security threat. The TSA and FAA deemed such regulations necessary "in order to minimize security threats and potential security vulnerabilities to the fullest extent possible." Given the respondents' legitimate concern over the threat of further terrorist acts involving aircraft in the aftermath of September 11, 2001, the agencies had "good cause" for not offering advance public participation.

It is self-evident that the regulations are related to the TSA's and FAA's goals of improving the safety of air travel. Nor is the court in a position to second-guess the respondents' judgment that imposing stricter procedures for coordinating security risks and restricting individuals who pose security threats from holding airman certificates was necessary to further that goal.

On the merits, the pilots' APA challenge fails. The court's review of agency rulemaking is highly deferential, limited to determining "whether the agency has considered the relevant factors and articulated a 'rational connection between the facts found and the choice made.'" Contrary to the pilots' position, the regulations are not arbitrary and capricious for bearing no rational connection to the problem identified by the FAA. It is self-evident that the regulations are related to the TSA's and FAA's goals of improving the safety of air travel. Nor is the court in a position to second-guess the respondents' judgment that imposing stricter procedures for coordinating security risks and restricting individuals who pose security threats from holding airman certificates was necessary to further that goal.

Moreover, the pilots' contention that the risk posed by the certificate holders alleged to be security threats was not remedied by providing fewer procedural protections to the certification holders and narrowing their right to NTSB review is to no avail because 49 U.S.C. § 46111 produces the same result. Section 46111 makes no provision for NTSB review even for citizens, and the Conference Report states that non-resident aliens "have the right to the appeal procedures that [TSA] has already provided for them." In addition, § 46111(a) requires the FAA to respond automatically to TSA threat assessments, providing that the FAA "shall issue an order amending, modifying, suspending, or revoking any part of a certificate issued under this title if the Administrator is notified by ... the Department of Homeland Security that the holder of the certificate poses, or is suspected of posing, a risk of air piracy or terrorism or a threat to airline or passenger safety."

Accordingly, if these pilots retain any right to NTSB review at all, it is no broader than the review for procedural regularity that they have received, and they would therefore garner no benefit from a remand. Indeed, an additional ground for rejecting the pilots' challenge to the promulgation of the FAA regulation without notice and comment exists precisely because § 46111 now provides an express statutory authorization for the automatic revocation that was previously predicated on the regulations alone; even were the court to invalidate the regulations for lack of notice and comment, the statute would compel the FAA to honor the TSA's notification and take immediate action against the pilots' certificates.

* * *

The scope of the court's review of the pilots' challenges to the TSA's actions is limited to determining whether the actions were "arbitrary, capricious, an abuse of discretion, or otherwise not in accordance with law." Under this standard, the court must consider whether those actions were "based on a consideration of the relevant factors and whether there has been a clear error of judgment." The court must affirm the agency's findings of fact if they are supported by "substantial evidence" and there is a "rational connection between the facts found and the choice made." "Substantial evidence" is simply such relevant evidence as a reasonable person might accept as proof of a conclusion.

Scope of Court's Review

In contending that the revocations of their airman certificates are unsupported by substantial evidence in the record, the pilots do not challenge the definition of "security threat" under the TSA regulations.

An individual poses a "security threat" if the individual "is suspected of posing, or is known to pose (1) A threat to transportation or national security; (2) A threat to air piracy or terrorism; (3) A threat to airline or passenger security; or (4) A threat to civil aviation security." 49 C.F.R. § 1540.117(c). Consistent with *Camp v. Pitts*, 411 U.S. 138 (1973), where the Supreme Court stated that when an agency official fails to adequately explain its decision, the agency should submit "either through affidavits or testimony, such additional explanation of the reasons for the agency decision as may prove necessary," the affidavit of TSA Deputy Administrator Stephen McHale provides an adequate basis for the TSA's determination that Jifry and Zarie each posed a "security threat" within the meaning of § 1540.117(c).

The unsealed affidavit recounts that the Deputy Administrator affirmed the TSA's determination on the basis of classified intelligence reports, combined with reports from the intelligence community that aircraft would continue to be used as weapons of terrorism, and consideration of "the ease with which an individual may obtain access to aircraft in the United States once he or she has a pilot license." The Deputy Administrator attested that "because it would be very difficult to avert harm once a terrorist had control of an aircraft, I concluded that it was important to err on the side of caution in determining whether [the two pilots] . . . pose a security threat . . ."

Viewing as a whole the record evidence before the TSA, including *ex parte* in camera review of the classified intelligence reports, we hold that there was substantial evidence to support the TSA's determination that the pilots were security risks. While we reject the pilots' contention that the court apply a *de novo* standard of review, we have carefully reviewed the classified intelligence reports on which TSA relied. The record is not lengthy and the basis for the TSA's conclusion is obvious.

* * *

The court reviews *de novo* the pilots' challenge to the constitutionality of the procedures under the January 2003 regulations. They contend that the TSA and FAA procedures violate the Fifth Amendment of the Constitution by depriving the pilots of their property interest in their airman certificates without due process of law.

Property Rights of Non-Resident Aliens

The Supreme Court has long held that non-resident aliens who have insufficient contacts with the United States are not entitled to Fifth Amendment protections. Exceptions may arise where aliens have come within the territory of the United States and established "substantial connections" with this country, or "accepted some societal obligations." In such situations, the Court has recognized that aliens may be accorded protections under the Constitution. This court has applied these principles in a series of cases concerning the designation of certain dissident organizations as "foreign terrorist organization[s]." We need not decide whether or not Jifry and Zarie are entitled to constitutional protections because, even assuming that they are, they have received all the process that they are due under our precedent. "The fundamental requirement of due process is the opportunity to be heard 'at a meaningful time and in a meaningful manner.' "

Generally, in determining whether administrative procedures are constitutionally adequate, courts weigh three factors:

First, the private interest that will be affected by the official action; second, the risk of an erroneous deprivation of such interest through the procedures used, and the probable value, if any, of additional or substitute procedural safeguards; and finally, the Government's interest, including the function involved and the fiscal and administrative burdens that the additional or substitute procedural requirement would entail.

The pilots' interests at stake here—their interest in possessing FAA airman certificates to fly foreign aircraft outside of the United States—pales in significance to the government's security interests in preventing pilots from using civil aircraft as instruments of terror. As the Supreme Court has noted, "It is 'obvious and unarguable' that no governmental interest is more compelling than the security of the Nation." *Haig v. Agee*, 453 U.S. 280 (1981).

The pilots' interests at stake here—their interest in possessing FAA airman certificates to fly foreign aircraft outside of the United States—pales in significance to the government's security interests in preventing pilots from using civil aircraft as instruments of terror.

Whatever the risk of erroneous deprivation, the pilots had the opportunity to file a written reply to the TSA's initial determination and were afforded independent de novo review of the entire administrative record by the Deputy Administrator of the TSA, and ex parte, in camera judicial review of the record.

Whatever the risk of erroneous deprivation, the pilots had the opportunity to file a written reply to the TSA's initial determination and were afforded independent *de novo* review of the entire administrative record by the Deputy Administrator of the TSA, and *ex parte*, in camera judicial review of the record. In light of the governmental interests at stake and the sensitive security information, substitute procedural safeguards may be impracticable, and in any event, are unnecessary under our precedent.

The TSA Assistant Administrator's Initial Notices informed the pilots that "[b]ased upon materials available to the [TSA], which I have personally reviewed, I have determined that you pose a security threat." The pilots were afforded an opportunity to respond to the designation and both filed written challenges to the TSA's Initial Notice, along with affidavits that they did not pose a threat to aviation or national security. These materials were considered by the TSA Deputy Administrator when he conducted a *de novo* review of the administrative record before issuing the Final Notice. While the pilots protest that without knowledge of the specific evidence on which TSA relied, they are unable to defend against the charge that they are security risks, the court has rejected the same argument in the terrorism listing cases. The due process protections afforded to them parallel those provided under similar circumstances are sufficient here.

EXERCISE 4-5. *JIFRY V. FED. AVIATION ADMIN.*—NATIONAL SECURITY AND THE ADMINISTRATIVE PROCEDURE ACT

1. When may the FAA reexamine the issuance of an airman certificate and what order(s), if any, might issue in connection as a result?

2. What are the functions that the Transportation Security Administration ("TSA") assumed from the FAA after September 11, 2001?

3. Does Congress distinguish between citizens and non-citizens for purposes of issuing an airman certificate? Explain.

4. Identify the three challenges made by the pilots with respect to the revocation of their FAA airman certificates and discuss how the court resolved each.

5. Describe the type of deference court's give to agency rulemaking.

Suggested Further Reading

Alan Armstrong, *Why Jurisdiction over Airmen Enforcement and Certificate Cases Should be Transferred from the National Transportation Safety Board to Federal District Court*, 83 J. Air L. & Com. 2018

Renee Martin-Nagle, *Diversity in Aviation: Between Takeoff and Landing*, 30 No. 3 Air and Space Law. 3 (2017)

Katherine Sharp Landdeck, *Experiment in the Cockpit: The Women Airforce Service Pilots of World War II in* THE AIRPLANE IN AMERICAN CULTURE (University of Michigan 2003)

Jill D. Snider, *"Great Shadow in the Sky"—The Airplane in the Tulsa Race Riot of 1921 and the Development of African American Visions of Aviation, 1921–1926 in* THE AIRPLANE IN AMERICAN CULTURE (University of Michigan 2003)

EUROPEAN UNION AVIATION SAFETY AGENCY, *Part-FCL—Flight Crew Licensing*, https://www.easa.europa.eu/acceptable-means-compliance-and-guidance-material-group/part-fcl-flight-crew-licensing

FEDERAL AVIATION ADMIN., *Pilot's Handbook of Aeronautical Knowledge*, https://www.faa.gov/regulations_policies/handbooks_manuals/aviation/phak/

CHAPTER 5

Federalism and Preemption

> The powers delegated by the proposed Constitution to the federal government are few and defined. Those which are to remain in the State governments are numerous and indefinite. The former will be exercised principally on external objects, as war, peace, negotiation, and foreign commerce; with which last the power of taxation will, for the most part, be connected. The powers reserved to the several States will extend to all the objects which, in the ordinary course of affairs, concern the lives, liberties, and properties of the people, and the internal order, improvement, and prosperity of the State.
>
> *The Federalist No. 45 (James Madison)*

A. OVERVIEW

In *Northwest Airlines, Inc. v. Minnesota*, 322 U.S. 292 (1944), a case of first impression about the constitutional limitations of state power to tax airplanes, Justice Robert H. Jackson wrote in a concurring opinion that "[p]lanes do not wander about in the sky like vagrant clouds." Rather, "[t]hey move only by federal permission, subject to federal inspection, in the hands of federally certified personnel and under an intricate system of federal commands." The "moment a ship taxies onto a runway it is caught up in an elaborate and detailed system of controls. It takes off only by instruction from the control tower, it travels on prescribed beams, it may be diverted from its intended landing, and it obeys signals and orders. Its privileges, rights, and protection, so far as transit is concerned, it owes to the Federal Government alone and not to any state government."

The point of Justice Jackson's concurrence was how pervasively aviation operations are regulated by the *federal* government. Indeed, at the heart of the *Northwest Airlines, Inc. v. Minnesota* is the concept of federalism—the constitutional

Federalism Defined

211

relationship between the 50 state governments and the national federal government. Understanding the dynamics of federalism and the breadth of the Supremacy Clause in the Constitution is critical in the context of aviation law in the United States. (The concept of federalism is important internationally also as different and multiple layers of governance are increasingly the norm in Europe and elsewhere within countries and among many countries.)

Each state has jurisdiction over local and intrastate aviation issues, including licensing airports, channeling federal funds to airports, imposing local taxes, legislating land use, and enacting laws allowing or disallowing guns in airport terminals. But, the national and international nature of air travel invites, if not requires, extensive federal oversight (particularly when safety is concerned, as discussed in Chapter 8, *supra*). In fact, as detailed below, whether there is any room for state law in an industry prevalently controlled by the federal government is an issue that is routinely litigated in courts around the nation under the heading of "preemption."

Express Preemption

The preemptive power of the federal government over state and local authorities—and to a lesser extent, state authorities over local officials—in matters involving the national airspace is a cornerstone of aviation law. (See Chapter 2 on Airspace.) In aviation and non-aviation contexts, courts have recognized two types of preemption, express and implied.

Express preemption exists when the language of a federal law communicates an *explicit* intent by Congress to preempt state law. Whether a federal law preempts a state law is a question of congressional intent. Thus, if Congress intended to govern an issue exclusively it need only say so as it has done in various areas. This preemptive power is based in the Supremacy Clause of the Constitution: "[t]he Constitution and the Laws of the United States which shall be made in Pursuance thereof . . . shall be the supreme Law of the Land." U.S. Const., art. VI, cl. 2. As interpreted by Chief Justice Marshall, "in every case, the act of Congress, or the treaty, is supreme; and the law of the state, though enacted in the exercise of powers not controverted, must yield to it." *Gibbons v. Ogden*, 22 U.S. (9 Wheat.) 1 (1824). Part B of this chapter features cases discussing express preemption (*Northwest Airlines, Inc. v. Minnesota* and *Bailey v. Rocky Mountain Holdings, LLC*), along with a case examining "complete" preemption (*Casey v. Goulian*).

Implied Preemption: Conflict and Field

Implied preemption is the other type of preemption and it consists of two subcomponents, "conflict preemption" and "field preemption." The former is said to exist either when compliance with both the federal and state laws is a "physical impossibility," or when the state law stands as an "obstacle" to the accomplishment and execution of the full purposes and objectives of Congress. The latter exists when a court determines that a federal regulatory scheme is so pervasive that Congress must have intended to leave no room for a state to supplement it. Courts generally understand field preemption to mean that federal law "thoroughly occupies" the "legislative field" in question, *e.g.*, the field of aviation safety. Field preemption analysis comes up frequently before courts, particularly in the arena of aviation safety. This type of preemption—and how state and federal laws coexist (or not)—is at the center of *Rowe v. New Hampshire Motor Transport, Ass'n* and *ABC Charters, Inc. v. Bronson*, which are discussed in Part C, *infra*. *U.S. Airways, Inc. v. O'Donnell, infra*, also is insightful about how courts decide between apparently competing state and federal laws. Moreover, the cases in Part C, *infra*, are some of the leading cases in which courts engage in a preemption analysis as applied to aviation safety and products liability.

A theme that runs throughout the cases in this chapter is that preemption jurisprudence is broadly guided by a well-established and uniformly accepted cornerstones:

Origin of Preemption

First, "the purpose of Congress is the ultimate touchstone in every pre-emption case," and "[s]econd, [i]n all pre-emption cases, and particularly those in which Congress has 'legislated in a field which the States have traditionally occupied' . . . we start with the assumption that the historic police powers of the States were not to be superseded by the Federal Act unless that was the clear and manifest purpose of Congress." *See Wyeth v. Levine*, 555 U.S. 555 (2009). In other words, there exists a "presumption against preemption" in litigation arising under the Airline Deregulation Act (discussed also in detail in Chapter 6, *supra*). *E.g.*, *Morales v. Trans World Airlines, Inc.*, 504 U.S. 374, 421 (1992) (Stevens, J. dissenting: "[a]lthough . . . the plain language of [the Airline Deregulation Act of 1978] pre-empts any state law that relates directly to rates, routes, or services, the presumption against pre-emption of traditional state regulation counsels that we not interpret [the law] to pre-empt every traditional state regulation that might have some indirect connection with, or relationship to, airline rates, routes or services unless there some indication that Congress intended that result.").

As you study the materials in this chapter, recognize how often the presumption against preemption is overcome in favor of carriers or against passengers, or in favor of passengers and against carriers and query whether this is consistent with the principles of federalism as articulated by the nation's founders. Is this fair? What can courts do about it?

B. EXPRESS PREEMPTION AND THE SUPREMACY CLAUSE

NORTHWEST AIRLINES, INC. V. MINNESOTA

322 U.S. 292 (1944)

MR. JUSTICE FRANKFURTER announced the conclusion and judgment of the Court.

The question before us is whether the Commerce Clause or the Due Process Clause of the Fourteenth Amendment bars the State of Minnesota from enforcing the personal property tax it has laid on the entire fleet of airplanes owned by the petitioner and operated by it in interstate transportation.

Northwest Airlines is a Minnesota corporation and its principal place of business is St. Paul. It is a commercial airline carrying persons, property and mail on regular fixed routes, with due allowance for weather, predominantly within the territory comprising Illinois, Minnesota, North Dakota, Montana, Oregon, Wisconsin and Washington. For all the planes St. Paul is the home port registered with the Civil Aeronautics Authority, under whose certificate of convenience and necessity Northwest operates. At six of its scheduled cities, Northwest operates maintenance bases, but the work of rebuilding and overhauling the planes is done in St. Paul. Details as to stopovers, other runs, the location of flying crew bases and of the usual facilities for aircraft, have no bearing on our problem.

The tax in controversy is for the year 1939. All of Northwest's planes were in Minnesota from time to time during that year. All were, however, continuously engaged in flying from State to State, except when laid up for repairs and overhauling for unidentified periods. On May 1, 1939, the time fixed by Minnesota for assessing personal property subject to its tax (Minn. Stat. 1941, § 273.01), Northwest's scheduled route mileage in Minnesota was 14% of its total scheduled route mileage, and the scheduled plane mileage was 16% of that scheduled. It based its personal property tax return for 1939 on the number of planes in Minnesota on May 1, 1939. Thereupon the appropriate taxing authority of Minnesota assessed a tax against Northwest on the basis of the entire fleet coming into Minnesota. For that additional assessment this suit was brought. The Supreme Court of Minnesota, with three judges dissenting, affirmed the judgment of a lower court in favor of the State. A new phase of an old problem led us to bring the case here.

Minnesota Tax on In-State Property

The tax here assessed by Minnesota is a tax assessed upon "all personal property of persons residing therein, including the property of corporations." Minn. Stat. 1941, § 272.01. It is not a charge laid for engaging in interstate commerce or upon airlines specifically; it is not aimed by indirection against interstate commerce or measured by such commerce. Nor is the tax assessed against planes which were "continuously without the state during the whole tax year," *New York Central & H.R.R. Co. v. Miller*, 202 U.S. 584, 594 (1906), and had thereby acquired "a permanent location elsewhere," *Southern Pacific Co. v. Kentucky*, 222 U.S. 63, 68 (1911).

Minnesota is here taxing a corporation for all its property within the State during the tax year no part of which receives permanent protection from any other State. The benefits given to Northwest by Minnesota and for which Minnesota taxes—its corporate facilities and the governmental resources which Northwest enjoys in the conduct of its business in Minnesota—are concretely symbolized by the fact that Northwest's principal place of business is in St. Paul and that St. Paul is the "home port" of all its planes. The relation between Northwest and Minnesota—a relation existing between no other State and Northwest—and the benefits which this relation affords are the constitutional foundation for the taxing power which Minnesota has asserted. *See State Tax Com. v. Aldrich*, 316 U.S. 174 (1942).

Justification for State Tax Over State Company

No other State can claim to tax as the State of the legal domicile as well as the home State of the fleet, as a business fact. No other State is the State which gave Northwest the power to be as well as the power to function as Northwest functions in Minnesota; no other State could impose a tax that derives from the significant legal relation of creator and creature and the practical consequences of that relation in this case. On the basis of rights which Minnesota alone originated and Minnesota continues to safeguard, she alone can tax the personalty which is permanently attributable to Minnesota and to no other State. It is too late to suggest that this taxing power of a State is less because the tax may be reflected in the cost of transportation.

Such being the case, it is clearly ruled by *New York Central & H.R.R. Co. v. Miller, supra*. Here, as in that case, a corporation is taxed for all its property within the State during the tax year none of which was "continuously without the state during the whole tax year." * * * This constitutional basis for what Minnesota did, reflects practicalities in the relations between the States and air transportation. "It has been customary to tax operating airplanes at their overhaul base." Cyril C. Thompson, *State and Local Taxation Affecting Air Transportation* 4 J. AIR L. 479, 483 (1933).

Who Owns the Sky in the Jet Age?

The doctrine of tax apportionment has been painfully evolved in working out the financial relations between the States and interstate transportation and communication conducted on land and thereby forming a part of the organic life of these States. Although a part of the taxing systems of this country, the rule of apportionment is beset with friction, waste and difficulties, but at all events it grew out of, and has established itself in regard to land commerce. To what extent it should be carried over to the totally new problems presented by the very different modes of transportation and communication that the airplane and the radio have already introduced, let alone the still more subtle and complicated technological facilities that are on the horizon, raises questions that we ought not to anticipate; certainly we ought not to embarrass the future by judicial answers which at best can deal only in a truncated way with problems sufficiently difficult even for legislative statesmanship.

Each new means of interstate transportation and communication has engendered controversy regarding the taxing powers of the States inter se and as between the States and the Federal Government. Such controversies and some conflict and confusion are inevitable under a federal system.

Each new means of interstate transportation and communication has engendered controversy regarding the taxing powers of the States inter se and as between the States and the Federal Government. Such controversies and some conflict and confusion are inevitable under a federal system. They have long been the source of difficulty and dissatisfaction for us, and have equally plagued the British federal systems. In response to arguments addressed also to us about the dangers of harassing state taxation affecting national transportation, the concurring judge below adverts to the power of Congress to incorporate airlines and to control their taxation. But insofar as these are matters that go beyond the constitutional issues which dispose of this case, they are not our concern. Affirmed.

MR. JUSTICE JACKSON, *concurring.*

This case considers for the first-time constitutional limitations upon state power to tax airplanes. Several principles of limitation have been judicially evolved in reference to ships and to railroad rolling stock. The question is which, if any of these should be transferred to air transport.

We are at a stage in development of air commerce roughly comparable to that of steamship navigation in 1824 when *Gibbons v. Ogden*, 9 Wheat. 1, came before this Court. Any authorization of local burdens on our national air commerce will lead to their multiplication in this country. Moreover, such an example is not likely to be neglected by other revenue-needy nations as international air transport expands.

> *Aviation has added a new dimension to travel and to our ideas. The ancient idea that landlordism and sovereignty extend from the center of the world to the periphery of the universe has been modified. Today the landowner no more possesses a vertical control of all the air above him than a shore owner possesses horizontal control of all the sea before him. The air is too precious as an open highway to permit it to be "owned" to the exclusion or embarrassment of air navigation by surface landlords who could put it to little real use.*

Aviation has added a new dimension to travel and to our ideas. The ancient idea that landlordism and sovereignty extend from the center of the world to the periphery of the universe has been modified. Today the landowner no more possesses a vertical control of all the air above him than a shore owner possesses horizontal control of all the sea before him. The air is too precious as an open highway to permit it to be "owned" to the exclusion or embarrassment of air navigation by surface landlords who could put it to little real use.

Students of our legal evolution know how this Court interpreted the Commerce Clause of the Constitution to lift navigable waters of the United States out of local controls and into the domain of federal control. Air as an element in which to navigate is even more inevitably federalized by the commerce clause than is navigable water. Local exactions and barriers to free transit in the air would neutralize its indifference to space and its conquest of time.

Congress has recognized the national responsibility for regulating air commerce. Federal control is intensive and exclusive. Planes do not wander about in the sky like vagrant clouds. They move only by federal permission, subject to federal inspection, in the hands of federally certified personnel and under an intricate system of federal commands. The moment a ship taxies onto a runway it is caught up in an elaborate and detailed system of controls. It takes off only by instruction from the control tower, it travels on prescribed beams, it may be diverted from its intended landing, and it obeys signals and orders. Its privileges, rights, and protection, so far as transit is concerned, it owes to the Federal Government alone and not to any state government.

Exclusive National Regulation

Congress has not extended its protection and control to the field of taxation, although I take it no one denies that constitutionally it may do so. It may exact a single uniform federal tax on the property or the business to the exclusion of taxation by the states. It may subject the vehicles or other incidents to any type of state and local taxation, or it may declare them tax-free altogether. Our function is to determine what rule governs in the absence of such legislative enactment.

> *Federal control is intensive and exclusive. Planes do not wander about in the sky like vagrant clouds. They move only by federal permission, subject to federal inspection, in the hands of federally certified personnel and under an intricate system of federal commands. The moment a ship taxies onto a runway it is caught up in an elaborate and detailed system of controls. It takes off only by instruction from the control tower, it travels on prescribed beams, it may be diverted from its intended landing, and it obeys signals and orders. Its privileges, rights, and protection, so far as transit is concerned, it owes to the Federal Government alone and not to any state government.*

Certainly today flight over a state either casually or on regular routes and schedules confers no jurisdiction to tax. Earlier ideas of a state's sovereignty over the air above it might argue for such a right to tax, but it is one of those cases where legal philosophy has to take account of the fact that the world does move.

Novel Issues of Jurisdiction

Does the act of landing within a state, even regularly and on schedule, confer jurisdiction to tax? Undoubtedly a plane, like any other article of personal property, could land or remain within a state in such a way as to become a part of the property within the state.

But when a plane lands to receive and discharge passengers, to undergo servicing or repairs, or to await a convenient departing schedule, it does not in my opinion lose its character as a plane in transit. Long ago this Court held that the landing of a ship within the ports of a state for similar purposes did not confer jurisdiction to tax. I cannot consider that to alight out of the skies onto a landing field and take off again into the air confers any greater taxing jurisdiction on a state than for a ship for the same purposes to come alongside a wharf on the water and get under way again.

What, then, remains as a basis for Minnesota's claim to tax this entire fleet of planes at their full value as property of the State of Minnesota? They have been within the state only transiently and in the same manner in which they have been in many states: to serve the public and to be serviced. The planes have received no "protection" or "benefit" from Minnesota that they have not received from many others. It might be difficult, in view of the complete control of this type of activity by the Federal Government, to find what benefits or protection any state extends. But no distinction whatever can be pointed out between those extended by Minnesota and those extended by any state where there is a terminal or a stopping place.

But it is said that Minnesota incorporated the company. Of course it is her right to tax the company she has created and the franchise she has granted. I suppose there are many ways that she might constitutionally measure the value of this privilege. If she chartered a corporation on condition that all property it might acquire, tangible or intangible, should be taxable under her laws, I do not think a company which accepted such a charter could appeal to the Constitution to give back what it voluntarily contracted away. But no such stipulation has been made in the charter in this case.

The tax imposed here is a general *ad valorem* property tax on the full value of every plane of the fleet operated by this company. Domicile of an owner is a usual test of power to tax intangibles, but has not generally been a conclusive test of taxability of tangible property situated elsewhere. If we should suppose that this corporation had a Delaware charter instead of a Minnesota one, and had nothing in Delaware except its agent, but operated otherwise in Minnesota exactly as it has done, would we say that the entire right to tax the fleet moved to Delaware because it was the corporation's state of domicile? I do not think that domicile, in the facts of this case, is decisive of Minnesota's claim to tax the tangible property of the company wherever situate.

Domicile as Basis for Tax?

It is strongly and plausibly advocated that the theory of apportionment of the total value among the several states of operation, heretofore applied to state taxation of railroad rolling stock, be transferred to air transportation. This would mean that each state of operation (no one ventures to say whether flight alone or both flight and landing would be required) could tax a proportion of the total value.

The apportionment theory is a mongrel one, a cross between desire not to interfere with state taxation and desire at the same time not utterly to crush out interstate commerce. It is a practical, but rather illogical, device to prevent duplication of tax burdens on vehicles in transit. It is established in our decisions and has been found more or less workable with more or less arbitrary formulate of apportionment. Nothing either in theory or in practice commends it for transfer to air commerce. A state has a different relation to rolling stock of railroads than it has to airplanes. Rolling stock is useless without surface rights and continuous structures on every inch of land over which it operates. Surface rights the railroad has acquired from the state or under its law. There is a physical basis within the state for the taxation of rolling stock which is lacking in the case of airplanes.

It seems more than likely that no solution of the competition among states to tax this transportation agency can be devised by the judicial process without legislative help. The best analogy that I find in existing decisions is the "home port" theory applied to ships. There is difficulty in the application of this doctrine to air commerce, I grant. There is no statutory machinery for fixing the home port. If federal registration established statehood as it establishes nationality, the home port doctrine would be easy to apply.

However, on the record before us it seems unquestioned that Minnesota is in an operational as well as in a domiciliary sense the home port of this fleet. On that doctrine Minnesota can tax the fleet, but its right to do so is exclusive, for no other state can acquire jurisdiction to tax merely because it provides a port of call. I therefore concur in the conclusion reached by the opinion of Mr. Justice Frankfurter. I do not accept the opinion because it falls short of commitment that Minnesota's right is exclusive of any similar right elsewhere. It is, I know, difficult to judge and dangerous to foreclose claims of other states that are not before us. That is the weakness of the judicial process in these tax questions where the total problem that faces an industry reaches us only in installments. If the reasoning should hereafter be extended to support full taxation everywhere, it would offend the commerce clause, as I see it, even more seriously than apportioned taxation everywhere.

The evils of local taxation of goods or vehicles in transit are not measured by the exaction of one locality alone, but by the aggregation of them. I certainly do not favor exemption of interstate commerce from its "just share of taxation." But history shows that fair judgment as to what exactions are just to the passerby cannot be left to local opinion. When local authority is taxing its own, the taxed ones may be assumed to be able to protect themselves at the polls. No such sanction enforces fair dealing to the transient. In all ages and climes those who are settled in strategic localities have made the moving world pay dearly. This the commerce clause was designed to end in the United States.

The rule I suggest seems most consonant with the purposes of the Commerce Clause among those found in our precedents. But the whole problem we deal with is unprecedented. I do not think we can derive from decisional law a satisfactory adjustment of the conflicting needs of the nation for free air commerce and the natural desire of localities to have revenue from the business that goes on about them.

I concur in the affirmance of the judgment below, but only because the record seems to me to establish Minnesota as a "home port" within the meaning of the old and somewhat neglected but to me wise authorities cited.

MR. CHIEF JUSTICE STONE, *dissenting.*

In my opinion the Minnesota levy imposed an unconstitutional tax on petitioner's vehicles of interstate transportation in violation of the Commerce Clause, and for that reason the judgment below should be reversed.

Commerce Clause Violation?

The case thus sharply presents in a new form the old question whether the Commerce Clause affords any protection against multiple state taxation of the physical facilities used in interstate transportation which, because they move from state to state, are exposed to full taxation in each, save only as the due process and commerce clauses may prevent. Although the question is new in form it is old in substance and this Court has considered it so often in other but similar relationships that the answer here seems plain. * * *

Minnesota cannot justify its imposition of an undue proportion of the total tax burden which can be imposed on an interstate carrier by saying that other states have taken or may take less than their share of the tax. It is enough that the tax exposes petitioner to "the risk of a multiple burden to which local commerce is not exposed." To hold otherwise would be to measure Minnesota's power to tax, not by constitutional standards, but by the action of other states over which neither Minnesota nor petitioner has any control and to leave petitioner's tax to be measured from year to year, not according to any legal standard, but by the unpredictable uncontrolled action of other states.

The judgment should be reversed and the case remanded for further proceedings in the course of which the state court would be free, if so advised, to inquire to what extent, if at all, the tax may, in harmony with state law, be apportioned in conformity to principles heretofore announced by this Court, and to that extent sustained.

EXERCISE 5-1. *NORTHWEST AIRLINES, INC. V. MINNESOTA—* STATE V. NATIONAL TAXING AUTHORITY

1. What is Minnesota seeking to tax?

2. What factors make Minnesota a "unique taxing authority" relative to the taxing power of every other state in which Northwest Airlines operates?

3. Some of Northwest Airlines, Inc.'s airplanes are in Minnesota for only a portion of the tax year. Are these airplanes thus exempted from Minnesota state tax? Or,

is tax "apportioned" based on the amount of time an airplane is physically located in Minnesota?

4.   Which branch of the federal government is best positioned to meet the national problems arising from state taxation upon interstate commerce, according to Justice Black's dissent? Why might that be important as the law adapts to emerging transportation modalities?

5.   Read in the context of Chapter 1, *supra*, does the tax in *Northwest Airlines, Inc. v. Minnesota* impede impermissibly on the constitutional right to travel? Why or why not.

CASEY V. GOULIAN

273 F. Supp. 2d 136 (D. Mass. 2003)

SARIS, DISTRICT JUDGE.

Plaintiffs bring state law nuisance claims, alleging that defendants are involved in noisy and dangerous stunt-airplane flights over their homes. Defendants removed this suit from state court on the ground that plaintiffs' claims fall within this Court's federal question jurisdiction. The Court holds it lacks jurisdiction over this suit, and allows plaintiffs' motion for remand.

Basis for Removal

A state court suit that includes at least one claim "arising under the Constitution, laws, or treaties of the United States" can be removed to federal court. *See* 28 U.S.C. § 1441 (allowing for removal of suits that fall within the federal district courts' original jurisdiction over federal question cases); 28 U.S.C. § 1331 (federal question statute). "[T]he question whether a claim 'arises under' federal law must be determined by reference to the 'well-pleaded complaint.' A defense that raises a federal question is inadequate to confer federal jurisdiction." *Merrell Dow Pharm. Inc. v. Thompson*, 478 U.S. 804, 808 (1986); *see also Rivet v. Regions Bank of La.*, 522 U.S. 470, 475 (1998) ("[A] case may not be removed to federal court on the basis of a federal defense . . . even if the defense is anticipated in the plaintiff's complaint, and even if both parties admit that the defense is the only question truly at issue in the case.").

Defendants argue that plaintiffs' state law claims fall within the Court's federal question jurisdiction, for two reasons. First, defendants contend that plaintiffs' state law claims necessarily turn on the construction of federal law. *See, e.g., City of Chicago v. Int'l Coll. of Surgeons*, 522 U.S. 156, 164 (1997) (stating that a federal question can arise through a state law claim "requir[ing] resolution of a substantial question of federal law"). Defendants maintain that plaintiffs' claims turn on federal aviation standards, in particular those set out in the Federal Aviation Act ("FAA"), 49 U.S.C. §§ 40101, and its enabling regulations applicable to aircraft flight and noise.

But the complaint itself does not contain any reference to the FAA or any other federal law. Even if FAA statutory or regulatory standards did provide a required element of plaintiffs' state law claims, defendants have failed to demonstrate that the FAA provides a private cause of action to enforce these standards. Under the weight of the caselaw, federal jurisdiction is not available absent such a showing. *See Merrell Dow*, 478 U.S. at 817 ("We conclude that a complaint alleging a violation of a federal statute as an element of a state cause of action, when Congress has determined that there should be no private, federal cause of action for the violation, does not state a claim 'arising under the Constitution, laws, or treaties of the United States.' ") (quoting 28 U.S.C. § 1331); *PCS 2000 LP v. Romulus Telecomms., Inc.*, 148 F.3d 32, 35 (1st Cir. 1998) ("Unless a federal statute bestows a private right of action, courts ought to presume that Congress did not intend the statute to confer federal jurisdiction."); *State of Montana v. Abbot Labs.*, 2003 WL 21356449 at *5 (D. Mass. 2003) (collecting cases interpreting *Merrell Dow*); *see also Vorhees v. Naper Aero Club, Inc.*, 272 F.3d 398, 404 (7th Cir. 2001) (noting that the FAA "has no civil enforcement provision or any provision allowing a private resident to sue for the property torts of an airline pilot or airport operator"). *But see Tipp City v. Dayton*, 204 F.R.D. 388, 395–96 (S.D. Ohio 2001) (finding, without the benefit of briefing, federal question jurisdiction where plaintiffs' state law nuisance claim based on airplane noise alleged that defendants had failed to comply with Federal Aviation Administration "Tower Orders").

Absence of Private Cause of Action

Second, defendants contend that federal aviation law "completely preempts" plaintiffs' claims. *See, e.g., Rivet*, 522 U.S. at 476 ("Although federal preemption is normally a defense, '[o]nce an area of state law has been completely pre-empted, any claim purportedly based on that pre-empted state law claim is considered, from its inception, a federal claim, and therefore arises under federal law.' ") (quoting *Caterpillar Inc. v. Williams*, 482 U.S. 386, 393 (1987)). Defendants argue that plaintiffs' claims seek to use state law to regulate the airspace over their homes, in contravention of the FAA, which expressly provides that "[t]he United States Government has exclusive sovereignty of airspace of the United States." 49 U.S.C. § 40103(a); *see also Burbank v. Lockheed Air Terminal Inc.*, 411 U.S. 624, 625–40 (1973) (finding federal preemption of a city ordinance imposing a curfew on jet-aircraft flights, given the "pervasive nature of the scheme of federal regulation of aircraft noise"; not addressing complete preemption).

Complete Preemption

But the Court is persuaded by the Seventh Circuit's recent rejection of a similar complete preemption argument in *Vorhees v. Naper Aero Club, Inc.* In *Vorhees*, the plaintiff owned property adjacent to an airport. Flights taking off and landing from the airport flew at low altitudes over plaintiff's property, preventing him from building high-rise buildings there. The plaintiff brought a state law trespass claim in state court, seeking an injunction preventing use of the runway adjacent to his property. The defendants removed the case on the ground of complete preemption:

> The defendants contended that because [plaintiff] Vorhees sought to prohibit the use of the runway at the Airport, and because regulation and operation of airports are matters exclusively within the purview of the federal government, federal law preempted state law with respect to all aspects of the complaint . . .

> [Defendants] point to the fact that 49 U.S.C. § 40103(a) provides that "[t]he United States Government has exclusive sovereignty of airspace of the United States." The injunction the plaintiff seeks would, at first blush, probably require the defendants to change their routes and flight patterns . . . The change in route and flight patterns would ultimately result in the regulation of airspace, in contravention of the rule that this regulation is solely within the sovereignty of the federal government. Because the requested state law recovery would interfere with federal authority, defendants argue, the claim must be completely preempted.

Complete Preemption vs. Preemption on the Merits

In addressing the defendants' arguments, the Seventh Circuit carefully distinguished "complete" preemption—a jurisdictional concept—from preemption on the merits:

> While [defendants'] arguments set forth a strong case for federal preemption, they do not answer the more subtle question of whether we are dealing with so-called "complete preemption" or its more ordinary cousin, "conflict preemption." Only "complete" preemption affects federal subject matter jurisdiction. "Conflict" preemption relates to the merits of a claim. It comes into play any time a state law allegedly conflicts with federal law. If such a conflict exists, then the state law is preempted and must necessarily give way to federal law. For present purposes, however, the key point is this: ordinary or conflict preemption is merely a defense to the merits of a claim. As such, according to the well-pleaded complaint rule, it does not provide a basis for federal question jurisdiction.

We agree with the defendants that the Illinois law claims Vorhees is trying to assert may very well be preempted by the Federal Aviation Act (although we make no ruling on that question at this time). But the fact that a federal statute creates a defense to a state law claim does not necessarily mean that "Congress has, by statute, taken the subject away from state tribunals and given it to federal courts." The question is whether, in enacting the Federal Aviation Act, Congress clearly intended completely to replace state law with federal law and create a federal forum, or, more likely, if it only intended to provide a federal defense to the application of state law.

The key point is this: ordinary or conflict preemption is merely a defense to the merits of a claim. As such, according to the well-pleaded complaint rule, it does not provide a basis for federal question jurisdiction.

The Seventh Circuit noted that "[t]here are only two areas in which the Supreme Court has found that Congress intended completely to replace state law with federal law for purposes of federal jurisdiction: the first is in the field of federal labor law and the second is in the area of federal pension law."

The Circuit Court refused to give a similarly expansive interpretation to the FAA, stating that "[t]here is no . . . broad language in the Federal Aviation Act specifically prohibiting state and local governments from regulating airflight in any way whatsoever" and "we have held that some state law claims relating to airflight may still have merit, notwithstanding the broad scope of the Federal Aviation Act." *See also Tipp City*, 204 F.R.D. at 393 (where plaintiffs brought a state law nuisance claim based on noise pollution caused by a neighboring airport, finding "no basis for concluding that Plaintiffs' nuisance claim is completely preempted by federal law"); *cf. also Kingsley v. Lania*, 221 F. Supp. 2d 93, 96 (D. Mass. 2002) (in dispute between passenger and airline over passenger's treatment at a security checkpoint, holding that "there is no indication that Congress intended to make a federal forum available for every case involving disputes with the airlines. There is no complete preemption of the field so as to allow removal on federal question grounds.").

Role of Local and State Government in Aviation?

The Court agrees with the Seventh Circuit that Congress, through the FAA, did not take the subject of airplane interference with property rights and give it exclusively to the federal courts. Perhaps defendants have a valid preemption defense on the merits, *see Burbank*, 411 U.S. at 625–40, perhaps not, *see Bieneman v. City of Chicago*, 864 F.2d 463, 472–73 (7th Cir. 1988) (stating that "Illinois has some role notwithstanding *Burbank* in governing the amount of noise and pollution that escapes from O'Hare [Airport]" and that state damages remedies are not preempted where they "enforce federal [aviation] requirements" or "regulate aspects of airport operation over which the state has discretionary authority"). In any event, defendants will have to address their arguments to the state court. Thus, the court allows plaintiffs' Motion to Vacate Removal and Remand to State Court and orders this suit remanded to Massachusetts Superior Court in Middlesex County.

EXERCISE 5-2. *CASEY V. GOULIAN*—"COMPLETE" PREEMPTION

1. The *Casey v. Goulian* case introduces important terms and concepts related to the jurisdiction of federal courts to adjudicate disputes. Look up the following terms in a legal dictionary to assist your reading of the case: (a) subject matter jurisdiction; (b) federal question jurisdiction, 28 U.S.C. § 1331; (c) removal, 28 U.S.C. § 1441; (d) remand; and (e) motion to vacate.

2. The defendants argued that a federal court should hear this case, not a federal court. What reasons do they assert in support of this position?

3. What is a private cause of action?

4. Describe the scope of authority the federal government has over airspace under 49 U.S.C. § 40103(a). Are state and local governments prohibited from regulating airflight in any way whatsoever?

5. What is the difference between "complete preemption" and "preemption on the merits"? Can "conflict preemption," when presented as a defense, serve as a basis for federal question jurisdiction?

BAILEY V. ROCKY MOUNTAIN HOLDINGS, LLC

136 F.Supp.3d 1376 (S.D. Fla. 2015)

WILLIAM J. ZLOCH, UNITED STATES DISTRICT JUDGE.

Part 135 Operator, Air Ambulance

Defendant Air Methods Corporation ("AMC") is authorized by the Federal Aviation Act ("FAA"), 49 U.S.C. §§ 40101 *et seq.*, to operate as a Part 135 air carrier providing on-demand and air ambulance services. AMC is registered with the Department of Transportation ("DOT") to operate as a Part 298 air taxi operator providing on-demand air ambulance services. Pursuant to their Part 135 certificate and their Part 298 registration, AMC doing business in the state of Florida as Rocky Mountain Holdings, LLC, ("RMH") is authorized to operate interstate flights as a common carrier for compensation. The DOT has expressly recognized AMC d/b/a RMH as an "air carrier" that is authorized to provide interstate transportation. As a Part 135 air carrier, AMC d/b/a RMH is pervasively regulated on safety and economic matters by the FAA.

On March 17, 2013, Plaintiff's son, Lemar Bailey, sustained fatal injuries in a motor vehicle accident in Martin County, Florida. He was ejected from the vehicle and transported by Defendants by helicopter from the accident scene to St. Mary's Medical Center in West Palm Beach, Florida. Plaintiff was thereafter invoiced for the air ambulance service provided by Defendants in an amount totaling $27,975.90.

Defendants also submitted an invoice to State Farm Insurance, the insurer for the motor vehicle involved in the accident. State Farm, pursuant to Florida's Personal Injury Protection statute ("PIP"), paid 80% of what it considered to be the allowable amount, or $6,911.54, which is 200% of the Medicare Part B fee. Thereafter, Defendants submitted a claim for payment to Mr. Lemar Bailey's health insurer, Aetna, which was secondary to the PIP coverage. Aetna then paid Defendants the sum of $3,681.60. Defendants applied the amounts paid by both State Farm and Aetna to Plaintiff's outstanding balance. Plaintiff did not make any payments to Defendants, and the remaining balance of $17,382.76 for air ambulance services was ultimately written off as a bad debt.

Lenworth Bailey, as Personal Representative of the Estate of Lemar Bailey, seeks a declaratory judgment that Defendants' billing practices violate the Florida PIP Statute and that Defendants' actions violate Florida's Deceptive and Unfair Trade Practices Act. Additionally, Plaintiff seeks damages for Defendants' alleged violations of FDUPTA. Plaintiff further alleges violations of the Florida Consumer Collection and Practices Act, and unjust enrichment.

ANALYSIS

The Supremacy Clause of the United States Constitution invalidates state and local laws that interfere with or are contrary to the laws of Congress. "[W]here Congress has legislated concerning a subject, on which it is authorized to act, all State legislation which interferes with it, is absolutely void." *Gibbons v. Ogden*, 22 U.S. (9 Wheat) 1 (1824). Federal law can preempt state and local laws either expressly or impliedly.

Voiding of State Law

Congress manifested its intent "to rest sole responsibility for supervising the aviation industry with the federal government" when it enacted the FAA:

> [A]viation is unique among transportation industries in its relation to the federal government—it is the only one whose operations are conducted almost wholly within federal jurisdiction, and are subject to little or no regulation by States or local authorities. Thus, the federal government bears virtually complete responsibility for the promotion and supervision of this industry in the public interest.

S. Rep. No. 1811 (85th Cong., 2d Sess. 5) (1985). In 1978, Congress amended the FAA and enacted the ADA. "To ensure that the States would not undo federal deregulation with regulation of their own," the ADA included an express preemption clause, codified at 49 U.S.C. § 41713(b). This clause states, in pertinent part, that:

> a State, political subdivision of a State, or political authority of at least 2 States may not enact or enforce a law, regulation, or other provision having the force and effect of law *related to a price, route, or service* of an air carrier that may provide air transportation under this subpart.

Reverse Preemption

Thus, States are expressly prohibited from enacting or enforcing any law, regulation, or other provision which relates to an air carrier's price, route, or service. "The purpose of the ADA's preemption provision was to increase 'reliance on competitive market forces rather than pervasive federal regulation.'" *Koutsouradis v. Delta Air Lines, Inc.*, 427 F.3d 1339 (11th Cir. 2005). In *Rowe v. N.H. Motor Transport Ass'n*, 552 U.S. 364 (2008), the Supreme Court described the goal of Congress in the ADA's preemption provision "as helping ensure transportation rates, routes, and services that reflect 'maximum reliance on competitive market forces,' thereby stimulating 'efficiency, innovation, and low prices,' as well as 'variety' and 'quality.'"

Notwithstanding the ADA's express preemption provision, Plaintiff contends that Florida's PIP Statute "reverse preempts" federal law in this case, pursuant to the McCarran-Ferguson Act ("MFA"). The MFA is a federal statute directed at insulating state insurance regulation from implied preemption by federal domestic commerce legislation. The MFA initially declares that "*silence* on the part of the Congress shall not be construed to impose any barrier" to state regulation or taxation of the business of insurance. It further provides that "[n]o Act of Congress shall be construed to invalidate, impair, or supersede any law enacted by any State for the purpose of regulating the business of insurance, or which imposes a fee or tax upon such business, unless such Act specifically relates to the business of insurance." Accordingly, the McCarran-Ferguson Act authorizes "reverse preemption" of federal statutes by state laws enacted to regulate the business of insurance. However, the Court finds that Congress has not been silent here, and the MFA therefore does not apply to reverse-preempt the ADA.

In enacting the ADA and including in it an express preemption provision, Congress made plain its intent to altogether preempt state laws that regulate an air carrier's prices, routes, or services. The MFA was intended only to protect state insurance regulation from inadvertent intrusion by the federal government, and not to insulate the same from every federal law. *See Humana Inc. v. Forsyth*, 525 U.S. 299 (1999) ("We reject any suggestion that Congress intended to cede the field of insurance regulation to the states, saving only instances in which Congress expressly orders otherwise. If Congress had meant generally to preempt the field for the States, Congress could have said . . . '[n]o federal statute that does not say so explicitly shall be construed to apply to the business of insurance.' "); *Barnett Bank of Marion Cnty., N.A. v. Nelson*, 517 U.S. 25 (1996) ("Particularly the word 'silence,' indicates that the Act does not seek to insulate state insurance regulation from the reach of all federal law.").

Intent of Congress

Rather, it seeks to protect state regulation primarily against inadvertent federal intrusion—say, through enactment of a federal statute that describes an affected activity in broad, general terms, of which the insurance business happens to constitute one part."). Indeed "when the intended effect of a federal statute is to displace state regulations, [the court] must give effect to this intent, regardless of whether an insurance company is involved." *Lander v. Hartford Life & Annuity Ins. Co.*, 251 F.3d 101 (2d Cir. 2001).

As stated above, the Parties agree that Defendant AMC is an "air carrier" within the meaning of the statute. Further, the Court finds that each of Plaintiff's state and common law claims can only be fairly characterized as directly challenging Defendants' rates for its air ambulance services. These claims, if permitted to proceed, would naturally affect the provision of Defendants' services in addition to the prices of and payment for those services. Consequently, the above-styled cause is essentially a state enforcement action having a very strong connection with or reference to a price, route, or service of an air carrier.

And the Court finds that this state and common law challenge is expressly disallowed by the ADA's express preemption provision, which intentionally leaves the price of such services to the competitive market. *See Crane v. Native Am. Ambulance, Inc.*, No. CV 06–092 (D. Ariz. Feb. 23, 2007) (finding class action regarding air ambulance fees was preempted by the ADA). Accordingly, the above-styled cause is altogether preempted as a matter of law and cannot proceed.

EXERCISE 5-3. *BAILEY V. ROCKY MOUNTAIN HOLDINGS, LLC*—EXPRESS PREEMPTION AND INTRODUCTION TO FAA OF 1958

1. What is a "Part 135" carrier and how does the FAA certify such a carrier? *See* Fed. Aviation Admin., 14 CFR Part 135 Air Carrier and Operator Certification, https://www.faa.gov/about/initiatives/atos/135_certification/.

2. What is an "air taxi operator" under 14 C.F.R. Part 298? *See* Part 298—Exemptions for Air Taxi and Commuter Air Carrier Operations, https://www.gpo.gov/fdsys/pkg/CFR-2018-title14-vol4/xml/CFR-2018-title14-vol4-part298.xml.

3. According to the court, the issues in *Bailey v. Rocky Mountain Holdings, LLC* present an example of "express preemption" under the Supremacy Clause of the United States Constitution. What is "express preemption" and what purpose or policy goal does it serve?

4. The plaintiff in *Bailey v. Rocky Mountain Holdings, LLC* claimed that a state insurance law "reverse preempts" federal domestic commerce legislation. Explain.

5. What is the holding of *Bailey v. Rocky Mountain Holdings, LLC* and what is the status of the state law at issue as a result?

NOTES ON *BAILEY V. ROCKY MOUNTAIN HOLDINGS, LLC*—PREEMPTION, NATIONAL VS. STATE VS. LOCAL

Courts are routinely asked to resolve matters involving explicitly or impliedly conflicting laws enacted at different levels of government:

1. *Federal Law v. Local Ordinance.*

Amerijet Int'l v. Miami-Dade County, 627 Fed. Appx. 744 (11th Cir. 2015) is an example of a conflict between federal law and a local ordinance. The case centered on whether a section of Miami-Dade County's Living Wage Ordinance, as applied to air carriers, was preempted by the federal Airline Deregulation Act of 1978. (*See generally* Chapter 4, "Airmen," *infra.*)

The ordinance, passed in 1999, was one of the first of its kind, and required that "certain individuals or entities that conduct business with the County or that use the facilities of Miami International Airport" pay a "living wage" to workers providing "covered services," which was defined as:

Guiding aircraft in and out of Airport; aircraft loading and unloading positions, designated by the Aviation Department; placing in position and operating passenger, baggage and cargo loading and unloading devices, as required for the safe and efficient loading and unloading of passengers, baggage and cargo to and from aircraft; performing such loading and unloading; providing aircraft utility services, such as air start and cabin air; fueling; catering; towing aircraft; cleaning of aircraft; delivering cargo, baggage and mail to and from aircraft to and from locations at any Miami-Dade County Aviation Department facility; and providing such other ramp services approved in writing by the Aviation Department.

An all-cargo airline (*i.e.* an airline that only carries property and mail) argued that the ordinance was preempted as an inappropriate attempt by the county to regulate the preempted field of air carrier regulation.

In a *per curiam* opinion, the Eleventh Circuit disagreed, ruling that "the ordinance resembles a law of general application, as opposed to a law that is designed to regulate the airline industry." As such, the ordinance was "not targeted at, and does not single out, airlines or carriers." In addition, the court reasoned that the "services" at issue—the provision of cargo handling services for other airlines—"are not the type that implicate the [Airline Deregulation Act's] preemption provision." Given *U.S. Airways, Inc. v. O'Donnell* (10th Cir. 2010), *supra*, would this result hold uniformly in other appellate circuits around the nation?

2. ***State Law v. Local Law: Drones.***

Some states have cut off the ability of cities, municipalities, and local governments to make laws by enacting state statutes with preemptive effect over local rules. Broadly, the power of a state to preempt and subordinate local law—referred to as Dillon's Rule—derives from a narrow interpretation of a local government's authority, in which a local or municipal government (*i.e.*, a "substate") may engage in an activity only if it is specifically sanctioned by the state government. *See* 1 J. DILLON, COMMENTARIES ON THE LAW OF MUNICIPAL CORPORATIONS § 237 (5th ed. 1911). Application of this rule is playing out in the arena of unmanned aerial vehicles—"UAVs" or "drones." *See* Chapter 2.

3. ***Federal Law v. Federal Law?***

Ray v. Spirit Airlines, Inc., 767 F.3d 1220 (11th Cir. 2014) required a federal appellate court to construe two federal laws that arguably conflicted. Specifically, a class of airline passengers sued Spirit Airlines, Inc. ("Spirit") under the Racketeer Influenced and Corrupt Organizations Act ("RICO"), 18 U.S.C. §§ 1961–68, alleging that Spirit conducted an enterprise by means of racketeering activity, *i.e.*, two or more predicate acts of mail and wire fraud involving the concealment and misrepresentation of airfares and user fees. The passengers alleged that Spirit concealed the existence and purpose of the Passenger Usage Fee and used the mails and wire to execute the scheme or artifice to defraud:

> Spirit holds itself out as an "Ultra Low Cost Carrier" offering airfares at rates far lower than other providers. These cheap fares disguise the total cost of travel because Spirit forces consumers to pay unbundled charges traditionally included in the price of an airline ticket. Specifically, Spirit charges a Passenger Usage Fee to all consumers who buy tickets through its website or call center. When searching for flights on Spirit's website, a consumer sees only the base fares. Once he has selected a flight, a webpage directs him to "confirm" the flight on a page that displays both the base fare and an undifferentiated amount labeled "Taxes & Fees." For a breakdown of these charges, the consumer then must click on an additional link, "more information," which lists "Passenger Usage Fee" alongside government taxes and fees.

> Spirit argued that permitting Plaintiffs' RICO action would thwart Congress's intent to delegate entirely the regulation of airline ticket prices and price advertising to the Department of Transportation ("DOT"). Spirit also argued that Plaintiffs' RICO claims were precluded by the Airline Deregulation Act's preemption provision. Alternatively, Spirit urged that Plaintiffs had failed to adequately plead RICO mail and wire fraud related to the Passenger Usage Fee. The Eleventh Circuit Court of Appeals reversed:

> Because federal laws do not preempt other federal laws, subsequent legislation could preclude Plaintiffs' claims only if Congress had repealed the provisions of RICO, at least insofar as they authorized Plaintiffs' actions. Congress did not do so expressly through the Airline Deregulation Act of 1978 ("ADA"). And we find no "repeal by implication" because Congress has not exhibited the requisite clear and manifest intent. *E.g.*, *Posadas v. Nat'l City Bank of N.Y.*, 296 U.S. 497 (1936). The ADA explicitly preempted state laws but, notably, said nothing about any federal cause of action. Moreover, a saving clause found in the ADA did not disturb any other remedies provided by law. Quite simply, the two laws are not irreconcilably in conflict, nor was the ADA clearly intended as a substitute for RICO. Applying the strong presumption against implied repeals, we are constrained to conclude that RICO supplements, rather than subverts, federal regulation of air carriers.

> Our decision in no way addresses whether Plaintiffs adequately alleged the elements of their civil RICO claim. Thus, we have no occasion today to pass any judgment on whether fraud is pled with particularity, or whether

Plaintiffs adequately pled the elements of mail and wire fraud, or indeed whether Plaintiffs sufficiently pled a RICO injury. All we hold today is that the federal regulatory scheme governing the airline industry does not preclude a claim founded on the civil provisions of RICO.

For further discussion of the Airline Deregulation Act of 1978 see Chapter 6 *supra.*

4.   *International Law v. U.S. Law.*

For a complete discussion of the way in which international treaties adopted by the United States impact (*e.g.* preempt) other domestic laws see Chapter 13.

C. IMPLIED PREEMPTION: CONFLICT AND FIELD

ROWE V. NEW HAMPSHIRE MOTOR TRANSPORT ASS'N
552 U.S. 364 (2008)

JUSTICE BREYER delivered the opinion of the Court.

We here consider whether a federal statute that prohibits States from enacting any law "related to" a motor carrier "price, route, or service" pre-empts two provisions of a Maine tobacco law, which regulate the delivery of tobacco to customers within the State. We hold that the federal law pre-empts both provisions.

In 1978, Congress "determin[ed] that 'maximum reliance on competitive market forces' " would favor lower airline fares and better airline service, and it enacted the Airline Deregulation Act. *Morales v. Trans World Airlines, Inc.*, 504 U.S. 374 (1992). In order to "ensure that the States would not undo federal deregulation with regulation of their own," that Act "included a pre-emption provision" that said "no State . . . shall enact or enforce any law . . . relating to rates, routes, or services of any air carrier."

In 1980, Congress deregulated trucking. *See* Motor Carrier Act of 1980, 94 Stat. 793. And a little over a decade later, in 1994, Congress similarly sought to pre-empt state trucking regulation. *See* Federal Aviation Administration Authorization Act of 1994, 108 Stat. 1605–1606; *see also* ICC Termination Act of 1995, 109 Stat. 899. In doing so, it borrowed language from the Airline Deregulation Act of 1978 and wrote into its 1994 law language that says: "[A] State . . . may not enact or enforce a law . . . related to a price, route, or service of any motor carrier . . . with respect to the transportation of property." *See* 49 U.S.C.

§ 14501(c)(1); § 41713(b)(4)(A) (similar provision for combined motor-air carriers).

The State of Maine subsequently adopted An Act to Regulate the Delivery and Sales of Tobacco Products and to Prevent the Sale of Tobacco Products to Minors, two sections of which are relevant here.

Section One, Maine Law

The first section forbids anyone other than a Maine-licensed tobacco retailer to accept an order for delivery of tobacco. It then adds that, when a licensed retailer accepts an order and ships tobacco, the retailer must "utilize a delivery service" that provides a special kind of recipient-verification service. The delivery service must make certain that (1) the person who bought the tobacco is the person to whom the package is addressed; (2) the person to whom the package is addressed is of legal age to purchase tobacco; (3) the person to whom the package is addressed has himself or herself signed for the package; and (4) the person to whom the package is addressed, if under the age of 27, has produced a valid government-issued photo identification with proof of age. Violations are punishable by civil penalties (first offense up to $1,500; subsequent offenses up to $5,000).

Section Two, Maine Law

The second section forbids any person "knowingly" to "transport" a "tobacco product" to "a person" in Maine unless either the sender or the receiver has a Maine license. It then adds that a "person is deemed to know that a package contains a tobacco product" (1) if the package is marked as containing tobacco and displays the name and license number of a Maine-licensed tobacco retailer; or (2) if the person receives the package from someone whose name appears on a list of un-licensed tobacco retailers that Maine's Attorney General distributes to various package-delivery companies. Violations are again punishable by civil penalties (up to $1,500 per violation against violator and/or violator's employer).

Respondents, several transport carrier associations, brought this lawsuit in federal court, claiming that federal law pre-empts several sections of Maine's statute. The District Court held (among other things) that federal law pre-empts the portions of the two sections we have described, namely the "recipient-verification" provision and the "deemed to know" provision. On appeal, the Court of Appeals for the First Circuit agreed that federal law pre-empted the two provisions. We granted *certiorari* to review these determinations.

II.

Morales Precedent

In *Morales*, this Court interpreted the pre-emption provision in the Airline Deregulation Act of 1978. And we follow *Morales* in interpreting similar language in the 1994 Act before us here. We have said that "when judicial interpretations have settled the meaning of an existing statutory provision, repetition of the same language in a new statute indicates, as a general matter, the intent to incorporate its judicial interpretations as well." Here, the Congress that wrote the language before us copied the language of the air-carrier pre-emption provision of the Airline Deregulation Act of 1978. And it did so fully aware of this Court's interpretation of that language as set forth in *Morales*. *See* H.R. Conf. Rep., at 83, U.S. CODE CONG. & ADMIN. NEWS 1994, pp. 1676, 1755 (motor carriers will enjoy "the identical intrastate preemption of prices, routes and services as that originally contained in" the Airline Deregulation Act).

In *Morales*, the Court determined: (1) that "[s]tate enforcement actions having a connection with, or reference to" carrier " 'rates, routes, or services' are pre-empted," (2) that such pre-emption may occur even if a state law's effect on rates, routes or services "is only indirect," (3) that, in respect to pre-emption, it makes no difference whether a state law is "consistent" or "inconsistent" with federal regulation, and (4) that pre-emption occurs at least where state laws have a "significant impact" related to Congress' deregulatory and pre-emption-related objectives. The Court described Congress' overarching goal as helping assure transportation rates, routes, and services that reflect "maximum reliance on competitive market forces," thereby stimulating "efficiency, innovation, and low prices," as well as "variety" and "quality." *Morales* held that, given these principles, federal law pre-empts States from enforcing their consumer-fraud statutes against deceptive airline-fare advertisements. *See American Airlines, Inc. v. Wolens*, 513 U.S. 219 (1995) (federal law pre-empts application of a State's general consumer-protection statute to an airline's frequent flyer program).

Finally, *Morales* said that federal law might not pre-empt state laws that affect fares in only a "tenuous, remote, or peripheral . . . manner," such as state laws forbidding gambling. But the Court did not say where, or how, "it would be appropriate to draw the line," for the state law before it did not "present a borderline question."

In light of *Morales*, we find that federal law pre-empts the Maine laws at issue here. Section 1555–C(3)(C) of the Maine statute forbids licensed tobacco retailers to employ a "delivery service" unless that service follows particular delivery procedures. In doing so, it focuses on trucking and other motor carrier services, which make up a substantial portion of all "delivery services," thereby creating a direct "connection with" motor carrier services.

At the same time, the provision has a "significant" and adverse "impact" in respect to the federal Act's ability to achieve its pre-emption-related objectives. The Solicitor General and the carrier associations claim (and Maine does not deny) that the law will require carriers to offer a system of services that the market does not now provide (and which the carriers would prefer not to offer). And even were that not so, the law would freeze into place services that carriers might prefer to discontinue in the future. The Maine law thereby produces the very effect that the federal law sought to avoid, namely, a State's direct substitution of its own governmental commands for "competitive market forces" in determining (to a significant degree) the services that motor carriers will provide.

We concede that the regulation here is less "direct" than it might be, for it tells shippers what to choose rather than carriers what to do. Nonetheless, the effect of the regulation is that carriers will have to offer tobacco delivery services that differ significantly from those that, in the absence of the regulation, the market might dictate. And that being so, "treating sales restrictions and purchase restrictions differently for pre-emption purposes would make no sense." If federal law pre-empts state efforts to regulate, and consequently to affect, the advertising about carrier rates and services at issue in *Morales*, it must pre-empt Maine's efforts to regulate carrier delivery services themselves.

Section 1555–D's "deemed to know" provision applies yet more directly to motor carrier services. The provision creates a conclusive presumption of carrier knowledge that a shipment contains tobacco when it is marked as originating from a Maine-licensed tobacco retailer or is sent by anyone Maine has specifically identified as an unlicensed tobacco retailer. That presumption means that the Maine law imposes civil liability upon the carrier, not simply for its knowing transport of (unlicensed) tobacco, but for the carrier's failure sufficiently to examine every package. The provision thus requires the carrier to check each shipment for certain markings and to compare it against the Maine attorney general's list of proscribed shippers. And it thereby directly regulates a significant aspect of the motor carrier's package pickup and delivery service. In this way it creates the kind of state-mandated regulation that the federal Act pre-empts.

Maine replies that the regulation will impose no significant additional costs upon carriers. But even were that so (and the carriers deny it), Maine's reply is off the mark. As with the recipient-verification provision, the "deemed to know" provision would freeze in place and immunize from competition a service-related system that carriers do not (or in the future might not) wish to provide.

> *To allow Maine to insist that the carriers provide a special checking system would allow other States to do the same. And to interpret the federal law to permit these, and similar, state requirements could easily lead to a patchwork of state service-determining laws, rules, and regulations. That state regulatory patchwork is inconsistent with Congress' major legislative effort to leave such decisions, where federally unregulated, to the competitive marketplace.*

To allow Maine to insist that the carriers provide a special checking system would allow other States to do the same. And to interpret the federal law to permit these, and similar, state requirements could easily lead to a patchwork of state service-determining laws, rules, and regulations. That state regulatory patchwork is inconsistent with Congress' major legislative effort to leave such decisions, where federally unregulated, to the competitive marketplace. If federal law pre-empts state regulation of the details of an air carrier's frequent flyer program, a program that primarily promotes carriage, *see Wolens*, it must pre-empt state regulation of the essential details of a motor carrier's system for picking-up, sorting, and carrying goods—essential details of the carriage itself.

Slippery Slope to Patchwork of Laws

* * *

Maine's primary arguments focus upon the reason why it has enacted the provisions in question. Maine argues for an exception from pre-emption on the ground that its laws help it prevent minors from obtaining cigarettes. In Maine's view, federal law does not pre-empt a State's efforts to protect its citizens' public health, particularly when those laws regulate so dangerous an activity as underage smoking.

Exception from Preemption?

Despite the importance of the public health objective, we cannot agree with Maine that the federal law creates an exception on that basis, exempting state laws that it would otherwise pre-empt. The Act says nothing about a public health exception. To the contrary, it explicitly lists a set of exceptions (governing motor vehicle safety, certain local route controls, and the like), but the list says nothing about public health.

Maine suggests that the provision's history indicates that Congress' primary concern was not with the sort of law it has enacted, but instead with state "economic" regulation. But it is frequently difficult to distinguish between a State's "economic"-related and "health"-related motivations, and, indeed, the parties vigorously dispute Maine's actual motivation for the laws at issue here. Consequently, it is not surprising that Congress declined to insert the term "economic" into the operative language now before us, despite having at one time considered doing so.

* * *

*Direct, Non-
Borderline
Case?*

In this case, the state law is not general, it does not affect truckers solely in their capacity as members of the general public, the impact is significant, and the connection with trucking is not tenuous, remote, or peripheral. The state statutes aim directly at the carriage of goods, a commercial field where carriage by commercial motor vehicles plays a major role. The state statutes require motor carrier operators to perform certain services, thereby limiting their ability to provide incompatible alternative services; and they do so simply because the State seeks to enlist the motor carrier operators as allies in its enforcement efforts.

Given these circumstances, from the perspective of pre-emption, this case is no more "borderline" than was *Morales*. Given *Morales*, where the Court held that federal law pre-empts state consumer-protection laws, we find that federal law must also pre-empt Maine's efforts directly to regulate carrier services.

JUSTICE GINSBURG, *concurring.*

Today's decision declares key portions of Maine's Tobacco Delivery Law incompatible with the Federal Aviation Administration Authorization Act of 1994 ("FAAAA"). The breadth of FAAAA's preemption language, coupled with our decisions closely in point, *Morales v. Trans World Airlines, Inc.* and *American Airlines, Inc. v. Wolens*, impel that conclusion. I write separately to emphasize the large regulatory gap left by an application of the FAAAA perhaps overlooked by Congress, and the urgent need for the National Legislature to fill that gap.

Tobacco use by children and adolescents, we have recognized, may be "the single most significant threat to public health in the United States." But no comprehensive federal law currently exists to prevent tobacco sellers from exploiting the underage market. Instead, Congress has encouraged state efforts. Congress has done so by providing funding incentives for the States to pass legislation making it unlawful to "sell or distribute any [tobacco] product to any individual under the age of 18."

State measures to prevent youth access to tobacco, however, are increasingly thwarted by the ease with which tobacco products can be purchased through the Internet. "As cyberspace acts as a risk-free zone where minors can anonymously purchase tobacco, unrestricted online tobacco sales create a major barrier to comprehensive youth tobacco control."

Maine and its *amici* maintain that, to guard against delivery of tobacco products to children, "the same sort of age verification safeguards [must be] used when tobacco is handed over-the-doorstep as . . . when it is handed over-the-counter." The FAAAA's broad preemption provisions, the Court holds, bar States from adopting this sensible enforcement strategy. While I join the Court's opinion, I doubt that the drafters of the FAAAA, a statute designed to deregulate the carriage of goods, anticipated the measure's facilitation of minors' access to tobacco. Now alerted to the problem, Congress has the capacity to act with care and dispatch to provide an effective solution.

JUSTICE SCALIA, concurring in part.

I join the opinion of the Court, except those portions that rely on the reports of committees of one House of Congress to show the intent of that full House and of the other—with regard to propositions that are apparent from the text of the law, unnecessary to the disposition of the case, or both.

Textual Judicial Philosophy

EXERCISE 5-4. *ROWE V. NEW HAMPSHIRE MOTOR TRANSPORT ASS'N*—INTERPRETING "RELATING TO"

1. What is the issue in *Rowe v. New Hampshire Motor Transport Ass'n*?

2. What does the Motor Carrier Act of 1980, as amended by the Federal Aviation Administration Authorization Act of 1994, say? What does Maine's Act to Regulate the Delivery of Tobacco Products and to Prevent the Sale of Tobacco Products to Minors state? Were these laws compatible?

3. The majority opinion found significance in the fact that the state law was not general and did not impact trucking in a "tenuous, remote, or peripheral" way. Explain.

4. In her concurrence in *Rowe v. New Hampshire Motor Transport Ass'n*, Justice Ginsburg noted that the court was bound by the language of the Federal Aviation Administration Act of 1994 and the precedent established in two Supreme Court decisions—*Morales v. Trans World Airlines, Inc.* and *American Airlines, Inc. v. Wolens* (she authored the latter). As a result the court was constrained to fill "the large regulatory gap left by an application of the FAAAA perhaps overlooked by Congress." What was needed in her view as a result? And, what does this say about the relationship between the judicial and legislative branch in matters of preemption?

5.   What is the main point of Justice Scalia's concurrence in *Rowe v. New Hampshire Motor Transport Ass'n*? Why is that important from the perspective of statutory interpretation?

ABC CHARTERS, INC. V. BRONSON

2009 WL 1010435 (S.D. Fla. 2009)

ALAN S. GOLD, DISTRICT JUDGE.

Travel agencies and charter companies providing services to individuals traveling to Cuba or who wish to send humanitarian aid or family remittances to Cuba advanced a facial challenge to the constitutionality of the amendments to the Florida Sellers of Travel Act effective July 1, 2008 ("Travel Act Amendments").

Elements of Travel Act Amendments

The Travel Act Amendments: (1) require companies providing lawful travel related services to Cuba to post a bond in an amount of $100,000 or $250,000 while requiring those companies not offering travel to Cuba or other "terrorist states" to post a bond of $25,000; (2) allow the state of Florida to use the bond to pay its own investigatory expenses without any limits to the exposure under the bond and prioritize the payment of the bond funds to the state over compensation to consumers; (3) permit the imposition of higher registration fees and fines on travel providers offering travel to Cuba; (4) automatically make any violation of federal law by Plaintiffs a third-degree felony under Florida law; and (5) require disclosure and identification by Plaintiffs of each company with whom each Plaintiff does any Cuba-related business or commerce, and make that information publicly available.

In my Preliminary Injunction Order, I concluded that:

(1)   The Travel Act Amendments are designed and structured to end or seriously hamper federally licensed travel from Florida to Cuba, and that such a law is more than just a state consumer protection decision but also a political statement of condemnation of Cuba;

(2)   The significant burdens on travel and charter service providers impair the ability of this Nation to choose between a range of policy options in developing its foreign relations with Cuba;

(3)   The Airline Deregulation Act, which extends to indirect air carriers such as Plaintiffs, expressly preempts the Travel Act Amendments

because they would have a significant effect on rates, routes or services;

(4) The Travel Act Amendments conflict with, and are therefore preempted by, federal laws and regulations including the Trading with the Enemy Act and the Office of Foreign Assets Control's ("OFAC") Cuba Asset Control Regulations;

(5) Federal laws and regulations occupy the field as to regulation interactions and transactions with Cuba by persons and businesses in the United States;

(6) The Travel Act Amendments impermissibly discriminate against the flow of foreign commerce and regulate conduct outside the borders of the United States; and

(7) Under the interstate commerce clause, the extensive web of federal laws regulating business with and travel to Cuba displaces state laws such as the Travel Act Amendments.

The United States is in substantial agreement with these conclusions. According to its Statement of Interest, the State of Florida enacted the Travel Act Amendments "in an attempt to conduct its own foreign policy," and "the very existence of the legislation . . . impairs the federal government's ability to present a single, unified foreign policy on behalf of the United States when dealing with other countries."

Recent developments further indicate our nation's changing foreign policy objectives with respect to Cuba, further counseling against permitting the Travel Act Amendments from going into effect. I take judicial notice that Office of Foreign Assets Control has recently issued, in response to the Omnibus Appropriations Act, 2009, a general license permitting an expanded range of family travel to permit visiting close relatives in Cuba from once every three years to once every year. Even more recently, President Barack Obama announced on April 13, 2009 that the restrictions on family travel, and remittances and gifts to Cuba will be lifted and Cuban Americans will now be permitted to travel freely to the island and send as much money as they want to their family members, in a marked reversal of the United States' prior policy. Such changes in foreign policy with respect to Cuba further demonstrate that the Travel Act Amendments interfere with this country's foreign policy objectives. As the United States represented at oral argument, these recent changes aptly demonstrate that the Travel Act Amendments would undermine the power of the federal government to act on behalf of the entire nation with respect to our relations with Cuba.

National Policy Changes

The State of Florida is not entitled to adopt a foreign policy under our Constitution or interfere with the exclusive prerogative of the United States to establish a carefully balanced approach to relations with foreign countries, including Cuba. The Travel Act Amendments are unconstitutional insofar as they are preempted by federal law and violate the foreign affairs power, the Foreign Commerce Clause, and the Interstate Commerce Clause.

NOTES ON *ABC CHARTERS, INC. V. BRONSON*—CONFLICT PREEMPTION

The Supremacy Clause of the United States Constitution invalidates state and local laws that interfere with or are contrary to the laws of congress. As stated in *Gibbons v. Ogden*, 22 U.S. (9 Wheat.) 1 (1824), "[w]here Congress has legislated concerning a subject, on which it is authorized to all, all State legislation which interferes with it, is absolutely void." Federal law can preempt state and local laws either expressly or impliedly.

Where Congress explicitly states its intention—as in in *Bailey v. Rocky Mountain Holdings, LLC*, 2015 WL 5885379 (S.D. Fla. 2015), *supra*—courts need only give effect to the explicit text or meaning of a law to preempt contrary state or local laws.

But sometimes Congress's intent is not explicit or unambiguous and courts must infer whether Congress intended a law to supersede a state or local law. This type of preemption analysis falls under the heading of "implied preemption." Implied preemption consists of "field preemption" and "conflict preemption." "Field preemption occurs when the federal scheme of regulation is so pervasive that Congress must have intended to leave no room for a State to supplement it. "Conflict preemption" occurs either when compliance with both the federal and state laws is a physical impossibility, or when the state law stands as an obstacle to the accomplishment and execution of the full purposes and objectives of Congress.

ABC Charters, Inc. v. Bronson fits under the heading "implied preemption." In that Florida law intruded on powers that are the exclusive prerogative of the federal government. While the Constitution did not explicitly prohibit enactment of the Travel Act Amendments at issue in the case, it is clear that those laws could not coexist with the foreign affairs power, the Foreign Commerce Clause, and the Interstate Commerce clause. As such, the court had little difficult finding the Travel Act Amendments void.

The following two cases—*U.S. Airways, Inc. v. O'Donnell* and *Abdullah v. American Airlines, Inc.*—involve implied preemption. Notice that such cases, unlike many express and conflict preemption cases, leave substantial room for differences in interpretation and result.

U.S. AIRWAYS, INC. V. O'DONNELL

627 F.3d 1318 (10th Cir. 2010)

BRISCOE, CHIEF JUDGE.

The New Mexico Liquor Control Act ("NMLCA"), N.M. Stat. § 60–3A–1 *et seq.*, regulates the sale, service and public consumption of alcoholic beverages in the State of New Mexico. NMLCA states, in relevant part, that "[e]very person selling alcoholic beverages to travelers on . . . airplanes within the state shall secure a public service license." Further, NMLCA prohibits any person from being "employed as a server on a licensed premises unless that person obtains within thirty days of employment alcohol server training."

US Airways, an interstate airline carrier regulated by the Federal Aviation Administration of the United States Department of Transportation, operates flights that travel to and from the State of New Mexico at the Albuquerque International Sunport Airport. These flights generally originate from or arrive at locations outside New Mexico. US Airways serves alcoholic beverages during its flights, including those that arrive in and depart from New Mexico. However, passengers are not permitted to remove from the aircraft the alcoholic beverages served during flight. Further, the U.S. Airways beverage carts containing the alcoholic beverages are not removed from the aircraft in New Mexico. US Airways does not stock its aircraft with alcoholic beverages and does not purchase or store such beverages in New Mexico. Prior to 2007, U.S. Airways provided alcoholic beverage service to passengers on flights departing from and arriving in New Mexico without possessing a public service license as required by NMLCA.

In November 2006, Dana Papst was a passenger on a U.S. Airways flight departing from Phoenix, Arizona and arriving in Albuquerque, New Mexico. He allegedly purchased and consumed alcoholic beverages during his U.S. Airways flight. During his drive home from the Albuquerque airport and approximately three hours after deplaning, he caused an automobile accident that resulted in his death and the death of five others. An analysis of Papst's blood drawn after the accident revealed that Papst's blood alcohol content was approximately 0.329. After conducting an investigation of the incident, the Federal Aviation Administration declined to take any action against U.S. Airways or its employees.

In January 2007, the Alcohol and Gaming Division ("AGD") of the New Mexico Regulation and Licensing Department served U.S. Airways with a citation asserting that U.S. Airways had served alcohol to an intoxicated person, namely Dana Papst. The AGD also served U.S. Airways with a cease-and-desist order directing U.S. Airways to "refrain from selling, serving and otherwise dispensing, storing or possessing alcoholic beverages of any kind in the State of New Mexico" without properly complying with the requirements of the New Mexico Liquor Control Act ("NMLCA"), N.M. Stat. § 60–3A–1 *et seq.*

In February 2007, while noting its belief that federal law preempted the application of NMLCA to an airline, U.S. Airways applied for a public service license to serve alcoholic beverages to passengers on aircraft in New Mexico. In response to the application, AGD issued U.S. Airways a ninety-day temporary license. However, in June 2007, AGD declined to extend U.S. Airways' temporary license explaining that U.S. Airways' alcohol server training did not comply with NMLCA's requirements. AGD ultimately rejected U.S. Airways' application for a license in November 2007 citing as reasons for the denial the Dana Papst incident and another incident which involved a passenger who had been served alcoholic beverages on a U.S. Airways flight and was apprehended for driving while intoxicated approximately an hour after he had deplaned at Albuquerque.

Injunction on Preemption Grounds

US Airways filed this action seeking to "enjoin New Mexico state officials [in the AGD and the New Mexico Regulation and Licensing Department] from enforcing laws that purport to govern U.S. Airways' alcoholic beverage service on flights departing from or arriving into New Mexico." US Airways asserted both express and implied preemption in support of its request for injunction.

Specifically, U.S. Airways argued that the enforcement of NMLCA against an airline violated the Supremacy Clause of the United States Constitution as the ADA expressly preempts state regulation of airline services, including the alcoholic beverage service provided to passengers on flights. Alternatively, U.S. Airways contended that federal law impliedly preempts the application of NMLCA to airlines as the application of NMLCA to an airline implicates the field of aviation safety, which federal law regulates to the exclusion of state regulation. Further, U.S. Airways asserted that New Mexico's regulatory efforts could not be otherwise authorized pursuant to the Twenty-first Amendment to the United States Constitution.

> *Specifically, U.S. Airways argued that the enforcement of NMLCA against an airline violated the Supremacy Clause of the United States Constitution as the ADA expressly preempts state regulation of airline services, including the alcoholic beverage service provided to passengers on flights. Alternatively, U.S. Airways contended that federal law impliedly preempts the application of NMLCA to airlines as the application of NMLCA to an airline implicates the field of aviation safety, which federal law regulates to the exclusion of state regulation.*

The parties filed cross-motions for summary judgment and the district court concluded that federal law neither expressly nor impliedly preempts New Mexico's regulation of the alcoholic beverage service that airlines provide. Specifically, the district court narrowly construed the explicit preemption provision in the ADA, concluding that the provision's reference to "service" did not include an airline's alcoholic beverage service. The district court reasoned that the narrow interpretation necessarily avoided rendering the ADA preemption provision violative of § 2 of the Twenty-first Amendment. Further, the district court addressed field preemption and concluded that federal law did not preempt the field of alcohol service on airlines. In reaching this decision, the district court reasoned that, when enacting the FAA, "Congress was addressing the need for exclusive and complete rules for the physical and mechanical operation of aircraft." The district court then denied U.S. Airways' motion for summary judgment and granted New Mexico's motion.

On appeal, U.S. Airways argues that the Airline Deregulation Act of 1978 ("ADA") expressly preempts state regulation of airlines' alcoholic beverage services provided to passengers. In addition to express preemption, U.S. Airways argues that federal law impliedly preempts the application of the NMLCA to U.S. Airways. Specifically, U.S. Airways contends that the Federal Aviation Act of 1958 ("FAA") and the federal regulations promulgated pursuant to the FAA occupy the field of aviation safety to the exclusion of state regulation and that NMLCA's application to an airline implicates the field of aviation safety. Exercising jurisdiction under 28 U.S.C. § 1291, we conclude that New Mexico's regulatory scheme is impliedly preempted as it falls within the field of aviation safety that Congress intended federal law to occupy exclusively, but that the Twenty-first Amendment of the United States Constitution requires a balancing of New Mexico's core powers and the federal interests underlying the FAA. Accordingly, we reverse and remand for the district court to conduct a Twenty-first Amendment balancing.

A. Preemption

The Supremacy Clause provides that the laws of the United States "shall be the supreme Law of the Land; . . . any Thing in the Constitution or Laws of any State to the Contrary notwithstanding." U.S. CONST. art. VI, cl. 2. Pursuant to this provision, Congress has the power to enact statutes that preempt state law. Thus, preemption is ultimately a question of congressional intent.

Types of Preemption

There are three types of preemption: (1) "express preemption, which occurs when the language of the federal statute reveals an express congressional intent to preempt state law;" (2) "field preemption, which occurs when the federal scheme of regulation is so pervasive that Congress must have intended to leave no room for a State to supplement it;" and (3) "conflict preemption, which occurs either when compliance with both the federal and state laws is a physical impossibility, or when the state law stands as an obstacle to the accomplishment and execution of the full purposes and objectives of Congress."

> *There are three types of preemption: (1) "express preemption, which occurs when the language of the federal statute reveals an express congressional intent to preempt state law;" (2) "field preemption, which occurs when the federal scheme of regulation is so pervasive that Congress must have intended to leave no room for a State to supplement it;" and (3) "conflict preemption, which occurs either when compliance with both the federal and state laws is a physical impossibility, or when the state law stands as an obstacle to the accomplishment and execution of the full purposes and objectives of Congress.*

In this case, U.S. Airways asserts that federal law expressly preempts NMLCA's application to an airline. Additionally, U.S. Airways asserts that the FAA, 49 U.S.C. § 40101 *et seq.*, and the federal regulations promulgated pursuant to the FAA occupy the field of aviation safety to the exclusion of state regulation, including the NMLCA. Because we conclude that applying New Mexico's regulatory scheme to U.S. Airways implicates the field of aviation safety that Congress intended federal law to regulate exclusively, we need not reach the question of express preemption.

1. Field Preemption

Field preemption occurs when a "state law . . . regulates conduct in a field that Congress intended the Federal Government to occupy exclusively." Congress's intent for federal law to occupy a field exclusively "may be inferred from a scheme of federal regulation so pervasive as to make reasonable the inference that Congress left no room for the States to supplement it, or where an

Act of Congress touches a field in which the interest is so dominant that the federal system will be assumed to preclude enforcement of state laws on the same subject."

When conducting a field preemption analysis, we must first identify the legislative field that the state law at issue implicates. In this case, the district court narrowly construed NMLCA as regulating the field of alcoholic beverage service provided on airplanes. In our view, however, the regulation of an airline's alcoholic beverage service necessarily implicates the field of airline safety. The FAA similarly recognized the safety considerations implicated when promulgating 14 C.F.R. § 121.575 to regulate the alcoholic beverage services provided on airplanes. *See* Drinking and Serving of Alcoholic Beverages, 25 Fed. Reg. 168, 168–69 (Jan. 9, 1960) (discussing the safety concerns associated with an airline's alcoholic beverage service). Additionally, NMLCA's regulatory scheme extends beyond the field of airline alcoholic beverage services. Specifically, NMLCA prescribes training and certification requirements for flight attendants and other airline crew members serving alcoholic beverages on aircraft. Thus, we conclude that New Mexico's regulatory scheme as applied to an airline generally implicates the field of aviation safety.

Having identified the legislative field at issue, we must next evaluate whether Congress intended to occupy the field to the exclusion of the states. Thus, in this case, we must determine whether Congress intended to occupy the field of aviation safety to the exclusion of the states. While recognizing that the purpose of Congress must be clear as we presume that "Congress does not cavalierly pre-empt state law causes of action," the field of aviation safety "has long been dominated by federal interests." *Montalvo v. Spirit Airlines*, 508 F.3d 464 (9th Cir. 2007). Thus, the presumption against preemption does not apply in this case.

Based on the FAA's purpose to centralize aviation safety regulation and the comprehensive regulatory scheme promulgated pursuant to the FAA, we conclude that federal regulation occupies the field of aviation safety to the exclusion of state regulations. The FAA was enacted to create a "uniform and exclusive system of federal regulation" in the field of air safety. Specifically, Congress enacted the FAA in response to a series of "fatal air crashes between civil and military aircraft operating under separate flight rules." H.R. Rep. No. 85-2360, at 2 (1958), *reprinted in* 1958 U.S.C.C.A.N. 3741, 3742 (noting that "[t]he magnitude and critical nature of [airspace use and air-safety problems] came . . . to general public notice . . . as a result of" a series of airplane crashes). In response to the air safety concerns, the House Report discussing the FAA indicated that the "Administrator of the new Federal Aviation Agency . . . would be given full

Exclusive Federal Control of Aviation Safety

responsibility and authority for the . . . promulgation and enforcement of safety regulations." Further, as documented in the House Report, a letter from a representative of the Executive Branch to the House Committee on International and Foreign Commerce explained that "[i]t is essential that one agency of government, and one agency alone, be responsible for issuing safety regulations."

The language of the FAA explicitly directs the FAA Administrator to promulgate regulations for the "safe flight of civil aircraft in air commerce." Beyond the types of regulations specifically enumerated, the FAA directs the Administrator to regulate any "other practices, methods, and procedure the Administrator finds necessary for safety in air commerce and national security." The Federal Aviation Administration has exercised its authority pursuant to the FAA to promulgate regulations addressing "virtually all areas of air safety." *Air Transp. Ass'n of Am., Inc. v. Cuomo*, 520 F.3d 218 (2d Cir. 2008); *see, e.g.,* 14 C.F.R. § 91.13(a) (identifying the general standard of care for operating an aircraft); 14 C.F.R. § 121.571 (specifying the mandatory briefings that must be provided to all passengers on aircraft); 14 C.F.R. pt. 121, app. A (identifying the minimum number of first-aid kits that must be stored on aircraft and the items that each first-aid kit must contain). Significantly, as relevant to the present case, the Federal Aviation Administration has promulgated a regulation pursuant to the FAA specifically addressing airlines' alcoholic beverage services. *See* 14 C.F.R. § 121.575.

We conclude that the comprehensive regulatory scheme promulgated pursuant to the FAA evidences the intent for federal law to occupy the field of aviation safety exclusively.

2.   NMLCA Related to Air Safety

Having addressed the field of aviation safety generally, we must consider whether the NMLCA implicates the field as occupied by federal law. Even if we narrowly define the field of aviation safety, we conclude that NMLCA's regulation of an airline's alcoholic beverage service directly implicates the field of aviation safety regulated by federal law. As noted, the FAA has promulgated a federal regulation specifically addressing airlines' alcoholic beverage services.

Section 121.575 provides in full:

(a)   No person may drink any alcoholic beverage aboard an aircraft unless the certificate holder operating the aircraft has served that beverage to him.

(b)   No certificate holder may serve any alcoholic beverage to any person aboard any of its aircraft who—(1) appears to be intoxicated; (2) is escorting a person or being escorted; or (3) has a deadly or dangerous weapon accessible to him while aboard the aircraft.

(c)   No certificate holder may allow any person to board any of its aircraft if that person appears to be intoxicated.

(d)   Each certificate holder shall, within five days after the incident, report to the Administrator the refusal of any person to comply with paragraph (a) of this section, or of any disturbance caused by a person who appears to be intoxicated aboard any of its aircraft.

Notably, the FAA promulgated this regulation to promote aviation safety. Specifically, the FAA balanced the safety concerns inherent in regulating airline alcoholic beverage service against the imposition of additional responsibilities on flight crew members by explaining that airline flight crew members would not have the responsibility to "restrain physically a passenger who wished to consume drinks that were not served to him by the carrier."

Additionally, the FAA considered whether the proposed provision adequately addressed safety concerns, noting that "flat prohibition [of alcohol on aircraft] has not proven successful" and "it might even work adversely, since passengers who wish to drink might . . . do so to excess in advance of the flight, knowing that they could not obtain a drink aboard an aircraft." Thus, NMLCA implicates the field of aviation safety as occupied by federal law.

Further, New Mexico's regulatory efforts extend beyond the alcoholic beverage service that airlines provide on flights. By requiring airlines to comply with NMLCA, New Mexico is seeking to impose additional training requirements on flight attendants and crew members serving alcoholic beverages on airplanes. *See* N.M. Stat. § 60–6E–4 ("No person shall be employed as a server on a licensed premises unless that person obtains within thirty days of employment alcohol server training pursuant to the provisions of [N.M. Stat. § 60–6E–1 *et seq.*]."); N.M. Stat. § 60–6E–5(B) (delineating the subjects that the training program for employees serving alcoholic beverages must cover). In fact, when New Mexico denied the renewal of U.S. Airways' temporary public service license, New Mexico noted that U.S. Airways "ha[d] done little if anything to consider implementing applicable portions of [New Mexico's] required alcohol server training."

However, federal law extensively regulates flight attendant and crew member training programs and certification requirements due to the aviation safety considerations involved. *See* 49 U.S.C. § 44728(a)(1) ("No person may serve as a flight attendant aboard an aircraft of an air carrier unless that person holds a certificate of demonstrated proficiency from the Administrator of the Federal Aviation Administration . . ."); 14 C.F.R. §§ 121.404 (requiring that flight attendants and aircraft dispatchers "complete[ ] approved crew resource management . . . or dispatcher resource management . . . initial training"), 121.405 (explaining the approval process for training programs or revisions to existing training programs), 121.415 (delineating the training program requirements), 121.421 (describing the initial and transition ground training requirements for flight attendants), 121.427 (explaining the recurrent training requirements for crew members and dispatchers), 121.433 (describing the mandatory crew member training requirements). Thus, NMLCA's regulatory scheme implicates the field occupied by federal law.

Based on the pervasive federal regulations concerning flight attendant and crew member training and the aviation safety concerns involved when regulating an airline's alcoholic beverage service, we conclude that NMLCA's application to an airline implicates the field of airline safety that Congress intended federal law to regulate exclusively. Thus, New Mexico's regulatory efforts are impliedly preempted.

Based on the pervasive federal regulations concerning flight attendant and crew member training and the aviation safety concerns involved when regulating an airline's alcoholic beverage service, we conclude that NMLCA's application to an airline implicates the field of airline safety that Congress intended federal law to regulate exclusively. Thus, New Mexico's regulatory efforts are impliedly preempted.

[The court went on to consider whether § 2 of the Twenty-first Amendment permitted New Mexico's regulatory scheme, as applied to an airline's alcoholic beverage service, to override federal policy. The district court never conducted any balancing of state and federal interests. Thus, the district court did not have the opportunity to evaluate the effectiveness of New Mexico's regulatory scheme in furtherance of its interests protected under the Twenty-first Amendment. As this inquiry may ultimately depend upon factual findings and conclusions, the court remanded this aspect of the case to the district court to conduct the balancing of state and federal interests.]

EXERCISE 5-5. APPLYING *U.S. AIRWAYS, INC. V. O'DONNELL*—FIELD PREEMPTION

1. What did the New Mexico Liquor Control Act at issue in *U.S. Airways, Inc. v. O'Donnell* regulate?

2. By suing officials of the Alcohol and Gaming Division of the New Mexico Regulation and Licensing Department, what legal relief did U.S. Airways seek? What arguments did U.S. Airways make in support of its lawsuit?

3. What is "field preemption"? What are the steps of a field preemption analysis?

4. What was the purpose of the Federal Aviation Act of 1958?

5. What was the holding of *U.S. Airways, Inc. v. O'Donnell*?

NOTES ON *U.S. AIRWAYS, INC. V. O'DONNELL*—LIMITS OF IMPLIED PREEMPTION ANALYSIS?

O'Donnell represents a continuing trend of courts taking an expansive view of implied preemption of commercial aviation. On the one hand, the Third and Ninth Circuit Courts of Appeal narrowly define the term "service" in the Airline Deregulation Act of 1978, the consequence of which is to find that most activities are not preempted. On the other hand, the Second, Fourth, Fifth, and Seventh Circuits have interpreted "service" broadly to encompass activities such as boarding procedures to food and drink provisions, resulting in preemption of most aviation passenger complaints.

As one commentator associated with the law firm that represented U.S. Airways suggests, "[a] desire to avoid taking sides in this circuit conflict may have prompted the Tenth Circuit in *O'Donnell* to begin (and end) with implied preemption, rather than express preemption." David S. Volchok, U.S. Airways v. O'Donnell: *The Tenth Circuit Upholds Broad Federal Preemption of State Regulation of* Airlines, 23 No. 4. AIR & SPACE L. 1, 21 n. 20 (2012).

Meanwhile, practically speaking, excessive alcohol misuse frequently is a contributor to passenger misconduct. *See* Keith L. Alexander, *Raising a Glass or Two—No More—To Safety in Flight*, WASH. POST, July 25, 2001, at E01 (discussing Senator Dianne Feinstein's (D-Cal.) letter to airline executives threatening to introduce legislation if the airlines did not "voluntarily" limit the number of alcoholic drinks served to passengers). *See also* Christian Giesecke, *Unruly Passengers: The Existing Legal System and Proposed Improvements*, 26 ANN. AIR & SPACE L. 45 (2001).

D. SAFETY AND PRODUCT LIABILITY

ABDULLAH V. AMERICAN AIRLINES, INC.
181 F.3d 363 (3d Cir. 1999)

ROTH, CIRCUIT JUDGE.

Plaintiffs Khaled Abdullah, Audrey James, Eardley James, and Velma George were passengers on American Airlines Flight 1473 from New York to San Juan, Puerto Rico, on August 28, 1991. En route, the aircraft encountered severe turbulence which caused serious injuries to a number of passengers, including the plaintiffs. The First Officer had noticed a weather system developing in the flight path and had illuminated the seatbelt sign. He had also gone to the back of the aircraft to warn the flight attendants that the ride could get choppy in ten minutes. None of the crew, however, alerted the passengers of the expected turbulence. Nor did the pilot change course in order to avoid the storm. Some of the injured passengers were wearing their seatbelts; some were not.

Negligence Allegations

Plaintiffs filed two separate lawsuits against defendant American Airlines, Inc., alleging negligence on the part of the pilot and flight crew in failing to take reasonable precautions to avoid the turbulent conditions known to them and in failing to give warnings reasonably calculated to permit plaintiffs to take steps to protect themselves. A jury found American liable, found plaintiffs to be without any contributory fault, and awarded monetary damages aggregating more than two million dollars.

American filed a post-trial motion which requested dismissal and/or a new trial plus attorney's fees and costs. Among the grounds asserted was that the District Court had improperly used territorial common law to establish the standards of care for the pilots, flight attendants, and passengers. American argued that the FAA implicitly preempts the standards for airline safety. The District Court issued an Opinion, holding that the FAA impliedly preempts state and territorial regulation of aviation safety and standards of care for pilots, flight attendants, and passengers, but that plaintiffs may recover under state and territorial law for violation of federal standards. The District Court held that its error of law regarding preemption, which resulted in admission of evidence regarding standards other than the federal standards, warranted a new trial. Upon motion of the plaintiffs, the District Court certified this issue for interlocutory review. We granted interlocutory review.

DISCUSSION

The instant case concerns the species of preemption known as field preemption. Field preemption occurs if federal law "thoroughly occupies" the "legislative field" in question, *i.e.*, the field of aviation safety. Our finding of implied field preemption here is based on our conclusion that the FAA and relevant federal regulations establish complete and thorough safety standards for interstate and international air transportation that are not subject to supplementation by, or variation among, jurisdictions. While some courts have found federal law to preempt discrete aspects of air safety we hold that federal law establishes the applicable standards of care in the field of air safety, generally, thus preempting the entire field from state and territorial regulation.

Field Preemption

Although the term "field preemption" suggests a broad scope, the scope of a field deemed preempted by federal law may be narrowly defined. For instance, we have held that federal regulation of nuclear safety preempted state tort law on the standard of care. Still, even though federal law controlled the standard of care, we held that the question whether causation and damages were federally preempted was a separate consideration. Similarly, in the instant case, we find that Congress, in enacting the FAA and relevant regulations, intended generally to preempt state and territorial regulation of aviation safety. Nevertheless, we find that plaintiffs may recover damages under state and territorial remedial schemes.

In coming to our answers to the certified question, we depart from the precedent established by a number of cases which hold that federal law does not preempt any aspect of air safety. As explained below, we find these cases to be unpersuasive, either because these courts presumed, without deciding through in-depth analysis, that the FAA did not preempt state or territorial air safety standards, or because these courts followed the preemption language of the Airline Deregulation Act ("ADA"), an economic deregulation statute that we find inapposite to resolving preemption questions relating to the safety of air operations. We conclude that Congress's intent to preempt state and territorial regulations of air safety is not affected by the language of the ADA.

A.   Federal Preemption of Air Safety Standards

The FAA was enacted in response to a series of "fatal air crashes between civil and military aircraft operating under separate flight rules." Congress's purpose in enacting the FAA was "to promote safety in aviation and thereby protect the lives of persons who travel on board aircraft." *In re Mexico City Air Crash of October 31, 1979*, 708 F.2d 400, 406 (9th Cir. 1983).

Congress found the creation of a single, uniform system of regulation vital to increasing air safety. By enacting the FAA, Congress intended to rest sole responsibility for supervising the aviation industry with the federal government:

> [A]viation is unique among transportation industries in its relation to the federal government—it is the only one whose operations are conducted almost wholly within federal jurisdiction, and are subject to little or no regulation by States or local authorities. Thus, the federal government bears virtually complete responsibility for the promotion and supervision of this industry in the public interest.

S. Rep. No. 1811, 85th Cong., 2d Sess. 5 (1958).

Similarly, the House Report accompanying the FAA indicates that one of the purposes of the Act is to give "[t]he Administrator of the new Federal Aviation Agency ... full responsibility and authority for the advancement and promulgation of civil aeronautics generally, including promulgation and enforcement of safety regulations." In addition, in a letter included as part of the House Report, the Airways Modernization Board Chairman wrote: "It is essential that one agency of government, and one agency alone, be responsible for issuing safety regulations if we are to have timely and effective guidelines for safety in aviation."

Thus, legislative history reveals that Congress intended the Administrator, on behalf of the Federal Aviation Administration, to exercise sole discretion in regulating air safety. And this is exactly what Congress accomplished through the FAA. Congress enacted Chapter 447, Safety Regulation, and directed the Administrator to "carry out this chapter in a way that best tends to reduce or eliminate the possibility or recurrence of accidents in air transportation."

Exclusive Federal Control of Flight Safety

To effectuate this broad authority to regulate air safety, the Administrator of the FAA has implemented a comprehensive system of rules and regulations, which promotes flight safety by regulating pilot certification, pilot pre-flight duties, pilot flight responsibilities, and flight rules. For example:

- 14 C.F.R. § 61.3 provides: "No person may act as pilot in command, or in any other capacity as a required pilot flight crew member of a civil aircraft of United States registry unless he has in his personal possession a current pilot certificate issued to him under this part."

- Before flight the pilot must review available information concerning the flight, 14 C.F.R. § 91.103, verify the aircraft's worthiness, 14 C.F.R. § 91.7, and ensure that passengers are briefed on the use of their seatbelts, 14 C.F.R. § 91.107.

- According to 14 C.F.R. § 91.13, "[n]o person may operate an aircraft in a careless or reckless manner so as to endanger the life or property of another."

- Furthermore 14 C.F.R. § 91.7 mandates that "[t]he pilot in command shall discontinue the flight when unairworthy mechanical, electrical, or structural conditions occur."

- And, 14 C.F.R. § 91.101 states: "This subpart prescribes flight rules governing the operation of aircraft within the United States and within 12 nautical miles from the coast of the United States."

The federal courts that adjudicated the first major cases involving the FAA interpreted its legislative history as evincing Congress's intent to exercise supremacy over the field of aviation safety. For instance, just after the passage of the FAA, the Second Circuit Court of Appeals remarked: "The Federal Aviation Act was passed by Congress for the purpose of centralizing in a single authority— indeed, in one administrator—the power to frame rules for the safe and efficient use of the nation's airspace." *Air Line Pilots Ass'n, Int'l v. Quesada*, 276 F.2d 892 (2d Cir. 1960).

Because the legislative history of the FAA and its judicial interpretation indicate that Congress's intent was to federally regulate aviation safety, we find that any state or territorial standards of care relating to aviation safety are federally preempted.

Because the legislative history of the FAA and its judicial interpretation indicate that Congress's intent was to federally regulate aviation safety, we find that any state or territorial standards of care relating to aviation safety are federally preempted. Our analysis is sustained by reference to the broad scope of the FAA, described above. It also is supported by decisions in which courts found federal preemption of discrete, safety-related matters, such as airspace management, flight operations, and aviation noise, because of the promulgation of specific federal regulations over those aspects of air safety. It follows from the evident intent of Congress that there be federal supervision of air safety and from the decisions in which courts have found federal preemption of discrete, safety-related matters, that federal law preempts the general field of aviation safety. Indeed, it would be illogical to conclude that, while federal law preempts state and territorial regulation of matters such as pilot licensing, it does not preempt regulations relating to the

Congressional Intent Regarding Air Safety

exercise of the specific skill for which licensing is necessary-pilots' operation of aircraft.

Moreover, our move from specific to general regulation is not without support in FAA regulations themselves. For example, 14 C.F.R. § 91.13(a), which governs "Careless or Reckless Operation," supplies a comprehensive standard of care to be exercised by pilots and flight crew. It provides, "No person may operate an aircraft in a careless or reckless manner so as to endanger the life or property of another." In a case then where there is no specific provision or regulation governing air safety, § 91.13(a) provides a general description of the standard required for the safe operation of aircraft.

In determining the standards of care in an aviation negligence action, a court must refer not only to specific regulations but also to the overall concept that aircraft may not be operated in a careless or reckless manner. The applicable standard of care is not limited to a particular regulation of a specific area; it expands to encompass the issue of whether the overall operation or conduct in question was careless or reckless.

Thus, in determining the standards of care in an aviation negligence action, a court must refer not only to specific regulations but also to the overall concept that aircraft may not be operated in a careless or reckless manner. The applicable standard of care is not limited to a particular regulation of a specific area; it expands to encompass the issue of whether the overall operation or conduct in question was careless or reckless. Moreover, when a jury is determining what constitutes careless or reckless operation of an aircraft, expert testimony on various aspects of aircraft safety may be helpful to the jury. In the present case, for example, the regulations on the use of seat belts and on the illumination of the "fasten seat belt" sign set the standard for determining both whether American operated the aircraft carelessly or recklessly and whether the passengers, who had not fastened their seatbelts, were contributorily negligent. In addition, expert testimony may help the jury to understand whether the way in which warnings of turbulence and/or illumination of seatbelt signs were conveyed to the passengers constituted careless or reckless operation.

We conclude, therefore, that because of the need for one, consistent means of regulating aviation safety, the standard applied in determining if there has been careless or reckless operation of an aircraft, should be federal; state or territorial regulation is preempted.

B.   Divergent Authority

Despite the legislative history and interpreting authority which have informed our decision, many courts have held that the field of aviation safety is not federally preempted. We find, however, that the rationales, on which these courts have relied in reaching this conclusion, are unpersuasive. As explained below, either the courts have presumed, without any in-depth analysis, that the FAA does not preempt state or territorial air safety standards, or they have followed precedent involving the ADA, an economic deregulation statute which is inapposite to resolving preemption questions relating to the FAA and air safety. We will deal with these various rationales in turn.

a.   Expressio Unius Est Exclusio Alterius

Expressio unius est exclusio alterius is a Latin maxim which means "to express one is to exclude the other." As with all easy answers, it should be taken with a grain of salt—or even better, with a grain of common sense. The maxim has been employed by some courts to justify a decision that air safety standards are not federally preempted. The main rationale for such a finding rests on Section 105(a)(1) of the ADA, which provides that the regulation of "rates, routes, and services" is expressly preempted. Based on the language of this section, some courts have observed that state tort law claims for personal injuries connected to airline operations are not preempted. *See, e.g., Hodges v. Delta Airlines, Inc.,* 44 F.3d 334 (5th Cir. 1995); *see also American Airlines, Inc. v. Wolens,* 513 U.S. 219 (1995) (noting that the United States as Amicus Curiae had conceded that "[i]t is unlikely that [the ADA] preempts safety-related personal injury claims relating to airplane operations").

A number of courts have, however, continued to use the state law standard of care, along with state remedies. They have concluded that the standards of care related to aviation safety by implication must not be preempted because *expressio unius est exclusio alterius.*

We agree with American that reliance on this maxim to determine whether safety standards are federally preempted is inappropriate. This maxim "stands on the faulty premise that all possible alternatives or supplemental provisions were necessarily considered and rejected by the legislative draftsmen." For that reason, it "can never override clear and contrary evidences of Congressional intent." As the District Court recognized in its comprehensive examination of the *exclusio unius maxim,* "the meaning of a statute is found in the evil which it is designed to remedy; and for this the court properly looks at contemporaneous events, the situation as it existed, and as it was pressed upon the attention of the legislative body." Thus, whether the maxim should be applied to the standards of care for pilots, flight attendants, and passengers depends on Congress's intent when it enacted the ADA-Congress's intent not only with respect to the ADA itself, but also regarding the ADA as it affected and interrelated with the earlier provisions of the FAA.

The ADA was enacted "[t]o ensure that the States would not undo federal deregulation with regulation of their own ... [by] prohibiting the States from enforcing any law 'relating to rates, routes, or services' of any air carrier." *Morales v. Trans World Airlines, Inc.*, 504 U.S. 374 (1992). Airlines compete against one another by attracting passengers through the rates, routes, and services that they offer. Congress did not want the states to hamper this competition by their own regulation of these areas. Safe operations, however, are a necessity for all airlines. Whether or not to conform to safety standards is not an option for airlines in choosing a mode of competition. For this reason, safety of an airline's operations would not appear to fall within the ambit of the ADA and its pro-competition preemption clause. The ADA was enacted 20 years after the FAA. Under the circumstances then of Congress's intent in adopting both the FAA and the ADA, we do not find the *exclusio unius* maxim helpful on the issue of federal preemption of aviation safety standards.

b.   Absence of Federal-State Law Conflict

Another rationale for finding that federal law does not preempt state and territorial safety standards rests upon the observation that Congress directed the Administrator to prescribe "minimum standards" to promote safety. 49 U.S.C. § 44701. Because the federal standards are "minimum," some courts have determined that a common law duty of safety may be owed beyond the FAA regulations. *See, e.g., In re Air Disaster at Lockerbie, Scotland*, 37 F.3d 804 (2d Cir. 1994).

We have a problem with applying the type of analysis to determine that there is no federal preemption of aviation safety. First, there is no gap in the federal standards to fill with a state common law standard. The § 91.13(a) prohibition of "careless or reckless" operation of an aircraft occupies the apparent void beyond the specified "minimum" standards. Therefore, because the Administrator has provided both general and specific standards, there is no need to look to state or territorial law to provide standards beyond those established by the Administrator.

Moreover, in a federally preempted area, the question whether state or territorial law conflicts with federal law is a pointless inquiry. If Congress has preempted a field—whether it be expressly or by implication—state laws attempting to regulate within that field "will be invalidated no matter how well they comport with substantive federal policies." L. TRIBE, AMERICAN CONSTITUTIONAL LAW § 6–27 at 497 (2d ed. 1988).

c.   The Savings and Insurance Clauses

The FAA's savings clause provides that, "[a] remedy under this part is in addition to any other remedies provided by law." 49 U.S.C. § 40120(c). The insurance clause requires that airlines maintain liability insurance "for bodily injury to, or death of, an individual . . . resulting from the operation or maintenance of the aircraft." 49 U.S.C. § 41112(a). These two sections have been interpreted to mean that state safety standards are not preempted because Congress provided for compensation of injured persons.

These two sections do demonstrate that Congress intended to allow for compensation of persons who were injured in aviation mishaps. As we point out in our answer to the second part of the certified question, however, we do not find that state and territorial law remedies are preempted, only the standards of care for the safe operation of aircraft. For that reason, the inclusion of the savings and insurance clauses in the FAA is not inconsistent with our decision. Their inclusion as a part of the FAA is in fact compatible with our determination that state and territorial damage remedies are preserved.

d.   Reserved State Power

Finally, as the District Court pointed out, some courts have found that federal law does not preempt state law in the field of aviation safety because they believe that states may regulate aviation safety under their traditional police powers. However, whether the states may invoke their police powers depends on whether the field is federally preempted. As a result, because we have found that the entire field of aviation safety is federally preempted, we need not consider whether the regulation of aviation safety falls within the traditional police powers of the states and territories.

C.   No Federal Preemption of State and Territorial Remedies

Even though we have found federal preemption of the standards of aviation safety, we still conclude that the traditional state and territorial law remedies continue to exist for violation of those standards. Federal preemption of the standards of care can coexist with state and territorial tort remedies.

Coexisting Remedies

In the present case, we find no "irreconcilable conflict between federal and state standards." Nor do we find that "imposition of a [territorial] standard in a damages action would frustrate the objectives of the federal law." Quite to the contrary, it is evident in both the savings and the insurance clauses of the FAA that Congress found state damage remedies to be compatible with federal aviation safety standards. The savings clause provides that "a remedy under this part is in addition to any other remedies provided by law." Clearly, Congress did not intend to prohibit state damage remedies by this language. Moreover, the insurance clause requires airlines to maintain liability insurance "for bodily injury to, or death of, an individual . . . resulting from the operation or maintenance of the aircraft." 49 U.S.C. § 41112(a). Congress could not have intended to abolish a damage remedy for injury or death if it required airlines to maintain insurance coverage to recompense injured persons. Furthermore, there is no federal remedy for personal injury or death caused by the operation or maintenance of aircraft to be found in the FAA itself. We must conclude, therefore, that the insurance proceeds are to be available as a remedy under state or territorial law.

CONCLUSION

Because we find Congress's intent to regulate interstate and international air safety to be unambiguous, we hold that state and territorial standards of care in aviation safety are federally preempted. Moreover, we find that state and territorial tort remedies can coexist with federal standards of care for air safety; thus, plaintiffs, who are injured during a flight as a result of the violation of federal air safety standards, may have a remedy in state or territorial law. We will remand this case to the District Court to evaluate whether the evidence on standards of care and the instructions given to the jury conformed to the federal aviation safety standards as we have described them, and for such further proceedings as it may deem necessary.

EXERCISE 5-6. *ABDULLAH V. AMERICAN AIRLINES, INC.*— PREEMPTION OF SAFETY STANDARDS

1. Why was the Federal Aviation Act of 1958 created and what was Congress's intent in enacting the law?

2. The court determined that state and territorial standards of care relating to safety are federal preempted. What examples does the court provide as evidence that Congress intended the FAA to exercise sole discretion in regulating air safety? Is this an example of express preemption or field preemption?

3. Congress directed the FAA to prescribe "minimum standards" to promote safety (49 U.S.C. § 44701). Because the federal standards are "minimum," does a common law duty of safety exist beyond the FAA regulations?

4. Explain the FAA Savings and Insurance clauses. Does the existence of these clauses support the conclusion that safety standards are not preempted by federal law?

5. According to the court, are federal standards of care and state and territorial tort remedies in conflict? Explain. Additionally, explain whether the *Abdullah v. American Airlines, Inc.* case is binding precedent outside of the Third Circuit?

SIKKELEE V. PRECISION AIRMOTIVE CORP.

822 F.3d 680 (3d Cir. 2016)

KRAUSE, CIRCUIT JUDGE.

This case presents the question whether *Abdullah v. American Airlines, Inc.*, 181 F.3d 363 (3d Cir. 1999), in which we held that federal law preempts the field of aviation safety, extends to state law products liability claims. We hold it does not.

In light of principles of federalism and the presumption against preemption, Congress must express its clear and manifest intent to preempt an entire field of state law. Here, none of the relevant statutes or regulations signals such an intent. To the contrary, the Federal Aviation Act, the General Aviation Revitalization Act of 1994, and the regulations promulgated by the Federal Aviation Administration reflect that Congress did not intend to preempt aircraft products liability claims in a categorical way. The District Court faithfully sought to apply our precedent, and while it concluded that state products liability claims are preempted by *Abdullah,* it also recognized the question was sufficiently unclear and important to certify its order for interlocutory review. Today, we clarify the scope of *Abdullah* and hold that neither the Act nor the issuance of a type certificate per se preempts all aircraft design and manufacturing claims. Rather, subject to traditional principles of conflict preemption, including in connection with the specifications expressly set forth in a given type certificate, aircraft products liability cases like Appellant's may proceed using a state standard of care. For these reasons, we will reverse the District Court's entry of summary judgment in favor of Appellees and remand for further proceedings.

I.   Background

A.   Overview of Federal Aviation Regulation

Almost immediately after the airplane became a viable means of transportation, it became clear that certain aspects of aviation, such as air traffic control, required uniform federal oversight. *See* Air Commerce Act of 1926.

Congress soon thereafter expanded federal control over aviation by enacting the Civil Aeronautics Act of 1938, which created the Civil Aeronautics Authority ("CAA") to oversee the regulatory aspects of aviation safety and to prescribe "minimum standards governing the design . . . of aircraft, aircraft engines, and propellers as may be required in the interest of safety." The 1938 Act also authorized the CAA to issue so-called "type certificates," "production certificate[s]," and "airworthiness certificate[s]" if an airplane or airplane part complied with the relevant safety regulations.

As the scope of federal involvement in regulating aviation expanded, so too did the number of governmental bodies regulating aviation, and by the 1950s, there had, at one point, been seventy-five different interagency groups with some responsibility in the field. To resolve this problem, Congress enacted the 1958 Federal Aviation Act to consolidate regulatory authority in a single entity: the Federal Aviation Administration ("FAA"). The Federal Aviation Act adopted verbatim from the Civil Aeronautics Act the statutory framework for the promulgation of minimum standards for design safety and the process for the issuance of certificates that indicated compliance with those regulations.

Type and Production Certificates

Pursuant to the statutory framework established in the Civil Aeronautics Act and adopted by the Federal Aviation Act, aircraft engine manufacturers must obtain from the FAA (1) a *type certificate,* which certifies that a new design for an aircraft or aircraft part performs properly and meets the safety standards defined in the aviation regulations, 49 U.S.C. § 44704(a); 14 C.F.R. § 21.31; and (2) a *production certificate,* which certifies that a duplicate part produced for a particular plane will conform to the design in the type certificate, 49 U.S.C. § 44704(c); 14 C.F.R. § 21.137. Before a new aircraft may legally fly, it must also receive (3) an *airworthiness certificate,* which certifies that the plane and its component parts conform to its type certificate and are in condition for safe operation. 49 U.S.C. §§ 44704(d), 44711(a)(1).

The FAA issues a type certificate when it has determined that a product "is properly designed and manufactured, performs properly, and meets the regulations and minimum standards prescribed under 49 U.S.C. § 44701(a)." A type certificate includes the type design, which outlines the detailed specifications, dimensions, and materials used for a given product; the product's operating limitations; a "certificate data sheet," which denotes the conditions and limitations necessary to meet airworthiness requirements; and any other conditions or limitations prescribed under FAA regulations. This certification process can be intensive and painstaking; for example, a commercial aircraft manufacturer seeking a new type certificate for a wide-body aircraft might submit 300,000 drawings, 2,000 engineering reports, and 200 other reports in addition to completing approximately 80 ground tests and 1,600 hours of flight tests. A type certificate remains in effect "until surrendered, suspended, revoked, or a termination date is otherwise established by the FAA." 14 C.F.R. § 21.51. A manufacturer may make both "major" and "minor" changes to a type certificated design, 14 C.F.R. § 21.93, but must obtain the appropriate regulatory approval to do so, which for "major changes" requires the issuance of an amended or supplemental type certificate by the FAA, and for "minor changes" requires the manufacturer to comply with a pertinent "method acceptable to the FAA."

B. Factual History

This case involves alleged manufacturing and design defects in a Textron Lycoming O-320-D2C engine ("the engine") manufactured in 1969 and installed "factory new" on a Cessna 172N aircraft ("the aircraft") in 1998. Lycoming holds both a type certificate and production certificate for the engine. The engine in the aircraft was overhauled in 2004 and installed with a MA-4SPA carburetor in accordance with Lycoming's type-certificated design.

David Sikkelee was piloting the aircraft when it crashed shortly after taking off from Transylvania County Airport in Brevard, North Carolina in July 2005. Sikkelee was killed as a result of serious injuries and burns he suffered in the crash. His wife, Jill Sikkelee, the Plaintiff-Appellant in this case, alleges that the aircraft lost power and crashed as a result of a malfunction or defect in the engine's carburetor. Specifically, she contends that, "due to the faulty design of the lock tab washers as well as gasket set," vibrations from the engine loosened screws holding the carburetor's throttle body to its float bowl. J.A. 643. When properly functioning, a carburetor regulates the mixture of fuel and air that enters the engine's cylinders. According to Sikkelee, however, the manner by which the throttle body was attached to the float bowl in the Textron Lycoming O-320-D2C engine allowed raw fuel to leak out of the carburetor into the engine and thereby caused the aircraft to crash.

Sikkelee initially filed a wrongful death and survival action in the Middle District of Pennsylvania in 2007 against seventeen defendants, asserting state law claims of strict liability, breach of warranty, negligence, misrepresentation, and concert of action. In 2010, the District Court granted defendants' motion for judgment on the pleadings, holding that Sikkelee's state law claims, which were premised on state law standards of care, fell within the preempted "field of air safety" described in *Abdullah*. Sikkelee subsequently filed an amended complaint, continuing to assert state law claims, but this time incorporating federal standards

Jury Instruction, Standards

of care by alleging violations of numerous FAA regulations. Following certain settlements and motion practice, Sikkelee narrowed her claims against Lycoming to defective design (under theories of both negligence and strict liability) and failure to warn.

As the trial date approached, the District Court expressed concern that Sikkelee's proposed jury instructions using federal standards of care were "all but completely unable to assist the Court in . . . formulating an intelligible statement of applicable law." On the one hand, the District Court asserted that, under *Abdullah,* it was bound to apply some federal standard of care and that compliance with the applicable design and construction regulations was the only identifiable, let alone articulable, federal standard. On the other hand, because it determined that the "FAA regulations relating to the design and manufacture of airplanes and airplane component parts were never intended to create federal standards of care," the District Court found it to be "arduous and impractical" to fashion the regulations themselves into such standards. Faced with this conundrum, the District Court ordered Sikkelee to submit additional briefing on the question of the appropriate standard of care and, after review of that briefing, invited Lycoming to file a motion for summary judgment.

In its ruling on that motion, the District Court concluded that the federal standard of care was established in the type certificate itself. Reasoning that the FAA issues a type certificate based on its determination that the manufacturer has complied with the pertinent regulations, the District Court held that the FAA's issuance of a type certificate for the Textron Lycoming O-320-D2C engine meant that the federal standard of care had been satisfied as a matter of law. *Id.* at 451–43, 456. The District Court therefore granted Lycoming's summary judgment motion, in part, on that basis. The District Court denied summary judgment, however, on Sikkelee's failure to warn claims, which were premised on Lycoming's alleged violation of 14 C.F.R. § 21.3 for failure to " 'report any failure, malfunction, or defect in any product, part, process, or article' " that Lycoming manufactured.

Recognizing that its grant of partial summary judgment raised novel and complex questions concerning the reach of *Abdullah* and the scope of preemption in the airlines industry, the District Court certified the order for immediate appeal, and we granted interlocutory review.

III. Discussion

The doctrine of preemption is a necessary but precarious component of our system of federalism under which the states and the federal government possess concurrent sovereignty, subject to the limitation that federal law is "the supreme Law of the Land . . . any Thing in the Constitution or Laws of any State to the Contrary notwithstanding." U.S. CONST. ART. VI, cl. 2. Consistent with this principle, Congress has the power to enact legislation that preempts state law. At the same time, with due respect to our constitutional scheme built upon a "compound republic," with power allocated between "two distinct governments," The Federalist No. 51, at 323 (James Madison) (Clinton Rossiter ed., 1961), there is a strong presumption against preemption in areas of the law that States have traditionally occupied. For that reason, all preemption cases "start with the assumption that the historic police powers of the States were not to be superseded by the Federal Act unless that was the clear and manifest purpose of Congress." Congressional intent is the "ultimate touchstone" of a preemption analysis. Thus, when confronted with the question of whether state claims are preempted, as we are here, we look to the language, structure, and purpose of the relevant statutory and regulatory scheme to develop a "reasoned understanding of the way in which Congress intended the statute and its surrounding regulatory scheme to affect business, consumers, and the law."

Congress may exert its supremacy by expressly preempting state law, but it may also do so implicitly, which we have recognized in limited circumstances in the doctrine of "field" preemption. For that doctrine to apply, "we must find that federal law leaves no room for state regulation and that Congress had a clear and manifest intent to supersede state law" in that field. Where Congress expresses an intent to occupy an entire field, States are foreclosed from adopting any regulation in that area, regardless of whether that action is consistent with federal standards.

In addition to field preemption, federal law may supersede state law through conflict preemption. This occurs when a state law conflicts with federal law such that compliance with both state and federal regulations is impossible, or when a challenged state law "stands as an obstacle to the accomplishment and execution of the full purposes and objectives of a federal law."

In this case, we are asked to analyze the extent to which federal aviation law preempts state tort law, specifically, products liability claims for defective design. We do not write on a blank slate, but rather, against the backdrop of our decision in *Abdullah v. American Airlines, Inc.*

A. Whether the Presumption Against Preemption Applies

Typically, our preemption analysis begins with the presumption that Congress does not preempt areas of law traditionally occupied by the states unless that is its clear and manifest intent. In this case, Appellees argue that the presumption against preemption should not apply in the aviation context given the history of federal involvement in the field. That argument turns, however, on a selective view of history.

In general, products liability claims are exemplars of traditional state law causes of action. Indeed, state law governed the earliest products liability claims in this country. More specifically, even aviation torts have been consistently governed by state law.

In general, products liability claims are exemplars of traditional state law causes of action. Indeed, state law governed the earliest products liability claims in this country. More specifically, even aviation torts have been consistently governed by state law. In *The Crawford Bros. No. 2*, 215 F. 269 (W.D. Wash. 1914), which appears to be the earliest tort case involving an aircraft, the court considered the effect of the "legal code of the air" that had been proposed by the International Juridic Committee on Aviation on a salvage claim related to an airplane crash in Puget Sound. The court posited that, if the code had become law, "it would be important to consider its provisions in determining what was reasonable and proper in a cause involving air craft in a common-law action," much like with rules governing water craft. The court ultimately dismissed the suit for lack of jurisdiction, as neither the proposed legal code of the air nor maritime law provided for jurisdiction, and instructed that such questions "must be relegated to the common-law courts." The decision in *Crawford Bros.* thus recognized that, absent specific legislation, the common law governed aviation tort claims.

Common Law Application to Aviation Torts

Years later, after Congress passed the 1926 Air Commerce Act but before the current type certification regime was imposed, Judge Buffington authored what appears to be this Court's first decision involving an aviation-related tort claim, *Curtiss-Wright Flying Service v. Glose,* 66 F.2d 710 (3d Cir. 1933). There, a widow brought suit against the Curtiss-Wright Flying Service, an early airline, after her husband was killed in a plane crash as a result of negligent operation. We analyzed the claims under common law negligence standards as no specific legislation or regulation governed those claims. Of course, because that decision preceded *Erie Railroad Co. v. Tompkins*, 304 U.S. 64 (1938), our analysis turned on federal, rather than state, common law, but the distinction is not important for our purposes here. Rather, our decision reflects that despite the emergence of federal statutes governing aviation, the common law continued to apply to aviation torts.

Since then, in the absence of applicable statutory or regulatory provisions, we have consistently applied state law to tort claims arising from airplane crashes. Only a month before the Federal Aviation Act was enacted, we were faced with a case involving three claims of defective design against an aircraft manufacturer after its plane broke apart in midair. *Prashker v. Beech Aircraft Corp.*, 258 F.2d 602 (3d Cir. 1958). In concluding that the aircraft manufacturer did not negligently design the plane, we did not exclusively rely on the Civil Aeronautics Board's certification of the relevant design, but rather methodically considered each design defect claim under a common law negligence standard, using the type certificate as but a part of that overall analysis.

We have done the same in the years since the Federal Aviation Act replaced the Civil Aeronautics Act. Consistent with the uniform treatment of aviation products liability cases as state law torts, we have expressly held that the presumption against preemption applies in the aviation context. Appellees' attempts to set the presumption aside are therefore unavailing.

With this presumption in mind, we must determine whether Congress expressed its clear and manifest intent to preempt aviation products liability claims. We do so by reviewing the text and structure of the Federal Aviation Act, and, to the extent necessary and relevant to this statute, examining subsequent congressional action that sheds light on its intent. We also consider relevant regulations that have been issued pursuant to the valid exercise of the FAA's delegated authority, which can have the same preemptive effect as federal statutes.

B. Indicia of Congressional Intent

1. The Federal Aviation Act

As we have explained, although the federal government has overseen certain aspects of aviation, such as air traffic control and pilot certification, since the early days of flight, *see* Air Commerce Act of 1926, there was little question when the Civil Aeronautics Act was adopted in 1938 that common law standards governed tort claims arising from plane crashes, *see, e.g., Curtiss-Wright Flying Serv.* (applying the common law standard for negligence). It is therefore significant that the Federal Aviation Act, which succeeded the Civil Aeronautics Act and remains the foundation of federal aviation law today, contains no express preemption provision. In fact, it says only that the FAA may establish "minimum standards" for aviation safety, 49 U.S.C. § 44701—statutory language the Supreme Court has held in other contexts to be insufficient on its own to support a finding of clear and manifest congressional intent of preemption.

> *It is significant that the Federal Aviation Act, which succeeded the Civil Aeronautics Act and remains the foundation of federal aviation law today, contains no express preemption provision. In fact, it says only that the FAA may establish "minimum standards" for aviation safety, 49 U.S.C. § 44701—statutory language the Supreme Court has held in other contexts to be insufficient on its own to support a finding of clear and manifest congressional intent of preemption.*

Further, the Federal Aviation Act contains a "savings clause," which provides that "[a] remedy under this part is *in addition* to any other remedies provided by law." 49 U.S.C. § 40120(c). The Supreme Court observed that this statutory scheme permits states to retain their traditional regulatory power over aspects of aviation. While the inclusion of the savings clause "is not inconsistent" with a requirement that courts apply federal standards of care when adjudicating state law claims, it belies Appellees' argument that Congress demonstrated a clear and manifest intent to preempt state law products liability claims altogether.

Whereas Appellees must show a clear and manifest congressional intent to overcome the presumption against preemption, they instead have mustered scant evidence and, at best, have demonstrated ambiguity. For example, they discuss § 601 of the Federal Aviation Act, which empowers the FAA to promulgate regulations "to promote safety of flight of civil aircraft in air commerce by prescribing . . . minimum standards governing the design, materials, workmanship, construction, and performance of aircraft, aircraft engines, and propellers as may be required in the interest of safety." Yet, that provision, along with § 603, which provides the statutory framework for the issuance of type certificates, was adopted verbatim from the 1938 Civil Aeronautics Act, which clearly did not preempt state law products liability claims. Neither the Federal Aviation Act nor subsequent amendments substantially changed this statutory framework.

Appellees thus present no evidence from the Federal Aviation Act's text or extensive legislative history that plausibly suggests Congress intended these same provisions to have a different meaning in the 1958 Act than they had in the 1938 Act. Simply put, if Congress had wanted to change the preemptive effect of the type certification process, it would have done so—or at least given some indication of that intention. It did not. The Federal Aviation Act itself therefore does not signal an intent to preempt state law products liability claims.

2.   Federal Aviation Regulations

The federal aviation design regulations are likewise devoid of evidence of congressional intent to preempt state law products liability claims. The FAA, in the letter brief it submitted as amicus curiae in this case, takes the position that the Act and these regulations so pervasively occupy the field of design safety that, consistent with *Abdullah,* they require state tort suits that survive a conflict preemption analysis to proceed under "federal standards of care found in the Federal Aviation Act and its implementing regulations."

We do not defer to an agency's view that its regulations preempt state law, but we do recognize that agencies are well equipped to understand the technical and complex nature of the subject matter over which they regulate and thus have a "unique understanding of the statutes they administer and an attendant ability to make informed determinations about how state requirements may pose an obstacle to the accomplishment and execution of the full purposes and objectives of Congress." We therefore consider the FAA's "explanation of state law's impact on the federal scheme" governing aircraft design and manufacture, but "[t]he weight we accord [its] explanation . . . depends on its thoroughness, consistency, and persuasiveness." Specifically, its views as presented in an amicus brief are " 'entitled to respect' only to the extent [they] ha[ve] the 'power to persuade.' "

Here, three fundamental differences between the regulations at issue in *Abdullah* and those concerning aircraft design, along with the agency's inability to specifically identify or articulate the proposed federal standard of care, lead us to disagree with this aspect of the FAA's submission. First, the regulations governing in-flight operations on their face "prescribe [ ] rules governing the operation of aircraft . . . within the United States." 14 C.F.R. § 91.1(a). In contrast, the manufacturing and design regulations prescribe "[p]rocedural requirements for issuing and changing—(i) Design approvals; (ii) Production approvals; (iii) Airworthiness certificates; and (iv) Airworthiness approvals" and "[r]ules governing applicants for, and holders of" such approvals and certificates. 14 C.F.R. § 21.1(a). That is, these regulations do not purport to govern the manufacture and design of aircraft per se or to establish a general standard of care but rather establish procedures for manufacturers to obtain certain approvals and certificates from the FAA, *see generally* 14 C.F.R. § 21, and in the context of those procedures, to "prescribe[ ] airworthiness standards *for the issue of type certificates,*" 14 C.F.R. § 33.1(a) (aircraft engines); *see also* 14 C.F.R. §§ 23.1(a), 25.1(a), 27.1(a), 29.1(a), 31.1(a), 35.1(a).

Abdullah
Distinguished

Of course, the issuance of a type certificate is a threshold requirement for the lawful manufacture and production of component parts and, at least to that extent, arguably reflects nationwide standards for the manufacture and design of such parts. But the fact that the regulations are framed in terms of standards to acquire FAA approvals and certificates—and not as standards governing manufacture generally—supports the notions that the acquisition of a type certificate is merely a baseline requirement and that, in the manufacturing context, the statutory language indicating that these are "minimum standards," 49 U.S.C. § 44701, means what it says.

Second, the standards that must be met for the issuance of type certificates cannot be said to provide the type of "comprehensive system of rules and regulations" we determined existed in *Abdullah* to promote in-flight safety "by regulating pilot certification, pilot pre-flight duties, pilot flight responsibilities, and flight rules." Rather, many are in the nature of discrete, technical specifications that range from simply requiring that a given component part work properly, *e.g.,* 14 C.F.R. § 33.71(a) (providing that a lubrication system "must function properly in the flight altitudes and atmospheric conditions in which an aircraft is expected to operate"), to prescribing particular specifications for certain aspects (and not even all aspects) of that component part, *e.g.,* 14 C.F.R. § 33.69 (providing that an electric engine ignition system "must have at least two igniters and two separate secondary electric circuits, except that only one igniter is required for fuel burning augmentation systems"). The regulation governing the fuel and induction system at issue in this case, for example, specifies that this part of the engine "must be designed and constructed to supply *an appropriate mixture* of fuel to the cylinders throughout the complete operating range of the engine under all flight and atmospheric conditions." 14 C.F.R. § 33.35(a). As the District Court observed, the highly technical and part-specific nature of these regulations makes them exceedingly difficult to translate into a standard of care that could be applied to a tort claim.

Third, the regulations governing in-flight operations "suppl[y] a comprehensive standard of care," *Abdullah,* that could be used to evaluate conduct not specifically prescribed by the regulations, i.e., that a person must not "operate an aircraft in a careless or reckless manner so as to endanger the life or property of another," 14 C.F.R. § 91.13(a). We recognized in *Abdullah* that § 91.13(a) sounds in common law tort, making it appropriate and practical to incorporate as a federal standard of care in state law claims concerning in-flight operations and rendering existing state law standards of care duplicative (if not conflicting with them outright). Neither the FAA nor Appellees have pointed us to any analogous provision for aircraft manufacture and design, nor have we identified one.

We therefore agree with the District Court that neither the Federal Aviation Act nor the associated FAA regulations "were [ever] intended to create federal standards of care" for manufacturing and design defect claims. However, the District Court proceeded from that accurate premise to a faulty conclusion (the one urged by Appellees), i.e., that because there is no federal standard of care for these claims in the statute or regulations, the issuance of a type certificate must both establish and satisfy that standard. Not so. In light of the presumption against preemption, absent clear evidence that Congress intended the mere issuance of a type certificate to foreclose all design defect claims, state tort suits using state standards of care may proceed subject only to traditional conflict preemption principles.

Besides preserving principles of federalism, this conclusion avoids interpreting the Federal Aviation Act in a way that would have "the perverse effect of granting complete immunity from design defect liability to an entire industry that, in the judgment of Congress, needed more stringent regulation." Conversely, were we to adopt Appellees' position, we would be holding, in effect, that the mere issuance of a type certificate exempts designers and manufacturers of defective airplanes from the bulk of liability for both individual and large-scale air catastrophes.

The Federal Aviation Act and its implementing regulations do not indicate a clear and manifest congressional intent to preempt state law products liability claims; Congress has not created a federal standard of care for persons injured by defective airplanes; and the type certification process cannot as a categorical matter displace the need for compliance in this context with state standards of care.

These observations lead us to conclude that the Federal Aviation Act and its implementing regulations do not indicate a clear and manifest congressional intent to preempt state law products liability claims; Congress has not created a federal standard of care for persons injured by defective airplanes; and the type certification process cannot as a categorical matter displace the need for compliance in this context with state standards of care.

3. GARA

Our conclusion is solidified by the General Aviation Revitalization Act of 1994 ("GARA") (codified at 49 U.S.C. § 40101 note). In that statute, Congress created a statute of repose that, with certain exceptions, bars suit against an aircraft manufacturer arising from a general aviation accident brought more than eighteen years after the aircraft was delivered or a new part was installed. GARA was adopted to limit the "long tail of liability" imposed on manufacturers of general aviation aircraft.

By barring products liability suits against manufacturers of these older aircraft parts, GARA necessarily implies that such suits were and are otherwise permitted. Indeed, GARA's eighteen-year statute of repose would be superfluous if all aviation products liability claims are preempted from day one. GARA reinforces what is now apparent: Federal law does not preempt state design defect claims. Rather, Congress left state law remedies in place when it enacted GARA in 1994, just as it did when it enacted the Civil Aeronautics Act in 1938 and the Federal Aviation Act in 1958.

Appellees argue that GARA would not be entirely superfluous because general aviation manufacturers would "remain subject to state tort remedies for actual violations of federal aviation safety standards," such as the failure to disclose defects discovered after a type certificate has been issued or the failure to comply with an airworthiness directive. Those kinds of claims, however, are already expressly exempted in § 2(b)(1) from GARA's statute of repose. In sum, if GARA and its § 2(b)(1) carveout are to serve their stated purpose, the state law claims to which GARA's statute of repose applies must not be preempted.

Our interpretation of the Federal Aviation Act is only bolstered by GARA's legislative history. We are mindful, of course, that "the authoritative statement is the statutory text, not the legislative history or any other extrinsic material," as legislative history can be "murky, ambiguous, and contradictory." *Exxon Mobil Corp. v. Allapattah Servs., Inc.*, 545 U.S. 546 (2005). Here, however, the legislative history is none of those things. GARA's legislative history states explicitly what is implied by the statutory text: Aviation products liability claims are governed by state law. The House Report begins by stating that "[t]he liability of general aviation aircraft manufacturers is governed by tort law" that "is ultimately grounded in the experiences of the legal system and values of the citizens of a particular State." In enacting GARA, Congress "voted to permit, in this exceptional instance, a very limited Federal preemption of State law," that is, only where GARA's statute of repose has run are state law claims preempted. "[I]n cases where the statute of repose has not expired, State law will continue to govern fully, unfettered by Federal interference."

> *The Federal Aviation Act itself neither states nor implies an intent to preempt state law products liability claims, and GARA confirms that Congress understood and intended that Act to preserve such claims. Thus, despite Appellees' exhortations, we cannot infer a clear and manifest congressional purpose to preempt these claims where the indicia of congressional intent, including in this case the assumptions underlying subsequent legislation, point overwhelmingly the other way.*

Here, the Federal Aviation Act itself neither states nor implies an intent to preempt state law products liability claims, and GARA confirms that Congress understood and intended that Act to preserve such claims. Thus, despite Appellees' exhortations, we cannot infer a clear and manifest congressional purpose to preempt these claims where the indicia of congressional intent, including in this case the assumptions underlying subsequent legislation, point overwhelmingly the other way.

D.   Relevant Preemption Precedent

We turn next to Appellees' contention that the Supreme Court's preemption jurisprudence compels us to find that federal law occupies the entire field of aircraft design and manufacture and that the issuance of a type certificate conclusively demonstrates compliance with the corresponding federal standard of care. Appellees argue that: (1) the Court has accorded broad field preemption to analogous statutory regimes governing oil tankers and locomotives; (2) the Court has given broad preemptive effect to analogous premarket approval processes in the medical device context; and (3) other Courts of Appeals have recognized preemption of the field of aviation safety. For its part, the FAA argues that the mere issuance of a type certificate does not preempt all design defect claims concerning the certificated part but that specifications expressly embodied in a type certificate may, in a given case, preempt such claims under traditional conflict preemption principles. We address Appellees' arguments below and conclude that the case law of the Supreme Court and our sister Circuits supports the application of traditional conflict preemption principles but not preemption of the entire field of aviation design and manufacture.

1.   Field Preemption in Analogous Statutory Regimes

Although they acknowledge that the Supreme Court has not addressed whether the Federal Aviation Act preempts the field of aviation design and manufacture, Appellees argue on the basis of other Supreme Court precedent that we should affirm the reasoning of the District Court. First, Appellees point to the Supreme Court's observation in *City of Burbank v. Lockheed Air Terminal, Inc.,* 411

U.S. 624 (1973) that the Federal Aviation Act "requires a uniform and exclusive system of federal regulation if the congressional objectives underlying [it] are to be fulfilled" as evidence that the Supreme Court has concluded the FAA occupies the entire field of aviation safety. That begs the question, however, of the scope of the field in question. In *City of Burbank,* the Court held only that Congress had preempted the field of aircraft noise regulation. Even in interpreting the express preemption clause of the Airline Deregulation Act, the Court has taken a cautious approach, holding that plaintiffs' claims under state consumer protection statutes are preempted but that related state law claims for breach of contract are not.

The Supreme Court also has observed in dicta that state tort law "plainly appl[ies]" to aviation tort cases and that Congress would need to enact legislation "[i]f federal uniformity is the desired goal with respect to claims arising from aviation accidents." *Exec. Jet Aviation, Inc. v. City of Cleveland*, 409 U.S. 249(1972). The Court's few pronouncements in the area of aviation preemption, in other words, offer little support for the broad field preemption Appellees seek.

Tankers and Locomotive Analogy

Appellees next compare aircraft to oil tankers and locomotives, urging that the broad scope of field preemption recognized by the Supreme Court in those industries should extend as well to aircraft design defect claims. As Appellees point out, the Supreme Court has found field preemption of oil tanker design, operation, and seaworthiness under Title II of the Ports and Waterways Safety Act and concluded state regulations that impose additional crew training requirements and mandate standard safety features on certain boats fall within this preempted field.

We do not find either of these analogies apt. As to tankers, the Supreme Court compared cases that invalidated state regulations that created positive obligations, and neither of those cases "purported to pre-empt possible common law claims" such as the aviation tort claims at issue here. As to locomotives, the Supreme Court and our own Court were bound to find such design defect claims preempted by the Supreme Court's ninety-year-old precedent in *Napier v. Atlantic Coast Line Railway Co.,* 272 U.S. 605 (1926), which held that the Locomotive Inspection Act preempts "the field of regulating locomotive equipment used on a highway of interstate commerce," including "the design, the construction, and the material of every part of the locomotive and tender and of all appurtenances."

Far more apropos in the transportation industry is the Supreme Court's conflict preemption approach in the context of automobiles and boats, for just as the Federal Aviation Act directs the FAA to "prescrib[e] minimum standards required in the interest of safety for appliances and for the design, material, construction, quality of work, and performance of aircraft, aircraft engines, and propellers," 49 U.S.C. § 44701(a)(1), the National Traffic and Motor Safety Act of 1966 ("NTMSA") empowers the National Highway Traffic Safety Administration to "prescribe motor vehicle safety standards for motor vehicles and motor vehicle equipment," 49 U.S.C. § 30101(1), and the Federal Boat Safety Act of 1971 ("FBSA") authorizes the Secretary of Transportation to issue regulations "establishing minimum safety standards for recreational vessels and associated equipment," 46 U.S.C. § 4302(a)(1). Moreover, like the Federal Aviation Act, the NTMSA and FBSA both contain savings clauses.

In assessing implied preemption under these statutory schemes, the Supreme Court has found that the statutory language and applicable regulations support not field preemption, but rather a traditional conflict preemption analysis. In the automobile context, for example, the Court held that a federal regulation governing air bag usage implicated a significant federal regulatory objective—maintaining manufacturer choice—and therefore preempted a state law tort claim, *Geier v. Am. Honda Motor Co.*, 529 U.S. 861 (2000), while another regulation governing seatbelt usage did not reflect a similarly significant federal objective and thus did not preempt state law claims.

Similarly, the Court held that the Federal Boat Safety Act did not preempt the field of "state common law relating to boat manufacture," but nonetheless applied a conflict preemption analysis to determine whether petitioner's tort law claims were preempted by the Federal Boat Safety Act ("FBSA") or the Coast Guard's decision not to promulgate a regulation requiring propeller guards on motorboats. The Court held that the Coast Guard's decision not to regulate did not preclude "a tort verdict premised on a jury's finding that some type of propeller guard should have been installed on this particular kind of boat equipped with respondent's particular type of motor" because the Coast Guard's decision "does not convey an 'authoritative' message of a federal policy against propeller guards."

In sum, the Supreme Court's preemption cases in the transportation context support that aircraft design and manufacture claims are not field preempted, but remain subject to principles of conflict preemption.

2.   Type Certification as Support for Field Preemption

Appellees also assert that because type certificates represent the FAA's determination that a design meets federal safety standards, allowing juries to impose tort liability notwithstanding the presence of a type certificate would infringe upon the field of aviation safety as defined in *Abdullah* and would fatally undermine uniformity in the federal regulatory regime. In support of this argument, Appellees rely on *Riegel v. Medtronic, Inc.*, 552 U.S. 312 (2008), in which state tort claims were deemed preempted by an express preemption clause where the plaintiff challenged the safety of a medical device that had received preapproval from the Food and Drug Administration. Although there is no express preemption clause here, Appellees posit that the FAA's type certification process should be accorded a similar field preemptive effect.

The FAA, on the other hand, argues that type certification is relevant only to an analysis under "ordinary conflict preemption principles." Thus, according to the FAA, "[i]t is . . . only where compliance with both the type certificate and the claims made in the state tort suit 'is a physical impossibility[ ]'; or where the claim 'stands as an obstacle to the accomplishment and execution of the full purposes and objectives of Congress,' that the type certificate will serve to preempt a state tort suit." This, the FAA contends, strikes the right balance in the interests of federalism because:

> to the extent that a plaintiff challenges an aspect of an aircraft's design that was expressly approved by the FAA as shown on the type certificate, accompanying operating limitations, underlying type certificate data sheet, or other form of FAA approval incorporated by reference into those materials, a plaintiff's state tort suit arguing for an alternative design would be preempted under conflict preemption principles . . . . because a manufacturer is bound to manufacture its aircraft or aircraft part in compliance with the type certificate.

> On the other hand, "to the extent that the FAA has not made an affirmative determination with respect to the challenged design aspect, and the agency has left that design aspect to the manufacturer's discretion, the claim would not be preempted."

We have no need here to demarcate the boundaries of those tort suits that will be preempted as a result of a conflict between state law and a given type certificate, nor which FAA documents incorporated by reference in a type certificate might give rise to such a conflict. While the parties responded to the FAA's submission by arguing for the first time in supplemental submissions whether the alleged design defect at issue in this case is a design aspect that was expressly incorporated into the type certificate for the Textron Lycoming O-320-D2C engine and what significance that might have for conflict preemption, we will leave those issues for the District Court to consider on remand. *See, e.g., Miller v. Mitchell*, 598 F.3d 139,

148 (3d Cir.2010) (remanding consideration of an issue discussed in supplemental briefing on appeal but not addressed by the district court in the first instance).

> *For today, we hold only that, consistent with the FAA's view, type certification does not itself establish or satisfy the relevant standard of care for tort actions, nor does it evince congressional intent to preempt the field of products liability; rather, because the type certification process results in the FAA's preapproval of particular specifications from which a manufacturer may not normally deviate without violating federal law, the type certificate bears on ordinary conflict preemption principles.*

For today, we hold only that, consistent with the FAA's view, type certification does not itself establish or satisfy the relevant standard of care for tort actions, nor does it evince congressional intent to preempt the field of products liability; rather, because the type certification process results in the FAA's preapproval of particular specifications from which a manufacturer may not normally deviate without violating federal law, the type certificate bears on ordinary conflict preemption principles.

Ordinary Preemption Principles

Indeed, when confronting an analogous preapproval scheme for pharmaceutical labeling, the Supreme Court has held that, where manufacturers are unable to simultaneously comply with both federal and state requirements, state law design defect claims are conflict preempted, not field preempted. Before a new drug may legally be distributed in the United States, both its contents and its labeling must be preapproved by the FDA. In a series of recent preemption cases, the Court has distinguished between brand-name drugs and their generic equivalents, determining that at least some state law tort claims may be brought against brand-name drug companies because such companies have the ability to make some *unilateral* changes to their labels without additional regulatory preapproval, but such claims against generic drug manufacturers cannot survive a conflict preemption analysis because the generic manufacturers are bound by federal law to directly mimic their brand-name counterparts. Ultimately, where a party cannot "independently do under federal law what state law requires of it," the state law is conflict preempted."

The same considerations apply to the case before us. The FAA's preapproval process for specifications embodied or incorporated into a type certificate, which precludes a manufacturer from making at least "major changes"[21] to a design aspect without further preapproval, means a manufacturer may well find it impossible to simultaneously comply with both a type certificate's specifications and a separate—and perhaps more stringent—state tort duty. Thus, there may be cases where a manufacturer's compliance with both the type certificate and a state law standard of care "is a physical impossibility," or would pose an obstacle to Congress's purposes and objectives. In such cases, the state law claim would be conflict preempted. For, even if an alternative design aspect would improve safety, the mere "possibility" that the FAA would approve a hypothetical application for an alteration does not make it possible to comply with both federal and state requirements: As the Supreme Court observed, if that were enough, conflict preemption would be "all but meaningless."

As for Appellees' reliance on *Riegel,* we agree that the FAA's type certification process resembles the " 'rigorous' " preapproval process for certain medical devices under the Federal Food, Drug, and Cosmetic Act ("FDCA"). Not unlike type certification, this approval process involves copious submissions and exhaustive review, and the FDA grants approval only if a device is deemed both safe and effective. In addition, just as aircraft manufacturers may not make major changes to or deviate from their type certificates without the FAA's sign-off, certain medical device manufacturers may not deviate from a federally sanctioned design without first obtaining supplemental approval from the FDA. However, unlike the Federal Aviation Act, the statute governing medical devices includes an express preemption clause that forbids states from imposing "requirements" that are "different from, or in addition to" federal requirements placed on medical devices. Because the Supreme Court's preemption analysis in *Riegel* hinged on its interpretation of this express preemption clause, the case provides no support for the general proposition that states may not regulate devices governed by a federal statutory scheme.

Moreover, in an important respect, *Riegel* cuts against a finding of field preemption in this case, particularly when read in conjunction with the Court's prior medical device decision in *Lohr.* Together these cases reflect a narrow, rather than sweeping, approach to analyzing the preemptive contours of a federal premarket approval scheme. In *Lohr,* finding that the "overarching concern" of the federal statutory and regulatory scheme was ensuring "that pre-emption occur only where a particular state requirement threatens to interfere with a specific federal interest," the Court preserved state common law requirements "equal to, or substantially identical to, requirements imposed under federal law." 518 U.S. at 497, 500–01, 116 S.Ct. 2240 (internal quotation marks omitted). Subsequently, in *Riegel,* although the Court held that state design defect claims were preempted where they imposed additional safety requirements on medical device manufacturers in violation of the express preemption clause, the Court left *Lohr* intact and took care to note that state duties that " 'parallel,' rather than add to, federal requirements" are not preempted by the statute. 552 U.S. at 330, 128 S.Ct. 999. Here, confronted with a similarly exhaustive preapproval process governing aircraft manufacture and design and no express preemption clause, we see no justification for going further than the Supreme Court elected to go in *Riegel* or *Lohr* by deeming categorically preempted even those state requirements that may be consistent with the federal regulatory scheme as embodied in the FAA's type certificates. We thus read *Riegel* not to bestow field preemptive effect on type certificates, but rather to counsel in favor of narrowly construing the effect of federal regulations on state law—much like the conflict preemption analysis undertaken in *Bartlett* and *PLIVA*.

3. Aviation Preemption Precedent in the Courts of Appeals

With a dearth of support for the proposition that the field of aircraft design and manufacture is preempted, Appellees attempt to muster support from select language in the opinions of other Courts of Appeals. Their efforts are unavailing.

Appellees observe that various Courts of Appeals have described the entire field of aviation safety as preempted, but, on inspection, even those courts have carefully circumscribed the scope of those rulings. The Second, Ninth, and Tenth Circuits all assess the scope of the field of aviation safety by examining the pervasiveness of the regulations in a particular area rather than simply determining whether the area implicated by the lawsuit concerns an aspect of air safety. *See Gilstrap v. United Air Lines, Inc.* (9th Cir. 2013) (inquiring as to "whether the particular area of aviation commerce and safety implicated by the lawsuit is governed by pervasive federal regulations"); *Goodspeed Airport L.L.C. v. E. Haddam Inland Wetlands & Watercourses Comm'n*, 634 F.3d 206, 210–11 (2d Cir. 2011) ("[C]oncluding that Congress intended to occupy the field of air safety does not end our task. . . . [T]he inquiry is twofold; we must determine not only Congressional intent to preempt, but also the scope of that preemption. 'The key question is thus at what point the state regulation sufficiently interferes with federal regulation that it should be deemed pre-empted[.]' ") *U.S. Airways, Inc. v. O'Donnell*, 627 F.3d 1318 (10th Cir. 2010) ("Based on the pervasive federal regulations concerning flight attendant and crew member training and the aviation safety concerns involved when regulating an airline's alcoholic beverage service, we conclude that NMLCA's application to an airline implicates the field of airline safety that Congress intended federal law to regulate exclusively.").

In any event, to date, the Courts of Appeals have held that aviation products liability claims are not preempted, although they have taken a variety of different approaches to reach that result. The Ninth Circuit has held that the entire field of aviation safety is preempted, *Montalvo v. Spirit Airlines,* 508 F.3d 464 (9th Cir. 2007), but that products liability claims are not within that preempted field, drawing a line between areas of law where the FAA *has* issued "pervasive regulations"—such as passenger warnings and pilot qualifications—and other areas where the FAA has not—such as products liability claims for allegedly defective airstairs.

The Tenth and Eleventh Circuits, in addressing products liability claims, have held that not only are those claims governed by state law, but also that the entire field of aviation safety is not preempted. While the basis for their broader holdings is now in doubt, both of those Circuits still hold that aviation products liability claims are governed by state law. The Sixth Circuit's approach is most difficult to decipher: In a single opinion, it relied on *Abdullah* for the proposition that "federal law establishes the standards of care in the field of aviation safety and thus preempts the field from state regulation" yet also applied Kentucky tort law to a design defect products liability claim involving a navigational instrument. The most logical reading of *Greene* is that it holds products liability claims not to be preempted, as any other interpretation would render futile its extensive analysis of the design defect claim under state law.

Even those Courts of Appeals that have not directly addressed the issue have adopted approaches to aviation preemption that suggest they would reach a similar result. The Seventh Circuit has clearly indicated its understanding that state law applies to aviation products liability claims. And the Fifth Circuit has found field preemption only of the narrower field of passenger safety warnings, *Witty v. Delta Air Lines, Inc.*, 366 F.3d. 380 (5th Cir. 2004), and otherwise has applied state law to aviation products liability claims.

Precedent?

In sum, no federal appellate court has held an aviation products liability claim to be subject to a federal standard of care or otherwise field preempted, and Appellees have been unable to identify a single decision from any court, other than the District Court here, that has held the mere issuance of a type certificate conclusively establishes a defendant's compliance with the relevant standard of care.

E.   The Parties' Policy Arguments

In addition to their legal arguments, the parties present various policy arguments in support of their respective positions. While we are not unsympathetic to those arguments, they carry no sway in face of clear evidence of congressional intent and the guidance we draw from the Supreme Court's preemption jurisprudence. Nonetheless, for the sake of completeness, we address those arguments briefly here.

First, in support of field preemption and a federal standard of care, Appellees and their *amici* warn that allowing state tort law to govern design defect claims will open up aviation manufacturers to tremendous potential liability and the unpredictability of non-uniform standards applied by juries throughout the states. Even if we accepted the premise that members of the aviation manufacturing industry would suffer more harm from exposure to tort liability than any other manufacturer that sells its products in all fifty states, this policy argument could not lead us to find field preemption without the requisite congressional intent. And as even the FAA acknowledges, "[a]lthough allowing a defendant to be held liable for a design defect in an engine that has received a type certificate from the FAA is in some tension with Congress's interest in national uniformity in safety standards with oversight by a single federal agency, Congress struck a balance between protecting these interests in uniformity and permitting States to compensate accident victims."

Nor are we moved by Appellees' predictions of the dire consequences to aircraft and component manufacturers of permitting products liability claims to proceed under state tort law, for our holding does not effect a sea change. On the contrary, it simply maintains the status quo that has existed since the inception of the aviation industry, preserving state tort remedies for people injured or killed in plane crashes caused by manufacturing and design defects. That status quo leaves intact the traditional deterrence mechanism of a state standard of care, with attendant remedies for its breach. Thus, while perhaps contrary to certain policies identified by Appellees and their *amici*, our holding furthers an overriding public policy and one we conclude is consistent with the Federal Aviation Act, FAA regulations, GARA, and decisions of the Supreme Court and our sister Circuits: promoting aviation safety.

On the other side of this debate, in arguing that type certificates should have no significance for conflict preemption, much less field preemption, Appellant contends that FAA preapproval of particular specifications provides no assurance of safety because the FAA delegates ninety percent of its certification activities to private individuals and organizations, known as designees, which can include the manufacturers themselves. We too have recognized that designees receive inconsistent monitoring and oversight from the FAA, and many have some association with the applicant, so that in essence "[s]ome manufacturers are able to grant themselves a type certificate." *Robinson v. Hartzell Propeller, Inc.*, 454 F.3d 163 (3d Cir. 2006). Even the FAA acknowledges that, "[i]n light of its limited resources," the agency designates outside organizations to perform some of the FAA's work in preparing a type certificate. From these alleged "flaws" in the review process, Appellant argues that the agency preapproval of specifications in the type certificate amounts to an unreliable self-policing regime that should play no role in even conflict preemption.

In sum, the parties' policy arguments notwithstanding, the case law of the Supreme Court and our sister Circuits confirm our conclusion: We are dealing with an area at the heart of state police powers, and we have no indication of congressional intent to preempt the entire field of aviation design and manufacture. We therefore decline the invitation to create a circuit split and to broaden the scope of *Abdullah's* field preemption to design defects when the statute, the regulations, and relevant precedent militate against it.

Conclusion

We conclude that the District Court erred in granting summary judgment on Sikkelee's design defect claims on the basis of field preemption. The field of aviation safety we identified as preempted in Abdullah does not include product manufacture and design, which continues to be governed by state tort law, subject to traditional conflict preemption principles. Accordingly, we will vacate and remand for further proceedings consistent with this opinion.

EXERCISE 5-7. *SIKKELEE V. PRECISION AIRMOTIVE CORP.*— PREEMPTION OF STATE LAW PRODUCTS LIABILITY CLAIMS

1. What is the scope of field preemption under the Federal Aviation Act of 1958? Specifically, does the preempted field include tort claims based on alleged defective design or manufacturing?

2. If the type of tort claims described in question 1, above, fall within the preempted field, may they proceed using a federal standard of care? If so, what is that standard and where is it found within the Act or its regulations?

3. What weight, if any, should be accorded to the issuance of a type certificate in determining whether the relevant standard of care has been met?

4. What fundamental differences exist between the regulations at issue in *Abdullah v. American Airlines, Inc.* and the issues presented in this case (*e.g.*, aircraft design and agency standards of care)?

5. Describe the precedent in the Court of Appeals on the issue of aircraft design and manufacture preemption and the policy reasons offered by the parties. Does the *Sikkelee* court find the precedent and policy persuasive to its conclusions? Why or why not?

Suggested Further Reading

Sarah E. Light, *Advisory Nonpreemption*, 95 WASH. U. L. REV. 327 (2017)

Alexander T. Simpson, *Standard of Care vs. Claim Preemption under the Federal Aviation Act*, 27 NO. 4 AIR & SPACE LAW. 4 (2014)

Caleb Nelson, *Preemption*, 86 VA. L. REV. 225 (2000)

Paul Wolfson, *Preemption and Federalism: The Missing Link*, 16 HASTINGS CONST. L.Q. 69 (1988)

CHAPTER 6

Airline Deregulation

> Fifty years ago, on September 30, 1968, the world's first 747 Jumbo Jet rolled out of Boeing's Everett plant in Seattle, Washington. It was hailed as the future of commercial air travel, complete with fine dining, live piano music and glamorous stewardesses. And perhaps we might still be living in that future, were it not for the 1978 Airline Deregulation Act signed into law by President Jimmy Carter.
>
> Deregulation was meant to increase the competitiveness of the airlines, while giving passengers more choice about the prices they paid. It succeeded in greatly expanding the accessibility of air travel, but at the price of making it a far less luxurious experience. Today, flying is a matter of "calculated misery," as Columbia Law School professor Tim Wu put it in a 2014 article in the New Yorker. Airlines deliberately make travel unpleasant in order to force economy passengers to pay extra for things that were once considered standard, like food and blankets.
>
> *Amanda Foreman, The Miseries of Travel, WALL ST. J., Sept. 22–23, 2018.*

A. OVERVIEW

While Chapter 7, *infra*, discusses the laws and regulations governing the rights of airline passengers in specific matters such as ticketing, delays, and baggage delivery, this chapter aims to present the legal authorities related to broader policy issues of passengers' rights under the Airline Deregulation Act of 1978, including consumer protection statutes (*Morales v. Trans World Airlines, Inc.*) and laws designed to re-regulate the industry (*e.g.,* Passengers' Bill of Rights and *Air Transport Ass'n of America v. Cuomo*).

A theme that will become quite clear to the reader is how few rights airline passengers actually enjoy and how apparently challenging interpreting the Airline Deregulation Act of 1978 can be for courts in matters of tort (*e.g.*, *Hodges v. Delta Airlines, Inc.*, *Witty v. Delta Air Lines, Inc.*, and *Charas v. Trans World Airlines, Inc.*) and contract (*American Airlines, Inc. v. Wolens* and *Northwest, Inc. v. Ginsberg*).

In reading the cases and materials that follow, consider whether the legacy of deregulation is positive, and if so, for whom (*e.g.* carrier or passengers). Consider, too, how to reconcile the interpretive splits of authority as to what airline "prices, routes, and services" legislators intended to prohibit states from regulating.

But first, read the two articles below (the first published in 1983 and the second in 2011) and query whether the law effects and impedes the business objectives of the Airline Deregulation Act and how, if at all, the law should be modified to achieve maximum reliance on competitive market forces that would best further efficiency, innovation, and low prices as well as variety and quality of air transportation services. Also, before evaluating the legacy of the Airline Deregulation Act, some background is important:

The origin of modern airline travel is traceable to the delivery of "airmail service," which began on Long Island, New York on September 23, 1911 on an experimental basis. Experience with airmail operations gave rise to important developments that would eventually support the safe carriage of passengers, including night flying, instrument flying, meteorological service, hard surface runways, radio communications, and multi-engine airplanes.

By the late 1920s, the use of airplanes to deliver mail was reliable and "airlines" bid competitively for contract airmail routes ("CAMs") pursuant to the Airmail Act of 1925, Pub. L. No. 68–359, 43 Stat. 805 (1925) ("Kelly Act"), An Act to Encourage Commercial Aviation and to Authorize the Postmaster General to Contract for the Mail Service."

Around the same time, Congress passed the Air Commerce Act of 1926, Pub. L. No. 69–254, 44 Stat. 568 (1926), creating a substantial role for the federal government to promote air commerce and safety (*e.g.*, aircraft registration and licensing, and pilot medical certification).

Figure 6-1. Airmail Act of 1935 (Kelly Act)

H.R. 7064 (The Kelly Act) *An act to encourage commercial aviation and to authorize the Postmaster General to contract for Air Mail Service.*

Be it enacted, etc., That this act may be cited as the Air Mail Act.

Sec. 2. That when used in this act the term "air mail" means first-class mail prepaid at the rates of postage herein prescribed.

Sec. 3. That the rates of postage on air mail shall be not less than 10 cents for each ounce or fraction thereof.

Sec. 4. That the Postmaster General is authorized to contract with any individual, firm, or corporation for the transportation of air mail by aircraft between such points as he may designate at a rate not to exceed four fifths of the revenues derived from such air mail, and to further contract for the transportation by aircraft of first-class mail other than air mail at a rate not to exceed four fifths of the revenues derived from such first-class mail.

Sec. 5. That the Postmaster General may make such rules, regulations, and orders as may be necessary to carry out the provisions of this act: *Provided,* That nothing in this act shall be construed to interfere with the postage charged or to be charged on Government operated air-mail routes.

Approved, February 2, 1925.

Source: https://en.wikipedia.org/wiki/Airmails_of_the_United_States#/media/File:HR7064.jpg or Here: https://commons.wikimedia.org/wiki/File:HR7064.jpg

In 1930, Congress enacted the Airmail Act of 1930 ("McNary-Watres Act"), which compensated airlines for airmail service on the basis of space instead of weight—an incentive that encouraged the use of aircraft suitable for commercial passenger purposes, not merely mail delivery. The 1930s legislation was favored by Postmaster General Walter Brown, a November 1928 political appointee of President Herbert Hoover. Brown aggressively sought the formation of a national, market-driven, federally regulated airline transportation system. Brown commanded great regulatory powers under the McNary-Watres Act through which

[r]oute certificates were promptly issued on several routes; numerous extensions were granted; routes were consolidated; several carriers were required to carry passengers; new schedules were authorized, partly with an eye to passenger needs; and mail rates were increased to help meet the costs incurred in the transition to passenger service. An elaborate rate formula was established, providing for "variables" in rates, based primarily on amount of mail space reserved in the plane, and taking into account the flying conditions over the particular route, equipment used, and passenger capacity furnished.

See Frederick A. Ballard, *Federal Regulation of Aviation*, 60 HARV. L. REV. 1235, 1245–48 (1947). The "Great Depression" and the election of Franklin D. Roosevelt cast doubt on Brown's conduct, however.

A congressional committee led by Hugo Black, an Alabama Senator and future Justice of the Supreme Court of the United States, suggested that Brown and several airlines were colluding to end-run the competitive bidding process used to award airmail routes under then-applicable airmail and commerce laws. *See generally* Comment, *Merger and Monopoly in Domestic Aviation*, 62 COLUM. L. REV. 851, 854–55 (1962).

Illustration 6-1. Contract Air Mail Routes

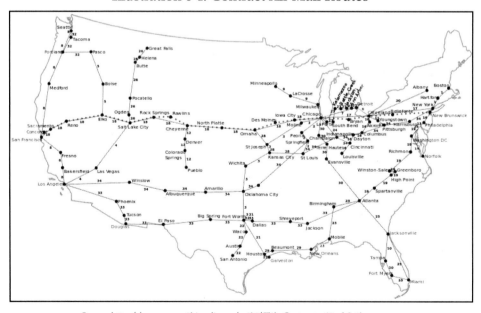

Source: https://commons.wikimedia.org/wiki/File:Contract_Air_Mail_routes.svg

In response, President Roosevelt ordered cancellation of all domestic airmail contracts and directed the army to transport airmail. *See* Exec. Order No. 6591,

Feb. 9, 1934. In contrast to more experienced airline pilots equipped to fly in day and night and variant weather conditions, pilots in the Air Corps were tragically underprepared. And, in fact the decision to use the Air Corps was disastrous, resulting in 66 crashes, 12 deaths, and government costs approaching $4 million; President Roosevelt ordered the Army to cease flying the airmail after only six months of operation. *See, e.g.*, ROBERT M. KANE, AIR TRANSPORTATION 110–11 (13th ed. Kendall/Hunt Publishing Co. 1999); *Civil Aeronautics Board Policy: An Evaluation*, 57 YALE L.J. 1053 (1948).

Enactment of the Airmail Act of 1934 ("Black-McKellar Act"), 48 Stat. 933 (1934), reestablished private air carriage and a comprehensive system of federal aviation regulation was introduced soon thereafter through the Civil Aeronautics Act of 1938 ("McCarran-Lea Act"), 52 Stat. 973 (1938). By 1936, airline revenue from passenger traffic exceeded airmail income.

Illustration 6-2. Seal of Civil Aeronautics Board ("CAB")

Source: https://commons.wikimedia.org/wiki/File:Civil_Aeronautics_Board_seal.svg

In 1938, Congress created the Civil Aeronautics Board ("CAB") to regulate interstate air transportation as a public utility. This meant that the CAB—not carriers themselves—established the rates airlines could charge and the routes airlines could fly. This framework was thought necessary to insulate the fledgling airline industry from the destructive competitive forces at work in other, more mature, sectors of the national economy. As a result, from 1938 to 1978, the U.S. airline industry essentially consisted of an oligopoly or cartel of four carriers.

Industrywide regulation of the U.S. airline industry began in 1938 in response to congressional concern over safety, airlines' financial health, and perceived inequities between airlines and other regulated forms of transportation. The Civil Aeronautics Act of 1938 (P.L. 706) applied to interstate operations of U.S. airlines and gave the Civil Aeronautics Authority, redesignated as the Civil Aeronautics Board ("CAB") in 1940, authority to regulate which airlines operated on each route and what fares they could charge. Airlines could not add or abandon routes or change fares without CAB approval.

CAB also limited the number of airlines in the industry. In 1938, the interstate U.S. airline industry consisted of 16 "trunk" airlines, but this number contracted to 10 by 1974, despite 79 applications from new airlines to initiate service. Competition was limited on a route to one airline unless the CAB determined that demand was sufficient to support an additional airline. Airfares were based on a complex cost-based formula used by the CAB, though the exact formulas and process varied over the life of the CAB. Generally, though, airlines during this time had little incentive to reduce costs, since each was assured a fixed rate of return. As a result, the competition that existed among airlines was largely based on the quality of service. Airlines operated largely a point-to-point system, more similar to railroads than the airline networks that we know today.

U.S. GEN. ACCOUNTING OFFICE, GAO–06–630, *Airline Deregulation: Reregulating the Airline Industry Would Likely Reverse Consumer Benefits and Not Save Airline Pensions* (2006). While CAB governance ostensibly insulated airlines from competition, its bureaucratic ways presented other difficulties. For example, Continental Airlines only began non-stop service between Denver and San Diego after more than eight years of administrative proceedings and a decision by the United States Court of Appeals for the District of Columbia requiring the CAB to approve service on the route. *See Continental Air Lines, Inc. v. Civil Aeronautics Bd.*, 519 F.2d 944 (D.C. Cir. 1975).

Perhaps unsurprisingly, then, deregulatory impulses in the late 1970s overtook the 40-year cartel-like operation of airlines under the CAB. In 1974, Senator Edward M. Kennedy (D-Mass.), then-Chair of the Senate Subcommittee on Administrative Practice and Procedure of the Committee on the Judiciary, set out to investigate the CAB's regulation. Senator Kennedy sought the advice of (eventual United States Supreme Court Justice) Stephen Breyer, a Harvard Law School professor, who was retained to head the subcommittee. (*See Airline Deregulation, Revisited, infra.*) President Jimmy Carter, meanwhile, had appointed Cornell economist Alfred Kahn—sometimes referred to as the "Father of Airline

Deregulations"—to the chairmanship of the CAB. Ultimately, on October 24, 1978, President Carter signed into law the Airline Deregulation Act. Originally introduced by Senator Howard W. Cannon (D. Nev.), the act, by amending the Federal Aviation Act of 1958, freed the airlines of federal regulation, and allowed, by-and-large, a market-driven commercial aviation system:

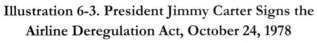

**Illustration 6-3. President Jimmy Carter Signs the
Airline Deregulation Act, October 24, 1978**

Source: https://commons.wikimedia.org/wiki/File:AirlineDeregulationAct.png

The Airline Deregulation Act phased out federal control over airline pricing and routes. Airline deregulation was premised on an expectation that an unregulated industry would attract entry and increase competition among airlines, thereby benefiting consumers with lower fares and improved service. The experience of unregulated (*i.e.*, state-regulated) intrastate service in Texas and California provided support for this expectation. Moreover, prior to deregulation, industry analysts—on the basis of conventional economic reasoning—expected that opportunities for increased competition would increase the number of airlines operating in many markets, thereby lowering fares and expanding service.

> The Airline Deregulation Act established specific goals of encouraging competition by attracting new entrant airlines and allowing existing airlines to expand. According to the act, competition was expected to lower fares and expand service, the chief aims of deregulation.

U.S. GEN. ACCOUNTING OFFICE, GAO–06–630, *Airline Deregulation: Reregulating the Airline Industry Would Likely Reverse Consumer Benefits and Not Save Airline Pensions* (2006) (noting that, "[a]long with the airline industry, Congress deregulated rail, trucking, and telecommunications to induce competition and thereby lower fares. In only a few cases, and in fairly narrow circumstances, has a deregulated industry been reregulated. For example, following cable television's deregulation, Congress established rate ceilings in cities that lacked sufficient competition.").

---

49 U.S.C. § 41713 (2018)

Preemption of Authority over Prices, Routes, and Service

Preemption. Except as provided in this subsection, a State, political subdivision of a State, or political authority of at least 2 States may not enact or enforce a law, regulation, or other provision having the force and effect of law related to a price, route, or service of an air carrier that may provide air transportation under this subpart.

To an extent, the Airline Deregulation Act of 1978 benefitted consumers as airlines—including low cost carriers such as Southwest Airlines and PEOPLExpress—set their own prices, routes, and services. Airline travel became routine, accessible, and less expensive on an almost yearly basis thanks to episodic "fare wars."

Figure 6-2. Annual U.S. Domestic Average Itinerary Fare (1995–2018)

Annual U.S. Domestic Average Itinerary Fare in Current and Constant Dollars

BTS reports average fares based on domestic itinerary fares. Itinerary fares consist of round-trip fares, unless the customer does not purchase a return trip. In that case, the one-way fare is included. Fares are based on the total ticket value, which consists of the price charged by the airlines plus any additional taxes and fees levied by an outside entity at the time of purchase. Fares include only the price paid at the time of the ticket purchase and do not include fees for optional services, such as baggage fees. Averages do not include frequent-flyer or "zero fares." Constant 2018 dollars are used for inflation adjustment.

| | Inflation-Adjusted (2018 constant dollars*) | | | Unadjusted (current dollars) | | |
| | | Percent Change | | | Percent Change | |
Year	Average Fare ($)	From Previous Year (%)	Cumulative from 1995 (%)	Average Fare ($)	From Previous Year (%)	Cumulative from 1995 (%)
1995	477			292		
1996	439	-8.0	-8.0	277	-5.3	-5.3
1997	445	1.5	-6.7	287	3.8	-1.7
1998	472	6.0	-1.1	309	7.6	5.8
1999	484	2.5	1.4	324	4.7	10.8
2000	490	1.3	2.7	339	4.7	16.0
2001	450	-8.0	-5.6	321	-5.4	9.7
2002	432	-4.1	-9.4	312	-2.6	6.9
2003	426	-1.3	-10.6	315	1.0	7.9
2004	402	-5.7	-15.7	305	-3.2	4.5
2005	392	-2.7	-17.9	307	0.6	5.2
2006	405	3.6	-15.0	329	6.9	12.4
2007	390	-3.7	-18.2	325	-1.0	11.3
2008	400	2.6	-16.1	346	6.5	18.5
2009	360	-10.1	-24.5	310	-10.4	6.2
2010	383	6.5	-19.6	336	8.3	15.0
2011	402	4.9	-15.6	364	8.3	24.5
2012	406	0.9	-14.9	375	3.0	28.3
2013	408	0.5	-14.5	382	1.9	30.7
2014	412	0.9	-13.7	392	2.5	34.1
2015	396	-3.9	-17.0	377	-3.8	29.0
2016	362	-8.5	-24.1	349	-7.4	19.5
2017	353	-2.5	-26.0	348	-0.4	19.0
2018	346	-1.8	-27.4	346	-0.3	18.6

SOURCE: Bureau of Transportation Statistics

Source: https://www.bts.gov/content/annual-us-domestic-average-itinerary-fare-current-and-constant-dollars.

Illustration 6-4. Annual U.S. Domestic Average Itinerary Fare, 1995–2018

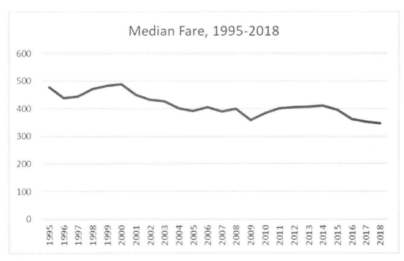

The emergence of low cost or "no frills" carriers such as Frontier Airlines and Spirit Airlines suggests robust competition in the commercial airline industry. But the quality of passenger service has deteriorated significantly since 1978 and the hallmark of deregulation—reduced barriers to entry—has gone largely unfulfilled as the 1980s saw the demise of numerous airlines through bankruptcy reorganization and liquidation (*See generally* U.S. Airlines for America, *Bankruptcies*, http://airlines.org/dataset/u-s-bankruptcies-and-services-cessations/), and arguably predatory marketplace behavior (*see generally United States v. AMR Corp.*, 335 F.3d 1109 (10th Cir. 2003)). In fact, just 40 years since deregulation, four airlines control more than 82% of domestic seats in the U.S. *See* Jack Nicas, *Airline Consolidation Hits Smallest Cities Hardest*, WALL ST. J., Sept. 10, 2015.

In 2015, the Department of Justice launched an investigation into alleged collusion between major airlines to keep ticket prices high. And, in August 2015, consumers had filed 75 lawsuits against airlines around the United States, alleging that the four major airlines conspired to hold down capacity in order to make airfares higher than they would otherwise be. *See* Terry Maxon, *Guess How Many Antitrust Lawsuits Have Been Filed against the Big 4 Airlines (No, More than That—Guess Again)*, DALLAS MORNING NEWS, Aug. 12, 2015. In this retrospective context, the fact that the airline industry did not favor deregulation may be unsurprising: "It was . . . the airlines themselves who invited the government to impose regulation in order to save them from competition, and only United among the then trunk carriers supported deregulation in 1978." *See* Michele McDonald, *Trouble on the Hill; Congress Considers Possible Airline Regulations*, AIR TRANSP. WORLD, June 1, 2001, at 95.

Figure 6-3. Delta Airlines: Opposition to Airline Deregulation

AIRLINE "DEREGULATION": "Wolf In Sheep's Clothing?"

Make no mistake about it. Everybody in the United States will be involved, directly or indirectly. The issue is clear enough, even if it is clouded sometimes by political rhetoric and academic confusion.

The issue is: "Will our nation's system of commercial aviation survive as a vital, private sector industry, serving the public interests?" Believe it or not, that survival could very well be in doubt. To be certain, the "patient," the airline industry, is anything but ill. Nonetheless, it is being dealt a dose of "airline deregulation medicine" by its "friendly deregulation doctors." Friends like that the airlines don't need, because the medicine might kill the patient.

"Wait a minute!" you say. "Why not get the government out of the airline business? Why not return the airlines to free enterprise?"

The theory's good, but the reality won't "wash." The "airline deregulation" bill, proposed by the Senate Commerce Committee, would mean more government regulation of the airlines than ever before.

Why is that so? Well, the core of the problem is the proposal in the Senate bill (sometimes called the Cannon/Kennedy bill) to give the airlines rights of "free entry" into airline markets. This proposal is the core of the more extreme "deregulation" proposals. Three years of debate in the Congress, however, have shown that the "free entry" concept, at least if accompanied by rights of "free exit" as originally proposed, pose some real dangers.

The greatest risk is that no one—in the Congress, the executive Branch of the federal government, or anyplace else—has a crystal ball which will let him foresee the results of experimentation with such an *untested* concept. In this respect, the American traveling and shipping public is being asked to take a tremendous gamble.

The debate has shown, however, that the "free entry" and "free exit" concept could very well result in concentrating the airline industry in the hands of only a few carriers, of causing service deterioration at smaller cities and in smaller markets, and of jeopardizing the financing of airport developments, among other problems.

In order to guard against these types of potential evils in the concept, the Senate has felt it necessary to retreat from the idea of "free exit" rights for airlines (indeed, would virtually eliminate the right for airlines to stop serving any markets), and to include many rigid rules and regulations in the proposed legislation itself and added regulatory responsibilities for the CAB. For example, for the first time the CAB would be given direct control over scheduling in small markets.

As Delta sees it, the Senate's proposal, if passed, would accomplish the very opposite of what it purports. Why "dress" more government regulation in the "clothes" of "deregulation"? Isn't this an attempt to deceive?

Source: https://airandspace.si.edu/exhibitions/america-by-air/online/jetage/jetage08.cfm.
Reproduced with and courtesy of Delta Air Lines.

The advent of "ancillary fees" for checked bags, increased seat space, and even bathroom use also suggests that while air fares are and have been quite low since airline deregulation—they are artificially low. As aviator and United States Bankruptcy Judge (Southern District of Florida) A.J. Cristol observed:

> Yes, we have lower fares on certain routes [but it is] because the airline industry, like the United States Congress, is unable to understand that if you sell your product for less than it costs you, you have a deficit. At the same time, we have astronomical airfares on other routes.
>
> Robert Crandall, the former president and CEO of American Airlines, used to make a speech where he opened up by asking his audience "How much did a Hershey Bar cost in 1945?" Members of the audience would volunteer, "a quarter," "a dime." Crandall would then point out that in 1945 you could buy a Hershey Bar for a nickel. A new Chevrolet could be purchased for $900. Roundtrip airfare from New York to Paris was $700.
>
> Today a Hershey bar is as much as a buck. A new Chevy Camaro is listed out as Chevy $33,600, and roundtrip airfare? New York to Paris can be $500 to $600, sometime less.
>
> Crandall's point is simple . . . Most airfares are too low. Airlines charge too much for first and business class and far too little for coach or economy . . . Each year they continue to lose more and more money and they try to make it up with charges for your suitcase or your seat assignment.
>
> In the irrational airline industry of today, the doctrine is sell your seats at a loss and make it up on volume. A few quarters ago, Delta announced a huge loss. Their solution: Reduce fares . . . and Pricing: It goes from the sublime to the ridiculous.

Hon. A.J. Cristol, United States Bankruptcy Judge, Southern District of Florida, Guest Lecture at the University of Miami School of Law (Sept. 12, 2013).

Hobart Rowen, Airline Deregulation: A Bankrupt Policy

Continental Airlines, the nation's eighth-largest, went belly-up the other day, the second major airline bankruptcy since Congress deregulated the industry in 1978. Labor unions charge that Continental is using the bankruptcy technique to bust the union contract.

Continental is not the only passenger carrier in trouble. Last week, Eastern Airlines appealed to its 37,500 employees to take a pay cut, part of an effort to slim spending by $300 million in 1984. Eastern boss Frank Borman, the former astronaut, is clearly eyeing Continental's initiative of using the courts to force lower pay scales for pilots and all other employees. Western Airlines, also seeking to control costs, is trying to get wage concessions by turning over 25 percent of the ownership of the company to employees. The list grows day by day.

Why are the skies so unfriendly to commercial aviation at a time when the economy seems to be recovering? Only three of the 10 top carriers in the nation are reported to be showing a profit. The answer, as this reporter has suggested on other occasions, is the predatory, cutthroat competition that was encouraged by over-eager deregulators, committed to Adam Smith but ignorant of what goes on in the real world.

When critics cited not only the rash of bankruptcies but the fact that many smaller communities no longer have adequate airline service, deregulators such as former CAB chairman Alfred Kahn shrugged it off: "That's the way the enterprise system works," Kahn says.

In a timely analysis to be published later this year in the Transportation Law Journal, Denver professor Paul Stephen Dempsey demonstrates that the nation was sold a bill of goods by deregulation zealots in the Carter administration. And the failed ideology hasn't been challenged by the Reagan administration.

"Deregulation was portrayed as offering Americans the best of all possible worlds," Dempsey says. The chief villain appears to be Kahn, named by Carter to be chairman of the Civil Aeronautics Board, but he had plenty of support from such liberals as Sen. Ted Kennedy. Kahn, who takes free-market philosophy quite literally, lowered entry barriers into the air passenger business, to encourage vigorous price competition.

With help from Kennedy and others, Carter and Kahn got the Air Cargo Deregulation Act of 1977 and the Airline Deregulation Act of 1978 through Congress. Motor-carrier deregulation was established in 1980, and rules covering railroads were liberalized with the Staggers Rail Act in 1980. In addition to saving consumers $8 billion, airline deregulation was to have other benefits: the industry would become more efficient without the intrusion of those pesky Washington bureaucrats.

When deregulation opponents warned that under an emasculated CAB the carriers could adopt whatever route and market practices they chose, pulling out of many small- and medium-sized markets, the free-marketeers were not impressed. When it was pointed out that fare "wars" create an unfair price structure, with passengers forced to pay much more to fly shorter distances than longer ones, the deregulators brushed off an economic contradiction for which there is no logical explanation. "To (these) arguments," Dempsey says, "they told us this was the way the invisible hand of the marketplace worked."

But as airline service deteriorated under deregulation, did the surviving deregulated airlines make money? Dempsey takes a look at the record: over the past three years, the airline industry has suffered operating losses of more than $1 million a day, or nearly $2 billion overall. The industry's debt has ballooned to 70 percent of capital.

Since the passage of the Airline Deregulation Act of 1978, Continental, Air New England, Braniff, El Al, Laker and 15 other carriers have gone bankrupt. Those in trouble from time to time, apart from those mentioned above, include Pan Am, Air Florida, Republic and World. A normally healthy operation like Delta in 1982 suffered its first deficit in 36 years.

In a way, the airlines are in a position analogous to the Third World countries: if the banks holding their long-term debt (which Dempsey estimates at $10.1 billion for the biggest 16 carriers) demanded timely payment, even more of them would join Continental in bankruptcy court.

Thomas G. Plaskett, vice president of American Airlines, sums it up well: "Deregulation has encouraged the concentration of services on major, dense routes, and this has led to excessive, destructive competition and overcapacity. . . . We find it difficult to reconcile such destructive competition with the overall public interest."

There's the key phrase—the public interest. Transportation is not just any old business. Basically, it's a public utility, which has to be regulated in the public interest. It's time to re-regulate the airlines.

Stephen Breyer, Airline Deregulation, Revisited

Supreme Court Justice Breyer Reflects on the Benefits of Competition—and Its Hazards

Thirty-five years ago this month, Senator Edward Kennedy (D-Mass.) held hearings on the federal government's regulation of the airlines. His primary focus was on fares. Why were they so high? Officials at the Federal Trade Commission believed that regulation itself was the primary reason. The Civil Aeronautics Board had forbidden price competition. The result was service competition instead: empty seats, steak sandwiches, Aloha bars near the galley, and sky-high prices. A business traveler may be pleased to find an empty seat for his briefcase, an FTC official said at the time, but probably doesn't realize he is paying full fare for the briefcase.

The hearings' objective was to determine if creating more competition—in fares and routes—would improve things. The answer seemed to be yes. In California and Texas, where fares were unregulated, they were much lower. The San Francisco-Los Angeles fare was about half that on the comparable, regulated Boston-Washington route. And an intra-Texas airline boasted that the farmers who used to drive across the state could fly for even less money—and it would carry any chicken coops for free.

Although the board, supported by the airlines, tried to find plausible explanations for high fares, it ultimately failed to do so. For example, were high fares on popular routes needed to support air service to small communities? If so, why should a grandmother flying New York-Los Angeles pay more to help the business traveler flying Utica-Albany pay less? Empirical investigation showed the amount of any such cross-subsidy was tiny and could take the form of a direct government transition payment instead.

When an East Boston constituent asked Kennedy, "Senator, why are you holding hearings about airlines? I've never been able to fly," Kennedy replied: "That's why I'm holding the hearings."

The hearings brought together a Democratic senator and a Republican President in Gerald Ford. They created alliances among consumer groups, pro-competition business groups, economists, and regulatory reformers. They helped make the "regulatory reform" issue politically visible. They showed that government regulation, being administered not by angels but by human beings, was itself imperfect. And they gave content to the notion of reform: In some areas where regulation was necessary—such as health, safety, and the environment—reform would mean "smarter" regulation, sometimes relying more heavily on incentives. In other areas of transportation regulation, reform would mean increased reliance on competition, sometimes to the point where government could abandon the effort to control prices.

Pressure from these broad alliances eventually brought change to the airline industry. President Jimmy Carter took up the theme and appointed as chairman of the Civil Aeronautics Board a Cornell economist, Alfred E. Kahn. Kahn knew regulation; he understood government; and he understood human nature. He began to dismantle fare and route controls and he supported deregulatory legislation, which, with the support of Kennedy and Senators Orrin Hatch (R-Utah) and Strom Thurmond (R-S.C.), became law in 1978. (Kahn, age 93, died last month, and was much mourned by all who knew him.)

What does the industry's history tell us? Was this effort worthwhile? Certainly it shows that every major reform brings about new, sometimes unforeseen, problems. No one foresaw the industry's spectacular growth, with the number of air passengers increasing from 207.5 million in 1974 to 721.1 million last year. As a result, no one foresaw the extent to which new bottlenecks would develop: a flight-choked Northeast corridor, overcrowded airports, delays, and terrorist risks consequently making air travel increasingly difficult. Nor did anyone foresee the extent to which change might unfairly harm workers in the industry. Still, fares have come down. Airline revenue per passenger mile has declined from an inflation-adjusted 33.3 cents in 1974, to 13 cents in the first half of 2010. In 1974 the cheapest round-trip New York-Los Angeles flight (in inflation-adjusted dollars) that regulators would allow: $1,442. Today one can fly that same route for $268. That is why the number of travelers has gone way up.

So we sit in crowded planes, munch potato chips, flare up when the loudspeaker announces yet another flight delay. But how many now will vote to go back to the "good old days" of paying high, regulated prices for better service? Even among business travelers, who wants to pay "full fare for the briefcase?"

As an aide to the late Senator Edward Kennedy, Justice Breyer helped pass the Airline Deregulation Act of 1978.

B. CONSUMER PROTECTION STATUTES

MORALES V. TRANS WORLD AIRLINES, INC.
504 U.S. 374 (1992)

JUSTICE SCALIA delivered the opinion of the Court.

The issue in this case is whether the Airline Deregulation Act of 1978, 49 U.S.C. § 1301 *et seq.*, preempts the States from prohibiting allegedly deceptive airline fare advertisements through enforcement of their general consumer protection statutes.

Prior to 1978, the Federal Aviation Act of 1958 ("FAA"), gave the Civil Aeronautics Board ("CAB") authority to regulate interstate airfares and to take administrative action against certain deceptive trade practices. It did not, however, expressly preempt state regulation, and contained a "saving clause" providing that "[n]othing . . . in this chapter shall in any way abridge or alter the remedies now existing at common law or by statute, but the provisions of this chapter are in addition to such remedies." As a result, the States were able to regulate intrastate airfares (including those offered by interstate air carriers), and to enforce their own laws against deceptive trade practices.

Savings Clause, FAA of 1958

In 1978, however, Congress, determining that "maximum reliance on competitive market forces" would best further "efficiency, innovation, and low prices" as well as "variety [and] quality . . . of air transportation services," enacted the Airline Deregulation Act ("ADA"). To ensure that the States would not undo federal deregulation with regulation of their own, the ADA included a preemption provision, prohibiting the States from enforcing any law "relating to rates, routes, or services" of any air carrier.

In 1978, however, Congress, determining that "maximum reliance on competitive market forces" would best further "efficiency, innovation, and low prices" as well as "variety [and] quality . . . of air transportation services," enacted the Airline Deregulation Act ("ADA"). To ensure that the States would not undo federal deregulation with regulation of their own, the ADA included a preemption provision, prohibiting the States from enforcing any law "relating to rates, routes, or services" of any air carrier. The ADA retained the CAB's previous enforcement authority regarding deceptive trade practices (which was transferred to the Department of Transportation ("DOT") when the CAB was abolished in 1985), and it also did not repeal or alter the saving clause in the prior law.

In 1987, the National Association of Attorneys General ("NAAG"), an organization whose membership includes the attorneys general of all 50 States, various Territories, and the District of Columbia, adopted Air Travel Industry Enforcement Guidelines (set forth in an Appendix to this opinion) containing detailed standards governing the content and format of airline advertising, the awarding of premiums to regular customers (so-called "frequent flyers"), and the payment of compensation to passengers who voluntarily yield their seats on overbooked flights. These guidelines do not purport to "create any new laws or regulations" applying to the airline industry; rather, they claim to "explain in detail how existing state laws apply to air fare advertising and frequent flyer programs." NAAG GUIDELINES, INTRODUCTION (1988).

Despite objections to the guidelines by the DOT and the Federal Trade Commission ("FTC") on preemption and policy grounds, the attorneys general of seven States, including petitioner's predecessor as attorney general of Texas, sent a memorandum to the major airlines announcing that "it has come to our attention that although most airlines are making a concerted effort to bring their advertisements into compliance with the standards delineated in the . . . guidelines for fare advertising, many carriers are still [not disclosing all surcharges]" in violation of § 2.5 of the guidelines.

The memorandum said it was the signatories " 'purpose . . . to clarify for the industry as a whole that [this practice] is a violation of our respective state laws on deceptive advertising and trade practices"; warned that this was an "advisory memorandum before [the] initiati[on of] any immediate enforcement actions"; and expressed the hope that "protracted litigation over this issue will not be necessary and that airlines will discontinue the practice . . . immediately." Several months later, petitioner's office sent letters to several respondents serving "as formal notice[s] of intent to sue."

Effect on General State Consumer Protection Law

Those respondents then filed suit in federal district court claiming that state regulation of fare advertisements is preempted by [the ADA]; seeking a declaratory judgment that, *inter alia*, § 2.5 of the guidelines is preempted; and requesting an injunction restraining Texas from taking any action under its law in conjunction with the guidelines that would regulate respondents' rates, routes, or services, or their advertising and marketing of the same. The District Court entered a preliminary injunction to that effect, determining that respondents were likely to prevail on their preemption claim. The Court of Appeals affirmed. Subsequently, the District Court, in an unreported order, permanently enjoined the States from taking "any enforcement action" which would restrict "any aspect" of respondents' fare advertising or operations relating to rates, routes, or services. The Court of Appeals once again affirmed. We granted *certiorari*.

* * *

We now turn to the question whether enforcement of the NAAG guidelines on fare advertising through a State's general consumer protection laws is preempted by the ADA. As we have often observed, "[p]re-emption may be either express or implied, and is compelled whether Congress' command is explicitly stated in the statute's language or implicitly contained in its structure and purpose." The question, at bottom, is one of statutory intent, and we accordingly " 'begin with the language employed by Congress and the assumption that the ordinary meaning of that language accurately expresses the legislative purpose.' " *Park 'N Fly, Inc. v. Dollar Park & Fly, Inc.*, 469 U.S. 189 (1985).

Section 1305(a)(1) expressly preempts the States from "enact[ing] or enforc[ing] any law, rule, regulation, standard, or other provision having the force and effect of law relating to rates, routes, or services of any air carrier . . ." For purposes of the present case, the key phrase, obviously, is "relating to."

The ordinary meaning of these words is a broad one—"to stand in some relation; to have bearing or concern; to pertain; refer; to bring into association with or connection with," BLACK'S LANGUAGE DICTIONARY 1158 (5th ed. 1979)—and the words thus express a broad preemptive purpose. We have repeatedly recognized that in addressing the similarly worded preemption provision of the Employee Retirement Income Security Act of 1974 ("ERISA"), which preempts all state laws "insofar as they . . . relate to any employee benefit plan."

The key phrase, obviously, is "relating to." The ordinary meaning of these words is a broad one—"to stand in some relation; to have bearing or concern; to pertain; refer; to bring into association with or connection with,"—and the words thus express a broad preemptive purpose.

We have said, for example, that the "breadth of [that provision's] preemptive reach is apparent from [its] language," that it has a "broad scope," and an "expansive sweep"; and that it is "broadly worded," "deliberately expansive," and "conspicuous for its breadth." True to our word, we have held that a state law "relates to" an employee benefit plan, and is preempted by ERISA, "if it has a connection with, or reference to, such a plan." Since the relevant language of the ADA is identical, we think it appropriate to adopt the same standard here: State enforcement actions having a connection with or reference to airline "rates, routes, or services" are preempted under 49 U.S.C. § 1305(a)(1).

Petitioner raises a number of objections to this reading, none of which we think is well taken. First, he claims that we may not use our interpretation of identical language in ERISA as a guide, because the sweeping nature of ERISA preemption derives not from the "relates to" language, but from "the wide and inclusive sweep of the comprehensive ERISA scheme," which he asserts the ADA does not have. This argument is flatly contradicted by our ERISA cases, which clearly and unmistakably rely on express preemption principles and a construction of the phrase "relates to."

Petitioner also stresses that the FAA "saving" clause, which preserves "the remedies now existing at common law or by statute," 49 U.S.C. § 1506, is broader than its ERISA counterpart. But it is a commonplace of statutory construction that the specific governs the general, a canon particularly pertinent here, where the "saving" clause is a relic of the pre-ADA/no preemption regime. A general "remedies" saving clause cannot be allowed to supersede the specific substantive preemption provision—unless it be thought that a State having a statute requiring "reasonable rates," and providing remedies against "unreasonable" ones, could actually set air fares. As in *Int'l Paper Co. v. Ouellette*, 479 U.S. 481 (1987), "we do not believe Congress intended to undermine this carefully drawn statute through a general saving clause."

Petitioner contends that § 1305(a)(1) only preempts the States from actually prescribing rates, routes, or services. This simply reads the words "relating to" out of the statute. Had the statute been designed to preempt state law in such a limited fashion, it would have forbidden the States to "regulate rates, routes, and services." Moreover, if the preemption effected by section 1305(a)(1) were such a limited one, no purpose would be served by the very next subsection, which preserves to the States certain proprietary rights over airports. It also bears mention that the rejected Senate bill did contain language that would have produced precisely the result the dissent desires: "No State shall enact any law . . . determining routes, schedules, or rates, fares, or charges in tariffs of . . ."

"Relating to"

The dissent is unperturbed by the full Congress' preference for "relating to" over "determining," because the Conference Report gave "no indication that the conferees thought the House's 'relating to' language would have a broader preemptive scope than the Senate's language,"—which is to say because the Conference Report failed to specify the completely obvious, that "relating to" is broader than "determining." The dissent evidently believes not only that plain statutory language cannot be credited unless specifically explained in legislative history, but also that the apparent import of legislative history cannot be credited unless specifically explained in legislative history.

Next, petitioner advances the notion that only state laws specifically addressed to the airline industry are preempted, whereas the ADA imposes no constraints on laws of general applicability. Besides creating an utterly irrational loophole (there is little reason why state impairment of the federal scheme should be deemed acceptable so long as it is effected by the particularized application of a general statute), this notion similarly ignores the sweep of the "relating to" language. We have consistently rejected this precise argument in our ERISA cases: "[A] state law may 'relate to' a benefit plan, and thereby be preempted, even if the law is not specifically designed to affect such plans, or the effect is only indirect."

Last, the State suggests that preemption is inappropriate when state and federal law are consistent. State and federal law are in fact inconsistent here—the DOT opposes the obligations contained in the guidelines, and Texas law imposes greater liability—but that is beside the point. Nothing in the language of § 1305(a)(1) suggests that its "relating to" preemption is limited to inconsistent state regulation; and once again our ERISA cases have settled the matter: " 'The preemption provision . . . displace[s] all state laws that fall within its sphere, even including state laws that are consistent with ERISA's substantive requirements.' "

It is hardly surprising that petitioner rests most of his case on such strained readings of § 1305(a)(1), rather than contesting whether the NAAG guidelines really "relat[e] to" fares. They quite obviously do. Taking them seriatim: Section 2.1, governing print advertisements of fares, requires "clear and conspicuous disclosure [defined as the lesser of one-third the size of the largest typeface in the ad or ten-point type] of restrictions such as" limited time availability, limitations on refund or exchange rights, time-of-day or day-of-week restrictions, length-of-stay requirements, advance-purchase and round-trip-purchase requirements, variations in fares from or to different airports in the same metropolitan area, limitations on breaks or changes in itinerary, limits on fare availability, and "[a]ny other material restriction on the fare."

Section 2.2 imposes similar, though somewhat less onerous, restrictions on broadcast advertisements of fares; and § 2.3 requires billboard fare ads to state clearly and conspicuously " 'Substantial restrictions apply' " if there are any material restrictions on the fares' availability. The guidelines further mandate that an advertised fare be available in sufficient quantities to "meet reasonably foreseeable demand" on every flight on every day in every market in which the fare is advertised; if the fare will not be available on this basis, the ad must contain a "clear and conspicuous statement of the extent of unavailability." *See* § 2.4.

Section 2.5 requires that the advertised fare include all taxes and surcharges; round-trip fares, under § 2.6, must be disclosed at least as prominently as the one-way fare when the fare is only available on round trips; and § 2.7 prohibits use of the words " 'sale,' 'discount,' [or] 'reduced' " unless the advertised fare is available only for a limited time and is "substantially below the usual price for the same fare with the same restrictions."

One cannot avoid the conclusion that these aspects of the guidelines "relate to" airline rates. In its terms, every one of the guidelines enumerated above bears a "reference to" airfares. And, collectively, the guidelines establish binding requirements as to how tickets may be marketed if they are to be sold at given prices. Under Texas law, many violations of these requirements would give consumers a cause of action for an airline's failure to provide a particular advertised fare—effectively creating an enforceable right to that fare when the advertisement fails to include the mandated explanations and disclaimers. This case therefore appears to us much like *Pilot Life Ins. Co. v. Dedeaux*, 481 U.S. 41 (1987), in which we held that a common-law tort and contract action seeking damages for the failure of an employee benefit plan to pay benefits "related to" employee benefit plans and was preempted by ERISA.

> *In any event, beyond the guidelines' express reference to fares, it is clear as an economic matter that state restrictions on fare advertising have the forbidden significant effect upon fares.*

Forbidden Significant Effect

In any event, beyond the guidelines' express reference to fares, it is clear as an economic matter that state restrictions on fare advertising have the forbidden significant effect upon fares. Advertising "serves to inform the public of the . . . prices of products and services, and thus performs an indispensable role in the allocation of resources." *Bates v. State Bar of Arizona*, 433 U.S. 350 (1977). Restrictions on advertising "serve to increase the difficulty of discovering the lowest cost seller . . . and [reduce] the incentive to price competitively." Accordingly, "where consumers have the benefit of price advertising, retail prices often are dramatically lower than they would be without advertising." As Judge Easterbrook succinctly put it, compelling or restricting "[p]rice advertising surely 'relates to' price." *Illinois Corporate Travel v. American Airlines, Inc.*, 889 F.2d 751 (7th Cir. 1989).

Although the State insists that it is not compelling or restricting advertising, but is instead merely preventing the market distortion caused by "false" advertising, in fact the dynamics of the air transportation industry cause the guidelines to curtail the airlines' ability to communicate fares to their customers. The expenses involved in operating an airline flight are almost entirely fixed costs; they increase very little with each additional passenger. The market for these flights is divided between consumers whose volume of purchases is relatively insensitive to price (primarily business travelers) and consumers whose demand is very price sensitive indeed (primarily pleasure travelers). Accordingly, airlines try to sell as many seats per flight as possible at higher prices to the first group, and then to fill up the flight by selling seats at much lower prices to the second group (since almost all the costs are fixed, even a passenger paying far below average cost is preferable to an empty seat). In order for this marketing process to work, and for it ultimately to redound to the benefit of price-conscious travelers, the airlines must be able to place substantial restrictions on the availability of the lower priced seats (so as to sell as many seats as possible at the higher rate), and must be able to advertise the lower fares.

The guidelines severely burden their ability to do both at the same time: The sections requiring "clear and conspicuous disclosure" of each restriction make it impossible to take out small or short ads, as does (to a lesser extent) the provision requiring itemization of both the one-way and round-trip fares. Since taxes and surcharges vary from State to State, the requirement that advertised fares include those charges forces the airlines to create different ads in each market. The section restricting the use of "sale," "discount," or "reduced" effectively prevents the airlines from using those terms to call attention to the fares normally offered to price-conscious travelers. As the FTC observed, "[r]equiring too much information in advertisements can have the paradoxical effect of stifling the information that consumers receive." Further, § 2.4, by allowing fares to be advertised only if sufficient seats are available to meet demand or if the extent of unavailability is disclosed, may make it impossible to use this marketing process at all.

All in all, the obligations imposed by the guidelines would have a significant impact upon the airlines' ability to market their product, and hence a significant impact upon the fares they charge. In concluding that the NAAG fare advertising guidelines are preempted, we do not, as Texas contends, set out on a road that leads to preemption of state laws against gambling and prostitution as applied to airlines. Nor need we address whether state regulation of the nonprice aspects of

Significant Impact

fare advertising (for example, state laws preventing obscene depictions) would similarly "relat[e] to" rates; the connection would obviously be far more tenuous.

All in all, the obligations imposed by the guidelines would have a significant impact upon the airlines' ability to market their product, and hence a significant impact upon the fares they charge.

Finally, we note that our decision does not give the airlines carte blanche to lie to and deceive consumers; the DOT retains the power to prohibit advertisements which in its opinion do not further competitive pricing, see 49 U.S.C. § 1381. We hold that the fare advertising provisions of the NAAG guidelines are preempted by the ADA, and affirm the judgment of the Court of Appeals insofar as it awarded injunctive and declaratory relief with respect to those provisions. Insofar as that judgment awarded injunctive relief directed at other matters, it is reversed and the injunction vacated.

JUSTICE STEVENS, *with whom* THE CHIEF JUSTICE *and* JUSTICE BLACKMUN *join, dissenting.*

Although I agree that the plain language of § 105(a) preempts any state law that relates directly to rates, routes, or services, the presumption against preemption of traditional state regulation counsels that we not interpret § 105(a) to preempt every traditional state regulation that might have some indirect connection with, or relationship to, airline rates, routes, or services unless there is some indication that Congress intended that result. To determine whether Congress had such an intent, I believe that a consideration of the history and structure of the ADA is more illuminating than a narrow focus on the words "relating to."

In 1938 Congress enacted two statutes that are relevant to today's inquiry. In March it broadened § 5 of the Federal Trade Commission Act by giving the Commission the power to prohibit "unfair or deceptive acts or practices in commerce" as well as "[u]nfair methods of competition in commerce." Three months later it enacted the Civil Aeronautics Act of 1938. That statute created the Civil Aeronautics Board and mandated that it regulate entry into the interstate airline industry, the routes that airlines could fly, and the fares that they could charge consumers. Moreover, the statute contained a provision, patterned after § 5 of the FTCA, giving the Civil Aeronautics Board the power to prohibit "unfair or deceptive practices or unfair methods of competition in air transportation." But the Board's power in this regard was not exclusive, for the statute also contained a "saving clause" that preserved existing common-law and statutory remedies for deceptive practices.

Although the 1938 Act was replaced by a similar regulatory scheme in 1958, the principal provisions of the statute remained in effect until 1978. In that year, Congress decided to withdraw economic regulation of interstate airline rates, routes, and services. Congress therefore enacted the ADA "to encourage, develop, and attain an air transportation system which relies on competitive market forces to determine the quality, variety, and price of air services." Because that goal would obviously have been frustrated if state regulations were substituted for the recently removed federal regulations, Congress thought it necessary to preempt such state regulation. Consequently, Congress enacted § 105(a) of the Act, which preempts any state regulation "relating to rates, routes, or services of any air carrier having authority under subchapter IV of this chapter to provide air transportation."

At the same time, Congress retained § 411, which gave the Civil Aeronautics Board the power to prohibit "unfair or deceptive practices or unfair methods of competition in air transportation." Congress also retained the saving clause that preserved common-law and statutory remedies for fraudulent and deceptive practices. Moreover, the state prohibitions against deceptive practices that had coexisted with federal regulation in the airline industry for 40 years, and had coexisted with federal regulation of unfair trade practices in other areas of the economy since 1914, were not mentioned in either the ADA or its legislative history.

> *Congress also retained the saving clause that preserved common-law and statutory remedies for fraudulent and deceptive practices. Moreover, the state prohibitions against deceptive practices that had coexisted with federal regulation in the airline industry for 40 years, and had coexisted with federal regulation of unfair trade practices in other areas of the economy since 1914, were not mentioned in either the ADA or its legislative history.*

Because the Department of Transportation has authority to prohibit unfair or deceptive practices and unfair methods of competition in air transportation, 49 U.S.C. § 1381, it, too, could promulgate regulations that would preempt inconsistent state laws and regulations. But the Court does not rest its holding on the fact that the state prohibitions of unfair and deceptive advertising conflict with federal regulations; instead, it relies on the much broader holding that the ADA itself preempts state prohibitions of deceptive advertising.

In short, there is no indication that Congress intended to exempt airlines from state prohibitions of deceptive advertising. Instead, this history suggests that the scope of the prohibition of state regulation should be measured by the scope of the federal regulation that was being withdrawn. This is essentially the position adopted by the Civil Aeronautics Board, which interpreted the scope of § 105 in light of its two underlying policies—to prevent state economic regulation from frustrating the benefits of federal deregulation, and to clarify the confusion under the prior law which permitted some dual state and federal regulation of the rates and routes of the same carrier. The Board thus explained:

> Section 105 forbids state regulation of a federally authorized carrier's routes, rates, or services. Clearly, states may not interfere with a federal carrier's decision on how much to charge or which markets to serve . . . Similarly, a state may not interfere with the services that carriers offer in exchange for their rates.

> Accordingly, we conclude that preemption extends to all of the economic factors that go into the provision of the *quid pro quo* for passenger's fare, including flight frequency and timing, liability limits, reservation and boarding practices, insurance, smoking rules, meal service, entertainment, bonding and corporate financing.

See also John W. Freeman, *State Regulation of Airlines and the Airline Deregulation Act of 1978*, 44 J. AIR L. & COM. 747, 766–67 (1979).

Because Congress did not eliminate federal regulation of unfair or deceptive practices, and because state and federal prohibitions of unfair or deceptive practices had coexisted during the period of federal regulation, there is no reason to believe that Congress intended § 105(a) to immunize the airlines from state liability for engaging in deceptive or misleading advertising.

* * *

The Court finds in Congress' choice of the words "relating to" an intent to adopt a broad preemption provision, analogous to the broad ERISA preemption provision. The legislative history does not support that assumption, however.

The bill proposed by the Civil Aeronautics Board provided that "[n]o State . . . shall enact any law . . . relating to rates, routes, or services in air transportation." *Hearings on H.R. 8813 before the Subcommittee on Aviation of the House Committee on Public Works and Transportation*, 95th Cong., 1st Sess., pt. 1, p. 200 (1977). Yet the Board's accompanying prepared testimony neither focused on the "relating to" language nor suggested that those words were intended to effect a broad scope of preemption; instead, the testimony explained that the preemption section was "added to make clear that no state or political subdivision may defeat the purposes of the bill by regulating interstate air transportation. This provision represents simply a codification of existing law and leaves unimpaired the states' authority over intrastate matters."

The "relating to" language in the bill that was finally enacted by Congress came from the House bill. But the House Committee Report—like the Civil Aeronautics Board—did not describe the preemption provision in the broad terms adopted by the Court today; instead, the Report described the scope of the preemption provision more narrowly, saying that it "provid[ed] that when a carrier operates under authority granted pursuant to title IV of the Federal Aviation Act, no State may regulate that carrier's routes, rates or services." U.S. CODE CONG. & ADMIN. NEWS, p. 3752. The preemption section in the Senate bill, on the other hand, did not contain the "relating to" language. That bill provided, "[n]o State shall enact any law, establish any standard determining routes, schedules, or rates, fares, or charges in tariffs of, or otherwise promulgate economic regulations for, any air carrier . . ." S. 2493, § 423(a)(1), *reprinted in* S. Rep. No. 95–631, p. 39 (1978). The Senate Report explained that this section "prohibits States from exercising economic regulatory control over interstate airlines."

The Conference Report explained that the Conference adopted the House bill (with an exception not relevant here), which it described in the more narrow terms used in the House Report. H.R. Conf. Rep. No. 95–1779, pp. 94–95 (1978). There is, therefore, no indication that the conferees thought the House's "relating to" language would have a broader preemptive scope than the Senate's "determining . . . or otherwise promulgate economic regulation" language. Nor is there any indication that the House and conferees thought that the preemption of state laws "relating to rates, routes, or services" preempted substantially more than state laws "regulating rates, routes, or services."

* * *

Even if I were to agree with the Court that state regulation of deceptive advertising could "relat[e] to rates" within the meaning of § 105(a) if it had a "significant impact" upon rates, I would still dissent.

The airlines' theoretical arguments have not persuaded me that the NAAG guidelines will have a significant impact upon the price of airline tickets. The airlines' argument (which the Court adopts) is essentially that (1) airlines must engage in price discrimination in order to compete and operate efficiently; (2) a modest amount of misleading price advertising may facilitate that practice; (3) thus compliance with the NAAG guidelines might increase the cost of price advertising or reduce the sales generated by the advertisements; (4) as the costs increase and revenues decrease, the airlines might purchase less price advertising; and (5) a reduction in price advertising might cause a reduction in price competition, which, in turn, might result in higher airline rates. This argument is not supported by any legislative or judicial findings.

Even on the assumption that the Court's economic reasoning is sound and restrictions on price advertising could affect rates in this manner, the airlines have not sustained their burden of proving that compliance with the NAAG guidelines would have a "significant" effect on their ability to market their product and, therefore, on their rates. Surely Congress could not have intended to preempt every state and local law and regulation that similarly increases the airlines' costs of doing business and, consequently, has a similar "significant impact" upon their rates. For these reasons, I respectfully dissent.

EXERCISE 6-1. *MORALES V. TRANS WORLD AIRLINES, INC.*— FORBIDDEN SIGNIFICANT EFFECT ON AIRLINE FARES

1. Describe the intent and objective of Congress in enacting the Airline Deregulation Act of 1978.

2. What does Section 2.5 of the National Association of Attorneys General Task Force on the Air Travel Industry, Revised Guidelines, state?

3. What state action does Section 1305(a)(1) of the Airline Deregulation Act "preempt"? Explain what "preemption" means in this context.

4. Explain what Justice Scalia may mean when stating that "state restrictions on fare advertising have the forbidden significant effect upon fares."

5. Summarize the dissenting opinion's discussion of the "relating to" language in the Airline Deregulation Act.

NOTES ON *MORALES V. TRANS WORLD AIRLINES, INC.*— MECHANISM AND LINKAGE QUESTIONS

At the center of disputes arising under the Airline Deregulation Act of 1978 is whether a claim "relates to" an airline's price, route, or service, with the overwhelming majority of cases focusing on the meaning of "service."

Tobin v. Federal Express Corp., 775 F.3d 448 (1st Cir. 2014), presents a helpful analytical framework that breaks preemption analysis into two questions—a mechanism question and a linkage question. *Tobin* is also striking in that it show just how far beyond traditional airline claims preemption cases under the Airline Deregulation Act go.

In *Tobin*, a federal court considered whether the Airline Deregulation Act of 1978 preempted common law claims of general negligence and intentional and negligent infliction of emotional distress at the summary judgment phase of trial. The case specifically arose from the incorrect delivery of a package containing marijuana, which was opened by an eleven-year-old girl. The girl's mother called the police, who in turn asked FedEx to flag the shipment and refrain from disclosing any information regarding the delivery address to anyone who might inquire about the package. On the same day, the intended recipient called FedEx to inquire about the status of the package. FedEx initiated a "trace."

Meanwhile, a man came to the unintended recipient's door asked whether she had received a package. The visitor's car was parked in the plaintiff's driveway with two men seated inside. Terrified, the plaintiff slammed the door shut and again contacted the police. In the aftermath of these events, the plaintiff and her minor daughter suffered fear and anxiety and manifested a range of symptoms. She bought suit, alleging that FedEx was responsible not only for mislabeling and misdelivering the package but also for wrongfully disclosing her address to the sender or intended recipient. FedEx, classified as a regulated air carrier under law, moved for summary judgment on grounds of preemption.

The First Circuit Court of Appeals agreed, framing the litigation in terms of two questions: (1) a "mechanism question," i.e., whether the claim was predicated on a law, regulation, or other provision having the force and effect of law; and if so, (2) a "linkage question," whether the claim is sufficiently "related to" an air carrier's prices, routes, or services to warrant preemption. The court found the "mechanism question" was "easily answered. The Supreme Court has made it pellucid that state common-law causes of action are provisions that have the force and effect of law for purposes of preemption under the Airline Deregulation Act.

Next, turning to the "linkage question," the court determined that FedEx's "services" were implicated and that the plaintiff's claims "related to" such services. Accordingly, they were barred as a matter of law:

> Stripped of rhetorical flourishes, the plaintiff's common-law claims all depend on FedEx's mislabeling and misdelivery of the package. In other words, they are claims about FedEx's package handling, address verification, and delivery procedures. Package handling, address verification, and package delivery plainly concern the contractual arrangement between FedEx and the users of its services (those who send

packages). Thus, they are necessary appurtenances of the contract of carriage. Seen in this light, Rowe leads inexorably to the conclusion that the plaintiff's claims implicate FedEx's services.

* * *

Having established that the plaintiff's claims implicate FedEx's services, we next must consider whether the plaintiff's claims are sufficiently "related to" those services to warrant preemption under the [Airline Deregulation Act ("ADA")]. The Supreme Court has instructed that the "related to" language of the ADA is meant to be construed broadly, consistent with Congress's intention that ADA preemption should have an expansive reach.

Thus, a state law claim having "connection with, or reference to," an airline's prices, routes, or services is preempted. That connection, however, cannot be de minimis—the challenged law must have a "forbidden significant effect" on prices, routes, or services in order to fall under the ADA's protective carapace. If the connection to an airline's prices, routes, and services is "tenuous, remote, or peripheral," preemption will not attach.

Against this background, is preemption just insofar as it might deprive private litigants of the proverbial day in court? Is preemption just insofar as it might require corporate litigants to defend themselves against creative, but ultimately unsuccessful lawsuits?

AIR TRANSPORT ASS'N OF AMERICA V. CUOMO

520 F.3d 218 (2d Cir. 2008)

PER CURIAM.

Appellant Air Transport Association of America ("Air Transport"), the principal trade and service organization of the United States airline industry, appeals from an order of the United States District Court for the Northern District of New York granting summary judgment to Appellees and dismissing its complaint seeking declaratory and injunctive relief against enforcement of the New York State Passenger Bill of Rights (the "PBR"). We hold that the PBR is preempted by the express preemption provision of the Airline Deregulation Act of 1978 (the "ADA") and therefore reverse.

Airline Passenger Bill of Rights

Following a series of well-publicized incidents during the winter of 2006–'07 in which airline passengers endured lengthy delays grounded on New York runways, some without being provided water or food, the New York legislature enacted the PBR. The substantive provisions of the PBR state as follows:

Whenever airline passengers have boarded an aircraft and are delayed more than three hours on the aircraft prior to takeoff, the carrier shall ensure that passengers are provided as needed with: (a) electric generation service to provide temporary power for fresh air and lights; (b) waste removal service in order to service the holding tanks for on-board restrooms; and (c) adequate food and drinking water and other refreshments.

N.Y. Gen. Bus. Law § 251–g(1). Taking effect on January 1, 2008, the law also requires all carriers to display consumer complaint contact information and an explanation of these rights.

Air Transport filed suit in the United States District Court for the Northern District of New York seeking declaratory and injunctive relief on the grounds that the PBR is preempted by the ADA and violates the Commerce Clause of the U.S. Constitution. Appellant Air Transport moved for summary judgment, and the district court granted summary judgment *sua sponte* to the appellees, holding that the PBR was not expressly preempted by the ADA because it is not "related to a price, route, or service of an air carrier" and was not impliedly preempted because Congress did not intend for the ADA to occupy the field of airplane safety. We granted Air Transport's motion for an expedited appeal.

Air Transport's complaint asserts a claim under the Supremacy Clause and a claim that the PBR violates § 41713(b)(1). Importantly, Section 41713(b)(1) does not provide an express private right of action, and we have held with regard to its predecessor statute, which is substantively identical, that no private right of action can be implied. *Western Air Lines, Inc. v. Port Auth. of N.Y. & N.J.*, 817 F.2d 222 (2d Cir. 1987). Air Transport therefore cannot sue for a violation of the statute.

Nevertheless, Air Transport is entitled to pursue its preemption challenge through its Supremacy Clause claim. The distinction between a statutory claim and a Supremacy Clause claim, although seemingly without a difference in this particular context, is important and is not a trifling formalism:

Supremacy Clause

A claim under the Supremacy Clause that a federal law preempts a state regulation is distinct from a claim for enforcement of that federal law . . . A claim under the Supremacy Clause simply asserts that a federal statute has taken away local authority to regulate a certain activity. In contrast, an implied private right of action is a means of enforcing the substantive provisions of a federal law. It provides remedies, frequently including damages, for violations of federal law by a government entity or by a private party. The mere coincidence that the federal law in question in this case contains its own preemption language does not affect this distinction.

Congress enacted the ADA in 1978, loosening its economic regulation of the airline industry after determining that " 'maximum reliance on competitive market forces' would best further 'efficiency, innovation, and low prices' as well as 'variety [and] quality . . . of air transportation.' " Recognizing this goal, the Supreme Court has repeatedly emphasized the breadth of the ADA's preemption provision. *See American Airlines, Inc. v. Wolens*, 513 U.S. 219 (1995).

> *Although this Court has not yet defined "service" as it is used in the ADA, we have little difficulty concluding that requiring airlines to provide food, water, electricity, and restrooms to passengers during lengthy ground delays relates to the service of an air carrier.*

Although this Court has not yet defined "service" as it is used in the ADA, we have little difficulty concluding that requiring airlines to provide food, water, electricity, and restrooms to passengers during lengthy ground delays relates to the service of an air carrier.

Matter of First Impression

A majority of the circuits to have construed "service" have held that the term refers to the provision or anticipated provision of labor from the airline to its passengers and encompasses matters such as boarding procedures, baggage handling, and food and drink—matters incidental to and distinct from the actual transportation of passengers. The Third and Ninth Circuits, in contrast, have construed service to refer more narrowly to "the prices, schedules, origins and destinations of the point-to-point transportation of passengers, cargo, or mail," but not to "include an airline's provision of in-flight beverages, personal assistance to passengers, the handling of luggage, and similar amenities." *Charas v. Trans World Airlines, Inc.* (9th Cir. 1998) (*en banc*).

Service, Interpreted

Charas's approach, we believe, is inconsistent with the Supreme Court's recent decision in *Rowe v. New Hampshire Motor Transport Ass'n*, 552 U.S. 364 (2008). There, the Court necessarily defined "service" to extend beyond prices, schedules, origins, and destinations. Indeed, in determining that the ADA's preemption provision reached, among other things, the imposition of recipient verification requirements on tobacco shipments, the Court stated expressly that "federal law must . . . preempt Maine's efforts directly to regulate carrier *services*." It noted further that to interpret the federal preemption provision not to reach such regulation "could easily lead to a patchwork of state service-determining laws, rules, and regulations," which would be "inconsistent with Congress' major legislative effort to leave such decisions, where federally unregulated, to the competitive marketplace."

We hold that requiring airlines to provide food, water, electricity, and restrooms to passengers during lengthy ground delays does relate to the service of an air carrier and therefore falls within the express terms of the ADA's preemption provision. As a result, the substantive provisions of the PBR, codified at section 251–g(1) of the New York General Business Law, are preempted. The PBR substitutes New York's commands for competitive market forces, requiring airlines to provide the services that New York specifies during lengthy ground delays, threatening a "patchwork of state service-determining laws, rules, and regulations."

The PBR substitutes New York's commands for competitive market forces, requiring airlines to provide the services that New York specifies during lengthy ground delays, threatening a "patchwork of state service-determining laws, rules, and regulations.

At least nine other states have proposed legislation regarding lengthy ground delays. *See* H.R. 2149, 48th Leg., 2d Reg. Sess. (Ariz. 2008); Assem. 1943, 2007–2008 Reg. Sess. (Cal. 2008); S. 2062, 110th Reg. Sess. (Fla. 2008); S. 161, 115th Gen. Assem., 2d Reg. Sess. (Ind. 2008); H.R. 5475, 94th Legis., 2007 Reg. Sess. (Mich. 2007); Assem. 967, 213th Leg., 1st Ann. Sess. (N.J. 2008); H.R.2055, 190th Gen. Assem., 2007 Sess. (Pa. 2007); S.2088, 2008 Legis. Sess. (R.I. 2008); S. 6269, 60th Legis., 2008 Reg. Sess. (Wash. 2008). These proposed laws would impose obligations ranging from a requirement that the airline accommodate passengers on the next available route, see Mich. H.R. 5475 § 5(2), to a requirement that passengers be permitted to disembark, see Pa. H.R. 2055 § 3(b).

It is irrelevant that these bills all seek to impose the same principal service obligations as the PBR—requiring airlines to provide food, water, electric generation, and waste removal after a three-hour ground delay—for state laws related to airline service are preempted regardless of whether they are consistent with each other and regardless of whether they are consistent with the ADA's objective. We note that the Department of Transportation has proposed and sought comment on several similar passenger protection measures that could provide uniform standards to deal with lengthy ground delays. *See* Enhancing Airline Passenger Protections, 72 Fed. Reg. 65,233 (Nov. 20, 2007) (to be codified at 14 C.F.R. pts. 234, 253, 259, 399).

Additionally, we note that the Supreme Court, in *Rowe*, declined to read into Section 14501(c)(1)'s preemption provision an exception that preserves state laws

Public Health Exception

protecting the public health. *Rowe* accordingly forecloses New York's argument and the district court's conclusion that classifying the PBR as a health and safety regulation or a matter of basic human necessities somehow shields it from the preemptive force of Section 41713(b)(1). Onboard amenities, regardless of whether they are luxuries or necessities, still relate to airline service and fall within the express terms of the preemption provision—a conclusion, we note, that even the drafters of the PBR appear to have been unable to escape. *See* N.Y. Gen. Bus. Law § 251–g(1)(a) (referring to "electric generation service"); *id.* § 251–g(1)(b) (referring to "waste removal service").

Standards of Airline Safety

Finally, insofar as the PBR is intended to prescribe standards of airline safety, we note that it may also be impliedly preempted by the FAA and regulations promulgated thereunder. The FAA was enacted to create a "uniform and exclusive system of federal regulation" in the field of air safety. Shortly after it became law, we noted that the FAA "was passed by Congress for the purpose of centralizing in a single authority—indeed, in one administrator—the power to frame rules for the safe and efficient use of the nation's airspace." Congress and the Federal Aviation Administration have used this authority to enact rules addressing virtually all areas of air safety. These regulations range from a general standard of care for operating requirements, see 14 C.F.R. § 91.13(a) ("No person may operate an aircraft in a careless or reckless manner so as to endanger the life or property of another"), to the details of the contents of mandatory onboard first-aid kits, to the maximum concentration of carbon monoxide permitted in "suitably vented" compartments, § 125.117. This power extends to grounded planes and airport runways. *See* § 91.123 (requiring pilots to comply with all orders and instructions of air traffic control); § 139.329 (requiring airlines to restrict movement of pedestrians and ground vehicles on runways).

The intent to centralize air safety authority and the comprehensiveness of these regulations pursuant to that authority have led several other circuits (and several courts within this Circuit) to conclude that Congress intended to occupy the entire field and thereby preempt state regulation of air safety. *See, e.g., Montalvo v. Spirit Airlines*, 508 F.3d 464 (9th Cir. 2007) ("[T]he FAA preempts the entire field of aviation safety through implied field preemption. The FAA and regulations promulgated pursuant to it establish complete and thorough safety standards for air travel, which are not subject to supplementation by . . . state laws."). Although we have not addressed this precise issue, we have acknowledged that the FAA does not preempt all state law tort actions. *See In re Air Crash Disaster at John F. Kennedy Int'l Airport on June 24, 1975*, 635 F.2d 67 (2d Cir. 1980). However, the FAA has a savings clause that specifically preserves these actions. *See* 49 U.S.C. § 40120(c).

If New York's view regarding the scope of its regulatory authority carried the day, another state could be free to enact a law prohibiting the service of soda on flights departing from its airports, while another could require allergen-free food options on its outbound flights, unraveling the centralized federal framework for air travel.

If New York's view regarding the scope of its regulatory authority carried the day, another state could be free to enact a law prohibiting the service of soda on flights departing from its airports, while another could require allergen-free food options on its outbound flights, unraveling the centralized federal framework for air travel. On this point, the decisions of the Fifth and Ninth Circuits finding preemption of state common law claims for failure to warn of the risk of deep vein thrombosis are instructive. *See Montalvo* ("[A] state [is not] free to require any announcement it wishe[s] on all planes arriving in, or departing from, its soil.").

In light of our determination that the PBR is preempted by the ADA, however, we need not address the scope of any FAA preemption, and we decline to do so here. Although the goals of the PBR are laudable and the circumstances motivating its enactment deplorable, only the federal government has the authority to enact such a law. We conclude, then, by reiterating our holding that the PBR's substantive provisions, codified at section 251–g(1) of the New York General Business Law, are preempted.

EXERCISE 6-2. *AIR TRANSPORT ASS'N OF AMERICA V. CUOMO—* AIRLINE PASSENGER BILL OF RIGHTS

1. Describe the motivation for and terms of the New York State Passenger Bill of Rights.

2. Explain how the Air Transport Association has no right to sue for a violation of 49 U.S.C. § 41713(b)(1) and yet is able to pursue a preemption challenge through the Supremacy clause?

3. What is the holding of the case? Does it matter if the New York State Passenger Bill of Rights at issue is classified as a health and safety regulation or a matter of basic human necessities? Explain.

4. Can the New York State Passenger Bill of Rights evade federal preemption on the basis that it is intended to prescribe standards of airline safety? Explain why or why not.

5.   To what branch of government (legislative, executive, or judicial) of which governmental authority (state or federal) must passengers turn to after *Air Transport Ass'n of America v. Cuomo* for relief?

NOTES ON *AIR TRANSPORT ASS'N OF AMERICA V. CUOMO*—THE LEGACY OF DEREGULATION

1.   *What Deregulation Isn't.*

Broad reference to the airline industry as "deregulated" is a bit of a misnomer. While aspects of the airline industry were deregulated *economically* in 1978, the airline industry itself remains among the most regulated industries in the United States, particularly within the context of safety. Indeed, the "dichotomization [between regulation and deregulation] is false . . . 'Deregulation' has in fact meant eliminating a few, specific controls while retaining all others. Air travel today, [for example,] as in the past, is totally dependent on the existence and effective operation of such industry specific controls as the FAA's air traffic system." Peter C. Carstensen, *Evaluating "Deregulation" of Commercial Air Travel: False Dichotomization, Untenable Theories, and Unimplemented Premises*, 46 WASH. & LEE L. REV. 109, 116 (1989).

2.   *Benefits and Drawbacks of the Airline Deregulation Act.*

Travelers have benefitted or were intended to benefit by airline deregulation policy vis-à-vis competition, discount fares, democratization of air travel, and frequent flyer programs. *See, e.g.*, Herbert D. Kelleher, *Deregulation and the Troglodytes—How the Airlines Met Adam Smith*, 50 J. AIR L. & COM. 299, 304 (1985) ("Deregulation has produced substantial societal benefits in the form of lower fares, increased service, diversity of service and price alternatives, reduced industry concentration, more efficient allocation of resources and, in the long run, a more healthy, efficient and innovative airline industry.")

"Hub premiums," airline bankruptcies, complex fare structures, and yield management have cast doubt on the policy decision to economically deregulate airlines in the United States, however. *See, e.g.*, Wesley G. Kaldahl, *Let the Process of Deregulation Continue*, 50 J. AIR L. & COM. 285, 295 (1985) ("The *public* has not benefited. There is less nonstop service, most lengthy trips require stops at intermediate hubs, and fares are widely inconsistent and tend to favor the few chosen markets."). *See also* LAURENCE E. GESELL, AIRLINE RE-REGULATION 17 (Coast Aire Publications 1990) (hypothesizing that "there has been an increase in finance-oriented managers during the airline deregulatory process . . . that . . . results in negative welfare interests."). Additionally, from a passenger's viewpoint, airlines may be charging low fares, but they otherwise are nickel-and-diming consumers for additional fees and surcharges, including upwards of $45 for checked luggage, fees for carry-on baggage,

$8 for pillows, fees for "advanced boarding," different costs for window, middle and aisle seats, and so on. *E.g.*, Glorida Goodale, *First It Was the Baggage Fees. What's Next? Pay Toilets?*, CHRISTIAN SCIENCE MONITOR, Apr. 26, 2010, at 2010 WL 8635095.

Commentary discussing the benefits and drawbacks of Airline Deregulation Act, Pub. L. 95–504 (codified as amended in scattered sections of 49 U.S.C.), is substantial. *See generally* Ann K. Wooster, Annotation, *Construction and Application of § 105 Airline Deregulation Act (49 U.S.C. § 41713), Pertaining to Preemption of Authority over Prices, Routes, and Services*, 149 A.L.R. FED. 299 (1998); GEORGE WILLIAMS, AIRLINE COMPETITION: DEREGULATION'S MIXED LEGACY (ASHGATE 2002); KENNETH BUTTON & ROGER STOUGH, AIR TRANSPORT NETWORKS (2000); GEORGE WILLIAMS, THE AIRLINE INDUSTRY AND THE IMPACT OF DEREGULATION (1993); PAUL STEPHEN DEMPSEY & ANDREW R. GOETZ, AIRLINE DEREGULATION AND LAISSEZ-FAIRE MYTHOLOGY (1992); Laurence E. Gesell & Martin T. Farris, *Airline Deregulation: An Evaluation of Goals and Objectives*, 21 TRANSP. L.J. 105 (1992); Theodore P. Harris, *The Disaster of Deregulation*, 20 TRANSP. L.J. 87 (1991); Alfred E. Kahn, *Deregulation: Looking Backward and Looking Forward*, 7 YALE J. ON REG. 325 (1990); Andrew R. Goetz & Paul Stephen Dempsey, *Airline Deregulation Ten Years After: Something Foul in the Air*, 54 J. AIR L. & COM. 927 (1989); Melvin A. Brenner, *Airline Deregulation—A Case Study in Public Policy Failure*, 16 TRANSP. L.J. 179 (1988); Alfred E. Kahn, *Airline Deregulation—A Mixed Bag, But a Clear Success Nevertheless*, 16 TRANSP. L.J. 229 (1988); Thomas G. Moore, *U.S. Airline Deregulation: Its Effects on Passengers, Capital and Labor*, 29 J.L. & ECON. 1 (1986); Edward A. Morash, *Airline Deregulation: Another Look*, 50 J. AIR L. & COM. 253 (1985); Michael E. Levine, *Revisionism Revised? Airline Deregulation and the Public Interest*, 44 L. & CONTEMP. PROBS. 179 (1981); C. Vincent Olson & John M. Trapani, III, *Who Has Benefited from Regulation of the Airline Industry?*, 24 J.L. & ECON. 75 (1981); *The Impact of Government Regulation on Air Transportation*, 9 AKRON L. REV. 629 (1976); Richard D. Gritta, *Profitability and Risk in Air Transport: A Case for Deregulation*, 7 TRANSP. L.J. 197 (1975); WILLIAM A. JORDAN, AIRLINE REGULATION IN AMERICA: EFFECTS AND IMPERFECTIONS (THE JOHNS HOPKINS PRESS 1970).

3. *Competition and Bankruptcy.*

The deregulated airline market was heralded as one that would be "perfectly contestable." *See* Elizabeth E. Bailey & William J. Baumol, *Deregulation and the Theory of Contestable Markets*, 1 YALE J. ON REG. 111, 113 (1984). But, just ten years after the Airline Deregulation Act of 1978 was enacted, Alfred Kahn—a Cornell University economist widely referred to as the "father of airline deregulation"—remarked:

> Just as one of the most pleasant surprises of the early deregulation experience was the large-scale entry of new, highly competitive carriers, so probably the most unpleasant one has been the reversal of that trend—the

departures of almost all of them, the reconcentration of the industry both nationally and at the major hubs, the diminishing disciplinary effectiveness of potential entry by totally new firms, and the increased likelihood, in consequence, of monopolistic exploitation . . . Were these developments surprises? Yes, to a large extent.

Alfred E. Kahn, *Surprises of Airline Deregulation*, 78 AM. ECON. REV. 316, 318 (1988) ("Most of us probably did not foresee the deterioration in the average quality of the flying experience, and in particular the congestion and delays that have plagued air travelers in recent years.").

Another commentator has noted that "[t]he vision of the deregulated airline industry as effectively competitive suggested that merger policies developed under antitrust laws would suffice for whatever mergers and acquisitions might transpire. In this the proponents [of airline deregulation] were wrong." Almarin Philips, *Airline Mergers in the New Regulatory Environment*, 129 U. PA. L. REV. 856, 857 (1981) ("The nation may be left with a really small number of large, quasi-monopolistic and not necessarily efficient carriers"). *See also* Yochi J. Dreazen et al., *Why the Sudden Rise in the Urge to Merge and Form Oligopolies?*, WALL. ST. J., Feb. 25, 2002, at A10 (quoting economist Carl Shapiro, "Twenty [competitors] to four is good. It's four to two that is much more dubious.").

In fact, the number of major airlines shrunk considerably in 1986 alone, from 18 to 8, many due to bankruptcy. Over the years since deregulation, Air California, Air Florida, Braniff, Eastern, National, New York Air, PEOPLExpress, Pan Am, Piedmont, Ozark, Republic, and Western Air Lines, among others, either stopped operations or were merged into American, Delta, Northwest, TWA, and/or Texas Air. *See generally* L. Milton Glisson, *Is U.S. Domestic Airline Competition on a Flight to Oblivion?*, 58 TRANSP. PRAC. J. 217, 218 (1991); Robert L. Thornton, *Airlines and Agents: Conflict and the Public Welfare*, 52 J. AIR L. & COM. 371, 396 (1986) (concluding "if [the DOT] fails to act soon, the number of effective competitors in the airline industry may fall below the point from which deconcentration is possible without a major crisis"); Paul Stephen Dempsey, *Antitrust Law and Policy in Transportation: Monopoly I$ the Name of the Game*, 21 GA. L. REV. 505, 514 (1987).

4. *Industry Consolidation.*

In 2008, Northwest Airlines merged into Delta Airlines to create the world's largest airline, and in 2010, United Airlines and Continental Airlines announced a merger between the two carriers that will become the world's largest airline. *See, e.g.,* Darren Shannon, *Fit to be Tied?*, AVIATION WK. & SPACE TECH., May 10, 2010, at 20. In 2015, American Airlines acquired U.S. Airways. Such mergers have raised the possibility of re-regulation of the airline industry. Representative James Oberstar (D-

Minn.), for example, voted for the Airline Deregulation Act of 1978, but threatened financial re-regulation of commercial airlines should the United States Department of Justice approve the United-Continental merger:

> Deregulation has been credited with making airline travel affordable for the average American. But Oberstar pointed to the $2.7 billion the airlines earned in baggage fees in 2009 as evidence that consumers are no longer benefiting from the system. He said he believes there's support in the House for re-regulation.
>
> "Hardly a day passes where I don't walk out on the [House] floor that someone asks me, 'When are we going to re-regulate the airlines?'" Oberstar told reporters after the hearing.
>
> The legislation would impose federal regulation of airline pricing and re-establish a government gatekeeper role similar to that played by the old Civil Aeronautics Board before deregulation in 1978, Oberstar said. * * *
>
> Airlines have suffered repeated shocks in recent years, including 9-11, the SARS virus, volatile oil prices and the recession. They have shed more than 158,000 full-time jobs since employment peaked in 2001 and lost an estimated $30 billion to $60 billion in recent years. At least 13 airlines have filed for bankruptcy in the past several years.

Congress to Revisit Airline Re-Regulation if Merger Goes Through, FORT WORTH-STAR TELEGRAM, June 17, 2010, at 2010 WLNR 12256952. *See also* Timothy M. Ravich, *Re-Regulation and Airline Passengers' Rights*, 67 J. AIR L. & COM. 935 (2002); Robert L. Crandall, *Bring Back Airline Regulation*, AVIATION WK. & SPACE TECH., June 16, 2008, at 62 ("Our airlines are now laggards in every category. Their financial health is precarious. . . . The solution is not consolidation. Mergers will not lower fuel prices. They will require major capital expenditures, are likely to increase labor costs and will disadvantage many employees."); Adrian Schofield, *Free to Fail*, AVIATION WK. & SPACE TECH., Oct. 27, 2008, at 48 (reporting concern by lawmakers that airline mergers will reduce consumer choice too much, which the very opposite of what deregulation was supposed to achieve).

That said, the actual impact of consolidation in the commercial airline marketplace "may be less harmful than is generally expected" as

> [c]onsolidation lowers competition, which tends to reduce welfare. At the same time, consolidation increases traffic densities in the networks of the surviving carriers. Since higher densities reduce costs, this effect tends to raise welfare. If the economies of density are sufficiently strong, the cost effect will overshadow the effect of lost competition, leading to a welfare gain. This outcome is in fact familiar from standard oligopoly models,

which show that industry consolidation in the presence of increasing returns can be welfare-improving.

Jan K. Brueckner & Pablo T. Spiller, *Economies of Traffic Density in the Deregulated Airline Industry*, 37 J.L. & ECON. 379, 408 (1994). *Contra* Melanie Trottman & Scott McCartney, *The Age of 'Wal-Mart' Airlines Crunches the Biggest Carriers*, WALL ST. J., June 18, 2002, at A1.

5.   ***Passenger-Centered Legislation.***

The legislation at the center of *Air Transport Ass'n v. Cuomo* was at least the third time in a decade—and first since multiple efforts undertaken in the 1980s—to regulate aspects of airline customer service.

In January 1999, Marti Sousanis was among thousands of post-holiday travelers at a crowded airport ready to go home. After waiting several hours in lines at Detroit Metropolitan Airport, she boarded Northwest Airlines flight 992 to San Francisco. Despite an announcement reporting that the flight was on time, the airplane sat on the tarmac for a seemingly interminable period. A blizzard covered the Detroit airport with over a foot of snow and stranded Sousanis's flight and more than two dozen other airplanes for up to eleven hours.

Conditions on the planes became nightmarish as the hours passed. Food and water ran out and toilets overflowed. Passengers "became physically ill [and were] exposed to the growing odor of [a] concentrated number of humans in an enclosed small space." *See Ex Parte* Amended Class Action Complaint, *Koczara et al. v. Wayne County et al.*, No. 99–900422 (MI Cir. Ct. Wayne County 1999), ¶ 19. The crew of flight 992 was rude. Each time Sousanis tried to stand to relieve her chronically-pained back, the flight crew threatened her with arrest and told her to obey an unrelenting "fasten seatbelt" sign.

In January, 2001, Northwest Airlines agreed to a settlement, paying $5 million among 700 class action plaintiffs based on the length of time each person was delayed. Plaintiffs' counsel remarked, "We've been working on this for two years and they were on the plane for 11 hours. That's the nature of our legal system." Michael Katz, *Airline Peanuts*, FORBES, Feb. 19, 2001, at 53.

The 1999 Detroit Blizzard prompted members of Congress—themselves commercial airline passengers—to propose various legislation under the title "Airline Passengers' Bill of Rights." One bill, for example, proposed the imposition of financial liability on airlines for "excessive departure or arrival delay," *i.e.*, a period of time excess of two hours—

(A)   in the case of departure, beginning when the door of an aircraft is closed at an airport and ending when the aircraft takes off from the airport or when the door of the aircraft is open for deplaning of passengers at the airport; and

(B)   in the case of arrival delay, beginning upon touchdown of an aircraft at an airport and ending when the door of the aircraft is open for deplaning of passengers at the airport.

Airline Passenger Bill of Rights, H.R. 700, 106th Cong. (1999). The penalty for a delay between two and three hours would have been 200 percent of the ticket purchase price, plus another 100 percent for each additional hour (or portion thereof) beyond a three hour delay. *See also* Biztravel.com, *Your Flight Arrives on Time or We Pay You Back*, WALL. ST. J., June 5, 2000, at A9 (advertising $100 refund if flight arrives thirty minutes late, $200 if one hour late, and the full ticket price if two hours late or cancelled).

Presuming that states cannot enact their own airline customer service laws, *inter alia*, pursuant to the precedent established in *Cuomo v. Air Transport Ass'n of Am.* and *Morales v. Trans World Airlines, Inc.* (1992), *supra*, should Congress enact a federal "Airline Passengers' Bill of Rights" to ensure a positive flying experience for the traveling public as a matter of law?

See, e.g., Timothy M. Ravich, *Re-Regulation and Airline Passengers' Rights*, 67 J. AIR L. & COM. 935 (2002); Daniel H. Rosenthal, Notes, *Legal Turbulence: The Courts's Miscontrual of the Airline Deregulation Act's Preemption Clause and the Effect on Passengers' Rights*, 51 DUKE L.J. 1857 (2002); Zachary Garsek, *Giving Power Back to the Passengers: The Airline Passengers' Bill of Rights*, 66 J. AIR L. & COM. 1187 (2001); Audrey Johnson, *Consumers and Congress Lobby for Airline Customer Service Improvements: Voluntary Action of Legislation*, 13 LOY. CONSUMER L. REV. 402 (2001). *See also Airline Passengers' Bill of Rights: Is It Time to Re-Regulate the Airline Industry with New Customer Protections?*, National Public Radio ("The Conversation" KUOW), Seattle, WA (2007). *See also* Chapter 7.

C. COMMON LAW TORT CLAIMS

HODGES V. DELTA AIRLINES, INC.

44 F.3d 334 (5th Cir. 1995)

EDITH H. JONES, CIRCUIT JUDGE.

During a flight from the Caribbean to Miami, Frances Hodges was injured when a fellow passenger opened an overhead compartment and dislodged a case containing several bottles of rum. The box fell and cut her arm and wrist. In her lawsuit against Delta Airlines, Hodges alleged that the airline's negligence caused her injury and medical expenses.

The question before this court *en banc* is whether her state law tort claim for physical injury based on alleged negligent operation of the aircraft is preempted by § 1305(a)(1) of the Airline Deregulation Act of 1978 ("ADA"). We hold that it is not and therefore overrule *Baugh v. Trans World Airlines, Inc.*, 915 F.2d 693 (5th Cir. 1990), an originally unpublished opinion that, as circuit precedent, compelled the opposite result in the panel opinion herein.

DISCUSSION

Section 1305(a)(1) provides in pertinent part:

> [N]o state . . . shall enact or enforce any law, rule, regulation, standard, or other provision having the force and effect of law relating to rates, routes or services of any air carrier having authority under Title IV of this Act to provide air transportation.

This provision originated in the ADA, an economic deregulation statute. The Federal Aviation Act of 1958 ("FAA"), 49 U.S.C. § 1301 *et seq.* (as amended), conferred on the Civil Aeronautics Board economic regulatory authority over interstate air transportation. The FAA did not expressly preempt state regulation of intrastate air transportation. In 1978, Congress amended the FAA after determining that efficiency, innovation, low prices, variety, and quality would be promoted by reliance on competitive market forces rather than pervasive federal regulation. Congress enacted the ADA to dismantle federal economic regulation. To prevent the states from frustrating the goals of deregulation by establishing or maintaining economic regulations of their own, Congress enacted § 1305(a)(1), which preempts the states from enforcing any law "relating to rates, routes or services" of any carrier.

Issue Presented

The question in this case is the breadth of that express preemption of state law. State law is displaced by federal law where (1) Congress expressly preempts state law; (2) Congressional intent to preempt is inferred from the existence of a pervasive regulatory scheme; or (3) state law conflicts with federal law or interferes with the achievement of federal objectives. Interpretation of the statutory language is the key to construing its preemptive force.

The Supreme Court has twice broached the subject of ADA preemption in a way that informs but does not squarely resolve this case. In the first decision the question was whether section 1305(a)(1), in providing that no state may enforce any law "relating to rates," overcame the attempts of several state attorneys general to apply state deceptive advertising laws against the airlines. *Morales v. Trans World Airlines, Inc.*, 504 U.S. 374 (1992), held that it did. *Morales* drew upon the broad construction of the phrase "relating to" in the ERISA cases. Thus, the phrase "relating to" means "to stand in some relation; to have bearing or concern; to pertain; refer; to bring to association with or connection with." Consequently, "[s]tate enforcement actions having a connection with or reference to airline 'rates, routes or services' are preempted" under § 1305(a)(1).

As a necessary consequence of its broad interpretation, the Court rejected the argument that § 1305(a)(1) preempts the states only from actually prescribing rates, routes, or services. The Court also rejected the notions that "only state laws specifically addressed to the airline industry are preempted" and that "preemption is inappropriate when state and federal law are consistent." Laws of general applicability, even those consistent with federal law, are preempted if they have the "forbidden significant effect" on rates, routes or services. The Court acknowledged, however, that "[s]ome state actions may affect [airline services] in too tenuous, remote or peripheral a manner" to be preempted. Refusing to state exactly where the line would be drawn in a close case, the Court observed that the facts before it presented no close question of the connection between the attempted regulation and air fares.

Morales commands that whatever state laws "relate to rates, routes or services" are broadly preempted, but it does not define "services." The panel opinion in this case concluded that:

"Service"

> "Services" generally represent a bargained—for or anticipated provision of labor from one party to another. If the element of bargain or agreement is incorporated in our understanding of services, it leads to a concern with the contractual arrangement between the airline and the user of the service.

> Elements of the air carrier service bargain include items such as ticketing, boarding procedures, provision of food and drink, and baggage handling, in addition to the transportation itself. These matters are all appurtenant and necessarily included with the contract of carriage between the passenger or shipper and the airline. It is these [contractual] features of air transportation that we believe Congress intended to de-regulate as "services" and broadly to protect from state regulation.

Hodges v. Delta Airlines, Inc., 4 F.3d 350 (5th Cir. 1993). The court adheres to this definition of services *en banc*, a definition inferentially reinforced by the Court's decision in *American Airlines, Inc. v. Wolens*, 513 U.S. 219 (1995) (describing claims concerning American Airlines' frequent flyer program as related to rates and "services," *i.e.*, access to flights and class-of-service upgrades.").

Thus, federal preemption of state laws, even certain common law actions "related to services" of an air carrier, does not displace state tort actions for personal physical injuries or property damage caused by the operation and maintenance of aircraft. This definition harmonizes § 1305(a)(1) with other sections of airline regulatory law, with Congressional intent underlying the ADA, with the regulatory agencies' understanding of the statute, and with general principles of federal preemption.

> *Federal preemption of state laws, even certain common law actions "related to services" of an air carrier, does not displace state tort actions for personal physical injuries or property damage caused by the operation and maintenance of aircraft.*

Under the regulatory framework established by the FAA, the term "service" or "services" had an established definition, consistent with dictionary usage. Webster's Third New International Dictionary (1976) includes some of the following definitions:

> An action or use that furthers some purpose; supply of needs [*e.g.*, a vending machine for the service of passersby]; railroads and telephone companies produce services—useful labor that does not produce a good; provision for conducting a public utility [*e.g.*, air freight service]; regularly scheduled trip on public transportation ([free air services]).

A vestige of this definition remains in what is left of the federal airline regulatory statutes: "All-cargo air service" means the carriage by aircraft in interstate or overseas air transportation of only property or mail, or both. 49 U.S.C. § 1301(11) ("Definitions"). "Air service" referred at the time of passage of the ADA to the point-to-point transportation of passengers, cargo or mail, and it encompassed the business of transportation as well as the schedules and type of contract (common carriage or charter). This court interpreted "service" to embody the airlines' quality of service in such a fashion as to authorize federal regulation of smoking on commercial flights. *Diefenthal v. Civil Aeronautics Bd.*, 681 F.2d 1039 (1982).

Following deregulation, the CAB's statements implementing the ADA strongly support the view that the ADA was concerned solely with economic deregulation, not with displacing state tort law. The Board concluded that:

preemption extends to all of the economic factors that go into the provision of the *quid pro quo* for passenger's [sic] fare, including flight frequency and timing, liability limits, reservation and boarding practices, insurance, smoking rules, meal service, entertainment, [and] bonding and corporate financing.

44 Fed. Reg. 9948, 9951 (Feb. 15, 1979). The CAB also opined:

[A] state may not interfere with the services that carriers offer in exchange for their rates and fares. For example, liquidated damages for bumping (denial of boarding), segregation of smoking passengers, minimum liability for loss, damages and delayed baggage, and ancillary charges for headsets, alcoholic beverages, entertainment, and excess baggage would clearly be "service" regulation within the meaning of section 105.

The Federal Aviation Agency, to which some of the Civil Aeronautics Board's powers were transferred by the ADA, *see* 49 U.S.C. § 1551(b), continues to identify "service" or "services" in its regulations to incorporate the accoutrements of the passenger- or shipper- and carrier contract. Specific references to the words "service" or "services" in the Code of Federal Regulations governing airlines are too numerous to incorporate here. Some examples include (all within 14 C.F.R.): § 201.1 (domestic all-cargo air service); § 201.4(d) (the type of service-passengers, property or mail to be rendered and whether such services are to be rendered on scheduled or charter operations); § 204.3(t) (a description of the service to be operated if an application is granted); § 207.1 (defining special "services"); § 207.13(b) (terms of service for charter trips); § 207.71(a) (terms of service for charter trips include those for ground accommodations and services); § 217.4(b) (listing classes of service including scheduled passengers/cargo; scheduled all-cargo, . . . non-scheduled services).

A facile analogy to *Morales* and the ERISA preemption cases could suggest that "services" includes all aspects of the air carrier's "utility" to its customers, hence, any state tort claim may "relate to" services as a result of its indirect regulatory impact on the airline's practices. Taken to its logical extreme, this argument would suggest that a lawsuit following a fatal airplane crash could relate to "services."

That Congress did not, however, intend § 1305(a)(1) to preempt all state claims for personal injury is evident from at least one other provision of the remaining airline regulatory statutes. Air carriers are required to maintain insurance or self-insurance as prescribed by the Federal Aviation Administration

Preemption of Personal Injury Claims

that covers "amounts for which . . . air carriers may become liable for bodily injuries to or the death of any person, or for loss of or damage to property of others, resulting from the operation or maintenance of aircraft." 49 U.S.C. § 1371(q) (1994); *see also*, 14 C.F.R. § 205.5(a) (1992) (insurance regulations.). The importance of § 1371(q) cannot be understated, for it can only be understood to qualify the scope of "services" removed from state regulation by § 1305(a)(1). A complete preemption of state law in this area would have rendered any requirement of insurance coverage nugatory.

The FAA further defines "operation of aircraft" as "the use of aircraft for the purpose of air navigation . . . includ[ing] the navigation of aircraft." 49 U.S.C. § 1301(31) (1988). One uses the overhead luggage racks or the food and beverages provided in aircraft operation just as one uses the cigarette lighter or built-in cooler compartment in an automobile, and all these devices are available to support the general purpose of navigation.

The FAA further defines "operation of aircraft" as "the use of aircraft for the purpose of air navigation . . . includ[ing] the navigation of aircraft." One uses the overhead luggage racks or the food and beverages provided in aircraft operation just as one uses the cigarette lighter or built-in cooler compartment in an automobile, and all these devices are available to support the general purpose of navigation.

Significantly, too, neither the ADA nor its legislative history indicates that Congress intended to displace the application of state tort law to personal physical injury inflicted by aircraft operations, or that Congress even considered such preemption. "This silence takes on added significance in light of Congress's failure to provide any federal remedy for persons injured by such conduct. It is difficult to believe that Congress would, without comment, remove all means of judicial recourse for those injured by illegal conduct." The Supreme Court has repeatedly cautioned that federal courts should not displace state police powers by federal law unless that was the "clear and manifest purpose of Congress." [Meanwhile], the Seventh Circuit noted that "[s]tate courts award damages every day in air crash cases, notwithstanding that federal law preempts the regulation of safety in air travel," confidently adding that "[t]he Federal Aviation Act does not expressly preempt state damages remedies."

Delta Airlines agrees that among the "services" deregulated under the ADA and covered by its preemption clause are the economic or contractual features of air transportation. Delta argues, however, that Mrs. Hodges' accident arose out of the "services" of baggage handling and boarding, not out of the "operation and maintenance of aircraft" covered by § 1371(q). The "services" that the state may not regulate under § 1305(a)(1) are distinct from the "operation and maintenance of aircraft," and all claims related to "services" are preempted.

> *Delta Airlines agrees that among the "services" deregulated under the ADA and covered by its preemption clause are the economic or contractual features of air transportation. Delta argues, however, that Mrs. Hodges' accident arose out of the "services" of baggage handling and boarding, not out of the "operation and maintenance of aircraft" covered by § 1371(q). The "services" that the state may not regulate under § 1305(a)(1) are distinct from the "operation and maintenance of aircraft," and all claims related to "services" are preempted.*

Service v. Aircraft Operation or Maintenance

This argument fails on two levels. First, if the statutory provisions created a strict dichotomy between services and operation or maintenance of aircraft, Hodges' injury more properly is laid at the door of operations. Whether certain luggage may be placed in overhead bins and whether the flight attendants properly monitor compliance with overhead rack regulations are matters that pertain to the safe operation of a flight. "Baggage handling" and "boarding," as referred to in the above-quoted CAB statement, concern the airline's policy for permitting baggage to be carried or passengers to be permitted to board. These are aspects of the "service" offered; they do not refer directly to the way in which the aircraft is operated.

Delta confuses its argument by contending that this state tort suit should not be permitted to proceed because it could impose duties that conflict with Federal Aviation Administration regulations governing carry-on baggage. There are no facts in the record that intimate the basis for such a conflict. Moreover, in *Cipollone v. Liggett Group, Inc.*, 505 U.S. 504 (1992), the Supreme Court held that when Congress has enacted an explicit preemption provision, courts should not usually imply broader preemption of state law. Therefore, this decision of our court does not address the possible preemptive effect of Federal Aviation Administration safety regulations governing aircraft and carriers. *See Public Health Trust of Dade Cty., Fla. v. Luke Aircraft, Inc.*, 992 F.2d 291 (11th Cir. 1993).

Second, as this example shows, the provinces of "services" and "operation and maintenance of aircraft" overlap somewhat conceptually; no strict dichotomy exists. There is not, however, a fundamental inconsistency between the two provisions. By means of § 1305(a)(1), Congress intended to prevent the states from regressing on economic deregulation by applying their own laws or rules concerning "services," but in § 1371(q), Congress explicitly preserved airlines' duty to respond to tort actions, inferentially state law actions, for physical injury or property damage.

Finally, unlike the NAAG Guidelines in *Morales*, enforcement of tort remedies for personal physical injury ordinarily has no "express reference" to services as defined above. Enforcement of such tort duties normally will not have "the forbidden significant effect" on airlines' services. *Morales* relied in part on the fact that the state restrictions on airfare advertising had a significant economic effect on fares. Generally, however, state tort laws concerning the operation and maintenance of aircraft can be enforced consistently with and distinctly from the services that Congress deregulated. Most cases will not pose as close a question as this one. But this general vindication of state tort claims arising from the maintenance or operation of aircraft does not extend to all conceivable state tort claims. Two examples of the continued scope of preemption are illustrative.

Generally, state tort laws concerning the operation and maintenance of aircraft can be enforced consistently with and distinctly from the services that Congress deregulated. Most cases will not pose as close a question as this one.

In *O'Carroll v. American Airlines, Inc.*, 863 F.2d 11 (5th Cir.1989), the plaintiff and his cousin were removed from a commercial airline flight because they were loud, boisterous, and intoxicated. O'Carroll sued, alleging that he was wrongfully evicted from the flight. This court vacated O'Carroll's sizeable jury verdict, holding that his state law claims were preempted by § 1305(a)(1). *O'Carroll* did not discuss the scope of § 1305(a)(1) because the state law claims arising from the alleged wrongful exclusion undeniably related only to the services provided by the airline. No claim was made that the airline breached any safety-related tort duty by bumping O'Carroll. Enforcement of O'Carroll's state law claims would result in significant *de facto* regulation of the airlines' boarding practices and, moreover, would interfere with federal law granting the airlines substantial discretion to refuse to carry passengers.

Similarly, the claims asserted by the plaintiff in *West v. Northwest Airlines*, 995 F.2d 148 (9th Cir. 1993), would be preempted under our interpretation of "services." Plaintiff West sued because he was "bumped" from the overbooked airline flight for which he had reserved a seat. After remand for reconsideration in light of *Morales*, the Ninth Circuit held, over a dissent, that West's state law claims were too tenuously connected to "rates, routes and services" to be preempted by § 1305(a)(1). The majority did find West's punitive damage claim preempted. Under either *Morales* or the analysis advanced here, it is difficult to see how a lawsuit for overbooking would not "relate to" the airline's contract for "services" with its passenger.

Hodges alleged that Delta was negligent in allowing the case of rum to be stowed in an overhead storage bin. This tort claim for personal injury has no specific "reference to" airline services, although it does derive from the operation of the aircraft. Nor would enforcement of her claim significantly affect Delta's services, as defined above. As other cases have recently held, this type of claim does not relate to Delta's services and is not preempted.

E. GRADY JOLLY, *specially concurring.*

I concur in the judgment in this case and its companion, *Smith v. America West Airlines*, 44 F.3d 344 (5th Cir. 1995). I cannot approve, however, of the rationale used to decide these cases. The majority and the dissent agree on the principle that a claim is preempted by the ADA express preemption provision if the claim relates to services that are not a part of the maintenance or operation of an airline; only the application of this rule prompts the dissent. The fact that the majority and the dissent disagree only on the application of this principle reveals that it promises uncertainty and inconsistent results.

I would have preferred that we give effect to the plain language of the ADA preemption provision. Plainly, it preempts only claims "related to a price, route, or service" that involve an instance of a "state . . . enact[ing] or enforc[ing] a law, regulation, or other provision having the force and effect of law." In my view, while these claims are unquestionably related to a service, they simply do not run afoul of the provision's prohibition of state-adopted legislation or regulation, or state enforcement of legislation or regulation. I would hold that claims by private individuals to obtain remedies for an asserted breach of the duty of reasonable care—traditional, well-settled common law tort remedies, in short—are not preempted by the ADA preemption provision either.

The majority and the dissent agree on the principle that a claim is preempted by the ADA express preemption provision if the claim relates to services that are not a part of the maintenance or operation of an airline; only the application of this rule prompts the dissent. The fact that the majority and the dissent disagree only on the application of this principle reveals that it promises uncertainty and inconsistent results ... I would hold that claims by private individuals to obtain remedies for an asserted breach of the duty of reasonable care—traditional, well-settled common law tort remedies, in short—are not preempted by the ADA preemption provision either.

I view as a mistake the majority's ascribing a broader sweep to the preemption provision than its language will admit, and then engrafting upon its own broad interpretation a series of narrowing distinctions that lack a basis in the words of the statute and are not susceptible of clear meaning or certain application. I would prefer, instead of erecting these tenuous and uncertain judge-made distinctions, to rely upon the plain language of the provision as Congress intended and enacted it and our other, well-settled, federal preemption principles.

The House Report accompanying the enactment of Section 1305 states that the lack of a clear delineation of state and federal jurisdiction over airlines had created "uncertainties and conflicts, including situations in which carriers have been required to charge different fares for passengers traveling between two cities, depending on whether these passengers were interstate passengers whose fares are regulated by the CAB, or intrastate passengers, whose fare is regulated by a state." 1978 U.S. CODE CONG. & ADMIN. NEWS. 3751–52. To that end, § 1305 would "prevent conflicts and inconsistent regulations by providing that when a carrier operates under authority granted pursuant to . . . the Federal Aviation Act, no state may regulate that carrier's routes, rates or services. The bill also eliminates Federal jurisdiction over certain service which is essentially intrastate in nature."

Similarly, the House Conference Report explains that § 1305 "prohibits a state from enacting any law, establishing any standard determining routes, schedules, or rates, fares, or charges in tariffs of, or otherwise promulgating economic regulations for, any air carrier certified by the Board." Nowhere, however, does Congress evidence an intent to relieve air carriers of their obligation to exercise reasonable care for the safety of their passengers.

A consideration of two cases referred to by the majority reveals the difficulties created by its departure from the plain language of the preemption provision. The majority today overrules *Baugh v. Trans World Airlines*, 915 F.2d 693 (5th Cir. 1990), and reaffirms *O'Carroll v. American Airlines*, 863 F.2d 11 (5th Cir.1989), but as far as I understand the majority's approach, it seems to compel an overruling of *O'Carroll* and a reaffirmance of *Baugh*. These cases bear out my expectation that confusion and uncertainty will ensue from the approach outlined in the majority's opinions.

In *Baugh*, a flight attendant stomped on a passenger's foot while engaged in some unspecified activity. We held that the passenger's claim was preempted because it related to the services afforded to the passengers on an airline. In *Hodges*, the majority specifically includes "provision of food and drink" in its open-ended definition of services that are preempted. As far as the majority knows, the flight attendant in *Baugh* was engaged in the provision of food and drink when the injury occurred, which means that one would assume under the majority's opinion that the cause of action in *Baugh* remains preempted. Why, then, does the majority assume that *Baugh* must be reversed?

Baugh relied upon *O'Carroll*. Although both this case and *Smith* reaffirm *O'Carroll*, I am convinced that under the majority's approach, *O'Carroll* would be overruled. In that case, the majority explains, we held that state claims stemming from an assertedly wrongful exclusion from an airplane were preempted. The majority states today that O'Carroll's claims are preempted by the express preemption provision because they "undeniably relate to services." Under *Smith*, however, the majority's explanation is not sufficient because the probability exists that, although the claim did relate to services, it implicated safety concerns, and thus would fall outside the preemption provision. *Smith* answers, in an oblique way, that O'Carroll's claims implicated economic practices as opposed to the safety of the flight. That answer, however, belies the fact that O'Carroll and his companion were excluded from the flight, and later jailed for disorderly conduct, because they were intoxicated and had been behaving so boisterously that at one point one of them offered his assistance to the pilot in flying the plane. O'Carroll's claims plainly implicated the safety of the flight. As a consequence, O'Carroll's suit should not be preempted under the approach announced by the majority today.

The result in *O'Carroll* can be reconciled with the plain language approach suggested by this concurring opinion. In *O'Carroll*, we determined that the claims were preempted for two reasons. First, 49 U.S.C. § 1511(a) granted broad discretion to refuse to transport any passenger if it "would or might be inimical to safety of flight." Clearly, transporting O'Carroll in his condition threatened the safety of the flight. O'Carroll's claims thus were impliedly preempted by the separate federal statute. A wholly convincing reason independent of the express preemption provision thus justified our determination that O'Carroll's claim was preempted. Seen in this light, our conclusory statement in *O'Carroll* that "[T]here is no need to rely upon inference alone as section 1305 . . . expressly preempts state law," and that "[i]n view of this explicit manifestation of congressional intent, we conclude that O'Carroll's common law claims are preempted under § 1305," is properly regarded as obiter dictum.

PATRICK E. HIGGINBOTHAM, CIRCUIT JUDGE, *with whom* EMILIO M. GARZA, CIRCUIT JUDGE, *joins, dissenting.*

While the term services must be given its ordinary meaning, it is clear that Congress did not intend operation or maintenance of an aircraft to fall within the statute's definition of services, despite its common sense relationship to provision of services. Section 1371(q)(1) requires each air carrier to maintain insurance to cover "amounts for which . . . such air carrier may become liable for bodily injuries to or the death of any person, or for loss of or damage to property of others, resulting from the operation or maintenance of aircraft." We cannot read § 1305(a)(1)'s use of the term services to include operation or maintenance of an aircraft and give meaning to § 1371(q)(1). If the claim relates to services, then it is preempted unless it also results from "the operation or maintenance of aircraft." If there is doubt as to whether the claim results from the operation or maintenance of the aircraft, that doubt is to be resolved in favor of the operation or maintenance category. Thus, preemption turns on whether judicial enforcement of a claim would regulate and whether the regulation was of the operation or maintenance of an aircraft.

Reflecting upon the practical reach of a tort claim sheds light on both inquiries. A mine run tort case from Louisiana makes the point. In *Schwamb v. Delta Air Lines, Inc.*, 516 So. 2d 452 (La. Ct. 1987), Schwamb was injured when a briefcase fell out of an overhead bin and struck him on the head. Schwamb introduced the testimony of Miller, an expert in aeronautical engineering, aviation accident investigation and reconstruction, human factors, crash survivability, safety engineering, and safety management. Miller testified that the following steps could have been taken to minimize a passenger's risk of being struck by objects falling from overhead bins:

(1)   A pre-boarding announcement to passengers about how to load the baggage; *e.g.*, "Put the heavy things on the bottom, the lighter things on top."

(2)   A pre-boarding announcement to passengers to stow their baggage but not to close the doors. If the doors were open, flight attendants could come down the aisle before takeoff and check each and every one of the bins without having to take the time to open closed bins.

(3)   A pre-boarding inspection of carry-on baggage, in which flight attendants check the volume of the luggage as well as its weight.

(4)   An on-board announcement by the flight attendant to passengers, *e.g.*, in conjunction with the safety briefing concerning oxygen masks and emergency exits.

(5)   A warning on the plastic safety card which says something such as: "Be careful; don't overload bins and use caution when you use them."

(6)   A warning or illustration depicting the proper way to pack an overhead bin.

(7)   A pre-landing announcement to passengers concerning the removal of baggage from the overhead bins.

(8)   An announcement or warning while taxiing to the arrival gate when the vast majority of passengers are still seated, to the effect that passengers need to be cautious when opening the bins.

The placement of baggage in an overhead compartment plainly relates to airline services. State enforcement of the claim plainly regulates. Hodges' claim is then preempted unless the activity she complains of constitutes operation or maintenance of an aircraft. "Operation of aircraft" means "the use of aircraft, for the purpose of air navigation and includes the navigation of aircraft." *See* 49 U.S.C. § 1301(31). The statute does not define "maintenance of aircraft." Nonetheless, I have little difficulty in concluding that stowing carry-on items in an overhead compartment is a service airlines provide for passengers who do not wish to check their baggage. It does not in any way relate to the navigation or maintenance of aircraft. Hodges' claim is preempted, and the judgment of the district court should be affirmed.

EXERCISE 6-3. *HODGES V. DELTA AIRLINES, INC.*—"SERVICES" VS. "OPERATION OR MAINTENANCE OF AIRCRAFT"

1.   What does *en banc* mean? What does this signify in terms of the ease with which the Airline Deregulation Act can be interpreted by judges?

2.   What are the three ways in which federal law might preempt state law and what is the key to construing preemption?

3. How are "services" defined under Section 1305(a)(1) of the Airline Deregulation Act? How does the court define the term? Does it include the "operation and maintenance of an aircraft"?

4. Did Congress intend the Airline Deregulation Act to preempt all state claims for personal injury? To what evidence does the court point to in resolving this question?

5. Detail the concern expressed in the concurring opinion? How would the dissenting judges have decided this case using the definition of "operation of aircraft" under 49 U.S.C. § 1301(31)?

WITTY V. DELTA AIR LINES, INC.

366 F.3d 380 (5th Cir. 2004)

REAVLEY, CIRCUIT JUDGE.

Milton Witty brought this diversity suit in Louisiana federal district court against Delta Air Lines, Inc. ("Delta"). He claims that he developed Deep Vein Thrombosis ("DVT") while on a Delta flight from Monroe, Louisiana to Hartford, Connecticut.

DVT occurs when a blood clot develops in a deep vein, usually in the leg. It can cause serious complications if the clot breaks off and travels to the lungs or brain. Witty alleged that Delta was negligent in failing to warn passengers about the risks of DVT. He asserts in his appellate brief that "[t]he warning should be that there is a high risk of developing [DVT] in pressurized cabins that exceed a certain length of time." The complaint also alleged that Delta was negligent in failing to provide adequate leg room to prevent DVT and in "failing to allow [passengers] to exercise their legs."

Delta filed a motion to dismiss, arguing that the state law claims were preempted. The district court denied the motion. The court reasoned that under *Hodges v. Delta Airlines, Inc.*, 44 F.3d 334 (5th Cir. 1995) (*en banc*), state regulation of airline "services" is preempted but that "state tort actions for personal physical injuries caused by the operation and maintenance of aircraft are not preempted by federal law." The court concluded that Witty's claim arose from the operation of Delta's aircraft and therefore was not preempted. The district court found that the order was appropriate for interlocutory appeal under 28 U.S.C. § 1292(b), and we permitted the appeal.

DISCUSSION

We review *de novo* the district court's ruling on preemption. Sitting *en banc* in *Hodges*, we held that a passenger's personal injury claim under state law was not preempted. The passenger "was injured when a fellow passenger opened an overhead compartment and dislodged a case containing several bottles of rum." We analyzed the effect of the preemption provision of Airline Deregulation Act of 1978 ("ADA"), which states that, subject to certain exceptions not relevant here, "a State . . . may not enact or enforce a law, regulation, or other provision having the force and effect of law related to a price, route or service of any air carrier that may provide air transportation under this subpart."

In *Hodges*, we held that the preemptive effect of § 41713(b)(1) is limited by a provision of the Federal Aviation Act of 1958 ("FAA"), which provides that air carriers must maintain insurance or self-insurance that covers liability "for bodily injury to, or death of, an individual . . . resulting from the operation or maintenance of the aircraft . . ." We reasoned that § 41112(a) "can only be understood to qualify the scope of 'services' removed from state regulation by [§ 41713(b)(1)]. A complete preemption of state law in this area would have rendered any requirement of insurance coverage nugatory . . . Thus, federal preemption of state laws, even certain common law actions 'related to services' of an air carrier, does not displace state tort actions for personal physical injuries or property damage caused by the operation and maintenance of aircraft."

We recognized in *Hodges* that there is no "strict dichotomy" between "services" and "operation or maintenance of aircraft," concluding instead that the terms "overlap somewhat conceptually," and thereby suggesting a case by case resolution of preemption questions. We ultimately concluded that the state personal injury claim was not related to the provision of airline services and did "derive from the operation of the aircraft," and accordingly was not preempted. Merely describing our analysis in *Hodges* demonstrates that preemption questions in this arena do not always submit to a simple analysis.

Insofar as plaintiff Witty in the pending case alleges that Delta should have provided more leg room, we hold that such a requirement would inexorably relate to prices charged by airlines . . . The failure to warn claim presents a closer question, but we conclude under implied preemption doctrines that Congress intended to preempt state standards for the warnings that must be given airline passengers.

Insofar as plaintiff Witty in the pending case alleges that Delta should have provided more leg room, we hold that such a requirement would inexorably relate to prices charged by airlines, and Witty does not seriously contend otherwise. Since requiring more leg room would necessarily reduce the number of seats on the aircraft, such a requirement would impose a standard "relating to a price" under § 41713(b)(1), and is accordingly preempted by the ADA. Section 41713(b)(1) not only preempts the direct regulation of prices by states, but also preempts indirect regulation "relating to" prices that have "the forbidden significant effect" on such prices. *Morales v. Trans World Airlines, Inc.* (1992). While the state regulation of leg room might not relate to prices as obviously as the state regulation of fare advertising at issue in *Morales*, the economic effect on prices would in our view be significant, perhaps much more so than the advertising rules at issue in *Morales*.

The failure to warn claim presents a closer question, but we conclude under implied preemption doctrines that Congress intended to preempt state standards for the warnings that must be given airline passengers. The complaint, by alleging that Delta was negligent in "failing to allow [passengers] to exercise their legs," might be construed as asserting a separate "failure to instruct" claim that passengers were not advised to move about the cabin or were instructed verbally or by the seat belt sign to remain in their seats. We conclude however that the preemption analysis of such a claim is essentially identical to the analysis of a failure to warn claim, and our discussion of the latter is intended to cover both claims.

At the outset, we note that *Hodges* described the ADA as "an economic deregulation statute," suggesting that the express preemption provision of that Act is not necessarily the only conceivable basis for finding preemption in a personal injury case based on inadequate safety warnings. There is a separate federal act, the FAA, which addresses air safety. The Supreme Court, after *Hodges*, has recognized that preemption under ordinary implied preemption principles is not necessarily foreclosed by the existence of an express preemption provision. Moreover, *Hodges* expressly did not reach the issue of "the possible preemptive effect of Federal Aviation Administration safety regulations governing aircraft and carriers." This issue is squarely raised in the pending case.

Preemption ultimately turns on congressional intent. Preemption may be express or implied. In the pending case, field preemption and conflict preemption are both applicable, because there exists a comprehensive scheme of federal regulation, and the imposition of state standards would conflict with federal law and interfere with federal objectives.

The FAA not only authorizes but affirmatively directs the Administrator of the Federal Aviation Administration to promulgate air safety standards and regulations, including standards and regulations relating to aircraft design, aircraft maintenance and inspections, "the maximum hours or periods of service of airmen and other employees of air carriers," and as a catchall provision, "other practices, methods, and procedure the Administrator finds necessary for safety in air commerce and national security." The administrator is generally charged with carrying out the FAA "in a way that best tends to reduce or eliminate the possibility or recurrence of accidents in air transportation."

Pursuant to its congressional charge to regulate air safety, the Federal Aviation Administration has issued a broad array of safety-related regulations codified in Title 14 of the Code of Federal Regulations. These regulations cover airworthiness standards, crew certification and medical standards, and aircraft operating requirements. The regulations include a general federal standard of care for aircraft operators, requiring that "[n]o person may operate an aircraft in a careless or reckless manner so as to endanger the life or property of another." 14 C.F.R. § 91.13(a) (2003).

Field and Conflict Preemption

There are a number of federal regulations governing the warnings and instructions which must be given to airline passengers. These regulations require, for example, that "no smoking" placards be placed in lavatories, that "no smoking" signs be illuminated during the entire flight on non-smoking flights, and that the "fasten seat belt" sign "shall be turned on during any movement on the surface, for each takeoff, for each landing, and at any other time considered necessary by the pilot in command." In addition, the Federal Aviation Administration has published regulations, 14 C.F.R. §§ 121.571 & 121.585, and an advisory circular setting out in detail the oral briefings, familiar to all domestic air travelers, which flight attendants or other flight personnel must give passengers, as well the information that must be included in passenger safety briefing cards.

We hold that federal regulatory requirements for passenger safety warnings and instructions are exclusive and preempt all state standards and requirements. Congress enacted a pervasive regulatory scheme covering air safety concerns that includes regulation of the warnings and instructions that must be given airline passengers. The Supreme Court has observed that the FAA "requires a delicate balance between safety and efficiency, and the protection of persons on the ground . . . The interdependence of these factors requires a uniform and exclusive system of federal regulation if the congressional objectives underlying the Federal Aviation Act are to be fulfilled." *City of Burbank v. Lockheed Air Terminal Inc.*, 411 U.S. 624 (1973).

Allowing courts and juries to decide under state law that warnings should be given in addition to those required by the Federal Aviation Administration would necessarily conflict with the federal regulations. In this case, the conflict is more than theoretical, since Witty claims that a DVT warning should have been given, while federal regulations do not require such a warning. And any warning that passengers should not stay in their seats, but should instead move about to prevent DVT, would necessarily conflict with any federal determination that, all things considered, passengers are safer in their seats. Warnings by their nature conflict, in the sense that the import of one warning is diluted by additional warnings that might be imposed under state law.

> *Allowing courts and juries to decide under state law that warnings should be given in addition to those required by the Federal Aviation Administration would necessarily conflict with the federal regulations. In this case, the conflict is more than theoretical, since Witty claims that a DVT warning should have been given, while federal regulations do not require such a warning.*

Ultimately, we need not decide whether a state claim for failure to warn passengers of air travel risks is entirely preempted, or, as another circuit has held, is preempted to the extent that a federal standard must be used but that state remedies are available. We hold that, at a minimum, any such claim must be based on a violation of federally mandated warnings. In this case, federal regulations do not require warnings to passengers about the risks of DVT or methods for preventing this condition. Delta therefore cannot be held liable for failing to provide warnings or instructions to Witty.

We hold that the leg room claim is preempted by the ADA. We further hold that federal law exclusively provides the safety warnings that airlines must give passengers, and that state law regarding air safety warnings is preempted. Since there is no federal requirement that airlines give DVT warnings, Witty's state claim for failure to warn fails. Accordingly, the order denying the motion to dismiss is reversed, and we render judgment in favor of Delta.

EXERCISE 6-4. *WITTY V. DELTA AIR LINES, INC.*—FAILURE TO WARN

1. Define the following procedural terms used in the *Witty v. Delta Air Lines, Inc.* case: (a) diversity jurisdiction; (b) interlocutory appeal; and (c) *de novo.*

2. What is Deep Vein Thrombosis ("DVT")?

3. Explain the procedural history of the case prior to reaching the Fifth Circuit.

4. How does the court rule on: (i) the plaintiff's negligent failure to provide adequate leg room claim; and (ii) the plaintiff's failure to warn claim? Explain the court's rationale.

5. Does *Witty v. Delta Air Lines, Inc.* fall under the heading of express or implied preemption? Explain.

CHARAS V. TRANS WORLD AIRLINES, INC.

160 F.3d 1259 (9th Cir. 1998)

SILVERMAN, CIRCUIT JUDGE.

These consolidated cases cause us to consider once again the circumstances under which the Airline Deregulation Act of 1978 ("ADA") preempts certain state law claims. We have taken these cases *en banc sua sponte* to rethink our previous decisions.

We now hold that in enacting the ADA, Congress intended to preempt only state laws and lawsuits that would adversely affect the economic deregulation of the airlines and the forces of competition within the airline industry. Congress did not intend to preempt passengers' run-of-the-mill personal injury claims. Accordingly, we hold that Congress used the word "service" in the phrase "rates, routes, or service" in the ADA's preemption clause to refer to the prices, schedules, origins and destinations of the point-to-point transportation of passengers, cargo, or mail. In the context in which it was used in the Act, "service" was not intended to include an airline's provision of in-flight beverages, personal assistance to passengers, the handling of luggage, and similar amenities. *[margin: Service Narrowly Defined]*

We expressly overrule our decisions in *Harris v. American Airlines, Inc.*, 55 F.3d 1472 (9th Cir. 1995), and *Gee v. Southwest Airlines*, 110 F.3d 1400 (9th Cir. 1997), to the extent that they are inconsistent with this interpretation.

FACTUAL AND PROCEDURAL BACKGROUND

1. *Beverage v. Continental Airlines*

Robert A. Beverage was a passenger on a Continental Airlines flight. He claims that a flight attendant hit his shoulder with a service cart and caused him serious injuries, including a dislocated shoulder and a cracked and detached scapular prosthesis. Beverage filed a state tort claim against Continental for negligence and breach of contract. The district court concluded that the ADA preempted Beverage's claims and granted Continental's motion to dismiss. Beverage timely appealed the district court's ruling.

2. *Jacoby v. Trans World Airlines*

Mildred Jacoby was a passenger on Trans World Airlines. After the plane landed, another passenger opened an overhead bin and a large piece of luggage fell on Jacoby's head, causing her injuries. Jacoby filed suit in state court against TWA; the airline removed the case and filed a motion to dismiss. Finding that the ADA preempted Jacoby's claims against TWA, the district court granted the motion to dismiss. Jacoby appealed.

3. *Charas v. Trans World Airlines*

Cherie Charas, a passenger on a TWA flight, tripped over a piece of luggage allegedly left in the aisle by a flight attendant. Due to the fall, Charas claims that she suffered a fractured humerus and required a shoulder joint replacement. Charas sued TWA for negligence. In granting TWA's motion for summary judgment, the district court concluded that Charas's claims were preempted by the ADA. Charas timely appealed the district court's ruling.

4. *Gulley v. American Airlines*

Bernice Gulley was a passenger aboard a small commuter airplane operated by American Airlines. Gulley has a bone condition that makes her susceptible to bone fractures. She claims that she advised American of her condition and informed the airline that she needed assistance in disembarking, but that American employees provided no help. Gulley exited the plane, unassisted, on a stairway with only a single, movable chain handhold. She alleges that she fell and sustained injuries. Gulley brought a state negligence action against American. The district court held that although Gulley's claim for negligent failure to provide safe equipment involved the "maintenance and operation" of the aircraft and was not preempted, Gulley's claim for negligent failure to assist her down the stairs involved the rendering of "service" and was preempted by the ADA. Gulley appealed the district court's order granting American's motion for summary judgment.

5. *Newman v. American Airlines, Inc.*

Elizabeth Newman's complaint stems from her attempt to fly from San Diego to Long Island on an American Airlines flight. Newman claims that in making her reservations, she informed American that she was blind, suffered from a heart condition, and required assistance in boarding the plane. She flew from Long Island to San Diego without incident. However, it is alleged that on her return flight to Long Island, a flight attendant attempted to check Newman's carry-on bags due to space constraints.

At that time, the flight attendant learned that the bags contained Newman's medications. The flight attendant then informed the captain that Newman might have a disability that would preclude her from flying. The captain asked the flight attendant to ask Newman about her medication and to ascertain the phone number of Newman's doctor to verify whether or not Newman was at risk for a heart attack during flight. When Newman could not remember her doctor's number, American denied her passage until she could provide a letter from her doctor certifying that it was safe for her to fly. Prior to obtaining the required certificate, Newman was required to stay overnight at a motel and suffered injuries when she fell upon boarding the shuttle bus transporting her there. She filed various claims, including state tort claims and federal statutory claims, against American. The district court granted American's motion for summary judgment, concluding that Newman's state law claims were preempted by the ADA and that American had "permissibly refused" boarding to Newman for the purposes of her federal claims. Newman timely appealed.

DISCUSSION

In 1978, Congress determined that efficiency, low prices, variety, and quality would be furthered by reliance on competitive market forces rather than pervasive federal regulation. To prevent states from "undo[ing] federal deregulation with regulation of their own," *Morales v. Trans World Airlines*, 504 U.S. 374 (1992), Congress enacted § 1305(a)(1) which preempts state laws "relating to the rates, routes, or service of any air carrier." However, the scope of this preemption has been a source of considerable dispute since its enactment.

In our own circuit, we have addressed the issue on several occasions. Prior to *Harris*, we held that the ADA did not preempt state law tort claims that were only "tenuously connected" with airline deregulation. *See Lathigra v. British Airways PLC*, 41 F.3d 535 (9th Cir. 1994) (looking to congressional intent, the panel concluded that the ADA did not preempt state tort actions for negligent reconfirmation because they did not undermine the goals of airline deregulation.); *West v. Northwest Airlines, Inc.*, 995 F.2d 148 (9th Cir. 1993) (holding that state law tort claim for compensatory damages was "too tenuously connected to airline regulation to trigger preemption under the ADA"). However, in 1995, we took a different approach.

Harris brought a tort suit against American Airlines for continuing to serve alcohol to an intoxicated passenger who was harassing her. In declining to look beyond the bare preemption language to congressional intent, the majority, over Judge Norris's dissent, concluded that the ADA preempted *Harris's* claim because it "relate[d] to [a] service" that the airline rendered, namely the provision of a drink. The panel did not discuss or distinguish *West* or *Lathigra*.

Two years later, we wrestled with this problem again in *Gee.* There, we expressed doubts about *Harris* and the validity of its analysis. However, in an attempt to mitigate the impact of *Harris*, we expressly adopted the Fifth Circuit's approach in *Hodges v. Delta Airlines, Inc.*, 44 F.3d 334 (5th Cir. 1995) (*en banc*). Under *Hodges*, claims related to an airline's "operations and maintenance" are not preempted by the ADA while claims related to a "service" provided by the airline are preempted. As Judges O'Scannlain and Jolly predicted in their respective concurrences in *Gee* and *Hodges*, the distinction between an airline's operations and its service turned out to be as elusive as it is unworkable.

Judge O'Scannlain noted that the operations-versus-service dichotomy invites nonsensical, inequitable, and inconsistent results, and in any event has nothing to do with the purpose of airline deregulation. For example, under the rule announced in *Gee*, a plaintiff injured when struck by a beverage cart door would be able to bring a tort action if the door swung open because a bolt was missing (because the injury arises out of the "operations and maintenance" of the aircraft), but not if the flight attendant negligently failed to latch the door properly (because the flight attendant's conduct relates to "service"). Judge O'Scannlain demonstrated the folly of the distinction between "operations and maintenance" and "service," and suggested instead that the court examine whether the state laws underlying the claims frustrate the goal of economic deregulation by interfering with the forces of competition. If they do, the claims would be preempted; otherwise, they would not.

In reconsidering our view of the scope of the ADA's preemption, we conclude that Judge Norris and Judge O'Scannlain got it right and that *Harris* is contrary to congressional intent. Further, although we recognize that we were bound by *Harris* when we decided *Gee*, we now believe that the rule we adopted in *Gee* was imprecise, difficult to apply, and inadequately reflective of the ADA's goal of economic deregulation. Accordingly, in defining the "service" that the ADA preempts, we adopt Judge O'Scannlain's approach, an approach consistent with Supreme Court precedent and the ADA's plain language and legislative history.

The Supreme Court twice has addressed the scope of § 1305(a)(1). In both decisions, the Supreme Court took great pains to articulate the boundaries of the preemption, indicating that the ADA would not preempt most state law tort claims. Although neither cases directly resolved whether the § 1305(a)(1) preemption encompasses state law tort claims, they certainly suggest that such claims are not within the intended reach of the preemption. Moreover, in its decisions interpreting § 1305(a)(1), the Supreme Court has not had occasion to define the term "service." In attempting to deduce its meaning, we are mindful that principles of statutory construction require us to consider the term within its context. Airlines' "rates" and "routes" generally refer to the point-to-point transport of passengers. "Rates" indicates price; "routes" refers to courses of travel. It therefore follows that "service," when juxtaposed to "rates" and "routes," refers to such things as the frequency and scheduling of transportation, and to the selection of markets to or from which transportation is provided (as in, "This airline provides service from Tucson to New York twice a day.")

To interpret "service" more broadly is to ignore the context of its use; and, it effectively would result in the preemption of virtually everything an airline does. It seems clear to us that that is not what Congress intended. Nowhere in the legislative history, or in what remains of the federal airline regulatory statutes, does Congress intimate that "service," in the context of deregulation, includes the dispensing of food and drinks, flight attendant assistance, or the like.

Like "rates" and "routes," Congress used "service" in § 1305(a)(1) in the public utility sense—i.e., the provision of air transportation to and from various markets at various times. In that context, "service" does not refer to the pushing of beverage carts, keeping the aisles clear of stumbling blocks, the safe handling and storage of luggage, assistance to passengers in need, or like functions.

We conclude that when Congress enacted federal economic deregulation of the airlines, it intended to insulate the industry from possible state economic regulation as well. It intended to encourage the forces of competition. It did not intend to immunize the airlines from liability for personal injuries caused by their tortious conduct. Like "rates" and "routes," Congress used "service" in § 1305(a)(1) in the public utility sense—i.e., the provision of air transportation to and from various markets at various times. In that context, "service" does not refer to the pushing of beverage carts, keeping the aisles clear of stumbling blocks, the safe handling and storage of luggage, assistance to passengers in need, or like functions.

We expressly overrule our decisions in *Harris* and *Gee* to the extent that they are inconsistent with this interpretation. Accordingly, we remand these cases to the panel for resolution consistent with this decision.

EXERCISE 6-5. *CHARAS V. TRANS WORLD AIRLINES, INC.*— "SERVICE" IN "PUBLIC UTILITY SENSE"

1. How does the *Charas v. Trans World Airlines, Inc.* court define "service" under the Airline Deregulation Act?

2. Summarize the different approaches the Ninth Circuit has taken when addressing the scope of preemption under the Airline Deregulation Act.

3. How does the court regard the "operations-versus-services" approach of *Hodges v. Delta Airlines, Inc.*? What example does the court provide to make its point.

4. How does the court define "service" and "rate." On the basis of those definition, what does the court hold?

5. Is the definition of "service" in *Charas v. Trans World Airlines, Inc.* broader or narrower than that of *Hodges v. Delta Airlines, Inc.*? Why might that matter?

NOTES ON *NORTHWEST AIRLINES, INC. V. DUNCAN*—PUTTING *HODGES*, *WITTY*, AND *CHARAS* TOGETHER: RESOLVING THE CIRCUIT SPLIT ON "SERVICE"

The cases presented in above, Part C, reflect a circuit split with respect to the meaning of the word "service" in the Airline Deregulation Act. The majority of circuits—the Fourth, Fifth, and Seventh Circuits—define service as referring to the provision of labor from an airline to a passenger, including matters incidental to and distinct from actual transportation (*e.g.*, boarding procedures, baggage handling, and food and drink). A minority of circuits, on the other hand—the Third and Ninth Circuits—interpret service quite narrowly as including prices, schedules, transportation from point-to-point. Notice how this narrow interpretation favors passengers, because it minimizes what can be characterized under the heading service, while the majority's reading is pro-carrier in that it is so broad as to swallow up many, if not most, matters arguably connected to airline economics.

Should the Supreme Court resolve this difference? If so, how?

In *Northwest Airlines, Inc. v. Duncan*, 531 U.S. 1058 (2000), *infra.* Justice O'Connor suggested the time for a uniform interpretation of service was at hand. By way of background, the underlying case, *Duncan v. Northwest Airlines, Inc.*, 208 F.3d 1112 (9th Cir. 2000), involved a class-action, personal injury lawsuit brought by flight attendants arguing that their employer-airline's allowance of smoking on international flights breached a Washington state law duty to provide a safe and healthy work environment for its employers. The airline moved to dismiss on preemption grounds and the case was dismissed, after which the airline banned smoking on all trans-Pacific flights. The dismissal was reversed on appeal:

> Given our holding in *Charas*, it is clear that allowing smoking on Northwest's trans-Pacific flights does not constitute a 'service.' An airline's decision to permit (or not to permit) smoking on a flight is not a decision dealing with 'the frequency and scheduling of transportation, [or] the selection of markets to or from which transportation is provided.' Rather, like the decision to offer in-flight beverages or prohibiting smoking deals with what we termed, for want of a better word, 'amenities.'

The flight attendant class appealed, but the Supreme Court denied *certiorari*:

NORTHWEST AIRLINES, INC. V. DUNCAN
531 U.S. 1058 (2000)

JUSTICE O'CONNOR, with whom THE CHIEF JUSTICE and JUSTICE THOMAS join, dissenting.

The petition for a *writ of certiorari* in this case presents an important issue that has divided the Courts of Appeals: the meaning of the term "service" in the portion of the Airline Deregulation Act of 1978 ("ADA") that pre-empts any state law "related to a price, route, or service of an air carrier." 49 U.S.C. § 41713(b)(1). I would grant the petition to resolve this issue and bring needed certainty to this area of the law.

We have addressed the scope of the ADA's pre-emption provision on two prior occasions. In *Morales v. Trans World Airlines, Inc.*, 504 U.S. 374, 383 (1992), we noted the "broad pre-emptive purpose" of the ADA. And while we have never directly addressed the definition of "service" within the meaning of § 41713(b)(1), we have suggested that this term encompasses "access to flights and class-of-service upgrades." *American Airlines, Inc. v. Wolens*, 513 U.S. 219, 226 (1995). The Courts of Appeals, however, have taken directly conflicting positions on this question of statutory interpretation.

The Ninth Circuit below, adhering to its decision in *Charas v. Trans World Airlines, Inc.*, 160 F.3d 1259 (1998) (*en banc*), held that the term "service" encompasses " 'the prices, schedules, origins and destinations of the point-to-point transportation of passengers, cargo, or mail,' " but not the " 'provision of in-flight beverages, personal assistance to passengers, the handling of luggage, and similar amenities.' " *Duncan v. Northwest Airlines, Inc.*, 208 F.3d 1112, 1114–1115 (2000). The Third Circuit has expressly agreed with this approach. *Taj Mahal Travel, Inc. v. Delta Airlines Inc.*, 164 F.3d 186, 194 (1998).

In contrast, three Courts of Appeals have adopted a much broader definition. *See Hodges v. Delta Airlines, Inc.*, 44 F.3d 334, 336 (5th Cir. 1995) (*en banc*) (defining "service" in terms of the " '[contractual] features of air transportation,' " including " 'ticketing, boarding procedures, provision of food and drink, and baggage handling' "); *Smith v. Comair, Inc.*, 134 F.3d 254, 259 (4th Cir. 1998) ("Undoubtedly, boarding procedures are a service rendered by an airline"); *Travel All Over The World, Inc. v. Kingdom of Saudi Arabia*, 73 F.3d 1423, 1433 (7th Cir. 1996) (adopting *Hodges* definition). *See also Chukwu v. Board of Directors British Airways*, 889 F. Supp. 12, 13 (D. Mass. 1995) (same).

Given these opposing interpretations, I believe we should hear this case. The legal issue is an important one, well suited for resolution by this Court. The two leading cases, *Charas* and *Hodges*, are both the product of *en banc* consideration. They have fully explored the relevant considerations, including the language and history of the ADA and its pre-emption clause, as well as the policies supporting the possible interpretations of the term "service." Resolution of this question would provide needed certainty to airline companies. While this case involves the potential pre-emption of a state law personal-injury claim based on an airline's smoking policy, the legal principle at stake has ramifications for a host of other tort actions against airlines. *See, e.g., Smith, supra* (false imprisonment and intentional infliction of emotional distress); Travel All Over The World, supra (defamation). Because airline companies operate across state lines, the divergent pre-emption rules formulated by the Courts of Appeals currently operate to expose the airlines to inconsistent state regulations. Cf. Morales, supra, at 378 (the ADA's pre-emption provision is intended "[t]o ensure that the States would not undo federal deregulation with regulation of their own").

A decision from this Court would provide needed clarification on this discrete and important issue of statutory interpretation. Accordingly, I respectfully dissent from the denial of the petition for *certiorari*.

D. CONTRACT CLAIMS

AMERICAN AIRLINES, INC. V. WOLENS
513 U.S. 219 (1995)

JUSTICE GINSBURG delivered the opinion of the Court.

The Airline Deregulation Act of 1978 ("ADA") prohibits States from "enact[ing] or enforc[ing] any law . . . relating to [air carrier] rates, routes, or services." This case concerns the scope of that preemptive provision, specifically, its application to a state-court suit, brought by participants in an airline's frequent flyer program, challenging the airline's retroactive changes in terms and conditions of the program. We hold that the ADA's preemption prescription bars state-imposed regulation of air carriers, but allows room for court enforcement of contract terms set by the parties themselves.

Plaintiffs (respondents here) are participants in American Airlines' frequent flyer program, AAdvantage. AAdvantage enrollees earn mileage credits when they fly on American. They can exchange those credits for flight tickets or class-of-service upgrades. Plaintiffs complained that AAdvantage program modifications, instituted by American in 1988, devalued credits AAdvantage members had already earned. Plaintiffs featured American's imposition of capacity controls (limits on seats available to passengers obtaining tickets with AAdvantage credits) and blackout dates (restrictions on dates credits could be used). Conceding that American had reserved the right to change AAdvantage terms and conditions, plaintiffs challenged only the retroactive application of modifications, *i.e.*, cutbacks on the utility of credits previously accumulated. These cutbacks, plaintiffs maintained, violated the Illinois Consumer Fraud and Deceptive Business Practices Act (Consumer Fraud Act or Act), and constituted a breach of contract. Plaintiffs currently seek only monetary relief.

In March 1992, several weeks before the U.S. Supreme Court's decision in *Morales v. Trans World Airlines, Inc.*, the Illinois Supreme Court rejected plaintiffs' prayer for an injunction. Such a decree, the Illinois court reasoned, would involve regulation of an airline's current rendition of services, a matter preempted by the ADA. That court, however, allowed the breach-of-contract and Consumer Fraud Act monetary relief claims to survive. The ADA's preemption clause, the Illinois court said, ruled out "only those State laws and regulations that specifically relate to and have more than a tangential connection with an airline's rates, routes or services."

American petitioned for *certiorari*. The airline charged that the Illinois court, in a decision out of sync with had narrowly construed the ADA's broadly preemptive § 1305(a)(1). We granted the petition, vacated the judgment of the Supreme Court of Illinois, and remanded for further consideration in light of *Morales v. Trans World Airlines, Inc.*, 504 U.S. 374 (1992). On remand, the Illinois Supreme Court, with one dissent, adhered to its prior judgment. Describing frequent flyer programs as not "essential," but merely "peripheral to the operation of an airline," the Illinois court typed plaintiffs' state law claims for money damages as "relat[ed] to American's rates, routes, and services" only "tangential[ly]" or "tenuous[ly]." We granted American's second petition for *certiorari*, and we now reverse the Illinois Supreme Court's judgment to the extent that it allowed survival of plaintiffs' Consumer Fraud Act claims; we affirm that judgment, however, to the extent that it permits plaintiffs' breach-of-contract action to proceed. In both respects, we adopt the position of the DOT, as advanced in this Court by the United States.

* * *

We need not dwell on the question whether plaintiffs' complaints state claims "relating to [air carrier] rates, routes, or services." *Morales*, we are satisfied, does not countenance the Illinois Supreme Court's separation of matters "essential" from matters unessential to airline operations. Plaintiffs' claims relate to "rates," *i.e.*, American's charges in the form of mileage credits for free tickets and upgrades, and to "services," *i.e.*, access to flights and class-of-service upgrades unlimited by retrospectively applied capacity controls and blackout dates.

"Enact or enforce any law"

But the ADA's preemption clause contains other words in need of interpretation, specifically, the words "enact or enforce any law" in the instruction: "[N]o State . . . shall enact or enforce any law . . . relating to [air carrier] rates, routes, or services." Taking into account all the words Congress placed in § 1305(a)(1), we first consider whether plaintiffs' claims under the Consumer Fraud Act are preempted, and then turn to plaintiffs' breach-of-contract claims.

The Consumer Fraud Act declares unlawful

[u]nfair methods of competition and unfair or deceptive acts or practices, including but not limited to the use or employment of any deception, fraud, false pretense, false promise, misrepresentation or the concealment, suppression or omission of any material fact, with intent that others rely upon the concealment, suppression or omission of such material fact, or the use or employment of any practice described in Section 2 of the 'Uniform Deceptive Trade Practices Act' . . . in the

conduct of any trade or commerce . . . whether any person has in fact been misled, deceived or damaged thereby.

Ill. Comp. Stat., ch. 815, § 505/2 (1992).

The Act is prescriptive; it controls the primary conduct of those falling within its governance. It serves as a means to guide and police the marketing practices of the airlines; the Act does not simply give effect to bargains offered by the airlines and accepted by airline customers. In light of the full text of the preemption clause, and of the ADA's purpose to leave largely to the airlines themselves, and not at all to States, the selection and design of marketing mechanisms appropriate to the furnishing of air transportation services, we conclude that § 1305(a)(1) preempts plaintiffs' claims under the Consumer Fraud Act.

We do not read the ADA's preemption clause to shelter airlines from suits alleging no violation of state-imposed obligations, but seeking recovery solely for the airline's alleged breach of its own, self-imposed undertakings.

Next, American maintains, and we agree, that "Congress could hardly have intended to allow the States to hobble [competition for airline passengers] through the application of restrictive state laws." We do not read the ADA's preemption clause, however, to shelter airlines from suits alleging no violation of state-imposed obligations, but seeking recovery solely for the airline's alleged breach of its own, self-imposed undertakings. As persuasively argued by the United States, terms and conditions airlines offer and passengers accept are privately ordered obligations and thus do not amount to a State's enactment or enforcement of any law, rule, regulation, standard, or other provision having the force and effect of law within the meaning of the ADA. A remedy confined to a contract's terms simply holds parties to their agreements—in this instance, to business judgments an airline made public about its rates and services.

Contract Not Preempted

The ADA, as we recognized in *Morales* was designed to promote "maximum reliance on competitive market forces." Market efficiency requires effective means to enforce private agreements. *See* Daniel Farber, *Contract Law and Modern Economic Theory*, 78 NW. U. L. REV. 303, 315 (1983) (remedy for breach of contract "is necessary in order to ensure economic efficiency"); RICHARD POSNER, ECONOMIC ANALYSIS OF LAW 90–91 (4th ed. 1992) (legal enforcement of contracts is more efficient than a purely voluntary system). As stated by the United States: "The stability and efficiency of the market depend fundamentally on the enforcement of agreements freely made, based on needs perceived by the contracting parties at the time." That reality is key to sensible construction of the ADA.

The FAA's text, we note, presupposes the vitality of contracts governing transportation by air carriers. Section 411(b), 49 U.S.C. § 1381(b), thus authorizes airlines to "incorporate by reference in any ticket or other written instrument any of the terms of the contract of carriage" to the extent authorized by the DOT. And the DOT's regulations contemplate that, upon the January 1, 1983, termination of domestic tariffs, "ticket contracts" ordinarily would be enforceable under "the contract law of the States." Correspondingly, the DOT requires carriers to give passengers written notice of the time period within which they may "bring an action against the carrier for its acts."

American does not suggest that its contracts lack legal force. American sees the DOT, however, as the exclusively competent monitor of the airline's undertakings. American points to the Department's authority to require any airline, in conjunction with its certification, to file a performance bond conditioned on the airline's "making appropriate compensation . . ., as prescribed by the [Department], for failure . . . to perform air transportation services in accordance with agreements therefor."

But neither the DOT nor its predecessor, the CAB, has ever construed or applied this provision to displace courts as adjudicators in air carrier contract disputes. Instead, these agencies have read the provision to charge them with a less taxing task: In passing on air carrier fitness, the DOT and the CAB have used their performance bond authority to ensure that, when a carrier's financial fitness is marginal, funds will be available to compensate customers if the carrier goes under before providing already-paid-for services. *See, e.g., U.S. Bahamas Service Investigation*, CAB Order 79–11–116, p. 3, 84 CAB Reports 73, 75 (1979) ("We . . . find that Southeast [Airlines] is fit to provide scheduled foreign air transportation. However, because of Southeast's current financial condition its operations present an unacceptable risk of financial loss to consumers. Therefore, we shall require the carrier . . . to procure and maintain a bond for the protection of passengers who have paid for transportation not yet performed.").

The United States maintains that the DOT has neither the authority nor the apparatus required to superintend a contract dispute resolution regime. Prior to airline deregulation, the CAB set rates, routes, and services through a cumbersome administrative process of applications and approvals. When Congress dismantled that regime, the United States emphasizes, the lawmakers indicated no intention to establish, simultaneously, a new administrative process for DOT adjudication of private contract disputes. We agree.

Nor is it plausible that Congress meant to channel into federal courts the business of resolving, pursuant to judicially fashioned federal common law, the range of contract claims relating to airline rates, routes, or services. The ADA contains no hint of such a role for the federal courts. In this regard, the ADA contrasts markedly with the ERISA, which does channel civil actions into federal courts, under a comprehensive scheme, detailed in the legislation, designed to promote "prompt and fair claims settlement."

> *The conclusion that the ADA permits state law-based court adjudication of routine breach-of-contract claims also makes sense of Congress' retention of the FAA's saving clause. The ADA's preemption clause, § 1305(a)(1), read together with the FAA's saving clause, stops States from imposing their own substantive standards with respect to rates, routes, or services, but not from affording relief to a party who claims and proves that an airline dishonored a term the airline itself stipulated.*

The conclusion that the ADA permits state law-based court adjudication of routine breach-of-contract claims also makes sense of Congress' retention of the FAA's saving clause, 49 U.S.C. § 1506 (preserving "the remedies now existing at common law or by statute"). The ADA's preemption clause, § 1305(a)(1), read together with the FAA's saving clause, stops States from imposing their own substantive standards with respect to rates, routes, or services, but not from affording relief to a party who claims and proves that an airline dishonored a term the airline itself stipulated.

This distinction between what the state dictates and what the airline itself undertakes confines courts, in breach-of-contract actions, to the parties' bargain, with no enlargement or enhancement based on state laws or policies external to the agreement. American suggests that plaintiffs' breach-of-contract and Consumer Fraud Act claims differ only in their labels, so that if Fraud Act claims are preempted, contract claims must be preempted as well. But a breach of contract, without more, "does not amount to a cause of action cognizable under the [Consumer Fraud] Act and the Act should not apply to simple breach of contract claims." *Golembiewski v. Hallberg Ins. Agency, Inc.*, 635 N.E. 2d 452 (Ill. App. Ct. 1994). The basis for a contract action is the parties' agreement; to succeed under the consumer protection law, one must show not necessarily an agreement, but in all cases, an unfair or deceptive practice.

* * *

Responding to our colleagues' diverse opinions dissenting in part, we add a final note. This case presents two issues that run all through the law. First, who decides (here, courts or the DOT, the latter lacking contract dispute resolution resources for the task)? On this question, all agree to this extent: None of the opinions in this case would foist on the DOT work Congress has neither instructed nor funded the Department to do.

Second, where is it proper to draw the line (here, between what the ADA preempts, and what it leaves to private ordering, backed by judicial enforcement)? Justice Stevens reads our *Morales* decision to demand only minimal preemption; in contrast, Justice O'Connor reads the same case to mandate total preemption. The middle course we adopt seems to us best calculated to carry out the congressional design; it also bears the approval of the statute's experienced administrator, the DOT. And while we adhere to our holding in *Morales*, we do not overlook that in our system of adjudication, principles seldom can be settled "on the basis of one or two cases, but require a closer working out." Roscoe Pound, *Survey of the Conference Problems*, 14 U. CIN. L. REV. 324, 339 (1940) (Conference on the Status of the Rule of Judicial Precedent).

For the reasons stated, the judgment of the Illinois Supreme Court is affirmed in part and reversed in part, and the case is remanded for proceedings not inconsistent with this opinion.

JUSTICE SCALIA *took no part in the decision of the case.*

JUSTICE STEVENS, *concurring in part and dissenting in part.*

Although I agree with the majority that the Airline Deregulation Act of 1978 ("ADA") does not preempt respondents' breach-of-contract claims, I do not agree with the Court's disposition of their consumer-fraud claims. In my opinion, private tort actions based on common-law negligence or fraud, or on a statutory prohibition against fraud, are not preempted. Under the broad (and in my opinion incorrect) interpretation of the words "law . . . relating to rates, routes, or services" that the Court adopted in *Morales*, direct state regulation of airline advertising is preempted; but I would not extend the holding of that case to embrace the private claims that respondents assert in this case.

Unlike the National Association of Attorneys General ("NAAG") guidelines reviewed in *Morales*, the Illinois Consumer Fraud and Deceptive Business Practices Act ("Consumer Fraud Act") does not instruct the airlines about how they can market their services. Instead, it merely requires all commercial enterprises—airlines included—to refrain from defrauding their customers. The *Morales* opinion said nothing about preempting general state laws prohibiting fraud. The majority's extension of the ADA's preemptive reach from airline-specific advertising standards to a general background rule of private conduct represents an alarming enlargement of *Morales'* holding.

I see no reason why a state law requiring an airline to honor its contractual commitments is any less a law relating to its rates and services than is a state law imposing a "duty not to make false statements of material fact or to conceal such facts." *Cipollone v. Liggett Group, Inc.*, 505 U.S. 504 (1992) (finding similar claim not to be preempted under Federal Cigarette Labeling and Advertising Act).

In this case, the two claims are grounded upon the exact same conduct and would presumably have an identical impact upon American's rates, routes, and services. I see no reason why the ADA should preempt a claim that the airline defrauded its customers in the making and performance of that very same agreement.

I would analogize the Consumer Fraud Act to a codification of common-law negligence rules. Under ordinary tort principles, every person has a duty to exercise reasonable care toward all other persons with whom he comes into contact. Presumably, if an airline were negligent in a way that somehow affected its rates, routes, or services, and the victim of the airline's negligence were to sue in state court, the majority would not hold all common-law negligence rules to be preempted by the ADA.

Like contract principles, the standard of ordinary care is a general background rule against which all individuals order their affairs. Surely Congress did not intend to give airlines free rein to commit negligent acts subject only to the supervision of the Department of Transportation, any more than it meant to allow airlines to breach contracts with impunity. And, if judge-made duties are not preempted, it would make little sense to find preemption of identical rules codified by the state legislature. The duty imposed by the Consumer Fraud Act is to refrain from committing fraud in commercial dealings—it is "the duty not to deceive." This is neither a novel nor a controversial proscription. It falls no more heavily upon airlines than upon any other business. It is no more or less a state-imposed "public policy" than a negligence rule. In sum, I see no difference between the duty to refrain from deception and the duty of reasonable care, and I see no meaningful difference between the enforcement of either duty and the enforcement of a private agreement.

The majority's extension of *Morales* is particularly untenable in light of the interpretive presumption against preemption. As in *Cipollone*, I believe there is insufficient evidence of congressional intent to supersede laws of general applicability to justify a finding that the ADA preempts either the contract or the fraud claim. Indeed, the presumption against preemption is especially appropriate to the ADA because Congress retained the "saving clause" preserving state "remedies now existing at common law or by statute." 49 U.S.C. § 1506.

JUSTICE O'CONNOR, with whom JUSTICE THOMAS joins, in part, concurring in the judgment in part and dissenting in part.

In permitting respondents' contract action to go forward, the Court arrives at what might be a reasonable policy judgment as to when state law actions against airlines should be preempted if we were free to legislate it. It is not, however, consistent with our controlling precedents, and it requires some questionable assumptions about the nature of contract law. I would hold that none of respondents' actions may proceed.

Applying *Morales* to this case, I agree with the Court that respondents' consumer fraud and contract claims are "related to" airline "rates" and "services." The Court says, however, that judicial enforcement of a contract's terms, in accordance with state contract law, does not amount to a "State . . . enforc[ing] any law," but instead is simply a State "hold[ing] parties to their agreemen[t]." It therefore concludes that § 1305 does not apply to respondents' contract actions. I cannot agree with that conclusion.

* * *

Congress has recently revisited § 1305, and said that it "d[id] not intend to alter the broad preemption interpretation adopted by the United States Supreme Court in *Morales*," H.R. Conf. Rep. No. 103–677, p. 83 (1994). If the Court nonetheless believes that *Morales* misread § 1305, the proper course of action would be to overrule that case, despite Congress' apparent approval of it. The Court's reading of § 1305 is not, in my view, a " 'closer working out' " of ADA preemption; rather, it is a new approach that does not square with our decisions in *Morales*.

Stare decisis has "special force" in the area of statutory interpretation. It sometimes requires adherence to a wrongly decided precedent. Here, however, Congress apparently does not think that our decision in *Morales* was wrong, nor do I. In the absence of any " 'special justification,' " for departing from *Morales*, I would recognize its import here, and render the decision that the language of § 1305, in light of those cases, compels. If, at the end of the day, Congress believes we have erred in interpreting § 1305, it remains free to correct our mistake.

* * *

Our decision in *Morales* suffice to decide this case along the lines I have described. In addition, however, I disagree with the Court's view that courts can realistically be confined, "in breach-of-contract actions, to the parties' bargain, with no enlargement or enhancement based on state laws or policies external to the agreement." When they are so confined, the Court says, courts are "simply hold[ing] parties to their agreements," and are not "enforcing" any "law." The Court also says that " '[s]ome state law principles of contract law might well be preempted to the extent they seek to effectuate the State's public policies, rather than the intent of the parties.' "

The doctrinal underpinnings of the notion that judicial enforcement of the "intent of the parties" can be divorced from a State's "public policy" have been in serious question for many years. As one author wrote some time ago:

A contract, therefore, between two or more individuals cannot be said to be generally devoid of all public interest. If it be of no interest, why enforce it? For note that in enforcing contracts, the government does not merely allow two individuals to do what they have found pleasant in their eyes.

Enforcement, in fact, puts the machinery of the law in the service of one party against the other. When that is worthwhile and how that should be done are important questions of public policy.

[T]he notion that in enforcing contracts the state is only giving effect to the will of the parties rests upon an . . . untenable theory as to what the enforcement of contracts involves.

Morris Cohen, *The Basis of Contract*, 46 HARV. L. REV. 553, 562 (1933).

More recent authors have expressed similar views. *See, e.g.,* Jean Braucher, *Contract Versus Contractarianism: The Regulatory Role of Contract Law*, 47 WASH. & LEE L. REV. 697, 699 (1990) ("Mediating between private ordering and social concerns, contract is a socioeconomic institution that requires an array of normative choices . . . The questions addressed by contract law concern what social norms to use in the enforcement of contracts, not whether social norms will be used at all").

Contract law is a set of policy judgments concerning how to decide the meaning of private agreements, which private agreements should be legally enforceable, and what remedy to afford for their breach. The Court fails to recognize that when a State decides to force parties to comply with a contract, it does so only because it is satisfied that state policy, as expressed in its contract law, will be advanced by that decision. Thus, the Court's allowance that " '[s]ome state law principles of contract law . . . might well be preempted to the extent they seek to effectuate the State's public policies, rather than the intent of the parties,' " threatens to swallow all of contract law.

For example, the Court observes that on remand, the state court will be required to decide whether petitioner reserved the right to alter the terms of its frequent flyer program retroactively, or instead only prospectively. The court will presumably decide that question by looking to the usual "rules" of contract interpretation to decide what the contract's language means. If the court finds the language to be ambiguous, it might invoke the familiar rule that the contract should be construed against its drafter, and thus that respondents should receive the benefit of the doubt. That rule of contract construction is not essential to a functional contract system. It is a policy choice that our contract system has made. Other such policy choices are that courts should not enforce agreements unsupported by consideration; that courts should supply "reasonable" terms to fill "gaps" in incomplete contracts; the method by which courts should decide what terms to supply; and that a breach of contract entitles the aggrieved party to expectation damages most of the time, but specific performance only rarely. If courts are not permitted to look to these aspects of contract law in airline-related actions, they will find the cases difficult to decide.

Even the doctrine of unconscionability, which the United States suggests as an aspect of contract law that "might well be preempted" because it "seek[s] to effectuate the State's public policies, rather than the intent of the parties" cannot be so neatly categorized. On the one hand, refusing to enforce a contract because it is "unfair" seems quintessentially policy oriented. But on the other, "[p]rocedural unconscionability is broadly conceived to encompass not only the employment of sharp practices and the use of fine print and convoluted language, but a lack of understanding and an inequality of bargaining power." 1 FARNSWORTH § 4.28, at 506–07. In other words, a determination that a contract is "unconscionable" may in fact be a determination that one party did not intend to agree to the terms of the contract. Thus, the unconscionability doctrine, far from being a purely "policy-oriented" doctrine that courts impose over the will of the parties, instead demonstrates that state public policy cannot easily be separated from the methods by which courts are to decide what the parties "intended."

"[T]he law itself imposes contractual liability on the basis of a complex of moral, political, and social judgments." The rules laid down by contract law for determining what the parties intended an agreement to mean, whether that agreement is legally enforceable, and what relief an aggrieved party should receive, are the end result of those judgments. Our legal system has decided to allow private parties to invoke the coercive power of the State in the effort to enforce those (and only those) private agreements that conform to rules set by those state policies known collectively as "contract law." Courts cannot enforce private agreements without reference to those policies, because those policies define the role of courts in deciding disputes concerning private agreements. For these reasons, I would reverse the judgment of the Illinois Supreme Court.

EXERCISE 6-6. *AMERICAN AIRLINES, INC. V. WOLENS*— ENFORCEMENT OF VOLUNTARY UNDERTAKINGS

1. Unlike many of the cases presented in this chapter, *American Airlines, Inc. v. Wolens* does not center on the interpretation of the language "relating to . . . rates, routes, or services" in the Airline Deregulation Act. What clause does the court focus on?

2. Is the Illinois Consumer Fraud Act preempted by the Airline Deregulation Act? Explain why or why not.

3. As between a court or the Department of Transportation, which is the authorized adjudicator of air carrier contract disputes, according to the parties in this case? Which party prevailed and why?

4. The majority opinion states that the "distinction between what the state dictates and what the airline itself undertakes confines courts, in breach-of-contract actions, to the parties' bargain, with no enlargement or enhancement based on state laws or policies external to the agreement." What does this mean? Reading *Northwest, Inc. v. Ginsberg*, 572 U.S. 273(2014), *infra*, may be instructive in responding.

5. Summarize the main points in the concurring and dissenting opinions. Which is most persuasive and why?

NOTES ON *AMERICAN AIRLINES, INC. V. WOLENS*—VOLUNTARY AIRLINE PASSENGERS' BILL OF RIGHTS

In 2007, hundreds of airline passengers were stranded aboard nine JetBlue Airways airplanes on the snow-covered tarmac of New York's JFK International Airport for almost 10 hours. To stave off Congressional action and repair its public image, JetBlue subsequently announced its own "Customer Bill of Rights," setting out self-imposed penalties and "major" rewards for passengers if that are inconvenienced beyond a "reasonable" amount of time. *See, e.g.*, Jeff Bailey, *Chief "Mortified" by JetBlue Crisis*, N.Y. Times, Feb. 19, 2007, at A1.

Subject to its own Contract of Carriage, JetBlue's "Customer Bill of Rights" (http://www.jetblue.com/about/ourcompany/promise/index.html) provides:

Above all else, JetBlue Airways is dedicated to bringing humanity back to air travel. We strive to make every part of your experience as simple and as pleasant as possible. Unfortunately, there are times when things do not go as planned. If you're inconvenienced as a result, we think it is important that you know exactly what you can expect from us. That's why we created our Customer Bill of Rights

These Rights will always be subject to the highest level of safety and security for our customers and crewmembers.

INFORMATION

JetBlue will notify customers of the following:

- Delays prior to scheduled departure

- Cancellations and their cause

- Diversions and their cause

CANCELLATIONS

All customers whose flight is cancelled by JetBlue will, at the customer's option, receive a full refund or re-accommodation on the next available JetBlue flight at no additional charge or fare. If JetBlue cancels a flight within 4 hours of scheduled departure and the cancellation is due to a Controllable Irregularity, JetBlue will also provide the customer with a $50 Credit good for future travel on JetBlue.

DEPARTURE DELAYS

Customers whose flight is delayed for 1–1:59 hours after scheduled departure time due to a *Controllable Irregularity* are entitled to a $25 Credit good for future travel on JetBlue.

Customers whose flight is delayed for 2–4:59 hours after scheduled departure time due to a *Controllable Irregularity* are entitled to a $50 Credit good for future travel on JetBlue.

Customers whose flight is delayed for 5–5:59 hours after scheduled departure time due to a *Controllable Irregularity* are entitled to a Credit good for future travel on JetBlue in the amount paid by the customer for the oneway trip less taxes and fees (or $50, whichever is greater).

Customers whose flight is delayed for 6 or more hours after scheduled departure time due to a *Controllable Irregularity* are entitled to a Credit good for future travel on JetBlue in the amount paid by the customer for the roundtrip (or the oneway trip, doubled) less taxes and fees.

DELAYS (DEPARTURE DELAYS AND ONBOARD GROUND DELAYS ON DEPARTURE)

For customers whose flight is delayed 3 hours or more after scheduled departure, JetBlue will provide free movies on flights that are 2 hours or longer.

OVERBOOKINGS

(As defined in JetBlue's [39-page] Contract of Carriage) Customers who are involuntarily denied boarding shall receive $1,000.

ONBOARD GROUND DELAYS

JetBlue will provide customers experiencing an Onboard Ground Delay with 36 channels of DIRECTV®, food and drink, access to clean restrooms and, as necessary, medical treatment. For customers who experience an Onboard Ground Delay for more than 5 hours, JetBlue will take necessary action so that customers may deplane.

Arrivals:

Customers who experience an Onboard Ground Delay on Arrival for 1–1:59 hours after scheduled arrival time are entitled to a $50 Credit good for future travel on JetBlue.

Customers who experience an Onboard Ground Delay on Arrival for 2 or more hours after scheduled arrival time are entitled to a Credit good for future travel on JetBlue in the amount paid by the customer for the roundtrip (or the oneway trip, doubled) less taxes and fees.

Departures:

Customers who experience an Onboard Ground Delay on Departure for 3–3:59 hours after scheduled departure time are entitled to a $50 Credit good for future travel on JetBlue.

Customers who experience an Onboard Ground Delay on Departure for 4–4:59 hours after scheduled departure time are entitled to a Credit good for future travel on JetBlue in the amount paid by the customer for the oneway trip less taxes and fees (or $50, whichever is greater).

Customers who experience an Onboard Ground Delay on Departure for 5 or more hours after scheduled departure time are entitled to a Credit good for future travel on JetBlue in the amount paid by the customer for the roundtrip (or the oneway trip, doubled) less taxes and fees.

IN-FLIGHT ENTERTAINMENT

JetBlue offers 36 channels of DIRECTV® service on its flights in the Continental U.S. If our LiveTV™ system is inoperable on flights in the Continental U.S., customers are entitled to a $15 Credit good for future travel on JetBlue.

NORTHWEST, INC. V. GINSBERG

572 U.S. 273 (2014)

ALITO, J., delivered the opinion for a unanimous Court.

We must decide in this case whether the Airline Deregulation Act preempts a state law claim for breach of the implied covenant of good faith and fair dealing. Following our interpretation of the Act in *American Airlines, Inc. v. Wolens*, 513 U.S. 219 (1995) we hold that such a claim is preempted if it seeks to enlarge the contractual obligations that the parties voluntarily adopt. And because the doctrine is invoked in the present case in an attempt to expand those obligations, we reverse the judgment of the Court of Appeals.

Like many airlines, petitioner Northwest, Inc. ("Northwest"), established a frequent flyer program, its WorldPerks Airline Partners Program, to attract loyal customers. Under this program, members are able to earn "miles" by taking flights operated by Northwest and other "partner" airlines. Members can then redeem these miles for tickets and service upgrades with Northwest or its airline partners. Respondent became a member of Northwest's WorldPerks program in 1999, and as a result of extensive travel on Northwest flights, he achieved "Platinum Elite" status (the highest level) in 2005. In 2008, however, Northwest terminated respondent's membership, apparently in reliance on a provision of the WorldPerks agreement that provided that "[a]buse of the . . . program (including . . . improper conduct as determined by [Northwest] in its sole judgment)] . . . may result in cancellation of the member's account." According to respondent, a Northwest representative telephoned him in June 2008 and informed him that his "Platinum Elite" status was being revoked because he had " 'abused' " the program. In a letter sent about two weeks later, Northwest wrote:

> You have contacted our office 24 times since December 3, 2007 regarding travel problems, including 9 incidents of your bag arriving late at the luggage carousel. Since December 3, 2007, you have continually asked for compensation over and above our guidelines. We have awarded you $1,925.00 in travel credit vouchers, 78,500 WorldPerks

bonus miles, a voucher extension for your son, and $491.00 in cash reimbursements. Due to our past generosity, we must respectfully advise that we will no longer be awarding you compensation each time you contact us.

Respondent requested clarification of his status, but a Northwest representative sent him an e-mail stating that "[a]fter numerous conversations with not only the Legal Department, but with members of the WorldPerks department, I believe your status with the program should be very clear."

Alleging that Northwest had ended his membership as a cost-cutting measure tied to Northwest's merger with Delta Air Lines, respondent filed a class action in the United States District Court for the Southern District of California on behalf of himself and all other similarly situated WorldPerks members. Respondent's complaint asserted four separate claims. Applying California choice-of-law rules, the District Court held that Minnesota law applies because respondent "was a resident of Minneapolis, appears to fly in and out of Minnesota, and Northwest's principal place of business is Minnesota." That determination was not challenged on appeal.

First, his complaint alleged that Northwest had breached its contract by revoking his "Platinum Elite" status without valid cause. Second, the complaint claimed that Northwest violated the duty of good faith and fair dealing because it terminated his membership in a way that contravened his reasonable expectations with respect to the manner in which Northwest would exercise its discretion. Third, the complaint asserted a claim for negligent misrepresentation, and fourth, the complaint alleged intentional misrepresentation. Respondent sought damages in excess of $5 million, as well as injunctive relief requiring Northwest to restore the class members' WorldPerks status and prohibiting Northwest from future revocations of membership.

The District Court held that respondent's claims for breach of the covenant of good faith and fair dealing, negligent misrepresentation, and intentional misrepresentation were preempted by the Airline Deregulation Act of 1978, as amended, 49 U.S.C. § 41713. These claims, the court concluded, were "relate[d] to" Northwest's rates and services and thus fell within the ADA's express preemption clause.

Respondent's remaining claim—for breach of contract—was dismissed without prejudice for failure to identify any material breach where the frequent flyer agreement gave Northwest sole discretion to determine whether a participant had abused the program. Respondent appealed the dismissal of his breach of the duty of good faith and fair dealing claim. The Ninth Circuit reversed. Relying on pre-*Wolens* Circuit precedent, the Ninth Circuit first held that a breach of implied covenant claim is " 'too tenuously connected to airline regulation to trigger preemption under the ADA.' " Such a claim, the Ninth Circuit wrote, "does not interfere with the [Act's] deregulatory mandate" and does not " 'force the Airlines to adopt or change their prices, routes or services—the prerequisite for . . . preemption.' " In addition, the Court held that the covenant of good faith and fair dealing does not fall within the terms of the Act's preemption provision because it does not have a "direct effect" on either "prices" or "services." We granted *certiorari*.

> *The first question we address is whether the ADA's preemption provision applies only to legislation enacted by a state legislature and regulations issued by a state administrative agency but not to a common-law rule like the implied covenant of good faith and fair dealing. We have little difficulty rejecting this argument.*

Preemption of Common Law Rules

The first question we address is whether, as respondent now maintains, the ADA's preemption provision applies only to legislation enacted by a state legislature and regulations issued by a state administrative agency but not to a common-law rule like the implied covenant of good faith and fair dealing. We have little difficulty rejecting this argument.

To begin, state common-law rules fall comfortably within the language of the ADA preemption provision. As noted above, the current version of this provision applies to state "law[s], regulation[s], or other provision[s] having the force and effect of law," 49 U.S.C. § 41713(b)(1). It is routine to call common-law rules "provisions." And a common-law rule clearly has "the force and effect of law." In *Wolens*, we noted that this phrase is most naturally read to " 'refe[r] to binding standards of conduct that operate irrespective of any private agreement,' " and we see no basis for holding that such standards must be based on a statute or regulation as opposed to the common law.

This understanding becomes even clearer when the original wording of the preemption provision is taken into account. When first enacted in 1978, this provision also applied to "rule[s]" and "standard[s]," and there surely can be no doubt that this formulation encompassed common-law rules. Indeed, we held in *CSX Transp., Inc. v. Easterwood*, 507 U.S. 658 (1993) that virtually identical language in the Federal Railroad Safety Act of 1970 includes "[l]egal duties imposed . . . by the common law." While "rule[s]" and "standard[s]" are not mentioned in the current version of the statute, this omission is the result of a recodification that was not meant to affect the provision's meaning. Those additional terms were deleted as part of a wholesale recodification of Title 49 in 1994, but Congress made it clear that this recodification did not effect any "substantive change."

In arguing that common-law rules fall outside the scope of the ADA preemption provision, respondent relies on our decision in *Sprietsma v. Mercury Marine*, 537 U.S. 51 (2002), which held that the Federal Boat Safety Act of 1971 did not preempt a common-law tort claim, but there are critical differences between the preemption provisions in the Boat Safety Act and the ADA. The Boat Safety Act provision applies only to "a law or regulation," whereas the ADA provision, as just explained, is much more broadly worded.

In addition, the relationship between the ADA's preemption provision and the saving provision carried over from the prior law is also quite different. The *Sprietsma* decision placed substantial weight on the Boat Safety Act's saving provision, which was enacted at the same time as the preemption provision, but we have described the Federal Aviation Act saving clause as "a relic of the pre-ADA/no preemption regime." *Morales v. Trans World Airlines, Inc.*, 504 U.S. 374, 385 (1992). That provision applies to the entire, sprawling Federal Aviation Act, and not just to the ADA, and as we held in *Morales*, this "general 'remedies' saving clause cannot be allowed to supersede the specific substantive preemption provision." *See also Wolens* (O'Connor, J., concurring in judgment in part and dissenting in part). For these reasons, respondent's interpretation of the ADA preemption provision cannot be squared with the provision's terms.

Exempting common-law claims would also disserve the central purpose of the ADA. The Act eliminated federal regulation of rates, routes, and services in order to allow those aspects of air transportation to be set by market forces, and the preemption provision was included to prevent the States from undoing what the Act was meant to accomplish.

What is important, therefore, is the effect of a state law, regulation, or provision, not its form, and the ADA's deregulatory aim can be undermined just as surely by a state common-law rule as it can by a state statute or regulation. As the First Circuit has recognized, "[i]t defies logic to think that Congress would disregard real-world consequences and give dispositive effect to the form of a clear intrusion into a federally regulated industry." *Brown v. United Airlines, Inc.*, 720 F.3d 60 (1st Cir. 2013).

Finally, if all state common-law rules fell outside the ambit of the ADA's preemption provision, we would have had no need in *Wolens* to single out a subcategory of common-law claims, *i.e.*, those based on the parties' voluntary undertaking, as falling outside that provision's coverage. Accordingly, we conclude that the phrase "other provision having the force and effect of law" includes common-law claims.

Whether Implied Covenant "Relates To" Rates, Routes or Services

We must next determine whether respondent's breach of implied covenant claim "relates to" "rates, routes, or services." A claim satisfies this requirement if it has "a connection with, or reference to, airline" prices, routes, or services, and the claim at issue here clearly has such a connection. That claim seeks respondent's reinstatement in Northwest's frequent flyer program so that he can access the program's "valuable . . . benefits," including "flight upgrades, accumulated mileage, loyalty program status or benefits on other airlines, and other advantages."

Like the frequent flyer program in *Wolens*, the Northwest program is connected to the airline's "rates" because the program awards mileage credits that can be redeemed for tickets and upgrades. When miles are used in this way, the rate that a customer pays, *i.e.*, the price of a particular ticket, is either eliminated or reduced. The program is also connected to "services," *i.e.*, access to flights and to higher service categories. Respondent argues that his claim differs from the claims in *Wolens* because he "does not challenge access to flights and upgrades or the number of miles needed to obtain air tickets" but instead contests "the termination of his WorldPerks elite membership," but this argument ignores respondent's reason for seeking reinstatement of his membership, *i.e.*, to obtain reduced rates and enhanced services.

Respondent and *amici* suggest that *Wolens* is not controlling because frequent flyer programs have fundamentally changed since the time of that decision. We are told that "most miles [are now] earned without consuming airline services" and are "spent without consuming airline services." But whether or not this alleged change might have some impact in a future case, it is not implicated here. In this case, respondent did not assert that he earned his miles from any activity other than taking flights or that he attempted to redeem miles for anything other than tickets and upgrades.

Implied Covenant: Legal Obligation or Voluntary Undertaking?

With these preliminary issues behind us, we turn to the central issue in this case, *i.e.*, whether respondent's implied covenant claim is based on a state-imposed obligation or simply one that the parties voluntarily undertook. Petitioners urge us to hold that implied covenant claims are always preempted, and respondent suggests that such claims are generally not preempted, but the reasoning of *Wolens* neither dooms nor spares all such claims.

While most States recognize some form of the good faith and fair dealing doctrine, it does not appear that there is any uniform understanding of the doctrine's precise meaning. "[T]he concept of good faith in the performance of contracts 'is a phrase without general meaning (or meanings) of its own.' " *Tymshare, Inc. v. Covell*, 727 F.2d 1145 (D.C. Cir. 1984) (Scalia, J.) (quoting Summers, "Good Faith" in *General Contract Law and the Sales Provisions of the Uniform Commercial Code*, 54 VA. L. REV. 195, 201 (1968)). Of particular importance here, while some States are said to use the doctrine "to effectuate the intentions of parties or to protect their reasonable expectations," other States clearly employ the doctrine to ensure that a party does not " 'violate community standards of decency, fairness, or reasonableness.' "

> *Whatever may be the case under the law of other jurisdictions, it seems clear that under Minnesota law, which is controlling here, the implied covenant must be regarded as a state-imposed obligation.*

Whatever may be the case under the law of other jurisdictions, it seems clear that under Minnesota law, which is controlling here, the implied covenant must be regarded as a state-imposed obligation. Respondent concedes that under Minnesota law parties cannot contract out of the covenant. And as a leading commentator has explained, a State's "unwillingness to allow people to disclaim the obligation of good faith . . . shows that the obligation cannot be implied, but is law imposed." 3A A. CORBIN, CORBIN ON CONTRACTS § 654A, p. 88 (L. Cunningham & A. Jacobsen eds. Supp. 1994). When the law of a State does not authorize parties to free themselves from the covenant, a breach of covenant claim is preempted under the reasoning of *Wolens*.

Implied Covenant is State-Imposed Obligation

Another feature of Minnesota law provides an additional, independent basis for our conclusion. Minnesota law holds that the implied covenant applies to "every contract," with the notable exception of employment contracts. The exception for employment contracts is based, in significant part, on "policy reasons," and therefore the decision not to exempt other types of contracts must be based on a policy determination, namely, that the "policy reasons" that support the rule for employment contracts do not apply (at least with the same force) in other contexts. When the application of the implied covenant depends on state policy, a breach of implied covenant claim cannot be viewed as simply an attempt to vindicate the parties' implicit understanding of the contract.

For these reasons, the breach of implied covenant claim in this case cannot stand, but petitioners exhort us to go further and hold that all such claims, no matter the content of the law of the relevant jurisdiction, are preempted. If preemption depends on state law, petitioners warn, airlines will be faced with a baffling patchwork of rules, and the deregulatory aim of the ADA will be frustrated. But the airlines have means to avoid such a result. A State's implied covenant rules will escape preemption only if the law of the relevant State permits an airline to contract around those rules in its frequent flyer program agreement, and if an airline's agreement is governed by the law of such a State, the airline can specify that the agreement does not incorporate the covenant. While the inclusion of such a provision may impose transaction costs and presumably would not enhance the attractiveness of the program, an airline can decide whether the benefits of such a provision are worth the potential costs.

Our holding also does not leave participants in frequent flyer programs without protection. The ADA is based on the view that the best interests of airline passengers are most effectively promoted, in the main, by allowing the free market to operate. If an airline acquires a reputation for mistreating the participants in its frequent flyer program (who are generally the airline's most loyal and valuable customers), customers can avoid that program and may be able to enroll in a more favorable rival program.

Federal law also provides protection for frequent flyer program participants. Congress has given the Department of Transportation ("DOT") the general authority to prohibit and punish unfair and deceptive practices in air transportation and in the sale of air transportation, 49 U.S.C. § 41712(a), and Congress has specifically authorized the DOT to investigate complaints relating to frequent flyer programs. See FAA Modernization and Reform Act of 2012, § 408(6), 126 Stat. 87. Pursuant to these provisions, the DOT regularly entertains and acts on such complaints.

We note, finally, that respondent's claim of ill treatment by Northwest might have been vindicated if he had pursued his breach-of-contract claim after its dismissal by the District Court. Respondent argues that, contrary to the holding of the District Court, the frequent flyer agreement did not actually give Northwest unfettered discretion to terminate his membership in the program, and the United States makes a related argument, namely, that even if the agreement gave Northwest complete discretion with respect to a determination regarding abuse of the program, the agreement did not necessarily bar a claim asserting that membership was ended for an ulterior reason, such as an effort to cut costs. If respondent had appealed the dismissal of his breach-of-contract claim, he could have presented these arguments to the Court of Appeals, but he chose not to press that claim. He voluntarily dismissed the breach-of-contract claim and instead appealed only the breach of implied covenant claim, which we hold to be preempted.

Because respondent's implied covenant of good faith and fair dealing claim seeks to enlarge his contractual agreement with petitioners, we hold that 49 U.S.C. § 41713(b)(1) preempts the claim. The judgment of the Court of Appeals for the Ninth Circuit is reversed, and the case is remanded for further proceedings consistent with this opinion.

EXERCISE 6-7. *NORTHWEST, INC. V. GINSBERG*—IMPLIED COVENANT OF GOOD FAITH AND FAIR DEALING

1. Define implied covenant of good faith and fair dealing.

2. Do common law claims fall outside the scope of preemption under the Airline Deregulation Act? Explain the court's reasoning.

3. Explain the court's analysis of the phrase "other provision having the force and effect of law" with respect to common law claims and preemption under the Airline Deregulation Act.

4. Does the breach of implied covenant claim here "relate to" an airline rate, route, or service? Detail.

5. Is the implied covenant applicable to the frequent flyer program a legal obligation (and thus preempted) or a voluntary undertaking (and thus not preempted)? What could the respondent have done to obtain a different result, according to Justice Alito?

Suggested Further Reading

Tim Wu, *Why Airlines Want to Make You Suffer*, NEW YORKER, Dec. 26, 2014

DEREGULATION AND THE AIRLINE BUSINESS IN EUROPE (ROUTLEDGE SEAN BARETT ED. 2009)

Timothy M. Ravich, *Re-Regulation and Airline Passengers' Rights*, 67 J. AIR L. & COM. 935 (2002)

RIGAS DOGANIS, FLYING OFF COURSE: THE ECONOMICS OF INTERNATIONAL AIRLINES (ROUTLEDGE, 2D ED. 1991)

Mark A. Katz, *The American Experience under the Airline Deregulation Act of 1978— An Airline Perspective*, 6 HOFSTRA LABOR AND EMPLOYMENT L.J. 87 (1988)

Airline Passenger Rights

H.R. 302—115TH CONGRESS (2017–2018)

FAA Reauthorization Act of 2018

SEC. 577.   MINIMUM DIMENSIONS FOR PASSENGER SEATS

[Seat Egress in Air Travel (SEAT) Act.]

In General.—Not later than 1 year after the date of enactment of this Act, and after providing notice and an opportunity for comment, the Administrator of the Federal Aviation Administration shall issue regulations that establish minimum dimensions for passenger seats on aircraft operated by air carriers in interstate air transportation or intrastate air transportation, including minimums for seat pitch, width, and length, and that are necessary for the safety of passengers.

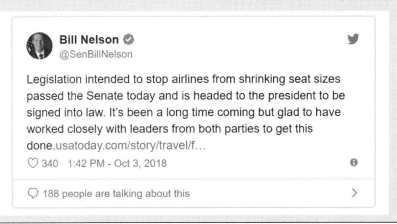

Bill Nelson ✔
@SenBillNelson

Legislation intended to stop airlines from shrinking seat sizes passed the Senate today and is headed to the president to be signed into law. It's been a long time coming but glad to have worked closely with leaders from both parties to get this done.usatoday.com/story/travel/f…

♡ 340   1:42 PM - Oct 3, 2018

💬 188 people are talking about this

A. OVERVIEW

In September 2019, Thomas Cook—a travel company created in 1841 and credited with inventing the package holiday—suddenly entered compulsory liquidation. The financial meltdown marooned 150,000 passengers around the world, triggering Britain's largest peacetime repatriation. *See* James Hookway & Denise Roland, *First Dunkirk. Now, The Collapse of Thomas Cook*, WALL ST. J., Sept. 23, 2019 (" 'Why were they still accepting payment for flights?' said an American passenger.").

While a sudden liquidation like this is rare, if not unprecedented, passenger complaints about airline practices are common, from inadequate seat size to unexplained delays and cancellations to ancillary charges for carry-on bags and schedule changes to policies that make it difficult for families to seat together. (But see Phil LeBeau, *Consumer Satisfaction in the Skies Soars to Record High in Annual Airline Travel Survey*, CNBC, May, 29, 2019.) But, does it have to be that way?

In his heralded book *Moments of Truth*, former Scandinavia Airlines President Jan Carlzon discussed the importance of a customer-driven company. With each of his airline's 10 million customers coming into contact with approximately 5 airline employees for an average of 15 seconds each time, the airline had 50 million moments of truth—"moments when we must prove to our customers that SAS is their best alternative." In this context, the cases in this chapter largely represent a failure from a customer facing perspective. Were the lawsuits in this chapter really necessary? Shouldn't the issues they involved been solved as a matter of business and customer service rather than as a matter of law? Were the airline defendants really unable to accommodate the passengers at the ticket counter as opposed to paying damages or defending themselves in court? Alternatively, were the passengers asking or expecting too much after already securing a low fare for convenient travel?

This chapter touches on many of the bread-and-butter issues that ostensibly pit passengers against carriers, including bumping, lost baggage, and refunds, as discussed in Part B (see *Stone v. Continental Airlines*, *Delta Airlines, Inc. v. Barnard*, and *Buck v. American Airlines, Inc.*, respectively). Part C, meanwhile, explores civil rights issues including discrimination, *i.e.,* an airline's legal right to refuse to transport a passenger (*Al-Watan v. American Airlines, Inc.*) or to accommodate passengers under the Air Carrier Access Act (*Deterra v. America West Airlines, Inc.*). Finally, Part D of this chapter concludes with a look at passenger rights in Europe, offering a stark juxtaposition to the way in which American lawmakers arbitrate passenger-carrier relations.

After reading this chapter, you should come away with some practical travel tips (*e.g.*, what can you do to insure the value of lost luggage, what are your legal rights if you are "bumped," etc.). Additionally, you can begin to analyze and critique the laws and policies related to airline passenger rights and develop his own preference for active government intervention or deregulation (see Chapter 6, *supra*).

Customer Service in the Deregulated Airline Marketplace

As detailed in Chapter 6, *supra*, and *Morales v. Trans World Airlines, Inc.*, 504 U.S. 374 (1992), only ten years after enactment of the Airline Deregulation Act of 1978, the National Association of Attorneys General recognized that consumer dissatisfaction with the industry had reached crisis proportions as federal agencies began focusing their attention on airline scheduling problems, on-time performance, safety, and other related issues. Today, more than thirty years later after liberalization of the commercial airline marketplace, the modern benefits of deregulation policy—competition, access, discount fares, and frequent flyer programs—are overshadowed by its drawbacks—hub premiums, congestion, decreased availability of non-stop service, limited airline service to rural and small communities, yield management (*i.e.*, where passengers sitting next to each other have paid vastly different amounts for the same service), bankruptcies, and industry consolidation leading to fewer traveling options.

The objective of deregulation—a free marketplace in which airlines would confront low barriers to entry in order to establish their own rates, routes, and services—arguably has been offset in some measure by the reality that many airline passengers are unhappy with commercial air travel. For many years after 1978, the economic benefits of deregulation represented an acceptable trade-off for airline passengers, namely a low fare in exchange for transportation, nothing more or less. Airline management cultivated a passenger culture that came to accept service limitations, including reduced seat pitch and limited or no in-flight meals. Airline passengers seemed to accept what airline deregulation proponents always understood airline passengers to be—variables in an equation based on the profit-driven saying of Alfred Kahn (the economist hailed as the "father of airline deregulation") that "airplanes are marginal costs with wings." But, even airline passengers who favor price over convenience sometimes reach a boiling point with delays, cancellations, diversions, and reduced market choices.

Airline Passenger Rights

In 1987, less than a decade after airline economics were deregulated in the United States, federal legislators sought to regulate issues of airline delays, truth-in-advertising, and flight cancellations. For example, Representative (and later Secretary of the Department of Transportation ("DOT")), Norman Y. Mineta (D-Cal.), introduced the "Air Passenger Protection Act of 1987," which directed the DOT Secretary to, among other things, establish: (1) a twenty-four hour toll-free airline consumer hotline; (2) regulations preventing air carriers from changing the requirements of a frequent flyer program to the detriment of program participants without reasonable notice; and (3) an advisory committee to report to the DOT and Congress about the appropriate capacity level in the air traffic control system. This proposal died in conference, along with an identical Senate version, but ultimately led to the current practice whereby the DOT compiles and publishes data relating to on-time performance and mishandled baggage.

Non-governmental entities developed passengers' rights proposals, too. A private group called "Airline Passengers of America" authored a passengers' rights proposal in 1987 to address poor airline service. It recommended the decongestion of hubs, enactment of consumer protection legislation aimed at increasing information available to passengers, and creation of a government program to provide real time reports of delays.

Two years later, in 1989, legislators presented more intrusive proposals meant to interpose the federal government between airlines and their passengers. Representative Fortney "Pete" Stark (D-Cal.) proposed an "Airline Passenger Bill of Rights" requiring airlines to make available, upon request, a fare not including food or beverage. Meanwhile, Senator Howard Metzenbaum (D-Ohio) introduced the "Airline Reregulation Act of 1989," which would have established an independent federal executive "to protect the public interest . . . to regulate the air fares and air routes of United States air carriers." Broadly, early passengers' rights proposals focused on airline accountability by demanding an increase in the substance and frequency of communication between airlines and their passengers.

The issue of airline passengers' rights reached an apex during a blizzard in January 1999. Then, almost two dozen airplanes and more than 7,000 passengers were stranded on airplanes at Detroit's Metropolitan Airport for up to 11 hours. Conditions on the planes were intolerable and disgusting. Food and water ran out and toilets overflowed. Passengers "became physically ill as they were exposed to the growing odor of a concentrated number of humans in an enclosed small space," according to the allegations in a lawsuit later filed by one of the passengers. Northwest Airlines paid millions of dollars to 700 class action plaintiffs based on the length of time each person was delayed during the winter storm in 1999. While the airline's balance sheet was impacted by this incident, the remedy for affected airline passengers was wanting and unsatisfactory. After settling with the air carrier in connection with the delays in 1999, lead class counsel remarked, "[w]e've been working on this for two years and they were on the plane for 11 hours. That's the nature of our legal system." *See* Michael Katz, *Airline Peanuts*, FORBES, Feb. 19, 2001, at 53. *See, e.g.*, Susan Carey, *Northwest Agrees to Pay $7.1 Million to Passengers Stranded in 1999 Blizzard*, WALL ST. J., Jan. 10, 2001, at B13. Indeed, where travel delays are measured in minutes and hours, civil lawsuits are measured in months and years, lending credence to the cliché that justice delayed is justice denied. It follows that remedying unpleasant airline travel by operation of law may generate more costs and aggravation for airline passengers than benefits.

Dating back to 1999, Congress has presented many different legislative proposals relating to airline passengers' rights. One plan guaranteed passengers a complete refund and right to exit an airplane that did not take off within two hours of the scheduled departure time or park within two hours of landing. An alternative proposal required airlines to allow passengers to exit an airplane that remained at its gate "more than 1 hour past its scheduled departure time." *See Move Toward Re-Regulation of Aviation Industry Gains Momentum*, WORLD AIRLINE NEWS, Feb. 2, 2001. A third proposal solicited regulations ensuring "access to necessary services and conditions, including food, water, restroom facilities, and emergency medical services for all passengers." *See* Passenger Entitlement and Competition Enhancement Act of 1999, H.R. 780, 106th Cong. (1999) (requiring airlines to submit an "emergency plan" to the DOT); Airline Deregulation and Disclosure Act of 1999, S. 603, 106th Cong. (1999). Other plans sought to improve, or provide in the first place, legal standards for better communication between airlines and passengers. Congress never voted on these various bills as airlines promised to improve their services voluntarily. Rather, after various tries to enact these laws, federal lawmakers and some airlines reached an agreement.

Specifically, in June 1999, the Air Transport Association ("ATA") announced that its member airlines would incorporate into their respective contracts of carriage (*i.e.*, the agreement between an airline and its customers that is printed on ticket jackets or available on the Internet) an "Airline Customer Service Commitment." That voluntary commitment included promises by the ATA airlines to offer the lowest fare available; notify customers of known delays, cancellations, and diversions; deliver baggage on time; support an increase in the baggage liability limit; allow reservations to be held or canceled; provide prompt ticket refunds; properly accommodate disabled and special-need passengers; meet a customer's essential needs during long on-aircraft delays; handle "bumped" passengers with fairness and consistency; disclose travel itinerary, cancellation policies, frequent flyer rules, and aircraft configuration; ensure good customer service from code-share partners; and be more responsive to customer complaints. In return for these promises, Congress did not enact an airline passenger bill of rights into law.

The airlines' voluntary promise and plans to self-improve were roundly discounted. Lawmakers dismissed such intentions as "legalistic gobbledygook which do nothing to protect passengers" and reflect only "vague promises to enforce policies already in place." Julia Malone, *Airlines Thwarted Passenger-Rights Legislation, Group Says*, PLAIN DEALER, Oct. 10, 1999, at 25A (quoting Sen. Ron Wyden). *E.g.*, Richard Williamson, *Airlines' Plans "Not Passing Laugh-ability Test,"* DENVER ROCKY MOUNTAIN NEWS, Sept. 16, 1999, at 2B; Robin Washington, *Airlines' Public Relations Bids Don't Fly with Critics*, BOSTON HERALD, Aug. 18, 1999, at 24.

United States Representative John Dingell (D-Mich.) similarly rejected airlines' assurances: "[V]oluntary commitments are only that—promises to do better." *See* James Pilcher, *Report: Airlines Broke Promises*, CINCINNATI ENQUIRER, Feb. 13, 2001, at A01. Passengers, too, predicted and realized no improvements in airline service. After spending 10 hours on an airplane on the tarmac at Hartsfield Atlanta International Airport, one passenger remarked, "Delta's attitude was like, '(Expletive) you, you're on our plane." *See* Bruce Mohl, *What about when the Airlines Render You Nearly Insensible?*, BOSTON GLOBE, Jan. 27, 2002, at M11 ("Throughout the ordeal, the pilot gave repeated updates on their progress toward de-icing stations, all of which turned out to be overly optimistic. [Passengers] were served no meals while the plane was on the ground. [Passengers] were not allowed to get off. By midnight, they felt as if they were about to snap . . . Delta ended up issuing a formal public apology to 50,000 customers and has since sent individual form letters of apology along with a $400 credit toward a future flight to . . . thousands of others who endured the longest delays.").

Several months later, the events of September 11, 2001 occurred. The terrorism of that day turned the issue of airline passengers' rights upside down. From January 1999 to September 11th, air travelers petitioned Congress to enlarge the law respecting airline passengers' rights. But after September 11th, travelers were less concerned with airline customer service than with actions by federal lawmakers and security officials to constrict airline passengers' rights with passenger profiling systems and other heightened anti-terrorism measures. Indeed, the terrorism of September 11th shifted the issue of airline passengers' rights from matters of comfort to matter of life and death. September 11th jolted the nation's focus from airline service to airline security, as the federal government—through the Transportation Security Administration and other departments—approached passengers' rights in terms of national security, not customer service or airline economics.

The push for enforceable rights has been led by a citizen's Coalition for an Airline Passengers' Bill of Rights, along with Senators Barbara Boxer (D.-Cal.) and Olympia Snowe (R-Me.), and U.S. Representative Mike Thompson (D-Cal.), who sponsored the "Airline Passenger Bill of Rights Act of 2007." Had it passed, the proposal would have codified an obligation by airlines to provide food and water to passengers on delayed airplanes. Moreover, the act would have created a legally enforceable "right to deplane" and required airlines to "provide passengers with the option to deplane safely" if a flight had not departed more than three hours after an airplane was boarded and its doors were closed. The "right to deplane" would not apply if the pilot of a delayed flight "reasonably determine[d] that such flight will depart not later than 30 minutes after the 3 hour delay . . . or, if the pilot of such flight reasonably determine[d] that permitting a passenger to deplane would jeopardize passenger safety or security." While sharing features of the Senate bill, Representative Thompson's proposed legislation also would have required airlines to provide a minimum level of customer service. For example, airlines would have been required to communicate fully with their passengers, including information relating to fares and the cause and timing of delays. Additionally, the Representative's proposal would have obligated airlines to provide passengers stranded aboard delayed airplanes with adequate food, safe drinking water, sanitary facilities and comfortable cabin temperatures.

Notwithstanding the federal government's apparent intention to regulate airline customer service more vigorously, JetBlue presented its own "Customer Bill of Rights" after its customer service failures in February, 2007. In addition to issuing a verbal and written apology by its CEO, JetBlue promised "necessary action" to deplane customers who experience a ground delay of more than five hours and further promised to provide delayed customers with food and drink, access to restrooms and, as necessary, medical treatment. Additionally, the airline promised $1,000 to customers who are involuntarily denied boarding and further promised to notify passengers of delays prior to scheduled departure, cancellations and their cause, and diversions and their cause. With respect to departure delays, JetBlue created a graduated schedule entitling passengers to vouchers for future travel; the amount of a voucher would correspond to the length of time that a flight is delayed, *e.g.*, $25 for a delay of 1–2 hours and a full roundtrip fare voucher for delays more than 6 hours. JetBlue's activism in trying to set things right with its customers illustrates well why airline service may best be reformed by the airlines themselves, not necessarily through federal legislation.

Bad Airline Service: Legal or Business Problem?

While domestic commercial airplane travel may not be as comfortable or convenient as it was decades ago it undoubtedly is a usual part of contemporary life for most Americans. Southwest Airlines founder (and lawyer) Herbert D. Kelleher once noted that, "[w]hen I started, only 15% of adults over 21 had ever flown on a single commercial flight. Today, [85%] of all adults over 21 have flown at least one commercial flight." *See* Del Jones, *Southwest CEO Tops This Year*, USA TODAY, July 12, 1999, at 5B. Airline travel is so routine, in fact, many travelers presume a legal right or freedom to it. As one federal judge put it, by the late 1980s:

> Commercial air travel, once a luxury, has become a staple of modern existence. For many Americans, boarding an airplane to travel across the state or across the country is as ordinary and commonplace an event as boarding a bus or train fifty years ago, or mounting a horse-drawn carriage around the turn of the century. Students going home for the holidays, corporate executives traveling on business, grandmothers visiting their grandchildren, federal judges riding circuit: Airplane travel has become the lifeblood of American society in the latter part of the twentieth century.

United States v. $124,570 U.S. Currency, 873 F.2d 1240 (9th Cir. 1989).

While air traffic has increased over time, the legal as opposed to business incentives for airlines to serve their customers effectively have not kept pace. This is explicable perhaps because airline service is a business matter not a legal one. As one television commentator said in 2001 while assessing the remarks of a former United Airlines CEO:

> He says, "We're in the service business. And if we don't find ways to provide that level of service, passengers will obviously find other airlines that can." Now, that's not just spin; that's a pretty good point. Why in the world would the airlines intentionally aggravate their customers? Congress doesn't need to tell restaurants to serve tasty food. Restaurants that serve bad food go out of business.

See CNN Crossfire, Is It Time for Congress to Give Airline Passengers More Rights? (CNN television broadcast Feb. 15, 2001). *Contra* James Higgins, *The Industry You Love to Hate*, WKLY. STANDARD, Mar. 19, 2001, at 24 ("the problem isn't that airlines have an incentive to antagonize their customers, but that the airlines lack an incentive not to antagonize their customers.").

In fact, unlike companies in other industries, airlines are immune from state regulations and consumer protection laws vis-à-vis the Airline Deregulation Act of 1978, which eliminated the federal government's control over airfares and routes and authorized the DOT to oversee and enforce air travel consumer protection requirements. The Airline Deregulation Act specifies that no state may enact or enforce any law, rule, regulation, standard, or other provision relating to prices, routes, or services of any air carrier. 49 U.S.C. § 41713(b). Although the Airline Deregulation Act displaces state consumer protection law, airline customers are not without legal recourse for deficient airline service.

In 1995, for example, in the case of *American Airlines v. Wolens*, 513 U.S. 219 (1995) (see Chapter 6, *supra*), the Supreme Court of the United States opined that the Airline Deregulation Act does not preempt "routine breach-of-contract claims." In other words, the Airline Deregulation Act does not "shelter airlines from suits alleging no violation of state-imposed obligations, but seeking recovery solely for the airline's alleged breach of its own, self-imposed undertakings . . . terms and conditions airlines offer and passengers accept are privately ordered obligations 'and thus do not amount to a State's "enact[ment] or enforce[ment] [of] any law, rule, regulation, standard, or other provision having the force and effect of law" within the meaning of [the ADA's preemption clause.]' " Therefore, the contracts between airlines and passengers afford airline passengers rights that are enforceable directly against an air carrier. Breach of contract actions could be at least as effective a way to discipline airlines for bad service as DOT regulations that may result in administrative or civil enforcement actions against an air carrier. In fact, because DOT regulations generally take years to promulgate, a contract dispute between an airline and its passengers may reflect a quicker mechanism for airlines and customers to address service problems. That said, courts are not necessarily expert in appraising bad airline service, whether arising from a breach of contract or violation of operational regulation.

From a practical perspective, too, when passengers purchase tickets for air travel, they do not imagine their final destination will be a court of law—with good reason. The inconvenience that passengers experience when stuck on airplanes for several hours will not be remedied immediately during the several months or longer that passengers may spend litigating customer service complaints in courts. And, it will be difficult for airline passengers to prove injury or obtain sufficient value for proven damages. For example, "[t]he judge is going to say 'What are your damages? . . . You had a long-distance phone-call to relatives, dinner in the airport—your damages are about $15.' " *See* Jayne O'Donnell, *Airline Chiefs Vow Customer-Service Plans Will Improve*, USA TODAY, June

8, 2001, at 2B. Even then, carriers often expressly insulate themselves from liability for service, disclaiming liability in their contracts of carriage, *e.g.*, "We are not responsible for any special, incidental, or consequential damages if we do not meet this commitment." Therefore, as proposed, federal legislation concerning airline passengers' rights may have no more force than airline policy. *But see Stop Finding Excuses, Ban Passenger Bumping*, AVIATION WK. & SPACE TECH., Sept. 17, 2005, at 98 (This magazine is not fan of a "passenger bill of rights" to regulate every facet of airline customer service, which ought for the most part to be left to the marketplace. But the mechanism of bumping—selling more seats than an airplane holds and then blocking access by ticketed passengers—smacks of illegality. If bumping isn't considered a unilateral breach of an airline's contract of carriage, it should be. It's an abuse whose time has come and gone.").

At a theoretical level, moreover, passengers' rights are difficult to enforce through legal process. While the recognition of legal rights should not turn on whether those rights are easy or difficult to effect, the recently proposed airline customer service laws will not placate an already hostile population of air travelers. Consider that rules already exist to protect airline passengers from poor airline service. For example, so-called "Rule 240," a vestige of older regulations, requires an airline to provide alternative travel or to arrange for transportation on another airline at no additional cost if it cancels, delays or causes a missed connection. The fact that this and other established rules have not soothed airline passenger upset forecasts the likely ineffectiveness of any new legal imperatives.

B. AVIATION CONSUMER PROTECTION

STONE V. CONTINENTAL AIRLINES

804 N.Y.S.2d 652 (N.Y.C. Civ. Ct. 2005)

DIANE A. LEBEDEFF, J.

This matter brings up a bread-and-butter airline issue the measure of damages governing the claims of passengers "bumped" from domestic airline flights an issue rarely explored in detail notwithstanding that more than 30,000 passengers a year could raise similar claims, as permitted by federal statute and regulations (49 U.S.C. § 41713, known as the "Airline Deregulation Act" or "ADA"; 14 C.F.R. part 250).

This case has simple facts. Claimant Thatcher A. Stone, a partner in a New York Law firm and a lecturer in aviation and airline industry law at the University of Virginia School of Law, made arrangements for a Colorado ski trip for himself and his 13-year old daughter for the 2004 Christmas season, to depart New York on December 25th and return from Telluride on January 1st. Their flights were booked with Continental Airlines ("Continental"). After their baggage was checked and when the father and daughter were at the airline gate, they were "bumped" from the flight. The Continental representative who testified at the trial stated that Continental records reveal claimant was offered an alternate flight two or more days later, but claimant only remembers clearly an offer of a flight departing one day before their scheduled return. Because the airline would not unload their luggage and could give no firm advice regarding how long the airline would take to return the baggage, which included cold-weather sportswear for both and the father's ski equipment, the father and daughter returned home and were unable to make any firm alternate ski or "getaway" plans. Continental refunded the price of the airline tickets while claimant was in the airline terminal.

Claimant seeks recovery for out-of-pocket losses and deprivation of the use of the contents of luggage, as well as damages under New York's consumer protection statutes and punitive damages. He testified that his loss included $1,360 for unrecoverable pre-paid ski lodge accommodations, lift tickets and his daughter's equipment rental, and that the entire experience involved inconveniences and stresses upon himself and his daughter because of the "bumping" and the scheduled holiday "that never was."

"Bumping" Claims and Federal Limitations

As any airline traveler knows, "bumping" of an unlucky passenger occurs when more passengers appear to take a flight than the number of seats available on a given flight, and it arises because tickets are sold above and beyond the airplane's seating capacity. The United States Supreme Court, addressing an instance in which consumer advocate Ralph Nader was "bumped" from a flight, described overbooking as "a common industry practice, designed to ensure that each flight leaves with as few empty seats as possible" (*Nader v. Allegheny Airlines, Inc.*, 426 U.S. 290 (1976)).

Bumping, Defined

The claims of "bumped" passengers are governed by federal regulation which require an airline to offer compensation to "bumped" passengers (14 C.F.R. part 250, entitled Oversales, originally published at 41 Fed. Reg. 16,478, and entitled Priority Rules, Denied-Boarding Compensation Tariffs and Reports of Unaccommodated Passengers [Apr. 19, 1976]).

Under 14 C.F.R. § 250.5, a "bumped" passenger is entitled to compensation . . . If a "bumped" passenger rejects an airline's offer, the passenger is entitled to "seek to recover damages in a court of law or in some other manner" under 14 C.F.R. § 250.9(b).

Compensation, 14 C.F.R. § 250.5

Under 14 C.F.R. § 250.5, a "bumped" passenger is entitled to compensation of $400 per passenger or a lower amount computed "at the rate of 200% of the sum of the value of the passenger's remaining flight coupons up the Passenger's next Stopover, or if none, to the Passenger's final destination"; an identical text appears in the Continental Contract of Carriage as paragraph (4)(a). This compensation rule applies only if a passenger is actually "bumped" from the flight because of overbooking. If a "bumped" passenger rejects an airline's offer, the passenger is entitled to "seek to recover damages in a court of law or in some other manner" under 14 C.F.R. § 250.9(b), which language is universally regarded as permitting a claim for contract damages which may exceed the amount of compensation offered by an airline.

All tickets for domestic flights embrace these same rights, for every airline's Contract of Carriage must be consistent with federal rules (14 C.F.R. § 253.4). As described in a comprehensive law review article with an analysis of the economics of overbooking by Elliott Blanchard, *Terminal 250: Federal Regulation of Airline Overbooking*, 79 N.Y.U. L. REV. 1799, 1807–1808 and n. 3 (2004), since 1990, on average, almost 900,000 domestic passengers are "bumped" annually, and 2003 study data developed by the United States Department of Transportation indicates that 96 per cent of such passengers accept the compensation offered by airlines, leaving approximately 36,000 "bumped" passengers per year who refuse such offers and are entitled to raise damages claims.

Preemption of Consumer Protection Claims

Any other claim which a passenger asserts arises from "bumping" must be parsed out and separately assessed. The bulk of other claims are barred by reasons of law, including federal preemption. Under the federal law, an airline may not be sued for many general matters touching upon airline operation, but an airline may be sued for some contract issues apart from "bumping" claims, frequent flyer program contractually adopted by airline). Following such a judicial review of the claims asserted in this case, the court is satisfied that New York State's consumer protection statutes cannot serve as the proper basis for claims against the airline. Additionally, a punitive damage claim against an airline is barred by federal preemption, even for a "bumped" passenger. Accordingly, the court severs and dismisses the consumer protection and punitive damages claims, which leaves only the contract damages claim before the court.

Contract Damages for a "Bumped" Passenger

A "bumped" passenger is entitled to contract damages upon no greater proof than facts establishing (1) ticket purchase, (2) involuntary denial of boarding within the meaning of the federal regulations, (3) non-acceptance of an airline's offer of compensation, and (4) damages. Such a claim for contract damages is measured under state law.

Elements of State Law Contract Claim

As the items to be embraced within contract damages for a passenger "bumped" from a domestic flight, only a handful of cases on point nationwide have granted relief on this issue (*see Smith v. Piedmont Aviation, Inc.*, 567 F.2d 290 (5th Cir. 1978), reciting as a factor in damages, inconvenience and a need to make alternate arrangements, including rental of a car to reach destination, $1,051.80 awarded).

In addition to case law, two sets of federal regulations give some guidance as to the dollar amount of damages which an airline should reasonably foresee in a "bumping" situation. The first regulation is the "bumping" regulation and airlines must contemplate that an impacted passenger would assert a claim exceeding the $400 per ticket lodestar compensation figure adopted in 1978 by the federal regulations, as well the fact that the $400 figure would be adjusted to its current economic value. Taking judicial notice of inflation, the inflation-adjusted equivalent to the 1978 figure of $400 is equal to $1,219.63 in 2005 dollars for each passenger, according to a U.S. Bureau of Labor Statistics inflation calculator.

And, still along general lines, it can be observed that the airline could also expect a somewhat increased claim where the "bumped" passenger has (1) a round trip scheduled with (2) a return flight date showing an appreciable layover period. The formula set forth in 14 C.F.R. § 250.5 ignores round-trip passengers, for it refers only to the ticket price to "the Passenger's next Stopover, or if none, to the Passenger's final destination. . . ." It would appear that Continental does not distinguish flyers on a return or one-way ticket from passengers on the first portion of a round-trip a distinction which an airline could add to its priority "bumping" rules, which each airline establishes independently under C.F.R. § 250.3 notwithstanding that such a distinction might reduce costs and inconvenience flowing from disruption of ground arrangements for a round-trip customer.

A second element is that a "bumped" passenger is also often exposed to the problem of lost or delayed luggage, which typically is checked before a passenger is denied boarding privileges. Under 14 C.F.R. § 254.4, an airline may be liable for "provable direct or consequential damages" for lost, destroyed, or delayed baggage up to the amount of $2,800 per passenger for domestic flights (see, discussing applicable law for claim when amount was $1,250 per passenger.

Accordingly, taking together both regulations regarding the loss of the flight boarding privileges and the deprivation of luggage and totaling the dollar figures, a working current economic figure of roughly $4,019 would appear to be within the expectation of an airline per "bumped" passenger, subject to proof of higher or lower damages. Plaintiff's claim of $4,000 in damages clearly is inside this recognizable ballpark.

Against this background, the court can turn to a New York definition of cognizable damages. A starting point is the basic consideration that contract damages can be "general, thus requiring only that plaintiff prove that they flowed naturally from the breach, or . . . special . . . which, to be compensable, must have been foreseeable and within the contemplation of the parties at the time the contract was made." There are three identifiable ingredients of such damages.

First, as to out-of-pocket expenses flowing from the loss of passage, claimant testified that he was unable to recoup $1,360 of pre-paid expenses. This item falls within the class of traditionally recognized damages for "bumped" passengers. Had claimant arranged a substitute trip, other supplemental calculations might be required, involving "overbooking" at a hotel, offsetting savings against increased costs, as well as recognizing an allowance for typical expenses involved in a change of travel plans, such as telephone calls to family members).

Second, it is well settled that an award for inconvenience, delay and uncertainty is cognizable under New York law. Here, a father and teenage daughter were bumped on the outward leg of a week-long round trip during the holiday season to a resort location, leaving the claimant father subject to the immediate upset of being denied boarding in a public setting, and with resulting inconvenience continuing for some period of time thereafter. Inconvenience damages represent compensation for normal reactions and are clearly distinguishable from, and definitively not a disguised award for, severe emotional distress as often pleaded in tort cases.

Although the basis for inconvenience damages was not explored closely in the cases which awarded them to New York passengers, this type of award stems from a well settled exception to the "general rule [that] mental suffering resulting from a breach of contract is not a subject of compensation * * * * [which] does not obtain, however, as between a common carrier or an innkeeper and an insulted and abused passenger or guest, or the proprietor of a public resort and a patron publicly ejected." On the record presented and the law, inconvenience damages of $1,000 are awarded.

Third, regarding the deprivation of use of the contents of checked luggage, this factor was also present and claimant testified that, had their baggage been made available, he would have arranged for a local substitute ski trip. This portion of the claim was unopposed in that the claimant testified, without protest or objection, that the luggage should have been removed from the flight. Further, given that the father and daughter were scheduled for a week-long trip and that their luggage had already been taken from them, the airline was on notice at the time of "bumping" that special damages could arise.

An allowance for the deprivation of use of the contents of the luggage is warranted, bearing in mind that "[m]oney damages are substitutional relief designed in theory 'to put the injured party in as good a position as he would have been put by full performance of the contract, at the least cost to the defendant and without charging him with harms that he had no sufficient reason to foresee when he made the contract.' " As to valuation, "the amount of the recovery ought not to be restricted to the price which could be realized by a sale in the market" but should consider the owner's "actual money loss, all the circumstances and conditions considered, resulting from his being deprived of the property, not including ... any sentimental or fanciful value he may ... place upon [the property]." The owner of the personal property may give testimony as to such value and clearly may also testify regarding the anticipated use of the items checked.

Recognizing that 14 C.F.R. § 254.4 sets a limit of $2,800 per passenger on claims for lost, destroyed, or delayed baggage, the court awards $750 as rough compensation, giving consideration of a replacement rental value of the father's ski equipment and the replacement cost of purchase of winter sports wear at a non-luxurious quality for temporary use. Such an amount would have placed claimant in a position that he could have arranged a substitute local ski trip or day-trips for himself and his daughter, as he stated he would have done had he not already been subject to an out-of-pocket loss over $1,000 by reason of defendant's conduct. Given that no such trips were arranged, the court will not attempt to fix a figure for the cost of anything more than adequate compensation for the deprivation of use of the checked materials.

Limitation of Liability

As to the damages testimony, this court had its opportunity to "view the witnesses, hear the testimony and observe demeanor." To the extent that there was a dispute as to the facts, the court found claimant credible and credits his version of the facts as true or that, given the explanation he received under pressing circumstances, he was left under the impression were true. It does appear that claimant was not given an offer of compensation in writing, as required by the federal regulations (14 C.F.R. § 250.9), and that the airline also failed to post the required information regarding its "bumping" policies (14 C.F.R. § 250.11).

Based on the foregoing, judgment shall enter for the total amount of $3,110.00, comprised of the three items as to which damages have been granted above, with interest from December 25, 2004, the date of the "bumping." The court determines that such award achieves substantial justice in this Small Claims matter. (Plaintiff did not assert a claim on behalf of the minor daughter.)

EXERCISE 7-1. *STONE V. CONTINENTAL AIRLINES*—DENIED BOARDING

1.   What is "bumping"?

2.   What are the legal obligations an airline has to "bumped" passengers bumped (a) voluntarily, and (b) involuntarily under 14 C.F.R. Pt. 250?

3.   Are the obligations to "bumped passengers" different for domestic and international flights? Explain. *See* https://www.transportation.gov/individuals/aviation-consumer-protection/bumping-oversales.

4.   What are the litigation rights of a "bumped" passenger who has declined airline compensation under 14 C.F.R. Pt. 250?

5.   The court notes that an accompanying inconvenience experienced by "bumped" passengers is lost, destroyed, or delayed baggage. To what extent (*i.e.*, limit) are airlines liable for this 14 C.F.R. § 254.4?

NOTES ON *STONE V. CONTINENTAL AIRLINES*—OVERSALES AND "BUMPING"

1.   *Carrier Liability—Limitation of Liability.*

The court in *Stone v. Continental Airlines* mentions that "14 C.F.R. § 254.4 sets a limit of $2,800 per passenger or claims for lost, destroyed, or delayed baggage." That is true, but the amount of compensation changes from time to time. The law was last updated in 2015 and caps damages at $3,500 as follows:

§ 254.4   Carrier liability.

On any flight segment using large aircraft, or on any flight segment that is included on the same ticket as another flight segment that uses large aircraft, an air carrier shall not limit its liability for provable direct or consequential damages resulting from the disappearance of, damage to, or delay in delivery of a passenger's personal property, including baggage, in its custody to an amount less than $3,500 for each passenger.

Recognize that this law—applicable to *domestic* baggage liability—does not mean that passengers are automatically entitled to $3,500 for lost, damaged, or delayed baggage. Rather, it sets a maximum amount of liability on the carrier and places the burden of proof on the passenger.

For further reading see M.R. Franks, *Airline Liability for Loss, Damage, or Delay of Passenger Baggage*, 12 FORDHAM J. CORP. & FIN. L. 735 (2007); Martin E. Rose & Beth E. McAllister, *The Effect of Post-Deregulation Court Decisions on Air Carrier Liability for Lost, Delayed, or Damaged Baggage*, 55 J. AIR L. & COM. 653 (1990).

2.   ***Limitation of Liability: Applied to the Transportation of Animals.***

Courts uphold liability limitations disclosed in airline passenger tickets even in rare situations. For example, in *Deiro v. American Airlines, Inc.*, 816 F.2d 1360 (9th Cir. 1987), a passenger sued to recover damages of approximately $900,000 for the death of seven greyhound racing dogs caused by heat exposure while the dogs were being transported in the cargo area of the jet on which the plaintiff was a passenger. The court found that the plaintiff was contractually bound to the legally valid $750 baggage liability limitation contained in his ticket coupon. *See also Gluckman v. American Airlines, Inc.*, 844 F. Supp. 151 (S.D.N.Y. 1994) (dismissing claims of emotional distress and loss of companionship arising out the death of an airline passenger's dog after it suffered heat stroke in the cargo hold of an airplane).

For further discussion of the transportation of animal by commercial aircraft see Note 3, *infra*.

3.   ***United Express Flight 3411.***

Perhaps the most dramatic example of denied boarding occurred in 2017 onboard a regional carrier operated by United Airlines. On April 9, 2017, United Airlines, in an effort to accommodate its own employees, needed to bump four passengers on the flight, from Chicago to Louisville. The airline offered $400 flight vouchers (and then doubled it) for passengers willing to voluntarily bump themselves from the flight, but nobody took the offer.

Four passengers were then selected for *in*voluntary bumping. All but Dr. David Dao of Louisville complied. He claimed that he needed to be at work at a hospital the next day and could not miss the flight. Airport security was then called. As captured in a video that went viral online, Dr. Dao was pulled out of his seat, screaming. His face hit an armrest during the struggle and yet he was dragged, unconscious and with a bloody mouth, down the aisle and off the plane.

Initially, United CEO Oscar Munoz issued a statement calling the incident "re-accommodating the customers". He also characterized Dr. Dao as "disruptive" and "belligerent." United ultimately issued an better received apology and said such an incident would never happen again. Munoz was also called to testify before Congress. *See* Michael Goldstein, *Biggest Travel Story of 2017: The Bumping and Beating of Dr. David Dao*, FORBES, Dec. 20, 2017. *See also* Lauren Zumbach, *A Year after a Passenger Was Dragged Off a United Flight, Everyday Indignities Remain*, CHI. TRIB., April 9, 2018.

4. ***Oversales—"Bumping."***

"Bumping"—essentially, denied boarding—may sound harsh, but it is legal. The U.S. Supreme Court confirmed this several decades ago in *Nader v. Allegheny Airlines, Inc.*, 426 U.S. 290 (1976), excerpted below:

> [O]verbooking is a common industry practice, designed to ensure that each flight leaves with as few empty seats as possible despite the large number of "no-shows" reservation-holding passengers who do not appear at flight time. By the use of statistical studies of no-show patterns on specific flights, the airlines attempt to predict the appropriate number of reservations necessary to fill each flight. In this way, they attempt to ensure the most efficient use of aircraft while preserving a flexible booking system that permits passengers to cancel and change reservations without notice or penalty. At times the practice of overbooking results in oversales, which occur when more reservation-holding passengers than can be accommodated actually appear to board the flight. When this occurs, some passengers must be denied boarding ("bumped").
>
> The chance that any particular passenger will be bumped is so negligible that few prospective passengers aware of the possibility would give it a second thought. In April 1972, the month in which petitioner's reservation was dishonored, 6.7 confirmed passengers per 10,000 enplanements were denied boarding on domestic flights.
>
> For all domestic airlines, oversales resulted in bumping an average of 5.4 passengers per 10,000 enplanements in 1972, and 4.6 per 10,000 enplanements in 1973. In domestic operations respondent oversold 6.3 seats per 10,000 enplanements in 1972 and 4.5 seats per 10,000 enplanements in 1973. Thus, based on the 1972 experience of all domestic airlines, there was only slightly more than one chance in 2,000 that any particular passenger would be bumped on a given flight. Nevertheless, the

total number of confirmed ticket holders denied seats is quite substantial, numbering over 82,000 passengers in 1972 and about 76,000 in 1973.

Board regulations require each airline to establish priority rules for boarding passengers and to offer "denied boarding compensation" to bumped passengers. These "liquidated damages" are equal to the value of the passenger's ticket with a $25 minimum and a $200 maximum. *See* 14 C.F.R. § 250.5 (1975). Passengers are free to reject the compensation offered in favor of a common-law suit for damages suffered as a result of the bumping.

Figure 7-1. Denied Boarding Compensation Scheme

Domestic - Denied Boarding Compensation (DBC)

Domestic - Denied Boarding Compensation (DBC)

Length of Delay	Compensation
0 to 1 hour arrival delay	No compensation
1 to 2 hour arrival delay	200% of one-way fare (but no more than $675)
Over 2 hour arrival delay	400% of one-way fare (but no more than $1,350)

International - Denied Boarding Compensation (DBC)

International - Denied Boarding Compensation (DBC)

Length of Delay	Compensation
0 to 1 hour arrival delay	No compensation
1 to 4 hour arrival delay	200% of one-way fare (but no more than $675)
Over 4 hour arrival delay	400% of one-way fare (but no more than $1,350)

Source: Dep't of Transp., Aviation Consumer Protection: Bumping & Oversales,
https://www.transportation.gov/individuals/aviation-consumer-protection/bumping-oversales.

U.S. airlines reduced the number of passengers involuntarily bumped to the lowest number of record in 2017, according to the U.S. Department of Transportation, bumping passengers at a rate of .34 per 10,000 passengers, which is nearly half of the rate of .62 per 10,000 set in 2016. *See Alana Wise, U.S. Airline Cut Involuntary Passenger Bumping to Lowest Rate on Record*, REUTERS, Feb. 8, 2018.

DELTA AIR LINES, INC. V. BARNARD

799 So. 2d 208 (Ala. Civ. 2001)

YATES, JUDGE.

On August 21, 1997, Dr. Henry H. Barnard II sued Delta Air Lines, Inc. ("Delta"), in the District Court of Mobile County, alleging a breach of contract, conversion, theft, negligent supervision, and reckless supervision and/or training. Dr. Barnard sought both compensatory and punitive damages. His claim arose out of the loss of his golf clubs while he was traveling by air from Brunswick, Georgia, to Mobile, Alabama.

On December 24, 1997, Delta moved for a summary judgment limiting its potential liability to a maximum of $1,250, pursuant to conditions it alleged had been made a part of its contract of carriage. Dr. Barnard, on February 4, 1998, amended his complaint to add Atlantic Southeast Airlines, Inc. ("ASA"), as a defendant. On February 17, the court granted Delta's motion for a summary judgment, limiting its liability to $1,250. On July 2, 1998, the court entered a judgment in favor of Dr. Barnard for $1,250.

Dr. Barnard appealed to the Circuit Court of Mobile County, on July 8, 1998, for a trial *de novo*. The case was tried before a jury on March 2, 1999. At trial, Dr. Barnard voluntarily dismissed ASA as a defendant. Delta moved for a judgment as a matter of law ("JML") at the close of Dr. Barnard's case. The court entered a JML in favor of Delta on all the claims except the claims alleging a breach of contract and conversion. Delta renewed its motion for a JML as to those claims at the close of all the evidence. The court denied the motion and submitted the case to the jury.

The jury returned a general verdict in favor of Dr. Barnard for $30,000. The court, in accordance with Rule 13(j), Ala. R. Civ. P., reduced the verdict to $10,000, which represents the jurisdictional limits of the district court. Delta appealed to this court, after the circuit court denied its postjudgment motion. This court affirmed the judgment of the trial court, without an opinion, on July 21, 2000. While this case was pending before this court on Delta's application for rehearing, our supreme court released *Ex parte Delta Air Lines, Inc.*, 785 So. 2d 327 (Ala. 2000). On October 17, 2000, this court requested the parties to the present appeal to brief the issues in light of the supreme court's opinion in *Ex parte Delta Air Lines, Inc.* The parties complied with that order.

* * *

Dr. Henry H. Barnard II and his wife purchased two Delta round-trip tickets from All Seasons Travel in Dothan, to fly on August 7, 1997, from Mobile to Brunswick, Georgia, with a return trip on August 10, 1997. The return trip required the Barnards to fly through Atlanta. The ticket Dr. Barnard purchased indicated that the return flight would be on Delta flight 7264; however, the Brunswick-to-Atlanta leg of the flight was to be operated by ASA. ASA flights from Brunswick fly only to Atlanta.

On the day of the return trip, Dr. Barnard and his wife arrived at the Brunswick airport between 5:00 P.M. and 5:30 P.M. for their flight, which was scheduled to depart Brunswick at 6:45 P.M. Upon arriving at the airport, Dr. Barnard checked two pieces of luggage to Mobile, and his wife checked her luggage to Dothan. This flight was the last scheduled flight of the day from Brunswick to Atlanta and was the only flight on which Dr. Barnard's luggage could be placed, because the previous flight had departed Brunswick for Atlanta at 2:45 P.M. Dr. Barnard's luggage consisted of a suitcase that contained clothing, and a hard-plastic carrying case that contained golf clubs and other golf equipment. He testified that each golf club carried a sticker showing his name, address, and telephone number. The clubs were first placed inside a soft carry bag, which had two attached tags bearing Dr. Barnard's name. He testified that the soft bag was then placed inside the hard case. He stated that he had placed a sticker and an identification tag on the hard case. Additionally, Dr. Barnard testified that he had watched the ASA representative affix the baggage seal to the case.

The airport in Brunswick is a small facility. Dr. Barnard testified that he actually watched the ticket agent push the hard-case carrier into the luggage chute that opened directly onto the tarmac. This was the last time Dr. Barnard saw the hard case. He boarded the plane and flew to Atlanta. He had a one-and-one-half hour layover in Atlanta and then flew to Mobile. When Dr. Barnard arrived in Mobile, he proceeded to the baggage-claim area, where he retrieved his suitcase from the baggage carousel. His carrying case containing his golf clubs did not arrive. He then filed a "Lost Bag Claim" with a Delta agent in Mobile and was told that he had been on the day's last flight to Mobile from Atlanta and therefore there was no chance that the carrying case would arrive that night. He was given a telephone number and told to call back the following morning to check the status of his claim.

Dr. Barnard called the following morning and was informed by Delta that the carrying case had not arrived and that Delta was attempting to locate it. He was given Delta's lost-baggage department's toll-free telephone number to follow up on his claim. He called, to no avail. Dr. Barnard testified that two days later he was told by someone at Delta, "[I]f we haven't found [the case] yet, we are not going to find it." He then spoke to a Delta manager, who informed him that after three days "[the case] is probably not going to show up, it's probably gone." The manager informed him that Delta's liability was limited to $1,250 and he offered to send Dr. Barnard a check for that amount. Dr. Barnard testified that the value of the clubs and equipment was $3,292.50. Dr. Barnard received a check for $1,250 two days later, but he returned it to Delta.

Beau Goss, a Delta customer-service agent, testified that Delta's baggage-tracking system is sophisticated. He stated that a "bag tag" containing an identification number, a three-letter abbreviation of the destination, and a bar-code number is attached to a passenger's luggage when it is checked. He said that Delta can track luggage nationwide by the "bag tag" number and the bar code, through its computer system. He also testified that the destination of any luggage is easily ascertainable by looking at the three-letter abbreviation on the "bag tag." Goss further testified that the baggage handling area is a Federal Aviation Administration ("FAA") restricted area, accessible by Delta employees with a security clearance. He had no explanation as to how the carrying case containing numerous pieces of identification could get lost on a flight from Brunswick to Mobile with a layover in Atlanta. The record indicates that at no time was Dr. Barnard referred to ASA regarding the missing case. Ronnie Edwards, an ASA representative, testified that only ASA employees would have access to the baggage-handling area in Brunswick, and that only ASA and Delta employees would have access to the baggage-handling area in Atlanta. Edwards also had no explanation as to how the carrying case could have been lost during the trip.

Delta argues that the trial court erred as a matter of law in refusing to enforce its baggage-liability limitation of $1,250, which it alleges was made part of the contract of carriage entered into between Dr. Barnard and Delta. In *Ex parte Delta Air Lines*, 785 So. 2d 327 (Ala. 2000), the plaintiff sued Delta in the district court, alleging negligence and a breach of contract. The plaintiff contended that Delta had negligently handled her luggage and that as a result she had suffered damage, including the loss of her family jewelry. The district court entered a judgment in favor of the plaintiff, awarding her damages of $5,000. Delta appealed to the circuit court.

In the circuit court, Delta moved for a summary judgment, contending that the plaintiff's claims were preempted by federal law. The court denied Delta's motion and conducted a bench trial. The plaintiff dismissed her breach-of-contract claim; thereafter, the court entered a judgment in favor of the plaintiff and awarded her damages in the amount of $6,327. Delta appealed to this court;

we affirmed the judgment of the trial court, without an opinion, on December 3, 1999. Delta petitioned the supreme court for *certiorari* review, which the court granted.

The supreme court examined the preemption clause found in the Airline Deregulation Act of 1978 and *American Airlines, Inc. v. Wolens*, 513 U.S. 219 (1995), and *Morales v. Trans World Airlines, Inc.*, 504 U.S. 374 (1992), two United States Supreme Court cases addressing the Airline Deregulation Act's preemption clause. In reversing this court's judgment, the Supreme Court concluded that the preemption clause applied and that the plaintiff's state-law negligence claim had been preempted. The court specifically stated, "Reading *Morales* and *Wolens* together with the language of the preemption provision, we conclude that a [state-law tort claim] is preempted if it is 'related' to an airline's rates, routes, or services and if pursuing the claim in a state court amounts to enforcing a state law." *Ex parte Delta Air Lines*, 785 So. 2d at 334. The court, however, concluded that state-law breach-of-contract claims were not preempted by the preemption clause of the Airline Deregulation Act. The court stated that "[a]s a result of *Morales* and *Wolens*, it is clear that general breach-of-contract claims may be resolved by state courts." *Id.*

In reaching its conclusion in *Ex parte Delta Air Lines*, our supreme court noted its holding in *Eastern Air Lines v. Williamson*, 211 So. 2d 912 (1968), a case decided before the adoption of the Airline Deregulation Act and the preemption clause; in that case, the court concluded that the plaintiff's claims arising from the destruction of her luggage were to be " 'determined by federal law.' " In *Williamson*, the plaintiff's luggage was lost when the plane carrying it crashed. The *Williamson* court noted that Eastern's tariff, which had been filed pursuant to 49 App. U.S.C. § 1373, part of the Federal Aviation Act of 1958, specifically limited to $250 its liability for the loss of, or damage to, luggage, unless the passenger declared a higher value for the luggage. The terms of the tariff were deemed by law to be incorporated into the contract of carriage, and the court held that Eastern's liability was limited by the terms of the tariff, *i.e.*, to $250 for the lost luggage.

The rules applicable to the carriage of baggage in interstate and overseas air transportation are found at 14 C.F.R. § 254. Section 254 sets permissible limitations of air-carrier liability for loss, damage, or delay in the carriage of a passenger's baggage and requires an air carrier to provide certain kinds of notice to passengers regarding its limitation of liability.

The rules applicable to the carriage of baggage in interstate and overseas air transportation are found at 14 C.F.R. § 254. Section 254 sets permissible limitations of air-carrier liability for loss, damage, or delay in the carriage of a passenger's baggage and requires an air carrier to provide certain kinds of notice to passengers regarding its limitation of liability. 14 C.F.R. § 254.4 provides:

> In any flight segment using large aircraft, or on any flight segment that is included on the same ticket as another flight segment that uses large aircraft, an air carrier shall not limit its liability for provable direct or consequential damages resulting from the disappearance of, damage to, or delay in delivery of a passenger's personal property, including baggage, in its custody to an amount less than $1,250 for each passenger.

Section 254.5 provides:

> In any flight segment using large aircraft, or on any flight segment that is included on the same ticket as another flight segment that uses large aircraft, an air carrier shall provide to passengers, by conspicuous written material included on or with its ticket, either: (a) notice of any monetary limitation on its baggage liability to passengers; or (b) the following notice: "Federal rules require any limit on an airline's baggage liability to be at least $1,250 per passenger."

The notice requirement that governs the incorporation of terms by reference into a contract of carriage and that makes such incorporation of terms effective is found at 14 C.F.R. § 253. Section 253.1 provides: "The purpose of this rule is to set uniform disclosure requirements, which preempt any State requirements on the same subject, for terms incorporated by reference into contracts of carriage for scheduled service in interstate and overseas passenger air transportation." Section 253.4 provides:

> A ticket or other written instrument that embodies the contract of carriage may incorporate contract terms by reference (*i.e.*, without stating their full text), and if it does so shall contain or be accompanied by notice to the passenger as required by this part. In addition to other remedies at law, an air carrier may not claim the benefit as against the passenger of, and the passenger shall not be bound by, any contract term incorporated by reference if notice of the term has not been provided to that passenger in accordance with this part.
>
> Each air carrier shall make the full text of each term that it incorporates by reference in a contract of carriage available for public inspection at each of its airport and city ticket offices. Each air carrier shall provide

free of charge by mail or other delivery service to passengers, upon their request, a copy of the full text of its terms incorporated by reference in the contract. Each carrier shall keep available at all times, free of charge, at all locations where its tickets are sold within the United States information sufficient to enable passengers to order the full text of such terms.

Section 253.5 provides, in part:

Contract of Carriage and Incorporation by Reference

> Except as provided in § 253.8, each air carrier shall include on or with a ticket, or other written instrument given to a passenger, that embodies the contract of carriage and incorporates terms by reference in that contract, a conspicuous notice that:

> Any terms incorporated by reference are part of the contract, passengers may inspect the full text of each term incorporated by reference at the carrier's airport or city ticket offices, and passengers have the right, upon request at any location where the carrier's tickets are sold within the United States, to receive free of charge by mail or other delivery service the full text of each such incorporated term.

> The incorporated terms may include and passengers may obtain from any location where the carrier's tickets are sold within the United States further information concerning: Limits on the air carrier's liability for personal injury or death of passengers, and for loss, damage, or delay of goods and baggage, including fragile or perishable goods.

As stated previously, Dr. Barnard and his wife had purchased their airline tickets from All Seasons Travel in Dothan. Dr. Barnard's ticket was prepared by Janet Lattime, the branch manager of All Seasons Travel. The back of the airline ticket issued to Dr. Barnard contained the following language:

> Air transportation to be provided between points in the U.S. (including its overseas territories and possessions) is subject to the individual contract terms (including rules, regulations, tariffs and conditions) of the transporting air carriers, which are herein incorporated by reference and made part of the contract of carriage.

Delta introduced into evidence a copy of its conditions of contract that are incorporated by reference into the terms of the contract of carriage. Section V pertains to baggage and contains language limiting to $1,250 Delta's liability for the loss of, or damage to, a passenger's baggage, unless a higher value is declared by the passenger.

Where this coupon is issued for transportation, or services other than air travel, specific terms and conditions may apply. These terms and conditions may be included in the ticket set or may be obtained from this issuing company or agent. Please make sure you have received the important legal notices entitled "Conditions of Contract," "Notice of Incorporated Terms," "Notice of Baggage Liability Limitations," and "Notice of Overbooking," or the specific terms and conditions relating to non-air transportation or services. If not, contact the nearest office of the company or agent to obtain copies.

Dr. Barnard testified that he never read the wording on the back of the ticket and did not obtain the legal notices referenced therein. Lattime testified that a two-page insert had accompanied Dr. Barnard's ticket when it was issued to him. Page one of the insert contained the following language:

NOTICE OF BAGGAGE LIABILITY LIMITATIONS

Liability for loss, delay, or damage to baggage is limited unless a higher value is declared in advance and additional charges are paid ... For travel wholly between U.S. points federal rules require any limit on an airline's baggage liability to be at least $1,250 per passenger. Excess valuation may be declared on certain types of articles. Some carriers assume no liability for fragile, valuable or perishable articles. Further information may be obtained from the carrier.

Page two of the insert contained the following language:

NOTICE OF INCORPORATED TERMS

Effective January 1, 1983, this notice forms part of the conditions of contract between the airline and the passenger. If there is any inconsistency between the incorporated terms described below and the terms and conditions in the passenger's ticket, these incorporated terms govern.

Air transportation to be provided between points in the U.S. (including its overseas territories and possessions) is subject to the individual terms of the transporting air carriers, which are herein incorporated by reference and made part of the contract of carriage. Incorporated terms may include, but are not restricted to: *Limits on liability for baggage, including fragile or perishable goods, and availability of excess valuation coverage.*

You can obtain additional information on items 1 through 6 above at any U.S. location where the transporting air carrier's tickets are sold.

You have the right to inspect the full text of each transporting air carrier's terms at its airport and city ticket offices. You also have the right upon request, to receive free of charge the full text of the applicable terms incorporated by reference from each of the transporting air carriers. Information on ordering the full text of each air carrier's terms is available at any U.S. location where the air carrier's tickets are sold.

Lattime testified that attached to every airline ticket issued by All Seasons is a copy of the above-mentioned insert, and she testified that she specifically recalls including the insert in the ticket packet issued to Dr. Barnard. Dr. Barnard testified that he did not recall seeing the insert in the ticket packet, but that he did not look at all of the information contained in the packet. He did state that it was possible that he had seen the insert before August 10, 1997. Additionally, Dr. Barnard stated that he had flown commercially approximately 30 to 40 times and that he was generally aware that airlines contractually limit their liability for baggage.

Dr. Barnard's conversion claim in this case relates to an airline's service and therefore must be determined in accordance with federal law . . . We conclude, from the evidence presented, that Delta complied with the notice requirements set forth in 14 C.F.R. §§ 253 and 254 and it was entitled, as a matter of law, to have its $1,250 limitation of liability enforced.

Based on our supreme court's holding in *Ex parte Delta Air Lines*, we conclude that Dr. Barnard's conversion claim in this case relates to an airline's service and therefore must be determined in accordance with federal law. We further note that Delta conceded at trial that a contract of carriage existed between the parties and that it had breached that contract; however, it argued that its liability was limited to $1,250, because, it contended, it had satisfied the notice requirements contained in 14 C.F.R. §§ 253 and 254. We conclude, from the evidence presented, that Delta complied with the notice requirements set forth in 14 C.F.R. §§ 253 and 254 and it was entitled, as a matter of law, to have its $1,250 limitation of liability enforced.

EXERCISE 7-2. *DELTA AIR LINES, INC. V. BARNARD*—LIMITATION OF LIABILITY

1. Delta Air Lines, Inc. is identified as the defendant in the caption of the case. What is ASA, then?

2. What is a contract of carriage? How can an airline passenger obtain a copy?

3.   What decision did the Alabama Supreme Court reach in *Ex parte Delta Air Lines, Inc.*, 785 So. 2d 327 (Ala. 2000), and how was it applied to this case?

4.   Explain the provisions of 14 C.F.R. §§ 253.4, 254.5.

5.   Discuss how the conversion and breach-of-contract claim were decided. Is this result fair? What should an airline passenger do to insure against the loss of or damage to baggage exceeding the limitation of liability?

NOTES ON *DELTA AIR LINES, INC. V. BARNARD*—AIRLINE BAGGAGE POLICIES

1.   *High-Value, Fragile, and Perishable Items.*

What remedy does a passenger have if the value of their checked luggage is damaged, lost, or delayed and *exceeds* the limitation of liability under 14 C.F.R. § 254.4? In this case, passengers can and should purchase excess valuation insurance at the ticket counter. American Airlines, for example, sells such insurance at the rate of $5 for every $1000 worth of checked baggage, up to $5,000 per passenger. *See* American Airlines, *Liability Limitations*, https://www.aa.com/i18n/travel-info/baggage/liability-limitations.jsp. *See generally* Eloisa C. Rodriguez-Dod, *"Lucy in the Sky with Diamonds"—Airline Liability for Checked-In Jewelry*, 69 J. AIR L. & COM. 743 (2004).

By comparison, United Airlines exculpates itself from some or all liability under its policy for some unexpected and unusual items of high-value, fragile or perishable items for which the airline disclaims liability (in the case of travel within the United States) or for which liability may be limited (in the case of most international travel). These includes items such as antiques, artifacts, heirlooms, collectibles, religious items and artifacts; antlers; jewelry and precious metals/stone; knives and swords; works of art such as paintings or sculptures; and "[a]ny other similar valuable property or irreplaceable property included in the passenger's checked or carry-on baggage with or without the knowledge of United." Also included under the heading of "high-value, fragile or perishable items" are human remains:

Cremated human remains

If you have recently lost a loved one, we're sorry for your loss and want to make your travel as easy as possible. If you're traveling with cremated human remains, they need to be transported as carry-on baggage. For travel within the U.S., it's highly recommended that you travel with appropriate documentation (such as a document from the funeral home or a death certificate) to present during TSA screening. Please visit the TSA website for details on acceptable containers. For travel outside of the U.S., you should check with a local consulate or burial advisor beforehand. If you prefer to have the remains shipped, we offer TrustUA, a specialized service designed to assist in the transportation of human remains.

2.   ***Carrier-Specific Baggage Policies.***

In addition to the law governing carrier liability for lost, damaged, or delayed baggage, airlines traditionally have their own baggage policies. For example, the policy of United Airlines reads:

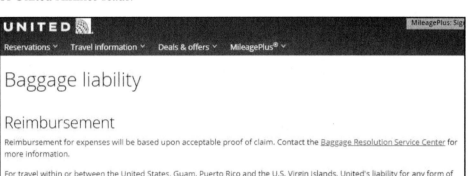

Baggage liability

Reimbursement

Reimbursement for expenses will be based upon acceptable proof of claim. Contact the Baggage Resolution Service Center for more information.

For travel within or between the United States, Guam, Puerto Rico and the U.S. Virgin Islands, United's liability for any form of damage as a result of loss, damage or delay in delivery of a customer's personal property shall be limited to the fair market value at the time of loss, damage or delay and will not exceed $3,500.00 USD/CAD per customer, except for wheelchairs and other assistive devices.

For international travel to which the Warsaw Convention applies (including domestic* portions of international travel), United's liability is limited to approximately $9.07 USD/CAD per pound up to $640.00 USD/CAD per bag for checked baggage and $400.00 USD/CAD per customer for unchecked baggage.

For international travel to which the Montreal Convention applies (including domestic* portions of international travel), United's liability is limited to 1,131 SDR (Special Drawing Rights) per customer for checked and unchecked baggage. Exchange rates are available online at imf.org ✎.

High-value, fragile or perishable items

If you're traveling with high-value, fragile or perishable items, we recommend keeping them in carry-on bags or personal items instead of checked bags. If you choose to pack high-value, fragile or perishable items in your checked bags or as checked bags for domestic* travel, we're not liable for the loss of, damage to or delay in delivery of such items.

Visit our page about high-value, fragile and perishable items for a detailed list of excluded items. For international travel, our liability is limited as per above.

Damaged bags

We know you count on us to handle your bags with care, and it's possible your checked bags may show signs of wear because of normal handling. However, if you believe we damaged your checked bags, please review our page about damaged bags to see how to submit a claim. You won't be able to report damaged bags by email or through our website.

We're not liable if you have a damaged bag because of:

— An existing defect with the bag

— The bag's poor quality

— Overpacking the bag

— Ordinary wear and tear

*Domestic travel includes travel within or between the United States, Guam, Puerto Rico and the U.S. Virgin Islands.

Source: United Airlines, Baggage Liability, https://www.united.com/ual/en/us/fly/travel/baggage/liability.html.

3. ***Animals.***

Increasingly controversial is the transportation of service or "therapy animals." Under 14 C.F.R. Part 382, airlines are required to allow passengers to fly with their service animals in the cabin on all U.S. airlines. Service animals are not pets, but working animals that assist persons with disabilities. There is no limit to the number of service animals that can be on any flight and service animals do not need any health certificates to travel, nor do they need to be confined in a container or cage. *See* Fed. Aviation Admin., *Pets in the Passenger Cabin. See generally* Laura Rothstein, *Puppies, Ponies, Pigs, and Parrots: Policies, Practices, and Procedures in Pubs, Pads, Planes, and Professions: Where We Live, Work, and Play, and How We Get There: Animal Accommodations in Public Places, Housing, Employment, and Transportation*, 24 ANIMAL L. 13 (2018); Brenda Goodman, *Pets on Planes: Emotional Support or Sham?*, WebMD.com, Dec. 21, 2017; Rebecca J. Huss, *Why Context Matters: Defining Service Animals under Federal Law*, 37 PEPP. L. REV. 1163 (2010).

4. ***Contract of Carriage.***

By purchasing a ticket from or accepting transportation on an airline, passengers agree to be bound by certain terms and conditions formalized in a "contract of carriage." An example of this contract—in the nature of a contract of adhesion—follows:

Figure 7-2. Contract of Carriage, Excerpt: Delta Airlines

CONTRACT OF CARRIAGE: UNITED STATES

When you buy a ticket for travel on Delta, you enter into a contract of carriage with us. The terms of your contract are set forth in:

- your ticket
- any tariffs that apply
- our Conditions of Carriage or General Rules Tariff

Delta Air Lines Conditions of Carriage: Domestic General Rules Tariff (PDF)

To view, save or print the documents that are in Portable Document Format (PDF) you'll need the free Adobe Acrobat Reader.

Download Adobe Acrobat Reader

For past date conditions of carriage, please email us specifying which tariff you are requesting and the date of your ticket purchase.

***A Note for Delta Customers Residing in Canada:** The plain language versions of Delta's Canadian General Rules Tariff and International Conditions of Carriage are posted to assist passengers in interpreting the tariffs filed with the Canadian Transportation Agency ("CTA"). To the extent there are discrepancies between the plain language versions and the tariffs filed with the CTA, the tariffs filed with the CTA shall prevail.

Most passengers do not bother to read the airline contract of carriage, which may span dozens and dozens of pages. The scope of such contracts is often extensive, touching on matters that passengers often want to know about, but sometimes only learn about after an issue or problem arises.

Figure 7-3. Domestic General Rules Tariff ("Contract of Carriage")—Delta Airlines (2018)

DELTA DOMESTIC GENERAL RULES TARIFF
[Last Modified JULY 11, 2018]

Consider the contract of carriage for United Airlines, Contract of Carriage, https://www.united.com/web/en-US/content/contract-of-carriage.aspx, and answer the following questions:

- What is the definition of "baggage"?
- How are "consequential damages" defined in United's Contract of Carriage? What does this mean—in your own words.
- Is a flight from Buffalo, New York, USA to Toronto, Canada "international" pursuant to United's Contract of Carriage? (Hint: See definition of "international sector.").
- Is "bumping" defined in United's Contract of Carriage? If so, what is the definition? (Hint: Oversales.)
- Is United Airlines permitted to refuse to transport pregnant passengers under its Contract of Carriage? Explain why or why not.

- Is United Airlines permitted to refuse to transport blind or deaf passengers under its Contract of Carriage? Explain why or why not.

- What about "malodorous" passengers—is the airline permitted to refuse their transportation? Explain, including detailing if any exceptions apply.

- What is a "force majeure event"? Provide three examples.

- Under what conditions will United accept the transportation of "service animals"?

- Read Rule 30 ("Consent to Use of Personal Data") and explain, in your own words, what this means?

BUCK V. AMERICAN AIRLINES, INC.

476 F.3d 29 (1st Cir. 2007)

SELYA, SENIOR CIRCUIT JUDGE.

On November 4, 2004, fifteen individuals filed suit against a number of airlines and related entities in a Massachusetts state court. The plaintiffs alleged that the defendants had wrongfully retained fees and taxes collected at the time of their purchase of nonrefundable tickets. This retention of funds was wrongful, the plaintiffs maintained, because they never used the tickets and, thus, the fees and taxes, which did not become due until the commencement of air travel, should have been returned.

The defendants removed the case to the federal district court. The plaintiffs, now reduced to nine in number, served an amended complaint that named six domestic and seven international airlines as the culprits. Of the domestic airlines, American Airlines, Alaska Airlines, Continental Airlines, and Southwest Airlines remain as defendants. Two other domestic carriers (Northwest and Delta) have been dismissed due to ongoing bankruptcy proceedings. The international airlines named in the suit are Aer Lingus, Alitalia, British Airways, China Eastern Airlines, China Southern Airlines, Lufthansa, and Olympic Airways. Of these, six remain (Olympic Airways appears to have been dropped as a party). The Federal Aviation Administration ("FAA") also was named, but the district court dismissed all claims against the FAA on grounds wholly unrelated to the issues raised on appeal.

Fees and Taxes

The fees and taxes said to have been wrongly withheld include passenger facility charges, see 14 C.F.R. § 158.5; customs fees, see 19 C.F.R. § 24.22(g)(1); immigration fees, see 8 C.F.R. § 286.2; agricultural quarantine fees, see 7 C.F.R.

§ 354.3(f); security fees, see 49 C.F.R. § 1510.5; and charges on behalf of foreign sovereigns (collectively, the "fees"). The plaintiffs averred that, in keeping the fees, the defendants violated a host of federal regulations, most notably a regulation that provides:

> A passenger shall not be bound by any terms restricting refunds of the ticket price, imposing monetary penalties on passengers, or permitting the carrier to raise the price, unless the passenger receives conspicuous written notice of the salient features of those terms on or with the ticket.

14 C.F.R. § 253.7. The plaintiffs claim that the retained fees constitute a forbidden monetary penalty, imposed without due notice. In this connection, they admit having had adequate notice that their tickets were nonrefundable; in their view, however, this only alerted them to the fact that they could not recover the base ticket price. They had no notice that the fees would be forfeit as well.

The plaintiffs cloaked this theory in pleochroic raiment; their multitudinous statements of claim included counts for declaratory judgment, rescission, breach of contract, unjust enrichment, breach of a covenant of good faith and fair dealing, breach of fiduciary duty, and civil conspiracy. In addition, the plaintiffs purposed to sue pursuant to an implied right of action arising under a federal regulation. Their prayer for relief requested certification of a class; a declaration that (i) the airlines had failed to provide adequate notice of an intention to withhold the fees and (ii) the airlines' retention of the fees was wrongful; treble damages; injunctive and other equitable remediation; and attorneys' fees.

A majority of the defendants moved to dismiss on the ground, *inter alia*, that all the claims were preempted by section 105(a) of the Airline Deregulation Act ("ADA"), 49 U.S.C. § 41713(b)(1). The district court granted the motion to dismiss. This timely appeal followed.

* * *

We begin our analysis with the plaintiffs' lone federal-law claim: their claim of an implied right of action under 14 C.F.R. § 253.4 and § 253.7. These provisions govern the disclosure of terms in contracts for air travel. Among other things, they prevent airlines from claiming the benefit of contract terms not incorporated by reference in a specified manner. *See* 14 C.F.R. § 253.4(a). They go on to restrict the authority of airlines to impose monetary penalties on passengers without clear notice. *See id.* § 253.7. In this instance, the plaintiffs argue that they were denied notice that they would forfeit the fees (in addition to the base fares) in the event that they did not use their nonrefundable tickets.

Implied Right of Action?

In support of this argument, the plaintiffs invoke the test formulated in *Cort v. Ash*, 422 U.S. 66 (1975), which they insist controls whether a private right of action is to be implied in connection with a federal statute. Under that test, courts are to ask four questions:

> [I]s the plaintiff a member of the class for whose "especial benefit" the statute was passed? Is there any cogent indication of legislative intent to create or deny the remedy sought? Would recognition of the remedy be "consistent with the underlying purposes' of the statutory scheme? Would it be inappropriate to infer a federal remedy because 'the cause of action [is] one traditionally relegated to state law?' "

Royal Business Group., Inc. v. Realist, Inc., 933 F.2d 1056 (1st Cir. 1991). The plaintiffs maintain that the regulations' goal is to protect consumers and, thus, that it is appropriate to imply a private right of action.

Source of Private Rights of Action

This argument cannot withstand scrutiny. In the first place, the plaintiffs misapprehend the relevant unit of analysis. Regulations alone cannot create private rights of action; the source of the right must be a statute. *See Alexander v. Sandoval* (2001). The regulations upon which the plaintiffs rely were promulgated pursuant to 49 U.S.C. § 41707—a statute that has its roots in the CAB Sunset Act, Pub. L. No. 98–443, § 7 (1984). The CAB Sunset Act embodies a series of amendments to the ADA, which six years earlier had significantly revamped the Federal Aviation Act. We recently rejected an entreaty to imply a private cause of action pursuant to other regulations implementing the ADA. In the process, we made clear that, for the purpose of implying private rights of action, the Federal Aviation Act (and, hence, the ADA) is barren soil. There is nothing about the case at bar that shakes our confidence in that assessment.

> *Regulations alone cannot create private rights of action; the source of the right must be a statute . . . thus, we hold that the consumer protection provisions of the ADA do not permit the imputation of a private right of action against an airline and that, therefore, the plaintiffs do not have an implied right of action under 14 C.F.R. § 253.4 or § 253.7.*

To cinch matters, "[e]very court faced with the question of whether a consumer protection provision of the ADA allows the implication of a private right of action against an airline has answered the question in the negative." *Casas v. American Airlines, Inc.*, 304 F.3d 517 (5th Cir. 2002). We see no justification for creating a circuit split. Thus, we hold that the consumer protection provisions of the ADA do not permit the imputation of a private right of action against an airline and that, therefore, the plaintiffs do not have an implied right of action under 14 C.F.R. § 253.4 or § 253.7.

Lacking a federal-law cause of action, the plaintiffs are relegated to their array of state-law claims. Yet, even though Massachusetts law offers them a cornucopia of vehicles for their theory that the fees should have been refunded, this bounty avails them naught; state-law claims premised on that theory cannot survive the ADA's broad preemptive sweep. We explain briefly.

Pertinently, the ADA declares that no state may "enact or enforce a law, regulation, or other provision having the force and effect of law related to a price, route, or service of an air carrier." 49 U.S.C. § 41713(b)(1). The Supreme Court has offered considerable guidance as to how this preemption provision should be construed. In *Morales v. Trans World Airlines, Inc.*, 504 U.S. 374 (1992), the Court referred to the "sweeping nature" of the preemption provision, emphasizing the reach of the provision's "relationship" language. The *Morales* Court held that the provision should be construed broadly. This court has explained that, under *Morales*, the ADA preempts both laws that explicitly refer to an airline's prices and those that have a significant effect upon prices.

Three years after *Morales*, the Supreme Court reaffirmed the breadth of the ADA's preemption provision. *See American Airlines, Inc. v. Wolens*, 513 U.S. 219 (1995). However, the Court carved out an exception for "suits alleging no violation of state-imposed obligations, but seeking recovery solely for the airline's alleged breach of its own, self-imposed undertakings." It follows that, in order to avoid preemption, the plaintiffs in this case must demonstrate either that their state-law claims do not constitute state enforcement related to airline prices or services, or that they can navigate the straits of the *Wolens* exception.

The plaintiffs' doctrinal starting point is the assertion that their claims are outside the ambit of ADA preemption because they seek to enforce federal, not state, regulatory requirements. At the heart of this assertion lies the dubious premise that since federal rules govern the airlines' collection of the fees and provide certain forms of passenger protection in the contracting process, only federal policies are being advanced by this litigation. On this telling, "[s]tate court enforcement of Federal law is not the same as enforcement of a State-imposed requirement," and the fact that the causes of action themselves spring from state law is less important than the source of the underlying policies. This is so, the plaintiffs asseverate, because federal preemption should not disrupt federal policies; after all, nationwide uniformity is the driver for preemption, see *Morales*, and that uniformity is not offended by enforcement of federal policies.

This sleight of hand will not work. While the plaintiffs strive to characterize their suit as one that invokes state remedies to right a federal wrong, that characterization does not ring true. More accurately, they are attempting to invoke state remedies to further a state policy: that those who are wronged should have individualized access to the courts in order to remediate that wrong. It is the imposition of this state policy that would constitute forbidden state enforcement, in violation of the ADA's preemption provision, because the ADA itself provides no private right of action.

As an alternative, the plaintiffs posit that allowing their suit to proceed "does not—and in fact cannot—affect the prices (or rates), routes, or services [of airlines], since the redress occurs only after the prices (or rates), routes, and services have been determined by the Air Industry." In their view, "[a]irline ticket prices (or rates) are composed of two separate components: (1) the fare prices (or rates) set by the airlines, which comprise the base cost of a ticket, and (2) the taxes, fees, and, charges imposed by the Government or other fee-levying authorities."

This dichotomy blurs when contextualized within the contours of the "significant effect" doctrine. Although the fees are in one sense separate from the base fare, the two are inextricably intertwined. In all events, an air traveler's concern is with the overall cost of his or her ticket. Thus, when an airline establishes the base fare, it must take cognizance of any surcharges that will be imposed by operation of law.

It is freshman-year economics that higher prices mean lower demand, and that consumers are sensitive to the full price that they must pay, not just the portion of the price that will stay in the seller's coffers. For that reason, an airline must account for the fees when setting its own rates. It follows that a finding for the plaintiffs in this case would impact base fares—and since past judgments affect future behavior, this is as true of the retrospective relief requested by the plaintiffs as it is of the prospective relief that they request.

It is freshman-year economics that higher prices mean lower demand, and that consumers are sensitive to the full price that they must pay, not just the portion of the price that will stay in the seller's coffers. For that reason, an airline must account for the fees when setting its own rates. It follows that a finding for the plaintiffs in this case would impact base fares—and since past judgments affect future behavior, this is as true of the retrospective relief requested by the plaintiffs as it is of the prospective relief that they request. In view of these practical realities, it is not surprising that most of the courts to have considered suits for refunds of government fees associated with air travel have found those suits preempted. We say "most" because at least one court has found to the contrary. *See In re Air Transp. Excise Tax. Litig.*, 37 F. Supp. 2d 1133 (D. Minn. 1999). We regard that decision as mistaken.

The plaintiffs next argue that their suit was improvidently dismissed because their contract-based claims fit within the *Wolens* exception. But the plaintiffs' amended complaint identifies only a single word—"nonrefundable"—as common to their contracts of carriage with a multitude of airlines. It seems fanciful to suggest, in the circumstances of this case, that the word "nonrefundable" alone can anchor a breach of contract claim. The same result would follow even if, as plaintiffs insist, the word "nonrefundable" is ambiguous. At best, an ambiguity would furnish a rejoinder to a claim that the airlines gave clear notice about fees being forfeit. It could not, without more, support a claim that the defendants have breached their duty to treat the tickets as "nonrefundable" by withholding both the fare and the fees.

The plaintiffs attempt to circumvent this conspicuous obstacle by latching onto the federal regulatory guidelines relating to the disclosure of terms in airline contracts. These guidelines, they suggest, are "federally mandated terms of their air travel contracts." In making this point, the plaintiffs again emphasize 14 C.F.R. § 253.7, the provision prohibiting the imposition of monetary penalties without clear notice. The plaintiffs allege that this regulation is written implicitly into every airline contract of carriage and thus, by retaining the fees, the airlines have breached their contractual duty not to levy an unwarned monetary penalty. The plaintiffs have not directed us to a single case holding that a federal regulation incapable of spawning an implied private right of action may be enforced between private parties as an implicit contract term. The precedent that they most loudly trumpet—the Texas Supreme Court's decision in *Delta Air Lines, Inc. v. Black* (Tex. 2003)—is inapposite. The contract at issue there explicitly incorporated federal regulations.

We conclude, without serious question, that the proposition asserted by the plaintiffs is untenable. As they conceded at oral argument, construing all federal regulations touching upon air travel as automatically incorporated into every airline's contracts of carriage would allow litigants freely to skirt the implied right of action doctrine. There is nothing to distinguish the regulation at issue here from the mine-run of federal regulations touching upon air travel, and we will not countenance the flagrant undermining of Supreme Court doctrine that the plaintiffs invite.

> *We conclude, without serious question, that the proposition asserted by the plaintiffs is untenable. As they conceded at oral argument, construing all federal regulations touching upon air travel as automatically incorporated into every airline's contracts of carriage would allow litigants freely to skirt the implied right of action doctrine. There is nothing to distinguish the regulation at issue here from the mine-run of federal regulations touching upon air travel, and we will not countenance the flagrant undermining of Supreme Court doctrine that the plaintiffs invite.*

Our reluctance is evidently shared by the Fifth Circuit, which confronted a similar problem in *Casas*. There, the plaintiff argued for a remedy under federal common law with respect to violations of regulations prescribed by the federal Department of Transportation. The court rejected this argument, observing that a contrary holding "would be, in substance, to craft a private right of action for violations of [the regulation]—and thus to circumvent the conclusion that the ADA, and therefore the regulations enacted pursuant to it, creates no private right of action." Like the Fifth Circuit, we refuse to abet a blatant evasion of the implied right of action doctrine.

To say more on this point would be supererogatory. At bottom, the plaintiffs would have us believe that the implied right of action doctrine contains a gaping aperture that allows federal regulations, promulgated pursuant to a statute that creates no right of private enforcement, to be privately enforced through state-law mechanisms. We cannot imagine that the Supreme Court, which has devoted nearly three decades to cabining the implied right of action doctrine would approve so vagarious a course.

> *To say more on this point would be supererogatory. At bottom, the plaintiffs would have us believe that the implied right of action doctrine contains a gaping aperture that allows federal regulations, promulgated pursuant to a statute that creates no right of private enforcement, to be privately enforced through state-law mechanisms. We cannot imagine that the Supreme Court, which has devoted nearly three decades to cabining the implied right of action doctrine would approve so vagarious a course. We hold instead that, because no implied right of action exists under the ADA and the regulation at issue here, the regulation cannot be read as an implied contract provision.*

We hold instead that, because no implied right of action exists under the ADA and the regulation at issue here, the regulation cannot be read as an implied contract provision. Next, the plaintiffs launch a naked appeal to public policy. They tell us that if state-law causes of action are denied them, there will be a wrong (the airlines' withholding of the fees) without a remedy. Put in more hyperbolic terms, a rejection of the plaintiffs' claims would render "almost all airline contracts and certain provisions of Federal law" meaningless.

The first half of this lament—that a finding for the defendants will jeopardize the enforceability of all airline contracts of carriage—is empty rhetoric. A finding for the defendants merely retains the configuration of the *Wolens* exception crafted by the Supreme Court, which limited that exception to "self-imposed undertakings." The second half of this lament—that a finding for the defendants will undercut the federal regulatory scheme—is equally baseless. Refusing to treat federal regulations as implied contract terms does not in any way diminish the efficacy of the regulatory scheme itself. Contrary to the plaintiffs' importunings, we do not think it "inexplicabl[e]" that Congress might view certain regulations as sufficiently important to warrant their promulgation, yet "not sufficiently important to permit [private] enforcement in any court."

What the plaintiffs fail to grasp is that the unavailability of private enforcement is not the same as the unavailability of any enforcement at all. We made that point in another case where we remarked upon the power of the Secretary of Transportation to conduct investigations and issue orders with respect to the airline industry. This led us to the conclusion that Congress's preference in this area is for public, rather than private, enforcement. In other words, Congress reasonably expected the regulations to be enforced by the Secretary.

EXERCISE 7-3. *BUCK V. AMERICAN AIRLINES, INC.*—PRIVATE RIGHT OF ACTION

1. Inventory the various fees at issue in this litigation and explain the plaintiffs' complaint in connection with them.

2. Explain the requirements of 14 C.F.R. § 253.4 and § 253.7.

3. What is a private right of action? Are they created by statute or regulation? What is the difference?

4. What is an *implied* private right of action?

5. How does a contract-based claim, under the precedent of *American Airlines, Inc. v. Wolens*, 513 U.S. 219 (1995), save (or not) plaintiffs' claim?

NOTES ON *BUCK V. AMERICAN AIRLINES, INC.*—U.S. DEPARTMENT OF TRANSPORTATION (DOT) AVIATION CONSUMER PROTECTION

1.   *DOT Aviation Consumer Protection Division.*

Judge Selya gives little weight to the claims of the plaintiffs in *Buck v. American Airlines, Inc.*, characterizing their theories as "cloaked in pleochroic raiment," a "sleight of hand," and against all precedent on the matters raised. So, what are airline passengers to do where no private right of action exists to vindicate explicit passenger rights—the U.S. Department of Transportation's Aviation Consumer Protection Division offers an outlet:

> If you can't resolve the problem at the airport, you may want to file a complaint with the airline. DOT requires airlines to acknowledge consumer complaints within 30 days of receiving them and to send consumers written responses addressing these complaints within 60 days of receiving them. DOT also requires airlines to let consumers know how to complain to them.

> It's often best to email or write to the airline's consumer office at its corporate headquarters. DOT requires airlines that fly to, from, or within the United States to state on their websites how and where complaints can be submitted. There may be a form on the airline's website for this purpose.

> If you feel that the airline does not resolve the issue to your satisfaction, you may want to file a complaint with DOT. You may also file a complaint with DOT if you feel that you experienced unlawful discriminatory treatment in air travel by airline employees or the airline's contractors on the basis of disability or on the basis of race, color, national origin, sex, religion, or ancestry.

The filing of a complaint with the U.S. DOT may not necessarily resolve or correct the complaining passenger's situation, but the U.S. DOT may decide to take enforcement action against the carrier and data about such complaints are reported monthly in an Air Travel Consumer Report that is divided into six sections: flight delays, mishandled baggage, oversales, consumer complaints, customer service reports to the Transportation Security Administration, and airline reports of the loss, injury, or death of animals during air transportation.

Below is a screenshot of the DOT's Aviation Consumer Protection website with guidance on how to complete a complaint. *See* https://www.transportation.gov/individuals/aviation-consumer-protection/air-travel-consumer-reports.

Figure 7-4. DOT Aviation Consumer Protection Complaint Process

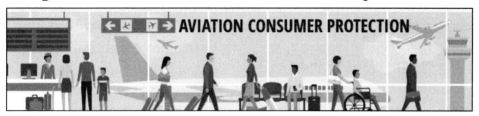

File a Consumer Complaint

Before you contact DOT for help with an air travel problem, you should give the airline a chance to resolve it. Airlines have trouble-shooters at the airports, usually called Customer Service Representatives, who can take care of many problems on the spot. They may be able to arrange meals and hotel rooms for stranded passengers, write checks if you're bumped from your flight, help with baggage issues, and settle other routine claims or complaints.

If you can't resolve the problem at the airport, you may want to file a complaint with the airline. DOT requires airlines to acknowledge consumer complaints within 30 days of receiving them and to send consumers written responses addressing these complaints within 60 days of receiving them. DOT also requires airlines to let consumers know how to complain to them.

It's often best to email or write to the airline's consumer office at its corporate headquarters. DOT requires airlines that fly to, from, or within the United States to state on their websites how and where complaints can be submitted. There may be a form on the airline's website for this purpose.

If you feel that the airline does not resolve the issue to your satisfaction, you may want to file a complaint with DOT. You may also file a complaint with DOT if you feel that you experienced unlawful discriminatory treatment in air travel by airline employees or the airline's contractors on the basis of disability or on the basis of race, color, national origin, sex, religion, or ancestry.

File a Consumer Complaint

Figure 7-5. Types of U.S. DOT Aviation Consumer Complaints

> **How the Complaint Process Works**
>
> **For Disability and Discrimination Complaints**
>
> - A Transportation Industry Analyst will forward your complaint to the airline, and the airline will be required to respond to you and the DOT.
>
> - Once the airline's response is received, a DOT analyst will review your complaint and the airline's response to determine if a violation occurred. After the analyst reviews your case, it will be given to an attorney for review. Once your case is reviewed by an attorney, an analysis with our findings will be mailed to you. Please note that due to the volume of cases received, and the thoroughness of this process, it may take some time to fully process your case.
>
> **For All Other Complaints**
>
> - A Transportation Industry Analyst will forward your complaint to the airline and the airline will be required to provide you with a response. The analyst will ask the airline to provide a copy of the response to DOT only if it falls under one of the areas DOT enforces. The DOT analyst will then review the case to determine whether a violation occurred. If your complaint does not appear to fall under any of the laws that we enforce, it will still be logged in our database.
>
> - Every month, DOT publishes its Air Travel Consumer Report, which contains information about the number of complaints we receive about each airline and what problems people are having. This report is made available to the public so that consumers and air travel companies can compare the complaint records of individual airlines and tour operators. In addition to complaints, the report also contains statistics that the airlines file with us on flight delays, cancellations, bumping, mishandled baggage, and other helpful information.
>
> **How Do Consumer Complaints Help DOT?**
>
> Complaints from consumers help DOT spot problem areas and trends in the airline industry. Complaints can lead to enforcement action against an airline when a serious violation of the law has occurred. Complaints may also be the basis for rulemaking actions.

Source: https://www.transportation.gov/airconsumer/file-consumer-complaint

2. ***Enabling Airline Passenger Protections.***

The upshot of cases like *Buck v. American Airlines, Inc.* finding that consumers have no private right of action to enforce passenger-centered regulations in the absence of an enabling statute means that improving airline customer service sometimes requires nothing less than an act of Congress—a substantial task. In 2010, Congress took action, enacting the "Enhancing Airliner Passenger Protections," 14 C.F.R. Pt. 259. Effective April 29, 2010, air carriers must adopt contingency plans for hours-long tarmac delays; develop and publish customer service plans, and respond to consumer problems. Through the new regulation, the United States Department of Transportation will consider continued delays on flights that are chronically late to be unfair and deceptive in violation of federal law. Highlights of the regulation include:

§ 259.1   Purpose.

The purpose of this part is to mitigate hardships for airline passengers during lengthy tarmac delays and otherwise to bolster air carriers' accountability to consumers.

§ 259.2   Applicability.

This rule applies to all the flights of a certificated or commuter air carrier if the carrier operates scheduled passenger service or public charter service using any aircraft originally designed to have a passenger capacity of 30 or more seats, except as provided in this part. This part does not apply to foreign carrier charters that operate to and from the United States if no new passengers are picked up in the United States.

§ 259.4   Contingency plan lengthy tarmac delays.

Adoption of Plan. Each covered carrier shall adopt a Contingency Plan for Lengthy Tarmac Delays for its scheduled and public charter flights at each large and medium hub U.S. airport at which it operates such air service and shall adhere to its plan's terms.

Contents of Plan. Each Contingency Plan for Lengthy Tarmac Delays shall include, at a minimum, the following:

(1)   For domestic flights, assurance that the air carrier will not permit an aircraft to remain on the tarmac for more than three hours unless: Pilot-in-command determines there is a safety-related or security-related reason (e.g., weather, a directive from an appropriate government agency) why the aircraft cannot leave its position on the tarmac to deplane passengers; or Air traffic control advises the pilot-in-command that returning to the gate or another disembarkation point elsewhere in order to deplane passengers would significantly disrupt airport operations.

(2)   For international flights that depart from or arrive at a U.S. airport, assurance that the air carrier will not permit an aircraft to remain on the tarmac at a large or medium hub U.S. airport for more than a set number of hours, as determined by the carrier and set out in its contingency plan, before allowing passengers to deplane, unless:

Pilot-in-command determines there is a safety-related or security-related reason why the aircraft cannot leave its position on the tarmac to deplane passengers; or

Air traffic control advises the pilot-in-command that returning to the gate or another disembarkation point elsewhere in order to deplane passengers would significantly disrupt airport operations.

(3) For all flights, assurance that the air carrier will provide adequate food and potable water no later than two hours after the aircraft leaves the gate (in the case of departure) or touches down (in the case of an arrival) if the aircraft remains on the tarmac, unless the pilot-in-command determines that safety or security considerations preclude such service;

(4) For all flights, assurance of operable lavatory facilities, as well as adequate medical attention if needed, while the aircraft remains on the tarmac;

(5) Assurance of sufficient resources to implement the plan; and

(6) Assurance that the plan has been coordinated with airport authorities at all medium and large hub airports that the carrier serves, including medium and large hub diversion airports.

Unfair and Deceptive Practice. An air carrier's failure to comply with the assurances required by this rule and as contained in its Contingency Plan for Lengthy Tarmac Delays will be considered an unfair and deceptive practice within the meaning of 49 U.S.C. § 41712 that is subject to enforcement action by the Department.

§ 259.5   Customer Service Plan.

Adoption of Plan. Each covered carrier shall adopt a Customer Service Plan applicable to its scheduled flights and shall adhere to this plan's terms.

Contents of Plan. Each Customer Service Plan shall, at a minimum, address the following subjects:

(1) Offering the lowest fare available;

(2) Notifying consumers of known delays, cancellations, and diversions;

(3) Delivering baggage on time;

(4) Allowing reservations to be held without payment or cancelled without penalty for a defined amount of time;

(5) Providing prompt ticket refunds;

(6) Properly accommodating passengers with disabilities and other special-needs, including during tarmac delays;

(7) Meeting customers' essential needs during lengthy tarmac delays;

(8) Handling "bumped" passengers with fairness and consistency in the case of oversales;

(9) Disclosing travel itinerary, cancellation policies, frequent flyer rules, and aircraft configuration;

(10) Ensuring good customer service from code-share partners;

(11) Ensuring responsiveness to customer complaints; and

(12) Identifying the services it provides to mitigate passenger inconveniences resulting from cancellations and misconnects.

§ 259.7   Response to consumer problems.

Informing consumers how to complain. Each covered carrier shall make available the mailing address and e-mail or Web address of the designated department in the airline with which to file a complaint about its scheduled service. This information shall be provided on the carrier's Web site (if any), on all e-ticket confirmations and, upon request, at each ticket counter and boarding gate staffed by the carrier.

Response to complaints. Each covered carrier shall acknowledge receipt of each complaint regarding its scheduled service to the complainant within 30 days of receiving it and shall send a substantive response to each complainant within 60 days of receiving the complaint. A complaint is a specific written expression of dissatisfaction concerning a difficulty or problem which the person experienced when using or attempting to use an airline's services.

Social networking sites. Each covered carrier that uses a social networking site (e.g. Facebook, Twitter) and that does not intend for that site to be a vehicle for receipt of written consumer complaints subject to this section shall clearly indicate on the carrier's primary page on that social networking site that it will not reply to consumer complaints on that site and shall direct consumers to the carrier's mailing address and e-mail or website location for filing written complaints.

§ 259.8 Notify passengers of known delays, cancellations, and diversions.

Each covered carrier for its scheduled flights to, from or within the U.S. must promptly provide to passengers who are ticketed or hold reservations, and to the public, information about a change in the status of a flight within 30 minutes after the carrier becomes aware of such a change in the status of a flight. A change in the status of a flight means, at a minimum, cancellation of a flight, a delay of 30 minutes or more in the planned operation of a flight, or a diversion. The flight status information must at a minimum be provided in the boarding gate area for the flight at a U.S. airport, on the carrier's website, and via the carrier's telephone reservation system upon inquiry by any person.

Are you surprised that it took an act of Congress to codify these customer-facing matters? Will this new rule achieve its objectives? *See, e.g.,* Kelly Yamanouchi, *Critics:*

Tarmac-Delay Rule Won't Fly, ATLANTA J.-CONST., Apr. 28, 2010, at A1; Susan Stellin, *Wider Protections for Travelers*, N.Y. TIMES, Mar. 23, 2010, at B6; David Koenig, *Continental Asks Tarmac Rules Exemption: Carrier Says It May Have to Speed Up Cancellations*, HOUS. CHRON., Mar. 19, 2010, at 3.

3. ***Fewer Regulations, Fewer Travel Rights?***

Within days of taking office, President Donald Trump signed an executive order requiring federal agencies to eliminate two regulations for every new one created. *E.g.*, Damian Paletta & Michael C. Bender, *Trump Signs Executive Order to Cut, Restrict Regulations*, WALL ST. J., Jan 30, 2017. What effect did this have on airline service?

Consider that on December 7, 2017, the DOT withdrew a proposal "to require air carriers, foreign air carriers, and ticket agents to clearly disclose to consumers at all points of sale customer-specific fee information, or itinerary-specific information if a customer elects not to provide customer-specific information, for a first checked bag, a second checked bag, and one carry-on bag wherever fare and schedule information is provided to consumers. The withdrawal of this rulemaking corresponds with the Department's and Administration's priorities and is consistent with Executive Order 13771, Reducing Regulation and Controlling Regulatory Costs, January 30, 2017." *See* https://www.transportation.gov/airconsumer/latest-news.

C. DISCRIMINATION

AL-WATAN V. AMERICAN AIRLINES, INC.
658 F. Supp. 2d 816 (E.D. Mich. 2009)

PAUL D. BORMAN, DISTRICT JUDGE.

On August 28, 2007, Plaintiffs were scheduled to take Defendant's flight 590 from San Diego to Chicago. Plaintiffs, employees of DTC, a security contractor, were returning together from a training session with the United States military. Plaintiffs are all of Iraqi descent.

Suspicious Activity?

Prior to boarding the flight, a passenger on the flight, while still at the gate spoke to one of Defendant's customer service managers, Anne Grove, and to the police, to express her concern about four men, identified as Middle Eastern, who appeared to be acting suspiciously. Grove and the police officers spoke to the passenger, who complained that the men were speaking to each other in their native language. The police officers told the passenger that they had no reason to question or detain the men, as they had cleared security without incident and were not displaying any cause for intervention. Grove reported that everything appeared normal to her, and no other passengers complained.

Plaintiffs boarded the plane without incident, and took their seats. Plaintiffs were not assigned to sit together. Upon boarding, the passenger who complained at the gate decided that she did not want to take the flight, and asked to deplane. She told the flight attendant that one of the men she complained about at the gate glared at her and her children, then went to the lavatory, and when he returned to his seat, he put a blanket over his head. The passenger and her children deplaned.

Flight Attendants Ann Saltzman and Anthony Kotsonis also saw the man, Plaintiff Al-Watan, go to the lavatory at the rear of the plane shortly before departure. All of the three flight attendants on board, Saltzman, Kotsonis and Lead Flight Attendant Kenneth Koc, saw Al-Watan sitting in his seat with his head covered with a blanket. Koc testified "It looked to me like a mummy. It was over and down around the—it was just strange." Kotsonis also testified that the blanket completely covered Al-Watan's entire body and Kotsonis believed "he was hiding or appeared to be hiding." Al-Watan testified that he used the bathroom while passengers were still boarding the plane, and that he had covered his head with a blanket because he was exhausted and wanted to take a nap.

The flight attendants informed Captain Plummer about the passenger who deplaned, the reasons for her departure, and Al-Watan's actions. Thus, the flight captain was aware Al-Watan was of Middle Eastern descent. After a discussion, during which the captain asked the flight attendants whether they "felt comfortable with the situation at the time," and the flight attendants stated that they did not have a problem, the captain decided to proceed with the flight.

First Call to Captain Plummer

As the plane began to taxi, Lead Flight Attendant Koc called Captain Plummer and told him that during the safety demonstration, Plaintiff Al-Watan, the individual who had been previously sitting in his seat with his head covered by a blanket, had removed the blanket and now had leaned out into the aisle and stared directly at him. Koc testified, "I was startled as I looked down the aisle to see the passenger in 14D, who was now uncovered by the blanket, leaned over with his head out in the middle of the aisle staring intently at us." Flight Attendant Saltzman also noticed Al-Watan leaning out into the aisle during the demonstration, and she "thought it was a little bit strange that we were being . . . tracked with his eyes . . . and the demeanor when we were getting the look, the evil eye, if you want to call it."

Second Call to Captain Plummer

Flight Attendant Koc called Captain Plummer a second time while the plane was taxiing and informed him that yet another man watched the flight attendants' safety demonstration in a way that disturbed the flight attendant. Flight attendant Anthony Kotsonis testified that during the demonstration he noted the passenger in seat 22F "glaring at [him] in a manner that actually scared me." Kotsonis stated that the passenger appeared agitated, flushed and was sweating. Kotsonis testified that the passenger glared at him—"agitated, mean facial expression." The passenger in 22F was Mr. Wessa Althwej, who is not a party in this case. Flight Attendant Kotsonis, who had observed Althwej directly, and had also heard about Al-Watan's actions, stated that when the flight attendants talked on the plane about the staring passengers, "[i]t was like each of those [Arabic] passengers had their assigned attendant."

Third Call to Captain Plummer

As the plane approached the runway, Captain Plummer received yet another call, this time from Flight Attendant Saltzman. Saltzman told the captain that a passenger, Paul Coslick, who identified himself as a Lieutenant in the U.S. Navy, told her that he was very concerned about the man sitting next to him because the man told him that he was traveling alone, while Coslick had seen the man with a group of other passengers, including Al-Watan, at the gate. Coslick testified that he noted that his seatmate came to the airport with five or six other men.

When Flight Attendant Saltzman was asked at her deposition why it alarmed her to learn that Coslick's seatmate was being inconsistent or untruthful about who he was traveling with, she testified:

> Well, because from past experience people—I mean, it's well-known now that a lot of terrorist groups are well-organized, they travel in groups and try to keep their identity hidden from other people by sitting in different parts of the aircraft, which is one of the things that we are aware of as flight attendants to be on the look out for.

The passenger to whom Coslick had spoken, the subject of his complaint, was Plaintiff Talal Cholagh. Cholagh told the San Diego Harbor Police that after he boarded the plane the passenger behind him, Coslick, " 'asked about 50 questions' about his work, where he lived, where he was going, and who he was flying with." Cholagh also told the police that he felt uncomfortable answering the questions posed by the stranger, and did not want to give out too much information because Cholagh is a contractor for the military.

Captain Plummer Decides to Return to the Gate

After the third phone call, Captain Plummer decided to return the plane to the gate to "sort everything out." Captain Plummer testified that he decided to return to the gate because of the information he received in the multiple calls from the flight attendants. This included the fact that Plaintiff Al-Watan was Middle Eastern and appeared to be traveling with three other males.

Captain Plummer was processing the previously noted phone call information in the context of his 20 years of experience as a pilot. Captain Plummer testified that he decided to return to the gate out of safety concerns:

- "I needed to know if there was any connection with these people traveling as a group but saying they were traveling alone."

- Something this bad never happened to him in twenty years of being a pilot. "I would have to say return to the gate because of the unusual behavior that we were being exposed to that evening."

- He felt that the safety of the plane and its passengers was threatened, "[b]y the odd behavior of the passengers that I received these calls about."

- "Their unusual behavior and the fact that they said they were traveling alone but they were actually in a group."

- Captain Plummer recounted the unusual behavior: First, place a blanket over his head at his seat. Second, stare intently at a flight attendant—gaze never left. Third, next to Coslick—not traveling with anyone. Coslick saw him with a group.

Once the plane returned to the gate, American Airlines Customer Service Manager Ann Grove called the police; either the first officer or the pilot or both had asked her to call the police. As all of the passengers exited the plane, the flight attendants pointed out the six Plaintiffs and one other man of Arabic descent on the flight, and the men were called over and talked to by the police. There is no evidence that Defendant's representatives or agents told the police to arrest the Plaintiffs.

The police officers questioned the men for up to two hours, after which they determined that no criminal activity had occurred, and released the men. Officer Adauto's report noted that Plaintiff Al-Watan "had red watery eyes and had the odor of an alcoholic beverage on his breath." The flight did not depart that evening because of a San Diego imposed late night curfew on flight activity. All passengers spent the night in San Diego. Flight Attendant Saltzman testified that the flight crew was "verbally accosted out at the front of the airport while we were waiting for our hotel pickup by man [Al-Watan] in 14D." Plaintiff Al-Watan was waiting in front of the airport for Fox News to show up for an interview. Flight 590 was rescheduled for the next morning. All of the Plaintiffs and the other passengers boarded the flight and flew to Chicago without incident.

On November 14, 2008, Defendant moved for summary judgment on the following grounds: (1) under 49 U.S.C. § 44902(b) it is immune from liability for the captain's decision to return the plane to the gate and remove Plaintiffs for questioning unless the captain's decision was arbitrary or capricious, and Plaintiffs cannot show that the captain's decision was arbitrary or capricious; (2) Plaintiffs' state law claims are based on the captain's decision; and therefore, are foreclosed because the captain's decision was not arbitrary or capricious; and (3) Plaintiff's state law claims are preempted by federal law.

III. ANALYSIS

A. Plaintiffs' Discrimination Claims

Plaintiffs allege that Defendant discriminated against them based on their race, color or national origin, in violation of 49 U.S.C. § 40127, prohibition on discrimination in air transportation and 42 U.S.C. § 2000a, prohibition against discrimination or segregation in places of public accommodation. Plaintiffs also allege that Defendant violated their civil rights, 42 U.S.C. § 1983, and denied them equal rights under the law, 42 U.S.C. § 1981, based on their race, color or national origin.

Discrimination in Air Transportation

The Airline Deregulation Act, 49 U.S.C. 40101, *et seq.* contains a provision prohibiting discrimination in air transportation. The provision reads: "(a) Persons in air transportation. An air carrier or foreign air carrier may not subject a person in air transportation to discrimination on the basis of race, color, national origin, religion, sex, or ancestry." Defendant argues that it is not subject to liability for its employees' actions, pursuant to 49 U.S.C. § 44902(b), unless Plaintiffs show that the captain's decision to refuse to transport Plaintiffs was arbitrary and capricious. Title 49 U.S.C. § 44902(b) states: "Permissive refusal.—Subject to regulations of the Under Secretary, an air carrier, intrastate air carrier, or foreign air carrier may refuse to transport a passenger or property the carrier decides is, or might be, inimical to safety."

Plaintiffs do not allege a claim for refusal to transport; instead, Plaintiffs allege illegal and discriminatory activity after the passengers disembarked from the plane. The Court's analysis, however, must include the activity on the airplane, which triggered the activity after the Plaintiffs and the rest of the passengers disembarked. In their Complaint, Plaintiffs allege that "without any proper justification, Defendants feared Plaintiffs as a threat to security," and "[a]s a result of Defendants' discrimination and unjustified actions, the passengers of flight 590 were required to deplane."

Plaintiffs further allege that upon disembarking they were "pulled aside," physically separated from the other passengers, "detained and interrogated." Plaintiffs do not allege that Defendant refused to transport them. In fact, Plaintiffs acknowledge that they completed their travel plans the next day—with the same passengers, on that very same flight. However, Plaintiffs' Complaint relates to Defendant's refusal to transport them that night. Plaintiffs argue that the captain's decision to return to the gate, which they assert "may" be protected by § 44902, is unrelated to "summoning police and interrogating suspected terrorists." The Court finds that this ignores the totality of the circumstances relevant to the instant case.

Defendant argues, "Captain Plummer's decision to have Plaintiffs questioned by law enforcement in the gate area is inextricably intertwined with, and the logical extension of, his decision to return the aircraft to the gate." Plaintiff's counsel conceded this in his argument to the Court at a discovery hearing:

> What I want is documents that deal—that deal with the decision to return to the gate. That is the gravamen of this entire lawsuit. We say the decision to return to the gate was based off of racial discrimination; they say it was something else . . . That's not that broad Judge, and it should be right in the heart of the case.

Plaintiffs ultimately were not refused transport, because all the passengers on the plane were required to deplane and wait overnight for the next flight because the airport curfew prevented a departure after the plane returned to the gate. The suspicious conduct involving some of the Plaintiffs was the reason Captain Plummer decided to return to the gate to further investigate the suspicious conduct.

* * *

The issues are, thus, two-fold: first, was the Captain's decision to return to the gate arbitrary and capricious; second, did Defendant's conduct upon returning to the gate violate the Plaintiffs' rights. The Court must separately evaluate Defendant's post-return conduct and the conduct of the police, unless there is evidence that Defendant controlled the police or ordered/requested the police to act in a specific manner that supports Plaintiffs' claims.

This Court's Opinion and Order Denying Defendant's Motion to Dismiss in the instant case adopted the arbitrary and capricious standard applied by the U.S. Court Appeals for the Second Circuit in *Williams v. Trans World Airlines*, 509 F.2d 942 (2d Cir. 1975):

> The test of whether or not the airline properly exercised its power under [§ 44902] to refuse passage to an applicant or ticket-holder rests upon the facts and circumstances of the case as known to the airline at the time it formed its opinion and made its decision and whether or not the opinion and decision were rational and reasonable and not capricious or arbitrary in the light of those facts and circumstances. They are not to be tested by other facts later discovered by hindsight.

This Court's Opinion and Order denying Defendant's Motion to Dismiss adopted this test, and then, after noting that the Sixth Circuit has not ruled on this issue, quoted approvingly at length from the recent First Circuit opinion in *Cerqueira v. American Airlines, Inc.*, 520 F.3d 1 (1st Cir. 2008). The Court's Opinion stated:

> The Sixth Circuit has not yet addressed the substantive analysis to be applied when a passenger alleges that an airline, citing security concerns, impermissibly removes him or her from an airplane on the base of race or national origin.
>
> > In the recent case *Cerqueira v. American Airlines, Inc.* the First Circuit utilized the following analysis when evaluating a claim of discrimination under § 1981 when the airline asserts its statutory authority under § 44902(b):
> >
> > > As a matter of federal policy, under the Federal Aviation Act, "assigning and maintaining safety [ranks] as the highest priority in air commerce." Thus, the highest priority is assigned to safety, even though the federal aviation statute also has a general prohibition on race and national origin discrimination."
> > >
> > > An air carrier may not subject a person in air transportation to discrimination on the basis of race, color, national origin, religion, sex or ancestry."

In 49 U.S.C. § 44902(a), which became effective in 1961, Congress mandated air carriers to refuse to transport passengers and property where a passenger does not consent to a search of his person or property for dangerous weapons, explosives, or destructive substances. In addition to mandating that some passengers be refused transport, Congress also authorized, at subsection (b), air carriers to engage in "permissive refusal":

> Subject to regulations of the Under Secretary, an air carrier, intrastate air carrier, or foreign air carrier may refuse to transport a passenger or property the carrier decides is, or might be, inimical to safety.

Thus Congress supplemented the discretion airlines already had under common law to exclude certain passengers, in light of their duty of utmost care to all passengers. It is obvious that § 44902(b) was enacted in furtherance of the first priority of safety in air traffic. The legislative history confirms this.

The permissive refusal authorization in § 44902(b) has several distinct components. The statute says the air carrier "may" refuse to transport, thus vesting discretion over the decision in the air carrier. That discretion is very broad. The carrier need not decide that the passenger or property is inimical to safety; the authorization extends to situations in which the carrier decides the passenger or property "might be" inimical to safety. The congressional authorization is granted to the air carrier to make the decision. The only limit contained in the statute on that discretion is that it be subject to regulations of the Under Secretary of Transportation for Security.

Permissive Refusal

The permissive refusal authorization in § 44902(b) has several distinct components. The statute says the air carrier "may" refuse to transport, thus vesting discretion over the decision in the air carrier. That discretion is very broad.

The carrier need not decide that the passenger or property is inimical to safety; the authorization extends to situations in which the carrier decides the passenger or property "might be" inimical to safety. The congressional authorization is granted to the air carrier to make the decision. The only limit contained in the statute on that discretion is that it be subject to regulations of the Under Secretary of Transportation for Security.

In turn, the Under Secretary has not promulgated regulations limiting the airline's discretion directly under 49 U.S.C. § 44902(b). However, one other regulation is directly pertinent, as it states that: "The pilot in command of an aircraft is directly responsible for, and is the final authority as to the operation of that aircraft." In other words, the pilot in command stands in the role of the air carrier for a decision to remove a passenger from a flight. The authorization in § 44902(b) also applies to decisions by others than the pilot not to rebook a passenger based on safety concerns. In this case, that decision was made by another person, based on information from the pilot.

Authority of Pilot in Command

While the statute refers to the air carrier's decision, the appropriate focus is on the actual decisionmaker: the pilot in command of the aircraft where the passenger is removed from the pilot's flight. That is so as a matter of law under 14 C.F.R. § 91.3. In practice in this context, it is not the air carrier that makes the decision to refuse transport to the passenger on the flight, but the pilot in command, who acts for the air carrier. Section 44902 itself does not provide for judicial review of decisions to refuse transportation by the pilot in command. Nonetheless, courts have entertained actions involving § 44902(b) brought under other general statutes which prohibit discrimination, such as § 1981 and Title VI of the Civil Rights Act.

Accordingly, the parties have assumed that the protections of 49 U.S.C. § 44901 and the U.S. Department of Transportation administrative enforcement mechanisms to protect the rights of passengers, 49 U.S.C. §§ 46101, 46301, do not preclude the filing of actions under 42 U.S.C. § 1981, and we will assume the same. It is clear that § 44902(b), being the more specific statute, applies to this case. Congress has, by statute, explicitly given safety the highest priority.

* * *

Some courts have described an air carrier's reliance on § 44902(b) as a defense in the nature of an immunity. In our view, § 44902(b) does not merely create a defense: the statute is an affirmative grant of permission to the air carrier. Congress specifically authorized permissive refusals by air carriers; Congress did not say § 44902 was merely creating a defense. It is the plaintiff who carries the burden to show that § 44902(b) is inapplicable.

In our view, § 44902(b) does not merely create a defense: the statute is an affirmative grant of permission to the air carrier. Congress specifically authorized permissive refusals by air carriers; Congress did not say § 44902 was merely creating a defense. It is the plaintiff who carries the burden to show that § 44902(b) is inapplicable.

Arbitrary or Capricious Standard

The courts, by judicial construction of § 44902(b), have adopted a standard for liability for an airline's permissive refusal to transport decisions. This standard reconciles the primary priority of safety with other important policies, such as § 1981's prohibitions on racial discrimination. The standard most frequently articulated is that developed by the Second Circuit in *Williams*: that the air carrier's decision to refuse air transport must be shown to be arbitrary or capricious. We agree with *Williams* and hold that an air carrier's decisions to refuse transport under § 44902(b) are not subject to liability unless the decision is arbitrary or capricious.

We also agree with *Williams* that Congress did not intend the nondiscrimination provisions of the FAA or of § 1981 to limit or to render inoperative the refusal rights of the air carrier. Congress left decisions to refuse passage to the air carrier, and any review in the courts is limited to review for arbitrariness or capriciousness. Congress was also well aware that the air carriers' decisions to deny transport have to be made very quickly and based on limited information. Section 44902(b) must be interpreted in that light. Congress "did not contemplate that the flight would have to be held up or cancelled until certainty was achieved."

In applying 49 U.S.C. § 44902(b), this Court will utilize the arbitrary and capricious standard in deciding whether to grant Defendant's Motion for Summary Judgment. Thus, this Court must decide whether Plaintiffs have proffered sufficient evidence to create a genuine issue of material fact that Captain Plummer's decision, given the facts he knew at the time he made the decision to return to the gate, was arbitrary and capricious.

In applying 49 U.S.C. § 44902(b), this Court will utilize the arbitrary and capricious standard in deciding whether to grant Defendant's Motion for Summary Judgment. Thus, this Court must decide whether Plaintiffs have proffered sufficient evidence to create a genuine issue of material fact that Captain Plummer's decision, given the facts he knew at the time he made the decision to return to the gate, was arbitrary and capricious. A decision to refuse to transport a passenger that is motivated by the passenger's race is "inherently arbitrary and capricious." A refusal to transport "cannot give rise to a claim for damages under . . . federal . . . law unless the carrier's decision was arbitrary and capricious." *Schaeffer v. Cavallero*, 54 F. Supp. 2d 350, 351 (S.D.N.Y. 1999). In support of its argument that the captain's decision was not arbitrary and capricious, Defendant relies primarily on two cases: *Cerqueira, supra,* and *Dasrath v. Continental Airlines, Inc.*, 467 F. Supp. 2d 431 (D.N.J. 2006). In both cases, after reviewing the information relayed to the captain by the crew, the courts held that the captain's decision to refuse transport was not arbitrary and capricious.

In *Cerqueira* three passengers were removed from the plane for questioning by the state police (to a secured location away from the gate and apart from the other passengers and were questioned by one of the State Police troopers) based on the following facts: (1) one of the passengers approached the captain before the flight and asked him if he was the captain for the flight and asked the same question when he boarded the flight; (2) a different passenger had been hostile to a flight attendant about a seat change, and then he boarded the plane with the first class passengers, even though he was in coach, and immediately went to the bathroom for an extended period of time; (3) two of the three passengers were acting "very bizarrely and asking questions such as 'Is this how you want me to do it?'; (4) one of the passengers asked strange questions during the exit row safety briefing and laughed; (5) one of the passengers stared at a flight attendant during the general safety demonstration; and (6) the three passengers wished the other passengers "Happy New Year" in a " 'very boisterous' manner."

The First Circuit concluded that "there is absolutely no evidence that the Captain himself or the [System Operations Control] manager had discriminatory animus, let alone that their decisions to refuse to transport a passenger, which were made under time pressure, were based on any discriminatory animus," and stated that the Captain's decision was justified given the safety concerns observed by the crew, which are recounted above. The First Circuit held:

> Review of a decision to refuse transport by the Captain is restricted to what information was actually known by the decisionmaker at the time of the decision. The test is not what the Captain reasonably should have known . . . The Captain (or other decisionmaker) is entitled to accept at face value the representations made to him by other air carrier employees. Thus, even mistaken decisions are protected as long as they are not arbitrary or capricious.

The First Circuit further held that the burden is on the plaintiff to show the decision not to transport was arbitrary and capricious.

In *Dasrath*, a female passenger alerted the gate agent to suspicious behavior by the plaintiff and two other male passengers, specifically that three men who apparently knew each other were pretending not to know each other and doing "funny things, talking on cell phones." After one of the male passengers identified by the female passenger boarded the plane, he reached down and felt underneath a seat in first class.

He then moved to the rear of the plane where he removed his duffel bag from the overhead bin and placed it behind the exit row. Shortly thereafter, the captain saw the three men conversing; one of the men was perspiring heavily and would not stop looking at the captain.

The District Court in New Jersey held that the Captain acted reasonably when he removed the plaintiff, having removed the plaintiff only after being alerted to suspicious behavior that caused security concerns among the crew. The court concluded that "there were many events that would have led a reasonable person to believe that the three men . . . were security risks." The court stated:

[T]he undisputed facts as perceived by Captain Harris would preclude a jury from finding that he removed Mr. Dasarath from the aircraft for racial reasons or for any reasons other than concern for the security of the aircraft and the passengers.

The court in *Dasrath* also noted that it was reasonable to remove additional passengers as well as the suspiciously-acting passengers because they were known to be flying together.

Defendant also cited to four other cases in which passengers were removed from a plane due to safety concerns. In all of the cases cited by Defendant, there is one common fact: the passengers removed from the plane engaged in behavior that drew the attention of the flight attendants and justifiably alarmed them to the point that they contacted the pilot. Such is the case here. The flight attendants noticed the unusual and threatening behavior of plaintiffs Al-Watan and Cholagh, and non-party Wessa Althwej, who was seated in 22F, became concerned for the safety of the flight, and alerted Captain Plummer.

The flight attendants saw Al-Watan use the restroom, while the plane door was still open, return to his seat, put a blanket over his head, and then lean out into the aisle during the safety demonstration and stare at flight attendant Koc. Although use of the restroom is not a reason for concern, the placing of a blanket over the head before takeoff is a basis for concern, as is the leaning over into the aisle and staring menacingly at the flight attendant during safety instructions.

During post-boarding pre-flight, another passenger, Althwej, stared at a flight attendant to the point of distracting him. In addition, a passenger reported his concern about the passenger sitting next to him because when he asked whether the passenger was traveling alone, the man responded that he was, but the reporting passenger had seen his seatmate with a group in the terminal, including Al-Watan. What the pilot had on his "plate" was three calls from three different flight attendants, regarding suspicious or threatening behavior on board the aircraft even before it was off the ground.

All of these unusual actions by the passengers reasonably concerned the flight attendants, and justified their calls to the pilot. Nothing in their calls can be regarded as evidencing discrimination. Captain Plummer emphasized in his deposition that the fact that the flight attendants called him at all was unusual because the flight attendants are not supposed to call the pilot when the doors are closed and the airplane is moving. The fact that Captain Plummer received not one, but three calls, from the flight attendants raised red flags about the safety of continuing the flight. It was only after the third call that Captain Plummer returned the plane to the gate.

> *All of these unusual actions by the passengers reasonably concerned the flight attendants, and justified their calls to the pilot . . . The fact that Captain Plummer received not one, but three calls, from the flight attendants raised red flags about the safety of continuing the flight. It was only after the third call that Captain Plummer returned the plane to the gate.*

Based on the facts as Captain Plummer knew them to be when he decided to return the airplane to the gate, this Court holds that his decision was not arbitrary and capricious. There is no evidence that it was based on Plaintiffs' race or ethnicity. While Captain Plummer knew that Al-Watan was Middle Eastern, and he appeared to be traveling with at least three other men, the Plaintiffs' actions that impelled the three phone calls clearly establishes a reasonable basis for returning to the gate, and calling the police to find out information about the individuals. It is noteworthy that although Captain Plummer knew that a passenger [Leigh Williams] had an earlier negative interaction with Al-Watan at the gate, which was carried over on to the airplane, and that the passenger had deboarded with her children, that incident did not factor into his ultimate decision. Plummer relied on the subsequent information about the incidents on the plane that the flight attendants reported to him in the three phone calls.

The most significant suspicious uncontested information was that passenger Al-Watan had put a blanket over his head. The actions of Al-Watan, Cholagh and Althwej reasonably appeared as linked in a rapidly evolving situation. The totality of the circumstances supports Captain Plummer's decision to return to the gate out of safety concerns and request that the police talk to the individuals engaged in the suspicious activity, and other members of the group. That all of these individuals were of Arabic ancestry is a factual reality.

However, Plaintiff has not presented any evidence of racial bias by Defendant. Captain Plummer is entitled, and must be able, to implicitly rely on the information relayed to him by his flight crew, assuming it is reasonable and believable. The flight attendants are his eyes and ears in the passenger area of the airplane, while he is closeted in the cockpit. Plaintiffs have not set forth evidence of racial bias by any of the flight attendants or the captain.

* * *

The Court must now examine for racial discrimination Defendant's actions after the plane returned to the gate. Plaintiffs argue that the arbitrary and capricious standard in § 44902(b) does not extend to Captain Plummer's decision to call the police. This Court disagrees. As the court explained in *Ruta v. Delta Airlines*, 322 F. Supp. 2d 391 (S.D.N.Y. 2014), "if . . . the Captain's decision to have Plaintiff removed was not arbitrary or capricious then it cannot have been arbitrary and capricious to call on law enforcement to enforce the Captain's decision." Indeed, in this case, there is even less activity by the Captain; Captain Plummer did not decide that Plaintiffs should be refused transport—just interviewed by police before reboarding, which turned out, for all passengers on the plane, to be the next morning.

Plaintiffs raised a related argument pointing to discrimination: the fact that all seven Arab men on the flight were identified by Defendant's employees for questioning by police, after the plane returned to the gate, even though only three men, Al-Watan, Cholagh and Althwej engaged in suspicious behavior. However, as noted before, there was evidence that the flight crew was aware that Plaintiffs were traveling together and this justified Defendant's identifying the group that included the suspicious individuals. Plaintiffs contend that Defendant's flight attendants identified individuals of Arabic descent to the police for questioning. Plaintiff Hasan Al-Zerej testified, "we were pointed at by the police and the flight attendants and separated from the rest [of the passengers]." Also, Al-Watan testified that an employee of Defendant pointed at him and, "delivered us to the police." The police proceeded to question the individuals.

This raises the issue of whether Defendant is responsible for conduct of the police, insofar as Plaintiffs allege that the police violated their rights. In addition, there is a question whether Defendant can be charged under 42 U.S.C. § 1983 as a state actor. There is no question that when a defendant reasonably believes that passengers have engaged in suspicious behavior, the passengers can be questioned by police.

The flight attendants' identification of a group of passengers they believed were traveling together raises the issue of whether the Defendant arbitrarily and capriciously identified all the Arab men on the flight for police questioning. To the extent that the six Plaintiffs were traveling together, there is no basis for finding the Defendant's decision to be arbitrary and capricious. As to the seventh individual of Arabic descent that was apparently identified to the police by Defendant, that individual was reported by the flight attendant to the captain as having exhibited strange and threatening behavior. There is no evidence supporting Plaintiffs' claim that Defendant acted in a discriminatory manner. Accordingly, this Court will enter summary judgment on Plaintiffs' discrimination claims.

A.   Plaintiffs' Claim under 42 U.S.C. § 1983

Title 42 U.S.C. § 1983 only provides a remedy against persons acting under color of state law. Plaintiffs have not presented any evidence or argument that Defendant's refusal to transport them is attributable to a "state actor." Defendant made the decision to cancel the flight and call the police. Although Defendant pointed out Plaintiffs to the police, there is no evidence that Defendant directed the police officers to arrest Plaintiffs or otherwise directed the conduct of the police officers.

C.   Plaintiffs' State Law Claims

Defendant argues that Plaintiffs' state law claims should also be dismissed because the Captain's decision was not arbitrary or capricious or, alternatively, because the state law claims are preempted by the Airline Deregulation Act, 49 U.S.C. § 41713(b). This Court holds that an airline's refusal to transport passengers cannot give rise to a claim for damages under either federal or state law unless the airline's decision was arbitrary and capricious. In this case, the Court finds that Defendant's action to return to the gate and call the police was not arbitrary and capricious; thus, Plaintiffs cannot prevail on their state law claims.

In addition, the Court agrees with the decision of the District Court in *Ruta*, that all of the state tort claims are preempted. Any alleged emotional and physical harm allegedly suffered by Plaintiffs was a direct result of the Captain's decision to remove them from the plane, as were the claims for negligence and intentional infliction of emotional distress.

There is no factual support for Plaintiffs' claim of false imprisonment. Defendant merely called the police to talk to Plaintiffs; there is no evidence that Defendant suggested that the police arrest Plaintiffs. This Court, therefore, enters summary judgment for Defendant on Plaintiffs' state law claims.

IV.   CONCLUSION

The Court concludes that information provided to Captain Plummer regarding the highly suspicious onboard conduct supports his decision to return to the terminal and to call the police to investigate. Plaintiff Al-Watan's placing a blanket over his head "mummy-like" prior to takeoff, leaning out into the aisle and staring menacingly at flight attendants, and the other actions discussed above is cause for concern; Captain Plummer's decision was not arbitrary and capricious. Certainly, the suspicious conduct at issue was not, as Plaintiffs' counsel characterized it at oral argument, "innocent" or "completely silly."

There is no evidence that supports Plaintiffs' claim of discrimination by Captain Plummer. There is no evidence that Captain Plummer's action was race-based. The fact that the individuals who engaged in the suspicious conduct were of Middle Eastern/Iraqi descent does not support the conclusion that the decision to return to the gate was race-based rather than fact-based.

The three passengers of concern, based on their suspicious conduct, were Plaintiff Al-Watan, seat 14B; non-party Althwej in seat 22F; and Cholagh, the person seated next to Lieutenant Coslick in 31 B. The six Plaintiffs were traveling together. The police questioning, which occurred as a result of the justified suspicions of Captain Plummer, was tied to the question of whether to refuse passage to these men. Thus, the applicable standard to be applied in this case against Defendant, is whether Captain Plummer's conduct was arbitrary and capricious. What the Captain, and the Defendant airline did, was seek more information about the Plaintiffs, some of whom had engaged in highly suspicious activity.

Nevertheless, given that Defendant American Airlines did remove the Plaintiffs (and all the other passengers) from the plane, the analysis of Defendant's conduct comes under 49 U.S.C. § 44902(b) whether it properly exercised its discretion to remove a passenger based on the facts and circumstances known to the decision-maker at the time he or she made the decision. "The decision is not to be tested by other facts later disclosed by hindsight." *Sedigh v. Delta Airlines* (E.D.N.Y. 1994).

The Court further concludes that Plaintiffs' state claims: false imprisonment; intentional infliction of emotional distress; and negligence, must be dismissed because they are preempted by federal law. The Court finds that the same safety concerns that justified Captain Plummer's return to the gate, are the same concerns that caused him to request assistance of police to talk to the Plaintiffs. Captain Plummer's decision to return to the gate, based on the information he received provided to him by the crew, to seek more information about the suspicious situation was not arbitrary and capricious, and not discriminatory.

EXERCISE 7-4. *AL-WATAN V. AMERICAN AIRLINES, INC.—* AUTHORITY TO REFUSE TO TRANSPORT

1. Detail the activity of the plaintiffs that gave the flight crew and other passengers cause for concern?

2. The Airline Deregulation Act prohibits discrimination in air transportation. Explain the provision of 49 U.S.C. § 40101 *et seq.*

3. Explain the authority of the pilot in command ("PIC") under 49 U.S.C. § 44902(b) and 14 C.F.R. § 91.3. Was this authority exercised properly in this case, according to the court?

4. Define "arbitrary" and "capricious." Did the court find the airline's conduct to be arbitrary or capricious in the circumstances of this case? Explain and, as part of your response, state the holdings of *Williams v. Trans World Airlines*, *Cerqueira v. American Airlines, Inc.*, and *Dasrath v. Continental Airlines, Inc.*, as stated by the court.

5. Why did the plaintiffs claim under Section 1983 fail?

DETERRA V. AMERICA WEST AIRLINES, INC.

226 F. Supp. 2d 298 (D. Mass. 2002)

LAWRENCE P. COHEN, UNITED STATES MAGISTRATE JUDGE.

As of August 7, 1999, plaintiff was wheelchair-bound due to a degenerative neuro-muscular disorder which rendered him a paraplegic. Together with his brother Daniel Deterra and sister-in-law, Catherine Deterra, plaintiff had reservations to travel on an America West flight to Boston, Massachusetts scheduled to depart from Las Vegas, Nevada at approximately 11:30 p.m. on August 7, 1999.

When plaintiff entered the ticket line at the Las Vegas Airport on August 7, 1999, to check in for his flight, plaintiff waited in line in his wheelchair for over an hour. He was not advanced to the front of the ticket line by America West as had occurred in Boston. Plaintiff arrived at the gate for boarding his flight at least 35 minutes before the flight's scheduled departure. At that time, the boarding of first class passengers from the terminal through the jetbridge, the tunnel-like structure leading from the terminal to the aircraft, had already begun.

Plaintiff attempted to communicate with the America West gate agents after they refused to stop the line to allow Plaintiff to board. He tried to tell the gate agents that he had to board first, because it would be too difficult to board him with all other passengers on the plane, but they ignored him, would not answer him and would not look directly at him. Instead of talking to him, they looked over him and talked to his brother and sister-in-law. When plaintiff's brother, Daniel, asked an America West agent named Jay to allow plaintiff to go to the front of the line and board ahead of the other passengers, Jay responded that they would need to wait until after the other passengers had boarded. In particular, according to plaintiff's brother, Daniel, when he and his wife and the plaintiff went to the counter in the gate area, they were told "We've already started boarding the people. It will have to be later. It will have to be done at the end." Deterra was not initiating any conversation with the airline personnel.

Plaintiff and/or his relatives disagreed with America West's response. Catherine Deterra claims that she asked to speak to a supervisor, was told by an America West agent named Robert that there was no supervisor available, and he gave her a telephone number to contact. She claims that she was told by the woman she spoke to at that number that the woman was "dismayed" at what was happening but that there was no one available to resolve the problem due to the late hour.

After it appeared that the other passengers had entered the jetbridge to board, Daniel Deterra addressed the America West employee who was standing in the gate area nearby and who had told them they would have to wait, saying "Are you fucking assholes ready to board him now?" Daniel Deterra admits that he was very upset and might have been mad when he made this remark. He admits that he said it "a little louder than normal" and in a "perturbed voice." Wayne DeMello, a friend traveling with the Deterras, recalls that when the group arrived at the gate to board the flight, other passengers were already boarding through the jetbridge and he heard one of the America West agents tell Daniel Deterra that they would have to wait and board last. He recalls that Daniel Deterra was loud and swore, and that DeMello told Daniel he wasn't supposed to be loud and told him, "you can't say that here." He told Daniel Deterra to calm down because there was no need for him to be screaming.

Plaintiff and Daniel Deterra both admit that if Daniel Deterra had not acted in the manner set forth above, plaintiff, his brother and sister-in-law could have boarded their original flight after the other passengers had boarded. According to plaintiff, the America West agents indicated that Daniel Deterra's words were too forceful and that plaintiff, his relatives, and the two friends with them, would not be allowed to board the flight. Plaintiff's brother immediately apologized to both gate agents, Jay and Robert, for his remarks. Robert stated that he understood Daniel Deterra's frustration regarding the boarding situation.

After general boarding had been completed, the gate agents advised plaintiff that he and his sister-in-law, Catherine, would be permitted to board the flight, but that plaintiff's brother, Daniel, would not be permitted to board that flight. Believing that he needed the assistance of his brother, Daniel, plaintiff chose not to take that flight. All three—plaintiff, Daniel Deterra, and Catherine Deterra, were rebooked for the next flight at 12:40 p.m., and they took that flight, arriving in Boston about three hours later than they would have had they been boarded on the original flight.

Plaintiff does not contend that he was denied a reasonable accommodation under the Air Carrier Access Act ("ACAA") on account of the fact that he had a long wait in the ticket line when he first arrived at the airport, or that he was denied a reasonable accommodation on account of the fact that he took the next flight out which arrived three hours later. Instead, he contends, as argued by counsel for plaintiff at the hearing on the motion for summary judgment, that he was denied a reasonable accommodation within the meaning of the ACAA only on account of the following: (1) because airline agents "talked over the plaintiff" directly to plaintiff's brother, Daniel; (2) because airline agents treated plaintiff in a humiliating and derogatory fashion by referring to him, on account of his handicap, as an "It"; and (3) because the airline did not have a "complaint resolution officer" present when the incident at the boarding area arose.

In the circumstances, vis-a-vis the three claims asserted by the plaintiff, this court finds and concludes that plaintiff cannot, on the basis of the undisputed material facts, make out a triable claim under the ACAA.

1. The "Talking Over Plaintiff's Head" Claim

As indicated above, plaintiff contends that agents of the defendant airline denied plaintiff a reasonable accommodation by "talking over his [plaintiff's] head" and directing their remarks to plaintiff's brother, Daniel, instead of to the plaintiff. In this court's view, this conduct, standing alone, does not constitute prohibited discrimination within the meaning of the ACAA.

The ACAA provides:

ACAA, Anti-Discrimination

§ 41705. Discrimination against handicapped individuals

(a) In general. *In providing air transportation*, an air carrier, including (subject to section 40105(b)) any foreign air carrier, may not discriminate against an otherwise qualified individual on the following grounds:

(1) the individual has a physical or mental impairment that substantially limits one or more major life activities.

(2) the individual has a record of such an impairment.

(3) the individual is regarded as having such an impairment.

Beyond the plain words of the statute, there is little legislative history surrounding the enactment of the ACAA—at least in terms of defining its scope. One court, however, has appropriately interpreted the ACAA as follows (*Rivera v. Delta Air Lines, Inc.*, 1997 WL 634500 * 7 (E.D. Pa. 1997)):

> The ACAA prohibits air carriers from discriminating against an individual because they have, or are regarded as having, a disability. The regulations promulgated in connection with the ACAA explain that the Act requires air carriers: (1) to provide *services and benefits* without discrimination on the basis of disability; and (2) to provide disabled individuals with certain services, equipment or assistance. 14 C.F.R. §§ 382.7, 382.39 (1996). In other words, all persons are entitled to be treated equally, but "qualified handicapped individuals" are further entitled to certain services. (Emphasis added).

In this case, plaintiff makes no argument that he was denied those certain services, equipment or assistance, beyond those provided to all travelers, specifically referred to in the implementing regulations. (The implementing regulations specifically set forth certain accommodations which must be provided to qualified handicapped travelers. Section 382.21 of Title 14 of the Code of Federal Regulations (referred to as Special Regulations.) And nothing in the implementing regulations suggest that qualified handicapped individuals should or must be boarded before all other boarders, or, at any particular time. Indeed, to the extent that the implementing regulations refer to boardings of aircraft at all, the implementing regulations suggest to the contrary—that is, that it is discriminatory to pre-board qualified handicapped individuals as a matter of policy.

Although the ACAA is otherwise silent as to what is, and what is not, discriminatory, Section 382.7 of Title 14 of the Code of Federal Regulations does provide the appropriate framework. Those regulations provide:

ACAA Regulations

§ 382.7   General prohibition of discrimination.

(a) A carrier shall not, directly or through contractual, licensing, or other arrangements:

    (1) Discriminate against any otherwise qualified individual with a disability, by reason of such disability, in the provision of air transportation;

    (2) Require a individual with a disability to accept special services (including, but not limited to, preboarding) not requested by the passenger;

    (3) Exclude a qualified individual with a disability from or deny the person the benefit of any air transportation or related services that are

available to other persons, even if there are separate or different services available for individuals with a disability except when specifically permitted by another section of this part; or,

(4) Take any action adverse to an individual because of the individual's assertion, on his or her own behalf or through or behalf of others, of rights protected by this part or the Air Carrier Access Act.

(b) If an indirect air carrier provides facilities or services for passengers that are covered for other carriers by sections §§ 382.21–382.55, the indirect air carrier shall do so in a manner consistent with those sections.

(c) Carriers shall, in addition to meeting the other requirements of this part, modify policies, practices, and facilities as needed to ensure nondiscrimination, consistent with the standards of section 504 of the Rehabilitation Act, as amended. Carriers are not required to make modifications that would constitute an undue burden or would fundamentally alter their program.

In addition to these general prohibitions, there are a series of specific regulations in Title 14 of the Code of Federal Regulations circumscribing that which is discriminatory, relating to, among other things, aircraft accessibility, a prohibition against "refusal" of transportation, a prohibition against requiring advance notice of travel by a handicapped person, a prohibition against requiring (with certain special exceptions) a handicapped person from traveling with his or her own "attendant," seating assignments, seating accommodation, provision of certain services and equipment (e.g., wheelchairs, etc.), boarding assistance on small and large aircrafts—none of which includes preboarding; assistance in stowage of personal equipment, treatment of mobility aids and assistive devices, passenger information (e.g., seating locations, lavatory information, etc.), accommodations for those with hearing impairments, security screening, prohibiting the refusal to provide transportation to those with communicable diseases (except where the health and safety of others would be endangered), prohibiting the requirement that handicapped persons have medical certificates, certain miscellaneous provisions, all of which relate to service and inflight accommodations; and prohibiting the charging of a fee to accommodate handicapped persons.

> *This court accordingly finds and concludes that, even if the airline agents ". . . talk[ed] over his [plaintiff's] head". . .directing their remarks to the plaintiff's brother, that isolated occurrence, not relating to the actual services provided by the airline, no matter how distasteful or uncivil it may well have been, does not warrant an action for damages under the ACAA.*

While not suggesting that these specific regulations are exclusive to other species or manners of discrimination falling with the ambit of the ACAA, those regulations are telling in one respect. All of those regulations relate to the manner in which handicapped persons are provided services, *e.g.*, seating, access to lavatories, wheelchair assistance—by the airlines. None suggest that demeanor of airline employees standing alone, uncivil as that demeanor may be, entitles the handicapped passenger to bring suit for damages under the ACAA. This court accordingly finds and concludes that, even if the airline agents ". . . talk[ed] over his [plaintiff's] head". . .directing their remarks to the plaintiff's brother, that isolated occurrence, not relating to the actual services provided by the airline, no matter how distasteful or uncivil it may well have been, does not warrant an action for damages under the ACAA. *Cf. Fitch v. Solipsys Corp.*, 94 F. Supp. 2d 670, 676–677 (D. Md. 2000).

Nothing in the statute or implementing regulations even remotely suggests that an isolated display of inappropriate demeanor on one single occasion, standing alone, is an act of discrimination within the meaning of the ACAA—much less an act of discrimination for which a complaining party may bring suit.

2. The "It" Reference

Plaintiff's second claim is that he is entitled to damages under the ACAA because airline agents treated plaintiff in a humiliating and derogatory fashion by referring to him, on account of his handicap, as an "It". That claim is predicated on the colloquy occurring at the airport as reported by plaintiff's sister-in-law, to wit:

> . . .when she [plaintiff's sister-in-law] told one of the America West agents at the gate that "He (Deterra) needs to get on so that we can get him safely into the chair," the agent said "It's going to have to wait until last." She also recalls that when she complained that she could not believe they were not going to be able to board, the agent said "We can't handle it now" and "Look, it's going to have to wait until last.

Even assuming that one could reasonably infer from the word "it" in the context of the in the above-referenced colloquy the sinister meaning ascribed to it by plaintiff, much less a reasonable inference that the speaker or speakers intended that reasonable inference on account of the handicap of the plaintiff, that, alone, for the reasons set forth immediately above, does not warrant damage relief under the ACAA.

In any event, based on the record before this court, this court concludes that no reasonable trier of fact could reasonably conclude that the agents, in using the word "it" as referred to above, intended anything demeaning whatsoever on account of the fact that the plaintiff was handicapped. In context, given the full colloquy, the use of the word "it" was grammatically correct and expected. That colloquy cannot reasonably support an inference, an inference which could be drawn by a reasonable trier of fact, that the agents of the airline demeaned the plaintiff on account of his handicap.

3.   *The Want of a Complaint Resolution Officer*

Plaintiff's final fallback is that he is entitled to bring suit for monetary damages on account of the fact that, at the time of the incident referred to in the complaint, the airlines did not immediately make a Complaint Resolutions Officer present.

Some four years after the enactment of the immediate predecessor to the ACAA, the Department of Transportation, in 1990, promulgated a series of regulations relating to discrimination, many of which are referred to above. Section 382.65 of those regulations promulgated in 1990 provides in pertinent part:

§ 382.65 Compliance procedures.

(a)   Each carrier providing scheduled service shall establish and implement a complaint resolution mechanism, including designating one or more complaint resolution official(s) ("CRO") to be available at each airport which the carrier serves.

   (1)   The carrier shall make a CRO available to any person who complains of alleged violations of this part during all times the carrier is operating at the airport.

   (2)   The carrier may make the CRO available via telephone, at no cost to the passenger, if the CRO is not present in person at the airport at the time of the complaint. If a telephone link to the CRO is used, TDD service shall be available so that persons with hearing impairments may readily communicate with the CRO.

Plaintiff can show: Plaintiff and/or his relatives disagreed with America West's response. Catherine Deterra claims that she asked to speak to a supervisor, was told by an America West agent named Robert that there was no supervisor available, and he gave her a telephone number to contact. She claims that she was told by the woman she spoke to at that number that the woman was "dismayed" at what was happening but that there was no one available to resolve the problem due to the late hour.

Based on this, plaintiff says that the defendant violated the provisions of Section 382.65 by not having a CRO available at the time of the incident, and based on this shortcoming, and this shortcoming alone, plaintiff says that he is entitled to money damages in an action brought under the ACAA.

In this court's view, plaintiff has not established to the satisfaction of this court that the violation of this particular regulation, standing alone, authorizes the plaintiff to repair to the federal courts to bring suit for an award of monetary damages. That is to say, plaintiff has not shown that Congress, in enacting the ACAA, and directing the Secretary of Transportation to "promulgate regulations to ensure non-discriminatory treatment of qualified handicapped individuals consistent with safe carriage of all passengers on air carriers," intended to grant the Secretary of Transportation the authority, explicitly or implicitly, to create a private right of action for conduct which is not, in and of itself discriminatory.

On this matter, in his memorandum in opposition to defendant's motion for summary judgment, as well as at the hearing on the motion, plaintiff asked the wrong question—begetting, of course, the wrong answer. All plaintiff says is that the Department of Transportation, in promulgating this particular regulation, created a substantive right favoring the plaintiff and those similarly situated. But that is only the first step in a two-step analysis.

As this court sees it, particularly in view of the holding in *Alexander v. Sandoval*, 532 U.S. 275 (2001), it is not enough to ask whether DOT, in promulgating Section 382.65, intended to confer a substantive right in favor of the plaintiff. To the contrary, the second, and far more important, question is whether Congress intended, by the language of the enabling statute, that a handicapped person such as plaintiff (and those similarly situated) could resort to the federal courts for compensatory damages for the violation of that alleged right. This second question looms, since, although Congress may grant an agency of the executive branch authority to promulgate the minutia and interstices of what may, and may not, be done under a broadly worded statute, consistent with Congressional intent, and, to that extent, "create" substantive rights, only Congress, and Congress alone, because of Article III constraints, can confer jurisdiction in the federal courts. That point is made clear in *Alexander v. Sandoval, supra,* where the majority observed, *inter alia*:

> Implicit in our discussion thus far has been a particular understanding of the genesis of private causes of action. Like substantive federal law itself, private rights of action to enforce federal law must be created by Congress. The judicial task is to interpret the statute Congress has passed to determine whether it displays an intent to create not just a private right *but also* a private remedy. Statutory intent on this latter point is determinative. Without it, a cause of action does not exist and courts may not create one, no matter how desirable that might be as a policy matter, or how compatible with the statute. "Raising up causes of action where a statute has not created them may be a proper function for common-law courts, but not for federal tribunals.

Private Right of Action

In this case, the operative statute (Section 41705 of Title 49) provides only that an air carrier ". . .may not *discriminate* against an otherwise qualified individual. . .," nothing more, and nothing less. For purposes of defendant's motion for summary judgment, we assume that, notwithstanding the failure of Congress to explicitly provide a remedy for acts of discrimination under the ACAA, Congress intended that a qualified handicapped person who was subjected to discrimination could bring suit in the federal courts for some sort of relief.

We also assume that under Section 3 of the predecessor to the current ACAA, Congress intended to confer upon the Department of Transportation the authority to promulgate rules and regulations defining that which should, or should not, be construed as discriminatory within the meaning of the intent of Congress, and that DOT complied with that mandate in a timely and appropriate fashion. And we finally assume that, in terms of the first of the four part of the analysis in *Cort v. Ash,* 422 U.S. 66 (1975), Section 382.65 was promulgated for the "especial benefit" of a class of persons (*i.e.,* qualified handicapped persons) to which plaintiff belongs and belonged.

All that having been said, however, in light of the teachings of *Cort v. Ash, supra,* and *Alexander v. Sandoval,* plaintiff has not established that Congress intended that, in a case, such as this particular case, where an air carrier fails to have a Complaint Resolution Officer present—unintentionally, that is, not for discriminatory purposes—and where that unintentional failure did not cause any discernible discrimination within the meaning of the language of the ACAA or the promulgated regulations scoping that which is, and that which is not, discrimination within the meaning of the ACAA, then that sort of failure, standing alone, was and is sufficient to invoke the jurisdiction of a federal court in pursuit of a remedy in the nature of compensatory (not to mention punitive) damages.

> *Nothing in the plain meaning of the statute suggests that Congress intended a federal court remedy. That plain language simply says that an airline ". . .may not discriminate against an otherwise qualified individual. . ." on account of a handicap. And nothing in the legislative history of the ACAA suggests that Congress intended a federal court remedy in circumstances such as those presented here.*

Nothing in the plain meaning of the statute suggests that Congress intended a federal court remedy. That plain language simply says that an airline ". . .may not discriminate against an otherwise qualified individual. . ." on account of a handicap. And nothing in the legislative history of the ACAA suggests that Congress intended a federal court remedy in circumstances such as those presented here. Senator Dole, the sponsor of the legislation which eventually became the ACAA (then under 49 U.S.C. App. § 1374(c)) observed:

> In fashioning remedial legislation two alternative approaches have been considered. The first was to add air carriers specifically to the coverage of section 504. Although this approach was simple and direct, substantial objections were posed by representatives of air carriers as well as those concerned with Grove City legislation. Once the scope of the legislation was expanded beyond those receiving direct assistance, the list [of those regulated under § 504] could become endless. Also, the airlines strongly felt that they should continue to be regulated under the control of the Aviation Act as the legislation providing the basic regulatory authority for their industry.

> For awhile it seemed that it would not be possible to reconcile these differences; however, a compromise has been reached and is reflected in S. 2703. This is now incorporated into the legislation which amends the Aviation Act and incorporates compromise definitions which rely heavily on language and precedents from the Rehabilitation Act. The bill also adds terminology from the FAA regulations and the Aviation Act.

132 Cong. Rec. S11784–08 (daily ed. Aug. 15, 1986) (statement of Sen. Dole).

Nothing in the language of Section 504 of the Rehabilitation Act suggests that a violation of a regulation, standing alone, which is not discriminatory in and of itself, and which does not result in discrimination, authorizes a person within the protected class to bring suit for a violation of that regulation in the federal courts. And insofar as this court has determined, no precedent interpreting Section 504 of the Rehabilitation Act has ever held or suggested that a violation of a regulation, standing alone, which is not discriminatory in and of itself, and which does not result in discrimination, authorizes a person within the protected class to bring suit for a violation of that regulation in the federal courts.

For these reasons, in the circumstances presented here, even though a Complaint Resolution Officer was not available at the time of the incident, contrary to the provisions of Section 382.65 of the applicable regulations, that, standing alone, is insufficient to state a claim upon which relief may be granted in the federal courts under the ACAA. Defendant's motion for summary judgment is allowed, and judgment shall enter against plaintiff for all claims set forth in the complaint, and in favor of defendant.

EXERCISE 7-5. *DETERRA V. AMERICA WEST AIRLINES, INC.*—AIR CARRIER ACCESS ACT ("ACAA")

1. What does the Air Carrier Access Act ("ACAA") prohibit?

2. What is (or is not) discriminatory under the ACAA? Do the regulations—14 C.F.R. § 382.7—offer more detail? Explain.

3. How does the court dispose of the plaintiff's second claim arising from alleged humiliating and derogatory conduct?

4. Describe the Compliance Procedures under 14 C.F.R. § 382.65.

5. According to the court, did Congress intend that a qualified handicapped person who was subjected to discrimination could bring suit in the federal courts for some sort of relief? Explain the court's reasoning.

NOTES ON *DETERRA V. AMERICA WEST AIRLINES, INC.*— PRIVATE RIGHT OF ACTION UNDER ACAA?

1. *"Individual with a Disability," Defined Under the ACAA.*

Travelers likely are familiar with the airline practice of boarding passengers who require special assistance in advance of other passengers. Less well-known is that it is discriminatory to require qualified handicapped individuals to board. Indeed, it is unlawful for an airline to require an individual with a disability to accept special services, including pre-boarding not requested by the passenger. This is so because Congress enacted the Air Carrier Access Act ("ACAA") to prohibit airlines from discriminating against disabled passengers.

The Air Carrier Access Act of 1986 ("ACAA") prohibits air carriers from discriminating against individuals with disabilities. 49 U.S.C. § 41705. Applicable regulations—Title 14, Part 382 of the Code of Federal Regulations—define an individual with a disability as "any individual who has a physical impairment that, on a permanent or temporary basis, substantially limits one or more major life activities, has a record of such an impairment, or is regarded as having such an impairment." 14 C.F.R. § 382.5. Physical or mental impairment includes "any psychological disorder or condition" and major life activities include "functions such as caring for one's self, performing manual tasks, walking . . . and working." *Id.*

2. *Split of Authority.*

The ACAA is peculiar in that a split in authority exists as to the question whether the ACAA creates a private right of action in federal district court. There is no question that the ACAA does not expressly provide a private entitlement to sue in district court. *Shinault v. American Airlines, Inc.*, 936 F.2d 796, 800 (5th Cir. 1991) ("The ACAA does not provide for a private right of action."); *Tallarico v. Trans World Airlines, Inc.*, 881 F.2d 566, 568 (8th Cir. 1989) ("The ACAA does not expressly provide for a cause of action to enable private citizens to seek a remedy for a violation of the Act."). Whether the ACAA *impliedly* provides a private right of action is less settled, however.

In particular, *Shinault* and *Tallarico* represent at least two decisions by federal courts of appeal interpreting the ACAA as conferring an implied private right of action in federal district court. *See also Adiutori v. Sky Harbor Int'l Airport*, 103 F.3d 137 (9th Cir. 1996) ("Although [the ACAA] does not expressly provide for a private right of action . . ., we are persuaded by the reasoning of other circuits which have held that [it] implies a private right of action . . ."). *Cf. Bower v. Fed. Express Corp.*, 156 F. Supp. 2d 678 (W.D. Tenn. 2001) (considering application of ACAA to all-cargo carrier).

Counsel prosecuting claims under the ACAA may argue in favor of a private right of action under the ACAA by emphasizing the fact courts may imply private remedies after considering the four factors articulated by the United States Supreme Court in *Cort v. Ash*, 422 U.S. 66, 78 (1975), namely: (1) whether the plaintiff is one of the class of persons whom the statute was intended to benefit; (2) whether the legislature intended to create a private remedy; (3) whether a private remedy is consistent with the underlying statutory scheme; and (4) whether the contemplated remedy traditionally has been relegated to state law. In *Shinault*, the Fifth Circuit Court of Appeals evaluated the factors set forth in *Ash* and reasoned that the legislative history of the ACAA indicates that Congress intended to provide a private cause of action, that such an action would be consistent with the statutory scheme, and that private remedies for discrimination by airlines traditionally emanated from federal legislation, including the Federal Aviation Act of 1958. *Shinhualt*, 958 F.2d at 800.

Oppositely, counsel defending against an ACAA claim may find support in a decision by the Eleventh Circuit Court of Appeals, *Love v. Delta Air Lines*, 310 F.3d 1347 (11th Cir. 2002). In *Love*, a passenger aboard an Alabama-to-Colorado flight who advised the airline of her "special needs" when making reservations, became ill onboard her flight and had to be carried to the restroom by her son. *Id.* The passenger ultimately sued, asserting claims under the Americans with Disabilities Act of 1990 and the ACAA. *Id.* She alleged that the airline engaged in discrimination by not ensuring that its facilities were accessible to a disabled person, and failed to provide an accessible "call button" to page a flight attendant, an aisle chair to assist her in accessing the restroom facilities, a restroom large enough to accommodate her, privacy in the restroom, or adequately trained flight personnel. *Id.* The federal trial court determined that the ACAA permitted private litigants to obtain declaratory and injunctive relief.

The Court of Appeals reversed, however, on the ground that several enforcement mechanisms written into the ACAA "strongly undermine[] the suggestion that Congress also intended to create by implication a private right of action in a federal district court but declined to say so expressly." *Id.* at 1357. Specifically, the *Love* court observed

> the ACAA and its attendant regulations provide three separate enforcement mechanisms. First, the [Department of Transportation] is required to investigate ACAA claims and is given broad powers to sanction air carriers for ACAA violations. Second, air carriers themselves are required to establish ACAA dispute resolution mechanisms. Finally, once the DOT has acted in response to an alleged ACAA violation, an individual "with a substantial interest" in that action may seek review in a court of appeals.

Id.

Therefore, the *Love* court opined that "the legislature instead [of creating a private right of action] opted to create an elaborate administrative enforcement scheme, augmented only by a *limited* form of judicial review of the DOT's actions in the court of appeals." *Id.* (italics in original). *See also Ruta v. Delta Airlines, Inc.*, 322 F. Supp. 2d 391 (S.D.N.Y. 2004) (no private right of action under ACAA); *Boswell v. Skywest Airlines, Inc.*, 361 F.3d 1263 (10th Cir. 2004) (same).

3. *Is the ACAA Preempted by Federal Law?*

Courts are divided on the preemptive effect of the Federal Aviation Act and the Airline Deregulation Act of 1978 on state law tort claims brought for alleged ACAA violations. Specifically, in enacting the Airline Deregulation Act Congress sought to foster "an air transportation system which relies on competitive market forces to determine the quality, variety and price of air services." H.R. Rep. No. 95–1779, at 53, *reprinted in* 1978 U.S.C.A.N.N. 3737. It follows logically then that Congress preempted any state regulation "related to a price, route or service of any air carrier." 49 U.S.C. § 41713(b). *See American Airlines, Inc. v. Wolens*, 513 U.S. 219 (1995); *Morales v. Trans World Airlines, Inc.*, 504 U.S. 374 (1992). Whether a particular claim arising under the ACAA relates to a price, route, or service is an open question.

Some courts have found that claims arising under the ACAA are not preempted because an award of damages would not contravene the goal of economically deregulating the nation's commercial airline industry and Congress did not intend to shield airlines from common law negligence claims. *E.g., Rowley v. American Airlines*, 875 F. Supp. 708 (D. Ore. 1995); *Jamerson v. Atlantic Southeast Airlines*, 860 F. Supp. 821 (M.D. Ala. 1994); *Moore v. Northwest Airlines, Inc*, 897 F. Supp. 313 (E.D. Tex. 1995). As one court noted, "[p]ermitting state law claims which seek to enforce provisions of the Air Carrier Access Act neither interferes nor conflicts with federal law." *Price v. Delta Airlines, Inc.*, 5 F. Supp. 2d 226 (D. Vt. 1998).

In contrast, some courts have found preemption. For example, in *Howard v. Northwest Airlines, Inc.*, 793 F. Supp. 129 (S.D. Tex. 1992), a wrongful death claim arising out of an airline's alleged failure to meet and assist an elderly passenger was adjudged preempted because the claim related to an airline service. Similarly, a federal court concluded that federal law preempted a false imprisonment claim by a passenger who alleged that he was falsely imprisoned by several airlines when he was prevented from boarding his flight when he was left in an immobile aisle chair for a substantial time. *Williams v. Express Airlines I, Inc.*, 825 F. Supp. 831 (W.D. Tenn. 1993).

Moreover, courts have held that discrimination claims under the ACAA are preempted under applicable treaties governing international carriage. *E.g., Turturro v. Continental Airlines*, 128 F. Supp. 2d. 170 (S.D.N.Y. 2001) (applying the Warsaw Convention); *Waters v. Port Authority of New York & New Jersey*, 158 F. Supp. 2d 415 (D.N.J. 2001) (same).

4.   *Damages Under the ACAA.*

Congress did not provide a remedial scheme in the ACAA. Therefore, putting aside preemption issues and assuming that claims are brought in a jurisdiction allowing a private action to enforce violations of the ACAA, counsel should note that even courts that recognize private enforcement of the ACAA have acknowledged "no significant evidence in the legislative history and the circumstances surrounding the passage of the ACAA to indicate what types of remedies Congress intended to provide for private litigants." *Shinault v. American Airlines, Inc.*, 936 F.2d 796, 800 (5th Cir. 1991). Indeed, one court that allows private lawsuits involving the ACAA has concluded that injunctive relief is not necessary because the DOT secures prospective relief through administrative remedies. *Id.*

Some courts have concluded that compensatory damages—including emotional distress damages—"are necessary and appropriate under the ACAA." *Id.* Punitive damages have not been recognized in ACAA claims, however, even by courts that find private suits cognizable under the ACAA. *Id. See generally Nader v. Allegheny Airlines, Inc.*, 512 F.2d 527, 549 (D.C. Cir. 1975), *rev'd on other grounds*, 426 U.S. 290 (1976) (standard for award of punitive damages for violation of Federal Aviation Act provision prohibiting discrimination by air carriers is proof of conduct evidencing "evil motive, actual malice, deliberate violence or oppression.").

On the other hand, practitioners are cautioned to evaluate the precedent established by *Americans Disabled for Accessible Public Transp. v. Skywest Airlines*, 762 F. Supp. 320 (D. Utah 1991), which dismissed claims for emotional distress damages and punitive damages alleged under the ACAA. *See also DeGirolamo v. Alitalia-Linee Aeree Italiane, S.p.A.*, 159 F. Supp. 2d 764 (D.N.J. 2001) (declining to award punitive damages for misinformation provided by airline in connection with ticket purchased by wheel-chair bound passenger).

For further information on application of the Air Carrier Access Act see Kristine Cordier Karnezis, *Recovery for Discriminatory Conduct under Air Carrier Access Act, 49 U.S.C.A. § 41705*, 188 A.L.R. Fed. 367 (2003); Curtis D. Edmonds, *When Pigs Fly: Litigation under the Air Carrier Access Act*, 78 N.D. L. REV. 687 (2002).

D. EUROPEAN UNION: REGULATION 261/2004

STURGEON V. CONDOR FLUGDIENST GMBH
(C–402/07 (2009))

These references for a preliminary ruling concern the interpretation of Articles 2(*l*), 5, 6 and 7 of Regulation ("EC") No. 261/2004 of the European Parliament and of the Council of 11 February 2004 establishing common rules on compensation and assistance to passengers in the event of denied boarding and of cancellation or long delay of flights, and repealing Regulation ("EEC") No 295/91.

The references were made in proceedings between (i) Mr. Sturgeon and his family and Condor Flugdienst GmbH and (ii) Mr. Bock and Ms. Lepuschitz and Air France SA, concerning the refusal of those airlines to pay compensation to the passengers concerned, whose arrival at the airport of destination was delayed by 25 and 22 hours respectively in relation to the scheduled arrival time.

The Sturgeons booked return tickets with Condor from Frankfurt am Main (Germany) to Toronto (Canada). The return flight from Toronto to Frankfurt was due to depart at 16.20 on 9 July 2005. Following check-in, passengers on that flight were informed that the flight was cancelled, as was indicated on the airport departures board. Their luggage was returned to them and they were then driven to a hotel where they spent the night. The following day, the passengers were checked in at another airline's counter for a flight with the same number as that on their booking. Condor did not schedule another flight with the same number for the day concerned. The passengers were given different seats from those they had been allocated on the previous day. The booking was not converted into a booking for a flight scheduled by another airline. The flight concerned arrived in Frankfurt at around 07.00 on 11 July 2005, some 25 hours after its scheduled arrival time.

The Sturgeons took the view that, in light of all the abovementioned circumstances, in particular the delay of more than 25 hours, the flight had been not delayed but cancelled. The Sturgeons brought an action against Condor before the Amtsgericht Rüsselsheim (Local Court, Rüsselsheim) (Germany), claiming compensation of EUR 600 per person plus damages, since, in their view, the damage sustained was the result not of a flight delay but of a cancellation.

Cancelled, Not Delayed

Condor contended that the action as framed should be dismissed on the ground that the flight in question was delayed and not cancelled. Prior to the proceedings before the national court, Condor claimed that the flight had been delayed as the result of a hurricane in the Caribbean but during the proceedings it attributed the delay to technical faults on the plane and illness among the crew.

The Amtsgericht Rüsselsheim concluded that the flight had been delayed not cancelled and, consequently, dismissed the Sturgeons' claim for compensation. The Sturgeons appealed to the Landgericht Darmstadt (Regional Court, Darmstadt) which upheld the decision of the lower court. The Sturgeons then appealed on a point of law ('Revision') to the Bundesgerichtshof (Federal Court of Justice). Taking the view that the outcome of the appeal depended on the interpretation of Articles 2(*l*) and 5(1)(c) of Regulation No. 261/2004, the Bundesgerichtshof decided to stay the proceedings and to refer the following questions to the Court for a preliminary ruling:

1. *Is it decisive for the interpretation of the term "cancellation" whether the original flight planning is abandoned, with the result that a delay, regardless of how long, does not constitute a cancellation if the air carrier does not actually abandon the planning for the original flight?*

2.   *If Question 1 is answered in the negative: in what circumstances is a delay of*
     the planned flight no longer to be regarded as a delay but as a cancellation? Is
     the answer to this question dependent on the length of the delay?

Mr. Böck and Ms. Lepuschitz booked return tickets with Air France from Vienna (Austria) to Mexico City (Mexico) via Paris (France). The Mexico City-Paris flight which Mr. Böck and Ms. Lepuschitz were due to take was scheduled to depart at 21.30 on 7 March 2005. When they came to check in, they were immediately informed, without the check-in taking place, that their flight was cancelled. The cancellation resulted from a change in the flight planning between Mexico City and Paris, which arose because of a technical breakdown on the aircraft due to fly from Paris to Mexico City and on account of the need to observe the rest period prescribed by law for the crew.

In order to get back earlier, Mr. Böck and Ms. Lepuschitz accepted Air France's offer of seats on a flight operated by Continental Airlines, which was scheduled to leave the following day, 8 March 2005, at 12.20. Their tickets were first cancelled and then new tickets were issued to them at the Continental Airlines counter. The other passengers on the Mexico City-Paris flight, who did not take the Continental Airlines flight, left Mexico City, with a number of additional passengers, on 8 March 2005 at 19.35. That flight, whose original number was followed by the letter "A," was operated in addition to the regular flight scheduled by Air France on the same day.

Mr. Böck and Ms. Lepuschitz arrived in Vienna almost 22 hours after the scheduled arrival time. Mr. Böck and Ms. Lepuschitz brought an action against Air France before the Bezirksgericht für Handelssachen Wien (District Commercial Court, Vienna) (Austria), claiming EUR 600 compensation per person for cancellation of their flight, on the basis of Articles 5 and 7(1)(c) of Regulation No. 261/2004. That court dismissed their claim on the ground that, despite the evident flight delay, Regulation No. 261/2004 did not support the conclusion that there was a flight cancellation. Mr. Böck and Ms. Lepuschitz appealed against that decision to the Handelsgericht Wien (Commercial Court, Vienna).

Before the national courts, the applicants in the main actions claim from Condor and Air France respectively the compensation provided for in Article 7 of Regulation No. 261/2004 on the ground that with those airlines they reached their airports of destination, in the first case, 25 and, in the second case, 22 hours after the scheduled arrival times. Condor and Air France assert that the applicants are not entitled to any compensation, since the flights concerned were not cancelled but delayed and Regulation No. 261/2004 provides for a right to compensation only in the case of flight cancellation. Furthermore, the airlines maintain that the late arrival of the flights was attributable to technical faults on the aircraft, which are covered by the concept of 'extraordinary circumstances' within the meaning of Article 5(3) of Regulation No. 261/2004, and that they are thus released from the obligation to pay compensation. In those circumstances, in order to give the national courts a useful answer, the questions referred should be understood as seeking, in essence, to ascertain:

1. *Whether a flight delay must be regarded as a flight cancellation for the purposes of Articles 2(l) and 5 of Regulation No. 261/2004 where the delay is long;*

2. *Whether Articles 5, 6 and 7 of Regulation No. 261/2004 must be interpreted as meaning that passengers whose flights are delayed may, for the purpose of the application of the right to compensation laid down in Article 7 of that regulation, be treated as passengers whose flights are cancelled, and*

3. *Whether a technical problem in an aircraft is covered by the concept of 'extraordinary circumstances' within the meaning of Article 5(3) of Regulation No. 261/2004.*

Concept of "Delay"

Regulation No. 261/2004 does not contain a definition of "flight delay." That concept may, however, be clarified in the light of the context in which it occurs. In that regard, it should be recalled, first, that a "flight" within the meaning of Regulation No. 261/2004 consists in an air transport operation, performed by an air carrier which fixes its itinerary. Thus, the itinerary is an essential element of the flight, as the flight is operated in accordance with the carrier's pre-arranged planning.

Flight Delay, Defined?

It is clear furthermore from Article 6 of Regulation No. 261/2004 that the Community legislature adopted a notion of "flight delay" which is considered only by reference to the scheduled departure time and which implies as a consequence that, after the departure time, the other elements pertaining to the flight must remain unchanged. Thus, a flight is "delayed" for the purposes of Article 6 of Regulation No. 261/2004 if it is operated in accordance with the original planning and its actual departure time is later than the scheduled departure time.

> *Regulation No. 261/2004 does not contain a definition of "flight delay." That concept may, however, be clarified in the light of the context in which it occurs. In that regard, it should be recalled, first, that a "flight" within the meaning of Regulation No. 261/2004 consists in an air transport operation, performed by an air carrier which fixes its itinerary. Thus, the itinerary is an essential element of the flight, as the flight is operated in accordance with the carrier's pre-arranged planning.*

Second, according to Article 2(l) of Regulation No. 261/2004, flight cancellation, unlike delay, is the result of non-operation of a flight which was previously planned. It follows that, in that regard, cancelled flights and delayed flights are two quite distinct categories of flights. It cannot therefore be inferred from Regulation No. 261/2004 that a flight which is delayed may be classified as a "cancelled flight" merely on the ground that the delay is extended, even substantially. Consequently, a flight which is delayed, irrespective of the duration of the delay, even if it is long, cannot be regarded as cancelled where there is a departure in accordance with the original planning.

When Cancelled?

In those circumstances, where passengers are carried on a flight whose departure time is later than the departure time originally scheduled, the flight can be classified as "cancelled" only if the air carrier arranges for the passengers to be carried on another flight whose original planning is different from that of the flight for which the booking was made. Thus, it is possible, as a rule, to conclude that there is a cancellation where the delayed flight for which the booking was made is "rolled over" onto another flight, that is to say, where the planning for the original flight is abandoned and the passengers from that flight join passengers on a flight which was also planned—but independently of the flight for which the passengers so transferred had made their bookings.

By contrast, it cannot, as a rule, be concluded that there is a flight delay or cancellation on the basis of a "delay" or a "cancellation" being shown on the airport departures board or announced by the air carrier's staff. Similarly, the fact that passengers recover their luggage or obtain new boarding cards is not, as a rule, a deciding factor. Those circumstances are not connected with the objective characteristics of the flight as such. They can be attributable to inaccurate classifications or to factors obtaining in the airport concerned or, yet again, they may be unavoidable given the waiting time and the fact that it is necessary for the passengers concerned to spend the night in a hotel.

> *Where passengers are carried on a flight whose departure time is later than the*
> *departure time originally scheduled, the flight can be classified as "cancelled" only if*
> *the air carrier arranges for the passengers to be carried on another flight whose original*
> *planning is different from that of the flight for which the booking was made.*

Nor, as a rule, is it conclusive that the composition of the group of passengers who initially held reservations is essentially identical to that of the group subsequently transported. Indeed, as the delay grows longer by reference to the departure time originally scheduled, the number of passengers in the first of those groups may decrease because some passengers have been offered re-routing on another flight and others, for personal reasons, have decided not to take the delayed flight. Conversely, to the extent that seats have become available on the flight for which the booking was made, there is nothing to prevent the carrier accepting, before departure of the plane which is delayed, additional passengers.

In view of the foregoing, the answer to the first part of the questions referred is that Articles 2(*l*), 5 and 6 of Regulation No. 261/2004 must be interpreted as meaning that a flight which is delayed, irrespective of the duration of the delay, even if it is long, cannot be regarded as cancelled where the flight is operated in accordance with the air carrier's original planning.

Right to Compensation in the Event of Delay

Article 5(1) of Regulation No. 261/2004 provides that in the event of cancellation of a flight, the passengers concerned are to have the right to compensation by the operating air carrier in accordance with Article 7 of the regulation. By contrast, it does not expressly follow from the wording of Regulation No. 261/2004 that passengers whose flights are delayed have such a right. Nevertheless, as the Court has made clear in its case-law, it is necessary, in interpreting a provision of Community law, to consider not only its wording, but also the context in which it occurs and the objectives pursued by the rules of which it is part. In that regard, the operative part of a Community act is indissociably linked to the statement of reasons for it, so that, when it has to be interpreted, account must be taken of the reasons which led to its adoption.

It must be stated that, even though the possibility of relying on "extraordinary circumstances," allowing air carriers to be released from the obligation to pay compensation under Article 7 of Regulation No. 261/2004, is provided for only in Article 5(3) thereof, which concerns flight cancellation, Recital 15 in the preamble to the regulation nevertheless states that that ground may also be relied on where an air traffic management decision in relation to a particular aircraft on a particular day gives rise to "a long delay [or] an overnight delay." As the notion of long delay is mentioned in the context of extraordinary circumstances, it must be held that the legislature also linked that notion to the right to compensation.

That is implicitly borne out by the objective of Regulation No. 261/2004, since it is apparent from Recitals 1 to 4 in the preamble, in particular from Recital 2, that the regulation seeks to ensure a high level of protection for air passengers regardless of whether they are denied boarding or whether their flight is cancelled or delayed, since they are all caused similar serious trouble and inconvenience connected with air transport. That is *a fortiori* the case since the provisions conferring rights on air passengers, including those conferring a right to compensation, must be interpreted broadly. In those circumstances it cannot automatically be presumed that passengers whose flights are delayed do not have a right to compensation and cannot, for the purposes of recognition of such a right, be treated as passengers whose flights are cancelled.

Next, it must be stated that, according to a general principle of interpretation, a Community act must be interpreted, as far as possible, in such a way as not to affect its validity. Likewise, where a provision of Community law is open to several interpretations, preference must be given to that interpretation which ensures that the provision retains its effectiveness. In that regard, all Community acts must be interpreted in accordance with primary law as a whole, including the principle of equal treatment, which requires that comparable situations must not be treated differently and that different situations must not be treated in the same way unless such treatment is objectively justified.

In view of the objective of Regulation No. 261/2004, which is to strengthen protection for air passengers by redressing damage suffered by them during air travel, situations covered by the regulation must be compared, in particular by reference to the type and extent of the various types of inconvenience and damage suffered by the passengers concerned. In this instance, the situation of passengers whose flights are delayed should be compared with that of passengers whose flights are cancelled.

Similarity in Damages

In that connection, Regulation No. 261/2004 seeks to redress damage in an immediate and standardised manner and to do so by various forms of intervention which are the subject of rules relating to denied boarding, cancellation and long flight delay. Regulation No. 261/2004 has, in those measures, the objective of repairing, *inter alia*, damage consisting, for the passengers concerned, in a loss of time which, given that it is irreversible, can be redressed only by compensation.

In that regard, it must be stated that that damage is suffered both by passengers whose flights are cancelled and by passengers whose flights are delayed if, prior to reaching their destinations, the latter's journey time is longer than the time which had originally been scheduled by the air carrier. Consequently, passengers whose flights have been cancelled and passengers affected by a flight delay suffer similar damage, consisting in a loss of time, and thus find themselves in comparable situations for the purposes of the application of the right to compensation laid down in Article 7 of Regulation No. 261/2004.

More specifically, the situation of passengers whose flights are delayed is scarcely distinguishable from that of passengers whose flights are cancelled, who are re-routed in accordance with Article 5(1)(c)(iii) of Regulation No. 261/2004 and who may be informed of the flight cancellation at the very last moment, when they actually arrive at the airport. First, both categories of passengers are informed, as a rule, at the same time of the incident which will make their journey by air more difficult. Second, even if they are transported to their final destination, they reach it after the time originally scheduled and, as a consequence, they suffer a similar loss of time.

That said, passengers who are re-routed under Article 5(1)(c)(iii) of Regulation No. 261/2004 are afforded the right to compensation laid down in Article 7 of the regulation where the carrier fails to re-route them on a flight which departs no more than one hour before the scheduled time of departure and reaches their final destination less than two hours after the scheduled time of arrival. Those passengers thus acquire a right to compensation when they suffer a loss of time equal to or in excess of three hours in relation to the duration originally planned by the air carrier.

If, by contrast, passengers whose flights are delayed did not acquire any right to compensation, they would be treated less favourably even though, depending on the circumstances, they suffer a similar loss of time, of three hours or more, in the course of their journey. There appears, however, to be no objective ground capable of justifying such a difference in treatment.

Given that the damage sustained by air passengers in cases of cancellation or long delay is comparable, passengers whose flights are delayed and passengers whose flights are cancelled cannot be treated differently without the principle of equal treatment being infringed. That is *a fortiori* the case in view of the aim sought by Regulation No. 261/2004, which is to increase protection for all air passengers. In those circumstances, the Court finds that passengers whose flights are delayed may rely on the right to compensation laid down in Article 7 of Regulation No.

261/2004 where they suffer, on account of such flights, a loss of time equal to or in excess of three hours, that is to say when they reach their final destination three hours or more after the arrival time originally scheduled by the air carrier. That solution is, moreover, consistent with Recital 15 in the preamble to Regulation No. 261/2004. As stated in this judgment, it must be held that the legislature, in that recital, also linked the notion of "long delay" to the right to compensation. That notion corresponds to a delay to which the legislature attaches certain legal consequences. As Article 6 of the regulation already accepts such legal consequences in the case of certain flights which are delayed for two hours, Recital 15 necessarily covers delays of three hours or more.

It is important to point out that the compensation payable to a passenger under Article 7(1) of Regulation No. 261/2004 may be reduced by 50% if the conditions laid down in Article 7(2) of the regulation are met. Even though the latter provision refers only to the case of re-routing of passengers, the Court finds that the reduction in the compensation provided for is dependent solely on the delay to which passengers are subject, so that nothing precludes the application mutatis mutandis of that provision to compensation paid to passengers whose flights are delayed. It follows that the compensation payable to a passenger whose flight is delayed, who reaches his final destination three hours or more after the arrival time originally scheduled, may be reduced by 50%, in accordance with Article 7(2)(c) of Regulation No. 261/2004, where the delay is—in the case of a flight not falling under points (a) or (b) of Article 7(2)—less than four hours.

The conclusion set out in paragraph 61 of this judgment is not undermined by the fact that Article 6 of Regulation No. 261/2004 provides for different forms of assistance under Articles 8 and 9 thereof for passengers whose flights are delayed. As the Court has already stated, Regulation No. 261/2004 provides for various forms of intervention in order to redress, in a standardised and immediate manner, the different types of damage constituted by the inconvenience that delay in the carriage of passengers by air causes. Those measures are autonomous in the sense that they address different aims and seek to make up for various types of damage caused by such delay.

That said, it should be recalled that, with the adoption of Regulation No. 261/2004, the legislature was also seeking to strike a balance between the interests of air passengers and those of air carriers. Having laid down certain rights for those passengers, it provided at the same time, in Recital 15 and Article 5(3) of the regulation, that air carriers are not obliged to pay compensation if they can prove that the cancellation or long delay is caused by extraordinary circumstances which could not have been avoided even if all reasonable measures had been taken, namely circumstances which are beyond the air carrier's actual control.

> *With the adoption of Regulation No. 261/2004, the legislature was seeking to strike a balance between the interests of air passengers and those of air carriers. Having laid down certain rights for those passengers, it provided at the same time, in Recital 15 and Article 5(3) of the regulation, that air carriers are not obliged to pay compensation if they can prove that the cancellation or long delay is caused by extraordinary circumstances which could not have been avoided even if all reasonable measures had been taken, namely circumstances which are beyond the air carrier's actual control.*

Moreover, the discharge of obligations pursuant to Regulation No. 261/2004 is without prejudice to air carriers' rights to seek compensation from any person who caused the delay, including third parties, as Article 13 of the regulation provides. Such compensation may accordingly reduce or even remove the financial burden borne by carriers in consequence of those obligations. Nor does it appear unreasonable for those obligations initially to be borne, subject to the abovementioned right to compensation, by the air carriers with which the passengers concerned have a contract of carriage that entitles them to a flight that should be neither cancelled nor delayed.

> *Articles 5, 6 and 7 of Regulation No. 261/2004 must be interpreted as meaning that passengers whose flights are delayed may be treated, for the purposes of the application of the right to compensation, as passengers whose flights are cancelled and they may thus rely on the right to compensation laid down in Article 7 of the regulation where they suffer, on account of a flight delay, a loss of time equal to or in excess of three hours, that is, where they reach their final destination three hours or more after the arrival time originally scheduled by the air carrier.*

In the light of the foregoing, the answer to the second part of the questions referred is that Articles 5, 6 and 7 of Regulation No. 261/2004 must be interpreted as meaning that passengers whose flights are delayed may be treated, for the purposes of the application of the right to compensation, as passengers whose flights are cancelled and they may thus rely on the right to compensation laid down in Article 7 of the regulation where they suffer, on account of a flight delay, a loss of time equal to or in excess of three hours, that is, where they reach their final destination three hours or more after the arrival time originally scheduled by the air carrier. Such a delay does not, however, entitle passengers to compensation if the air carrier can prove that the long delay was caused by extraordinary

When Delay Is Equal to Cancellation

circumstances which could not have been avoided even if all reasonable measures had been taken, namely circumstances beyond the actual control of the air carrier.

Extraordinary Circumstances resulting from Technical Problem

The Court has already held that Article 5(3) of Regulation No. 261/2004 must be interpreted as meaning that a technical problem in an aircraft which leads to the cancellation of a flight is not covered by the concept of "extraordinary circumstances" within the meaning of that provision, unless that problem stems from events which, by their nature or origin, are not inherent in the normal exercise of the activity of the air carrier concerned and are beyond its actual control. The same conclusion applies when Article 5(3) of Regulation No. 261/2004 is pleaded in the case of flight delay.

> *Article 5(3) of Regulation No. 261/2004 must be interpreted as meaning that a technical problem in an aircraft which leads to the cancellation or delay of a flight is not covered by the concept of "extraordinary circumstances" within the meaning of that provision, unless that problem stems from events which, by their nature or origin, are not inherent in the normal exercise of the activity of the air carrier concerned and are beyond its actual control.*

Thus, the answer to the third question in Case C–432/07 is that Article 5(3) of Regulation No. 261/2004 must be interpreted as meaning that a technical problem in an aircraft which leads to the cancellation or delay of a flight is not covered by the concept of "extraordinary circumstances" within the meaning of that provision, unless that problem stems from events which, by their nature or origin, are not inherent in the normal exercise of the activity of the air carrier concerned and are beyond its actual control. On those grounds, the Court (Fourth Chamber) hereby rules:

1.   Articles 2(*l*), 5 and 6 of Regulation (EC) No. 261/2004 of the European Parliament and of the Council of 11 February 2004 establishing common rules on compensation and assistance to passengers in the event of denied boarding and of cancellation or long delay of flights, and repealing Regulation (EEC) No 295/91, must be interpreted as meaning that a flight which is delayed, irrespective of the duration of the delay, even if it is long, cannot be regarded as cancelled where the flight is operated in accordance with the air carrier's original planning.

2.   Articles 5, 6 and 7 of Regulation No. 261/2004 must be interpreted as meaning that passengers whose flights are delayed may be treated, for the purposes of the application of the right to compensation, as passengers whose flights are cancelled and they may thus rely on the right to compensation laid down

in Article 7 of the regulation where they suffer, on account of a flight delay, a loss of time equal to or in excess of three hours, that is, where they reach their final destination three hours or more after the arrival time originally scheduled by the air carrier. Such a delay does not, however, entitle passengers to compensation if the air carrier can prove that the long delay was caused by extraordinary circumstances which could not have been avoided even if all reasonable measures had been taken, namely circumstances beyond the actual control of the air carrier.

3.   Article 5(3) of Regulation No. 261/2004 must be interpreted as meaning that a technical problem in an aircraft which leads to the cancellation or delay of a flight is not covered by the concept of 'extraordinary circumstances' within the meaning of that provision, unless that problem stems from events which, by their nature or origin, are not inherent in the normal exercise of the activity of the air carrier concerned and are beyond its actual control.

EXERCISE 7-6. *STURGEON V. CONDOR FLUGDIENST GMBH*— CONCEPT OF "DELAY"

1.   This case involves two different proceedings, *i.e.*, Mr. Sturgeon and his family, and Mr. Bock and Ms. Lepuschitz. Explain the factual basis and legal issues for each of their respective cases.

2.   How is each term below defined by the court under Regulation No. 261/2004? (a) flight; (b) flight delay; (c) flight cancellation; (d) cancelled; (e) extraordinary circumstances.

3.   How does the tribunal resolve the issue of whether a flight delay is a flight cancellation under applicable regulations where the delay is long?

4.   Are passengers of cancelled flights compensated differently than passengers of delayed flights? Explain.

5.   What are the goals of Regulation 261/2004 as expressed in its Recitals 1 to 4 of its preamble? How should the regulations be interpreted?

GERMANWINGS GMBH V. HENNING
(C–452/13 (2014))

This request for a preliminary ruling concerns the interpretation of the concept of "arrival time" within the meaning of Articles 2, 5 and 7 of Regulation ("EC") No. 261/2004 of the European Parliament and of the Council of 11 February 2004 establishing common rules on compensation and assistance to passengers in the event of denied boarding and of cancellation or long delay of flights, and repealing Regulation ("EEC") No 295/91 (OJ 2004 L 46, p. 1). The request has been made in proceedings between Germanwings GmbH ("Germanwings"), an air carrier, and Mr. Henning concerning that carrier's refusal to compensate Mr. Henning for the alleged delay with which his flight arrived at Cologne/Bonn airport (Germany).

Mr. Henning purchased an aeroplane ticket from Germanwings in order to go from Salzburg (Austria) to Cologne/Bonn. That ticket specified a take-off from Salzburg airport at 13.30 on 11 May 2012 and an arrival at Cologne/Bonn airport at 14.40 on the same day. The flight distance between those two airports is, according to the great circle route method, less than 1,500 kilometres.

On 11 May 2012, Mr. Henning's aircraft was delayed in taking off from Salzburg airport. On arrival, the aircraft touched down on the tarmac of the runway at Cologne/Bonn airport at 17.38. The aircraft did not, however, reach its parking position until 17.43, that is to say three hours and three minutes after the scheduled arrival time. The doors of the aircraft were opened shortly afterwards.

Mr. Henning takes the view that the final destination was reached with a delay of more than three hours in relation to the scheduled arrival time. He thus considers that he has the right to compensation of EUR 250 on the basis of Articles 5 to 7 of Regulation No. 261/2004. Germanwings submits that, as the actual arrival time was the time at which the plane touched down on the tarmac at Cologne/Bonn airport, the delay in relation to the scheduled arrival time is only two hours and 58 minutes, with the result that no compensation is payable.

The first-instance court held that the actual arrival time to be taken into account was the time at which the first door of the aircraft was opened to enable the passengers to leave. Consequently, that court ordered Germanwings to pay compensation of EUR 250 to Mr. Henning. That company lodged an appeal against that judgment before the referring court. In those circumstances the Landesgericht Salzburg (Regional Court, Salzburg) decided to stay the proceedings and to refer the following question to the Court of Justice for a preliminary ruling:

> *What time is relevant for the term "time of arrival" used in Articles 2, 5 and 7 of Regulation [No. 261/2004]: (a) the time that the aircraft lands on the runway ("touchdown"); (b) the time that the aircraft reaches its parking position and the parking brakes are engaged or the chocks have been applied ("in-block time"); (c) the time that the aircraft door is opened; or (d) a time defined by the parties in the context of party autonomy?*

By its question the referring court asks, in essence, whether Articles 2, 5 and 7 of Regulation No. 261/2004 are to be interpreted as meaning that the concept of "arrival time," which is used to determine the length of the delay to which passengers on a flight have been subject, refers to (a) the time at which the aircraft touches down on the runway of the destination airport; (b) the time at which the aircraft reaches its parking position and the parking brakes are engaged or the chocks have been applied; (c) the time at which the aircraft door is opened or (d) a time defined by the parties by common accord.

It must be pointed out at the outset that that regulation envisages two different types of flight delay. First, in some cases, such as the flight delay described in Article 6 of Regulation No. 261/2004, that regulation refers to a flight's being delayed beyond its scheduled departure time. Secondly, in other cases, such as those referred to in Articles 5 and 7 of that regulation, the regulation refers to the situation where arrival has been delayed. It is apparent from those articles that, in order to establish the length of such a delay, it is necessary to compare the scheduled arrival time of the aircraft with the time at which it actually arrived at its destination.

Arrival Time?

Regulation No. 261/2004 does not define the actual arrival time. That being the case, the need for a uniform application of EU law and the principle of equal treatment require that the terms of a provision of EU law which makes no express reference to the law of the Member States for the purpose of determining its meaning and scope must normally be given an independent interpretation throughout the European Union. It follows that that concept of "actual arrival time" must be interpreted in such a way as to apply uniformly throughout the European Union. In those circumstances, one of the possibilities envisaged by the referring court, namely that according to which that concept is defined by the parties concerned on a contractual basis, must, in the absence of any indication to that effect in Regulation No. 261/2004, be rejected at the outset.

Compensation for Delay over Three Hours

It must also be noted that the Court has held that when their flights are subject to long delay, that is delay equal to or in excess of three hours, passengers of such flights are entitled to compensation on the basis of Article 7 of Regulation No. 261/2004, like those passengers whose original flights have been cancelled and whom an air carrier is not able to offer re-routing in accordance with the conditions laid down in Article 5(1)(c)(iii) of that regulation, given that they also suffer an irreversible loss of time. During a flight, passengers remain confined in an enclosed space, under the instructions and control of the air carrier, in which, for technical and safety reasons, their possibilities of communicating with the outside world are considerably restricted. In such circumstances, passengers are unable to carry on, without interruption, their personal, domestic, social or business activities. It is only once the flight has ended that they are able to resume their normal activities.

Although such inconveniences must be regarded as unavoidable as long as a flight does not exceed the scheduled duration, the same is not true if there is a delay, since the time by which, in the circumstances described in the preceding paragraph, the scheduled duration of the flight has been exceeded, represents 'lost time' in the light of the fact that the passengers concerned cannot use it to achieve the objectives which led them to go at the desired time to the destinations of their choice. It follows that the concept of "actual arrival time" must be understood, in the context of Regulation No. 261/2004, as corresponding to the time at which the situation described in paragraph 20 of the present judgment comes to an end.

In that regard, it must be stated that, in principle, the situation of passengers on a flight does not change substantially when their aircraft touches down on the runway at the destination airport, when that aircraft reaches its parking position and the parking brakes are engaged or when the chocks are applied, as the passengers continue to be subject, in the enclosed space in which they are sitting, to various constraints. It is only when the passengers are permitted to leave the aircraft and the order is given to that effect to open the doors of the aircraft that the passengers may in principle resume their normal activities without being subject to those constraints.

Articles 2, 5 and 7 of Regulation No. 261/2004 must be interpreted as meaning that the concept of "arrival time," which is used to determine the length of the delay to which passengers on a flight have been subject, corresponds to the time at which at least one of the doors of the aircraft is opened, the assumption being that, at that moment, the passengers are permitted to leave the aircraft.

Arrival Time, Defined

It is apparent from the foregoing considerations that Articles 2, 5 and 7 of Regulation No. 261/2004 must be interpreted as meaning that the concept of "arrival time," which is used to determine the length of the delay to which passengers on a flight have been subject, corresponds to the time at which at least one of the doors of the aircraft is opened, the assumption being that, at that moment, the passengers are permitted to leave the aircraft. That finding is not invalidated by the fact that a number of European Regulations and also certain International Air Transport Association ("IATA") documents refer to the concept of "actual arrival time" as the time at which an aircraft reaches its parking position. Those regulations and documents pursue objectives relating to air navigation rules and, in particular, to the allocation of slots, which are different from those of Regulation No. 261/2004. Consequently, the definitions that they give cannot be regarded as relevant for the interpretation of corresponding terms in the context of Regulation No. 261/2004, which is aimed exclusively at conferring minimum rights on passengers who are subject to various inconveniences because they are denied boarding against their will or have their flights cancelled or delayed.

In the light of all of the foregoing considerations, the answer to the referring court's question is that Articles 2, 5 and 7 of Regulation No. 261/2004 must be interpreted as meaning that the concept of "arrival time," which is used to determine the length of the delay to which passengers on a flight have been subject, refers to the time at which at least one of the doors of the aircraft is opened, the assumption being that, at that moment, the passengers are permitted to leave the aircraft.

On those grounds, the Court (Ninth Chamber) hereby rules: Articles 2, 5 and 7 of Regulation (EC) No. 261/2004 of the European Parliament and of the Council of 11 February 2004 establishing common rules on compensation and assistance to passengers in the event of denied boarding and of cancellation or long delay of flights, and repealing Regulation (EEC) No 295/91, must be interpreted as meaning that the concept of "arrival time," which is used to determine the length of the delay to which passengers on a flight have been subject, refers to the time at which at least one of the doors of the aircraft is opened, the assumption being that, at that moment, the passengers are permitted to leave the aircraft.

EXERCISE 7-7. *GERMANWINGS GMBH V. HENNING*— CANCELLATION: ARRIVAL TIME, DEFINED

1. Detail how the actual arrival and departure time of the flight at issue differed from the ticketed arrival and departure time.

2. Describe the competing arguments of the passenger and carrier respecting the actual arrival time and explain how the first-instance court ruled.

3. How does Regulation No. 261/2004 define "arrival time"?

4. How does the court interpret "actual arrival time?" Is this consistent with the definition of other European regulations and certain International Air Transport Association ("IATA") documents? Explain.

5. How does the court ultimately rule?

MCDONAGH V. RYANAIR, LTD.
(C–12/11 (2013))

This request for a preliminary ruling concerns the interpretation and assessment of the validity of Articles 5(1)(b) and 9 of Regulation (EC) No. 261/2004 of the European Parliament and of the Council of 11 February 2004 establishing common rules on compensation and assistance to passengers in the event of denied boarding and of cancellation or long delay of flights, and repealing Regulation (EEC) No 295/91.The request has been made in proceedings between Ms. McDonagh and Ryanair Ltd ("Ryanair") regarding the airline company's refusal to give Ms. McDonagh the care provided for in Article 5(1)(b) of Regulation No. 261/2004 after the eruption of the Icelandic volcano Eyjafjallajökull had caused the cancellation of her flight and, more generally, closure of part of European airspace.

On 11 February 2010, Ms. McDonagh booked a flight with Ryanair from Faro (Portugal) to Dublin (Ireland) scheduled for 17 April 2010, for EUR 98. On 20 March 2010, the Eyjafjallajökull volcano in Iceland began to erupt. On 14 April 2010, it entered an explosive phase, casting a cloud of volcanic ash into the skies over Europe. On 15 April 2010, the competent air traffic authorities closed the airspace over a number of Member States because of the risks to aircraft. On 17 April 2010, Ms. McDonagh's flight was cancelled following the closure of Irish airspace. Ryanair flights between continental Europe and Ireland resumed on 22 April 2010 and Ms. McDonagh was not able to return to Dublin until 24 April 2010. During the period between 17 and 24 April 2010, Ryanair did not provide Ms. McDonagh with care in accordance with the detailed rules laid down in Article 9 of Regulation No. 261/2004.

Ms. McDonagh brought an action against Ryanair before the referring court for compensation in the amount of EUR 1 129.41, corresponding to the costs which she had incurred during that period on meals, refreshments, accommodation and transport. Ryanair claims that the closure of part of European airspace following the eruption of the Eyjafjallajökull volcano does not constitute "extraordinary circumstances" within the meaning of Regulation No. 261/2004 but "super extraordinary circumstances," releasing it not only from its obligation to pay compensation but also from its obligations to provide care under Articles 5 and 9 of that regulation.

In light of its doubts as to whether the obligation to provide that care may be subject to limitations in circumstances such as those at issue in the main proceedings and taking the view that the Court of Justice has not yet ruled on that matter, the Dublin Metropolitan District Court decided to stay the proceedings and to refer the following questions to the Court of Justice for a preliminary ruling:

(1) Do circumstances such as the closures of European airspace as a result of the eruption of the Eyjafjallajökull volcano in Iceland, which caused widespread and prolonged disruption to air travel, go beyond "extraordinary circumstances" within the meaning of Regulation No. 261/2004?

(2) If the answer to Question 1 is yes, is liability for the duty to provide care excluded under Articles 5 and 9 [of Regulation No. 261/2004] in such circumstances?

(3) If the answer to Question 2 is no, are Articles 5 and 9 [of Regulation No. 261/2004] invalid in so far as they violate the principles of proportionality and non-discrimination, the principle of an "equitable balance of interests" enshrined in the Montreal Convention, and Articles 16 and 17 of the Charter of Fundamental Rights of the European Union ["the Charter"]?

(4) Is the obligation in Articles 5 and 9 [of Regulation No. 261/2004] to be interpreted as containing an implied limitation, such as a temporal and/or a monetary limit, to provide care in cases where cancellation is caused by "extraordinary circumstances"?

(5) If the answer to Question 4 is no, are Articles 5 and 9 [of Regulation No. 261/2004] invalid in so far as they violate the principles of proportionality and non-discrimination, the principle of an "equitable balance of interests" enshrined in the Montreal Convention, and Articles 16 and 17 of the [Charter]?

"Extraordinary Circumstances"

By its first question the referring court asks, in essence, whether Article 5 of Regulation No. 261/2004 must be interpreted as meaning that circumstances such as the closure of part of European airspace as a result of the eruption of the Eyjafjallajökull volcano constitute "extraordinary circumstances" within the meaning of that regulation which do not release air carriers from their obligation laid down in Articles 5(1)(b) and 9 of the regulation to provide care or, on the contrary and because of their particular scale, go beyond the scope of that notion, thus releasing air carriers from that obligation.

At the outset, it should be noted that the term "extraordinary circumstances" is not defined in Article 2 of Regulation No. 261/2004 or in the other provisions of that regulation, even though a non-exhaustive list of those circumstances can be derived from recitals 14 and 15 in the preamble to the regulation. European Union law provides no definition must be determined by considering their usual

Extraordinary Circumstances, Defined?

meaning in everyday language, while also taking into account the context in which they occur and the purposes of the rules of which they are part. In accordance with everyday language, the words "extraordinary circumstances" literally refer to circumstances which are "out of the ordinary."

> *In the context of air transport, the words "extraordinary circumstances" refer to an event which is not inherent in the normal exercise of the activity of the carrier concerned and is beyond the actual control of that carrier on account of its nature or origin. In other words, they relate to all circumstances which are beyond the control of the air carrier, whatever the nature of those circumstances or their gravity.*

In the context of air transport, they refer to an event which is not inherent in the normal exercise of the activity of the carrier concerned and is beyond the actual control of that carrier on account of its nature or origin. In other words, they relate to all circumstances which are beyond the control of the air carrier, whatever the nature of those circumstances or their gravity. Regulation No. 261/2004 contains nothing that would allow the conclusion to be drawn that it recognises a separate category of "particularly extraordinary" events, beyond 'extraordinary circumstances' referred to in Article 5(3) of that regulation, which would lead to the air carrier being exempted from all its obligations, including those under Article 9 of the regulation.

Next, as for the context of and the aims pursued by Article 5 of Regulation No. 261/2004, which prescribes the obligations of an air carrier in the event of cancellation of a flight, it must be noted, first, that when exceptional circumstances arise, Article 5(3) exempts the air carrier only from its obligation to pay compensation under Article 7 of that regulation. The European Union legislature thus took the view that the obligation on the air carrier to provide care under Article 9 of that regulation is necessary whatever the event which has given rise to the cancellation of the flight. Second, it is clear from recitals 1 and 2 of Regulation No. 261/2004 that the regulation aims at ensuring a high level of protection for passengers and takes account of the requirements of consumer protection in general, inasmuch as cancellation of flights causes serious inconvenience to passengers.

If circumstances such as those at issue in the main proceedings went beyond the scope of "extraordinary circumstances" within the meaning of Regulation No. 261/2004 due in particular to their origin and scale, such an interpretation would go against not only the meaning of that notion in everyday language but also the objectives of that regulation. Such an interpretation would in fact mean that air carriers would be required to provide care pursuant to Article 9 of Regulation No. 261/2004 to air passengers who find themselves, due to cancellation of a flight, in a situation causing limited inconvenience, whereas passengers, such as the plaintiff in the main proceedings, who find themselves in a particularly vulnerable state in that they are forced to remain at an airport for several days would be denied that care.

In the light of the foregoing, the answer to the first question is that Article 5 of Regulation No. 261/2004 must be interpreted as meaning that circumstances such as the closure of part of European airspace as a result of the eruption of the Eyjafjallajökull volcano constitute "extraordinary circumstances" within the meaning of that regulation which do not release air carriers from their obligation laid down in Articles 5(1)(b) and 9 of the regulation to provide care. It follows from the answer given to the first question that there is no need to answer the second and third questions.

Limitations on Obligation to Provide Passenger Care

By its fourth and fifth questions, which should be examined together, the referring court asks, in essence, whether Articles 5(1)(b) and 9 of Regulation No. 261/2004 must be interpreted as meaning that, in the event of cancellation of a flight due to "extraordinary circumstances" such as those at issue in the main proceedings, the obligation to provide care to passengers laid down in those provisions is limited in temporal or monetary terms and, if not, whether those provisions thus interpreted are invalid in the light of the principles of proportionality and non-discrimination, the principle of an "equitable balance of interests" referred to in the Montreal Convention or Articles 16 and 17 of the Charter.

It should be noted that, in the case of cancellation of a flight on account of "extraordinary circumstances," the European Union legislature sought to modify the obligations of air carriers laid down in Article 5(1) of Regulation No. 261/2004. Under recital 15 and Article 5(3) of Regulation No. 261/2004, by way of derogation from the provisions of Article 5(1), the air carrier is thus exempted from its obligation to compensate passengers under Article 7 of that regulation if it can prove that the cancellation is caused by extraordinary circumstances which could not have been avoided even if all reasonable measures had been taken, namely circumstances which are beyond the air carrier's actual control (Nelson and Others, paragraph 39). In that regard, the Court has held that, in such circumstances, the air carrier is only released from its obligation to provide compensation under Article 7 of Regulation No. 261/2004 and that, consequently, its obligation to provide care in accordance with Article 9 of that regulation remains. Furthermore, no limitation, whether temporal or monetary, of the obligation to provide care to passengers in extraordinary circumstances such as those at issue in the main proceedings is apparent from the wording of Regulation No. 261/2004.

> *Under recital 15 and Article 5(3) of Regulation No. 261/2004, by way of derogation from the provisions of Article 5(1), the air carrier is thus exempted from its obligation to compensate passengers under Article 7 of that regulation if it can prove that the cancellation is caused by extraordinary circumstances which could not have been avoided even if all reasonable measures had been taken, namely circumstances which are beyond the air carrier's actual control.*

It follows from Article 9 of Regulation No. 261/2004 that all the obligations to provide care to passengers whose flight is cancelled are imposed, in their entirety, on the air carrier for the whole period during which the passengers concerned must await their re-routing. To that effect, it is clear from Article 9(1)(b) that hotel accommodation is to be offered free of charge by the air carrier during the "necessary" period. Moreover, any interpretation seeking the recognition of limits, whether temporal or monetary, on the obligation of the air carrier to provide care to passengers whose flight has been cancelled would have the effect of jeopardising the aims pursued by Regulation No. 261/2004 recalled in paragraph 31 of this judgment, in that, beyond the limitation adopted, passengers would be deprived of all care and thus left to themselves.

As the Advocate General noted in his Opinion, the provision of care to such passengers is particularly important in the case of extraordinary circumstances which persist over a long time and it is precisely in situations where the waiting period occasioned by the cancellation of a flight is particularly lengthy that it is necessary to ensure that an air passenger whose flight has been cancelled can have access to essential goods and services throughout that period. Consequently, and contrary to what Ryanair claims, it cannot be deduced from Regulation No. 261/2004 that, in circumstances such as those at issue in the main proceedings, the obligation referred to in Articles 5 and 9 of that regulation to provide care to passengers must be subject to a temporal or monetary limitation.

Principles of Proportionality

However, it is necessary to ensure that the interpretation in the preceding paragraph does not conflict with the principles of proportionality, of an "equitable balance of interests" referred to in the Montreal Convention and of non-discrimination, or with Articles 16 and 17 of the Charter. Under a general principle of interpretation, a European Union measure must be interpreted, as far as possible, in such a way as not to affect its validity and in conformity with primary law as a whole.

As regards, first, the principle of proportionality, it must be noted that the Court has already had occasion to find that Articles 5 to 7 of Regulation 543No. 261/2004 are not invalid by reason of infringement of the principle of proportionality. There is nothing to justify, even on the basis of the lack of a temporal or monetary limit on the obligation to provide care in circumstances such as those at issue in the main proceedings, the finding of validity made by the Court in that case being called into question.

The fact that the obligation defined in Article 9 of Regulation No. 261/2004 to provide care entails, as Ryanair claims, undoubted financial consequences for air carriers is not such as to invalidate that finding, since those consequences cannot be considered disproportionate to the aim of ensuring a high level of protection for passengers. The importance of the objective of consumer protection, which includes the protection of air passengers, may justify even substantial negative economic consequences for certain economic operators. In addition, as the Advocate General noted, air carriers should, as experienced operators, foresee costs linked to the fulfilment, where relevant, of their obligation to provide care and, furthermore, may pass on the costs incurred as a result of that obligation to airline ticket prices. It follows that Articles 5(1)(b) and 9 of Regulation No. 261/2004 are not contrary to the principle of proportionality.

Air carriers should, as experienced operators, foresee costs linked to the fulfilment, where relevant, of their obligation to provide care and, furthermore, may pass on the costs incurred as a result of that obligation to airline ticket prices. It follows that Articles 5(1)(b) and 9 of Regulation No. 261/2004 are not contrary to the principle of proportionality.

None the less, an air passenger may only obtain, by way of compensation for the failure of the air carrier to comply with its obligation referred to in Articles 5(1)(b) and 9 of Regulation No. 261/2004 to provide care, reimbursement of the amounts which, in the light of the specific circumstances of each case, proved necessary, appropriate and reasonable to make up for the shortcomings of the air carrier in the provision of care to that passenger, a matter which is for the national court to assess.

As regards, second, the principle of an "equitable balance of interests" referred to in the last paragraph of the preamble to the Montreal Convention, suffice it to note that the standardised and immediate compensatory measures laid down by Regulation No. 261/2004, which include the obligation to provide care to passengers whose flight has been cancelled, are not among those whose institution is governed by the Montreal Convention. Therefore, there is no need to assess the validity of the aforesaid provisions in the light of the principle of an "equitable balance of interests" referred to in that Convention.

Principle of Non-Discrimination

As regards, third, the general principle of non-discrimination or equal treatment, Ryanair claims that the obligation laid down in Articles 5(1)(b) and 9 of Regulation No. 261/2004 to provide care in a situation such as that as issue in the main proceedings imposes obligations on air carriers which, in circumstances similar to those at issue in the main proceedings, do not fall upon other modes of transport governed by Regulation ("EC") No 1371/2007 of the European Parliament and of the Council of 23 October 2007 on rail passengers' rights and obligations, Regulation (EU) No 1177/2010 of the European Parliament and of the Council of 24 November 2010 concerning the rights of passengers when travelling by sea and inland waterway and amending Regulation (EC) No 2006/2004 and Regulation ("EU") No 181/2011 of the European Parliament and of the Council of 16 February 2011 concerning the rights of passengers in bus and coach transport and amending Regulation (EC) No 2006/2004, even though passengers stranded by widespread and prolonged disruption of transport find themselves in an identical situation whatever their mode of transport. In that respect, it should be noted that the Court has already held in IATA and ELFAA, paragraphs 93 to 99, that Articles 5 to 7 of Regulation No. 261/2004 do not infringe the principle of equal treatment.

The situation of undertakings operating in the different transport sectors is not comparable since the different modes of transport, having regard to the manner in which they operate, the conditions governing their accessibility and the distribution of their networks, are not interchangeable as regards the conditions of their use. In those circumstances, the European Union legislature was able to establish rules providing for a level of customer protection that varied according to the transport sector concerned. It follows that Articles 5(1)(b) and 9 of Regulation No. 261/2004 do not infringe the principle of non-discrimination.

As regards, fourth, Articles 16 and 17 of the Charter, guaranteeing freedom to conduct a business and the right to property respectively, Ryanair claims that the obligation to provide care to passengers imposed on air carriers in circumstances such as those at issue in the main proceedings has the effect of depriving air carriers of part of the fruits of their labour and of their investments. In that regard, it must be noted, first, that freedom to conduct a business and the right to property are not absolute rights but must be considered in relation to their social function.

Next, Article 52(1) of the Charter accepts that limitations may be imposed on the exercise of rights enshrined by it as long as the limitations are provided for by law, respect the essence of those rights and freedoms, and, subject to the principle of proportionality, are necessary and genuinely meet objectives of general interest recognised by the European Union or the need to protect the rights and freedoms of others. Lastly, when several rights protected by the European Union legal order clash, such an assessment must be carried out in accordance with the need to reconcile the requirements of the protection of those various rights and striking a fair balance between them.

In this case, the referring court mentions Articles 16 and 17 of the Charter. However, it is also necessary to take account of Article 38 thereof which, like Article 169 TFEU, seeks to ensure a high level of protection for consumers, including air passengers, in European Union policies. As has been noted in paragraph 31 of this judgment, protection of those passengers is among the principal aims of Regulation No. 261/2004. It follows from paragraphs 45 to 49 of this judgment relating to the principle of proportionality that Articles 5(1)(b) and 9 of Regulation No. 261/2004, as interpreted in paragraph 43 of this judgment, must be considered to comply with the requirement intended to reconcile the various fundamental rights involved and strike a fair balance between them. Therefore, those provisions do not breach Articles 16 and 17 of the Charter.

Consequently, the answer to the fourth and fifth questions is that Articles 5(1)(b) and 9 of Regulation No. 261/2004 must be interpreted as meaning that, in the event of cancellation of a flight due to "extraordinary circumstances" of a duration such as that in the main proceedings, the obligation to provide care to air passengers laid down in those provisions must be complied with, and the validity of those provisions is not affected. However, an air passenger may only obtain, by way of compensation for the failure of the air carrier to comply with its obligation referred to in Articles 5(1)(b) and 9 of Regulation No. 261/2004 to provide care, reimbursement of the amounts which, in the light of the specific circumstances of each case, proved necessary, appropriate and reasonable to make up for the shortcomings of the air carrier in the provision of care to that passenger, a matter which is for the national court to assess.

EXERCISE 7-8. *MCDONAGH V. RYANAIR, LTD.*—CANCELLATION: EXTRAORDINARY CIRCUMSTANCES

1.   Why was Ms. McDonagh's flight cancelled?

2.   Describe the damages claim of Ms. McDonagh and the airline's initial defense.

3.   How does Regulation No. 261/2004 define "extraordinary circumstances"? Did the facts of this case constitute "extraordinary circumstances"?

4.   Explain what the court means by "principle of proportionality."

5.   How does the court ultimately rule with respect to the passenger's claim for damages?

Suggested Further Reading

David Heffernan, *Department of Transportation's "Aggressive" Approach to Consumer Protection Regulation and Enforcement*, 80 J. AIR L. & COM. 347 (2015)

Timothy M. Ravich, *National Airline Policy*, 23 U. MIAMI BUS. L. REV. 1 (2014)

Matthew Schoonover, *Oversold, Delayed, Rescheduled: Airline Passenger Rights and Protections*, 35 WASH. U. J.L. & POL'Y 519 (2011)

Daniel H. Rosenthal, *Legal Turbulence: The Court's Misconstrual of the Airline Deregulation Act's Preemption Clause and the Effect on Passengers' Rights*, 51 DUKE L.J. 1857 (2002)

Air Piracy and Crime

National Transportation Safety Board
Aviation Accident Preliminary Report

Location:	Steilacoom, WA	**Accident Number:**	WPR18FA220
Date & Time:	08/10/2018, 2043 PDT	**Registration:**	N449QX
Aircraft:	De Havilland DHC8	**Injuries:**	1 Fatal
Flight Conducted Under:	Unknown		

On August 10, 2018, about 2043 Pacific daylight time, a De Havilland DHC-8-402, N449QX, was destroyed when it impacted trees on Ketron Island, near Steilacoom, WA. The non-certificated pilot was fatally injured. The airplane was registered to Horizon Air Industries Inc. and operated by the individual as an unauthorized flight. Visual meteorological conditions prevailed in the area at the time of the accident, and no flight plan was filed. The airplane departed from the Seattle-Tacoma International Airport, Seattle, Washington, about 1932 for an unknown destination.

Horizon Air personnel reported that the individual was employed as a ground service agent and had access to the airplanes on the ramp.

The investigation of this event is being conducted under the jurisdiction of the Federal Bureau of Investigation (FBI). The NTSB provided requested technical assistance to the FBI, and any material generated by the NTSB is under the control of the FBI. The NTSB does not plan to issue a report or open a public docket.

See also Alex Horton & Nick Miroff, *Authorities Identify Man Who Stole Horizon Airplane from Seattle Airport and Crashed it into an Island*, WASH. POST, Aug. 11, 2018.

A. OVERVIEW

Terrorism has always shadowed aviation. The first documented airline hijacking occurred as early as 1931, for example, when Peruvian revolutionaries overtook a domestic flight to distribute propaganda. Hijackers since have seized commercial airplanes to bargain for the exchange of political prisoners or to escape to a particular destination like Cuba. In contrast, the objective of the

September 11th hijackers was to kill Americans and to destroy national icons of American economic, military, and political might. To some degree, then, the terrorism of September 11, 2001 represented a departure from historical conceptions of aviation terrorism. At the same time, September 11th also represented a failure of aviation security policy makers to appreciate the history of aviation terrorism. A former United States Department of Transportation ("DOT") Inspector General recounted:

> There was a plot . . . to take four jetliners, maybe it was five, depending on if you count the plane that escaped. Anyway, there was a plot to take four jetliners. They hijacked them in a jihad to protest America's role in Israel. In this jihad, they would take the planes and crash them into something to do maximum harm to a nation and government at which they were very displeased. Sorry, but they would have casualties. They would not even give them a second thought . . . You think I am talking about September Eleventh, don't you? I am not.

> I happen to be talking about September Twelfth, September 12, 1970. The same thing happened. The four planes were taken to the Middle East and blown up. In that case, they allowed the passengers—a very bizarre way that they did it, but they allowed the passengers to scramble to get off the plane.

Mary Schiavo, *Flying Right: What it Takes to Make Aviation Safer and More Secure after 2001*, 14 DePaul Bus. L.J. 279, 294–95 (2001–2002). Whatever the novelty or precedence of the tactics of September 11th, the terrorist threat confronting today's airlines is conceptually different from national security concerns that previously confronted aviation security policy makers. Whereas the Soviet Union created "things" during the Cold War that could be observed and countered, for example, terrorism is an indefinite threat, as "the terrorists only create transactions that can be sifted from the noise of everyday activity only with great difficulty."

In the foregoing context, this chapter examines both *ex post* and *ex ante* statutory and decisional laws whose objective is to fashion criminal law remedies by operation of law—for often irreparably injured victims.

———————

B. TERRORISM

STETHEM V. ISLAMIC REPUBLIC OF IRAN

201 F. Supp. 2d 78 (D.D.C. 2002)

JACKSON, DISTRICT JUDGE.

On the morning of Friday, June 14, 1985, Trans World Airlines ("TWA") Flight No. 847, a Boeing 727, took off from Athens, Greece, bound for Rome, Italy, with a full complement of 143 passengers and a crew of eight. On board were U.S. citizens Robert Stethem, Kurt Carlson, Stuart Dahl, Jeffery Ingalls, Clinton Suggs, Tony Watson, and Kenneth Bowen. All were U.S. military personnel, enroute back to the United States from various assignments abroad and coincidentally aboard the same plane traveling in civilian dress.

Shortly after takeoff the plane was commandeered at gunpoint by at least two hijackers, also armed with hand grenades, who forced the plane to divert first to a landing for fuel in Beirut, then on to Algiers, and back once more to Beirut, finally landing dramatically at night in Beirut about 16 hours after the flight had commenced. During the journey several of the servicemen were brutally beaten by their captors. One was executed by gunshot to the head and his body shoved from the plane onto the tarmac at the Beirut airport. Eventually debarked from the plane as prisoners of a local militia in Beirut, the surviving servicemen were held captive by confederates of the hijackers until June 30, 1985, when they were released to Syrian military personnel and ultimately flown home. The airborne portion of their ordeal was characterized for some of them by excruciating pain from repeated beatings, and for all of them by stark terror in expectation of either an imminent violent death or prolonged captivity. While imprisoned in Beirut they were confined under execrable conditions, tormented with daily threats of torture and death, and vilified as citizens of a despised nation, all the while uncertain of their fate.

These two consolidated actions by the servicemen and their spouses, and by the personal representatives of the murder victim, seek to recover damages from the parties they hold ultimately responsible for these terrorist acts, the Islamic Republic of Iran and its Ministry of Information and Security, pursuant to the Foreign Sovereign Immunities Act ("FSIA"), 28 U.S.C. §§ 1602 *et seq.* Defaults were taken against defendants in both cases. Judgments will consequently be entered for plaintiffs.

BACKGROUND

Robert Dean Stethem (Deceased)

Robert Stethem, the murder victim, was identified by the hijackers early in the flight as a U.S. serviceman. He was, in fact, a 23-year-old U.S. Navy petty officer, trained as a diver and underwater construction specialist. In June, 1985, Stethem and fellow divers assigned to Underwater Construction Team No. 1 ("UCT1"), stationed in Norfolk, Virginia, were aboard TWA 847 enroute back to the U.S. from Athens where they had spent several weeks repairing an underwater structure at a U.S. military installation nearby.

First thought to be a U.S. Marine by the hijackers (who never totally abandoned their suspicions), Stethem was taken to the front of the aircraft, his arms tightly bound, and beaten about the head and shoulders repeatedly with a pistol or an armrest wrenched from a passenger seat. He bled profusely. Although only semi-sensible, losing blood, and in obvious pain for much of the trip, he apparently never lost consciousness altogether. Upon the second landing in Beirut, Stethem was the hostage the hijackers selected for their first execution, partly to emphasize their insistence that their various demands be taken seriously, partly to manifest their hostility to Americans generally. The forward passenger door was thrown open, and one of the hijackers placed his gun to Stethem's head and fired a shot through his skull. As he was about to die he was heard to mutter an exclamation—"Oh, God"—indicating that he was aware of what was happening. His body was pushed from the open doorway to fall upon the pavement beneath the plane where it remained for several hours.

Stethem's survivors include his father and mother, Richard and Patricia Stethem; a sister, Sheryl (Stethem) Sierralta; and two brothers, Kenneth and Patrick Stethem. Although none were his dependents, the family is a remarkably close one. Filial and fraternal affection between Robert, his parents, and siblings was both mutual and intense.

The Stethems are a Navy family. Richard Stethem retired as a Senior Chief Petty Officer after a 25-year career, most of it on sea duty, and worked thereafter as a civilian employee of the Navy Department until 1995. Patricia met Richard while she herself was a sailor. Kenneth joined the Navy at age 19, became a SEAL, and retired in April, 2000, after 20 years. Patrick enlisted the day before TWA 847 was hijacked, followed his deceased brother into underwater construction, and remained a Navy diver for nearly 10 years.

The surviving Stethems last saw Robert at a family reunion in May, 1985, but were together again in June, 1985, to follow the saga of TWA 847 on CNN at the family home in Waldorf, Maryland, all the while besieged by an insatiable media horde at their doorstep. They first learned that Robert was the murdered U.S. serviceman thrown from the plane when Kenneth identified the distinctive shirt on the body on the tarmac shown on television as a shirt he had given his younger brother. All of the Stethem family have been diagnosed as suffering from post-traumatic stress syndrome. According to the psychologist who made the diagnosis, their grief at Robert's death remains unresolved to the present and will probably never subside.

> *All of the Stethem family have been diagnosed as suffering from post-traumatic stress syndrome. According to the psychologist who made the diagnosis, their grief at Robert's death remains unresolved to the present and will probably never subside.*

Plaintiffs Richard Stethem and Patricia Stethem, as father and mother of Robert Stethem, are the duly appointed co-personal representatives of Robert's estate. Both are U.S. citizens, as are his brothers and sister. They bring this action in the nature of a wrongful death and survival action for such damages as may be recoverable from defendants under the FSIA by reason of Robert's false imprisonment as a hostage aboard TWA 847, his torture by beating prior to his death, and his extrajudicial killing that can only be characterized as an intentional, deliberate and premeditated act of murder. These damages include, as established by numerous prior decisions under the FSIA, the net economic loss to Robert's estate; compensation for his ante mortem pain and suffering; solatium for his immediate surviving kin; and punitive damages to chasten the perpetrators of these acts of terrorism and deter their repetition by others.

Kurt and Cheryl Carlson

Kurt and Cheryl Carlson are U.S. citizens, married since 1969, who reside in Illinois, where Kurt Carlson is a building contractor. In 1985, Carlson was a major in the U.S. Army Reserve, and he volunteered for an active duty assignment in Cairo, Egypt, to make a preliminary survey of facilities in preparation for forthcoming joint U.S.-Egyptian military exercises. On June 14, 1985, Carlson was enroute home from Egypt aboard TWA 847 when it landed in Athens where Robert Stethem and his companions boarded. (TWA 847 originated in Cairo.) Carlson, traveling alone, had acquired a standby seat in the first class cabin. Ten minutes into the flight the hijackers stormed the forward section of the plane, assaulted a flight attendant, and, brandishing both a pistol and hand grenades, shouted in English, "Americans come to die!"

Carlson surreptitiously slipped his military identification out of his pocket into the seat cushion, but was eventually discovered to be in the U.S. armed forces by the hijackers following an enforced passport collection in which the absence of a passport in his name was noted. (All U.S. military personnel were eventually identified, and as such treated with special hostility. Had they been U.S. Marines, they would all likely have been killed.) At first, however, he was forced into a seat in the aft cabin with all other passengers, and, like them, compelled to assume an excruciatingly uncomfortable position Carlson describes to this day as the "847 position"—hands behind head; head down, with elbows on knees—and to remain so, in total silence, whenever the plane was airborne.

Not until TWA 847 had landed in Algiers, some six hours into the flight, was Carlson singled out for special treatment. He and Stethem were marched at gunpoint to the forward cabin. His hands were bound behind him; he was blindfolded, and prodded to the cabin floor. He was then (as was Stethem) beaten at intervals about the head, shoulders, back and arms with a club. The hijackers intermittently shouted "one American must die," and they identified Carlson as the first who would do so if their demand that the plane be refueled was not complied with within successive 10- or 15-minute deadlines. Carlson fully expected to be killed. He was spared by the eventual arrival of a fuel truck, and TWA 847, once refueled, took off again for Beirut.

Following Stethem's death on the ground in Beirut, Carlson and all but one of the Navy divers were turned over to a contingent of local militia (known as Amal) who were confederated with the hijackers. They were held captive—and periodically tormented—for approximately two weeks in a filth-ridden basement dungeon in a combat zone somewhere in West Beirut.

Like most of the rest of the U.S. population, Cheryl Carlson followed the saga of TWA 847 on television, apprehensive that she would never see her husband again. When he did return she became aware of how profoundly the experience had affected him, and she has suffered with him through the manifestations of the post-traumatic stress syndrome with which he remains afflicted to the present—irrational fear, sleeplessness, nightmares, extreme irritability—and which has had a markedly deleterious effect on their marriage relationship.

Stuart and Martha Dahl

Stuart and Martha Dahl are U.S. citizens, have been married since 1974, and live in Virginia. Stuart Dahl retired from the U.S. Navy in 1997. In June of 1985 Stuart Dahl was the senior Navy petty officer and in charge of the diver detachment returning from Greece aboard TWA 847. Although he was never singled out for physical mistreatment by the hijackers (other than a blow to the head for breaking the "847 position"), he was aware that his shipmates Stethem and Suggs were being beaten, and overheard (from his "847 position") the sounds associated with Stethem's murder. While a captive in Beirut, as the senior enlisted man he maintained military discipline among his fellow prisoners who, under Kurt Carlson's command as the only commissioned officer present, governed themselves as if they were prisoners-of-war.

Tony and Pamala Watson

Tony and Pamala Watson have been married since 1975. Both are U.S. citizens and live in North Carolina. Tony Watson retired from a 20-year naval career in 1998 and owns a woodworking business. His experience was consistent with that of the other divers of UCT1, and Pamala Watson endured both the nationally televised vigil for the TWA 847 hostages, as did the other wives, and her husband's acute and chronic suffering at the memory of his ordeal once he returned home.

Kenneth and Vicki Bowen

The Bowens did not marry until 1988. Both are U.S. citizens. Kenneth Bowen left active duty with the Navy before the end of 1985, although he remained in the Reserve. He currently works as a bridge inspector for the U.S. Department of Transportation. Bowen was briefly confronted by one of the hijackers on the plane who accused him, with a gun to his forehead, of being a "U.S. Marine." Bowen demurred: "U.S. Navy." The hijacker said, "We kill Marines," and turned away.

Clinton Suggs and Chantal Gautier

Clinton Suggs, an American citizen, married Chantal Gautier, a Canadian, in 1982. He and Stethem were the closest of friends among the UCT1 divers, and were brought forward together by the hijackers to the first class cabin of TWA 847, and became the first to be bound, blindfolded, and beaten. Suggs overheard, at close range, the final moments of Stethem's life, including the fatal gunshot, and a hijacker's threat to execute another hostage in five minutes if his demands of the moment were not met. Suggs knew he would be next and resigned himself to die. Suggs and Gautier first separated in 1986 and ultimately divorced in 1991, a consequence they both attribute directly to the personality changes Suggs underwent as a result of the events of June, 1985.

Jeffrey Ingalls

Ingalls' identity was not discovered until after the other divers and Carlson had left the plane in Beirut. Consequently, he was separated from his shipmates and held captive elsewhere in the city, but only after being forced to lie on the ground and threatened with execution for having eluded earlier identification. He was confined in a 6 by 8 closet with three other American men—all Jewish civilians—for nine days. Ingalls remained in the Navy until 1998, retiring as a Master Chief Petty Officer and Master Diver. He now suffers from depression and lives as a recluse in New Hampshire.

"847 Position"

Aside from the physical abuse inflicted upon some of them, each of the men aboard TWA 847 share a common memory of other particularly horrific details of the ordeal. They remember the acute discomfort associated with the "847 position" and the anticipation of a blow to the head if they changed posture or tried to communicate with another passenger. They recall the odor of overflowing lavatories covered with ordure; the ignominy of relieving themselves while being observed at gunpoint by a hijacker standing at the open door; the stifling heat while the plane sat motionless for hours, un-airconditioned, on a runway in the Algerian desert at midday; the virulent anti-American hatred spewed by the hijackers, especially at U.S. military personnel, and the brutality it provoked against certain of their companions. They remember expecting to die in a plane crash when the passengers were told by the pilot that the control tower at Beirut refused permission to land the second time and had darkened the runway.

Once off the plane in Beirut, they were herded into a line by their guards. Each remembers expecting an imminent execution by a firing squad. Then, imprisoned somewhere in the city, they recall their vermin-infested cells; the taunting guards who would awaken them at night for verbal abuse and would on occasion pretend to shoot them, then laugh at their discomfiture. The guards also proudly displayed photographs of the murdered Stethem's body lying beneath the plane. Another common memory is of being forced to witness the beating death of another unknown prisoner. They remember the spoiled food they were served, and the epidemic of dysentery that beset them all as a result. Each of them remembers, as do the wives, the onset and persistence of the symptoms of his own peculiar case of post-traumatic stress disorder: the constant anxiety and irritability; insomnia, followed by slumber with nightmares reprising the events of June, 1985; the unexpiated guilt at having survived, yet done nothing to prevent the murder of a shipmate whom they could not possibly have saved; the irrational idiosyncrasies each has developed, such as refusing to board planes with "Arabic-looking" co-passengers, carrying a tennis racket aboard a plane to be used as a weapon against any future hijackers, or sleeping on the floor, armed against nighttime intruders.

The hijackers—known only by the sobriquets "Crazy" and "Hitler" by the TWA passengers at the time—have been reliably identified as belonging to Hizballah, a radical Shi'ite paramilitary organization recruited, trained and financially supported by the Ministry of Information and Security ("MOIS") of the Islamic Republic of Iran. Originally affiliated with Amal, the Lebanese militia supported by Syria during the Lebanese civil war, and a frequent collaborator with Amal even after shifting allegiance to Iran following the Israeli invasion of Lebanon in 1982, Hizballah has been implicated in numerous acts of terrorism for which this district court has held its patron state Iran liable under the FSIA.

The record in this case contains extensive documentary evidence from U.S. intelligence sources connecting Hizballah to Iran and its Ministry of Information and Security. According to the testimony of U.S. Ambassador Robert Oakley who, as Director of Counterterrorism for the Department of State at the time, was directly involved in efforts to effect a military rescue or to induce the Lebanese or Algerian governments to secure the release of the passenger-hostages, the hijackers' initial demands—the release of prisoners in Israel and Kuwait—gave reason to believe they were agents of Amal. As later proved to be the case, however, Amal had employed Hizballah to undertake the actual hijacking, with support from Amal militia on the ground and in control of the Beirut airport. Further testimony from Robert McFarlane, U.S. National Security Advisor, established that his direct discussions with the leader of Amal (which had taken custody of all the hostage—save Ingalls—from the hijackers in Beirut) had been ineffectual in procuring their release. Not until approval had been given by Iranian President Rafsanjani from Tehran were they turned over to Syrian authorities in Damascus to be released.

DISCUSSION

While a foreign state is generally immune from the jurisdiction of the courts of the United States under the FSIA, *see* 28 U.S.C. § 1604, plaintiffs bring this action against defendants pursuant to section 1605(a)(7) of the Act. That section explicitly authorizes, as an exception to the general grant of sovereign immunity to foreign nations, suits against foreign states that sponsor terrorism for certain acts that cause personal injury or death if either the claimant or victim was a citizen of the United States at the time of the act. *See* 28 U.S.C. § 1605(a)(7).

FSIA Exception to Sovereign Immunity

A foreign state is generally immune from the jurisdiction of the courts of the United States under the FSIA, [but] section 1605(a)(7) of the Act explicitly authorizes, as an exception to the general grant of sovereign immunity to foreign nations, suits against foreign states that sponsor terrorism for certain acts that cause personal injury or death if either the claimant or victim was a citizen of the United States at the time of the act.

In numerous suits preceding this action, private claimants have successfully invoked this statutory exception to establish a basis by which federal district courts may exercise subject matter jurisdiction over claims similar to those brought by plaintiffs here against these same defendants. Plaintiffs' causes of action in this case are predicated on the unlawful detention and torture of plaintiffs, and, in the case of Robert Stethem, his summary execution—acts which unequivocally beget claims eligible for relief under section 1605(a)(7).

Conditions for FSIA Subject Matter Jurisdiction

The FSIA imposes two preconditions upon the exercise of subject matter jurisdiction by district courts over foreign states: the foreign state must have been designated a state sponsor of terrorism at the time the acts occurred, unless later so designated as a result of such act, and a plaintiff (either claimant or victim) must have been a United States citizen at the time of the incident. *See* 28 U.S.C. § 1605(a)(7)(A) and (B).

Both of these requirements are clearly satisfied here. Iran was designated as a state sponsor of terrorism pursuant to section 6(j) of the Export Administration Act of 1979 on January 19, 1984, and remains so designated today. The multiple plaintiffs bringing this action (except Chantal Gautier) have always been United States citizens. Accordingly, the Court finds that it has jurisdiction over the subject matter of this suit and the named defendants. And as the Court has previously found in so many similar cases before it, the evidence conclusively establishes that the Islamic Republic of Iran and its MOIS provided "material support or resources" to Hizballah, and Hizballah and its co-conspirator Amal were the perpetrators of these heinous acts of terrorism. Having concluded that defendants are liable for the tortious conduct alleged, the Court next considers the extent to which the plaintiffs should be compensated for the injuries they sustained as a result of their client organization's unconscionable behavior.

Consistent with its approach in previous FSIA cases involving claims for personal injury or death resulting from state-sponsored terrorism, this Court will evaluate plaintiffs' claims under the federal common law. While the Court will separately analyze the individual claims for compensatory damages brought by each plaintiff below, plaintiffs' claims for punitive damages will be dealt with in the aggregate.

Compensatory Damages—The Stethem Plaintiffs

Plaintiffs Richard and Patricia Stethem, in their own right, and as personal representatives of the Estate of Robert Dean Stethem, seek compensatory damages for Robert Stethem's wrongful death, his pain and suffering, and solatium for themselves and his surviving brothers and sister. Pursuant to their claim for wrongful death under federal common law, the Estate of Robert Stethem is entitled to monetary damages for funeral expenses and loss of prospective income if Robert's premature death was wrongful and proximately caused by an act of terrorism. As previously shown, agents of the defendants intentionally caused Robert's death. Moreover, it goes with saying that his summary execution was wrongful in that it was carried out by members of a terrorist organization with no legally cognizable basis for taking a life. Therefore, a calculation of the monetary damages actually suffered by Robert's estate is all that remains.

Loss of accretion damages are calculated by estimating a decedent's future earning potential based on the individual's work and education and adjusting that amount to account for inflation, rise in productivity, job advancement, and personal consumption. Dr. Herman Miller, an economic consultant, testified at trial that Robert's estate experienced economic losses of $904,665.00. In coming to this conclusion, Dr. Miller assumed that, following his service in the Navy, Robert would then attend and successfully complete college to become a civil engineer specializing in underwater construction. The Court finds these assumptions and Dr. Miller's corresponding estimation of accretion reasonable; therefore, it will enter an award for pecuniary loss in the amount of $904,665.00 in favor of the Estate of Robert Stethem.

As his personal representatives, the estate is also entitled to recover any damages Robert himself would have been entitled to for the extensive pain he suffered at the hands of the hijackers prior to and in the course of his death. The record is replete with evidence substantiating the Stethems' contention that Robert suffered excruciating pain while being viciously beaten and tortured over the course of fifteen hours. Known to those closest to him as an extremely virile and stoic young man who was able to endure pain without outwardly manifesting discomfort, witnesses testified that Robert cried out on several occasions throughout his ordeal. Particularly telling is the fact that Robert had to be dragged to the front of the plane by his tormentors because of his inability to walk just prior to his being shot in the back of the head. Even then, his suffering did not end. Based upon his finding at autopsy that Robert's lungs continued to function after he had been shot—significant quantities of blood were found to have been aspirated into his lungs—the forensic pathologist Dr. Michael Clark opined that Robert survived the gunshot wound for several minutes.

While pain and suffering is particularly difficult to quantify in terms of assessing damages, the Court can certainly award damages to Robert's estate commensurate with those awards for pain and suffering provided in prior FSIA cases. For purposes of comparison, Robert's suffering occurred in two distinct stages: (1) the pain he experienced from beatings prior to being shot in the head; and (2) the anguish of his final moments anticipating certain death and the pain he experienced after being shot while drowning in his own blood on the tarmac.

Damages Computation

With respect to the former, this district court has typically compensated a plaintiff hostage (or his representative) in a FSIA case at a rate of $10,000 per day of captivity accompanied by physical torture. This formulaic approach has not precluded a greater or lesser award in a case where the evidence establishes that the victim of the maltreatment suffered more or less than the hostages in the preceding cases. Notwithstanding, the $10,000 per diem amount serves as a useful benchmark for beginning the damages calculus in a manner that is both just and consistent with previous awards.

In this case, the Court finds that while the time in which Robert was tortured (*i.e.,* fifteen hours) was comparatively much shorter than that of other hostage victims previously considered by this district court, the sheer intensity and frequency of abuse caused Robert to experience a degree of suffering that exceeded that of previous hostages. The hijackers were both uncertain and insecure about their ability to control the volatile circumstances inherent in their hijacking of the plane. As a result, they chose to impose an inordinate amount of pain and suffering on Robert as an example to the other passengers should any have been contemplating resistance or revolt. As the uncertainty of the situation escalated, so did the intensity and frequency of the beatings to which Robert was subjected. The Court concludes that Robert's estate is entitled to $500,000.00 for the pain and suffering he endured prior to being singled out for execution.

With respect to the several minutes of anguish and pain Robert endured as and immediately after being shot by Hamadi and thrown from the plane, this district court has previously awarded the estates of terrorist victims suffering similarly brief yet intense pain an amount of $1,000,000. Likewise, this Court awards Robert's estate the sum of $1,000,000 for this terminal stage of his pain and suffering. In total, the Court will enter a judgment in favor of the Estate of Robert Stethem in the amount of $2,404,665.00.

The Stethem parents also seek loss of solatium damages on behalf of all the Stethems for the bereavement and grief attendant upon their loss of Robert's society and companionship. Because the District of Columbia does not recognize claims for loss of solatium, this Court has recognized this cause of action under the federal common law by relying upon the SECOND RESTATEMENT OF TORTS: " '[O]ne who by extreme and outrageous conduct intentionally or recklessly causes severe emotional distress to another is subject to liability for such emotional distress.' " All acts of terrorism are by their very definition extreme and outrageous and intended to cause the highest degree of emotional distress, literally, terror, in their targeted audience: The more extreme and outrageous, the greater the resulting distress. In this case, the agents of Hizballah and Amal engaged in conduct no less extreme than that of their fellow terrorists in earlier cases. Because the Stethems have consequently experienced grave emotional distress from having lost a beloved son and brother, they are entitled to damages for loss of solatium.

Solatium Damages

In calculating damages for loss of solatium in the case of a deceased family member, this district court has considered a variety of factors to include: (1) whether the decedent's death was sudden and unexpected; (2) whether the death was attributable to negligence or malice; (3) whether the claimants have sought medical treatment for depression and related disorders resulting from the decedent's death; (4) the nature (*i.e.*, closeness) of the relationship between the claimant and the decedent; and (5) the duration of the claimants' mental anguish in excess of that which would have been experienced following the decedent's natural death. Here, Robert's death was both sudden and unforeseen by his loved ones and the consequences of the terrorists' actions upon them all the more intense. While the Stethems have sought little in the way of professional help to assist them in coping with Robert's death, the enormity of their emotional distress remains evident even to this day.

There is no question based on the evidence presented at trial and the presence and testimony of members of the Stethem family in court that the Stethems have always enjoyed an extraordinarily close familial relationship. Each of the Stethems had a unique and special relationship with Robert and continues to mourn his death on a daily basis in his or her own way. Even 16 years later, the Stethems are unable, in many ways, to move beyond Robert's death. Indeed, the Court accepts Dr. Clark's conclusion that the Stethems will likely remain in the loss and loneliness stage of grief until their own deaths. Moreover, even were they to come to terms with Robert's death, continued media coverage of the events surrounding the hijacking from June 14–15, 1985 (most recently revived in connection with the events of September 11, 2001), serve as constant reminders of their loss.

Depending on the duration of captivity, this district court has on occasion awarded greater judgments for claims of loss of solatium to those family members of terrorism victims who were tortured over a prolonged period of time but not killed than to those family members of terrorist victims who expired relatively quickly (although usually suffering intense pain for several minutes) after a single deadly terrorist attack (*i.e.*, bombing, gunshot wound). The Stethems grieve not only the absence of Robert in their lives, but the knowledge that he suffered greatly prior to being executed. Their grief is tempered only by the knowledge that his suffering was of relatively brief duration, and that he died bravely. Accordingly, the Court will award the Stethem parents $5,000,000 each and the Stethem siblings $3,000,000 each for the loss of Robert's society and companionship.

Compensatory Damages—The Carlson plaintiffs

Plaintiffs Kurt Carlson, Stuart Dahl, Jeffery Ingalls, Clinton Suggs, Tony Watson, and Kenneth Bowen ("Carlson hostages") seek compensatory damages upon claims in the nature of kidnapping, false imprisonment, torture, assault, battery, intentional infliction of severe emotional distress, and violation of international human rights. Plaintiffs Cheryl Carlson, Martha Dahl, Chantal Gautier, and Pamala Watson ("Carlson spouses") seek compensatory damages for loss of consortium and solatium. As determined above, this Court holds the defendants responsible for the hijacking of TWA 847 and the attendant hostage taking and torture of the plaintiff hostages.

Although plaintiff hostages were detained for a period of days as opposed to months or years, they arguably remained captive under conditions entailing even more frequent physical and emotional trauma than that of some of the other plaintiff hostages to come before this Court. Indeed, because the hijackers felt compelled to assert and maintain complete control over the situation, they were tireless and unrelenting in their physical and emotional abuse of their hostages. As evidenced by the summary execution of Robert Stethem in their presence, many of the plaintiff hostages feared the imminent loss of their own lives and were themselves subjected to mock executions (*e.g.*, by firing squad or the dry firing of weapons pointed at their heads) several times during their detention. Even after being removed from the plane, the plaintiff hostages were held under armed guard in inhumane surroundings, witnessed acts of torture and brutality inflicted upon other prisoners, and lived in constant fear for their lives. Because of the terrifying intensity associated with the hijacking itself, as well as their subsequent detention, and the resulting permanent psychic damage they exhibit today, the Court concludes that a per diem calculation of damages is less appropriate than a lump sum award embracing the totality of their experience. Accordingly, this Court will award Kurt Carlson and Clinton Suggs $1,500,000.00 each, and Stuart Dahl, Jeffery Ingalls, Tony Watson, and Kenneth Bowen $1,000,000 apiece for injuries suffered at the hands of the agents of the defendants.

With regard to the claims for loss of consortium by the Carlson spouses, while they were without their husbands for a relatively short period of time, it is clear that the experience has had a detrimental and disturbing effect on their relationships. Their formerly healthy husbands returned estranged and incapable of participating in the marriage with the same physical and emotional warmth they previously displayed. To varying degrees, each of the plaintiff hostages continues to suffer from post-traumatic stress disorder and related behavioral disorders (*e.g.*, violent nightmares, hyper vigilance, uncontrollable tempers, impatience) that serve to interfere with their ability to function normally within any social relationship, including marriage. Therefore, this Court concludes that the Carlson spouses are entitled to damages for loss of consortium and solatium and will award them $200,000 each.

Punitive Damages

Plaintiffs also request an award of punitive damages against defendant MOIS for its role in providing support and resources to Hizballah and Amal. As in previous cases, the evidence clearly inculpates MOIS as the instigator and financier of terrorist acts by Hizballah and Amal in this case. The hostage taking, torture, and killing of innocent non-belligerents for political ends constitutes unconscionable conduct in any civilized society.

Accordingly, the Court finds that not only are punitive damages authorized under the FSIA to punish the MOIS for its continued role in fomenting terrorist activity, and to the extent possible deter it from future criminal behavior, *see* 28 U.S.C. § 1606, but that the MOIS's role in sponsoring the agents responsible for the instant acts of terrorism warrants such an award. Consistent with this Court's prior experience and a calculation equivalent to approximately three times the estimated annual budget of MOIS for support of terrorism as testified to by Dr. Richard Clausen, the Court will assess punitive damages in the amount of $300,000,000 against the MOIS, to be awarded to all plaintiffs jointly and severally.

EXERCISE 8-1. *STETHEM V. ISLAMIC REPUBLIC OF IRAN*—FOREIGN SOVEREIGN IMMUNITIES ACT ("FSIA")

Illustration 8-1. Hezbollah Hijackers TWA Flight 847

Source: https://commons.wikimedia.org/wiki/File:Hezbollah_hijackers_TWA_Flight_847.png

1. Define sovereign immunity.

2. Describe the Foreign Sovereign Immunities Act ("FSIA").

3. Explain the exception allowed under Section 1605(a)(7) of the FSIA.

4. The FSIA imposes two preconditions upon the exercise of subject matter jurisdiction by district courts over foreign states. What are they?

5. What are punitive damages? Are they recoverable under the FSIA? Explain in the context of the facts of *Stethem v. Islamic Republic of Iran*.

NOTES ON *STETHEM V. ISLAMIC REPUBLIC OF IRAN*—PROFILING

The court in *Stethem v. Islamic Republic of Iran* described the onset and persistence of post-traumatic stress disorders experienced by hijacking victims, including "irrational idiosyncrasies each has developed, such as refusing to board planes with 'Arabic-looking' co-passengers . . ." Is that view an "irrational idiosyncrasy" and racist, or experience-based? Are the two mutually exclusive? Consider one appeal to common sense: "Nobody is suggesting using ethnicity or religion as the only—or even the primary—factors in profiling terrorists. But it also makes no sense to take zero account of the fact that every suicide attack against U.S. aviation to date has been perpetrated by men of Muslim origin."

The 'Profiling' Debate, WALL. ST. J., Aug. 19, 2006, at A10 (arguing that avoiding screening on the basis of ethnic and religious background has resulted in "a policy of random searches that focuses scarce screening resources as much on eight-year-old girls as on 22-year old men with Pakistani passports.").

See also Richard Lowry, *How to Deal with the Terrorist Threat—and How Not To*, NAT'L REV., Jan. 28, 2002, at 32 ("Arab-American groups still scream at any suggestion of commonsense security at airports, while the Bush administration still cowers at any association with 'racial profiling.' It has become clear in recent weeks that the pieties of American racial politics will remain unchanged—even after contributing to a mass murder."). *Contra* Debra J. Saunders, *Go Ahead, Search Granny*, S.F. CHRON., Aug. 17, 2006, at B7 ("Why . . . search little old white ladies when young Arab and Muslim men were behind the Sept. 11, 2001, attacks and other terrorist plots? The answer is: The feds should avoid racial profiling because it breeds discontent without enhancing security.")

Stated another way:

The mathematical probability that a randomly chosen Arab passenger might attempt a mass-murder-suicide hijacking—while tiny—is considerably higher than the probability that a randomly chosen white, black, Hispanic, or Asian passenger might do the same. In constitutional-law parlance, while racial profiling may be presumptively unconstitutional, that presumption is overcome in the case of airline passengers, because the government has a compelling interest in preventing mass-murder-suicide hijackings, and because close scrutiny of Arab-looking people is narrowly tailored to protect that interest.

Stuart Taylor, Jr., *The Case for Using Racial Profiling at Airports*, NAT'L J., Sept. 22, 2001, at 2877. *Contra* Naureen Kamdar, *Muslim Americans are Americans, Too*, ATL. J.-CONST., Feb. 20, 2007, at A11 (editorial by American college student of Pakistani heritage selected for heightened airport screening: "I even understand that suspicion of Muslims is inevitable . . . What I don't understand is why of any of that—beards or scarves included—allows bullying of American Muslims by airport security officials.").

ALEJANDRE V. REPUBLIC OF CUBA

996 F. Supp. 1239 (S.D. Fla. 1997)

JAMES LAWRENCE KING, DISTRICT JUDGE.

The government of Cuba, on February 24, 1996, in outrageous contempt for international law and basic human rights, murdered four human beings in international airspace over the Florida Straits. The victims were Brothers to the Rescue pilots, flying two civilian, unarmed planes on a routine humanitarian mission, searching for rafters in the waters between Cuba and the Florida Keys.

As the civilian planes flew over international waters, a Russian built MiG-29 of the Cuban Air Force, without warning, reason, or provocation, blasted the defenseless planes out of the sky with sophisticated air-to-air missiles in two separate attacks. The pilots and their aircraft disintegrated in the mid-air explosions following the impact of the missiles. The destruction was so complete that the four bodies were never recovered.

The personal representatives of three of the deceased instituted this action against the Republic of Cuba ("Cuba") and the Cuban Air Force to recover monetary damages for the killings. One of the victims was not a U.S. citizen and his family therefore could not join in the suit. This is the first lawsuit to rely on recent legislative enactments that strip foreign states of immunity for certain acts of terrorism. Neither Cuba nor the Cuban Air Force has defended this suit, asserting through a diplomatic note that this Court has no jurisdiction over Cuba or its political subdivisions. A default was thus entered against both Defendants on April 23, 1997 pursuant to Rule 55(a) of the Federal Rules of Civil Procedure. Because this is a lawsuit against a foreign state, however, the Court may not enter judgment by default. Rather, the claimants must establish their "claim or right to relief by evidence that is satisfactory to the Court." 28 U.S.C. § 1608(e) (1994).

The Congressional purpose behind this section was to protect foreign states from "unfounded default judgments rendered solely upon a procedural default." As detailed more fully below, the abundant evidence offered at trial more than satisfies the Court that Plaintiffs are entitled to relief. Moreover, it bears mention that Cuba's default has been willful, as evidenced by its diplomatic note rejecting this Court's jurisdiction, further bolstering the entry of a default judgment.

These three consolidated cases proceeded to trial on November 13, 14, and 20, 1997, on the issues of liability and damages. Because the Court finds that neither Cuba nor the Cuban Air Force is immune from suit for the killings, and because the facts amply prove both Defendants' liability and Plaintiffs' damages, the Court will enter judgment against Defendants.

FINDINGS OF FACT

At trial, Plaintiffs presented extensive testimonial and documentary evidence in support of their claims. Because Cuba has presented no defense, the Court will accept as true Plaintiffs' uncontroverted factual allegations. The pertinent facts are as follows.

A.   The Victims

Armando Alejandre was forty-five years old at the time of his death. Although born in Cuba, Alejandre made Miami, Florida his home at an early age and became a naturalized U.S. citizen. Alejandre served an active tour of duty for eight months in Vietnam, completed his college education at Florida International University, and worked as a consultant to the Metro-Dade Transit Authority at the time of his death. He is survived by his wife of twenty-one years, Marlene Alejandre, who serves as the Personal Representative of his estate, and his daughter Marlene, a college student. Both are Plaintiffs in this lawsuit.

Carlos Alberto Costa was born in the United States in 1966 and resided in Miami. He was only twenty-nine years old when the Cuban government ended his life. Always interested in aviation and hoping to someday oversee the operations of a major airport, Costa earned his bachelor's degree at Embry-Riddle Aeronautical University and worked as a Training Specialist for the Dade County Aviation Department. He is survived by his parents, Mirta Costa and Osvaldo Costa, and by his sister, Mirta Mendez, all of whom sue on his behalf.

Mario Mañuel De la Peña was also born in the United States and was a mere twenty-four years old at the time of his death. Working toward his goal of being an airline pilot, De la Peña was in his last semester at Embry-Riddle when he was killed. During that semester he had obtained a coveted and highly competitive internship with American Airlines. Embry-Riddle granted De la Peña a bachelor's degree in Professional Aeronautics posthumously. He is survived by a younger brother, Michael De La Peña, and his parents, Mario T. De la Peña and Miriam De la Peña, both of whom are Plaintiffs in this case.

B.   The Shootdown

Alejandre, Costa, and De la Peña were all members of a Miami-based humanitarian organization known as Hermanos al Rescate, or Brothers to the Rescue. The organization's principal mission was to search the Florida Straits for rafters, Cuban refugees who had fled the island nation on precarious inner tubes or makeshift rafts, often perishing at sea. Brothers to the Rescue would locate the rafters and provide them with life-saving assistance by informing the U.S. Coast Guard of their location and condition.

On the morning of February 24, 1996, two of Brothers to the Rescue's civilian Cessna 337 aircraft departed from Opa Locka Airport in South Florida. (A third Brothers to the Rescue, Cessna 337 aircraft also departed on the mission. That plane returned safely to the United States.) Costa piloted one plane, accompanied by Pablo Morales, a Cuban national who had once been a rafter himself. De la Peña piloted the second plane, with Alejandre as his passenger. Before departing, the planes notified both Miami and Havana traffic controllers of their flight plans, which were to take them south of the 24th parallel. The 24th parallel, well north of Cuba's twelve-mile territorial sea, is the northernmost boundary of the Havana Flight Information Region. Commercial and civilian aircraft routinely fly in this area, and aviation practice requires that they notify Havana's traffic controllers when crossing south through the 24th parallel. Both Brothers to the Rescue planes complied with this custom by contacting Havana, identifying themselves, and stating their position and altitude.

While the two planes were still north of the 24th parallel, the Cuban Air Force launched two military aircraft, a MiG-29 and a MiG-23, operating under the control of Cuba's military ground station. The MiGs carried guns, close range missiles, bombs, and rockets and were piloted by members of the Cuban Air Force experienced in combat. Excerpts from radio communications between the MiG-29 and Havana Military Control detail what transpired next:

MiG-29:	OK, the target is in sight; the target is in sight. It's a small aircraft. Copied, small aircraft in sight.
MiG-29:	OK, we have it in sight, we have it in sight.
MiG-29:	The target is in sight.
Military Control:	Go ahead.
MiG-29:	The target is in sight.
Military Control:	Aircraft in sight.
MiG-29:	Come again?
MiG-29:	It's a small aircraft, a small aircraft.
MiG-29:	It's white, white.
Military Control:	Color and registration of the aircraft?
Military Control:	Buddy.

MiG-29:	Listen, the registration also?
Military Control:	What kind and colour?
MiG-29:	It's white and blue.
MiG-29:	White and blue, at a low altitude, a small aircraft.
MiG-29:	Give me some instructions.
MiG-29:	Instructions!
MiG-29:	Listen, authorize me . . .
MiG-29:	If we give it a pass, it will complicate things. We are going to give it a pass. Because some vessels are approaching there, I am going to give it a pass.
MiG-29	Talk, talk.
MiG-29:	I have it in lock-on, I have it in lock-on.
MiG-29:	We have it in lock-on. Give us authorization.
MiG-29:	It is a Cessna 337. That one. Give us authorization, damn it!
Military Control:	Fire.
MiG-29:	Give us authorization, damn it, we have it.
Military Control:	Authorized to destroy.
MiG-29:	I'm going to pass it.
Military Control:	Authorized to destroy.
MiG-29:	We already copied. We already copied.
Military Control:	Authorized to destroy.
MiG-29:	Understood, already received. Already received. Leave us alone for now.
Military Control:	Don't lose it.
MiG-29:	First launch.
MiG-29:	We hit him! Damn. We hit him! We hit him! We retired him!
MiG-29:	Wait to see where it fell.
MiG-29:	Come on in, come on in! Damn, we hit. F—s!

MiG-29:	Mark the place where we took it out.
MiG-29:	We are over it. This one won't mess around anymore.
Military Control:	Congratulations to the two of you.
MiG-29:	Mark the spot.
MiG-29:	We're climbing and returning home.
Military Control:	Stand by there circling above.
MiG-29:	Over the target?
Military Control:	Correct.
MiG-29:	S—t, we did tell you, Buddy.
Military Control:	Correct, the target is marked.
MiG-29:	Go ahead.
Military Control:	OK, climb to 3200, 4000 meters above the destroyed target and maintain economical speed.
MiG-29:	Go ahead.
Military Control:	I need you to stand by . . . there. What heading did the launch have?
MiG-29:	I have another aircraft in sight.
MiG-29:	We have another aircraft.
Military Control:	Follow it.
MiG-29:	Don't lose the other small aircraft.
MiG-29:	We have another aircraft in sight. It's in the area where (the first aircraft fell. It's in the area where it fell.
MiG-29:	We have the aircraft.
Military Control:	Stand by.
MiG-29:	Comrade, it's in the area of the event.
MiG-29:	Did you copy?
MiG-29:	OK, this aircraft is headed 90 degrees now.
MiG-29:	It's in the area of the event, where the target fell. They're going to have to authorize us.

MiG-29:	Hey, the SAR isn't needed. Nothing remains, nothing.
Military Control:	Correct, keep following the aircraft. You're going to stay above it.
MiG-29:	We're above it.
Military Control:	Correct . . .
MiG-29:	For what?
MiG-29:	Is the other authorized?
Military Control:	Correct.
MiG-29:	Great. Let's go Alberto.
MiG-29:	Understood; we are now going to destroy it.
Military Control:	Do you still have it in sight?
MiG-29:	We have it, we have it, we're working. Let us work.
MiG-29:	The other is destroyed; the other is destroyed. Fatherland or death, s—t! The other is down also.

The missiles disintegrated the Brothers to the Rescue planes, killing their occupants instantly and leaving almost no recoverable debris. Only a large oil slick marked the spot where the planes went down. The Cuban Air Force never notified or warned the civilian planes, never attempted other methods of interception, and never gave them the opportunity to land. The MiGs' first and only response was the intentional and malicious destruction of the Brothers to the Rescue planes and their four innocent occupants. Such behavior violated clearly established international norms requiring the exhaustion of all measures before resort to aggression against any aircraft and banning the use of force against civilian aircraft altogether.

These norms have been codified in various international instruments. *See, e.g.,* Convention on International Civil Aviation, Dec. 7, 1944, 61 Stat. 1180, 15 U.N.T.S. 295 (both the United States and Cuba are parties to the Convention). The proscription on using force against civilian planes attaches even if they penetrate foreign airspace. *See, e.g.,* Kay Hailbronner, *Freedom of the Air and the Convention on the Law of the Sea*, 77 AM. J. INT'L L. 490, 514 (1983) ("Even if an order to land is deliberately disregarded, a civil unarmed aircraft that intrudes into foreign airspace may not be fired upon."). Common sense dictates that the negligible threat civilian planes may pose does not justify the possible loss of life.

C. The International Reaction

The international community moved quickly and in unison to condemn the murders. The United Nations Security Council, the European Union, and the International Civil Aviation Organization ("ICAO") were among the many to issue statements deploring Cuba's excessive use of force. The French Ministry of Foreign Affairs stated that, "France regrets the use of such brutal methods which nothing can justify, regardless of the circumstances, toward aircraft presenting no threat to the safety of the population." Following an extensive investigation, the ICAO issued a report in June 1996 concluding that the planes were shot down over international waters. The ICAO also adopted a resolution reaffirming the prohibition of the use of weapons against civilian aircraft in flight and declaring such practices incompatible with elementary considerations of humanity and the dictates of customary international law.

The shootdown elicited a similar reaction from the United States and even precipitated the enactment of the Cuban Liberty and Democratic Solidarity ("LIBERTAD") Act of 1996, 22 U.S.C. §§ 6021–6091 (1997), which includes an entire section devoted to a condemnation of the Cuban attack. Among other findings, Congress characterized the shootdown as wholly disproportionate: "The response chosen by Fidel Castro, the use of lethal force, was completely inappropriate to the situation presented to the Cuban Government, making such actions a blatant and barbaric violation of international law and tantamount to cold-blooded murder." Finally, Congress concluded: "The Congress strongly condemns the act of terrorism by the Castro regime in shooting down the Brothers to the Rescue aircraft on February 24, 1996."

CONCLUSIONS OF LAW

A. Jurisdiction and Liability

District courts have original jurisdiction to hear suits, not barred by foreign sovereign immunity, that are brought against foreign states.

Under the Foreign Sovereign Immunities Act of 1976 ("FSIA"), 28 U.S.C. §§ 1602–1611, a federal court lacks subject matter jurisdiction to hear a claim against a foreign state unless the claim falls within one of the FSIA's enumerated exceptions. For example, if a foreign state commits a tortious act or engages in commercial activities in the United States, it may fall into one of the FSIA's exceptions and be stripped of immunity from suit in U.S. courts.

The Anti-Terrorism and Effective Death Penalty Act of 1996 ("AEDPA"), Pub. L. No. 104–132, § 221, amended the FSIA to allow suits in U.S. courts against a foreign state that engages in acts of terrorism under certain specified circumstances.

Most recently, Congress crafted an additional, narrow exception to foreign sovereign immunity through the Anti-Terrorism and Effective Death Penalty Act of 1996 ("AEDPA"), Pub. L. No. 104–132, § 221. AEDPA amended the FSIA to allow suits in U.S. courts against a foreign state that engages in acts of terrorism under certain specified circumstances. As a result, the FSIA now provides that a foreign state shall not be immune from the jurisdiction of U.S. courts in any case

AEDPA Exception to FSIA

> in which money damages are sought against a foreign state for personal injury or death that was caused by an act of torture, extrajudicial killing, aircraft sabotage, hostage taking, or the provision of material support or resources . . . for such an act if such act or provision of material support is engaged in by an official, employee, or agent of such foreign state while acting within the scope of his or her office, employment, or agency.

In addition, section 1605(a)(7) imposes the following requirements: (1) the U.S. must have designated the foreign state as a state sponsor of terrorism pursuant to section 6(j) of the Export Administration Act of 1979; (2) the act must have occurred outside the foreign state; and (3) the claimants and victims must have been U.S. nationals at the time the acts occurred.

Designation as State Sponsor of Terrorism

The record of this trial clearly establishes that all of these requirements have been met. First, the unprovoked firing of deadly rockets at defenseless, unarmed civilian aircraft undoubtedly comes within the statute's meaning of "extrajudicial killing." That term is defined in reference to its use in the Torture Victim Protection Act of 1991 ("TVPA"), which states that "the term 'extrajudicial killing' means a deliberated killing not authorized by a previous judgment pronounced by a regularly constituted court affording all the judicial guarantees which are recognized as indispensable by civilized peoples." 28 U.S.C. § 1350.

Cuba's actions in this case easily come within this definition. The occupants of the two civilian, unarmed planes received no warning whatsoever of their imminent destruction, much less the judicial process contemplated by the TVPA. *See Lafontant v. Aristide*, 844 F. Supp. 128 (E.D.N.Y. 1994) (finding that assassination of political opponent fell within statute's definition of extrajudicial killing).

Second, the Cuban Air Force was acting as an agent of Cuba when it committed the killings. The Cuban Air Force is clearly an agent of the Cuban state, as it acts on Cuba's behalf and subject to Cuba's control. The evidence adduced at trial demonstrated how the pilots of the Cuban MiGs obtained authorization from state officials prior to the shootdown of each plane and hearty congratulations from those officials after the planes were destroyed.

Third, section 1605(a)(7)'s requirement that the foreign state have been designated as a state sponsor of terrorism has also been satisfied. Cuba was one of only seven states so designated at the time pursuant to the authority of the Export Administration Act of 1979.

Fourth, the act occurred outside of Cuban territory. Plaintiffs have presented undisputed and competent evidence that the planes were shot down over international waters. As discussed above, the ICAO Report concluded that the planes were over international waters when they were destroyed. Congress reached the same conclusion, finding that the first plane was "18 miles from the Cuban coast" when it was shot down, and that the second plane was "30.5 miles from the Cuban coast" when it was fired upon. These numbers place the planes well outside the twelve-mile territorial sea claimed by Cuba and permitted under international law. In addition, evidence from the crew and passengers on a nearby cruise ship, the Majesty of the Seas, and private fishing vessel, the Triliner, established beyond any doubt that the civilian aircraft were flying in international air space toward Florida (and away from Cuba) when the Defendants committed this brutal act of terrorism.

Finally, Plaintiffs and three of the four murdered pilots were U.S. citizens at the time of the shootdown. De la Peña and Costa were born in the United States, and Alejandre was a naturalized U.S. citizen. Plaintiffs were also U.S. citizens when the incident took place. Consequently, the facts of this case fall squarely within the requirements of section 1605(a)(7). Indeed, this is precisely the type of action for which Congress meant to provide redress by stripping terrorist states of immunity from the judgment of U.S. courts.

The Civil Liability Act creates a cause of action against agents of a foreign state that act under the conditions specified in FSIA section 1605(a)(7). It thus serves as an enforcement provision for acts described in section 1605(a)(7). If Plaintiffs prove an agent's liability under this Act, the foreign state employing the agent would also incur liability under the theory of respondeat superior.

Having established an exception to foreign sovereign immunity, Plaintiffs base their substantive cause of action on a different statute, also enacted in 1996, entitled Civil Liability for Acts of State Sponsored Terrorism ("Civil Liability Act"). The Civil Liability Act creates a cause of action against agents of a foreign state that act under the conditions specified in FSIA section 1605(a)(7). It thus serves as an enforcement provision for acts described in section 1605(a)(7). If Plaintiffs prove an agent's liability under this Act, the foreign state employing the agent would also incur liability under the theory of *respondeat superior*.

Because, as detailed above, Plaintiffs have presented compelling evidence that all of the relevant statutory requirements have been met, the Court finds that both the Cuban Air Force and Cuba are liable for the murders of Alejandre, Costa, and De la Peña.

B. Damages

The amount of damages that Plaintiffs may recover in this case is specified in the Civil Liability Act. It provides that an agent of a foreign state who commits an extrajudicial killing as described in FSIA section 1605(a)(7) shall be liable for "money damages which may include economic damages, solatium, pain and suffering, and punitive damages." Thus, the Cuban Air Force is liable for both compensatory and punitive damages. Under the theory of *respondeat superior*, Cuba is liable for the same amount of damages as its agent, with the exception of punitive damages, which the FSIA prohibits against foreign states.

Civil Liability Act

Section 1606 of the FSIA, which determines the extent of liability in suits against a foreign state, provides in pertinent part: "[T]he foreign state shall be liable in the same manner and to the same extent as a private individual under like circumstances; but a foreign state except for an agency or instrumentality thereof shall not be liable for punitive damages." Thus, although punitive damages may not be assessed against the Republic of Cuba, they may be assessed against the Cuban Air Force.

1. Compensatory Damages

To support their claim for compensatory damages, Plaintiffs presented the testimony of Dr. David Williams, an expert economist. Using widely-accepted methodology, Dr. Williams calculated the present value of De la Peña's and Costa's lost wages and benefits. He also calculated the present value of Alejandre's lost wages, benefits, and services to his family. The Court finds Dr. Williams's calculations to be reasonable and therefore adopts his figures for lost wages, benefits, and services.

In addition, Plaintiffs request damages for pain and suffering. The record is replete with testimony from Plaintiffs and other family members of the deceased, which attests in painful detail to the grief they have suffered as a result of the killings. The Court finds this evidence more than sufficient to justify the awards for pain and suffering that Plaintiffs request.

2.   Punitive Damages

In addition to compensatory damages, punitive damages are explicitly permitted by the Civil Liability Act. The Court observes again that it may impose judgment and damages retroactively. First, Congress expressed its clear intent in AEDPA to allow suits against terrorist states for acts occurring before AEDPA's effective date. Second, the Civil Liability Act and AEDPA's amendments to the FSIA are jurisdictional provisions, and as the Supreme Court has explained, "We have regularly applied intervening statutes conferring or ousting jurisdiction, whether or not jurisdiction lay when the underlying conduct occurred or when the suit was filed." Finally, compensatory damages were already available against foreign states, and punitive damages were available against foreign governmental entities, long before changes to the FSIA made this suit possible.

Because this is the first case to proceed to trial under this Act, however, there is no precedent to guide the Court in determining whether punitive damages are appropriate in this particular case, and if so, in what amount. Thus, the Court will look both to the traditional purpose behind awarding punitive damages and to analogous federal court cases addressing the role of punitive damages in cases of egregious international human rights violations.

> *The purpose of punitive, or exemplary, damages has traditionally been twofold. First, they may serve as a tool to punish truly reprehensible conduct. In this way, the aggrieved plaintiff is given a socially acceptable avenue of retaliation . . . Punitive damages are also an appropriate remedy in international law. As the Supreme Court has observed, "[A]n attack from revenge and malignity, from gross abuse of power, and a settled purpose of mischief . . . may be punished by all the penalties which the law of nations can properly administer."*

The purpose of punitive, or exemplary, damages has traditionally been twofold. First, they may serve as a tool to punish truly reprehensible conduct. In this way, the aggrieved plaintiff is given a socially acceptable avenue of retaliation, and, perhaps more importantly, the "punitive nature of exemplary awards also affords society a means of retribution for wrongs against the community interest." *See* Judith Camile Glasscock, *Emptying the Deep Pocket in Mass Tort Litigation*, 18 ST.

MARY'S L.J. 977, 982 (1987). Punitive damages are also an appropriate remedy in international law. As the Supreme Court has observed, "[A]n attack from revenge and malignity, from gross abuse of power, and a settled purpose of mischief . . . may be punished by all the penalties which the law of nations can properly administer."

The law also provides for awards of punitive damages upon the sound reasoning that they will deter others from committing similar acts. Courts reason that if a sizeable monetary sum over and above compensatory damages is assessed against the wrongdoer, he and others may be prevented from engaging in similar behavior in the future. As acknowledged in the RESTATEMENT (SECOND) OF TORTS, punitive damages are meant both "to punish [a defendant] for his outrageous conduct and to deter him and others like him from similar conduct in the future."

Most courts faced with gross violations of international human rights have employed the tool of punitive damages to achieve these dual purposes. By granting large exemplary awards, courts have both expressed their condemnation of human rights abuses and attempted to deter other international actors from engaging in similar practices. Most of these cases have been brought pursuant to the authority of the Alien Tort Claims Act ("ATCA"), 28 U.S.C. § 1350, which allows aliens to sue in U.S. federal court for torts that violate "the law of nations or a treaty of the United States," and the more recently enacted TVPA, which establishes a cause of action against individuals for torture.

Part of the reason why punitive damages have been extensively awarded in cases brought under the ATCA is that they serve to redress conduct so heinous that it has been condemned by the world community. Punitive damages help reinforce "the consensus of the community of humankind" that horrific abuses against the person will not be tolerated. Although, unlike claimants proceeding under the ATCA, Plaintiffs in this case do not have to prove a violation of international law in order to be entitled to damages, the Court finds that such an inquiry would be helpful in assessing the amount of punitive damages that should be awarded.

The practice of summary execution has been consistently condemned by the world community. A multitude of international agreements and declarations proclaim every individual's right not to be deprived of life wantonly and arbitrarily. So widespread is the consensus against extrajudicial killing that "every instrument or agreement that has attempted to define the scope of international human rights has 'recognized a right to life coupled with a right to due process to protect that right.' " The ban on extrajudicial killing thus rises to the level of *jus cogens*, a norm of international law so fundamental that it is binding on all members of the world community.

> *Cuba's extrajudicial killings of Mario T. De la Peña, Carlos Alberto Costa, and Armando Alejandre violated clearly established principles of international law. More importantly, they were inhumane acts against innocent civilians. The fact that the killings were premeditated and intentional, outside of Cuban territory, wholly disproportionate, and executed without warning or process makes this act unique in its brazen flouting of international norms. There appears to be no precedent for a military aircraft intentionally shooting down an unarmed, civilian plane.*

Cuba's extrajudicial killings of Mario T. De la Peña, Carlos Alberto Costa, and Armando Alejandre violated clearly established principles of international law. More importantly, they were inhumane acts against innocent civilians. The fact that the killings were premeditated and intentional, outside of Cuban territory, wholly disproportionate, and executed without warning or process makes this act unique in its brazen flouting of international norms. There appears to be no precedent for a military aircraft intentionally shooting down an unarmed, civilian plane.

KAL 007   The only conceivable parallel may be the shootdown of KAL Flight 007 by the former Soviet Union in 1983. That incident can be distinguished, however, by two keys facts: First, the Soviets were arguably under the impression that the KAL plane was a military aircraft, and, second, the plane had strayed into Soviet airspace. Neither of these facts is true in this case. Despite the fact that the KAL plane was in Soviet airspace, a commentator studying the incident concluded that the lethal use of force was completely inappropriate: " 'Exclusive sovereignty' over airspace above a state was not enough to justify employing force." CRAIG A. MORGAN, THE SHOOTING OF KOREAN AIR LINES FLIGHT 007: RESPONSES TO UNAUTHORIZED AERIAL INCURSIONS, IN INTERNATIONAL INCIDENTS: THE LAW THAT COUNTS IN WORLD POLITICS, 202, 210 (W. Michael Reisman & Andrew R. Willard eds., 1988). International consensus is clear:

> [W]hen measures of force are employed to protect territorial sovereignty, whether on land, on sea, or in the air, their employment is subject to the duty to take into consideration the elementary obligations of humanity, and not to use a degree of force in excess of what is commensurate with the reality and gravity of the threat (if any).

The Court must therefore fashion a remedy consistent with the unprecedented nature of this act. The Court finds that Plaintiffs have proven their clear entitlement to punitive damages. Based upon this record, the Court would be shirking its duty were it to refrain from entering a substantial punitive damage award for the dual purpose of (1) expressing the strongest possible condemnation of the Cuban government for its responsibility for commission of this monstrous act, and (2) deterring Defendants from ever again committing other crimes of terrorism.

In addition to considerations of the heinousness of Cuba's act, the Court will follow the traditional approach of considering the Cuban Air Force's assets in its assessment of punitive damages. *See* RESTATEMENT (SECOND) OF TORTS § 908(2) (1977) ("In assessing punitive damages, the trier of fact can properly consider the character of the defendant's act, the nature and extent of the harm to the plaintiff that the defendant caused or intended to cause and the wealth of the defendant.").

Of course, it would be impossible for the Court to calculate precisely the assets of the Cuban Air Force. The record contains, however, testimony as to the value and number of the MiG fighter jets in the Cuban Air Force. Because this testimony is both uncontroverted and credible, the Court will accept it as true. The record reflects that each MiG is worth approximately $45 million, and that the Cuban Air Force owns approximately 102 MiGs. The total value of this fleet, which is undoubtedly only a fraction of the Cuban Air Force's total assets, is therefore approximately $4.59 billion. The Court finds that 1% of this total, or $45.9 million, should be assessed against the Cuban Air Force for each of the killings. This figure is dictated by the unparalleled nature of Cuba's actions and comports with similar judgments against individual, non-governmental defendants. Monetary damages, in whatever amount, can never adequately express the revulsion of this Court, and every civilized society, over these callous murders. Perhaps, however, this decision may serve in some small way as a deterrent to others in the future.

Accordingly, after a careful review of the record, and the Court being otherwise fully advised, it is ordered and adjudged that judgment is hereby entered on behalf of Plaintiffs and against Defendants the Republic of Cuba and the Cuban Air Force for total compensatory damages of $49,927,911. Further, judgment is hereby entered for Plaintiffs and against the Defendant the Cuban Air Force (only) as punitive damages, the sum of One Hundred Thirty Seven Million, Seven Hundred Thousand Dollars ($137,700,000).

The total compensatory and punitive damages herewith awarded to Plaintiffs are $187,627,911, for which sum execution may issue forthwith against the Defendants Cuba and the Cuban Air Force and against any of their assets wherever situated.

EXERCISE 8-2. *ALEJANDRE V. REPUBLIC OF CUBA*—ANTI-TERRORISM AND EFFECTIVE DEATH PENALTY ACT OF 1996 ("AEDPA")

1. Describe the purpose and effect of the Foreign Sovereign Immunities Act of 1976 ("FSIA"), 28 U.S. §§ 1602–1611.

2. What exception to the FSIA did Congress create by enacting the Anti-Terrorism and Effective Death Penalty Act of 1996 ("AEDPA")?

3. What does Section 1605(a)(7) of the AEDPA provide and how did it apply in *Alejandre v. Republic of Cuba*?

4. Explain how the Civil Liability for Acts of State Sponsored Terrorism Act and theory of *respondeat superior* worked to promote the plaintiffs cause in this case.

5. Detail the type and amount of damages awarded? Is recovery likely? Explain why or why not.

C. AIRCRAFT SABOTAGE AND HIJACKING

UNITED STATES V. MCGUIRE

706 F.3d 1333 (11th Cir. 2013)

O'CONNOR, SUPREME COURT JUSTICE (RET.) (sitting by designation).

Inebriated and distraught because of losing his girlfriend and his job, McGuire took his father's loaded .38-caliber revolver from an unlocked safe and out into the driveway of his home. He called several friends on his cell phone, attempting to vent his distress, but could not find a ready ear. He was contemplating suicide, he says, but he could not bring himself to it. Instead, he fired off several rounds: one into a tree near the driveway, and several down the empty street. Neighbors called the police. McGuire, meanwhile, went back inside.

Witness Testimony

When he came out again, the police had responded. By then, there were officers on the ground and a police helicopter in the air, shining its spotlight in his direction. McGuire raised his arm and fired one round into the sky. One witness testified that he saw McGuire fire directly into the spotlight and at the helicopter;

another said that he raised his arm to an 80-degree angle and fired; and yet others testified that he had surely fired into the air and in the general direction of the helicopter, but could not say whether he had fired at the helicopter or not.

McGuire's story at trial was that, having abandoned his thoughts of suicide, he merely came back outside to empty the gun of its final bullet, as he had intended when firing into the empty night before. He had fired the bullet off "randomly," without meaning to hit the helicopter or even knowing it was there. That was not the same story he told when he was arrested, however: Then he had said that he had been inside sleeping, had heard nothing, and had never fired a gun at all. Other witnesses had also undermined the suggestion that McGuire could somehow have failed to appreciate the helicopter's presence at the time that he fired, attesting to the loud noise and vibrant spotlight it produced.

Inconsistent Testimony

In closing, McGuire told the jury that "there [wa]s just one issue and that [wa]s whether [he had] intentionally, willfully and knowingly shot at the sheriff's office helicopter." Evidently believing that he had, the jury found McGuire guilty on Count One: attempting to wreck, damage, or destroy an aircraft in the special aircraft jurisdiction of the United States. See 18 U.S.C. § 32(a)(1). It also found that McGuire had used or possessed a firearm in connection with that crime, which the judge determined to be a crime of violence. This appeal followed.

* * *

We review the sufficiency of the evidence supporting the jury's verdict *de novo*, but in so doing, we must draw all reasonable inferences in favor of the verdict. *United States v. Mercer*, 541 F.3d 1070, 1074 (11th Cir. 2008). If "a reasonable jury could have found the defendant guilty beyond a reasonable doubt," then we cannot overturn the jury's determination. *Id.*

This standard, which entrusts the resolution of disputed factual issues to the jury, resolves McGuire's sufficiency challenge. McGuire admits, as he must, that "one witness, Deputy Nicholas Paul, testified that he witnessed a stationary Jason McGuire shoot a pistol skyward 'right toward the spotlight' where a helicopter orbited." The jury was entitled to believe Deputy Paul, and conflicting testimony about whether McGuire aimed at the helicopter or the sky was for the jury to resolve.

McGuire counters that a reasonable jury could not have accepted Deputy Paul's testimony because the testimony indicated that the helicopter was circling and McGuire was standing still "without moving to follow the path of the helicopter" or otherwise tracking it when he fired. He views this as a physical impossibility that makes Paul's testimony that McGuire fired at the helicopter "so inherently incredible, so contrary to the teachings of basic human experience, so completely at odds with ordinary common sense, that no reasonable person would believe it beyond a reasonable doubt." *United States v. Chancey*, 715 F.2d 543, 546 (11th Cir.1983). We cannot agree.

To begin with, we are not convinced that any real inconsistency exists between these two elements of the testimony—at least to the degree that would make Paul's testimony "completely at odds with ordinary common sense." Any person who has ever hunted anything—even electronic ducks—knows that a person can fire a round quickly in the direction of a moving object without tracking it first; they might well miss, but they would still mean to hit the target.

More importantly, such evidentiary points are classic jury arguments about McGuire's likely intentions, not a reason to disregard the jury's determination of his intent. Indeed, at the heart of the case is a contested inference; McGuire offers reason to infer from his body position that he meant only to empty his gun of its final bullet; the prosecution offers reasons to infer from his firing into the sky where a police helicopter circled that he meant to hit the police helicopter. We must draw every inference in favor of the jury's verdict, however, and some evidence clearly supports the prosecution's theory. Thus, we cannot accept McGuire's sufficiency challenge.

* * *

Crime of Violence Under Title 18, U.S.C

McGuire also maintains that, even if he did attempt to damage, destroy, disable, or wreck an aircraft, that is not a crime of violence within the ambit of 18 U.S.C. § 924(c). This is a question of law we review *de novo*, and that we must answer "categorically"—that is, by reference to the elements of the offense, and not the actual facts of McGuire's conduct. We employ this categorical approach because of the statute's terms: It asks whether McGuire committed "an offense" that "has *as an element* the use, attempted use, or threatened use of physical force against the person or property of another," or that "*by its nature*, involves a substantial risk that physical force against the person or property of another may be used." 18 U.S.C. § 924(c)(3)(A)–(B) (emphasis added). Thus, even though firing a gun at a flying helicopter is unmistakably violent, we must ask whether the crime, in general, plausibly covers any non-violent conduct. *See Gonzales v. Duenas-Alvarez*, 549 U.S. 183, 193, 127 S.Ct. 815, 166 L.Ed.2d 683 (2007) (requiring "a realistic probability, not a theoretical possibility, that the State would apply its statute to conduct that falls outside" the standard). Only if the plausible applications of the statute of conviction all require the use or threatened use of force can McGuire be held guilty of a crime of violence.

> *A special fact about McGuire's conviction is that that it requires attempting to damage*
> *or disable an aircraft in the "special aircraft jurisdiction of the United States." 18*
> *U.S.C. § 32(a)(1). This is defined as an "aircraft in flight," 49 U.S.C. § 46501(2),*
> *which is further defined as encompassing the time "from the moment all external doors*
> *are closed following boarding through the moment when one external door is opened to*
> *allow passengers to leave." Id. § 46501(1)(A). In other words, McGuire was*
> *necessarily convicted of attempting to damage or disable an aircraft that was either flying*
> *or else ready to take off or arriving at a destination with people on board.*

We begin this analysis by noting a special fact about McGuire's conviction—namely, that it requires attempting to damage or disable an aircraft in the "special aircraft jurisdiction of the United States." 18 U.S.C. § 32(a)(1). This is defined as an "aircraft in flight," 49 U.S.C. § 46501(2), which is further defined as encompassing the time "from the moment all external doors are closed following boarding through the moment when one external door is opened to allow passengers to leave." *Id.* § 46501(1)(A). In other words, McGuire was necessarily convicted of attempting to damage or disable an aircraft that was either flying or else ready to take off or arriving at a destination with people on board.

Special Aircraft Jurisdiction

In that context, we have no trouble concluding that most of the separately stated versions of the offense can be readily recognized as crimes of violence. Attempting to "set[ ] fire to, damage[ ], destroy[ ] . . . or wreck [ ]" an aircraft with people on board is unmistakably violent. At a minimum, each of these actions has "as an element, the use, attempted use, or threatened use of physical force against the . . . property of another." 18 U.S.C. § 924(c)(3)(A). Because each necessarily involves the attempted or threatened destruction of very sensitive property—and quite probably lives as well—they are crimes of violence, and properly accounted predicates for the firearms enhancement under § 924(c).

Understandably, McGuire focuses on the sole remaining version of the offense—"disabl[ing] an aircraft"—and argues that it does not necessarily involve the use of force or a serious risk that force will be involved. To that end, he cites such possibilities as "deflating the tires, disabling the ignition, or disengaging the fuel lines" while the airplane is on the ground, or "disconnecting the onboard circuitry, disabling the radio transponder . . . and interfering with the aircraft's radio equipment" while the plane is in the air. He correctly cites to *Leocal v. Ashcroft*, 543 U.S. 1 (2004), in which the Supreme Court held that drunk driving is not a crime of violence, for the proposition that we must determine whether the crime involves the risk that force will be used, not the risk that an injury might result. *Id.* at 10–11 & n. 7. Accordingly, he says, it is not enough that attempting

"Disabling an Aircraft"

to disable an aircraft risks danger to the people on board; it must involve the risk that an act of force will be done against them.

This argument misses twice.

First, we think that attempting to disable an aircraft while people are on board is itself an act of force in the meaningful sense. It involves an "active crime" done "intentionally" against the property of another, with extreme and manifest indifference to the owner of that property and the wellbeing of the passengers. *See Leocal*, 543 U.S. at 7, 9. Unlike drunk driving, where any harm to others or their property is an accident, a serious interference with the freedom, safety and security of others is a natural and probable consequence of sabotaging an airplane with people aboard. It makes little difference that the physical act, in isolation from the crime, can be done with a minimum of force; we would not say that laying spikes across a roadway is a non-violent crime because laying something upon the ground is not a forceful act. It still involves an intentional act against another's property that is calculated to cause damage and that is exacerbated by indifference to others' wellbeing. Likewise, the fact that deflating an airplane's tire or rewiring its onboard systems are minimally forceful acts does not mean that such acts of sabotage against a loaded plane are not crimes that involve the use of force against that plane or its passengers.

Second, attempting to disable a plane in flight or during takeoff or landing is a crime of violence for the same reason that the Supreme Court gave in Leocal regarding burglary: it, "by its nature, involves a substantial risk that the burglar will use force against a victim in completing the crime." *Leocal*, 543 U.S. at 10. The Court has explained that the risk of violence from burglary comes

> not from the simple physical act of wrongfully entering onto another's property, but rather from the possibility of a face-to-face confrontation between the burglar and a third party—whether an occupant, a police officer, or a bystander—who comes to investigate. That is, the risk arises not from the completion of the burglary, but from the possibility that an innocent person might appear while the crime is in progress.

James v. United States, 550 U.S. 192, 203. The same is true of attempting to disable an aircraft that is full of people and about to take off, landing, or already in flight. If, at such a time, a person attempts to disable the craft, there is, at a minimum, a serious risk of "a face-to-face confrontation between the [perpetrator] and a third party—whether an occupant, a police officer," an air marshal, federal safety personnel, the crew, or a bystander. This is especially true given the heightened level of security that is now entailed by air travel. Accordingly, disabling a plane in the special aircraft jurisdiction of the United States at least involves a serious risk that force will be used in its completion.

Accordingly, we determine that there was sufficient evidence to convict McGuire of attempting to damage or disable an aircraft in flight under 18 U.S.C. § 32(a)(1), and that this is categorically a crime of violence. His conviction and sentence are affirmed.

EXERCISE 8-3. *UNITED STATES V. MCGUIRE*—SPECIAL AIRCRAFT JURISDICTION, CRIME OF VIOLENCE

Amendments to 18 U.S.C. § 32 enacted in 1984 expanded United States jurisdiction over aircraft sabotage to include destruction of any aircraft in the "special aircraft jurisdiction" of the United States or any civil aircraft used, operated or employed in interstate, overseas, or foreign air commerce. This statute makes it a Federal offense to commit an act of violence against any person on the aircraft, not simply crew members, if the act is likely to endanger the safety of the aircraft. In addition, the United States is authorized under the statute to prosecute any person who destroys a foreign civil aircraft outside of the United States if the offender is later found in the United States a national of the United States was aboard such aircraft (or would have been aboard if such aircraft had taken off) or a national of the United States was a perpetrator of the offense.

U.S. DEP'T OF JUSTICE, *Aircraft Sabotage (18 U.S.C. 32)*, https://www.justice.gov/usam/criminal-resource-manual-2-aircraft-sabotage-18-usc-32. *See also* USAM 9–63.221, et seq.

1. Describe the facts of the case—what happened and why?

2. Summarize the testimony about the round of ammunition that McGuire fired into the sky.

3. Explain the accused's argument respecting the sufficiency of the evidence introduced against him. How did the court rule?

4. Define the "special aircraft jurisdiction of the United States" and explain its relevance to this case.

5. Did a "crime of violence" occur here under 18 U.S.C. § 924. Explain the court's reasoning.

UNITED STATES V. HUME

453 F.2d 339 (5th Cir. 1972)

PER CURIAM.

Appellant Hume was convicted by the district court sitting without a jury of violating Title 18 U.S.C. § 32. Hume asserts error in that (1) there is a total lack of jurisdiction; (2) there is insufficient evidence that the aircraft was damaged; and (3) that there was not sufficient evidence that he acted willfully.

The evidence presented at the trial was not in dispute. One Castleberry owned and operated an aircraft used for dusting. On the morning of July 26, 1970, Castleberry took off in his aircraft and dusted three fields near Gadsden High School in New Mexico. After dusting the fields, he returned to his residence in nearby Texas, refueled his poison tanks, and was spraying in Texas very near to appellant Hume's residence when Hume came out of his residence and shot the aircraft with his .22 caliber rifle on two different runs that the dusting aircraft was making.

18 U.S.C. § 32

Hume's shots made a small hole in the aircraft wing and also hit the fuel pump bracket. Appellant contends that these facts failed to establish that the plane was being used, operated, or employed in interstate commerce at the time of the shooting, and that it was not damaged as a result of the shooting. Title 18, U.S.C. § 32, provides that, "[w]hoever willfully sets fire to, damages, destroys, disables, or wrecks any civil aircraft used, operated, or employed in interstate, overseas, or foreign air commerce . . ." shall be punished according to law.

Title 18, U.S.C. § 32, provides that, "[w]hoever willfully sets fire to, damages, destroys, disables, or wrecks any civil aircraft used, operated, or employed in interstate, overseas, or foreign air commerce" shall be punished according to law.

Interstate Commerce, Defined

The indictment in this case alleges that the defendant wilfully damaged and disabled a civil aircraft being used, operated, and employed in interstate commerce. Title 49 U.S.C. § 1301, defines "air commerce" as meaning

> . . . interstate . . . air commerce or the transportation of mail by aircraft or any operation or navigation of aircraft within the limits of any Federal airway or any operation or navigation of aircraft which directly affects, or which may endanger safety in, interstate, overseas, or foreign air commerce.

The term "interstate air commerce" is defined as meaning *inter alia*

. . . the operation or navigation of aircraft in the conduct or furtherance of a business or vocation, in commerce between, respectively—

(a) a place in any State of the United States, or the District of Columbia, and a place in any other State of the United States, or the District of Columbia; or between places in the same State of the United States through the airspace over any place outside thereof . . .

The wording of the statute makes it clear that Congress intended not only to protect civil aircraft while actually operating in interstate commerce, but also to protect such aircraft as is used or employed in interstate commerce, and also the parts, materials and facilities used by such aircraft.

This interpretation gives to the words as used in the statute their fair meaning and is in accord with the obvious intent of Congress. The purpose of the bill as stated in the House Committee report is, "[t]o provide suitable punishment, first, for the willful damaging or destruction of air-carrier aircraft *used* in interstate, overseas, or foreign air commerce." U. S. CONGRESSIONAL AND ADMINISTRATIVE NEWS, 84th Congress, 2d Session, page 3145.

We conclude that the district court was not without jurisdiction. There is no merit in Hume's other assertions of error as the photographs introduced in evidence clearly show that the aircraft sustained damage from the .22 caliber rifle, and the appellant freely admitted in his testimony at the trial that his intentions were to hit the plane but not the pilot. There being substantial evidence to support the findings of the district court, the judgment is affirmed.

EXERCISE 8-4. *UNITED STATES V. HUME*—DESTRUCTION OF AIRCRAFT AND AIRCRAFT FACILITIES

1. What are the facts in *United States v. Hume*? Are they undisputed?

2. Title 18, U.S.C. § 32 is entitled "Destruction of Aircraft or Aircraft Facilities." What does it prohibit and how does it apply to this case?

3. What is "air commerce" under 49 U.S.C. § 1301.

4. Was the aircraft described in the case flying in "*interstate* air commerce"? Explain how that is so given that the airplane flew in New Mexico and never crossed state lines.

5. What is holding of the case and what impact does it have on the conviction entered by the district court judge?

UNITED STATES V. SMITH

756 F.3d 1070 (8th Cir. 2014)

RILEY, CHIEF JUDGE.

This case calls upon us to interpret 18 U.S.C. § 39A(a) for the first time. This subsection imposes criminal liability on anyone who "knowingly aims the beam of a laser pointer at an aircraft in the special aircraft jurisdiction of the United States, or at the flight path of such an aircraft." 18 U.S.C. § 39A(a). A jury convicted Michael A. Smith of violating § 39A(a) after which the district court sentenced him to 24 months in prison and 3 years of supervised release. Smith challenges his conviction, arguing the district court should have read § 39A(a) to provide Smith a mistake-of-fact defense based upon his reasonable belief that his laser would not reach the targeted aircraft. Claiming the word "aims" "carries with it an 'intent to hit' the object," Smith argues the district court erred in (1) excluding expert testimony as to the perceived range of a laser, and (2) rejecting his defense instructions. Because we do not read § 39A(a) to require an "intent to hit," we affirm.

Factual Background

In the early morning hours of July 11, 2012, authorities in Omaha, Nebraska, learned the cockpit of an inbound Boeing 737 had been illuminated by a laser. The local police department dispatched a helicopter to locate the laser. As the police helicopter approached the approximate location of the laser's source, Smith, standing in his backyard, directed his laser pointer's green beam at the helicopter, illuminating its cockpit. Smith's beam struck the helicopter several times, but when the helicopter got close, his beam disappeared. Unable to pinpoint Smith's location, the helicopter was forced to depart. But as the helicopter began to do so, Smith again shone his laser's beam on the helicopter. The helicopter resumed its approach until, again, the beam disappeared. In what the helicopter pilots described as a back-and-forth game of "cat-and-mouse," the helicopter approached Smith when the laser was visible and feigned departure when it was not. Ultimately, the pilots were able to identify Smith's exact location and dispatched a ground officer.

The ground officer found Smith standing in his backyard pointing a green laser pointer skyward in the direction of the helicopter. The officer handcuffed Smith and removed him for questioning. According to the arresting officer's testimony, Smith "stated that earlier he had been shining [the laser] at aircraft that he thought were far enough away that it wouldn't actually reach those aircraft." Smith "denied actually shining [the laser] at the police" helicopter.

Procedural History

A grand jury indicted Smith of knowingly aiming a laser pointer's beam at the police helicopter in violation of 18 U.S.C. § 39A(a). The day before trial, Smith submitted proposed jury instructions, including a theory-of-defense instruction proposing he could not have " 'knowingly' aimed the beam at the aircraft" if he "mistakenly believed that the laser beam could not travel the distance necessary to reach the aircraft."

On the first day of trial, the parties asked the district court to provide its preliminary interpretation of § 39A(a) and asked, in particular, whether the statute required the government to prove Smith believed his laser's beam would strike the aircraft. The district court concluded, "[§] 39A is violated whenever a person points a laser pointer at what the person knows to be an aircraft, regardless of that person's belief, whether it be reasonable or not, that the laser pointer will not reach the aircraft or affect its crew." First, the district court noted "the term 'knowingly' . . . clearly applies to what the laser is pointed at"—that is, "the defendant has to know that he's aiming . . . a laser beam at an aircraft" as opposed to believing the target is "a shooting star" or "a satellite." The district court then reasoned the central question revolved around the meaning of "knowingly aim." The district court read "to aim at" as simply meaning "to point[ ] at," reasoning this definition was supported by the statutory text's common meaning, its legislative history, and the circumstances underlying the statute's enactment. Based on this interpretation, the district court ultimately refused Smith's proposed theory-of-defense instruction.

Knowledge as Element of Crime

During the second day of trial, Smith called a physics professor, Dr. David Sidebottom. Following the government's objection, Dr. Sidebottom testified during an offer of proof that a layer of atmosphere close to the ground contains dust which reflects the laser's beam. Dr. Sidebottom explained that once the beam clears this dust layer, there can be fewer particles to reflect the laser, making it sometimes appear as if the beam stops abruptly when it actually continues on. The district court excluded Dr. Sidebottom's testimony because under the district court's interpretation of § 39A(a), it did not matter whether Smith believed— reasonable or not—that the beam could reach the helicopter. The jury found Smith guilty of violating § 39A(a). Smith now appeals his conviction.

Expert Testimony

Discussion

Smith's appeal targets the district court's exclusion of Dr. Sidebottom's testimony and rejection of Smith's proposed jury instructions. As both parties agree, the foundation of these challenges and the crux of this appeal is the definition of the phrase "knowingly aim." Section 39A(a) covers an offender who "knowingly aims the beam of a laser pointer at an aircraft . . . or at the flight path of such an aircraft." Smith contends this language requires a defendant to knowingly point a laser beam intending the beam to strike the targeted object, whereas the government defends the district court's understanding by arguing an offender need only direct the beam towards the target. We review *de novo* this question of statutory interpretation.

"As in all such cases, we begin by analyzing the statutory language," *Hardt v. Reliance Standard Life Ins. Co.*, 560 U.S. 242 (2010), "giv[ing] words their 'ordinary, contemporary, common meaning' unless they are otherwise defined in the statute itself," *Hennepin Cnty. v. Fed. Nat'l Mortg. Ass'n*, 742 F.3d 818, 821 (8th Cir. 2014). If the language's meaning is unambiguous when "read in its proper context," *McCarthy v. Bronson*, 500 U.S. 136, 139 (1991), "then, this first canon is also the last: 'judicial inquiry is complete,' " *Conn. Nat'l Bank v. Germain*, 503 U.S. 249, 254 (1992). Here, our inquiry begins and ends with this first step.

1.   Knowingly

Smith's opening salvo is his argument that "the district court only applied 'knowingly' to the 'aircraft' element of § 39A and did not apply 'knowingly' to the 'aim the beam of a laser pointer at' element." This argument misses its mark. The district court never suggested "knowingly" modifies only the "aircraft" element but instead recognized there was no question the *mens rea* requirement modified the "aircraft" element and then moved on to explain the real task at hand was determining "how 'knowingly' modifies 'aims' " and, more importantly, what "Congress meant by the word 'aim.' " Thus, contrary to Smith's contention, the district court correctly recognized "knowingly" modifies both the "aim" and "aircraft" elements. *See, e.g., United States v. Bruguier*, 735 F.3d 754, 758 (8th Cir. 2013) (*en banc*) (noting our presumption is to read " 'a phrase in a criminal statute that introduces the elements of a crime with the word "knowingly" as applying that word to each element,' " unless " 'special contexts or . . . background circumstances' " call for a different reading).

Nor does the district court's interpretation of "to aim at"—that is, "to point at"—wash away the "knowingly" requirement. Under the district court's interpretation, "knowingly" still modifies "aim" to require that an offender understand he or she is pointing or directing the laser's beam at an aircraft, regardless whether the offender intends to strike the aircraft. There is thus no real disagreement as to whether "knowingly" modifies "aim." Smith's real argument, as the district court correctly observed, comes down to the proper construction of the word "aim."

2. Aim

Smith contends the statute's use of "aim" unambiguously "carries with it an 'intent to hit' the object" targeted. This word's common American usage necessitates no such intent requirement. See, e.g., New Oxford American Dictionary 33 (3d ed.2010) (defining "aim" paired with a direct object as "point or direct (a weapon or camera) at a target: aim the camcorder at some suitable object"); The American Heritage Dictionary of the English Language 36 (5th ed.2011) (defining the verb as "[t]o direct (a weapon or camera) toward a point" and "[t]o direct or propel (an object, such as a ball) toward a point").

The district court looked to Webster's Third New International Dictionary 45 (1993), which defines the verb "to aim" as "to point in a particular direction or at a particular object." Smith asserts "the district court read the wrong definition from Webster's Third New International." In his brief and at oral argument, Smith proposed one of the dictionary's other definitions: "to direct or point (as a weapon or missile) at or so as to hit an object." This, Smith vigorously asserts, is the "proper" definition and the one which "Congress intended to be used." But even if that were true (and we see nothing in the statute mandating the use of this particular definition), Smith's preferred definition still falls short. Under this disjunctive definition, a defendant can "aim" by directing the beam "at . . . an object" or "so as to hit an object." *See also* Random House Webster's Unabridged Dictionary 42 (2d ed.2001) (providing the transitive definition: "to position or direct (a firearm, ball, arrow, rocket, etc.) so that, on firing or release, the discharged projectile will hit a target or travel along a certain path" (emphasis added)). The usage examples for this definition show that "a small cannon" can be "aimed into space" and "a camera" can be "aimed at the scene." Webster's Third New International. Thus, aiming may accompany an intent to strike the target, but the word's common meaning is not limited to such instances.

Ordinary use of the word "aim" confirms this understanding. Consider the familiar phrase "Ready, aim, fire!" A ceremonial commander at a military memorial orders the riflemen to ready their rifles, aim the barrels, and then pull the triggers. The riflemen dutifully obey the second of these three orders not by manifesting any present intent for either barrel or bullet to strike any target, but instead by directing the rifle's gaze. By using the term "aim at" rather than some result or contact oriented term—for instance, "knowingly illuminating an aircraft"—Congress specified the act of directing the active laser pointer's beam, not of manifesting one's intent to strike the target.

> *By using the term "aim at" rather than some result or contact oriented term—for instance, "knowingly illuminating an aircraft"—Congress specified the act of directing the active laser pointer's beam, not of manifesting one's intent to strike the target ... Relying on plain text and common usage, we conclude § 39A(a)'s requirement that the laser beam be "knowingly aim[ed]" does not require an offender to intend the beam to strike the aircraft or flight path in question.*

Congress's clear choice is amplified by the " 'the design of the statute as a whole and . . . its object and policy.' " *Dada v. Mukasey*, 554 U.S. 1, 16 (2008). By also criminalizing the act of knowingly aiming at an aircraft's "flight path," Congress illustrates its intent to discourage those who would direct the beam so as to harry the aircraft without necessarily intending to strike it—including the individual who knowingly directs the laser toward a recognized aircraft, but neglects to consider the power of his device or the effective range of his laser.

Relying on plain text and common usage, we conclude § 39A(a)'s requirement that the laser beam be "knowingly aim[ed]" does not require an offender to intend the beam to strike the aircraft or flight path in question.

Rule of Lenity

The rule of lenity requires a criminal statute be construed in a defendant's favor where, " 'after considering text, structure, history, and purpose, there remains a grievous ambiguity or uncertainty in the statute, such that the Court must simply guess as to what Congress intended.' " *United States v. Castleman*, 134 S.Ct. 1405, 1416. This rule is based on the need to provide "fair warning[,] . . . in language that the common world will understand, of what the law intends to do if a certain line is passed." *United States v. Bass*, 404 U.S. 336, 348 (1971). Yet penal laws "should not be construed so strictly as to defeat the obvious intention of the legislature." *United States v. Warren*, 149 F.3d 825, 828 (8th Cir. 1998) ("[G]rievous ambiguity or uncertainty" necessary to invoke lenity requires more than "[t]he simple existence of some statutory ambiguity" because "most statutes are ambiguous to some degree.").

Smith does not invoke this rule, instead contending the statute is unambiguous in his favor. As we have already explained, § 39A(a)'s common and ordinary meaning gave Smith "fair warning" his conduct violated the law. Because the district court correctly interpreted 18 U.S.C. § 39A(a), it did not err in excluding Dr. Sidebottom's irrelevant testimony and rejecting Smith's inapposite proposed instructions. We affirm.

EXERCISE 8-5. *UNITED STATES V. SMITH*—AIMING LASER POINTER AT AIRCRAFT

1. Describe 18 U.S.C. § 39A and the conduct it criminalizes.

2. What are the facts of the case and was the accused convicted? Explain.

3. The defendant contended that the trial court misinterpreted the word "aim" in the applicable statute. Explain his position and the appellate court's resolution of the issue.

4. What is the "rule of lenity"?

5. Are laser beams pointed at aircraft a narrow or widespread problem? While 18 U.S.C. § 32 represents a domestic legal response, what is being done internationally? *See, e.g.,* Gordon Lubold, *Laser Beam Attack Bedevil U.S. Military Pilots in Mideast,* WALL ST. J., Aug. 17, 2018.

STANFORD V. KUWAIT AIRWAYS CORP.

89 F.3d 117 (2d Cir. 1996)

McLAUGHLIN, CIRCUIT JUDGE.

Four terrorists boarded Middle Eastern Airlines ("MEA") flight 426 in Beirut, Lebanon. The flight ended in Dubai, United Arab Emirates where the four terrorists disembarked, and connected with Kuwait Airways flight KU221, bound for Karachi, Pakistan. Three American diplomats, William Stanford, Charles Hegna, and Charles Kapar were also on board KU221. Shortly after take-off from Dubai, the terrorists hijacked KU221, forcing the pilot to turn north. The plane landed in Tehran, Iran and sat on the airport tarmac for days while the terrorists tortured the three American diplomats, finally murdering Hegna and Stanford.

Plaintiffs, Charles Kapar and the estates of the two deceased diplomats, brought this suit alleging that MEA's negligence was a proximate cause of the injuries and deaths occurring aboard KU221. After a jury trial in the United States District Court for the Southern District of New York, the jury deadlocked, and the court declared a mistrial. MEA then filed a motion for judgment as a matter of law, arguing that MEA owed no duty to the three diplomats, and that MEA's actions (in Beirut) were not a proximate cause of the injuries and deaths aboard KU221 (in Tehran). The court granted MEA's motion.

Plaintiffs appeal, arguing that MEA owed them a duty to use due care to avoid the known risk of hijacking, MEA breached that duty by failing to screen passengers adequately in Beirut, and this breach was a proximate cause of their injuries. We reverse and remand for a new trial.

BACKGROUND

In the Fall of 1983, the Da'Wa, a group of Shiite extremists, was imprisoned in Kuwait for deadly attacks on the United States and French embassies in Beirut. A year later, the Shiite Muslim group Hezbollah, an Islamic terror organization based in Beirut, increased its violent opposition to the incarceration of the Da'Wa prisoners. With the first suicide car bombing of the American embassy in Beirut in 1983, Hezbollah embarked on large scale terrorist activities, kidnapping American journalists, diplomats and academics, and murdering scores of people in suicide car bombings. This Shiite Muslim terror group threatened continued attacks on Kuwaiti, French, and American citizens unless the Da'Wa prisoners were released.

IATA

In May, 1983, the International Air Transport Association ("IATA") held its 21st Security Advisory Committee meeting in Montreal, Canada to discuss security measures among member airlines. IATA, of which MEA is a member, is "a private organization of domestic and foreign air carriers engaged in scheduled international air transportation. One of IATA's major purposes set out in its Articles of Association is 'to provide means for collaboration among the air transport enterprises engaged directly or indirectly in international air transport services.' "

At this meeting, IATA discussed new techniques terror groups were using to circumvent airport security measures to infiltrate an airport or airline. The meeting discussed one particular method for terrorists to capitalize on the lax security at a "dirty" airport and board a plane bound for a more secure airport. Upon arrival at the more secure airport, the terrorists would transfer to a "target" airline and then hijack the target plane: "[T]he would be terrorist may well have traveled on the original Carrier without any intention of committing a terrorist act against that Carrier, but with the object of a transfer to another target Carrier." Minutes of the IATA 21st Security Advisory Committee Meeting, Montreal, May 4–5, 1983. IATA cautioned its members that "the only solution to this situation is to create circumstances where some degree of reliance can be placed on the security measures of other States."

Interline Ticketing

MEA, Kuwait Airways, and other members of IATA, participated in a program of "interline" ticketing, a reciprocal arrangement whereby a single ticket written by one airline for a flight on that airline will also accommodate the same passenger's flight on a second airline with the revenues to be allocated *pro tanto* between the airlines. Passengers need only one ticket and one baggage check to travel on both airlines.

An MEA official admitted that he knew, in December 1984, that the security measures at Beirut airport were minimal. Specifically, MEA knew that X-ray machines for checking passengers' luggage were not operating and that metal detectors were apparently functioning but "locked" and not in use. In addition, MEA was aware or, in the exercise of reasonable prudence, should have been aware that many airlines had ceased all operations out of Beirut because of the threats of violence coming from Islamic militants in Beirut.

MEA maintained, however, that it was helpless to offer additional security measures because airport security was under the sole control of the Lebanese army. An MEA official testified that the military conducted searches of passengers and luggage by hand, but did not employ any more sophisticated forms of security screening. He also testified that MEA never asked the Lebanese military to strengthen the security measures at the Beirut airport.

MEA's employees at the Beirut airport were responsible for selling and examining passengers' tickets, checking the information on the tickets against visas and passports, and receiving baggage from the passengers. These employees were the first line of defense between hijackers who slipped through the ludicrous security at Beirut Airport and innocent passengers aboard MEA and connecting flights. Nevertheless, they did not perform any other searches, known as "secondary screening," of passengers or their bags. Also in place was a communications network within MEA, allowing MEA employees to relay information between its stations in Beirut and Dubai. There is no evidence, however, that MEA ever used this information network to contact its agents in Dubai to have them relay information to other IATA members about suspicious passengers; and its employees certainly did not do so in this case.

On December 2, 1984, in the eye of the political hurricane roaring through the Middle East, four Hezbollah hijackers purchased interline tickets for travel from Beirut to Bangkok, Thailand, via Dubai and Karachi. They began their journey by presenting their interline tickets to the MEA agents at the Beirut airport, where they boarded MEA flight 426 to Dubai.

> *The hijackers' tickets had a stench about them. They had been purchased on very*
> *short notice with cash, and the flight traced an outlandish route: the passengers were*
> *to fly on MEA from Beirut to Dubai, where they were then to connect with Kuwait*
> *Airways to Karachi, and from there continue on to Bangkok. This itinerary was*
> *bizarre.*

The hijackers' tickets had a stench about them. They had been purchased on very short notice with cash, and the flight traced an outlandish route: the passengers were to fly on MEA from Beirut to Dubai, where they were then to connect with Kuwait Airways to Karachi, and from there continue on to Bangkok. This itinerary was bizarre because: (1) there were regularly scheduled direct flights between Beirut and Bangkok; (2) the four terrorists were the only passengers aboard MEA 426 to connect with a Kuwaiti airline—every other passenger aboard who happened to be traveling to Karachi connected in Dubai with a Pakistani International Airlines flight; and (3) there was another scheduled MEA flight from Beirut directly to Karachi on December 4th, a day after the hijackers' actual departure. If the hijackers had waited for this next flight, they would have avoided (a) the stop at Dubai, and (b) an unnecessary twenty-hour layover in Karachi while waiting for the same December 4th plane that would eventually take them to Bangkok. Still another suspicious feature of the journey was that the men were traveling one-way, a very long distance, without any checked baggage. None of this apparently raised the eyebrow of any MEA employee.

Upon arrival in Dubai, the hijackers alighted MEA flight 426 and headed for their target: Kuwait Airways flight KU221. KU221 had originated in Kuwait City, bound for Karachi with a fateful stop in Dubai. It carried William Stanford, Charles Hegna and Charles Kapar. The three were employed by the United States Department of State, Agency for International Development, and were en route from Kuwait City to their base of operations in Karachi. KU221 stopped in Dubai to refuel and to pick up additional passengers heading for Karachi. Passengers connecting to KU221 from other flights were required to take a bus on the tarmac to KU221 and climb a set of stairs to enter the jet through the forward door of the plane.

A Kuwait Airlines official placed a table at the top of the stairs leading to the forward door of flight KU221, where he checked connecting passengers' carry-on luggage as they boarded. One witness, Neil Beeston, testified that he saw three of the four hijackers standing on the tarmac near the unguarded—and not in use—rear stairs of the airplane during the boarding process. Other testimony established that the tarmac, in general, was poorly lit and not well guarded.

Once KU221 was airborne, and over the Gulf of Oman, two hijackers burst into the cockpit, pressed a grenade against the flight commander's neck and ordered him to fly the plane to Mehrabad Airport in Tehran. The flight crew complied, landing in Tehran in the early morning of December 4th.

Events of KU221

The four hijackers were armed with pistols, explosives, and other weapons. They released the women and children passengers, but singled out Hegna, Stanford, Kapar and a fourth American, John Costa, and forced them into the first-class cabin. Over the next six days the hijackers murdered Hegna and Stanford and beat and tortured Kapar and Costa, using them as pawns to gain the release of the Da'Wa prisoners in Kuwait. Iranian commandos raided the aircraft on December 9th, rescued the remaining passengers, and captured the hijackers.

No one knows how the hijackers got their weapons on board flight KU221. There was no direct evidence that they had weapons in their possession on board MEA flight 426 or, later, when they boarded flight KU221. On the other hand, there was also no evidence that the weapons were already on board flight KU221 when the hijackers boarded. Plaintiffs showed that no weapons were found when KU221 was routinely cleaned at Dubai, that no passengers disembarked while the plane waited for about an hour on the tarmac at Dubai, and that all panels in the plane remained undisturbed. In addition, there was evidence that it was a common practice in the Middle East to allow one passenger to check in for a number of other passengers, thus allowing armed passengers to avoid contact with airline officials.

Plaintiffs brought this action against MEA, IATA, Kuwait Airways, Pan American World Airways, and Northwest Airlines. The claims against Kuwait Airways, Pan Am, and Northwest have been dismissed. The parties stipulated to the dismissal of claims against IATA.

The case against MEA went to trial but the jury was unable to reach a verdict. The court declared a mistrial. Later, MEA moved for judgment as a matter of law under Rule 50(b) of the Federal Rules of Civil Procedure, and the court granted the motion. The court reasoned that: (1) there was insufficient evidence for the jury to conclude that MEA owed plaintiffs a duty of care to avoid the risk of hijacking on another airline; (2) MEA's inaction was not a proximate cause of any of the injuries; and (3) the failure of (a) security at the Dubai airport and (b) Kuwait Airways's secondary screening measures were independent intervening acts breaking the causal chain that might have linked MEA's actions to the injury and deaths aboard flight KU221.

Plaintiffs appeal arguing that: (1) MEA had a duty to use due care to avoid the risk of hijacking within the interline system; (2) there was sufficient evidence for a jury to conclude that the failure of MEA to use due care was a proximate cause of the injuries; and (3) the foreseeable negligence of (a) the security officials at Dubai and (b) Kuwait Airways were not intervening acts breaking the causal link between MEA and the injuries and deaths. We reverse and remand the proceedings to the district court for a new trial.

NEGLIGENCE

A.   Duty

It is elementary that to find a party liable in negligence, there must have been a duty—a relationship between the two parties such that society imposes an obligation on one to protect the other from an unreasonable risk of harm. The question here is: did the circumstances in this case create a duty on the part of MEA to protect Kapar, Hegna, and Stanford? We think they did, and hold, as a matter of law, that MEA had a duty to protect the plaintiffs from unreasonable risk of foreseeable harm.

Duty is a relative concept. Whether an individual must protect another from the unreasonable risk of foreseeable harm depends on the nature of the risk and the particular level of knowledge of the alleged tortfeasor. Thus, "[t]he duty which one person may owe in a particular situation for the protection of another person is measured by the exigencies of the occasion." STUART M. SPEISER, ET AL., 2 THE AMERICAN LAW OF TORTS, § 9:4, at 1011 (1985). The alleged tortfeasor "must exercise such attention . . . of the circumstances . . . [and] knowledge of other pertinent matters, intelligence, and judgment as a 'reasonable person' would have—and, such superior attention . . . knowledge, intelligence, and judgment as the actor himself happens to possess." 2 THE AMERICAN LAW OF TORTS, § 9:4, at 1012.

In determining whether a duty exists, a court should examine: (1) the relationship between the parties; and (2) the reasonable foreseeability of harm to the person injured.

1.   *Relationship between MEA and the Victims*

Privity?

Although the plaintiffs were not passengers on an MEA flight, it is too late in the day to suggest that contractual privity is a prerequisite to the existence of a duty. Indeed, "[t]he duty of vigilance to prevent injury has its source in the law applicable to human relations rather than in a narrow conception of privity." 57A AM. JUR. 2d *Negligence* § 93 (1989). Thus, even without contractual privity,

[w]henever one person is by circumstances placed in such a position with regard to another that every one of ordinary sense who did think would at once recognize that if he did not use ordinary care and skill in his own conduct with regard to the circumstances he would cause danger of injury to the person or property of the other, a duty arises to use ordinary care and skill to avoid such danger.

Stagl v. Delta Airlines, Inc., 52 F.3d 463 (2d Cir. 1995).

Plaintiffs demonstrated that MEA joined an enterprise with interline airlines, including Kuwait Airways, to facilitate travel among the cooperating carriers. MEA's participation in interline arrangements with other IATA airlines was a lucrative venture. It expanded the reach of their routes, and facilitated inter-airline travel. Interline carriers shared the profits resulting from this cooperative endeavor.

In addition, based on evidence produced at trial, a jury could properly find that: as early as May, 1983, the Security Advisory Committee of IATA issued a warning that terrorists would board airlines at airports with poor security, and transfer to target airlines at other airports with tighter security. *See* Minutes of the IATA 21st Security Advisory Committee Meeting, Montreal, May 4–5, 1983. While it is unclear from the record to whom IATA issued the warning, MEA, as a member of IATA, knew or, in the exercise of reasonable care should have known, of the warning. In addition, MEA was fully aware of the poor security measures at the Beirut airport. MEA's Assistant Vice President at the Beirut station testified that he knew that the Lebanese military had, but did not use, metal detectors, that X-ray equipment was unavailable, and that security checks consisted only of personal searches over which MEA exercised no control.

IATA concluded that a critical way to protect passengers aboard target flights was to place increased reliance on security measures directed toward passengers upon their initial entry into the interline system. Thus, IATA implicitly recognized the principle that "[d]uty is largely grounded in the natural responsibilities of societal living and human relations, such as have the recognition of reasonable men." Accordingly, a jury could reasonably find that when MEA accepted interline passengers aboard its planes in Beirut, it knew or should have known that there was a danger that terrorists would try to board their airline only to transfer later to a vulnerable, interline target airplane. MEA operated out of Beirut airport, amidst heightened political tensions, an ongoing terrorist campaign that posed continuing threats against American and Kuwaiti citizens and establishments, and lax airport security. In addition, MEA was armed with information regarding unique terrorist hijacking tactics. Accepting interline passengers, while perhaps not normally a function implicating the safety of third parties, became such a function under the perilous circumstances existent at that time in Beirut.

If MEA, in the exercise of ordinary care, should have recognized that under these circumstances, knowing what it knew, there was an unreasonable risk of hijacking to passengers aboard its flight and other connecting flights, then the jury could find that MEA should have implemented secondary screening measures or warned other interline members of a possible threat of hijacking.

If MEA, in the exercise of ordinary care, should have recognized that under these circumstances, knowing what it knew, there was an unreasonable risk of hijacking to passengers aboard its flight and other connecting flights, then the jury could find that MEA should have implemented secondary screening measures or warned other interline members of a possible threat of hijacking.

MEA argued that it could not put secondary screening measures in place because security was under the sole control of the Lebanese military. The district court concluded that plaintiffs failed to adduce proof that MEA could have conducted secondary screening procedures. This was an erroneous allocation of the burden of proof. It is not incumbent upon the plaintiff to disprove every possible defense to a negligence theory. If MEA's contention was that it had no duty because it was barred by the Lebanese military from instituting secondary screening procedures in Beirut, it was MEA's responsibility to prove this, not the plaintiffs' responsibility to disprove it. In any event, even if MEA's hands were tied by the Lebanese military, precluding secondary screening measures, nothing prevented MEA officials in Beirut from contacting connecting airlines to warn them of the danger of hijacking.

2. *The Reasonable Foreseeability of Harm to the Persons Injured*

In determining the existence of a duty, a court may examine the reasonable foreseeability of harm to the party injured. MEA argues that this erroneously conflates the concepts of duty and foreseeability. What MEA fails to recognize, however, is that there are two concepts of foreseeability, the one specific, the other general. The first concerns the foreseeability of the specific injury the plaintiff suffered, and focuses on whether the defendant's actions are a proximate cause of the harm. The second, and the one at issue here, concerns the general foreseeable risk which is crucial to determining the existence of a duty and helps to limit its scope.

In the second, or risk-defining sense, Judge Cardozo early recognized, "[t]he risk reasonably to be perceived defines the duty to be obeyed, and risk imports relation; it is risk to another or to others within the range of apprehension." *Palsgraf v. Long Island R.R. Co.*, 162 N.E. 99 (N.Y. 1928). Hence,

> [t]he duty element of negligence focuses on whether the defendant's conduct foreseeably created a broader "zone of risk" that poses a general threat of harm to others . . . The proximate causation element, on the other hand, is concerned with whether and to what extent the defendant's conduct foreseeably and substantially caused the specific injury that actually occurred . . . As to *duty*, the proper inquiry for the reviewing appellate court is whether the defendant's conduct created a foreseeable zone of risk, not whether the defendant could foresee the specific injury that actually occurred.

McCain v. Florida Power Corp., 593 So. 2d 500 (Fla. 1992).

There was evidence that MEA knew: (1) of the threatened attacks by Hezbollah terrorists; (2) that terrorists were boarding flights in dirty airports to infiltrate other airlines; (3) that the Beirut airport had extraordinarily poor security; and (4) that the four hijackers who boarded in Beirut had tickets which teemed with suspicion. A jury could reasonably find, under these circumstances, that if MEA did nothing, it would create a zone of risk that stretched at least as far as the innocent passengers aboard flights with which the four hijackers would eventually connect. It lay well within ordinary prudence for an airline to realize that persons at the dirty Beirut airport who purchased tickets on short notice with cash, checked no luggage for a flight from the Middle East to the Far East, and took a circuitous route aboard flights which (a) they did not have to take to reach their destination, (b) created inordinate delays and layovers, and (c) no other passenger aboard MEA flight 426 took, posed a hijacking threat.

Evidence of MEA Knowledge

In sum, the duty is dictated and measured by the exigencies of the situation, and the risk reasonably to be perceived defines the duty to be obeyed. We conclude that MEA, as a first leg interline carrier, had a duty to protect passengers on other interline connecting flights from unreasonable risk of harm through the use of reasonable precautions in the face of reasonably foreseeable risks. MEA was faced with a set of circumstances that a jury could reasonably find created a foreseeable risk, necessitating some action to protect others from an unreasonable threat of hijacking.

B.   Breach

On the evidence presented a jury could reasonably find that MEA failed to take reasonable precautions in the face of foreseeable risks. This question should be left for the jury to decide on retrial.

C.   Proximate Cause

The district court held that plaintiffs failed to prove that MEA's inaction was a proximate cause of the deaths of Hegna and Stanford, and the injuries sustained by Kapar. The court reasoned that: (1) there was no evidence of what the Lebanese military could have done if MEA had alerted them to the four suspicious men; (2) the evidence showed only that the weaponry emerged on board the Kuwait Airways plane, leaving open the possibility that the hijackers procured their weapons in Dubai; and (3) even if a causal link were established, the negligence of the Kuwait Airways employees and the Dubai airport security officials were intervening acts, breaking the chain of causation between MEA and the resultant harm.

We disagree with this analysis. Plaintiffs made at least a *prima facie* showing of causation, and this record does not present such an overwhelming amount of evidence that fair minded jurors "could not arrive at a verdict against [MEA]." Considering the evidence in the light most favorable to plaintiffs, and resolving all inferences that a jury might draw in their favor, it cannot be said that no rational juror could find in plaintiffs' favor.

The district court concluded that plaintiffs failed to establish proximate cause, in part, because "there [was] no evidence of what, if anything, the army would have done" if alerted by the MEA ticket agents of the threat posed by the four hijackers. We disagree.

First, as a practical matter, warning the Lebanese military was not the only option open to MEA. Even assuming that the Lebanese military, after receiving a warning of the possible threat, would do nothing, plaintiffs contend that MEA could have warned the connecting airlines on which MEA knew the hijackers had reservations. Consequently, the fact that there was no evidence of what, if anything, the military would have done, is not determinative. Second, the district court impermissibly substituted its judgment for that of the jury. We cannot say that the district court's doubts regarding the possible lack of concern of the Lebanese military amounts to such overwhelming evidence in favor of MEA that reasonable and fair-minded jurors would have to conclude that there was no causal link between MEA's inaction and the resultant injuries and deaths. The district court also noted that, even if MEA employees or the Lebanese military conducted a search, there was no evidence that they would have found the weapons used in the hijacking of KU221. The court concluded that it was possible that the hijackers did not get their weapons until they reached Dubai. Again, this is a case where reasonable minds can differ. The plaintiffs presented testimony and circumstantial evidence from which a reasonable person could infer that MEA's failure to act proximately caused Kapar's injuries and the deaths of Stanford and Hegna.

First, the plaintiffs offered the testimony of Neil Beeston, an engineer at Kuwait Airways and passenger aboard flight KU221, who witnessed three of the hijackers trying to use the unguarded rear stairs of the Kuwait Airways jet during the boarding process. Plaintiffs showed that it was common in the Middle East to allow one passenger to check in for several others, thus allowing armed cohorts to avoid detection. Also, the Kuwait Airways jet was cleaned at Dubai and no passengers were allowed to leave the aircraft. Furthermore, no passenger had access to any area of the plane, other than the toilets and overhead bins, where one could stash weapons. Plaintiffs showed that there was no evidence of tampering with any of the panels in the aircraft bathrooms. Finally, there was an IATA warning describing the *modus operandi* of some armed terrorists, who board airlines at dirty airports.

From this evidence a reasonable juror could conclude that the terrorists had the weapons in their possession at the very beginning of their journey in Beirut. One could reasonably conclude that the hijackers boarded the MEA flight armed (consistent with the *modus operandi* outlined in the IATA circular) and, once in Dubai, one "clean" hijacker checked in for the other three who attempted to bypass the Kuwait Airways official at the forward door by entering the rear stairwell. One could infer from the facts that (1) the cleaning crew discovered nothing, (2) no one left the plane, and (3) the plane's panels were not disturbed, that the weapons were not already aboard KU221 when it arrived in Dubai.

Plaintiffs were not required to prove causation beyond a reasonable doubt. It was sufficient to present evidence "from which reasonable persons may conclude that it [was] more probable that [the hijacking] was caused by [MEA] than that it was not." PROSSER AND KEETON, § 41, at 269. While reasonable minds could differ on this evidence, there is not such a dearth of proof on the issue of causation as to justify taking the matter away from the jury.

Proof of Causation, Standard

Finally, the district court concluded that plaintiffs failed to establish a proximate link between MEA and the injuries and deaths aboard flight KU221, because the negligence of the security officials and of the Kuwait Airways employees in Dubai were independent intervening acts breaking the causative chain. Again, we must disagree. The causative link is not broken by the negligent conduct of a third person when such conduct is normal or foreseeable under the circumstances. Questions regarding what is normal or foreseeable, like other questions of proximate cause, are generally issues for the trier of fact. Here, the evidence at trial, bathed in a light most favorable to plaintiffs, was sufficient to carry to the jury the issue of foreseeability of third party negligence. There was evidence that the airport at Dubai had poor tarmac security. Also, MEA had notice, from the IATA warning issued in May, 1983, that there were differing standards of security in airports across the Middle East, and that even those airports engaging in security measures were potentially lax due to the "delays in facilitation and escalating security costs . . . [and the difficulty in meeting] the manning requirements for sufficient, trained personnel to operate a gate search system." Minutes of the IATA 21st Security Advisory Committee Meeting, Montreal, May 4–5, 1983.

Although it is arguable whether it was "foreseeable" that security measures would be insufficient in Dubai to respond to the heightened threat, such matters are properly left to the trier of fact. There was enough evidence to allow the jury to decide whether the actions of the Kuwait Airways employees and security officials in Dubai were "closely and reasonably associated with the immediate consequences of the defendant's act, and form a normal part of its aftermath . . ." PROSSER & KEETON § 44, at 307. Just as a tortfeasor who negligently breaks a victim's leg must reasonably anticipate negligence on the part of the doctor setting that leg, so too an airline which does nothing to prevent potential hijackers from traveling aboard its aircraft may reasonably have to anticipate that other airlines will be lax in their security measures.

CONCLUSION

We recognize, as the district court did, that this is an "anguishingly distressing case." And we concede it is a close call. We conclude, however, that MEA was not so far removed from the actions aboard the ill-fated Kuwait Airways flight as to be entitled to judgment as a matter of law. MEA took on responsibilities in the clouded atmosphere of threatened terrorist attacks, with knowledge of terrorist hijacking tactics. With this awareness and knowledge it had a commensurate duty to protect those within a foreseeable scope of danger. Accordingly, we reverse the district court's grant of MEA's Rule 50(b) motion, and remand for a new trial.

EXERCISE 8-6. *STANFORD V. KUWAIT AIRWAYS CORP.*—NEGLIGENCE

1. Define "interline" ticketing and the new terror techniques identified at the 21st Security Advisory Committee of the International Air Transport Association ("IATA").

2. Give examples of how the airport in Beirut, Lebanon was a "dirty" airport?

3. Describe why the hijackers' tickets were suspicious.

4. In defining the tort of negligence, how does the law define "duty"? Did MEA owe a duty to the passenger-victims? Explain.

5. Was MEA's conduct the proximate cause of the deaths at issue? Who should decide, according to the court?

D. INTERFERENCE WITH CREW AND CO-PASSENGER TORTS

UNITED STATES V. SPELLMAN

243 F. Supp. 2d 285 (E.D. Pa. 2003)

DALZELL, DISTRICT JUDGE.

On January 7, 2003, defendant Alonzo Spellman pleaded guilty to interference with flight attendants and crew members and to two counts of simple assault on an aircraft, all arising from what can only be described as every air passenger's and crew member's nightmare on Delta Flight 2038 on July 23, 2002. At Spellman's sentencing yesterday, we were presented with the unusual coincidence of (a) the Government's motion for upward departure and (b) the defendant's motion for downward departure.

It is undisputed that Alonzo Spellman is a veteran of the National Football League. After graduating from Ohio State University, where he was first-team AP All-Big Ten, Spellman starting in 1993 played with the Chicago Bears, where as a defensive end in 1995 he set a club record for sacks in consecutive games. He later signed with the Dallas Cowboys, and then played for the Detroit Lions until his release for tardiness at practices. As one might expect from his impressive career in football defense, Spellman is something of a man-mountain. Not only is he six feet, six inches tall, but he now weighs 330 pounds, and can be so formidable-looking that Philadelphia police officers were afraid to arrest him.

At the sentencing hearing, we heard the testimony of seven passengers and crew members who on July 23, 2002 shared the misfortune of flying on Delta Flight 2038 from Cincinnati, Ohio to Philadelphia, Pennsylvania. Shortly after sitting in Row 21 of the aircraft, Spellman began speaking loudly about a variety of subjects, including the plane crashing. He made remarks such as, "I hope we make it to Philadelphia before this plane crashes into a building." After the aircraft was airborne for about twenty minutes, Spellman added obscenities to his verbal barrage, including in a loud voice, "motherfucker," "fuck you," "shit," and "bitch."

When flight attendant Danielle Eller spoke to Spellman, he asked her if she was a Christian. Upon quietly answering in the affirmative, Spellman commanded her to say out loud that she was a Christian. Ms. Eller tried to ignore this behavior, and shortly thereafter she saw Spellman swinging his arms in the air and saying in a loud voice, "I'll smash your fucking head with my cleats, I will."

Flight attendants told Spellman that this kind of behavior was unacceptable, especially with families on the plane, and told him he was scaring many of the other over 130 passengers. Spellman ignored these requests. Ms. Eller reported that all of the passengers around Spellman remained frozen in their seats, frightened even to get up and go to the bathroom for fear of attracting Spellman's attention.

About a half hour into the flight, Karen Weaver, who sat in the seat in front of Spellman and who was traveling with her two small sons, turned around and requested that Spellman not use such vulgar language, explaining that she was traveling with small children. Spellman's response to Mrs. Weaver's polite request was, "Oh, you're going to tell me to mind my tongue, you Jew."

Although Mrs. Weaver tried to ignore Spellman, his verbal barrage continued with, "You hear me, Mom, now you're not going to talk to me." Commenting on Mrs. Weaver's skirt, he said, "Where do you get off wearing your miniskirt and showing your pussy to everyone?" He added that she "could show her body to everybody dressed like a whore in front of [her] kids." Spellman referred to Mrs. Weaver's two- and three-year-old sons as "sorry white boys." Mrs. Weaver remained quiet, but began crying. Her husband, Stephen, who was seated in a different row, tried to intervene. Spellman kept up his verbal assaults on Mrs. Weaver and taunted her husband, saying, "What are you going to do about it, Dad?"

Flight attendant Lane Stephens tried to accomplish what flight attendant Eller had failed to achieve, but Spellman immediately challenged her with loud and insulting comments about her appearance. When Ms. Stephens told Spellman that he couldn't use such language, and that police would meet the plane, Spellman responded that he didn't care and predicted that the police wouldn't do anything to him.

As Ms. Stephens was taking down the names of people in seats around Spellman as witnesses to give to the police, Spellman said to her, "You got a problem with me, you want me to take you down?" Since Spellman showed no signs of calming down, the flight attendants thrice advised the pilot, Captain Robert Freund, of what was happening. Captain Freund ultimately made an announcement requesting that the passenger stop his conduct and stating that it would result in his arrest. In response, Spellman yelled that he would "get off" because he was "bipolar." Spellman's conduct worsened after the Captain's admonition.

Passenger Arthur Daemmrich had the bad luck to sit next to Spellman. Mr. Daemmrich was so frightened that he spent much of the flight in the galley area without a seat (all other seats on the aircraft being occupied). Because he was so afraid, and notwithstanding Federal Aviation Administration regulations requiring all passengers to be seated and restrained by a seatbelt, flight attendant Anne Chase granted permission to Mr. Daemmrich to sit in the bathroom stall during the landing.

Perhaps most dramatic of all, several passengers reported that Spellman, according to the account of passenger John Liebenthal, "talked out loud about opening the door while in flight." Passenger Matthew Lynch, who testified that he takes about one hundred Delta flights per year, reported that he had "never experienced anything close to this," *i.e.*, statements about opening the door during flight. Passenger Carol McAdam recalled Spellman's words as, "Give me a parachute and I'll jump off this plane," and said that she believed, "This could be another incident similar to the hijackings that occurred on September 11." Passenger Sally Schulz reported that she "was particularly scared when Spellman said that he wanted to open the door so he could get out."

As a direct result of Spellman's conduct, Captain Freund contacted air traffic control at Philadelphia International Airport to request a "priority handling." The tower granted the Captain's request, and other planes that were ahead of Delta Flight 2038 were ordered to clear the way. Captain Freund testified that he had only "broken out" of an orderly landing pattern four times in his twenty-two years as a commercial airline pilot. He explained that this "hazardous procedure" created danger for the two aircraft ahead of Flight 2038 because in three to four seconds the planes automatically go at full power from a ten degree descending pitch to a thirty degree ascent, which is "very disconcerting for passengers—they scream out." Because his aircraft was landing before he and his crew could complete their normal protocol, Captain Freund also reported that there was "no tolerance for error" in his landing. Flight 2038 then landed ahead of the other planes.

Captain Freund directed all the passengers to remain seated until such time as Spellman was removed from the aircraft. But because of Mr. Weaver's fear for his children, as soon as the plane was on the ground, he "scooped up" his sons in each arm and ran up the narrow aisle to the galley while the aircraft taxied to the gate, a very dangerous act. Karen Weaver followed close behind.

Once the plane was near the gate, Captain Freund entered the passenger compartment to escort Spellman out of the plane. While the aft aircraft door was still closed and locked, Captain Freund approached Spellman and observed that it was "obvious" that the passengers around him "were terrified." On the Captain's approach, Spellman raised his hands to him and said, "You see this, I can feel the adrenaline rushing through my hands, I'm about to rip your throat out." Notwithstanding this ghastly and highly credible threat, (Captain Freund confessed that "I was shaking in my shoes. I was very, very scared.") Captain Freund continued to attempt to keep Spellman calm, but Spellman said that if the police came aboard, "they are going to carry me off in a body bag." The Captain testified that "I was certain people were going to be hurt."

At this point matters reached a level bordering on the surreal. When the Captain and Spellman finally got to the front of the plane, the aircraft door was not fully open. Captain Freund asked why the ground crew had not opened the door and was informed that the Philadelphia police had told the ground personnel not to open the door until more police arrived. Not wanting to keep over 130 people hostage to this evident danger, the Captain commanded the crew to open the aircraft door.

When Spellman and his mother and sister left the aircraft, the armed Philadelphia police—perhaps as many as six of them—did nothing. At all times Spellman continued to act aggressively, cursing all the while and frightening everyone in his path. The passengers reported that when they complained to the Philadelphia police about their inaction, the officers, displaying indifference and abject cowardice, responded to them, "You want to help?"

After menacing about in the baggage area for upwards of forty-five minutes with the Philadelphia police at all times giving him a wide berth, Spellman eventually left the airport, unimpeded by local law enforcement. We believe that a sentence of eighteen months is on this record warranted. The government's motion is granted and the defendant's motion is denied.

MUSTAFA V. CITY OF CHICAGO

442 F.3d 544 (7th Cir. 2006)

WILLIAMS, CIRCUIT JUDGE.

Anna Mustafa sued the defendant police officers for false arrest and violation of her civil rights following an incident at Chicago's O'Hare Airport. The district court granted summary judgment in favor of the defendants because it found that there was probable cause to arrest Mustafa, and even in the absence of probable cause, the defendants were protected by qualified immunity. Because we agree with the district court that the defendant officers acted upon probable cause and, in any event, acted within the scope of their immunity, we reject Mustafa's argument that summary judgment was improperly granted and affirm the district court's ruling.

BACKGROUND

Anna Mustafa is a 56-year-old American citizen of Palestinian descent and Muslim faith. On December 28, 2001, just three months after the attacks of September 11, Mustafa received word that her father had died in Israel. That afternoon, Mustafa arrived at the Swissair ticket counter at O'Hare, intending to fly to Tel Aviv by way of Zurich, Switzerland to attend her father's funeral. Mustafa was accompanied to the counter by nineteen members of her immediate family. Mustafa ordered a "Muslim" meal for the flight. Moments later, the Swissair clerk took Mustafa to a bomb-detection machine to have her two pieces of luggage inspected for weapons. Mustafa suspected that this was an instance of discriminatory religious or ethnic profiling.

Passenger Demographics

Following the inspection, Mustafa complained about her treatment to a Swissair manager, Muhammad Qadeer, who offered to escort her to the gate because the screening was complete. During this exchange, Mustafa was screaming and the area was crowded. Mustafa realized that security personnel had failed to inspect her purse. She did not realize that carry-on bags would be screened at another checkpoint, and she was concerned that if Swissair later realized it had not checked the purse, she would be delayed and miss her flight. Mustafa tried to point out that her purse had not been inspected, saying, "You already checked my luggage. Maybe I have a bomb in my purse. Nobody has checked that." In response to the word "bomb," an employee working at a nearby United Airlines counter began to yell that she had heard the "B-word" and that security should be called. Another manager, Mauricio Penaranda, called the police to report an "unruly" passenger saying the word "bomb."

Within two to three minutes, defendant Officer Susan Schober arrived and observed what she later described as a "commotion." Qadeer informed her that Mustafa had made a statement like "Maybe I have a bomb in my purse." Officer Schober, Qadeer, Mustafa, and one of Mustafa's sons, Murad Mustafa, spent 20 to 30 minutes in conversation that focused on calming Mustafa down so that she could get on the flight to Zurich. Following this conversation, defendants Sergeant Gawlik and Officer Burke arrived and asked Officer Schober if she had checked Mustafa's purse. Since the answer was no, the two new officers checked the purse, shouting abusively at Mustafa. Sergeant Gawlik placed Mustafa under arrest. Mustafa, her son Murad, and Sergeant Gawlik engaged in a screaming argument during which Sergeant Gawlik insulted Mustafa's family and made a racist reference to the September 11 terrorist attacks three months earlier.

Mustafa spent two days in jail before being released on $50,000 bond; she missed her father's funeral. Mustafa was indicted on a charge of Felony Disorderly Conduct—Bomb Threat pursuant to 720 Ill. Comp. Stat. 5/26–1(a)(3), but acquitted following a bench trial. The statute under which Mustafa was charged applies to any person who "Transmits or causes to be transmitted in any manner to another a false alarm to the effect that a bomb . . . is concealed in such place that its explosion or release would endanger human life, knowing at the time of such transmission that there is no reasonable ground for believing that such bomb . . . is concealed in such place."

After Mustafa was acquitted, she filed the instant suit against the City of Chicago and four police officers, which originally contained seven counts. A number of claims, including all those stated against the city, were dismissed. The defendant police officers moved for summary judgment on the surviving counts, false arrest and violation of Mustafa's right to equal protection under the law pursuant to 18 U.S.C. § 1983. The district court granted summary judgment for the defendants on both counts. This appeal followed.

II. ANALYSIS

A. There was Probable Cause to Arrest Mustafa

We review a district court's grant of summary judgment *de novo*, viewing the facts in the light most favorable to the non-moving party. Probable cause to arrest is an absolute defense to any claim under Section 1983 against police officers for wrongful arrest, false imprisonment, or malicious prosecution. This is so even where the defendant officers allegedly acted upon a malicious motive (such as the racism that Mustafa suggests motivated the defendants here).

Police officers have probable cause to arrest an individual when "the facts and circumstances within their knowledge and of which they have reasonably trustworthy information are sufficient to warrant a prudent person in believing that the suspect had committed" an offense. The court evaluates probable cause "not on the facts as an omniscient observer would perceive them," but rather "as they would have appeared to a reasonable person in the position of the arresting officer." *See Woods v. City of Chicago*, 234 F.3d 979 (7th Cir. 2000).

Probable Cause

Here, there were at least two separate facts that could have led a reasonable person to believe that a crime had been committed. First, the earliest arriving officer, Officer Schober, observed "commotion" and "agitation" in progress, with Mustafa at its center, at a crowded ticket counter at an international airport. *See* 720 Ill. Comp. Stat. 5/26–1(a)(1) ("A person commits disorderly conduct when he knowingly does any act in such an unreasonable manner as to alarm or disturb another and to provoke a breach of the peace"). Second, Qadeer, the Swissair manager, told the officers that the plaintiff had said, "Maybe I have a bomb." Once a reasonably credible witness informs an officer that a suspect has committed a crime, the police have probable cause to arrest the suspect. Qadeer's apparent credibility as a manager of Swissair at O'Hare has not been questioned here. Therefore, based on the undisputed facts, a prudent person might have believed that Mustafa committed the crime of making a false bomb threat.

Mustafa makes much of the fact that Qadeer never actually believed that Mustafa had a bomb in her purse. This argument misapprehends the focus of our review of the circumstances surrounding her arrest. The existence of probable cause does not depend on the actual truth of the complaint. The officers were entitled to take Qadeer at his word as to Mustafa's actions. Furthermore, the statute under which Mustafa was later charged applies categorically to all false bomb threats; it contains no element limiting its application to credible bomb threats or to those threats that convince the listener.

Particularly in light of the time and place of the event, which occurred in an international airport three months after the September 11 attacks, and the understandable sensitivity of air travelers and airport security personnel at that time, it was reasonable for the officers to conclude that Mustafa had committed disorderly conduct by stating that she might have a bomb in her purse.

Likewise, the fact that Mustafa's statement was phrased conditionally, prefaced by the word "maybe," is irrelevant under the plain language of the statute, which forbids any "false alarm to the effect that a bomb . . . is concealed." Particularly in light of the time and place of the event, which occurred in an international airport three months after the September 11 attacks, and the understandable sensitivity of air travelers and airport security personnel at that time, it was reasonable for the officers to conclude that Mustafa had committed disorderly conduct by stating that she might have a bomb in her purse.

Finally, Mustafa erroneously suggests that the defendant officers were derelict in their duty to investigate the circumstances surrounding the incident before arresting her. But police officers have no duty to investigate extenuating circumstances or search for exculpatory evidence once probable cause has been established via the accusation of a credible witness. They may simply arrest the accused suspect.

B.   The Defendants were Protected by Qualified Immunity

Even if we were to find that there was insufficient probable cause to justify Mustafa's arrest, the doctrine of qualified immunity would nonetheless ensure a ruling in favor of the defendants.

Qualified immunity protects officers performing discretionary functions from civil liability so long as their conduct does not violate clearly established statutory or constitutional rights that a reasonable person would know about. A plaintiff seeking to defeat this defense in a Section 1983 action must show, first, that the plaintiff's rights were violated. Second, the plaintiff must show that the law concerning the plaintiff's asserted right was clearly established at the time the challenged conduct occurred. Finally, the court must determine whether a reasonably competent official would know that the conduct was unlawful in the situation he confronted. Here, Mustafa certainly had a right to be free from an arrest that lacked probable cause, and that right is clearly established, so the only remaining question is whether a reasonable officer could believe that it was lawful to arrest Mustafa.

As discussed above, Mustafa argues that it was unreasonable to believe she had committed a crime because her statement about a bomb was phrased as a possibility rather than a fact ("maybe I have a bomb in my purse"), because any reasonable person would have realized that she was not serious, and because she did not actually frighten or convince anyone that she had a real bomb. However, even if we accepted this argument, this would not disturb the defendants' qualified immunity defense.

The Illinois statute at issue applies to implausible and unconvincing bomb threats. *See People v. Barron*, 348 Ill. App. 3d 109 (Ill. App. Ct. 2004) (upholding the felony disorderly conduct conviction of an individual who joked about having a bomb in his shoe at Midway Airport, because the statute applies to false threats "regardless of the intention of the speaker or the effect the words have upon the person receiving them"). At the time of the arrest, prior to *Barron*, the application of the bomb threat statute to circumstances involving jokes, sarcasm, etc., was, perhaps, arguable; a court might theoretically read a limitation into the statute and apply it only to credible or convincing bomb threats. But where the law is open to interpretation, qualified immunity protects police officers who reasonably interpret an unclear statute. Reviewing courts must ask "whether X is a crime under the statute that the police arrested the plaintiff for violating. If the answer to that question was unclear when the arrest was made, the police are entitled to their immunity." *Northern v. City of Chicago*, 126 F.3d 1024 (7th Cir. 1997).

Here, the most Mustafa can plausibly claim is that the criminality of her conditional statement was unclear; no case clearly established that implausible threats fall outside of its reach. Furthermore, even if no reasonable person could have believed that Mustafa had made a genuine bomb threat, the officers might reasonably have believed that Mustafa had committed the closely related offense of nonspecific disorderly conduct under 720 Ill. Comp. Stat. 5/26–1(a)(1), which covers any unreasonable activity which alarms or disturbs another and provokes a breach of the peace. It is undisputed that Mustafa disturbed employees at the airport and that a noisy confrontation ensued. Officers may arrest individuals suspected of any crime; the fact that Mustafa was prosecuted under only the bomb threat section of the disorderly conduct statute does not mean that she could only properly be arrested under that section. Thus, the officers are protected by qualified immunity, and the district court's ruling in their favor is affirmed.

EXERCISE 8-7. *MUSTAFA V. CITY OF CHICAGO*—BOMB THREAT

1. What, if anything, do Mrs. Mustafa's name, age, nationality and purpose for travel indicate about the threat she presents to her flight?

2. What are the terms of the Illinois bomb threat statute, 720 Ill. Comp. Stat. 5/26–1(a)(3), and how was it applied in this case?

3. What is a Section 1983 claim and what defenses apply to it?

4. What is "qualified immunity"?

5. Was Mrs. Mustafa the victim of racial profiling in this case?

NOTES ON *MUSTAFA V. CITY OF CHICAGO*—PROBABLE CAUSE

On Christmas Day 2009, Umar Farouk Abdulmutallab, attempted to destroy an Amsterdam-Detroit flight by detonating plastic explosives hidden in his underwear. He was known to American intelligence analysts because his father, a banker in Nigeria, had reported him to the authorities, yet he had not been placed on the watch list. *E.g.*, Mike McIntire, *Ensnared by Error on Growing U.S. Watch List, With No Way Out*, N.Y. TIMES, Apr. 7, 2010, at A1. Consider this situation side-by-side the facts of *Mustafa v. City of Chicago* in answering the question what threats should aviation security officials regard as creditable as opposed to incredible? Can practical considerations be harmonized with the law in this respect? *See also U.S. v. Mendoza*, 244 F.3d 1037 (9th Cir. 2001) (prosecution of bomb threat that endangered the safety of an aircraft in flight in violation of 18 U.S.C. § 32(a)(6)).

RUBIN V. UNITED AIR LINES, INC.

117 Cal. Rptr. 2d 109 (Cal. Ct. 2002)

JOHNSON, ACTING P.J.

An airline passenger brought suit against an airline and others after Los Angeles Police Department officers removed her from a commercial flight about to depart for Hawaii. Her suit alleged causes of action for false arrest, false imprisonment, assault, battery and emotional distress. The airline claimed it was entitled to summary judgment as a matter of law because a provision of the Airline Deregulation Act of 1978 expressly preempted her state law tort claims. In the alternative, the airline claimed it was also entitled to judgment as a matter of law because it acted within its statutory discretion by refusing to transport a passenger it decided was, or might be, inimical to airline safety. The trial court granted summary judgment in favor of the airline.

Lawful Grounds for Expulsion of Passenger

We hold a passenger whom the airline believes is, or might become, inimical to the safety of the aircraft or its passengers may be ejected from a flight without subjecting the airline to tort liability if at the time airline personnel had a reasonable basis for believing the passenger presented a safety risk. We further conclude the airline's actions in this case were reasonable as a matter of law. Accordingly, we affirm the summary judgment.

FACTS AND PROCEEDINGS BELOW

Appellant, Ms. Adrienne Rubin, decided to join her husband, Stanford Rubin, a trusts and estates attorney who was then in Hawaii. She purchased an airline ticket from respondent United Airlines, Inc. ("United"). She paid for a coach ticket and upgraded the ticket to first class by using her husband's frequent flyer miles.

On October 28, 1998, Ms. Rubin arrived at the Los Angeles International Airport approximately an hour before the plane was scheduled to depart. She went directly to the gate with her bags. She waited in line a long time before she could present her ticket to the agent at the gate. Ms. Rubin had a first class itinerary card with a seat designation of 2F. However, the United computer showed no first-class reservation for her. The agent explained Ms. Rubin needed to surrender an additional 3,000 frequent flyer miles to qualify for a first class upgrade because, for some reason, 3,000 miles had been recredited to her husband's account. The agent directed Ms. Rubin to the customer service counter nearby.

Approximately 30 minutes remained before the flight for Hawaii was to depart. It took nearly 15 minutes for Ms. Rubin to reach the front of the line at the customer service counter. When the United agent finally located Ms. Rubin's frequent flyer account on the computer she discovered Ms. Rubin did not have the needed 3,000 miles in her account. Ms. Rubin told the agent to take the miles from her husband's account. Only 10 or so minutes remained before the plane was due to take off. The agent told Ms. Rubin to go to the gate while she continued to try to locate Mr. Rubin's frequent flyer account number.

Ms. Rubin went to the gate and told the gate agent she had a first class seat and wanted to board. The agent responded all first class seats on the flight had already been assigned. He explained the flight was very full but two or three seats were available in the coach section. The agent offered Ms. Rubin the option of taking one of the seats in coach or flying first class on a later flight. He apparently did not indicate a specific coach seat assignment. Ms. Rubin explained she had to leave on this flight because she and her husband had an engagement later in the day she did not want to miss. Ms. Rubin was adamant about wanting a first class seat, and on this particular flight. The gate agent notified the service director on board there was a person about to board who was insisting on leaving on this flight and insisting on a first class seat. The service director decided he would at least accommodate Ms. Rubin's wishes to leave on this flight.

The service director met Ms. Rubin in the jetway. Ms. Rubin told the service director she had a first class ticket, a seat assignment of 2F, and could not understand why the airline had given her seat away. Ms. Rubin told the service director she had to fly first class because she had a special diet. The director reiterated all first class seats were now assigned and occupied. He explained if she wanted to take this fight she would have to fly coach in seat 26B.

Ms. Rubin entered the plane. She did not go to seat 26B in coach. According to Ms. Rubin, the service director did not specify any particular seat but told her she could sit anywhere in coach. Instead, Ms. Rubin entered (or attempted to enter) the first class cabin to determine for herself whether seat 2F was in fact occupied. As the service director put it, "that's when the hair came up on the back of my neck, because, . . . you're violating everything that it's about, because it was clearly stated to Mrs. Rubin that the first-class seats were full."

The purser of an aircraft has primary responsibility for the safety of the passengers and has ultimate authority over the other flight attendants. When she saw Ms. Rubin enter (or attempt to enter) the first class cabin, the purser, according to Ms. Rubin, "went ballistic." Ms. Rubin got into a lengthy and loud discussion with the purser. The service director intervened and again directed Ms. Rubin to take her seat in 26B. Instead, Ms. Rubin dropped her luggage in the doorway of the aircraft and took a bulkhead emergency row seat immediately behind the first class section. The service director told Ms. Rubin to store her bag. Ms. Rubin refused and told the director he could do it himself or have someone else store the bag if he wished. The service director and another stewardess repeatedly told Ms. Rubin she could not sit in row 9 either, both because she had been assigned seat 26B, and because she was not "emergency row qualified."

The service director left to consult with the purser. The purser, in the meantime, had already talked to the captain. The purser told the captain she had an irate passenger on board who refused to follow directions and who had attempted to make an unauthorized entry into the first class section. Based on the purser's representations, the captain agreed Ms. Rubin's demeanor and refusal to follow directions had the potential to create a safety problem in flight. The purser told the service director she would not fly if Ms. Rubin remained on board. The captain, purser and service director decided Ms. Rubin should be deplaned.

When the service director returned to the cabin Ms. Rubin was no longer sitting in row 9. She was instead sitting in another person's seat who had been in the lavatory. The person whose seat Ms. Rubin occupied was now sitting on the armrest of an aisle seat. The service director told Ms. Rubin she would have to deplane. In response, she instead finally took her assigned seat in 26B. By this time the flight was at least 15 minutes past schedule for takeoff. The other passengers were becoming impatient and unruly. Some yelled at United personnel suggesting they do something to regain control of the situation. A gate agent came on board to take Ms. Rubin off the plane. Ms. Rubin was talking loudly on her cell phone. She refused to acknowledge his presence or mission. He could not get Ms. Rubin to pay attention to him or to stop talking on the telephone. He left the plane in frustration. Now the flight was some 20 to 25 minutes past departure time. United personnel decided to call the Los Angeles Airport Police.

Passengers started applauding when the police officers boarded the plane. The Los Angeles police officers asked Ms. Rubin to leave the plane. Ms. Rubin kept interrupting to explain she believed she had a first class seat assignment and could not understand why United had given her seat away. The officers told Ms. Rubin the airplane was not going to take off with her on it. Ms. Rubin refused to leave the plane voluntarily. She refused to leave her seat, refused to stand up and refused to walk. The officers had to pick Ms. Rubin up out of her seat and carry her by her shoulders off the plane. As they proceeded in this fashion through the aisles passengers applauded and whistled. They also yelled and hurled wads of paper at Ms. Rubin. In the view of one officer, the situation on board was "a mob scene." He believed the other passengers were so frustrated and upset with Ms. Rubin because of the trouble and delay, he believed if United had permitted Ms. Rubin to stay on the flight "it could have gotten ugly."

"A Mob Scene"

The officers took Ms. Rubin off the plane. Her luggage was still where she had dropped it in the doorway. The service director removed her bag to the jetway. The officers detained Ms. Rubin at the police station for several hours. The officers contacted the Federal Aviation Administration and the Federal Bureau of Investigation as is required when investigating a potential federal charge of obstructing a flight crew. A representative from the Federal Aviation Administration arrived and interviewed Ms. Rubin, as did a sergeant from the Los Angeles Police Department. Ultimately, Ms. Rubin was not charged. The officers returned Ms. Rubin to the airport and she flew first class on the next flight to Hawaii.

Ms. Rubin filed suit against United, the City of Los Angeles, and the Los Angeles police officers who removed her from the plane. Her complaint alleged causes of action for false arrest, false imprisonment, unlawful search and seizure, assault, battery, and emotional distress. United moved for summary judgment claiming Ms. Rubin's state tort law causes of action were expressly preempted by the Airline Deregulation Act. In the alternative, United claimed it was entitled to judgment as a matter of law in any event, asserting it had acted within the broad discretion accorded airlines by federal law to decide when a passenger presents a security risk sufficient to be removed from a flight. United argued there were no material factual disputes and asserted it was thus entitled to judgment as a matter of law. The trial court granted United's motion and this appeal followed.

DECISIONAL LAW IS UNSETTLED, AND THUS INCONCLUSIVE, WHICH STATE LAW TORT CLAIMS ARE PREEMPTED BY FEDERAL LAW

The Airline Deregulation Act of 1978 ("ADA") prohibits states from "enact[ing] or enforc[ing] a law, regulation, or other provision having the force and effect of law related to a price, route, or service of an air carrier . . ." This case concerns the scope of this preemptive provision as applied to a suit raising state tort law claims regarding, as United alleges, claims arising from its boarding procedures.

United claims "boarding procedures" are classified as a "service" and state claims challenging this airline service are expressly preempted by federal law. Ms. Rubin, by contrast, claims the airline gives a too all-encompassing reading to the term "service." She argues Congress used "service" in the public utility sense to only refer to the provision of air transportation to and from various markets at various times. She asserts her claims do not affect these services and thus are not preempted by the ADA.

Preemption Analysis Unnecessary

We need not decide which of the competing definitions of "service" most accurately reflects Congress's intent in adopting section 41713. Regardless of the types of state claims which should be preempted under the rubric of "services" in the ADA, we conclude United properly exercised the discretion given it in section 44902 of the FAA to refuse Ms. Rubin passage in the circumstances presented in this case.

THE UNDISPUTED FACTS ESTABLISH AS A MATTER OF LAW UNITED HAD A REASONABLE BELIEF MS. RUBIN WAS OR COULD BE INIMICAL TO THE SAFETY OF THE FLIGHT WHICH JUSTIFIED UNITED IN REFUSING HER PASSAGE

Section 44902 of the FAA was originally enacted by Congress in 1961. This provision authorizes an airline to "refuse to transport a passenger or property the carrier decides is, or might be, inimical to safety." It provides:

(a) *Mandatory refusal.*

The Administrator of the Federal Aviation Administration shall prescribe regulations requiring an air carrier, intrastate air carrier, or foreign air carrier to refuse to transport—(1) a passenger who does not consent to a search under section 44901(a) of this title establishing whether the passenger is carrying unlawfully a dangerous weapon, explosive, or other destructive substance; or (2) property of a passenger who does not consent to a search of the property establishing whether the property unlawfully contains a dangerous weapon, explosive, or other destructive substance.

(b) Permissive refusal.

Subject to regulations of the Administrator, an air carrier, intrastate air carrier, or foreign air carrier may refuse to transport a passenger or property the carrier decides is, or might be, inimical to safety.

(c) Agreeing to consent to search.

An agreement to carry passengers or property in air transportation or intrastate air transportation by an air carrier, intrastate air carrier, or foreign air carrier is deemed to include an agreement that the passenger or property will not be carried if consent to search the passenger or property for a purpose referred to in this section is not given.

Congress originally enacted this provision to help combat an air piracy problem. However, section 44902 is not, as Ms. Rubin suggests, reserved strictly for would-be terrorists and hijackers. Airlines have also invoked their discretion under this statute, as they have under common law, to exclude passengers in any number of circumstances.

As the Second Circuit noted in *Williams v. Trans World Airlines*, 509 F.2d 942 (2d Cir. 1975), an airline's duty to perform its services with the highest possible degree of safety in the public interest has both a statutory and common law basis. All commercial airlines are common carriers, and as such, owe a duty of utmost care for their safety. On the other hand, although the discretion given an airline under this provision to refuse to transport a passenger for safety reasons is "decidedly expansive, [it] is not unfettered." *O'Carroll v. American Airlines, Inc.*, 863 F.2d 11 (5th Cir. 1989). If an airline's refusal of transportation is arbitrary or capricious, its refusal can give rise to a claim by the offended passenger for damages. Stated another way, the decision to accept or refuse transport to a passenger based on considerations of safety and security "lies exclusively with the air carrier" and if such discretion is "exercised in good faith and for a rational reason" it will be upheld.

Carrier's Duty to Perform Services

In the present case, the record evidence establishes as a matter of law Ms. Rubin presented a safety risk which justified United's decision to remove her from the plane. Unlike other situations, Ms. Rubin was not simply loudly belligerent about a non-safety matter. Also unlike other cases, this was not a case of misidentifying the objectionable passenger. Nor did Ms. Rubin present any evidence tending to suggest United ejected her from the flight simply to retaliate against her for arguing with the purser. Instead the evidence demonstrates Ms. Rubin committed what in the industry is considered a serious breach of security by making or attempting to make an unauthorized entry into the first class cabin. In addition, the evidence demonstrates Ms. Rubin deliberately and repeatedly refused to follow directions from any of the uniformed airline personnel regarding the safety issues of proper stowing of luggage and emergency row seating.

The evidence demonstrates Ms. Rubin committed what in the industry is considered a serious breach of security by making or attempting to make an unauthorized entry into the first class cabin. In addition, the evidence demonstrates Ms. Rubin deliberately and repeatedly refused to follow directions from any of the uniformed airline personnel regarding the safety issues of proper stowing of luggage and emergency row seating.

In his deposition testimony the service director explained airlines had developed a heightened sensitivity to safety issues after events such as the Gulf War, the Oklahoma City bombing, the bombing of the World Trade Towers, and the explosion of Pam Am flight 103 over Lockerbie, Scotland. As a result of these events airlines learned they had become potential targets, and at the direction of the Federal Aviation Administration, airlines and airports started taking safety issues much more seriously. According to the service director, it was for this reason the purser perceived Ms. Rubin's unauthorized intrusion, or attempted intrusion, into the first class area as a threatening act. All seats in first class were occupied thus all the purser knew was someone was attempting to enter the forward cabin who clearly had no business being there. The service director stated "the hair came up on the back of his neck" as he watched Ms. Rubin drop her bag and "run into" first class. Instead of leaving the area as directed Ms. Rubin argued loudly with the purser for several minutes and insisted she be permitted to fly in the fully occupied first class cabin. Even Ms. Rubin described the argument as a "confrontation."

Although the service director intervened in an attempt to accommodate Ms. Rubin she refused to follow his directions as well. She refused to stow her bag as directed, and in fact told the director if he did not want the bag in the doorway, he could stow it himself. The director told Ms. Rubin her assigned seat was 26B. Ms. Rubin refused to go to the back of the plane and instead sat in an empty seat immediately behind the first class cabin. United personnel told Ms. Rubin she could not sit in the emergency row bulkhead seat and repeatedly asked her to move. According to the service director, given her demonstrated unwillingness to follow directions, Ms. Rubin was not considered "emergency row qualified." It was only after much pleading Ms. Rubin finally moved. However, she still refused to follow orders to sit in seat 26B. She instead moved a bit further back and sat in someone's seat who was then in the lavatory. When the person returned from the lavatory, United personnel had to again request Ms. Rubin to leave the seat.

In the meantime the purser alerted the pilot who came out of the cockpit to assess the situation. The flight was already considerably delayed and many passengers were becoming upset and unruly. The pilot, purser and service director conferred and decided Ms. Rubin should be removed from the flight. As the service director described the situation, "it was unacceptable behavior, it was unsafe behavior. I had a riot going on, just about, and this is where I draw the line."

Although a pilot necessarily relies in part on the purser and operations director in making the decision to deplane a passenger, a pilot has ultimate responsibility for the overall safety of the aircraft, its crew and passengers. *See* 14 C.F.R. § 121.537, subd. (d) (pilot has complete control over and responsibility for all passengers and crew "without limitation."). The Federal Aviation Administration has enacted numerous regulations granting considerable discretion to airlines and pilots to control dangerous or unruly behavior. For example, regulations grant authority (1) to the pilot and crew members to prohibit anyone from interfering, intimidating or threatening a crew member or interfering with his or her duties; (2) jointly to the pilot and director of operations for the initiation, continuation, diversion or termination of a flight; (3) to the pilot to ensure no flight crewmember is engaged in any activity which might distract the person from his or her duties during a critical phase of the flight. *See generally*, Tory A. Weigand, *Air Rage and Legal Pitfalls for State Based Claims Challenging Airline Regulation of Passenger Conduct During Flight*, 45 BOSTON. B.J. 10 (2001).

Ms. Rubin refused to comply with the gate agent's request to leave the plane voluntarily. In fact, she refused to stop talking on her cell phone long enough to even acknowledge his presence. The gate agent testified he thought Ms. Rubin could have been a danger to other passengers on the airplane because of her "aggressive behavior." The gate agent reasoned, "She wouldn't listen. She wouldn't listen to the uniform[ed] crew member[s], she wouldn't listen to the service director. She was very loud. And in her conversation on the phone, that was very loud, and completely ignoring my presence less than 20 inches from her, looking her dead in the eye . . ."

United personnel then summoned the assistance of the Los Angeles Airport Police Department. Given the length of the delay of 20 to 25 minutes, and the volatile situation they discovered on board, the police officers were ready to arrest Ms. Rubin and file charges against her for obstructing a flight crew. The FAA makes it a criminal offense for a person to assault or intimidate a member of the flight crew in any way which interferes with his or her ability to perform his or her duties. 49 U.S.C. § 46504 provides:

> An individual on an aircraft in the special aircraft jurisdiction of the United States who, by assaulting or intimidating a flight crew member or flight attendant of the aircraft, interferes with the performance of the duties of the member or attendant or lessens the ability of the member or attendant to perform those duties, shall be fined under title 18, imprisoned for not more than 20 years, or both. However, if a dangerous weapon is used in assaulting or intimidating the member or attendant, the individual shall be imprisoned for any term of years or for life."

See also cases collected in William Mann, *All The (Air) Rage: Legal Implications Surrounding Airline and Government Bans on Unruly Passengers in the Sky*, 65 J. AIR. L. & COM. 857 (2000). Indeed, one of the officers believed because so many of the passengers were angry at Ms. Rubin her own personal safety would have been at risk had she remained on the flight.

In short, the undisputed evidence establishes Ms. Rubin did, or at least attempted to, make an unauthorized entry into the first class forward cabin area, which airline personnel consider a threatening act. Moreover, the undisputed evidence establishes Ms. Rubin repeatedly and deliberately refused to comply with any of the directions from any of the airline personnel regarding safety issues. This evidence in combination, coupled with the unruly and potentially dangerous situation she helped create on board, is sufficient as a matter of law to establish United when it made its decision had a reasonable basis for believing Ms. Rubin, was, "or might be, inimical to safety," which in turn justified removing her from this particular flight.

Ms. Rubin's allegedly triable issues of fact, for example, whether the flight was already somewhat delayed, whether the outraged purser unilaterally decided to have her ejected, or whether the passengers instead applauded because they were promised a free movie, are too immaterial to alter this conclusion. Accordingly, we further conclude the trial court correctly granted judgment in United's favor and dismissed the action. The judgment is affirmed.

EXERCISE 8-8. *RUBIN V. UNITED AIR LINES, INC.*—REFUSAL TO TRANSPORT

1. Describe the facts of the case and the situation caused by the passenger onboard the airplane during the boarding process. Do they seem inimical to the safety of the flight?

2. Identify the passenger's common law claims. Are they preempted by the Airline Deregulation Act?

3. What authority does 49 U.S.C. § 44902 confer on an airline? What was its original purpose and can it lawfully be extended beyond that? Give examples.

4. Under the precedent of *Williams v. Trans World Airlines*, 509 F.2d 942 (2d Cir. 1975), cited in *Rubin v. United Air Lines, Inc.*, what duty does an airline owe its passenger(s) as a matter of law, and in what circumstances will an airline's decision to transport a passenger give rise to a claim for damages?

5. What authority does the "pilot in command" have under 14 C.F.R. § 121.537?

NOTES ON *SPELLMAN, MUSTAFA,* AND *RUBIN*—AIR AND GROUND RAGE

1. *Airline-Passenger Relations.*

A bitter Internet culture exists with respect to airline customer service, *e.g.*, AirlinesSuck.com, AmericanAirlinesSucks.org, NorthWorstAir.org, Passengerrights.com, SkyRage.com, Ticked.com, TravelProblems.com and Untied.com. *See generally*, Marilyn Adams, *More Fliers Land on the Internet to Air Complaints*, USA TODAY, Apr. 18, 2000, at 12B. As illustrated in *United States v. Spellman*, (E.D. Pa. 2003), and *Rubin v. United Air Lines, Inc.* (Cal. Ct. 2002), *infra*, an airplane cabin commingles passengers with different psychological impulses, travel phobias, and other propensities for inappropriate and threatening behavior—even without alcohol service.

2. *"Air Rage," Generally.*

"Road rage," "ground rage," and "air rage," represent a sampling of new terms in the modern transportation lexicon, expressing the sometimes antisocial reaction of travelers en route. *See generally* Joan Fleischman, *Miami Lawyer Yanked off Flight to Colorado*, THE MIAMI HERALD, Mar. 27, 2002, at 4A; Jo Bowman, *How 747 Pilot Knocked Out Drunken Pop Star*, SOUTH CHINA MORNING POST, Feb. 23, 2000, at 1; Complaint, Elabiad v. Schuller, No. 97–4907 (E.D.N.Y. 1997); Complaint, United States v. Robert Schuller, No. 97–1194M (E.D.N.Y. 1997) (alleging "Hour of Power" televangelist Reverend Robert Schuller placed a flight attendant in a head lock). In

2000, the Federal Aviation Administration reported 314 cases of "unruly passengers" while the airline industry contended over 4,000 air rage incidents occur per year. Marshall Wilson, *Airline Rage Policies Assailed, Unruly Passengers often Unprosecuted, Crews Say*, S.F. CHRON., July 7, 2001, at A13.

> "Air rage" is a general intent crime defined and punishable by federal law:
>
> An individual on an aircraft in the special aircraft jurisdiction of the United States who, by assaulting or intimidating a flight crew member or flight attendant of the aircraft, interferes with the performance of the duties of the member or attendant or lessens the ability of the member or attendant to perform those duties, attempts or conspires to do such an act, shall be fined under title 18, imprisoned for not more than 20 years, or both.

49 U.S.C. § 46504. *See also* 14 C.F.R. §§ 91.11, 121.580, and 135.120. *See also* Nancy Lee Firak & Kimberly A. Schmaltz, *Air Rage: Choice of Law for Intentional Torts Occurring Over International Waters*, 63 ALB. L. REV. 1, 7 (1999) (defining air rage as "intentional acts that are highly disproportionate to motivating factors, which endanger the flight crew and/or other passengers and potentially jeopardize the safety of the aircraft itself.").

3.   *Air Rage, Globally.*

Air rage is not a phenomenon peculiar to airline travel within the United States. For example, before September 11, 2001, the United Kingdom's Civil Aviation Authority estimated that air rage incidents occurred an average of once out of every 870 flights. *Air Rage Incidents Four Times a Day*, BIRMINGHAM POST, Feb. 19, 2000, at 8. *See also Off-Duty SAA Steward Goes Berserk on Plane*, THE STAR (South Africa), Feb. 26, 2002 (reporting a drunk attendant on board a Bangkok to Johannesburg flight who, for thirty minutes, "tore down the aisles, swearing and taking swipes at passengers. . . biting some on their arms and hands. . . and forcing himself on a Chinese woman and kissing her," until restrained by fellow passengers).

Instances of air rage and interference with flight crew include:

- A passenger on a flight from London to Miami said to the passenger seated next to him, "If you give me a knife, I'll kill everyone on the plane." He then attempted to touch and kiss a female flight attendant and grabbed her arms several times and continued to try to kiss her before the Flight Service Manager told him to return to his seat. He then took several swings at the Flight Service Manager before the crew was able to get him to his seat. Before they got him in his seat, the passenger placed his hands on another female flight attendant and pushed her head to the side. Before two male flight attendants were able to restrain the passenger, he bit the first flight attendant on the arm. *United States v. Ahmed* (11th Cir. 2007).

- A banker on an international flight tried "to talk to the captain" by applying several "kung fu" kicks to the reinforced cockpit door. Martin Merzer et al., *Crew's Ax Stops Cockpit Intruder*, THE MIAMI HERALD, Feb. 8, 2002, at 1A (reporting that the co-pilot subdued the panicked passenger by hitting him in the head with the blunt end of an ax).

- From August 1, 1993, until his arrest on September 22, 1993, a Virginia resident broadcast unauthorized radio messages to aircraft and air traffic controllers, pretending to be an air traffic controller at the Roanoke Regional Airport. Among other messages, he gave instructions to pilots who were preparing to land, including instructing incoming pilots to change frequencies, or to break off their approach. He told pilots they were not clear to land after they had been cleared to land by the tower, told pilots their runway was closed because of a disabled aircraft on the runway, and told landing pilots to hold short of a runway intersection. *United States v. Bocook* (4th Cir. 1995).

- A businessman defecated on an in-use service cart. Complaint, United States v. Gerard B. Finneran, No. 95–1744M (E.D.N.Y. 1995).

- Federal Express began investigating irregularities in the reporting of flight hours by one its flight engineers. One day before he was to appear at a company hearing, the engineer boarded a cargo plane flight in full flight gear and with carry-on items though he was not a member of the flight crew; he entered the cockpit and began adjusting instruments and controls. The real crew members arrived later, and assumed the engineer was a "jump-seater" (*i.e.,* an employee passenger). After the plane took off, the troubled engineer entered the cockpit and began attacking the crew with a hammer, spear gun, spear, claw hammers, and sledgehammers, severely injuring the crew. *United States v. Calloway* (6th Cir. 1997).

For further reading on unlawful airline passenger behavior see ANGELA DAHLBERG, AIR RAGE: THE UNDERESTIMATED SAFETY RISK (2001); Tory A. Weigand, *Air Rage and Legal Pitfalls for State-Based Claims Challenging Airline Regulation of Passenger Conduct During Flight*, BOSTON B. J., May/June 2001, at 10; *See generally* William Mann, Comment, *All the (Air) Rage: Legal Implications Surrounding Airline and Government Bans on Unruly Passengers in the Sky*, 65 J. AIR L. & COM. 857 (2000); John A. Glenn, Annotation, *Validity, Under Commerce Clause of Federal Constitution, of State Tolls or Taxes*

On, Or Affecting, Interstate or Foreign Air Carriers or Passengers, 31 L. Ed. 2d 975 (1999). *See also* ELLIOTT HESTER, PLANE INSANITY: A FLIGHT ATTENDANT'S TALES OF SEX, RAGE AND QUEASINESS AT 30,000 FEET (St. Martin's Press 2002).

4. ***Saying Bomb on an Airplane.***

Consider a flight attendant's description of Southwest Airlines Flight 2466, bound for Ontario, California, from Las Vegas, Nevada:

> The cabin was total chaos, . . . when [a passenger] said "I have [a] bomb." I saw many of our male passengers unbuckle their seatbelts and they stood up and they—I remember seeing the people throwing punches and everybody, you know, they were all on top of Mr. Gonzalez . . . [The passenger] was hysterical and he was swinging and kicking and he was just—he was hitting and kicking passengers and the passengers were trying to take him down and hold him down.
>
> Many of the female passengers were screaming and yelling and crying. The cabin was total chaos. They were yelling, "We're going to die. We're going to crash. We're going down." And a lot of the women were hysterical. They were—they were thinking we were going to crash. Thinking they—when the passengers heard Mr. Gonzalez say, "I have a bomb," and at that point it was just all hell broke loose.

United States v. Gonzalez, 492 F.3d 1031 (9th Cir. 2007). Ultimately, FBI agents arrested the passenger, who told them that "he knew what he was doing was wrong but felt he had to do something to land the plane." At the change of plea hearing, Gonzalez acknowledged that, although he had used methamphetamine the day before the incident, he was aware of his actions and understood and knew what he was doing at the time of the incident.

Prior to the enactment of the "Uniting and Strengthening America by Providing Appropriate Tools Required to Intercept and Obstruct Terrorism Act of 2001" ("USA PATRIOT Act"), Pub. L. No. 107–56, 115 Stat. 272 (2001), referred to recklessly endangering the safety of the "aircraft *and passengers*." Effective November 1, 2002, § 2A5.2(a)(2) was amended to refer to "endangering the safety of . . . an airport or an aircraft; or . . . a mass transportation facility, a mass transportation vehicle, or a ferry." U.S.S.G. § 2A5.2(a)(2) (2003). Thus, sentencing now does not require a showing of endangerment to the passengers and even a threat to detonate an empty aircraft is punishable.

WALLACE V. KOREAN AIR

214 F.3d 293 (2d Cir. 2000)

MCLAUGHLIN, CIRCUIT JUDGE:

Plaintiff Brandi Wallace was sexually assaulted while on a Korean Air Lines Co., Ltd. ("KAL") international flight. Her attacker was a fellow passenger. She sued KAL to recover for the assault under the Warsaw Convention, which makes air carriers liable for passenger injuries caused by an "accident." Warsaw Convention Art. 17. The United States District Court for the Southern District of New York (Patterson, J.) dismissed the suit, concluding that the sexual assault was not "a risk characteristic of air travel," and therefore was not an "accident" for purposes of the Convention. *Wallace v. Korean Air*, 1999 WL 187213 (S.D.N.Y. 1999). Because we disagree with that conclusion, we vacate and remand.

BACKGROUND

The facts are undisputed. On the evening of August 17, 1997, Brandi Wallace boarded KAL flight 61 in Seoul, Korea, destination Los Angeles, California. It being the middle of summer, Ms. Wallace wore a T-shirt and jean shorts with a belt. Initially, the flight passed uneventfully. Ms. Wallace was seated in a window seat in economy class, and fell asleep shortly after finishing her in-flight meal.

Two male passengers sat between Ms. Wallace's window seat and the aisle of the airliner's cabin. Seated closest to Ms. Wallace was Mr. Kwang-Yong Park. Before she fell asleep, Ms. Wallace had neither spoken to Mr. Park, nor given him the slightest indication that familiarity would be welcome. Nevertheless, about three hours into the flight, Ms. Wallace awoke in the darkened plane to find that Mr. Park had unbuckled her belt, unzipped and unbuttoned her jean shorts, and placed his hands into her underpants to fondle her. Ms. Wallace woke with a start and immediately turned her body toward the window causing Mr. Park to withdraw his hands. When Mr. Park resumed his unwelcome amours, however, Ms. Wallace recovered from her shock and hit him hard. She then climbed out of her chair and jumped over the sleeping man in the aisle seat to make her escape.

At the back of the plane, Ms. Wallace found a flight attendant and complained about the assault. The attendant reassigned her to another seat. When the plane arrived in Los Angeles, Ms. Wallace told airport police about the incident, and they arrested Mr. Park. He subsequently pled guilty in the United States District Court for the Central District of California to the crime of engaging in unwelcome sexual conduct with another person in violation of 18 U.S.C. § 2244(b).

In February 1998, Wallace brought this action against KAL in the United States District Court for the Southern District of New York (Patterson, J.), alleging that KAL was liable for Park's sexual assault under the Warsaw Convention, which applies to "all international transportation of persons, baggage, or goods performed by aircraft for hire." Warsaw Convention Art. 1(1). As modified by the Montreal Agreement, the Warsaw Convention makes airlines liable (up to a $75,000 limit per passenger) "if *the accident* which caused the damage so sustained took place on board the aircraft or in the course of any of the operations of embarking or disembarking" from an international air flight. Warsaw Convention Art. 17.

Following discovery, Wallace moved for summary judgment on her Warsaw Convention claim. The district court denied the motion and dismissed that claim. Relying on its reading of *Air France v. Saks*, 470 U.S. 392 (1985), the district court reasoned that because the sexual assault was not "a risk characteristic of air travel," it therefore did not constitute an "accident" for purposes of the Warsaw Convention. Wallace now appeals.

DISCUSSION

The proper interpretation of the Warsaw Convention is an issue of law, which we review *de novo*. A brief history of the evolution of the liability regime fostered by the Warsaw Convention will help to elucidate the issue on this appeal. The Convention was drafted at two international conferences, the first in Paris in 1925, and the second in Warsaw in 1929. The United States became a signatory in 1934. *See* 78 Cong. Rec. 11,582 (1934).

Goals of Warsaw Convention

The Convention had two goals: to establish uniform rules for international air travel and to limit potential carrier liability for passenger injuries so as not to frighten away potential investors from the fledgling air industry. To achieve these goals, the Convention capped the airlines' potential liability to each passenger at 125,000 gold french francs, or approximately $8,300. *See* Warsaw Convention Art. 22. At the same time, however, the Convention made the airlines subject to Article 17, which provides in its entirety:

> The carrier shall be liable for damage sustained in the event of the death or wounding of a passenger or any other bodily injury suffered by a passenger, if the accident which caused the damage so sustained took place on board the aircraft or in the course of any of the operations of embarking or disembarking.

Article 17 created what the courts have characterized as a "presumption" that air carriers are liable for passenger injuries. There was a counterweight to the presumption: carriers could avoid Article 17 liability altogether by establishing the so-called "due care" defense provided by Article 20(1). See Warsaw Convention Art. 20(1) ("The carrier shall not be liable if he proves that he and his agents have taken all necessary measures to avoid the damage or that it was impossible for him or them to take such measures.").

From the beginning, the United States was hostile to the "stringent" limitations on liability imposed by the Convention. In particular, the $8,300 liability cap was regarded as too stingy. In November 1965, the United States announced its intention to withdraw from the Warsaw system if an international agreement could not be reached to raise the limits on liability. *See* 31 Fed. Reg. 7302 (1966). This notice of denunciation led to intense negotiations which ultimately culminated in the Montreal Agreement of 1966. Through that Agreement, the air carriers agreed to raise the limit of liability to $75,000 for flights originating, terminating, or having a stopping point in the United States. In addition, the carriers agreed to eliminate the "due care" defense they had enjoyed under Article 20.

The rationale for the new regime was straightforward. In exchange for the cap on liability at the new level of $75,000, the air carriers consented to a system under which they assumed "virtual strict liability" for death or injury to passengers. *In re Korean Air Lines Disaster of Sept. 1, 1983*, 932 F.2d 1475, 1485 (D.C. Cir. 1991). As Lowenfeld and Mendelsohn, who represented the United States at Montreal, explained, this arrangement made sense because: "[i]n terms of distribution of risk, the carrier would seem, in nearly every case, to be in the best position to . . . spread the risk most economically" regardless of fault. 80 HARV. L.REV. at 599–600. In sum, a fundamental reason for the abandonment of the fault-based "due care" defense available under the Warsaw Convention was to guarantee to passengers the prospect of quicker and less expensive settlements.

* * *

The essential predicate of carrier liability is the occurrence of an "accident" contemplated by Article 17 of the Convention. The issue presented here is whether Park's sexual molestation of Ms. Wallace constituted such an "accident." We hold that it did.

Although the Convention itself does not define an "accident," the Supreme Court addressed the meaning of that term in *Air France v. Saks*, 470 U.S. 392 (1985). There, Valerie Saks sued an airline because she became deaf as a result of changes in air pressure during a flight. After extensive discovery established that the aircraft's pressurization system had operated in the usual manner, the district court dismissed the case, holding that Saks could not recover under the Convention without evidence of some malfunction in the aircraft's operation.

On appeal, the Ninth Circuit rejected this rationale, "hold[ing] that a showing of a malfunction or abnormality in the aircraft's operation is not a prerequisite for liability under the Warsaw Convention." Reviewing the history of the Convention, the circuit court emphasized that the air carriers had surrendered their due care defense when they entered into the Montreal Agreement. This contractual modification, the court reasoned, imposed "absolute liability [on the air carriers] for injuries proximately caused by the risks inherent in air travel." Applying this standard of absolute liability, the Ninth Circuit found that the normal pressurization changes that caused Saks's deafness constituted an Article 17 "accident."

The Ninth Circuit recognized that its absolute liability approach differed from the approach adopted by the Third Circuit. The Supreme Court granted *certiorari* to resolve the circuit split. According to the Court, "the narrow issue presented" was whether Saks could prove an "accident" for purposes of the Convention "by showing that her injury was caused by the normal operation of the aircraft's pressurization system." The Court's answer to that question was no.

The Court rejected as "not entirely accurate" the Ninth Circuit's characterization of the Montreal Agreement as imposing "absolute" liability on air carriers. While acknowledging that the carriers had waived their due care defense by entering the Montreal Agreement, the Court pointed out that "[t]hey did not waive other provisions in the Convention that operate to qualify liability, such as . . . the 'accident' requirement of Article 17."

Accident, Defined

In addressing what constitutes an "accident," the Supreme Court essentially adopted the Third Circuit's language, defining the term as an injury "caused by an unexpected or unusual event or happening that is external to the passenger." The Court announced that "[t]his definition should be flexibly applied" and, as examples, cited with approval to "lower courts in this country [that] have interpreted Article 17 broadly enough to encompass torts committed by terrorists or fellow passengers." With respect to Saks herself, however, the Court concluded that no accident had occurred because her deafness indisputably resulted from her own "internal reaction to the usual, normal, and expected operation of the aircraft." This was no "accident."

* * *

Courts have wrestled with the *Saks* definition of "accident" since it was announced. That struggle is particularly difficult in cases like ours where the putative injuries are caused by torts committed by fellow passengers.

In one camp, courts hold that an "accident" under Article 17 must arise from "such risks that are characteristic of air travel." *Stone v. Continental Airlines, Inc.*, 905 F. Supp. 823, 827 (D. Haw. 1995) (injury caused by being punched without provocation by another passenger not an accident because it was not "derived from air travel"); (quoting *Price v. British Airways*, 1992 WL 170679 (S.D.N.Y. July 7, 1992) (injury caused by a fistfight between two passengers not an "accident" because "a fracas is not a characteristic risk of air travel nor may carriers easily guard against such a risk through the employment of protective security measures.")); *see Curley v. American Airlines, Inc.*, 846 F. Supp. 280, 283 (S.D.N.Y.1994) (same standard).

Another camp has cast a wider net. For example, in *Barratt v. Trinidad & Tobago (BWIA Int'l) Airways Corp.*, 1990 WL 127590 (E.D.N.Y. 1990), the court rejected the contention that a stumble and fall inside an airline terminal could never come within the scope of Article 17 because such an accident is not caused by a risk inherent in aviation. The court reasoned:

> In *Air France v. Saks*, the Supreme Court held that an "accident," for purposes of Article 17, is an injury caused by "an unexpected or unusual event or happening that is external to the passenger." This definition is in no way limited to those injuries resulting from dangers exclusive to aviation. [Article 17] itself limits liability for accidents, not by reference to risks inherent in aviation, but by whether they occur "on board the aircraft or in the course of any of the operations of embarking or disembarking."

Obviously, under this reading of *Saks*, an airline presumably would be liable for all passenger injuries, including those caused by co-passenger torts, regardless of whether they arose from a characteristic risk of air travel.

This Circuit has yet to choose definitively between these competing interpretations of the term "accident." The issue is not an easy one, for as one of our sister circuits has noted, the *Saks* opinion does not make it "clear whether an event's relationship to the operation of an aircraft is relevant to whether the event is an 'accident.'" *Gezzi v. British Airways PLC*, 991 F.2d 603, 605 n. 4 (9th Cir. 1993).

To be sure, in the lower court cases cited with approval in *Saks*, all the passenger injuries seem to have arisen out of risks that are inherent to air travel, or out of the operation of the aircraft itself. *See Saks*, 470 U.S. at 405 (citing *Evangelinos v. Trans World Airlines, Inc.*, 550 F.2d 152 (3rd Cir. 1977) (*en banc*) (terrorist attack); *Day v. Trans World Airlines, Inc.*, 528 F.2d 31 (2d Cir. 1975) (same); *Krystal v. British Overseas Airways Corp.*, 403 F. Supp. 1322 (C.D. Cal. 1975) (hijacking); *Oliver v. Scandinavian Airlines Sys.*, 17 CCH Av. Cas. 18,283 (D. Md. 1983) (drunken passenger who was continually served alcohol fell and injured fellow passenger)).

Despite these citations, however, the *Saks* court did not address whether an event must relate to air travel to be an Article 17 "accident." Instead, the *Saks* opinion expressly limited itself to the *"narrow issue"* of whether the "normal " (as opposed to abnormal) operation of an aircraft could give rise to an "accident." *Saks*, 470 U.S. at 396. This language, which expressly limits the scope of the Court's holding, clearly was chosen carefully. As Humpty Dumpty explained to Alice: "When I use a word . . . it means just what I choose it to mean—neither more nor less." LEWIS CARROLL, THROUGH THE LOOKING-GLASS ch. 6 at 106–09 (SCHOCKEN BOOKS 1987) (1872). Thus, while we share our concurring colleague's preference for simplicity, we cannot agree that *Saks* resolved ("implicitly" or otherwise) the issue of whether all co-passenger torts must be "accidents." Neither do we see any need to address that issue today.

Happily, this Talmudic debate is academic in the unique circumstances of this case. Indeed, we have no occasion to decide whether all co-passenger torts are necessarily accidents for purposes of the Convention. This is so because we conclude that an Article 17 "accident" occurred here even under the narrower characteristic risk of air travel approach. Though a close question, we reach that conclusion mindful of the "virtual strict liability" imposed on air carriers by the Warsaw regime, and in deference to the *Saks* Court's admonition to interpret the term "accident" both "flexibly" and "broadly."

> *It is plain that the characteristics of air travel increased Ms. Wallace's vulnerability to Mr. Park's assault. When Ms. Wallace took her seat in economy class on the KAL flight, she was cramped into a confined space beside two men she did not know, one of whom turned out to be a sexual predator. The lights were turned down and the sexual predator was left unsupervised in the dark. It was then that the attack occurred.*

Turning to the particular facts that give rise to an "accident" in this case, it is plain that the characteristics of air travel increased Ms. Wallace's vulnerability to Mr. Park's assault. When Ms. Wallace took her seat in economy class on the KAL flight, she was cramped into a confined space beside two men she did not know, one of whom turned out to be a sexual predator. The lights were turned down and the sexual predator was left unsupervised in the dark. It was then that the attack occurred.

Equally important was the manner in which Mr. Park was able to carry out his assault. While Ms. Wallace lay sleeping, Mr. Park: (1) unbuckled her belt; (2) unbuttoned her shorts; (3) unzipped her shorts; and (4) squeezed his hands into her underpants. These could not have been five-second procedures even for the nimblest of fingers. Nor could they have been entirely inconspicuous. Yet it is undisputed that for the entire duration of Mr. Park's attack not a single flight attendant noticed a problem. And it is not without significance that when Ms. Wallace woke up, she could not get away immediately, but had to endure another of Mr. Park's advances before clambering out to the aisle.

In sum, recognizing the flexibility called for by *Saks*, we are satisfied that Mr. Park's assault on Ms. Wallace was, in the language of *Saks*, "an unexpected or unusual event or happening that [was] external to the passenger." As such, it constituted an "accident" for purposes of Article 17 of the Warsaw Convention.

CONCLUSION

The district court's decision that Mr. Park's assault of Ms. Wallace did not constitute an "accident" under Article 17 of the Convention is vacated and this case is remanded for further proceedings. We express no opinion on any other aspect of Ms. Wallace's Warsaw Convention claim.

POOLER, CIRCUIT JUDGE, concurring.

I concur in the result and in the majority's able discussion of the Warsaw Convention, but I write separately because I would decide the case on a ground the majority avoids. At issue in this case is whether a tort committed by a fellow passenger constitutes an "accident" under Article 17 of the Warsaw Convention. The district court dismissed the case holding that airlines are only "liable for torts that are proximately caused by the abnormal or unexpected operation of the aircraft ... the abnormal or unexpected conduct of airline personnel," or that involve "a risk characteristic of air travel." *Wallace v. Korean Air*, 1999 WL 187213 *4 (S.D.N.Y. 1999).

The majority now reverses, assuming without deciding that the district court's interpretation of "accident" was correct, but holding that the sexual assault Wallace suffered met that definition—a factual issue neither briefed nor argued by counsel.

I would reverse in more straightforward fashion, because I believe that the lower court's holding contradicts Supreme Court precedent. We need not reach the complicated, always fact laden, and irrelevant question of what constitutes a risk characteristic of air travel.

For example, one might argue that being strapped into one's seat next to a stranger is not so much a characteristic of air travel as it is a characteristic of any form of public transportation. If we adopt, even provisionally, the district court's approach, an even more "Talmudic" question arises than the one the majority avoids: how associated with air travel need a hazard be before it can fairly be described as "characteristic"?

"Inherent in Air Travel" Not an Element of "Accident"

Imposing an "inherent in air travel" requirement does not comport with the plain meaning of the Supreme Court's decision in *Air France v. Saks*, 470 U.S. 392 (1985). A co-passenger's tort satisfies the Supreme Court's interpretation of "accident" as "an unexpected or unusual event or happening that is external to the passenger," and the Court did not also include a "characteristic of air travel" requirement in the definition. Although the Court stated that its definition should "be flexibly applied," the Court did not thereby authorize courts to add more hurdles for a plaintiff to overcome. Rather, the Court approved lower court decisions that had already read Article 17 "broadly enough to encompass torts committed by terrorists or fellow passengers."

When the Supreme Court partially restated its holding, it again avoided any mention of the inherent risks of air travel: "[a]ny injury is the product of a chain of causes, and we require only that the passenger be able to prove that some link in the chain was an unusual or unexpected event external to the passenger." What the Court left to district courts to decide is "whether an 'accident' as here defined caused the passenger's injury." The majority mistakes this for an invitation to decide what is an accident.

When the Supreme Court partially restated its holding, it again avoided any mention of the inherent risks of air travel: "[a]ny injury is the product of a chain of causes, and we require only that the passenger be able to prove that some link in the chain was an unusual or unexpected event external to the passenger."

What the Court left to district courts to decide is "whether an 'accident' as here defined caused the passenger's injury." The majority mistakes this for an invitation to decide what is an accident.

The context of the Court's holding in *Saks* also supports the view that "characteristic of air travel" is not a necessary element of an Article 17 accident.

Valerie Saks's unfortunate left-ear deafness was caused by the normal operation of the airplane pressurization system. Article 17 of the Warsaw Convention makes air carriers liable for injuries sustained by a passenger, "if the accident which caused the damage so sustained took place on board the aircraft. . . ." At the district court, Air France argued that "accident" means an "abnormal, unusual or unexpected occurrence" aboard the aircraft. Ms. Saks argued for a "hazard of air travel" definition. *See id.* The district court agreed with Air France. The Ninth Circuit disagreed and concluded that absolute liability attached "for injuries proximately caused by the risks inherent in air travel."

I recite this history to put in context the two competing constructions the Court had before it when it held, "We conclude that liability under Article 17 of the Warsaw Convention arises only if a passenger's injury is caused by an unexpected or usual event or happening that is external to the passenger." *Saks,* 470 U.S. at 405. The Court adopted the view advanced by Air France at the district court and rejected the view advanced by Ms. Saks—the "inherent in air travel" view. Conspicuously absent from the Court's decision is language concerning air travel and its inherent risks. Nonetheless, the district court in this case saw fit to engraft an "inherent in air travel" requirement into the Saks test when it dismissed Ms. Wallace's claim. The majority, like the district court, fails to recognize that the Supreme Court has already implicitly rejected that interpretation.

The majority concludes that we need not reach the interpretation of "accident," and that we should not do so. I disagree, because I believe the Supreme Court has spoken to the issue and resolved it. We, therefore, have an obligation to address the Supreme Court's interpretation of Article 17. *Saks* is the law as explained to us by the Court, and it is our duty to implement the Court's articulation of Article 17, not the district court's. This duty looms especially large since other courts have misinterpreted Article 17 and *Saks.* In the instant case, the district court's addition of a prong to the definition demonstrates the need for a clearly understood rule in our circuit. Our decision today will leave district courts wondering what to do in future cases with respect to a question the Supreme Court has already answered.

EXERCISE 8-9. *WALLACE V. KOREAN AIR*—P2P ASSAULT

1. What actions, if any, did the airline take to remedy the situation as it was occurring?

2. How did the district court rule and why?

3. What are the goals of the Warsaw Convention? What does Article 17 provide?

4.   How does the Warsaw Convention define "accident"?

5.   Explain the court's rationale in deciding whether an accident occurred under the specific facts of *Wallace v. Korean Air*? What does the concurrence say about this?

Suggested Further Reading

Alex Fitzpatrick, *Here's What Happens when a Crime is Committed on a Plane*, TIME, Sept. 23, 2016

Timothy M. Ravich, *Is Airline Passenger Profiling Necessary?*, 62 U. MIAMI L. REV. 1 (2007)

Jason Binimow, *Validity, Construction, and Application of 18 U.S.C.A. § 2333(a), Which Allows U.S. Nationals who have been Injured "By Reason of Act of International Terrorism" to Sue Therefor and Recover Treble Damages*, 195 A.L.R. Fed. 217 (2004)

Charu A. Chandrasekhar, *Flying While Brown: Federal Civil Rights Remedies to Post-9/11 Airline Racial Profiling of South Asians*, ASIAN L.J. 215 (2003)

Aircraft Transactions

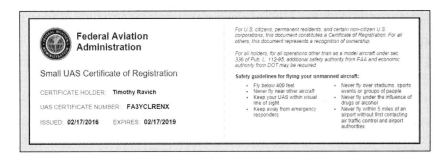

A. OVERVIEW

Chapter 3 introduced how regulators and courts define and distinguish "aircraft" from vessels and vehicles and other types of conveyances. Chapter 3 also examined how lawmakers prosecuted and/or adjudicated liability arising from the operation of airplanes. This chapter compliments that material by focusing on private transactions involving aircraft, particularly aircraft ownership.

Aircraft transactions are cross border dealings that often involve state, national, and international laws relating to jurisdiction, taxation, and contract. In fact, the purchase and sale of aircraft involves not only a seller and buyer, but also sometimes third parties who might finance, lease, or use the aircraft. Airplanes are also a unique type of property in that they are mobile assets that can be flown away from creditors. As such, the legal regimes that govern aircraft transactions are particularly important from an economic and security standpoint.

In this context, all airplanes are registered in much the same way automobiles bear a vehicle identification number or "VIN." In fact, internationally, pursuant to the Convention on International Civil Aviation—the Chicago Convention—all civil aircraft must be registered with a national aviation authority following the procedures of that country.

In the United States, all civil aircraft registered in the nation are given serial numbers prefixed by the letter N. The registration number, apart from the N prefix, is made up of one to five symbols, the last two of which may be alphabetical. This alphabetical suffix must be preceded by at least one numerical symbol, with the lowest possible number is N1. A zero never precedes the first number. For example: N1 through N99999, all symbols are numeric, and N1A through N9999Z, single alphabetical suffix, and N1AA through N999ZZ, double alphabetical suffix. To a large extent the "N" registration mark gives creditors confidence that airplane is registered in a nation that has a robust aviation financing and tracking system that will safeguard their investment and ownership in an airplane.

Illustration 9-1 below shows the registration number painted onto an American Airlines Boeing 737. You will see a similar registration number on any commercial airliner you fly. This registration number corresponds to an FAA online registry (Illustration 9-2, below), which shows detailed information about the airplane.

Illustration 9-1. Aircraft Registration, American Airlines 737

More specifically, the FAA Registration below discloses important information in three categories: aircraft description, registered owner, and airworthiness. Here, you can learn such as the manufacture date of the airplane (2010) the owner (*not* the airline, but the Wilmington Trust Company Trustee), and details about its engines (transport category).

Illustration 9-2. FAA Registry

FAA REGISTRY
N-Number Inquiry Results

N845NN is Assigned

Data Updated each Federal Working Day at Midnight

Aircraft Description

Serial Number	40579	Status	Valid
Manufacturer Name	BOEING	Certificate Issue Date	08/05/2010
Model	737-823	Expiration Date	02/28/2021
Type Aircraft	Fixed Wing Multi-Engine	Type Engine	Turbo-fan
Pending Number Change	None	Dealer	No
Date Change Authorized	None	Mode S Code (base 8 / oct)	52711645
MFR Year	2010	Mode S Code (base 16 / hex)	AB93A5
Type Registration	Corporation	Fractional Owner	NO

Registered Owner

Name	WILMINGTON TRUST CO TRUSTEE		
Street	ATTN: CORPORATE TRUST ADMIN		
	1100 N MARKET ST		
City	WILMINGTON	State	DELAWARE
County	NEW CASTLE	Zip Code	19891-1605
Country	UNITED STATES		

Airworthiness

Engine Manufacturer	CFM INTL	Classification	Standard
Engine Model	CFM56-7B24/3	Category	Transport
A/W Date	07/17/2010	Exception Code	No

The information contained in this record should be the most current Airworthiness information available in the historical aircraft record. However, this data alone does not provide the basis for a determination regarding the airworthiness of an aircraft or the current aircraft configuration. For specific information, you may request a copy of the aircraft record at http://aircraft.faa.gov/e.gov/ND/

Importantly, registration is a precondition of aircraft operation in the United States as a matter of law. Pursuant to 49 U.S.C. § 44101(a), a person may not operate a civil aircraft that is not registered with the FAA. An aircraft may be registered only by and in the legal name of its owner by transmitting certain information and documents to the Aircraft Registration Branch: (1) an Aircraft Registration Application; (2) an original AC Form 8050-1; (3) evidence of ownership (such as a bill of sale); and (4) a $5.00 registration fee made payable to the Federal Aviation Administration. What is more, an aircraft is eligible for U.S. registration *only* if it is not registered in another country and it is owned by:

(1)   A U.S. citizen as defined in 14 C.F.R. § 47.2;

(2)   A resident alien (foreign individual lawfully admitted for permanent U.S. residence);

(3)   A U.S. governmental unit or subdivision; or

(4)   A non-citizen corporation lawfully organized and doing business under the laws of the U.S. or one of the States as long as the aircraft is based and primarily used in the U.S. (*i.e.*, 60% of all flight hours must be from flights starting and ending within the U.S.).

In the foregoing context, this chapter proceeds in two parts:

- Part B explores how aircraft are purchased and sold, including by auction, *Godwin Aircraft, Inc. v. Houston*; the aircraft registration scheme managed by the Federal Aviation Administration, *Philko Aviation, Inc. v. Shacket*; and how aircraft ownership is established as a matter of law, *United States v. Malago* and *United States v. Starcher.*

- Part C examines how an ownership interest in an airplane (including partial—fractional—ownership) is enforced by operation of law, whether by statutory lien, *Lewistown Propane Co. v. Ford* and *Commercial Jet, Inc. v. U.S. Bank*, or replevin and judicial sale, *PNCEF, LLC v. South Aviation, Inc.* The final case, *U.S. Acquisition, LLC v. Tabas, Freedman, Soloff, Miller & Brown, P.A.*, underscores the financial consequences borne by aviation lawyers and airplane owners who do not comply strictly with the letter of the law respecting aircraft ownership.

After reading these materials, you should come away from this chapter with some practical knowledge about aircraft transactions, including the terms of an aircraft purchase and sale agreement, the standard forms used in an aircraft transaction, how to register and secure a financial interest in an aircraft, and how to get assert and effect an ownership interest in an airplane.

Federal Aviation Administration, *Where do N-Numbers Come From?*

The U.S. received the "N" as its nationality designator under the International Air Navigation Convention, held in 1919. The Convention prescribed an aircraft-marking scheme of a single letter indicating nationality followed by a hyphen and four identity letters (for example, G-REMS). The five letters together were to be the aircraft's radio call sign.

In the original 1919 allotment, most of the nations shared first letters. Only U.S. and four other nations were assigned a unique first letter to be followed by any combination of four letters. In each case, that first letter was the same as a radio call letter that had been previously assigned to that nation by an evolving series of international agreements. As of April 1913, for example, Great Britain had complete rights to the radio letters B, G, and M, while sharing certain other letters. Not surprisingly, Great Britain received G as its aircraft nationality identifier under the 1919 agreement.

During this era, the U.S. had complete rights to the radio letters N and W, and to combinations of K from KDA to KZZ. Why these particular letters? The assignments of W and K appear to have been arbitrary, according to articles on early radio call signs by Thomas H. White. In the case of N, Whites notes that the U.S. Navy had used this radio letter since November 1909.

This still leaves the question of why N was chosen over W for the U.S. aircraft identifier. The answer may lie in the fact that the Government had reserved N for itself, while assigning combinations beginning with K and W to various radio stations along geographic lines. N would therefore be less confusing as a single national marking for aircraft.

The choice was not universally popular. The Journal Aviation wanted the U.S. to adopt W in honor of the Wright brothers. Use of the letter N in the early days seems to have been restricted to aircraft that made international flights. Compliance was voluntary at this time, since the U.S. did not ratify the 1919 Convention.

No mention of N numbers appeared in the initial Air Commerce Regulations placed in effect by FAA's first predecessor agency in December 1926. The letter markings that this original set of rules specified were C (commercial), S (state), and P (private), which were to precede the numbers assigned to licensed aircraft. Unlicensed aircraft had numbers, but no letters, at this time.

The earliest legal requirement for the N marking is found in the first general amendments to the Air Commerce Regulations on March 22,1927. These amendments mandated that U.S. aircraft engaged in foreign air commerce display the N at the beginning of its identification markings. Later, this requirement was extended to all U.S. aircraft, regardless of whether they operated beyond the Nation's borders.

A second letter indicating the aircraft's airworthiness category followed the N and preceded the identification numbers. These airworthiness indicators were; "C" for standard, "R" for restricted, "X" for experimental, and later an "L" for limited, (for example, NC1234). This was standard until December 31, 1948, when aircraft registered for the first time were required to display identification marks consisting of only the Roman capital letter "N" followed by the registration number. Existing aircraft operated solely within the United States could continue to display an airworthiness symbol until the first time such aircraft were recovered or refinished to an extent necessitating the reapplication of the identification marks. After December 31, 1950, all aircraft of United States registry operated outside of the United States were required to display identification marks consisting of the Roman capital letter "N" followed by the registration number.

Until December 31, 1960, the required location for display of nationality and identification marks for fixed-wing aircraft was the wing surfaces, and the vertical surface of either the tail or fuselage. Effective January 1, 1960, all fixed-wing aircraft were required to display identification marks on the vertical surfaces or either the tail or fuselage. Wing surface markings were no longer required.

Current standards for the display of nationality and registration identification marks on U.S. civil aircraft can be found in the Code of Federal Regulations, Title 14, Part 45, Subpart C.

Source: Fed. Aviation Aircraft N-Number History https://www.faa.gov/licenses_certificates/aircraft_certification/aircraft_registry/aircraft_nnumber_history/.

B. OWNERSHIP AND REGISTRATION

GODWIN AIRCRAFT, INC. V. HOUSTON

851 S.W.2d 816 (Tenn. Ct. App. 1992)

CRAWFORD, JUDGE.

This case involves the purchase of an airplane by plaintiff-appellee, Godwin Aircraft, Inc., ("Godwin") from a Georgia resident, Ray R. Houston, d/b/a Washington County Air Service ("Houston").

Godwin filed a complaint against Houston in the Chancery Court of Shelby County, Tennessee. The complaint seeks damages allegedly caused by defendant's fraud, misrepresentation and breach of contract in the purchase of an aircraft. Defendant first filed a motion to dismiss for lack of personal jurisdiction, which was denied. Defendant's answer, in addition to relying on lack of jurisdiction, joined issue in the material allegations of the complaint.

The plane was sold at a national auction held in Oklahoma City, Oklahoma on June 19, 20, and 21, 1991, under the terms of a contract between Oklahoma Aircraft Dealers Association and the defendant-appellant, Ray Houston. *Auction, Sale Terms*

The auction catalog set out the terms of the auction which includes the following:

> The aircraft listed in this catalog have been submitted by the owner. In no way is the Oklahoma Aircraft Dealers Association responsible for their accuracy. Understand you buy "as is" "where is". Inspect aircraft and log books prior to bidding. If you are high bidder and bid is accepted by the owner, aircraft is considered *sold!* (emphasis in original).

The procedure used at the auction was for the individual planes to be rolled out for potential bidders to inspect and then the bidding begins. The potential bidder has the opportunity to inspect the log book for each particular aircraft. In the instant case, Houston not only was the owner of the subject aircraft, but was also an authorized inspector for the Federal Aviation Administration ("FAA"). *Logbook Certification*

On December 22, 1989, Houston, as the authorized inspector, made the following certification in the aircraft log book. "I CERTIFY THAT THIS AIRCRAFT HAS BEEN INSPECTED IN ACCORDANCE WITH THE ANNUAL INSPECTION AND FOUND TO BE IN AN AIRWORTHY CONDITION. I.A. 255921619 R. Ray Houston." The certification on December 22, 1989, was made when the aircraft had 2,601 hours, and the aircraft at the time of the sale had 2,728.8 hours. Godwin became the successful bidder and Houston provided clear title to the aircraft and the bill of sale to Godwin.

Houston flew the plane from Oklahoma City to the General Dewitt Spain Airport on Second Street in Memphis. Houston testified that he offered to fly the plane to Memphis as a convenience to himself in order to save air fare on his return flight to Georgia. Godwin and several witnesses in his behalf testified that Houston insisted upon flying the aircraft to Memphis himself. The plane was left on Godwin's ramp at the airport.

A few days after the plane arrived at the Spain airport, the plane was flown to Jonesboro, Arkansas, for an examination by a prospective purchaser, a company owned by Mark Haggenmacher. Haggenmacher had the plane inspected by Dale Sharp, an A & P Mechanic with 22 years experience. After a preliminary inspection by Sharp, the plane was returned to Godwin at the Spain airport. After the plane was returned, Godwin learned that Sharp's preliminary inspection indicated that several airworthiness directives ("AD") issued by the FAA had not been complied with, such as inspection of turbo charges, inspection of exhaust system, inspection of fuel cells, inspection of hoses in the engine compartment, and inspection of the heater. In addition, the preliminary report also noted inoperable flaps.

A&P Inspection

After the plane was returned to Memphis, a more detailed inspection was made by two A & P mechanics, Steve Wallace and Glen Mitchell. Wallace testified that the inoperable flaps were caused because there was no flap motor and transmission in the airplane. There was also evidence of a disregard of an AD concerning cracks in the engine casing where repairs were attempted instead of required replacement. Wallace further testified that parts of the turbo charger and exhaust system were cracked and missing and exhaust gasses had scarred the left engine support beam which could cause the engine to fail. In his opinion, this scarring of the beam was a result of at least 200 hours of operation and that this condition would have been evident on inspection at the time of the Houston inspection 127 hours earlier as noted in the aircraft log. Wallace further testified about a bent elevator push rod and evidence that an attempt had been made to repair the push rod, both of which should have been evident upon an annual inspection. Wallace opined that at the time the aircraft was sold at auction it was not airworthy.

Glen Mitchell, an aircraft inspector and pilot testified that the bent elevator push rod could have caused loss of control of the aircraft. He likewise found the cause of the inoperable flaps to be the absence of a flap motor. Mitchell also testified concerning the disregard of the engine casing AD. He testified that the majority of all the parts on the exhaust and turbo were cracked and deteriorated beyond repair, and that the engine support beam was corroded and severely damaged which could cause a crash. He opined that damage to the support beam occurred over a 150 to 200 hour period and that this damage had to have been evident in an inspection 127 hours previous to the time he inspected it.

Alan Godwin, President of Godwin Aircraft, testified that he had 19 years experience in the aircraft business. He stated that although the auction was "as is—where is," this aircraft was represented as being in an airworthy condition by virtue of the annual inspection signed off by Houston himself. The only time Godwin saw the aircraft before the auction was when it was run through the auction block. He had time to inspect the log book and read the certification that the plane was airworthy. He testified that Houston insisted on flying the aircraft to Memphis, although Godwin had five extra pilots available who could have flown the plane. This testimony was corroborated by Mark Haggenmacher.

An expert for the United States Testing Company also testified concerning physical testing done to the engine support beam to determine the extent of the damage done and the period of time over which it had occurred. He reached the conclusion that the damage occurred over a long period of time and that his company could not replicate the corrosion by test in twelve cycles of 180 hours.

Houston's testimony did not specifically contradict the existence of the defects in the aircraft. He testified that mistakes do happen in aircraft logs, but he did not deny that the aircraft was defective and unairworthy. He is a pilot and aircraft inspector licensed by the FAA and was the owner and operator of the subject aircraft. During the time that he owned the aircraft, he maintained the plane and fulfilled federal regulations regarding required inspections. As a licensed aircraft inspector, he conducted the required inspections and signed the plane's log indicating that the inspections had been completed. He flew the plane to Oklahoma City for the auction and listed it for sale. He further testified that the catalog made no express representation as to the condition of the aircraft, except that it contained language by which it was noted that the plane's auto pilot was inoperable, which fact was known to the buyer prior to the auction. He testified that he made no warranties, express or implied to anyone and he had no contact with the plaintiff until after the auction.

Houston further testified that the plane was located at the airport in Oklahoma City for approximately three days prior to the auction and available for buyer inspection at any time. He stated that after the bid was made and accepted, the completion of the sales transfer took place while the parties were in Oklahoma. Houston noted in his testimony that Godwin's mechanics discovered the defects through visual inspection, which visual inspection could have been made by Godwin prior to making a bid on the aircraft. He further testified that with regard to his inspection prior to the auction which is recorded in the log book, he was the owner and sole operator of the plane and that he had not contemplated plans to sell the plane at that time. He indicated that the defects subsequently discovered could have occurred during the time period between his last inspection and the purchase at the auction.

After a bench trial, the chancellor awarded plaintiff compensatory damages in the amount of $41,171.88 and punitive damages in the amount of $10,375.00. Defendant has appealed.

[An] issue for review is whether the "as is, where is" disclaimer, and Godwin's opportunity to inspect the aircraft prior to the sale, should relieve the seller of liability for the misrepresentation that the aircraft was airworthy.

Airworthy?

In the case at bar, the log book certified by Houston declared the aircraft to be in airworthy condition. The evidence supports the trial court's findings that the certification was untrue, and that Houston intended to keep this information from Godwin until after delivery of the aircraft in Memphis. The record also contains proof that Godwin specifically inspected the log book to determine whether the aircraft was airworthy and that he relied upon the certification made to that effect. There is also proof that several of the more serious defects would not have been revealed unless the aircraft had been partially dismantled.

Effective "As Is, Where Is" Clause?

Houston further argues that the "as is, where is" disclaimer absolves him from liability. We must respectfully disagree. In the case at bar, the trial court found, and we have agreed, that the evidence does not preponderate against the finding that specific misrepresentations were made which were relied upon by the purchaser. In *Morris v. Mack's Used Cars*, 824 S.W.2d 538 (Tenn. 1992), our Supreme Court held that disclaimers permitted by the Uniform Commercial Code do not constitute a defense under the Tennessee Consumer Protection Act. The court noted that the Act created a separate and distinct cause of action for unfair or deceptive acts or practices. While we do not have a Consumer Protection Act case here, we do have a tortious misrepresentation case, which likewise is a distinct and separate cause of action from breach of warranty cases under the Uniform Commercial Code. In the case at bar, the action for tortious misrepresentation is analogous to an action for deceptive trade practices under the Consumer Protection Act.

The trial court found that defendant Houston made material misrepresentation and that he willfully continued these representations until delivery of the aircraft in Memphis. The evidence does not preponderate against the trial court's findings in this regard. The judgment of the trial court is affirmed and this case is remanded to the trial court for such further proceedings as may be necessary. Costs of the appeal are assessed against the appellant.

EXERCISE 9-1. *GODWIN AIRCRAFT V. HOUSTON*—CONTRACT TERMS, "AS IS, WHERE IS"

1. Describe the auction involved in *Godwin Aircraft v. Houston.*

2. What is an Airworthiness Directive ("AD")? Detail what import does it have, if any, in this case.

3. Define: (i) express warranty; and (ii) implied warranty.

4. Does the buyer's opportunity to inspect the aircraft prior to sale relieve the seller of liability for any misrepresentation that the aircraft is airworthy? Should it as a matter of policy? Does your answer change if the seller merely omitted—rather than misrepresented—a fact about the aircraft for sale? Explain.

5. Do contractual disclaimers exculpate the seller of an airplane from liability for tortious misrepresentation under Tennessee law? Explain.

Figure 9-1. Aircraft Security Agreement (Form AC 8050-98)

OMB Control No. 2120-0042
Exp. 09/30/2020

PRA Public Burden Statement: A federal agency may not conduct or sponsor, and a person is not required to respond to, nor shall a person be subject to a penalty for failure to comply with a collection of information subject to the requirements of the Paperwork Reduction Act unless that collection of information displays a currently valid OMB Control Number. The OMB Control Number for this information collection is 2120-0042. Public reporting for this collection of information is estimated to be approximately 45 minutes per response, including the time for reviewing instructions, searching existing data sources, gathering and maintaining the data needed, completing and reviewing the collection of information. All responses to this collection of information are required for recordation of security interest, in aircraft, engines, propellers and spare parts, in accordance with 14 CFR Part 49. Send comments regarding this burden estimate or any other aspect of this collection of information, including suggestions for reducing this burden to: Information Collection Clearance Officer, Federal Aviation Administration, 10101 Hillwood Parkway, Fort Worth, TX 76177-1524.

DEPARTMENT OF TRANSPORTATION
FEDERAL AVIATION ADMINISTRATION
CIVIL AVIATION REGISTRY
AIRCRAFT REGISTRATION BRANCH
P. O. Box 25504
Oklahoma City, Oklahoma 73125
AIRCRAFT SECURITY AGREEMENT

NAME & ADDRESS OF DEBTOR	
NAME & ADDRESS OF SECURED PARTY/ASSIGNOR	
ASSIGNED/NAME & ADDRESS OF ASSIGNEE	**ABOVE SPACE FOR FAA USE ONLY**

Date: ____________________

A security interest is hereby granted to the secured party on the following described collateral:
AIRCRAFT (FAA registration number, manufacturer, model, and serial number):

NOTICE: ENGINES LESS THAN 550 HORSEPOWER AND PROPELLERS NOT CAPABLE OF ABSORBING 750 OR MORE RATED SHAFT HORSEPOWER ARE NOT ELIGIBLE FOR RECORDING.

ENGINES (manufacturer, model, and serial number):

PROPELLERS (manufacturer, model, and serial number):

SPARE PARTS LOCATIONS (air carrier's name, city, and state):

together with all equipment and accessories attached thereto or used in connection therewith, including engines of ______ horsepower, or the equivalent, and propellers capable of absorbing ________ rated takeoff shaft horsepower, described above, all of which are included in the term aircraft as used herein.
The above described aircraft is hereby mortgaged to the secured party for the purpose of securing in the order named:

FIRST: The payment of all indebtedness evidenced by and according to the terms of that certain promissory note, herein below described, and all renewals and extensions thereof.

Note bearing date _________ executed by the debtor and payable to the order of ___________________________ in the aggregate sum of $________ with interest thereon at the rate of ___________ per centum per annum, from date, payable in installments as follows: The principal and interest of said note is payable in _______ installments of $ ________ each on _______day of each successive month beginning with the _______ day of _________. The last payment of $ _________ is due on the ________ day of _________

AC 8050-98 (10/18)

OMB Control No. 2120-0042
Exp. 09/30/2020

SECOND: The prompt and faithful discharge and performance of each agreement of the debtor herein contained made with or for the benefit of the secured party in connection with the indebtedness to secure which this instrument is executed, and the repayment of any sums expended or advanced by the secured party for the maintenance or preservation of the property mortgaged hereby or in enforcing their rights hereunder. Said debtor hereby declares and hereby warrants to the said secured party that they are the absolute owner of the legal and beneficial title to the said aircraft and in possession thereof, and that the same is free and clear of all liens, encumbrances, and adverse claims whatsoever, except as follows: (If no liens other than this mortgage, indicate "none".)
It is the intention of the parties to deliver this instrument in the state of _____.

Provided, however, that if the debtor, their heirs, administrators, successors, or assignees shall pay said note and the interest thereon in accordance with the terms thereof and shall keep and perform all and singular the terms, covenants, and agreements in this security agreement, then this security agreement shall be null and void.

Time is of the essence of this security agreement. It is hereby agreed that, if default be made in the payment of any part of the principal or interest of the promissory note secured hereby at the time and in the manner therein specified, or if any breach be made of any obligation or promise of the debtor herein contained or secured hereby, or if any or all of the property covered hereby be hereafter sold, leased, transferred, mortgaged, or otherwise encumbered without the written consent of the secured party may deem himself insecure, then the whole principal sum unpaid upon said promissory note, with the interest accrued thereon, or advanced under the terms of this security agreement, or secured thereby, and the interest thereon shall immediately become due and payable at the option of the secured party.

Upon default, secured party may at once proceed to foreclose this mortgage in any manner provided by law, or the secured party may at its option, and they are hereby empowered so to do, with or without foreclosure action, enter upon the premises where the said aircraft may be and take possession thereof; and remove and sell and dispose of the same at public or private sale, and from the proceeds of such sale retain all costs and charges incurred by secured party in the taking or sale of said aircraft, including any reasonable attorney's fees incurred; also all sums due him on said promissory note, under any provisions thereof, or advanced under the terms of this security, and interest thereon, or due or owing to the said secured party, under any provisions of this security agreement, or secured hereby, with the interest thereon, and any surplus of such proceeds remaining shall be paid to the debtor, or whoever may be lawfully entitled to receive the same. If a deficiency occurs, the debtor agrees to pay such deficiency forthwith.

Said secured party or his agent may bid and purchase at any sale made under this mortgage or herein authorized, or at any sale made upon foreclosure of this security agreement.

In witness whereof, the debtor has hereunto set _____ hand and seal on the day and year first above

ACKNOWLEDGMENT:
(If required by applicable local law)

NAME OF DEBTOR _____

SIGNATURE(S) (IN INK) _____
(If executed for co-ownership, all must sign)

TITLE _____
(If signed for a corporation, partnership, owner, or agent)

ASSIGNMENT BY SECURED PARTY

For value received, the undersigned secured party does hereby sell, assign, and transfer all right, title, and interest in and to the foregoing note and security agreement and the aircraft covered thereby, unto the assignee named on the face of this instrument at the address given, and hereby authorizes the said assignee to do every act and thing necessary to collect and discharge the same. The undersigned secured party warrants and agrees to defend the title of said aircraft hereby conveyed against all lawful claims and demands except the rights of the maker. The undersigned secured party warrants that the secured party is the owner of a valid security interest in the said aircraft. (A Guaranty Clause or any other provisions which the parties are desirous of making a part of this assignment should be included in the following space.)

Dated this _____ day of _____.

ACKNOWLEDGMENT:
(If required by applicable local law)

NAME OF SECURED PARTY (ASSIGNOR) _____

SIGNATURE(S) (IN INK) _____
(If executed for co-ownership, all must sign)

TITLE _____
(If signed for a corporation, partnership, owner, or agent)

THIS FORM IS ONLY INTENDED TO BE A SUGGESTED FORM OF SECURITY AGREEMENT WHICH MEETS THE RECORDING REQUIREMENTS OF TITLE 49, UNITED STATES CODE, AND THE REGULATIONS ISSUED THEREUNDER. IN ADDITION TO THESE REQUIREMENTS, THE FORM OF SECURITY AGREEMENT SHOULD BE DRAFTED IN ACCORDANCE WITH THE PERTINENT PROVISIONS OF LOCAL STATUTES AND OTHER APPLICABLE FEDERAL STATUTES. THIS FORM MAY BE REPRODUCED.

SEND, WITH APPROPRIATE FEE, TO: AIRCRAFT REGISTRATION BRANCH
P.O. BOX 25504
OKLAHOMA CITY, OKLAHOMA 73125-0504

AC 8050-98 (10/18)

Source: https://www.faa.gov/documentLibrary/media/Form/ac8050-98.pdf

Figure 9-2. Aircraft Bill of Sale

```
                    UNITED STATES OF AMERICA                    OMB Control No. 2120-0042
    U.S. DEPARTMENT OF TRANSPORTATION FEDERAL AVIATION ADMINISTRATION   Exp. 09/30/2020

                    AIRCRAFT BILL OF SALE

        FOR AND IN CONSIDERATION OF $           THE
        UNDERSIGNED OWNER(S) OF THE FULL LEGAL AND
        BENEFICIAL TITLE OF THE AIRCRAFT  DESCRIBED
        AS FOLLOWS:

        UNITED STATES            N
        REGISTRATION NUMBER
    AIRCRAFT MANUFACTURER & MODEL

    AIRCRAFT SERIAL NO.

        DOES THIS              DAY OF          ,
        HEREBY SELL, GRANT, TRANSFER AND
        DELIVER ALL RIGHTS, TITLE, AND INTERESTS
        IN AND TO SUCH AIRCRAFT UNTO:                  Do Not Write In This Block
                                                        FOR FAA USE ONLY
            NAME AND ADDRESS
            (IF INDIVIDUAL(S), GIVE LAST NAME, FIRST NAME, AND MIDDLE INITIAL.)

P
U
R
C
H
A
S
E
R
            DEALER CERTIFICATE NUMBER
    AND TO                         EXECUTORS, ADMINISTRATORS, AND ASSIGNS TO HAVE AND TO HOLD
    SINGULARLY THE SAID AIRCRAFT FOREVER, AND WARRANTS THE TITLE THEREOF:

    IN TESTIMONY WHEREOF        HAVE SET        HAND AND SEAL THIS      DAY OF
            NAME(S) OF SELLER       SIGNATURE(S)           TITLE
            (TYPED OR PRINTED)      (IN INK) (IF EXECUTED FOR  (TYPED OR PRINTED)
                                    CO-OWNERSHIP, ALL MUST SIGN.)
S
E
L
L
E
R

    ACKNOWLEDGMENT (NOT REQUIRED FOR PURPOSES OF FAA RECORDING: HOWEVER, MAY BE REQUIRED BY LOCAL LAW FOR
    VALIDITY OF THE INSTRUMENT.)

    ORIGINAL:  TO FAA:
    AC Form 8050-2 (10/18)
```

Source: https://www.faa.gov/documentLibrary/media/form/ac8050-2.pdf.

Figure 9-3. FAA Aircraft Registration Form

UNITED STATES OF AMERICA – DEPARTMENT OF TRANSPORTATION
FEDERAL AVIATION ADMINISTRATION – MIKE MONRONEY AERONAUTICAL CENTER

AIRCRAFT REGISTRATION APPLICATION

UNITED STATES REGISTRATION NUMBER	N	TYPE OF REGISTRATION (Check one box.)	☐ 1. Individual ☐ 2. Partnership ☐ 3. Corporation ☐ 4. Co-Owner ☐ 5. Government ☐ 7. Limited Liability Company (LLC) ☐ 8. Non-Citizen Corporation ☒ 9. Non-Citizen Corporation Co-Owner
AIRCRAFT MANUFACTURER AND MODEL			
AIRCRAFT SERIAL NUMBER			

NAME(S) OF APPLICANT(S) (Person(s) shown on evidence of ownership. If individual, give last name, first name and middle initial.)

TELEPHONE NUMBER: (   )

MAILING ADDRESS (Permanent mailing address for first applicant on list.)

NUMBER AND STREET: _____

RURAL ROUTE: _____ P.O. BOX _____

CITY: _____ STATE: _____ ZIP: _____

PHYSICAL ADDRESS/LOCATION IF P.O. BOX OR RURAL ROUTE BOX USED FOR MAILING ADDRESS

NUMBER AND STREET: _____
DESCRIPTION OF LOCATION: _____

CITY: _____ STATE: _____ ZIP: _____

☐ CHECK HERE IF YOU ARE ONLY REPORTING A CHANGE OF ADDRESS

CERTIFICATION

I/WE CERTIFY:

(1) That the above aircraft is owned by the undersigned applicant who is: (MUST CHECK AND/OR COMPLETE a, b, c, or d)

☐ a. A citizen of the United States as defined by 49 USC 40102(15).

☐ b. A resident alien with alien registration (Form I-551) No. _____

☐ c. A non-citizen corporation organized and doing business under the laws of (state) _____ and said aircraft is based and primarily used in the United States. Records of flight hours are available for inspection at (provide complete physical address) _____

☐ d. A corporation using a voting trust to qualify. Enter name of trustee _____

(2) If box c or d above is checked, I, the below signed, certify that I am authorized, by the applicant shown above, to sign corporate documents and to seek aircraft registration on behalf of the entity and that I will provide the same authorization if requested;

(3) That the aircraft is not registered under the laws of any foreign country; and

(4) That legal evidence of ownership is attached or has been filed with the Federal Aviation Administration.

ANY AND ALL SIGNATORIES OF THIS APPLICATION MUST READ THE FOLLOWING AND UNDERSTAND THAT, BY APPLYING A SIGNATURE TO THIS DOCUMENT, THEY ARE SUBJECT TO THE REFERENCED STATUTES AND ASSOCIATED PENALTIES.

I hereby certify that the information provided herein and in any attachments to the application for aircraft registration is true, accurate and correct to the best of my knowledge and belief. I understand that the information provided by me will be relied on by the FAA administrator in his/her determination of qualification for aircraft registration. I understand that whoever, in any matter within the jurisdiction of any department or agency of the United States, knowingly and willfully falsifies, conceals or covers up (by any trick, scheme or device) a material fact or who makes any false, misleading or fraudulent statements or representations or entry, may be fined up to $250,000 or imprisoned not more than five (5) years or both (18 U.S.C. Sections 1001 and 3571). I understand that, should I intentionally provide any inaccurate or false information, registration of the subject aircraft may be revoked.

NOTE: If executed for co-ownership, all applicants must sign. Use next page and add page(s) if necessary.

1	SIGNATURE:		DATE:
	TYPED/PRINTED NAME:	TITLE:	
2	SIGNATURE:		DATE:
	TYPED/PRINTED NAME:	TITLE:	

NOTE: Except when the most recent registration of the subject aircraft is expired or cancelled, 14 CFR 47.31(c) provides for an airworthy U.S. aircraft to be operated for up to 90 days within the United States when a copy of the signed application for its registration is carried in the aircraft while awaiting issuance and receipt of the new registration certificate.

AC Form 8050-1 (10/18)

Source: https://www.faa.gov/documentLibrary/media/Form/AC8050-1.pdf.

PHILKO AVIATION, INC. V. SHACKET

462 U.S. 406 (1983)

JUSTICE WHITE delivered the opinion of the Court.

This case presents the question whether the Federal Aviation Act of 1958 ("Act"), 49 U.S.C. §§ 1301 *et seq.*, prohibits all transfers of title to aircraft from having validity against innocent third parties unless the transfer has been evidenced by a written instrument, and the instrument has been recorded with the Federal Aviation Administration ("FAA"). We conclude that the Act does have such effect.

On April 19, 1978, at an airport in Illinois, a corporation operated by Roger Smith sold a new airplane to respondents. Respondents, the Shackets, paid the sale price in full and took possession of the aircraft, and they have been in possession ever since. Smith, however, did not give respondents the original bills of sale reflecting the chain of title to the plane. He instead gave them only photocopies and his assurance that he would "take care of the paperwork," which the Shackets understood to include the recordation of the original bills of sale with the FAA. Insofar as the present record reveals, the Shackets never attempted to record their title with the FAA.

Fraudulent Scheme

Unfortunately for all, Smith did not keep his word but instead commenced a fraudulent scheme. Shortly after the sale to the Shackets, Smith purported to sell the same airplane to petitioner, Philko Aviation. According to Philko, Smith said that the plane was in Michigan having electronic equipment installed. Nevertheless, Philko and its financing bank were satisfied that all was in order, for they had examined the original bills of sale and had checked the aircraft's title against FAA records. (It is perhaps noteworthy, however, that Philko's title search did not even reveal that the seller, Smith's corporation, owned or ever had owned the subject airplane.) At closing, Smith gave Philko the title documents, but, of course, he did not and could not have given Philko possession of the aircraft. Philko's bank subsequently recorded the title documents with the FAA.

After the fraud became apparent, the Shackets filed the present declaratory judgment action to determine title to the plane. Philko argued that it had title because the Shackets had never recorded their interest in the airplane with the FAA. Philko relied on § 503(c) of the Act, 49 U.S.C. § 1403(c), which provides that no conveyance or instrument affecting the title to any civil aircraft shall be valid against third parties not having actual notice of the sale, until such conveyance or other instrument is filed for recordation with the FAA. However, the District Court awarded summary judgment in favor of the Shackets, and the

Court of Appeals affirmed, reasoning that § 503(c) did not preempt substantive state law regarding title transfers, and that, under the Illinois Uniform Commercial Code, the Shackets had title but Philko did not. We granted *certiorari*, and we now reverse and remand for further proceedings.

Section 503(a)(1) of the Act, 49 U.S.C. § 1403(a)(1), directs the Secretary of Transportation to establish and maintain a system for the recording of any "conveyance which affects the title to, or any interest in, any civil aircraft of the United States." Section 503(c), 49 U.S.C. § 1403(c), states:

Federal Recording System

> No conveyance or instrument the recording of which is provided for by [§ 503(a)(1)] shall be valid in respect of such aircraft . . . against any person other than the person by whom the conveyance or other instrument is made or given, his heir or devisee, or any person having actual notice thereof, until such conveyance or other instrument is filed for recordation in the office of the Secretary of Transportation."

The statutory definition of "conveyance" defines the term as "a bill of sale, contract of conditional sale, mortgage, assignment of mortgage, or other instrument affecting title to, or interest in, property." 49 U.S.C. § 1301(20) (Supp. V, 1981). If § 503(c) were to be interpreted literally in accordance with the statutory definition, that section would not require every transfer to be documented and recorded; it would only invalidate unrecorded title instruments, rather than unrecorded title transfers.

Conveyance Defined

Under this interpretation, a claimant might be able to prevail against an innocent third party by establishing his title without relying on an instrument. In the present case, for example, the Shackets could not prove their title on the basis of an unrecorded bill of sale or other writing purporting to evidence a transfer of title to them, even if state law did not require recordation of such instruments, but they might still prevail, since Illinois law does not require written evidence of a sale "with respect to goods for which payment has been made and accepted or which have been received and accepted."

> *§ 503(c) means that every aircraft transfer must be evidenced by an instrument, and every such instrument must be recorded, before the rights of innocent third parties can be affected. Furthermore, because of these federal requirements, state laws permitting undocumented or unrecorded transfers are preempted, for there is a direct conflict between § 503(c) and such state laws, and the federal law must prevail.*

We are convinced, however, that Congress did not intend § 503(c) to be interpreted in this manner. Rather, § 503(c) means that every aircraft transfer must be evidenced by an instrument, and every such instrument must be recorded, before the rights of innocent third parties can be affected. Furthermore, because of these federal requirements, state laws permitting undocumented or unrecorded transfers are preempted, for there is a direct conflict between § 503(c) and such state laws, and the federal law must prevail.

Legislative History

These conclusions are dictated by the legislative history. The Senate, House, and Conference committee reports, and the section-by-section analysis of one of the bill's drafters, all expressly declare that the federal statute "requires" the recordation of "every transfer . . . of any interest in a civil aircraft." The Senate report explains: "This section requires the recordation with the Authority of every transfer made after the effective date of the section, of any interest in a civil aircraft of the United States.

The conveyance evidencing each such transfer is to be recorded with an index in a recording system to be established by the Authority." Thus, since Congress intended to require the recordation of a conveyance evidencing each transfer of an interest in aircraft, Congress must have intended to preempt any state law under which a transfer without a recordable conveyance would be valid against innocent transferees or lienholders who have recorded.

Any other construction would defeat the primary congressional purpose for the enactment of § 503(c), which was to create "a central clearing house for recordation of titles so that a person, wherever he may be, will know where he can find ready access to the claims against, or liens, or other legal interests in an aircraft." Hearings before the House Comm. on Interstate and Foreign Commerce, 75 Cong., 3d Sess., p. 407 (April 1, 1938) (testimony of F. Fagg, Director of Air Commerce, Dept. of Commerce).

Here, state law does not require any documentation whatsoever for a valid transfer of an aircraft to be effected. An oral sale is fully valid against third parties once the buyer takes possession of the plane. If the state law allowing this result were not preempted by § 503(c), then any buyer in possession would have absolutely no need or incentive to record his title with the FAA, and he could refuse to do so with impunity, and thereby prevent the "central clearing house" from providing "ready access" to information about his claim. This is not what Congress intended.

Here, state law does not require any documentation whatsoever for a valid transfer of an aircraft to be effected. An oral sale is fully valid against third parties once the buyer takes possession of the plane. If the state law allowing this result were not preempted by § 503(c), then any buyer in possession would have absolutely no need or incentive to record his title with the FAA, and he could refuse to do so with impunity, and thereby prevent the "central clearing house" from providing "ready access" to information about his claim. This is not what Congress intended.

Although the recording system ideally should allow any transferee who has checked the FAA records to acquire his interest with the certain knowledge that the transferor's title is clear, we recognize that the present system does not allow for such certainty, because there is a substantial lag from the time at which an instrument is mailed to the FAA to the time at which the FAA actually records the instrument. Thus, if the owner of an airplane grants a lien on it to Doe on one day and attempts to sell it to Roe on the following day, Roe might erroneously assume, based on a search of the FAA records, that his vendor has clear title to the plane, even if Doe had promptly mailed the documents evidencing his lien to the FAA for recordation.

In the absence of the statutory definition of conveyance, our reading of § 503(c) would be by far the most natural one, because the term "conveyance" is first defined in the dictionary as "the action of conveying," *i.e.*, "the act by which title to property . . . is transferred." Webster's Third New International Dictionary 499 (P. Gove ed. 1976). Had Congress defined "conveyance" in accordance with this definition, then § 503(c) plainly would have required the recordation of every transfer. Congress' failure to adopt this definition is not dispositive, however, since the statutory definition is expressly not applicable if "the context otherwise requires." 49 U.S.C. § 1301. Even in the absence of such a caveat, we need not read the statutory definition mechanically into § 503(c), since to do so would render the recording system ineffective and thus would defeat the purpose of the legislation. A statutory definition should not be applied in such a manner. Accordingly, we hold that state laws allowing undocumented or unrecorded transfers of interests in aircraft to affect innocent third parties are preempted by the federal Act.

In support of the judgment below, respondents rely on *Matter of Gary Aircraft Corp.*, 681 F.2d 365 (5th Cir. 1981). *Gary Aircraft* involved a contest between the holder of a security interest in two airplanes and a subsequent purchaser. Although the security interest holder recorded its interest in the planes prior to the time that the purchaser did so, the Court of Appeals held in favor of the purchaser, because

Validity v. Priority

Texas law governed priorities and, under Texas law, the purchaser was a buyer in the ordinary course of business who took free of the security interest. The security interest holder argued that Texas law was preempted by § 503(d) of the Act, 49 U.S.C. § 1403(d), which states that all instruments recorded with the FAA shall be "valid" without further recordation, but the court found that "validity" did not mean "priority." Instead, it only meant such "validity" as granted by state law. *Gary Aircraft* thus dealt with the question of the effect of recording under § 503(d), unlike the present case, which concerns the effect of nonrecording under § 503(c).

Moreover, the court in *Gary Aircraft* rejected the contention that § 503 preempted all state laws dealing with priority of interests in aircraft. The Court of Appeals held that the first person to record his interest with the FAA is not assured of priority, which is determined by reference to state law. We are inclined to agree with this rationale, but it does not help the Shackets.

Although state law determines priorities, all interests must be federally recorded before they can obtain whatever priority to which they are entitled under state law. As one commentator has explained, "The only situation in which priority appears to be determined by operation of the [federal] statute is where the security holder has failed to record his interest. Such failure invalidates the conveyance as to innocent third persons. But recordation itself merely validates; it does not grant priority."

Although state law determines priorities, all interests must be federally recorded before they can obtain whatever priority to which they are entitled under state law.

In view of the foregoing, we find that the courts below erred by granting the Shackets summary judgment on the basis that if an unrecorded transfer of an aircraft is valid under state law, it has validity as against innocent third parties. Of course, it is undisputed that the sale to the Shackets was valid and binding as between the parties. Hence, if Philko had actual notice of the transfer to the Shackets or if, under state law, Philko failed to acquire or perfect the interest that it purports to assert for reasons wholly unrelated to the sale to the Shackets, Philko would not have an enforceable interest, and the Shackets would retain possession of the aircraft. Furthermore, we do not think that the federal law imposes a standard with which it is impossible to comply. There may be situations in which the transferee has used reasonable diligence to file and cannot be faulted for the failure of the crucial documents to be of record. But because of the manner in which this case was disposed of on summary judgment, matters such as these were not considered, and these issues remain open on remand. The judgment of the

Court of Appeals is reversed, and the case is remanded for further proceedings consistent with this opinion.

JUSTICE O'CONNOR, *concurring in part and concurring in the judgment.*

I join the opinion of the Court except to the extent that it might be read to suggest this Court's endorsement of the view that one who makes a reasonably diligent effort to record will obtain the protections ordinarily reserved for recorded interests. I would express no opinion on that question, for it is not before us and has not been addressed in brief or in argument or, indeed, in the statute.

EXERCISE 9-2. *PHILKO AVIATION, INC. V. SHACKET*—PRIORITY

1. Identify the following parties and the relationship of each to the litigation: (a) Roger Smith; (b) the Shackets; and (c) Philko Aviation.

2. Detail the facts and claims of the case. What happened? Alternatively, what did not happen that should have?

3. What interpretation, according to the court, did Congress intend of Section 503(a)(1) of the Federal Aviation Act of 1958?

4. What is the relationship between "validity" and priority." Discuss *Matter of Gary Aircraft Corp.* as part of your answer.

5. What is the holding of the case? What would happen if Philko had actual notice of the transfer or if, under state law, Philko failed to acquire or perfect its interest in the airplane? Is this fair?

UNITED STATES V. STARCHER

883 F. Supp. 2d 1175 (M.D. Fla. 2012)

DAVID A. BAKER, *UNITED STATES MAGISTRATE JUDGE.*

Defendant Starcher was indicted on May 18, 2011 and arrested on May 25, 2011 for criminal drug conspiracy activity that took place from May 2009 to January 2010. Prior to the indictment, in October 2010, Homeland Security Investigations agents seized a Cessna 206 aircraft, Tail No. 8065Z from a private residence located on Sand Lake Shores Court in Orlando, Florida for violations of 49 U.S.C. § 46306. Petitioners, James and Sharon Hoots, do not own the residence; the owner of the residence is a friend of Defendant Starcher's who agreed to allow him to keep the Aircraft on his property. The work that was performed on the Aircraft to make it "seaplane-ready" between approximately

March to May 2010 was conducted in Gobles, Michigan by a mechanic hired by Petitioners. Petitioners had direct authority in overseeing the work performed by the mechanic and were monetarily responsible for all work completed by the mechanic during that time period. After the work was completed in Michigan, the plane was returned to Florida and kept at Defendant's friend's residence. Petitioners do not maintain that they had actual possession of the Aircraft either before or after the repairs to the plane were made in Michigan.

On October 3, 2011, Defendant Randall Starcher pled guilty to conspiracy to possess with intent to distribute marijuana in violation of 21 U.S.C. § 841(a)(1), in violation of 21 U.S.C. § 846. Defendant entered into a plea agreement, which required him to "forfeit all of his interest in any and all property constituting or derived from proceeds traceable to the offense," including the Aircraft titled in the name of Mile High Adventures LLC, pursuant to 21 U.S.C. § 853.

Starcher agreed to forfeit the Aircraft, admitting that it was used to facilitate drug offenses that were committed between May 2009 and January 2010, and that the Aircraft was purchased with proceeds obtained from the drug conspiracy. The Government sought a Preliminary Order of Forfeiture, which the Court granted on November 3, 2011. The Court required the Government to notify in writing all known third parties who allegedly had a legal interest in the aircraft.

Conditional Verbal Sale Agreement

On December 6, 2011, Petitioners received a written notice of forfeiture of the Aircraft, to which they timely filed a claim alleging that they had fifty percent ownership. Petitioners assert that they entered into an oral "conditional sale agreement" with Defendant, on behalf of Mile High Adventures, LLC. They alleged the oral conditional agreement provided that if Petitioners spent money and labor to convert the Aircraft into a seaplane, in return, Mile High Adventures, LLC, would provide sightseeing services to tourists and give a fifty percent interest in the Aircraft to Petitioners. Petitioners assert that in May 2010 they completed their obligations under the "verbal conditional sale agreement."

According to Federal Aviation Administration ("FAA") records, on May 23, 2009, Web Thomas Aircraft Sales Inc. sold the subject aircraft to Mile High Adventures, LLC and the Bill of Sale and Aircraft Registration Application were filed at the FAA Registry on May 29, 2009. However, because Mile High Adventures, LLC's Bill of Sale failed to properly provide proof of its United States citizenship, the company never obtained a Certificate of Aircraft Registration from the FAA. According to Special Agent Steve Tochterman of the FAA, a review of FAA aircraft registration records indicates that no other documents evidencing a conveyance of the Aircraft—by Petitioners or anyone else—have been submitted and/or recorded at the FAA Registry since May/June 2009, when Mile High Adventures, LLC submitted its paperwork to the FAA.

Under 21 U.S.C. § 853(n)(6), the petitioner must establish by a preponderance of the evidence that:

(A)   the petitioner has a legal right, title, or interest in the property, and such right, title, or interest renders the order of forfeiture invalid in whole or in part because the right, title, or interest was vested in the petitioner rather than the defendant or was superior to any right, title, or interest of the defendant at the time of the commission of the acts which gave rise to the forfeiture of the property under this section; or

(B)   the petitioner is a bona fide purchaser for value of the right, title, or interest in the property and was at the time of purchase reasonably without cause to believe that the property was subject to forfeiture under this section.

The Government moves to dismiss Petitioners' claim of interest. Petitioners do not seriously dispute that they failed to properly perfect their interest (if any) in the Aircraft under 21 U.S.C. § 853(n)(6)(A), arguing repeatedly that Petitioners are *bona fide* purchasers under § 853(n)(6)(B) as the "very basis of the Petition." The majority of Petitioners' argument is that they have a fifty percent interest in the Aircraft under § 853(n)(6)(B) as *bona fide* purchasers who, at the time of purchase, were "reasonably without cause to believe that the property was subject to forfeiture."

Legal Interest

The Government seeks to dismiss Petitioners' asserted interest in the Aircraft under their "verbal conditional sale agreement." It is undisputed that the Petitioners filed their petition on January 4, 2012, after they received a Notice of Forfeiture by certified mail on December 6, 2011 and following Government publication of the Notice of Forfeiture.

The Government moves to dismiss Petitioners' claim of interest because they failed to (1) record their ownership with the FAA; (2) failed to reduce the alleged "verbal conditional sales agreement" to writing; and (3) they are not bona fide purchasers.

Grounds for Dismissal

The Eleventh Circuit has held "federal law decides what interests are subject to forfeiture under § 853." *United States v. Kennedy*, 201 F.3d 1324, 1334 (11th Cir. 2000). In this case, the Federal Aviation Act decides whether an oral contract such as Petitioners' "verbal conditional sale agreement" is enforceable. *See* 49 U.S.C. § 40101.

Petitioners argue that, because they met the terms and conditions of their verbal conditional agreement with Defendant Starcher as of May 2010, they gained a 50% interest in the Aircraft at that time. However, Title 49 U.S.C. § 44108 provides, "[u]ntil a conveyance, lease, or instrument executed for security purposes that may be recorded under section 44107(a)(1) or (2) of this title is filed for recording, the conveyance, lease, or instrument is valid only against-(1) the person making the conveyance, lease, or instrument; (2) that person's heirs and devisees; and (3) a person having actual notice of the conveyance, lease, or instrument." 49 U.S.C. § 44108. Thus, Petitioners' interest is not effective until they have recorded it.

The Supreme Court in *Philko Aviation Inc. v. Shacket* prohibited "all transfers of title to aircraft from having validity against innocent third parties unless the transfer has been evidenced by a *written* instrument, and the instrument *has been recorded* with the Federal Aviation Administration." *Philko Aviation, Inc. v. Shacket,* 462 U.S. 406, 407 (1983) (emphasis added). Petitioners failed to reduce their oral "conditional sale agreement" with Defendant Starcher into writing. Although Petitioners spent time and money (approximately $35,000) to convert the Airplane into a seaplane, under § 44108, the oral conditional agreement would not be an enforceable interest against third parties because a written instrument was never executed or recorded. Thus, Petitioners acquired no legal interest through their transaction with Defendant preceding the forfeiture.

Aircraft Ownership— State of Federal Law?

> *Although Petitioners spent time and money (approximately $35,000) to convert the Airplane into a seaplane, under § 44108, the oral conditional agreement would not be an enforceable interest against third parties because a written instrument was never executed or recorded. Thus, Petitioners acquired no legal interest through their transaction with Defendant preceding the forfeiture*

Petitioners argue that their interest in the Aircraft should be construed under the "application of state law" applying the Uniform Commercial Code. The Supreme Court has expressly rejected that approach, holding that any "state laws allowing undocumented or unrecorded transfers of interests in aircraft to affect innocent third parties are preempted by the federal Act." *Philko Aviation, Inc.,* 462 U.S. at 412. Moreover, Florida Statute § 329.01 adopts the language, nearly verbatim, from § 44108 of the United States Code requiring recording with the FAA to effect an interest in an aircraft. Fla. Stat. § 329.01.

In addition, Petitioners contend that their 50% interest began in *May 2010,* after completion of their obligations under the verbal agreement and would not be superior to the Government's interest in the aircraft which vested in May 2009, when Defendant's drug conspiracy began, under the "relation back doctrine."

In *United States v. Watkins,* 320 F.3d 1279, 1282 (11th Cir. 2003), the Eleventh Circuit held that Petitioners could not recover any interest because they gave money to the defendant *after* the conspiracy that prompted the forfeiture had already ended. The court recognized that petitioners had no interest in the property "at the time of the commission of the acts which gave rise to the forfeiture," as § 853(n)(6)(A) requires, and their interest against the assets would be as unsecured creditors. *Id.* at 1282 (holding claimants were unsecured creditors who could not qualify as a bona fide purchaser for value under § 853(n)(6)(B), as "their interest lies against the debtor personally as opposed to any specific property that they purchased from the debtor").

Similarly, here, Petitioners assert that they acquired interest in the aircraft in May 2010, however, the Government's interest began at least one year prior in May 2009, when the drug conspiracy began. Thus, because Petitioners had no interest *at the time* Defendant's drug conspiracy began, Petitioners cannot recover any interest under § 853(n)(6)(A).

Bona Fide Purchaser for Value

The bulk of Petitioners' argument is that, rather than acquiring a legal interest in the aircraft before the conspiracy, they acquired an interest in the aircraft after the criminal activity as bona fide purchasers for value as defined in § 853(n)(6)(B). Section 853(n)(6)(B) protects petitioners who are "bona fide purchasers for value without knowledge of the forfeitability of the defendant's assets." *Kennedy,* 201 F.3d at 1328–29.

Petitioners assert that they had no knowledge of Defendant's previous criminal conduct that led to his indictment and conviction when they entered into the verbal contract with him on behalf of Mile High Adventures, LLC. The Eleventh Circuit has defined "the term bona fide purchaser" as "generally understood to mean 'one who has purchased property for value without notice of any defects in the title of the seller.' " *United States v. Watkins,* 320 F.3d at 1283.

Petitioners did not purchase an interest directly in the Aircraft that they ever perfected; they filed no lien and recorded no bill of sale under the FAA regulations to protect their interest. As such, their interest against the Aircraft is as unsecured creditors and "their interest lies against the debtor personally as opposed to any specific property." *See Watkins,* 320 F.3d at 1284 (holding claimants were unsecured creditors who could not qualify as bona fide purchasers for value under § 853(n)(6)(B)); *United States v. Carmichael*, 440 F. Supp. 2d 1280 (M.D. Ala. 2006) (holding that claimant was not a "bona fide purchaser" where it had no lien against the real property for materials supplied for construction and untimely filed its judgment lien).

In order to qualify as a bona fide purchaser for value under the language of the statute, a person must not have known that the property purchased was subject to forfeiture.

Bona Fide Purchaser and Timing of Lien

Petitioners also do not qualify as bona fide purchasers "without knowledge of the forfeitability of" the Airplane. In order to qualify as a bona fide purchaser for value under § 853(n)(6)(B), under the language of the statute, a person must not have known that the property purchased was subject to forfeiture. 21 U.S.C. § 853(n)(6)(B). Petitioners did not assert their written claim or lien to the airplane until January 23, 2012, after the Government had published the notice of forfeiture in November–December 2011 and provided notice to Petitioners directly. Any registration or lien on the airplane that Petitioners would file at this juncture would clearly be after Petitioners learned of the forfeiture and negate an objectively reasonable belief they have in the property. *Carmichael*, 440 F. Supp. 2d at 1280 (holding that claimant was not a "bona fide purchaser" where it had no lien against property and government's publication of order of forfeiture before it filed claim put it on notice of forfeiture); *cf. United States v. One Parcel of Real Estate Located at 6640 SW 48th Street*, 41 F.3d 1448, 1452–53 (11th Cir. 1995) (person who acquires property knowing that it was used to commit an illegal act is not an innocent owner under "innocent owner" defense in § 881(a)(7)).

As the Supreme Court has held, "every aircraft transfer must be evidenced by an instrument, and every such instrument must be recorded, before the rights of innocent third parties can be affected." *Philko Aviation, Inc.*, 462 U.S. at 409–10. Given the circumstances before the Court in this case, Petitioners failed to perfect any interest they might have had in the aircraft in compliance with federal and state regulations, and as unsecured creditors, they do not qualify as bona fide purchasers.

EXERCISE 9-3. *UNITED STATES V. STARCHER*—LEGAL INTEREST

1. Identify the following: (a) James and Sharon Hoots; (b) Randall Starcher; and (c) Mile High Adventures LLC.

2. What were the "terms" of the alleged oral conditional sale agreement?

3. How is an interest in an airplane perfected under 21 U.S.C. § 853(n)(6)? How do the petitioners claim an interest in the Cessna at issue?

4. What is the petitioner's argument that they have a legal interest in the airplane? Does the court accept that argument? Explain.

5. What is a "bona fide purchaser for value"? Do the petitioners qualify as such purchasers here? Explain.

NOTES ON *UNITED STATES V. STARCHER*—FRACTIONAL OWNERSHIP

United States v. Starcher, supra, introduces you to the idea that several different stakeholders can hold different legal interests in an airplane. Such "fractional ownership" arrangements have become common as described in Eileen M. Gleimer, *The Regulation of Fractional Ownership: Have the Wings of the Future Been Clipped,* 67 J. AIR L. & COM. 321 (2002) ("In general terms, fractional ownership programs are multi-year programs covering a pool of aircraft, most of which are owned by more than one party and all of which are placed in a dry lease exchange pool and available to any program participant when the aircraft in which such participant owns an interest is not available."). *See also Regulation of Fractional Aircraft Ownership Programs and On-Demand Operations,* 66 Fed. Reg. 37,520 (July 18, 2001).

UNITED STATES V. MALAGO
2012 WL 4378102 (S.D. Fla. 2012)

ROBERT N. SCOLA, JR. DISTRICT JUDGE.

This matter is before the Court on the Defendant's Motion to Dismiss Courts 3 and 12–16 of the Indictment. The Defendant seeks to dismiss Count 3 and 12–16 which alleges that the Defendant violated 49 USC. § 46306(b)(4) by knowingly and willfully falsifying and concealing a material fact by asserting that North Atlantic Aircraft Services Corporation was the true owner of several aircraft when he knew that it was not.

The Defendant argues that the term "true owner" as contained in the superceding indictment is so fundamentally ambiguous as to preclude a conviction as a matter of law. The Government has filed a Response to Defendant's Motion.

49 U.S.C. § 46306(b)(4), Registration violations involving aircraft not providing air transportation, reads as follows:

Registration Violations

(b) General criminal penalty—Except as provided by subsection (c) of this section, a person shall be fined under title 18, imprisoned for not more than 3 years, or both, if the person—

   (4) obtains a certificate authorized to be issued under this part by knowingly and willfully falsifying or concealing a material fact, making a false, fictitious, or fraudulent statement, or making or using a false document knowing it contains a false, fictitious or fraudulent statement or entry;

In counts 3 and 12–16 of the Superseding Indictment, the Defendant is charged with "knowingly and willfully falsifying and concealing a material fact by asserting that North Atlantic Aircraft Services Corporation was the true owner of [five aircrafts], when in truth and in fact, and as the defendant then and there well knew, North Atlantic Aircraft Services Corporation was not the true owner," in violation of 49 U.S.C. § 46306(b)(4).

For each of these counts, the Government must prove that the Defendant knowingly and willfully made a materially false statement as to ownership of the aircrafts in his submission of a Form 8050-1 Aircraft Registration Application to the Federal Aviation Administration ("FAA"). In its response to the Defendant's Motion to Dismiss, the Government alleges that the evidence will show two materially false statements on each Form 8050-1:(1) that the defendant knew he was not the owner of the aircraft, but at most was the broker for the sale of the aircraft; and (2) that the corporation he was signing on behalf of was not a U.S. citizen corporation, but rather a non-citizen corporation. The Defendant asserts that Counts 3 and 12–16 of the Superseding Indictment should be dismissed because the use of the term "true owner" in the indictment is so fundamentally ambiguous as to preclude conviction as a matter of law.

FACTUAL BACKGROUND

The facts supporting Counts 3 and 12–16 of the Superseding Indictment are as follows: The Defendant was listed as the President of North Atlantic Aircraft Services Corporation ("NAASC") during the time period specified in these counts, September 2010 through May 2011. The Defendant served as a broker, purchasing planes in NAASC's name in order to eventually sell and deliver them to his international customers who usually provided the funding and specifications for the planes purchased. He would then take possession and ownership of the planes, file the appropriate registration paperwork, and take responsibility for the plane's maintenance, repairs and custody until the plane could be safely sold and delivered to the customer. His responsibilities included filing customs paperwork to the United States regarding the individual to whom he was selling the plane, to whom he was delivering the plane and to where he was exporting the plane. From March 16, 2009 through August 24, 2010, the Defendant executed five purchase contracts on behalf of NAASC for five different planes, and for each plane submitted an application for Aircraft Registration Form 8050-1 signed by the Defendant.

Whether the term "true owner" is fundamentally ambiguous

The Defendant argues that the term "true owner" in Counts 3 and 12–16 of the Superceding Indictment is fundamentally ambiguous and therefore precludes conviction as a matter of law. The Government responds that the term requires no subjective assessment and can be understood under standard, legal terms. Moreover, the Government argues that the indictment properly charges the Defendant and that to the extent the motion seeks dismissal of these Counts based on alleged evidentiary failures, such an argument is procedurally improper at this stage and should instead be made under Fed. R. Crim. P. 29 after the Government has presented its evidence at trial.

In supporting its motion, the Defendant relies heavily upon *United States v. Manapat,* 928 F.2d 1100 (11th Cir. 1991) in which the Eleventh Circuit affirmed the granting of a motion to dismiss on the basis of an ambiguity in another FAA form. In *Manapat,* the Defendant was charged with knowingly and willfully making false statements in the form by falsely answering "no" to questions of whether she had a record of traffic convictions or other convictions. The Eleventh Circuit agreed that the two questions were ambiguous in the context of the form because the two questions were included within a medical history section that asked whether the applicant had any of twenty-four medical conditions. The court found that a reasonable application could be "confused by this configuration of questions" and that it was "conceivable that an applicant might believe that the form was asking for convictions somehow related to medical conditions." *Id.*

Ambiguity

The Defendant's motion provides examples of other perjury charges that were dismissed as fundamentally ambiguous. In *United States v. Lattimore,* 127 F. Supp. 405, 406 (D.D.C.1955), the district court dismissed the defendant's perjury charged for answering "no" to the question of whether he was a "follower of the Communist line." The court found that the question was too vague because it provided an "open invitation to the jury to substitute, by conjecture, their understanding of the phrase for that of the defendant." In *United States v. Ryan,* the court dismissed a perjury charged based on false statements in a banking application that asked for the defendant's "previous address (last 5 years)." *Ryan,*

828 F.2d at 1010. The court found the term "previous address" to be ambiguous because it could mean a business address, a residential address or a mailing address, and that "address" was not synonymous with "domicile" or "primary residence."

Drawing from the ambiguities found in *Manapat, Lattimore* and *Ryan,* the Defendant in the instant case argues that the term "owner" in the indictment and in FAA Form 8050-1 is fundamentally ambiguous. The Defendant argues that the term is susceptible to many meanings and has been defined differently depending on the context and area of law. Under some of these definitions, the Defendant could qualify as an owner of the planes identified in the indictment because he bought the planes under his company's name and was in possession of them. For example, Black's Law Dictionary defines "owner" as "[o]ne who has the right to possess, use, and convey something; a person in whom one or more interests are vested." BLACK'S LAW DICTIONARY (9th ed. 2009).

Ownership Defined

Ownership is defined as "[t]he bundle of rights allowing one to use, manage, and enjoy property, including the right to convey it to others. Alternatively, the Code of Federal Regulations' chapter on Federal Aviation Administration, owner is defined as "a buyer in possession, a bailee, or a lessee of an aircraft under a contract of conditional sale, and the assignee of that person."

Ownership is defined as "[t]he bundle of rights allowing one to use, manage, and enjoy property, including the right to convey it to others." *Id.* Alternatively, in the Code of Federal Regulations' chapter on Federal Aviation Administration, owner is defined as "a buyer in possession, a bailee, or a lessee of an aircraft under a contract of conditional sale, and the assignee of that person." 14 C.F.R. § 47.5(d).

Defendant argues another possible definition of the term "owner" can be found in aircraft forfeiture law regarding what individuals would qualify as the "owner" of an aircraft subject to forfeiture. In these types of forfeiture cases, courts have used various factors to determine whether an individual is the "owner" of an aircraft, such as "showings of actual possession, control, title and financial stake." *United States v. One 1945 Douglas C-54 (DC-4) Aircraft, Serial No. 22186,* 647 F.2d 864, 866 (8th Cir. 1981).

Evidence of Ownership

Under these cases, even having a certificate of aircraft registration is not conclusive as to ownership for forfeiture purposes. *See id.* at 866, 867 n. 3 ("The mere fact that the certificate of aircraft registration was issued to Stumpff does not determine rights of ownership in the aircraft as between Kammerer and Stumpff. Such certificates are issued for registration purposes only and are not certificates of title. . . . In other circumstances, it is possible that a bill of sale and registration certificate might be sufficient to establish an ownership interest.").

Finally, federal statutory law regarding forfeiture in general uses a definition that allows for more than one owner at any given time. 18 U.S.C. § 983, General Rules for Civil Forfeiture Proceedings, defines "owner" as "a person with an ownership interest in the specific property sought to be forfeited," and excludes an individual who "exercises no dominion or control over the property." 18 U.S.C. § 983(d)(6). Thus, the Defendant argues that under statutory forfeiture law and forfeiture common law, he could qualify as an "owner" of the planes in addition to other individuals who could be concurrent owners.

The Defendant's argument that the term "owner" is fundamentally ambiguous falls short. The Defendant may be able to prove at trial that he was in fact an owner of the planes in question and therefore may be entitled to an acquittal on these counts. However, several portions of the form and the accompanying instructions provide clear direction as to the importance of the applicant being the owner of the plane being registered, and even provide contextual and specific explanations of who is an owner. The Form 8050-1 employs clear language that eliminates the contextual confusion caused by the FAA form in *Manapat*. The instructions for completing the 8050-1 states as follows:

AIRCRAFT REGISTRATION INFORMATION

PREPARATION: [. . .] The name of the applicant should be identical to the name of the purchaser shown on the applicant's evidence of ownership.

EVIDENCE OF OWNERSHIP: The applicant for registration of an aircraft must submit evidence of ownership that meets the requirements prescribed in Part 47 of the Federal Aviation Regulations. AC Form 8050-2, Aircraft Bill of Sale, or its equivalent may be used as evidence of ownership.

The "Evidence of Ownership" instruction puts the applicant on notice of the definition of ownership used in Federal Aviation Regulations, Part 47: "a buyer in possession, a bailee, or a lessee of an aircraft under a contract of conditional sale, and the assignee of that person." In the body of the Form 8050-1, the box asking for the "NAME OR APPLICANT" specifies that this entry should be completed with the name of the "Person(s) shown on evidence of ownership." And in the CERTIFICATION section, among the certifications required of the applicant is "(3) That legal evidence of ownership is attached with the Form or has been filed with the FAA." Finally, the Form 8050-1 warns that "A false or dishonest answer to any question in this application may be grounds for punishment by fine and/or imprisonment."

As a whole, the form makes repeated references to the importance of proof of ownership and the requirement that only an owner may complete the form. When the use of the term "owner" is examined in the context of the form, including the explanations and instructions contained in the form, and taking into account the extrinsic evidence of the Defendant's extensive familiarity and experience in the aviation business, there is no viable argument that the term is so fundamentally ambiguous as to preclude conviction as a matter of law. While the Defendant may be able to argue at trial that the Government's evidence does not prove that he knowingly stated he was the owner of the planes in question when he was not, such an argument is properly made at the end of the Government's presentation of evidence and not in a motion to dismiss. For the reasons stated, the Defendant's Motion to Dismiss Counts 3 and 12–16 is denied.

EXERCISE 9-4. *UNITED STATES V. MALAGO*—PROOF OF OWNERSHIP

1. What conduct is prohibited by 49 U.S.C. § 46306(b)(4) and what penalties are associated with violation of this statute?

2. What is FAA Form 8050-1? What is the defendant accused of doing wrong?

3. Summarize the defendant's argument under *United States v. Manapat*, 928 F.2d 1100 (11th Cir. 1991).

4. Define "owner" under 14 C.F.R. § 47.5.

5. What is the next step in the prosecution given the court's ruling on the motion to dismiss?

TAYLOR V. HUERTA

856 F.3d 1089 (D.C. Cir. 2017)

KAVANAUGH, CIRCUIT JUDGE.

Congress has charged the Federal Aviation Administration ("FAA") with maintaining the safety of the Nation's air traffic. As small unmanned aircraft (sometimes known as drones) have become more popular, the number of unmanned aircraft-related safety incidents has increased. In 2015, in an effort to address that trend, the FAA promulgated a rule known as the Registration Rule. That Rule requires the owners of small unmanned aircraft operated for recreational purposes to register with the FAA. Unmanned aircraft operated for recreational purposes are known as "model aircraft," and we will use that term throughout this opinion. Separately, the FAA published a notice, known as Advisory Circular 91–57A, announcing that model aircraft would be subject to certain flight restrictions in the Washington, D.C., area.

Petitioner John Taylor is a model aircraft hobbyist who is now required to register with the FAA. He has operated model aircraft from his home in the Washington, D.C., area, and he wants to continue to do so without registering or complying with the new flight restrictions. Taylor filed petitions in this Court to challenge the FAA's Registration Rule and the Advisory Circular.

To begin, Taylor does not think that the FAA had the statutory authority to issue the Registration Rule and require him to register. Taylor is right. In 2012, Congress passed, and President Obama signed the FAA Modernization and Reform Act. Section 336(a) of that Act states that the FAA "may not promulgate any rule or regulation regarding a model aircraft." Pub. L. No. 112–95, § 336(a), 126 Stat. 11, 77 (2012) (codified at 49 U.S.C. § 40101 note). The FAA's 2015 Registration Rule, which applies to model aircraft, directly violates that clear statutory prohibition. We therefore grant Taylor's petition and vacate the Registration Rule to the extent it applies to model aircraft.

Taylor challenges Advisory Circular 91–57A on the ground that the Circular likewise violates Section 336(a). That Circular prohibits the operation of model aircraft in various restricted areas, including the Flight Restricted Zone around Washington, D.C. But Taylor's petition challenging the Advisory Circular is untimely. By statute, a petitioner must challenge an FAA order within 60 days of the order's issuance unless there are reasonable grounds for delay. 49 U.S.C. § 46110(a). Taylor acknowledges that he filed his petition challenging the Advisory Circular outside the 60-day window. He did not have reasonable grounds for the late filing. His petition for review of Advisory Circular 91–57A is therefore denied.

AC 91–57A

Congress has directed the FAA to "promote safe flight of civil aircraft" and to set standards governing the operation of aircraft in the United States. 49 U.S.C. § 44701(a). Congress has also required "aircraft" to be registered before operation. See id. §§ 44101, 44103. To register, aircraft owners must complete a registration process that is quite extensive, as one would imagine for airplanes.

But the FAA has not previously interpreted the general registration statute to apply to model aircraft. Instead, the FAA has issued an optional set of operational guidelines for model aircraft. The FAA's Advisory Circular 91–57, titled Model Aircraft Operating Standards and published in 1981, provided suggestions for the safe operation of model aircraft. Under that Advisory Circular, compliance with the Circular by operators of model aircraft was voluntary. See J.A. 1.

As unmanned aircraft technology has advanced, small unmanned aircraft have become increasingly popular. In response, the FAA has taken a more active regulatory role. In 2007, the FAA promulgated a notice announcing a new regulatory approach to unmanned aircraft. See Unmanned Aircraft Operations in the National Airspace System, 72 Fed. Reg. 6689 (Feb. 13, 2007). In the notice, the FAA distinguished between commercial and recreational unmanned aircraft. Under the new regulatory approach, commercial unmanned aircraft are subject to mandatory FAA regulations. Those regulations require operators to report the aircraft's intended use, time or number of flights, and area of operation, among other things. *Id.* at 6690. By contrast, this notice did not alter the longstanding voluntary regulatory approach for model aircraft. *Id.*

FMRA   In 2012, Congress weighed in on the debate over regulation of unmanned aircraft. Congress passed and President Obama signed the FAA Modernization and Reform Act of 2012, Pub. L. No. 112–95, 126 Stat. 11 (codified at 49 U.S.C. § 40101 note). The Act codified the FAA's longstanding hands-off approach to the regulation of model aircraft. Specifically, Section 336 of the Act, called the "Special Rule for Model Aircraft," provides that the FAA "may not promulgate any rule or regulation regarding a model aircraft." *Id.* § 336(a). The Act defines "model aircraft" as "an unmanned aircraft that is—(1) capable of sustained flight in the atmosphere; (2) flown within visual line of sight of the person operating the aircraft; and (3) flown for hobby or recreational purposes." *Id.* § 336(c).

Notwithstanding that clear statutory restriction on FAA regulation of model aircraft, in December 2015 the FAA issued a final rule requiring owners of all small unmanned aircraft, including model aircraft, to register with the FAA. *See* Registration and Marking Requirements for Small Unmanned Aircraft, 80 Fed. Reg. 78,594 (Dec. 16, 2015). The Registration Rule requires model aircraft owners to provide their names; physical, mailing, and email addresses; and any other information the FAA chooses to require. *Id.* at 78,595–96. The Registration Rule also creates an online platform for registration, establishes a $5 per-individual registration fee, sets compliance deadlines, and requires all small unmanned aircraft to display a unique identifier number issued by the FAA. *Id.* Model aircraft owners who do not register face civil or criminal monetary penalties and up to three years' imprisonment. *Id.* at 78,630.

Also in 2015, the FAA withdrew Advisory Circular 91–57 and replaced it with Advisory Circular 91–57A. See J.A. 3–5. Among other things, the revised Circular provided that model aircraft could not fly within the Flight Restricted Zone covering Washington, D.C., and the surrounding areas without specific authorization. *See id.* at 5.

Petitioner Taylor is a model aircraft hobbyist living in the Washington, D.C., area. Taylor argues that Section 336 of the FAA Modernization and Reform Act bars both the FAA's Registration Rule and Advisory Circular 91–57A.

* * *

We first consider Taylor's challenge to the Registration Rule.

Section 336 of the FAA Modernization and Reform Act of 2012 provides that the FAA "may not promulgate any rule or regulation regarding a model aircraft." Pub. L. No. 112–95, § 336(a), 126 Stat. 11, 77 (2012) (codified at 49 U.S.C. § 40101 note). The FAA's 2015 Registration Rule is undoubtedly a rule. By requiring the prospective registration of all model aircraft, the Registration Rule announces an FAA "statement of general or particular applicability and future effect designed to implement, interpret, or prescribe law or policy." 5 U.S.C. § 551(4) (defining "rule" for purposes of the Administrative Procedure Act). In addition, the Registration Rule is a rule "regarding a model aircraft." FAA Modernization and Reform Act § 336(a). The Registration Rule sets forth requirements for "small unmanned aircraft, including small unmanned aircraft operated as *model aircraft*." Registration and Marking Requirements for Small Unmanned Aircraft, 80 Fed. Reg. 78,594, 78,594 (Dec. 16, 2015) (emphasis added). Lest there be any doubt about whether the Registration Rule is a rule "regarding a model aircraft" for purposes of Section 336, the Registration Rule states that its "definition of 'model aircraft' is identical to the definition provided in section 336(c) of Public Law 112–95," the FAA Modernization and Reform Act. *Id.* at 78,604.

Statutory interpretation does not get much simpler. The Registration Rule is unlawful as applied to model aircraft.

Interpreting the FMRA

In short, the 2012 FAA Modernization and Reform Act provides that the FAA "may not promulgate any rule or regulation regarding a model aircraft," yet the FAA's 2015 Registration Rule is a "rule or regulation regarding a model aircraft."

Statutory interpretation does not get much simpler. The Registration Rule is unlawful as applied to model aircraft.

The FAA's arguments to the contrary are unpersuasive. First, the FAA contends that the Registration Rule is authorized by pre-existing statutory provisions that are unaffected by the FAA Modernization and Reform Act. Specifically, the FAA notes that, under longstanding statutes, aircraft are statutorily required to register before operation. See 49 U.S.C. §§ 44101, 44103. But the FAA has never previously interpreted that registration requirement to apply to model aircraft. The FAA responds that nothing in the 2012 FAA Modernization and Reform Act prevents the FAA from changing course and applying that registration requirement to model aircraft now. The FAA claims that the Registration Rule is therefore not a new requirement at all, but merely a "decision to cease its exercise of enforcement discretion."

We disagree. The Registration Rule does not merely announce an intent to enforce a pre-existing statutory requirement. The Registration Rule is a rule that creates a new regulatory regime for model aircraft. The new regulatory regime includes a "new registration process" for online registration of model aircraft. 80 Fed. Reg. at 78,595. The new regulatory regime imposes new requirements—to register, to pay fees, to provide information, and to display identification—on people who previously had no obligation to engage with the FAA. Id. at 78,595–96. And the new regulatory regime imposes new penalties—civil and criminal, including prison time—on model aircraft owners who do not comply. *See id.* at 78,630.

In short, the Registration Rule is a rule regarding model aircraft.

We note that Section 336(b) expressly preserves the FAA's authority to "pursue enforcement action against persons operating model aircraft who endanger the safety of the national airspace system." FAA Modernization and Reform Act § 336(b). That provision, however, is tied to safety. It does not authorize the FAA to enforce any pre-existing registration requirement.

Second, the FAA argues that the Registration Rule is consistent with one of the general directives of the FAA Modernization and Reform Act: to "improve aviation safety." FAA Modernization and Reform Act preamble. Aviation safety is obviously an important goal, and the Registration Rule may well help further that goal to some degree. But the Registration Rule is barred by the text of Section 336 of the Act. *See Central Bank of Denver, N.A. v. First Interstate Bank of Denver, N.A.*, 511 U.S. 164, 188 (1994) ("Policy considerations cannot override our interpretation of the text and structure of the Act. . . ."). Congress is of course always free to repeal or amend its 2012 prohibition on FAA rules regarding model aircraft. Perhaps Congress should do so. Perhaps not. In any event, we must follow the statute as written.

In short, Section 336 of the FAA Modernization and Reform Act prohibits the FAA from promulgating "any rule or regulation regarding a model aircraft." The Registration Rule is a rule regarding model aircraft. Therefore, the Registration Rule is unlawful to the extent that it applies to model aircraft.

In short, Section 336 of the FAA Modernization and Reform Act prohibits the FAA from promulgating "any rule or regulation regarding a model aircraft." The Registration Rule is a rule regarding model aircraft. Therefore, the Registration Rule is unlawful to the extent that it applies to model aircraft.

The FAA's Registration Rule violates Section 336 of the FAA Modernization and Reform Act. We grant Taylor's petition for review of the Registration Rule, and we vacate the Registration Rule to the extent it applies to model aircraft. Because Taylor's petition for review of Advisory Circular 91–57A is untimely, that petition is denied.

[The court then considered Taylor's challenge to FAA Advisory Circular 91–57A. The Circular prohibits the operation of model aircraft in certain areas, including in the Washington, D.C., Flight Restricted Zone. Taylor argues, among other things, that the Circular violates Section 336(a) of the FAA Modernization and Reform Act of 2012 because it too is a rule regarding model aircraft. The court did not consider this question, however, because Taylor's challenge was untimely.]

EXERCISE 9-5. *TAYLOR V. HUERTA*—DRONE REGISTRATION RULE

1. Describe the purpose and requirements of the FAA's Registration Rule for unmanned aerial vehicles.

2. Explain the arguments of the petitioner, John Taylor, under the FAA Modernization and Reform Act of 2012 and Advisory Circular 91–57A.

3. Listen to oral argument in the matter of *Taylor v. Huerta* at https://www.cadc. uscourts.gov/recordings/recordings2017.nsf/469F0B57EDA3C53A852580E3 00577ED7/$file/15-1495.mp3. What is the FAA's position? How does Judge Brett Kavanaugh (now U.S. Supreme Court Justice) react (listen at time mark 20:36 "you're just making this stuff up")?

4. What is the *Chevron* doctrine and what is its relevance to this case? *See Grounding Chevron*, https://droninglawyer.com/2017/06/15/grounding-chevron/.

5. Is the Registration Rule still a requirement after the decision in *Taylor v. Huerta*? *See How Can We Approve This?*, https://droninglawyer.com/2018/07/17/how-can-we-approve-this/.

C. POSSESSION: LIENS, REPLEVIN, AND JUDICIAL SALE

COMMERCIAL JET, INC. V. U.S. BANK

45 So. 3d 887 (Fla. 3d DCA 2010)

CORTIÑAS, J.

Commercial Jet filed this action to foreclose a purported mechanic's lien on a Boeing 767 aircraft for which it had provided maintenance and repairs. Despite an outstanding balance, Commercial Jet returned the aircraft to Silver Jet, its operator, which put it back into service. After it relinquished possession of the aircraft, Commercial Jet recorded a claim of lien under sections 713.58 and 329.51, Florida Statutes, for the unpaid balance against Silver Jet and U.S. Bank, the aircraft's owner. Since the purported lien is a possessory lien under section 713.58, and Commercial Jet was no longer in possession of the aircraft at the time it filed the lien, the trial court granted U.S. Bank's motion for summary judgment. We affirm the trial court's order and reject Commercial Jet's argument that section 329.51 modifies section 713.58 by eliminating the requirement that one must have possession of the property in order to claim a lien.

Fla. Stat.
§ 713.58

Section 713.58 creates a lien "[i]n favor of persons performing labor or services for any other person, upon the personal property of the latter upon which the labor or services is performed. . . ." § 713.58(1), Fla. Stat. This lien exists only as long as the person entitled to the lien retains possession of the property upon which the lien is claimed: the statute expressly provides that "the possessory right and lien of the person performing labor or services under this section is released, relinquished, and lost by the removal of such property. . . ." § 713.58(3), Fla. Stat.

Possessory
Lien

Therefore, there is no question that the lien right afforded by section 713.58 is possessory in nature and that a repairman's right to claim a lien under section 713.58 is extinguished when he relinquishes possession of the property on which the lien is asserted. See *State v. Miller*, 373 So.2d 677 (Fla. 1979) (explaining that a section 713.58 "lien entitles the lienholder to possession of a customer's property for three months," which "is a form of leverage looking solely toward full payment"); *Eastern Airlines Empls. Fed. Credit Union v. Lauderdale Yacht Basin, Inc.*, 334 So. 2d 175 (Fla. 4th DCA 1976) (finding that "a mechanic's possessory lien against personal property (under a provision such as Fla. Stat. § 713.58) . . . continued as long as [the lienor] continued in possession thereof").

Commercial Jet agrees that section 713.58 "has been interpreted to" require possession but argues that section 329.51 amended section 713.58 by providing that a valid lien can be created simply by recording a claim of lien within ninety days. However, section 329.51 does not create any new lien rights. Instead, it is manifestly a notice statute, as is apparent by its title ("Liens for labor, services, fuel, or material expended upon aircraft; notice"), and it specifically states that it applies to "[a]ny lien claimed on an aircraft *under § 329.41 or § 713.58* . . . ." § 329.51, Fla. Stat. Section 329.41 creates a lien right for fuel furnished to aircraft; section 713.58 creates a lien right for labor or services performed on aircraft and other personal property. Section 329.51 details how, once a fuel or service provider acquires a lien on an aircraft pursuant to section 329.41 or 713.58, he may perfect his lien and establish priority of enforcement as it relates to third parties. Thus, section 329.51 has no application here because Commercial Jet never acquired a valid lien under sections 713.58 or 329.41.

As Commercial Jet did not have possession of the aircraft when it attempted to claim a possessory lien under section 713.58, it cannot proceed in its attempt to foreclose on the purported lien. Therefore, we affirm the trial court's grant of summary judgment in favor of U.S. Bank.

SCHWARTZ, SENIOR JUDGE, (dissenting).

Section 329.51, Florida Statutes provides:

Any lien claimed on an aircraft under § 329.41 or § 713.58 is enforceable when the lienor records a verified lien notice with the clerk of the circuit court in the county where the aircraft was located at the time the labor, services, fuel, or material was last furnished. The lienor must record such lien notice within 90 days after the time the labor, services, fuel, or material was last furnished. The notice must state the name of the lienor; the name of the owner; a description of the aircraft upon which the lienor has expended labor, services, fuel, or material; the amount for which the lien is claimed; and the date the expenditure was completed. This section does not affect the priority of competing interests in any aircraft or the lienor's obligation to record the lien under s. 329.01.

It clearly provides that a lien for repairs on an aircraft such as the one in this case is perfected simply by recording a claim of lien within ninety days of the services rendered, as the appellant did in this case. The majority holding that following that provision did not have the effect specifically provided by the legislature is in conflict with just about every canon of legislative interpretation there is, including: that statutory words must be accorded their plain meaning; that every statute must be deemed to have some meaning and accomplish something (here, the court's ruling renders the filing of the lien of no effect whatever); that a statute dealing with a specific subject, such as aircraft, must be deemed to control over a general one such as section 713.58, which applies to all personal property, and no doubt other general rules which no one has thought it necessary to devise-until now. I would reverse.

EXERCISE 9-6. *COMMERCIAL JET, INC. V. U.S. BANK*— MECHANIC'S LIEN AND LIEN PERFECTION

1. Identify: (a) Commercial Jet; (b) Silver Jet; and (c) U.S. Bank.

2. Explain the lien rights created by Fla. Stat. § 713.58. Further, explain how a valid lien is created pursuant to the statute.

3. How does the court describe Fla. Stat. § 329.51? What relevance does it have to Commercial Jet's argument?

4. Is Commercial Jet authorized to foreclose on its lien, according to the court? Explain.

5. What is the dissent's position about? Is the majority so obviously or clearly wrong? Explain.

NOTES ON *COMMERCIAL JET, INC. V. U.S. BANK*—CAPE TOWN CONVENTION

From 1996 to 2001, states participated in negotiations under the auspices of the UN International Institute for the Unification of Private Law to draft a convention that would establish an international legal regime for the creation, perfection, and priority of security, title-retention, and leasing interests in such equipment. In November 2001, the convention was adopted by fifty-three states, including the United States, at Cape Town, South Africa (and thus is commonly referred to as the "Cape Town Convention").

The convention is designed to address three types of equipment: aircraft equipment, railway rolling stock, and outer space assets. While the convention contains provisions that apply generally to such equipment, more specific provisions concerning each of the three types of equipment are to be included in protocols to the convention. The first protocol, on aircraft equipment (including airframes, aircraft engines, and helicopters above certain thresholds), was completed at the same time as the Cape Town Convention, while the other two protocols remain under negotiation.

On May 9, 2003, the United States signed the convention. In November, President Bush transmitted the convention to the Senate for advice and consent, subject to seven declarations (three for the convention and four for the protocol). In testimony before the Senate Foreign Relations Committee, the U.S. Department of Transportation's general counsel explained the benefits of the convention and its first protocol as follows:

> As a general matter, the Convention adopts the asset-based financing practices already widely used in the United States and weaves them into an international agreement. Specifically, the Convention establishes an "international interest" which is a secured credit or leasing interest with defined rights in a piece of equipment. These rights consist primarily of 1) the ability to repossess or sell or lease the equipment in case of default; and 2) the holding of a transparent finance priority in the equipment.
>
> Priority will be established when a creditor files, on a first-in-time basis, a notice of its security interest, in a new high-technology international registry. Once an international interest has been filed by a creditor and becomes searchable at the international registry, that creditor's interest will have priority over all subsequent registered interests and all unregistered interests, with a few exceptions. The Federal Aviation Administration (FAA), which currently operates an aircraft registry, will serve as the authorized entry point into the International Registry.

Sean D. Murphy, *Cape Town Convention on Financing of High-Value, Mobile Equipment*, 98 AM. J. INT'L L. 852, 852–53 (2004).

PNCEF, LLC v. SOUTH AVIATION, INC.

60 So. 3d 1120 (Fla. 4th DCA 2011)

GERBER, J.

The appellant lender moved for a prejudgment writ of replevin pursuant to Fla. Stat. § 78.055, to recover four aircraft which the borrowers' lessee maintained in Broward County. The circuit court denied the motion. We reverse, concluding that the lender met its burden of showing that its motion for a prejudgment writ of replevin should have been granted.

The lender initially filed an action to recover the aircraft from the borrowers in Illinois, where the borrowers were based. In response, the borrowers alleged that they had leased the aircraft to appellee South Aviation, Inc. ("lessee") which maintained the aircraft in Broward County. According to the borrowers, the lessee filed liens against the aircraft and refused to return the aircraft because of the liens.

Based on the borrowers' response, the lender and the borrowers agreed to submit a proposed order to the Illinois court. The order provided that the lender and the borrowers would establish a joint escrow account into which the lessee would be required to "deposit all sums payable to the [b]orrowers pursuant to [the lessee's] use of the Aircraft." The order further provided: "Nothing contained herein shall constitute a waiver of any right or remedy of [the lender] to pursue its legal and equitable rights against the [borrowers], the [lessee], and/or the [aircraft] to the full extent permitted under all applicable agreements and laws." The Illinois court entered the order.

Allegations   The lender then sued the lessee and its owner, appellee Machado, in Broward County for replevin, conversion, and injunctive relief. The lender's verified complaint:

(1)   Described the four aircraft by model number, serial number, and registration number, and stated that, to the best knowledge, information, and belief of the lender, the aircraft's value was between $9,749,000 and $11,200,000, and that the aircraft's location was the Fort Lauderdale/Hollywood International Airport;

(2)   Stated that the lender is entitled to possession of the aircraft pursuant to notes and mortgages which the borrowers executed in favor of the lender or its predecessor, copies of which the lender attached to the complaint;

(3)   Stated that the aircraft are being wrongfully detained by the lessee or its owner, who came into possession thereof by virtue of lease agreements between the borrowers and the lessee, and that the cause of such detention is that the lessee's owner has refused, upon the borrowers' request, to return possession of the aircraft to the borrowers;

(4)   Stated that the aircraft have not been taken for a tax, assessment, or fine pursuant to law; and

(5)   Stated that the aircraft have not been taken under an execution or attachment against the lender's property.

The verified complaint further alleged that the Broward action was necessary because the Illinois court questioned whether it had jurisdiction to order the lessee and its owner to surrender the aircraft.

Along with the complaint, the lender moved for an order directing the lessee to show cause why the court should not enter a prejudgment writ of replevin by which the aircraft would be taken from the lessee's possession and delivered to the lender. The Broward court entered the order to show cause.

In response to the order to show cause, the lessee raised three material arguments: (1) the lessee's liens on the aircraft were superior to the lender's liens; (2) the Broward court lacked jurisdiction due to the Illinois court first exercising jurisdiction over the aircraft; and (3) the Broward court lacked jurisdiction over two aircraft which were not located in Broward County for the entire day on which the lender filed the verified complaint and over one aircraft which was not located in Broward County at any time that day. *Lessee's Arguments*

In rebuttal, the lender argued that it was entitled to possession of the aircraft pursuant to the following section in the borrowers' mortgages: *Mortgage Terms*

6.6 Return of Aircraft.

Upon the occurrence of an Event of Default and demand by Lender, Borrower [sic] shall return the Aircraft by delivering the same forthwith to Lender. . . .

The lender also relied on two sections in the leases between the borrowers and the lessee:

13.2 Quiet Enjoyment.

So long as no Event of Default shall have occurred and be continuing[,] Lessor[s] shall not disturb Lessee's quiet and peaceful use and enjoyment of the Aircraft for its intended purpose. NOTWITHSTANDING THE FOREGOING OR ANY OTHER PROVISION HEREOF, IT IS EXPRESSLY UNDERSTOOD BY [THE LESSEE] THAT ITS QUIET ENJOYMENT OF THE AIRCRAFT IS AT ALL TIMES, EVEN WHEN NO EVENT OF DEFAULT EXISTS HEREUNDER, SUBJECT AND

SUBORDINATE TO THE RIGHTS OF [THE LENDER] IN AND
TO THE AIRCRAFT.

. . . .

16.4 No Lessee Liens.

Lessee shall not create or suffer to exist any Liens on the Aircraft or any
of its rights under the Lease except, . . . (iii) inchoate material men's,
workmen's, repairmen's . . . or other like Liens. . . . All Liens created by
repairers or vendors in the ordinary course of Lessee's business shall be
cleared by Lessee. . . .

After the hearing, the Broward court entered an order denying the lender's motion
for a prejudgment writ of replevin. The order did not contain any findings of fact
or conclusions of law.

The lender then filed this appeal. Our review is *de novo*. We conclude that the
Broward court erred in denying the lender's motion for a prejudgment writ of
replevin. We base our conclusion on three grounds. First, the lender's verified
complaint recited and showed all of the information required to obtain an order
authorizing the issuance of a prejudgment writ of replevin.

Replevin,
Elements

Section 78.055, Florida Statutes, provides that "[t]o obtain an order
authorizing the issuance of a writ of replevin prior to final judgment, the plaintiff
shall first file . . . a complaint reciting and showing the following information":

(1) A description of the claimed property that is sufficient to make
possible its identification and a statement, to the best knowledge,
information, and belief of the plaintiff of the value of such property
and its location.

(2) A statement that the plaintiff is the owner of the claimed property
or is entitled to possession of it, describing the source of such title
or right. If the plaintiff's interest in such property is based on a
written instrument, a copy of said instrument must be attached to
the complaint.

(3) A statement that the property is wrongfully detained by the
defendant, the means by which the defendant came into possession
thereof, and the cause of such detention according to the best
knowledge, information, and belief of the plaintiff.

(4) A statement that the claimed property has not been taken for a tax,
assessment, or fine pursuant to law.

(5) A statement that the property has not been taken under an
execution or attachment against the property of the plaintiff or, if
so taken, that it is by law exempt from such taking, setting forth a
reference to the exemption law relied upon.

Here, the lender's verified complaint, which we outlined earlier in this opinion,
recited and showed the required information to support all five of these
statements.

Second, at the show cause hearing, the lender met its burden of proof.
Section 78.067(2), Florida Statutes, provides, in pertinent part:

[T]he court shall at the hearing on the order to show cause consider the
affidavits and other showings made by the parties appearing and make
a determination of which party, *with reasonable probability, is entitled to the
possession of the claimed property pending final adjudication of the claims of the
parties.* This determination shall be based on a finding as to *the probable
validity of the underlying claim alleged against the defendant.* If the court
determines that the plaintiff is entitled to take possession of the claimed
property, it shall issue an order directing the clerk of the court to issue
a writ of replevin.

Here, the lender proved, with reasonable probability, that it is entitled to
possession of the aircraft pending final adjudication of the parties' claims. Section
6.6 of the underlying mortgages provides that upon the occurrence of an event of
default and the lender's demand, the borrowers "shall return the Aircraft by
delivering the same forthwith to Lender." The lender further proved the probable
validity of its underlying claim alleged against the lessee. In Section 13.2 of the
lease between the borrowers and the lessee, the lessee expressed its understanding
that its quiet enjoyment of the aircraft is subordinate to the lender's rights in the
aircraft. In section 16.4 of the lease, the lessee agreed not to create any liens on
the aircraft.

Third, the lender satisfied the additional requirements of Fla. Stat. § 78.068,
which provides, in pertinent part:

(1) A prejudgment writ of replevin may be issued and the property
seized delivered forthwith to the petitioners when the nature of the
claim and the amount thereof, if any, and the grounds relied upon
for the issuance of the writ clearly appear from specific facts shown
by the verified petition or by separate affidavit of the petitioner.

(2) This prejudgment writ of replevin may issue if the court finds, pursuant to subsection (1), that the defendant is engaging in, or is about to engage in, conduct that may place the claimed property in danger of destruction, concealment, waste, removal from the state, removal from the jurisdiction of the court, or transfer to an innocent purchaser during the pendency of the action or that the defendant has failed to make payment as agreed.

Here, the lender's verified complaint alleges specific facts which clearly show the nature of the lender's claim, the amount thereof, and the grounds relied upon for the issuance of the writ. The lender further proved at the show cause hearing that the lessee is engaging in conduct that may place the aircraft in danger of removal from the state and the court's jurisdiction by removing the aircraft from Broward County.

We reject the three arguments which the lessee raised in the circuit court. First, we are unconvinced by the lessee's argument that its liens on the aircraft were superior to the lender's liens. We conclude that the lessee waived any priority which its liens may have had because it agreed in sections 13.2 and 16.4 of the leases that its quiet enjoyment of the aircraft would be subordinate to the lender's rights in the aircraft and that it would not create any liens on the aircraft. *See Bueno v. Workman*, 20 So. 3d 993, 998 (Fla. 4th DCA 2009) (elements of waiver are: existence of a right which may be waived; actual or constructive knowledge of the right; and intent to relinquish the right).

Second, we are unconvinced by the lessee's argument that the Broward court lacked jurisdiction due to the Illinois court first exercising jurisdiction over the aircraft. We conclude that the Illinois court did not exercise jurisdiction over the aircraft. Rather, the Illinois court merely exercised jurisdiction over the "sums payable" to the borrowers pursuant to the lessee's use of the aircraft. As such, the principle of priority, which requires the identity of subject matter, does not apply. Further, the Illinois court agreed that nothing in its order constituted a waiver of the lender's ability to pursue its rights against the lessee or the aircraft. Consistent with that order, the lender's Broward action supplements the Illinois action instead of conflicting with it.

Third, we are unconvinced by the lessee's argument that the Broward court lacked jurisdiction over the two aircraft which allegedly were not located in Broward County for the entire day on which the lender filed the verified complaint and over the one aircraft which allegedly was not located in Broward County at any time that day. "It has long been established in this and other jurisdictions that a court which has obtained in personam jurisdiction over a defendant may order that defendant to act on property that is outside of the court's jurisdiction, provided that the court does not directly affect the title to the property while it remains in the foreign jurisdiction." *Gen. Elec. Capital Corp. v. Advance Petroleum, Inc.*, 660 So. 2d 1139, 1142 (Fla. 3d DCA 1995).

We conclude that the third district's reasoning and directions apply here. We reverse and remand for the Broward court to enter an order granting the lender's motion for a prejudgment writ of replevin. Based on that order, the Broward court shall have the power to require the lessee and its owner to locate and return the subject aircraft to Broward County, so as to proceed with the court's replevin order. If the lessee and its owner do not do so, then the Broward court may do whatever is necessary, including issuing civil contempt and indirect criminal contempt orders, to compel the lessee and its owner to acquiesce to the court's demands. However, the court may not issue any further orders which directly act on the aircraft until the court confirms that the aircraft are within its in rem or quasi in rem jurisdictional domain.

EXERCISE 9-7. *PNCEF, LLC V. SOUTH AVIATION, INC.*—REPLEVIN

1. Define: (a) replevin; (b) conversion; and (c) injunctive relief.

2. What is an escrow account? How was an escrow account used in this case?

3. What is a prejudgment writ of replevin, and what are the elements under Fla. Stat. § 78.055?

4. How was "reasonable probability" of a right to possession demonstrated to the court's satisfaction here?

5. What jurisdictional argument did the lessee raise? Did the court agree? Explain.

U.S. ACQUISITION, LLC v. TABAS, FREEDMAN, SOLOFF, MILLER & BROWN, P.A.

87 So. 3d 1229 (Fla. 4th DCA 2012)

POLEN, J.

US Acquisition, LLC ("US Acquisition"), appeals the trial court's order granting Tabas, Freedman, Soloff, Miller & Brown, P.A.'s ("Tabas Freedman") motion to enforce attorney's charging lien. Tabas Freedman also appeals the trial court's final order determining attorney's fees and costs.

Due to Tabas Freedman's failure to record the charging lien with the Federal Aviation Administration ("FAA"), the lien was not perfected, pursuant to title 49, United States Code, section 44108(a). As a result, we reverse the trial court's order enforcing the attorney's charging lien which was attached to an aircraft.

Rockbridge Commercial Bank ("Rockbridge") was the lender in a transaction with Kaizen Aviation, LLC ("Kaizen") where Kaizen borrowed over five million dollars from Rockbridge. A promissory note was executed and delivered and Kaizen defaulted on the obligations therein by failing to make monthly payments. The loan was secured by an aircraft as collateral. Tabas Freedman was retained by Rockbridge to file an action in replevin to recover the collateral aircraft. An order granting the request for a writ of replevin was granted, stating that there was a perfected security interest in the aircraft and the owner of the collateral aircraft undisputedly defaulted. A separate order directing clerk of court to issue writ of replevin was also issued.

Subsequent to filing the replevin action, Rockbridge was taken over by the Federal Deposit Insurance Corporation ("FDIC") and FDIC was substituted for Rockbridge in the action. Tabas Freedman filed a notice and claim of attorney's charging lien, alleging its representation of Rockbridge, as well as the unpaid amount of $56,425.21. (Tabas Freedman stated at a related hearing that "all [they] have to do is provide notice of the charging lien.") In other words, Tabas Freedman concedes that the lien was not recorded with the FAA.

Tabas Freedman soon withdrew as counsel from the action, while the outstanding debt remained unpaid by the bank to the law firm. It also filed a motion to enforce attorney's charging lien and an order granting the motion was entered. US Acquisition became a party to this action when it was substituted for FDIC after it acquired the loan at an auction sale.

This appeal followed the order granting the motion to enforce the charging lien, as U.S. Acquisition argues the validity of the lien due to Tabas Freedman's failure to record the lien with the FAA.

"The charging lien is an equitable right to have costs and fees due an attorney for services in the suit secured to him in the judgment or recovery in that particular suit. It serves to protect the rights of the attorney." *Sinclair, Louis, Siegel, Heath, Nussbaum & Zavertnik, P.A. v. Baucom*, 428 So. 2d 1383, 1384 (Fla. 1983). To impose such a lien, there must be: an express or implied contract between the attorney and client; an express or implied understanding that payment depends upon recovery; and to recover, there must be a failure to pay fees and/or a dispute to the amount of those fees. To perfect a charging lien, the only requirement is timely notice.

The charging lien is an equitable right to have costs and fees due an attorney for services in the suit secured to him in the judgment or recovery in that particular suit. It serves to protect the rights of the attorney. To impose such a lien, there must be: an express or implied contract between the attorney and client; an express or implied understanding that payment depends upon recovery; and to recover, there must be a failure to pay fees and/or a dispute to the amount of those fees. To perfect a charging lien, the only requirement is timely notice.

In this case of first impression, U.S. Acquisition argues that because Tabas Freedman did not record the charging lien with the FAA, pursuant to the Federal Aviation Act of 1958, the lien was not perfected and, therefore, invalid. Tabas Freedman contends that U.S. Acquisition bases its arguments on inapplicable case law and that it put U.S. Acquisition on notice, thereby perfecting the lien. U.S. Acquisition relies heavily on *Creston Aviation, Inc. v. Textron Financial Corp.*, 900 So. 2d 727 (Fla. 4th DCA 2005), which provides that "[u]ntil a lien or other interest affecting title in a civil aircraft is recorded in the federal registry, it is valid only against those with actual notice." The purpose of recordation when aircraft title is affected is to "create a central clearing house for recordation of title and liens affecting civil aircraft . . . so that a person would know where to find ready access to this type of information." *Id.*

Creston Precedent

The lien at issue in *Creston Aviation* was a mechanic's lien which was placed on the aircraft for services to the actual aircraft. The notice and claim of attorney's charging lien in this case states that the lien is in the amount of $56,425.21 for unpaid compensation for legal services rendered. Section 713.58, Florida Statutes, explains that a lien for labor, or a mechanic's lien as in *Creston Aviation,* is placed on the property of the person for whom labor or services are being performed, in favor of the person performing the labor or services. Fla. Stat. § 713.58. Such a lien is a possessory right of the serviceman's and once he relinquishes possession, the lien is extinguished. A charging lien attaches to the judgment to ensure an attorney is compensated for his services.

Mechanic's Lien

Title 49, United States Code, section 44108(a) requires that a conveyance, lease or instrument securing an aircraft is recorded in order to achieve validity against anybody but the parties involved or those having actual notice thereof. The lien in this case claims "entitlement to the aircraft" to the extent of "whatever the plaintiff's rights are in the aircraft or the proceeds of the aircraft based upon the work that [the] firm did in procuring the aircraft for this plaintiff." We hold that the lien in this case is not a mechanic's lien, thus distinguishing *Creston Aviation;* however, the lien in this case is also not a typical charging lien that requires only timely notice because, if granted, it grants "entitlement to the aircraft" to the lienor.

The explanation offered by Tabas Freedman at its hearing stated that the law firm was claiming entitlement to the aircraft to the extent of the plaintiff's rights or entitlement to the proceeds from the aircraft. The notice and claim of attorney's charging lien filed by Tabas Freedman also expressed that its lien attached to "all of the Plaintiff's rights, title and interest in any property or judgment that Plaintiff recovers." Plaintiff's entitlement could include possession of the aircraft itself or its parts and/or "any and all logs, manuals and other technical records documents relating thereto, and together with any and all other associated items."

In *Creston Aviation,* this court explained that the purpose of recording the interests in aircrafts with the FAA "is operative to the extent that if the title or lien interest is not recorded in the FAA Aircraft Registry, then it will not be valid as against third parties without notice." *Creston Aviation,* 900 So. 2d at 731.

The Supreme Court of the United States held in *Philko Aviation, Inc. v. Shacket,* 462 U.S. 406 (1983), that Congress intended to protect innocent third parties from unknowingly accepting the transfer of an aircraft which has some claim, lien, or other legal interest attached. The recording system creates a centralized location for all potential transferees to search the FAA records before acquiring an interest in an aircraft without clear title. Failure to record results in the misconception that title is clear when, in fact, the transferee is taking the aircraft subject to some lien, or other claim or interest.

Perfection, Charging Lien

While it is true that a charging lien requires only timely notice for perfection, the charging lien in this case does not only attach to a monetary judgment, but also to the actual aircraft and/or its parts. Therefore, the lien which is attached to the aircraft should be recorded with the FAA, pursuant to federal law, to protect any third parties from subsequently purchasing an interest in the aircraft which inaccurately appears to have free and clear title. US Acquisition purchased the loan to the aircraft without notice, actual or constructive, that a lien was attached by Tabas Freedman. This is the exact situation which recordation would prevent, thereby shifting responsibility to the transferee to diligently search the FAA's registry before obtaining an interest in the aircraft.

While it is true that a charging lien requires only timely notice for perfection, the charging lien in this case does not only attach to a monetary judgment, but also to the actual aircraft and/or its parts. Therefore, the lien which is attached to the aircraft should be recorded with the FAA, pursuant to federal law, to protect any third parties from subsequently purchasing an interest in the aircraft which inaccurately appears to have free and clear title.

Tabas Freedman alleges that it attempted to record the lien, but the FAA refused to record because the lien did not affect the aircraft and only directs payment of money. However, the language in the letter from the FAA states that "The Order Granting Tabas, Freedman, Soloff, Miller & Brown PA's Motion to Enforce Attorney's Charging Lien" need not be recorded because it does not affect the aircraft itself. The correspondence does not support Tabas Freedman's assertion that it did not have to record the actual charging lien and only shows the ineligibility of the court's order referring to the enforcement thereof.

Based on current statutory and case law, as well as the facts of this case, we reverse the trial court's order enforcing the charging lien which attached to the aircraft because the lien was not perfected through the act of recordation with the FAA, pursuant to title 49, United States Code, section 44108(a).

EXERCISE 9-8. *U.S. ACQUISITION, LLC V. TABAS, FREEDMAN, SOLOFF, MILLER & BROWN, P.A.*—ATTORNEYS' CHARGING LIEN

1. Identify the following:(a) Rockbridge Commercial Bank; (b) Kaizen Aviation, LLC; (c) Tabas, Freedman, Soloff, Miller & Brown, P.A.; (d) Federal Deposit Insurance Corporation ("FDIC"); and (e) U.S. Acquisition, LLC.

2. What is action in replevin?

3. What is an attorney's charging lien? How is it perfected?

4. Explain the appellant's argument made on the basis of *Creston Aviation, Inc. v. Textron Financial Corp.*

5. As a practical matter, what is the result of this case?

Suggested Further Reading

Annotation, *Situs of Aircraft, Rolling Stock, and Vessels for Purposes of Property Taxation,* 3 A.L.R.4th 837 (1981 & 2004 Supp.)

P.G. Guthrie, Annotation, *Construction and Effect of 49 US Code § 1403, Governing Recordation of Ownership, Conveyances, and Encumbrances on Aircraft*, 22 A.L.R.3d 1270 (1968 & 2005 Supp.)

James L. Burt, III, *Bogus Aircraft: Offenses and Defenses*, 61 J. AIR L. & COM. 859 (1996)

Labor and Employment

"They are in violation of the law and if they do not report for work within 48 hours they have forfeited their jobs and will be terminated." President Ronald Reagan, 1981.

Source: https://commons.wikimedia.org/wiki/File:Reagan_speaks_on_ air_traffic_controllers_strike_1981.jpg.

A. OVERVIEW

The uninterrupted movement of goods and people depends on effective relations between airline managers and employees. When those relations are strained, commerce potentially suffers. For example, when asked about ongoing negotiations with management in 2001, an American Airlines flight attendant said, "When I see they are not willing to pacify us, and we're not asking for a huge chunk of change, it makes me ask: 'Do I want to do a good job for them' "?" *See*

Ina Paiva Cordle, *"We're Not Asking for the World,"* MIAMI HERALD, June 3, 2001, at 6E.

Almost a decade later, Spirit Airlines pilots declared a strike at 5 A.M. and walked-out on labor contract negotiations after more than three years of bargaining for better salaries and benefits. It was the first by pilots at a commercial U.S. carrier since 2001 and the first strike since Northwest Airlines mechanics walked out in 2005. *See, e.g.,* Jaclyn Giovis & Jerome Burdi, *Spirit Airlines Pilots Declare Strike and Walk Out on Negotiations,* S. FLA. SUN-SENTINEL, June 12, 2010, at 2010 WLNR 12001298. Later still, in 2019, workers for Lufthansa staged a walkout ahead of pay talks, forcing the airline to cancel 1,600 scheduled flights, affecting 90,000 passengers. Meanwhile, airlines across Europe braced for a summer of flight disruption as French air traffic controllers prepared for a strike, following their 35th walkout, in 2019. To say that labor relations impact airline operations both nationally and internationally is an understatement.

Perhaps most famous, in 1981, the Professional Air Traffic Controllers Organization ("PATCO") called an illegal strike. As captured by the photo at the outset of this chapter, President Ronald Reagan ordered all striking air traffic controllers back to work. After they also refused to comply with a court order requiring them to return to work, President Reagan promptly fired more than 11,000 air traffic controllers and banned them from federal service for life. This harsh result and the law's intolerance for this sort of labor disruption was based on the still-prevailing view that, given the importance of aviation to the nation's (and the world's) economy and security, such a strike by public employees was a peril to national safety.

Interestingly, the labor laws applicable to other modes of transportation serve as precedent for labor and employment relations in the aviation industry. Specifically, to govern disputes in air transportation, lawmakers in the United States have looked to the precedent of railroads. In fact, Congress enacted the Railway Labor Act ("RLA") in 1926 to encourage collective bargaining by railroads and their employees in order to prevent wasteful strikes and interruptions of interstate commerce. Designed to sustain uninterrupted transportation operations, the RLA created an intricate alternative dispute regime that obligates employers and employees' union representatives to mediate or arbitrate their labor disputes.

In 1936, the RLA was extended to the airline industry and it has governed labor-management relations within the airline industry since. Broadly, the RLA provides remedies for the resolution of employee disputes arising out of the interpretation of collective bargaining agreements and requires all parties to "exert every reasonable effort to make and maintain" collectively bargained agreements, and to abide by the terms of the most recent agreement until all the dispute resolution procedures have been exhausted. *See Detroit & Toledo Shore Line R.R. v. United Transp. Union*, 396 U.S. 142 (1969).

In this context, this chapter sets out the seminal labor and employment cases in both the public and private spheres that influence the airline industry, including collective bargaining agreements ("CBAs"). *Goodwin v. Ridge* bridges earlier discussion from Chapter 4 about airmen qualifications with the law of employment discrimination. *Hawaiian Airlines v. Norris* goes on to explain the intricate procedures by which employment discrimination and labor disputes are mediated and resolved under the RLA. And, *Air Line Pilots Ass'n v. Eastern Air Lines* features the substantive aspects of airline collective bargaining—namely *how* airline labor and employment disputes are resolved under the RLA.

After reading this chapter, readers should have an appreciation for the RLA and be able to define a "major" dispute from a "minor" one. Readers, too, should understand the interplay between national and state law respecting employee rights and how that impacts the airline passenger experience.

B. LABOR RELATIONS: DISCRIMINATION, COLLECTIVE BARGAINING, AND THE RAILWAY LABOR ACT

GOODWIN V. RIDGE
2005 WL 2176936 (E.D. Ark. 2005)

HOLMES, J.

This is an employment discrimination case. Kenny E. Goodwin, an African American male, brought a race discrimination claim pursuant to 42 U.S.C. § 2000e *et seq.* (Title VII of the Civil Rights Act of 1964) against Thomas J. Ridge in his official capacity as Secretary of the United States Department of Homeland Security. The defendant has moved for summary judgment. For the reasons stated below, this motion is granted.

Following the terrorist attacks of September 11, 2001, Congress passed the Aviation and Transportation Security Act ("ATSA") and created the Transportation Security Administration ("TSA") to protect our nation's civil air

Privatization of Airport Security

transportation system. Section 110 of the ATSA requires the TSA to recruit and hire federal employees to provide security screening of passengers and cargo at commercial airports. Before the ATSA was passed, private firms performed airport security screening functions. Goodwin was employed by one of these private firms, Wackenhut, as an airport screener at the Little Rock National Airport. After the ATSA was enacted the TSA began the federalization process for airport security personnel.

Credentials   To ensure the qualifications of security screeners, all applicants were required to meet specific job requirements and pass a series of tests. The minimum requirements were (1) a high school diploma, a GED, or equivalent, or (2) one year of work experience performing security work or as an aviation screener or x-ray technician. Applicants meeting these requirements were then required to complete an assessment process successfully.

In the assessment process, job candidates first took Phase I, a battery of computerized tests. Candidates who passed Phase I moved to Phase II, which consisted of a structured interview, physical performance tests, medical evaluations, and a background check. When candidates completed each portion of the assessment, the tester for that station initialed or checked off that the candidate had been to the station. These checklists did not indicate whether the candidate passed or failed that portion of the assessment.

All screener candidates were required to pass two physical performance tests, a luggage/box-lift test and a baggage-search test, which were separate and independent from any medical evaluations. Both physical performance tests were pass/fail tests intended to measure candidates' abilities to perform essential job functions. TSA standardized these tests by providing scripts for testers to use when giving instructions to candidates and conducting the tests. One of the physical performance tests, the baggage-search test, required candidates to put their hands in a covered box, identify objects by feeling them, and indicate the identified items on a preprinted answer sheet by circling them. The covered box contained 5 items, and the answer sheet listed 20 items. To pass the test, candidates had to correctly identify 4 of the 5 items in the box. All applicants were provided with the same instructions and completed the tests in the same exact manner.

Each candidate was given only one chance to take the physical performance portion of the assessment. Those who failed one or both of the physical performance tests were disqualified from consideration as a screener, and candidates were not informed which of the two tests they failed. None of the candidates was allowed to repeat these tests, and no candidate who failed either of the two physical performance tests was hired. TSA policy allows disqualified candidates to retest for a position after six months, however, if a vacancy is available.

In contrast, candidates who did not meet TSA's medical standards for vision and hearing were told what standards they did not meet and were allowed to attempt to obtain medical clearance by going to a private physician. Any applicant who passed both physical performance tests but did not demonstrate compliance with TSA medical standards at the assessment center could later submit documentation from a personal physician or specialist. Medical documentation demonstrating that a candidate satisfied TSA's medical standards was considered, and some applicants who had failed the medical evaluation at the assessment center were later hired after submitting such documentation.

Goodwin applied for a TSA position and attended a screener assessment. He passed Phase I and the structured interview component of Phase II but failed the baggage-search test in the physical performance portion of Phase II because he correctly identified only three items on the answer sheet. Goodwin was not hired as a TSA screener.

The defendant asserts that Goodwin was not hired because he failed the baggage-search test. Goodwin admits that he failed the baggage-search test, that none of the applicants at the assessment center was allowed to retake this test, and that no applicant who failed this test was hired by TSA as a screener. Goodwin argues, however, that he failed the baggage-search test because he was not wearing his eyeglasses and could not see the answer sheet. Goodwin further contends that he was not allowed to retake the baggage search test because of his race and that he was therefore not selected as a TSA screener due to racial discrimination.

Defenses

Under the burden-shifting framework set out in McDonnell Douglas Corp. v. Green, 411 U.S. 792 (1973), a plaintiff typically must demonstrate the following four elements: (1) that he belonged to a protected class, (2) that he applied and met the minimum qualifications for the job, (3) that he was rejected, and (4) that after rejecting him the employer continued to seek applicants with the plaintiff's qualifications.

Because there is no direct evidence of discriminatory intent, Goodwin's failure-to-hire claim is analyzed under the burden-shifting framework set out in *McDonnell Douglas Corp. v. Green*, 411 U.S. 792 (1973), which means that a plaintiff typically must demonstrate the following four elements: (1) that he belonged to a

Burden Shifting Framework

protected class, (2) that he applied and met the minimum qualifications for the job, (3) that he was rejected, and (4) that after rejecting Goodwin the employer continued to seek applicants with Goodwin's qualifications.

The Supreme Court has recognized, however, that facts vary in Title VII cases and the *prima facie* proof required of a plaintiff may differ according to the situation. Accordingly, federal courts in some cases have held that, as an alternative to the fourth element stated above, the plaintiff may show that he was treated differently from similarly-situated members of the unprotected class. This element of disparate treatment in comparison to similarly-situated members of the unprotected class is most appropriate to apply under the circumstances of this case.

If the plaintiff establishes a *prima facie* case, a rebuttable presumption of discrimination is created. The employer may rebut this presumption by articulating one or more nondiscriminatory reasons for the employment decision. When the *prima facie* case has been successfully rebutted, the presumption of discrimination drops out of the picture, and the burden shifts back to the plaintiff to present evidence sufficient to support two findings. First, the plaintiff must present evidence that creates a fact issue as to whether the employer's proffered reasons are mere pretext. Second, he must present evidence that creates a reasonable inference that the adverse employment decision was an act of intentional discrimination based on race.

The parties in this case do not dispute the first and third elements: Goodwin is an African-American, a member of a protected class, and the TSA did not hire him. Goodwin asserts, however, that he was qualified for the screener job and that he was treated differently than other similarly-situated persons in the hiring process. Because Goodwin has failed to produce any evidence to establish that any material fact relevant to these issues is actually in dispute, he has not stated a *prima facie* case of racial discrimination.

Job Qualifications

As to the first issue, whether Goodwin was qualified for the job, he does not dispute that one of the job qualifications established by TSA was successful completion of the physical performance tests, including the baggage-search test. Goodwin does not dispute that he failed this test; rather, he contends that the test itself should be disregarded and that he was qualified for the job based on other factors not required by the TSA.

An employer is not required to hire an applicant who does not possess basic skills essential to performance of a particular job, regardless of the color of his skin. When the stated qualifications for the job at issue are objective, such as passing a certain test, the plaintiff must show that he meets the stated qualifications. An employer has wide discretion to establish its requirements and qualifications for particular positions, so long as these requirements do not discriminate based upon impermissible characteristics such as race. In the normal course of business, employers will hire the most qualified candidates, and an employer, not a federal court, is in the best position to identify those strengths that constitute the best qualifications. The Eighth Circuit has often noted that " 'the employment-discrimination laws have not vested in the federal courts the authority to sit as super-personnel departments reviewing the wisdom or fairness of the business judgments made by employers, except to the extent that those judgments involve intentional discrimination.' "

Employer Discretion

The stated job qualifications in this case were both objective and nondiscriminatory. The purpose of the baggage-search test was to determine whether applicants could identify objects by feeling them, a job function relevant to the TSA screener positions. Goodwin admits that all applicants were provided with the same instructions and completed the test in the same exact manner. The activity of touching and identifying concealed objects would in no way directly discriminate between candidates of different races. Moreover, Goodwin has neither alleged nor offered any evidence to show that the test had a discriminatory impact upon African-Americans. Accordingly, TSA acted within its discretion as an employer in establishing the baggage-search test as a job qualification and rejecting applicants who failed the test.

Instead of offering any evidence or argument that the baggage-search test itself was racially discriminatory, Goodwin argues that he was qualified based upon other factors and that the test should be disregarded because it was poorly designed. Specifically, Goodwin states that he was qualified for the screener position because he had previously worked as a contract security screener, he continued to work as private contract screener until the federalization process of the airport security personnel was completed, he has an aviation management degree, and he is a veteran of the United States Army.

None of these factors was a qualification sought by the TSA for the airport screeners. Goodwin further argues that because job applicants had to read an answer sheet to indicate which items they had felt in the box, the test measured more than ability to tactually identify objects; it also measured an applicant's ability to see or read the answer sheet, *i.e.*, vision. Goodwin contends that he failed the test because he had forgotten his eyeglasses on the assessment day and could not see the answer sheet, not because he could not identify the objects by touch.

Even if Goodwin is correct that he possessed other job qualifications and that the baggage-search test had a design flaw, however, these facts are irrelevant. The TSA, as an employer, has the authority to establish its job qualifications, so long as its requirements do not discriminate based upon race or other improper factors. Goodwin, as a job applicant, is not at liberty to establish his own criteria for the TSA screener position and demand that TSA follow them.

Disparate Treatment

The remaining issue is whether Goodwin was treated differently than similarly-situated job candidates who were not members of the protected class. At the *prima facie* stage, a plaintiff's burden to show that he is similarly situated to other job applicants is not onerous. Goodwin admits that all screener candidates were required to successfully complete the assessment process and that no candidate who failed either of the two physical performance tests, which included the baggage-search test, was hired. Goodwin alleges that he received disparate treatment in the testing process, however, for two reasons.

First, Goodwin alleges that he informed the test proctors at the assessment center that he could not see the answer sheet but was denied the opportunity to either leave the center to get his eyeglasses and return to finish testing later or to retake the baggage-search test after failing it. Goodwin has shown no evidence that he was treated differently from any other job candidate in this regard. The TSA asserts that, to ensure the integrity of the assessment process, none of the job candidates was allowed to leave the assessment center after starting the physical performance tests and then return to complete them. Goodwin has produced no evidence to the contrary.

Instead, Goodwin complains that job candidates who failed the medical evaluations were later allowed to submit documentation from private physicians to establish that they met TSA's medical standards for vision and hearing. That candidates who failed the medical evaluation were permitted to submit later documentation to show that they met the qualifications while candidates who failed the baggage-search test were not in no way establishes disparate treatment based upon race.

The candidates who initially failed the medical evaluations were not similarly situated to Goodwin. He failed a proficiency test; they failed a medical evaluation. Goodwin has produced no evidence that TSA's different treatment of those who failed a proficiency test and those who failed a medical evaluation was a subterfuge for race discrimination. To the contrary, the undisputed evidence shows that both

African-American and white applicants who initially failed the medical evaluations were later allowed to submit further medical documentation and were hired.

Goodwin complains that the baggage-search test was poorly designed and that his disqualification was unfair because some candidates who initially failed the medical vision tests were later hired. The wisdom or fairness of an employer's hiring practices is not subject to review by a federal court unless improper discrimination is involved. Although Goodwin insists that TSA's refusal to allow him to leave during the assessment to get his eyeglasses must have been due to some racial animus, he has produced no evidence to support that allegation. Bald allegations alone cannot create an issue of material fact to withstand a motion for summary judgment. There is no genuine issue of material fact. The defendant has established a *prima facie* case of entitlement to summary judgment. Goodwin has failed to meet proof with proof. The defendant's motion for summary judgment is granted.

EXERCISE 10-1. *GOODWIN V. RIDGE*—EMPLOYMENT DISCRIMINATION

1. Explain Section 110 of the Aviation and Transportation Security Act ("ATSA").

2. Detail the qualifications and "assessment process" for security screeners under the ATSA, and summarize the plaintiff's claims.

3. What is the burden-shifting framework established by *McDonnell Douglas Corp. v. Green*, 411 U.S. 792 (1973)?

4. According to the court, what role, if any, do courts play in establishing the job qualifications for employers and employees?

5. Was the plaintiff treated differently than similarly-situated job candidates as a matter of law?

NOTES ON *GOODWIN V. RIDGE*—TRANSPORTATION SECURITY ADMINISTRATION ("TSA")

Congress federalized the aviation security system after September 11, 2001. In addition to creating the Department of Homeland Security (of which the Transportation Security Administration is a part) in November, 2001, the government also assumed responsibility for screening passengers, a task historically managed by private airlines through independent contractors. As a result, all airport screeners now are federal employees. Aviation & Transportation Security Act, Pub. L. No. 107–071, 115 Stat. 597 (codified as amended in scattered sections of 49 U.S.C.). *See also* Andrew

Hessick, *The Federalization of Airport Security: Privacy Implications*, 24 WHITTIER L. REV. 43–69 (2002–2003).

Whether to allow airport screeners to bargain collectively is a subject of great debate among federal lawmakers. *See* Joe Davidson, *TSA Nominee is Urged to Reject Airport Screeners' Push for Collective Bargaining*, WASH. POST, June 11, 2010. Which viewpoint should prevail as the better policy?

HAWAIIAN AIRLINES, INC. V. NORRIS
512 U.S. 246 (1994)

JUSTICE BLACKMUN delivered the opinion of the Court.

Railway Labor Act of 1926

This action involves the scope of federal preemption under the Railway Labor Act (RLA), 45 U.S.C. § 151 *et seq.* The RLA, which was extended in 1936 to cover the airline industry, sets up a mandatory arbitral mechanism to handle disputes "growing out of grievances or out of the interpretation or application of agreements concerning rates of pay, rules, or working conditions," 45 U.S.C. § 153 First (i).

State or Federal Remedy?

The question in this case is whether an aircraft mechanic who claims that he was discharged for refusing to certify the safety of a plane that he considered unsafe and for reporting his safety concerns to the Federal Aviation Administration may pursue available state-law remedies for wrongful discharge, or whether he may seek redress only through the RLA's arbitral mechanism. We hold that the RLA does not preempt his state-law causes of action.

* * *

Respondent Grant Norris is an aircraft mechanic licensed by the Federal Aviation Administration ("FAA"). His aircraft mechanic's license authorizes him to approve an airplane and return it to service after he has made, supervised, or inspected certain repairs performed on that plane. *See* Certification: Airmen Other Than Flight Crewmembers, 14 C.F.R. §§ 65.85 and 65.87 (1987). If he were to approve any aircraft on which the repairs did not conform to FAA safety regulations, the FAA could suspend or revoke his license. *See* Maintenance, Preventive Maintenance, Rebuilding and Alteration, 14 C.F.R. § 43.12 (1992).

On February 2, 1987, respondent was hired by petitioner Hawaiian Airlines, Inc. ("HAL"). Many of the terms of his employment were governed by a collective-bargaining agreement ("CBA") negotiated between the carrier and the International Association of Machinists and Aerospace Workers. Under the CBA, respondent's duties included inspecting and repairing all parts of a plane and its engine. On July 15, 1987, during a routine preflight inspection of a DC-9 plane, he noticed that one of the tires was worn. When he removed the wheel, respondent discovered that the axle sleeve, which should have been mirror smooth, was scarred and grooved. This damaged sleeve could cause the landing gear to fail.

Respondent recommended that the sleeve be replaced, but his supervisor ordered that it be sanded and returned to the plane. This was done, and the plane flew as scheduled. At the end of the shift, respondent refused to sign the maintenance record to certify that the repair had been performed satisfactorily and that the airplane was fit to fly. *See* 14 C.F.R. § 43.9(a) (1992). The supervisor immediately suspended him pending a termination hearing. Respondent immediately went home and called the FAA to report the problem with the sleeve. In response, the FAA initiated a comprehensive investigation, proposed a civil penalty of $964,000 against HAL, proposed the revocation of the license of the supervisor who terminated respondent, and ultimately settled all charges for a substantial fine.

Respondent then invoked the grievance procedure outlined in the CBA, and a "Step 1" grievance hearing was held on July 31, 1987. Petitioner HAL accused respondent of insubordination, claiming that his refusal to sign the record violated the CBA's provision that an aircraft mechanic "may be required to sign work records in connection with the work he performs." Respondent relied on the CBA's guarantees that an employee may not be discharged without just cause and may not be disciplined for refusing to perform work that is in violation of health or safety laws. The hearing officer terminated respondent for insubordination.

Still conforming to the CBA procedures, respondent appealed his termination, seeking a "Step 3" grievance hearing. Before this hearing took place, HAL offered to reduce respondent's punishment to suspension without pay, but warned him that "any further instance of failure to perform [his] duties in a responsible manner" could result in discharge. Respondent did not respond to this offer, nor, apparently, did he take further steps to pursue his grievance through the CBA procedures.

On December 18, 1987, respondent filed suit against HAL in Hawaii Circuit Court. His complaint included two wrongful-discharge torts—discharge in violation of the public policy expressed in the Federal Aviation Act of 1958 and implementing regulations, and discharge in violation of Hawaii's Whistleblower Protection Act.

The Hawaii Whistleblower Protection Act forbids an employer to "discharge, threaten, or otherwise discriminate against an employee . . . because . . . [t]he employee . . . reports or is about to report to a public body . . . a violation or a suspected violation of a law or rule adopted pursuant to law of this State, a political subdivision of this State, or the United States, unless the employee knows that the report is false." The Act authorizes an employee to file a civil action seeking injunctive relief and actual damages.

He also alleged that HAL had breached the CBA agreement. HAL removed the action to the United States District Court for the District of Hawaii, which dismissed the breach-of-contract claim as preempted by the RLA, and remanded the other claims to the state trial court. The trial court then dismissed respondent's claim of discharge in violation of public policy, holding that it, too, was preempted by the RLA's provision of exclusive arbitral procedures. The state court certified its order as final to permit respondent to take an immediate appeal.

In the meantime, respondent had filed a second lawsuit in state court, naming as defendants three of HAL's officers who allegedly directed, confirmed, or ratified the claimed retaliatory discharge. He again sought relief for, among other things, discharge in violation of public policy and of the Hawaii Whistleblower Protection Act. The Hawaii trial court dismissed these two counts as preempted by the RLA and certified the case for immediate appeal.

The Supreme Court of Hawaii reversed in both cases, concluding that the RLA did not preempt respondent's state tort actions. That court concluded that the plain language of § 153 First (i) does not support preemption of disputes independent of a labor agreement and interpreted the opinion in *Consolidated Rail Corporation (Conrail) v. Railway Labor Executives' Assn.*, 491 U.S. 299 (1989), to limit RLA preemption to "disputes involving contractually defined rights."

The court rejected petitioners' argument that the retaliatory discharge claims were preempted because determining whether HAL discharged respondent for insubordination, and thus for just cause, required construing the CBA. The court pointed to *Lingle v. Norge Div. of Magic Chef, Inc.*, 486 U.S. 399 (1988), a case involving § 301 of the Labor-Management Relations Act, 1947 ("LMRA"), in which the Court held that a claim of wrongful termination in retaliation for filing a state worker's compensation claim did not require interpretation of a CBA, but depended upon purely factual questions concerning the employee's conduct and the employer's motive. Because the same was true in this action, said the Supreme Court of Hawaii, respondent's state tort claims were not preempted. We granted *certiorari* in these consolidated cases.

* * *

Whether federal law preempts a state law establishing a cause of action is a question of congressional intent. Preemption of employment standards "within the traditional police power of the State" "should not be lightly inferred." Congress' purpose in passing the RLA was to promote stability in labor-management relations by providing a comprehensive framework for resolving labor disputes. To realize this goal, the RLA establishes a mandatory arbitral mechanism for "the prompt and orderly settlement" of two classes of disputes.

Intent and Purpose of RLA

The RLA establishes a mandatory arbitral mechanism for "the prompt and orderly settlement" of two classes of disputes.

The first class, those concerning "rates of pay, rules or working conditions," are deemed "major" disputes. Major disputes relate to " 'the formation of collective [bargaining] agreements or efforts to secure them.' "

The second class of disputes, known as "minor" disputes, "gro[w] out of grievances or out of the interpretation or application of agreements covering rates of pay, rules, or working conditions." Minor disputes involve "controversies over the meaning of an existing collective bargaining agreement in a particular fact situation."

Thus, "major disputes seek to create contractual rights, minor disputes to enforce them."

Disputes— Major and Minor

The first class, those concerning "rates of pay, rules or working conditions," are deemed "major" disputes. Major disputes relate to " 'the formation of collective [bargaining] agreements or efforts to secure them.' " *Conrail* (quoting *Elgin, J. & E.R. Co. v. Burley*, 325 U.S. 711 (1945)). The second class of disputes, known as "minor" disputes, "gro[w] out of grievances or out of the interpretation or application of agreements covering rates of pay, rules, or working conditions." Minor disputes involve "controversies over the meaning of an existing collective bargaining agreement in a particular fact situation." Thus, "major disputes seek to create contractual rights, minor disputes to enforce them."

Petitioners contend that the conflict over respondent's firing is a minor dispute. If so, it must be resolved only through the RLA mechanisms, including the carrier's internal dispute-resolution processes and an adjustment board established by the employer and the unions. Thus, a determination that respondent's complaints constitute a minor dispute would preempt his state-law actions.

* * *

The Court's inquiry into the scope of minor disputes begins, of course, with the text of the statute. Petitioners point out that the statute defines minor disputes to include "disputes . . . growing out of grievances, or out of the interpretation or application of [CBA's]." Petitioners argue that this disjunctive language must indicate that "grievances" means something other than labor-contract disputes, else the term "grievances" would be superfluous. Accordingly, petitioners suggest that "grievances" should be read to mean all employment-related disputes, including those based on statutory or common law.

Even if we were persuaded that the word "or" carried this weight, petitioners' interpretation produces an overlap not unlike the one it purports to avoid. Their expansive definition of "grievances" necessarily encompasses disputes growing out of "the interpretation or application" of CBA's. Thus, in attempting to save the term "grievances" from superfluity, petitioners would make the phrase after the "or" mere surplusage.

We think it more likely that "grievances," like disputes over "the interpretation or application" of CBA's, refers to disagreements over how to give effect to the bargained-for agreement. The use of "grievance" to refer to a claim arising out of a CBA is common in the labor-law context in general, and it has been understood in this way in the RLA context. *See* H.R. Rep. No. 1944, 73d Cong., 2d Sess., 2–3 (1934) (referring to RLA settlement of "minor disputes known as 'grievances,' which develop from the interpretation and/or application of the contracts between the labor unions and the carriers"). Significantly, too, the adjustment boards charged with administration of the minor-dispute provisions have understood these provisions as pertaining only to disputes invoking contract-based rights.

Accordingly, we believe that the most natural reading of the term "grievances" in this context is as a synonym for disputes involving the application or interpretation of a CBA. Nothing in the legislative history of the RLA or other sections of the statute undermines this conclusion. But even accepting that § 151a is susceptible of more than one interpretation, no proposed interpretation demonstrates a clear and manifest congressional purpose to create a regime that broadly preempts substantive protections extended by the States, independent of any negotiated labor agreement. * * *

Our case law confirms that the category of minor disputes contemplated by § 151a are those that are grounded in the CBA. We have defined minor disputes as those involving the interpretation or application of existing labor agreements.

See e.g., Conrail ("The distinguishing feature of [a minor dispute] is that the dispute may be conclusively resolved by interpreting the existing [CBA]").

But it cannot be said that the minimum requirements laid down by state authority are all set aside. We hold that the enactment by Congress of the [RLA] was not a preemption of the field of regulating working conditions themselves.

---

*Interpreting
Existing CBA*

Moreover, we have held that the RLA's mechanism for resolving minor disputes does not preempt causes of action to enforce rights that are independent of the CBA. More than 60 years ago, the Court rejected a railroad's argument that the existence of the RLA arbitration scheme preempted a state statute regulating the number of workers required to operate certain equipment. Not long thereafter, the Court rejected a claim that the RLA preempted an order by the Illinois Commerce Commission requiring cabooses on all trains; the operative CBA required cabooses only on some of the trains. Although the Court assumed that a railroad adjustment board would have jurisdiction under the RLA over this dispute, it concluded that the state law was enforceable nonetheless:

> State laws have long regulated a great variety of conditions in transportation and industry, such as sanitary facilities and conditions, safety devices and protections, purity of water supply, fire protection, and innumerable others. Any of these matters might, be the subject of a demand by work[ers] for better protection and upon refusal might, we suppose, be the subject of a labor dispute which would have such effect on interstate commerce that federal agencies might be invoked to deal with some phase of it. But it cannot be said that the minimum requirements laid down by state authority are all set aside. We hold that the enactment by Congress of the [RLA] was not a preemption of the field of regulating working conditions themselves.

Thus, substantive protections provided by state law, independent of whatever labor agreement might govern, are not preempted under the RLA.

The Court has taken a consistent approach in the context of state actions for wrongful discharge. In *Andrews v. Louisville & Nashville R. Co.*, 406 U.S. 320 (1972), the Court held that a state-law claim of wrongful termination was preempted, not because the RLA broadly preempts state-law claims based on discharge or discipline, but because the employee's claim was firmly rooted in a breach of the CBA itself. He asserted no right independent of that agreement:

> Here it is conceded by all that the only source of [Andrews'] right not to be discharged, and therefore to treat an alleged discharge as a

'wrongful' one that entitles him to damages, is the [CBA] . . . [T]he disagreement turns on the extent of [the railroad's] obligation to restore [Andrews] to his regular duties following injury in an automobile accident. The existence and extent of such an obligation in a case such as this will depend on the interpretation of the [CBA]. Thus [Andrews'] claim, and [the railroad's] disallowance of it, stem from differing interpretations of the [CBA]. His claim is therefore subject to the Act's requirement that it be submitted to the Board for adjustment.

RLA Preemption and State Law

Here, in contrast, the CBA is not the "only source" of respondent's right not to be discharged wrongfully. In fact, the "only source" of the right respondent asserts in this action is state tort law. Wholly apart from any provision of the CBA, petitioners had a state-law obligation not to fire respondent in violation of public policy or in retaliation for whistle-blowing. The parties' obligation under the RLA to arbitrate disputes arising out of the application or interpretation of the CBA did not relieve petitioners of this duty.

* * *

The preemption standard—that a state-law cause of action is not preempted by the RLA if it involves rights and obligations that exist independent of the CBA—is virtually identical to the preemption standard the Court employs in cases involving § 301 of the LMRA.

In a case remarkably similar to the case before us now, this Court made clear that the existence of a potential CBA-based remedy did not deprive an employee of independent remedies available under state law. In *Lingle v. Norge Div. of Magic Chef, Inc.*, 486 U.S. 399 (1988), an employee covered by a labor agreement was fired for filing an allegedly false worker's compensation claim. After filing a grievance pursuant to her CBA, which protected employees against discharge except for "proper" or "just" cause, she filed a complaint in state court, alleging that she had been discharged for exercising her rights under Illinois worker's compensation laws. The state court had held her state-law claim preempted because "the same analysis of the facts" was required in both the grievance proceeding and the state-court action. This Court reversed.

It recognized that where the resolution of a state-law claim depends on an interpretation of the CBA, the claim is preempted. It observed, however, that "purely factual questions" about an employee's conduct or an employer's conduct and motives do not "requir[e] a court to interpret any term of a collective-bargaining agreement." The state-law retaliatory discharge claim turned on just this sort of purely factual question: whether the employee was discharged or threatened with discharge, and, if so, whether the employer's motive in discharging her was to deter or interfere with her exercise of rights under Illinois worker's compensation law.

While recognizing that "the state-law analysis might well involve attention to the same factual considerations as the contractual determination of whether Lingle was fired for just cause," the Court disagreed that

> such parallelism render[ed] the state-law analysis dependent upon the contractual analysis. For while there may be instances in which the National Labor Relations Act preempts state law on the basis of the subject matter of the law in question, § 301 preemption merely ensures that federal law will be the basis for interpreting collective-bargaining agreements, and says nothing about the substantive rights a State may provide to workers when adjudication of those rights does not depend upon the interpretation of such agreements.

> In other words, even if dispute resolution pursuant to a collective-bargaining agreement, on the one hand, and state law, on the other, would require addressing precisely the same set of facts, as long as the state-law claim can be resolved without interpreting the agreement itself, the claim is "independent" of the agreement for § 301 preemption purposes.

We conclude that *Lingle* provides an appropriate framework for addressing preemption under the RLA, and we adopt the *Lingle* standard to resolve claims of RLA preemption.

The question under *Lingle* is whether respondent's state-law wrongful-discharge claims are independent of the CBA. Petitioners argue that resort to the CBA is necessary to determine whether respondent, in fact, was discharged. This argument is foreclosed by *Lingle* itself. *Lingle* teaches that the issue to be decided in this action—whether the employer's actions make out the element of discharge under Hawaii law—is a "purely factual questio[n]."

Nor are we persuaded by petitioners' contention that the state tort claims require a determination whether the discharge, if any, was justified by respondent's failure to sign the maintenance record, as the CBA required him to do. Although such a determination would be required with regard to respondent's separate allegation of discharge in violation of the CBA, the District Court dismissed that count as preempted by the RLA, and respondent does not challenge that dismissal. The state tort claims, by contrast, require only the purely factual inquiry into any retaliatory motive of the employer. Accordingly, we agree with the Supreme Court of Hawaii that respondent's claims for discharge in violation of public policy and in violation of the Hawaii Whistleblower Protection Act are not preempted by the RLA, and we affirm that court's judgment.

EXERCISE 10-2. *HAWAIIAN AIRLINES, INC. V. NORRIS*—RAILWAY LABOR ACT

1. What is a collective-bargaining agreement ("CBA") and how is it at issue in *Hawaiian Airlines, Inc. v. Norris?*

2. Since when did the Railway Labor Act apply to airlines, and what is its purpose?

3. The Railway Labor Act covers two classes of disputes—"major" and "minor." Describe both and the process for resolving each.

4. How does the court define "grievances"?

5. The court notes that the Railway Labor Act's "mechanism for resolving disputes does not preempt causes of action to enforce rights that are independent of the CBA." Explain the court's rationale and what preemption standard it establishes in this case for state law wrongful discharge claim.

NOTES ON *HAWAIIAN AIRLINES, INC. V. NORRIS*—WHISTLEBLOWERS

The federal Whistleblower Protection Program ("WPP") was enacted as part of the Wendell H. Ford Aviation Investment and Reform Act for the 21st Century, Pub. L. No. 106–181, Title V, § 519(a), 114 Stat. 61, 145–49 (2000) ("AIR21"). In addition to state whistleblower statutes, the federal program was designed to "provide protection for airline employee whistleblowers by prohibiting the discharge or other discrimination against an employee who provides information to its employer or the Federal government about air safety or files or participates in a proceeding related to air safety." H.R. Rep. No. 106–167, pt. 1, at 100 (1999).

Section 519 of AIR21prevents an airline from discriminating against an employee because he or she "provided . . . to the employer or Federal Government information relating to any violation or alleged violation of any order, regulation, or standard of the [FAA] or any other provision of law relating to air carrier safety under [Title 49] or any other law of the United States . . ." 49 U.S.C. § 42121(a). AIR21 thus was designed to protect not only those who report air safety violations to the government, but also those who make such reports to their employers. *See* 49 U.S.C. § 42121(a).

Consistent with this goal, the WPP established a detailed administrative scheme for the investigation and resolution of claims brought by airline employees. *See* 49 U.S.C. § 42121(b); 29 C.F.R. Part 1979. An aggrieved employee may file a complaint with the Secretary of Labor ("Secretary") within 90 days after the date on which a violation of the WPP occurs. Once an employee files a complaint and presents a *prima facie* case, the Secretary must conduct an investigation and issue a final order. *See id.* §§ 42121(b)(2)(A), (b)(3)(A). The statute explicitly provides for review of the Secretary's final order in the courts of appeal. In the event of non-compliance with the Secretary's final order, either the Secretary or the employee may bring a civil action in a federal district court to compel compliance with the Secretary's order.

———————

AIR LINE PILOTS ASS'N, INT'L V. EASTERN AIR LINES
701 F. Supp. 865 (D.D.C. 1988)

BARRINGTON D. PARKER, SENIOR DISTRICT JUDGE.

In separate verified complaints alleging violations of the Railway Labor Act ("RLA" or "Act"), the Air Line Pilots Association, International ("ALPA"), the International Machinists & Aerospace Workers ("IAM") and Local 553 Transport Workers Union of America ("TWU") have sued Eastern Air Lines, Inc. ("Eastern") and request both injunctive and declaratory relief.

In a joint motion for a preliminary injunction, filed on November 18, 1988, the three unions seek to halt the proposed sale of Eastern's Air Shuttle ("Shuttle") operations to Trump Shuttle, Inc. ("Trump Shuttle" or "Trump"). They claim that Eastern's proposed sale of the Shuttle to Trump violates both Eastern's *status quo* and collective bargaining obligations under the RLA, triggers a "major dispute" under the RLA because the proposed action was not based on any express or arguable contractual right or consistent past practice, and was undertaken with the express intent of undermining the unions and violates the statutory obligation to refrain from interfering with certified bargaining representatives. For the reasons stated below the Court determines that the sale of the Shuttle should not be halted. Accordingly, plaintiffs' motion for a preliminary injunction is denied.

* * *

Eastern is the nation's sixth largest air carrier and a wholly-owned subsidiary of the Texas Air Corporation ("Texas Air"). It provides scheduled passenger and cargo service out of hubs located in Atlanta, Miami, Philadelphia, and San Juan, Puerto Rico. It also operates passenger and other services extending through Central and South America.

Eastern Shuttle Operations and Assets

Eastern operates a shuttle service, on an hourly basis, between LaGuardia Airport, New York City, and both Logan Airport, Boston, and National Airport, Washington, D.C. The Shuttle has operated for more than 25 years and is a well-established and profitable division of Eastern Air Lines. It provides employment for approximately 700 full-time employees, including 200 pilots, 146 machinists and approximately 250 flight attendants. It has no single permanent group of employees, rather, Eastern's workers bid for positions on basis of seniority. An employee's assignment to the Shuttle on a month-to-month basis depends upon the bids of more senior employees.

The Shuttle division employs 2.3% of Eastern's 30,500 employees, utilizes 6.7% of the company's 255 aircraft, accounts for approximately 1.5% of the company's total available seat miles ("ASM's"), and generates approximately 4.3% of the total operating revenue. The division accounts for approximately 2.9% of Eastern's total assets at net book value, and approximately 7% of its assets at fair market value.

The Shuttle's traffic is virtually limited to passengers who travel only between the three named cities. The passengers do not continue to other Eastern destinations. In recent years the Shuttle's market share has declined, primarily because of competition from Pan American which has penetrated the New York, Boston, and Washington shuttle market.

* * *

In early 1988, Eastern sought to dispose of the Shuttle when it attempted to spin off the division to Air Shuttle, L.P., a newly formed subsidiary of Texas Air. The transaction was challenged by the IAM and the carrier was enjoined from taking any steps to spin off the Shuttle operation, pending exhaustion of the dispute resolution procedures of the RLA. His ruling was subsequently vacated on procedural grounds. Meanwhile, Eastern withdrew its proposed plans.

This Memorandum Opinion involves Eastern's second attempt to dispose of the Shuttle when on October 12, 1988, Texas Air officials publicly announced a Purchase and Sale Agreement ("Agreement") between Eastern and Trump Shuttle, Inc. The Agreement provided for sale of the Shuttle division for $365 million in cash to be paid at the closing.

Trump Shuttle was formed in October 1988, by Donald J. Trump. He is the sole stockholder, board chairman and chief executive officer of Trump Shuttle which was formed to effect the purchase from Eastern. Mr. Trump is a successful entrepreneur engaged in real estate developments, hotel operations, and a variety of other enterprises.

* * *

Terms of Agreement

Plaintiffs do not contest the fairness of the $365 million sale price and it is estimated that the proceeds will provide Eastern with approximately $315 to $320 million net cash. The terms of the Agreement provide that Eastern sell its entire Shuttle division to Trump Shuttle. This includes all ground equipment, airport gate positions, 17 Boeing 727 aircraft, 92 airport landing and take-off slots, 14 airport gates, and related terminal facilities at LaGuardia, Logan, and National airports.

The Agreement provides that the Shuttle may not be resold to any of Eastern's six principal competitors (American, Delta, Northwest, United, USAir, or TWA) for a period of ten years. It also provides that for five years after the sale, Eastern will retain a right of first refusal if Trump decides to sell the Shuttle to those airlines, or if other potential purchasers attempt to buy it. The Agreement further provides that Trump Shuttle shall continue to participate in Eastern's OnePass, frequent flyer program for three years, and that for twelve years thereafter, Trump shall not participate in the frequent flyer program of any other airline.

Deposition testimony and declarations from various witnesses showed that following the sale, Eastern would continue to have substantial flight operations, assets and employees through the LaGuardia, Logan, and National airports. Expert witnesses, James F. Chadbourne and Daniel M. Kasper, agreed that the Shuttle sale would not have a significant impact on Eastern's non-shuttle operations.

Of great concern to plaintiffs is the impact of the Shuttle sale on Eastern's employees. Mr. Trump made it clear in his testimony on behalf of Trump Shuttle, that he extended to Eastern employees an opportunity to work for his company, that he would recognize the three unions, and support the present collective bargaining agreements.

Terms of Employment and Union Status

The October 12 Agreement provides, *inter alia*, that Mr. Trump will offer guaranteed employment, in order of seniority, to Eastern's employees in the same numbers presently utilized, will establish wages and work rules identical to those in effect at Eastern—with full credit for seniority, and will not change existing wage rates and work rules without compliance with the Railway Labor Act. Employees would not be hired from any other source unless an insufficient number of Eastern's employees were willing to accept the employment offers. The Agreement also requires Trump to recognize Eastern's unions as the bargaining representative and as Captain John Bavis, an Eastern pilot and ranking

ALPA official, testified to "assume as a successor" all rights and obligations of Eastern under any labor contract or the Railway Labor Act, "to the full extent permitted by law." No Eastern employee is required to accept the offer of employment; the choice is entirely optional.

Mr. Trump's job offers have been accepted by more than a sufficient number of Eastern employees to fully staff the Shuttle. Thus, no employee furloughs are likely as a result of the transaction. Employees who choose not to accept the employment option with Trump may remain with Eastern, employed and treated in accord with the seniority-based employment provisions of their respective collective bargaining agreement.

* * *

History of Asset Sales and Bargaining

The record shows that historically, Eastern has had a record of selling assets and eliminating services without prior bargaining with the unions. Such changes have taken place within the framework of the existing agreements. Captain John Bavis and others, whose deposition testimony or declarations are a part of this record, readily admitted that the following operations were terminated without union bargaining: The 1986 hub in Charlotte, North Carolina, the Moonlight Special between Houston and Chicago, operating between 1984–1987, the Military Airlift Command operations ("MAC flights") from 1974–1977, the Montreal, Canada-New York City shuttle operating in the mid-1970s, and the 1980–86 Contract Maintenance Center in Miami.

The Charlotte hub closing resulted in a substantial reduction of flights from 110 to 14 per day accompanied by a nearly 60% reduction within two months of the 176 IAM-represented employees. The Moonlight Special, a late night cargo service, commenced in Houston and was unilaterally transferred to Chicago and then unilaterally discontinued several months later. As a result of that decision IAM-represented employees, in addition to pilots and flight attendants, were displaced. While some of the employees preferred those work opportunities, Eastern did not bargain with the unions but made the unilateral decisions on its own. The MAC flights were chartered services for the United States military. Those non-scheduled operations carried premium pay together with seniority-based crew assignments for pilots and flight attendants. Between 1974 and 1977, there were high averages of MAC departures—38 per month. Since then the operations have been intermittent. In 1987, there were no operations and in 1988, there have been an average of only 11 per month. Again, Eastern's management alone made the decisions. As to the Miami Contract Maintenance Center, the deposition testimony of IAM representative, Charles Bryan showed that the operation was discontinued and employees' bumping and bidding rights were exercised in accordance with the IAM-Eastern collective bargaining agreement.

Several union witnesses testified that the above situations could be distinguished from the Shuttle sale since the Shuttle offered unique and unusual opportunities and personal conveniences for many. However, their testimony while interesting, did not alter the fact that past practices support a finding that significant changes affecting personnel and airline facilities have been made unilaterally by management without collective bargaining over such changes. Nor was their testimony sufficient to overcome the substantial corroboration of such practices otherwise found in the record, upon which the Court has relied.

The impact of the sale to Trump Shuttle pales in comparison to the impact of the September 1988 schedule change. The latter included the elimination and reduction of two major hub services, termination of all services to 14 cities, closure of a pilot domicile center, and disposition of more than 30 aircraft. But even more interesting, is the comparison between several particular items.

Elimination of the Shuttle involves approximately 700 employees, compared with the more than 3,000 affected by the fall schedule. The Shuttle sale results in a curtailment of only 62 departure flights per day from three cities, compared with a net curtailment of 143 daily flights under the fall schedule. Beyond the 62 departures, Eastern will continue its regular flight service to and from Boston, New York, and Washington, D.C., even though the Shuttle division is eliminated. Clearly, the fall schedule resulted in a reduction of far more services. Only 17 aircraft are eliminated by the Shuttle close down, compared to 30 from the fall schedule changes. Finally, there is a decrease of only 1.5% of total available seat miles as compared with the 15.4% decrease associated with the fall schedule.

Consequences of the Sale

Our Circuit Court recognized the fall schedule as changes consistent with past practices and consistent with the provisions of the Railway Labor Act. The changes resulting from the Trump sale are far less drastic than those resulting from the fall schedule. Several witnesses offered testimony presenting what they considered to be important distinctions from the Shuttle transaction. Their testimony, while not entirely discounted, is lacking and is insufficient to support a finding that the Railway Labor Act has been violated.

* * *

As before, plaintiffs urge that the underlying reason and motive for the decision to sell the Shuttle is Eastern's bias or animus toward unions. After this Court found some merit in their position, our Circuit Court found otherwise and held that there were no forbidden purposes behind Eastern's decision and that

Union Animus?

there was no basis for a finding of union animus. That Court made its own judgment from a written record and without benefit of the witnesses' testimony.

Plaintiffs rely substantially on the showing in the earlier preliminary injunction proceedings to support a finding of bias and unlawful interference with union activity. However, they did attempt to strengthen their reliance on the 1987 "CHUNKS" memorandum. They claim that the memorandum was an overt manifestation of union bias, a deliberate plotting by Eastern management and Texas Air to block so-called "oppressive" demands of the IAM and ALPA. That claim, however, was based in large measure on hearsay testimony. After a careful review of plaintiffs' supporting testimony and documentation, the Court finds that their reliance on the CHUNKS memorandum is overdrawn and inconclusive. They have not made a sufficient showing beyond their original effort, which the Circuit Court rejected.

The principal reason advanced by Eastern for the Shuttle sale is a critical and deteriorating financial condition which could prove fatal to the company's existence. The situation has been ongoing. Since the early 1980s Eastern has been faced with continual financial losses. In 1987, the company faced $194 million in losses before adjustments were made for the sale of certain assets. For the first half of 1988, losses approached $120 million. For the third quarter alone losses approached $349 million before capital gains were reported. More than $100 million in losses are anticipated for the present quarter.

Rationale for Sale

The Eastern witnesses who testified clearly recognized that the company was experiencing a loss of cash and liquidity balances that impacted severely on the company's overall financial health, particularly its dwindling net worth. It is estimated that the Trump Shuttle sale will net at least $315 million after certain debt and expense obligations are discharged. Management maintains that the transaction will offset cash now absorbed by Eastern's large losses, allow it to remain in business, permit it to stem rumors of near insolvency, and stop the growing erosion of consumer confidence. Management testified that the net proceeds from the sale would serve to meet those problems.

Eastern officials also testified that available alternatives to the sale were limited and uncertain. In their judgment, the sale would provide much needed liquidity with relatively little, if any, negative impact on the company's remaining core operations; the net cash acquired would allow consideration of long delayed preventive maintenance projects, modernization of operating assets, and improvement of the general quality of service. Absent such efforts, they felt that there was an increasing likelihood that Eastern would be unable to survive the competition which had been accelerated by the Air Line Deregulation Act of 1978 and the entry of Pan American in the shuttle market.

The testimony also showed that Eastern's core business was in dire need. The added cash assets would enable the company to develop its principal operations and generally, it would become a more profitable and upscale business.

Eastern officials were aware of the company's problems and recently undertook certain corrective measures. Current advertisements in the press rank the carrier as outstanding in on-time performance. Advertising budgets, in general, have been increased. Incentive programs to improve both customer service and market penetration have been introduced. New facilities and the upgrading of existing facilities in San Juan and Miami, respectively, have been accomplished. New flight kitchens have been considered and in fact, building operations are underway. With such improvements, Eastern's management contends that it has made a thoughtful and prudent decision to employ the proceeds from the Shuttle sale in a manner that will allow them to continue those and other overdue changes.

* * *

The unions challenge Eastern's claim that there is a critical need for cash and that the Shuttle sale would improve the company's cash position. The bottom line of their challenge, is that selling the Air Shuttle is simply not prudent. They claim that over the past several years, the Shuttle has returned sizable annual profits and that the indications are that it will continue to earn such profits. They also assert that any financial justification for the sale is belied by the fact that the company has failed to place in operation or even blueprint a well-defined recovery or profit improvement plan. Therefore, they claim, it is inconsistent for Eastern to argue that the sale will help the airline return to profitability when it has not even taken the fundamental planning steps. Based upon these considerations, the unions ask the Court to find that union animus and bias rather than the Company's financial condition serve as the impetus for the proposed sale.

After hearing hours of contradictory testimony by the "experts," the Court feels that Eastern has the better argument. There is no doubt that an ongoing struggle has and will continue to exist between Eastern and its certified bargaining representatives. However, the Court feels that equally plausible is the idea that management is seeking to rebuild the company and place it on a sound financial footing.

> *Eastern has the better argument. There is no doubt that an ongoing struggle has and will continue to exist between Eastern and its certified bargaining representatives. However, the Court feels that equally plausible is the idea that management is seeking to rebuild the company and place it on a sound financial footing.*

The unions claim that management is developing plans to liquidate the company and lead it into bankruptcy. If in fact Eastern is not committed to fighting its deferred maintenance problems but is only half-heartedly engaged in improving the core of its carrier system, then Eastern's executives are acting out a cruel hoax upon the legislative, executive, and judicial branches of our federal government and the general public as well. The passage of time should prove whether this is true.

II.   CONCLUSIONS OF LAW

A.   APPLICATION OF THE RAILWAY LABOR ACT MAJOR AND MINOR DISPUTES

The Railway Labor Act of 1926 was enacted in an effort to promote stability in labor management relations within the railroad industry. Since 1936, it has governed labor-management relations within the airline industry. The Act provides remedies for the resolution of employee disputes arising out of the interpretation of collective bargaining agreements and requires all parties to "exert every reasonable effort to make and maintain" collectively bargained agreements, and to abide by the terms of the most recent agreement until all the dispute resolution procedures have been exhausted. *See Detroit & Toledo Shore Line R.R. v. United Transp. Union*, 396 U.S. 142 (1969) ("Shore Line").

Type of RLA Disputes

The resolution procedures depend on whether the dispute is classified as "major" or "minor." A major dispute arises from the formation or change of collective agreements covering rates of pay, rules, or working conditions. *Elgin, J. & E.R. Co. v. Burley*, 325 U.S. 711 (1945). The RLA establishes elaborate machinery for negotiation and mediation of major disputes. The exhaustive bargaining process is designed to force the parties into serious negotiation and to encourage compromise.

A minor dispute, on the other hand, arises from the interpretation or application of an existing agreement. "The dispute relates either to the meaning or proper application of a particular provision with reference to a specific situation or to an omitted case." Such a dispute is one that "arguably" can be covered by the existing collective bargaining agreement. *Maine Central R.R. Co. v. United Transp. Union*, 787 F.2d 780 (1st Cir. 1986) ("Maine Central"). Minor disputes are resolved through a formal grievance process that culminates in binding arbitration by the National Railroad Adjustment Board.

A major dispute arises from the formation or change of collective agreements covering rates of pay, rules, or working conditions. The RLA establishes elaborate machinery for negotiation and mediation of major disputes. The exhaustive bargaining process is designed to force the parties into serious negotiation and to encourage compromise.

A minor dispute, on the other hand, arises from the interpretation or application of an existing agreement. "The dispute relates either to the meaning or proper application of a particular provision with reference to a specific situation or to an omitted case." Such a dispute is one that "arguably" can be covered by the existing collective bargaining agreement. Minor disputes are resolved through a formal grievance process that culminates in binding arbitration by the National Railroad Adjustment Board.

A major dispute triggers a *status quo* obligation. Both the carrier and the union must preserve the "actual, objective working conditions and practices, broadly conceived, which were in effect before the pending dispute arose and which are involved in or related to that dispute." Once a party proposes a change in the collective bargaining agreement, that party is required to serve notice of its intentions (a "section 6 notice"), and both parties must maintain the *status quo* until the bargaining processes have been exhausted. The Supreme Court has described those processes as "almost interminable." Once the process is exhausted without reaching agreement, the parties are released from their *status quo* obligations, and can resort to "self-help"-management may implement its proposed changes and the unions may strike.

In a minor dispute, however, the parties are not precluded from changing the *status quo*; management is free to implement its interpretation of the agreement and a union cannot make a minor dispute the subject of a strike. The changes made by management remain in effect unless declared invalid by the National Railroad Adjustment Board.

B. THE SHUTTLE SALE IS JUSTIFIED BY PAST AGREEMENTS AND PRACTICES

Whether the sale of the Shuttle is classified as a major or minor dispute depends on whether it involves "the acquisition of rights for the future," *Elgin*, or is "arguably comprehended within an already existing collective bargaining agreement." As our Circuit and other circuit courts have held, they look to the parties' settled past practices to determine whether disputed actions fall within a bargaining agreement.

1.   *The Shuttle Sale is Contemplated by Past Agreements*

Eastern's collective bargaining agreement with Local 553 of the TWU clearly contemplates that Eastern may cut back or relocate its flight attendants. Obviously, one reason Eastern would implement such changes would be to reduce the number of flights or alter its schedule. The reason for the work reduction, whether the abandonment of a hub or the sale of an asset, is immaterial. As our Circuit held:

> [T]he [TWU-Eastern] contract's language is quite broad and evidences an awareness that work reductions might be necessary in the future; it does not specify what forces might cause such reductions.

As stated previously, the agreements between Eastern and ALPA and IAM have expired and the parties have exchanged section 6 notices. Our Circuit Court's recent decision refused to recognize the expiration of the agreements and the filing of section 6 notices as a major dispute. Rather, it looked to provisions in expired contracts as evidence of settled past practice.

The Eastern-ALPA collective bargaining agreement contemplates domicile closures, flight reductions, pilot displacements, and furloughs. Similarly, the Eastern-IAM agreement contains provisions dealing with reductions in force, employee furloughs, and transfers. These provisions not only "indicate that furloughs were contemplated by the parties," but also show that the unions recognized that their employees would be affected by domicile closings and flight reductions. It makes no difference that pilots, mechanics, and ground service personnel were laid off or relocated because planes were sold or because schedules were trimmed back. The collective bargaining agreements themselves serve as evidence of actual working conditions and practices. Because the sale of an asset, such as the Shuttle, is "arguably" within the labor contracts, the dispute may not be characterized as major.

2.   *The Shuttle Sale is Consistent with Past Practices*

As discussed in this Court's findings, Eastern has a well-established history of selling airplanes and cutting back its flight operations. These past practices and working conditions may become part of a collective bargaining agreement even if the agreement is silent regarding the causes of work reductions and furloughs. While the agreements between Eastern and the unions fail to specify the procedures to be followed when assets are sold, the Supreme Court has recognized that it would be "virtually impossible to include all working conditions in a collective-bargaining agreement."

Courts must determine whether actions similar to a present disputed action had "occurred for a sufficient period of time with the knowledge and acquiescence of the employees to become in reality a part of the actual working conditions." The court is limited to determining whether the action is supported by past practice-it does not decide whether such action is prudent for the carrier's future:

> If [the carrier] presented instances of past practice accepted by the unions which, arguably, could support its contention, the court's inquiry must end; it is not for it to weigh, and decide who has the better of the argument. If the court did this, it overstepped its bounds and usurped the arbitrator's function.

Our Circuit Court recently held that Eastern's past practices included the continued exercise of management rights to discontinue service, sell assets, and reassign or furlough employees. Prior to the Circuit's determination, this Court also found in its August 30, 1988 Memorandum Opinion that Eastern's practices of schedule changes, hub closures and asset sales were part of the actual, objective working conditions and practices followed by the airline. In that August 30, 1988 Memorandum Opinion, this Court held that Eastern's proposed September schedule changes were similar to past actions taken by the airline and concluded that "Eastern should be permitted to implement such changes without first bargaining with plaintiffs."

In reviewing Eastern's record, the Court is reminded that "[p]ast practice is . . . not part of the total contract, unless it was accepted." Eastern has engaged in numerous sales or lease-outs of the same type of assets to be conveyed in the Shuttle sale. In addition, Eastern has frequently changed the size and scope of its operations, reassigned employees, and otherwise engaged in a wide range and variety of changes relating to personnel, facilities and services. Those decisions were not preceded by bargaining with plaintiff unions concerning the decisions or their effects, except as was provided in Eastern's pre-existing labor contracts.

Plaintiff unions have repeatedly tried to distinguish the facts of the Shuttle sale from previous sales or changes in service. They argue that the Shuttle provides unique employment opportunities and working conditions and that the transfer to Trump of a separate operating division is unprecedented. The Court is not persuaded by plaintiffs' attempt to differentiate the Trump deal from other business decisions of Eastern. Employment opportunities have been changed in the past; working conditions have frequently changed, arising from hub closures or discontinuance of service. Bumping and bidding rights have been frequently exercised by Eastern's employees, schedules have varied and the airlines' employees have adjusted and adapted. The unions have failed to identify any legal cognizable difference between the Shuttle sale and Eastern's repeated closures of principal hubs, elimination of discrete operating units, and sales of assets.

This Circuit has stated that "if the shuttle sale is analogous to the closing of a hub, the abandonment of a route or the sale of assets, then a question may be raised whether, under the parties' established bargaining tradition, the proposed action is subject to bargaining." After carefully examining Eastern's past practices, the Court holds that the proposed Shuttle sale is similar to prior actions in which the unions acquiesced; therefore, it falls within their bargaining agreements.

Not a Major Dispute

Since Eastern has no obligation to bargain with the plaintiff unions over its decision to sell the Shuttle, the proposed action does not create a major dispute. The collective bargaining provisions of the RLA do not prevent consummation of the Shuttle transaction. *See Japan Air Lines Co. v. IAM*, 538 F.2d 46 (2d Cir. 1976) (no duty to bargain over decision to continue practice of subcontracting); *IAM v. Northeast Airlines, Inc.*, 473 F.2d 549 (1st Cir. 1973) (no duty to bargain over decision to merge); *ALPA v. Transamerica Airlines, Inc.*, 123 L.R.R.M (BNA) 2682 (E.D.N.Y. 1986) (no obligation to bargain over decision to shut down airline and lease 12 aircraft to another carrier). The Supreme Court has consistently held that fundamental management decisions concerning the scope and direction of an employer's business fall outside the area of mandatory bargaining subjects.

The unions argue that Eastern must bargain over the effects of the proposed Shuttle sale before the airline can close the deal. The Court disagrees. First, Eastern's actions are "arguably comprehended" on the terms of its agreements with the plaintiffs; therefore, any dispute with respect to the impacts of the Shuttle sale upon employees must be considered minor. When this Court in its August 30, 1988 ruling instructed Eastern to "comply with the intricate RLA bargaining process" before it could furlough 4,000 employees in September 1988, this Circuit reversed, finding that the pre-existing provisions of Eastern's collective bargaining agreements contemplated work reductions even though they did not specify what forces might cause such reductions.

Secondly, while the Third Circuit in *Railway Labor Executive Ass'n v. Pittsburgh & Lake Erie R.R.*, 845 F.2d 420 (3d Cir. 1988) held that a carrier must bargain over the effects of its business decisions before implementing any changes, this Circuit and others have disagreed. As our Circuit recently held, the agreements and the course of dealing contemplated the effects of such proposals. In *ALPA v. Transamerica Airlines, Inc.*, where the issue of effects bargaining was not even litigated, the Ninth Circuit recognized as a general principle that effects bargaining could continue after the carrier ceased operations. In *Northeast Airlines*, the First Circuit stated that "[w]here it is clear, as in the case of a merger, that bargaining about some effects of the decision would be ineffective unless the company could be required to renegotiate the merger, we believe that the duty to bargain about those effects does not arise at all."

In *Pittsburgh & Lake Erie R.R.*, the Third Circuit affirmed the district court's *status quo* injunction, enjoining the sale of the entire business only "to the extent that such sale does not include provisions for the maintenance of the *status quo* . . ." In contrast to the present case, that court enjoined the sale because there was no past practice and the preexisting labor agreement did not provide for the effects of the transaction.

Finally, the Supreme Court made it absolutely clear that a company need not secure the agreement of its unions or exhaust bargaining before it carries out a decision to close its business. The company's only obligation is to offer "meaningful bargaining at a meaningful time" over the effects of the decision. From the outset, Eastern has offered to bargain over its decision to sell the Shuttle to Donald Trump. When it announced the Trump deal, an Eastern executive wrote that the airline was "prepared to bargain about the effects of such decisions, as it has in the past, and to entertain any proposals the IAM might present on this subject." Eastern has never bargained over possible effects to its unions prior to closing a sale of assets or terminating flights. However, it has engaged in effects bargaining after the transactions and new schedules have been completed. These post-transaction negotiations have been "meaningful" as required by the Supreme Court. For example, Eastern initiated bargaining about the effects of the September 1988 schedule change, offering union members a new early-out option with pass privileges. Eastern reached agreement with the TWU on September 1, 1988, and the IAM on October 3, 1988, on extended leave programs to limit the employee impact of the downsizing.

3. *The Shuttle Sale is a Minor Dispute*

Eastern has met its "relatively light" burden of demonstrating that the Shuttle sale is a minor dispute. Eastern's position cannot be said to constitute the type of clear departure from its past practices necessary to trigger a finding of a major dispute under the RLA format.

Our Circuit's recent ruling holds true in this case:

Given the express contractual terms and the similarity between the proposed [action by Eastern] and previous ones, the record compels a finding that Eastern's proposal [is] covered by the collective bargaining agreement and the course of dealing between the company and [its unions]. This [proposed action] is a minor dispute for purposes of resolution through the RLA, and the district court lack[s] jurisdiction to enjoin Eastern's [proposed action].

ALPA v. Eastern, 863 F.2d 891 (D.C. Cir. 1988). The precedent clearly dictates that in a circumstance such as the present, this Court must deem the matter a minor dispute.

C. THE SHUTTLE SALE DOES NOT UNLAWFULLY INTERFERE WITH THE UNIONS

Plaintiffs contend that the sale of the Shuttle violates Sections 2 Third and Fourth of the RLA because it undermines the representative status of ALPA, IAM and Local 553 of TWU. They also claim that the sale is unlawful because its purpose is to discourage union activity at Eastern's remaining operations. Eastern counters that the unions have not shown that the airline's decision to sell the Shuttle was motivated by a desire to interfere with the unions. Eastern also contends that under the "mixed motive" *Wright Line* there is no labor law violation because Eastern has shown a compelling business need for selling the Shuttle.

Under the *Wright Line* test, *NLRB v. WrightLine*, 662 F.2d 899 (1st Cir. 1981), plaintiff must make a *prima facie* showing sufficient to support the inference that the employer's anti-union bias was a "motivating factor." Once this is established, the burden shifts to the employer to demonstrate that it would have taken the same action even in the absence of union animus. This Circuit recently held in *ALPA v. Eastern*, that attacks on Eastern's flight reductions and employee furloughs as manifesting animus, are subject to analysis under *Wright Line*:

We are persuaded that the Wright Line principle is applicable here . . . Application of the Wright Line principle will provide full protection for the union activity protected by § 2 Third and Fourth and will avoid creating perverse incentives in either management or labor.

1. *New Evidence of Anti-Union Bias is Lacking*

Plaintiff unions cannot show a likelihood of success on their claim that Eastern's decision to sell the Shuttle was motivated by anti-union animus. In *ALPA v. Eastern*, our Court of Appeals recently ruled that the record provided little support for any finding that "forbidden purposes" controlled Eastern's decision. Because plaintiffs have failed to present new facts of union animus, the record has not changed since these parties were before this Court in August 1988. They have failed to make out a *prima facie* case in support of their allegations. They cannot satisfy their burden merely by proffering evidence of generalized anti-union bias. The unions have the burden of establishing a causal connection between the employer's hostility and the challenged action. Evidence of that causal connection is missing here.

It is not enough that the decision to sell the Shuttle may have an adverse impact on the unions. There must be a specific motive to chill unionism. The "CHUNKS" memorandum relied upon to prove that the decision to sell the Shuttle was part of a grand anti-union scheme was rejected by our Court of Appeals as evidence of labor law violations. The Circuit characterized the memorandum as evidence that management wanted to exert "economic pressure," which would not constitute unlawful interference with union rights. In view of these circumstances, this Court concludes that plaintiffs have not met their burden of proving unlawful motivation to pressure the unions.

2. *Eastern Has Shown a Financial Necessity to Sell Shuttle*

Even if there is some evidence that the Shuttle sale was motivated in part by a desire to undermine the unions' representative status, Eastern has met its burden by showing that it would have arranged to sell the Shuttle in the absence of union hostility. More than ten years ago, the Supreme Court held that once the plaintiff carried his burden of persuasion, the burden shifted to the employer to show by a preponderance of evidence that he would have reached the same decision even if, hypothetically, he had not been motivated by a desire to punish the plaintiff for exercising his rights. Since then the Court has applied this allocation of burdens of proof to labor law situations where anti-union sentiment was involved. In *NLRB v. Transportation Management Corp.*, 462 U.S. 393 (1983), the Supreme Court held that an employer need only prove that "absent the improper motivation he would have acted in the same manner for wholly legitimate reasons."

As set forth in this Court's factual findings, there is credible testimony relating to Eastern's serious financial problems and desperate need for a cash infusion. Eastern's officials and several industry experts, claim that the airline needs several hundreds of million dollars in cash to stay in business. Because compelling business reasons exist for Eastern's sale of the Shuttle, this Court finds that regardless of anti-union bias, the Trump deal "would have occurred in any event and for valid reasons."

D. THE SHUTTLE SALE IS NOT A SALE OF "SUBSTANTIALLY ALL" OF EASTERN'S ASSETS AND DOES NOT VIOLATE IAM'S STOCK RIGHTS

The IAM claims that its members, as owners of certain preferred stock issued by Eastern under the 1984 Wage Investment Program ("WIP"), are entitled to vote on Eastern's decision to sell the Shuttle. Recognizing that the preferred stock requires a shareholder vote only on a sale of "all or substantially all" of Eastern's assets, the IAM contends that because the Shuttle is Eastern's only profitable operation, its sale amounts to the liquidation of the airline.

The IAM and the other unions have failed to show that the sale of the Shuttle constitutes a sale of "all or substantially all" of Eastern's assets. As the Court wrote in its findings, the Shuttle constitutes only 2.9% of Eastern's total assets at net book value (approximately 7.0% at fair market value), only 1.5% of Eastern's total operation, and only 4.3% of Eastern's total operating revenue. Clearly, the Shuttle cannot be considered "substantially all" of Eastern's assets.

Shareholder approval is not necessary in the ordinary course of business, nor is it usually mandatory in a major restructuring of a corporation. A leading case in this area explains that shareholder approval is not required "simply because an independent, important branch of a corporate business is sold." *Gimbel v. Signal Cos.*, 316 A.2d 599 (Del. Ch. 1974). The Delaware court did state, however, that:

> If the sale is of assets quantitatively vital to the operation of the corporation and is out of the ordinary and substantially affects the existence and purpose of the operations, then it is beyond the power of the Board of Directors.

At this point, plaintiffs have failed to show that the Shuttle sale will substantially affect Eastern's corporate existence or purpose. There was evidence that after the sale, Eastern will remain a major airline, employing approximately 30,000 people and utilizing over 220 aircraft. The IAM has not established that the Shuttle transaction violates any provision of the WIP.

E. THE SHUTTLE SALE SHOULD NOT BE ENJOINED

Under the law of this Circuit, this Court does not have subject matter jurisdiction to enter an injunction in a minor dispute. The parties must attempt to negotiate their differences and if negotiations fail, the dispute must be submitted to an arbitration board for resolution. As our Circuit recently declared, "[T]he arbitration board's jurisdiction over minor disputes is exclusive; the courts do not have jurisdiction to issue *status quo* injunctions."

The First Circuit has repeatedly held that when disputes are classified as minor under the RLA, a district court does not have jurisdiction to enter *status quo* injunctions. That Circuit has pointed to the strong presumption that a minor dispute is the type of controversy mandated by Congress to be resolved outside the judicial system. The Supreme Court has addressed the policy against judicial involvement in labor disputes by way of injunctive relief: "An injunction does not settle a dispute-it simply disables one of the parties." Given this policy and the Circuit's recent decision, the Court finds itself without jurisdiction to issue equitable relief in this case.

III. CONCLUSION

Plaintiff unions have failed to meet their burden in this regard. They have failed to establish either by virtue of the facts or the law that they are likely to succeed on the merits. Further, the balance of equities weighs in favor of Eastern.

In issuing this opinion, the Court holds that the sale of the Shuttle to Donald Trump is a minor dispute under the Railway Labor Act. Under the law of this Circuit, the Court is deprived of the jurisdiction to enter a preliminary injunction. Accordingly, this conflict must be resolved through negotiation and arbitration. Hopefully, the management of Eastern will not see this decision as an invitation to undervalue the interests of its unions. In selling the airline's premier financial asset, Eastern management leaves itself a special obligation to provide a future for the company and its workers. If management is serious about rebuilding Eastern, now is a good time to start.

EXERCISE 10-3. *AIR LINE PILOTS ASS'N, INT'L V. EASTERN AIR LINES*—UNIONS

1. Describe the terms of the acquisition deal by Trump Shuttle of Eastern Airlines Shuttle, *e.g.,* value of the deal, number of airplanes, gate positions, etc.

2. What guarantees, if any, did the October 12, 1981 Memorandum Opinion offer to Eastern Shuttle employees?

3. What is "major" and "minor" dispute under the Railway Labor Act of 1926 and which dispute is at issue here?

4. Was the acquisition consistent with past agreements and practices of the airline, according to the court.

5. How does the court resolve the claim that the shuttle sale unlawfully interfered with union rights?

NOTES ON *AIR LINE PILOTS ASS'N, INT'L V. EASTERN AIR LINES*—MAJOR AND MINOR DISPUTES

Is an airline pilot required to clean and prepare and secure an airplane cabin before or after a flight? Can an airline unilaterally impose a comprehensive, mandatory drug testing program for its employees? While certain issues that arise between airline management and labor are answerable by reference to a controlling collective bargaining agreement, many aviation labor and employment disputes require judicial application of the Railway Labor Act, 45 U.S.C. § 151 *et seq.*

1. ***Major vs. Minor Disputes.***

As shown by *Hawaiian Airlines, Inc. v. Norris* (1994) and *Air Line Pilots Ass'n, Int'l v. Eastern Air Lines* (D.D.C. 1988), *supra*, courts are designed to play an extraordinarily limited role in aviation labor disputes in favor of extended rounds of alternative dispute resolution. Indeed, the forum for resolution depends upon the characterization of the dispute. The United States Supreme Court has differentiated "minor" and "major" disputes:

> [A] major dispute relates to disputes over formation of collective agreements or efforts to secure them. They arise when there is no such agreement or where it is sought to change the terms of one.

> [A] minor dispute contemplates the existence of a collective agreement already concluded or, at any rate, a situation in which no effort is made to bring about a formal change in terms or to create a new one. The dispute relates either to the meaning or proper allocation of a particular provision with reference to a specific situation or to an omitted case.

Elgin J & E. Ry. Co. v. Burley, 325 U.S. 711 (1945). Stated another way, " '[m]ajor and 'minor' disputes do not necessarily refer to important and unimportant disputes, or significant and insignificant issues; rather, the terms refer to the bargaining context in which a dispute arises." *Int'l Brotherhood of Teamsters, Chauffeurs, Warehousemen & Helpers of America-Airline Division and Teamsters Local 19 v. Southwest Airlines Co.*, 875 F.2d 1129 (5th Cir. 1989).

2. ***Resolving Major Disputes Under the RLA.***

The process for resolving "major disputes" follows statutorily-staged events:

1. Written notice of proposed changes in agreements affecting rates of pay, rules or working conditions ("Section 6 notices") must be given at least 30 days in advance.

2. Within ten days after receipt of the Section 6 notice, the parties shall agree to the time and place for the beginning of conferences;

3.   The parties engage in direct negotiations in connection with the Section 6 notices;

4.   If, during the course of direct negotiations, an agreement is reached, the parties are obliged to execute that agreement;

5.   If no agreement is reached in direct negotiations and an "impasse" is reached, either party may request mediation by the National Mediation Board within ten days of termination of conferences (Section 5, First).

6.   If mediation is invoked, the [National Mediation Board] is required to promptly put itself in communication with the parties and use its best efforts, by mediation, to bring them to agreement.

7.   Whenever the Mediation Board concludes that an amicable settlement through mediation is not available, it proffers binding arbitration to the parties to resolve their disputes.

8.   If arbitration is refused by one or both parties, the Board is required "at once" to notify both parties in writing that its mediation efforts have failed (the issuance of a "release") and advise the parties that for a period of 30 days thereafter, except in certain limited circumstances, the *status quo* must be maintained (the 30-day "cooling off period").

9.   During the 30-day cooling off period, the President may, in his discretion, establish an Emergency Board to investigate and report regarding the dispute, and while the Emergency Board is in existence and for 30 days after its report to the President is issued, the parties are required to maintain the *status quo*.

10.   At the end of the cooling off period, if no Emergency Board is established, the parties are free to engage in economic action to attempt to resolve the dispute. Congress may legislate a resolution of the dispute, which legislation is presumptively valid and constitutional. If such legislation includes binding arbitration of the dispute, normal standards of judicial review of the award will apply.

Roger H. Briton & Christopher Valentino, *Airline Collective Bargaining under the Railway Labor Act: The Management Perspective*, SR035 ALI-ABA 353 (2010).

3.   *Duty to Represent.*

Unions have a duty to represent fairly all employees subject to a collective bargaining agreement. This putatively clear directive creates dispute on occasion, however, particularly when carriers merge and their company seniority lists are merged into a single list. *See, e.g., Addington v. U.S. Airlines Pilots Ass'n* (9th Cir. 2010) (evaluating when a duty of fair representation claim based on a union's representation becomes ripe). *See also Air Line Pilots Ass'n, Int'l v. O'Neill* (1991) (clarifying the standard that governs a claim that a union has breached its duty of fair representation in its negotiation of a back-to-work agreement terminating a strike, holding that (i) the rule that a union breaches its duty of fair representation if its actions are either "arbitrary, discriminatory, or in bad faith" applies to all union activity, including contract negotiation, and (ii) a union's actions are arbitrary only if, in light of the factual and legal landscape at the time of the union's actions, the union's behavior is so far outside a "wide range of reasonableness" as to be irrational).

Outsourcing, like consolidation of carriers, presents opportunities and challenges for contemporary airline management. Many major airlines feed their hub operations with passengers transported by partner or subsidiary regional carriers from mid- to small-sized markets, *e.g.*, American Airlines though American Eagle, which generally operates aircraft of 50 seats or fewer. As part of their collective bargaining agreement, airmen value "scope clauses," which limit how much flying the major carrier can outsource to the regional carriers. *See* Andrew Compart, *The Scope of Hope*, AVIATION WK. & SPACE TECH., May 24, 2010, at 46. *See also Air Line Pilots Ass'n v. Guilford Transp. Industries, Inc.* (1st Cir. 2005).

4.   *Amendment to Railway Labor Act?*

On May 11, 2010, the National Mediation Board formally announced its intention to amend the Railway Labor Act, 45 U.S.C. §§ 151 *et seq.*, to change the way unions are elected at airlines and rail lines. The Final Rule, making it easier for unions to win representation elections, states:

> As part of its ongoing efforts to further the statutory goals of the Railway Labor Act, the National Mediation Board (NMB or Board) is amending its Railway Labor Act rules to provide that, in representation disputes, a majority of valid ballots cast will determine the craft or class representative. This change to its election procedures will provide a more reliable measure/indicator of employee sentiment in representation disputes and provide employees with clear choices in representation matters.

75 Fed. Reg. 26,062 (May 11, 2010). On May 17, 2010, the Air Transport Association of America ("ATA"), the trade organization for major airlines, brought suit in the United District Court for the District of Columbia, seeking to prevent changes to a 75-year-old rule that a union would be certified as the collective bargaining representative only if a majority of the total eligible employees in a relevant work group (*e.g.*, "class" or "craft") voted in favor of union representation—not just the votes cast. *Air Transport Ass'n of America, Inc. v. National Mediation Bd.*, Case No. 10–CV–804 (PLF). *See generally* Jennifer Michels, *Precedent-Setting Case*, AVIATION WK. & SPACE TECH., May 24, 2010, at 43 (ruling in favor of National Mediation Board).

Suggested Further Reading

JOSEPH A. MCCARTIN, COLLISION COURSE (OXFORD UNIVERSITY PRESS 2011)

Katherine Van Wezel Stone, *Labor Relations on the Airlines: The Railway Labor Act in the Era of Deregulation*, 47 STAN. L. REV. 1485 (1990)

Neil Fox, *PATCO and the Courts: Public Sector Labor Law as Ideology*, 1985 U. ILL. L. REV. 245 (1985)

Bernard D. Meltzer & Cass R. Sunstein, *Public Employee Strikes, Executive Discretion, and the Air Traffic Controllers*, 50 U. CHI. L. REV. 731 (1983)

CHAPTER 11

Airports

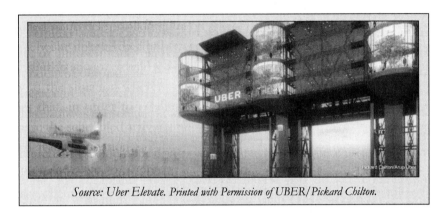

Source: Uber Elevate. Printed with Permission of UBER/Pickard Chilton.

A. OVERVIEW

Airports are extraordinary places. They are dynamic environments unto themselves and often major economic engines of the communities in which they are situated. As the materials in this chapter show, integrating an airport within the world around it presents significant legal challenges. For that matter, a new type of airport—a "skyport" or "vertiport"—may be on the horizon as companies like Uber are planning to launch fleets of small, electric VTOL (vertical takeoff and landing) aircraft for aerial ride-sharing. (*See* illustration above.) In this context, the legal antecedents applicable to airports will be important as new and emerging technologies test local, state, national, and international development and operation of new types of transportation nodes. *See generally Urban Air Mobility Adds a New Dimension to Travel*, MITRE, July 2018, https://www.mitre.org/publications/project-stories/urban-air-mobility-adds-a-new-dimension-to-travel.

Like the issues relating to airspace (Chapter 2), airports challenge lawmakers to balance traditional property rights with the unique operational issues airports present. In the 1920s-era case *Dysart v. City of St. Louis*, 11 S.W. 2d 1045 (Mo. 1928), for example, a Missouri taxpayer attempted to enjoin the development of a publicly-funded airport on the basis that the concept of an airport ran counter to the general or public welfare:

> It will afford a starting and landing place for a few wealthy, ultra-reckless persons, who own planes and who are engaged in private pleasure flying. They may pay somewhat for the privilege.

> It will afford a starting and landing place for pleasure tourists from other cities, alighting in St. Louis while flitting here and yon. It will offer a passenger station for the very few persons who are able to afford, and who desire to experience, the thrill of a novel and expensive mode of luxurious transportation.

> The number of persons using the airport will be about equal to the total number of persons who engage in big-game hunting, trips to the African wilderness, and voyages of North Pole exploration. * * *

> In the very nature of things, the vast majority of the inhabitants of the city, a 99 per cent. majority, cannot now and never can, reap any benefit from the existence of an airport. True it may be permitted to the ordinary common garden variety of citizen to enter the airport free of charge, so that he may press his face against some restricting barrier, and sunburn his throat gazing at his more fortunate compatriots as they sportingly navigate the empyrean blue. But beyond that, beyond the right to hungrily look on, the ordinary citizen gets no benefit from the taxes he is forced to pay.

The Supreme Court of Missouri rejected this view, recognizing that, by 1928, "[it was] unquestionably true that the airplane [was] not in general use as a means of travel or transportation, either in the city of St. Louis or elsewhere; [but] *it never will be unless properly equipped landing fields are established.*"

In *Hesse v. Rath*, 164 N.E. 342 (N.Y. App. 1928), also decided in 1928, Judge Benjamin N. Cardozo, then a New York appellate judge, similarly embraced the era of modern aviation, recognizing that "[a]viation today is an established method of transportation." In doing so, the eventual U.S. Supreme Court Justice cautioned against shortsighted urban planners and politicians:

> The city that is without the foresight to build the ports for the new traffic may soon be left behind in the race of competition. Chalcedon was called the city of the blind, because its founders rejected the nobler site of Byzantium lying at their feet. The need for vision of the future in the governance of cities has not lessened with the years. The dweller within

the gates, even more than the stranger from afar, will pay the price of blindness.

Legislatures around the nation embraced this message as courts recognized airport development as a valid municipal purpose. For example, the Florida Legislature enacted Ch. 13569, General Acts of 1929, authorizing municipal corporations to purchase (including by way of a right of condemnation), establish, construct, and operate airports and landing fields. Courts upheld such laws on constitutional grounds, including in *State v. Dade County*, 27 So. 2d 283 (Fla. 1946), in which the Supreme Court of Florida stated:

> [T]his Court knows that air transportation is one of the great innovations of the age, that Miami is potentially one of the greatest air distribution points in the World, and that Florida is the port of entry for air transportation from South and Central America, the West Indies, and Africa.
>
> It is quite true that there were no Jules Verns or Wright Brothers in the Constitutional Convention to portend the marvelous changes the future had in store, but it was not intended by those present that the dead hand of the past should shape the destiny of the future. Constitutional mandates are wise in proportion to the manner in which they respond to the public welfare and should be construed to effectuate that purpose when possible. The law does not look with favor on social or progressive stalemates ... [and] extension of political controls should keep pace with physical changes, and collective ingenuity should not be hobbled by the Constitution in a way to be outclassed by collective design to overreach and serve a selfish purpose.

Between the time of these court decisions and the end of World War II, private, public, and commercial aviation was becoming routine, so much so that state courts, again such as the Supreme Court of Florida in the decision of *Brooks v. Patterson*, 31 So. 2d 472 (Fla. 1946), rejected claims sounding in nuisance and trespass in connection with airplane operations:

> The City should be mindful at all times of the admonition which comes to us from the days of the Roman Empire, '*sicutere tuo ut alienum non laedas*'—so use your own property as not to injure another's.
>
> That aviation is as much a part of modern civilization is as the railroad, steamship and automobile as a means of transportation of both freight and passengers is too obvious for serious discussion.

In the foregoing context, the decisions and materials in this chapter introduce the complex airport ecosystem. Some practitioners consider airport law to be a subject matter that stands apart from aviation law. Indeed, key areas of airport law span a wide range of issues, including airport governance and control such as financing, funding and taxation (*see Griggs v. County of Allegheny* from Chapter 2); zoning and airside obligations (*e.g.,* road, runway, and taxi-way construction); tenant rights, including food and beverage concessions and parking fees; and airport and community improvement. Environmental concerns are also at play, including safety and noise pollution and abatement (*see City of Burbank v. Lockheed Air Terminal, Inc.* and *Goodspeed Airport, LLC v. East Haddam Inland Wetlands and Watercourses Comm'n*). Issues of constitutional magnitude, such as the right of assembly and speech under the First Amendment, also arise from the operation of airports (*see Int'l Soc. for Krishna Consciousness, Inc. v. Lee*).

B. THE AIRPORT ENVIRONMENT

INT'L SOC. FOR KRISHNA CONSCIOUSNESS, INC. V. LEE

505 U.S. 672 (1992)

CHIEF JUSTICE REHNQUIST delivered the opinion of the Court.

In this case we consider whether an airport terminal operated by a public authority is a public forum and whether a regulation prohibiting solicitation in the interior of an airport terminal violates the First Amendment.

The relevant facts in this case are not in dispute. Petitioner International Society for Krishna Consciousness, Inc. ("ISKCON"), is a not-for-profit religious corporation whose members perform a ritual known as *sankirtan*. The ritual consists of " 'going into public places, disseminating religious literature and soliciting funds to support the religion.' " The primary purpose of this ritual is raising funds for the movement.

Respondent Walter Lee, now deceased, was the police superintendent of the Port Authority of New York and New Jersey and was charged with enforcing the regulation at issue. The Port Authority owns and operates three major airports in the greater New York City area: John F. Kennedy International Airport ("Kennedy"), La Guardia Airport ("La Guardia"), and Newark International Airport ("Newark"). The three airports collectively form one of the world's busiest metropolitan airport complexes. They serve approximately 8% of this country's domestic airline market and more than 50% of the trans-Atlantic market. By decade's end they are expected to serve at least 110 million passengers annually.

The airports are funded by user fees and operated to make a regulated profit. Most space at the three airports is leased to commercial airlines, which bear primary responsibility for the leasehold. The Port Authority retains control over unleased portions, including La Guardia's Central Terminal Building, portions of Kennedy's International Arrivals Building, and Newark's North Terminal Building (we refer to these areas collectively as the "terminals"). The terminals are generally accessible to the general public and contain various commercial establishments such as restaurants, snack stands, bars, newsstands, and stores of various types. Virtually all who visit the terminals do so for purposes related to air travel. These visitors principally include passengers, those meeting or seeing off passengers, flight crews, and terminal employees.

User Fees

The Port Authority has adopted a regulation forbidding within the terminals the repetitive solicitation of money or distribution of literature. The regulation states:

> The following conduct is prohibited within the interior areas of buildings or structures at an air terminal if conducted by a person to or with passers-by in a continuous or repetitive manner: (a) the sale or distribution of any merchandise, including but not limited to jewelry, food stuffs, candles, flowers, badges and clothing; (b) the sale or distribution of flyers, brochures, pamphlets, books or any other printed or written material; (c) the solicitation and receipt of funds.

The regulation governs only the terminals; the Port Authority permits solicitation and distribution on the sidewalks outside the terminal buildings. The regulation effectively prohibits ISKCON from performing *sankirtan* in the terminals. As a result, ISKCON brought suit seeking declaratory and injunctive relief under 42 U.S.C. § 1983, alleging that the regulation worked to deprive its members of rights guaranteed under the First Amendment.

The suit was filed in 1975. ISKCON originally sought access to both the airline controlled areas and to the terminals and as a result sued both respondent and various private airlines. The regulation at issue was not formally promulgated until 1988 although it represents a codification of presuit policy. Respondent concedes that sankirtan may be performed on the sidewalks outside the terminals.

* * *

_"Forum Based"
Approach to
Speech
Restriction_

It is uncontested that the solicitation at issue in this case is a form of speech protected under the First Amendment. But it is also well settled that the government need not permit all forms of speech on property that it owns and controls. Where the government is acting as a proprietor, managing its internal operations, rather than acting as lawmaker with the power to regulate or license, its action will not be subjected to the heightened review to which its actions as a lawmaker may be subject.

The parties disagree whether the airport terminals here are public _fora_ or nonpublic _fora_. They also disagree whether the regulation survives the "reasonableness" review governing nonpublic _fora_, should that prove the appropriate category. We conclude that the terminals are nonpublic _fora_ and that the regulation reasonably limits solicitation.

Reflecting the general growth of the air travel industry, airport terminals have only recently achieved their contemporary size and character. _See_ H. HUBBARD, M. MCCLINTOCK, & F. WILLIAMS, AIRPORTS: THEIR LOCATION, ADMINISTRATION AND LEGAL BASIS 8 (1930) (noting that the United States had only 807 airports in 1930). But given the lateness with which the modern air terminal has made its appearance, it hardly qualifies for the description of having "immemorially . . . time out of mind" been held in the public trust and used for purposes of expressive activity.

_Speech in
Airport
Terminals,
Historically_

Moreover, even within the rather short history of air transport, it is only "[i]n recent years [that] it has become a common practice for various religious and non-profit organizations to use commercial airports as a forum for the distribution of literature, the solicitation of funds, the proselytizing of new members, and other similar activities." 45 Fed. Reg. 35,314 (1980). Thus, the tradition of airport activity does not demonstrate that airports have historically been made available for speech activity. Nor can we say that these particular terminals, or airport terminals generally, have been intentionally opened by their operators to such activity; the frequent and continuing litigation evidencing the operators' objections belies any such claim. In short, there can be no argument that society's time-tested judgment, expressed through acquiescence in a continuing practice, has resolved the issue in petitioners' favor.

_Airport as
Transport
Node?_

Petitioners attempt to circumvent the history and practice governing airport activity by pointing our attention to the variety of speech activity that they claim historically occurred at various "transportation nodes" such as rail stations, bus stations, wharves, and Ellis Island. Even if we were inclined to accept petitioner's historical account describing speech activity at these locations, an account respondent contests, we think that such evidence is of little import for two reasons.

First, much of the evidence is irrelevant to public *fora* analysis, because sites such as bus and rail terminals traditionally have had private ownership. *See United Transportation Union v. Long Island R. Co.*, 455 U.S. 678 (1982). The development of privately owned parks that ban speech activity would not change the public *fora* status of publicly held parks. But the reverse is also true. The practices of privately held transportation centers do not bear on the government's regulatory authority over a publicly owned airport.

Second, the relevant unit for our inquiry is an airport, not "transportation nodes" generally. When new methods of transportation develop, new methods for accommodating that transportation are also likely to be needed. And with each new step, it therefore will be a new inquiry whether the transportation necessities are compatible with various kinds of expressive activity. To make a category of "transportation nodes," therefore, would unjustifiably elide what may prove to be critical differences of which we should rightfully take account. The "security magnet," for example, is an airport commonplace that lacks a counterpart in bus terminals and train stations. And public access to air terminals is also not infrequently restricted—just last year the Federal Aviation Administration required airports for a 4-month period to limit access to areas normally publicly accessible. To blithely equate airports with other transportation centers, therefore, would be a mistake.

The differences among such facilities are unsurprising since airports are commercial establishments funded by users fees and designed to make a regulated profit, and where nearly all who visit do so for some travel related purpose. As commercial enterprises, airports must provide services attractive to the marketplace. In light of this, it cannot fairly be said that an airport terminal has as a principal purpose promoting "the free exchange of ideas." To the contrary, the record demonstrates that Port Authority management considers the purpose of the terminals to be the facilitation of passenger air travel, not the promotion of expression. Even if we look beyond the intent of the Port Authority to the manner in which the terminals have been operated, the terminals have never been dedicated (except under the threat of court order) to expression in the form sought to be exercised here: *i.e.*, the solicitation of contributions and the distribution of literature.

The terminals here are far from atypical. Airport builders and managers focus their efforts on providing terminals that will contribute to efficient air travel. *See, e.g.*, R. Horonjeff & F. McKelvey, Planning and Design of Airports 326 (3d ed. 1983) ("The terminal is used to process passengers and baggage for the interface with aircraft and the ground transportation modes."). The Federal Government is in accord; the Secretary of Transportation has been directed to publish a plan for airport development necessary "to anticipate and meet the needs of civil aeronautics, to meet requirements in support of the national defense . . . and to meet identified needs of the Postal Service." 49 U.S.C. § 2203(a)(1); *see also* 45 Fed. Reg. 35,317 (1980) ("The purpose for which the [Dulles and National airport] terminal[s] [were] built and maintained is to process and serve air travelers efficiently").

Although many airports have expanded their function beyond merely contributing to efficient air travel, few have included among their purposes the designation of a forum for solicitation and distribution activities. Thus, we think that neither by tradition nor purpose can the terminals be described as satisfying the standards we have previously set out for identifying a public forum. The restrictions here challenged, therefore, need only satisfy a requirement of reasonableness.

Although many airports have expanded their function beyond merely contributing to efficient air travel, few have included among their purposes the designation of a forum for solicitation and distribution activities. Thus, we think that neither by tradition nor purpose can the terminals be described as satisfying the standards we have previously set out for identifying a public forum. The restrictions here challenged, therefore, need only satisfy a requirement of reasonableness. We reiterate that the restriction " 'need only be reasonable; it need not be the most reasonable or the only reasonable limitation.' " We have no doubt that under this standard the prohibition on solicitation passes muster.

Standard of Review: Reasonableness

We have on many prior occasions noted the disruptive effect that solicitation may have on business. "Solicitation requires action by those who would respond: The individual solicited must decide whether or not to contribute (which itself might involve reading the solicitor's literature or hearing his pitch), and then, having decided to do so, reach for a wallet, search it for money, write a check, or produce a credit card." Passengers who wish to avoid the solicitor may have to alter their paths, slowing both themselves and those around them. The result is that the normal flow of traffic is impeded. This is especially so in an airport, where "[a]ir travelers, who are often weighted down by cumbersome baggage . . . may be hurrying to catch a plane or to arrange ground transportation." Delays may be particularly costly in this setting, as a flight missed by only a few minutes can result in hours' worth of subsequent inconvenience.

In addition, face-to-face solicitation presents risks of duress that are an appropriate target of regulation. The skillful, and unprincipled, solicitor can target the most vulnerable, including those accompanying children or those suffering physical impairment and who cannot easily avoid the solicitation. The unsavory solicitor can also commit fraud through concealment of his affiliation or through deliberate efforts to shortchange those who agree to purchase. Compounding this problem is the fact that, in an airport, the targets of such activity frequently are on tight schedules. This in turn makes such visitors unlikely to stop and formally complain to airport authorities. As a result, the airport faces considerable difficulty in achieving its legitimate interest in monitoring solicitation activity to assure that travelers are not interfered with unduly.

The Port Authority has concluded that its interest in monitoring the activities can best be accomplished by limiting solicitation and distribution to the sidewalk areas outside the terminals. This sidewalk area is frequented by an overwhelming percentage of airport users [no more than 3% of air travelers passing through the terminals are doing so on intraterminal flights, *i.e.*, transferring planes]. Thus the resulting access of those who would solicit the general public is quite complete. In turn we think it would be odd to conclude that the Port Authority's terminal regulation is unreasonable despite the Port Authority having otherwise assured access to an area universally traveled.

The inconveniences to passengers and the burdens on Port Authority officials flowing from solicitation activity may seem small, but viewed against the fact that "pedestrian congestion is one of the greatest problems facing the three terminals," the Port Authority could reasonably worry that even such incremental effects would prove quite disruptive. The congestion problem is not unique to these airports. Moreover, "[t]he justification for the Rule should not be measured by the disorder that would result from granting an exemption solely to ISKCON." For if ISKCON is given access, so too must other groups. "Obviously, there would be a much larger threat to the State's interest in crowd control if all other religious, nonreligious, and noncommercial organizations could likewise move freely. As a result, we conclude that the solicitation ban is reasonable [and] for the foregoing reasons, the judgment of the Court of Appeals sustaining the ban on solicitation in Port Authority terminals is affirmed.

———————

EXERCISE 11-1. *INT'L SOC. FOR KRISHNA CONSCIOUSNESS, INC. V. LEE*—AIRPORT TERMINALS AND THE FIRST AMENDMENT

1. What is the function and scope of operations of the Port Authority of New York and New Jersey?

2. How many people and how many operations are served by the airports at the subject of the litigation?

3. Explain in your own words what the regulation at issue is designed to do, where it applies, and how it was applied in this case?

4. What is the "traditional public forum" doctrine? Does it apply here?

5. Identify the specific drawbacks the court equates with face-to-face solicitation inside the airport terminal? Is this persuasive?

NOTES ON *INT'L SOC. FOR KRISHNA CONSCIOUSNESS, INC. V. LEE*—AIRPORT LAW

1. ***At the Epicenter of Political Controversy.***

Protestors descended on airports across the country in 2017, giving rare insight into the ways in which airports are (and are not) equipped to manage such events. For example, protests occurred at Denver International Airport ("DIA") in an interior area of Jeppesen Terminal colloquially known as the "Great Hall." The protests were in response to President Donald Trump's Executive Order 13769 ("Protecting the Nation from Foreign Terrorist Entry into the United States") which, *inter alia*, temporarily suspended entry into the United States of nationals from seven predominantly Muslim countries. With respect to such protests, the Denver Revised Municipal Code provides:

> DIA requires any person or organization intent on engaging in speech-related activity at DIA for religious, charitable, or political purposes to first obtain a permit "at least seven (7) days prior to the commencement of the activity for which the permit is sought." The protestors were allowed to continue without a permit, but they were eventually moved from the Great Hall to an outdoor plaza. They later sued, challenging the permitting process DIA had in place pursuant to the Denver Revised Municipal Code, which states:

>> The manager of aviation shall have the power and authority, and is hereby empowered and authorized, upon the basis of passenger flow or where necessitated by the peculiar character of Denver Municipal Airport System as an airport, to adopt rules and regulations pertaining

to the exercise of First Amendment rights, including by way of
example, but not by way of limitation, solicitation of contributions for
charitable or religious purposes and the dissemination of printed
material upon Denver Municipal Airport System. Such rules and
regulations shall establish reasonable time, place and manner
guidelines for the exercise of such First Amendment rights.

See also Denver Revised Mun. Code § 50.01 (regulating "all leafleting, display of signs,
signature gathering, solicitations of funds and other speech related activity conducted
at Denver International Airport for religious, charitable, or political purposes, or in
connection with labor disputes."). *See McDonnell v. City and County of Denver*, 878 F.3d
1247 (10th Cir. 2018).

2. ***Extending Non Public Fora Analysis Beyond Airport Terminals.***

Legislators and judges have extended the non-public forum doctrine expressed
in *Int'l Soc. for Krishna Consciousness, Inc. v. Lee, supra*, beyond airport terminals to include
areas outside the terminals.

*Airspace Is Not a Public Fora. Center for Bio-Ethical Reform, Inc. v. City and Cty. Of
Honolulu*, 455 F.3d 910 (9th Cir. 2006) involved a challenge to an ordinance that
prohibited aerial tow-banners over the beaches of Honolulu. Honolulu's aerial
advertising ordinance was part of a long-standing scheme aimed at regulating outdoor
advertising in order to protect the critical visual landscape that has made the area
famous. A pro-life advocacy group that intended to fly 100-foot-long banners that dis
ed graphic photographs of aborted fetuses sued to prevent enforcement of the
ordinance. The ordinance was upheld as viewpoint neutral and reasonable and non-
violative of any constitutional right. Moreover, the court noted that airspace does not
fit the public forum category:

> [L]ike the airport terminal, highway overpass fences, and the interstate rest
> stops, the use of the airspace for banner towing is a relatively modern
> creation that "hardly qualifies for the description of having 'immemorially
> . . . time out of mind' been held in the public trust and used for purposes
> of expressive activity." In fact, one would be hard pressed to find another
> forum that has had its access as historically restricted as U.S. airspace. The
> FAA has strict regulations governing the airspace and for more than
> twenty-five years Honolulu has regulated aerial advertising. In light of the
> numerous restrictions placed on the use of the airspace in and around
> Honolulu, its principal purpose can hardly be characterized as "promoting
> 'the free exchange of ideas.' "

The physical characteristics of the airspace also underscore that it is not a
public forum. The airspace is not, as the Center argues, an extension of the

fora below, namely the beaches. We do not express any opinion as to whether the beaches are public fora because the record is not developed on this point and this categorization is not necessary to our analysis. But even assuming that the beaches are public fora, the airspace above is not a public forum by extension.

For other examples of the extension of the non-public forum status to other areas of an airport see *Wickersham v. City of Columbia*, 371 F. Supp. 2d 1061 (W.D. Mo. 2005) (air show was not a public forum); *Air Line Pilots Ass'n Int'l v. Dep't of Aviation of the City of Chicago*, 45 F.3d 1144 (7th Cir. 1995) (diorama display cases at Chicago's O'Hare International Airport may be a public fora such that refusal to display an advertisement by Air Line Pilots Association critical of United Airlines was unconstitutional.)

Advertising Prohibited in Outer Space. Federal law (51 U.S.C. § 50911 ("Space Advertising")) prohibits the launch of a payload that contains any material to be used for purposes of "obtrusive space advertising," i.e., "advertising in outer space that is capable of being recognized by a human being on the surface of the Earth without the aid of a telescope or other technological device." 51 U.S.C. § 50902(12).

3. *Categories of Airports.*

Whether an airport terminal was a public forum was uncertain until *Int'l Soc. for Krishna Consciousness, Inc. v. Lee, supra,* but the legal definition of "airport" is definite—albeit nuanced. An airport is defined in the law as any area of land or water used or intended for landing or takeoff of aircraft including appurtenant area used or intended for airport buildings, facilities, as well as rights of way together with the buildings and facilities. *See* 14 C.F.R. § 1.1. Special types of facilities such as seaplane bases and heliports are included in the airport categories.

Altogether, the law categorizes airports by type of activities, including commercial service, primary, cargo service, reliever, and general aviation airports, as follows:

- **Commercial Service Airports** are publicly owned airports that have at least 2,500 passenger boardings each calendar year and receive scheduled passenger service. Passenger boardings refer to revenue passenger boardings on an aircraft in service in air commerce whether or not in scheduled service. The definition also includes passengers who continue on an aircraft in international flight that stops at an airport in any of the 50 States for a non-traffic purpose, such as refueling or aircraft maintenance rather than passenger activity. Passenger boardings at airports that receive scheduled passenger service are also referred to as Enplanements.

- **Nonprimary Commercial Service Airports** are Commercial Service Airports that have at least 2,500 and no more than 10,000 passenger boardings each year.

- **Primary Airports** are Commercial Service Airports that have more than 10,000 passenger boardings each year. Hub categories for Primary Airports are defined as a percentage of total passenger boardings within the United States in the most current calendar year ending before the start of the current fiscal year. For example, calendar year 2014 data are used for fiscal year 2016 since the fiscal year began 9 months after the end of that calendar year. The table above depicts the formulae used for the definition of airport categories based on statutory provisions cited within the table, including Hub Type described in 49 U.S.C. § 47102.

- **Cargo Service Airports** are airports that, in addition to any other air transportation services that may be available, are served by aircraft providing air transportation of only cargo with a total annual landed weight of more than 100 million pounds. "Landed weight" means the weight of aircraft transporting only cargo in intrastate, interstate, and foreign air transportation. An airport may be both a commercial service and a cargo service airport.

- **Reliever Airports** are airports designated by the FAA to relieve congestion at Commercial Service Airports and to provide improved general aviation access to the overall community. These may be publicly or privately-owned.

- **General Aviation** Airports are public-use airports that do not have scheduled service or have less than 2,500 annual passenger boardings (49 U.S.C. § 47102(8)). Approximately 88 percent of airports included in the NPIAS are general aviation.

See Fed. Aviation Admin., Airport Categories, https://www.faa.gov/airports/ planning_capacity/passenger_allcargo_stats/categories/.

4. *Airport Advocacy.*

While cases like *Int'l Soc. for Krishna Consciousness, Inc. v. Lee, supra,* focus on the expression of constitutional and legal rights at airports, a number of organizations and entities exist for the purpose of advocating *for* airports themselves. Examples include:

Airports Council International-North America ("ACI-NA"). The Airports Council International-North America (ACI-NA) represents local, regional and state governing bodies that own and operate commercial airports in the United States and Canada. Approximately 380 aviation-related businesses are also members of ACI-NA, providing goods and services to airports. ACI-NA's members enplane more than 95 percent of the domestic and virtually all the international airline passenger and cargo traffic in North America. The mission of ACI-NA is to advocate policies and provide services that strengthen the ability of commercial airports to serve their passengers, customers and communities. ACI-NA is one of the five worldwide regions of Airports Council International (ACI). https://www.aci-na.org/content/who-we-are.

American Association of Airport Executives, Inc. ("AAAE"). Founded in 1928, AAAE is the world's largest professional organization for airport executives, representing thousands of airport management personnel at public-use commercial and general aviation airports. AAAE's members represent nearly 875 airports and authorities, in addition to hundreds of companies and organizations that support airports. AAAE serves its membership through results-oriented representation in Washington, D.C. and delivers a wide range of industry services and professional development opportunities including training, meetings and conferences, and a highly respected accreditation program. *See* https://www.aaae.org/aaae/AAAEMBR/About/AAAEMemberResponsive/About_AAAE/About_AAAE.aspx?hkey=17fa23bc-bfe6-4589-9c8b-c362c1e7c303.

Florida Airports Council ("FAC"). FAC is an association of publicly-owned and operated airports, airport professionals, and experts in the fields of airport design, development, and improvement, as well as aviation trades that support the airport industry in Florida. FAC provides up-to-date information to its members about key issues affecting Florida's airports through bi-weekly newsletters, presentations, publications, specialty conferences and on this web-page. FAC has relationships with each legislator in the state, as well as Florida's congressional delegation. FAC's annual conference is the largest and most successful statewide airport event in the country with more than 700 industry professionals in attendance and outstanding world-renowned speakers. *See* http://www.floridaairports.org/.

The FAA also has its own staff dedicated to airport and environmental law issues (see https://www.faa.gov/about/office_org/headquarters_offices/agc/practice_areas/airports_environmental_law/).

The Airports and Environmental Law practice provides legal advice on all airport matters and on environmental matters for all lines of business. Its environmental law practice area supports: environment and energy; airport environment program; air traffic organization environmental program; commercial space transportation environmental program; and the national parks air tour management program. The FAA also review environmental impact statements and other environmental documents for airport development projects and projects proposed to enhance safety and/or efficiency in the national airspace system. Moreover, the FAA maintains relationships with state and local governments on environmental concerns.

The FAA's airports law practice area supports the following programs: airport improvement program ("AIP"); passenger facility charge ("PFC") program; airport compliance program; airport safety program; and airport engineering and design program

The FAA also appears in administrative proceedings concerning airport grant assurance compliance and it provides legal support to the Airport Civil Rights Programs (Title VI of the Civil Rights Act of 1964, Americans with Disabilities Act, Limited English Proficiency, Environmental Justice, and Disadvantaged Business Enterprise).

Finally, the Airports and Environmental Law practice area works closely with the U.S. Department of Justice to represent the FAA in federal court litigation concerning airport and environmental matters. It also supports rulemaking on airport and environmental law matters and provide legal support for airport noise compatibility planning and the national program for review of airport noise and access restrictions under the Airport Noise and Capacity Act of 1990.

5. *Ground Transportation: Ridesharing and Transportation Network Providers ("TNPs")*

In addition to managing traditional constitutional and legal issues such as those discussed in *Int'l Soc. for Krishna Consciousness, Inc. v. Lee, supra,* airport owners, users, and managers increasingly are confronted with the regulatory challenges presented by ridesharing services such as Uber and Lyft. Federal law does not address the various issues presented by these new methods of ground transportation to and from airports, including revenue collection, safety, service, and congestion. As such, several states and localities have adopted restrictions to regulate these entities. Colorado legislated the first such law—the "Transportation Network Company Act." Colo. Rev. Stat. §§ 40–10.1–601–608 (2014). *See also Illinois Transp. Trade Ass'n v. City of Chicago,* 839 F.3d 594 (7th Cir. 2016); Katrina M. Wyman, *Taxi Regulation in the Age of Uber,* 20 N.Y.U. J. Legis. & Pub. Pol'y 1 (2017).

CITY OF BURBANK V. LOCKHEED AIR TERMINAL, INC.

411 U.S. 624 (1973)

MR. JUSTICE DOUGLAS delivered the opinion of the Court.

This suit brought by appellees asked for an injunction against the enforcement of an ordinance adopted by the City Council of Burbank, California, which made it unlawful for a so-called pure jet aircraft to take off from the Hollywood-Burbank Airport between 11 p.m. of one day and 7 a.m. the next day, and making it unlawful for the operator of that airport to allow any such aircraft to take off from that airport during such periods. The only regularly scheduled flight affected by the ordinance was an intrastate flight of Pacific Southwest Airlines originating in Oakland, California, and departing from Hollywood-Burbank Airport for San Diego every Sunday night at 11:30.

The District Court found the ordinance to be unconstitutional on both Supremacy Clause and Commerce Clause grounds. The Court of Appeals affirmed on the grounds of the Supremacy Clause both as respects pre-emption and as respects conflict. We affirm the Court of Appeals.

The Federal Aviation Act of 1958, 49 U.S.C. § 1301 et seq., as amended by the Noise Control Act of 1972, 86 Stat. 1234, and the regulations under it, 14 C.F.R. pts. 71, 73, 75, 77, 91, 93, 95, 97, are central to the question of pre-emption.

Fed. Aviation Act of 1958

Section 1108(a) of the Federal Aviation Act, 49 U.S.C. § 1508(a), provides in part, "The United States of America is declared to possess and exercise complete and exclusive national sovereignty in the airspace of the United States . . ." The Administrator of the Federal Aviation Administration ("FAA") has been given broad authority to regulate the use of the navigable airspace, "in order to insure the safety of aircraft and the efficient utilization of such airspace . . ." and "for the protection of persons and property on the ground."

Problems with Nationwide Curfew

The Solicitor General, though arguing against pre-emption, concedes that as respects "airspace management" there is pre-emption. That, however, is a fatal concession, for as the District Court found: "The imposition of curfew ordinances on a nationwide basis would result in a bunching of flights in those hours immediately preceding the curfew. This bunching of flights during these hours would have the twofold effect of increasing an already serious congestion problem and actually increasing, rather than relieving, the noise problem by increasing flights in the period of greatest annoyance to surrounding communities. Such a result is totally inconsistent with the objectives of the federal statutory and regulatory scheme." It also found "(t)he imposition of curfew ordinances on a nationwide basis would cause a serious loss of efficiency in the use of the navigable airspace."

Curfews such as Burbank has imposed would, according to the testimony at the trial and the District Court's findings, increase congestion, cause a loss of efficiency, and aggravate the noise problem. FAA has occasionally enforced curfews. But the record shows that FAA has consistently opposed curfews, unless managed by it, in the interests of its management of the "navigable airspace."

As stated by Judge Dooling in *American Airlines v. Hempstead*, D.C., 272 F. Supp. 226, 230 (E.D.N.Y 1967):

> The aircraft and its noise are indivisible; the noise of the aircraft extends outward from it with the same inseparability as its wings and tail assembly; to exclude the aircraft noise from the Town is to exclude the aircraft; to set a ground level decibel limit for the aircraft is directly to exclude it from the lower air that it cannot use without exceeding the decibel limit.

The Noise Control Act of 1972, which was approved October 27, 1972, provides that the Administrator "after consultation with appropriate Federal, State, and local agencies and interested persons" shall conduct a study of various facets of the aircraft noise problems and report to the Congress within nine months." The 1972 Act, by amending § 611 of the Federal Aviation Act, also involves the Environmental Protection Agency ("EPA") in the comprehensive scheme of federal control of the aircraft noise problem.

There is, to be sure, no express provision of pre-emption in the 1972 Act. That, however, is not decisive. As we stated in *Rice v. Santa Fe Elevator Corp.*, 331 U.S. 218, 230 (1947):

> Congress legislated here in a field which the States have traditionally occupied . . . So we start with the assumption that the historic police powers of the States were not to be superseded by the Federal Act unless that was the clear and manifest purpose of Congress . . . Such a purpose may be evidenced in several ways. The scheme of federal regulation may be so pervasive as to make reasonable the inference that Congress left no room for the States to supplement it . . . Or the Act of Congress may touch a field in which the federal interest is so dominant that the federal system will be assumed to preclude enforcement of state laws on the same subject . . . Likewise, the object sought to be obtained by the federal law and the character of obligations imposed by it may reveal the

same purpose . . . Or the state policy may produce a result inconsistent with the objective of the federal statute.

It is the pervasive nature of the scheme of federal regulation of aircraft noise that leads us to conclude that there is pre-emption. As Mr. Justice Jackson stated, concurring in *Northwest Airlines, Inc. v. Minnesota*, 322 U.S. 292, 303(1944):

> Federal control is intensive and exclusive. Planes do not wander about in the sky like vagrant clouds. They move only by federal permission, subject to federal inspection, in the hands of federally certified personnel and under an intricate system of federal commands. The moment a ship taxis onto a runway it is caught up in an elaborate and detailed system of controls.

When the President signed the bill he stated that "many of the most significant sources of noise move in interstate commerce and can be effectively regulated only at the federal level." Our prior cases on pre-emption are not precise guidelines in the present controversy, for each case turns on the peculiarities and special features of the federal regulatory scheme in question.

State Police Powers

Control of noise is of course deep-seated in the police power of the States. Yet the pervasive control vested in EPA and in FAA under the 1972 Act seems to us to leave no room for local curfews or other local controls. What the ultimate remedy may be for aircraft noise which plagues many communities and tens of thousands of people is not known. The procedures under the 1972 Act are under way. In addition, the Administrator has imposed a variety of regulations relating to takeoff and landing procedures and runway preferences.

The Federal Aviation Act requires a delicate balance between safety and efficiency and the protection of persons on the ground. Any regulations adopted by the Administrator to control noise pollution must be consistent with the "highest degree of safety." The interdependence of these factors requires a uniform and exclusive system of federal regulation if the congressional objectives underlying the Federal Aviation Act are to be fulfilled.

The Federal Aviation Act requires a delicate balance between safety and efficiency, 49 U.S.C. § 1348(a), and the protection of persons on the ground. 49 U.S.C § 1348(c). Any regulations adopted by the Administrator to control noise pollution must be consistent with the "highest degree of safety." 49 U.S.C. § 1431(d)(3). The interdependence of these factors requires a uniform and exclusive system of federal regulation if the congressional objectives underlying the Federal Aviation Act are to be fulfilled.

Slippery Slope

If we were to uphold the Burbank ordinance and a significant number of municipalities followed suit, it is obvious that fractionalized control of the timing of takeoffs and landings would severely limit the flexibility of FAA in controlling air traffic flow. The difficulties of scheduling flights to avoid congestion and the concomitant decrease in safety would be compounded. In 1960 FAA rejected a proposed restriction on jet operations at the Los Angeles airport between 10 p.m. and 7 a.m. because such restrictions could "create critically serious problems to all air transportation patterns." 25 Fed. Reg. 1764. The complete FAA statement said:

> The proposed restriction on the use of the airport by jet aircraft between the hours of 10 p.m. and 7 a.m. under certain surface wind conditions has also been reevaluated and this provision has been omitted from the rule. The practice of prohibiting the use of various airports during certain specific hours could create critically serious problems to all air transportation patterns. The network of airports throughout the United States and the constant availability of these airports are essential to the maintenance of a sound air transportation system. The continuing growth of public acceptance of aviation as a major force in passenger transportation and the increasingly significant role of commercial aviation in the nation's economy are accomplishments which cannot be inhibited if the best interest of the public is to be served. It was concluded therefore that the extent of relief from the noise problem which this provision might have achieved would not have compensated the degree of restriction it would have imposed on domestic and foreign Air Commerce.

This decision, announced in 1960, remains peculiarly within the competence of FAA, supplemented now by the input of EPA. We are not at liberty to diffuse the powers given by Congress to FAA and EPA by letting the States or municipalities in on the planning. If that change is to be made, Congress alone must do it.

MR. JUSTICE REHNQUIST, *with whom* MR. JUSTICE STEWART, MR. JUSTICE WHITE, *and* MR. JUSTICE MARSHALL *join, dissenting.*

The Court concludes that congressional legislation dealing with aircraft noise has so "pervaded" that field that Congress has impliedly pre-empted it, and therefore the ordinance of the city of Burbank here challenged is invalid under the Supremacy Clause of the Constitution. The Court says that the 1972 "Act reaffirms and reinforces the conclusion that FAA, now in conjunction with EPA, has full control over aircraft noise, pre-empting state and local control."

Considering the language Congress enacted into law, the available legislative history, and the light shed by these on the congressional purpose, Congress did not intend either by the 1958 Act or the 1968 Amendment to oust local governments from the enactment of regulations such as that of the city of Burbank. The 1972 Act quite clearly intended to maintain the status quo between federal and local authorities. The legislative history of the 1972 Act, quite apart from its concern with avoiding additional pre-emption, discloses a primary focus on the alteration of procedures within the Federal Government for dealing with problems of aircraft noise already entrusted by Congress to federal competence. The 1972 Act set up procedures by which the Administrator of EPA would have a role to play in the formulation and review of standards promulgated by FAA dealing with noise emissions of jet aircraft. But because these agencies have exclusive authority to reduce noise by promulgating regulations and implementing standards directed at one or several of the causes of the level of noise, local governmental bodies are not thereby foreclosed from dealing with the noise problem by every other conceivable method.

A local governing body that owns and operates an airport is certainly not, by the Court's opinion, prohibited from permanently closing down its facilities. A local governing body could likewise use its traditional police power to prevent the establishment of a new airport or the expansion of an existing one within its territorial jurisdiction by declining to grant the necessary zoning for such a facility. Even though the local government's decision in each case were motivated entirely because of the noise associated with airports, I do not read the Court's opinion as indicating that such action would be prohibited by the Supremacy Clause merely because the Federal Government has undertaken the responsibility for some aspects of aircraft noise control. Yet if this may be done, the Court's opinion surely does not satisfactorily explain why a local governing body may not enact a far less "intrusive" ordinance such as that of the city of Burbank.

The history of congressional action in this field demonstrates, I believe, an affirmative congressional intent to allow local regulation. But even if it did not go that far, that history surely does not reflect 'the clear and manifest purpose of Congress' to prohibit the exercise of 'the historic police powers of the States' which our decisions require before a conclusion of implied preemption is reached. Clearly Congress could pre-empt the field to local regulation if it chose, and very likely the authority conferred on the Administrator of FAA by 49 U.S.C. § 1431 is sufficient to authorize him to promulgate regulations effectively pre-empting local action. But neither Congress nor the Administrator has chosen to go that route. Until one of them does, the ordinance of the city of Burbank is a valid exercise of its police power.

EXERCISE 11-2. *CITY OF BURBANK V. LOCKHEED AIR TERMINAL, INC.*—LOCAL AIRPORT CONTROL AND MANAGEMENT

1. Explain what was outlawed by the ordinance adopted by the City Council of Burbank, California. Did the district court determine the law to be constitutional or unconstitutional—on what ground?

2. What findings did the district court make about the "imposition of curfew ordinances on a nationwide basis"?

3. How does the court reconcile the potential conflict between state police powers respecting noise (which the court describes as "deep-seated") and the provisions of the Federal Aviation Act, which "requires a delicate balance between safety and efficiency."? In other words, does state law preempt federal law (or vice-versa) and why?

4. The dissenting opinion posits that the laws at issue intended to maintain the "status quo between federal and local authorities." What evidence supports this argument? Is it persuasive?

5. The dissenting opinion acknowledges that the FAA and EPA "have exclusive authority to reduce noise by promulgating regulations and implementing standards at one or several of the causes of the level of noise," but that "local government bodies are not . . . foreclosed from dealing with the noise problem by every other conceivable method." Explain.

NOTES ON *CITY OF BURBANK V. LOCKHEED AIR TERMINAL, INC.*—NOISE REGULATION

1. *Aircraft and Airport Noise Control, Generally.*

The FAA has recognized and studied the issue of aircraft and airport noise for decades, noting:

> The FAA recognizes that aircraft noise issues can be highly technical and complex. We have developed a variety of programs aimed at increasing the understanding of noise impacts, identifying solutions to reduce those impacts, and educating the public on the issues and our ongoing efforts. The website Noise Quest was specifically developed to offer the public a source of information on aviation and airport noise. This resource provides access to educational material as well as updated content, new publications

on noise projects and research, and informational videos and audio. It also features an interactive mapping application, NQ Explorer, which allows the user to search for a specific airport and find the related airport website links as well as view the latest airport noise contours, if available. Results of our research can be found on our Environment and Energy Research and Development web page.

The FAA [further] pursues a program of aircraft noise control in cooperation with the aviation community. Noise control measures include noise reduction at the source, i.e., development and adoption of quieter aircraft, soundproofing and buyouts of buildings near airports, operational flight control measures, and land use planning strategies.

The FAA's primary mission is to ensure the safety and efficiency of our nation's navigable airspace. The agency does not have the authority to prohibit aircraft overflights of a particular geographic area unless the operation is unsafe, or the aircraft is operated in a manner inconsistent with Federal Aviation Regulations. In order to handle high air traffic demands, runway configurations are used in accordance with runway selection criteria. Air Traffic's runway selection is based on several factors which include the following: runway availability, wind, weather, operational efficiency, and noise considerations.

See Fed. Aviation Admin., Aircraft Noise Issues, https://www.faa.gov/about/office_org/headquarters_offices/apl/noise_emissions/airport_aircraft_noise_issues/. See also Fed. Aviation Admin., Noise Mitigation, https://www.faa.gov/about/office_org/headquarters_offices/apl/research/science_integrated_modeling/noise_mitigation/.

2. ***Regulating Noise: FAA Noise Levels, Stages, and Prohibitions.***

The FAA regulates aircraft noise through internationally set "standards" that are applied to an aircraft during the airworthiness certification. According to the FAA:

The standard requires that the aircraft meet or fall below designated noise levels. For civil jet aircraft, there are four stages identified, with Stage 1 being the loudest and Stage 4 being the quietest. For helicopters, two different stages exist, Stage 1 and Stage 2. As with civil jet aircraft, Stage 2 is quieter than Stage 1. In addition, the FAA is currently working to adopt the latest international standards for helicopters, which will be called Stage 3 and will be quieter than Stage 2.

The FAA has undertaken a phase out of older, noisier civil aircraft, resulting in some stages of aircraft no longer being in the fleet. Currently within the contiguous US, civil jet aircraft over 75,000 pounds maximum take-off weight must meet Stage 3 and Stage 4 to fly. In addition, aircraft at or under 75,000 pounds maximum take-off weight must meet Stage 2, 3, or 4 to operate within the U.S. In addition, by December 31, 2015, all civil jet aircraft, regardless of weight must meet Stage 3 or Stage 4 to fly within the contiguous U.S. Both Stage 1 and Stage 2 helicopters are allowed to fly within the U.S.

The FAA has further explained how it regulates aircraft noise, as follows: (*see* https://www.faa.gov/about/office_org/headquarters_offices/apl/noise_emissions/ airport_aircraft_noise_issues/levels/).

Details on FAA Noise Levels, Stages, and Phaseouts

Noise Levels

The U.S. noise standards are defined in the Code of Federal Regulations (CFR) Title 14 Part 36—Noise Standards: Aircraft Type and Airworthiness Certification (14 C.F.R. Part 36). The FAA publishes certificated noise levels in the advisory circular, Noise Levels for U.S. Certificated and Foreign Aircraft. This advisory circular provides noise level data for aircraft certificated under 14 C.F.R. Part 36 and categorizes aircraft into their appropriate "stages." Any aircraft that is certified for airworthiness in the U.S. needs to also comply with noise standard requirements to receive a noise certification. The purpose of the noise certification process is to ensure that the latest available safe and airworthy noise reduction technology is incorporated into aircraft design and enables the noise reductions offered by those technologies to be reflected in reductions of noise experienced by communities. As noise reduction technology matures, the FAA works with the international community to determine if a new stringent noise standard is needed. If so, the international community through the International Civil Aviation Organization ("ICAO") embarks on a comprehensive analysis to determine what that new standard will be.

Noise Stages

The current FAA noise standards applicable to new type certifications of jet and large turboprop aircraft is Stage 4. It is equivalent to the ICAO Annex 16, Volume 1 Chapter 4 standards. Recently, the international community has established and approved a more stringent standard within the ICAO Annex 16, Volume 1 Chapter 14, which became effective July 14, 2014. The FAA is adopting this standard and promulgating the rule for Stage 5 that is anticipated to be effective for new type certificates after December 31, 2017 and December 31, 2020, depending on the weight of the aircraft. The Notice of Proposed Rule Making ("NPRM") for Stage 5 was published on January 14, 2016.

For helicopters, the FAA has noise standards for a Stage 3 helicopter that became effective on May 5, 2014. These more stringent standards apply to new type helicopters and are consistent with ICAO Annex 16, Volume 1 Chapter 8 and Chapter 11.

Prohibitions

The FAA Modernization and Reform Act of 2012, in Section 513, had a prohibition on operating certain aircraft weighing 75,000 pounds or less not complying with Stage 3 noise levels, and on July 2, 2013, the FAA published a Final Rule in the Federal Register for the Adoption of Statutory Prohibition the Operation of Jets Weighing 75,000 Pounds or Less That Are Not Stage 3 Noise Compliant. In 1990, Congress passed the Aviation Noise and Capacity Act, which required that by the year 2000 all jet and large turboprop aircraft at civilian airports be Stage 3.

3. ### Noise Compatibility Planning Program.

Part 150 of the Federal Aviation Regulations is the primary federal regulation guiding and controlling planning for aviation noise compatibility of an around airports. It was issued under the authority of the Aviation Safety and Noise Abatement Act of 1979. Notably, The FAA's Part 150 Airport Noise Compatibility Program ("ANCP") under 14 C.F.R. Pt. 150 is a voluntary program through which federally funded airports—called "sponsors"—to show what measures the airport operator has taken or proposes to take to reduce noncompatible land uses and for preventing the introduction of additional noncompatible uses.

Illustration 11-1. Comparative Noise Level

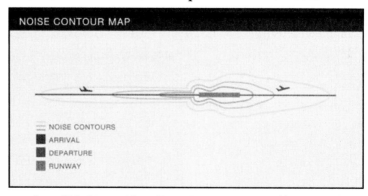

Source: Fed. Aviation Admin., FAA History of Noise, https://www.faa.gov/ regulations_policies/policy_guidance/noise/history/.

Noise Exposure Maps—or "NEMs"—are an important part of the ANCP. As the FAA has explained:

> [NEMs] are designed to identify clearly an airport's present and future noise patterns and the land uses that are not compatible with those noise patterns. When received and found in compliance with applicable rules and regulations, an airport's NEM serves as a standard reference to the airport's existing and future noise impacts for anyone propose noise sensitive development in the vicinity of the airport.
>
> An NEM consists of two maps of the airport with noise contours plotted over land uses, plus supporting documentation. The noise contours for the DNL 65, 70, and 75 noise levels are shown on these maps. The first map indicates the current conditions and, in effect, identifies the airport's noise compatibility problems. The second map projects the noise contours which can reasonably be predicted five years in the future taking into account changes in land use and in airport operations, plus any improvement in compatibility from noise mitigation actions which may be planned for that five-year period. An NEM is prepared in consultation with airport users, the public, local governments, land use control agencies, and the FAA.

Fed. Aviation Admin., The FAR Part 150 Airport Noise Compatibility Planning Program, https://www.faa.gov/about/office_org/headquarters_offices/apl/noise_emissions/planning_toolkit/media/II.B.pdf.

John Wayne Airport in Orange County, California, claims to have "one of the most stringent aircraft access and noise monitoring programs in the United States and, perhaps, the world," as follows:

> Commercial Air Carrier operations at John Wayne Airport are regulated by the Phase 2 Commercial Airline Access Plan and Regulation ("Access Plan"). The Access Plan places restrictions on operational capacity, hours of operations, and noise levels at the County's ten (10) noise monitoring stations. General Aviation operations are permitted 24 hours daily subject to compliance with the daytime noise limits and the more restrictive curfew noise limits, as documented in the General Aviation Noise Ordinance (GANO).
>
> In order to monitor and enforce these restrictions, the Access and Noise Office utilizes a state-of the-art noise monitoring system that enables us to track each and every one of the approximate 248,000 air carrier and general aviation operations that occur each year at John Wayne Airport. The noise monitoring stations transmit noise events instantaneously to the Access and Noise Office, enabling the staff to have up-to-the-second data on aircraft

operations. The newest addition to our system is VOLANS, an aircraft flight tracking system which shows flights around John Wayne Airport.

In 2006, the County of Orange and the City of Newport Beach entered into a "Cooperative Agreement" to promote compatibility between operations at John Wayne Airport and land uses within and in proximity to the City.

Noise and Access staff responds to approximately 2,500 calls a year. The staff strives to provide outstanding customer service by listening and responding to noise complaints, concerns of the community, and requests for information. *See* John Wayne Airport Orange County, Access & Noise, https://www.ocair.com/aboutjwa/accessandnoise/default.

Illustration 11-2. Noise Compatibility Study: Chicago Midway International Airport

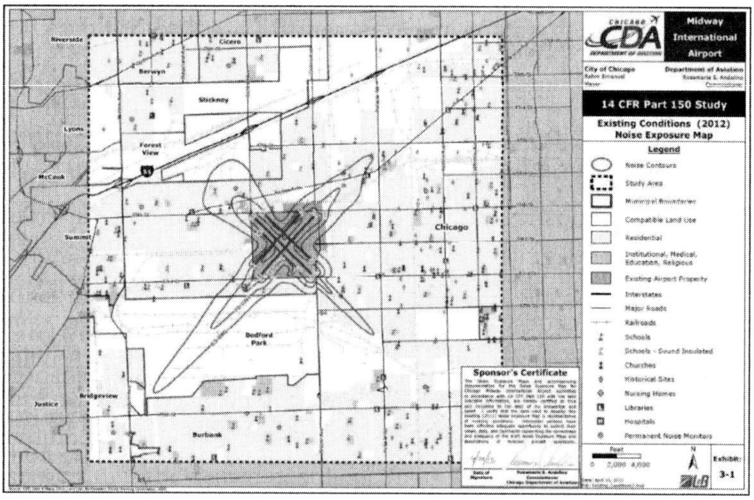

Source: Chicago Midway International Airport, FAR Part 150 Noise Compatibility Study Update (Draft), http://www.airportsites.net/env/mdw/downloads/Chapter3.pdf; See also Chicago Department of Aviation, Noise 101, https://www.flychicago.com/community/ORDnoise/Noise101/Pages/default.aspx.

FAA approval of flight paths is at the center of many lawsuits. See, e.g., Citizens Ass'n of Georgetown v. Fed. Aviation Admin., 896 F.3d 425 (D.C. Cir. 2018) (allegations that FAA failed to comply with environmental and historical preservation laws when assessing noise impacts of new routes).

4. *Reporting Aircraft Noise.*

According to the FAA, airport noise issues and concerns should first be addressed with the local airport manager or staff who respond to airport noise issues. Many airports also have noise abatement information and contact information published on their website.

The FAA has also noted that helicopters generally fly under visual flight rules ("VFR"), where they are not under the control of Air Traffic Control ("ATC"), resulting in ATC not controlling where the helicopter flies. Additionally, while some metropolitan areas have defined helicopter routes, many are voluntary and helicopter pilots can deviate from those routes. Thus, the FAA advises that helicopter operators should be contacted directly for information regarding noise-related complaints.

But, where contacting the local airport manager or helicopter operator is unproductive, the FAA offers the help of an FAA Aviation Noise Ombudsman, who serves as a liaison with the public on issues regarding aircraft noise. *See* Fed. Aviation Admin., *Who to Contact if You're Impacted by Aircraft Noise*, https://www.faa.gov/about/office_org/headquarters_offices/apl/noise_emissions/airport_aircraft_noise_issues/noise/.

Alternatively, people annoyed by the sound of airplanes flying over their homes have turned to litigation and digital solutions, including the "Airnoise Button," a software program that allows complainants to automatically file a noise-based complaint with the correct regional airport authority. *See* Katy McLaughlin, *Airplane Noise Complaints are Skyrocketing: "I Start Pushing that Button at 6:33 a.m.,"* WALL ST. J., Aug. 24, 2018; Katy McLaughlin, *Affluent—and Angry—Homeowners Raise Ruckus over Roar of Overhead Planes*, WALL ST. J., July 5, 2018.

GOODSPEED AIRPORT, LLC V. EAST HADDAM INLAND WETLANDS AND WATERCOURSES COMM'N

681 F. Supp. 2d 182 (D. Conn. 2010)

MARK R. KRAVITZ, DISTRICT JUDGE.

This case raises important questions regarding the extent to which Congress intended federal regulation of aviation safety to preempt generally applicable state and local environmental laws.

Plaintiff Goodspeed Airport, LLC, the owner and operator of Goodspeed Airport ("Goodspeed" or "Airport") in East Haddam, Connecticut, seeks a declaration that the Connecticut environmental laws—the Inland Wetlands and Watercourses Act ("Wetlands Act"), and the Connecticut Environmental Protection Act (the "CEPA")—are preempted by federal aviation law insofar as the state statutes require Goodspeed to obtain a permit before removing certain trees located at the Airport.

State License

Goodspeed claims that the trees are "obstructions to air navigation" under Federal Aviation Administration ("FAA") regulations, making them potential hazards to aeronautical safety that the Airport is obligated to remediate. However, because the trees are located in wetlands protected by the Wetlands Act and the CEPA, Goodspeed is required to obtain permission of the Town of East Haddam's Inland Wetlands and Watercourses Commission (the "Wetlands Commission") before trimming or removing the trees. If Goodspeed undertakes the trimming or removal of these trees without the required permit, the Airport could be subjected to civil liability and substantial fines under the Wetlands Act and the CEPA.

After considering evidence presented at a bench trial, and as explained below, the Court concludes that in the particular circumstances of this case, federal regulation of airport safety does not preempt state and local environmental laws in the manner in which Goodspeed asserts. The Court emphasizes that it does not take the Airport's safety concerns lightly, and it does not mean to suggest that the obstructing trees ought to be ignored—there do appear to be a number of trees that pose legitimate safety concerns. But if Goodspeed wishes to remove the trees that it believes are obstructions, it will need to seek a permit to do so from the Wetlands Commission, which may, consistent with state law, impose conditions designed to mitigate degradation of the wetlands.

FINDINGS OF FACT

Part 139 Airport, Scheduled Operations

Goodspeed Airport, located in East Haddam, Connecticut, is a small, privately-owned airport open for public use, as defined by 14 C.F.R. § 77.2. The Airport was established in 1964 and maintains a "utility runway," which is intended to accommodate propeller-driven aircraft weighing 12,500 pounds or less. Approaches to the Airport are governed solely by visual (as opposed to instrument) flight rules. The Airport does not provide regularly-scheduled passenger service and does not receive any federal funds or aid. As a consequence, the Airport does not have (and is not required to have) a certificate issued by the FAA under Part 139 of the Federal Aviation Regulations.

In fact, because Goodspeed does not serve scheduled air carrier operations, the FAA apparently does not have the statutory authority to directly license or certify Goodspeed Airport at all. *See* 49 U.S.C. § 44706(a)(2) (granting the FAA the authority to certificate airports serving scheduled air carrier operations using aircraft of at least 10 passenger seats, except in Alaska); *see also id.* § 44706(a)(3) ("Nothing in this title may be construed as requiring a person to obtain an airport operating certificate if such person does not desire to operate an airport [serving scheduled air carrier operations].").

Instead, Goodspeed Airport is licensed and regulated by the State of Connecticut. Within Connecticut, jurisdiction over and responsibility for airports have been entrusted to the Commissioner of the Department of Transportation ("Commissioner"). The Commissioner is given the authority to issue and renew airport licenses, which are effective for three years and to revoke licenses upon a determination that an airport "is not being maintained or used in accordance with" Connecticut's statutes and regulations regarding aviation.

The Connecticut General Assembly gave the Commissioner the authority to require landowners to remove obstacles that "constitute a hazard to aerial navigation or to the efficient or safe use of any airport." Conn. Gen. Stat. § 15–74(a). An "airport hazard" is defined as "any structure, object of natural growth or use of land which obstructs the air space required for the flight of aircraft in landing or taking off at any airport, heliport or restricted landing area or is otherwise hazardous to such landing or taking-off." *Id.* § 15–34(8). The Commissioner also may condition the approval of an airport license on the removal of an obstacle "at or near the landing area." *Id.* § 15–74(b). If such a condition is imposed, the applicant for the airport license is required to compensate the owner of the obstacle for its removal. *See id.* Goodspeed has not provided any evidence that the Commissioner has ever required Goodspeed or any nearby landowner to remove any obstacle or airport hazard.

The definitions and standards for determining what constitutes an "obstruction to air navigation" are found in Part 77 of the Federal Aviation Regulations ("FAR"), 14 C.F.R. Part 77. The FAA promulgated these regulations pursuant to a Congressional directive. The Part 77 regulations—which explicitly apply to "objects of natural growth," 14 C.F.R. §§ 77.5(a), 77.21—state in relevant part that an object is considered "an obstruction to air navigation" if it is of greater height than any one of several imaginary surfaces.

Obstructions in Air Navigation, Part 77

One of those imaginary surfaces is called the "primary surface." The length of the primary surface extends 200 feet beyond each end of the runway. For utility airports with only visual approaches such as Goodspeed, the primary surface is 250 feet wide, longitudinally centered on the center of the runway (that is, extending 125 feet on either side of the center line of the runway). Since the runway at Goodspeed is 50 feet wide, this means that the primary surface is 75 feet wider on each side of the paved portion of Goodspeed's runway.

Also relevant here are the "approach surface" and the "transitional surface." The "approach surface" is applied to each end of the primary surface, and for an airport such as Goodspeed, it is 1250 feet wide and extends for a horizontal distance of 5,000 feet at a slope of 20-to-1 (that is, 20 feet up for every 1 foot out). The "transitional surface" is shaped like a trapezoid; it flares upwards and outwards at right-angles from the edge of the primary surface to 1250 horizontal feet at a slope of 7-to-1. Together, the primary surface, approach surface, and the transitional surface create what is, in essence, a "bowl" of airspace, and any object—including a tree—that penetrates any of these imaginary surfaces is considered, by definition, an "obstruction to air navigation." *See id.* § 77.23(a)(5).

The parties have stipulated that certain of the trees at Goodspeed penetrate both the "primary surface" and the "transitional surface" such that they are "obstructions to air navigation" under Part 77. A review of the DOT inspections of Goodspeed over the past 30 years reveals that the Airport has long experienced substantial tree obstructions. However, Goodspeed is not unique in this regard, even within Connecticut; in fact, the vast majority of airports in the State have obstructions (mostly trees), which appear to be a chronic problem for all airports. *See Conn. Statewide Airport System Plan* (2006), (discussing obstructions at each of Connecticut's public-use airports).

Significantly, nothing in either Part 77 or its authorizing statute, 49 U.S.C. § 44718, grants the FAA the power to regulate how land is used insofar as structures that may penetrate navigable airspace are concerned. In other words, the FAA cannot require that a structure or object be altered or removed, even if it is an obstruction; instead, the regulations focus on studying potential hazards and giving notice to interested individuals.

The crux of this case turns in large part on the import of the determination that the trees at Goodspeed are "obstructions" under Part 77. Significantly, nothing in either Part 77 or its authorizing statute, 49 U.S.C. § 44718, grants the FAA the power to regulate how land is used insofar as structures that may penetrate navigable airspace are concerned. In other words, the FAA cannot require that a structure or object be altered or removed, even if it is an obstruction; instead, the regulations focus on studying potential hazards and giving notice to interested individuals. Thus, for example, Part 77 requires notice to be given to the FAA of any proposed structure that would be more than 200 feet above ground level at its site, see 14 C.F.R. § 77.13(a)(1), as well as any proposed construction or alteration that would be of greater height than an imaginary surface extending outward and upward from any public use airport's runway at certain slopes (depending on the length of the runway).

In the ordinary case, of course, an airport owner is generally free to remove or lower trees that are on airport property without an order from DOT. In this case, however, the parties have stipulated that the trees at Goodspeed Airport, including those that constitute Part 77 obstructions, are located within wetlands protected by the State of Connecticut through the Wetlands Act and the CEPA.

Under Conn. Gen. Stat. § 22a–42, the East Haddam Wetlands Commission is charged with administering the Wetlands Act within East Haddam. As a consequence, before undertaking any "regulated activity" within the wetlands— including removing trees and other vegetation—Goodspeed is required to obtain a permit from the East Haddam Wetlands Commission. The failure to secure a permit before undertaking regulated activity is punishable by a fine. Additionally, removing trees or other vegetation from protected wetlands can constitute "pollution" and/or "destruction" of the wetlands under the CEPA, which grants standing to a variety of individuals to bring claims for equitable relief against the responsible individual(s).

It is undisputed that no one affiliated with Goodspeed has applied to the Wetlands Commission for a permit to remove any trees or vegetation on Airport property. Therefore, it is not possible to speculate as to how the Wetlands Commission would treat such an application. However, testimony was introduced that the Wetlands Commission has granted permits to applicants wishing to cut or trim certain trees within protected wetlands in the past. Goodspeed has not produced any examples of the Wetlands Commission denying a permit request outright, and Mr. Ventres testified that, in his experience, the Wetlands Commission has never done so. That is to say, by its history, the Wetlands Commission does not have a flat prohibition on all trimming or cutting of trees in protected wetlands. In fact, the record suggests that the Wetlands Commission allowed Goodspeed to trim trees and vegetation in the protected wetlands on numerous occasions in the past, apparently without a permit and without consequence (at least until Goodspeed went beyond merely trimming).

Based on the record presented, the Court finds no evidence that the Wetlands Commission would prohibit all trimming or removal of the obstructing trees, although it may impose conditions on such activity to ameliorate damage to the protected wetlands. And, the results of all of the many inspections of Goodspeed after 1983 do not contain any suggestion whatsoever that the Airport's license is in danger of revocation, even while the trees have continued growing and have reduced the approach to the runway's southern end to a 7-to-1 ratio. Moreover, the DOT letters from 1977, 1978 and 1983 are all explicit that the primary threat to Goodspeed's license was the poor condition of its runway, and not any Part 77 obstructions.

To be sure, many of the more recent DOT Landing Area Inspection Reports recommend that Goodspeed continue to trim the surrounding vegetation—as it clearly had been doing, and which it could potentially resume with the permission of the Wetlands Commission—but none of the Inspection Reports suggests that the Airport's license is in any danger if it did not do so, even as the trees continued to encroach further and further into the imaginary surfaces established by Part 77. Finally, and not insignificantly, both Goodspeed's expert on airport safety and the pilot with presumably the most experience flying into and out of Goodspeed Airport testified that the Airport is not unsafe. Indeed, the pilot testified that he has every intention of continuing to base the operation of Action Airlines—the only "air carrier" currently operating out of Goodspeed—at the Airport into the foreseeable future.

On the basis of the evidence presented, the Court finds that the obstructing trees that Goodspeed wishes to lower or remove do not pose a present-day threat to its continued operation as an airport.

CONCLUSIONS OF LAW

Goodspeed has brought claims of field preemption and express preemption only. First, it argues that because the Wetlands Act and the CEPA regulate the removal of obstructions in navigable airspace, they are facially preempted by the Federal Aviation Act and the Part 77 regulations promulgated thereunder. Second, Goodspeed argues that the express preemption clause of the federal Airline Deregulation Act ("ADA") applies to invalidate the two state statutes because they have an impermissible effect on air carriers utilizing the airport. Goodspeed is not pursuing any claim of conflict preemption in this case, and therefore the Court expresses no view on that subject. However, as is explained below, the Court disagrees with Goodspeed, and holds that the neither the Wetlands Act nor the CEPA is either field preempted or expressly preempted.

A. Implied (Field) Preemption

Goodspeed's field preemption argument is based on the Federal Aviation Act, 49 U.S.C. § 40101 *et seq.*, and the FAA's regulations on obstructions, codified at 14 C.F.R. Part 77. The task of this Court, then, is two-fold: first, to determine whether Congress intended to occupy the entire field of aviation safety, as Goodspeed argues; and, if so, to determine whether the Wetlands Act and the CEPA are within the scope of the preempted field. As explained below, the Court answers the former question in the affirmative, but reaches the opposite conclusion with regard to the latter.

Courts have long distinguished between state laws that directly affect aeronautical safety, on the one hand, and facially neutral laws of general application that have merely an incidental impact on aviation safety.

The essence of Goodspeed's argument is that since the trees it wishes to remove penetrate "navigable airspace," over which the federal government has exclusive dominion, Connecticut is powerless to interfere in any way with whatever the Airport wishes to do to remove or lower the trees. The scope of Congress's preemption of state law does not necessarily sweep this broadly. Courts have long distinguished between state laws that directly affect aeronautical safety, on the one hand, and facially neutral laws of general application that have merely an incidental impact on aviation safety.

Logically, there must be a limit to the preemptive effect of federal law, even in an area, like aeronautical safety, where Congress has expressed an intention to occupy the "entire" field. Otherwise, a virtually unlimited number of state and local laws and regulations that might conceivably touch upon the operation of airports, even to a negligible degree, could be said to have some impact on aviation safety, assuming one is willing to retreat far enough up the chain of causation. As the Supreme Court has repeatedly emphasized, the limiting principle is the intent of Congress. Consideration of the issues raised by this case, and application of the presumption against finding federal preemption of state laws on health and safety, leads inexorably to the conclusion that neither the Wetlands Act nor the CEPA fall within the preemptive scope of federal law regulating aviation safety.

The state laws challenged by Goodspeed—environmental laws that make no reference whatsoever to aviation or aviation safety—are certainly deserving of the presumption against preemption. Neither statute expresses any intent to directly regulate airport operations or aeronautical safety. Instead, the Wetlands Act was passed to prevent a variety of deleterious effects brought about by the unregulated use of Connecticut's wetlands and watercourses—"an indispensable and irreplaceable but fragile natural resource with which the citizens of the state have been endowed"—that were occurring through the "deposition, filling or removal of material, the diversion or obstruction of water flow, the erection of structures and other uses, all of which have despoiled, polluted and eliminated wetlands and watercourses." Wetlands Act, Conn. Gen. Stat. § 22a–36 ("Legislative finding"). The CEPA evidences a complementary intent to protect the "public trust in the

Presumption Against Preemption

air, water and other natural resources of the state of Connecticut." CEPA, Conn. Gen. Stat. § 22a–15 ("Declaration of Policy").

Goodspeed has not argued, and nor could it, that Congress's intent in enacting the Federal Aviation Act was to preempt all state laws, such as these, whose express purpose are environmental protection. Rather, Goodspeed argues that, in this case, "[t]he relevant inquiry is whether the effect of the state law is such that it impacts the field of air safety and aircraft operations." The crux of Goodspeed's argument is that "state environmental laws that prohibit the removal of obstructions to air navigation, obstructions which are situated directly at the end of a runway, surely have an effect on air safety and aircraft operations, two areas solely within the province of the federal government," and are thereby preempted.

While Goodspeed is no doubt correct that, in the abstract, state laws that prohibit the removal of such obstructions would "have an effect on air safety and aircraft operations," Goodspeed's argument suffers a fatal flaw. The argument is misleadingly premised on "state environmental laws that prohibit the removal of obstructions to air navigation." But neither the Wetlands Act nor the CEPA contains such a prohibition. Rather, the Wetlands Act merely requires that Goodspeed obtain a permit before attempting to remove or trim the trees in question. The statute contains no outright prohibition on undertaking regulated activity and the East Haddam Wetlands Commission has never applied the law in that manner. Similarly, the CEPA simply prohibits the Airport from "unreasonabl[y] pollut[ing], impair[ing] or destr[oying]" the "air, water and other natural resources of the state." Thus, the "relevant inquiry" is not as Goodspeed presents it, but rather, whether state environmental laws that impose a permitting requirement on the removal of trees in protected wetlands and prohibit unreasonable environmental degradation are field preempted by federal law that is meant to ensure aviation safety. Presented appropriately, the answer to this question is certainly "no."

Intent of Congress

There is nothing in the text or legislative history of the Federal Aviation Act that even hints at the congressional intent that Goodspeed asserts can be found therein. For sure, Congress intended that safety be "the highest priority in air commerce." 49 U.S.C. § 40101(1). But accepting Goodspeed's field preemption argument would require the conclusion that Congress intended to completely eviscerate all attempts by states to protect their own environmental integrity whenever those attempts would have an indirect, incidental, or even speculative impact on the operations of an airport within its boundaries.

In this case, it would mean Congress intended to preempt state wetlands protections regardless of whether, for example, the protected trees pose an actual threat to air safety and/or the Airport's continued operation, and regardless of the impact Goodspeed's actions may have on the surrounding environment. There is absolutely no indication that this is what Congress intended when it passed the Federal Aviation Act—and nor would Congress have needed to intend such a dramatic alteration of the federal/state balance of power to effectuate its purpose in passing the Act.

Rather, it is much more consistent with the values inherent in our federal system for Congress to have intended for its regulation of aviation safety to preempt only those state laws that either (a) have the purpose or effect of directly regulating an aspect of air safety; or (b) are actually shown, on an as-applied basis, to impact the unified regulation of air safety. The Court has already explained that the state laws at issue here do not have the purpose of directly regulating any aspect of air safety, and Goodspeed has not shown that the permitting requirement of the Wetlands Act or the CEPA's prohibition on environmental degradation have that impermissible effect, either. Therefore, since Goodspeed has chosen not to bring an as-applied challenge, there is no basis for concluding that either state law is preempted.

The Court has already explained that the state laws at issue here do not have the purpose of directly regulating any aspect of air safety, and Goodspeed has not shown that the permitting requirement of the Wetlands Act or the CEPA's prohibition on environmental degradation have that impermissible effect, either. Therefore, since Goodspeed has chosen not to bring an as-applied challenge, there is no basis for concluding that either state law is preempted.

In this case, there is no federal or state mandate; no federal funding; and no federal or state approval for the lowering or removal of any of the obstructing trees at Goodspeed Airport. Instead, Goodspeed contends that even though the FAA has no authority to license the Airport or to order it to remove the trees, as soon as a tree at the Airport grows tall enough that it penetrates one of the imaginary surfaces established by the notice provisions of Part 77, that tree's growth preempts the Wetlands Act and the CEPA such that Goodspeed can—without any federal, state or local agency oversight or approval—cut the tree to the ground if it so chooses, and to do so in any manner that Goodspeed sees fit. There is no basis in law or in the evidence in this case to support such an assertion. Therefore, the Court holds that, at least in the particular circumstances of this case—which involves trees located in protected wetlands at Goodspeed

Airport—the Wetlands Act and the CEPA are not field preempted by federal law on air safety.

The Court also rejected Goodspeed's argument that the Wetlands Act and the CEPA are expressly preempted by the Airline Deregulation Act, at least insofar as they regulate the removal of trees that are "obstructions"

C.   Deference to the Federal Government

Prior to trial, and with the blessing and aid of the parties, the Court requested the views of the federal government on Goodspeed's preemption arguments [which it supplied in the form of a Statement of Interest of the United States.

The Statement, consistent with this Court's own independent analysis, examines the text, purpose, legislative history of the Federal Aviation Act to conclude that it "provides the Federal Aviation Administrator with exclusive authority in the field of air safety and airspace management." It then discusses relevant case law, explaining that:

> While the [Federal Aviation Act's] preemptive authority is well established, courts have distinguished between state regulation that directly affects air safety and airspace management, and facially neutral laws that have only a tangential impact. Generally applicable laws that do not regulate in the areas of aircraft operation, safety, or the use of navigable airspace are not preempted by the federal scheme.

The Statement of Interest confirms that the Part 77 regulations "do not authorize the FAA to order the removal of an obstruction," and therefore, the Statement concludes, these regulations "are irrelevant for purposes of Plaintiff's field preemption claim." Nonetheless, "the agency has alternatives to ensure air safety once an obstruction has been identified." And, the Statement notes that "[t]rees constituting obstructions to navigable airspace are very common[,] and the FAA will, in these cases, alert aircraft operators of the obstruction so that they take necessary precautions."

Extent of FAA Safety Authority

"In sum," the Statement concludes, "tall trees affecting navigable airspace are commonplace, and the FAA will take the necessary steps to ensure safe operation . . . [but][t]he FAA's authority to intervene is limited, . . . and Goodspeed may not claim facial preemption of state environmental laws such as the [Wetlands Act] and [the] CEPA." The Court agrees.

Finally, the Court also finds it significant that while the Statement acknowledges that "[t]he FAA has a strong interest in terrain growth at privately-owned and operated commercial airports" like Goodspeed, and that "it is the

FAA's responsibility to mitigate" any unsafe conditions that result from tree growth, the Statement is also candid about the limitations of federal law generally and the authority of the FAA specifically. The fact that the FAA has chosen not to attempt to aggrandize its own authority here—even while agreeing that federal law completely preempts the field of aviation safety—lends additional support to the conclusion that the Statement "reflect[s] the agency's fair and considered judgment on the matter in question." *Auer v. Robbins*, 519 U.S. 452, 462 (1997). In summary, the Statement of Interest is worthy of deference under *Skidmore v. Swift & Co.*, 323 U.S. 134 (1944), and the fact that its conclusions match those of the Court lends additional certainty to the holding that the Wetlands Act and the CEPA are not preempted in the circumstances of this case.

Based on the foregoing, the Court concludes that the Defendants' actions in regulating the removal of trees at Goodspeed Airport that are within the protected wetlands are neither field preempted by federal aviation law nor expressly preempted by the ADA.

EXERCISE 11-3. *GOODSPEED AIRPORT, LLC V. EAST HADDAM INLAND WETLANDS AND WATERCOURSES COMM'N*—OBSTRUCTIONS

1. What situation is preventing Goodspeed Airport, LLC from simply cutting down the trees apparently posing "obstructions to air navigation"?

2. How is a small, privately-owned airport for public use defined under 14 C.F.R. § 77.3?

3. Did the obstructing trees at issue actually pose a threat to continued operation of the airport?

4. Assuming the trees at issue were "obstructions," could the FAA require that they be altered or removed? Explain.

5. Are the state laws at issue preempted by federal law? Explain the court's reasoning in detail.

NOTES ON *GOODSPEED AIRPORT, LLC V. EAST HADDAM INLAND WETLANDS AND WATERCOURSES COMM'N*—AVIATION AND THE ENVIRONMENT

In terms of aviation law, "environment" connotes at least four different, but intertwined, settings: the actual physical environment (discussed in this chapter); the legal and regulatory environment (discussed throughout this text book particularly,

Chapters 1, 2, 3, and 5); local, state, and national, and global business realities (Chapters 6 and 7); and the safety and security climate (Chapters 8 through 10). The FAA's Airport Environmental Programs assist airports implement the National Environmental Policy Act ("NEPA") and other federal environmental laws and regulations, including airport noise compatibility planning (Part 15), airport noise and access restrictions (Part 161), environmental review for airport development, and the application of the Uniform Relocation Assistance and Real Property Acquisition Policies Act of 1970. *See* Fed. Aviation Admin., *Airport Environmental Programs*, https://www.faa.gov/airports/environmental/.

1.   ***The Environment on September 11, 2001.***

With respect to the natural environment, climatologists have long wondered whether contrails (*e.g.*, condensation or vapor trails) from the thousands of jetliners airborne over the United States each day cool or heat the atmosphere. When all airline activity in the nation was grounded on September 11, 2001, climatologists had an unprecedented opportunity to study that issue. Several studies now suggest that "contrails can suppress both daytime highs (by reflecting sunlight back to space) and nighttime lows (by trapping radiated heat). That is, they can be both cooling and warming clouds." *See* Peter Tyson, *Diming the Sun—Inquiry: The Contrail Effect*, NOVA ONLINE, Apr. 2006. http://www.pbs.org/wgbh/nova/sun/contrail.html.

2.   ***Volcanoes and Air Safety.***

Volcanic ash presents particular peril for aviation operations. In April 2010, for example, all commercial aviation operations to-and-from Europe were shut down for six days as the Eyjafjallajokull volcano in Iceland erupted, throwing volcanic ash several kilometers into the atmosphere, creating a humongous ash cloud over Europe, and causing the biggest closure of airspace in peacetime. Pierre Sparaco, *Europe's Volcanic Failure*, AVIATION WK. & SPACE TECH., May 3, 2010, at 53 (noting that "individual [European] countries still 'own' their airspace and no cross-border agreement is required to implement local decisions, including the temporary creation of a no-fly zone. Individual decisions resulting from volcano fears [ ] were coordinated, but the EU's 27 member states nevertheless could not speak with a single voice for nearly a week.").

Once operations normalized, airlines and passengers alike demanded compensation for the extensive delay and disruption caused by the air space ban (estimated to have cost the industry more than £1 billion). On a smaller scale, Hawaii's Kilauea volcano erupted in June 2018, impacting many flight schedules. *See, e.g.*, *Hawaiian Airlines Says Volcanic Eruption Led to Modest Drop in Bookings*, REUTERS, June 4, 2018. *See also* Daniel Glover, FAA Office of Communications, *Mount St. Helens: 38 Years Later*, https://spark.adobe.com/page/T8cqpgWnneHsi/.

3. *Prevailing Winds.*

The airport environment consists of airside operations and landside operations. As the Chicago Department of Aviation has explained with respect to one of the world's busiest airports—O'Hare International—they very layout of an airport is linked to environmental conditions:

**Illustration 11-3. Runway Configuration for
Chicago O'Hare Airport (2018)**

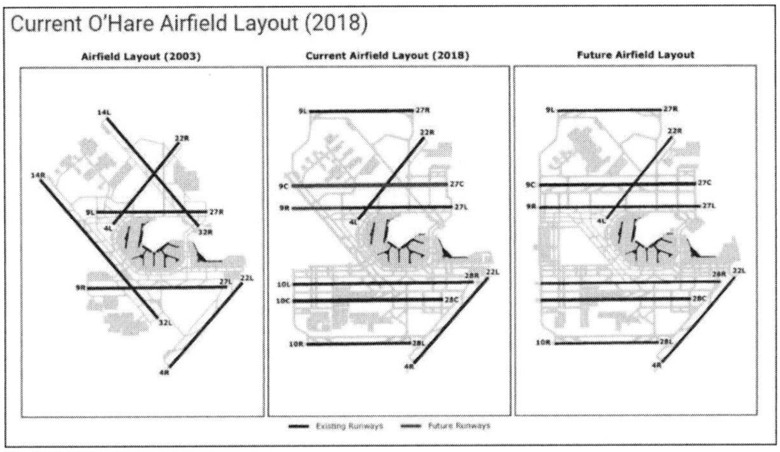

Aircraft take off and land into the prevailing winds. Federal Aviation Administration Air Traffic Control determines which runway will be used based on wind and other weather conditions as well as ground conditions, such as runway closures due to periodic maintenance. At O'Hare, the primary runways face east to west. In east flow, aircraft depart the primary runways to the east; arriving aircraft approach from the west. Generally, east flow conditions occur during periods of inclement weather. Conversely, in west flow, aircraft depart the primary runways to the west and arrivals come from the east.

Due to prevailing winds, the FAA Air Traffic Control Tower can sometimes use the same runways for an extended period of time. At times one may notice a shift in the way airplanes fly over an area, and this is usually because the "flow" has changed and different runways are in use.

Runway usage is primarily dictated by the prevailing winds, although it is important to note that winds aloft can vary in speed and direction from winds at ground level. During calm wind conditions and air traffic permitting, it is not uncommon for FAA Air Traffic Control to approve a pilot's request to depart in the opposite direction. This is done in accordance with FAA Order JO 7110.65X.

Chicago Dep't of Aviation, *Airport Operations 101*, *Prevailing Winds* https://www. flychicago.com/community/ORDnoise/AirportOperations/pages/default.aspx# winds.

4. ***Accidents.***

Where weather is a contributing factor to an aviation accident (see Chapter 12 and discussion of Delta Air Lines Flight 191, *infra*), litigation frequently centers on issues of weather reporting, air traffic control, and responsibility for weather forecasting. *See, e.g., United States Aviation Underwriters, Inc. v. United States*, 682 F. Supp. 2d 761 (S.D. Tex. 2010) (concluding that the National Weather Service must issue Significant Meteorological Information ("SIGMENT") warnings to pilots, whenever moderate to severe clear air turbulence ("CAT") is forecast, but the underlying determination of whether severe CAT is occurring is discretionary, insulating the federal government from liability under the discretionary function exception of the Federal Tort Claims Act, 28 U.S.C. § 2680(a).)

5. ***Wildlife and Bird Strikes.***

According to the FAA, wildlife-aircraft strikes have resulted in the loss of hundreds of lives and billions of dollars in aircraft damages during the past century. The FAA maintains a comprehensive program to address wildlife hazards, including a Wildlife Strike Database that contains records of reported wildlife strikes since 1990. *See* Fed. Aviation Admin., *Wildlife Hazard Mitigation*, https://www.faa.gov/airports/ airport_safety/wildlife/.

See also Fed. Aviation Admin.*, Submit a Wildlife Strike Report*, https://wildlife.faa. gov/strikenew.aspx; Fed. Aviation Admin. & U.S. Dep't of Agriculture, *Wildlife Strikes to Civil Aircraft in the United States (1990–2018)*, Serial Report Number 25, July 2019, https://www.faa.gov/airports/airport_safety/wildlife/media/Wildlife-Strike-Report-1990-2018.pdf.

Figure 11-1. FAA Wildlife Strike Database

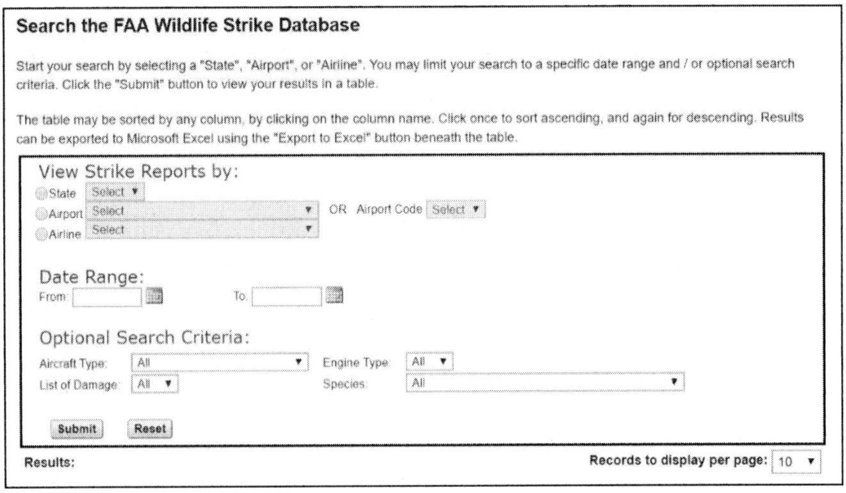

Source: https://wildlife.faa.gov/databaseSearch.aspx.

6. ***Emissions Trading.***

Airlines are a natural target of public concern about the emission of carbon dioxide (CO_2) and other greenhouse gases. Some officials report that the transportation sector contributes 32 percent of all CO_2 emissions, 12 percent of which (*e.g.*, 3 to 4 percent of total CO_2) are attributable to aviation. UNITED STATES ENVIRONMENTAL PROTECTION AGENCY, INVENTORY OF U.S. GREENHOUSE GAS EMISSIONS AND SINKS: 1990–2005 (2007). *See also* Daniel H. Conrad, Note, *Into the Wild Green Yonder: Applying the Clean Air Act to Regulate Emissions of Greenhouse Gases from Aircraft*, 34 N.C. J. INT'L L. & COM. REG. 919 (2009).

To address climate change and reduce aviation's "footprint," European Union ("EU") regulators have instituted a market-based cap-and-trade and emissions trading scheme ("ETS"). *See generally* Ruwantissa Abeyratne, *The Authority of the European Union to Unilaterally Impose an Emissions Trading Scheme*, 21 AIR & SPACE LAW. 5 (2008).

> Consider two companies, A and B, both of which emit significant quantities of a given pollutant. Their emissions may damage air quality, and the relevant authorities may decide that emissions should be reduced by a given amount, say by 10 per cent. At first glance, the solution seems simple: both A and B cut their emissions by 10 per cent. But in the real world, this may impose very different burdens on the two companies. For example, company A may, by the nature of its activities, be able to reduce its emissions by 10 per cent or even more at relatively low cost. Company B, on the other hand, may find this a difficult and costly process. It is this

potential difference in reduction cost between A and B that creates a market opportunity.

UNITED NATIONS ENVIRONMENT PROGRAM, AN EMERGING MARKET FOR THE ENVIRONMENT: A GUIDE TO EMISSIONS TRADING; UNITED NATIONS ENVIRONMENT PROGRAMME DIVISION OF TECHNOLOGY, INDUSTRY AND ECONOMICS 4 (2002). *See generally* Carl Burleson, *The EU Emissions Trading System Proposal*, 21 AIR & SPACE LAW. 1 (2007); Allen Pei-Jan Tsai & Annie Petsonk, *The Skies: An Airline-Based System for Limiting Greenhouse Gas Emissions from International Civil Aviation*, 6 ENVT. LAW. 763 (2000).

Application of the EU's ETS globally is controversial, raising issues of extraterritorial jurisdiction. For example, under ETS, if a U.S.-operated airliner travels from Los Angeles, California, across the entire United States, over the Atlantic Ocean, over Great Britain, and through the airspace over mainland Europe, to its final destination in Ankara, Turkey, should the carrier be taxed over the entire journey or for those emissions discharged over Europe only?

7. ***Committee on Aviation Environmental Protection ("CAEP").***

In February 2013, the International Civil Aviation Organization's ("ICAO's") Committee on Aviation Environmental Protection (CAEP) agreed to a new global noise reduction standard. The FAA participates in the CAEP meetings and supports this new standard. The most beneficial area of future noise reduction is technology development to reduce source noise. The FAA has an active program, The Continuous Lower Energy, Emissions, and Noise ("CLEEN") program, to advance the development of technologies to further reduce noise from aircraft. This program supports FAA's technology and alternative jet fuel solution sets.

Illustration 11-4. Noise Exposure v. Traffic Growth (1975–2012)

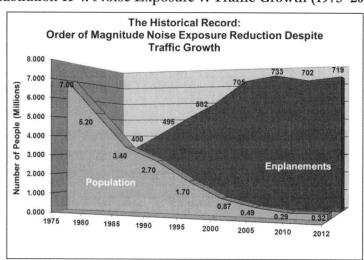

CLEEN will develop and mature environmentally-friendly technologies for civil subsonic jet aircraft. These technologies will help achieve NextGen goals to reduce aviation noise and emissions impacts. One of the goals of the CLEEN program is to develop certifiable aircraft technology that reduces noise levels by 32dB cumulative, relative to the ICAO noise standards. The program also focuses on maturing and demonstrating aircraft and alternative jet fuel technologies to accelerate commercialization of these technologies into current and future aircraft.

Fed. Aviation Admin., *Continuous Lower Energy, Emissions, and Noise (CLEEN) Program,* https://www.faa.gov/about/office_org/headquarters_offices/apl/noise_emissions/ airport_aircraft_noise_issues/.

8. ***Noise in NextGen.***

"NextGen" refers to an ongoing multibillion-dollar modernization of the national airspace system. As explained by the FAA:

> The movement to the next generation of aviation is possible by a shift to smarter, satellite-based and digital technologies and new procedures that combine to make air travel more convenient, predictable and environmentally friendly. The environmental vision for NextGen is to provide environmental protection that allows sustained aviation growth. Noise, air quality, climate, and energy are the most significant potential environmental constraints to increasing aviation capacity, efficiency, and flexibility.

> The FAA has established several programs and activities aimed at addressing these constraints. For noise, that involves limiting the number of people exposed to significant noise levels. Significant noise is defined as Day Night Average Sound Level (DNL) 65 decibels (dB). The number of people exposed to significant noise levels was reduced by approximately 90 percent between 1975 and 2000. This is due primarily to the legislatively mandated transition of airplane fleets to newer generation aircraft that produce less noise. Most of the gains from quieter aircraft were achieved by 2000. There have been incremental improvements since that time. Absent further advances in noise reduction technologies and fleet evolution, the remaining problem must be addressed primarily through operational procedures and airport-specific noise compatibility programs.

Fed. Aviation Admin., *Noise in NextGen,* https://www.faa.gov/about/office_org/ headquarters_offices/apl/noise_emissions/airport_aircraft_noise_issues/.

9.   ***The Future of Airports—and Urban Air Transport.***

Airports, as currently conceptualized, may be a relic of the past if companies like Uber create a future of on-demand urban air transportation produce a network of small, electric aircraft that take off and land vertically in a ridesharing scheme. *See* Uber Elevate, *Air Transport*, https://www.uber.com/info/elevate/.

Even if viable, is this desirable from a legal point of view? *See* Uber, *Fast-Forwarding to a Future of On-Demand Urban Air Transportation*, Oct. 27, 2016, https://www.uber.com/elevate.pdf/.

––––––––––

Suggested Further Reading

J.L. Horwick, Transportation Research Board, Airport Cooperative Research Program, Legal Digest 10: *Analysis of Federal Laws, Regulations, and Case Law Regarding Airport Proprietary Rights* (2010)

ALASTAIR GORDON, NAKED AIRPORT: A CULTURAL HISTORY OF THE WORLD'S MOST REVOLUTIONARY STRUCTURE (METROPOLITAN BOOKS 2004)

CHAPTER 12

Accident Litigation

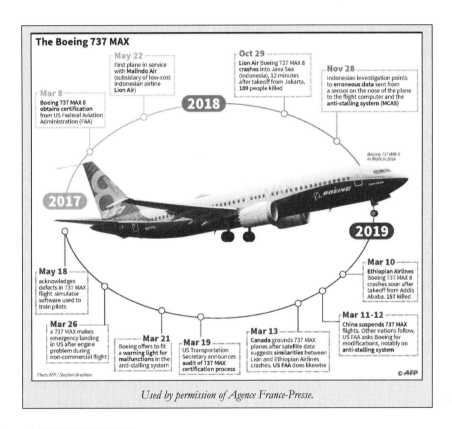

The Boeing 737 MAX

Mar 8 — Boeing 737 MAX 8 obtains certification from US Federal Aviation Administration (FAA)

May 22 — First plane in service with **Malindo Air** (subsidary of low-cost Indonesian airline **Lion Air**)

Oct 29 — **Lion Air** Boeing 737 MAX 8 crashes into Java Sea (Indonesia), 12 minutes after takeoff from Jakarta. 189 people killed

Nov 28 — Indonesian investigation points to **erroneous data** sent from a sensor on the nose of the plane to the flight computer and the **anti-stalling system (MCAS)**

2018

2017

2019

Boeing 737 MAX 8 in flight in 2016

May 18 — acknowledges defects in 737 MAX flight simulator software used to train pilots

Mar 26 — a 737 MAX makes emergency landing in US after engine problem during non-commercial flight

Mar 21 — Boeing offers to fit a **warning light for malfunctions** in the anti-stalling system

Mar 19 — US Transportation Secretary announces **audit of 737 MAX certification process**

Mar 13 — **Canada** grounds 737 MAX planes after satellite data suggests **similarities between** Lion and Ethiopian Airlines crashes. **US FAA does likewise**

Mar 10 — Ethiopian Airlines Boeing 737 MAX 8 crashes soon after takeoff from Addis Ababa. 157 killed

Mar 11-12 — China suspends 737 MAX flights. Other nations follow. US FAA asks Boeing for modifications, notably on **anti-stalling system**

Photo AFP / Stephen Drazheo

© AFP

Used by permission of Agence France-Presse.

A. OVERVIEW

In July 2013 Asiana Airlines Flight 214 crash landed in San Francisco, California following a failed visual approach—its pilots reportedly were confused in working with autopilot systems. In March 2014, Malaysia Flight 370 mysteriously disappeared after somebody turned off the airplane's transponder. In February 2015, TransAsia Airways grounded most of its fleet after flight data indicated that pilots mistakenly cut off fuel to the left engine after the right engine of a twin turboprop malfunctioned after takeoff. In 2018, the engine of Southwest

Airlines Boeing 737 exploded at 32,000 feet, sending shrapnel smashing into a window and killing a woman who was nearly sucked out of the airplane. And, shockingly, these tragedies somehow pale in comparison to events of March 2015, when a Germanwings copilot locked himself in the flight deck of an airliner, which he programmed to crash into the French Alps, killing all 150 people onboard. Independently and taken together, these tragedies make clear that few events more than aviation accidents invoke the phrase "mass torts."

Indeed, to the extent a commercial aviation disaster might be attributed to negligence or intentional wrongdoing on the part of an operator or manufacturer, aviation accident litigation generates many complex administrative, evidentiary, procedural, and substantive concerns for courts. Lawsuits arising from airplane accidents routinely involve dozens of parties, lawyers, governmental authorities, witnesses, experts, insurers, and airplane and component producers. This chapter overviews the main legal and ethical themes arising from catastrophic commercial airplane disasters, including the seminal jurisdictional and choice-of-law issues (*see Executive Jet Aviation, Inc. v. City of Cleveland, Ohio* and *Piper Aircraft Co. v. Reyno*), together with an introduction to the Federal Tort Claims Act (*United States v. S.A. Empresa de Viacao Aerea Rio Grandense (Varig Airlines)*) and the General Aviation Revitalization Act ("GARA") (*Inmon v. Air Tractor, Inc.*), in Parts C and D, respectively.

As with most legal texts, many of the cases and materials presented in this chapter are *ex post*, representing judicial decisions and laws rendered *after* a tragedy has occurred. But, the role that the law plays *prospectively* to ensure air safety should not be lost to readers. While regulators and regulations cannot prevent every accident, they have gone a long way to encouraging safety. In fact, 2017 was the safest year on record ever with no commercial jet fatalities—there had not been a fatal crash of a major U.S. passenger airliner since 2009. *See* Scott McCartney, *Why Flying Has Never Been Safer*, WALL ST. J., Jan. 24, 2018. A Dutch aviation consulting firm estimates that the fatal accident rate for large commercial passenger flights is 0.06 per million flights, or one fatal accident for every 16 million flights. *See, e.g.,* David Shepardson, *2017 Safest Year on Record for Commercial Passenger Air Travel*, REUTERS, Jan. 1, 2018.

The safety record for "general aviation" is also improving. *See* Flight Safety Foundation, *FAA: 2017 Shaping Up as GA's Safest Year*, Oct. 26, 2017. Regulators and the regulatory environment deserve great credit for this as the statistics show that flying really is safer than driving. *But see* Nancy L. Rose, *Fear of Flying? Economic Analyses of Airline Safety*, 6 J. ECON. PERSPECTIVES (1992).

Figure 12-1. NTSB: Transportation Fatalities by Mode

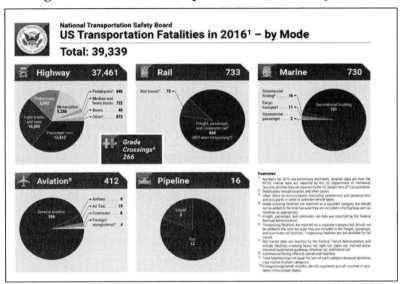

But, the law is not a perfect safeguard to accidents nor is it a comprehensive vehicle for compensating survivors of air disasters. And, as Part B of this chapter, *infra*, develops, jurists and lawmakers have approached liability for aviation accidents in different ways over time—initially regarding aviation as an ultrahazardous activity subject to the *res ipsa loquitur* standard of liability (*Crosby v. Cox Aircraft Co. of Washington*) and now consisting of a sophisticated administrative process by which regulators try to determine the probable cause of an accident (*Graham v. Teledyne-Continental Motors*) independent of a judicial finding of liability.

The fact that a particular problem or type of accident rarely happens more than once is a testament to the work regulators do to create an operational culture predicated on safety and accountability. And, it is a testament to the remedial steps aviators take in light of court decisions imposing liability for accidents. The truth is that there is no remedy that can fully compensate families for the pain and suffering following an aviation disaster. Yet, the statutory and common law framework presented in this chapter should inspire some confidence in the ability of regulators and courts to fashion remedies for victims of air disasters while also advancing rules and policies that make future air transportation safer.

Recent crashes are troubling in this context, however, as 347 people died when two Boeing 737 MAX aircraft crashed within months of each other, one in 2018 (Lion Air Flight 610) and another in 2019 (Ethiopian Airlines Flight 302), in connection with a computerized program known as MCAS. The aftermath of the crash brought allegations that the aircraft manufacturer rushed an airplane to market to get ahead of a competitor and failed to inform pilots about both the existence of and override procedures for the new automated MCAS system. As a result, the aircraft type was grounded worldwide (see illustration at the outset of this chapter). This significant action brought into focus not only the conduct of regulated entities such as a major airplane manufacturer, but also on regulators themselves and their relationship with regulated entities. This included fresh focus on the Federal Aviation Administration's Organization Designation Authorization Program ("ODA") through which FAA may delegate to a qualified private person a matter related to issuing certificates, or related to the examination, testing, and inspection necessary to issue a certificate on behalf of the FAA Administrator—in other words, a program that some critics, in the aftermath of the Boeing 737 Max grounding, argued could allow an airplane manufacturer to self-certify its product.

Figure 12-2. FAA Statement on Boeing 737 MAX

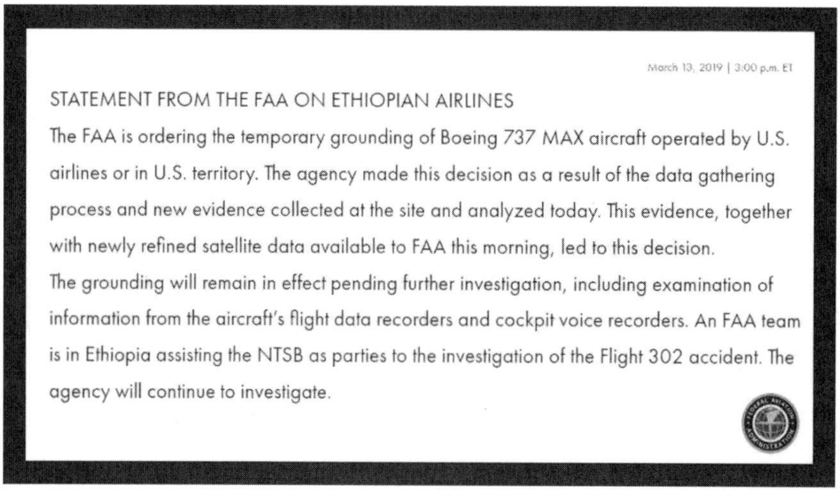
March 13, 2019 | 3:00 p.m. ET

STATEMENT FROM THE FAA ON ETHIOPIAN AIRLINES

The FAA is ordering the temporary grounding of Boeing 737 MAX aircraft operated by U.S. airlines or in U.S. territory. The agency made this decision as a result of the data gathering process and new evidence collected at the site and analyzed today. This evidence, together with newly refined satellite data available to FAA this morning, led to this decision.

The grounding will remain in effect pending further investigation, including examination of information from the aircraft's flight data recorders and cockpit voice recorders. An FAA team is in Ethiopia assisting the NTSB as parties to the investigation of the Flight 302 accident. The agency will continue to investigate.

The cases and materials in this chapter should be read with the emergence of autonomous and autonomous technologies in mind. Software onboard airplanes is are apparently outpacing the abilities of human aviators. How should the law anticipate—not just respond to—scenarios like the Boeing 737 MAX which involved failures in human-machine interfacing (along with more traditional problems of agency and corporate behavior). Readers should consider whether doctrines like *res ipsa loquitur* or common law negligence or strict liability should or will suffice in a new era of digital and smart airplanes. Against this background, this chapter presents the seminal precedents that inform the majority of accident cases in many courts around the world.

B. LIABILITY VS. PROBABLE CAUSE

CROSBY V. COX AIRCRAFT COMPANY OF WASHINGTON
746 P.2d 1198 (Wash. 1987)

CALLOW, JUSTICE.

Should owners and operators of flying aircraft be held strictly liable for ground damage caused by operation of the aircraft, or should their liability depend on a finding of negligence? The trial court determined that strict liability was applicable and awarded judgment in favor of the plaintiff landowners. We find that the general principles of negligence should control. We reverse and remand for trial.

The case involves a claim for property damage caused when a plane owned by Cox Aircraft Co. and piloted by Hal Joines (the pilot) crash-landed onto Douglas Crosby's property. The plane was a DeHavilland DHC-3 Otter aircraft. Its engine had recently been converted from piston-driven to turbine and the conversion had been undertaken in strict conformity with Federal Aviation Administration ("FAA") requirements. FAA certification of the plane's fuel system was still pending at the time of the accident.

On December 19, 1984, the pilot flew the airplane over the Olympic Peninsula and then turned back to Seattle, intending to land at Boeing Field. However, the engine ran out of fuel in mid-flight, and the pilot was forced to crash land the plane at Alki Point in West Seattle. The plane landed on the roof of Crosby's garage, causing $3,199.89 in damages.

Crosby sued both the pilot and Cox Aircraft. His complaint raised the following alternative allegations: (1) that the pilot was negligent in his operation of the plane; (2) that Cox Aircraft was negligent in its maintenance of the plane; (3) that Cox Aircraft, the alleged employer of the pilot, should be held vicariously liable for all negligence of the pilot under the doctrine of *respondeat superior*; and (4) that both the pilot and Cox Aircraft should be held strictly liable for all damages caused by the crash landing. The pilot and Cox Aircraft denied liability and filed a third-party complaint against Parker Hannifin Corporation alleging that Parker had equipped the plane with a defective fuel system control valve which failed to operate properly, thus causing the plane's engine to run out of fuel and forcing the pilot to make the crash landing.

The trial court granted partial summary judgment for Crosby, holding that both the pilot and Cox Aircraft were strictly liable for all damage done to Crosby's property. The court did not address Crosby's negligence claims, nor the third-party complaint against Parker. The pilot and Cox Aircraft appealed. We accepted certification.

The Boeing Company and the Washington State Trial Lawyer's Association ("WSTLA") have both filed *amicus curiae* briefs regarding the appropriate standard of liability to be imposed. Boeing argues that the liability of aircraft owners and operators for ground damage should be governed by a negligence standard. WSTLA contends (as does plaintiff Crosby), on the other hand, that strict liability should be applied. The defendants argue for yet a third standard—a "rebuttable presumption" of negligence on the part of the aircraft owner and operator. We hold that the general principles of negligence control.

* * *

This is the first case in this State to directly deal with the standard of liability governing ground damage caused by aircraft. *Mills v. Orcas Power & Light Co.*, 355 P.2d 781 (Wash. 1960), alluded to this issue, but only in *dicta*. No subsequent cases have considered the question, and the Legislature has enacted no statute on the matter.

Plaintiff Crosby and *amicus* party WSTLA urge us to adopt RESTATEMENT (SECOND) OF TORTS § 520A (1977):

§ 520A. Ground Damage from Aircraft

If physical harm to land or to persons or chattels on the ground is caused by the ascent, descent or flight of aircraft, or by the dropping or falling of an object from the aircraft,

(a)   the operator of the aircraft is subject to liability for the harm, even though he has exercised the utmost care to prevent it, and

(b)   the owner of the aircraft is subject to similar liability if he has authorized or permitted the operation.

This provision establishing strict liability is said to be a "special application" of §§ 519–20, the Restatement sections governing liability for "abnormally dangerous" activities. (*See* § 520A, Comment (a)). Sections 519–20 provide:

§ 519.   General Principle

(1)   One who carries on an abnormally dangerous activity is subject to liability for harm to the person, land or chattels of another resulting from the activity, although he has exercised the utmost care to prevent the harm.

(2)   This strict liability is limited to the kind of harm, the possibility of which makes the activity abnormally dangerous.

§ 520.   Abnormally Dangerous Activities

In determining whether an activity is abnormally dangerous, the following factors are to be considered:

(a)   existence of a high degree of risk of some harm to the person, land or chattels of others;

(b)   likelihood that the harm that results from it will be great;

(c)   inability to eliminate the risk by the exercise of reasonable care;

(d)   extent to which the activity is not a matter of common usage;

(e)   inappropriateness of the activity to the place where it is carried on; and

(f)   extent to which its value to the community is outweighed by its dangerous attributes.

The defendants urge us to reject RESTATEMENT § 520A. They contend that aviation can no longer be designated an "abnormally dangerous activity" requiring special rules of liability. We agree.

In the early days of aviation, the cases and treatises were replete with references to the hazards of "aeroplanes." The following assessment is typical:

[E]ven the best constructed and maintained aeroplane is so incapable of complete control that flying creates a risk that the plane even though carefully constructed, maintained and operated, may crash to the injury of persons, structures and chattels on the land over which the flight is made.

RESTATEMENT (FIRST) OF TORTS, § 520, Comment b (1938). As colorfully stated in *Prosser & Keeton on Torts* § 78, at 556 (5th ed. 1984): "Flying was of course regarded at first as a questionable and highly dangerous enterprise, the province exclusively of venturesome fools."

In 1922 the Commission on Uniform State Laws proposed a new Uniform Aeronautics Act which, *inter alia,* made owners of aircraft strictly liable for all ground damage caused by the "ascent, descent or flight of the aircraft." Twenty-three states originally adopted this act by statute. By 1943, however, the Commissioners recognized that the act had become "obsolete," and it was removed from the list of uniform laws.

The number of states imposing strict liability has diminished significantly. At present, only six states retain the rule, and even these states apply it only to the owner of the aircraft. The aircraft operator remains liable only for damages caused by his own negligence. *See* Del. Code Ann., title 2, § 305 (1985); Hawaii Rev. Stat. § 263–5 (1985); Minn. Stat. § 360.012, subd. 4 (1986); N.J. Stat. Ann. § 6:2–7 (West 1973); S.C. Code § 55–3–60 (1977); Vt. Stat. Ann., title 5, §§ 224–225 (1972).

The modern trend followed by a majority of states is to impose liability only upon a showing of negligence by either the aircraft owner or operator. Several states have legislated this rule by providing that ordinary tort law (or the law applicable to torts on land) applies to aviation accidents. Moreover, a number of courts have expressly disavowed the notion that aviation is an "ultrahazardous activity" requiring special rules of liability.

The modern trend followed by a majority of states is to impose liability only upon a showing of negligence by either the aircraft owner or operator. Several states have legislated this rule by providing that ordinary tort law (or the law applicable to torts on land) applies to aviation accidents. *See e.g.* Ark. Stat. Ann., § 74–110 (1979); Idaho Code § 21–205 (1977); N.D. Cent. Code § 2–03–05 (1975); Pa. Con. Stat. Ann., title 74, § 5502 (Purdom Supp. 1987); Tenn. Code Ann. § 42–1–105 (1980). Other jurisdictions have case law to this effect. *See, e.g., Daley v. United States*, 792 F.2d 1081 (11th Cir. 1986) (applying Florida law); *Brooks v. United States*, 695 F.2d 984 (5th Cir.1983) (applying Texas law); *Mackey v. Miller*, 273 S.E.2d 550 (Va. 1981). Moreover, a number of courts have expressly disavowed the notion that aviation is an "ultrahazardous activity" requiring special rules of liability. As observed in *Boyd v. White* (Cal. App. Ct. 1954):

> The courts and the law formerly looked upon aviation with the viewpoint still expressed in the American Law Institute, Restatement, Torts, Vol. 3, § 520, holding that aviation is an ultra-hazardous activity, similar to the operation of automobiles in the early days of the horseless carriage, and requiring those who take part in it to observe the highest degree of care.

> The Uniform Aeronautic Act, adopted in time by twenty-three states, imposed absolute liability on the owner, as well as the operator or lessee, of every aircraft for any damage to person or property caused by its operation provided there was no contributory negligence on the part of him who was thus harmed. With the passage of time, however, this view

came to be modified, and the trend of decisions established it to be the general rule that, properly handled by a competent pilot exercising reasonable care, an airplane is not an inherently dangerous instrument, so that in the absence of statute the ordinary rules of negligence control, and the owner (or operator) of an airship is only liable for injury inflicted upon another when such damage is caused by a defect in the plane or its negligent operation.

By 1945, coincident with the opening of the postwar civilian aviation period, the number of states retaining the portions of the Uniform Aeronautic Act dealing with an owner's liability had dropped to eighteen.

We have discovered no cases relying on RESTATEMENT (SECOND) OF TORTS § 520A. That section is said to be a "special application" of § 519 and § 520(a–f), which impose strict liability on persons engaging in abnormally dangerous activities. An analysis of the individual factors listed in § 520 further persuades us that strict liability is inappropriate here.

Factor (a) of § 520 requires that the activity in question contain a "high degree of risk of some harm to the person, land or chattels of others." No such showing has been made. Indeed, statistics indicate that air transportation is far safer than automobile transportation. *See, e.g.,* 3 Harper, James & Gray, *The Law of Torts* § 14.13 at 309–10 n. 64 (1986); Comment, *Aviation Law: Owner-Lessor Liability— The Need for Uniformity,* 36 MAINE L. REV. 93, 98–99 (1984).

Factor (b) speaks to the gravity of the harm—that is, in the unlikely event that an airplane accident occurs, whether there is a "likelihood that the [resulting harm] will be great." It is apparent that this possibility is present. However, this must be further evaluated in light of factor (c), which speaks of the "inability to eliminate the risk by the exercise of reasonable care." Given the extensive governmental regulation of aviation, *see generally* 14 C.F.R. Ch. I (1978) (Federal Aviation Administration regulations), and the continuing technological improvements in aircraft manufacture, maintenance and operation, we conclude that the *overall* risk of serious injury from ground damage can be sufficiently reduced by the exercise of due care.

Finally, factors (d), (e), and (f) do not favor the imposition of strict liability. Aviation is an activity of "common usage", it is appropriately conducted over populated areas, and its value to the community outweighs its dangerous attributes. Indeed, aviation is an integral part of modern society.

> *The causes of aircraft accidents are legion and can come from a myriad of sources . . .*
> *Any listing of the causes of such accidents undoubtedly would fall short of the*
> *possibilities. In such circumstances the imposition of liability should be upon the*
> *blameworthy party who can be shown to be at fault.*

The causes of aircraft accidents are legion and can come from a myriad of sources. Every aircraft that flies is at risk from every bird, projectile and other aircraft. Accidents may be caused by improper placement of wires or buildings or from failure to properly mark and light such obstructions. The injury to the ground dweller may have been caused by faulty engineering, construction, repair, maintenance, metal fatigue, operation or ground control. Lightning, wind shear and other acts of God may have brought about a crash. Any listing of the causes of such accidents undoubtedly would fall short of the possibilities. In such circumstances the imposition of liability should be upon the blameworthy party who can be shown to be at fault.

In *King v. United States*, 178 F.2d 320 (5th Cir. 1949), a United States Army Air Force student pilot got drunk and took off in a training plane at midnight. Shortly thereafter he crashed into the plaintiff's home causing damages. The plaintiff brought suit under the Federal Tort Claims Act against the United States. The court found that the act of the student pilot was without the knowledge or consent of the Air Force, was unauthorized and that the pilot was acting outside of the scope of his duties. The court held that there should be no recovery against the government, stating succinctly:

> In a case of this nature, the United States cannot escape liability if a private person under similar circumstances should be held liable.

> There are no special statutory provisions that regulate or govern the responsibility of persons owning and operating airplanes. In the absence of such statutes, the rules of law applicable generally to torts govern. The ordinary rules of negligence and due care are invoked.

Special Rule for Ground Damage?

We are not persuaded that we should create a special rule of liability governing only ground damage caused by aircraft accidents. We note, for example, that passengers of airplanes involved in accidents must prove negligence to recover damages. As stated in *Rathvon v. Columbia P. Airlines*, 633 P.2d 122 (Wash. App. Ct. 1981):

> A carrier's failure to discover a latent defect is not negligence if it exercised the highest degree of care reasonably consistent with the practical operation of its business, and used the best precautions that

were in common, practical use in the same business and had proved to be effective in discovering defects. We conclude that whether or not CPA failed to exercise the highest degree of care according to the standards expressed above remains a genuine issue of material fact.

This is true even though the likelihood of serious injury to a passenger is at least as great as is the case with persons or property on the ground.

We also emphasize that, although the plaintiff's recovery will depend on a showing of negligence, the plaintiff may of course employ the doctrine of *res ipsa loquitur,* if appropriate, to establish his negligence claim. *Res ipsa* is now frequently used in aviation crash cases and is widely recognized as an acceptable means of proving negligence. *See generally* Annot., *Res Ipsa Loquitur in Aviation Accidents,* 25 A.L.R.4th 1237 (1983).

Res Ipsa
Loquitur

Finally, the plaintiff raises an alternative argument that we apply the rule of strict liability to ground damages arising out of "test flights" of aircraft. We decline to do so. Plaintiff has cited no authority to support his claim that test flights of aircraft qualify as "abnormally dangerous" under Restatement (Second) of Torts § 519–20. The question is not whether test flights are more dangerous than routine aviation flights, but rather, whether they are so inherently dangerous that a "high degree of risk of harm" cannot be eliminated by the exercise of reasonable care. § 520(a), (c). In light of the extensive government regulation regarding the design, development, and testing of new and modified aircraft, *see generally* 14 CFR Ch. I, Subchapter C (1978) (Federal Aviation Administration certification procedures and airworthiness standards), we conclude that test flights are not abnormally dangerous.

We hold that owners and operators of flying aircraft are liable for ground damage caused by such aircraft only upon a showing of negligence. The partial summary judgment entered in favor of the plaintiff is reversed and the cause is remanded for trial.

BRACHTENBACH, JUSTICE *(dissenting).*

What a peculiar, aberrant twist of tort law is created by the majority. Almost a decade ago we held that when a wine glass shatters in the hands of a wine drinker, the seller of the wine, who merely supplied the glass, is strictly liable. The law demanded and gave compensation without proof of fault. Today the majority tells the wholly innocent, inactive homeowner into whose home an airplane suddenly crashes "you must prove by a preponderance of the evidence that someone was at fault; never mind that you had no part in this damage, go forth and prove negligence and if you cannot, the loss is all yours." How can that be? The majority's answer is that it cannot fit these facts into a magic phrase—abnormally dangerous—which started in an 1868 case from England, *Rylands v. Fletcher*, 3 L.R.-E&I App. 330 (1868)

In fact and theory, it is a policy question whether to impose liability upon the pilot and owner of an airplane which crashes into the person or property of a wholly innocent person on the ground. Compelling, persuasive policy reasons exist to impose such strict liability. Those reasons should be explored and evaluated rather than simply accepting the pigeonhole conclusion that aviation is not abnormally dangerous as defined by the black letter rule of the RESTATEMENT (SECOND) OF TORTS, therefore, *ipso facto*, strict liability cannot be imposed. If the RESTATEMENT (SECOND) OF TORTS, is to be followed, as the majority proposes, strict liability should result as discussed hereafter.

Unfortunately, the majority totally fulfills the prophecy of one text writer:

It is predictable that some courts will be less likely to impose strict liability as a matter of common law development if the case cannot be fitted into some familiar mold such as trespass or abnormally dangerous activity. While this fact must be recognized, it should be regretted. Surely the step so clearly called for here is a small one as compared with many that courts have taken without aid of statute.

3 F. Harper, F. James & O. Gray, *Torts* § 14.13, at 311 n. 68 (2d ed. 1986). My position is summarized by the same text:

As the science of aviation has advanced, there seems to have been increasing reluctance to characterize it as an abnormally dangerous activity. But unwillingness to call aviation abnormally dangerous would not by any means prove that strict liability is inappropriate here. Ample justification for imposing it may be found in frequent difficulties of proof and the fact that these risks are properly allocated to aviation, especially where the victim is no participant in the enterprise.

3 F. Harper, F. James & O. Gray, *Torts* § 14.13, at 311 (2d ed. 1986).

If we assume that the aircraft operator is without legal fault, *i.e.,* is not negligent, the policy issue is then clear. Which of two persons should bear the loss? In this case we have a totally innocent, nonacting homeowner whose property is suddenly invaded and damaged by an airplane—operated by the person who voluntarily chose to fly that airplane, for his own purpose and benefit. The result of the majority is that the wholly innocent, nonactive, nonbenefited, but damaged person must shoulder the burden of proving that the person who set in motion the forces which caused the damage was negligent.

I suggest that were it not for the historical development of the concept of abnormally dangerous activity, there would be no reason or justification for denying strict liability for aircraft damage to persons or property on the ground. The philosophy which led to strict product liability should be and is equally relevant to aircraft liability.

In summary, I would affirm the trial court which held that strict liability applies. The able trial judge saw the obvious policy reasons for strict liability which the majority rejects. Adoption of strict liability for ground damage from aircraft is justified on either of the two theories set forth, *i.e.,* (1) policy reasons and (2) the literal language of RESTATEMENT (SECOND) OF TORTS § 520A (1977). Under either theory liability would apply to the operator and to the owner of the aircraft if the owner authorized or permitted the operation. Section 520A(b). I would affirm.

EXERCISE 12-1. *CROSBY V. COX AIRCRAFT COMPANY OF WASHINGTON*—NEGLIGENCE OR STRICT LIABILITY?

1. Define the following terms: (a) intentional tort; (b) negligence; (c) strict liability; (d) respondeat superior; (e) third party complaint; (f) amicus curiae.

2. What standard of liability is established by the RESTATEMENT (SECOND) OF TORTS § 520A (1977)? Does the court adopt this—explain.

3. Describe the doctrine of *res ipsa loquitur*. What does it mean, what are its elements, and who bears the burden of persuasion? Finally, why might it be "frequently used in aviation crash cases," as the court suggests.

4. Explain the central concern expressed by the dissenting judge. Is this position persuasive? Explain.

5. After *Crosby v. Cox Aircraft Company of Washington*, is airplane travel an "abnormally dangerous activity" as a matter of law? Familiarize yourself with the Boeing 737 MAX tragedies previewed at the outset of this chapter—does your answer to this question change?

NOTES ON *CROSBY V. COX AIRCRAFT CO. OF WASHINGTON*— LIABILITY MATTERS

The burden of persuasion and standard of liability, as introduced in *Crosby v. Cox Aircraft of Washington*, is extraordinarily important in aviation accidents. One commentator, echoing *Crosby*, noted, that "[t]here is virtually always someone who is liable for an aviation accident … [t]ypically, the defendants either agree among themselves about how to divide expenditures for compensation and litigation, or they agree to let the outcome of one trial decide the division of liability." JAMES S. KAKALIK ET AL., COSTS AND COMPENSATION PAID IN AVIATION ACCIDENT LITIGATION 88 (1988).

Damages are also a driving factor for litigants in aviation accident cases. Notably, where plaintiffs may receive 50 percent of funds expended in mass tort litigation generally, they may attain a more significant 71 percent in aviation torts. *Compare id.* at 93–94, *with* JAMES S. KAKALIK ET AL., COSTS OF ASBESTOS LITIGATION 39–40 (1983) (finding that plaintiffs received 37% of funds expended in early stages of asbestos litigation). *See also* R. Daniel Truitt, *Hints of Uneven Playing Field in Aviation Torts: Is There Proof?*, 61 J. AIR L. & COM. 577 (1996).

Indeed, on average, aviation accident litigation is more lucrative than other mass tort litigation. For example, in the average award from a 1987 Northwest Airlines crash in Detroit, Michigan was projected to be $1 million. Eric S. Roth, Note, *Confronting Solicitation of Mass Disaster Victims*, 2 GEO. J. LEGAL ETHICS 967, 976, n.46 (1989) (citing Andrew Blum, *The Aviation Bar Splits Over Turf*, NAT'L L.J., Mar. 20, 1989, at 1, 29). In tort cases that proceeded to trial in federal district court in 1996–97, of 41 cases described as "personal injury—airplane," the median award was $937,000, far higher than the median for "product liability" cases, and of the 16 plaintiff verdicts in "airplane" cases, 43.8 percent were $1 million or more. *See* BUREAU OF JUSTICE STATISTICS, BULLETIN: FEDERAL TORT TRIALS AND VERDICTS, 1996–97 5 (1999), *available at* https://www.bjs.gov/content/pub/pdf/fttv97.pdf.

Given the potential for significant damages, lawyer ethics and professionalism in the arena of aviation disaster litigation sometimes is wanting. Truly, a small number of lawyers in the world specialize in the area of aviation law, including accident cases. Yet, solicitation by unqualified lawyers has become commonplace, particularly in the Internet age, where a search of "aviation lawyer" may generate a list of lawyers who, other than listing "aviation" as a practice area, have had scant, if any, experience in the subject matter. *See generally* Wendell K. Smith, *The General Aviation Case*, UTAH B.J., Feb. 1999 at 17; Charles Maher, *Crashes & Disasters*, 5 CALIF. LAW. 39, 41 (1985). *See also Matter of Anis*, 599 A.2d 1265 (N.J. 1992), *cert. denied*, 504 U.S. 956 (1992).

Moreover, anecdotal evidence exists that lawyers who do not practice aviation law, but who secure aviation accidents clients through aggressive advertising refer the aviation accident cases to specialized aviation attorneys after demanding as much as one-half the total fee. KAKALIK ET AL., at 46.

To stem this and other opportunistic conduct related to airplane accidents, Congress enacted the Aviation Disaster Family Assistance Act of 1996 ("ADFAA") to prohibit lawyers from soliciting clients during the first 30 days following an aviation accident. In 2000, Congress expanded the ADFAA's "black out" period to 45 days. *See* 49 U.S.C. § 1136(g)(2) (2003). *See generally* Lester Brickman, *The Market for Contingent-Fee Financed Tort Litigation: Is It Price Competitive?*, 25 CARDOZO L. REV. 65, 107–08 (2003).

GRAHAM V. TELEDYNE-CONTINENTAL MOTORS
805 F.2d 1386 (9th Cir. 1986)

KOZINSKI, CIRCUIT JUDGE.

James Graham was the pilot of a twin-engine Beechcraft Baron aircraft that crashed into the Sun Valley Mall in Concord, California on December 23, 1985. The accident resulted in five fatalities, numerous injuries and extensive property damage. Appellant Dorothy Graham, the executrix of James Graham's estate, has been named a defendant in several lawsuits arising from this event.

As charged by the Independent Safety Board Act of 1974, 49 U.S.C. §§ 1901 *et seq.* (1982), the National Transportation Safety Board ("NTSB") began an immediate investigation into the cause of the accident. To this end, the NTSB directed that the aircraft's two engines be shipped to their manufacturer, Teledyne Industries, Inc. ("Teledyne"). There the agency planned to conduct a complete teardown analysis. In accordance with NTSB practice, the proposed inspection and disassembly was to be conducted by Teledyne engineers working in conjunction with, and under the supervision of, NTSB officials.

NTSB and Independent Safety Board Act of 1974

The practice of disassembling airplane engines and other component parts on the premises of their manufacturer, with the assistance and participation of the manufacturer's personnel, grows out of the NTSB's belief that the manufacturer and its staff are best equipped to perform such functions. Each manufacturer uses somewhat different designs and specifications, requiring somewhat different tools and techniques for disassembly. The NTSB has determined that use of the manufacturer's facilities and personnel will maximize its ability to determine the cause of the accident while minimizing cost. Cost is minimized because this practice saves the NTSB from maintaining staff and facilities capable of disassembling every type of airplane component used in U.S. civil aviation.

On learning that the NTSB was shipping the engines to Teledyne for inspection and testing, appellant requested permission to have her technical representative participate in, or at least observe, the teardown inspection. Appellant asserted an interest because of the related civil litigation; she expressed fears about possible destructive testing and spoliation of evidence. The NTSB and Teledyne refused appellant's demands.

Appellant then brought this action seeking interlocutory and permanent injunctive relief. She alleged that the NTSB examination would cause irreparable harm due to the destruction of evidence, deprive her of due process by impairing her legal rights and remedies, and take her property (consisting of these rights) without just compensation. The district court denied a temporary restraining order, holding that the NTSB did not abuse its discretion under applicable statutes and regulations in deciding who shall participate in the accident investigation. In addition, the district court determined that appellant had failed to establish that any constitutional right would be violated by the pending engine examination. Graham immediately appealed, challenging the denial of the temporary restraining order. [T]his court enjoined appellees from conducting destructive testing pending resolution of the appeal.

Appellant bases her claim for relief on two sources of authority. First, she argues that the regulations promulgated by the NTSB pursuant to the Independent Safety Board Act give her a right to participate in the inspection and disassembly procedures, or at least render it an abuse of discretion for the NTSB to refuse her request to participate. Second, she argues that the NTSB's refusal denies her the constitutionally guaranteed right to due process.

The Regulations

Appellant bases her claim on 49 C.F.R. §§ 831.9(a) and 831.10(a), which govern who will participate in the investigation and who may have access to the aircraft wreckage. However, neither of these sections gives appellant the rights she seeks.

IIC Powers

Section 831.9(a) provides that NTSB's "investigator-in-charge may . . . designate parties to participate in the field investigation." The section is written in the permissive. It gives no one a right to participate; it merely authorizes the investigator to designate parties to the investigation. Section 831.10(a) is even less helpful to appellant. That section restricts access to the wreckage to "the Board's accident investigation personnel and persons authorized . . . to participate in any particular investigation, examination or testing." Since appellant's representative is not so authorized, he simply does not qualify under this regulation.

Appellant argues, however, that the NTSB's refusal to designate her representative as a participant in the investigation constitutes an abuse of discretion. In appellant's view, the NTSB was not entitled to exclude an entity with "legitimate interests" in the outcome of the investigation, while at the same time permitting Teledyne, a party with similar interests, to participate. Appellant argues quite plausibly that her interests are antithetical to those of Teledyne.

The plane crash was most likely caused either by mechanical failure or pilot error. Establishing one would tend to exclude the other. Graham believes that, by having its technical representatives present when the engines are torn down, Teledyne is given a substantial advantage in any subsequent adjudication of liability.

Appellant's attempt to impose upon the NTSB investigation rules of procedural fairness reflects a misconception of the Board's mission. The NTSB's authorizing statute provides that the Board shall "investigate or cause to be investigated (in such detail as it shall prescribe), and determine the facts, conditions, and circumstances and the cause or probable cause or causes of any . . . aircraft accident." These investigations are not primarily for the purpose of determining civil liability; indeed, the Board has no authority to adjudicate the rights of private parties. The NTSB's function is "to promote transportation safety by conducting independent accident investigations and by formulating safety improvement recommendations."

NTSB Mission

The NTSB's authorizing statute provides that the Board shall "investigate or cause to be investigated (in such detail as it shall prescribe), and determine the facts, conditions, and circumstances and the cause or probable cause or causes of any . . . aircraft accident."

These investigations are not primarily for the purpose of determining civil liability; indeed, the Board has no authority to adjudicate the rights of private parties.

Wherever the parties may stand with respect to each other under applicable tort law, they stand on much different footing vis-a-vis the NTSB's investigation. The use of Teledyne's facilities and expertise in disassembling its own engines could be indispensable in enabling the NTSB to carry out its mission.

We conclude that the NTSB did not abuse its discretion by deputizing Teledyne to participate in the investigation but refusing to accord Graham's representative the same status. Wherever the parties may stand with respect to each other under applicable tort law, they stand on much different footing vis-a-vis the NTSB's investigation. The use of Teledyne's facilities and expertise in disassembling its own engines could be indispensable in enabling the NTSB to carry out its mission.

By contrast, there is nothing unique appellant's expert could add to the investigation, or so the NTSB could rationally decide. The only one connected with appellant who might have had unique insight into what happened was James Graham, the pilot, who is dead. The NTSB did not abuse its discretion by determining that it did not require appellant's representative as a participant or observer in the teardown of the engines. [Moreover,] the district court determined, as an alternate ground for denying access to appellant, that Graham's representative also represented an insurance company. Under the regulations, this would render him entirely ineligible to participate in the investigation. *See* 49 C.F.R. § 831.9(c). Appellant contends this finding was clearly erroneous. Given our ruling, we need not reach this issue.

The Constitution

Appellant next argues that denying her access to the teardown inspection violates her right to due process. She contends that her right to contribution or indemnity from others involved in the accident is a property right that will be impaired if appellees are allowed to conduct destructive testing. Although appellant's interest in the investigation may be substantial, we conclude that her exclusion does not rise to the level of a due process violation.

Assuming appellant has a property interest in her contribution/indemnity cause of action, she will suffer no deprivation of that right. At most, appellant may be deprived of certain evidence that could assist her in litigation. Courts have consistently rejected arguments that deprivation of evidence constitutes a denial of due process. *See, e.g., Samuelson v. Susen*, 576 F.2d 546 (3d Cir. 1978) (medical review committee privilege denying plaintiff information central to defamation action does not violate due process).

Deprivation of Evidence?

In addition, it is highly speculative whether appellant will in fact be deprived of any evidence. While having her representative present at the teardown is one way to ascertain what went wrong, other avenues are open to appellant to obtain substantially similar proof. Appellant will have access to the NTSB factual reports from the investigation.

Moreover, although the expert testimony of Board employees is inadmissible, Graham may secure the testimony of NTSB investigators concerning the factual information they gathered during the course of the accident investigation. Finally, she will presumably have access to the physical evidence itself after the engines have been released by the NTSB.

Appellant has expressed concern that Teledyne may alter or destroy vital evidence. This case, however, is not much different from those where an adverse party retains possession of key elements of proof, *e.g.*, purloined trade secrets, documents proving fraud, or machinery involved in personal injury accidents. The presumptions and sanctions available to punish those who alter or destroy evidence must be considered sufficient to deter any misconduct and Teledyne is no doubt aware that its handling of the materials may come under intense scrutiny. In any case, as we understand the NTSB's procedures, the engines will be handled by Teledyne employees only under the supervision of NTSB investigators.

Graham's remaining claim for a taking of property is premature. If and when she suffers a deprivation, she may bring an inverse condemnation claim under the Tucker Act, 28 U.S.C. §§ 1346(a)(2), 1491. Such a suit, brought after the NTSB's investigation is completed, would avoid much of the speculation inherent in appellant's current action. It would also allow the NTSB to proceed with its investigation, unencumbered by concerns extraneous to—and inconsistent with—the important mission entrusted it by Congress.

Appellant is not the only one who can claim a legitimate interest in the NTSB's investigation; presumably the estates of others killed in the Sun Valley Mall crash, as well as those who were injured or suffered property damage, could assert that their rights will be impaired if their representatives are not allowed to observe the teardown. If appellant's claim were sustained on constitutional grounds, it would be difficult to exclude these others.

The problem would be infinitely multiplied in a crash involving an airliner where literally hundreds of interested parties may be in the position of having some interest potentially affected by the NTSB's investigation. The NTSB would be rendered entirely ineffective in carrying out its mission if it were required to allow all of these parties access to every critical step of the investigation. The government must be allowed to carry out its responsibilities; if private property is taken in the process, the appropriate remedy is a suit for compensation.

EXERCISE 12-2. *GRAHAM V. TELEDYNE-CONTINENTAL MOTORS*—NATIONAL TRANSPORTATION SAFETY BOARD ("NTSB")

1. Describe the accident at the center of *Graham v. Teledyne-Continental Motors* and identify the most likely cause of the crash, according to the court's understanding of the event.

2. What is an "executrix"?

3. Explain what authority the National Transportation Safety Board has under 49 C.F.R. § 831.9. How was that power was exercised in this case, according to the executrix?

4. According to the court, what is the primary purpose of NTSB accident investigations? What is it *not*?

5. The executrix asserted several property-based rights. How does the court decide each of the following claims: (a) Due Process violation related to contribution or indemnity cause of action; (b) deprivation of evidence; (c) alteration or destruction of vital evidence; and (d) inverse condemnation.

NOTES ON *GRAHAM V. TELEDYNE-CONTINENTAL MOTORS*—SAFETY CULTURE

1. ***NTSB Most Wanted List.***

Consider that the NTSB has a "Most Wanted List" of safety issues to which it grades the FAA's response as "acceptable response, progressing in a timely manner," "acceptable response, progressing slowly," or "unacceptable response." In mid-2010, pilot proficiency, flying in icing conditions, and accidents and incidents caused by human fatigue were identified as issues to which the FAA had provided an "unacceptable response." *See generally* https://www.ntsb.gov/safety/mwl/Pages/default.aspx.

Should the Federal Aviation Administration be required to adopt and enforce the NTSB's "recommendations" as a matter of law? *See, e.g.,* Richard H. Fallon, Jr., *Enforcing Aviation Safety Regulations: The Case for Split-Enforcement Model of Agency Adjudication*, 4 ADMIN. L.J. 389 (1991).

2. ***Criminalization of Aircraft Accidents?***

Graham v. Teledyne-Continental Motors raises the interesting prospect of involving (or not) a potentially liable party as part of an accident investigation. This touches on a different issue of liability, namely whether aviation accidents might be criminalized.

Consider that on July 25, 2000, a Continental Airlines DC-10 departed from Charles de Gaulle Airport in France. A 17-inch-long titanium wear strip was shed by the jumbo-jet and left on the runway. Air France Flight 4590—Concorde—departed next, bound for New York. The supersonic jet hit the strip, which punctured a tire, throwing rubber debris into the delta wing. A fuel tank ruptured and the airplane was ignited into a catastrophic fire. After a 90 second attempt to gain speed and altitude, the Concorde crashed into a nearby hotel, killing 113 people. In 2010, a French court tried Continental Airlines and two of its employees for manslaughter while prosecutors accused French officials of neglecting to fix known design defects in the airplane.

For further reading see generally Roderick D. van Dam, *Preserving Safety in Aviation: "Just Culture" and the Administration of Justice*, 22 AIR & SPACE LAW. 1 (2009); Richard M. Dunn et al., *Criminalization in Aviation*, 38–SPG BRIEF 10 (2009); Phillip J. Kolczynski, *The Criminal Liability of Aviators and Related Issues of Mixed Criminal-Civil Litigation: "A Venture in the Twilight Zone,"* 51 J. AIR L. & COM. 1 (1985); Pierre Sparaco, *An Icon on Trial*, AVIATION WK. & SPACE TECH., Mar. 29/Apr. 5, 2010, at 45. Pierre Sparaco, *Elusive Denouement*, AVIATION WK. & SPACE TECH., June 14/21, 2010, at 71 ("The trial . . . further confirms that accident investigations and judiciary probes are largely incompatible."). *See also United States v. Sabretech, Inc.*, 271 F.3d 1018 (11th Cir. 2001).

Case Study—NTSB Probable Cause Report

The National Transportation Safety Board ("NTSB") was established in 1967 to conduct independent investigations of all civil aviation accidents in the United States and major accidents in the other modes of transportation. It is not part of the Department of Transportation, nor organizationally affiliated with any of DOT's modal agencies, including the Federal Aviation Administration. The Safety Board has no regulatory or enforcement powers.

One of the main products of the NTSB are Accident Reports, which "provide details about the accident, analysis of the factual data, conclusions and the probable cause of the accident, and the related safety recommendations.

The NTSB also maintains an aviation accident database that contains information from 1962 and later about civil aviation accidents and selected incidents within the United States, its territories and possessions, and in international waters. *See* Aviation Accident Database & Synopses, https://www.ntsb.gov/_layouts/ntsb.aviation/index.aspx.

Importantly, an accident is different than an incident for NTSB investigation purposes. An incident is "[a]n occurrence other than an accident associated with the operation of an aircraft, which affects or could affect the safety of operations." 49 C.F.R. § 830.2. An accident is an occurrence associated with the operation of an aircraft that: (1) takes place between the time any person boards the aircraft with the intention flight and all such persons have disembarked, and in which (2) any person suffers death or serious injury, or in which the aircraft suffers substantial damages.

- Examples of "serious injury" in this context include something that requires hospitalization for more than 48 hours, commencing within seven days of the date of the injury, a fracture of any bone (but not fractures of fingers, toes, or nose), or second or third degree burns affecting more than five percent of the body surface.

- Examples of "substantial damage," meanwhile includes damage or failure that adversely affects the structural strength, performance, or flight characteristics of the aircraft, and which would normally require major repair or replacement of the affected component. Substantial damage does *not* include bent fairings or cowling, dented skin, small punctured holes, or damage to landing gear, wheels, tires, flaps, engine accessories.

Where an accident has occurred, the NTSB is charged with determining the probable cause of the event. The probable cause report is the last stage in a rigorous investigative process:

> To ensure that Safety Board investigations focus only on improving transportation safety, the Board's analysis of factual information and its determination of probable cause cannot be entered as evidence in a court of law.

The NTSB "Go Team"

At the core of NTSB investigations is the "Go Team." The purpose of the Safety Board Go Team is simple and effective: Begin the investigation of a major accident at the accident scene, as quickly as possible, assembling the broad spectrum of technical expertise that is needed to solve complex transportation safety problems.

The team can number from three or four to more than a dozen specialists from the Board's headquarters staff in Washington, D.C., who are assigned on a rotational basis to respond as quickly as possible to the scene of the accident. Go Teams travel by commercial airliner or government aircraft depending on circumstances and availability. Such teams have been winging to catastrophic airline crash sites for more than 35 years.

During their time on the "duty" rotation, members must be reachable 24 hours a day by telephone at the office or at home, or by pager. Most Go Team members do not have a suitcase pre-packed because there's no way of knowing whether the accident scene will be in Florida or Alaska, but they do have tools of their trade handy— carefully selected wrenches, screwdrivers and devices peculiar to their specialty. All carry flashlights, tape recorders, cameras, and lots of extra tape and film.

The Go Team's immediate boss is the Investigator-in-Charge (IIC), a senior investigator with years of NTSB and industry experience. Each investigator is a specialist responsible for a clearly defined portion of the accident investigation. In aviation, these specialties and their responsibilities are:

Operations. The history of the accident flight and crewmembers' duties for as many days prior to the crash as appears relevant.

Structures. Documentation of the airframe wreckage and the accident scene, including calculation of impact angles to help determine the plane's pre-impact course and attitude.

Powerplants. Examination of engines (and propellers) and engine accessories.

Systems. Study of components of the plane's hydraulic, electrical, pneumatic and associated systems, together with instruments and elements of the flight control system.

Air Traffic Control. Reconstruction of the air traffic services given the plane, including acquisition of ATC radar data and transcripts of controller-pilot radio transmissions.

Weather. Gathering of all pertinent weather data from the National Weather Service, and sometimes from local TV stations, for a broad area around the accident scene.

Human Performance: Study of crew performance and all before-the-accident factors that might be involved in human error, including fatigue, medication, alcohol. Drugs, medical histories, training, workload, equipment design and work environment.

Survival Factors. Documentation of impact forces and injuries, evacuation, community emergency planning and all crash-fire-rescue efforts.

Under direction of the IIC, each of these NTSB investigators heads what is called a "working group" in one area of expertise. Each is, in effect, a subcommittee of the overall investigating team. The groups are staffed by representatives of the "parties" to the investigation—the Federal Aviation Administration, the airline, the pilots' and flight attendants' unions, airframe and engine manufacturers, and the like. Pilots would assist the operations group; manufacturers' experts, the structures, systems and power plants groups; etc. Often, added groups are formed at the accident scene—aircraft performance, maintenance records, and eyewitnesses, for example. Flight data recorder and cockpit voice recorder teams assemble at NTSB headquarters. * * *

At least once daily during the on-scene phase of an investigation, one of the five Members of the Safety Board itself, who accompanies the team, briefs the media on the latest factual information developed by the team. While a career investigator runs the inquiry as Investigator-in-Charge, the Board Member is the primary spokesperson for the investigation. A public affairs officer also maintains contact with the media. Confirmed, factual information is released. There is no speculation over cause.

At major accidents, transportation disaster assistance specialists also accompany the team to fulfill the Board's responsibilities under the Aviation Disaster Family Assistance Act of 1996 and the Rail Passenger Disaster Family Assistance Act of 2008. See the Disaster

Assistance section of the NTSB' web site for details on this activity.

The individual working groups remain as long as necessary at the accident scene. This varies from a few days to several weeks. Some then move on—power plants to an engine teardown at a manufacturer or overhaul facility; systems to an instrument manufacturer's plant; operations to the airline's training base, for example. Their work continues at Washington headquarters, forming the basis for later analysis and drafting of a proposed report that goes to the Safety Board itself perhaps 12 to 18 months from the date of the accident. Safety recommendations may be issued at any time during the course of an investigation.

Aviation Go Teams respond only to accidents that occur on U.S. territory or in international waters. Elsewhere, the investigator is the government in whose territory the accident occurs, usually assisted by a U.S. "accredited representative" from the NTSB's staff of IICs if a U.S. carrier or U.S. manufactured plane is involved.

Source: https://www.ntsb.gov/investigations/process/Pages/default.aspx.

The title page of the NTSB Accident Report arising from the "Miracle on the Hudson" in 2009 follows:

Illustration 12-1. "Miracle on the Hudson"— NTSB Probable Cause Report

Loss of Thrust in Both Engines After Encountering a Flock of
Birds and Subsequent Ditching on the Hudson River
US Airways Flight 1549
Airbus A320-214, N106US
Weehawken, New Jersey
January 15, 2009

Accident Report

NTSB/AAR-10/03
PB2010-910403

 **National
Transportation
Safety Board**

EXERCISE 12-3. AIR FLORIDA 90

See the NTSB report relating to the accident of Air Florida Flight 90 on January 13, 1982 and explain what happened and the probable cause of the accident:

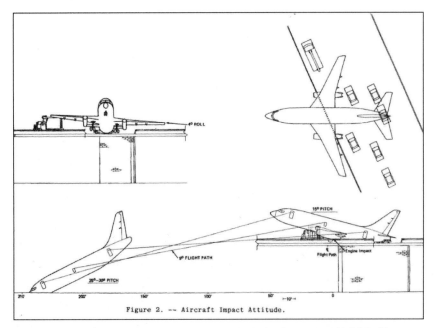

Figure 2. -- Aircraft Impact Attitude.

Source: NAT'L TRANSP. SAFETY BD., Air Florida, Inc. Boeing 737-222, N62AF, Collision with 14th Street Bridge, NTSB No. AAR8208, January 13, 1982, https://www.ntsb.gov/investigations/AccidentReports/Pages/AAR8208.aspx.

Is the report admissible in court? Explain.

C. JURISDICTION

EXECUTIVE JET AVIATION, INC. V. CITY OF CLEVELAND, OHIO
409 U.S. 249 (1972)

MR. JUSTICE STEWART delivered the opinion for a unanimous Court.

On July 28, 1968, a jet aircraft, owned and operated by the petitioners, struck a flock of seagulls as it was taking off from Burke Lakefront Airport in Cleveland, Ohio, adjacent to Lake Erie. As a result, the plane lost its power, crashed, and ultimately sank in the navigable waters of Lake Erie, a short distance from the airport. The question before us is whether the petitioner's suit for property damage to the aircraft, allegedly caused by the respondents' negligence, lies within federal admiralty jurisdiction.

When the crash occurred, the plane was manned by a pilot, a co-pilot, and a stewardess, and was departing Cleveland on a charter flight to Portland, Maine, where it was to pick up passengers and then continue to White Plains, New York. After being cleared for takeoff by the respondent Dicken, who was the federal air traffic controller at the airport, the plane took off, becoming airborne at about half the distance down the runway. The takeoff flushed the seagulls on the runway, and they rose into the airspace directly ahead of the ascending plane. Ingestion of the birds into the plane's jet engines caused an almost total loss of power. Descending back toward the runway in a semi-stalled condition, the plane veered slightly to the left, struck a portion of the airport perimeter fence and the top of a nearby pickup truck, and then settled in Lake Erie just off the end of the runway and less than one-fifth of a statute mile offshore. There were no injuries to the crew, but the aircraft soon sank and became a total loss.

Invoking federal admiralty jurisdiction under 28 U.S.C. § 1333(1), the petitioners brought this suit for damages in the District Court for the Northern District of Ohio against Dicken and the other respondents alleging that the crash had been caused by the respondents' negligent failure to keep the runway free of the birds or to give adequate warning of their presence. The District Court, in an unreported opinion, held that the suit was not cognizable in admiralty and dismissed the complaint for lack of subject matter jurisdiction.

Locality and Maritime Relationship Criteria

Relying primarily on the Sixth Circuit precedent of *Chapman v. City of Grosse Pointe Farms*, 385 F.2d 962 (6th Cir. 1967), the District Court held that admiralty jurisdiction over torts may properly be invoked only when two criteria are met: (1) the locality where the alleged tortious wrong occurred must have been on navigable waters; and (2) there must have been a relationship between the wrong and some maritime service, navigation, or commerce on navigable waters. The District Court found that the allegations of the petitioners' complaint satisfied neither of these criteria. With respect to the locality of the alleged wrong, the court stated that "the alleged negligence became operative upon the aircraft while it was over the land; and in this sense the 'impact' of the alleged negligence occurred with the gulls disabled the plane's engines (over the land) . . . From this point on the plane was disabled and was caused to fall. Whether it came down upon land or upon water was largely fortuitous." Alternatively, the court concluded that the wrong bore no relationship to maritime service, navigation, or commerce.

The Court of Appeals for the Sixth Circuit affirmed on the ground that "the alleged tort in this case occurred on land before the aircraft reached Lake Erie . . ." Hence, that court found it "not necessary to consider the question of maritime relationship or nexus." We granted *certiorari* to consider a seemingly important question affecting the jurisdiction of the federal courts.

* * *

Determination of the question whether a tort is "maritime" and thus within the admiralty jurisdiction of the federal courts has traditionally depended upon the locality of the wrong. If the wrong occurred on navigable waters, the action is within admiralty jurisdiction; if the wrong occurred on land, it is not.

Locality Test, Origin and Challenges

This locality test, of course, was established and grew up in an era when it was difficult to conceive of a tortious occurrence on navigable waters other than in connection with a waterborne vessel. Indeed, for the traditional types of maritime torts, the traditional test has worked quite satisfactorily. As a leading admiralty text has put the matter:

> It should be stressed that the important cases in admiralty are not the borderline cases on jurisdiction; these may exercise a perverse fascination in the occasion they afford for elaborate casuistry, but the main business of the (admiralty) court involves claims for cargo damage, collision, seamen's injuries and the like-all well and comfortably within the circle, and far from the penumbra.

G. GILMORE & C. BLACK, THE LAW OF ADMIRALTY 24 n.88 (1957). But it is the perverse and casuistic borderline situations that have demonstrated some of the problems with the locality test of maritime tort jurisdiction.

In *Smith & Son v. Taylor* (1928), for instance, a longshoreman unloading a vessel was standing on the pier when he was struck by a cargo laden sling from the ship and knocked into the water where he was later found dead. This Court held that there was no admiralty jurisdiction in that case, despite the fact that the longshoreman was knocked into the water, because the blow by the sling was what gave rise to the cause of action, and it took effect on the land. Hence, the Court concluded, "(t)he substance and consummation of the occurrence which gave rise to the cause of action took place on land." In the converse factual setting, however, where a longshoreman working on the deck of a vessel was struck by a hoist and knocked onto the pier, the Court upheld admiralty jurisdiction because the cause of action arose on the vessel.

Other serious difficulties with the locality test are illustrated by cases where the maritime locality of the tort is clear, but where the invocation of admiralty jurisdiction seems almost absurd. If a swimmer at a public beach is injured by another swimmer or by a submerged object on the bottom, or if a piece of machinery sustains water damage from being dropped into a harbor by a land-based crane, a literal application of the locality test invokes not only the jurisdiction of the federal courts, but the full panoply of the substantive admiralty law as well. In cases such as these, some courts have adhered to a mechanical application of the strict locality rule and have sustained admiralty jurisdiction despite and lack of any connection between the wrong and traditional forms of maritime commerce and navigation. Other courts, however, have held in such situations that a maritime locality is not sufficient to bring the tort within federal admiralty jurisdiction, but that there must also be a maritime nexus—some relationship between the tort and traditional maritime activities, involving navigation or commerce on navigable waters.

Apart from the difficulties involved in trying to apply the locality rule as the sole test of admiralty tort jurisdiction, another indictment of that test is to be found in the number of times the federal courts and the Congress, in the interests of justice, have had to create exceptions to it in the converse situation, *i.e.*, when the tort has no maritime locality, but does bear a relationship to maritime service, commerce, or navigation.

In sum, there has existed over the years a judicial, legislative, and scholarly recognition that, in determining whether there is admiralty jurisdiction over a particular tort or class of torts, reliance on the relationship of the wrong to traditional maritime activity is often more sensible and consonant with the purposes of maritime law than a purely mechanical application of the locality test.

* * *

One area in which locality as the exclusive test of admiralty tort jurisdiction has given rise to serious problems in application is that of aviation. We have concluded that maritime locality alone is not a sufficient predicate for admiralty jurisdiction in aviation tort cases.

In one of the earliest aircraft cases brought in admiralty, *The Crawford Bros., No. 2,* 215 F. 269 (W.D. Wash. 1914), in which a libel *in rem* for repairs was brought against an airplane that had crashed into Puget Sound, the federal court declined to assume jurisdiction, reasoning that an airplane could not be characterized as a maritime vessel. *The Crawford Bros.* was followed by a number of cases dealing with seaplanes, in which the courts restricted admiralty jurisdiction to occurrences involving planes that were afloat on navigable waters.

Continuing doubt as to the applicability of admiralty law to aircraft was illustrated by cases in the 1930's and 1940's holding that aircraft owners could not invoke the benefits of the maritime doctrine of limitation of liability, and that crimes committed on board aircraft flying over international waters were not punishable under criminal statutes proscribing acts committed on the high seas. Moreover, Congress exempted all aircraft from conformity with United States navigation and shipping laws under the Federal Aviation Act of 1958.

In 1952, however, Congress amended the criminal jurisdiction of admiralty to include crimes committed aboard aircraft while in flight over the high seas or any other waters within the admiralty jurisdiction of the United States except waters within the territorial jurisdiction of any State. The first major extension of admiralty jurisdiction to land-based aircraft came in wrongful-death actions arising out of aircraft crashes at sea and brought under the Death on the High Seas Act, 46 U.S.C. § 761 *et seq.* The federal courts took jurisdiction of such cases because the literal provisions of that statute appeared to be clearly applicable.

The Death on the High Seas Act, enacted in 1920, provides:

> Whenever the death of a person shall be caused by wrongful act, neglect, or default occurring on the high seas beyond a marine league from the shore of any State, or the District of Columbia, or the Territories or dependencies of the United States, the personal representative of the decedent may maintain a suit for damages in the district courts of the United States, in admiralty.

The first aviation case brought pursuant to the Death on the High Seas Act was apparently *Choy v. Pan American Airways Co.*, 1941 A.M.C. 483 (S.D.N.Y. 1941), where death was caused by the crash of a seaplane into the Pacific Ocean during a transoceanic flight. The District Court upheld admiralty jurisdiction on the ground that the language of the Act was broad and made no reference to surface vessels. According to the court:

> The statute certainly includes the phrase 'on the high seas' but there is no reason why this should make the law operable only on a horizontal plane. The very next phrase 'beyond a marine league from the shore of any State' may be said to include a vertical sense and another dimension.

Since *Choy*, many actions for wrongful death arising out of aircraft crashes into the high seas beyond one marine league from shore have been brought under the Death on the High Seas Act, and federal jurisdiction has consistently been sustained in those cases. Indeed, it may be considered as settled today that this specific federal statute gives the federal admiralty courts jurisdiction of such wrongful-death actions.

* * *

These latter cases graphically demonstrate the problems involved in applying a locality-alone test of admiralty tort jurisdiction to the crashes of aircraft. Airplanes, unlike waterborne vessels, are not limited by physical boundaries and can and do operate over both land and navigable bodies of water. As Professor Moore and his colleague Professor Pelaez have stated, "In both death and injury cases . . . it is evident that while distinctions based on locality often are in fact quite relevant where water vessels are concerned, they entirely lose their significance where aircraft, which are not geographically restrained, are concerned." 7A J. MOORE, FEDERAL PRACTICE, ADMIRALTY, .330(5), at 3772–73.

Admiralty Jurisdiction Based on Accident Site?

In flights within the continental United States, which are principally over land, the fact that an aircraft happens to fall in navigable waters, rather than on land, is wholly fortuitous. The ALI STUDY observed:

> If a plane takes off from Boston's Logan Airport bound for Philadelphia, and crashes on takeoff, it makes little sense that the next of kin of the passengers killed should be left to their usual remedies, ordinarily in state court, if the plane crashes on land, but that they have access to a federal court, and the distinctive substantive law of admiralty applies, if the wrecked plane ends up in the waters of Boston Harbor.

Moreover, not only is the locality test in such cases wholly adventitious, but it is sometimes almost impossible to apply with any degree of certainty. Under the locality test, the tort "occurs" where the alleged negligence took effect, and in the case of aircraft that locus is often most difficult to determine.

The case before us provides a good example of these difficulties. The petitioners contend that since their aircraft crashed into the navigable waters of Lake Erie and was totally destroyed when it sank in those waters, the locality of the tort, or the place where the alleged negligence took effect, was there. The fact that the major damage to their plane would not have occurred if it had not landed in the lake indicates, they say, that the substance and consummation of the wrong took place in navigable waters.

The respondents, on the other hand, argue that the alleged negligence took effect when the plane collided with the birds-over land. Relying on cases such as *Smith & Son v. Taylor, supra,* where admiralty jurisdiction was denied in the case of a longshoreman struck by a ship's sling while standing on a pier, and knocked into the water, the respondents contend that a tort "occurs" at the point of first impact of the alleged negligence. Here, they say, the cause of action arose as soon as the plane struck the birds; from then on, the plane was destined to fall, and whether it came down on land or water should not affect "the locality of the act."

In the view we take of the question before us, we need not decide who has the better of this dispute. It is enough to note that either position gives rise to the problems inherent in applying the strict locality test of admiralty tort jurisdiction in aviation accident cases. The petitioners' argument, if accepted, would make jurisdiction depend on where the plane ended up—a circumstance that could be wholly fortuitous and completely unrelated to the tort itself.

The anomaly is well illustrated by the hypothetical case of two aircraft colliding at a high altitude, with one crashing on land and the other in a navigable river. If, on the other hand, the respondents' position were adopted, jurisdiction would depend on whether the plane happened to be flying over land or water when the original impact of the alleged negligence occurred. This circumstance, too, could be totally fortuitous. If the plane in the present case struck the birds over Cleveland's Lakefront Airport, admiralty jurisdiction would not lie; but if the plane had just crossed the shoreline when it struck the birds, admiralty jurisdiction would attach, even if the plane were then able to make it back to the airport and crash land there. These are hardly the types of distinctions with which admiralty law was designed to deal.

The mere fact that the alleged wrong "occurs" or "is located" on or over navigable waters—whatever that means in an aviation context—is not of itself sufficient to turn an airplane negligence case into a "maritime tort." It is far more consistent with the history and purpose of admiralty to require also that the wrong bear a significant relationship to traditional maritime activity. We hold that unless such a relationship exists, claims arising from airplane accidents are not cognizable in admiralty in the absence of legislation to the contrary.

All these and other difficulties that can arise in attempting to apply the locality test of admiralty jurisdiction to aeronautical torts are, of course, attributable to the inherent nature of aircraft. Unlike waterborne vessels, they are not restrained by one—dimensional geographic and physical boundaries. For this elementary reason, we conclude that the mere fact that the alleged wrong "occurs" or "is located" on or over navigable waters—whatever that means in an aviation context—is not of itself sufficient to turn an airplane negligence case into a "maritime tort." It is far more consistent with the history and purpose of admiralty to require also that the wrong bear a significant relationship to traditional maritime activity. We hold that unless such a relationship exists, claims arising from airplane accidents are not cognizable in admiralty in the absence of legislation to the contrary.

This conclusion, however, does not end our inquiry, for there remains the question of what constitutes, in the context of aviation, a significant relationship to traditional maritime activity.

The petitioners argue that any aircraft falling into navigable waters has a sufficient relationship to maritime activity to satisfy the test. The relevant analogy, they say, is not between flying aircraft and sailing ships, but between a downed plane and a sinking ship. Quoting from the *Weinstein v. Eastern Airlines, Inc.*, 316 F.2d 758 (3d Cir. 1963), opinion, they contend: "When an aircraft crashes into navigable waters, the dangers to persons and property are much the same as those arising out of the sinking of a ship or a collision between two vessels." The dissenting opinion in the Court of Appeals in the present case made the same argument:

> I believe that there are many comparisons between the problems of aircraft over navigable waters and those of the ships which the aircraft are rapidly replacing.

> Problems posed for aircraft landing on, crashing on, or sinking into navigable waters differ markedly from landings upon land. In such instances, wind and wave and water, the normal problems of the mariner, become the approach or survival problems of the pilot and his passengers. What I would hold is that tort cases arising out of aircraft crashes into navigable waters are cognizable in admiralty jurisdiction even if the negligent conduct is alleged to have happened wholly on land.

We cannot accept that definition of traditional maritime activity. It is true that in a literal sense there may be some similarities between the problems posed for a plane downed on water and those faced by a sinking ship. But the differences between the two modes of transportation are far greater, in terms of their basic qualities and traditions and consequently in terms of the conceptual expertise of the law to be applied. Moreover, if the mere happenstance that an aircraft falls into navigable waters creates a maritime relationship because of the maritime dangers to a sinking plane, then the maritime relationship test would be the same as the petitioners' view of the maritime-locality test, with the same inherent fortuity.

The law of admiralty has evolved over many centuries, designed and molded to handle problems of vessels relegated to ply the waterways of the world, beyond whose shores they cannot go. That law deals with navigational rules-rules that govern the manner and direction those vessels may rightly move upon the waters. When a collision occurs or a ship founders at sea, the law of admiralty looks to those rules to determine fault, liability, and all other questions that may arise from such a catastrophe. Through long experience, the law of the sea knows how to determine whether a particular ship is seaworthy, and it knows the nature of maintenance and cure. It is concerned with maritime liens, the general average, captures and prizes, limitation of liability, cargo damage, and claims for salvage.

Aviation's Relationship to Traditional Maritime Activity?

Rules and concepts such as these are wholly alien to air commerce, whose vehicles operate in a totally different element, unhindered by geographical boundaries and exempt from the navigational rules of the maritime road. The matters with which admiralty is basically concerned have no conceivable bearing on the operation of aircraft, whether over land or water. Indeed, in contexts other than tort, Congress and the courts have recognized that, because of these differences, aircraft are not subject to maritime law. Although dangers of wind and wave faced by a plane that has crashed on navigable waters may be superficially similar to those encountered by a sinking ship, the plane's unexpected descent will almost invariably have been attributable to a cause unrelated to the sea—be it pilot error, defective design or manufacture of airframe or engine, error of a traffic controller at an airport, or some other cause; and the determination of liability will thus be based on factual and conceptual inquiries unfamiliar to the law of admiralty. It is clear, therefore, that neither the fact that a plane goes down on navigable waters nor the fact that the negligence "occurs" while a plane is flying over such waters is enough to create such a relationship to traditional maritime activity as to justify the invocation of admiralty jurisdiction.

We need not decide today whether an aviation tort can ever, under any circumstances bear a sufficient relationship to traditional maritime activity to come within admiralty jurisdiction in the absence of legislation. But, one commentator has posited:

> What possible rational basis is there in holding that the personal representative of a passenger killed in the crash of an airplane traveling from Shannon, Ireland to Logan Field in Boston has a cause of action within the admiralty jurisdiction if the plane goes down three miles from shore; may have a cause of action within the admiralty jurisdiction if the plane goes down within an area circumscribed by the shore and the three-mile limit; and will not have a cause of action within the admiralty jurisdiction if the plane managed to remain airborne until reaching the Massachusetts coast? And this notwithstanding that the plane may have developed engine trouble or been the victim of pilot error at an identical site far out over the Atlantic.

It could be argued, for instance, that if a plane flying from New York to London crashed in the mid-Atlantic, there would be admiralty jurisdiction over resulting tort claims even absent a specific statute. An aircraft in that situation might be thought to bear a significant relationship to traditional maritime activity because it would be performing a function traditionally performed by waterborne vessels. Apart from transoceanic flights, the Government's brief suggests that another example where admiralty jurisdiction might properly be invoked in an airplane accident case on the ground that the plane was performing a function traditionally performed by waterborne vessels, is shown in *Hornsby v. Fish Meal Co.*, 431 F.2d 865 (5th Cir. 1970), which involved the mid-air collision of two light aircraft used in spotting schools of fish and the crash of those aircraft into the Gulf of Mexico within one marine league of the Louisiana shore.

Moreover, other factors might come into play in the area of international air commerce-choice-of-forum problems, choice of law problems, international-law problems, problems involving multi-nation conventions and treaties, and so on In such a situation, it has been stated: "Were the maritime law not applicable, it is argued that the recovery would depend upon a confusing consideration of what substantive law to apply, *i.e.*, the law of the forum, the law of the place where each decedent (or injured party) purchased his ticket, the law of the place where the plane took off, or, perhaps, the law of the point of destination."

But none of these considerations is of concern in the case before us. The flight of the petitioners' land-based aircraft was to be from Cleveland to Portland, Maine, and thence to White Plains, New York—a flight that would have been almost entirely over land was within the continental United States. After it struck the flock of seagulls over the runway, the plane descended the settled in Lake Erie within the territorial waters of Ohio. We can find no significant relationship between such an even befalling a land-based plane flying from one point in the continental United States to another, and traditional maritime activity involving navigation and commerce on navigable waters.

In the situation before us, which is only fortuitously and incidentally connected to navigable waters and which bears no relationship to traditional maritime activity, the Ohio courts could plainly exercise jurisdiction over the suit, (there is no diversity of citizenship between petitioners and the City of Cleveland) and could plainly apply familiar concepts of Ohio tort law without any effect on maritime endeavors. The possibility that the petitioners would have to litigate the same claim in two forums is the same possibility that would exist if their plane had stopped on the shore of the lake, instead of going into the water, and is the same possibility that exists every time a plane goes down on land, negligence of the federal air traffic controller is alleged, and there is no diversity of citizenship. This problem cannot be solved merely by upholding admiralty jurisdiction in cases where the plane happens to fall on navigable waters.

It may be, as the petitioners argue, that aviation tort cases should be governed by uniform substantive and procedural laws and that such actions should be heard in the federal courts so as to avoid divergent results and duplicitous litigation in multi-party cases. But for this Court to uphold federal admiralty jurisdiction in a few wholly fortuitous aircraft cases would be a most quixotic way of approaching that goal. If federal uniformity is the desired goal with respect to claims arising from aviation accidents, Congress is free under the Commerce Clause to enact legislation applicable to all such accidents, whether occurring on land or water, and adapted to the specific characteristics of air commerce.

For the reasons stated in this opinion we hold that, in the absence of legislation to the contrary, there is no federal admiralty jurisdiction over aviation tort claims arising from flights by land-based aircraft between points within the continental United States. (Some such flights, *e.g.*, New York City to Miami, Florida, no doubt involve passage over "the high seas beyond a marine league from the shore of any State." To the extent that the terms of the Death on the High Seas Act become applicable to such flights, that Act, of course, is "legislation to the contrary.") The judgment is affirmed.

EXERCISE 12-4. *EXECUTIVE JET AVIATION, INC. V. CITY OF CLEVELAND, OHIO*—SUBJECT MATTER JURISDICTION (ADMIRALTY)

1. What is federal admiralty jurisdiction under 28 U.S.C. § 1333?

2. What is the "locality test" and identify the legal problems it has presented for courts?

3. Explain the concept of "a significant relationship to traditional maritime activity" for purposes of jurisdiction over an airplane accident.

4. State the holding of *Executive Jet Aviation, Inc. v. City of Cleveland, Ohio*.

5. What role, according to the court, has (and perhaps, should) Congress play in establishing admiralty jurisdiction for aviation accidents? Consider, for example, that in 2002, Congress passed the Multiparty, Multiforum Trial Jurisdiction Act of 2002, which greatly expanded the original and removal jurisdiction of the federal courts by granting federal district courts original jurisdiction over mass tort cases involving at least 75 deaths in a discrete location arising from a single

accident where there is only minimal diversity between adverse parties. *See* Kristine Cordier Karnezis, *Construction and Application of Multiparty, Multiforum, Trial Jurisdiction Act of 2002 (MMTJA), 28 U.S.C. § 1369*, 32 A.L.R. Fed. 2d 263 (2008).

NOTES ON *EXECUTIVE JET AVIATION, INC. V. CITY OF CLEVELAND, OHIO*—EXTENSION OF ADMIRALTY JURISDICTION ACT

While the "locality test" may not be sufficient for admiralty jurisdiction to attach to aviation accident litigation, the "significant relationship test" presented in the seminal case of *Executive Jet Aviation, Inc. v. City of Cleveland* (1972), *supra*, shows that the impact of an aviation incident, if any, on maritime commerce is an appropriate consideration. In that context, courts have found that the sinking of an aircraft in navigable waters creates a "potentially disruptive impact on maritime commerce" such that admiralty jurisdiction generally applies. *E.g., In re Air Crash at Belle Harbor New York on November 12, 2001*, 2006 WL 1288298 (S.D.N.Y. 2006).

The Extension of Admiralty Jurisdiction Act ("AEA"), 46 U.S.C. § 30101 (2006), originally enacted in 1948, extends the admiralty and maritime jurisdiction of the United States "to include all cases of damage or injury, to person or property, caused by a vessel on navigable water, notwithstanding that such damage or injury be done or consummated on land." The AEA was designed to "end the concern over the sometimes confusing line between land and water" by affording litigants a potential remedy in "all cases" in which a vessel causes an injury. *E.g., Gutierrez v. Waterman S.S. Corp.*, 373 U.S. 206 (1963) (finding vessel liable in admiralty for injuries to longshoremen who slipped on beans spilled on pier while cargo was being unloaded). The AEA will apply only to damage or injury that is caused by a "vessel on navigable water." *E.g., Pearson v. Northeast Airlines, Inc.*, 309 F.2d 553 (S.D.N.Y. 1961) (declining to apply AEA to an airplane crash occurring on an island, where the decedent "[s]ustained no injury of any kind contributing to his death while the airplane was in flight over the sea.").

For example, in considering whether a crane on a barge afloat in navigable waters could be a vessel under the AEA, the United Supreme Court considered a "connection test," *e.g.*, (1) whether the "general features" of an incident had "a potentially disruptive impact on maritime commerce," and (2) whether "the general character" of the "activity giving rise to the incident" showed a "substantial relationship to traditional maritime activity." *Jerome B. Grubart, Inc. v. Great Lakes Dredge & Dock Co.*, 513 U.S. 527 (1995).

PIPER AIRCRAFT CO. V. REYNO

454 U.S. 235 (1981)

JUSTICE MARSHALL delivered the opinion of the Court.

In July 1976, a small commercial aircraft crashed in the Scottish highlands during the course of a charter flight from Blackpool to Perth. The pilot and five passengers were killed instantly. The decedents were all Scottish subjects and residents, as are their heirs and next of kin. There were no eyewitnesses to the accident. At the time of the crash the plane was subject to Scottish air traffic control.

The aircraft, a twin-engine Piper Aztec, was manufactured in Pennsylvania by petitioner Piper Aircraft Co. ("Piper"). The propellers were manufactured in Ohio by petitioner Hartzell Propeller, Inc. ("Hartzell"). At the time of the crash the aircraft was registered in Great Britain and was owned and maintained by Air Navigation and Trading Co., Ltd. ("Air Navigation"). It was operated by McDonald Aviation, Ltd. ("McDonald"), a Scottish air taxi service. Both Air Navigation and McDonald were organized in the United Kingdom. The wreckage of the plane is now in a hangar in Farnsborough, England.

The British Department of Trade investigated the accident shortly after it occurred. A preliminary report found that the plane crashed after developing a spin, and suggested that mechanical failure in the plane or the propeller was responsible. At Hartzell's request, this report was reviewed by a three-member Review Board, which held a 9-day adversary hearing attended by all interested parties. The Review Board found no evidence of defective equipment and indicated that pilot error may have contributed to the accident. The pilot, who had obtained his commercial pilot's license only three months earlier, was flying over high ground at an altitude considerably lower than the minimum height required by his company's operations manual.

In July 1977, a California probate court appointed respondent Gaynell Reyno administratrix of the estates of the five passengers. Reyno is not related to and does not know any of the decedents or their survivors; she was a legal secretary to the attorney who filed this lawsuit. Several days after her appointment, Reyno commenced separate wrongful-death actions against Piper and Hartzell in the Superior Court of California, claiming negligence and strict liability. Air Navigation, McDonald, and the estate of the pilot are not parties to this litigation. The survivors of the five passengers whose estates are represented by Reyno filed a separate action in the United Kingdom against Air Navigation, McDonald, and the pilot's estate.

Ethics?

Reyno candidly admits that the action against Piper and Hartzell was filed in the United States because its laws regarding liability, capacity to sue, and damages are more favorable to her position than are those of Scotland. Scottish law does not recognize strict liability in tort. Moreover, it permits wrongful-death actions only when brought by a decedent's relatives. The relatives may sue only for "loss of support and society."

On petitioners' motion, the suit was removed to the United States District Court for the Central District of California. Piper then moved for transfer to the United States District Court for the Middle District of Pennsylvania, pursuant to 28 U.S.C. § 1404(a), which provides: "For the convenience of parties and witnesses, in the interest of justice, a district court may transfer any civil action to any other district or division where it might have been brought." Hartzell moved to dismiss for lack of personal jurisdiction, or in the alternative, to transfer. The District Court quashed service on Hartzell and transferred the case to the Middle District of Pennsylvania. Respondent then properly served process on Hartzell.

After the suit had been transferred, both Hartzell and Piper moved to dismiss the action on the ground of *forum non conveniens*. The District Court granted these motions, relying on the balancing test set forth by this Court in *Gulf Oil Corp. v. Gilbert*, 330 U.S. 501 (1947), and its companion case, *Koster v. Lumbermens Mut. Cas. Co.*, 330 U.S. 518 (1947).

In those decisions, the Court stated that a plaintiff's choice of forum should rarely be disturbed. However, when an alternative forum has jurisdiction to hear the case, and when trial in the chosen forum would "establish . . . oppressiveness and vexation to a defendant . . . out of all proportion to plaintiff's convenience," or when the "chosen forum [is] inappropriate because of considerations affecting the court's own administrative and legal problems," the court may, in the exercise of its sound discretion, dismiss the case. To guide trial court discretion, the Court provided a list of "private interest factors" affecting the convenience of the litigants, and a list of "public interest factors" affecting the convenience of the forum.

Private Interest Factors

The factors pertaining to the private interests of the litigants included the "relative ease of access to sources of proof; availability of compulsory process for attendance of unwilling, and the cost of obtaining attendance of willing, witnesses; possibility of view of premises, if view would be appropriate to the action; and all other practical problems that make trial of a case easy, expeditious and inexpensive."

The public factors bearing on the question included the administrative difficulties flowing from court congestion; the "local interest in having localized controversies decided at home"; the interest in having the trial of a diversity case in a forum that is at home with the law that must govern the action; the avoidance of unnecessary problems in conflict of laws, or in the application of foreign law; and the unfairness of burdening citizens in an unrelated forum with jury duty.

Public Factors

After describing our decisions in *Gilbert* and *Koster*, the District Court analyzed the facts of these cases. It began by observing that an alternative forum existed in Scotland; Piper and Hartzell had agreed to submit to the jurisdiction of the Scottish courts and to waive any statute of limitations defense that might be available. It then stated that plaintiff's choice of forum was entitled to little weight. The court recognized that a plaintiff's choice ordinarily deserves substantial deference. It noted, however, that Reyno "is a representative of foreign citizens and residents seeking a forum in the United States because of the more liberal rules concerning products liability law," and that "the courts have been less solicitous when the plaintiff is not an American citizen or resident, and particularly when the foreign citizens seek to benefit from the more liberal tort rules provided for the protection of citizens and residents of the United States."

The District Court next examined several factors relating to the private interests of the litigants, and determined that these factors strongly pointed towards Scotland as the appropriate forum. Although evidence concerning the design, manufacture, and testing of the plane and propeller is located in the United States, the connections with Scotland are otherwise "overwhelming." The real parties in interest are citizens of Scotland, as were all the decedents. Witnesses who could testify regarding the maintenance of the aircraft, the training of the pilot, and the investigation of the accident—all essential to the defense—are in Great Britain. Moreover, all witnesses to damages are located in Scotland. Trial would be aided by familiarity with Scottish topography, and by easy access to the wreckage.

The District Court reasoned that because crucial witnesses and evidence were beyond the reach of compulsory process, and because the defendants would not be able to implead potential Scottish third-party defendants, it would be "unfair to make Piper and Hartzell proceed to trial in this forum." The survivors had brought separate actions in Scotland against the pilot, McDonald, and Air Navigation. "[I]t would be fairer to all parties and less costly if the entire case was presented to one jury with available testimony from all relevant witnesses." Although the court recognized that if trial were held in the United States, Piper and Hartzell could file indemnity or contribution actions against the Scottish defendants, it believed that there was a significant risk of inconsistent verdicts. The District Court explained that inconsistent verdicts might result if petitioners were held liable on the basis of strict liability here, and then required to prove negligence in an indemnity action in Scotland. Moreover, even if the same standard of liability applied, there was a danger that different juries would find different facts and produce inconsistent results.

The District Court concluded that the relevant public interests also pointed strongly towards dismissal. The court determined that Pennsylvania law would apply to Piper and Scottish law to Hartzell if the case were tried in the Middle District of Pennsylvania. As a result, "trial in this forum would be hopelessly complex and confusing for a jury." In addition, the court noted that it was unfamiliar with Scottish law and thus would have to rely upon experts from that country. The court also found that the trial would be enormously costly and time-consuming; that it would be unfair to burden citizens with jury duty when the Middle District of Pennsylvania has little connection with the controversy; and that Scotland has a substantial interest in the outcome of the litigation.

In opposing the motions to dismiss, respondent contended that dismissal would be unfair because Scottish law was less favorable. The District Court explicitly rejected this claim. It reasoned that the possibility that dismissal might lead to an unfavorable change in the law did not deserve significant weight; any deficiency in the foreign law was a "matter to be dealt with in the foreign forum."

* * *

On appeal, the United States Court of Appeals for the Third Circuit reversed and remanded for trial. The decision to reverse appears to be based on two alternative grounds. First, the Court held that the District Court abused its discretion in conducting the *Gilbert* analysis. Second, the Court held that dismissal is never appropriate where the law of the alternative forum is less favorable to the plaintiff.

The Court of Appeals began its review of the District Court's *Gilbert* analysis by noting that the plaintiff's choice of forum deserved substantial weight, even though the real parties in interest are nonresidents. It then rejected the District Court's balancing of the private interests. It found that Piper and Hartzell had failed adequately to support their claim that key witnesses would be unavailable if trial were held in the United States: they had never specified the witnesses they would call and the testimony these witnesses would provide. The Court of Appeals gave little weight to the fact that Piper and Hartzell would not be able to implead potential Scottish third-party defendants, reasoning that this difficulty would be "burdensome" but not "unfair." Finally, the court stated that resolution of the suit would not be significantly aided by familiarity with Scottish topography, or by viewing the wreckage.

The Court of Appeals also rejected the District Court's analysis of the public interest factors. It found that the District Court gave undue emphasis to the application of Scottish law: " 'the mere fact that the court is called upon to determine and apply foreign law does not present a legal problem of the sort which would justify the dismissal of a case otherwise properly before the court.' " In any event, it believed that Scottish law need not be applied. After conducting its own choice-of-law analysis, the Court of Appeals determined that American law would govern the actions against both Piper and Hartzell. The same choice-of-law analysis apparently led it to conclude that Pennsylvania and Ohio, rather than Scotland, are the jurisdictions with the greatest policy interests in the dispute, and that all other public interest factors favored trial in the United States.

The Court of Appeals concluded as part of its choice-of-law analysis that the United States had the greatest policy interest in the dispute. It apparently believed that this conclusion necessarily implied that the *forum non conveniens* public interest factors pointed toward trial in the United States. In any event, it appears that the Court of Appeals would have reversed even if the District Court had properly balanced the public and private interests. The court stated:

> [I]t is apparent that the dismissal would work a change in the applicable law so that the plaintiff's strict liability claim would be eliminated from the case. But . . . a dismissal for *forum non conveniens*, like a statutory transfer, "should not, despite its convenience, result in a change in the applicable law." Only when American law is not applicable, or when the foreign jurisdiction would, as a matter of its own choice of law, give the plaintiff the benefit of the claim to which she is entitled here, would dismissal be justified."

In other words, the court decided that dismissal is automatically barred if it would lead to a change in the applicable law unfavorable to the plaintiff.

We granted *certiorari* in these cases to consider the questions they raise concerning the proper application of the doctrine of *forum non conveniens*, specifically: (1) whether, in an action in federal district court brought by foreign plaintiffs against American defendants, the plaintiffs may defeat a motion to dismiss on the ground of *forum non conveniens* merely by showing that the substantive law that would be applied if the case were litigated in the district court is more favorable to them than the law that would be applied by the courts of their own nation, and (2) whether a motion to dismiss on grounds of *forum non conveniens* [should] be denied whenever the law of the alternate forum is less favorable to recovery than that which would be applied by the district court.

* * *

Change in Substantive Law—Ground for Dismissal

The Court of Appeals erred in holding that plaintiffs may defeat a motion to dismiss on the ground of *forum non conveniens* merely by showing that the substantive law that would be applied in the alternative forum is less favorable to the plaintiffs than that of the present forum. The possibility of a change in substantive law should ordinarily not be given conclusive or even substantial weight in the *forum non conveniens* inquiry. *Gilbert* implicitly recognized that dismissal may not be barred solely because of the possibility of an unfavorable change in law.

Under *Gilbert*, dismissal will ordinarily be appropriate where trial in the plaintiff's chosen forum imposes a heavy burden on the defendant or the court, and where the plaintiff is unable to offer any specific reasons of convenience supporting his choice. If substantial weight were given to the possibility of an unfavorable change in law, however, dismissal might be barred even where trial in the chosen forum was plainly inconvenient.

The Court of Appeals' decision is inconsistent with this Court's earlier *forum non conveniens* decisions in another respect. Those decisions have repeatedly emphasized the need to retain flexibility. In *Gilbert*, the Court refused to identify specific circumstances "which will justify or require either grant or denial of remedy." Similarly, in *Koster*, the Court rejected the contention that where a trial would involve inquiry into the internal affairs of a foreign corporation, dismissal was always appropriate. "That is one, but only one, factor which may show convenience." And in *Williams v. Green Bay & Western R. Co.*, 326 U.S. 549 (1946), we stated that we would not lay down a rigid rule to govern discretion, and that "[e]ach case turns on its facts." If central emphasis were placed on any one factor, the *forum non conveniens* doctrine would lose much of the very flexibility that makes it so valuable.

In fact, if conclusive or substantial weight were given to the possibility of a change in law, the *forum non conveniens* doctrine would become virtually useless. Jurisdiction and venue requirements are often easily satisfied. As a result, many plaintiffs are able to choose from among several forums. Ordinarily, these plaintiffs will select that forum whose choice-of-law rules are most advantageous. Thus, if the possibility of an unfavorable change in substantive law is given substantial weight in the *forum non conveniens* inquiry, dismissal would rarely be proper.

The Court of Appeals' approach is not only inconsistent with the purpose of the *forum non conveniens* doctrine, but also poses substantial practical problems. If the possibility of a change in law were given substantial weight, deciding motions to dismiss on the ground of *forum non conveniens* would become quite difficult. Choice-of-law analysis would become extremely important, and the courts would frequently be required to interpret the law of foreign jurisdictions. First, the trial court would have to determine what law would apply if the case were tried in the chosen forum, and what law would apply if the case were tried in the alternative forum. It would then have to compare the rights, remedies, and procedures available under the law that would be applied in each forum. Dismissal would be appropriate only if the court concluded that the law applied by the alternative forum is as favorable to the plaintiff as that of the chosen forum.

The doctrine of *forum non conveniens*, however, is designed in part to help courts avoid conducting complex exercises in comparative law. As we stated in *Gilbert*, the public interest factors point towards dismissal where the court would be required to "untangle problems in conflict of laws, and in law foreign to itself."

Upholding the decision of the Court of Appeals would result in other practical problems. At least where the foreign plaintiff named an American manufacturer as defendant, a court could not dismiss the case on grounds of *forum non conveniens* where dismissal might lead to an unfavorable change in law. In fact, the defendant might not even have to be American. A foreign plaintiff seeking damages for an accident that occurred abroad might be able to obtain service of process on a foreign defendant who does business in the United States. Under the Court of Appeals' holding, dismissal would be barred if the law in the alternative forum were less favorable to the plaintiff—even though none of the parties are American, and even though there is absolutely no nexus between the subject matter of the litigation and the United States.

The American courts, which are already extremely attractive to foreign plaintiffs, would become even more attractive. First, all but 6 of the 50 American States—Delaware, Massachusetts, Michigan, North Carolina, Virginia, and Wyoming—offer strict liability. Rules roughly equivalent to American strict liability are effective in France, Belgium, and Luxembourg. West Germany and Japan have a strict liability statute for pharmaceuticals. However, strict liability remains primarily an American innovation. Second, the tort plaintiff may choose, at least potentially, from among 50 jurisdictions if he decides to file suit in the

United States. Each of these jurisdictions applies its own set of malleable choice-of-law rules. Third, jury trials are almost always available in the United States, while they are never provided in civil law jurisdictions. Even in the United Kingdom, most civil actions are not tried before a jury. Fourth, unlike most foreign jurisdictions, American courts allow contingent attorney's fees, and do not tax losing parties with their opponents' attorney's fees. Fifth, discovery is more extensive in American than in foreign courts.

The flow of litigation into the United States would increase and further congest already crowded courts. In holding that the possibility of a change in law unfavorable to the plaintiff should not be given substantial weight, we also necessarily hold that the possibility of a change in law favorable to defendant should not be considered.

Respondent suggests that Piper and Hartzell filed the motion to dismiss, not simply because trial in the United States would be inconvenient, but also because they believe the laws of Scotland are more favorable. She argues that this should be taken into account in the analysis of the private interests. We recognize, of course, that Piper and Hartzell may be engaged in reverse forum-shopping. However, this possibility ordinarily should not enter into a trial court's analysis of the private interests. If the defendant is able to overcome the presumption in favor of plaintiff by showing that trial in the chosen forum would be unnecessarily burdensome, dismissal is appropriate—regardless of the fact that defendant may also be motivated by a desire to obtain a more favorable forum.

We do not hold that the possibility of an unfavorable change in law should never be a relevant consideration in a *forum non conveniens* inquiry. Of course, if the remedy provided by the alternative forum is so clearly inadequate or unsatisfactory that it is no remedy at all, the unfavorable change in law may be given substantial weight; the district court may conclude that dismissal would not be in the interests of justice. At the outset of any *forum non conveniens* inquiry, the court must determine whether there exists an alternative forum. Ordinarily, this requirement will be satisfied when the defendant is "amenable to process" in the other jurisdiction.

In rare circumstances, however, where the remedy offered by the other forum is clearly unsatisfactory, the other forum may not be an adequate alternative, and the initial requirement may not be satisfied. Thus, for example, dismissal would not be appropriate where the alternative forum does not permit litigation of the subject matter of the dispute. In these cases, however, the remedies that would be provided by the Scottish courts do not fall within this category. Although the relatives of the decedents may not be able to rely on a strict liability theory, and although their potential damages award may be smaller, there is no danger that they will be deprived of any remedy or treated unfairly.

* * *

The Court of Appeals also erred in rejecting the District Court's *Gilbert* analysis. The Court of Appeals stated that more weight should have been given to the plaintiff's choice of forum, and criticized the District Court's analysis of the private and public interests. However, the District Court's decision regarding the deference due plaintiff's choice of forum was appropriate. Furthermore, we do not believe that the District Court abused its discretion in weighing the private and public interests.

When the home forum has been chosen, it is reasonable to assume that this choice is convenient. When the plaintiff is foreign, however, this assumption is much less reasonable. Because the central purpose of any forum non conveniens inquiry is to ensure that the trial is convenient, a foreign plaintiff's choice deserves less deference.

The District Court acknowledged that there is ordinarily a strong presumption in favor of the plaintiff's choice of forum, which may be overcome only when the private and public interest factors clearly point towards trial in the alternative forum. It held, however, that the presumption applies with less force when the plaintiff or real parties in interest are foreign. The District Court's distinction between resident or citizen plaintiffs and foreign plaintiffs is fully justified. In *Koster*, the Court indicated that a plaintiff's choice of forum is entitled to greater deference when the plaintiff has chosen the home forum. When the home forum has been chosen, it is reasonable to assume that this choice is convenient. When the plaintiff is foreign, however, this assumption is much less reasonable. Because the central purpose of any *forum non conveniens* inquiry is to ensure that the trial is convenient, a foreign plaintiff's choice deserves less deference.

Additionally, the *forum non conveniens* determination is committed to the sound discretion of the trial court. It may be reversed only when there has been a clear abuse of discretion; where the court has considered all relevant public and private interest factors, and where its balancing of these factors is reasonable, its decision deserves substantial deference. Here, the Court of Appeals expressly acknowledged that the standard of review was one of abuse of discretion. In examining the District Court's analysis of the public and private interests, however, the Court of Appeals seems to have lost sight of this rule, and substituted its own judgment for that of the District Court.

Court Discretion

In analyzing the private interest factors, the District Court stated that the connections with Scotland are "overwhelming." This characterization may be somewhat exaggerated. Particularly with respect to the question of relative ease of access to sources of proof, the private interests point in both directions. As respondent emphasizes, records concerning the design, manufacture, and testing of the propeller and plane are located in the United States. She would have greater access to sources of proof relevant to her strict liability and negligence theories if trial were held here. However, the District Court did not act unreasonably in concluding that fewer evidentiary problems would be posed if the trial were held in Scotland. A large proportion of the relevant evidence is located in Great Britain.

The Court of Appeals found that the problems of proof could not be given any weight because Piper and Hartzell failed to describe with specificity the evidence they would not be able to obtain if trial were held in the United States. It suggested that defendants seeking *forum non conveniens* dismissal must submit affidavits identifying the witnesses they would call and the testimony these witnesses would provide if the trial were held in the alternative forum. Such detail is not necessary. Piper and Hartzell have moved for dismissal precisely because many crucial witnesses are located beyond the reach of compulsory process, and thus are difficult to identify or interview. Requiring extensive investigation would defeat the purpose of their motion. Of course, defendants must provide enough information to enable the District Court to balance the parties' interests. Our examination of the record convinces us that sufficient information was provided here. Both Piper and Hartzell submitted affidavits describing the evidentiary problems they would face if the trial were held in the United States.

The District Court correctly concluded that the problems posed by the inability to implead potential third-party defendants clearly supported holding the trial in Scotland. Joinder of the pilot's estate, Air Navigation, and McDonald is crucial to the presentation of petitioners' defense. If Piper and Hartzell can show that the accident was caused not by a design defect, but rather by the negligence of the pilot, the plane's owners, or the charter company, they will be relieved of all liability. It is true, of course, that if Hartzell and Piper were found liable after a trial in the United States, they could institute an action for indemnity or contribution against these parties in Scotland. It would be far more convenient, however, to resolve all claims in one trial. The Court of Appeals rejected this argument. Forcing petitioners to rely on actions for indemnity or contributions would be "burdensome" but not "unfair." Finding that trial in the plaintiff's chosen forum would be burdensome, however, is sufficient to support dismissal on grounds of *forum non conveniens.*

The District Court's review of the factors relating to the public interest was also reasonable. On the basis of its choice-of-law analysis, it concluded that if the case were tried in the Middle District of Pennsylvania, Pennsylvania law would apply to Piper and Scottish law to Hartzell. It stated that a trial involving two sets of laws would be confusing to the jury. It also noted its own lack of familiarity with Scottish law. Consideration of these problems was clearly appropriate under *Gilbert*; in that case we explicitly held that the need to apply foreign law pointed towards dismissal. The Court of Appeals found that the District Court's choice-of-law analysis was incorrect, and that American law would apply to both Hartzell and Piper. Thus, lack of familiarity with foreign law would not be a problem. Even if the Court of Appeals' conclusion is correct, however, all other public interest factors favored trial in Scotland.

Scotland has a very strong interest in this litigation. The accident occurred in its airspace. All of the decedents were Scottish. Apart from Piper and Hartzell, all potential plaintiffs and defendants are either Scottish or English. As we stated in *Gilbert*, there is "a local interest in having localized controversies decided at home." Respondent argues that American citizens have an interest in ensuring that American manufacturers are deterred from producing defective products, and that additional deterrence might be obtained if Piper and Hartzell were tried in the United States, where they could be sued on the basis of both negligence and strict liability. However, the incremental deterrence that would be gained if this trial were held in an American court is likely to be insignificant. The American interest in this accident is simply not sufficient to justify the enormous commitment of judicial time and resources that would inevitably be required if the case were to be tried here.

American Interest in Accident?

The Court of Appeals erred in holding that the possibility of an unfavorable change in law bars dismissal on the ground of *forum non conveniens*. It also erred in rejecting the District Court's *Gilbert* analysis. The District Court properly decided that the presumption in favor of the respondent's forum choice applied with less than maximum force because the real parties in interest are foreign. It did not act unreasonably in deciding that the private interests pointed towards trial in Scotland. Nor did it act unreasonably in deciding that the public interests favored trial in Scotland.

JUSTICE STEVENS, with whom JUSTICE BRENNAN joins, dissenting.

I would simply remand the case to the Court of Appeals for further consideration of the question whether the District Court correctly decided that Pennsylvania was not a convenient forum in which to litigate a claim against a

Pennsylvania company that a plane was defectively designed and manufactured in Pennsylvania.

EXERCISE 12-5. *PIPER AIRCRAFT CO. V. REYNO—FORUM NON CONVENIENS*

1. Create a chart detailing which parties, events, and things were located in the United States and which were located in the United Kingdom. Do your results suggest where venue should lie? If so, where? And, why?

2. What is an administratrix? Who is she and what role did she serve in this litigation?

3. Why was this lawsuit filed in the United States according to the plaintiff?

4. Detail the analysis set out in *Gulf Oil Corp. v. Gilbert* with respect to forum.

5. What error did the Supreme Court in *Piper Aircraft Co. v. Reyno* find in the underlying opinion by the Court of Appeals for the Third Circuit?

NOTES ON *PIPER AIRCRAFT V. REYNO*—VENUE AND DEATH ON THE HIGH SEAS ACT ("DOHSA")

1. ***Why Jurisdiction Matters—Damages.***

On March 27, 1977, almost 600 people died when two Boeing 747 jumbo-jets collided on a runway in Tenerife in the Canary Islands. It was the worst aviation disaster prior to September 11, 2001. In litigation arising out of the tragedy, Dutch plaintiffs sued U.S.-based Pan American Airways and two of its New York-based crew members in American courts. Because all of the evidence was located in the Netherlands and Dutch civil law applied, the case was dismissed from an American court on grounds of *forum non conveniens. Bouvy-Loggers v. Pan American World Airways, Inc.*, 1978 U.S. Dist. LEXIS 18792 (S.D.N.Y. 1978). The case epitomizes the fact that United States courts are attractive forums for non-U.S. plaintiffs to try aviation cases for accidents occurring outside the United States.

American juries generally award higher damages awards—including punitive damages—than fact finders in foreign jurisdictions. Additionally, plaintiffs are advantaged by the liberal discovery regime, availability of legal theories including strict liability, and contingency fee arrangements permitted under federal and state rules of civil procedure. *See generally* Lory Barsdate Easton, *Getting out of Dodge: Defense Pointers on Jurisdictional Issues in Aviation Torts Litigation*, 20–WTR Air & Space Law. 9, 9 (2006). When considering whether to move for dismissal on grounds of *forum non conveniens*, therefore, aviation defense counsel consider the causes of action available to plaintiff, potential ranges of damages awards, the civil procedure and appeal process, the typical time from filing to disposition of a complex civil action, local attitudes toward U.S. corporate defendants, the availability of documents and witnesses, the procedures (if any) for nonparty discovery, the viability of contribution or indemnity claims against other potentially responsible parties, the methods for enforcement of judgments and risks of asset seizure, and any potential for criminal prosecution arising from torts liability claims.

Id. See also Ronald A. Brand, *Comparative Forum Non Conveniens and the Hague Convention on Jurisdiction and Judgments*, 37 TEX. INT'L L.J. 467 (2002); James L. Baudino, Comment, *Venue Issues against Negligent Carriers—International and Domestic Travel; The Plaintiff's Choice?*, 62 J. AIR L. & COM. 163 (1996); Alexander Reus, *Judicial Discretion: A Comparative View of the Doctrine of Forum Non Conveniens in the United States, the United Kingdom, and Germany*, 16 LOY. L.A. INT'L & COMP. L.J. 455 (1994).

2. *Choice of Law and the Restatement (Second) of Torts.*

Choice-of-law may be the most important preliminary issue in an aviation injury and wrongful death case, potentially representing the difference between multi-million-dollar and no recovery. As one authority stated, however, the law of conflicts generally is a "dismal swamp, filled with quaking quagmires, and inhabited by learned but eccentric professors who theorize about mysterious matters in a strange and incomprehensible jargon." William Prosser, *Interstate Publication*, 51 MICH. L. REV. 959, 971 (1953).

In diversity actions, federal courts apply the choice-of-law rules of the forum state, and in multi-district litigation, the court in which jurisdiction ultimately rests must apply the choice-of-law rules of the state that applied in the court from which the case was transferred. In addition to these scenarios, the aviation practitioner must recognize several choice-of-law approaches, including the traditional or *lex loci delicti* doctrine articulated in the Restatement (First) of Conflict of Law, the *lex fori* doctrine, the analysis recommended by the Restatement (Second), or the "most significant contacts," "better law," or "combined modern" approaches.

Most courts generally apply the "most significant relationship" test under the Second Restatement in resolving choice-of-law issues. Section 175 of the Restatement (Second) provides that, "[i]n an action for wrongful death, the local law of the state where the injury occurred determines the rights and liabilities of the parties unless, with respect to the particular issue, some other state has a more significant relationship." RESTATEMENT (SECOND) OF CONFLICTS OF LAWS (1971). *See also Trumpet Vine Investments, N.V. v. Union Capital Partners I, Inc.*, 92 F.3d 110, 1115 (11th Cir. 1996). The careful practitioner will be aware that the Second Restatement approach is not uniformly applied, even if it is the majority approach. *See* James P. George, *False Conflicts and Faulty Analyses: Judicial Misuse of Government Interests in the Second Restatement of Conflict of Laws*, 23 REV. LITIG. 489, 490–91 (2004).

Under the doctrine of *dépeçage*, a state's own interests and policies concerning a precise issue in an aviation accident merit critical attention. For example, with respect to damages, a court must attempt to determine which of multiple states having some relationship to the parties or the crash has the most significant interest in the application of its own substantive law to the merits of a claim for punitive damages. Section 145 of the Second Restatement reinforces the point that "[t]he rights and liabilities of the parties with respect to an issue in tort are determined by the local law of the state which, with respect to that issue, has the most significant relationship to the occurrence and the parties . . ."

In the absence of any statutory directive of a state's own choice of law, Section 6 of the Restatement (Second) sets out several administrative factors relevant to choice-of-law: (a) the needs of the interstate and international systems; (b) the relevant policies of the forum; (c) the relevant policies of other interested states and the relative interests of those states in the determination of the particular issue; (d) the protection of justified expectations; (e) the basic policies underlying the particular field of law; (f) certainty, predictability, and uniformity of result; and (g) ease in the determination and application of the law to be applied.

Moreover, Section 145 of the Second Restatement identifies four contacts to be taken into account in applying the principles of Section 6: (1) the place where the injury occurred; (2) the place where the conduct causing the injury occurred; (3) the domicile, residence, nationality, place of incorporation and place of business of the parties; and (4) the place where the relationship, if any, the parties is centered. These contacts are to be evaluated according to their relative importance with respect to a particular issue. Where choice-of-law-issues present, therefore, it is the court's primary function "to determine which, if any, of the states having some relationship to the parties or to the crash has the most significant interest in the application of its own substantive law to the merits of the [case]." *In re Air Crash Disaster Near Chicago, Illinois, on May 25, 1979*, 644 F.2d 594, 601–11 (7th Cir.), *cert. denied*, 454 U.S. 878 (1981) ("The application of choice-of-law rules is not a mechanical process of cranking various factors through a formula.").

Experienced aviation practitioners keep in mind the different burdens and presumptions parties bear in choice-of-law determinations. In diversity actions, "unless the parties argue otherwise, it is assumed that the law of the forum and the laws of the applicable jurisdictions are in substance the same." *National Ass'n of Sporting Goods Wholesalers, Inc. v. F.T.L. Marketing Corp.*, 779 F.2d 1281, 1285 (7th Cir. 1985). When a litigant asserts the law of a state other than the forum, courts must evaluate the forum's choice-of-law rules and, in this context, plaintiff's counsel should be aware that some courts have declined to give the place of injury much weight:

> In cases involving aircraft accidents, the general rule is that little weight is given to the place of injury in choice-of-law determinations. The usual explanation is that, given an airplane's mobility, the location of an unexpected event such as an airplane crash is almost always fortuitous.

Wert v. McDonnell Douglas Corp., 634 F. Supp. 401, 404 (E.D. Mo. 1986).

Indeed, the RESTATEMENT (SECOND) provides that "[w]hen certain contacts involving a tort are located in two or more states with identical local law rules on the same issue in question, the case will be treated for choice-of-law purposes as if those contacts were grouped in a single state."

In all, aviation counsel should carefully and thoroughly evaluate the choice-of-law approach of each of the jurisdictions to which an air crash lawsuit might relate. In arguing why a particular approach should be employed over another, counsel should be careful to appeal to the court's sense of reason and equity and avoid appearing opportunistic in choosing the appropriate choice-of-law methodology.

3. *The Death on the High Seas Act ("DOHSA").*

The Death on the High Seas Act ("DOHSA") is a federal statute that creates a private cause of action to recover for wrongful death, neglect, or default occurring on the high seas, and provides a remedy for wrongful death at sea where none otherwise existed, specifically:

> When the death of an individual is caused by wrongful act, neglect, or default occurring on the high seas beyond 3 nautical miles from the shore of the United States, the personal representative of the decedent may bring a civil action in admiralty against the person or vessel responsible. The action shall be for the exclusive benefit of the decedent's spouse, parent, child, or dependent relative.

46 U.S.C. § 30302 ("Causes of action"). *See, e.g., In re Air Crash Off Long Island, New York, on July 17, 1996,* 209 F.3d 200 (2d Cir. 2000); *Zicherman v. Korean Air Lines Co., Ltd.,* 516 U.S. 217 (1996). In this context, nonpecuniary damages are available if "the death resulted from a commercial aviation accident occurring on the high seas beyond 12 nautical miles from the shore of any State, or the District of Columbia, or the Territories or dependencies of the United States." Wendell H. Ford Aviation Investment & Reform Act for the 21st Century, H.603, 106th Cong., § 404 (2000). Consequently, if admiralty jurisdiction applies, state law recoveries—except for punitive damages—will control claims brought under DOHSA.

4. *DOHSA and Korean Air Lines Flight 007.*

July 3, 2018 marked the 30th anniversary of the downing of Iran Air Flight 655 enroute to Dubai from Tehran. The airplanes was shot down by a missile fired by the U.S. Navy operating the USS Vincennes in the Persian Gulf, killing 250 people. *See* Jon Gambrell, *30 Years Later, US Downing of Iran Flight Haunts Relations*, NAVYTIMES, July 3, 2018. In 1996, the United States and Iran reached a settlement agreement stating, in part, "the United States recognized the aerial incident of 3 July 1988 as a terrible human tragedy and expressed deep regret over the loss of lives caused by the incident." The U.S. government did not admit legal liability or formally apologize, though it agreed to pay $61.8 million on an *ex gratia* basis (*i.e.*, approximately $213,000 per passenger) to compensate the families of the passengers.

Interestingly, events five years earlier involving the shoot down of a commercial airliner prompted enactment of DOHSA:

> Eighteen years before 9/11, there was 9/1—a Cold War event so tragic and catastrophic that, like the attacks on the World Trade Center and the Pentagon by Arab fanatics in the new millennium, it seared itself into the consciousness of three nations. On August 31, 1983, a Boeing 747 aircraft, operated by Korean Air Lines (KAL) and carrying 269 passengers, departed New York City at approximately 11:50 P.M. After a fuel stop in Anchorage, Alaska, the flight would proceed to its final destination, Seoul, Korea, where it would land on September 1, 1983.

> The pilots, however, inadvertently failed to program the aircraft's inertial navigation system properly. Flying in the dark over the North Pacific at 35,000 feet, the aircraft slowly drifted off course, until it entered Soviet airspace near Sakhalin Island. With the belief that a spy plane was approaching, the Soviet air force scrambled three fighter jets to intercept the wayward aircraft.

> Within minutes, and without warning, the Soviet jets fired heat-seeking missiles at the aircraft. The exploding missiles damaged the aircraft's hydraulic systems, and shrapnel penetrated the cabin, causing a rapid decompression. The crippled aircraft entered a long, spiraling descent before it slammed into the Sea of Japan and was destroyed. All 269 passengers and crew on board the aircraft perished, including 105 Koreans, 28 Japanese, and 62 Americans.

> Although it was impossible to foresee at the time, the KAL Flight 007 disaster would permanently change the body of jurisprudence under the federal maritime wrongful death statute, The Death on the High Seas Act (DOHSA). Not only did the disaster have a significant impact on Cold War

relations between the United States and the Soviet Union, it spawned two decisions by the U.S. Supreme Court that swept away recovery of non-pecuniary damages in DOHSA cases.

Those decisions were handed down in the mid-1990s against the backdrop of another noteworthy mass airline disaster: TWA Flight 800. In response to an outpouring of sympathy for the families of the victims of TWA Flight 800, Congress took up the question of compensation for non-pecuniary damages in cases governed by DOHSA. The result was an amendment to DOHSA known as the "Commercial Aviation Exception," which allows recovery of loss of society damages in actions arising from a "commercial aviation accident."

Stephen R. Ginger & Will S. Skinner, *DOHSA's Commercial Aviation Exception: How Mass Airline Disasters Influenced Congress on Compensation for Deaths on the High Seas*, 75 J. AIR L. & COM. 137, 137–38 (2010).

5. ***TWA 800, DOHSA, and "Beyond a Marine League."***

In *In re Air Crash off Long Island, New York, on July 17, 1996*, 209 F.3d 200 (2d Cir. 2000) arose from tragedy of TWA Flight 800, a 747 that exploded and crashed in the Atlantic Ocean. The panel majority *In re Air Crash off Long Island, New York, on July 17, 1996*, held that although the crash occurred beyond a marine league—approximately three miles—from shore, the DOHSA did not apply (and thus the plaintiffs could recover for non-pecuniary damages) because the crash did not occur on the "high seas," which it defined as "international waters beyond both state and federal territorial waters. *See also Eberli v. Cirrus Design Corp.* (S.D. Fla. 2009) (evaluating post-TWA Flight 800 amendments to the DOHSA, 46 U.S.C. § 30307(b).)

Judge Sonia Sotomayor dissented from the panel majority holding, reasoning the DOHSA "applies to all deaths occurring 'beyond a marine league [three nautical miles] from the shore of any State,' and not only to deaths occurring beyond the U.S. territorial sea." Judge Sotomayor emphasized that Congress in 1920 had enacted the DOHSA to "preserve state remedies in state waters, and to provide a separate remedy . . . to waters subject only to federal jurisdiction." She explained that when the DOHSA was enacted, the "high seas" started at the three-mile mark, and that this did not change when President Ronald Reagan signed a 1988 Proclamation that extended the U.S. territorial waters to twelve nautical miles. Judge Sotomayor acknowledged that the majority's holding will create "a more generous remedial scheme" for the victims' families, but countered that "[t]he appropriate remedial scheme for deaths occurring off the United States coast is clearly a legislative policy choice, which should not be made by the courts."

Appointed by President Barack Obama, Judge Sotomayor joined the Supreme Court of the United States as an Associate Justice in August 2009. What might Justice Sotomayor's presence on the Supreme Court signify, if anything, with respect to the future of DOHSA legislation and jurisprudence?

D. STATUTORY CAUSES OF ACTION

UNITED STATES V. S.A. EMPRESA DE VIACAO AEREA RIO GRANDENSE (VARIG AIRLINES)
467 U.S. 797 (1984)

CHIEF JUSTICE BURGER delivered the opinion of the Court.

On July 11, 1973, a commercial jet aircraft owned by respondent S.A. Empresa De Viacao Aerea Rio Grandense ("Varig Airlines") was flying from Rio de Janeiro to Paris when a fire broke out in one of the aft lavatories. The fire produced a thick black smoke, which quickly filled the cabin and cockpit. Despite the pilots' successful effort to land the plane, 124 of the 135 persons on board died from asphyxiation or the effects of toxic gases produced by the fire. Most of the plane's fuselage was consumed by a post-impact fire.

The aircraft involved in this accident was a Boeing 707, a product of the Boeing Co. In 1958 the Civil Aeronautics Agency ("CAA"), a predecessor of the FAA, had issued a type certificate for the Boeing 707, certifying that its designs, plans, specifications, and performance data had been shown to be in conformity with minimum safety standards. * * *

After the accident respondent Varig Airlines brought an action against the United States under the Federal Tort Claims Act seeking damages for the destroyed aircraft. Respondents asserted that the fire originated in the towel disposal area located below the sink unit in one of the lavatories and alleged that the towel disposal area was not capable of containing fire. In support of their argument, respondents pointed to an air safety regulation requiring that waste receptacles be made of fire-resistant materials and incorporate covers or other provisions for containing possible fires.

Respondents claimed that the CAA had been negligent when it inspected the Boeing 707 and issued a type certificate to an aircraft that did not comply with CAA fire protection standards. The District Court granted summary judgment for the United States on the ground that California law does not recognize an actionable tort duty for inspection and certification activities. The District Court also found that, even if respondents had stated a cause of action in tort, recovery against the United States was barred by two exceptions to the Act: the discretionary function exception and the misrepresentation exception.

* * *

In the Federal Aviation Act of 1958 Congress directed the Secretary of Transportation to promote the safety of flight of civil aircraft in air commerce by establishing minimum standards for aircraft design, materials, workmanship, construction, and performance. Congress also granted the Secretary the discretion to prescribe reasonable rules and regulations governing the inspection of aircraft, including the manner in which such inspections should be made. Congress emphasized, however, that air carriers themselves retained certain responsibilities to promote the public interest in air safety: the duty to perform their services with the highest possible degree of safety, the duty to make or cause to be made every inspection required by the Secretary, and the duty to observe and comply with all other administrative requirements established by him.

Minimum Safety Standards for Aircraft Manufacturers

Congress also established a multistep certification process to monitor the aviation industry's compliance with the requirements developed by the Secretary. Acting as the Secretary's designee, the FAA has promulgated a comprehensive set of regulations delineating the minimum safety standards with which the designers and manufacturers of aircraft must comply before marketing their products.

At each step in the certification process, FAA employees or their representatives evaluate materials submitted by aircraft manufacturers to determine whether the manufacturer has satisfied these regulatory requirements. Upon a showing by the manufacturer that the prescribed safety standards have been met, the FAA issues an appropriate certificate permitting the manufacturer to continue with production and marketing. The first stage of the FAA compliance review is type certification. A manufacturer wishing to introduce a new type of aircraft must first obtain FAA approval of the plane's basic design in the form of a type certificate. After receiving an application for a type certificate, the Secretary must "make, or require the applicant to make, such tests during manufacture and upon completion as the Secretary ... deems reasonably necessary in the interest of safety." 49 U.S.C. § 1423(a)(2). By regulation, the FAA has made the applicant itself responsible for conducting all inspections and tests necessary to determine that the aircraft comports with FAA airworthiness requirements. The applicant submits to the FAA the designs, drawings, test reports, and computations necessary to show that the aircraft sought to be certificated satisfies FAA regulations.

One major manufacturer of commercial aircraft estimated that in the course of obtaining a type certificate for a new wide-body aircraft it would submit to the FAA approximately 300,000 engineering drawings and changes, 2,000 engineering reports, and 200 other reports. In addition, it would subject the aircraft to about 80 major ground tests and 1,600 hours of flight tests. In the course of the type certification process, the manufacturer produces a prototype of the new aircraft and conducts both ground and flight tests. FAA employees or their representatives then review the data submitted by the applicant and make such inspections or tests as they deem necessary to ascertain compliance with the regulations. If the FAA finds that the proposed aircraft design comports with minimum safety standards, it signifies its approval by issuing a type certificate.

Production may not begin, however, until a production certificate authorizing the manufacture of duplicates of the prototype is issued. To obtain a production certificate, the manufacturer must prove to the FAA that it has established and can maintain a quality control system to assure that each aircraft will meet the design provisions of the type certificate. When it is satisfied that duplicate aircraft will conform to the approved type design, the FAA issues a production certificate, and the manufacturer may begin mass production of the approved aircraft.

Before any aircraft may be placed into service, however, its owner must obtain from the FAA an airworthiness certificate, which denotes that the particular aircraft in question conforms to the type certificate and is in condition for safe operation. It is unlawful for any person to operate an aircraft in air commerce without a valid airworthiness certificate. An additional certificate is required when an aircraft is altered by the introduction of a major change in its type design. To obtain this supplemental type certificate, the applicant must show the FAA that the altered aircraft meets all applicable airworthiness requirements.

With fewer than 400 engineers, the FAA obviously cannot complete this elaborate compliance review process alone. Accordingly, 49 U.S.C. § 1355 authorizes the Secretary to delegate certain inspection and certification responsibilities to properly qualified private persons. By regulation, the Secretary has provided for the appointment of private individuals to serve as designated engineering representatives to assist in the FAA certification process. These representatives are typically employees of aircraft manufacturers who possess detailed knowledge of an aircraft's design based upon their day-to-day involvement in its development. The representatives act as surrogates of the FAA in examining, inspecting, and testing aircraft for purposes of certification. In determining whether an aircraft complies with FAA regulations, they are guided by the same requirements, instructions, and procedures as FAA employees. FAA employees may briefly review the reports and other data submitted by representatives before certificating a subject aircraft.

* * *

The Federal Tort Claims Act, 28 U.S.C. § 1346(b), authorizes suits against the United States for damages

> for injury or loss of property, or personal injury or death caused by the negligent or wrongful act or omission of any employee of the Government while acting within the scope of his office or employment, under circumstances where the United States, if a private person, would be liable to the claimant in accordance with the law of the place where the act or omission occurred.

The Act further provides that the United States shall be liable with respect to tort claims "in the same manner and to the same extent as a private individual under like circumstances."

The Act did not waive the sovereign immunity of the United States in all respects, however; Congress was careful to except from the Act's broad waiver of immunity several important classes of tort claims. Of particular relevance here, 28 U.S.C. § 2680(a) provides that the Act shall not apply to

FTCA, Sovereign Immunity

> [a]ny claim based upon an act or omission of an employee of the Government, exercising due care, in the execution of a statute or regulation, whether or not such statute or regulation be valid, or based *upon the exercise or performance or the failure to exercise or perform a discretionary function or duty on the part of a federal agency or an employee of the Government, whether or not the discretion involved be abused.*

The discretionary function exception, embodied in the second clause of § 2680(a), marks the boundary between Congress' willingness to impose tort liability upon the United States and its desire to protect certain governmental activities from exposure to suit by private individuals. * * *

Discretionary Function Exception

The discretionary function exception, embodied in the second clause of § 2680(a), marks the boundary between Congress' willingness to impose tort liability upon the United States and its desire to protect certain governmental activities from exposure to suit by private individuals.

While it is unnecessary—and indeed impossible—to define with precision every contour of the discretionary function exception, from the legislative and judicial materials, it is possible to isolate several factors useful in determining when the acts of a Government employee are protected from liability. First, it is the nature of the conduct, rather than the status of the actor, that governs whether the discretionary function exception applies in a given case. Thus, the basic inquiry concerning the application of the discretionary function exception is whether the challenged acts of a Government employee—whatever his or her rank—are of the nature and quality that Congress intended to shield from tort liability. Second, whatever else the discretionary function exception may include, it plainly was intended to encompass the discretionary acts of the Government acting in its role as a regulator of the conduct of private individuals.

* * *

We now consider whether the discretionary function exception immunizes from tort liability the FAA certification process involved in [this case]. Respondent argues that the CAA was negligent in issuing a type certificate for the Boeing 707 aircraft in 1958 because the lavatory trash receptacle did not satisfy applicable safety regulations. From the records in these cases there is no indication that the Boeing 707 trash receptacle was actually inspected or reviewed by an FAA inspector or representative. Respondent thus argues in effect that the negligent failure of the FAA to inspect certain aspects of aircraft type design in the process of certification gives rise to a cause of action against the United States under the Act.

"Spot-Check" Delegation

The Government, on the other hand, urges that the basic responsibility for satisfying FAA air safety standards rests with the manufacturer, not with the FAA. The role of the FAA, the Government says, is merely to police the conduct of private individuals by monitoring their compliance with FAA regulations. According to the Government, the FAA accomplishes its monitoring function by means of a "spot-check" program designed to encourage manufacturers and operators to comply fully with minimum safety requirements. Such regulatory activity, the Government argues, is the sort of governmental conduct protected by the discretionary function exception to the Act. We agree that the discretionary function exception precludes a tort action based upon the conduct of the FAA in certificating these aircraft for use in commercial aviation.

* * *

In the exercise of his discretion, the FAA, as the Secretary's designee, has devised a system of compliance review that involves certification of aircraft design and manufacture at several stages of production. The FAA certification process is founded upon a relatively simple notion: the duty to ensure that an aircraft conforms to FAA safety regulations lies with the manufacturer and operator, while the FAA retains the responsibility for policing compliance. This premise finds ample support in the statute and regulations. *See, e.g.,* 49 U.S.C. § 1421(b) (duty rests on air carriers to perform their services with highest possible degree of safety); 49 U.S.C. § 1425(a) (air carrier has duty to make or cause to be made inspections required by Secretary and duty to comply with regulations); 14 C.F.R. § 21.17 (1983) (applicant for type certificate must show that aircraft meets applicable requirements); § 21.33 (applicant for type certificate must conduct all tests and inspections necessary to determine compliance); § 21.35 (specifying tests that must be made by applicants for type certificates).

Thus, the manufacturer is required to develop the plans and specifications and perform the inspections and tests necessary to establish that an aircraft design comports with the applicable regulations; the FAA then reviews the data for conformity purposes by conducting a "spot check" of the manufacturer's work. The operation of this "spot-check" system is outlined in detail in the handbooks and manuals developed by the CAA and FAA for the use of their employees.

* * *

As to the engineering review of an application for a type certificate, the CAA materials note that only a "relatively small number of engineers" are available to evaluate for compliance with air safety regulations the data submitted by applicants. In a recent report, the National Academy of Sciences recognized that because "FAA engineers cannot review each of the thousands of drawings, calculations, reports, and tests involved in the type certification process," the agency must place great reliance on the manufacturer. The report also noted that "in most cases the FAA staff performs only a cursory review of the substance of th[e] overwhelming volume of documents" submitted for its approval.

Respondents' contention that the FAA was negligent in failing to inspect certain elements of aircraft design before certificating the Boeing 707 necessarily challenges two aspects of the certification procedure: the FAA's decision to implement the "spot-check" system of compliance review, and the application of that "spot-check" system to the particular aircraft involved in these cases. In our view, both components of respondents' claim are barred by the discretionary function exception to the Act.

The FAA's implementation of a mechanism for compliance review is plainly discretionary activity of the "nature and quality" protected by § 2680(a). When an agency determines the extent to which it will supervise the safety procedures of private individuals, it is exercising discretionary regulatory authority of the most basic kind. Decisions as to the manner of enforcing regulations directly affect the feasibility and practicality of the Government's regulatory program; such decisions require the agency to establish priorities for the accomplishment of its policy objectives by balancing the objectives sought to be obtained against such practical considerations as staffing and funding.

> *The FAA has determined that a program of "spot-checking" manufacturers' compliance with minimum safety standards best accommodates the goal of air transportation safety and the reality of finite agency resources. Judicial intervention in such decision-making through private tort suits would require the courts to "second-guess" the political, social, and economic judgments of an agency exercising its regulatory function. It was precisely this sort of judicial intervention in policymaking that the discretionary function exception was designed to prevent.*

Here, the FAA has determined that a program of "spot-checking" manufacturers' compliance with minimum safety standards best accommodates the goal of air transportation safety and the reality of finite agency resources. Judicial intervention in such decision-making through private tort suits would require the courts to "second-guess" the political, social, and economic judgments of an agency exercising its regulatory function. It was precisely this sort of judicial intervention in policymaking that the discretionary function exception was designed to prevent.

It follows that the acts of FAA employees in executing the "spot-check" program in accordance with agency directives are protected by the discretionary function exception as well. The FAA employees who conducted compliance reviews of the aircraft involved in this case were specifically empowered to make policy judgments regarding the degree of confidence that might reasonably be placed in a given manufacturer, the need to maximize compliance with FAA regulations, and the efficient allocation of agency resources. In administering the "spot-check" program, these FAA engineers and inspectors necessarily took certain calculated risks, but those risks were encountered for the advancement of a governmental purpose and pursuant to the specific grant of authority in the regulations and operating manuals. Under such circumstances, the FAA's alleged negligence in failing to check certain specific items in the course of certificating a particular aircraft falls squarely within the discretionary function exception. * * *

FAA Safety Duty

In rendering the United States amenable to some suits in tort, Congress could not have intended to impose liability for the regulatory enforcement activities of the FAA challenged in this case. The FAA has a statutory duty to promote safety in air transportation, not to insure it. We hold that these actions against the FAA for its alleged negligence in certificating aircraft for use in commercial aviation are barred by the discretionary function exception of the Federal Tort Claims Act. Accordingly, the judgments of the United States Court of Appeals for the Ninth Circuit are reversed.

EXERCISE 12-6. *UNITED STATES V. S.A. EMPRESA DE VIACAO AEREA RIO GRANDENSE (VARIG AIRLINES)*—FEDERAL TORT CLAIMS ACT ("FTCA")

1. Detail the accident at issue and identify the plaintiff and defendant.

2. Explain the concept of "minimum standards" set out in the Federal Aviation Act of 1958 and further explain the following concepts within the context of the multistep certification process associated with the design, construction, and performance of aircraft; (a) type certificate; (b) production certificate; and (c) airworthiness certificate.

3. Describe the types of lawsuits permitted against the government under 28 U.S.C. § 1346(b) of the Federal Tort Claims Act ("FTCA").

4. Under what circumstances will the government be found liable for tort claims under the FTCA?

5. What is the "discretionary function exception" under the FTCA generally and how was it applied to this case specifically.

NOTES ON *UNITED STATES V. S.A. EMPRESA DE VIACAO AEREA RIO GRANDENSE (VARIG AIRLINES)*—SOVEREIGN IMMUNITY

The federal government plays a significant and wide-ranging role in promoting, managing, and ensuring the safe operation of aircraft in the national airspace system. This has been the case since the beginning of commercial aviation in the United States. In 1936, Congress first appropriated funds to establish an air traffic control system. Five years later, in 1941, Congress passed legislation empowering the Civil Aeronautics Administration ("CAA")—the predecessor agency to the Federal Aviation Administration ("FAA")—to construct and operate air traffic control ("ATC") towers. But, what happens if, or more likely when, the government, through its employees or agents, makes a mistake? For example, who is liable if an FAA air traffic controller orders a pilot to take a heading that causes or contributes to a fatal collision with another airplane? Until the mid-1940s, the law totally protected the

United States from liability arising from the negligent acts or omissions on the part of its ATC employees.

Why this was so dates back to the ancient common law maxim, "Rex non potest peccare"—"the King can do no wrong"—pursuant to which English subjects were barred from commencing or prosecuting suit against the monarch or his agents. This concept—encompassed in the doctrine of *sovereign immunity*—was in part enshrined by the Eleventh Amendment of the Constitution, which renders the United States, its departments, and its employees in their official capacities as agents of the federal government, immune from suit except as the United States consents to be sued. The doctrine of sovereign immunity was judicially recognized in America in the 1830s in *United States v. Clarke*, 33 U.S. (8 Pet.) 436 (1834), to protect the federal and state governments from suit. Under this precedent, absent a waiver of sovereign immunity, the United States is immune from liability for its wrongful acts—a circumstance that the Supreme Court, in *Nichols v. United States*, 74 U.S. (7 Wall.) 122 (1868), noted was intended to prevent litigation from interfering with public acts that are *essential* to governing the nation.

But, as stated in *Interfirst Bank Dallas, N.A. v. United States*, 769 F.2d 299 (5th Cir.1985), the doctrine of sovereign immunity has been "[d]ecried as irrational and immoral by some, . . . criticized on historical grounds by others, . . . [and] recognized by all to have little doctrinal coherence." The policy and protections afforded the government under the guise of absolute sovereign immunity were softened in 1946 when, after nearly thirty years of consideration, Congress passed the Federal Tort Claims Act ("FTCA"). As the Supreme Court stated in *Dalehite v. United States*, 346 U.S. 15 (1953), the adoption of the FTCA was the "offspring of a feeling that the Government should assume the obligation to pay damages for the misfeasance of employees carrying out its work." Moreover, the FTCA prevents courts from second-guessing legislative and administrative decisions grounded in social, economic, and political policy through the medium of action in tort.

Notably, the FTCA law now allows private litigants to sue the government for money damages arising from the negligence of its employees in certain situations. Under 28 U.S.C. § 1346(b), the government can be sued for money damages

> for injury or loss of property, or personal injury or death caused by the negligent or wrongful act or omission of any employee of the Government while acting within the scope of his office or employment, under circumstances where the United States, if a private person, would be liable to the claimant in accordance with the law of the place where the act or omission occurred.

Under 28 U.S.C. §§ 2671–80, then, the United States may be liable for *unintentional torts*—negligence—committed by its employees or agents to the same extent and in the same manner as liability would attach to a private individual in similar circumstances.

While the United States maintains the ability to assert any defense based on judicial or legislative immunity that otherwise would have been available to a federal employee whose act or omissions gave rise to the claim, as well as any other defenses available to the United States, the FTCA, in effect, partially ameliorated traditional sovereign immunity by imposing responsibility on the United States for its negligent conduct and allowing American citizens who were injured as a result of the negligence of the United States to sue for damages. As stated in *Figueroa v. United States*, 64 F. Supp. 2d 1125 (D. Utah 1999), before the FTCA was enacted, the only way a person could be compensated for an injury negligently caused by the United States was to have a private claim bill presented in and passed by Congress and signed into law by the President. The FTCA avoided this clumsy (and likely partisan) approach in favor of an easier and simpler practice that gives federal district courts the power to hear claims against the United States under 28 U.S.C. § 1346(b)(1) "for money damages . . . for injury . . . or death caused by the negligent or wrongful act or omission of any employee of the Government."

Importantly, while the FTCA broadly effectuates a legislative aim of putting private parties and federal government on equal footing, it is a *limited* waiver of sovereign immunity. Thus, as expressed in *Dept. of Army v. Blue Fox, Inc.*, 525 U.S. 255 (1999), the limitations and conditions upon which the government consents to be sued under the FTCA must be strictly construed and observed. For starters, under 28 U.S.C. § 2679(b)(1), "the remedy against the United States provided by [the FTCA] is *exclusive* of any other civil action or proceeding for money damages by reason of the same subject matter against the same employee."

An FTCA claim may lie where: (1) facts exist to support a cause of action of negligence against the federal government; (2) the U.S. employee(s) involved acted within the course and scope of employment with a federal agency; and (3) the law of the place where the alleged negligence occurred supports the cause of action.

An FTCA claim may lie where: (1) facts exist to support a cause of action of negligence against the federal government; (2) the U.S. employee(s) involved acted within the course and scope of employment with a federal agency; and (3) the law of the place where the alleged negligence occurred supports the cause of action.

The FTCA confers federal district courts with *exclusive* jurisdiction of civil actions on claims against the United States for money damages, for injury or loss of property, or personal injury or death caused by the negligent or wrongful act or omission of any government employee acting within the scope of his office or employment of the government, if a private person would be liable to the claimant in accordance with the law of the place where the act or omission occurred. In aviation cases, the FTCA may pose special venue and choice-of-law considerations. As to venue, FTCA actions may be brought "only in the judicial district where the plaintiff resides or wherein the act or omission complained of occurred." 28 U.S.C. § 1402(b). Courts have interpreted the phrase "where the plaintiff resides" to mean the residence of the administrator of the decedent's estate. *See, e.g., Lopez v. United States*, 68 F. Supp. 2d 688, 691 (M.D.N.C. 1999).

ADMINISTRATIVE CLAIM UNDER THE FTCA

Because the FTCA provides a limited opportunity to seek redress from the federal government for particular actions or inactions, claimants and their counsel must take care to comply strictly with the conditions precedent to instituting suit. In fact, a critical and unique aspect of the FTCA is the requirement that potential litigants present an *administrative claim* to the appropriate federal agency *before* initiating a lawsuit against the government in court. This requirement is jurisdictional in nature in that a district court may not exercise jurisdiction over an FTCA claim unless the claimant has timely filed an administrative claim with the appropriate federal agency *and* six months have elapsed since the agency received the claim. These two requirements exist "to encourage prompt settlement of claims and to ensure fairness to FTCA litigants . . . and ease court congestion and avoid unnecessary litigation." *Burchfield v. United States*, 168 F.3d 1252 (11th Cir. 1999). Moreover, regulations promulgated by the Department of Justice—28 C.F.R. § 14.6(a)—reflect the fact that Congress intended the administrative processes of the FTCA "to serve as an efficient effective forum for rapidly resolving tort claims with low costs to all participants."

The mechanics of presenting an administrative claim under the FTCA are relatively simple, reflecting a policy choice to encourage the speedy and inexpensive determination of negligence claims against the government. However, inattention to two details—*how* and *when* to present and provide notice of a claim—can seriously delay or derail an FTCA proceeding.

First, although the FTCA itself does not define the term "claim, the Seventh Circuit Court of Appeals, in *Kanar v. United States*, 118 F.3d 527 (7th Cir. 1997), identified four elements of an FTCA administrative "claim," *e.g.*, (1) notification of the accident or incident; (2) a demand for a sum certain; (3) the title or capacity of the person signing; and (4) evidence of the signatory's authority to represent the claimant.

Typically, claimants present an FTCA administrative claim by submitting a Standard Form 95 ("SF-95"):

Figure 12-3. FTCA: Standard Form 95

CLAIM FOR DAMAGE, INJURY, OR DEATH	INSTRUCTIONS: Please read carefully the instructions on the reverse side and supply information requested on both sides of this form. Use additional sheet(s) if necessary. See reverse side for additional instructions.	FORM APPROVED OMB NO. 1105-0008

1. Submit to Appropriate Federal Agency:

2. Name, address of claimant, and claimant's personal representative if any. (See instructions on reverse). Number, Street, City, State and Zip code.

3. TYPE OF EMPLOYMENT ☐ MILITARY ☐ CIVILIAN	4. DATE OF BIRTH	5. MARITAL STATUS	6. DATE AND DAY OF ACCIDENT	7. TIME (A.M. OR P.M.)

8. BASIS OF CLAIM (State in detail the known facts and circumstances attending the damage, injury, or death, identifying persons and property involved, the place of occurrence and the cause thereof. Use additional pages if necessary).

9. PROPERTY DAMAGE

NAME AND ADDRESS OF OWNER, IF OTHER THAN CLAIMANT (Number, Street, City, State, and Zip Code).

BRIEFLY DESCRIBE THE PROPERTY, NATURE AND EXTENT OF THE DAMAGE AND THE LOCATION OF WHERE THE PROPERTY MAY BE INSPECTED. (See instructions on reverse side).

10. PERSONAL INJURY/WRONGFUL DEATH

STATE THE NATURE AND EXTENT OF EACH INJURY OR CAUSE OF DEATH, WHICH FORMS THE BASIS OF THE CLAIM. IF OTHER THAN CLAIMANT, STATE THE NAME OF THE INJURED PERSON OR DECEDENT.

11. WITNESSES

NAME	ADDRESS (Number, Street, City, State, and Zip Code)

12. (See instructions on reverse). AMOUNT OF CLAIM (in dollars)

12a. PROPERTY DAMAGE	12b. PERSONAL INJURY	12c. WRONGFUL DEATH	12d. TOTAL (Failure to specify may cause forfeiture of your rights).

I CERTIFY THAT THE AMOUNT OF CLAIM COVERS ONLY DAMAGES AND INJURIES CAUSED BY THE INCIDENT ABOVE AND AGREE TO ACCEPT SAID AMOUNT IN FULL SATISFACTION AND FINAL SETTLEMENT OF THIS CLAIM.

13a. SIGNATURE OF CLAIMANT (See instructions on reverse side).	13b. PHONE NUMBER OF PERSON SIGNING FORM	14. DATE OF SIGNATURE

CIVIL PENALTY FOR PRESENTING FRAUDULENT CLAIM	CRIMINAL PENALTY FOR PRESENTING FRAUDULENT CLAIM OR MAKING FALSE STATEMENTS
The claimant is liable to the United States Government for a civil penalty of not less than $5,000 and not more than $10,000, plus 3 times the amount of damages sustained by the Government. (See 31 U.S.C. 3729).	Fine, imprisonment, or both. (See 18 U.S.C. 287, 1001.)

Authorized for Local Reproduction
Previous Edition is not Usable
95-109

NSN 7540-00-634-4046

STANDARD FORM 95 (REV. 2/2007)
PRESCRIBED BY DEPT. OF JUSTICE
28 CFR 14.2

INSURANCE COVERAGE

In order that subrogation claims may be adjudicated, it is essential that the claimant provide the following information regarding the insurance coverage of the vehicle or property.

15. Do you carry accident insurance? ☐ Yes   If yes, give name and address of insurance company (Number, Street, City, State, and Zip Code) and policy number.   ☐ No

16. Have you filed a claim with your insurance carrier in this instance, and if so, is it full coverage or deductible? ☐ Yes ☐ No   17. If deductible, state amount.

18. If a claim has been filed with your carrier, what action has your insurer taken or proposed to take with reference to your claim? (It is necessary that you ascertain these facts).

19. Do you carry public liability and property damage insurance? ☐ Yes   If yes, give name and address of insurance carrier (Number, Street, City, State, and Zip Code).   ☐ No

INSTRUCTIONS

Claims presented under the Federal Tort Claims Act should be submitted directly to the "appropriate Federal agency" whose employee(s) was involved in the incident. If the incident involves more than one claimant, each claimant should submit a separate claim form.

Complete all items - Insert the word NONE where applicable.

A CLAIM SHALL BE DEEMED TO HAVE BEEN PRESENTED WHEN A FEDERAL AGENCY RECEIVES FROM A CLAIMANT, HIS DULY AUTHORIZED AGENT, OR LEGAL REPRESENTATIVE, AN EXECUTED STANDARD FORM 95 OR OTHER WRITTEN NOTIFICATION OF AN INCIDENT, ACCOMPANIED BY A CLAIM FOR MONEY

Failure to completely execute this form or to supply the requested material within two years from the date the claim accrued may render your claim invalid. A claim is deemed presented when it is received by the appropriate agency, not when it is mailed.

If instruction is needed in completing this form, the agency listed in item #1 on the reverse side may be contacted. Complete regulations pertaining to claims asserted under the Federal Tort Claims Act can be found in Title 28, Code of Federal Regulations, Part 14. Many agencies have published supplementing regulations. If more than one agency is involved, please state each agency.

The claim may be filed by a duly authorized agent or other legal representative, provided evidence satisfactory to the Government is submitted with the claim establishing express authority to act for the claimant. A claim presented by an agent or legal representative must be presented in the name of the claimant. If the claim is signed by the agent or legal representative, it must show the title or legal capacity of the person signing and be accompanied by evidence of his/her authority to present a claim on behalf of the claimant as agent, executor, administrator, parent, guardian or other representative.

If claimant intends to file for both personal injury and property damage, the amount for each must be shown in item number 12 of this form.

DAMAGES IN A **SUM CERTAIN** FOR INJURY TO OR LOSS OF PROPERTY, PERSONAL INJURY, OR DEATH ALLEGED TO HAVE OCCURRED BY REASON OF THE INCIDENT. THE CLAIM MUST BE PRESENTED TO THE APPROPRIATE FEDERAL AGENCY WITHIN **TWO YEARS** AFTER THE CLAIM ACCRUES.

The amount claimed should be substantiated by competent evidence as follows:

(a) In support of the claim for personal injury or death, the claimant should submit a written report by the attending physician, showing the nature and extent of the injury, the nature and extent of treatment, the degree of permanent disability, if any, the prognosis, and the period of hospitalization, or incapacitation, attaching itemized bills for medical, hospital, or burial expenses actually incurred.

(b) In support of claims for damage to property, which has been or can be economically repaired, the claimant should submit at least two itemized signed statements or estimates by reliable, disinterested concerns, or, if payment has been made, the itemized signed receipts evidencing payment.

(c) In support of claims for damage to property which is not economically repairable, or if the property is lost or destroyed, the claimant should submit statements as to the original cost of the property, the date of purchase, and the value of the property, both before and after the accident. Such statements should be by disinterested competent persons, preferably reputable dealers or officials familiar with the type of property damaged, or by two or more competitive bidders, and should be certified as being just and correct.

(d) **Failure to specify a sum certain will render your claim invalid and may result in forfeiture of your rights.**

PRIVACY ACT NOTICE

This Notice is provided in accordance with the Privacy Act, 5 U.S.C. 552a(e)(3), and concerns the information requested in the letter to which this Notice is attached.
  A. *Authority:* The requested information is solicited pursuant to one or more of the following: 5 U.S.C. 301, 28 U.S.C. 501 et seq., 28 U.S.C. 2671 et seq., 28 C.F.R. Part 14.

B. *Principal Purpose:* The information requested is to be used in evaluating claims.
C. *Routine Use:* See the Notices of Systems of Records for the agency to whom you are submitting this form for this information.
D. *Effect of Failure to Respond:* Disclosure is voluntary. However, failure to supply the requested information or to execute the form may render your claim "invalid."

PAPERWORK REDUCTION ACT NOTICE

This notice is solely for the purpose of the Paperwork Reduction Act, 44 U.S.C. 3501. Public reporting burden for this collection of information is estimated to average 6 hours per response, including the time for reviewing instructions, searching existing data sources, gathering and maintaining the data needed, and completing and reviewing the collection of information. Send comments regarding this burden estimate or any other aspect of this collection of information, including suggestions for reducing this burden, to the Director, Torts Branch, Attention: Paperwork Reduction Staff, Civil Division, U.S. Department of Justice, Washington, DC 20530 or to the Office of Management and Budget. Do not mail completed form(s) to these addresses.

STANDARD FORM 95 REV. (2/2007) BACK

Source: https://www.va.gov/OGC/docs/SF-95.pdf.

Use of the Standard Form 95 is not required, but the template has proven useful for presenting the type of minimal notice and information that federal agencies need to conduct a full investigation of the alleged accident or event upon and process FTCA claim. Whether made via SF-95 or "other written notification of an incident," an FTCA administrative claim should contain a detailed account of the facts and circumstances that form the basis for liability (*e.g.*, date, place, nature or injury or damage, and names of witnesses), as well as the basis for the sum certain of the damages claimed for loss or damage to property or for personal injury or death.

While the FTCA requires a claimant to provide minimal notice rather than a comprehensive exposition of every theory of liability, stating a "sum certain" is essential. For example, a claim for "more than $100,000" will be limited to $100,000 should the claimant win more at trial. Similarly, a claim for "$1 million and other amount as may be shown" will be limited to $1 million. *Martinez v. United States*, 728 F.2d 694 (5th Cir. 1984). A claim for "an amount to be determined," meanwhile, is a nullity. Finally, an FTCA claimant cannot claim in a district court complaint against the United States *more* than the amount of damages initially set forth in the administrative claim unless "the increased amount is based upon newly discovered evidence not reasonably discoverable at the time of presenting the claim to the federal agency, or upon allegation and proof of intervening facts, relating to the amount of the claim." 28 U.S.C. § 2675(b).

Aside from the substantive requirements of an FTCA claim, *when* a claim is initially presented is critically important. An administrative claim is deemed presented when, pursuant to 28 C.F.R. § 14.2, the proper federal agency *receives* written notification of the incident from the claimant. *Kanar v. United States*, 118 F.3d 527 (7th Cir. 1997). A claim is not "presented" until the appropriate federal agency *receives* the claim—not the date of mailing or delivery to a delivery service. Moreover, an FTCA claim must be presented to the appropriate federal agency *within two years* of the date on which a claim arose—usually the date of the accident or injury. If it is not, the consequences are serve—the claim "shall be forever barred" under the limitations statute, 28 U.S.C. § 2401(b).

Once timely presented with a proper administrative claim, the head of the responding federal agency or his designee has six months to "consider, ascertain, adjust, determine, compromise, and settle any claim for money damages against the United States." In doing so, federal authorities may request additional information probative of the claim, including a death certificate, medical information, proof of property ownership, damage estimates, and "[a]ny other evidence or information which may have a bearing on either the responsibility of the United States for the injury to or loss of property or the damages claimed." 15 C.F.R. § 15.7. During this six-month review period, a claimant is prohibited from filing suit against the United States on the basis of the FTCA claim. 28 U.S.C. § 2675(a). Once the claim is "finally denied," however, the claimant has six months after the date of the denial within which to file suit. 28 U.S.C. § 2401(b). An FTCA claimant is "finally denied" when either: (1) the claim is explicitly denied by the responding federal agency in writing and sent by certified or registered mail; or (2) the responding agency fails "to make final disposition of a claim within six months after it is filed." If the FAA denies the claim, but does so after the expiration of six months, the six-month period within which to file a district court complaint begins to run from the date of that denial.

DISCRETIONARY FUNCTION EXCEPTION

Although the federal government has waived its sovereign immunity under the FTCA, and has consented to be sued for "the negligent or wrongful act or omission' by an officer or employee of the federal government acting within the scope of his employment," the FTCA is peppered with exceptions under 28 U.S.C. § 2672.

- **Scope of Employment.** Under 28 U.S.C. § 2679(b)(2), the FTCA does not permit a claim against the United States if the employee or agent was not acting within the scope of employment with the federal agency.

- **Intentional Torts.** The FTCA applies to *un*intentional torts (*i.e.,* negligence) only. Under 28 U.S.C. § 2680, the FTCA does *not* apply to claims arising out of *intentional* torts such as assault, battery, false imprisonment, false arrest, malicious prosecution, abuse of process, libel, slander, misrepresentation, deceit or interference with contract rights.

- **Independent Contractors.** The term "federal agency" in the FTCA includes the executive departments, the judicial and legislative branches, the military departments, independent establishments of the United States, and corporations primarily acting as instrumentalities or agencies of the United States. Under 28 U.S.C. § 2671, it does *not* include "any contractor with the United States."

- **Damages.** Under 28 U.S.C. § 2674, the FTCA does not permit the recovery of prejudgment interest or punitive damages against the government. This is so even if, in any case wherein death was caused, the law of the place where the act or omission complained of occurred provides, or has been construed to provide, for damages only punitive in nature. In that case, the United States will be liable for actual or compensatory damages, measured by the pecuniary injuries resulting from such death to the persons respectively, for whose benefit the action was brought, in lieu thereof.

- **Attorneys' Fees.** Attorney's fees are recoverable under the FTCA, but the law prohibits the charge, demand, receipt, or collection of attorney's fees that are *more than 25 percent* of any judgment rendered or settlement reached under the FTCA.

The most widely litigated exception under the FTCA is the so-called discretionary function exception, by which a claim that is based upon the performance or failure to perform "a discretionary function or duty" is unassailable under 28 U.S.C. § 2680(a). It provides:

> Any claim . . . based upon the exercise or performance or the failure to exercise or perform a discretionary function or duty on the part of a federal agency or an employee of the Government, whether or not the discretion involved be abused.

What this means practically is that the United States government is immune from a claim based on a government employee's act or omission that is exercised with due care in the execution of a statute of regulation, whether or not the statute or regulation is valid, or based upon the exercise or performance or the failure to exercise or perform a discretionary function or duty on the part of the federal agency or a government employee. 28 U.S.C. § 2680.

Reduced to its component parts, the discretionary function exception consists of a two-part test. *Berkowitz v. United States*, 486 U.S. 531 (1988). First, in examining the nature of the challenged conduct, a court must first consider whether the action is a matter of choice for the acting employee. This inquiry is mandated by the language of the FTCA exception; conduct cannot be discretionary unless it involves an element of judgment or choice. Thus, the discretionary function exception will *not* apply when a federal statute, regulation, or policy specifically prescribes a course of action for an employee to follow. In this event, the employee has no rightful option but to adhere to the directive. And if the employee's conduct cannot appropriately be the product of judgment or choice, then there is no discretion in the conduct for the discretionary function exception to protect. Second, assuming the challenged conduct involves an element of judgment, a court must determine whether that judgment is of the kind that the discretionary function exception was designed to shield.

FTCA CASE STUDY: DELTA 191, AIR TRAFFIC CONTROL ERROR?

Airplane accident cases regularly include computer-generated visual evidence and interactive video drawn from event data recorders, more commonly referred to as flight data recorders, cockpit voice recorders, and "black boxes." *See, e.g.*, Mark Joye, *Big Brother or Big Savior? Here Comes the Black Box*, S.C. LAW. MAG., Sept. 2004 (discussing use of "event data recorders" in the automobile industry). Courts routinely admit into evidence or reject information taken from computerized data recorders used in various modes of transportation, including maritime, rail, and automobile. *See* Optical *Commc'ns Grp., Inc. v. M/V Ambassador*, 558 Fed. Appx. 94 (2d Cir. 2014) (reviewing summary judgment based on a vessel's Simplified Vessel Data Radar—the maritime equivalent of an airplane's black box); *Waisonovitz v. Metro-N. Commuter R.R.*, 350 Fed. Appx. 497 (2d Cir. 2009) (evaluating arguments based on data collected from a train's "event recorder").

The presentation of simulations and accident reconstruction is indispensably powerful for aviation plaintiff and defense counsel explaining aerodynamics, air traffic control, meteorological conditions, and other aspects of aerospace science. Indeed, "[c]omputer technology provides litigators the means to depict not only why an accident happened, but also alternate scenarios of how the accident could have been avoided, in an attempt to show who or what was responsible." Kathlynn G. Fadely, *Use of Computer-Generated Visual Evidence in Aviation Litigation: Interactive Video Evidence Comes to Court*, 55 J. AIR & L. COM. 839, 840 (1990).

Litigation arising from the crash of Delta Flight 191 was one of the most important cases to incorporate courtroom technology in complex aviation disputes and is an apt case study of the usefulness of computer technology in aviation accident litigation.

Delta 191: Cockpit Voice Recorder Transcript

On August 2, 1985, Delta Air Lines flight 191 crashed while approaching to land on runway 17L at the Dallas/Fort Worth International Airport, Texas. While passing through the rain shaft beneath a thunderstorm, flight 191 entered a microburst, which the pilot was unable to traverse successfully. The airplane struck the ground about 6,300 feet north of the approach end of runway 17L, hit a car on a highway north of the runway killing the driver, struck two water tanks on the airport, and broke apart. Except for a section of the airplane containing the aft fuselage and empennage, the remainder of the airplane disintegrated during the impact sequence, and a severe fire erupted during the impact sequence. Of the 163 persons aboard, 134 passengers and crewmembers were killed; 26 passengers and 3 cabin attendants survived.

The National Transportation Safety Board determined that the probable causes of the accident were the flight crew's decision to initiate and continue the approach into a cumulonimbus cloud which they observed to contain visible lightening; the lack of specific guidelines, procedures, and training for avoiding and escaping from low-altitude wind shear; and the lack of definitive, real-time wind shear hazard information. This resulted in the aircraft's encounter at low altitude with a microburst-induced, severe wind shear from a rapidly developing thunderstorm located on the final approach course.

The cockpit voice recorder ("CVR") captured the final moments of the flight:

Tower:	Delta one ninety one heavy regional tower one seven left cleared to land, win zero nine zero at five gusts to one five
First Officer ("FO"):	Lightning coming out of that one.
Captain:	What?
First Officer:	Lightning coming out of that one.
Captain:	Where?
First Officer	Right ahead of us.
Flight Engineer:	You get the good legs don't ya?

(Sound similar to rain begins and continues to impact)

Captain:	Watch your speed . . . You're gonna lose it all of sudden, there it is. . . Push it up, push it way up . . . Way up . . . Way up . . . That's it.

(Sound of engines high RPM)

Captain:	Hang on to the sonofabitch.
First Officer:	Whats's vee ref?

Ground Proximity Warning System ("GPWS"):

WHOOP WHOOP PULL UP. WHOOP WHOOP PULL UP

Captain:	Toga.

(Sound of radio altimeters)

Unknown:	Push it way up.

WHOOP WHOOP PULL UP. WHOOP WHOOP PULL UP

(Sound of first impact)

Unknown:	Shit.
Unknown:	Oh Shit.

(Sound of second impact)

Tower:	Delta go around.

Source: National Transp. Safety Bd., Aircraft Accident Report, Delta Air Lines, Inc., Lockheed L–1011–385–1, N726DA, Dallas/Fort-Worth-International Airport, Texas, August 2, 1985, NTSB/AAR-86/05. See also Delta Airlines Flight 191 Crash Animation + CVR, https://www.youtube.com/watch?v=dKwyU1RwPto.

The airline, together with its insurers and two of the three cockpit crew members' estates sued the federal government for the loss of the jetliner, contribution and indemnity, and wrongful death. *See In re Air Crash at Dallas/Fort Worth Airport on August 2, 1985,* 720 F. Supp. 1258, 1290–91 (N.D. Tex. 1989) ("Defendant, the United States of America, is entitled to a judgment in its favor inasmuch as Plaintiffs have failed to prove that the United States of America, through its agents, servants or employees, was guilty of any negligence that proximately caused the air crash of DL 191 on August 2, 1985.").

The central contention in the consolidated lawsuits was that the Federal Aviation Administration and the National Weather Service failed to provide the airline's crew with reports of severe weather and to warn them to fly around the airport or change runways.

The resulting trial—considered the longest in aviation history—generated more than 18,000 pages of transcribed testimony, included 49 expert witnesses, and featured the use of computer-generated simulations to support their cases. *See* Paul Marcotte, *Animated Evidence: Delta 191 Crash Re-Created through Computer Simulations at Trial,* 75 A.B.A. J. 52 (1989). The government's defense emphasized that the Delta crew failed to use their own onboard radar to detect the storm and avoid it. *In re Air Crash at Dallas/Fort Worth Airport,* 720 F. Supp. at 1290.

To support its theory, the government produced computer-generated graphics pertaining to the relevant weather conditions, showing a "recreation of the location and development of weather cells near the airport and cells that would have been depicted on the airborne weather radar of the L-1011 aircraft, had the radar been utilized at any of three different tilt settings," lead counsel for the Department of Justice attorney involved in the litigation recounted. *See* Fadely, *Computer-Generated Visual Evidence in Aviation Litigation,* 55 J. Air & L. Com., at 843. While computer animation had become somewhat common in litigation up to that time, "the Justice Department's presentation at the Delta Flight 191 trial marked a new milestone in terms of length, sophistication and technology used." Marcotte, *Animated Evidence,* at 53.

> The U.S. used a disc player and a laptop computer equipped with custom-designed software in its presentation. By using the laptop computer, a witness could display on television monitors facing the judge and lawyers any image on the disc almost instantly—also freeze-action animation without distortion. *Id.* at 54 ("Just as consumers mix and match components to create their own stereo systems, the U.S. lawyers were among the first to adapt laserdisc technology for courtroom use. The process is called interactive video and has been widely used in industrial and military training.").

It took nearly two years for the government to prepare its 55-minute presentation. Crucial to the simulations was a new generation of digital flight-data recorder on board Delta 191—the first commercial flight to crash in a microburst with such a recorder.

The Justice Department used 40 different parameters, such as acceleration, roll, pitch and heading, to recreate the plane's flight. The plane's cockpit-voice recorder, ground radar images, weather photos and other pilots' statements helped complete the government's picture of what happened

. . .

Three witnesses for the Justice Department were on the stand for several days using the simulations, charts and photos to illustrate points to the judge . . . the flight synchronized to the cockpit-voice recorder most effectively illustrated the government's contentions. Not only could the judge see the plane's movement in relation to the storm, he could see the data displayed on Delta 191's instruments at the time. The various animations created an eerie feeling of being there, of seeing and hearing what the crew experienced.

Id. Significantly, the animation used in the Delta Flight 191 litigation was admitted not as demonstrative evidence, but as substantive evidence, meaning it had independent probative value. *Id.* at 55. Given the stakes, the parties attacked each other's computer animations as inaccurate, inappropriate, prejudicial, and thus inadmissible. As such, the computerized evidence offered by the parties was subjected to a battery of evidentiary tests, including the then-applicable general-acceptance standard under *Daubert v. Merrell Dow Pharm., Inc.* 509 U.S. 579 (1993), and the requirements of Federal Rules of Evidence 401, 402, 403, 702, and 901 dealing with issues of authenticity, relevancy, expert testimony, and possible prejudicial or cumulative aspects of the evidence, respectively.

INMON V. AIR TRACTOR, INC.

74 So. 3d 534 (4th DCA 2011)

MAY, C.J.

Having had his negligence complaint dismissed on two grounds, the plaintiff appeals both an adverse summary judgment and the dismissal order. He argues the trial court erred in applying the applicable statutes of repose and in dismissing the action as a sanction for violation of multiple court orders. We find no error and affirm.

While the plaintiff was dusting crops, the right wing of his airplane suddenly failed. The plaintiff was injured and the plane was destroyed. The airplane was not considered airworthy at the time because the plaintiff had failed to obtain a required annual inspection.

Two years later, the plaintiff sued the plane manufacturer. He alleged the crash was caused by a defective wing assembly and a factory modification kit manufactured and designed by the manufacturer. The plaintiff specifically claimed that the plane's right wing cracked at the "lower spar cap."

The plane manufacturer ultimately moved for summary judgment based on the eighteen-year federal statute of repose and the twelve-year Florida statute of repose. The primary issue was whether the plane manufacturer's design and sale of a new part for the wing assembly in 1993 restarted the respective periods of repose.

The record established the following facts. The plane had been manufactured in 1982. The plaintiff purchased the plane from a third party in 1998 with no warranty. The airframe was originally rated with a useable or "safe life" of 5,000 hours.

The safe life of an airframe represents the maximum number of hours the airplane can be flown before the accumulated stresses of ordinary flight make continued flying dangerous. If, on a particular aircraft, the first fatigue critical location ("FFCL") can be modified or replaced and thereby increase the safe life of the FFCL, then the safe life of the entire airframe will likewise increase by the same amount (not to exceed the safe life of any other airframe component).

The plane manufacturer's president, who had also designed the plane, agreed that the FFCL on the plane is the outermost of four bolt holes on the "spar splice." The spar splice connects the right wing to the left wing at the airplane's centerline. The spar, including its lower spar cap, is an original component of the plane. The lower spar cap on the right side fractured in the accident, resulting in the wing separating.

To extend the safe life of that FFCL on a similar airplane, the plane manufacturer issued Service Letter 55, which was made applicable to this model by Service Letter 70. By designing a new spar splice with an additional fifth bolt hole further out from the centerline of the aircraft and installing it on the existing lower wing spar cap, the plane manufacturer purportedly extended the safe life of the FFCL (and thus the entire airframe) by an additional 2,000 hours.

The work specified in Service Letters 55 and 70 was performed on the airplane by a mechanic—not affiliated with the plane manufacturer—nine years before the accident and while the plane was owned by another individual. The mechanic did not replace the original spar cap, which already had four bolt holes. Instead, he modified the spar cap by drilling a fifth bolt hole and adding a new five-bolt spar splice (replacing the original four-bolt spar splice) and bolts.

The owner of the dealership that sold the airplane confirmed that the parts required by Service Letter 55 were "factory parts" supplied by the plane manufacturer to its dealers as part of the modification kit. An engineer from the plane manufacturer testified that the spar splice modification kit included the five-bolt spar splice sold by the plane manufacturer as a replacement part for the original four-bolt spar splice.

Service Letter 161 subsequently advised that, if Service Letters 55 and 70 were followed, and certain additional inspections and maintenance were performed, the safe life of this model's airframe could be extended from 7,000 to 10,000 hours. That additional work was completed by the dealer at the time the airplane was sold to the plaintiff. When the plane crashed less than four years later, it had reached approximately 8,200 hours on the airframe.

New Part Toll Statute of Repose?

In its motion for summary judgment, the plane manufacturer argued that the spar splice did not cause the accident and therefore the addition of the new part could not restart the applicable statutes of repose. The plaintiff argued in opposition that installation of the new five-bolt spar splice should restart the clock because the defective design of the new part was the cause of the crash. The plaintiff's expert testified that the crash resulted from the failure of the right wing during flight.

The trial court granted the motion for summary judgment, finding that the "service letters and inspections referred to in [the] Complaint did not toll the applicable statute of repose." The court also rendered an order dismissing the complaint as a sanction for violating numerous court orders.

On appeal, the plaintiff argues that the trial court erred in granting summary judgment because the design and manufacture of the replacement five-bolt spar splice restarted the repose period. Furthermore, the plaintiff argues expert testimony established that the defective design of this new part caused the crash. The plane manufacturer responds that the plaintiff sued over an alleged defect in the plane's wing, which was over twenty years old and beyond the statute of repose. The plane manufacturer further argues that any modification to an original part does not restart the statute of repose.

This court has *de novo* review of a trial court's application of a statute of repose in a products liability action because it involves an issue of law.

Congress passed the General Aviation Revitalization Act ("GARA") in an effort to curb the enormous product liability costs imposed on manufacturers of general aviation aircraft. *Lyon v. Agusta S.P.A.*, 252 F.3d 1078, 1084 (9th Cir. 2001). GARA provides:

> Except as provided in subsection (b), no civil action for damages for death or injury to persons or damage to property arising out of an accident involving a general aviation aircraft may be brought against the manufacturer of the aircraft or the manufacturer of any new component, system, subassembly, or other part of the aircraft, in its capacity as a manufacturer if the accident occurred—
>
> (1)   after the applicable limitation period [18 years] beginning on—
>
>> (A)   the date of delivery of the aircraft to its first purchaser or lessee, if delivered directly from the manufacturer; or
>>
>> (B)   the date of first delivery of the aircraft to a person engaged in the business of selling or leasing such aircraft;

Id. (citing General Aviation Revitalization Act of 1994, Pub. L. No. 103–298, 108 Stat. 1552 (1994)) (provisions at 49 U.S.C. § 40101 notes). It is considered a "classic statute of repose." *Id.* (citing *Caldwell v. Enstrom Helicopter Corp.*, 230 F.3d 1155, 1156 (9th Cir.2000)). "[I]t runs from what amounts to the date of the first transfer from the manufacturer." *Id.*

Section 2(a)(2) of GARA, known as the "rolling provision," states that an eighteen-year repose period must be applied separately to " 'any new component, system, subassembly, or other part which replaced another component, system, subassembly, or other part originally in, or which was added to, the aircraft . . .' "

The "rolling statute of repose applies only with respect to a new item that replaces an original item . . . Modification of an item, whether it is a component, system, subassembly, or other part, does not restart the limitation period under GARA."

Section 2(a)(2) of GARA, known as the "rolling provision," states that an eighteen-year repose period must be applied separately to " 'any new component, system, subassembly, or other part which replaced another component, system, subassembly, or other part originally in, or which was added to, the aircraft . . .' " *Alter v. Bell Helicopter Textron, Inc.*, 944 F. Supp. 531, 538 (S.D. Tex. 1996) (quoting GARA § 201, 114 Stat. 91). However, "[t]he language of the statute including 'component, system, subassembly, or other part' is not accompanied by any modifier or reference to 'design' thereby indicating that 'replacement' means replacement of a physical item, '*i.e.*, a piece of hardware, and not a new intangible concept or design.' " *Holliday v. Extex,* 457 F. Supp. 2d 1112, 1117 (D. Hawai'i 2006) (quoting *Hiser v. Bell Helicopter Textron, Inc.,* 111 Cal. App. 4th 640 (2003)).

The "rolling statute of repose applies only with respect to a new item that replaces an original item." *Hiser,* 4 Cal. Rptr. 3d at 257. "Modification of an item, whether it is a component, system, subassembly, or other part, does not restart the limitation period under GARA." *Id.*

Service bulletins do not constitute a "new part" and do not qualify under the rolling provision of GARA to extend the repose period; as one court wrote, "given the continual issuance of service bulletins pertaining to a variety of topics, 'if the statute of repose [were] triggered every time a service bulletin was issued, the intent of GARA would be eviscerated.' " *Moyer v. Teledyne Cont'l Motors, Inc.,* 979 A.2d 336, 344 (Pa. Super. Ct. 2009) (quoting the opinion issued by the trial court).

Service Bulletin as "New Part"?

We agree with the trial court that the eighteen-year and twelve-year repose periods did not restart with the replacement of the five-bolt spar splice. Although the plaintiff established a new part was installed, it did not replace an item, but rather modified the original design. Further, the plaintiff failed to demonstrate that the new part actually caused the accident. We therefore affirm the summary judgment in favor of the manufacturer. Because we affirm on the statutes of repose, we need not address the alternative basis upon which the trial court dismissed the plaintiff's complaint.

EXERCISE 12-7. *INMON V. AIR TRACTOR, INC.*—GENERAL AVIATION REVITALIZATION ACT ("GARA")

1. What is a statute of repose?

2. Define the following terms (a) Safe Life; and (b) First Fatigue Critical Location ("FFCL").

3. Summarize the issues on appeal as to timing.

4. Explain the purpose the General Aviation Revitalization Act ("GARA").

5. How does the "rolling provision" of GARA function? How are calculations under GARA impacted, if at all, by Service Bulletins? Explain.

NOTES ON *INMON V. AIR TRACTOR, INC.*—GENERAL AVIATION ("GA")

1.   *General Aviation, Defined.*

General aviation aircraft may be defined as all aviation other than military and scheduled commercial airplanes, including airplanes generally having a maximum seating capacity of fewer than twenty passengers that are not engaged in regularly scheduled airline operations. General Aviation Revitalization Act of 1994, Pub. L. No. 103–298, § 2(c), 108 Stat. 1552, 1553 (codified at 49 U.S.C. § 40101 (2006)). There were 210,030 such aircraft in active use in 2015, including piston-engine airplanes, turboprops, business jets, rotocraft, gliders, lighter-than-air aircraft, and experimental and special light-sport airplanes. *See, e.g.,* GEN. AVIATION MFRS. ASS'N, 2008 GENERAL AVIATION STATISTICAL DATABOOK & INDUSTRY OUTLOOK 28 (2008). In 2008, general aviation aircraft accounted for approximately forty-four percent of all aviation fatalities in the United States. *See* NAT'L TRANSP. SAFETY BD., AVIATION ACCIDENT STATISTICS, https://www.ntsb.gov/_layouts/ntsb.aviation/index. aspx. *See also* A. Mitchell Polinsky & Steven Shavell, *The Uneasy Case for Product Liability,* 123 HARV. L. REV. 1437, 1455–56 & n.68 (2010).

General aviation sometimes is a target of lawmakers. In November 2009, automobile industry executives appeared before Congress to request taxpayer bailout money to survive the Great Recession that began manifested in 2008. They flew to Washington, D.C. in corporate jets, drawing the ire of politicians and citizens alike by perpetuating the perception that equates general aviation with wealth and luxury. To blunt this perception, the National Business Aviation Association ("NBAA") emphasized that "[t]he vast majority of the passengers who fly on a business airplane are salespeople, engineers, technicians, and other mid-level employees." *See generally* Ed Bolen, *Business Aviation is Essential to Local Economies and the National Interest,* Jan. 28, 2009, https://nbaa.org/advocacy/legislative-and-regulatory-issues/business-aviation-essential-to-local-economies-and-national-interest/. *See also Fay Vincent, Corporate Jets and Congress,* WALL ST. J., Nov. 26, 2008, at A13.

2.   *The Policy Underlying GARA.*

The General Aviation Revitalization Act ("GARA") is the product of many competing business, political, procedural, and equitable considerations. GARA was implemented to rejuvenate the general aviation market in light of litigation costs arising from product liability lawsuits. *See, e.g.,* William J. Woodward, Jr., *The Third Way: Mediation of Products Claims in the Piper Aircraft Trust,* 17 AM. BANKR. INST. L. REV. 463 (2009).

In considering GARA legislation, the United States Senate noted that "[t]he rationale for this time limitation is that general aviation manufacturers should not be exposed to liability for harm caused by their products for an unlimited period of time . . . Accidents involving general aviation aircraft which have been in use, for example, 25 years or more, are not likely to be due to any defect in the design or manufacture of the product because the product has operated safely for a long period of time." S. Rep. No. 202, 103d Cong. 1st Sess. (1993).

More specifically, in the mid-1990s Congress was deeply concerned about staggering product liability costs that United States manufacturers of general aviation aircraft confronted. Lawmakers believed that manufacturers were being "driven to the wall," among other things, because of the long tail of liability attached to those aircraft, which could be used for decades after they were first manufactured and sold. *See* H.R. Rep. No. 103–525, pt. I, at 1–4 (1994), *reprinted in* 1994 U.S.C.C.A.N. 1638, 1638–41. In other words, general aviation manufacturers could be sued today for airplanes made many years ago. Accordingly, Congress enacted GARA, which formally is a federal statute of repose that prescribes an 18-year limitation on claims against general aviation aircraft manufacturers of any new component, system, subassembly, or other part of the aircraft, from the time of the first delivery of the airplane, with certain exceptions discussed below.

3.   *Exceptions to GARA.*

Four circumstances exist in which GARA's 18-year statute of repose will not bar a claim against a general aviation manufacturer:

- **Misrepresentation.** A claimant will avoid GARA's time-bar upon pleading and proving injuries causally related to a manufacturer's knowing misrepresentation, concealment, or withholding of information that is material and relevant to the performance, maintenance, or operation of an aircraft.

- **Medical or Emergency Treatment.** Under the "air ambulance" exception, a "patient" will not be barred from bringing a claim for injuries sustained while the claimant was a passenger aboard an aircraft while receiving treatment for a medical or "other emergency."

- **Aboard the Aircraft**. GARA will not apply to claimants who were *not* aboard the aircraft at the time of the accident. For example, GARA does not apply to accidents resulting in injury or death to persons on the ground or aboard other aircraft in the event of a mid-air collision.

- **Written Warranty.** Courts will give effect to a written manufacturer's warranty of a product for a definite period of time beyond 18 years from delivery.

Suggested Further Reading

Lauren Haertlein, *An Alternative Liability System for Autonomous Aircraft*, 31 NO. 2 AIR & SPACE LAW. 1 (2018)

Mark C. Niles, *On the Hijacking of Agencies (and Airplanes): The Federal Aviation Administration, "Agency Capture," and Airline Security*, 10 AM. U. J. GENDER SOC. POL'Y & L. 381 (2002)

Van Stewart, *"Privileged Communications?" The Bright Line Rule in the Use of Cockpit Voice Recorder Tapes*, 11 COMMLAW CONSPECTUS 389 (2003)

NTSB Bar Ass'n, *Aviation Professionals and the Threat of Criminal Liability—How do We Maximize Aviation Safety*, 67 J. AIR L. & COM. 875 (2002)

Marc S. Moller & Lori B. Lasson, *Handling the Turbulence Case*, 64 J. AIR L. & COM. 1057 (1999)

CHAPTER 13

International Accident Litigation: Warsaw and Montreal Convention

Press Statement
Richard Boucher, Spokesman
Washington, DC
September 5, 2003

Ratification of the 1999 Montreal Convention

Earlier today, the United States deposited with the International Civil Aviation Organization the U.S. instrument of ratification of the 1999 Convention for the Unification of Certain Rules for International Carriage by Air, known as the "Montreal Convention". The Senate gave its advice and consent to ratification on July 31. The United States is the thirtieth state to consent to be bound by the Convention, which will bring the Convention into force sixty days from today.

The Montreal Convention is the culmination of over four decades of efforts by the United States to eliminate the unconscionably low limits of liability provided under the 1929 Warsaw Convention when passengers are killed or injured in international air carrier accidents.

The significant new benefits of the Montreal Convention include:

- Completely eliminating liability limits for death or injury of passengers.

- Allowing lawsuits in cases of passenger death or injury to be brought in the courts of the passenger's "principal and permanent residence" where the carrier has a commercial presence in that state, which will in almost all cases ensure that U.S. citizens and permanent residents can bring an action in U.S. courts.

- Retaining, in all important substantive respects, the cargo provisions of Montreal Protocol No. 4, which updated the Warsaw Convention's outdated rules for cargo documentation.

- Clarifying the joint liability of the ticketing carrier and operating carrier in code-share operations, which are now widely used in international air transportation.

Source: https://2001-2009.state.gov/r/pa/prs/ps/2003/23851.htm.

A. OVERVIEW

This chapter, which can be read in tandem with Chapter 12 on Accident Litigation, centers on two of the most important and litigated treaties that apply to accidents involving commercial flights engaged in international carriage—the Warsaw Convention and the Montreal Convention. To a large degree understanding how international treaties function in the context of litigation arising from international aviation accidents involves recalling and extending the principle of preemption presented in Chapter 5 (see *El Al Israel Airlines, Ltd. v. Tseng*, Part A, *infra*). But, studying the Warsaw and Montreal conventions also requires students, lawyers, judges, and lawmakers to think about everyday terms in newly critical ways. For example, the cases in this chapter, such as *Air France v. Saks* and *Olympic Airways v. Husain*, examine the meaning of the word "accident" while *Eastern Airlines, Inc. v. Floyd* and *Doe v. Etihad Airways, P.J.S.C.*, evaluate whether mental or psychic injuries are compensable "bodily injuries" associated with aviation accidents. Finally, *Aziz v. Air India Ltd.* and *Watts v. American Airlines, Inc.* feature original ways in which counsel for aviation accidents define the duties of carriers engaged in international carriage. These issues are surprisingly complex.

To resolve the matters at issue in these and other cases, litigants and jurists give great weight to the history and purpose of the treaties. An exegesis presented by the United States Court of Appeals for the Sixth Circuit (*Doe v. Etihad Airways, P.J.S.C., infra*) presents this history aptly, tracking the pendulum-like evolution of international aviation treaty law, from the 1920s when delegates from nations around the world convened to create a uniform body of rules governing international air liability that was favorable to carriers, to the modern era of broader passenger rights:

> The Warsaw Convention, by which it is now referred, was opened for signature in 1929, just two years after Charles Lindbergh famously flew his Spirit of St. Louis solo from New York to Paris, and eight years before Amelia Earhart disappeared over the Pacific Ocean. The original parties to the Warsaw Convention had the "primary purpose of . . . limiting the liability of air carriers in order to foster the growth of the fledgling commercial aviation industry." *Eastern Airlines, Inc. v. Floyd*, 499 U.S. 530 (1991). The Warsaw Convention was the product of four years of work by a committee of experts that was appointed in 1925 at an international conference in Paris at which an early draft protocol was circulated. That draft protocol included an expansive liability provision, holding the carrier "liable for accidents, losses, breakdowns, and delays"

without imposing any requirement of death or bodily injury. Ministère des Affaires Étrangères, Conférence Internationale de Droit Privé Aérien (27 Octobre–6 Novembre 1925), 79 (1926), as translated in *Floyd.*

By the time the conference in Warsaw began in 1929, the committee had divided the protocol on liability into three separate provisions (one for injury to passengers, one for damage to goods, and one for losses from delays). This text was then further developed in Warsaw until the final version of the Warsaw Convention was agreed upon. The Warsaw Convention imposed a cap on damages at 125,000 gold French francs (at the time, approximately $8,300) per passenger, which carriers could reduce to zero upon showing that they had exercised due care by taking "all necessary measures to avoid the damage or that it was impossible" to do so. The cap on damages was lifted (so as to allow potentially unlimited liability) only if the carrier's "willful misconduct" caused the injury or death. "In 1929 the parties were more concerned with protecting air carriers and fostering a new industry rather than providing a full recovery to injured passengers." *Floyd,* 499 U.S. at 543.

The Warsaw Convention entered into force in 1933, and the United States became a party to it in 1934. The United States subsequently led various efforts to modernize it and raise its liability limits. In the early 1950s, the newly created International Civil Aviation Organization ("ICAO") began evaluating a potential increase to the liability limits at international conferences in Rio de Janeiro and The Hague.

At The Hague, the United States proposed raising the personal-liability limits to approximately $25,000, but the majority of other participants resisted; the United States countered with a reduced proposal of approximately $20,000, which was also met with disapproval. "It was not until the United States began to threaten denunciation" that any agreement to increase the personal-liability limits was reached, and even then, the United States "succeeded only in doubling the original Warsaw Convention liability limit to $16,600," in a proposed amendment to the Warsaw Convention known as the Hague Protocol. The United States, dissatisfied with the low liability limits, refused to ratify the Hague Protocol. (In 2003, the United States finally did ratify the Hague Protocol.)

In 1965, in response to what some courts have described as the "unconscionably low" liability limits under the Warsaw Convention,

Dunn v. Trans World Airlines, Inc., 589 F.2d 408, 411 (9th Cir. 1978), United States Secretary of State Dean Rusk gave Poland six months' notice that the United States intended to denounce the Warsaw Convention. The notice included a proviso that the United States would retract its notice of denunciation if personal-liability limits were raised to $75,000 to $100,000 per passenger.

As a result of this notice, the ICAO held a conference in Montreal in 1966 at which the United States unsuccessfully sought to increase the personal-liability limits. The airlines themselves, however—including all major air carriers that served the United States—entered into a private intercarrier agreement (the Montreal Agreement) that made two broad changes to the Warsaw Convention's limitations. First, the Montreal Agreement increased the personal-liability limit to $75,000 per passenger. Second, the Montreal Agreement imposed strict liability up to the $75,000 limit (while retaining the preexisting provision that allowed liability beyond that limit upon a showing of willful misconduct by the airline). The United States retracted its notice of denunciation. The Montreal Agreement remained in force among its signatories for approximately thirty years, and was applicable to all carriage to, from, or through the United States.

In the wake of the Montreal Agreement of 1966, various other international agreements were also reached to increase liability. In 1974, various European and Japanese carriers agreed to increase passenger liability in an informal "Malta Agreement." In 1992, Japanese carriers agreed to strict liability for personal injury up to 100,000 Special Drawing Rights per passenger. And in 1995, a dozen airlines signed a "Washington Intercarrier Agreement," endorsed by the International Air Transport Association, to which the United States Department of Transportation had given antitrust immunity to facilitate discussion of the modernization of international air-carrier liability. This Washington Intercarrier Agreement, signed in Kuala Lumpur, imposed strict liability up to 100,000 SDRs per passenger and removed the "willful misconduct" provision for liability beyond the cap, replacing that provision with something more like a negligence standard that imposes unlimited liability above the 100,000-SDR cap if the airline cannot prove that it took "all necessary measures" to avoid the injury. The major United States-based airlines joined the Washington Intercarrier Agreement within a week of its initial signing in Kuala Lumpur.

Also in the wake of the Montreal Agreement of 1966, aside from the private intercarrier agreements that were negotiated, the United States continued to seek amendments to the Warsaw Convention that would impose higher personal-liability limits. In 1971, the Guatemala City Protocol came close to achieving a limit of 1,500,000 gold francs (then equivalent to approximately $100,000) per passenger, but that Protocol would have imposed an absolute limitation on liability, even in cases of willful misconduct. The United States Senate refused to ratify the Guatemala City Protocol in part because it used the gold standard for liability limits and because it would have imposed an absolute, unbreakable limitation on liability. In 1975, various "Montreal Protocols" were proposed at a diplomatic conference as part of an initiative to replace the Warsaw Convention's gold standard with the SDR. But the only protocol that entered into force worldwide was Protocol No. 4, which affected only cargo liability and not personal-injury liability.

Against that backdrop, the Montreal Convention of 1999 was revolutionary: it replaced not only the Warsaw Convention but also "all of its related instruments and . . . eliminate[d] the need for the patchwork of regulation and private voluntary agreements" that then dominated the world's air-carrier liability regime. The Montreal Convention imposes strict liability for injuries that are compensable under Article 17(1), up to 100,000 SDRs per passenger, with a decennial adjustment for inflation. (The first official adjustment came in 2009, increasing the strict-liability limit to 113,100 SDRs—or approximately $160,000—per passenger. Montreal Convention arts. 21, 24; *see* Inflation Adjustments to Liability Limits Governed by the Montreal Convention Effective Dec. 30, 2009, 74 Fed. Reg. 59,017 (Nov. 16, 2009).)

Above that strict-liability limit, a carrier remains liable for all damage sustained, with no limit, unless the carrier can prove either that "such damage was not due to the negligence or other wrongful act or omission of the carrier or its servants or agents," or that "such damage was solely due to the negligence or other wrongful act or omission of a third party." Montreal Convention art. 21. Finally, an exoneration provision allows a reduction in compensation for injuries caused by or contributed to by the plaintiff, in the same manner as a pure-comparative-negligence or pure-comparative-fault scheme; this exoneration provision applies to all claimed damages including those falling under the strict-liability limit.

Montreal Convention art. 20. In short, the Montreal Convention replaced a "restrictive," "pro-airline industry" regime, with "a treaty that favors passengers rather than airlines." And it did so on terms that reflected decades of effort by the United States to abolish the outdated limitations of the Warsaw Convention.

Moreover, by 1999, when the Montreal Convention was opened for signature, the aviation industry was anything but "fledgling," and the purpose of the Montreal Convention was not to protect the aviation industry, but rather to provide a "modernized uniform liability regime for international air transportation." Letter of Submittal, 1999 WL 33292734, at *6.

Doe v. Etihad Airways, P.J.S.C., 870 F.3d 406, 420–423 (6th Cir. 2017).

B. EXCLUSIVITY OF REMEDY

EL AL ISRAEL AIRLINES, LTD. V. TSENG

525 U.S. 155 (1999)

JUSTICE GINSBURG delivered the opinion of the Court.

Plaintiff-respondent Tsui Yuan Tseng was subjected to an intrusive security search at John F. Kennedy International Airport in New York before she boarded an El Al Israel Airlines May 22, 1993 flight to Tel Aviv. Tseng seeks tort damages from El Al for this occurrence.

Her case presents a question of the Convention's exclusivity: When the Convention allows no recovery for the episode-in-suit, does it correspondingly preclude the passenger from maintaining an action for damages under another source of law, in this case, New York tort law?

The case presents a question of the Convention's exclusivity: When the Convention allows no recovery for the episode-in-suit, does it correspondingly preclude the passenger from maintaining an action for damages under another source of law, in this case, New York tort law?

The exclusivity question before us has been settled prospectively in a Warsaw Convention protocol (Montreal Protocol No. 4) recently ratified by the Senate. Montreal Protocol No. 4 to Amend the Convention for the Unification of Certain Rules Relating to International Carriage By Air, signed at Warsaw on October 12,

1929, as amended by the Protocol Done at the Hague on September 8, 1955 ("Montreal Protocol No. 4"), *reprinted in* S. Exec. Rep. No. 105–20, pp. 21–32 (1998). In accord with the protocol, Tseng concedes, a passenger whose injury is not compensable under the Convention (because it entails no "bodily injury" or was not the result of an "accident") will have no recourse to an alternate remedy. We conclude that the protocol, to which the United States has now subscribed, clarifies, but does not change, the Convention's exclusivity domain. We therefore hold that recovery for a personal injury suffered "on board [an] aircraft or in the course of any of the operations of embarking or disembarking," Art. 17, 49 Stat. 3018, if not allowed under the Convention, is not available at all.

At the outset, we highlight key provisions of the treaty we are interpreting. Chapter I of the Warsaw Convention, entitled "SCOPE-DEFINITIONS," declares in Article 1(1) that the "[C]onvention shall apply to all international transportation of persons, baggage, or goods performed by aircraft for hire." Chapter III, entitled "LIABILITY OF THE CARRIER," defines in Articles 17, 18, and 19 the three kinds of liability for which the Convention provides. Article 17 establishes the conditions of liability for personal injury to passengers:

> The carrier shall be liable for damage sustained in the event of the death or wounding of a passenger or any other bodily injury suffered by a passenger, if the accident which caused the damage so sustained took place on board the aircraft or in the course of any of the operations of embarking or disembarking.

Article 18 establishes the conditions of liability for damage to baggage or goods. Article 18 provides, in relevant part:

> The carrier shall be liable for damage sustained in the event of the destruction or loss of, or of damage to, any checked baggage or any goods, if the occurrence which caused the damage so sustained took place during the transportation by air.

Article 19 establishes the conditions of liability for damage caused by delay. *Id.* Article 19 provides, "[t]he carrier shall be liable for damage occasioned by delay in the transportation by air of passengers, baggage, or goods." Article 24, referring back to Articles 17, 18, and 19, instructs:

> In the cases covered by articles 18 and 19 any action for damages, however founded, can only be brought subject to the conditions and limits set out in this convention.

In the cases covered by article 17 the provisions of the preceding paragraph shall also apply, without prejudice to the questions as to who are the persons who have the right to bring suit and what are their respective rights.

Chapter III of the Convention sets forth a number of other rules governing air carrier liability. Among these, Article 20 relieves a carrier of liability if it has "taken all necessary measures to avoid the damage." Article 22 sets monetary limits on a carrier's liability for harm to passengers and baggage. Article 23 invalidates "[a]ny [contract] provision tending to relieve the carrier of liability or to fix a lower limit than that which is laid down in th[e] [C]onvention." Article 25(1) renders the Convention's limits on liability inapplicable if the damage is caused by a carrier's "willful misconduct."

* * *

On May 22, 1993, Tsui Yuan Tseng arrived at John F. Kennedy International Airport ("JFK") to board an El Al Israel Airlines flight to Tel Aviv. In conformity with standard El Al preboarding procedures, a security guard questioned Tseng about her destination and travel plans. The guard considered Tseng's responses "illogical," and ranked her as a "high risk" passenger. Tseng was taken to a private security room where her baggage and person were searched for explosives and detonating devices. She was told to remove her shoes, jacket, and sweater, and to lower her blue jeans to midhip. A female security guard searched Tseng's body outside her clothes by hand with an electronic security wand.

After the search, which lasted 15 minutes, El Al personnel decided that Tseng did not pose a security threat and allowed her to board the flight. Tseng later testified that she "was really sick and very upset" during the flight, that she was "emotionally traumatized and disturbed" during her month-long trip in Israel, and that, upon her return, she underwent medical and psychiatric treatment for the lingering effects of the body search.

Tseng filed suit against El Al in 1994 in a New York state court of first instance. Her complaint alleged a state-law personal injury claim based on the May 22, 1993 episode at JFK. Tseng's pleading charged, *inter alia*, assault and false imprisonment, but alleged no bodily injury.

Article 24

Our inquiry begins with the text of Article 24, which prescribes the exclusivity of the Convention's provisions for air carrier liability. "[I]t is our responsibility to give the specific words of the treaty a meaning consistent with the shared expectations of the contracting parties." "Because a treaty ratified by the United States is not only the law of this land, *see* U.S. Const., Art. II, § 2, but also an agreement among sovereign powers, we have traditionally considered as aids to its interpretation the negotiating and drafting history (travaux préparatoires) and the postratification understanding of the contracting parties."

Article 24 provides that "cases covered by article 17"—or in the governing French text, "les cas prévus à l'àrticle 17"—may "only be brought subject to the conditions and limits set out in th[e] [C]onvention." That prescription is not a model of the clear drafter's art. We recognize that the words lend themselves to divergent interpretation. In Tseng's view, and in the view of the Court of Appeals, "les cas prévus à l'àrticle 17" means those cases in which a passenger could actually maintain a claim for relief under Article 17. So read, Article 24 would permit any passenger whose personal injury suit did not satisfy the liability conditions of Article 17 to pursue the claim under local law.

In El Al's view, on the other hand, and in the view of the United States as *amicus curiae*, "les cas prévus à l'àrticle 17" refers generically to all personal injury cases stemming from occurrences on board an aircraft or in embarking or disembarking, and simply distinguishes that class of cases (Article 17 cases) from cases involving damaged luggage or goods, or delay (which Articles 18 and 19 address). So read, Article 24 would preclude a passenger from asserting any air transit personal injury claims under local law, including claims that failed to satisfy Article 17's liability conditions, notably, because the injury did not result from an "accident," or because the "accident" did not result in physical injury or physical manifestation of injury.

Respect is ordinarily due the reasonable views of the Executive Branch concerning the meaning of an international treaty. We conclude that the Government's construction of Article 24 is most faithful to the Convention's text, purpose, and overall structure. * * *

The cardinal purpose of the Warsaw Convention is to "achiev[e] uniformity of rules governing claims arising from international air transportation." The Convention signatories, in the treaty's preamble, specifically "recognized the advantage of regulating in a uniform manner the conditions of . . . the liability of the carrier." To provide the desired uniformity, Chapter III of the Convention sets out an array of liability rules which, the treaty declares, "apply to all international transportation of persons, baggage, or goods performed by aircraft."

> *The cardinal purpose of the Warsaw Convention is to "achiev[e] uniformity of rules governing claims arising from international air transportation" . . . To provide the desired uniformity, Chapter III of the Convention sets out an array of liability rules which, the treaty declares, "apply to all international transportation of persons, baggage, or goods performed by aircraft.*

In that Chapter, the Convention describes and defines the three areas of air carrier liability (personal injuries in Article 17, baggage or goods loss, destruction, or damage in Article 18, and damage occasioned by delay in Article 19), the conditions exempting air carriers from liability (Article 20), the monetary limits of liability (Article 22), and the circumstances in which air carriers may not limit liability (Articles 23 and 25). Given the Convention's comprehensive scheme of liability rules and its textual emphasis on uniformity, we would be hard put to conclude that the delegates at Warsaw meant to subject air carriers to the distinct, non-uniform liability rules of the individual signatory nations.

Balancing Recovery Against Liability

A complementary purpose of the Convention is to accommodate or balance the interests of passengers seeking recovery for personal injuries, and the interests of air carriers seeking to limit potential liability. Before the Warsaw accord, injured passengers could file suits for damages, subject only to the limitations of the forum's laws, including the forum's choice-of-law regime. This exposure inhibited the growth of the then-fledgling international airline industry. Many international air carriers at that time endeavored to require passengers, as a condition of air travel, to relieve or reduce the carrier's liability in case of injury. The Convention drafters designed Articles 17, 22, and 24 of the Convention as a compromise between the interests of air carriers and their customers worldwide. In Article 17 of the Convention, carriers are denied the contractual prerogative to exclude or limit their liability for personal injury. In Articles 22 and 24, passengers are limited in the amount of damages they may recover, and are restricted in the claims they may pursue by the conditions and limits set out in the Convention.

Construing the Convention to allow passengers to pursue claims under local law when the Convention does not permit recovery could produce several anomalies. Carriers might be exposed to unlimited liability under diverse legal regimes, but would be prevented, under the treaty, from contracting out of such liability. Passengers injured physically in an emergency landing might be subject to the liability caps of the Convention, while those merely traumatized in the same mishap would be free to sue outside of the Convention for potentially unlimited damages. * * *

The drafting history of Article 17 is consistent with our understanding of the preemptive effect of the Convention. The preliminary draft of the Convention submitted to the conference at Warsaw made air carriers liable "in the case of death, wounding, or any other bodily injury suffered by a traveler." In the later draft that prescribed what is now Article 17, airline liability was narrowed to encompass only bodily injury caused by an "accident." It is improbable that, at the same time the drafters narrowed the conditions of air carrier liability in Article 17, they intended, in Article 24, to permit passengers to skirt those conditions by pursuing claims under local law. Sir Alfred Dennis of Great Britain stated at the Warsaw Conference that Article 24 is "a very important stipulation which touches the very substance of the Convention, because [it] excludes recourse to common law."

* * *

Montreal Protocol No. 4, ratified by the Senate on September 28, 1998, amends Article 24 to read, in relevant part: "In the carriage of passengers and baggage, any action for damages, however founded, can only be brought subject to the conditions and limits set out in this Convention." Article 24, as amended by Montreal Protocol No. 4, provides:

> In the carriage of passengers and baggage, any action for damages, however founded, can only be brought subject to the conditions and limits set out in this Convention, without prejudice to the question as to who are the persons who have the right to bring suit and what are their respective rights.

> In the carriage of cargo, any action for damages, however founded, whether under this Convention or in contract or in tort or otherwise, can only be brought subject to the conditions and limits of liability set out in this Convention without prejudice to the question as to who are the persons who have the right to bring suit and what are their respective rights.

> Such limits of liability constitute maximum limits and may not be exceeded whatever the circumstances which gave rise to the liability.

Both parties agree that, under the amended Article 24, the Convention's preemptive effect is clear: The treaty precludes passengers from bringing actions under local law when they cannot establish air carrier liability under the treaty. Revised Article 24, El Al urges and we agree, merely clarifies, it does not alter, the Convention's rule of exclusivity. Supporting the position that revised Article 24 provides for preemption not earlier established, Tseng urges that federal preemption of state law is disfavored generally, and particularly when matters of health and safety are at stake. Tseng overlooks in this regard that the nation-state, not subdivisions within one nation, is the focus of the Convention and the perspective of our treaty partners. Our home-centered preemption analysis, therefore, should not be applied, mechanically, in construing our international obligations.

Decisions of the courts of other Convention signatories corroborate our understanding of the Convention's preemptive effect. The British House of Lords considered and decided the very question we now face concerning the Convention's exclusivity when a passenger alleges psychological damages, but no physical injury, resulting from an occurrence that is not an "accident" under Article 17.

Reviewing the text, structure, and drafting history of the Convention, the Lords concluded that the Convention was designed to "ensure that, in all questions relating to the carrier's liability, it is the provisions of the [C]onvention which apply and that the passenger does not have access to any other remedies, whether under the common law or otherwise, which may be available within the particular country where he chooses to raise his action." Courts of other nations bound by the Convention have also recognized the treaty's encompassing preemptive effect. The "opinions of our sister signatories," we have observed, are "entitled to considerable weight." The text, drafting history, and underlying purpose of the Convention, in sum, counsel us to adhere to a view of the treaty's exclusivity shared by our treaty partners.

For the reasons stated, we hold that the Warsaw Convention precludes a passenger from maintaining an action for personal injury damages under local law when her claim does not satisfy the conditions for liability under the Convention.

JUSTICE STEVENS, dissenting.

I agree with the Court that the drafters of the Convention intended that the treaty largely supplant local law. The Convention, however, does not preempt local law in cases arising out of "willful misconduct." Article 25 expressly provides that a carrier shall not be entitled to avail itself of the provisions of the Convention that "exclude or limit" its liability if its misconduct is willful. Moreover, the question whether the carrier's wrongful act "is considered to be equivalent to willful misconduct" is determined by "the law of the court to which the case is submitted." Accordingly, the vast majority of the potential claims by passengers against international air carriers are either preempted by Article 24 or unequivocally governed by local law under Article 25. I firmly believe that a treaty, like an Act of Congress, should not be construed to preempt state law unless its intent to do so is clear. For this reason, I respectfully dissent.

EXERCISE 13-1. *EL AL ISRAEL AIRLINES, LTD. V. TSENG—*
PREEMPTION OF "LOCAL" LAW

1. Summarize what Articles 17, 18, 19, 20, and 22, and 24 of the Warsaw Convention provide.

2. Detail each party's view of Article 24 of the Warsaw Convention and explain which view prevailed in the court's view.

3. Identify the main purposes of the Warsaw Convention. Is it more carrier- or passenger-friendly?

4. Explain how the court resolved the exclusivity and preemption questions. In practical terms, what does this mean for plaintiffs?

5. What does the dissent argue? *See, e.g., In re Air Disaster at Lockerbie, Scotland on Dec. 21, 1988*, 37 F.3d 804 (2d Cir. 1994) for an extraordinary opinion detailing the limitation of liability under the Warsaw Convention in connection with the bombing of Pan Am 103 over Lockerbie, Scotland a few days before Christmas Day in 1988.

NOTES ON *EL AL AIRLINES, LTD. V. TSENG*—INTERNATIONAL CARRIAGE

1. ***Convention Signatories.***

The Montreal Convention is the product of a meeting sponsored by the United Nations in 1999 of delegates from 121 different states via the International Civil Aviation Organization—ICAO. The Montreal Convention has been ratified by more than 95 nations to date. The United States adopted the treaty in November, 2003, as a replacement to the Warsaw Convention. *See* Convention for the Unification of Certain Rules for International Carriage by Air, https://www.state.gov/documents/organization/122936.pdf.

What law applies to an international aviation accident that occurred prior to ratification of the Montreal Convention by a particular state, *e.g.*, an accident involving an American passenger pre-2003? To what law should courts look in resolving disputes arising out of international transportation involving nations that ratified neither the Warsaw nor the Montreal Convention? What treaty applies where one nation applies the Warsaw Convention and another nation employs the Montreal Convention? The scenarios are knowable:

- If both countries are signatories to the Montreal Convention then that convention applies.

- If both countries are *not* signatories to the Montreal Convention, then the inquiry is whether one country is a signatory to both Conventions but the other country is signatory to Warsaw Convention only. If so, the Warsaw Convention applies.

2. *What Is "International Carriage"?*

The Montreal Convention—like its predecessor, the Warsaw Convention—applies only to "international carriage." Whether a claimant under the Montreal Convention was traveling internationally is not always obvious, however. For example, the Montreal Convention may apply to a domestic flight that is but a part of an international itinerary (*e.g.*, Illinois to New York to Ireland). Consider:

> ***Single Operation.*** A Denver-to-Chicago flight was "international transportation" under the Warsaw Convention where the passenger-plaintiff's layover in Denver was to make a connection after a flight from London, tickets were sold by the same travel agent, and the parties had knowledge of the trip as a single operation. *See Robertson v. American Airlines, Inc.*, 401 F.3d 499 (D.C. Cir. 2005).

> ***"Domestic" Operations.*** A domestic flight constitutes international transportation if it is part of an international itinerary regarded by the parties—the passenger and the carrier—as a single operation. Art. 1(2)–(3). *See Haldimann v. Delta Airlines, Inc.*, 168 F.3d 1324 (D.C. Cir. 1999).

The intent of the parties is a critical consideration in determining the international character of air carriage, therefore. Does a stop-over in a foreign country qualify as international carriage under the Montreal Convention? *See, e.g., Gustafson v. American Airlines, Inc.*, 658 F. Supp. 2d 276 (D. Mass. 2009). *See also Jones v. USA 3000 Airlines*, 2009 WL 330596 (E.D. Mo. Feb. 9, 2009) ("for round-trip international travel, the place of destination is the same as the place of departure.").

3. *The "Fifth Jurisdiction."*

Jurisdiction is a primary consideration in Montreal Convention cases. In fact, the Montreal Convention applies only to international carriage where the place of departure and destination are situated within the territories of two different countries, or within the territory of one country if there is an agreed stopping place within the territory of another country. There are four forums in which a plaintiff can sue a carrier for damages resulting in the death or injury of passengers in international transportation:

- The carrier's domicile;

- The carrier's principal place of business;

- The place of business where the contract was made; and

- The passenger's destination.

Importantly, Article 33 of the Montreal Convention adds a "fifth jurisdiction," namely the country in which a passenger has his or her "principal and permanent residence" at the time of the accident. The Montreal Convention specifically defines this residence as "the one fixed and permanent abode of the passenger at the time of the accident." Because "[t]he nationality of the passenger shall not be the determining factor in this regard," it is now possible for American citizens to seek relief in United States courts for international carriage arising under the Montreal Convention.

C. "ACCIDENT"

AIR FRANCE V. SAKS

470 U.S. 392 (1985)

JUSTICE O'CONNOR delivered the opinion of the Court.

Article 17 of the Warsaw Convention makes air carriers liable for injuries sustained by a passenger "if the accident which caused the damage so sustained took place on board the aircraft or in the course of any of the operations of embarking or disembarking." We granted *certiorari* to resolve a conflict among the Courts of Appeals as to the proper definition of the word "accident" as used in this international air carriage treaty.

On November 16, 1980, respondent Valerie Saks boarded an Air France jetliner in Paris for a 12-hour flight to Los Angeles. The flight went smoothly in all respects until, as the aircraft descended to Los Angeles, Saks felt severe pressure and pain in her left ear. The pain continued after the plane landed, but Saks disembarked without informing any Air France crew member or employee of her ailment. Five days later, Saks consulted a doctor who concluded that she had become permanently deaf in her left ear.

Saks filed suit against Air France in California state court, alleging that her hearing loss was caused by negligent maintenance and operation of the jetliner's pressurization system. The case was removed to the United States District Court for the Central District of California. After extensive discovery, Air France moved for summary judgment on the ground that respondent could not prove that her injury was caused by an "accident" within the meaning of the Warsaw Convention.

The term "accident," according to Air France, means an "abnormal, unusual or unexpected occurrence aboard the aircraft." All the available evidence, including the post-flight reports, pilot's affidavit, and passenger testimony, indicated that the aircraft's pressurization system had operated in the usual manner. Accordingly, the airline contended that the suit should be dismissed because the only alleged cause of respondent's injury—normal operation of a pressurization system—could not qualify as an "accident." In her opposition to the summary judgment motion, Saks acknowledged that "[t]he sole question of law presented . . . by the parties is whether a loss of hearing proximately caused by normal operation of the aircraft's pressurization system is an "accident" within the meaning of Article 17 of the Warsaw Convention . . ." She argued that "accident" should be defined as a "hazard of air travel," and that her injury had indeed been caused by such a hazard.

Relying on precedent which defines the term "accident" in Article 17 as an "unusual or unexpected" happening, the District Court granted summary judgment to Air France. A divided panel of the Court of Appeals for the Ninth Circuit reversed. The appellate court reviewed the history of the Warsaw Convention and its modification by the 1966 Montreal Agreement, a private agreement among airlines that has been approved by the United States Government. The court concluded that the language, history, and policy of the Warsaw Convention and the Montreal Agreement impose absolute liability on airlines for injuries proximately caused by the risks inherent in air travel. The court found a definition of "accident" consistent with this history and policy in Annex 13 to the Convention on International Civil Aviation: "an occurrence associated with the operation of an aircraft which takes place between the time any person boards the aircraft with the intention of flight and all such persons have disembarked." Normal cabin pressure changes qualify as an "accident" under this definition. A dissent agreed with the District Court that "accident" should be defined as an unusual or unexpected occurrence. We disagree with the definition of "accident" adopted by the Court of Appeals, and we reverse.

* * *

Liberal
Interpretation
of Treaties

Air France is liable to a passenger under the terms of the Warsaw Convention only if the passenger proves that an "accident" was the cause of her injury. The narrow issue presented is whether respondent can meet this burden by showing that her injury was caused by the normal operation of the aircraft's pressurization system. The proper answer turns on interpretation of a clause in an international treaty to which the United States is a party. "[T]reaties are construed more liberally than private agreements, and to ascertain their meaning we may look beyond the written words to the history of the treaty, the negotiations, and the practical construction adopted by the parties." The analysis must begin, however, with the text of the treaty and the context in which the written words are used.

Article 17 of the Warsaw Convention establishes the liability of international air carriers for harm to passengers. Article 18 contains parallel provisions regarding liability for damage to baggage. The governing text of the Convention is in the French language.

Two significant features of these provisions stand out in both the French and the English texts. First, Article 17 imposes liability for injuries to passengers caused by an "accident" whereas Article 18 imposes liability for destruction or loss of baggage caused by an "occurrence." This difference in the parallel language of Articles 17 and 18 implies that the drafters of the Convention understood the word "accident" to mean something different than the word "occurrence," for they otherwise logically would have used the same word in each article. The language of the Convention accordingly renders suspect the opinion of the Court of Appeals that "accident" means "occurrence."

Accident vs. Occurrence

Second, the text of Article 17 refers to an accident which caused the passenger's injury, and not to an accident which is the passenger's injury. In light of the many senses in which the word "accident" can be used, this distinction is significant. As Lord Lindley observed in 1903:

> The word "accident" is not a technical legal term with a clearly defined meaning. Speaking generally, but with reference to legal liabilities, an accident means any unintended and unexpected occurrence which produces hurt or loss. But it is often used to denote any unintended and unexpected loss or hurt apart from its cause; and if the cause is not known the loss or hurt itself would certainly be called an accident. The word "accident" is also often used to denote both the cause and the effect, no attempt being made to discriminate between them."

In Article 17, the drafters of the Warsaw Convention apparently did make an attempt to discriminate between "the cause and the effect"; they specified that air carriers would be liable if an accident caused the passenger's injury. The text of the Convention thus implies that, however we define "accident," it is the cause of the injury that must satisfy the definition rather than the occurrence of the injury alone. American jurisprudence has long recognized this distinction between an accident that is the cause of an injury and an injury that is itself an accident.

While the text of the Convention gives these two clues to the meaning of "accident," it does not define the term. Nor is the context in which the term is used illuminating. To determine the meaning of the term "accident" in Article 17 we must consider its French legal meaning. This is true not because "we are forever chained to French law" by the Convention, *see Rosman v. Trans World Airlines, Inc.*, 314 N.E.2d 848 (N.Y. Ct. App. 1974), but because it is our responsibility to give the specific words of the treaty a meaning consistent with the shared expectations of the contracting parties. We look to the French legal meaning for guidance as to these expectations because the Warsaw Convention was drafted in French by continental jurists.

While the text of the Convention gives these two clues to the meaning of "accident," it does not define the term. Nor is the context in which the term is used illuminating.

A survey of French cases and dictionaries indicates that the French legal meaning of the term "accident" differs little from the meaning of the term in Great Britain, Germany, or the United States. Thus, while the word "accident" is often used to refer to the event of a person's injury, it is also sometimes used to describe a cause of injury, and when the word is used in this latter sense, it is usually defined as a fortuitous, unexpected, unusual, or unintended event. This parallels British and American jurisprudence. The text of the Convention consequently suggests that the passenger's injury must be caused by an unexpected or unusual event.

* * *

This interpretation of Article 17 is consistent with the negotiating history of the Convention, the conduct of the parties to the Convention, and the weight of precedent in foreign and American courts. In interpreting a treaty it is proper, of course, to refer to the records of its drafting and negotiation. In part because the "travaux preparatoires" of the Warsaw Convention are published and generally available to litigants, courts frequently refer to these materials to resolve ambiguities in the text.

The treaty that became the Warsaw Convention was first drafted at an international conference in Paris in 1925. The protocol resulting from the Paris Conference contained an article specifying: "The carrier is liable for accidents, losses, breakdowns, and delays. It is not liable if it can prove that it has taken reasonable measures designed to pre-empt damage . . ." The protocol drafted at Paris was revised several times by a committee of experts on air law, and then submitted to a second international conference that convened in Warsaw in 1929. The draft submitted to the conference stated:

The carrier shall be liable for damage sustained during carriage: (a) in the case of death, wounding, or any other bodily injury suffered by a traveler; (b) in the case of destruction, loss, or damage to goods or baggage; (c) in the case of delay suffered by a traveler, goods, or baggage.

Article 22 of this draft, like the original Paris draft, permitted the carrier to avoid liability by proving it had taken reasonable measures to avoid the damage. None of the early drafts required that an accident cause the passenger's injury.

At Warsaw, delegates from several nations objected to the application of identical liability rules to both passenger injuries and damage to baggage, and the German delegation proposed separate liability rules for passengers and baggage. The need for separate rules arose primarily because delegates thought that liability for baggage should commence upon delivery to the carrier, whereas liability for passengers should commence when the passengers later embark upon the aircraft. The Reporter on the Preliminary Draft of the Convention argued it would be too difficult to draft language specifying this distinction, and that such a distinction would be unnecessary because "Article 22 establishes a very mitigated system of liability for the carrier, and from the moment that the carrier has taken the reasonable measures, he does not answer for the risks, nor for the accidents occur[r]ing to people by the fault of third parties, nor for accidents occur [r]ing for any other cause." The delegates were unpersuaded, and a majority voted to have a drafting committee rework the liability provisions for passengers and baggage.

A few days later, the drafting committee proposed the liability provisions that became Articles 17 and 18 of the Convention. Article 20(1) of the final draft contains the "necessary measures" language which the Reporter believed would shield the carrier from liability for "the accidents occur[r]ing to people by the fault of third parties" and for "accidents occur[r]ing for any other cause." Nevertheless, the redrafted Article 17 also required as a prerequisite to liability that an accident cause the passenger's injury, whereas the redrafted Article 18 required only that an occurrence cause the damage to baggage.

Although Article 17 and Article 18 as redrafted were approved with little discussion, the President of the drafting committee observed that "given that there are entirely different liability cases: death or wounding, disappearance of goods, delay, we have deemed that it would be better to begin by setting out the causes of liability for persons, then for goods and baggage, and finally liability in the case of delay."

This comment at least implies that the addition of language of causation to Articles 17 and 18 had a broader purpose than specification of the time at which liability commenced. It further suggests that the causes of liability for persons were intended to be different from the causes of liability for baggage. The records of the negotiation of the Convention accordingly support what is evident from its text: "A passenger's injury must be caused by an accident, and an accident must mean something different than an 'occurrence' on the plane." Like the text of the Convention, however, the records of its negotiation offer no precise definition of "accident." Reference to the conduct of the parties to the Convention and the subsequent interpretations of the signatories helps clarify the meaning of the term.

At a Guatemala City International Conference on Air Law in 1971, representatives of many of the Warsaw signatories approved an amendment to Article 17 which would impose liability on the carrier for an "event which caused the death or injury" rather than for an "accident which caused" the passenger's injury, but would exempt the carrier from liability if the death or injury resulted "solely from the state of health of the passenger." The Guatemala City Protocol of 1971 and the Montreal Protocols Nos. 3 and 4 of 1975 include this amendment, but have yet to be ratified by the Senate, and therefore do not govern the disposition of this case. The statements of the delegates at Guatemala City indicate that they viewed the switch from "accident" to "event" as expanding the scope of carrier liability to passengers. The Swedish Delegate, for example, in referring to the choice between the words "accident" and "event," emphasized that the word "accident" is too narrow because a carrier might be found liable for "other acts which could not be considered as accidents."

In determining precisely what causes can be considered accidents, we "find the opinions of our sister signatories to be entitled to considerable weight." *Benjamins v. British European Airways*, 572 F.2d 913 (2d Cir. 1979). While few decisions are precisely on point, we note that, in *Air France v. Haddad*, Judgment of June 19, 1979, Cour d'appel de Paris, Première Chambre Civile, 1979 Revue Francaise de Droit Aérien, at 328, a French court observed that the term "accident" in Article 17 of the Warsaw Convention embraces causes of injuries that are fortuitous or unpredictable.

European legal scholars have generally construed the word "accident" in Article 17 to require that the passenger's injury be caused by a sudden or unexpected event other than the normal operation of the plane. *See, e.g.*, O. Riese & LaCour, Précis de Droit Aérien 264 (1951) (noting that Swiss and German law require that the damage be caused by an accident, and arguing that an accident should be construed as an event which is sudden and independent of the will of the carrier); 1 C. Shawcross & K. Beaumont, Air Law ¶ VII(148) (4th ed. 1984) (noting that the Court of Appeals for the Third Circuit's definition of accident accords with some English definitions and "might well commend itself to an English court"). These observations are in accord with American decisions which, while interpreting the term "accident" broadly nevertheless refuse to extend the term to cover routine travel procedures that produce an injury due to the peculiar internal condition of a passenger. * * *

We conclude that liability under Article 17 of the Warsaw Convention arises only if a passenger's injury is caused by an unexpected or unusual event or happening that is external to the passenger. This definition should be flexibly applied after assessment of all the circumstances surrounding a passenger's injuries.

We conclude that liability under Article 17 of the Warsaw Convention arises only if a passenger's injury is caused by an unexpected or unusual event or happening that is external to the passenger. This definition should be flexibly applied after assessment of all the circumstances surrounding a passenger's injuries. For example, lower courts in this country have interpreted Article 17 broadly enough to encompass torts committed by terrorists or fellow passengers. In cases where there is contradictory evidence, it is for the trier of fact to decide whether an "accident" as here defined caused the passenger's injury. But when the injury indisputably results from the passenger's own internal reaction to the usual, normal, and expected operation of the aircraft, it has not been caused by an accident, and Article 17 of the Warsaw Convention cannot apply. The judgment of the Court of Appeals in this case must accordingly be reversed. We recognize that any standard requiring courts to distinguish causes that are "accidents" from causes that are "occurrences" requires drawing a line, and we realize that "reasonable [people] may differ widely as to the place where the line should fall."

We draw this line today only because the language of Articles 17 and 18 requires it, and not because of any desire to plunge into the "Serbonian bog" that accompanies attempts to distinguish between causes that are accidents and injuries that are accidents. Any injury is the product of a chain of causes, and we require only that the passenger be able to prove that some link in the chain was an unusual or unexpected event external to the passenger. Until Article 17 of the Warsaw Convention is changed by the signatories, it cannot be stretched to impose carrier liability for injuries that are not caused by accidents. It remains "[o]ur duty . . .to enforce the . . .treaties of the United States, whatever they might be, and . . .the Warsaw Convention remains the supreme law of the land." The judgment of the

Court of Appeals is reversed, and the case is remanded for further proceedings consistent with this opinion.

EXERCISE 13-2. *AIR FRANCE V. SAKS*—"UNUSUAL OR UNEXPECTED EVENT OR HAPPENING THAT IS EXTERNAL TO THE PASSENGER"

1. The facts of *Air France v. Saks* are not complicated, but they are striking to many students. What are they?

2. Identify where in the Warsaw Convention the word "accident" is defined. Is it synonymous with "occurrence"?

3. What definition of "accident" does the court announce in *Air France v. Saks*? How is it to be applied to different factual scenarios; for example, are torts committed by terrorists or fellow passengers encompassed by Article 17 of the Warsaw Convention. Why or why not?

4. According to the court, is the focus of Article 17 on the accident that causes the passenger's injury or the accident that is the passenger's injury. What is the difference?

5. Using the definition from Question 3, *supra*, did an accident occur in this case? Explain.

NOTES ON *AIR FRANCE V. SAKS*—DEFINING ACCIDENT

The definition of "accident" under both the Warsaw Convention and its successor, the Montreal Convention, has generated a substantial body of decisional law. An "accident" under either treaty has been defined generally as an "unexpected or unusual event that is external to the passenger" occurring during the embarking or disembarking of an aircraft, but its application is case-specific.

One federal district court has noted that, "as the causal balance shifts towards acts and conditions that are independent of the knowledge or will of the carrier, or not associated with the operation of the aircraft or airline nor arising from risks characteristic of air travel, and instead are more unique to the passenger alleging injury, the lesser the claimant's probability of recovery." *Fulop v. Malev Hungarian Airlines*, 175 F. Supp. 2d 651 (S.D.N.Y. 2001). *See generally Sethy v. Malev-Hungarian Airlines, Inc.*, 2000 WL 1234660 (S.D.N.Y. Aug. 31, 2000); *Price v. British Airways*, 1992 WL 170679 (S.D.N.Y. July 7, 1992); *Margrave v. British Airways*, 643 F. Supp. 510 (S.D.N.Y. 1986); *Warshaw v. Trans World Airlines, Inc.*, 442 F. Supp. 400 (E.D. Pa. 1977); *Potter v. Delta Air Lines, Inc.*, 1996 WL 603941 (5th Cir. 1996) (no "accident" where the alleged injury arose from an altercation between two passengers without any involvement of flight crew); *Stone v. Continental Airlines, Inc.*, 905 F. Supp. 823 (D. Haw. 1995) (same); *Tsevas v. Delta Air Lines, Inc.*, 1997 WL 767278 (N.D. Ill. Dec. 1, 1997) (finding injuries were caused by an "accident" where assault by one passenger on another occurred after the flight attendant excessively served drinks to the attacker and refused to intervene or to change plaintiff's seat assignments). *See also Schneider v. Swiss Air Transp. Co., Ltd.*, 686 F. Supp. 15 (D. Me. 1988) (finding "accident" where plaintiff was injured in moving from her seat when another passenger refused to put his seat upright and flight crew denied assistance).

Other courts have construed "accident" quite narrowly, finding no liability in situations where the circumstances indicate no causal involvement or relationship of the carrier in the events constituting the alleged accident, as demonstrated by the absence of evidence of any abnormal aircraft operations; departures from recognized industry standards, carrier policies or procedures; or aberrant conduct of employees in some way related to the operation of the aircraft or airline. In those situations, courts seem to emphasize occurrences outside the airline's control or ability to prevent, or that are not related to hazards inherently associated with aviation, but rather are risks incident to "living in a world such as ours," may not be classified as accidents under the Convention. *Martinez Hernandez v. Air France*, 545 F.2d 279 (1st Cir. 1976) (rejecting an argument that a terrorist attack within an airport was a "characteristic of air travel" to which Article 17 liability should apply). *See, e.g., Maxwell v. Aer Lingus Ltd.*, 122 F. Supp. 2d 210 (D. Mass. 2000); *Gotz v. Delta Airlines, Inc.*, 12 F. Supp. 2d 199 (D. Mass. 1998) (finding no accident where a passenger was injured by another engaged in removing an overhead bag, where there was no failure by the flight attendant to intervene and no request for assistance). *But cf. Pittman v. Grayson*, 869 F. Supp. 1065 (S.D.N.Y.1994) (finding no accident, because the events did not constitute risks inherent in air travel, even though plaintiff alleged that airline personnel had assisted in smuggling and transporting a passenger on a flight out of the country in violation of a court order); *Curley v. American Airlines, Inc.*, 846 F. Supp. 280 (S.D.N.Y. 1994) (no accident even where plaintiff claimed that the flight captain falsely identified him to Mexican police officials as having smoked marijuana while aboard the aircraft, resulting in plaintiff's alleged injuries from detention and search by the Mexican police; the court concluded that being suspected and falsely accused of smoking marijuana in the airplane's lavatory was not a risk inherent in air travel).

How does (or will) the decision of *Doe v. Etihad Airways, P.J.S.C., infra,* impact the foregoing precedent?

OLYMPIC AIRWAYS V. HUSAIN

540 U.S. 644 (2004)

JUSTICE THOMAS delivered the opinion of the Court.

Article 17 of the Warsaw Convention ("Convention") imposes liability on an air carrier for a passenger's death or bodily injury caused by an "accident" that occurred in connection with an international flight. In *Air France v. Saks*, 470 U.S. 392 (1985), the Court explained that the term "accident" in the Convention refers to an "unexpected or unusual event or happening that is external to the passenger," and not to "the passenger's own internal reaction to the usual, normal, and expected operation of the aircraft. The issue we must decide is whether the "accident" condition precedent to air carrier liability under Article 17 is satisfied when the carrier's unusual and unexpected refusal to assist a passenger is a link in a chain of causation resulting in a passenger's pre-existing medical condition being aggravated by exposure to a normal condition in the aircraft cabin. We conclude that it is.

The issue we must decide is whether the "accident" condition precedent to air carrier liability under Article 17 is satisfied when the carrier's unusual and unexpected refusal to assist a passenger is a link in a chain of causation resulting in a passenger's pre-existing medical condition being aggravated by exposure to a normal condition in the aircraft cabin. We conclude that it is.

In December 1997, respondent, Dr. Abid Hanson and his wife, Rubina Husain, traveled with their children and another family from San Francisco to Athens and Cairo for a family vacation. During a stopover in New York, Dr. Hanson learned for the first time that petitioner allowed its passengers to smoke on international flights. Because Dr. Hanson had suffered from asthma and was sensitive to secondhand smoke, respondent requested and obtained seats away from the smoking section. Dr. Hanson experienced no problems on the flights to Cairo.

For the return flights, Dr. Hanson and respondent arrived early at the Cairo airport in order to request nonsmoking seats. Respondent showed the check-in agent a physician's letter explaining that Dr. Hanson "has [a] history of recurrent anaphylactic reactions," and asked the agent to ensure that their seats were in the nonsmoking section. The flight to Athens was uneventful. After boarding the plane for the flight to San Francisco, Dr. Hanson and respondent discovered that their seats were located only three rows in front of the economy-class smoking section.

Respondent advised Maria Leptourgou, a flight attendant for petitioner, that Dr. Hanson could not sit in a smoking area, and said, " 'You have to move him.' " The flight attendant told her to " 'have a seat.' " After all the passengers had boarded but prior to takeoff, respondent again asked Ms. Leptourgou to move Dr. Hanson, explaining that he was " 'allergic to smoke.' " Ms. Leptourgou replied that she could not reseat Dr. Hanson because the plane was " 'totally full' " and she was "too busy" to help.

Shortly after takeoff, passengers in the smoking section began to smoke, and Dr. Hanson was soon surrounded by ambient cigarette smoke. Respondent spoke with Ms. Leptourgou a third time, stating, " 'You have to move my husband from here.' " Ms. Leptourgou again refused, stating that the plane was full. Ms. Leptourgou told respondent that Dr. Hanson could switch seats with another passenger, but that respondent would have to ask other passengers herself, without the flight crew's assistance. Respondent told Ms. Leptourgou that Dr. Hanson had to move even if the only available seat was in the cockpit or in business class, but Ms. Leptourgou refused to provide any assistance. Dr. Hanson and respondent did not know at the time that, despite Ms. Leptourgou's representations, the flight was actually not full. There were 11 unoccupied passenger seats, most of which were in economy class, and 28 "non-revenue passengers," 15 of whom were seated in economy class rows farther away from the smoking section than Dr. Hanson's seat.

About two hours into the flight, the smoking noticeably increased in the rows behind Dr. Hanson. Dr. Hanson asked respondent for a new inhaler because the one he had been using was empty. Dr. Hanson then moved toward the front of the plane to get some fresher air. While he was leaning against a chair near the galley area, Dr. Hanson gestured to respondent to get his emergency kit. Respondent returned with it and gave him a shot of epinephrine. She then awoke Dr. Umesh Sabharwal, an allergist, with whom Dr. Hanson and respondent had been traveling. Dr. Sabharwal gave Dr. Hanson another shot of epinephrine and began to administer CPR and oxygen. Dr. Hanson died shortly thereafter. (For religious reasons, no autopsy was performed to determine the cause of death.)

Respondents filed a wrongful-death suit in California state court. Petitioner removed the case to federal court, and the District Court found petitioner liable for Dr. Hanson's death. The District Court held that Ms. Leptourgou's refusal to reseat Dr. Hanson constituted an "accident" within the meaning of Article 17. Applying *Saks'* definition of that term, the court reasoned that the flight attendant's conduct was external to Dr. Hanson and, because it was in "blatant disregard of industry standards and airline policies," was not expected or usual.

The Ninth Circuit affirmed. Applying *Saks'* definition of "accident," the Ninth Circuit agreed that the flight attendant's refusal to reseat Dr. Hanson "was clearly external to Dr. Hanson, and it was unexpected and unusual in light of industry standards, Olympic policy, and the simple nature of Dr. Hanson's requested accommodation." We granted *certiorari* and now affirm.

We begin with the language of Article 17 of the Convention, which provides:

> The carrier shall be liable for damage sustained in the event of the death or wounding of a passenger or any other bodily injury suffered by a passenger, if the accident which caused the damage so sustained took place on board the aircraft or in the course of any of the operations of embarking or disembarking.

The Warsaw Convention's governing text is in French. We cite to the official English translation of the Convention, which was before the Senate when it consented to ratification of the Convention in 1934.

Burden Shifting Under Arts. 17 and 20 Treaties

After a plaintiff has established a *prima facie* case of liability under Article 17 by showing that the injury was caused by an "accident," the air carrier has the opportunity to prove under Article 20 that it took "all necessary measures to avoid the damage or that it was impossible for [the airline] to take such measures." Thus, Article 17 creates a presumption of air carrier liability and shifts the burden to the air carrier to prove lack of negligence under Article 20. Article 22(1) caps the amount recoverable under Article 17 in the event of death or bodily injury, and Article 25(1) removes the cap if the damage is caused by the "willful misconduct" of the airline or its agent, acting within the scope of his employment. Additionally, Article 21 enables an air carrier to avoid or reduce its liability if it can prove the passenger's comparative negligence.

In *Saks*, the Court recognized that the text of the Convention does not define the term "accident" and that the context in which it is used is not "illuminating." The Court nevertheless discerned the meaning of the term "accident" from the Convention's text, structure, and history as well as from the subsequent conduct of the parties to the Convention.

Neither party here contests *Saks'* definition of the term "accident" under Article 17 of the Convention. Rather, the parties differ as to which event should be the focus of the "accident" inquiry. The Court's reasoning in *Saks* sheds light on whether the flight attendant's refusal to assist a passenger in a medical crisis is the proper focus of the "accident" inquiry. In *Saks*, the Court addressed whether a passenger's " 'loss of hearing proximately caused by normal operation of the aircraft's pressurization system' " was an " 'accident.' " The Court concluded that it was not, because the injury was her "own internal reaction" to the normal pressurization of the aircraft's cabin. The Court noted two textual clues to the meaning of the term "accident."

First, the Convention distinguishes between liability under Article 17 for death or injuries to passengers caused by an "accident" and liability under Article 18 for destruction or loss of baggage caused by an "occurrence." The difference in these provisions implies that the meaning of the term "accident" is different from that of "occurrence."

Second, the Court found significant the fact that Article 17 focuses on the "accident which caused" the passenger's injury and not an accident that is the passenger's injury. The Court explained that it is the cause of the injury—rather than the occurrence of the injury—that must satisfy the definition of "accident." And recognizing the Court's responsibility to read the treaty in a manner "consistent with the shared expectations of the contracting parties," the Court also looked to the French legal meaning of the term "accident," which when used to describe the cause of an injury, is usually defined as a "fortuitous, unexpected, unusual, or unintended event." Accordingly, the Court held in *Saks* that an "accident" under Article 17 is "an unexpected or unusual event or happening that is external to the passenger," and not "the passenger's own internal reaction to the usual, normal, and expected operation of the aircraft."

The Court emphasized that the definition of "accident" "should be flexibly applied after assessment of all the circumstances surrounding a passenger's injuries." The Court further contemplated that intentional conduct could fall within the "accident" definition under Article 17, an interpretation that comports with another provision of the Convention. As such, *Saks* correctly characterized the term "accident" as encompassing more than unintentional conduct. The term "accident" has at least two plausible yet distinct definitions. On the one hand, as noted in *Saks*, "accident" may be defined as an unintended event. *See* WEBSTER'S NEW WORLD COLLEGE DICTIONARY 8 (4th ed. 999) ("a happening that is not . . . intended"); *see also* AMERICAN HERITAGE DICTIONARY 10 (4th ed. 2000) ("[l]ack of intention; chance").

On the other hand, as noted in *Saks*, the term "accident" may be defined as an event that is "unusual" or "unexpected," whether the result of intentional action or not. *See* BLACK'S LAW DICTIONARY 15 (6th ed.1990) ("an unusual, fortuitous, unexpected, unforeseen, or unlooked for event, happening or occurrence" and "if happening wholly or partly through human agency, an event which under the circumstances is unusual and unexpected by the person to whom it happens"); *see also* AMERICAN HERITAGE DICTIONARY, *supra*, at 10 ("[a]n unexpected and undesirable event," "[a]n unforeseen incident"). Although either definition of "accident" is at first glance plausible, neither party contests the definition adopted by the Court in *Saks*, which after careful examination discerned the meaning of "accident" under Article 17 of the Convention as an "unexpected or unusual event or happening that is external to the passenger."

The Court focused its analysis on determining "what causes can be considered accidents," and observed that Article 17 "embraces causes of injuries" that are "unexpected or unusual." The Court did not suggest that only one event could constitute the "accident," recognizing that "[a]ny injury is the product of a chain of causes." Thus, for purposes of the "accident" inquiry, the Court stated that a plaintiff need only be able to prove that "some link in the chain was an unusual or unexpected event external to the passenger."

* * *

Petitioner argues that the "accident" inquiry should focus on the "injury producing event," which, according to petitioner, was the presence of ambient cigarette smoke in the aircraft's cabin. Because petitioner's policies permitted smoking on international flights, petitioner contends that Dr. Hanson's death resulted from his own internal reaction—namely, an asthma attack—to the normal operation of the aircraft. Petitioner also argues that the flight attendant's failure to move Dr. Hanson was inaction, whereas Article 17 requires an action that causes the injury.

We disagree. As an initial matter, we note that petitioner did not challenge in the Court of Appeals the District Court's finding that the flight attendant's conduct in three times refusing to move Dr. Hanson was unusual or unexpected in light of the relevant industry standard or petitioner's own company policy. Petitioner instead argued that the flight attendant's conduct was irrelevant for purposes of the "accident" inquiry and that the only relevant event was the presence of the ambient cigarette smoke in the aircraft's cabin. Consequently, we need not dispositively determine whether the flight attendant's conduct qualified as "unusual or unexpected" under *Saks*, but may assume that it was for purposes of this opinion.

Petitioner's "injury producing event" inquiry—which looks to "the precise factual 'event' that caused the injury"—neglects the reality that there are often multiple interrelated factual events that combine to cause any given injury.

Petitioner's focus on the ambient cigarette smoke as the injury producing event is misplaced. We do not doubt that the presence of ambient cigarette smoke in the aircraft's cabin during an international flight might have been "normal" at the time of the flight in question. But petitioner's "injury producing event" inquiry—which looks to "the precise factual 'event' that caused the injury"—neglects the reality that there are often multiple interrelated factual events that combine to cause any given injury. In *Saks,* the Court recognized that any one of these factual events or happenings may be a link in the chain of causes and—so long as it is unusual or unexpected—could constitute an "accident" under Article 17. Indeed, the very fact that multiple events will necessarily combine and interrelate to cause any particular injury makes it difficult to define, in any coherent or non-question-begging way, any single event as the "injury producing event."

Petitioner's only claim to the contrary here is to say: "Looking to the purely factual description of relevant events, the aggravating event was Dr. Hanson remaining in his assigned non-smoking seat and being exposed to ambient smoke, which allegedly aggravated his pre-existing asthmatic condition leading to his death," and that the "injury producing event" was "not the flight attendant's failure to act or violation of industry standards." Petitioner ignores the fact that the flight attendant's refusal on three separate occasions to move Dr. Hanson was also a "factual 'event,'" that the District Court correctly found to be a " 'link in the chain' " of causes that led to Dr. Hanson's death, Petitioner's statement that the flight attendant's failure to reseat Dr. Hanson was not the "injury producing event" is nothing more than a bald assertion, unsupported by any law or argument.

An example illustrates why petitioner's emphasis on the ambient cigarette smoke as the "injury producing event" is misplaced. Suppose that petitioner mistakenly assigns respondent and her husband to seats in the middle of the smoking section, and that respondent and her husband do not notice that they are in the smoking section until after the flight has departed. Suppose further that, as here, the flight attendant refused to assist respondent and her husband despite repeated requests to move. In this hypothetical case, it would appear that, "[l]ooking to the purely factual description of relevant events, the aggravating event was [the passenger] remaining in his assigned seat and being exposed to ambient smoke, which allegedly aggravated his pre-existing asthmatic condition leading to his death." To argue otherwise, petitioner would have to suggest that the misassignment to the smoking section was the "injury producing event," but this would simply beg the question.

The fact is, the exposure to smoke, the misassignment to the smoking section, and the refusal to move the passenger would all be factual events contributing to the death of the passenger. In the instant case, the same can be said: The exposure to the smoke and the refusal to assist the passenger are happenings that both contributed to the passenger's death.

And petitioner's argument that the flight attendant's failure to act cannot constitute an "accident" because only affirmative acts are "event[s] or happening[s]" under *Saks* is unavailing. The distinction between action and inaction, as petitioner uses these terms, would perhaps be relevant were this a tort law negligence case. But respondents do not advocate, and petitioner vigorously rejects, that a negligence regime applies under Article 17 of the Convention. The relevant "accident" inquiry under *Saks* is whether there is "an unexpected or unusual event or happening." The rejection of an explicit request for assistance would be an "event" or "happening" under the ordinary and usual definitions of these terms. *See* AMERICAN HERITAGE DICTIONARY 635 (3d ed. 1992) ("event": "[s]omething that takes place; an occurrence"); BLACK'S LAW DICTIONARY 554–55 (6th ed. 1990) ("event": "Something that happens"); WEBSTER'S NEW INTERNATIONAL DICTIONARY 885 (2d ed. 1949) ("event": "The fact of taking place or occurring; occurrence" or "[t]hat which comes, arrives, or happens").

International Precedent

The dissent cites two cases from our sister signatories England and Australia—*Deep Vein Thrombosis and Air Travel Group Litigation*, [2004] Q.B. 234, and *Qantas Ltd. v. Povey*, [2003] VSCA 227, ¶ 17 (Dec. 23, 2003), respectively—and suggests that we should simply defer to their judgment on the matter. But our conclusion is not inconsistent with *Deep Vein Thrombosis and Air Travel Group Litigation*, where the England and Wales Court of Appeals commented on the District Court and Court of Appeal opinions in this case, and agreed that Dr. Hanson's death had resulted from an accident. The English court reasoned: "The refusal of the flight attendant to move Dr. Hanson cannot properly be considered as mere inertia, or a non-event. It was a refusal to provide an alternative seat which formed part of a more complex incident, whereby Dr. Hanson was exposed to smoke in circumstances that can properly be described as unusual and unexpected."

To the extent that the precise reasoning used by the courts in *Deep Vein Thrombosis and Air Travel Group Litigation* is inconsistent with our reasoning, we reject the analysis of those cases for the reasons stated in the body of this opinion. In such a circumstance, we are hesitant to "follo[w]" the opinions of intermediate appellate courts of our sister signatories. This is especially true where there are substantial factual distinctions between these cases or to advise on precautions which would avoid or minimise that risk and where the respective courts of last resort—the House of Lords and High Court of Australia—have yet to speak.

Moreover, the fallacy of petitioner's position that an "accident" cannot take the form of inaction is illustrated by the following example. Suppose that a passenger on a flight inexplicably collapses and stops breathing and that a medical doctor informs the flight crew that the passenger's life could be saved only if the plane lands within one hour. Suppose further that it is industry standard and airline policy to divert a flight to the nearest airport when a passenger otherwise faces imminent death. If the plane is within 30 minutes of a suitable airport, but the crew chooses to continue its cross-country flight, "[t]he notion that this is not an unusual event is staggering."

We do not suggest—as the dissent erroneously contends—that liability must lie because otherwise "harsh results," (opinion of Scalia, J.), would ensue. This hypothetical merely illustrates that the failure of an airline crew to take certain necessary vital steps could quite naturally and, in routine usage of the language, be an "event or happening."

Confirming this interpretation, other provisions of the Convention suggest that there is often no distinction between action and inaction on the issue of ultimate liability. For example, Article 25 provides that Article 22's liability cap does not apply in the event of "willful misconduct or . . . such default on [the carrier's] part as, in accordance with the law of the court to which the case is submitted, is considered to be equivalent to willful misconduct." The Montreal Protocol No. 4 to Amend the Convention for the Unification of Certain Rules relating to International Carriage by Air (1975) amends Article 25 by replacing "willful misconduct" with the language "done with intent to cause damage or recklessly and with knowledge that damage would probably result," as long as the airline's employee or agent was acting "within the scope of his employment." In 1998, the United States gave its advice and consent to ratification of the protocol, and it entered into force in the United States on March 4, 1999. Because the facts here took place in 1997–1998, Montreal Protocol No. 4 does not apply.

Because liability can be imposed for death or bodily injury only in the case of an Article 17 "accident" and Article 25 only lifts the caps once liability has been found, these provisions read together tend to show that inaction can give rise to liability. Moreover, Article 20(1) makes clear that the "due care" defense is unavailable when a carrier has failed to take "all necessary measures to avoid the damage." These provisions suggest that an air carrier's inaction can be the basis for liability.

Because liability can be imposed for death or bodily injury only in the case of an Article 17 "accident" and Article 25 only lifts the caps once liability has been found, these provisions read together tend to show that inaction can give rise to liability. Moreover, Article 20(1) makes clear that the "due care" defense is unavailable when a carrier has failed to take "all necessary measures to avoid the damage." These provisions suggest that an air carrier's inaction can be the basis for liability.

Finally, petitioner contends that the Ninth Circuit improperly created a negligence-based "accident" standard under Article 17 by focusing on the flight crew's negligence as the "accident." The Ninth Circuit stated: "The failure to act in the face of a known, serious risk satisfies the meaning of 'accident' within Article 17 so long as reasonable alternatives exist that would substantially minimize the risk and implementing these alternatives would not unreasonably interfere with the normal, expected operation of the airplane." Admittedly, this language does seem to approve of a negligence-based approach. However, no party disputes the Ninth Circuit's holding that the flight attendant's conduct was "unexpected and unusual," which is the operative language under *Saks* and the correct Article 17 analysis. For the foregoing reasons, we conclude that the conduct here constitutes an "accident" under Article 17 of the Warsaw Convention. Accordingly, the judgment of the Court of Appeals is affirmed.

JUSTICE BREYER took no part in the consideration or decision of this case.

JUSTICE SCALIA, with whom JUSTICE O'CONNOR join and dissent, in part.

When we interpret a treaty, we accord the judgments of our sister signatories " 'considerable weight.' " True to that canon, our previous Warsaw Convention opinions have carefully considered foreign case law. Today's decision stands out for its failure to give any serious consideration to how the courts of our treaty partners have resolved the legal issues before us.

This sudden insularity is striking, since the Court in recent years has canvassed the prevailing law in other nations (at least Western European nations) to determine the meaning of an American Constitution that those nations had no part in framing and that those nations' courts have no role in enforcing. One would have thought that foreign courts' interpretations of a treaty that their governments adopted jointly with ours, and that they have an actual role in applying, would be (to put it mildly) all the more relevant.

The Court's new abstemiousness with regard to foreign fare is not without consequence: Within the past year, appellate courts in both England and Australia have rendered decisions squarely at odds with today's holding. Because the Court offers no convincing explanation why these cases should not be followed, I respectfully dissent.

* * *

The Court holds that an airline's mere inaction can constitute an "accident" within the meaning of the Warsaw Convention. It derives this principle from our definition of "accident" in *Saks* as "an unexpected or unusual event or happening that is external to the passenger." The Court says this definition encompasses failures to act like the flight attendant's refusal to reseat Hanson in the face of a request for assistance.

That is far from clear. The word "accident" is used in two distinct senses. One refers to something that is unintentional, not "on purpose"—as in, "the hundred typing monkeys' verbatim reproduction of War and Peace was an accident." The other refers to an unusual and unexpected event, intentional or not: One may say he has been involved in a "train accident," for example, whether or not the derailment was intentionally caused. As the Court notes, *Saks* adopted the latter definition rather than the former. That distinction is crucial because, while there is no doubt that inaction can be an accident in the former sense ("I accidentally left the stove on"), whether it can be so in the latter sense is questionable.

Two of our sister signatories have concluded that it cannot. In *Deep Vein Thrombosis and Air Travel Group Litigation*, [2004] Q.B. 234, England's Court of Appeal, in an opinion by the Master of the Rolls that relied heavily on *Abramson v. Japan Airlines Co.*, 739 F.2d 130 (3d Cir. 1984), and analyzed more than a half-dozen other non-English decisions, held as follows:

Majority Opinion Cuts Against International Precedent

> A critical issue in this appeal is whether a failure to act, or an omission, can constitute an accident for the purposes of article 17. Often a failure to act results in an accident, or forms part of a series of acts and omissions which together constitute an accident. In such circumstances it may not be easy to distinguish between acts and omissions. I cannot see, however, how inaction itself can ever properly be described as an accident. It is not an event; it is a non-event. Inaction is the antithesis of an accident.

Six months later, the appellate division of the Supreme Court of Victoria, Australia, in an opinion that likewise gave extensive consideration to American and other foreign decisions, agreed:

The allegations in substance do no more than state a failure to do something, and this cannot be characterised as an event or happening, whatever be the concomitant background to that failure to warn or advise. That is not to say that a failure to take a specific required step in the course of flying an aircraft, or in picking up or setting down passengers, cannot lead to an event or happening of the requisite unusual or unexpected kind and thus be an accident for the purpose of the article.

A failure by a pilot to use some device in the expected and correct manner, such as a failure to let down the landing wheels or a chance omission to adjust the level of pressurisation, may lead, as has been held, to an accident contemplated by Article 17, but I would venture to suggest that it is not the failure to take the step which is properly to be characterised as an accident but rather its immediate and disastrous consequence whether that be the dangerous landing on the belly of the aircraft or an immediate unexpected and dangerous drop in pressurisation.

Qantas Ltd. v. Povey, [2003] VSCA 227, ¶ 17 (Dec. 23, 2003).

We can, and should, look to decisions of other signatories when we interpret treaty provisions. Foreign constructions are evidence of the original shared understanding of the contracting parties. Moreover, it is reasonable to impute to the parties an intent that their respective courts strive to interpret the treaty consistently. (The Warsaw Convention's preamble specifically acknowledges "the advantage of regulating in a uniform manner the conditions of . . . the liability of the carrier.") Finally, even if we disagree, we surely owe the conclusions reached by appellate courts of other signatories the courtesy of respectful consideration.

The Court nonetheless dismisses *Deep Vein Thrombosis* and *Povey* (in a footnote) responding to this dissent. As to the former, it claims (choosing its words carefully) that the "conclusion "it reaches is "not inconsistent" with that case. The reader should not think this to be a contention that the Master of the Rolls' opinion might be read to agree with today's holding that inaction can constitute an "accident." (To repeat the conclusion of that opinion: "Inaction is the antithesis of an accident." [2004] Q.B., at 247, ¶ 25.) What it refers to is the fact that the Master of the Rolls distinguished the Court of Appeals' judgment below (announced in an opinion that assumed inaction was involved, but did not at all discuss the action-inaction distinction) on the ground that action was involved—namely, "insistence that [Hanson] remain seated in the area exposed to smoke." The Court quotes only part of the relevant discussion.

Here is what the Master of the Rolls said about our case in full:

> I have no difficulty with the result in this case but, with respect, I question the reasoning of the judge in both events. The refusal of the flight attendant to move Dr. Hanson cannot properly be considered as mere inertia, or a non-event. It was a refusal to provide an alternative seat which formed part of a more complex incident, whereby Dr. Hanson was exposed to smoke in circumstances that can properly be described as unusual and unexpected. The existence of the non-smoking zone provided the opportunity for Dr. Hanson, if suitably placed within it, to avoid exposure to the smoke that threatened his health and, as it proved, his life.

> The direct cause of his death was the unnecessary exposure to the smoke. The refusal of the attendant to move him could be described as insistence that he remain seated in the area exposed to smoke. The exposure to smoke in these circumstances could, in my view, properly be described as an unusual or unexpected event.

Deep Vein Thrombosis and Air Travel Group Litigation, [2004] Q.B. 234.

As I explain below, that theory does not quite work because, in fact, the flight attendant did not insist that Hanson remain seated. But we can ignore this detail for the time being. The point is that the English court thought Husain could recover, not because the action-inaction distinction was irrelevant, but because, even though action was indispensable, it had in fact occurred.

The Court charts our course in exactly the opposite direction, spending three pages explaining why the action-*inaction* distinction is irrelevant. If the Court agrees with the Master of the Rolls that this case involves action, why does it needlessly place us in conflict with the courts of other signatories by deciding the then-irrelevant issue of whether inaction can constitute an accident? It would suffice to hold that our case involves action and end the analysis there. Whether inaction can constitute an accident under the Warsaw Convention is a significant issue on which international consensus is important; whether Husain can recover for her husband's death in this one case is not. As they stand, however, the core holdings of this case and Deep Vein Thrombosis—their *rationes decidendi*—are not only not "not inconsistent"; they are completely opposite.

To the extent the Court implies that *Deep Vein Thrombosis* and *Povey* merit only slight consideration because they were not decided by courts of last resort, I note that our prior Warsaw Convention cases have looked to decisions of intermediate appellate foreign courts as well as supreme courts. Moreover, *Deep Vein Thrombosis* was no ordinary decision. It was *authored* by the Master of the Rolls, the chief judge of England's civil appellate court—a position thought by many to be even more influential than that of a Law Lord.

That there are "substantial factual distinctions" between the cases, is surely beside the point. A legal rule may arise in different contexts, but the differences are relevant only if the logic of the rule makes them so. *Deep Vein Thrombosis* and *Povey* hold in no uncertain terms that inaction cannot be an accident; not that inaction consisting of failure to warn of deep vein thrombosis cannot be an accident. Maintaining a coherent international body of treaty law requires us to give deference to the legal rules our treaty partners adopt. It is not enough to avoid inconsistent decisions on factually identical cases.

I would follow the holdings of *Deep Vein Thrombosis* and *Povey*, since the Court's analysis today is no more convincing than theirs. Merely pointing to dictionaries that define " 'event' " as an " 'occurrence' " or " '[s]omething that happens,' " hardly resolves the problem; it only reformulates one question (whether "accident" includes nonevents) into an equivalent one (whether "accident" includes nonoccurrences and nonhappenings).

Equally unavailing is the reliance, on Article 25 of the Warsaw Convention (which lifts liability caps for injury caused by a "default" of the airline equivalent to willful misconduct) and Article 20 (which precludes the airline's due-care defense if it fails to take "all necessary measures" to avoid the injury). The Court's analytical error in invoking these provisions is to assume that the inaction these provisions contemplate is the accident itself. The treaty imposes no such requirement. If a pilot negligently forgets to lower the landing gear, causing the plane to crash and killing all passengers on board, then recovery is presumptively available (because the crash that caused the deaths is an accident), and the due-care defense is inapplicable (because the pilot's negligent omission also caused the deaths), even though the omission is not the accident. Similarly, if a flight attendant fails to prevent the boarding of an individual whom she knows to be a terrorist, and who later shoots a passenger, the damages cap might be lifted even though the accident (the shooting) and the default (the failure to prevent boarding) do not coincide. Without the invented restriction that the Article 20 or 25 default be the accident itself, the Court's argument based on those provisions loses all force.

As for the Court's hypothetical of the crew that refuses to divert after a passenger collapses: This would be more persuasive as a *reductio ad absurdum* if the Eleventh Circuit had not already ruled out Article 17 liability in substantially these very circumstances. *See Krys v. Lufthansa German Airlines*, 119 F.3d 1515 (11th Cir. 1997). A legal construction is not fallacious merely because it has harsh results. The Convention denies a remedy, even when outrageous conduct and grievous injury have occurred, unless there has been an "accident." Whatever that term means, it certainly does not equate to "outrageous conduct that causes grievous injury." It is a mistake to assume that the Convention must provide relief whenever traditional tort law would do so.

To the contrary, a principal object of the Convention was to promote the growth of the fledgling airline industry by limiting the circumstances under which passengers could sue. Unless there has been an accident, there is no liability, whether the claim is trivial, *cf. Lee v. American Airlines Inc.*, 355 F.3d 386 (5th Cir. 2004) (suit for "loss of a 'refreshing, memorable vacation'"), or cries out for redress.

Were we confronting the issue in the first instance, perhaps the Court could persuade me to its view. But courts in two other countries have already rejected it, and their reasoning is no less compelling than the Court's. I would follow *Deep Vein Thrombosis* and *Povey* and hold that mere inaction cannot be an "accident" under Article 17.

* * *

Respondents argue that, even if the Convention distinguishes action from inaction, this case involves sufficient elements of action to support recovery. That argument is not implausible; as noted earlier, the court in *Deep Vein Thrombosis* suggested that "[t]he refusal of the attendant to move [Hanson] could be described as insistence that he remain seated in the area exposed to smoke." I cannot agree with this analysis, however, because it miscomprehends the facts of this case. That the flight attendant explicitly refused Husain's pleas for help after the third request, rather than simply ignoring them, does not transform her inaction into action. The refusal acknowledged her inaction, but it was the inaction, not the acknowledgment, that caused Hanson's death. Unlike the previous responses, the third was a mere refusal to assist, and so cannot be the basis for liability under Article 17.

But even if the flight attendant's insistence that Hanson remain seated before takeoff was unusual or unexpected, and hence an accident, it was not a compensable cause of Hanson's death. It was perhaps a but for cause (had the flight attendant allowed him to move before takeoff, he might have lived, just as he might have lived if he had taken a different flight); but it was not a proximate cause, which is surely a predicate for recovery. Any early insistence that Hanson remain seated became moot once the attendant later told Husain and her husband they were free to move about.

There is, however, one complication, which I think requires us to remand this case to the District Court: Although the flight attendant, once the plane was aloft, invited Husain to find another passenger willing to switch seats, she did not invite Husain to find an empty seat, but to the contrary affirmatively represented that the plane was full. If such a misrepresentation is unusual and unexpected; and (the more difficult question) if it can reasonably be said that it caused Hanson's death—*i.e.*, that Husain would have searched for and found an empty seat, although unwilling to ask another passenger to move—then a cause of action might lie. I would remand so that the District Court could consider in the first instance whether the flight attendant's misrepresentation about the plane's being full, independent of any failure to reseat, was an accident that caused Hanson's death. Tragic though Dr. Hanson's death may have been, it does not justify the Court's putting us in needless conflict with other signatories to the Warsaw Convention. I respectfully dissent.

EXERCISE 13-3. *OLYMPIC AIRWAYS V. HUSAIN*—INACTION AS ACCIDENT

1. Detail the procedural history of this case, focusing on how the lower courts ruled.

2. Explain the burden shifting procedure set out by the court under Article 17 of the Warsaw Convention.

3. Identify the several "link[s] in the chain" causing the respondent's death, according to the majority opinion?

4. Justice Thomas suggests that inaction or failure to act can be an "unusual event or happening" under the Warsaw Convention? Give an example and discuss whether this is persuasive or not.

5. In a dissenting opinion, Justices Scalia and O'Connor criticize the majority in three main ways. Elaborate on each:

   a. Departure from international precedent.

   b. Wrongly assuming that the Warsaw Convention must provide relief whenever traditional tort law would do so.

c.   Failure to remand the issue of flight attendant misrepresentation about the airplane being fully occupied.

EASTERN AIRLINES, INC. V. FLOYD
499 U.S. 530 (1991)

MARSHALL, J., delivered the opinion for a unanimous Court.

Article 17 of the Warsaw Convention sets forth conditions under which an international air carrier can be held liable for injuries to passengers. This case presents the question whether Article 17 allows recovery for mental or psychic injuries unaccompanied by physical injury or physical manifestation of injury.

On May 5, 1983, an Eastern Airlines flight departed from Miami, bound for the Bahamas. Shortly after takeoff, one of the plane's three jet engines lost oil pressure. The flight crew shut down the failing engine and turned the plane around to return to Miami. Soon thereafter, the second and third engines failed due to loss of oil pressure. The plane began losing altitude rapidly, and the passengers were informed that the plane would be ditched in the Atlantic Ocean. Fortunately, after a period of descending flight without power, the crew managed to restart an engine and land the plane safely at Miami International Airport.

Respondents, a group of passengers on the flight, brought separate complaints against petitioner, Eastern Airlines, Inc. ("Eastern"), each claiming damages solely for mental distress arising out of the incident. Eastern conceded that the engine failure and subsequent preparations for ditching the plane amounted to an "accident" under Article 17 of the Convention but argued that Article 17 also makes physical injury a condition of liability. Relying on another federal court's analysis of the French authentic text and negotiating history of the Convention, the District Court concluded that mental anguish alone is not compensable under Article 17.

We granted *certiorari* to resolve a conflict between the Eleventh Circuit's decision in this case and the New York Court of Appeals' decision in *Rosman v. Trans World Airlines, Inc.*, 314 N.E.2d 848 (N.Y. 1974), which held that purely psychic trauma is not compensable under Article 17. We now hold that Article 17 does not allow recovery for purely mental injuries.

Because the only authentic text of the Warsaw Convention is in French, the French text must guide our analysis. The text reads as follows:

> Le transporteur est responsable du dommage survenu en cas de mort, *de blessure ou de toute autre lésion corporelle* subie par un voyageur lorsque l'accident qui a causé le dommage s'est produit à bord de l'aéronef ou au cours de toutes opérations d'embarquement et de débarquement.

The American translation of this text, employed by the Senate when it ratified the Convention in 1934, reads:

> The carrier shall be liable for damage sustained *in the event of the death or wounding of a passenger or any other bodily injury* suffered by a passenger, if the accident which caused the damage so sustained took place on board the aircraft or in the course of any of the operations of embarking or disembarking.

Thus, under Article 17, an air carrier is liable for passenger injury only when three conditions are satisfied: (1) there has been an accident, in which (2) the passenger suffered "mort," "blessure," "ou . . . toute autre lésion corporelle," and (3) the accident took place on board the aircraft or in the course of operations of embarking or disembarking. As petitioner concedes, the incident here took place on board the aircraft and was an "accident" for purposes of Article 17. Moreover, respondents concede that they suffered neither "mort" nor "blessure" from the mishap. Therefore, the narrow issue presented here is whether, under the proper interpretation of "lésion corporelle," condition (2) is satisfied when a passenger has suffered only a mental or psychic injury.

Thus, under Article 17, an air carrier is liable for passenger injury only when three conditions are satisfied: (1) there has been an accident, in which (2) the passenger suffered "mort," "blessure," "ou . . . toute autre lésion corporelle," and (3) the accident took place on board the aircraft or in the course of operations of embarking or disembarking.

Lésion Corporelle

We must consider the "French legal meaning" of "lésion corporelle" for guidance as to the shared expectations of the parties to the Convention because the Convention was drafted in French by continental jurists. Perhaps the simplest method of determining the meaning of a phrase appearing in a foreign legal text would be to consult a bilingual dictionary. Such dictionaries suggest that a proper translation of "lésion corporelle" is "bodily injury." These translations, if correct, clearly suggest that Article 17 does not permit recovery for purely psychic injuries. Although we have previously relied on such French dictionaries as a primary method for defining terms in the Warsaw Convention, we recognize that dictionary definitions may be too general for purposes of treaty interpretation.

Our concerns are partly allayed when, as here, the dictionary translation accords with the wording used in the "two main translations of the 1929 Convention in English." As we noted earlier, the translation used by the United States Senate when ratifying the Warsaw Convention equated "lésion corporelle" with "bodily injury." The same wording appears in the translation used in the United Kingdom Carriage by Air Act of 1932. We turn, then, to French legal materials to determine whether French jurists' contemporary understanding of the term "lésion corporelle" differed from its translated meaning.

In 1929, as in the present day, lawyers trained in French civil law would rely on the following principal sources of French law: (1) legislation, (2) judicial decisions, and (3) scholarly writing. Our review of these materials indicates neither that "lésion corporelle" was a widely used legal term in French law nor that the term specifically encompassed psychic injuries.

Turning first to legislation, we find no French legislative provisions in force in 1929 that contained the phrase "lésion corporelle." The principal provision of the French Civil Code relating to the scope of compensable injuries appears to be Article 1382, which provides in very general terms: "Tout fait quelconque de l'homme, qui cause à autrui un dommage, oblige celui par la faute duquel il est . . . arrivé, à le réparer."

Turning next to cases, we likewise discover no French court decisions in or before 1929 that explain the phrase "lésion corporelle," nor do the parties direct us to any. Indeed, we find no French case construing Article 17 of the Warsaw Convention to cover psychic injury. The only reports of French cases we did find that used the term "lésion corporelle" are relatively recent and involve physical injuries caused by automobile accidents and other incidents. These cases tend to support the conclusion that, in French legal usage, the term "lésion corporelle" refers only to physical injuries. However, because they were decided well after the drafting of the Warsaw Convention, these cases do not necessarily reflect the contracting parties' understanding of the term "lésion corporelle."

Turning finally to French treatises and scholarly writing covering the period leading up to the Warsaw Convention, we find no materials (and the parties have brought none to our attention) indicating that "lésion corporelle" embraced psychic injury. Subsequent to the adoption of the Warsaw Convention, some scholars have argued that "lésion corporelle" as used in Article 17 should be interpreted to encompass such injury. These scholars draw on the fact that, by 1929, France—unlike many other countries—permitted tort recovery for mental distress. However, this general proposition of French tort law does not demonstrate that the specific phrase chosen by the contracting parties—"lésion corporelle"—covers purely psychic injury.

We find it noteworthy, moreover, that scholars who read "lésion corporelle" as encompassing psychic injury do not base their argument on explanations of this term in French cases or French treatises or even in the French Civil Code; rather, they chiefly rely on the principle of French tort law that any damage can "giv[e] rise to reparation when it is real and has been verified." We do not dispute this principle of French law. However, we have been directed to no French case prior to 1929 that allowed recovery based on that principle for the type of mental injury claimed here—injury caused by fright or shock—absent an incident in which someone sustained physical injury. Since our task is to "give the specific words of the treaty a meaning consistent with the shared expectations of the contracting parties," we find it unlikely that those parties' apparent understanding of the term "lésion corporelle" as "bodily injury" would have been displaced by a meaning abstracted from the French law of damages. Particularly is this so when the cause of action for psychic injury that evidently was possible under French law in 1929 would not have been recognized in many other countries represented at the Warsaw Convention.

Nor is this conclusion altered by our examination of Article 17's structure. In the decision below, the Court of Appeals found that the Article's wording "suggests that the drafters did not intend to exclude any particular category of damages," because if they had intended "to refer only to injury caused by physical impact," they "would not have singled out and specifically referred to a particular case of physical impact such as blessure ('wounding')." This argument, which has much the same force as the surplusage canon of domestic statutory construction, is plausible.

Yet one might draw a contrary inference from the same language. As noted, one meaning of "lésion" is a change in the structure of an organ due to injury or disease. If "blessure" refers to injuries causing visible ruptures in the body (a common meaning of a "wounding"), "lésion corporelle" might well refer to a more general category of physical injuries that includes internal injuries caused, for example, by physical impact, smoke or exhaust inhalation, or oxygen deprivation. Admittedly, this inference still runs afoul of the Court of Appeals' surplusage argument. However, because none of the other sources of French legal meaning noted above support the Court of Appeals' construction, we are reluctant to give this argument dispositive weight.

The same structural argument offered by the Court of Appeals was advanced by one of the German delegates to the Warsaw Convention. Accordingly, the official German translation of "lésion corporelle" adopted by Austria, Germany, and Switzerland uses German terms whose closest English translation is apparently "infringement on the health." See Mankiewicz 146. We are reluctant, however, to place much weight on an English translation of a German translation of a French text, particularly when we have been unable to find (and the parties have not cited) any German, Austrian, or Swiss cases adhering to the broad interpretation of Article 17 that the German delegate evidently espoused.

In sum, neither the Warsaw Convention itself nor any of the applicable French legal sources demonstrates that "lésion corporelle" should be translated other than as "bodily injury"—a narrow meaning excluding purely mental injuries. However, because a broader interpretation of "lésion corporelle" reaching purely mental injuries is plausible, and the term is both ambiguous and difficult, we turn to additional aids to construction.

In sum, neither the Warsaw Convention itself nor any of the applicable French legal sources demonstrates that "lésion corporelle" should be translated other than as "bodily injury"—a narrow meaning excluding purely mental injuries. However, because a broader interpretation of "lésion corporelle" reaching purely mental injuries is plausible, and the term is both ambiguous and difficult, we turn to additional aids to construction.

* * *

Translating "lésion corporelle" as "bodily injury" is consistent, we think, with the negotiating history of the Convention. The treaty that became the Warsaw Convention was first drafted at an international conference in Paris in 1925. The final protocol of the Paris Conference contained an article specifying that: " 'The carrier is liable for accidents, losses, breakdowns, and delays. It is not liable if it can prove that it has taken reasonable measures designed to pre-empt damage. . . .' " It appears that "[t]his expansive provision, broadly holding carriers liable in the event of an accident, would almost certainly have permitted recovery for all types of injuries, including emotional distress."

The Paris Conference appointed a committee of experts, the Comité International Technique d'Experts Juridiques Aériens ("CITEJA"), to revise its final protocol for presentation to the Warsaw Conference. The CITEJA draft split the liability article of the Paris Conference's protocol into three provisions with one addressing damages for injury to passengers, the second addressing injury to goods, and the third addressing losses caused by delay. The CITEJA subsection on injury to passengers introduced the phrase "en cas de mort, de blessure ou de toute autre lésion corporelle." This language was retained in Article 17 ultimately adopted by the Warsaw Conference. Although there is no definitive evidence explaining why the CITEJA drafters chose this narrower language, we believe it is reasonable to infer that the Conference adopted the narrower language to limit the types of recoverable injuries.

Our review of the documentary record for the Warsaw Conference confirms—and courts and commentators appear universally to agree—that there is no evidence that the drafters or signatories of the Warsaw Convention specifically considered liability for psychic injury or the meaning of "lésion corporelle."

Two explanations commonly are offered for why the subject of mental injuries never arose during the Convention proceedings: (1) many jurisdictions did not recognize recovery for mental injury at that time, or (2) the drafters simply could not contemplate a psychic injury unaccompanied by a physical injury. Indeed, the unavailability of compensation for purely psychic injury in many common and civil law countries at the time of the Warsaw Conference persuades us that the signatories had no specific intent to include such a remedy in the Convention. Because such a remedy was unknown in many, if not most, jurisdictions in 1929, the drafters most likely would have felt compelled to make an unequivocal reference to purely mental injury if they had specifically intended to allow such recovery.

In this sense, we find it significant that, when the parties to a different international transport treaty wanted to make it clear that rail passengers could recover for purely psychic harms, the drafters made a specific modification to this effect. The liability provision of the Berne Convention on International Rail, drafted in 1952, originally conditioned liability on "la mort, les blessures et toute autre atteinte, à l'intégrité corporelle." The drafters subsequently modified this provision to read "l'intégrité physique ou mentale."

Primary Purpose of Warsaw Convention

The narrower reading of "lésion corporelle" also is consistent with the primary purpose of the contracting parties to the Convention: limiting the liability of air carriers in order to foster the growth of the fledgling commercial aviation industry. Indeed, it was for this reason that the Warsaw delegates imposed a maximum recovery of $8,300 for an accident—a low amount even by 1929 standards. Whatever may be the current view among Convention signatories, in 1929 the parties were more concerned with protecting air carriers and fostering a new industry than providing full recovery to injured passengers, and we read "lésion corporelle" in a way that respects that legislative choice. * * *

We also conclude that, on balance, the evidence of the post-1929 "conduct" and "interpretations of the signatories" supports the narrow translation of "lésion corporelle."

In the years following adoption of the Convention, some scholars questioned whether Article 17 extended to mental or emotional injury. In 1951, a committee composed of 20 Warsaw Convention signatories met in Madrid and adopted a proposal to substitute "affection corporelle" for "lésion corporelle" in Article 17. The French delegate to the committee proposed this substitution because, in his view, the word "lésion" was too narrow, in that it "presupposed a rupture in the tissue, or a dissolution of continuity" which might not cover an injury such as mental illness or lung congestion caused by a breakdown in the heating apparatus of the aircraft. The United States delegate opposed this change if it "implied the inclusion of 1,500 mental injury or emotional disturbances or upsets which were not connected with or the result of bodily injury," but the committee adopted it nonetheless. Although the committee's proposed amendment was never subsequently implemented, its discussion and vote in Madrid suggest that, in the view of the 20 signatories on the committee, "lésion corporelle" in Article 17 had a distinctly physical scope.

In finding that the signatories' post-1929 conduct supports the broader interpretation of "lésion corporelle," the Court of Appeals relied on three international agreements: The Hague Protocol of 1955, The Montreal Agreement of 1966, and the Guatemala City Protocol of 1971. For each of these agreements, the Court of Appeals emphasized that English translations rendered "lésion corporelle" as "personal injury," instead of "bodily injury." In our view, none of these agreements support the broad interpretation of "lésion corporelle" reached by the Court of Appeals.

The Hague Protocol amended Article 3 of the Warsaw Convention, which sets forth the particular information a passenger's ticket must contain, to require notice of the limitation upon the carrier's liability for passenger injuries under the Convention. While the authentic French version of Article 3 retained the phrase "lésion corporelle," the authentic English version of the Hague Protocol, which was proposed by the United States delegation, used the phrase "personal injury."

Citing *Air France v. Saks*, 470 U.S. 392 (1985), the Court of Appeals treated the Hague Protocol's use of "personal injury" as a " 'subsequent interpretation of the signatories' " that "helps clarify the meaning" of "lésion corporelle."

However, we do not accept the argument that the Hague Protocol signatories intended "personal injury" to be an interpretive translation of "lésion corporelle" where there is no evidence that they intended the authentic English text to effect a substantive change in, or clarification of that term. Moreover, the portion of Article 3 of the Hague Protocol in which "personal injury" appears is concerned solely with informing passengers that when the convention "governs" it "in most cases limits the liability of carriers for death or personal injury." It may be, therefore, that the signatories used "personal injury" not as an interpretive translation of "lésion corporelle" but merely as a way of giving a summary description of the limitations of liability imposed by the Convention.

The Montreal Agreement of 1966 is similarly inconclusive. The Agreement, which affects only international flights with connecting points in the United States, raised the limit of accident liability to $75,000 and waived due-care defenses. The Court of Appeals noted that, under the Montreal Agreement, the notice appearing on passenger tickets used the term "personal injury" rather than "bodily injury" and that the United States Civil Aeronautics Board used these terms interchangeably in approving the Agreement. For two reasons, we do not believe that this evidence bears on the signatories' understanding of "lésion corporelle" in Article 17.

First, as the Court of Appeals acknowledged, "[t]he Montreal Agreement is not a treaty, but rather an agreement among all major international air carriers that imposes a quasi-legal and largely experimental system of liability essentially contractual in nature." Therefore, the Montreal Agreement does not and cannot purport to speak for the signatories to the Warsaw Convention. Second, the Montreal Agreement does not purport to change or clarify the provisions of Article 17.

We likewise do not believe that the Guatemala City Protocol of 1971 sheds any light upon the intended scope of Article 17. The Protocol was drafted in three authentic texts, English, French, and Spanish, but the French text was to control in cases of conflict. The Protocol amended the French text of Article 17 by deleting the word "blessure," while retaining "lésion corporelle." Additionally, the English text of the Protocol substituted "personal injury" for "wounding or other bodily injury" in Article 17. The Court of Appeals read the changes in both the French and English versions of Article 17 as supporting an interpretation of "lésion corporelle" broader than "bodily injury."

For several reasons, however, we disagree. First, there is no evidence that the changes to the English or French text were intended to effect a substantive change or clarification. Neither mental injuries nor the minor drafting changes were discussed at the Guatemala City Conference. Second, of the approximately 120 signatories to the Warsaw Convention, only a few countries have actually ratified the Guatemala City Protocol, and therefore the Protocol is not in effect in the international arena. Likewise, we have stated that because the United States Senate has not ratified the Protocol we should not consider it to be dispositive.

We must also consult the opinions of our sister signatories in searching for the meaning of a "lésion corporelle." The only apparent judicial decision from a sister signatory addressing recovery for purely mental injuries under Article 17 is that of the Supreme Court of Israel. That court held that Article 17 does allow recovery for purely psychic injuries. *See Cie Air France v. Teichner*, 39 Revue Française de Droit Aérien.

Teichner arose from the hijacking in 1976 of an Air France flight to Entebbe, Uganda. Passengers sought compensation for psychic injuries caused by the ordeal of the hijacking and detention at the Entebbe Airport. While acknowledging that the negotiating history of the Warsaw Convention was silent as to the availability of such compensation, the court determined that "desirable jurisprudential policy" ("la politique jurisprudentielle souhaitable") favored an expansive reading of Article 17 to reach purely psychic injuries. In reaching this conclusion, the court emphasized the post-1929 development of the aviation industry and the evolution of Anglo-American and Israeli law to allow recovery for psychic injury in certain circumstances. In addition, the court followed the view that this expansive construction was desirable to avoid an apparent conflict between the French and English versions of the Guatemala City Protocol. See GEORGETTE MILLER, LIABILITY IN INTERNATIONAL AIR TRANSPORT 128 (1977) (arguing that "a liberal interpretation of [Article 17] would be more in line with the spirit of the Convention").

Although we recognize the deference owed to the Israeli court's interpretation of Article 17, we are not persuaded by that court's reasoning. Even if we were to agree that allowing recovery for purely psychic injury is desirable as a policy goal, we cannot give effect to such policy without convincing evidence that the signatories' intent with respect to Article 17 would allow such recovery. As discussed, neither the language, negotiating history, nor post-enactment interpretations of Article 17 clearly evidences such intent. Nor does the Guatemala City Protocol support the Israeli court's conclusion because nothing in the Protocol purports to amend Article 17 to reach mental injuries. Moreover, although the Protocol reflects a liberalization of attitudes toward passenger recovery in that it provides for strict liability, see Article IV, reprinted in

Goldhirsch 320, the fact that the Guatemala City Protocol is still not in effect after almost 20 years since it was drafted should caution against attaching significance to it.

Moreover, we believe our construction of Article 17 better accords with the Warsaw Convention's stated purpose of achieving uniformity of rules governing claims arising from international air transportation. As noted, the Montreal Agreement subjects international carriers to strict liability for Article 17 injuries sustained on flights connected with the United States. Recovery for mental distress traditionally has been subject to a high degree of proof, both in this country and others. We have no doubt that subjecting international air carriers to strict liability for purely mental distress would be controversial for most signatory countries. Our construction avoids this potential source of divergence.

We conclude that an air carrier cannot be held liable under Article 17 when an accident has not caused a passenger to suffer death, physical injury, or physical manifestation of injury.

We conclude that an air carrier cannot be held liable under Article 17 when an accident has not caused a passenger to suffer death, physical injury, or physical manifestation of injury. Although Article 17 renders air carriers liable for "damage sustained in the event of" ("dommage survenu en cas de") such injuries, we express no view as to whether passengers can recover for mental injuries that are accompanied by physical injuries. That issue is not presented here because respondents do not allege physical injury or physical manifestation of injury. Eastern urges us to hold that the Warsaw Convention provides the exclusive cause of action for injuries sustained during international air transportation. The Court of Appeals did not address this question, and we did not grant certiorari to consider it. We therefore decline to reach it here. The judgment of the Court of Appeals is reversed.

EXERCISE 13-4. *EASTERN AIRLINES V. FLOYD*—MENTAL OR PSYCHIC INJURIES

1. What is "lesion corporelle" and why is it significant under Article 17 of the Warsaw Convention?

2. What is the "narrow" issue presented in *Eastern Airlines v. Floyd*?

3. To what three sources of French civil law does the court turn to decide if "bodily injury" includes mental injuries in addition to bodily injuries? What does the court conclude about each source?

4. What two explanations are commonly offered for why the subject of mental injuries did not arise during the drafting of the Warsaw Convention? Did this represent a pro-carrier or pro-passenger perspective?

5. Explain the purpose of each of the following international agreements and what each provides with respect to the recovery of psychic injuries related to aviation accidents: (a) Hague Protocol; (b) Montreal Agreement of 1966; and (c) Guatemala Protocol of 1971.

DOE V. ETIHAD AIRWAYS, P.J.S.C.

870 F.3d 406 (6th Cir. 2017)

BOGGS, CIRCUIT JUDGE.

Plaintiff Jane Doe and her eleven-year-old daughter flew aboard Etihad Airways from Abu Dhabi to Chicago. For the duration of the fourteen-hour journey, Doe's tray table remained open in her lap because a knob that was meant to hold it in place had fallen to the floor. During the flight, Doe's daughter found the knob on the floor and gave it to Doe, who placed it in a seatback pocket. When it came time to descend, an Etihad flight attendant (unaware of the detached knob) gave Doe the familiar reminder to place her tray table in the upright and locked position for landing. Doe, of course, could not comply. To aid in explaining her problem, she reached into the seatback pocket to retrieve the fallen knob. But when she stuck her hand into the pocket, she was unexpectedly pricked by a hypodermic needle that lay hidden within. She gasped, and the needle drew blood from her finger.

Doe claims damages from Etihad for both her physical injury and her "mental distress, shock, mortification, sickness and illness, outrage and embarrassment from natural sequela of possible exposure to" various diseases. Her husband claims loss of consortium.

The Montreal Convention of 1999, an international treaty under which these claims arise, imposes strict liability (up to a monetary cap) upon Etihad "for damage sustained in case of death or bodily injury of a passenger upon condition only that the accident which caused the death or injury took place on board the aircraft." Etihad concedes that an accident onboard its aircraft caused Doe to suffer a bodily injury. But Etihad argues that "damage sustained in case of . . .

bodily injury" means only "damage caused by bodily injury," and thus does not include Doe's fear of contagion and other emotional-distress and mental-anguish damages—damages that Etihad claims were caused not by Doe's bodily injury (the small hole in her finger) but by the nature of the instrumentality of that injury (the needle).

The district court agreed and granted partial summary judgment for Etihad. But the district court erred both in reading the additional "caused by" requirement into the treaty and in concluding that Doe's bodily injury didn't cause her emotional and mental injuries. The plain text of the Montreal Convention allows Doe to recover all her "damage sustained" from the incident, which includes damages for both physical injury and accompanying emotional or mental harm. So, for the reasons that follow, we reverse and remand.

* * *

When Doe was pricked by the needle, the passenger seated in the aisle seat to her right heard Doe exclaim, "ouch," and saw her finger bleeding. The Etihad flight attendant who had come to Doe's seat picked up the needle and what was later determined to be its accompanying insulin syringe, both of which Doe had placed on her tray table. But the flight attendant then returned the items to the tray table and left to summon the assistance of her supervisor. Because the airplane had begun its descent, the flight attendants did not have access to the flight deck, which was where the only onboard sharps box was located, nor were the flight attendants permitted to call the flight deck absent a more pressing emergency.

The flight attendant returned with her supervisor. The flight attendant took the needle and syringe, placed them in an empty water bottle, capped the bottle, and later turned the bottle over to her cabin manager. The supervisor, meanwhile, gave Doe an antiseptic wipe, which Doe used to wipe her finger, and a Band-Aid, which the supervisor himself wrapped around her finger. The cabin manager wrote a report of the incident and told Doe that Etihad would contact her. A flight attendant recommended that Doe see a doctor, but Etihad provided no medical assistance other than the antiseptic wipe and Band-Aid.

The next day, Doe saw a family physician, who noted a "small needle poke" on Doe's finger. Doe was prescribed medication for possible exposure to hepatitis, tetanus, and HIV, and she underwent several rounds of testing over the following year. Thankfully for Doe, all the tests came back negative. Nevertheless, Doe claims that she refrained from sexual intercourse with her husband and from sharing food with her daughter until one year after the incident, when her doctor told her that she could be certain that she had not contracted a disease from the needlestick.

Two days after the flight, Doe sent an email to Etihad to follow up because Etihad had neither sent her a copy of the incident report nor offered her any further assistance. One week later, Etihad replied by email to offer a "purely goodwill gesture" of "possible reimbursement" of Doe's medical expenses, "without any admission of liability." This litigation followed.

* * *

Plaintiffs filed suit against Etihad in the United States District Court for the Eastern District of Michigan. At first blush, the Eastern District of Michigan seems an unlikely venue for this action. Plaintiffs reside in Grand Rapids, in the Western District of Michigan, and no part of Plaintiffs' itinerary included travel to points in the Eastern District of Michigan. But Plaintiffs' counsel is based in Oakland County, Michigan (in the Eastern District), and, as we discuss in this paragraph, venue was proper in the Eastern District of Michigan because of Etihad's status as a "foreign state."

Etihad, an entity wholly owned by the Government of Abu Dhabi, United Arab Emirates, is a "foreign state" within the meaning of the Foreign Sovereign Immunities Act, 28 U.S.C. § 1603(a). But as a condition of Etihad's Foreign Air Carrier Permit—issued by the United States Department of Transportation to permit Etihad to fly to United States airports—Etihad waived sovereign immunity from suit in United States courts and could thus be sued "in any judicial district in which [Etihad] is licensed to do business or is doing business," which includes the Eastern District of Michigan because of Etihad's codeshare and other business agreements with airlines operating from points within that district. 28 U.S.C. § 1391(f); see 49 U.S.C. § 41301.

Following discovery, Etihad moved for, and the district court granted, partial summary judgment in favor of Etihad as to Doe's claims for mental-anguish and emotional-distress damages, including fear of contagion. (For simplicity, we will refer to these various claims collectively as Doe's claims for mental anguish. Mental anguish and emotional distress are distinct harms under Michigan damages laws. *See, e.g., McClain v. Univ. of Mich. Bd. of Regents*, 665 N.W.2d 484, 488 (2003) (*per curiam*). But this distinction does not affect the determination of whether Etihad may be subject to liability for such harms under the Montreal Convention; the distinction matters, if at all, only in our discussion of the measure of damages, *infra*.)

We first discuss whether the district court erred in holding that Doe's mental-anguish damages were not recoverable under Article 17(1) of the Montreal Convention, and—after analyzing both the plain text of the treaty and relevant persuasive authorities—we conclude that the district court did so err. Then, because the Montreal Convention provides rules for liability but looks to local law for the measure of damages, we conduct a choice-of-law analysis and hold that Michigan damages law governs both the amount of any damages Etihad comes to owe Doe and the ability of Doe's husband to recover loss-of-consortium damages.

* * *

The parties agree that Article 17(1) of the Montreal Convention, a multilateral treaty to which the United States is a signatory, provides Plaintiffs' only avenue for recovery against Etihad. See Convention for the Unification of Certain Rules for International Carriage by Air, art. 17, May 28, 1999, S. Treaty Doc. 106–45, (entered into force Nov. 4, 2003) ("Montreal Convention"). More than 125 countries, including the United Arab Emirates, have signed, ratified, or acceded to the Montreal Convention since 1999.

The interpretation of a treaty is a question of law that we review *de novo*. Under the Supremacy Clause, treaties are "the supreme Law of the Land." U.S. Const. art. VI, cl. 2. Neither our court nor the Supreme Court has yet interpreted any provision of the Montreal Convention. The Warsaw Convention (the Montreal Convention's longstanding predecessor treaty), however, has been the subject of much litigation over the past eighty years, and interpretations of the Warsaw Convention have at least some persuasive value in interpreting parallel provisions of the Montreal Convention.

Our analysis of Article 17(1) of the Montreal Convention "must begin . . . with the text of the treaty and the context in which [its] written words are used." *Air France v. Saks*, 470 U.S. 392 (1985). The text of Article 17(1) provides:

> The carrier is liable for damage sustained in case of death or bodily injury
> of a passenger upon condition only that the accident which caused the
> death or injury took place on board the aircraft or in the course of any
> of the operations of embarking or disembarking.

The contested language here is "in case of." Etihad's argument has two components: its understanding of what "in case of" means, and its application of that understanding to the facts of this case.

First, Etihad argues that "in case of" means "caused by," or perhaps "caused directly by." If we impose Etihad's reading of Article 17(1) back onto the text of the treaty, Etihad is then "liable for damage sustained [caused directly by] death or bodily injury of a passenger upon condition only that the accident which caused the death or injury took place on board the aircraft. . . ." Thus, according to Etihad, in order for Doe to recover for her mental anguish under Article 17(1), Doe would have to prove that (1) an "accident" caused her "bodily injury" on board an aircraft and (2) her "bodily injury" (*i.e.*, the small hole in her finger) directly caused her "damage sustained" (*i.e.*, her mental anguish).

Second, Etihad concedes that an accident caused Doe to suffer a bodily injury on board its aircraft, but Etihad argues that Doe's bodily injury *did not* directly cause her mental anguish: according to Etihad, Doe's anguish was caused not by her "bodily injury" (*i.e.*, the needlestick, the physical puncture wound) but rather by the "accident" that caused the injury (*i.e.*, being stuck by a needle, as opposed to being stuck by something else). It is not the physical needle prick itself that caused Plaintiff's distress, but the possibility that she may have been exposed to an infectious disease.") A simple diagram helps to illustrate Etihad's curious understanding:

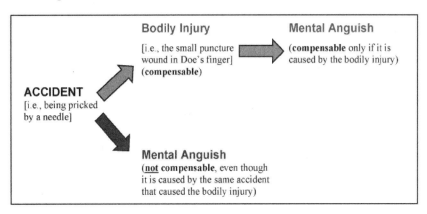

As this diagram indicates, according to Etihad, mental anguish caused directly by the bodily injury is recoverable, but mental anguish that merely *accompanies* the bodily injury, and which is instead caused more generally by the *accident*, is not recoverable.

But "in case of" does not mean "caused by." Rather, the plain meaning of "in case of" is "if there is" or "in the event of" or "during a case in which there is." The Oxford English Dictionary, for example, defines "in case" (as a conjunction) as, "In the event that; if it should happen that; if," and defines "in case of" (as an adverb) as "in the event of (esp. something untoward). Now frequently in in case of emergency." The Canadian Oxford Dictionary has similar definitions and is a seemingly apt dictionary for identifying the contemporaneous

Meaning of "in Case of"

meaning of terms in the Montreal Convention, given that the dictionary was first published in 1998 and then updated in 2004, while the treaty was signed in 1999 (in Canada) and entered into force in 2003.

Clearly, the plain meaning of "in case of" is conditional, not causal. To say in case of X, do Y is to say "if X happens, then do Y"—none of which means that there is a causal relationship between X and Y—just as to say *in case of a compensable bodily injury*, the passenger may recover damage sustained is to say "if there is a compensable bodily injury, the passenger may recover damage sustained." But to adopt Etihad's meaning of "in case of," we would impose an additional causal restriction onto the text of Article 17(1) that the plain text does not contemplate. Indeed, imposing such an additional causal restriction would contradict the plain text, which states that "[t]he carrier is liable for damage sustained in case of . . . bodily injury . . . *upon condition* only that the accident which caused the death or bodily injury took place on board the aircraft or [while] embarking or disembarking." Montreal Convention art. 17(1) (emphasis added).

"Upon
Condition
Only"

The phrase "upon condition only" is new to the Montreal Convention—it is not found in the Warsaw Convention (either in English or in the official French version)—and it makes clear that the passenger's recovery is conditioned only on the occurrence of an accident that causes death or bodily injury either on board the aircraft or during boarding or deplaning. Surely, the drafters of the Montreal Convention could have used a word or phrase with causal meaning instead of "in case of" if they wanted to impose such a causal restriction on the kinds of "damage sustained" that are recoverable when an accident on board an aircraft causes a passenger to incur a bodily injury. Indeed, the drafters did impose such a causal requirement in stating that the accident must have "caused" the death or bodily injury. The drafters' use of "caused" to express that an accident must have caused the bodily injury thus provides additional support for our conclusion that the drafters did not, in the very same sentence, use "in case of" also to mean "caused by."

The Underpinnings of Etihad's Argument

Admittedly, in light of the foregoing discussion, Etihad's position—that "in case of" does mean "caused by"—may seem absurd. But it is not, and that is because Etihad's argument is rooted in a Warsaw Convention decision of the Second Circuit Court of Appeals in which that court held that American Airlines was *not* liable under the Warsaw Convention "for mental injuries that were not caused by physical injuries." *Ehrlich v. Am. Airlines, Inc.*, 360 F.3d 366, 368 (2d Cir. 2004) (emphasis added). Etihad asks us to adopt the Second Circuit's Warsaw

Convention decision in *Ehrlich* to decide the Montreal Convention case before us. But the Montreal Convention is a new treaty that we interpret as a matter of first impression, and there is no legal authority that would require us to import *Ehrlich's* Warsaw Convention determination to govern this Montreal Convention claim.

In *Ehrlich*, an American Eagle aircraft overshot its designated runway upon landing at New York's JFK International Airport. An arrestor bed—a bed of material made of water, foam, and cement that crushes under the weight of an airplane, increasing drag and helping bring the airplane to a stop—saved the plane from plunging into the waters of Thurston Bay, which lay 200 feet beyond where the plane came to a halt. To evacuate the aircraft, passengers had to jump six to eight feet from its doorway.

Gary and Maryanne Ehrlich were passengers on the flight. They contended that they suffered bodily injuries (neck, back, shoulder, hip, and knee injuries; hypertension; and a heart problem) during the abnormal landing and subsequent evacuation. They also alleged mental injuries including a fear of flying, nightmares, and trouble sleeping. The district court granted partial summary judgment for the airline defendant as to the mental injuries on the basis that "a plaintiff may only recover for emotional damages *caused by* physical injuries." The Second Circuit affirmed, noting that "the Ehrlichs had offered no evidence demonstrating a causal connection between their mental and physical injuries."

Ehrlich reached its conclusion only after grappling at length with the original French text of the Warsaw Convention, finding it ambiguous as to whether it held airlines liable for mental injuries that are not caused by a compensable bodily injury, and inquiring into the original purpose of the Warsaw Convention when it was signed in 1929. Indeed, *Ehrlich* discussed the Montreal Convention as well: the Montreal Convention was signed just weeks after the Ehrlichs' emergency landing, and the Montreal Convention entered into force after the Second Circuit heard argument in *Ehrlich* but before it issued its opinion. But *Ehrlich* expressly rejected the argument that the Montreal Convention had any retroactive applicability to the Ehrlichs' claim, and the Second Circuit based its decision entirely on its interpretation of the Warsaw Convention.

In reaching its conclusion, *Ehrlich* followed the lead of *Jack v. Trans World Airlines*, 854 F. Supp. 654, 663–68 (N.D. Cal. 1994), a district-court decision that also concluded that "only emotional distress *flowing from* the bodily injury is recoverable" under Article 17 of the Warsaw Convention. *Jack* expressly acknowledged (after rejecting other possible interpretations of the Warsaw Convention) that its interpretation "does read a causal component into the phrase 'damage sustained in the event of,' " but nevertheless went ahead with such an interpretation because that interpretation was "not prohibited" by the United States Supreme Court's Warsaw Convention precedents.

But "to alter, amend, or add to any treaty, by inserting any clause, whether small or great, important or trivial, [is] an usurpation of power, and not an exercise of judicial functions." *The Amiable Isabella*, 19 U.S. (6 Wheat.) 1 (1821) (holding that the 1795 U.S.-Spain Treaty for safe passage of ships did not protect a Spanish claimant from United States condemnation of a schooner during the War of 1812 when the requisite passport mandated by the treaty was not affixed to the vessel).

Both *Ehrlich* and *Jack* interpolated a causal component into the Warsaw Convention that was not required by the text, and both did so expressly to serve the Warsaw Convention's purpose of "limiting the liability of air carriers in order to foster the growth of the fledgling commercial aviation industry." To be sure, both *Ehrlich* and *Jack* found ambiguity in the original French text of the Warsaw Convention before inquiring into the purpose of that treaty and seeking to give effect to that purpose. But what that should mean for us is not, as Etihad would have it, that we should blindly adopt *Ehrlich* as the law of our circuit for claims under Article 17(1) of the Montreal Convention, but rather that we should grapple with the text of the Montreal Convention itself, and then, to the extent that we find any ambiguity therein, look to relevant persuasive authority—which may include evidence of the purpose of the Montreal Convention, but almost certainly not the nearly century-old purpose of the Warsaw Convention—to assist us in resolving that ambiguity.

Ehrlich recognized that "the Montreal Convention is an entirely new treaty that unifies and replaces the system of liability that derives from the Warsaw Convention." So do we.

The Montreal Convention was signed in 1999, in six languages including English, and we are charged with interpreting that English text in the first instance rather than clinging to the Second Circuit's purposivist interpretation of a French-language predecessor treaty signed in 1929. To fortify our textual analysis of Article 17(1), we will discuss more fully the relative purposes of the Warsaw and the Montreal Conventions, and we will address relevant decisions of the United States Supreme Court and other courts, which provide useful context for both *Ehrlich* and our decision here. But for now, it suffices to say that *Ehrlich* and *Jack* do not provide insight into meaning of the plain text of Article 17(1) of the Montreal Convention.

Our Textual Interpretation

Here, then, is a fairer illustration of what damages are recoverable under Article 17(1) according to the plain text of the Montreal Convention:

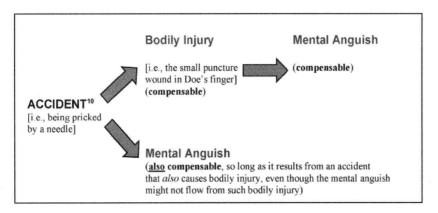

As this diagram makes clear, because an accident onboard Etihad's aircraft caused Doe to suffer a bodily injury (a fact that Etihad concedes), Doe may therefore recover damages for her mental anguish, regardless of whether that anguish was caused directly by her bodily injury or more generally by the accident that caused the bodily injury. That is because, either way, Doe's mental anguish is "damage sustained in case of"—*i.e.*, "in the event of" a compensable bodily injury.

What the plain text of Article 17(1) also makes clear is that a passenger cannot recover damages for mental anguish if there is no requisite accident or if the accident does not cause a bodily injury.

What the plain text of Article 17(1) also makes clear is that a passenger cannot recover damages for mental anguish if there is no requisite accident or if the accident does not cause a bodily injury. For example, if ordinary turbulence causes a passenger to suffer an anxiety attack, the Montreal Convention would not allow the passenger to recover damages for the anxiety attack because ordinary turbulence is not an "accident." Likewise, if there is an accident, such as an emergency landing, and a passenger escapes physically unscathed but mentally harmed, the passenger is barred from recovering mental-anguish damages for want of the required bodily injury. This understanding is supported by the plain text of Article 17(1) of the Montreal Convention—and it also happens to have the advantage of being simpler than *Ehrlich's* approach.

Admittedly, however, the text of Article 17(1) is still not entirely clear as to what connection must exist between the required bodily injury and claimed mental anguish. The plain text of Article 17(1) is sufficient on its own to reject Etihad's interpretation of it. And the plain text of Article 17(1) allows our conclusion that when a single "accident" causes both bodily injury and mental anguish, that mental anguish is sustained "in case of" the bodily injury. But the plain text on its own does not necessarily require that a single accident cause both the required bodily injury and the claimed mental anguish in order for that mental anguish to be "sustained in case of" the bodily injury, as our conclusion suggests.

What if, for example, there are two accidents: first, unusually rough turbulence (which causes a passenger mental anguish but no bodily injury), and second, an unrelated emergency landing, during which every passenger sustains at least some bodily injury. Does the bodily injury sustained in the emergency landing allow the passenger who had previously suffered severe emotional distress to recover for that distress? That is, is mental anguish from the first accident considered "damage sustained in case of bodily injury" because it was sustained during the same flight as the second accident, which caused bodily injury?

On the one hand, it seems reasonable to read the "in case of" language as precluding recovery of damages for mental anguish in the example presented in the preceding paragraph, and our interpretation of Article 17(1) implicitly supports such a conclusion; but on the other hand, the text of the treaty does not explicitly prohibit such recovery. So, both to bolster our conclusion that mental anguish is "sustained in case of" a bodily injury when it arises from the same accident that caused that bodily injury, and to reinforce the proposition that *Ehrlich* and *Jack* does not control this case, we review relevant persuasive authorities that provide insight into the meaning of Article 17(1) in the context of its ratification by its signatories. *See, e.g., Saks*, 470 U.S. at 396 ("[T]reaties are construed more liberally than private agreements, and to ascertain their meaning we may look beyond the written words to the history of the treaty [and] the negotiations" that produced the treaty).

We therefore turn next to the history of the negotiations that culminated in the signing of the Montreal Convention and to evidence of the signatories' purpose in ratifying the Montreal Convention. This historical inquiry is important because the question before us is important. And the question before us is important for several reasons. First, Article 17(1) governs not only claims for needlesticks, snakebites, and the like, but also claims for injuries and fatalities sustained in plane crashes. Second, "uniformity is an important goal of treaty interpretation," *Sanchez-Llamas v. Oregon*, 548 U.S. 331, 383 (2006), so we look to the history of the Montreal Convention to ensure that the conclusion we draw today is consistent with how our sister signatories would understand the text of Article 17(1). Third, the Warsaw Convention's analogue to the question before us was expressly left unanswered by the United States Supreme Court in *Eastern Airlines* v. *Floyd*, 499 U.S. 530 (1991) when it ruled that mental injury standing alone was not recoverable under the Warsaw Convention because of the absence of the required death or bodily injury:

> We conclude that an air carrier cannot be held liable under Article 17 when an accident has not caused a passenger to suffer death, physical injury, or physical manifestation of injury. Although Article 17 renders air carriers liable for "damage sustained in the event of" . . . such injuries, we express no view as to whether passengers can recover for mental injuries that are accompanied by physical injuries. That issue is not presented here because respondents do not allege physical injury or physical manifestation of injury.

Fourth, although we have expended considerable effort explaining that the Montreal Convention is a new treaty that we should interpret independently of the Warsaw Convention, such that *Ehrlich* does not inform our decision here, there is nonetheless evidence that the drafters of the Montreal Convention intended Article 17(1) to be construed consistently with well-settled Warsaw Convention precedents of the United States Supreme Court. These precedents, as we will discuss, include the United States Supreme Court's decision defining "accident" (in *Saks*, a decision from 1985 that has gained global currency). But these precedents do not include *Ehrlich*, which was decided well after the Montreal Convention was signed and which was not a decision of a signatory's highest court, in any event, *see, e.g., Husain*, 540 U.S. 644, 655 n.9 (2003).

And finally, while *Ehrlich* was a Warsaw Convention decision, we recognize that our conclusion today is directly contrary to *Ehrlich's* conclusion as to a similarly worded provision. The history behind the Montreal Convention will make clear why the conclusion we reach today is correct, and why we cannot use the same lines of reasoning that *Ehrlich* and *Jack* used in reaching their holdings that denied recovery for mental injuries that accompanied but did not directly flow from a bodily injury.

* * *

Relevant Warsaw Convention Litigation

We turn next to (1) relevant decisions of our Supreme Court under the Warsaw Convention; (2) a brief summary of our reasons for rejecting *Ehrlich* in light of the foregoing discussion of the history and purpose of the Montreal Convention; and (3) a brief discussion of relevant district-court cases.

United States Supreme Court Decisions Under the Warsaw Convention

From 1984 to 2004, the United States Supreme Court handed down a series of seven opinions clarifying various aspects of the Warsaw Convention, most of which involved Article 17. The first of these, *Trans World Airlines, Inc. v. Franklin Mint Corp.*, 466 U.S. 243 (1984), upheld the Convention's liability limit for cargo and is not particularly relevant to our case. More relevant is the Court's 1985 decision in *Air France v. Saks*, in which it held that "accident" in Article 17 of the Warsaw Convention means "an unexpected or unusual event or happening that is external to the passenger."

A year later, the Court decided *Chan v. Korean Air Lines, Ltd.*, 490 U.S. 122 (1989), holding that the Warsaw Convention's limitations applied even if an airline defendant failed to provide notice of the Convention in at least 10-point type as the airline defendant agreed to in the Montreal Agreement of 1966.

In 1991, the Court decided *Eastern Airlines v. Floyd*, which as we noted earlier held that "bodily injury" in Article 17 of the Warsaw Convention does not allow for the recovery of mental injuries on their own (that is, with no physical injury incurred whatsoever), but which "express[ed] no view as to whether passengers can recover for mental injuries that are accompanied by physical injuries." Next came *Zicherman v. Korean Air Lines*, 516 U.S. 217 (1996), in which the Court held that although the Warsaw Convention provided rules for liability and limitations of liability, it did not govern the measure (or calculation, so to speak) of damages, which was instead a matter to be determined in each case by applicable domestic law.

In 1999, the Court decided *El Al Israel Airlines, Ltd. v. Tsui Yuan Tseng*, 525 U.S. 155 (1999), in which it held that the Warsaw Convention provided the sole remedy for personal-injury claims arising from injuries sustained during international air travel, even if the injured party could not state a claim for relief under the Warsaw Convention, in which case no remedy was available at all.

Finally, in 2004, the Court decided *Olympic Airways v. Husain*, 540 U.S. 644 (2003), in which it clarified that finding an "accident" to have occurred for the purpose of applying Article 17 does not require identifying a single "injury producing event" but may rather involve a chain of causation that results in death or bodily injury, so long as there is an unexpected or unusual happening external to the passenger in that chain, following

Saks, Chan, Floyd, and *Zicherman* were all decided unanimously, and *Franklin Mint* and *Tseng* were both decided eight to one over the dissent of Justice Stevens.

Husain was decided six to two, with Justice Scalia dissenting, arguing that because two other Warsaw Convention signatories (England and Australia) had rejected the proposition that an airline's inaction could constitute an "accident" under Article 17, and because the text of Article 17 did not clearly resolve that issue, the Court should instead have followed the English and Australian decisions.

These opinions have enjoyed wide acceptance among our sister signatories, which have given them (especially *Saks*, *Tseng*, and *Floyd*) at least some deference and have developed their own jurisprudence using these opinions as guideposts.

Because these Supreme Court cases analyzed aspects of the Warsaw Convention that we have no reason to believe have changed following the ratification of the Montreal Convention (and that neither party has argued have changed following the ratification of the Montreal Convention), it is reasonable to conclude that these cases form part of the "precedent" consistent with which, according to the Explanatory Note, the drafters expected signatories to construe Article 17(1) of the Montreal Convention. Accordingly, we have adopted *Saks's* definition of "accident," and our discussion of damages will be guided by *Zicherman's* deference to the forum jurisdiction's choice-of-law rules.

Why the Second Circuit's *Ehrlich* Decision Does Not Govern Montreal Convention Claims

In light of the discussion above, there are several reasons why we decline to adopt *Ehrlich* to govern Doe's claims. First, Etihad's argument that we should adopt *Ehrlich* is unconvincing in part because of how thorough *Ehrlich* itself is: *Ehrlich* reaches its conclusion only after plumbing the depths of the original French meaning of the Warsaw Convention, French legal materials, the purpose of the Warsaw Convention, and the "negotiating history" of the Convention. Indeed, if *Ehrlich* is persuasive, it is persuasive not for the conclusion it reached but for how it got there, and our similarly searching analysis leads us to a conclusion opposite *Ehrlich's*.

Second, *Ehrlich* interpreted the authoritative French text of the Warsaw Convention, and found ambiguity in that text (in the original French) that *Ehrlich* thought could accommodate a causal meaning. Specifically, *Ehrlich* examined French-language dictionaries and found that the word "cas" in "en cas de" (the French phrase that was the Warsaw Convention analogue to the Montreal Convention's "in case of") could actually mean "cause."

Setting aside the fact that the French word cas does not actually mean "cause" except perhaps in the same way that we might say a "hopeless case" is a "lost cause," the range of ambiguity in the English "in case of" is far, far narrower than the range of ambiguity that *Ehrlich* found in the French "en cas de" and, as we concluded in Section III.A, notwithstanding any ambiguity in the English "in case of," the plain text of the English "in case of" does not contain a requirement that "damages sustained" be "caused by" bodily injury.

Third, as we discussed, the purpose of the Montreal Convention vastly differs from the purpose of the Warsaw Convention, such that we have no reason to interpret Article 17(1) of the Montreal Convention in such a way as to serve the purposes of the Warsaw Convention, as *Ehrlich* did.

Fourth, although the *Ehrlich* court stated that its ruling was necessary to avoid anomalous results, it appears that under the Montreal Convention, following *Ehrlich* would be more rather than less likely to lead to anomalous results. *Ehrlich* explained its reasoning as follows:

> The interpretation of Article 17 favored by the [plaintiffs] would give rise to anomalous and illogical consequences because "similarly situated passengers [would be] treated differently from one another on the basis of an arbitrary and insignificant difference in their experience." For example, a passenger who sustained a mental injury but no bodily injury would be unable to look to Article 17 for relief whereas a co-passenger who suffered the same mental injury yet fortuitously pinched his little finger in his tray table while evacuating and thereby suffered an unrelated bodily injury would be able to hold the carrier liable under the Warsaw Convention.

But our interpretation of Article 17(1) of the Montreal Convention does not necessarily imply this result. *Ehrlich* hypothetical here presumably involves some sort of crash or emergency landing (no context is provided in *Ehrlich* itself for the portion quoted above).

Under our interpretation of the Montreal Convention, if an airplane crash-landed, then any passenger who sustained a bodily injury caused by that crash-landing would also be permitted to recover for mental anguish sustained in that crash-landing—*i.e.*, anguish sustained "in case of" a compensable bodily injury. If a passenger sustained a broken leg, that passenger would be able to recover for the broken leg, for mental anguish caused by the broken leg, and for mental anguish arising from the crash-landing that accompanied the broken leg—all of that would be "damage sustained in case of" the broken leg. True, another passenger escaping the same crash-landing physically unscathed would be barred from recovering damages for mental anguish alone, but that's not an "anomalous" result. Rather, it is a result that is fully consistent with (and compelled by) the text of the Montreal Convention.

Returning to *Ehrlich* hypothetical of the passenger who escapes the same crash-landing entirely unscathed except for a pinched pinky finger: what result? As we read the Montreal Convention, so long as that passenger can prove that the accident (*i.e.*, the crash-landing) caused the injury to the pinky finger, that passenger would be able to recover both for the physical injury to the finger and for mental anguish sustained—and that passenger would be able to recover mental anguish sustained on the same terms as the passenger who suffered the broken leg.

None of these outcomes produce an "illogical or unreasonable result" that might caution against our ruling today. *Int'l Union, United Auto., Aerospace & Agric. Implement Workers of Am. v. Brock*, 816 F.2d 761, 766 (D.C. Cir. 1987). Thus, we are not persuaded by *Ehrlich* that we must read in an additional causation requirement to avoid interpreting the Montreal Convention in a manner that would produce absurd results.

To the contrary, it would be odd to require the passenger to prove which mental injuries in fact were caused by the physical injury as opposed to being caused more generally by the accident. In our crash-landing hypothetical, a passenger might, for example, be conscious for the duration of the crash-landing and then realize that he has suffered a grievous injury to his leg. Perhaps the passenger fears losing the leg for hours or days while he is in the hospital. And perhaps the passenger, who has a compensable bodily injury (bruised ribs and a broken leg), suffers mental anguish and other emotional damages—some as a result of the fear of losing the leg (which surely would be caused by the bodily injury, even if the leg was ultimately not lost), and some as a result of having experienced the crash-landing.

It would not "favor[ ] passengers," *Ehrlich*, 360 F.3d at 371 n.4, to require the passenger to prove which mental harms were caused directly by the broken leg as opposed to being caused more generally by the accident. After all, causation is difficult. Surely, for example, harm such as insomnia, fear of flying (or other fears), or emotional distress might initially result from the crash-landing but then be exacerbated by the bodily injury. Would only the portion of harm traceable and subsequent to the bodily injury be recoverable? Or, what if some of the harm resulted from the realization of an imminent crash-landing—should that harm be excluded from recovery because its cause preceded the accident, while harm occurring together with or flowing from the crash-landing would be recoverable?

Thus, at the end of the day, adopting *Ehrlich* would mean requiring Doe and other Montreal Convention plaintiffs to prove causation in a way that burdens the injured passenger far more than the text requires; that would be an anomalous result. For all these reasons, we decline to adopt *Ehrlich*.

Relevant District Court Cases

We now turn to *Jack*, the district-court opinion that *Ehrlich* followed, and which was the first district-court opinion to analyze the text and history of the Warsaw Convention at any serious length. *Jack* followed on the heels of the Supreme Court's decision in *Floyd*.

In the *Jack* case, where fire consumed a plane following an aborted takeoff and crash but all the passengers survived, the court addressed the question whether *Floyd's* bar to recovering purely mental damages under the Warsaw Convention also meant that mental anguish was recoverable only if caused by bodily injury. The court posited four theories for the recovery of emotional-distress damages under Article 17:

1. Emotional-distress damages are never recoverable.

2. Emotional-distress damages are always recoverable as long as the plaintiff has a bodily injury, even if the bodily injury is wholly unrelated to the emotional distress. *Id.* at 665–66 (notably, the court found that this approach "would read emotional distress as damages resulting from the accident (as opposed to the injury), which is difficult to do under the wording of Article 17," although the court did not explain the difficulty). This theory is broader than our interpretation, in that it allows recovery for mental injuries that are wholly unrelated to a compensable bodily injury, which would seem to capture more than just those mental injuries "sustained in case of" a compensable bodily injury.

3. Emotional-distress damages are recoverable as "an element of the damages for bodily injury," but "need not be about the injury," so long as the distress occurs "at the same time or later than the bodily injury." *Id.* at 666–67 (noting that in a plane crash that caused an injury, distress about the plane crash would be recoverable so long as it occurred after the injury, just as federal common law would allow the victim of a racially motivated false arrest to recover for emotional distress subsequent to physical injuries sustained, and not only for the minor physical injuries). This theory attempts to limit the scope of recovery to something narrower than what the

second theory would allow, but it does so by reading in a temporal element, which is not supported by the text of the treaty.

4.   Emotional-distress damages are recoverable only if they are "caused by the bodily injury." This was the approach *Jack* settled on and that *Ehrlich* adopted.

The problem with this purported tetralemma is that it omits a plausible fifth option—namely, our conclusion that mental injuries are recoverable if they are caused either by a compensable bodily injury or by the accident that causes a compensable bodily injury. Thus, while Jack's theoretical framework produces an elegant syllogism in support of Jack's fourth theory, it is not one that we have reason to follow in interpreting the Montreal Convention. Plus, as we noted above, *Jack* expressly acknowledged that its fourth theory "read a causal component into" the Warsaw Convention.

Etihad relies not only on *Jack* but also on *Rothschild v. Tower Air, Inc.*, 1995 WL 71053 (E.D. Pa. Feb. 22, 1995). In *Rothschild*, a passenger (Joan Rothschild) bound for New York from Tel Aviv reached into a seatback pocket and—just like Doe—was pricked on the finger by a hypodermic needle that lay hidden within. Mrs. Rothschild sued the airline for damages under the Warsaw Convention and Pennsylvania state law. The airline removed the case from Pennsylvania state court to federal district court, where Mrs. Rothschild proceeded to jury trial and won a $10,000 verdict for her injuries. But, although Mrs. Rothschild had been "permitted to testify about, and recover for, her pain and suffering flowing from the needle prick, such as any pain and suffering she experienced from the various tests that were performed on her," Mrs. Rothschild "was not permitted to testify about her fear of contracting AIDS and/or hepatitis because she did not show any exposure to these diseases, and permitting recovery under these circumstances would be purely speculative." Mrs. Rothschild contended that the court improperly prevented her from testifying about her fear of AIDS and hepatitis and she thus moved for a new trial, presumably in pursuit of a larger damages award; her motion was denied.

Etihad relies on the denial of Mrs. Rothschild's motion for new trial to support its contention that "fear of AIDS/contagion is too speculative to be recoverable absent actual exposure." But, for several reasons, *Rothschild* does not help Etihad. First, the *Rothschild* court expressly applied Pennsylvania state law, rather than the Warsaw Convention, in determining whether Mrs. Rothschild could recover for fear of contagion. The court noted that the parties "agree[d] that

Rothschild Distinguished

the Warsaw Convention [was] applicable" but that they had nevertheless based their arguments on Pennsylvania state law.

"Due to this apparent uncertainty of the parties as to the applicable law," the court stated its intention to "analyze this matter under both the Warsaw Convention and Pennsylvania law." But the court did not actually apply the Warsaw Convention to determine which of Mrs. Rothschild's claims were cognizable; rather, the court cited *Jack* for the general proposition that emotional distress was recoverable only if it "related to and flow[ed] from" physical injury, and the court then turned to various cases decided under Pennsylvania state law to hold that "in order to recover for the fear of contracting a disease, a plaintiff must show that there has been some exposure to the disease." Whether Pennsylvania state law does or does not require a plaintiff to prove actual exposure to a disease to recover for fear of contagion is a question that is not relevant to the matter before us, so this line of reasoning from *Rothschild* does not help Etihad.

Second, unlike Doe, Mrs. Rothschild was tested for AIDS only once—the day after the incident—and the *Rothschild* court's denial of her motion for new trial relied on the fact that "[d]uring the seven months between the injury and trial, Mrs. Rothschild was never again tested." The *Rothschild* court might thus have had good reason to find, as a matter of fact, that Mrs. Rothschild's claimed fear of contagion was too speculative to support additional damages.

Third, the fact that Mrs. Rothschild proceeded to trial at all would seemingly help Doe more than it helps Etihad, especially in light of the fact that we are reviewing the district court's grant of partial summary judgment. How reasonable or speculative Doe's fear of contagion was is not a question of whether Etihad may be liable to Doe but is rather a question of fact (and a damages question, at that) that is properly resolved at trial rather than at summary judgment.

In sum, neither *Jack* nor *Rothschild* provides any basis on which to affirm the grant of partial summary judgment for Etihad.

The Montreal Convention in Our Sister Circuits

We now turn to recent Montreal Convention decisions of our sister circuits. Since the ratification of the Montreal Convention, some of our sister circuits have applied *Ehrlich* in deciding Montreal Convention cases, but—so far, at least—they have done so without seriously considering either the text or the purpose of the Montreal Convention, and they have done so only in cases in which the outcome was not materially affected by the decision to apply *Ehrlich* rather than our interpretation of the text of Article 17(1).

The Eleventh Circuit, for example, affirmed a grant of summary judgment against a Montreal Convention plaintiff who traveled from Hawaii to Mumbai, India, and was refused entry (and ordered to return to the United States) by the Indian government for lack of proper immigration documentation. He subsequently claimed that Korean Air Lines was liable for various alleged "accidents" including (1) an alleged theft of $2000 cash from him; (2) denial of access to medicine while his luggage was checked; (3) failure to call a doctor for him while in Mumbai or in transit in South Korea; (4) failure to provide diabetic meals on the return flight from Mumbai; (5) "detention" and lack of "proper hydration" in a holding area in South Korea; and (6) failure to assist him when his legs swelled and caused him to fall. *Jacob v. Korean Air Lines*, 606 Fed. Appx. 478, 482 (11th Cir. 2015) (*per curiam*) (first holding that plaintiff had failed to prove that any "accident" had happened on board that had caused him a bodily injury, then holding alternatively that plaintiff's damages were unrecoverable emotional damages). In denying recovery for "subsequent physical manifestations of an earlier emotional injury," the court quoted *Ehrlich's* statement that "mental injuries are recoverable under Article 17 only to the extent that they have been caused by bodily injuries."

Jacob does not conduct any analysis of the text of the Montreal Convention; in a footnote, the opinion notes that "[c]ourts interpreting the Montreal Convention may rely on authority concerning its predecessor, the Warsaw Convention, where provisions of both conventions are similar." *Id.* (citing *Campbell v. Air Jam. Ltd.*, 760 F.3d 1165, 1177 (11th Cir. 2014)). Notably, in *Campbell*, on which *Jacob* relies to support its adoption of Warsaw caselaw, the plaintiff had failed to state a claim under Article 17(1) of the Montreal Convention because his only claimed damages were economic losses arising from a delay.

Thus, neither *Jacob* nor *Campbell* had reason to consider whether mental damages accompanying a compensable bodily injury were recoverable under Article 17(1) of the Montreal Convention. Nor did *Jacob's* use of *Ehrlich* amount to a reasoned decision to adopt *Ehrlich* as opposed to a competing approach to recovery for mental anguish under the Montreal Convention, because there was no "accident" in *Jacob* in the first place.

Finally, it is worth noting that some courts have looked to the relative histories of the Warsaw and Montreal Conventions to support reaching a different conclusion under the Montreal Convention than what the Warsaw Convention might have dictated. *See Pierre-Louis v. Newvac Corp.*, 584 F.3d 1052, 1058, 1058 n.7 (11th Cir. 2009) (affirming the dismissal of Montreal Convention claims on *forum non conveniens* grounds when parallel Warsaw Convention claims would not have been subject to such dismissal; distinguishing the instant case from "cases [that] involved interpretation of the Warsaw Convention, a predecessor to the Montreal Convention drafted in 1929, at which time forum non conveniens, in its current form, was not recognized under U.S. law").

Relevant Foreign Law

When we interpret a treaty provision, "the opinions of our sister signatories [are] entitled to considerable weight." *Saks*, 470 U.S. at 404; *see also Husain*, 540 U.S. at 660 (Scalia, J., dissenting) ("We can, and should, look to decisions of other signatories when we interpret treaty provisions. Foreign constructions are evidence of the original shared understanding of the contracting parties.").

Most Montreal Convention litigation in the European courts has involved the interplay between the Convention and various European Union Regulations, specifically in cases of delays and lost baggage. *See, e.g.*, Case C–94/14, *Flight Refund Ltd v. Deutsche Lufthansa AG*, 2016 E.C.R. 148 (Court of Justice) (delay-compensation claim); Case C–63/09, *Walz v. Clickair SA*, 2010 E.C.R. I–4239 (Court of Justice) (lost-baggage claim). But some cases have involved the interpretation of Article 17(1). The Supreme Court of the United Kingdom has reaffirmed, for example, that "injury to feelings ... related to [a passenger's] treatment during the process of embarkation and during the flight, which made him feel humiliated" is not a "bodily injury" under Article 17(1) of the Montreal Convention. *Hook v. British Airways Plc* [2014] UKSC 15, 2014 WL 795206, at *6.

One Canadian court, engaging in a mode of analysis substantially similar to ours in this case, applied *Floyd* and considered *Ehrlich* in declining to interpret "bodily injury" in Article 17(1) of the Montreal Convention to include purely psychological injuries caused by an emergency landing. Plourde, 2007 QCCA 739, at para. 29.

None of these cases, however, confronted the question of whether mental anguish that accompanies a compensable bodily injury, rather than only mental anguish caused by a bodily injury, is recoverable under Article 17(1).

Indeed, the only foreign case we can find that has confronted that question is a decision of a trial court in British Columbia, which—citing *Floyd* and *Ehrlich* favorably—required a "sufficient causal link" between the bodily injury and the mental injury in order for the mental injury to be compensable:

> In some cases, the causal link between the bodily injury and the mental injury will be clear. For example, an airline passenger who suffers burns on his or her face as a result of an aircraft fire will undoubtedly suffer

mental anguish. So long as the bodily injury is proven, the mental injury proven to have been caused by it will be compensable.

Wettlaufer v. Air Transat A.T. Inc., 2013 BCSC 1245, para. 82 (2013) (where a passenger aboard an Air Transat flight from Vancouver to Cancun was struck by "an unsecured food cart" upon landing, the passenger recovered money damages under Article 17(1) to compensate her for both her bodily injury and the emotional damages resulting from her fear of being "bumped" while driving or walking in public, but not to compensate for fear of flying "because there is not a sufficient causal link between such a fear and the whiplash-type injury" sustained).

Despite *Wettlaufer's* "sufficient causal link" language, the relief ordered in *Wettlaufer* is entirely consistent with the relief Doe seeks here and with our interpretation of Article 17(1): the "accident" that harmed Wettlaufer was being struck by the food cart, her "bodily injury" included the resulting bruises on her back and neck, and her recoverable emotional damages—fear of being "bumped"—seemingly must have been caused not by the bruises themselves, but from the fact that she was bumped by a food cart (that is—again, despite the language used by the court—her emotional damages were caused by the accident that caused the bodily injury, and those emotional damages were nevertheless recoverable). Further, denying Wettlaufer's recovery for fear of flying is consistent with the text of Article 17(1) as well, because fear of flying might not be the sort of fear "sustained in case of" bruises caused by a runaway food cart. *Wettlaufer* does not seriously explore the language "damage sustained in case of," and it is only the decision of a provincial trial court rather than a sister signatory's high court. Even if we were to accord it the same weight as a decision of a high court, however, it would not give us reason to believe that our decision today is at odds with the "shared understanding of the contracting parties" to the Montreal Convention. *Husain*, 540 U.S. at 660.

The Montreal Convention Imposes Liability for Emotional and Mental Harms Accompanying a Compensable Bodily Injury

In light of the foregoing discussion, we now provide a brief summary of our decision and its application to Doe's case. For ease of reference, we state again the full text of Article 17(1) of the Montreal Convention:

> The carrier is liable for damage sustained in case of death or bodily injury of a passenger upon condition only that the accident which caused the death or injury took place on board the aircraft or in the course of any of the operations of embarking or disembarking.

Montreal Convention art. 17(1).

To prevail on a claim for damages under Article 17(1), a plaintiff must prove that (1) there was an "accident," defined as "an unexpected or unusual event or happening that is external to the passenger," *Saks*, 470 U.S. at 405; (2) the accident happened either "on board the aircraft" or during "the operations of embarking or disembarking"; and (3) the accident caused "death or bodily injury of a passenger." The carrier is then liable for damage sustained, which we interpret to include emotional or mental damages, so long as they are traceable to the accident, regardless of whether they are caused directly by the bodily injury.

A simple example serves to illustrate our understanding. Consider a case in which an overhead bin unexpectedly opens in flight, causing a suitcase to fall out and strike a passenger in the eye. The passenger might sustain bodily injury—bruises, broken or fractured bones, a concussion, etc.—and the passenger might sustain mental anguish such as the fear of losing sight in the injured eye or a fear of being struck by flying objects. The "accident" would be the suitcase striking the passenger. (The faulty overhead bin or latch, like the airline's failure to clean out the seatback pocket in Doe's case, might be underlying negligence that precipitated the accident.) The accident happened on board the aircraft. And the accident caused bodily injury. Thus, the carrier would be liable for the passenger's damage sustained as the result of being struck by the suitcase—including such mental anguish as fear of losing sight, even if the passenger ultimately did not suffer a loss of vision, and even if the fear of losing sight was not caused directly by a bodily injury. The following diagram illustrates this result:

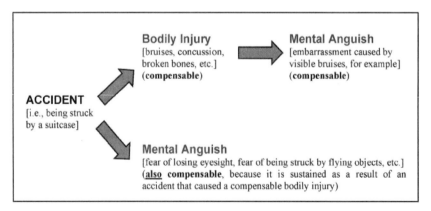

Under Etihad's framework, a plaintiff seeking to recover damages for mental anguish would instead have to prove that an accident caused bodily injury, which in turn caused the mental anguish. But that framework is neither found in the text of the Montreal Convention nor supported by the history and purpose of the

Montreal Convention, nor do relevant decisions of the courts of the United States or sister signatories give us reason to adopt Etihad's understanding.

> *Here, the accident was the needle pricking Doe's finger. The accident happened on board Etihad's aircraft. And the accident caused bodily injury, as Etihad has conceded. Etihad is therefore liable for Doe's damage sustained, which includes both her physical injury and the mental anguish that she is able to prove that she sustained.*

Here, the accident was the needle pricking Doe's finger. The accident happened on board Etihad's aircraft. And the accident caused bodily injury, as Etihad has conceded. Etihad is therefore liable for Doe's damage sustained, which includes both her physical injury and the mental anguish that she is able to prove that she sustained. Assuming that, on remand, Doe is able to prove fear of contagion or other mental anguish, Etihad is liable for damages arising from that anguish regardless of whether the anguish was directly caused by the physical hole in Doe's finger or by the fact that Doe was pricked by a needle. The diagram, *supra*, illustrates this result.

Michigan Damages Laws Govern the Measure of Doe's Recovery and Any Recovery by Doe's Husband for Loss of Consortium

Having determined that the Montreal Convention does not preclude Etihad's liability for Doe's mental-anguish claims, we turn to the choice-of-law question of whose law governs the measure of any recovery to which Doe is entitled. Although the district court did not expressly (or implicitly) address this question in its order granting partial summary judgment, the question was raised in the parties' summary-judgment pleadings below. On appeal, Plaintiffs' brief includes a lengthy discussion of whether federal common law or Michigan law determines the extent of Doe's recovery for mental anguish. Etihad responds at even greater length in its brief. For the reasons that follow, Michigan law governs both the measure of Doe's recovery and the ability of Doe's husband to recover damages for loss of consortium.

Article 29 of the Montreal Convention clarifies that actions under Article 17(1), such as Plaintiffs' action, are brought "without prejudice to the question as to who are the persons who have the right to bring suit and what are their respective rights." Montreal Convention art. 29 (emphasis added). As we discussed, *supra*, the United States Supreme Court has held that the effect of the parallel provision in the Warsaw Convention (Article 24) is to leave to the domestic law of the contracting parties the determination of how a successful plaintiff's damages are measured. See *Zicherman*, 516 U.S. at 224–26.

Lower courts have consistently applied *Zicherman* to hold that the measure of damages is to be fixed according to whatever law (*i.e.*, according to whatever choice-of-law rules) would apply in a domestic-law case, and *Zicherman* is one of the Warsaw Convention "precedents" that guides our interpretation of the Montreal Convention.

In this case, then, the district court should measure Doe's damages by whatever law would apply to an analogous case in the Eastern District of Michigan. An analogous case would be a diversity action for personal-injury damages. A federal court exercising diversity jurisdiction applies the choice-of-law rules of the state in which it sits. And "a federal court in a diversity action is obligated to apply the law it believes the highest court of the state would apply if it were faced with the issue." *Mahne v. Ford Motor Co.*, 900 F.2d 83, 86 (6th Cir. 1990).

Our court has previously recognized Michigan's strong presumption in favor of applying Michigan law in Michigan courts:

> Michigan's choice of law framework is established in two Michigan Supreme Court decisions: *Olmstead v. Anderson*, 400 N.W.2d 292, 302 (1987), and *Sutherland v. Kennington Truck Serv.*, Ltd., 562 N.W.2d 466, 471 (1997). In a tort action, Michigan courts recognize a presumption in favor of *lex fori* and apply Michigan law "unless a 'rational reason' to do otherwise exists." *Sutherland*, 562 N.W.2d at 471. The two-step test for determining whether such a rational reason exists was distilled in *Sutherland* from *Olmstead* as follows:
>
> > First, we must determine if any foreign state has an interest in having its law applied. If no state has such an interest, the presumption that Michigan law will apply cannot be overcome. If a foreign state does have an interest in having its law applied, we must then determine if Michigan's interests mandate that Michigan law be applied, despite the foreign interests.

Neither party here has asserted a "rational reason" for us to hold that any law other than Michigan's damages laws should apply to govern the measure of Plaintiffs' recovery, including any recovery by Doe's husband for loss of consortium. Plaintiffs are Michigan residents, so there is no reason to apply the substantive law of any state in the United States other than Michigan. And Etihad has not argued that the law of the United Arab Emirates should apply.

Michigan's substantive damages laws therefore govern the measure of any recovery that Plaintiffs win. On remand, assuming Doe wins a judgment, the district court is free to determine, within the bounds of what Michigan damages laws allow, what specific kinds of damages—such as emotional distress, mental anguish, fear of contagion, loss of consortium, and so on—Plaintiffs are entitled to recover, in "grant[ing] the relief to which each party is entitled." Fed. R. Civ. P. 54(c).

* * *

The Warsaw Convention ruled aviation law for more than seventy-five years. Over the decades, despite various amendments, courts have routinely interpreted the Warsaw Convention in line with its purpose as drafted in 1929. Etihad urges us to interpret the Montreal Convention in line with that same purpose.

But the Montreal Convention is not an amendment to the Warsaw Convention. The Warsaw Convention provided limitations of liability to protect fledgling airlines from litigious passengers; the Montreal Convention provides limitations of liability to protect (still litigious) passengers from the not-so-fledgling airlines. To adopt Etihad's reading of the Montreal Convention would distort the treaty's text and would frustrate rather than serve its purpose.

Having determined that the Montreal Convention imposes liability for the damages that Doe has alleged, and that the damages laws of Michigan govern the measure of any judgment Plaintiffs win, we reverse the district court's partial-summary-judgment order and remand this matter for further proceedings consistent with this opinion.

EXERCISE 13-5. *DOE V. ETIHAD AIRWAYS, P.J.S.C.*—THE MONTREAL CONVENTION: AN ENTIRELY NEW TREATY

1. Detail the factual allegations in *Doe v. Etihad Airways, P.J.S.C.* and identify the specific type of damages sought.

2. Summarize Etithad's arguments as presented by the court and discuss how the court decided each issue.

3. The court examines *Ehrlich v. American Airlines* extensively. Discuss how the court applied this precedent to the facts of the case before it.

4. In what way does the court apply foreign law to the issue before it?

5. Explain what choice-of-law question arose in this case for damages purposes and how the court resolved it.

NOTES ON *DOE V. ETIHAD AIRWAYS, P.J.S.C.*—WHAT IS THE ACCIDENT?

In a footnote, the court in *Doe v. Ethihad, P.J.S.C.* elaborated on the parties' litigation of the word "accident," as follows:

> At oral argument, there was some confusion about what the "accident" was in this case: was it the airline's failure to clean out the seatback pocket, or was it the moment at which the needle in the seatback pocket pricked Doe's finger?

> Under *Husain*, it is not terribly important to identify the moment of the accident so long as there was an accident. That said, it seems clear in our case that the "unexpected or unusual happening" was the moment when the needle pricked Doe's finger; the airline's failure to clean the pocket was perhaps underlying negligence that allowed the accident to happen. The confusion can be traced to a line from *Saks*, in which the Court stated that "the text of Article 17 [of the Warsaw Convention] refers to an accident which caused the passenger's injury, and not to an accident which is the passenger's injury."

> What the Court meant there was that the mere fact of an unexpected or unusual injury (such as a passenger, for example, suffering a sudden heart attack during a flight) is not itself an accident—something unexpected and external to the passenger must itself cause an injury. At oral argument, presumably in response to Etihad's argument that attempted to separate Doe's injury of bring pricked from the fact that Doe was pricked by a needle, see Section III.A.1, supra, Doe's counsel argued that Etihad's failure to clean the airplane was the accident and the needlestick was the bodily injury. Both of those arguments are misplaced: the needlestick was simply an accident that caused a contemporaneous bodily injury. Nothing in the Montreal Convention or in the Warsaw Convention caselaw requires us to separate the accident from the bodily injury in cases like this one where there is no temporal gap between the accident and the bodily injury.

> Of course, in most cases, there is such a gap, as when an accident such as a crash landing causes subsequent and separately identifiable injuries—but in cases like ours, or perhaps in cases of insect bites or physical assaults by flight crewmembers, the accident and the bodily injury may logically be one and the same.

D. INDUSTRY STANDARDS

Aziz v. Air India, Ltd.

658 F. Supp. 2d 1144 (C.D. Cal. 2009)

Stephen G. Larson, District Judge.

This case involves the tragic story of a passenger suffering cardiac arrest onboard a lengthy international flight and later being pronounced dead by paramedics at the arrival gate. The question before the Court is whether the airline's failure to have onboard an automated external defibrillator ("AED") renders it liable for the passenger's death under international law, as established by treaty. For the reasons set forth below, the Court holds that, under the law governing this case, the aircraft is not required to have such a device in place and, therefore, awards summary judgment in favor of the airline.

I.   UNDISPUTED FACTS

Air India Limited, d/b/a Air India ("Air India"), is a foreign air carrier, organized under the laws of and with its principal place of business in India, that operates aircraft in the United States pursuant to a certificate issued under Part 129 of the Federal Aviation Regulations.

On June 27, 2007, Ramazan Aziz was a passenger on board Air India Flight 137 from Frankfurt, Germany, to Los Angeles, California, traveling on a round-trip ticket on Air India originating in Los Angeles. After landing at Los Angeles International Airport, and while the airplane was still in the process of taxiing to the gate, a passenger seated next to Aziz noticed that he had collapsed and was not breathing. The passenger called the flight attendant and alerted her to Aziz's condition. Another passenger seated nearby reported to the flight attendant that, an hour earlier, she had spoken to Aziz, and that after that conversation the passenger presumed Aziz had fallen asleep.

Air India's procedures for assisting medically ill passengers are as follows: (1) The In-Flight Supervisor ("IFS") shall be informed; (2) a suitable announcement shall be made requesting the help of a qualified medical practitioner; (3) the cabin crew shall render every assistance to the doctor treating the sick passenger by ensuring that the doctor has privacy to conduct the examination and that a bed is prepared if necessary; (4) the IFS or Flight Purser shall indicate in the flight report the doctor's name, address, registration number, seat number, and the sector on which assistance was sought; (5) if a doctor is not available on board and the passenger's condition appears serious, the IFS shall inform the Commander so that a message can be sent for a doctor to meet the flight at the next port of call;

and (6) the Commander shall be informed in all cases where the passenger's illness appears serious.

When Air India Flight 137's flight crew was alerted to Aziz's condition, the flight attendant immediately summoned an on-board doctor, a passenger who identified himself as Dr. Gautam Mittal, and then notified the IFS and the plane's captain. Dr. Mittal examined Aziz and took his vital signs. Dr. Mittal found that Aziz was not breathing, did not have a pulse, and was very pale. As Dr. Mittal was treating Aziz, the flight crew contacted the airport for paramedics and requested that they respond to the aircraft at the arrival gate. The flight crew initially provided Dr. Mittal with a stethoscope and a blood pressure apparatus. Later, a flight attendant also brought him an oxygen mask and tank. Dr. Mittal had another passenger standing nearby administer oxygen to Aziz while the doctor performed CPR on Aziz.

At no time did Dr. Mittal ask the flight crew for a defibrillator or any other equipment or medicine. Paramedics boarded the aircraft after it arrived at the gate fifteen minutes later and the door was opened. Upon entering the aircraft the paramedics spotted Aziz lying in his seat, (and for reasons never explained) unattended and with no medical services being provided by anyone.

Although the paramedics found that Aziz was not breathing and had no pulse, they noted that he was not yet asystolic (no heart contractions) and their EKG monitor initially showed that he did emulate ventricular fibrillation ("V-fib") waves. The paramedics attempted CPR and employed an AED to administer a defibrillation shock on Aziz. Thereafter, the monitor showed that Aziz became asystolic. Epinephrine and Atrophine were administered intravenously at which point Aziz's heart temporarily resumed ventricular fibrillation waves on the monitor. Continuing attempts to revive Aziz's heart were unsuccessful and Aziz thereafter remained asystolic. Aziz was pronounced dead on board the airplane at 5:45 P.M. No autopsy of Aziz's body was performed.

Aziz's wife and his four children eventually filed suit against Air India alleging a state law tort claim of wrongful death based on the contention that, if the aircraft was equipped with an AED, Aziz would have survived.

II. ANALYSIS

Neither party disputes that the Montreal Convention applies to the allegations leveled by the Aziz family, and thereby preempts their state common law wrongful death claim. Aziz's round-trip international flight unquestionably constitutes "international carriage" as that phrase is defined in the Montreal Convention, and therefore "any action for damages" arising from such a "carriage of passengers[,] . . . however founded, whether . . . in contract or in tort or otherwise, can only be brought subject to the conditions and such limits of liability as are set out in" the convention.

The question, then, is whether the Aziz family can establish a viable claim against Air India under the framework set forth in the Montreal Convention. The circumstances under which an airline carrier may be liable for injury to a passenger during an international flight are set forth in Article 17 of the Montreal Convention:

> The carrier shall be liable for damage sustained in the event of the death or wounding of a passenger or any other bodily injury suffered by a passenger, if the accident which caused the damage so sustained took place on board the aircraft or in the course of any of the operations of embarking or disembarking.

The United States Supreme Court has interpreted this treaty language as requiring that, for a passenger to hold an airline carrier liable for any injury he or she sustains, the passenger must establish that (1) there has been an "accident," (2) that caused the passenger's injury, and (3) that said accident occurred while on board the aircraft or in the course of embarking or disembarking the aircraft. Here, the parties' spar over whether an "accident" occurred and, if it did, whether such an accident "caused" Aziz's death.

Nowhere does the convention define the term "accident," but the United States Supreme Court later supplied meaning to the term (as it was used in the predecessor to the present convention—the Warsaw Convention) in the case of *Air France v. Saks*, 470 U.S. 392 (1985). There, the court held that "accident" means "an unexpected or unusual event or happening that is external to the passenger." As explained by the court, although "this definition should be flexibly applied after assessment of all the circumstances surrounding a passenger's injuries," at its core, "when the injury indisputably results from the passenger's own internal reaction to the usual, normal, and expected operation of the aircraft, it has not been caused by an accident." Questions of negligence are not implicated or even relevant; instead the focus of the inquiry is on "the nature of the event which caused the injury rather than the care taken by the airline to avert the injury." Thus, for there to have been an "accident", the Aziz family must show that the asserted act or omission was unexpected or an unusual event that was external to Aziz, and that actually caused his death.

A.   *Whether the Occurrence was "External" to the Passenger*

Air India takes the position that, because Aziz's heart attack was nothing more than his own "internal" reaction to an otherwise uneventful, routine flight (as opposed to being something "external" to him), it cannot form the basis for an "accident" under the Montreal Convention. The airline reads the Aziz family's complaint too narrowly. Their complaint is not with simply their husband and father suffering a medical emergency while onboard the aircraft; instead their complaint is directed at the airline's failure to stock a particular medical device on the plane, characterizing that failure as the "event" which was the "unusual or unexpected" occurrence that "caused" his death. No serious argument can be advanced that the airline's decision on whether to stock its aircraft with AEDs was something external to Aziz.

> *The complaint is not with simply their husband and father suffering a medical emergency while onboard the aircraft; instead their complaint is directed at the airline's failure to stock a particular medical device on the plane, characterizing that failure as the "event" which was the "unusual or unexpected" occurrence that "caused" his death.*

The Supreme Court has held that a flight attendant's repeated refusal to honor a request to reseat a passenger who was severely allergic to tobacco smoke further away from the plane's smoking section was external to the passenger, see *Olympic Airways v. Husain*, 540 U.S. 644 (2004); in much the same way an airline's decision on what medical equipment to place onboard its aircraft is external to the passenger. Indeed, in nearly all the cases cited to by Air India in support of its legal proposition regarding externality, the courts have simply held that the fact of a passenger suffering a heart attack or some other physical ailment, by itself, was not an "external" occurrence under the convention.

Failure to Stock AED as Accident

Here, however, the Aziz family is arguing that there was something more that caused his death separate and apart from the heart attack itself, namely, Air India's failure to stock an AED on its aircraft. That something else was "external" to Aziz and thus could qualify as an "accident" under the Montreal Convention depending upon whether the other requirements are met.

B.   *Whether Failure to have AED Onboard Airplane was an "Event"*

With respect to the failure to have an AED onboard, Air India argues that such an omission was not an "event" as defined in the Montreal Convention. Air India makes the argument that, without a specific plea made to flight attendants for an AED by the on-board doctor, any inaction on its or the flight crew's part (or in this case, the affirmative decision not to stock the plane with said AED) was simply an act of omission for which no liability may attach. In Air India's view, only a failure to act in the face of either explicit requests by the passenger (or a doctor in his or her stead if the passenger is unconscious), or regulatory requirements to provide certain aid or provisions, can constitute an "event" for which it can be held liable. Using this reading, Air India notes that no event occurred here, as the airline followed all of its own internal procedures and Dr. Mittal did not make a request for an AED during the incident in question on Flight 137.

Here, there is no dispute that Aziz did not make a "specific health based request" for an AED; a result that is not surprising given that he was comatose and suffering from a heart attack at the time. Nor did the physician who treated him onboard the plane, Dr. Mittal, make such a request. However, in a later interview with private investigators, Dr. Mittal downplayed the significance of his failure to ask for an AED, explaining that "his whole attention was on the cardiac massage and CPR efforts," not making requests for particular items of medical equipment. Indeed, from the interview with Dr. Mittal, it appears that at no point did he make a request for any of the medical equipment that was onboard the airplane and that he did in fact use to treat Aziz; instead, flight attendants simply brought, unsolicited, such equipment to him. Thus, it would appear that if an AED was onboard Flight 137 the flight attendant would have brought it to Dr. Mittal unsolicited. Nonetheless, the Court agrees that there is, in fact, no evidence of a request for an AED being made.

This then leaves the question as to whether having an AED onboard an international flight was either required by a public agency or was an industry standard at the time.

Breach of Industry Standard?

For its part, Air India labels the Aziz family's call for the provision of an AED onboard international flights as asking for the airline to do something more than what Dr. Mittal sought, and states that the Ninth Circuit rejected in *Caman v. Continental Airlines, Inc.*, 455 F.3d 1087 (9th Cir. 2006), such a basis for liability. That court did provide that "[a]ttributing liability to an air carrier for failing to do all it can to prevent an injury that is inherent in air travel . . . improperly shifts the focus of the inquiry from the nature of the event which caused the injury to the alleged failure of the air carrier to avert the same." On that basis, Air India labels the Aziz family as seeking to impose liability on account of the "risk inherent in air travel" where there are "limited resources available to respond to medical emergencies." This contention, however, assumes that there was no legal requirement that airlines carry AEDs on board international flights or an industry standard for the same, an assumption to which the Court now turns.

The Aziz family points to FAA regulations which state that, "for treatment of injuries, medical events or minor accidents that might occur during flight time [,] each airplane must have the following equipment[:] . . . in airplanes for which a flight attendant is required and with a maximum payload capacity of more than 7,500 pounds, an approved automated external defibrillator as of April 12, 2004." *See* 14 C.F.R. § 121.803. The Aziz family also note that the Office of the Director of Civil Aviation for the Indian government promulgated a regulation in 2002 that mirrors the requirements contained in the FAA regulation quoted above. Specifically, the Indian regulation provided that, effective April 12, 2004, "all scheduled airlines operating transport category aircraft capable of carrying more than 30 passengers including crew when engaged in commercial flights shall carry one approved automated external defibrillators to provide the option to treat any serious medical events during flight time." Air India responds by arguing that both regulations cited to by the Aziz family are irrelevant to international flights.

Insofar as the FAA regulation is concerned, Air India notes that the cited provisions only apply to domestic U.S. air carriers. A separate section to the FAA regulations contained in the Code of Federal Regulations—part 129 of Title 14 of the C.F.R. (as opposed to part 121 cited to by the Aziz family)—applies to foreign air carriers. Indeed, Air India operates aircraft in the United States pursuant to a certificate issued under part 129 of the Federal Aviation Regulations. Section 129.11 of part 129 of the regulations, in contrast, provides that "each foreign air carrier shall conduct its operations within the United States in accordance with operations specifications issued by the Administrator under this part and in accordance with the Standards and Recommended Practices contained in part I (International Commercial Air Transport) of Annex 6 (Operation of Aircraft) to the Convention on International Civil Aviation Organization ("ICAO")." *See* 14 C.F.R. § 129.11. There are no operation specifications under part 129 (as opposed to those found in part 121 for domestic carriers) requiring foreign air carriers to equip their aircraft with AEDs. This the Aziz family does not contest.

Nor, at the time of the incident in question, Air India argues was there any requirement for onboard AEDs found in part I of Annex 6 to the ICAO. On this point, the Aziz family takes exception. They note that section 6.2.2 to Part I Annex 6 of the ICAO requires (using the word "shall") that airplanes be "equipped with a) accessible and adequate medical supplies appropriate to the number of passengers the aeroplane is authorized to carry" and recommends that such "medical supplies" consist of "one or more first-aid kits, and a medical kit, for the use of medical doctors or other qualified persons in treating in-flight medical emergencies for aeroplanes authorized to carry more than 250 passengers." According to the Aziz family, such a requirement may have compelled that an AED be onboard an international flight "in order for [the] medical supplies onboard to be adequate."

Air India responds that the same provision requiring "adequate medical supplies" also notes that "[g]uidance on the types, number, location and contents of the medical supplies is given in Attachment B," and then provides that attachment. An AED is not among the list of required medical supplies and equipment in Attachment B to the ICAO. Indeed, that attachment contains a specific statement regarding AEDs and their presence on international flights:

> Based on the limited available evidence, only a very small number of passengers are likely to benefit from the carriage of ... AED on aeroplanes. However, many operators carry them because they offer the only effective treatment for cardiac fibrillation. The likelihood of use, and therefore of potential benefit to a passenger, is greatest in aircraft carrying a large number of passengers, over long duration sector lengths. The carriage of AEDs should be determined by operators on the basis of a risk assessment taking into account the particular needs of the operation.

Although this statement would appear to strongly recommend that an AED be carried onboard a long flight such as that which occurred here (noting that the dangers inherent in failing to have such a device onboard are for flights "carrying a large number of passengers over a long duration sector lengths"), as explained above, the Ninth Circuit has made plain that failure to heed recommendations or suggestions made by governmental or international agencies is not enough to constitute an "event" under the Montreal Convention. Given that this "recommendation" is all that the ICAO provides with regards to AEDs, the Court holds that Air India's failure to heed the ICAO's suggestion is insufficient to constitute an "event" as understood under the Montreal Convention.

As far as the requirement of the Indian government cited to by the Aziz family, Air India represents that, on November 12, 2003, (after the regulation's effective date), the Indian government expressly retracted its directive for Air India to carry an AED on board its domestic passenger flights. The letter in question from the Director of Airworthiness for the Indian Director General of Civil Aviation begins by noting the requirements cited to by the Aziz family, and then observes that "[s]ome of the scheduled airlines had expressed reservations about installation of such equipment on the aircraft with the plea that cabin crew need to be trained for use of such equipment and there are chances that airline may be sued in the court for negligence in case of any death of passenger."

The letter also observed that, outside of the United States FAA regulations mandating AEDs onboard domestic flights, no other governmental agency had made the presence of such equipment "mandatory." In light of these concerns, the letter concluded that "this requirement [for the provision of AEDs onboard aircraft] would be deferred until the JAA makes it mandatory to European operators." Neither side has submitted any evidence as to whether the JAA has ever mandated that European operators of aircraft carry AEDs onboard. Thus, the Court is in no position to ignore the import from the Indian government's decision to suspend its requirement that an AED be placed onboard domestic flights.

On this point, all that the Aziz family argues is that they "cannot at this moment ascertain the propriety of the letter['s]" effect on abrogating what would otherwise be the clear mandate contained in the regulation. As expressed by their counsel, "it seems utterly impracticable that a letter from the government of India to the airline wholly owned by the government of India, can suffice as a rescission of an obligation of a law." What is missing, however, is any evidence or argument (other than the personal supposition of counsel) that the letter cannot do as it proclaims—to suspend an airline regulation issued earlier by the Indian government. In the absence of such proof, and without any other evidence on the question, the Court takes the letter on its face as accomplishing what it claims to have done. Thus, as with the ICAO's suggestion, the Court finds this failure to comply with a rescinded regulation insufficient to constitute an event under the Montreal Convention.

C. *Whether the Lack of an AED Onboard the Airplane was Unexpected or Unusual*

Air India further argues that, even were the Court to find that an "event" did occur, the lack of an AED onboard an international flight was not an "unexpected or unusual" occurrence. Thus, the question of industry standards vis-a-vis whether an "event" occurred bleeds into resolution of the "unexpected or unusual" occurrence question as well.

Air India asserts that conformity with its own policies and compliance with applicable laws and regulations is sufficient, foreclosing any contention that the occurrence at issue was unusual or unexpected. In essence, Air India seeks for a court to shy away from reference to industry standards in establishing whether an occurrence is unusual or unexpected. There is case law outside the Ninth Circuit to support such an approach; the Fifth Circuit in *Blansett v. Continental Airlines, Inc.*, 379 F.3d 177 (5th Cir. 2004), held that an airline's decision to merely cleave to the requirements of a public agency (as opposed to conforming to industry standards) was not an unusual or unexpected occurrence.

Failure to conform to regulatory recommendations—which are akin to industry standards—is not sufficient to constitute an "event," this Court is of the view that applying such a rationale to what is to be expected from an airline carrier goes beyond the boundaries of what the phrase "unusual or unexpected" is ordinarily understood to mean.

Although such an approach is consistent with the analysis that failure to conform to regulatory recommendations—which are akin to industry standards—is not sufficient to constitute an "event," this Court is of the view that applying such a rationale to what is to be expected from an airline carrier goes beyond the boundaries of what the phrase "unusual or unexpected" is ordinarily understood to mean.

Nevertheless, the Court need not resolve this question, as the Aziz family has failed to proffer any evidence establishing that there was in fact an industry standard to provide such AED devices on board international flights. In this regard, Air India correctly observes that the Aziz family has "presented . . . no evidence that an industry standard among foreign airlines regarding onboard AEDs exist," that no evidence has been presented showing "that any governing body recommended or required AEDs," and there has been no showing that "at least one of the many other foreign or international airlines carried onboard AEDs at the time of the incident."

Air India not only correctly identifies what the Aziz family has failed to proffer, but also that the missing evidence would be of the type needed to establish an industry standard. This does not mean that such evidence does not in fact exist to substantiate each of those points, but the duty to provide such evidence rests with the Aziz family, and it is a burden they have not met.

Indeed, certain periodicals would appear to address some of the factual deficits pointed to by Air India. *See* MEDICAL GUIDELINES FOR AIRLINE TRAVEL, SECOND EDITION, AEROSPACE MEDICAL ASSOCIATION MEDICAL GUIDELINES TASK FORCE, Vol. 74, No. 5, section II (May 2003 supplement) (noting "[m]any of the world's airlines have greatly increased their capacity for providing medical care to passengers in-flight by enhancing their onboard emergency medical kits

("EMKs"). One of the more significant changes is the greater availability of automatic external defibrillators ("AEDs")" and that "[t]he European Joint Aviation Authority already mandates similar requirements"). None of this evidence was ever offered, much less submitted, to the Court. Moreover, the Court cannot analyze the import (or lack thereof) of such information contained in a periodical.

The Aziz family seeks to reframe the point, arguing that the domestic requirements in both the United States and India to have AEDs onboard was instructive of a "shift" in industry standards "towards implementing AEDs," which thereby demonstrates that Air India Flight 137 taking off from Frankfurt, Germany, without such equipment onboard was unusual or unexpected. Even assuming that domestic regulatory requirements could be considered in establishing an international norm, a growing shift toward something is not the same as an established standard to provide the same.

In the absence of such proof, the Court finds that there is insufficient evidence to establish that there is an industry standard upon which a showing of an "unusual or unexpected" occurrence can be made regarding the lack of an AED onboard Air India Flight 137. Thus, in the final analysis, the Aziz family cannot show that their husband and father's death was a result of an "accident" as that term is understood under the Montreal Convention.

III. CONCLUSION

Accordingly, the Court denies the Aziz family's motion for summary judgment and grants Air India's motion for summary judgment, finding that Aziz's death onboard Flight 137 was neither an "event" nor an "unusual or unexpected" occurrence in light of the lack of evidence on industry standards regarding the latter, and the affirmative proof by Air India that provision of such AED devices was neither requested by Dr. Mittal nor was it required by governmental or international regulatory agencies at the relevant time for international flights.

EXERCISE 13-6. *AZIZ V. AIR INDIA, LTD.*—OCCURRENCE OF AN "EVENT"

1. Air India operates under Part 129 of the Federal Aviation Regulations ("FARs"), according to the court. Briefly summarize this part of the FARs. *See* https://www.gpo.gov/fdsys/pkg/CFR-2012-title14-vol3/pdf/CFR-2012-title14-vol3-part129.pdf.

2.   Was the airline's decision to stock (or not) its aircraft with AEDs something "external" to its passengers under the Montreal Convention, according to the court? Is this conclusion persuasive?

3.   What is "ICAO"? Is the failure by Air India to heed the recommendations of ICAO an "event" or an "unusual or unexpected" happening under the Montreal Convention, according to the court? Explain.

4.   The court seems to leave open the possibility that the plaintiffs could have defeated the airline's motion for summary judgment. How?

5.   What is the holding of the case?

WATTS V. AMERICAN AIRLINES, INC.

2007 WL 3019344 (S.D. Ind. 2007)

RICHARD L. YOUNG, UNITED STATES DISTRICT JUDGE.

Plaintiff, Carolyn D. Watts ("Plaintiff"), as the personal representative of the estate of Taisuke Matsuo ("Matsuo"), brings the instant suit against American Airlines, Inc. and AMR Corporation (collectively "American Airlines"), under Article 17 of the Montreal Convention. American Airlines now moves to dismiss the Complaint. For the reasons explained below, the court denies the motion.

Matsuo lived in Indianapolis, Indiana, with his wife, the Plaintiff herein. On April 6, 2005, Matsuo flew from the Indianapolis International Airport ("IND") to Tokyo Narita International Airport ("NRT") on an American Airlines flight with an en route connection at Chicago O'Hare International Airport ("ORD"). Matsuo returned from NRT to ORD on April 13, 2005, on American Airlines flight 154. During the flight, Matsuo left his seat to use the lavatory on the aircraft and locked the door. Matsuo suffered a heart attack while in the lavatory. Flight 154 landed at ORD with Matsuo locked in the lavatory, and upon arrival at the gate, the passengers and crew exited the aircraft. Matsuo was discovered locked in the lavatory by cleaning personnel and later pronounced dead by the Chicago Police Department.

Plaintiff alleges American Airlines violated industry standards of care and their own policies and procedures by, *inter alia*, failing to respond to a medical emergency involving Matsuo, and by failing to recognize and/or respond to visible or verbal indications that Matsuo was having a heart attack aboard the aircraft. * * *

Plaintiff has included an allegation in her Complaint that American Airlines violated "industry standards of care and the airline's own policies and procedures by failing to attend to a medical emergency involving Mr. Matsuo which occurred aboard an American Airlines aircraft; and failed to recognize and/or respond to visible or verbal indications that Mr. Matsuo was having a heart attack aboard the aircraft."

Although Matsuo's heart attack was caused by his own internal condition and was unrelated to the operation of the American Airlines aircraft, American Airlines' unusual or unexpected failure to recognize and/or respond to Matsuo's heart attack, and its failure to conform to industry custom and practices by responding to his medical emergency, could constitute a link in the chain of the events causing the ill-fated "accident" on board Flight 154.

Taking these allegations of Plaintiff's Complaint as true, the court finds that there are a set of facts which would entitle Plaintiff to relief. Although Matsuo's heart attack was caused by his own internal condition and was unrelated to the operation of the American Airlines aircraft, American Airlines' unusual or unexpected failure to recognize and/or respond to Matsuo's heart attack, and its failure to conform to industry custom and practices by responding to his medical emergency, could constitute a link in the chain of the events causing the ill-fated "accident" on board Flight 154. Accordingly, American Airlines' Motion to Dismiss must be denied.

EXERCISE 13-7. *WATTS V. AMERICAN AIRLINES, INC.*—INDUSTRY CUSTOM AND PRACTICES

1. Detail the allegations of plaintiff's complaint. How does it compare with *Aziz v. Air India, Ltd.*?

2. Did an "accident" occur here, according to the court?

3. Would the Montreal Convention apply if the event at issue took place on the Indianapolis-Chicago leg of the trip? Why or why not?

4. What defenses might be available to the defendant?

5. Given the court's ruling, who "won," what did they "win," and what is the next step in the litigation process?

Suggested Further Reading

David M. Krueger, *Mental Distress for Airline Lawyers: The Sixth Circuit's Decision in Doe v. Etihad*, 31 No. 2 AIR & SPACE LAW. 4 (2018)

Philip Weissman, *The Warsaw and Montreal Conventions: Ending the Complete Preemption Debate*, 30 No. 3 AIR & SPACE LAW. 12 (2017)

Jae Woon Lee & Joseph Charles Wheeler, *Air Carrier Liability for Delay: A Plea to Return to International Uniformity*, 77 J. AIR L. & COM. 43 (2012)

National Association of Attorneys General Task Force on the Air Travel Industry Revised Guidelines

INTRODUCTION

In June 1987, the National Association of Attorneys General ("NAAG") directed the appointment of a Task Force of states to study the advertising and marketing practices of the airline industry in the United States. In addition to the study, the Task Force was directed to determine the nature and extent of existing unfair and deceptive airline advertising practices and to report a recommended course of action to NAAG at its meeting in December 1987.

The Task Force Report and Recommendations were adopted by NAAG at its winter meeting on December 12, 1987, with a continuing direction to the Task Force (1) to receive and examine any comments from industry, consumer groups, federal agencies, and other interested parties; (2) to evaluate these comments; and (3) to report to NAAG at its Spring 1988 meeting on the advisability of any modifications of the Guidelines.

The Task Force received written comments from the Air Transport Association, the American Association of Advertising Agencies, American Airlines, the Association of National Advertisers, the Council of Better Business Bureaus, the Federal Trade Commission, the National Association of Broadcasters, Southwest Airlines, United Airlines, USAir, and the U.S. Department of Transportation. Assistant attorneys general of the Task Force states evaluated these comments, and reported their recommendations to NAAG. It is important to note that these Guidelines do not create any new laws or regulations regarding the advertising practices or other business practices of the airline industry. They merely explain in detail how existing state laws apply to air fare advertising and frequent flyer programs.

Section 1—Definitions

1.0 Advertisement means any oral, written, graphic or pictorial statement made in the course of solicitation of business. Advertisement includes, without limitation, any statement or representation made in a newspaper, magazine or other public publication, or contained in any notice, sign, billboard, poster, display, circular, pamphlet, or letter (collectively called "print advertisements"), or on radio or television ("broadcast commercials").

Comment: This definition *encompasses those materials and media covered by most states' false advertising statutes. "Print advertisements" and "broadcast commercial" are separated into different categories because they are afforded slightly different treatment under these Guidelines. This represents a change from an earlier draft of the Guidelines and is an attempt to address some of the airlines' concerns regarding the difficulties of lengthy disclosures in broadcast commercials.*

1.1 Award means any coupon, certificate, voucher, benefit or tangible thing which is promised, given, sold or otherwise transferred by an airline or program partner to a program member in exchange for mileage, credits, bonuses, segments or other units of value credited to a consumer as an incentive to fly on any airline or to do business with any program partner.

*Comment: This definition, [and] definitions 1.2, 1.3, 1.4, 1.6, 1.9, and 1.10, is self-*explanatory.

1.2 Award level means a specified amount of mileage or number of credits, bonuses, segments or other units which a program member must accumulate in order to receive an award.

1.3 Blackout date means any date on which travel or use of other program benefits is not permitted for program members seeking to redeem their award levels. This is a form of capacity control.

1.4 Capacity control means the practice by which an airline or program partner restricts or otherwise limits the opportunity of program members to redeem their award levels for travel or other benefits offered in the program.

1.5 Clear and conspicuous means that the statement, representation or term ("statement") being disclosed is of such size, color contrast, and audibility and is so presented as to be readily noticed and understood by the person to whom it is being disclosed. All language and terms should be used in accordance with their common or ordinary usage and meaning. For example, "companion" should be used only when it means any companion (*i.e.*, any person traveling with the program member), not solely family members. Without limiting the requirements of the preceding sentences:

(a) A statement in a print advertisement is considered clear and conspicuous if a type size is used which is at least one-third the size of the largest type size used in the advertising. However, it need not be larger than: 10-point type in advertisements that are 200 square inches or smaller, and 12-point type in advertisements that are larger than 200 square inches. If the statement is in the body copy of the advertisement, it may be in the same size type as the largest type used in the body copy, and does not have to meet these type-size requirements.

(b) A statement in a broadcast commercial is considered clear and conspicuous if it is made orally and is as clear and understandable in place and volume as the fare information.

(c) A statement on any billboard is considered clear and conspicuous if a type is used which is at least one-third the size of the largest one size used on the billboard.

(d) A statement required by Section 3, relating to frequent flyer programs, is considered clear and conspicuous if it is prominently located directly adjacent to the materials to which it applies. Type size should be no smaller than the most commonly-used print size in the document, but in no event smaller than 10-point type. Any reservation of any right to make future changes in the program or award levels should be located prominently at the beginning of printed materials.

Comment: One of the most deceptive aspects of current air fare advertisements is the completely inadequate manner in which those advertisements disclose the restrictions and limitations which apply to the advertised fares. The restrictions disclosed in print advertisements are rarely located near the fare advertised and often appear only in extremely small type at the bottom of the advertisement. In broadcast commercials, such disclosures are generally absent from radio advertisements, and if included at all in television commercials appear as written disclosures flashed on the screen much too quickly for the average person to read. On billboards any mention of restrictions on advertised fares is unusual.

Given this background, NAAG believes that it is necessary to define clearly for the airlines what constitutes clear and adequate disclosure in all advertising media. The type-size minima for print advertisements are aimed at making the disclosures both easy to read and noticeable. Consequently, a slightly larger size print is suggested in larger size advertisements. These type-size minima are not absolute. That is, print disclosures do not in every instance have to be in at least 10-point type, as long as they are clear and conspicuous regardless of the size of the type. The type size suggestions are merely examples of advertising practices which give an airline a reasonable expectation that it will not be sued if it follows the Guidelines. In the Task Force's meetings with the airlines last summer, one common note expressed was that the airlines could abide by disclosure guidelines, as long as they were clear and enforced uniformly. If an airline does not choose this safe harbor and instead ventures into untested waters, it may run aground and it may not. But it is free to do so.

The comments to this Guideline were critical largely because NAAG singled out airline advertisements for this treatment. However, on the whole, the airlines indicated they could meet the type size standard relatively easily in print advertisements.

NAAG elected to encourage oral disclosures in broadcast media, because written disclosures are difficult if not impossible to read and because many people listen to, rather than watch television commercials. We continue to believe that oral disclosure is the best method of conveying information in a television commercial. However, the converse of this Guideline is not true—a disclosure in a television commercial is not necessarily deceptive if it is instead made in a video super or crawl, as long as it is still clear and conspicuous. For safety reasons, very large type is provided for billboards.

1.6 Frequent flyer program means any program offered by an airline or program partner in which awards are offered to program members.

1.7 Limited-time availability means that the fare is only available for a specific period of time or that the fare is not available during certain blackout periods.

Comment: This definition applies to air fares that are only available certain times of the year (e.g., available December 15 through April 15), are not available at certain times at all (not available December 23 through January 5), or are only available until a date certain (available only until January 15). It does not apply to fares that are unavailable only on certain days of the week or times of the day.

1.8 Material restriction means a restriction, limitation, or other requirement which affects the use or refundability of a ticket, and which is not generally applicable to all classes of fares or tickets (such as standard conditions of carriage).

Comment: Due to the numerous standard conditions applicable to most airline tickets, NAAG has confined the definition of "material restrictions" to those restrictions and limitations that are specific and unique to certain fare categories (i.e., those that are different from the restrictions and limitations that apply to a standard coach ticket).

1.9   Program member means any consumer who has applied and been accepted for membership in an airline's frequent flyer program, regardless of whether he or she has accrued mileage, credits, bonuses, segments or other units of value on an airline or with any program partner.

1.10 Program partner means any business entity which provides awards as part of an airline's frequent flyer program.

1.11 Vested member means a member of a frequent flyer program who is enrolled in an existing program and has provided consideration to the airline or its partners, and who has not received adequate notice of program changes such as set forth in Sections 3.2 and 3.9. For example, consideration includes purchasing tickets on an airline, renting a car or using a specific credit card.

Comment: This definition separates out those consumers who joined a frequent flyer program without receiving adequate notice of how that program could change prospectively. The Guidelines afford some special protections to vested members and miles. There is sound reason for this.

After reviewing the travel reward promotional materials for most of the major airlines, NAAG concluded that currently vested members have not received adequate disclosure of the potential for significant increases in award levels or imposition of other restrictions which may result in the airlines' unilateral devaluation of awards. Therefore, the Guidelines treat vested members and the miles which members accrued before receiving adequate notice of prospective changes differently.

1.12 Vested mile means program mileage (or other credits) accumulated by a vested member before that person receives adequate notice of program changes, as set forth in Sections 3.2 and 3.9.

Comment: This definition identifies any mileage or credit accrued by a vested member before he or she received adequate notice regarding the possibility of future detrimental changes in the program. See the comments to the definition of vested member.

Section 2—Fare Advertisements

2.0 General guideline

Any advertisement which provides air fares or other price information must be in plain language, clear and conspicuous, and non-deceptive. Deception may result not only from a direct statement in the advertisement and from reasonable inferences therefrom, but also omitting or obscuring a material restriction.

Comment: This Guideline and the following Guidelines restate individual states' false advertising and deceptive practices statutes as they apply to air fare and price advertising.

2.1 Disclosure in print advertisements

Print advertisements for fares must make clear and conspicuous disclosure of restrictions such as:

- **Limited-time availability.**

- **Limitations on right to refund or exchange of ticket.**

- **Time of day or day of week restrictions.**

- **Length of stay requirements.**

- **Advance purchase requirements.**

- **Round trip purchase requirements.**

- **Variations in fares to or from two or more airports serving the same metropolitan area.**

- **Limitations on, or extra charges for, breaks or changes in itinerary, such as failure to travel on every leg as scheduled.**

- **The statement, if any, required by Guideline 2.4.**

- **Any other material restriction on the fare.**

Comment: The advantage to consumers of print advertisements over television or radio advertisements is that they give consumers something tangible to use as a reference when shopping for low cost air fares. Because consumers can take their time and carefully read a print advertisement it is especially important that this type of advertisement contain the most accurate and complete information possible regarding any advertised air fares. The restrictions singled out by NAAG in this Guideline for disclosure are those NAAG believes are the most significant to a consumer contemplating purchasing a ticket. An advertisement that complies with this Guideline will give a consumer three crucial pieces of information:

1. Eligibility—consumers will know if they are eligible for the fare (i.e., can a consumer meet advance purchase requirements or other restrictions affecting time or date of travel?);

2. Availability—consumers can accurately gauge the likelihood that they will be able to obtain a ticket at the advertised price; and

3. Risk—consumers will know the risks associated with purchasing a ticket at the advertised price (i.e., is the ticket non-refundable or do other penalties apply upon cancellation or changes in itinerary?).

This particular Guideline received a great deal of negative comment because the airlines and government agencies misunderstood it to mean that it required full disclosure of all of the restrictions that apply to each specific flight. This is not correct. The Guideline only requires that if any of the restrictions listed in the Guideline apply to any of the air fares advertised then the advertisement must disclose the existence of that restriction and the fact that the restriction applies to one or more of the air fares advertised. To clear up this misunderstanding, NAAG included specific examples of the disclosures required by the revised Guidelines. There was also some misunderstanding that disclosure in a box was required. As the Guideline states, this is just one option.

The comments made to the December Guidelines evidenced another misconception about the wording of the disclosures on fare restrictions. This Guideline provides suggested wording, again to assist the airlines in determining how to meet the disclosures, but the language is by no means sacrosanct. The best creative minds in the advertising business are available to the airlines through their advertising agencies. The airlines are free to avail themselves of these talents, who are certainly adept at phrasing a message the advertiser wants to get across to the consumer.

The essence of the Guidelines is that consumers must be advised of the limits which the airlines has [sic] chosen to impose on consumers' ability to buy tickets at the advertised price.

2.2 Disclosure in broadcast commercials

Broadcast commercials for fares must make clear and conspicuous disclosure of limited-time availability; limitations on right to refund or exchange of ticket; the statement, if any, required by Guideline 2.4.

In addition, if the following seven disclosures are not made in a clear and conspicuous manner in the commercial, any that are applicable must be disclosed orally to the passenger before reservations are actually made:

- Time of day or day of week restrictions.
- Length of stay requirements.
- Advance purchase requirements.
- Round trip purchase requirements.
- Variations in fares to or from two or more airports serving the same metropolitan area.
- Limitations on, or extra charges for, breaks or changes in itinerary, such as failure to travel on every leg as scheduled.
- Any other material restriction in the fare.

As to these seven types of disclosure, the airline may include any or all in the commercial or may choose to defer disclosure until the time reservations are actually made.

If any of these seven disclosures applies to the fare advertised and the airline chooses to defer disclosure until the time the reservations are actually made, the commercial must give clear and conspicuous disclosure that "Other substantial restrictions apply," or similar language. The statement "Restrictions apply" is not sufficient.

Comment: In an earlier draft, the Guidelines required that radio and television advertisements include all the same disclosures required in print advertisements. The airline industry unanimously responded that such detailed disclosures would be impossible to include in the 15 and 30 second advertising spots generally purchased for radio and television ads, and argued that, even if time allowed this much oral disclosure, the resulting commercial would provide too much information for a consumer to absorb usefully. They concluded that such a requirement would eliminate airline price advertising on television and radio.

The provision of fare information, without stating the most significant restrictions that apply to the fare advertised, is deceptive and ultimately harmful to consumers and the airline industry alike.

The Guideline as revised provides a compromise. It suggests disclosure of the three most serious restrictions that can apply to an airline ticket—limited time availability, nonrefundability or exchangeability and limitations on fare availability. Disclosure of all of these restrictions can be accomplished by something as simple as the following statement: "Tickets are nonrefundable, are not available on all flights, and must be purchased by December 15. Other significant restrictions apply." These 20 words can easily be read in a 30 second commercial. In addition, some or all of this information may be clearly and conspicuously disclosed in a video super or crawl in television commercials. Of course, this option is not available for radio commercials. However, commenting airlines confirmed that the typical radio spot is 60 seconds, making the concern about time less crucial.

Airlines then have the option of disclosing any additional material restrictions in the advertisement itself or deferring such disclosure until a consumer makes a reservation. Of course, if an airline does not choose to restrict its fare severely, fewer words (and thus, less air time) is needed.

This compromise position also recognizes that print advertising lends itself more readily to detailed information in a form which the consumer can retain and refer to at his own pace. For this reason, NAAG has chosen to require less disclosure in broadcast, allowing print to be the medium for full disclosure.

2.3 Disclosure on billboards

Any billboard which provides air fare or other price information on a fare to which any material restrictions apply must have clear and conspicuous language such as "Substantial restrictions apply." The statement "Restrictions apply" is not sufficient.

Comment: For safety reasons, NAAG concluded that lengthy written disclosures on billboards are inappropriate and potentially hazardous to drivers. We disagree with the DOT that this special treatment of price advertising on billboards will result in a proliferation of billboards on our nation's highways.

2.4 Fare availability

Any advertised fare must be available in sufficient quantity so as to meet reasonably foreseeable demand on *every* flight each day for the market in which the advertisement appears, beginning on the day on which the advertisement appears and continuing for at least three days after the advertisement terminates. However, if the advertised fare is not thus available, the advertisement must contain a clear and conspicuous statement to the extent of unavailability of the advertised fare.

Statements such as "Seats limited" and "Restrictions apply" do not meet this Guideline. These examples do meet this Guideline:

- This fare may not be available when you call.

- This fare is not available on all flights.

- This fare is only available on some Saturday and Sunday flights.

Comment: This Guideline elicited the greatest amount of negative comments from the airline industry, the ATA, FTC and the DOT. They argue that this Guideline is impossible to implement because, due to the complexity of airline pricing systems, the number of seats available at a particular low fare on a particular flight is not a fixed number. It is continuously modified up to the point of departure. They suggest that it is acceptable for the airlines to communicate a general invitation to the public to buy low fare seats, but then reduce the number of seats available to zero or close to zero for the most popular flights, because the possibility that a consumer can purchase a seat at the advertised price exists at the time the advertisement is placed.

The complexity of the airlines' system cannot justify the unfairness of such an approach. No other retailer would be allowed to justify a failure to stock an advertised item on the grounds that, at the last minute the retailer decided it was less costly not to stock the item it had just advertised. The availability of an item advertised, at the price advertised, goes to the very heart of truthful advertising. If an airline advertises an air fare that is not available on each and every flight to the destination advertised, and this fact is not disclosed, then the advertisement is deceptive on its face.

While NAAG appreciates the difficulty of disclosing the specific number of seats available on each flight advertised, a disclosure that "This fare is not available on all flights" or "This fare may not be available when you call" is not particularly onerous. Absent such disclosure, airlines, as all other retailers, should be required to have sufficient stock available to meet reasonable demand for any fare advertised.

2.5 Surcharges

Any fuel, tax, or other surcharge to a fare must be included in the total advertised price of the fare.

Comment: Recently, several airlines considered the possibility of passing along an increase in the cost of fuel to consumers by imposing a "fuel surcharge" rather than simply raising air fares to reflect their increased costs. The air fare advertised was to remain the same, but a footnote would be added to the advertisement in the "mice type" disclosing that, for instance, a $16 fuel surcharge would be tacked on to the advertised fare. The potential for abuse, if this type of price advertising is permitted, is obvious. It would only be a matter of time before $19 air fares from New York to California could be advertised with $300 meal, fuel, labor, and baggage surcharges added in a footnote. The total advertised price of the fare must include all such charges in order to avoid these potential abuses. However, this Guideline should not be construed to require an airline to do the impossible. We do not believe that such minimal tour-related charges fall within the meaning of "fare" and therefore do not believe that unknown charges must be disclosed as a surcharge (if the amounts are not in fact known). This of course does not mean that charges which are known—either as an exact amount or as a percentage—do not have to be disclosed in advertisements.

2.6 Round-trip fare advertising

If an airline elects to advertise the one-way portion of a fare that is only available as a round-trip purchase, this restriction, together with the full round-trip fare, must be advertised in a clear and conspicuous manner, at least as prominently as the one-way fare.

Comment: Airlines routinely advertise one-half of the price (i.e., the alleged "one-way" price) for tickets that are only available if a consumer makes a round-trip purchase. Under this Guideline, if an airline elects to continue this advertising practice, it must also disclose that the fare is only available if a consumer purchases a round trip ticket and the actual price of the full round trip ticket. The disclosure must be made in a type size and location as prominent as the fare advertised.

The airlines have, for the most part, stated a willingness to advertise the full round trip air fare if all of the airlines do the same. This Guideline is intended to encourage all airlines to adopt this practice.

2.7 Deceptive use of "sale," "discount," "reduced," or similar terms. A fare may be advertised by use of the words "sale," "discount," "reduced," or other such words that suggest that the fare advertised is a temporarily reduced fare and is not a regularly-available fare only if that fare is: available only for a specified, limited period of time, and substantially below the usual price for the same fare with the same restrictions.

Comment: The majority of airline tickets sold each year sell at prices significantly lower than the full "Y" or standard regular coach fare. These lower fares are offered year round and airlines in theory allocate a certain amount of seats to each fare "bucket." As a result, the regular coach fare has ceased to have any meaning as a starting point for determining whether or not a ticket is being offered for a "sale" price as consumers have come to understand that term.

In this Guideline NAAG has attempted to prevent consumer confusion by limiting the use of such words as "sale," "discount," or "reduced," to describe only those fares that represent a true savings over regularly available air fares—those that are available only for short periods of time and are substantially below any regularly offered fare for a ticket carrying identical restrictions.

Section 3—Frequent Flyer Programs

General Comments to Section 3

Frequent flyer programs have been widely acknowledged as the most successful marketing programs in airline industry history. The bargain struck between customers and the airlines has proven to be very costly to many of the airlines. Customers who have accrued the necessary mileage are expecting to collect the awards which led them to join and fly in the programs in the first place. Some airlines are now disturbed by the cost of keeping their side of the bargain and the real possibility that they may lose revenue because passengers flying on frequent flyer awards may begin displacing paying customers. The solution contemplated by some carriers has been to raise award thresholds and implement restrictions to decrease the cost to them of the award program. The effect of these actual and/or potential changes is to significantly devalue vested members' accrued mileage or other credits in the program. Although various frequent flyer program awards materials have contained some obscure mention of the possibility of future program changes, these disclosures have been wholly inadequate to inform program members of the potentially major negative changes which are contemplated by *many* airlines.

These Guidelines cover frequent flyer programs including any partner airlines or other providers of goods or services such as rental cars and hotel rooms. They are intended to protect those consumers who have participated in these programs in good faith, without adequate notice that the programs could change, and to advise the airlines of how they can reserve this right in the future by adequately providing this information to all members in a nondeceptive manner consistent with state law.

3.0 Capacity controls

1.   **If an airline or its program partners employ capacity controls, the airline must clearly and conspicuously disclose in its frequent flyer program solicitations, newsletters, rules and other bulletins the specific techniques used by the airline or program partner to control capacity in any solicitation which states a specific award. This includes blackout dates, limits on percentage of seats (for example, "the number of seats on any flight allocated to award recipients is limited"), maximum number of seats or rooms allocated or any other mechanism whereby the airline or program partner limits the opportunities of program members redeeming frequent flyer award levels. To meet this Guideline, all blackout dates must be specifically disclosed.**

2.   **As to awards for vested miles, the airline or program partner must provide the award to the vested member without capacity controls or provide the award with capacity controls within a reasonable period of time. A reasonable period would be within 15 days before or after the date originally requested. If all seats within this 31-day period were sold at the time the vested member requested a reservation, so that the member could not be accommodated without displacing a passenger to whom a seat has been sold, then a reasonable period would be the period to the first available date on which every seat was not sold to the requested destination at the time the program member requests a reservation.**

Comment: All of the airlines that met with the Task Force stated that they intended to retain the right to impose capacity controls, in the future, to limit the number of seats available to consumers purchasing tickets with frequent flyer award certificates. The imposition of capacity controls, including blackout dates, has the potential for unreasonably restricting the supply of seats or other benefits in such a way as to significantly devalue the awards due vested program members. NAAG found that this potential limitation has not been adequately disclosed to program members in the frequent flyer promotional materials we reviewed. This Guideline puts the airlines on notice as to what information they should provide to consumers if they want to impose capacity controls on the use of frequent flyer awards at some future date.

In earlier drafts of the Guidelines the Task Force took the position that capacity controls could not be applied to awards based on any mileage or credits accrued by vested members before they received adequate notice that capacity controls could be imposed. However, as a compromise, and to permit the airlines reasonable flexibility around holiday or other peak travel times, the revised Guideline provides for a reasonable time to accommodate passengers with award tickets: a 31-day "time window"—15 days before and 15 days after the date requested for ticketing. This "time window" allows the airlines to allocate capacity to meet demand over a reasonable, yet defined period of time. In the event all flights to a certain destination are sold out during the entire 31-day time window, ticketing on the next available seat would be reasonable. This approach has the additional benefit of being simple and straightforward to implement with less possibility of customer confusion and frustration.

3.1 Program changes affecting vested members

1.   Any airline or program partner that has not reserved the right to make future changes in the manner required by Sections 3.2 and 3.9 of these Guidelines and that changes any aspect of its program (for example, imposition of capacity controls, increases in award levels, or any other mechanism whereby a vested member's ability to redeem any award will be adversely affected) must protect vested program members. Examples which meet this Guideline are:

(a)   All vested members may not be adversely affected by that change for a reasonable period. A reasonable period would be one year following mailing of notice of that change.

(b)   The airline or program partner may allow vested members to lock in any award level which is in effect immediately preceding any change in the program. That award level would be guaranteed for a period of one year after mailing notice of any increase in award levels. A vested member would also be permitted to change his or her selection to lock in a different award in existence at any time prior to an increase in award levels.

(c)   The airline or program partner may credit vested program members with miles or other units sufficient to assume that, at the time of any change in the program, the member will be able to claim the same awards he or she could have claimed under the old program.

Comment: This Guideline institutes corrective measures to protect vested members and the mileage they accrued before receiving adequate notice that a program could change to their detriment at some point in the future. The Guideline sets forth three acceptable alternative approaches to allow airlines to change existing programs without unreasonably altering the rights and expectations of vested members. For example, an airline may wish to create a new program with higher award levels for persons who join in the future. Guideline 3.1.1(a) grandfathers in vested members for a one-year period after notice. Guideline 3.1.1(b) grandfathers only a specified locked-in award for a one-year period after the effective date of the change and thereby gives the member an additional year to accrue mileage or units toward a specific award. Guideline 3.1.1(c) allows the program to avoid the administrative problems of distinguishing between old and new members and old and new award levels by equitably adjusting the award levels of the vested members. These examples are not the only ways in which airlines can reasonably protect vested members when changing existing programs. They are intended to delineate minimum acceptable standards.

3.2   Notice of changes

1.   Adequate notice of changes in current frequent flyer program award levels must be provided to vested program members by the airline or program partner to allow a reasonable time for the vested member to obtain and use an award. For example, a notice no less than one year prior to the effective date of such change would be reasonable. Reduction in award levels would not require such notice.

2.   Any airline which has a policy of deleting program members from its mailing list for notices and statements must clearly and conspicuously disclose that policy in plain language in its rules and regulations.

3.   To reserve the right to make future changes in the award levels and program conditions or restrictions in a manner providing reasonable notice consistent with state law, which notice is less than the notice set forth in Guideline 3.2.1, an airline must first clearly and conspicuously disclose that reservation and the nature of such future changes, in plain language. This disclosure should include examples which make clear the outer limits within which program awards may be changed. For example, the following is not adequate disclosure: "Program rules, regulations and mileage levels are subject to change without notice."

This example is adequate disclosure: "(Airline) reserves the right to terminate the program with six months' notice. This means that regardless of the amount you participate in this program, your right to accumulate mileage and claim awards can be terminated six months after we give you notice."

Or: "(Airline) reserves the right to change the program rules, regulations, and mileage level. This means that (Airline) may raise mileage levels, add an unlimited number of blackout days, or limit the number of seats available to any or all destinations with notice. Program members may not be able to use awards to certain destinations, or may not be able to obtain certain types of awards such as cruises."

Or, if the airline so intends, the disclosure might also say: "In any case, (Airline) will make award travel available within—days of a program member's requested date, except for blackout dates listed here."

The airline's right to make future changes, in a manner other than that provided in Guideline 3.1, shall apply only to mileage accrued after members receive the notice required by this Guideline.

Comment: In the past, airlines have attempted to reserve the right to make radical future changes in their programs by using such vague and uncertain blanket language as "Subject to additions, deletions, or revisions at any time." The consumer outrage that ensued when several of the major airlines attempted unilaterally to change their programs in the winter of 1986–87 makes it clear that consumers were not adequately told, when they joined and participated in frequent flyer programs, that they were taking a gamble that the award they were striving for would still be available, at the mileage level originally advertised by the time they accrued the necessary miles.

To avoid a recurrence of this same problem in the future, this Guideline provides that the potential for such extensive program changes must be clearly and conspicuously disclosed to the public by specific example. It also puts the airlines on notice that (1) their previous attempts to disclose this critical information have been inadequate, (2) if they intend to reserve the right to make such changes in the future, they must give members new and different notice, and (3) as to vested members, airlines cannot implement any adverse changes until one year after notice is given. One year is deemed reasonable because many consumers can only travel during particular periods of the year due to work or family constraints, and therefore notice of less than a year may impact unduly harshly on a particular class of program members.

If an airline wants to reserve the rights to change the terms of its program without giving its members one year's notice (1) it can do so only after clear and adequate notice has been given to the program members and (2) this reduced standard can apply only to mileage accrued after clear and adequate notice has been given.

NAAG discovered that many airlines delete program members from their mailing lists if they are determined to be "inactive." Inactive is defined differently by each airline, but generally includes some formula requiring active participation in the program within a six to ten-month period prior to any given mailing. Because crucial information regarding changes is included in program mailings, the Guidelines require that any airline with a policy of deleting program members from its mailing list clearly and conspicuously disclose that policy in the rules and regulations distributed to all program members when they join.

3.3   Fare or passenger class limitations

Any limitation upon the type or class of fare with which an upgrade certificate, discount flight coupon, or free companion coupon may be used must be clearly and conspicuously disclosed before the program member claims the award. Disclosure of the fare by airline terminology (for example, "Y Class") is not deemed sufficient.

Comment: Many airlines are encouraging consumers to use their accrued mileage or credits to obtain upgrade certificates or free campaign coupons, rather than free tickets because this is more cost effective for the airlines. Many of these coupons and certificates can be used only in conjunction with a regular coach fare ticket. Because of the high cost of a full coach ticket (often disclosed only as "Y Class") many of these coupons and certificates represent no real savings and therefore are useless to consumers. This Guideline requires that any such restriction be clearly disclosed to consumers before the award is claimed.

3.4   Certificates issued for vested miles

Certificates, coupons, vouchers, or tickets issued by an airline for awards redeemed for vested miles must be valid for a reasonable period of time. One year is deemed to be reasonable. Any restrictions on use, redeposit, extension, or re-issuance of certificates must be clearly and conspicuously disclosed on the certificate and in any rules, regulations, newsletter or other program materials.

Comment: Again, because many consumers may only travel during certain periods of the year, fairness requires that awards be valid for at least a full twelve month cycle.

3.5   Fees

Any airline which charges a fee for enrollment in its frequent flyer program must fully disclose at airline ticket counters and in all advertisements, solicitations or other materials distributed to prospective members prior to enrollment all terms and conditions of the frequent flyer program. Such disclosure must be made prior to accepting payment for enrollment in the airline's program.

Comment: Some airlines have required that consumers fill out a membership application and pay a membership fee before obtaining a copy of the program rules and regulations. Because of the serious restrictions that can apply to a travel reward program, it is essential that all consumers have an opportunity to review all of the program rules and regulations before paying an enrollment fee.

3.6   Redemption time

All airlines must disclose clearly and conspicuously the actual time necessary for processing award redemption requests where such requests are not normally processed promptly. An example of prompt processing would be within 14 days of processing the request. An example of a disclosure would be "processing of awards may take up to 30 days."

Comment: The airlines indicated that full disclosure of redemption time will not be a problem.

3.7   Termination of program affecting vested members

In the event a frequent flyer program is terminated, adequate notice of termination must be sent to all vested members so that vested members have a reasonable time to obtain awards and use them. Adequate notice would be notice at least one year prior to the termination of the program. Award levels in existence prior to such notice should remain in effect for one year. Program members should then have one year to use certificates, coupons, vouchers or tickets. Any applicable capacity controls should be modified as necessary to meet the demand for all award benefits due program members.

Comment: The airlines uniformly take the position that because participation in travel reward programs is "free," an airline should be able to terminate a travel reward program at any time without notice. NAAG strenuously disagrees. Consumers pay significant consideration for the airlines' promise to award them "free tickets" and other awards. Program members fly on a particular airline to accrue mileage in a travel reward program often foregoing a more convenient departure time, a more direct flight, and even a less expensive ticket. Those consumers who kept their part of the bargain have a right to expect the airlines to keep theirs, regardless of the cost. This Guideline affords consumers reasonable protection against unilateral changes. It gives consumers one year to accrue the mileage to reach a desired award level and one year to use the award.

This Guideline is intended to apply to programs that are terminated due to mergers or for any other reason. It would be unconscionable to permit airlines, which have reaped the rewards of these travel incentive programs, to walk away from their obligations to consumers under any circumstances.

3.8 Restrictions

All material restrictions on frequent flyer programs must be clearly and conspicuously disclosed to current program members and to prospective members at the time of enrollment.

Comment: This Guideline is intended as a corrective measure. Any airline that has not clearly and conspicuously disclosed material program restrictions to vested members should do so now. New members are entitled to full disclosure at the time of enrollment.

3.9 Method of disclosure

Disclosures referred to in these Guidelines should be made in frequent flyer program solicitations, newsletters, rules, and other bulletins in a clear and conspicuous manner so as to assure that all program members receive adequate notice. As used in these Guidelines, disclosure also refers to information on program partners.

Comment: The brochures containing the rules and regulations for airlines' frequent flyer programs have been as long as 52 pages. Extremely important restrictions are often buried under inappropriate topic headings or hidden on the back of the last inside pages of the brochure. This Guideline requires that restrictions be disclosed in reasonable print size in a location that will be most helpful and informative to consumers.

Any reservation of the right to make future changes in a program is so significant to consumers that it should be disclosed prominently to insure that the maximum number of people see and read this restriction. The Guideline permits the airlines flexibility to determine when and how often a disclosure must be made so long as the airline discloses the information in a manner which gives meaningful notice to all affected members.

One airline complained that Guideline 3.9 is unreasonable because it proposes that all the restrictions be disclosed at the beginning of the program brochure. In fact, the only disclosure the Guidelines suggested listing at the beginning of a brochure is the reservation of the right to change the program prospectively. The significance of such a restriction—that the terms and conditions of the program can change at any moment—is so critical that potential members should be made aware of it immediately. All other disclosures can be made in the text of the brochure.

Section 4—Compensation for Voluntary Denied Boarding

4.0 Disclosure of policies

If an airline chooses to offer ticketed passengers incentives to surrender their tickets on overbooked flights, the airline must clearly and conspicuously disclose all terms and conditions of the proposal—including any restrictions on offers of future air travel—to the person to whom the

offer is made, and in the same manner in which the offer is made, before the person accepts the offer.

Comment: Federal regulations offer specific protections and certain rights to individuals who are involuntarily bumped from a flight. Airlines, however, are free to offer whatever compensation they want to people who voluntarily give up their seat on an airplane because of overbooking. For economic reasons, airlines prefer to offer vouchers good for free tickets on future flights, instead of cash compensation to these passengers. While these vouchers may seem very attractive to a consumer who has the flexibility to wait for a later flight, many carry serious restrictions on their use or are subject to lengthy blackout periods when they cannot be used.

This Guideline requires that airlines fully disclose any and all restrictions on offers for future air travel, before a consumer agrees to give up his or her seat. It does not, as several airlines and government agencies argued in their responsive comments, set any standards for the type of compensation that airlines must offer to these passengers.

CONCLUSION

Consumer dissatisfaction with the airline industry has reached crisis proportions. Federal agencies have focused their attention on airline scheduling problems, on-time performance, safety, and other related issues, but have not addressed airline advertising and frequent flyer programs. Unchecked, the airlines have engaged in practices in these areas that are unfair and deceptive under state law. The individual states through NAAG can play an important role in eliminating such practices through these Guidelines.

Convention on International Civil Aviation ("Chicago Convention")

CONVENTION

ON

INTERNATIONAL

CIVIL AVIATION

DONE

AT CHICAGO

ON THE

7TH DAY OF DECEMBER

1944

CONVENTION ON INTERNATIONAL CIVIL AVIATION

PREAMBLE

WHEREAS the future development of international civil aviation can greatly help to create and preserve friendship and understanding among the nations and peoples of the world, yet its abuse can become a threat to the general security; and

WHEREAS it is desirable to avoid friction and to promote that cooperation between nations and peoples upon which the peace of the world depends;

THEREFORE, the undersigned governments having agreed on certain principles and arrangements in order that international civil aviation may be developed in a safe and orderly manner and that international air transport services may be established on the basis of equality of opportunity and operated soundly and economically;

Have accordingly concluded this Convention to that end.

PART I. AIR NAVIGATION

CHAPTER I
GENERAL PRINCIPLES AND APPLICATION OF THE CONVENTION
Article 1

Sovereignty   The contracting States recognize that every State has complete and exclusive sovereignty over the airspace above its territory.

Article 2

Territory   For the purposes of this Convention the territory of a State shall be deemed to be the land areas and

territorial waters adjacent thereto under the sovereignty, suzerainty, protection or mandate of such State.

Article 3

Civil and state air-craft

(a) This Convention shall be applicable only to
civil aircraft, and shall not be applicable to state
aircraft.

(b) Aircraft used in military, customs and police
services shall be deemed to be state aircraft.

(c) No state aircraft of a contracting State
shall fly over the territory of another State or land
thereon without authorization by special agreement or
otherwise, and in accordance with the terms thereof.

(d) The contracting States undertake, when issuing regulations for their state aircraft, that they
will have due regard for the safety of navigation of
civil aircraft.

Article 4

Misuse of civil aviation

Each contracting State agrees not to use civil
aviation for any purpose inconsistent with the aims of
this Convention.

CHAPTER II

FLIGHT OVER TERRITORY OF CONTRACTING STATES

Article 5

Right of non-scheduled flight

Each contracting State agrees that all aircraft
of the other contracting States, being aircraft not
engaged in scheduled international air services shall
have the right, subject to the observance of the terms
of this Convention, to make flights into or in transit
non-stop across its territory and to make stops for

non-traffic purposes without the necessity of obtaining prior permission, and subject to the right of the
State flown over to require landing. Each contracting
State nevertheless reserves the right, for reasons of
safety of flight, to require aircraft desiring to proceed over regions which are inaccessible or without
adequate air navigation facilities to follow prescribed
routes, or to obtain special permission for such
flights.

Such aircraft, if engaged in the carriage of passengers, cargo, or mail for remuneration or hire on
other than scheduled international air services, shall
also, subject to the provisions of Article 7, have the
privilege of taking on or discharging passengers,
cargo, or mail, subject to the right of any State
where such embarkation or discharge takes place to
impose such regulations, conditions or limitations as
it may consider desirable.

Article 6

Scheduled
air services
No scheduled international air service may be
operated over or into the territory of a contracting
State, except with the special permission or other
authorization of that State, and in accordance with
the terms of such permission or authorization.

Article 7

Cabotage
Each contracting State shall have the right to
refuse permission to the aircraft of other contracting States to take on in its territory passengers,
mail and cargo carried for remuneration or hire and

destined for another point within its territory. Each contracting State undertakes not to enter into any arrangements which specifically grant any such privilege on an exclusive basis to any other State or an airline of any other State, and not to obtain any such exclusive privilege from any other State.

Article 8

Pilotless
aircraft

No aircraft capable of being flown without a pilot shall be flown without a pilot over the territory of a contracting State without special authorization by that State and in accordance with the terms of such authorization. Each contracting State undertakes to insure that the flight of such aircraft without a pilot in regions open to civil aircraft shall be so controlled as to obviate danger to civil aircraft.

Article 9

Prohibited
areas

(a) Each contracting State may, for reasons of military necessity or public safety, restrict or prohibit uniformly the aircraft of other States from flying over certain areas of its territory, provided that no distinction in this respect is made between the aircraft of the State whose territory is involved, engaged in international scheduled airline services, and the aircraft of the other contracting States likewise engaged. Such prohibited areas shall be of reasonable extent and location so as not to interfere unnecessarily with air navigation. Descriptions of such prohibited areas in the territory of a contracting State, as well as any subsequent alterations

therein, shall be communicated as soon as possible to
the other contracting States and to the International
Civil Aviation Organization.

(b) Each contracting State reserves also the
right, in exceptional circumstances or during a period
of emergency, or in the interest of public safety, and
with immediate effect, temporarily to restrict or prohibit flying over the whole or any part of its territory, on condition that such restriction or prohibition
shall be applicable without distinction of nationality
to aircraft of all other States.

(c) Each contracting State, under such regulations as it may prescribe, may require any aircraft
entering the areas contemplated in subparagraphs (a)
or (b) above to effect a landing as soon as practicable thereafter at some designated airport within its
territory.

Article 10

Landing at
customs
airport

Except in a case where, under the terms of this
Convention or a special authorization, aircraft are
permitted to cross the territory of a contracting State
without landing, every aircraft which enters the territory of a contracting State shall, if the regulations
of that State so require, land at an airport designated
by that State for the purpose of customs and other
examination. On departure from the territory of a
contracting State, such aircraft shall depart from a
similarly designated customs airport. Particulars
of all designated customs airports shall be published

by the State and transmitted to the International
Civil Aviation Organization established under Part II
of this Convention for communication to all other contracting States.

Article 11

Applicability
of air regu-
lations

Subject to the provisions of this Convention, the
laws and regulations of a contracting State relating
to the admission to or departure from its territory of
aircraft engaged in international air navigation, or
to the operation and navigation of such aircraft while
within its territory, shall be applied to the aircraft
of all contracting States without distinction as to
nationality, and shall be complied with by such aircraft upon entering or departing from or while within
the territory of that State.

Article 12

Rules of the
air

Each contracting State undertakes to adopt measures to insure that every aircraft flying over or
maneuvering within its territory and that every aircraft carrying its nationality mark, wherever such aircraft may be, shall comply with the rules and regulations relating to the flight and maneuver of aircraft
there in force. Each contracting State undertakes to
keep its own regulations in these respects uniform, to
the greatest possible extent, with those established
from time to time under this Convention. Over the
high seas, the rules in force shall be those established under this Convention. Each contracting State

undertakes to insure the prosecution of all persons
violating the regulations applicable.

Article 13

Entry and
clearance
regulations
The laws and regulations of a contracting State
as to the admission to or departure from its territory of passengers, crew or cargo of aircraft, such
as regulations relating to entry, clearance, immigration, passports, customs, and quarantine shall be
complied with by or on behalf of such passengers,
crew or cargo upon entrance into or departure from,
or while within the territory of that State.

Article 14

Prevention of
spread of
disease
Each contracting State agrees to take effective
measures to prevent the spread by means of air navigation of cholera, typhus (epidemic), smallpox, yellow
fever, plague, and such other communicable diseases
as the contracting States shall from time to time
decide to designate, and to that end contracting
States will keep in close consultation with the agencies concerned with international regulations relating to sanitary measures applicable to aircraft.
Such consultation shall be without prejudice to the
application of any existing international convention
on this subject to which the contracting States may
be parties.

Article 15

Airport and
similar
charges
Every airport in a contracting State which is
open to public use by its national aircraft shall
likewise, subject to the provisions of Article 68,

be open under uniform conditions to the aircraft of
all the other contracting States. The like uniform
conditions shall apply to the use, by aircraft of
every contracting State, of all air navigation facilities, including radio and meteorological services,
which may be provided for public use for the safety
and expedition of air navigation.

Any charges that may be imposed or permitted to
be imposed by a contracting State for the use of such
airports and air navigation facilities by the aircraft
of any other contracting State shall not be higher,

(a) As to aircraft not engaged in scheduled international air services, than those that
would be paid by its national aircraft of the
same class engaged in similar operations, and

(b) As to aircraft engaged in scheduled
international air services, than those that would
be paid by its national aircraft engaged in similar international air services.

All such charges shall be published and communicated
to the International Civil Aviation Organization:
provided that, upon representation by an interested
contracting State, the charges imposed for the use of
airports and other facilities shall be subject to
review by the Council, which shall report and make
recommendations thereon for the consideration of the
State or States concerned. No fees, dues or other
charges shall be imposed by any contracting State in
respect solely of the right of transit over or entry

into or exit from its territory of any aircraft of a contracting State or persons or property thereon.

Article 16

Search of aircraft

The appropriate authorities of each of the contracting States shall have the right, without unreasonable delay, to search aircraft of the other contracting States on landing or departure, and to inspect the certificates and other documents prescribed by this Convention.

CHAPTER III
NATIONALITY OF AIRCRAFT
Article 17

Nationality of aircraft

Aircraft have the nationality of the State in which they are registered.

Article 18

Dual registration

An aircraft cannot be validly registered in more than one State, but its registration may be changed from one State to another.

Article 19

National laws governing registration

The registration or transfer of registration of aircraft in any contracting State shall be made in accordance with its laws and regulations.

Article 20

Display of marks

Every aircraft engaged in international air navigation shall bear its appropriate nationality and registration marks.

Article 21

Report of registrations

Each contracting State undertakes to supply to any other contracting State or to the International Civil Aviation Organization, on demand, information concerning the registration and ownership of any particular aircraft registered in that State. In addition, each contracting State shall furnish reports to the International Civil Aviation Organization, under such regulations as the latter may prescribe, giving such pertinent data as can be made available concerning the ownership and control of aircraft registered in that State and habitually engaged in international air navigation. The data thus obtained by the International Civil Aviation Organization shall be made available by it on request to the other contracting States.

CHAPTER IV
MEASURES TO FACILITATE AIR NAVIGATION
Article 22

Facilitation of formalities

Each contracting State agrees to adopt all practicable measures, through the issuance of special regulations or otherwise, to facilitate and expedite navigation by aircraft between the territories of contracting States, and to prevent unnecessary delays to aircraft, crews, passengers and cargo, especially in the administration of the laws relating to immigration, quarantine, customs and clearance.

Article 23

Customs and immigration procedures

Each contracting State undertakes, so far as it may find practicable, to establish customs and

immigration procedures affecting international air
navigation in accordance with the practices which may
be established or recommended from time to time, pursuant to this Convention. Nothing in this Convention
shall be construed as preventing the establishment of
customs-free airports.

Article 24

Customs
duty

(a) Aircraft on a flight to, from, or across
the territory of another contracting State shall be
admitted temporarily free of duty, subject to the
customs regulations of the State. Fuel, lubricating
oils, spare parts, regular equipment and aircraft
stores on board an aircraft of a contracting State,
on arrival in the territory of another contracting
State and retained on board on leaving the territory
of that State shall be exempt from customs duty,
inspection fees or similar national or local duties
and charges. This exemption shall not apply to any
quantities or articles unloaded, except in accordance
with the customs regulations of the State, which may
require that they shall be kept under customs supervision.

(b) Spare parts and equipment imported into the
territory of a contracting State for incorporation in
or use on an aircraft of another contracting State
engaged in international air navigation shall be
admitted free of customs duty, subject to compliance
with the regulations of the State concerned, which
may provide that the articles shall be kept under
customs supervision and control.

Article 25

Aircraft in
distress

Each contracting State undertakes to provide such
measures of assistance to aircraft in distress in its
territory as it may find practicable, and to permit,
subject to control by its own authorities, the owners
of the aircraft or authorities of the State in which
the aircraft is registered to provide such measures
of assistance as may be necessitated by the circumstances. Each contracting State, when undertaking
search for missing aircraft, will collaborate in
coordinated measures which may be recommended from
time to time pursuant to this Convention.

Article 26

Investigation
of accidents

In the event of an accident to an aircraft of a
contracting State occurring in the territory of another contracting State, and involving death or serious
injury, or indicating serious technical defect in the
aircraft or air navigation facilities, the State in
which the accident occurs will institute an inquiry
into the circumstances of the accident, in accordance,
so far as its laws permit, with the procedure which
may be recommended by the International Civil Aviation
Organization. The State in which the aircraft is
registered shall be given the opportunity to appoint
observers to be present at the inquiry and the State
holding the inquiry shall communicate the report and
findings in the matter to that State.

Article 27

Exemption
from
seizure
on patent
claims

(a) While engaged in international air navigation, any authorized entry of aircraft of a contracting State into the territory of another contracting
State or authorized transit across the territory of
such State with or without landings shall not entail
any seizure or detention of the aircraft or any
claim against the owner or operator thereof or any
other interference therewith by or on behalf of such
State or any person therein, on the ground that the
construction, mechanism, parts, accessories or operation of the aircraft is an infringement of any patent,
design, or model duly granted or registered in the
State whose territory is entered by the aircraft, it
being agreed that no deposit of security in connection
with the foregoing exemption from seizure or detention of the aircraft shall in any case be required in
the State entered by such aircraft.

(b) The provisions of paragraph (a) of this
Article shall also be applicable to the storage of
spare parts and spare equipment for the aircraft and
the right to use and install the same in the repair
of an aircraft of a contracting State in the territory of any other contracting State, provided that
any patented part or equipment so stored shall not be
sold or distributed internally in or exported commercially from the contracting State entered by the
aircraft.

(c) The benefits of this Article shall apply
only to such States, parties to this Convention, as
either (1) are parties to the International Convention
for the Protection of Industrial Property and to any
amendments thereof; or (2) have enacted patent laws
which recognize and give adequate protection to
inventions made by the nationals of the other States
parties to this Convention.

Article 28

Air navigation
facilities
and standard
systems

Each contracting State undertakes, so far as
it may find practicable, to:

(a) Provide, in its territory, airports,
radio services, meteorological services and
other air navigation facilities to facilitate
international air navigation, in accordance
with the standards and practices recommended
or established from time to time, pursuant to
this Convention;

(b) Adopt and put into operation the appropriate standard systems of communications
procedure, codes, markings, signals, lighting
and other operational practices and rules which
may be recommended or established from time to
time, pursuant to this Convention;

(c) Collaborate in international measures to secure the publication of aeronautical
maps and charts in accordance with standards
which may be recommended or established from
time to time, pursuant to this Convention.

CHAPTER V

CONDITIONS TO BE FULFILLED WITH RESPECT TO AIRCRAFT

Article 29

Documents
carried in
aircraft

Every aircraft of a contracting State, engaged in international navigation, shall carry the following documents in conformity with the conditions prescribed in this Convention:

(a) Its certificate of registration;

(b) Its certificate of airworthiness;

(c) The appropriate licenses for each member of the crew;

(d) Its journey log book;

(e) If it is equipped with radio apparatus, the aircraft radio station license;

(f) If it carries passengers, a list of their names and places of embarkation and destination;

(g) If it carries cargo, a manifest and detailed declarations of the cargo.

Article 30

Aircraft
radio
equipment

(a) Aircraft of each contracting State may, in or over the territory of other contracting States, carry radio transmitting apparatus only if a license to install and operate such apparatus has been issued by the appropriate authorities of the State in which the aircraft is registered. The use of radio transmitting apparatus in the territory of the contracting State whose territory is flown over shall be in accordance with the regulations prescribed by that State.

(b) Radio transmitting apparatus may be used
only by members of the flight crew who are provided
with a special license for the purpose, issued by
the appropriate authorities of the State in which
the aircraft is registered.

Article 31

Certificates
of airworthi-
ness

Every aircraft engaged in international navigation shall be provided with a certificate of airworthiness issued or rendered valid by the State in
which it is registered.

Article 32

Licenses of
personnel

(a) The pilot of every aircraft and the other
members of the operating crew of every aircraft
engaged in international navigation shall be provided
with certificates of competency and licenses issued
or rendered valid by the State in which the aircraft
is registered.

(b) Each contracting State reserves the right
to refuse to recognize, for the purpose of flight
above its own territory, certificates of competency
and licenses granted to any of its nationals by
another contracting State.

Article 33

Recognition
of certifi-
cates and
licenses

Certificates of airworthiness and certificates
of competency and licenses issued or rendered valid
by the contracting State in which the aircraft is
registered, shall be recognized as valid by the
other contracting States, provided that the

requirements under which such certificates or licenses
were issued or rendered valid are equal to or above
the minimum standards which may be established from
time to time pursuant to this Convention.

Article 34

Journey
log books

There shall be maintained in respect of every
aircraft engaged in international navigation a journey log book in which shall be entered particulars of
the aircraft, its crew and of each journey, in such
form as may be prescribed from time to time pursuant
to this Convention.

Article 35

Cargo
restrictions

(a) No munitions of war or implements of war may
be carried in or above the territory of a State in
aircraft engaged in international navigation, except
by permission of such State. Each State shall determine by regulations what constitutes munitions of war
or implements of war for the purposes of this Article,
giving due consideration, for the purposes of uniformity, to such recommendations as the International
Civil Aviation Organization may from time to time
make.

(b) Each contracting State reserves the right,
for reasons of public order and safety, to regulate
or prohibit the carriage in or above its territory
of articles other than those enumerated in paragraph
(a): provided that no distinction is made in this
respect between its national aircraft engaged in
international navigation and the aircraft of the

other States so engaged; and provided further that
no restriction shall be imposed which may interfere
with the carriage and use on aircraft of apparatus
necessary for the operation or navigation of the aircraft or the safety of the personnel or passengers.

Article 36

Photographic
apparatus

Each contracting State may prohibit or regulate
the use of photographic apparatus in aircraft over
its territory.

CHAPTER VI
INTERNATIONAL STANDARDS AND RECOMMENDED PRACTICES
Article 37

Adoption of
international
standards and
procedures

Each contracting State undertakes to collaborate
in securing the highest practicable degree of uniformity in regulations, standards, procedures, and
organization in relation to aircraft, personnel, airways and auxiliary services in all matters in which
such uniformity will facilitate and improve air
navigation.

To this end the International Civil Aviation
Organization shall adopt and amend from time to time,
as may be necessary, international standards and recommended practices and procedures dealing with:

(a) Communications systems and air navigation aids, including ground marking;

(b) Characteristics of airports and landing areas;

(c) Rules of the air and air traffic
control practices;

(d) Licensing of operating and mechanical personnel;

(e) Airworthiness of aircraft;

(f) Registration and identification of aircraft;

(g) Collection and exchange of meteorological information;

(h) Log books;

(i) Aeronautical maps and charts;

(j) Customs and immigration procedures;

(k) Aircraft in distress and investigation of accidents;

and such other matters concerned with the safety, regularity, and efficiency of air navigation as may from time to time appear appropriate.

Article 38

Departures from international standards and procedures

Any State which finds it impracticable to comply in all respects with any such international standard or procedure, or to bring its own regulations or practices into full accord with any international standard or procedure after amendment of the latter, or which deems it necessary to adopt regulations or practices differing in any particular respect from those established by an international standard, shall give immediate notification to the International Civil Aviation Organization of the differences between its own practice and that established by the international standard. In the case of amendments to international standards, any State which does not make the

appropriate amendments to its own regulations or practices shall give notice to the Council within sixty
days of the adoption of the amendment to the international standard, or indicate the action which it
proposes to take. In any such case, the Council
shall make immediate notification to all other states
of the difference which exists between one or more
features of an international standard and the corresponding national practice of that State.

Article 39

Endorsement
of certifi-
cates and
licenses

(a) Any aircraft or part thereof with respect
to which there exists an international standard of
airworthiness or performance, and which failed in any
respect to satisfy that standard at the time of its
certification, shall have endorsed on or attached
to its airworthiness certificate a complete enumeration of the details in respect of which it so failed.

(b) Any person holding a license who does not
satisfy in full the conditions laid down in the international standard relating to the class of license
or certificate which he holds shall have endorsed on
or attached to his license a complete enumeration of
the particulars in which he does not satisfy such
conditions.

Article 40

Validity of
endorsed
certificates
and licenses

No aircraft or personnel having certificates or
licenses so endorsed shall participate in international navigation, except with the permission of the
State or States whose territory is entered. The

registration or use of any such aircraft, or of any certificated aircraft part, in any State other than that in which it was originally certificated shall be at the discretion of the State into which the aircraft or part is imported.

Article 41

Recognition of existing standards of airworthiness

The provisions of this Chapter shall not apply to aircraft and aircraft equipment of types of which the prototype is submitted to the appropriate national authorities for certification prior to a date three years after the date of adoption of an international standard of airworthiness for such equipment.

Article 42

Recognition of existing standards of competency of personnel

The provisions of this Chapter shall not apply to personnel whose licenses are originally issued prior to a date one year after initial adoption of an international standard of qualification for such personnel; but they shall in any case apply to all personnel whose licenses remain valid five years after the date of adoption of such standard.

PART II. THE INTERNATIONAL CIVIL AVIATION ORGANIZATION

CHAPTER VII

THE ORGANIZATION

Article 43

Name and composition

An organization to be named the International Civil Aviation Organization is formed by the Convention. It is made up of an Assembly, a Council, and such other bodies as may be necessary.

Article 44

Objectives   The aims and objectives of the Organization are
to develop the principles and techniques of international air navigation and to foster the planning
and development of international air transport so as
to:

(a) Insure the safe and orderly growth of
international civil aviation throughout the
world;

(b) Encourage the arts of aircraft design
and operation for peaceful purposes;

(c) Encourage the development of airways,
airports, and air navigation facilities for
international civil aviation;

(d) Meet the needs of the peoples of the
world for safe, regular, efficient and economical
air transport;

(e) Prevent economic waste caused by unreasonable competition;

(f) Insure that the rights of contracting
States are fully respected and that every contracting State has a fair opportunity to operate
international airlines;

(g) Avoid discrimination between contracting States;

(h) Promote safety of flight in international air navigation;

(i) Promote generally the development of
all aspects of international civil aeronautics.

Article 45

Permanent
seat

The permanent seat of the Organization shall be at such place as shall be determined at the final meeting of the Interim Assembly of the Provisional International Civil Aviation Organization set up by the Interim Agreement on International Civil Aviation signed at Chicago on December 7, 1944. The seat may be temporarily transferred elsewhere by decision of the Council.

Article 46

First meet-
ting of
Assembly

The first meeting of the Assembly shall be summoned by the Interim Council of the above-mentioned Provisional Organization as soon as the Convention has come into force, to meet at a time and place to be decided by the Interim Council.

Article 47

Legal
capacity

The Organization shall enjoy in the territory of each contracting State such legal capacity as may be necessary for the performance of its functions. Full juridical personality shall be granted wherever compatible with the constitution and laws of the State concerned.

CHAPTER VIII

THE ASSEMBLY

Article 48

Meetings of
Assembly
and voting

(a) The Assembly shall meet annually and shall be convened by the Council at a suitable time and place. Extraordinary meetings of the Assembly may

be held at any time upon the call of the Council or
at the request of any ten contracting States addressed
to the Secretary General.

(b) All contracting States shall have an equal
right to be represented at the meetings of the
Assembly and each contracting State shall be entitled
to one vote. Delegates representing contracting
States may be assisted by technical advisers who may
participate in the meetings but shall have no vote.

(c) A majority of the contracting States is
required to constitute a quorum for the meetings of
the Assembly. Unless otherwise provided in this
Convention, decisions of the Assembly shall be taken
by a majority of the votes cast.

Article 49

Powers and
duties of
Assembly

The powers and duties of the Assembly shall be
to:

(a) Elect at each meeting its President
and other officers;

(b) Elect the contracting States to be
represented on the Council, in accordance with
the provisions of Chapter IX;

(c) Examine and take appropriate action on
the reports of the Council and decide on any matter referred to it by the Council;

(d) Determine its own rules of procedure
and establish such subsidiary commissions as it
may consider to be necessary or desirable;

(e) Vote an annual budget and determine the financial arrangements of the Organization, in accordance with the provisions of Chapter XII;

(f) Review expenditures and approve the accounts of the Organization;

(g) Refer, at its discretion, to the Council, to subsidiary commissions, or to any other body any matter within its sphere of action;

(h) Delegate to the Council the powers and authority necessary or desirable for the discharge of the duties of the Organization and revoke or modify the delegations of authority at any time;

(i) Carry out the appropriate provisions of Chapter XIII;

(j) Consider proposals for the modification or amendment of the provisions of this Convention and, if it approves of the proposals, recommend them to the contracting States in accordance with the provisions of Chapter XXI;

(k) Deal with any matter within the sphere of action of the Organization not specifically assigned to the Council.

CHAPTER IX

THE COUNCIL

Article 50

Composition and election of Council

(a) The Council shall be a permanent body responsible to the Assembly. It shall be composed of twenty-one contracting States elected by the Assembly. An

election shall be held at the first meeting of the
Assembly and thereafter every three years, and the members of the Council so elected shall hold office until
the next following election.

(b) In electing the members of the Council, the
Assembly shall give adequate representation to (1) the
States of chief importance in air transport; (2) the
States not otherwise included which make the largest
contribution to the provision of facilities for international civil air navigation; and (3) the States not
otherwise included whose designation will insure that
all the major geographic areas of the world are represented on the Council. Any vacancy on the Council
shall be filled by the Assembly as soon as possible;
any contracting State so elected to the Council shall
hold office for the unexpired portion of its predecessor's term of office.

(c) No representative of a contracting State on
the Council shall be actively associated with the
operation of an international air service or financially interested in such a service.

Article 51

President
of Council

The Council shall elect its President for a term
of three years. He may be reelected. He shall have
no vote. The Council shall elect from among its members one or more Vice Presidents who shall retain their
right to vote when serving as acting President. The
President need not be selected from among the representatives of the members of the Council but, if a

representative is elected, his seat shall be deemed
vacant and it shall be filled by the State which he
represented. The duties of the President shall be
to:

> (a) Convene meetings of the Council, the
> Air Transport Committee, and the Air Navigation
> Commission;
>
> (b) Serve as representative of the
> Council; and
>
> (c) Carry out on behalf of the Council the
> functions which the Council assigns to him.

Article 52

Voting in
Council

Decisions by the Council shall require approval
by a majority of its members. The Council may delegate authority with respect to any particular matter
to a committee of its members. Decisions of any committee of the Council may be appealed to the Council
by any interested contracting State.

Article 53

Participation
without a
vote

Any contracting State may participate, without
a vote, in the consideration by the Council and by
its committees and commissions of any question which
especially affects its interests. No member of the
Council shall vote in the consideration by the Council
of a dispute to which it is a party.

Article 54

Mandatory
functions
of Council

The Council shall:

> (a) Submit annual reports to the Assembly;

(b) Carry out the directions of the Assembly and discharge the duties and obligations which are laid on it by this Convention;

(c) Determine its organization and rules of procedure;

(d) Appoint and define the duties of an Air Transport Committee, which shall be chosen from among the representatives of the members of the Council, and which shall be responsible to it;

(e) Establish an Air Navigation Commission, in accordance with the provisions of Chapter X;

(f) Administer the finances of the Organization in accordance with the provisions of Chapters XII and XV;

(g) Determine the emoluments of the President of the Council;

(h) Appoint a chief executive officer who shall be called the Secretary General, and make provision for the appointment of such other personnel as may be necessary, in accordance with the provisions of Chapter XI;

(i) Request, collect, examine and publish information relating to the advancement of air navigation and the operation of international air services, including information about the costs of operation and particulars of subsidies paid to airlines from public funds;

(j) Report to contracting States any infraction of this Convention, as well as any failure to carry out recommendations or determinations of the Council;

(k) Report to the Assembly any infraction of this Convention where a contracting State has failed to take appropriate action within a reasonable time after notice of the infraction;

(l) Adopt, in accordance with the provisions of Chapter VI of this Convention, international standards and recommended practices; for convenience, designate them as Annexes to this Convention; and notify all contracting States of the action taken;

(m) Consider recommendations of the Air Navigation Commission for amendment of the Annexes and take action in accordance with the provisions of Chapter XX;

(n) Consider any matter relating to the Convention which any contracting State refers to it.

Article 55

The Council may:

Permissive functions of Council

(a) Where appropriate and as experience may show to be desirable, create subordinate air transport commissions on a regional or other basis and define groups of states or airlines with or through which it may deal to facilitate the carrying out of the aims of this Convention;

(b) Delegate to the Air Navigation Commission duties additional to those set forth in the Convention and revoke or modify such delegations of authority at any time;

(c)   Conduct research into all aspects of air transport and air navigation which are of international importance, communicate the results of its research to the contracting States, and facilitate the exchange of information between contracting States on air transport and air navigation matters;

(d)   Study any matters affecting the organization and operation of international air transport, including the international ownership and operation of international air services on trunk routes, and submit to the Assembly plans in relation thereto;

(e)   Investigate, at the request of any contracting State, any situation which may appear to present avoidable obstacles to the development of international air navigation; and, after such investigation, issue such reports as may appear to it desirable.

CHAPTER X
THE AIR NAVIGATION COMMISSION
Article 56

Nomination and appointment of Commission

The Air Navigation Commission shall be composed of twelve members appointed by the Council from among persons nominated by contracting States. These persons shall have suitable qualifications and experience in the science and practice of aeronautics. The Council shall request all contracting States to submit nominations. The President of the Air Navigation Commission shall be appointed by the Council.

Article 57

Duties of Commission

The Air Navigation Commission shall:

(a) Consider, and recommend to the Council for adoption, modifications of the Annexes to this Convention;

(b) Establish technical subcommissions on which any contracting State may be represented, if it so desires;

(c) Advise the Council concerning the collection and communication to the contracting States of all information which it considers necessary and useful for the advancement of air navigation.

CHAPTER XI
PERSONNEL

Article 58

Appointment of personnel

Subject to any rules laid down by the Assembly and to the provisions of this Convention, the Council shall determine the method of appointment and of termination of appointment, the training, and the salaries, allowances, and conditions of service of tne Secretary General and other personnel of the Organization, and may employ or make use of the services of nationals of any contracting State.

Article 59

International character of personnel

The President of the Council, the Secretary General, and other personnel shall not seek or receive instructions in regard to the discharge of their responsibilities from any authority external to the

Organization. Each contracting State undertakes
fully to respect the international character of the
responsibilities of the personnel and not to seek to
influence any of its nationals in the discharge of
their responsibilities.

Article 60

**Immunities
and priv-
ileges of
personnel**

Each contracting State undertakes, so far as
possible under its constitutional procedure, to accord
to the President of the Council, the Secretary
General, and the other personnel of the Organization,
the immunities and privileges which are accorded to
corresponding personnel of other public international
organizations. If a general international agreement
on the immunities and privileges of international
civil servants is arrived at, the immunities and
privileges accorded to the President, the Secretary
General, and the other personnel of the Organization
shall be the immunities and privileges accorded under
that general international agreement.

CHAPTER XII
FINANCE
Article 61

**Budget and
apportion-
ment of
expenses**

The Council shall submit to the Assembly an
annual budget, annual statements of accounts and
estimates of all receipts and expenditures. The
Assembly shall vote the budget with whatever modification it sees fit to prescribe, and, with the
exception of assessments under Chapter XV to States
consenting thereto, shall apportion the expenses

of the Organization among the contracting States on the basis which it shall from time to time determine.

Article 62

Suspension
of voting
power

The Assembly may suspend the voting power in the Assembly and in the Council of any contracting State that fails to discharge within a reasonable period its financial obligations to the Organization.

Article 63

Expenses of
delegations
and other
repre-
sentatives

Each contracting State shall bear the expenses of its own delegation to the Assembly and the remuneration, travel, and other expenses of any person whom it appoints to serve on the Council, and of its nominees or representatives on any subsidiary committees or commissions of the Organization.

CHAPTER XIII

OTHER INTERNATIONAL ARRANGEMENTS

Article 64

Security
arrange-
ments

The Organization may, with respect to air matters within its competence directly affecting world security, by vote of the Assembly enter into appropriate arrangements with any general organization set up by the nations of the world to preserve peace.

Article 65

Arrangements
with other
inter-
national
bodies

The Council, on behalf of the Organization, may enter into agreements with other international bodies for the maintenance of common services and for common arrangements concerning personnel and, with the approval of the Assembly, may enter into such other arrangements as may facilitate the work of the Organization.

Article 66

Functions relating to other agreements

(a) The Organization shall also carry out the functions placed upon it by the International Air Services Transit Agreement and by the International Air Transport Agreement drawn up at Chicago on December 7, 1944, in accordance with the terms and conditions therein set forth.

(b) Members of the Assembly and the Council who have not accepted the International Air Services Transit Agreement or the International Air Transport Agreement drawn up at Chicago on December 7, 1944 shall not have the right to vote on any questions referred to the Assembly or Council under the provisions of the relevant Agreement.

PART III.   INTERNATIONAL AIR TRANSPORT

CHAPTER XIV
INFORMATION AND REPORTS
Article 67

File reports with Council

Each contracting State undertakes that its international airlines shall, in accordance with requirements laid down by the Council, file with the Council traffic reports, cost statistics and financial statements showing among other things all receipts and the sources thereof.

CHAPTER XV

AIRPORTS AND OTHER AIR NAVIGATION FACILITIES

Article 68

Designation
of routes
and airports

Each contracting State may, subject to the provisions of this Convention, designate the route to be followed within its territory by any international air service and the airports which any such service may use.

Article 69

Improvement
of air
navigation
facilities

If the Council is of the opinion that the airports or other air navigation facilities, including radio and meteorological services, of a contracting State are not reasonably adequate for the safe, regular, efficient, and economical operation of international air services, present or contemplated, the Council shall consult with the State directly concerned, and other States affected, with a view to finding means by which the situation may be remedied, and may make recommendations for that purpose. No contracting State shall be guilty of an infraction of this Convention if it fails to carry out these recommendations.

Article 70

Financing of
air naviga-
tion facili-
ties

A contracting State, in the circumstances arising under the provisions of Article 69, may conclude an arrangement with the Council for giving effect to such recommendations. The State may elect to bear all of the costs involved in any such arrangement.

If the State does not so elect, the Council may
agree, at the request of the State, to provide for
all or a portion of the costs.

Article 71

Provision
and main-
tenance of
facilities
by Council

If a contracting State so requests, the
Council may agree to provide, man, maintain, and
administer any or all of the airports and other air
navigation facilities, including radio and meteorological services, required in its territory for the
safe, regular, efficient and economical operation
of the international air services of the other
contracting States, and may specify just and reasonable charges for the use of the facilities provided.

Article 72

Acquisition
or use
of land

Where land is needed for facilities financed in
whole or in part by the Council at the request of
a contracting State, that State shall either provide the land itself, retaining title if it wishes,
or facilitate the use of the land by the Council on
just and reasonable terms and in accordance with
the laws of the State concerned.

Article 73

Expenditure
and assess-
ment of
funds

Within the limit of the funds which may be
made available to it by the Assembly under Chapter
XII, the Council may make current expenditures for
the purposes of this Chapter from the general funds
of the Organization. The Council shall assess the

capital funds required for the purposes of this
Chapter in previously agreed proportions over a reasonable period of time to the contracting States
consenting thereto whose airlines use the facilities.
The Council may also assess to States that consent
any working funds that are required.

Article 74

Technical
assistance
and utili-
zation of
revenues

When the Council, at the request of a contracting State, advances funds or provides airports or
other facilities in whole or in part, the arrangement may provide, with the consent of that State, for
technical assistance in the supervision and operation
of the airports and other facilities, and for the
payment, from the revenues derived from the operation
of the airports and other facilities, of the operating expenses of the airports and the other facilities,
and of interest and amortization charges.

Article 75

Taking over
of facili-
ties from
Council

A contracting State may at any time discharge
any obligation into which it has entered under
Article 70, and take over airports and other facilities which the Council has provided in its territory pursuant to the provisions of Articles 71 and
72, by paying to the Council an amount which in the
opinion of the Council is reasonable in the circumstances. If the State considers that the amount
fixed by the Council is unreasonable it may appeal
to the Assembly against the decision of the Council

and the Assembly may confirm or amend the decision
of the Council.

Article 76

Return
of
funds

Funds obtained by the Council through reimbursement under Article 75 and from receipts of
interest and amortization payments under Article 74
shall, in the case of advances originally financed
by States under Article 73, be returned to the
States which were originally assessed in the proportion of their assessments, as determined by the
Council.

CHAPTER XVI

JOINT OPERATING ORGANIZATIONS AND POOLED SERVICES

Article 77

Joint oper-
ating organ-
izations
permitted

Nothing in this Convention shall prevent two
or more contracting States from constituting joint
air transport operating organizations or international operating agencies and from pooling their air
services on any routes or in any regions, but such
organizations or agencies and such pooled services
shall be subject to all the provisions of this
Convention, including those relating to the registration of agreements with the Council. The Council
shall determine in what manner the provisions of
this Convention relating to nationality of aircraft
shall apply to aircraft operated by international
operating agencies.

Article 78

Function of
Council

The Council may suggest to contracting States concerned that they form joint organizations to operate air services on any routes or in any regions.

Article 79

Partici-
pation in
operating
organiza-
tions

A State may participate in joint operating organizations or in pooling arrangements, either through its government or through an airline company or companies designated by its government. The companies may, at the sole discretion of the State concerned, be state-owned or partly state-owned or privately owned.

PART IV. FINAL PROVISIONS

CHAPTER XVII
OTHER AERONAUTICAL AGREEMENTS AND ARRANGEMENTS

Article 80

Paris and
Habana
Conventions

Each contracting State undertakes, immediately upon the coming into force of this Convention, to give notice of denunciation of the Convention relating to the Regulation of Aerial Navigation signed at Paris on October 13, 1919 or the Convention on Commercial Aviation signed at Habana on February 20, 1928, if it is a party to either. As between contracting States, this Convention supersedes the Conventions of Paris and Habana previously referred to.

Article 81

Registration
of existing
agreements

All aeronautical agreements which are in existence on the coming into force of this Convention, and

which are between a contracting State and any other
State or between an airline of a contracting State and
any other State or the airline of any other State,
shall be forthwith registered with the Council.

Article 82

Abrogation
of incon-
sistent
arrangements

The contracting States accept this Convention as
abrogating all obligations and understandings between
them which are inconsistent with its terms, and undertake not to enter into any such obligations and understandings. A contracting State which, before becoming a member of the Organization has undertaken any
obligations toward a non-contracting State or a
national of a contracting State or of a non-contracting
State inconsistent with the terms of this Convention,
shall take immediate steps to procure its release
from the obligations. If an airline of any contracting State has entered into any such inconsistent
obligations, the State of which it is a national shall
use its best efforts to secure their termination forthwith and shall in any event cause them to be terminated as soon as such action can lawfully be taken
after the coming into force of this Convention.

Article 83

Registration
of new
arrangements

Subject to the provisions of the preceding
Article, any contracting State may make arrangements
not inconsistent with the provisions of this Convention. Any such arrangement shall be forthwith
registered with the Council, which shall make it
public as soon as possible.

CHAPTER XVIII

DISPUTES AND DEFAULT

Article 84

Settlement
of disputes

If any disagreement between two or more contracting States relating to the interpretation or application of this Convention and its Annexes cannot be
settled by negotiation, it shall, on the application
of any State concerned in the disagreement, be decided
by the Council. No member of the Council shall vote
in the consideration by the Council of any dispute to
which it is a party. Any contracting State may,
subject to Article 85, appeal from the decision of the
Council to an ad hoc arbitral tribunal agreed upon
with the other parties to the dispute or to the
Permanent Court of International Justice. Any such
appeal shall be notified to the Council within sixty
days of receipt of notification of the decision of
the Council.

Article 85

Arbitration
procedure

If any contracting State party to a dispute in
which the decision of the Council is under appeal has
not accepted the Statute of the Permanent Court of
International Justice and the contracting States
parties to the dispute cannot agree on the choice of
the arbitral tribunal, each of the contracting States
parties to the dispute shall name a single arbitrator
who shall name an umpire. If either contracting
State party to the dispute fails to name an arbitrator
within a period of three months from the date of the
appeal, an arbitrator shall be named on behalf of

that State by the President of the Council from a
list of qualified and available persons maintained by
the Council. If, within thirty days, the arbitrators
cannot agree on an umpire, the President of the
Council shall designate an umpire from the list previously referred to. The arbitrators and the umpire
shall then jointly constitute an arbitral tribunal.
Any arbitral tribunal established under this or the
preceding Article shall settle its own procedure and
give its decisions by majority vote, provided that the
Council may determine procedural questions in the
event of any delay which in the opinion of the Council
is excessive.

Article 86

Appeals

Unless the Council decides otherwise, any decision by the Council on whether an international airline is operating in conformity with the provisions
of this Convention shall remain in effect unless reversed on appeal. On any other matter, decisions of
the Council shall, if appealed from, be suspended
until the appeal is decided. The decisions of the
Permanent Court of International Justice and of an
arbitral tribunal shall be final and binding.

Article 87

Penalty for
non-conform-
ity of air-
line

Each contracting State undertakes not to allow
the operation of an airline of a contracting State
through the airspace above its territory if the
Council has decided that the airline concerned is not
conforming to a final decision rendered in accordance
with the previous Article.

Article 88

Penalty for non-conform-ity by State

The Assembly shall suspend the voting power in the Assembly and in the Council of any contracting State that is found in default under the provisions of this Chapter.

CHAPTER XIX
WAR
Article 89

War and emergency conditions

In case of war, the provisions of this Convention shall not affect the freedom of action of any of the contracting States affected, whether as belligerents or as neutrals. The same principle shall apply in the case of any contracting State which declares a state of national emergency and notifies the fact to the Council.

CHAPTER XX
ANNEXES
Article 90

Adoption and amendment of Annexes

(a) The adoption by the Council of the Annexes described in Article 54, subparagraph (l), shall require the vote of two-thirds of the Council at a meeting called for that purpose and shall then be submitted by the Council to each contracting State. Any such Annex or any amendment of an Annex shall become effective within three months after its submission to the contracting States or at the end of such longer period of time as the Council may prescribe, unless in the meantime a majority of the contracting States register their disapproval with the Council.

(b)   The Council shall immediately notify all contracting States of the coming into force of any Annex or amendment thereto.

CHAPTER XXI

RATIFICATIONS, ADHERENCES, AMENDMENTS, AND DENUNCIATIONS

Article 91

Ratification of Convention

(a)   This Convention shall be subject to ratification by the signatory States.   The instruments of ratification shall be deposited in the archives of the Government of the United States of America, which shall give notice of the date of the deposit to each of the signatory and adhering States.

(b)   As soon as this Convention has been ratified or adhered to by twenty-six States it shall come into force between them on the thirtieth day after deposit of the twenty-sixth instrument.   It shall come into force for each State ratifying thereafter on the thirtieth day after the deposit of its instrument of ratification.

(c)   It shall be the duty of the Government of the United States of America to notify the government of each of the signatory and adhering States of the date on which this Convention comes into force.

Article 92

Adherence to Convention

(a)   This Convention shall be open for adherence by members of the United Nations and States associated with them, and States which remained neutral during the present world conflict.

(b) Adherence shall be effected by a notification addressed to the Government of the United States
of America and shall take effect as from the thirtieth day from the receipt of the notification by the
Government of the United States of America, which
shall notify all the contracting States.

Article 93

Admission of
other States

States other than those provided for in Articles
91 and 92(a) may, subject to approval by any general
international organization set up by the nations of
the world to preserve peace, be admitted to participation in this Convention by means of a four-fifths
vote of the Assembly and on such conditions as the
Assembly may prescribe: provided that in each case
the assent of any State invaded or attacked during
the present war by the State seeking admission shall
be necessary.

Article 94

Amendment
of
Convention

(a) Any proposed amendment to this Convention
must be approved by a two-thirds vote of the Assembly
and shall then come into force in respect of States
which have ratified such amendment when ratified by
the number of contracting States specified by the
Assembly. The number so specified shall not be less
than two-thirds of the total number of contracting
States.

(b) If in its opinion the amendment is of such
a nature as to justify this course, the Assembly in

its resolution recommending adoption may provide that
any State which has not ratified within a specified
period after the amendment has come into force shall
thereupon cease to be a member of the Organization
and a party to the Convention.

Article 95

Denunciation
of
Convention

(a) Any contracting State may give notice of
denunciation of this Convention three years after its
coming into effect by notification addressed to the
Government of the United States of America, which
shall at once inform each of the contracting States.

(b) Denunciation shall take effect one year
from the date of the receipt of the notification and
shall operate only as regards the State effecting the
denunciation.

CHAPTER XXII
DEFINITIONS
Article 96

For the purpose of this Convention the expression:

(a) "Air service" means any scheduled air
service performed by aircraft for the public
transport of passengers, mail or cargo.

(b) "International air service" means an
air service which passes through the air space
over the territory of more than one State.

(c) "Airline" means any air transport
enterprise offering or operating an international air service.

(d)   "Stop for non-traffic purposes" means a landing for any purpose other than taking on or discharging passengers, cargo or mail.

SIGNATURE OF CONVENTION

IN WITNESS WHEREOF, the undersigned plenipotentiaries, having been duly authorized, sign this Convention on behalf of their respective governments on the dates appearing opposite their signatures.

DONE at Chicago the seventh day of December 1944, in the English language. A text drawn up in the English, French, and Spanish languages, each of which shall be of equal authenticity, shall be open for signature at Washington, D. C. Both texts shall be deposited in the archives of the Government of the United States of America, and certified copies shall be transmitted by that Government to the governments of all the States which may sign or adhere to this Convention.

Convention on Offences and Certain Other Acts Committed on Board Aircraft ("Tokyo Convention")

No. 10106

MULTILATERAL

Convention on offences and certain other acts committed on board aircraft. Signed at Tokyo on 14 September 1963

Authentic texts: English, French and Spanish.
Registered by the International Civil Aviation Organization on 22 December 1969.

MULTILATÉRAL

Convention relative aux infractions et à certains autres actes survenant à bord des aéronefs. Signée à Tokyo le 14 septembre 1963

Textes authentiques : anglais, français et espagnol.
Enregistrée par l'Organisation de l'aviation civile internationale le 22 décembre 1969.

CONVENTION [1] ON OFFENCES AND CERTAIN OTHER ACTS COMMITTED ON BOARD AIRCRAFT

The States Parties to this Convention

---

[1] Came into force on 4 December 1969 between the following States, i.e., on the ninetieth day after the date of deposit with the International Civil Aviation Organization of the twelfth instrument of ratification by the said States, in accordance with article 21:

State	Date of deposit of the instrument
Portugal	25 November 1964 [a]
Philippines	26 November 1965
Republic of China	28 February 1966
Denmark	17 January 1967 [b]
Norway	17 January 1967 [c]
Sweden	17 January 1967
Italy	18 October 1968
United Kingdom of Great Britain and Northern Ireland (With a declaration.) [d]	29 November 1968
Mexico	18 March 1969 [e]
Upper Volta	6 June 1969
Niger	27 June 1969 [f]
United States of America	5 September 1969

Subsequently, in accordance with article 21, the Convention came into force for the following State on the ninetieth day after the deposit of its instrument of ratification:

State	Date of deposit of the instrument
Israel	19 September 1969 (With effect from 18 December 1969).

[a] Signature affixed on 11 March 1964: Ed. Brazão.
[b] Signature affixed on 21 November 1966: Mogens Juhl.
[c] Signature affixed on 19 April 1966: Bredo Stabell.
[d] See p. 254 of this volume for the text of the declaration made upon ratification.
[e] Signature affixed on 24 December 1968: José Rodríguez Torres.
[f] Signature affixed on 14 April 1969: Adamou Mayaki.

No. 10106

Have agreed as follows:

CHAPTER I
SCOPE OF THE CONVENTION

Article 1

1. This Convention shall apply in respect of:

(*a*) offences against penal law;

(*b*) acts which, whether or not they are offences, may or do jeopardize the safety of the aircraft or of persons or property therein or which jeopardize good order and discipline on board.

2. Except as provided in Chapter III, this Convention shall apply in respect of offences committed or acts done by a person on board any aircraft registered in a Contracting State, while that aircraft is in flight or on the surface of the high seas or of any other area outside the territory of any State.

3. For the purposes of this Convention, an aircraft is considered to be in flight from the moment when power is applied for the purpose of take-off until the moment when the landing run ends.

4. This Convention shall not apply to aircraft used in military, customs or police services.

Article 2

Without prejudice to the provisions of Article 4 and except when the safety of the aircraft or of persons or property on board so requires, no provision of this Convention shall be interpreted as authorizing or requiring any action in respect of offences against penal laws of a political nature or those based on racial or religious discrimination.

CHAPTER II
JURISDICTION

Article 3

1. The State of registration of the aircraft is competent to exercise jurisdiction over offences and acts committed on board.

No. 10106

2. Each Contracting State shall take such measures as may be necessary to establish its jurisdiction as the State of registration over offences committed on board aircraft registered in such State.

3. This Convention does not exclude any criminal jurisdiction exercised in accordance with national law.

Article 4

A Contracting State which is not the State of registration may not interfere with an aircraft in flight in order to exercise its criminal jurisdiction over an offence committed on board except in the following cases:

(*a*) the offence has effect on the territory of such State;

(*b*) the offence has been committed by or against a national or permanent resident of such State;

(*c*) the offence is against the security of such State;

(*d*) the offence consists of a breach of any rules or regulations relating to the flight or manœuvre of aircraft in force in such State;

(*e*) the exercise of jurisdiction is necessary to ensure the observance of any obligation of such State under a multilateral international agreement.

CHAPTER III
POWERS OF THE AIRCRAFT COMMANDER

Article 5

1. The provisions of this Chapter shall not apply to offences and acts committed or about to be committed by a person on board an aircraft in flight in the airspace of the State of registration or over the high seas or any other area outside the territory of any State unless the last point of take-off or the next point of intended landing is situated in a State other than that of registration, or the aircraft subsequently flies in the airspace of a State other than that of registration with such person still on board.

2. Notwithstanding the provisions of Article 1, paragraph 3, an aircraft shall for the purposes of this Chapter, be considered to be in flight at any

time from the moment when all its external doors are closed following embarkation until the moment when any such door is opened for disembarkation. In the case of a forced landing, the provisions of this Chapter shall continue to apply with respect to offences and acts committed on board until competent authorities of a State take over the responsibility for the aircraft and for the persons and property on board.

Article 6

1. The aircraft commander may, when he has reasonable grounds to believe that a person has committed, or is about to commit, on board the aircraft, an offence or act contemplated in Article 1, paragraph 1, impose upon such person reasonable measures including restraint which are necessary:

(*a*) to protect the safety of the aircraft, or of persons or property therein; or

(*b*) to maintain good order and discipline on board; or

(*c*) to enable him to deliver such person to competent authorities or to disembark him in accordance with the provisions of this Chapter.

2. The aircraft commander may require or authorize the assistance of other crew members and may request or authorize, but not require, the assistance of passengers to restrain any person whom he is entitled to restrain. Any crew member or passenger may also take reasonable preventive measures without such authorization when he has reasonable grounds to believe that such action is immediately necessary to protect the safety of the aircraft, or of persons or property therein.

Article 7

1. Measures of restraint imposed upon a person in accordance with Article 6 shall not be continued beyond any point at which the aircraft lands unless:

(*a*) such point is in the territory of a non-Contracting State and its authorities refuse to permit disembarkation of that person or those measures have been imposed in accordance with Article 6, paragraph 1 (*c*) in order to enable his delivery to competent authorities;

(*b*) the aircraft makes a forced landing and the aircraft commander is unable to deliver that person to competent authorities; or

No. 10106

(c) that person agrees to onward carriage under restraint.

2. The aircraft commander shall as soon as practicable, and if possible before landing in the territory of a State with a person on board who has been placed under restraint in accordance with the provisions of Article 6, notify the authorities of such State of the fact that a person on board is under restraint and of the reasons for such restraint.

Article 8

1. The aircraft commander may, in so far as it is necessary for the purpose of subparagraph (*a*) or (*b*) of paragraph 1 of Article 6, disembark in the territory of any State in which the aircraft lands any person who he has reasonable grounds to believe has committed, or is about to commit, on board the aircraft an act contemplated in Article 1, paragraph 1 (*b*).

2. The aircraft commander shall report to the authorities of the State in which he disembarks any person pursuant to this Article, the fact of, and the reasons for, such disembarkation.

Article 9

1. The aircraft commander may deliver to the competent authorities of any Contracting State in the territory of which the aircraft lands any person who he has reasonable grounds to believe has committed on board the aircraft an act which, in his opinion, is a serious offence according to the penal law of the State of registration of the aircraft.

2. The aircraft commander shall as soon as practicable and if possible before landing in the territory of a Contracting State with a person on board whom the aircraft commander intends to deliver in accordance with the preceding paragraph, notify the authorities of such State of his intention to deliver such person and the reasons therefor.

3. The aircraft commander shall furnish the authorities to whom any suspected offender is delivered in accordance with the provisions of this Article with evidence and information which, under the law of the State of registration of the aircraft, are lawfully in his possession.

Article 10

For actions taken in accordance with this Convention, neither the aircraft commander, any other member of the crew, any passenger, the owner or operator of the aircraft, nor the person on whose behalf the flight was performed shall be held responsible in any proceeding on account of the treatment undergone by the person against whom the actions were taken.

CHAPTER IV
UNLAWFUL SEIZURE OF AIRCRAFT

Article 11

1. When a person on board has unlawfully committed by force or threat thereof an act of interference, seizure, or other wrongful exercise of control of an aircraft in flight or when such an act is about to be committed, Contracting States shall take all appropriate measures to restore control of the aircraft to its lawful commander or to preserve his control of the aircraft.

2. In the cases contemplated in the preceding paragraph, the Contracting State in wich the aircraft lands shall permit its passengers and crew to continue their journey as soon as practicable, and shall return the aircraft and its cargo to the persons lawfully entitled to possession.

CHAPTER V
POWERS AND DUTIES OF STATES

Article 12

Any Contracting State shall allow the commander of an aircraft registered in another Contracting State to disembark any person pursuant to Article 8, paragraph 1.

Article 13

1. Any Contracting State shall take delivery of any person whom the aircraft commander delivers pursuant to Article 9, paragraph 1.

2. Upon being satisfied that the circumstances so warrant, any Contracting State shall take custody or other measures to ensure the presence of any person suspected of an act contemplated in Article 11, paragraph 1 and of any person of whom it has taken delivery. The custody and other

measures shall be as provided in the law of that State but may only be continued for such time as is reasonably necessary to enable any criminal or extradition proceedings to be instituted.

3. Any person in custody pursuant to the previous paragraph shall be assisted in communicating immediately with the nearest appropriate representative of the State of which he is a national.

4. Any Contracting State, to which a person is delivered pursuant to Article 9, paragraph 1, or in whose territory an aircraft lands following the commission of an act contemplated in Article 11, paragraph 1, shall immediately make a preliminary enquiry into the facts.

5. When a State, pursuant to this Article, has taken a person into custody, it shall immediately notify the State of registration of the aircraft and the State of nationality of the detained person and, if it considers it advisable, any other interested State of the fact that such person is in custody and of the circumstances which warrant his detention. The State which makes the preliminary enquiry contemplated in paragraph 4 of this Article shall promptly report its findings to the said States and shall indicate whether it intends to exercise jurisdiction.

Article 14

1. When any person has been disembarked in accordance with Article 8, paragraph 1, or delivered in accordance with Article 9, paragraph 1, or has disembarked after committing an act contemplated in Article 11, paragraph 1, and when such person cannot or does not desire to continue his journey and the State of landing refuses to admit him, that State may, if the person in question is not a national or permanent resident of that State, return him to the territory of the State of which he is a national or permanent resident or to the territory of the State in which he began his journey by air.

2. Neither disembarkation, nor delivery, nor the taking of custody or other measures contemplated in Article 13, paragraphe 2, nor return of the person concerned, shall be considered as admission to the territory of the Contracting State concerned for the purpose of its law relating to entry or admission of persons and nothing in this Convention shall affect the law of a Contracting State relating to the expulsion of persons from its territory.

Article 15

1. Without prejudice to Article 14, any person who has been disembarked in accordance with Article 8, paragraph 1, or delivered in accordance with Article 9, paragraph 1, or has disembarked after committing an act contemplated in Article 11, paragraph 1, and who desires to continue his journey shall be at liberty as soon as practicable to proceed to any destination of his choice unless his presence is required by the law of the State of landing for the purpose of extradition or criminal proceedings.

2. Without prejudice to its law as to entry and admission to, and extradition and expulsion from its territory, a Contracting State in whose territory a person has been disembarked in accordance with Article 8, paragraph 1, or delivered in accordance with Article 9, paragraph 1 or has disembarked and is suspected of having committed an act contemplated in Article 11, paragraph 1, shall accord to such person treatment which is no less favourable for his protection and security than that accorded to nationals of such Contracting State in like circumstances.

CHAPTER VI
OTHER PROVISIONS

Article 16

1. Offences committed on aircraft registered in a Contracting State shall be treated, for the purpose of extradition, as if they had been committed not only in the place in which they have occurred but also in the territory of the State of registration of the aircraft.

2. Without prejudice to the provisions of the preceding paragraph, nothing in this Convention shall be deemed to create an obligation to grant extradition.

Article 17

In taking any measures for investigation or arrest or otherwise exercising jurisdiction in connection with any offence committed on board an aircraft the Contracting States shall pay due regard to the safety and other interests of air navigation and shall so act as to avoid unnecessary delay of the aircraft, passengers, crew or cargo.

Article 18

If Contracting States establish joint air transport operating organizations or international operating agencies, which operate aircraft not registered in any one State those States shall, according to the circumstances of the case, designate the State among them which, for the purposes of this Convention, shall be considered as the State of registration and shall give notice thereof to the International Civil Aviation Organization which shall communicate the notice to all States Parties to this Convention.

CHAPTER VII

FINAL CLAUSES

Article 19

Until the date on which this Convention comes into force in accordance with the provisions of Article 21, it shall remain open for signature on behalf of any State which at that date is a Member of the United Nations or of any of the Specialized Agencies.

Article 20

1. This Convention shall be subject to ratification by the signatory States in accordance with their constitutional procedures.

2. The instruments of ratification shall be deposited with the International Civil Aviation Organization.

Article 21

1. As soon as twelve of the signatory States have deposited their instruments of ratification of this Convention, it shall come into force between them on the ninetieth day after the date of the deposit of the twelfth instrument of ratification. It shall come into force for each State ratifying thereafter on the ninetieth day after the deposit of its instrument of ratification.

2. As soon as this Convention comes into force, it shall be registered with the Secretary-General of the United Nations by the International Civil Aviation Organization.

Article 22

1. This Convention shall, after it has come into force, be open for accession by any State Member of the United Nations or of any of the Specialized Agencies.

2. The accession of a State shall be effected by the deposit of an instrument of accession with the International Civil Aviation Organization and shall take effect on the ninetieth day after the date of such deposit.

Article 23

1. Any Contracting State may denounce this Convention by notification addressed to the International Civil Aviation Organization.

2. Denunciation shall take effect six months after the date of receipt by the International Civil Aviation Organization of the notification of denunciation.

Article 24

1. Any dispute between two or more Contracting States concerning the interpretation or application of this Convention which cannot be settled through negotiation, shall, at the request of one of them, be submitted to arbitration. If within six months from the date of the request for arbitration the Parties are unable to agree on the organization of the arbitration, any one of those Parties may refer the dispute to the International Court of Justice by request in conformity with the Statute of the Court.

2. Each State may at the time of signature or ratification of this Convention or accession thereto, declare that it does not consider itself bound by the preceding paragraph. The other Contracting States shall not be bound by the preceding paragraph with respect to any Contracting State having made such a reservation.

3. Any Contracting State having made a reservation in accordance with the preceding paragraph may at any time withdraw this reservation by notification to the International Civil Aviation Organization.

Article 25

Except as provided in Article 24 no reservation may be made to this Convention.

No. 10106

240 *United Nations — Treaty Series* 1969

Article 26

The International Civil Aviation Organization shall give notice to all States Members of the United Nations or of any of the Specialized Agencies:

(*a*) of any signature of this Convention and the date thereof;

(*b*) of the deposit of any instrument of ratification or accession and the date thereof;

(*c*) of the date on which this Convention comes into force in accordance with Article 21, paragraph 1;

(*d*) of the receipt of any notification of denunciation and the date thereof; and

(*e*) of the receipt of any declaration or notification made under Article 24 and the date thereof.

IN WITNESS WHEREOF the undersigned Plenipotentiaries, having been duly authorized, have signed this Convention.

DONE at Tokyo on the fourteenth day of September One Thousand Nine Hundred and Sixty-three in three authentic texts drawn up in the English, French and Spanish languages.

This Convention shall be deposited with the International Civil Aviation Organization with which, in accordance with Article 19, it shall remain open for signature and the said Organization shall send certified copies thereof to all States Members of the United Nations or of any Specialized Agency.

Convention for the Unification of Certain Rules for International Carriage by Air ("Montreal Convention")

S. Treaty Doc. No. 106–45, 1999 WL 33292734

THE STATES PARTIES TO THIS CONVENTION

RECOGNIZING the significant contribution of the Convention for the Unification of Certain Rules Relating to International Carriage by Air signed in Warsaw on 12 October 1929, hereinafter referred to as the "Warsaw Convention," and other related instruments to the harmonization of private international air law;

RECOGNIZING the need to modernize and consolidate the Warsaw Convention and related instruments;

RECOGNIZING the importance of ensuring protection of the interests of consumers in international carriage by air and the need for equitable compensation based on the principle of restitution;

REAFFIRMING the desirability of an orderly development of international air transport operations and the smooth flow of passengers, baggage and cargo in accordance with the principles and objectives of the Convention on International Civil Aviation, done at Chicago on 7 December 1944;

CONVINCED that collective State action for further harmonization and codification of certain rules governing international carriage by air through a new Convention is the most adequate means of achieving an equitable balance of interests;

HAVE AGREED AS FOLLOWS:

CHAPTER I

GENERAL PROVISIONS

ARTICLE 1

SCOPE OF APPLICATION

1.   This Convention applies to all international carriage of persons, baggage or cargo performed by aircraft for reward. It applies equally to gratuitous carriage by aircraft performed by an air transport undertaking.

2.   For the purposes of this Convention, the expression international carriage means any carriage in which, according to the agreement between the parties, the place of departure and the place of destination, whether or not there be a break in the carriage or a transhipment, are situated either within the territories of two States Parties, or within the territory of a single State Party if there is an agreed stopping place within the territory of another State, even if that State is not a State Party. Carriage between two points within the territory of a single State Party without an agreed stopping place within the territory of another State is not international carriage for the purposes of this Convention.

3.   Carriage to be performed by several successive carriers is deemed, for the purposes of this Convention, to be one undivided carriage if it has been regarded by the parties as a single operation, whether it had been agreed upon under the form of a single contract or of a series of contracts, and it does not lose its international character merely because one contract or a series of contracts is to be performed entirely within the territory of the same State.

4.   This Convention applies also to carriage as set out in Chapter V, subject to the terms contained therein.

ARTICLE 2

CARRIAGE PERFORMED BY STATE AND CARRIAGE OF POSTAL ITEMS

1.   This Convention applies to carriage performed by the State or by legally constituted public bodies provided it falls within the conditions laid down in Article 1.

2.   In the carriage of postal items, the carrier shall be liable only to the relevant postal administration in accordance with the rules applicable to the relationship between the carriers and the postal administrations.

3.   Except as provided in paragraph 2 of this Article, the provisions of this Convention shall not apply to the carriage of postal items.

CHAPTER II

DOCUMENTATION AND DUTIES OF THE PARTIES RELATING TO THE CARRIAGE OF PASSENGERS, BAGGAGE AND CARGO

ARTICLE 3

PASSENGERS AND BAGGAGE

1.   In respect of carriage of passengers, an individual or collective document of carriage shall be delivered containing:

(a)   an indication of the places of departure and destination;

(b)   if the places of departure and destination are within the territory of a single State Party, one or more agreed stopping places being within the territory of another State, an indication of at least one such stopping place.

2.   Any other means which preserves the information indicated in paragraph 1 may be substituted for the delivery of the document referred to in that paragraph. If any such other means is used, the carrier shall offer to deliver to the passenger a written statement of the information so preserved.

3.   The carrier shall deliver to the passenger a baggage identification tag for each piece of checked baggage.

4.   The passenger shall be given written notice to the effect that where this Convention is applicable it governs and may limit the liability of carriers in respect of death or injury and for destruction or loss of, or damage to, baggage, and for delay.

5.   Non-compliance with the provisions of the foregoing paragraphs shall not affect the existence or the validity of the contract of carriage, which shall, nonetheless, be subject to the rules of this Convention including those relating to limitation of liability.

ARTICLE 4

CARGO

1.   In respect of the carriage of cargo, an air waybill shall be delivered.

2.   Any other means which preserves a record of the carriage to be performed may be substituted for the delivery of an air waybill. If such other means are used, the carrier shall, if so requested by the consignor, deliver to the consignor a cargo receipt permitting identification of the consignment and access to the information contained in the record preserved by such other means.

ARTICLE 5

CONTENTS OF AIR WAYBILL OR CARGO RECEIPT

The air waybill or the cargo receipt shall include: (a) an indication of the places of departure and destination; (b) if the places of departure and destination are within the territory of a single State Party, one or more agreed stopping places being within the territory of another State, an indication of at least one such stopping place; and (c) an indication of the weight of the consignment.

ARTICLE 6

DOCUMENT RELATING TO THE NATURE OF THE CARGO

The consignor may be required, if necessary to meet the formalities of customs, police and similar public authorities, to deliver a document indicating the nature of the cargo. This provision creates for the carrier no duty, obligation or liability resulting therefrom.

ARTICLE 7

DESCRIPTION OF AIR WAYBILL

1.   The air waybill shall be made out by the consignor in three original parts.

2.   The first part shall be marked "for the carrier"; it shall be signed by the consignor. The second part shall be marked "for the consignee"; it shall be signed by the consignor and by the carrier. The third part shall be signed by the carrier who shall hand it to the consignor after the cargo has been accepted.

3.   The signature of the carrier and that of the consignor may be printed or stamped.

4.   If, at the request of the consignor, the carrier makes out the air waybill, the carrier shall be deemed, subject to proof to the contrary, to have done so on behalf of the consignor.

ARTICLE 8

DOCUMENTATION FOR MULTIPLE PACKAGES

When there is more than one package: (a) the carrier of cargo has the right to require the consignor to make out separate air waybills; (b) the consignor has the right to require the carrier to deliver separate cargo receipts when the other means referred to in paragraph 2 of Article 4 are used.

ARTICLE 9

NON-COMPLIANCE WITH DOCUMENTARY REQUIREMENTS

Non-compliance with the provisions of Articles 4 to 8 shall not affect the existence or the validity of the contract of carriage, which shall, nonetheless, be subject to the rules of this Convention including those relating to limitation of liability.

ARTICLE 10

RESPONSIBILITY FOR PARTICULARS OF DOCUMENTATION

1.   The consignor is responsible for the correctness of the particulars and statements relating to the cargo inserted by it or on its behalf in the air waybill or furnished by it or on its behalf to the carrier for insertion in the cargo receipt or for insertion in the record preserved by the other means referred to in paragraph 2 of Article 4. The foregoing shall also apply where the person acting on behalf of the consignor is also the agent of the carrier.

2.   The consignor shall indemnify the carrier against all damage suffered by it, or by any other person to whom the carrier is liable, by reason of the irregularity, incorrectness or incompleteness of the particulars and statements furnished by the consignor or on its behalf.

3.   Subject to the provisions of paragraphs 1 and 2 of this Article, the carrier shall indemnify the consignor against all damage suffered by it, or by any other person to whom the consignor is liable, by reason of the irregularity, incorrectness or incompleteness of the particulars and statements inserted by the carrier or on its behalf in the cargo receipt or in the record preserved by the other means referred to in paragraph 2 of Article 4.

ARTICLE 11

EVIDENTIARY VALUE OF DOCUMENTATION

1.   The air waybill or the cargo receipt is prima facie evidence of the conclusion of the contract, of the acceptance of the cargo and of the conditions of carriage mentioned therein.

2.   Any statements in the air waybill or the cargo receipt relating to the weight, dimensions and packing of the cargo, as well as those relating to the number of packages, are prima facie evidence of the facts stated; those relating to the quantity, volume and condition of the cargo do not constitute evidence against the carrier except so far as they both have been, and are stated in the air waybill

or the cargo receipt to have been, checked by it in the presence of the consignor, or relate to the apparent condition of the cargo.

ARTICLE 12

RIGHT OF DISPOSITION OF CARGO

1. Subject to its liability to carry out all its obligations under the contract of carriage, the consignor has the right to dispose of the cargo by withdrawing it at the airport of departure or destination, or by stopping it in the course of the journey on any landing, or by calling for it to be delivered at the place of destination or in the course of the journey to a person other than the consignee originally designated, or by requiring it to be returned to the airport of departure. The consignor must not exercise this right of disposition in such a way as to prejudice the carrier or other consignors and must reimburse any expenses occasioned by the exercise of this right.

2. If it is impossible to carry out the instructions of the consignor, the carrier must so inform the consignor forthwith.

3. If the carrier carries out the instructions of the consignor for the disposition of the cargo without requiring the production of the part of the air waybill or the cargo receipt delivered to the latter, the carrier will be liable, without prejudice to its right of recovery from the consignor, for any damage which may be caused thereby to any person who is lawfully in possession of that part of the air waybill or the cargo receipt.

4. The right conferred on the consignor ceases at the moment when that of the consignee begins in accordance with Article 13. Nevertheless, if the consignee declines to accept the cargo, or cannot be communicated with, the consignor resumes its right of disposition.

ARTICLE 13

DELIVERY OF THE CARGO

1. Except when the consignor has exercised its right under Article 12, the consignee is entitled, on arrival of the cargo at the place of destination, to require the carrier to deliver the cargo to it, on payment of the charges due and on complying with the conditions of carriage.

2. Unless it is otherwise agreed, it is the duty of the carrier to give notice to the consignee as soon as the cargo arrives.

3. If the carrier admits the loss of the cargo, or if the cargo has not arrived at the expiration of seven days after the date on which it ought to have arrived,

the consignee is entitled to enforce against the carrier the rights which flow from the contract of carriage.

ARTICLE 14

ENFORCEMENT OF THE RIGHTS OF CONSIGNOR AND CONSIGNEE

The consignor and the consignee can respectively enforce all the rights given to them by Articles 12 and 13, each in its own name, whether it is acting in its own interest or in the interest of another, provided that it carries out the obligations imposed by the contract of carriage.

ARTICLE 15

RELATIONS OF CONSIGNOR AND CONSIGNEE OR MUTUAL RELATIONS OF THIRD PARTIES

1.   Articles 12, 13 and 14 do not affect either the relations of the consignor and the consignee with each other or the mutual relations of third parties whose rights are derived either from the consignor or from the consignee.

2.   The provisions of Articles 12, 13 and 14 can only be varied by express provision in the air waybill or the cargo receipt.

ARTICLE 16

FORMALITIES OF CUSTOMS, POLICE OR OTHER PUBLIC AUTHORITIES

1.   The consignor must furnish such information and such documents as are necessary to meet the formalities of customs, police and any other public authorities before the cargo can be delivered to the consignee. The consignor is liable to the carrier for any damage occasioned by the absence, insufficiency or irregularity of any such information or documents, unless the damage is due to the fault of the carrier, its servants or agents.

2.   The carrier is under no obligation to enquire into the correctness or sufficiency of such information or documents.

CHAPTER III

LIABILITY OF THE CARRIER AND EXTENT OF COMPENSATION FOR DAMAGE

ARTICLE 17

DEATH AND INJURY OF PASSENGERS—DAMAGE TO BAGGAGE

1.   The carrier is liable for damage sustained in case of death or bodily injury of a passenger upon condition only that the accident which caused the death or

injury took place on board the aircraft or in the course of any of the operations of embarking or disembarking.

2.   The carrier is liable for damage sustained in case of destruction or loss of, or of damage to, checked baggage upon condition only that the event which caused the destruction, loss or damage took place on board the aircraft or during any period within which the checked baggage was in the charge of the carrier. However, the carrier is not liable if and to the extent that the damage resulted from the inherent defect, quality or vice of the baggage. In the case of unchecked baggage, including personal items, the carrier is liable if the damage resulted from its fault or that of its servants or agents.

3.   If the carrier admits the loss of the checked baggage, or if the checked baggage has not arrived at the expiration of twenty-one days after the date on which it ought to have arrived, the passenger is entitled to enforce against the carrier the rights which flow from the contract of carriage.

4.   Unless otherwise specified, in this Convention the term "baggage" means both checked baggage and unchecked baggage.

ARTICLE 18

DAMAGE TO CARGO

1.   The carrier is liable for damage sustained in the event of the destruction or loss of, or damage to, cargo upon condition only that the event which caused the damage so sustained took place during the carriage by air.

2.   However, the carrier is not liable if and to the extent it proves that the destruction, or loss of, or damage to, the cargo resulted from one or more of the following:

    (a)   inherent defect, quality or vice of that cargo;

    (b)   defective packing of that cargo performed by a person other than the carrier or its servants or agents;

    (c)   an act of war or an armed conflict;

    (d)   an act of public authority carried out in connection with the entry, exit or transit of the cargo.

3.   The carriage by air within the meaning of paragraph 1 of this Article comprises the period during which the cargo is in the charge of the carrier.

4.   The period of the carriage by air does not extend to any carriage by land, by sea or by inland waterway performed outside an airport. If, however, such

carriage takes place in the performance of a contract for carriage by air, for the purpose of loading, delivery or transhipment, any damage is presumed, subject to proof to the contrary, to have been the result of an event which took place during the carriage by air. If a carrier, without the consent of the consignor, substitutes carriage by another mode of transport for the whole or part of a carriage intended by the agreement between the parties to be carriage by air, such carriage by another mode of transport is deemed to be within the period of carriage by air.

ARTICLE 19

DELAY

The carrier is liable for damage occasioned by delay in the carriage by air of passengers, baggage or cargo. Nevertheless, the carrier shall not be liable for damage occasioned by delay if it proves that it and its servants and agents took all measures that could reasonably be required to avoid the damage or that it was impossible for it or them to take such measures.

ARTICLE 20

EXONERATION

If the carrier proves that the damage was caused or contributed to by the negligence or other wrongful act or omission of the person claiming compensation, or the person from whom he or she derives his or her rights, the carrier shall be wholly or partly exonerated from its liability to the claimant to the extent that such negligence or wrongful act or omission caused or contributed to the damage. When by reason of death or injury of a passenger compensation is claimed by a person other than the passenger, the carrier shall likewise be wholly or partly exonerated from its liability to the extent that it proves that the damage was caused or contributed to by the negligence or other wrongful act or omission of that passenger. This Article applies to all the liability provisions in this Convention, including paragraph 1 of Article 21.

ARTICLE 21

COMPENSATION IN CASE OF DEATH OR INJURY OF PASSENGERS

1. For damages arising under paragraph 1 of Article 17 not exceeding 100,000 Special Drawing Rights for each passenger, the carrier shall not be able to exclude or limit its liability.

2. The carrier shall not be liable for damages arising under paragraph 1 of Article 17 to the extent that they exceed for each passenger 100,000 Special Drawing Rights if the carrier proves that: (a) such damage was not due to the

negligence or other wrongful act or omission of the carrier or its servants or agents; or (b) such damage was solely due to the negligence or other wrongful act or omission of a third party.

ARTICLE 22

LIMITS OF LIABILITY IN RELATION TO DELAY, BAGGAGE AND CARGO

1.   In the case of damage caused by delay as specified in Article 19 in the carriage of persons, the liability of the carrier for each passenger is limited to 4,150 Special Drawing Rights.

2.   In the carriage of baggage, the liability of the carrier in the case of destruction, loss, damage or delay is limited to 1,000 Special Drawing Rights for each passenger unless the passenger has made, at the time when the checked baggage was handed over to the carrier, a special declaration of interest in delivery at destination and has paid a supplementary sum if the case so requires. In that case the carrier will be liable to pay a sum not exceeding the declared sum, unless it proves that the sum is greater than the passenger's actual interest in delivery at destination.

3.   In the carriage of cargo, the liability of the carrier in the case of destruction, loss, damage or delay is limited to a sum of 17 Special Drawing Rights per kilogramme, unless the consignor has made, at the time when the package was handed over to the carrier, a special declaration of interest in delivery at destination and has paid a supplementary sum if the case so requires. In that case the carrier will be liable to pay a sum not exceeding the declared sum, unless it proves that the sum is greater than the consignor's actual interest in delivery at destination.

4.   In the case of destruction, loss, damage or delay of part of the cargo, or of any object contained therein, the weight to be taken into consideration in determining the amount to which the carrier's liability is limited shall be only the total weight of the package or packages concerned. Nevertheless, when the destruction, loss, damage or delay of a part of the cargo, or of an object contained therein, affects the value of other packages covered by the same air waybill, or the same receipt or, if they were not issued, by the same record preserved by the other means referred to in paragraph 2 of Article 4, the total weight of such package or packages shall also be taken into consideration in determining the limit of liability.

5.   The foregoing provisions of paragraphs 1 and 2 of this Article shall not apply if it is proved that the damage resulted from an act or omission of the carrier, its servants or agents, done with intent to cause damage or recklessly and with

knowledge that damage would probably result; provided that, in the case of such act or omission of a servant or agent, it is also proved that such servant or agent was acting within the scope of its employment.

6. The limits prescribed in Article 21 and in this Article shall not prevent the court from awarding, in accordance with its own law, in addition, the whole or part of the court costs and of the other expenses of the litigation incurred by the plaintiff, including interest. The foregoing provision shall not apply if the amount of the damages awarded, excluding court costs and other expenses of the litigation, does not exceed the sum which the carrier has offered in writing to the plaintiff within a period of six months from the date of the occurrence causing the damage, or before the commencement of the action, if that is later.

ARTICLE 23

CONVERSION OF MONETARY UNITS

1. The sums mentioned in terms of Special Drawing Right in this Convention shall be deemed to refer to the Special Drawing Right as defined by the International Monetary Fund. Conversion of the sums into national currencies shall, in case of judicial proceedings, be made according to the value of such currencies in terms of the Special Drawing Right at the date of the judgment. The value of a national currency, in terms of the Special Drawing Right, of a State Party which is a Member of the International Monetary Fund, shall be calculated in accordance with the method of valuation applied by the International Monetary Fund, in effect at the date of the judgment, for its operations and transactions. The value of a national currency, in terms of the Special Drawing Right, of a State Party which is not a Member of the International Monetary Fund, shall be calculated in a manner determined by that State.

2. Nevertheless, those States which are not Members of the International Monetary Fund and whose law does not permit the application of the provisions of paragraph 1 of this Article may, at the time of ratification or accession or at any time thereafter, declare that the limit of liability of the carrier prescribed in Article 21 is fixed at a sum of 1,500,000 monetary units per passenger in judicial proceedings in their territories; 62,500 monetary units per passenger with respect to paragraph 1 of Article 22; 15,000 monetary units per passenger with respect to paragraph 2 of Article 22; and 250 monetary units per kilogramme with respect to paragraph 3 of Article 22. This monetary unit corresponds to sixty-five and a half milligrammes of gold of millesimal fineness nine hundred. These sums may be converted into the national currency concerned in round figures. The conversion

of these sums into national currency shall be made according to the law of the State concerned.

3.   The calculation mentioned in the last sentence of paragraph 1 of this Article and the conversion method mentioned in paragraph 2 of this Article shall be made in such manner as to express in the national currency of the State Party as far as possible the same real value for the amounts in Articles 21 and 22 as would result from the application of the first three sentences of paragraph 1 of this Article. States Parties shall communicate to the depositary the manner of calculation pursuant to paragraph 1 of this Article, or the result of the conversion in paragraph 2 of this Article as the case may be, when depositing an instrument of ratification, acceptance, approval of or accession to this Convention and whenever there is a change in either.

ARTICLE 24

REVIEW OF LIMITS

1.   Without prejudice to the provisions of Article 25 of this Convention and subject to paragraph 2 below, the limits of liability prescribed in Articles 21, 22 and 23 shall be reviewed by the Depositary at five-year intervals, the first such review to take place at the end of the fifth year following the date of entry into force of this Convention, or if the Convention does not enter into force within five years of the date it is first open for signature, within the first year of its entry into force, by reference to an inflation factor which corresponds to the accumulated rate of inflation since the previous revision or in the first instance since the date of entry into force of the Convention. The measure of the rate of inflation to be used in determining the inflation factor shall be the weighted average of the annual rates of increase or decrease in the Consumer Price Indices of the States whose currencies comprise the Special Drawing Right mentioned in paragraph 1 of Article 23.

2.   If the review referred to in the preceding paragraph concludes that the inflation factor has exceeded 10 per cent, the Depositary shall notify States Parties of a revision of the limits of liability. Any such revision shall become effective six months after its notification to the States Parties. If within three months after its notification to the States Parties a majority of the States Parties register their disapproval, the revision shall not become effective and the Depositary shall refer the matter to a meeting of the States Parties. The Depositary shall immediately notify all States Parties of the coming into force of any revision.

3.   Notwithstanding paragraph 1 of this Article, the procedure referred to in paragraph 2 of this Article shall be applied at any time provided that one-third

of the States Parties express a desire to that effect and upon condition that the inflation factor referred to in paragraph 1 has exceeded 30 per cent since the previous revision or since the date of entry into force of this Convention if there has been no previous revision. Subsequent reviews using the procedure described in paragraph 1 of this Article will take place at five-year intervals starting at the end of the fifth year following the date of the reviews under the present paragraph.

ARTICLE 25

STIPULATION ON LIMITS

A carrier may stipulate that the contract of carriage shall be subject to higher limits of liability than those provided for in this Convention or to no limits of liability whatsoever.

ARTICLE 26

INVALIDITY OF CONTRACTUAL PROVISIONS

Any provision tending to relieve the carrier of liability or to fix a lower limit than that which is laid down in this Convention shall be null and void, but the nullity of any such provision does not involve the nullity of the whole contract, which shall remain subject to the provisions of this Convention.

ARTICLE 27

FREEDOM TO CONTRACT

Nothing contained in this Convention shall prevent the carrier from refusing to enter into any contract of carriage, from waiving any defences available under the Convention, or from laying down conditions which do not conflict with the provisions of this Convention.

ARTICLE 28

ADVANCE PAYMENTS

In the case of aircraft accidents resulting in death or injury of passengers, the carrier shall, if required by its national law, make advance payments without delay to a natural person or persons who are entitled to claim compensation in order to meet the immediate economic needs of such persons. Such advance payments shall not constitute a recognition of liability and may be offset against any amounts subsequently paid as damages by the carrier.

ARTICLE 29

BASIS OF CLAIMS

In the carriage of passengers, baggage and cargo, any action for damages, however founded, whether under this Convention or in contract or in tort or otherwise, can only be brought subject to the conditions and such limits of liability as are set out in this Convention without prejudice to the question as to who are the persons who have the right to bring suit and what are their respective rights. In any such action, punitive, exemplary or any other non-compensatory damages shall not be recoverable.

ARTICLE 30

SERVANTS, AGENTS—AGGREGATION OF CLAIMS

1.   If an action is brought against a servant or agent of the carrier arising out of damage to which the Convention relates, such servant or agent, if they prove that they acted within the scope of their employment, shall be entitled to avail themselves of the conditions and limits of liability which the carrier itself is entitled to invoke under this Convention.

2.   The aggregate of the amounts recoverable from the carrier, its servants and agents, in that case, shall not exceed the said limits.

3.   Save in respect of the carriage of cargo, the provisions of paragraphs 1 and 2 of this Article shall not apply if it is proved that the damage resulted from an act or omission of the servant or agent done with intent to cause damage or recklessly and with knowledge that damage would probably result.

ARTICLE 31

TIMELY NOTICE OF COMPLAINTS

1.   Receipt by the person entitled to delivery of checked baggage or cargo without complaint is prima facie evidence that the same has been delivered in good condition and in accordance with the document of carriage or with the record preserved by the other means referred to in paragraph 2 of Article 3 and paragraph 2 of Article 4.

2.   In the case of damage, the person entitled to delivery must complain to the carrier forthwith after the discovery of the damage, and, at the latest, within seven days from the date of receipt in the case of checked baggage and fourteen days from the date of receipt in the case of cargo. In the case of delay, the complaint must be made at the latest within twenty-one days from the date on which the baggage or cargo have been placed at his or her disposal.

3.   Every complaint must be made in writing and given or dispatched within the times aforesaid.

4.   If no complaint is made within the times aforesaid, no action shall lie against the carrier, save in the case of fraud on its part.

ARTICLE 32

DEATH OF PERSON LIABLE

In the case of the death of the person liable, an action for damages lies in accordance with the terms of this Convention against those legally representing his or her estate.

ARTICLE 33

JURISDICTION

1.   An action for damages must be brought, at the option of the plaintiff, in the territory of one of the States Parties, either before the court of the domicile of the carrier or of its principal place of business, or where it has a place of business through which the contract has been made or before the court at the place of destination.

2.   In respect of damage resulting from the death or injury of a passenger, an action may be brought before one of the courts mentioned in paragraph 1 of this Article, or in the territory of a State Party in which at the time of the accident the passenger has his or her principal and permanent residence and to or from which the carrier operates services for the carriage of passengers by air, either on its own aircraft, or on another carrier's aircraft pursuant to a commercial agreement, and in which that carrier conducts its business of carriage of passengers by air from premises leased or owned by the carrier itself or by another carrier with which it has a commercial agreement.

3.   For the purposes of paragraph 2, (a) "commercial agreement" means an agreement, other than an agency agreement, made between carriers and relating to the provision of their joint services for carriage of passengers by air; (b) "principal and permanent residence" means the one fixed and permanent abode of the passenger at the time of the accident. The nationality of the passenger shall not be the determining factor in this regard.

4.   Questions of procedure shall be governed by the law of the court seised of the case.

ARTICLE 34

ARBITRATION

1.   Subject to the provisions of this Article, the parties to the contract of carriage for cargo may stipulate that any dispute relating to the liability of the carrier under this Convention shall be settled by arbitration. Such agreement shall be in writing.

2.   The arbitration proceedings shall, at the option of the claimant, take place within one of the jurisdictions referred to in Article 33.

3.   The arbitrator or arbitration tribunal shall apply the provisions of this Convention.

4.   The provisions of paragraphs 2 and 3 of this Article shall be deemed to be part of every arbitration clause or agreement, and any term of such clause or agreement which is inconsistent therewith shall be null and void.

ARTICLE 35

LIMITATION OF ACTIONS

1.   The right to damages shall be extinguished if an action is not brought within a period of two years, reckoned from the date of arrival at the destination, or from the date on which the aircraft ought to have arrived, or from the date on which the carriage stopped.

2.   The method of calculating that period shall be determined by the law of the court seised of the case.

ARTICLE 36

SUCCESSIVE CARRIAGE

1.   In the case of carriage to be performed by various successive carriers and falling within the definition set out in paragraph 3 of Article 1, each carrier which accepts passengers, baggage or cargo is subject to the rules set out in this Convention and is deemed to be one of the parties to the contract of carriage in so far as the contract deals with that part of the carriage which is performed under its supervision.

2.   In the case of carriage of this nature, the passenger or any person entitled to compensation in respect of him or her can take action only against the carrier which performed the carriage during which the accident or the delay occurred, save in the case where, by express agreement, the first carrier has assumed liability for the whole journey.

3.   As regards baggage or cargo, the passenger or consignor will have a right of action against the first carrier, and the passenger or consignee who is entitled to delivery will have a right of action against the last carrier, and further, each may take action against the carrier which performed the carriage during which the destruction, loss, damage or delay took place. These carriers will be jointly and severally liable to the passenger or to the consignor or consignee.

ARTICLE 37

RIGHT OF RECOURSE AGAINST THIRD PARTIES

Nothing in this Convention shall prejudice the question whether a person liable for damage in accordance with its provisions has a right of recourse against any other person.

CHAPTER IV

COMBINED CARRIAGE

ARTICLE 38

COMBINED CARRIAGE

1.   In the case of combined carriage performed partly by air and partly by any other mode of carriage, the provisions of this Convention shall, subject to paragraph 4 of Article 18, apply only to the carriage by air, provided that the carriage by air falls within the terms of Article 1.

2.   Nothing in this Convention shall prevent the parties in the case of combined carriage from inserting in the document of air carriage conditions relating to other modes of carriage, provided that the provisions of this Convention are observed as regards the carriage by air.

CHAPTER V

CARRIAGE BY AIR PERFORMED BY A PERSON OTHER THAN THE CONTRACTING CARRIER

ARTICLE 39

CONTRACTING CARRIER—ACTUAL CARRIER

The provisions of this Chapter apply when a person (hereinafter referred to as "the contracting carrier") as a principal makes a contract of carriage governed by this Convention with a passenger or consignor or with a person acting on behalf of the passenger or consignor, and another person (hereinafter referred to as "the actual carrier") performs, by virtue of authority from the contracting carrier, the whole or part of the carriage, but is not with respect to such part a successive carrier within the meaning of this Convention. Such authority shall be presumed in the absence of proof to the contrary.

ARTICLE 40

RESPECTIVE LIABILITY OF CONTRACTING AND ACTUAL CARRIERS

If an actual carrier performs the whole or part of carriage which, according to the contract referred to in Article 39, is governed by this Convention, both the contracting carrier and the actual carrier shall, except as otherwise provided in this Chapter, be subject to the rules of this Convention, the former for the whole of the carriage contemplated in the contract, the latter solely for the carriage which it performs.

ARTICLE 41

MUTUAL LIABILITY

1.   The acts and omissions of the actual carrier and of its servants and agents acting within the scope of their employment shall, in relation to the carriage performed by the actual carrier, be deemed to be also those of the contracting carrier.

2.   The acts and omissions of the contracting carrier and of its servants and agents acting within the scope of their employment shall, in relation to the carriage performed by the actual carrier, be deemed to be also those of the actual carrier. Nevertheless, no such act or omission shall subject the actual carrier to liability exceeding the amounts referred to in Articles 21, 22, 23 and 24. Any special agreement under which the contracting carrier assumes obligations not imposed by this Convention or any waiver of rights or defences conferred by this Convention or any special declaration of interest in delivery at destination contemplated in Article 22 shall not affect the actual carrier unless agreed to by it.

ARTICLE 42

ADDRESSEE OF COMPLAINTS AND INSTRUCTIONS

Any complaint to be made or instruction to be given under this Convention to the carrier shall have the same effect whether addressed to the contracting carrier or to the actual carrier. Nevertheless, instructions referred to in Article 12 shall only be effective if addressed to the contracting carrier.

ARTICLE 43

SERVANTS AND AGENTS

In relation to the carriage performed by the actual carrier, any servant or agent of that carrier or of the contracting carrier shall, if they prove that they acted within the scope of their employment, be entitled to avail themselves of the conditions and limits of liability which are applicable under this Convention to the carrier whose servant or agent they are, unless it is proved that they acted in a manner that prevents the limits of liability from being invoked.

ARTICLE 44

AGGREGATION OF DAMAGES

In relation to the carriage performed by the actual carrier, the aggregate of the amounts recoverable from that carrier and the contracting carrier, and from their servants and agents acting within the scope of their employment, shall not exceed the highest amount which could be awarded against either the contracting carrier or the actual carrier under this Convention, but none of the persons mentioned shall be liable for a sum in excess of the limit applicable to that person.

ARTICLE 45

ADDRESSEE OF CLAIMS

In relation to the carriage performed by the actual carrier, an action for damages may be brought, at the option of the plaintiff, against that carrier or the contracting carrier, or against both together or separately. If the action is brought against only one of those carriers, that carrier shall have the right to require the other carrier to be joined in the proceedings, the procedure and effects being governed by the law of the court seised of the case.

ARTICLE 46

ADDITIONAL JURISDICTION

Any action for damages contemplated in Article 45 must be brought, at the option of the plaintiff, in the territory of one of the States Parties, either before a court in which an action may be brought against the contracting carrier, as provided in Article 33, or before the court having jurisdiction at the place where the actual carrier has its domicile or its principal place of business.

ARTICLE 47

INVALIDITY OF CONTRACTUAL PROVISIONS

Any contractual provision tending to relieve the contracting carrier or the actual carrier of liability under this Chapter or to fix a lower limit than that which is applicable according to this Chapter shall be null and void, but the nullity of any such provision does not involve the nullity of the whole contract, which shall remain subject to the provisions of this Chapter.

ARTICLE 48

MUTUAL RELATIONS OF CONTRACTING AND ACTUAL CARRIERS

Except as provided in Article 45, nothing in this Chapter shall affect the rights and obligations of the carriers between themselves, including any right of recourse or indemnification.

CHAPTER VI

OTHER PROVISIONS

ARTICLE 49

MANDATORY APPLICATION

Any clause contained in the contract of carriage and all special agreements entered into before the damage occurred by which the parties purport to infringe the rules laid down by this Convention, whether by deciding the law to be applied, or by altering the rules as to jurisdiction, shall be null and void.

ARTICLE 50

INSURANCE

States Parties shall require their carriers to maintain adequate insurance covering their liability under this Convention. A carrier may be required by the State Party into which it operates to furnish evidence that it maintains adequate insurance covering its liability under this Convention.

ARTICLE 51

CARRIAGE PERFORMED IN EXTRAORDINARY CIRCUMSTANCES

The provisions of Articles 3 to 5, 7 and 8 relating to the documentation of carriage shall not apply in the case of carriage performed in extraordinary circumstances outside the normal scope of a carrier business.

ARTICLE 52

DEFINITION OF DAYS

The expression "days" when used in this Convention means calendar days, not working days.

CHAPTER VII

FINAL CLAUSES

ARTICLE 53

SIGNATURE, RATIFICATION AND ENTRY INTO FORCE

1. This Convention shall be open for signature in Montreal on 28 May 1999 by States participating in the International Conference on Air Law held at Montreal from 10 to 28 May 1999. After 28 May 1999, the Convention shall be open to all States for signature at the Headquarters of the International Civil Aviation Organization in Montreal until it enters into force in accordance with paragraph 6 of this Article.

2. This Convention shall similarly be open for signature by Regional Economic Integration Organisations. For the purpose of this Convention, a "Regional Economic Integration Organisation" means any organisation which is constituted by sovereign States of a given region which has competence in respect of certain matters governed by this Convention and has been duly authorized to sign and to ratify, accept, approve or accede to this Convention.

A reference to a "State Party" or "States Parties" in this Convention, otherwise than in paragraph 2 of Article 1, paragraph 1(b) of Article 3, paragraph (b) of Article 5, Articles 23, 33, 46 and paragraph (b) of Article 57, applies equally to a Regional Economic Integration Organisation. For the purpose of Article 24, the references to "a majority of the States Parties" and "one-third of the States Parties" shall not apply to a Regional Economic Integration Organisation.

3. This Convention shall be subject to ratification by States and by Regional Economic Integration Organisations which have signed it.

4. Any State or Regional Economic Integration Organisation which does not sign this Convention may accept, approve or accede to it at any time.

5. Instruments of ratification, acceptance, approval or accession shall be deposited with the International Civil Aviation Organization, which is hereby designated the Depositary.

6.   This Convention shall enter into force on the sixtieth day following the date of deposit of the thirtieth instrument of ratification, acceptance, approval or accession with the Depositary between the States which have deposited such instrument. An instrument deposited by a Regional Economic Integration Organisation shall not be counted for the purpose of this paragraph.

7.   For other States and for other Regional Economic Integration Organisations, this Convention shall take effect sixty days following the date of deposit of the instrument of ratification, acceptance, approval or accession.

8.   The Depositary shall promptly notify all signatories and States Parties of: (a) each signature of this Convention and date thereof; (b) each deposit of an instrument of ratification, acceptance, approval or accession and date thereof; (c) the date of entry into force of this Convention; (d) the date of the coming into force of any revision of the limits of liability established under this Convention; (e) any denunciation under Article 54.

ARTICLE 54

DENUNCIATION

1.   Any State Party may denounce this Convention by written notification to the Depositary.

2.   Denunciation shall take effect one hundred and eighty days following the date on which notification is received by the Depositary.

ARTICLE 55

RELATIONSHIP WITH OTHER WARSAW CONVENTION INSTRUMENTS

This Convention shall prevail over any rules which apply to international carriage by air:

1.   Between States Parties to this Convention by virtue of those States commonly being Party to:

(a)   the Convention for the Unification of Certain Rules Relating to International Carriage by Air Signed at Warsaw on 12 October 1929 (hereinafter called the Warsaw Convention);

(b)   the Protocol to Amend the Convention for the Unification of Certain Rules Relating to International Carriage by Air Signed at Warsaw on 12 October 1929, Done at The Hague on 28 September 1955 (hereinafter called The Hague Protocol);

(c)   the Convention, Supplementary to the Warsaw Convention, for the Unification of Certain Rules Relating to International Carriage by Air Performed by a Person Other than the Contracting Carrier, signed at Guadalajara on 18 September 1961 (hereinafter called the Guadalajara Convention);

(d)   the Protocol to Amend the Convention for the Unification of Certain Rules Relating to International Carriage by Air Signed at Warsaw on 12 October 1929 as Amended by the Protocol Done at The Hague on 28 September 1955 Signed at Guatemala City on 8 March 1971 (hereinafter called the Guatemala City Protocol);

(e)   Additional Protocol Nos. 1 to 3 and Montreal Protocol No. 4 to amend the Warsaw Convention as amended by The Hague Protocol or the Warsaw Convention as amended by both The Hague Protocol and the Guatemala City Protocol Signed at Montreal on 25 September 1975 (hereinafter called the Montreal Protocols); or

2.   within the territory of any single State Party to this Convention by virtue of that State being Party to one or more of the instruments referred to in sub-paragraphs (a) to (e) above.

ARTICLE 56

STATES WITH MORE THAN ONE SYSTEM OF LAW

1.   If a State has two or more territorial units in which different systems of law are applicable in relation to matters dealt with in this Convention, it may at the time of signature, ratification, acceptance, approval or accession declare that this Convention shall extend to all its territorial units or only to one or more of them and may modify this declaration by submitting another declaration at any time.

2.   Any such declaration shall be notified to the Depositary and shall state expressly the territorial units to which the Convention applies.

3.   In relation to a State Party which has made such a declaration: (a) references in Article 23 to "national currency" shall be construed as referring to the currency of the relevant territorial unit of that State; and (b) the reference in Article 28 to "national law" shall be construed as referring to the law of the relevant territorial unit of that State.

ARTICLE 57

RESERVATIONS

No reservation may be made to this Convention except that a State Party may at any time declare by a notification addressed to the Depositary that this Convention shall not apply to: (a) international carriage by air performed and operated directly by that State Party for non-commercial purposes in respect to its functions and duties as a sovereign State; and/or (b) the carriage of persons, cargo and baggage for its military authorities on aircraft registered in or leased by that State Party, the whole capacity of which has been reserved by or on behalf of such authorities.

IN WITNESS WHEREOF the undersigned Plenipotentiaries, having been duly authorized, have signed this Convention.

DONE at Montreal on the 28th day of May of the year one thousand nine hundred and ninety-nine in the English, Arabic, Chinese, French, Russian and Spanish languages, all texts being equally authentic. This Convention shall remain deposited in the archives of the International Civil Aviation Organization, and certified copies thereof shall be transmitted by the Depositary to all States Parties to this Convention, as well as to all States Parties to the Warsaw Convention, The Hague Protocol, the Guadalajara Convention, the Guatemala City Protocol, and the Montreal Protocols.

Multilateral Agreement on the Liberalization of International Air Transportation

Overview

On October 31–November 2, 2000, the United States, Brunei Darussalam, Chile, New Zealand and Singapore met in Kona, Hawaii to negotiate the MALIAT. The MALIAT entered into force on December 21, 2001, and is open to accession. Key features of the MALIAT include:

- an open route schedule;
- open traffic rights, including seventh freedom cargo services;
- open capacity;
- airline investment provisions which focus on effective control and principal place of business, but protect against flag of convenience airlines;
- multiple airline designation;
- third-country code-sharing; and
- a minimal tariff filing regime.

Updated: Wednesday, August 29, 2012

Done at Washington, D.C., May 21, 2001

Entered in Force, December 21, 2001

Effective in United States, December 21, 2001

The Parties to this Agreement (hereinafter, "the Parties");

Desiring to promote an international aviation system based on competition among airlines in the marketplace with minimum interference and regulation;

Desiring to facilitate the expansion of international air transport opportunities;

Recognizing that efficient and competitive international air services enhance trade, benefit consumers, and promote economic growth;

Recognizing the contribution made by the Asia-Pacific Economic Cooperation forum in facilitating discussions on the liberalization of air services;

Desiring to make it possible for airlines to offer the traveling and shipping public a variety of service options and wishing to encourage individual airlines to develop and implement innovative and competitive prices;

Desiring to ensure the highest degree of safety and security in international air transport and reaffirming their grave concern about acts or threats against the security of aircraft, which jeopardize the safety of persons or property, adversely affect the operation of air transportation, and undermine public confidence in the safety of civil aviation; and

Noting the Convention on International Civil Aviation, opened for signature at Chicago on December 7, 1944;

Have agreed as follows:

Article 1—Definition

For the purposes of this Agreement, unless otherwise stated, the term:

1. "Agreement" means this Agreement, its Annex and Appendix, and any amendments thereto;

2. "Air transportation" means the public carriage by aircraft of passengers, baggage, cargo, and mail, separately or in combination, for remuneration or hire;

3. "Convention" means the Convention on International Civil Aviation, opened for signature at Chicago on December 7, 1944, and includes:

    1. any amendment that has entered into force under Article 94(a) of the Convention and has been ratified by all Parties to this Agreement, and

    2. any Annex or any amendment thereto adopted under Article 90 of the Convention, insofar as such Annex or amendment is at any given time effective for all Parties to this Agreement;

4. "Designated airline" means an airline designated and authorized in accordance with Article 3 of this Agreement;

5. "Full cost" means the cost of providing service, including a reasonable amount for administrative overhead;

6. "International air transportation" means air transportation that passes through the airspace over the territory of more than one State or APEC member economy as identified in the Appendix to the Annex;

7. "Price" means any fare, rate or charge for the carriage of passengers, baggage and/or cargo (excluding mail) in air transportation, including surface transportation in connection with international air transportation, if applicable, charged by airlines, including their agents, and the conditions governing the availability of such fare, rate or charge;

8. "Stop for non-traffic purposes" means a landing for any purpose other than taking on or discharging passengers, baggage, cargo and/or mail in air transportation;

9. "Territory" means the land areas under the sovereignty, jurisdiction, authority, administration, protection, or trusteeship of a Party, and the territorial waters adjacent thereto; and

10. "User charge" means a charge imposed on airlines for the provision of airport, air navigation, or aviation security facilities or services including related services and facilities.

Article 2—Grant of Rights

1. Each Party grants to the other Parties the following rights for the conduct of international air transportation by the airlines of the other Parties:

   a. the right to fly across its territory without landing;

   b. the right to make stops in its territory for non-traffic purposes;

   c. the right, in accordance with the terms of their designations, to perform scheduled and charter international air transportation between points on the following route:

      i. From points behind the territory of the Party designating the airline via that Party and intermediate points to any point or points in the territory of any other Party and beyond;

      ii. For all-cargo service or services, between the territory of the Party granting the right and any point or points; and

    d.   the rights otherwise specified in this Agreement.

2.   Each designated airline may on any or all flights and at its option:

    a.   operate flights in either or both directions;

    b.   combine different flight numbers within one aircraft operation;

    c.   serve behind, intermediate, and beyond points and points in the territories of the Parties on the routes in any combination and in any order;

    d.   omit stops at any point or points;

    e.   transfer traffic from any of its aircraft to any of its other aircraft at any point on the routes;

    f.   serve points behind any point in its territory with or without change of aircraft or flight number and hold out and advertise such services to the public as through services;

    g.   make stopovers at any points whether within or outside the territory of any Party;

    h.   carry transit traffic through any other Party's territory; and

    i.   combine traffic on the same aircraft regardless of where such traffic originates;

without directional or geographic limitation and without loss of any right to carry traffic otherwise permissible under this Agreement.

3.   The provisions of paragraph 2 of this Article shall apply subject to the requirement that, with the exception of all-cargo services, the service serves a point in the territory of the Party designating the airline.

4.   On any segment or segments of the routes above, any designated airline may perform international air transportation without any limitation as to change, at any point on the route, in type or number of aircraft operated; provided that, with the exception of all-cargo services, in the outbound direction, the transportation beyond such point is a continuation of the transportation from the territory of the Party that has designated the airline and, in the inbound direction, the transportation to the territory of the Party that has designated the airline is a continuation of the transportation from beyond such point.

5.   Nothing in this Agreement shall be deemed to confer on the airline or airlines of one Party the right to take on board, in the territory of another Party,

passengers, baggage, cargo, or mail carried for compensation and destined for another point in the territory of that other Party.

Article 3—Designation and Authorization

1. Each Party shall have the right to designate as many airlines as it wishes to conduct international air transportation in accordance with this Agreement and to withdraw or alter such designations. Such designations shall be transmitted to the concerned Parties in writing through diplomatic or other appropriate channels and to the Depositary.

2. On receipt of such a designation, and of applications from the designated airline, in the form and manner prescribed for operating authorizations and technical permissions, each Party shall grant appropriate authorizations and permissions with minimum procedural delay, provided that:

   a. effective control of that airline is vested in the designating Party, its nationals, or both;

   b. the airline is incorporated in and has its principal place of business in the territory of the Party designating the airline;

   c. the airline is qualified to meet the conditions prescribed under the laws, regulations, and rules normally applied to the operation of international air transportation by the Party considering the application or applications; and

   d. the Party designating the airline is in compliance with the provisions set forth in Article 6 (Safety) and Article 7 (Aviation Security).

3. Notwithstanding paragraph 2, a Party need not grant authorizations and permissions to an airline designated by another Party if the Party receiving the designation determines that substantial ownership is vested in its nationals.

4. Parties granting operating authorizations in accordance with paragraph 2 of this Article shall notify such action to the Depositary

5. Nothing in this Agreement shall be deemed to affect a Party's laws and regulations concerning the ownership and control of airlines that it designates. Acceptance of such designations by the other Parties shall be subject to paragraphs 2 and 3 of this Article.

Article 4—Revocation of Authorization

1. Each Party may withhold, revoke, suspend, limit or impose conditions on the operating authorizations or technical permissions of an airline designated by another Party where:

    a. effective control of that airline is not vested in the designating Party, its nationals, or both;

    b. the first Party determines that substantial ownership is vested in its nationals;

    c. the airline is not incorporated or does not have its principal place of business in the territory of the party designating the airline;

    d. the airline has failed to comply with the laws, regulations, and rules referred to in Article 5 (Application of Laws) of this Agreement; or

    e. the other Party is not maintaining and administering the standards as set forth in Article 6 (Safety).

2. Unless immediate action is essential to prevent further noncompliance with subparagraphs 1(d) or 1(e) of this Article, the rights established by this Article shall be exercised only after consultation with the Party designating the airline.

3. A Party that has exercised its right to withhold, revoke, suspend, limit or impose conditions on the operating authorizations of an airline or airlines in accordance with paragraph 1 of this Article shall notify its action to the Depositary.

4. This Article does not limit the rights of any Party to withhold, revoke, suspend, limit or impose conditions on the operating authorization or technical permission of an airline or airlines of other Parties in accordance with the provisions of Article 7 (Aviation Security).

Article 5—Application of Laws

1. While entering, within, or leaving the territory of one Party, its laws, regulations and rules relating to the operation and navigation of aircraft shall be complied with by the airlines designated by any other Party.

2. While entering, within, or leaving the territory of one Party, its laws, regulations and rules relating to the admission to or departure from its territory of passengers, crew or cargo on aircraft (including regulations relating to entry, clearance, aviation security, immigration, passports, customs and quarantine or, in the case of mail, postal regulations) shall be complied

with by, or on behalf of, such passengers, crew or cargo of the airlines of any other Party.

3. No Party shall give preference to its own or any other airline over a designated airline of the other Parties engaged in similar international air transport in the application of its customs, immigration and quarantine regulations.

4. Passengers, baggage and cargo in direct transit through the territory of any Party and not leaving the area of the airport reserved for such purpose shall not undergo any examination except for reasons of aviation security, narcotics control, prevention of illegal entry or in special circumstances.

Article 6—Safety

1. Each Party shall recognize as valid, for the purpose of operating the air transportation provided for in this Agreement, certificates of airworthiness, certificates of competency, and licenses issued or validated by the other Parties and still in force, provided that the requirements for such certificates or licenses at least equal the minimum standards that may be established pursuant to the Convention. Each Party may, however, refuse to recognize as valid for the purpose of flight above its own territory, certificates of competency and licenses for its own nationals granted or validated by another Party.

2. Each Party may request consultations with another Party concerning the safety standards maintained by that other Party relating to aeronautical facilities, aircrews, aircraft, and operation of the designated airlines. If, following such consultations, the first Party finds that the other Party does not effectively maintain and administer safety standards and requirements in these areas that at least equal the minimum standards that may be established pursuant to the Convention, the other Party shall be notified of such findings and the steps considered necessary to conform with these minimum standards, and the other Party shall take appropriate corrective action. Each Party reserves the right to withhold, revoke, suspend, or limit or impose conditions on the operating authorization or technical permission of an airline or airlines designated by the other Party in the event the other Party does not take such appropriate corrective action within a reasonable time.

Article 7—Aviation Security

1. In accordance with their rights and obligations under international law, the Parties reaffirm that their obligation to each other to protect the security of

civil aviation against acts of unlawful interference forms an integral part of this Agreement. Without limiting the generality of their rights and obligations under international law, the Parties shall in particular act in conformity with the provisions of the Convention on Offenses and Certain Other Acts Committed on Board Aircraft, done at Tokyo on September 14, 1963, the Convention for the Suppression of Unlawful Seizure of Aircraft, done at The Hague on December 16, 1970, the Convention for the Suppression of Unlawful Acts against the Safety of Civil Aviation, done at Montreal on September 23, 1971, and the Protocol for the Suppression of Unlawful Acts of Violence at Airports Serving International Civil Aviation, done at Montreal on February 24, 1988.

2.   Each Party shall provide upon request of another Party all necessary assistance to that other Party to prevent acts of unlawful seizure of civil aircraft and other unlawful acts against the safety of such aircraft, of their passengers and crew, and of airports and air navigation facilities, and to address any other threat to the security of civil air navigation.

3.   Each Party shall, in its relations with the other Parties, act in conformity with the aviation security standards and appropriate recommended practices established by the International Civil Aviation Organization and designated as Annexes to the Convention; it shall require that operators of aircraft of its registry, operators of aircraft who have their principal place of business or permanent residence in its territory, and the operators of airports in its territory act in conformity with such aviation security provisions.

4.   Each Party shall observe the security provisions required by the other Parties for entry into, for departure from, and while within their respective territories and each Party shall ensure that adequate measures are effectively applied within its territory to protect aircraft and to inspect passengers, crew, and their baggage and carry-on items, as well as cargo and aircraft stores, prior to and during boarding or loading. Each Party shall also give positive consideration to any request from another Party for special security measures to meet a particular threat.

5.   When an incident or threat of an incident of unlawful seizure of aircraft or other unlawful acts against the safety of passengers, crew, aircraft, airports or air navigation facilities occurs, the Parties shall assist each other by facilitating communications and other appropriate measures intended to terminate rapidly and safely such incident or threat.

6.   When a Party has reasonable grounds to believe that another Party has departed from the aviation security provisions of this Article, the aeronautical authorities of that Party may request immediate consultations with the aeronautical authorities of the other Party. Failure to reach a satisfactory agreement within 15 days from the date of such request shall constitute grounds to withhold, revoke, suspend, limit, or impose conditions on the operating authorization and technical permissions of an airline or airlines of the other Party. When required by an emergency, a Party may take interim action prior to the expiry of 15 days.

7.   Any Party that has exercised its right to withhold, revoke, suspend, or limit or impose conditions on the operating authorization of an airline or airlines in accordance with paragraph 6 of this Article shall notify such action to the Depositary.

Article 8—Commercial Opportunities

1.   The airlines of each Party shall have the right to:

    a.   establish offices in the territory of the other Parties for the promotion and sale of air transportation;

    b.   engage in the sale of air transportation in the territory of the other Parties directly and, at the airlines' discretion, through their agents. The airlines shall have the right to sell such transportation, and any person shall be free to purchase such transportation, in local currency or in freely convertible currencies;

    c.   convert and remit to the territory of its incorporation, on demand, local revenues in excess of sums locally disbursed. Conversion and remittance shall be permitted promptly without restrictions or taxation in respect thereof at the rate of exchange applicable to current transactions and remittance on the date the carrier makes the initial application for remittance; and

    d.   pay for local expenses, including purchases of fuel, in the territories of the other Parties in local currency. At their discretion, the airlines of each Party may pay for such expenses in the territory of the other Parties in freely convertible currencies according to local currency regulation.

2.   The designated airlines of each Party shall have the right:

    a.   in accordance with the laws, regulations and rules of the other Parties relating to entry, residence, and employment, to bring in and maintain in the territories of the other Parties managerial, sales, technical, operational, and other specialist staff required for the provision of air transportation;

b. to perform their own ground-handling in the territory of the other Parties ("self-handling") or, at their option, select among competing agents for such services in whole or in part. The rights shall be subject only to physical constraints resulting from considerations of airport safety. Where such considerations preclude self-handling, ground services shall be available on an equal basis to all airlines; charges shall be based on the costs of services provided; and such services shall be comparable to the kind and quality of services as if self-handling were possible; and

c. in operating or holding out the authorized services on the agreed routes, to enter into cooperative marketing arrangements such as blocked-space, code-sharing or leasing arrangements, with:

    i.   an airline or airlines of any Party;

    ii. an airline or airlines of any State or APEC member economy as identified in the Appendix to the Annex that is not party to this Agreement; and

    iii. a surface transportation provider of any State or APEC member economy as identified in the Appendix to the Annex;

provided that all participants in such arrangements hold the appropriate authority and meet the requirements applied to such arrangements.

3. Notwithstanding any other provision of this Agreement, airlines and indirect providers of cargo transportation of the Parties shall be permitted without restriction to employ in connection with international air transportation any surface transportation for cargo to or from any points within or outside the territories of the Parties, including transport to and from all airports with customs facilities, and including, where applicable, the right to transport cargo in bond under applicable laws and regulations. Such cargo, whether moving by surface or by air, shall have access to airport customs processing and facilities. Airlines may elect to perform their own surface transportation or to provide it through arrangements with other surface carriers, including surface transportation operated by other airlines and indirect providers of cargo air transportation. Such intermodal cargo services may be offered at a single, through price for the air and surface transportation combined,

provided that shippers are not misled as to the facts concerning such transportation.

Article 9—Customs Duties and Charges

1. On arriving in the territory of one Party, aircraft operated in international air transportation by the designated airline or airlines of any other Party, their regular equipment, ground equipment, fuel, lubricants, consumable technical supplies, spare parts (including engines), aircraft stores (including but not limited to such items of food, beverages and liquor, tobacco and other products destined for sale to or use by passengers in limited quantities during flight), and other items intended for or used solely in connection with the operation or servicing of aircraft engaged in international air transportation shall be exempt, on the basis of reciprocity, from all import restrictions, property taxes and capital levies, customs duties, excise taxes, and similar fees and charges that are (i) imposed by the national or central authorities, and (ii) not based on the cost of services provided, provided that such equipment and supplies remain on board the aircraft.

2. There shall also be exempt, on the basis of reciprocity, from the taxes, levies, duties, fees and charges referred to in paragraph 1 of this Article, with the exception of charges based on the cost of the service provided:

    a. aircraft stores introduced into or supplied in the territory of a Party and taken on board, within reasonable limits, for use on outbound aircraft of airlines of the other Parties engaged in international air transportation, even when these stores are to be used on a part of the journey performed over the territory of the Party in which they are taken on board;

    b. ground equipment and spare parts (including engines) introduced into the territory of a Party for the servicing, maintenance, or repair of aircraft of airlines of the other Parties used in international air transportation;

    c. fuel, lubricants and consumable technical supplies introduced into or supplied in the territory of a Party for use in an aircraft of airlines of the other Parties engaged in international air transportation, even when these supplies are to be used on a part of the journey performed over the territory of the Party in which they are taken on board; and

    d. promotional and advertising materials introduced into or supplied in the territory of one Party and taken on board, within reasonable limits, for use on outbound aircraft of an airline of the other Parties engaged in international air transportation, even when these stores are to be used on a part of the journey performed over the territory of the Party in which they are taken on board.

3. Equipment and supplies referred to in paragraphs 1 and 2 of this Article may be required to be kept under the supervision or control of the appropriate authorities.

4. The exemptions provided by this Article shall also be available where the designated airlines of one Party have contracted with another airline, which similarly enjoys such exemptions from another Party or Parties, for the loan or transfer in the territory of the other Party or Parties of the items specified in paragraphs 1 and 2 of this Article.

Article 10—User Charges

1. User charges that may be imposed by the competent charging authorities or bodies of each Party on the airlines of the other Parties shall be just, reasonable, not unjustly discriminatory, and equitably apportioned among categories of users. In any event, any such user charges shall be assessed on the airlines of the other Parties on terms not less favorable than the most favorable terms available to any other airline at the time the charges are assessed.

2. User charges imposed on the airlines of the other Parties may reflect, but shall not exceed, the full cost to the competent charging authorities or bodies of providing the appropriate airport, airport environmental, air navigation, and aviation security facilities and services at the airport or within the airport system. Such charges may include a reasonable return on assets, after depreciation. Facilities and services for which charges are made shall be provided on an efficient and economic basis.

3. Each Party shall encourage consultations between the competent charging authorities or bodies in its territory and the airlines using the services and facilities, and shall encourage the competent charging authorities or bodies and the airlines to exchange such information as may be necessary to permit an accurate review of the reasonableness of the charges in accordance with the principles of paragraphs (1) and (2) of this Article. Each Party shall encourage the competent charging authorities to provide users with reasonable notice of any proposal for changes in user charges to enable users to express their views before changes are made.

4. No Party shall be held, in dispute resolution procedures pursuant to Article 14, to be in breach of a provision of this Article, unless (i) it fails to undertake a review of the charge or practice that is the subject of complaint by another Party within a reasonable amount of time; or (ii) following such a review it fails to take all steps within its power to remedy any charge or practice that is inconsistent with this Article.

Article 11—Fair Competition

1. Each Party shall allow a fair and equal opportunity for the designated airlines of all Parties to compete in providing the international air transportation governed by this Agreement.

2. Each Party shall allow each designated airline to determine the frequency and capacity of the international air transportation it offers based upon commercial considerations in the marketplace. Consistent with this right, no Party shall act to limit the volume of traffic, frequency or regularity of service, or the aircraft type or types operated by the designated airlines of the other Parties, except as may be required for customs, technical, operational, or environmental reasons under uniform conditions consistent with Article 15 of the Convention.

3. No Party shall impose on another Party's designated airlines a first-refusal requirement, uplift ratio, no-objection fee, or any other requirement with respect to capacity, frequency or traffic.

4. No Party shall require the filing of schedules, programs for charter flights, or operational plans by airlines of the other Parties for approval, except as may be required on a non-discriminatory basis to enforce the uniform conditions foreseen by paragraph 2 of this Article. If a Party requires filings to enforce the uniform conditions as foreseen by paragraph 2 of this Article or requires filings for informational purposes, it shall minimize the administrative burdens of filing requirements and procedures on air transportation intermediaries and on designated airlines of the other Parties.

5. Subject to the provisions of this Agreement, no Party may apply its laws, regulations, and rules to restrict the operation or sale of the charter international air transportation provided for in this Agreement, except that the Parties may require compliance with their own requirements relating to the protection of charter passenger funds and charter passenger cancellation and refund rights.

6. Pursuant to paragraph 1 of this Article, the airlines of each Party shall be entitled to market their services on a fair and nondiscriminatory basis through computer reservations systems (CRSs) used by travel agencies or travel companies in the territories of the Parties. In addition, CRS vendors of each Party that are not in violation of the CRS rules, if any, that apply in the territories of the Parties in which they are operating shall be entitled to non-discriminatory, effective, and unimpaired access to market, maintain, operate and freely make available their CRSs to travel agencies or travel companies in the territories of the Parties. In particular, if any airline of any Party chooses to participate in a CRS offered to travel agents or travel companies in the territory of another Party, that airline shall participate in CRSs of that other Party operated in the territory of its incorporation as fully as it does in any CRS in the territory of that other Party, unless it can show that the fees charged by that CRS for participation in the territory of its incorporation are not commercially reasonable (fees are presumed to be commercially reasonable if the fees charged the airline for participation in the territory of its incorporation by any other CRS that is used by travel agents or travel companies equal or exceed those charged by the CRS of the other Party for such participation). Airlines and CRS vendors of one Party shall not discriminate against travel agencies or travel companies in that Party's territory because of their use of a CRS of another Party.

Article 12—Pricing

Prices for international air transportation operated pursuant to this Agreement shall not be subject to the approval of any Party, nor may they be required to be filed with any party, provided that a Party may require that they be filed for informational purposes for so long as the laws of that Party continue to so require.

Article 13—Consultations

Each Party shall have the right to request consultations with one or more other Parties relating to the implementation or application of this Agreement. Unless otherwise agreed, such consultations shall begin at the earliest possible date, but not later than 60 days from the date the other Party or Parties receive, through diplomatic or other appropriate channels, a written request, including an explanation of the issues to be raised. When the date for consultations has been agreed, the requesting Party shall also notify all other Parties of the consultations and the issues to be raised. Any Party may attend, subject to the consent of the Parties involved in the consultations. Once the consultations have been concluded, all Parties shall be notified of the results.

Article 14—Settlement of Disputes

1. Any dispute arising under this Agreement that is not resolved by a first round of consultations may be referred by agreement of the Parties involved for decision to some person or body. If the Parties involved do not so agree, the dispute shall at the request of one Party be submitted to arbitration with respect to another Party in accordance with the procedures set forth below. The Party submitting the dispute to arbitration shall notify all other Parties of the dispute at the same time that it submits its arbitration request.

2. Arbitration shall be by a panel of three arbitrators to be constituted as follows:

    a. Within 30 days after the receipt of a request for arbitration, each Party to the dispute shall name one arbitrator. Within 60 days after these two arbitrators have been named, the Parties to the dispute shall by agreement appoint a third arbitrator, who shall act as President of the arbitral panel;

    b. If either Party to the dispute fails to name an arbitrator, or if the third arbitrator is not appointed in accordance with subparagraph (a) of this paragraph, either Party may request the President of the Council of the International Civil Aviation Organization to appoint the necessary arbitrator or arbitrators within 30 days. If the President of the Council is of the same nationality as one of the Parties to the dispute, the most senior Vice President who is not disqualified on that ground shall make the appointment.

3. Except as otherwise agreed by the Parties to the dispute, the arbitral panel shall determine the limits of its jurisdiction in accordance with this Agreement and shall establish its own procedural rules. The arbitral panel, once formed, may recommend interim measures pending its final determination. At the direction of the arbitral panel or at the request of either of the Parties to the dispute, a conference concerning the precise issues to be arbitrated and the specific procedures to be followed shall be held on a date determined by the arbitral panel, in no event later than 15 days after the third arbitrator has been appointed. If the Parties to the dispute are unable to reach agreement on these issues, the arbitral panel shall determine the precise issues to be arbitrated and the specific procedures to be followed.

4. Except as otherwise agreed by the Parties to the dispute or as directed by the panel, the complaining Party shall submit a memorandum within 45 days of the time the third arbitrator is appointed, and the reply of the responding

Party shall be due 60 days after the complaining Party submits its memorandum. The complaining Party may submit a pleading in response to such reply within 30 days after the submission of the responding Party's reply and the responding Party may submit a pleading in response to the complaining Party's pleading within 30 days after the submission of such pleading. The arbitral panel shall hold a hearing at the request of either Party or on its own initiative within 15 days after the last pleading is due.

5.   The arbitral panel shall attempt to render a written decision within 30 days after completion of the hearing or, if no hearing is held, after the date the last pleading is submitted. The decision of the majority of the arbitral panel shall prevail.

6.   The parties to the dispute may submit requests for clarification of the decision within 15 days after it is rendered, and any clarification given shall be issued within 15 days of such request.

7.   In the case of a dispute involving more than two Parties, multiple Parties may participate on either or both sides of a proceeding described in this Article. The procedures set out in this Article shall be applied with the following exceptions:

   a.   with respect to paragraph 2(a), the Parties on each side of a dispute shall together name one arbitrator;

   b.   with respect to paragraph 2(b), if the Parties on one side of a dispute fail to name an arbitrator within the permitted time, the Party or Parties on the other side of the dispute may utilize the procedures in paragraph 2(b) to secure the appointment of an arbitrator;

   c.   with respect to paragraphs 3, 4, and 6, each of the Parties on either side of the dispute has the right to take the action provided to a Party.

8.   Any other Party that is directly effected by the dispute has the right to intervene in the proceedings, under the following conditions:

   a.   A Party desiring to intervene shall file a declaration to that effect with the arbitral panel no later than 10 days after the third arbitrator has been named;

   b.   The arbitral panel shall notify the Parties to the dispute of any such declaration, and the Parties to the dispute shall each have 30 days from the date such notification is sent to submit to the arbitral panel any objection to an intervention under this paragraph. The arbitral panel shall decide whether to allow any intervention within 15 days after the date such objections are due;

c. If the arbitral panel decides to allow an intervention, the intervening Party shall notify all other Parties to the Agreement of the intervention, and the arbitral panel shall take the necessary steps to make the documents of the case available to the intervening Party, who may file pleadings of a type and within a time limit to be set by the arbitral panel, within the timetable set out in paragraph 4 of this Article to the extent practical, and may participate in any subsequent proceedings; and

d. The decision of the arbitral panel will be equally binding upon the intervening Party.

9. All Parties to the dispute, including intervening Parties, shall, to the degree consistent with their law, give full effect to any decision or award of the arbitral panel.

10. The arbitral panel shall transmit copies of its decision or award to the Parties to the dispute, including any intervening Parties. The arbitral panel shall provide to the Depositary a copy of the decision or award, provided that appropriate treatment shall be accorded to confidential business information.

11. The expenses of the arbitral panel, including the fees and expenses of the arbitrators, shall be shared equally by all of the Parties to the dispute, including intervening Parties. Any expenses incurred by the President of the Council of the International Civil Aviation Organization in connection with the procedures of paragraph 2(b) of this Article shall be considered to be part of the expenses of the arbitral panel.

Article 15—Relationship to other Agreements

Upon entry into force of this Agreement between one Party and any other Party, any bilateral air transport agreement existing between them at the time of such entry into force shall be suspended and shall remain suspended for so long as this Agreement shall remain in force between them.

Article 16—Relationship to Annex

The Annex is an integral part of this Agreement and, unless expressly provided otherwise, a reference to this Agreement includes a reference to the Annex relating thereto.

Article 17—Amendment

1. Any Party may propose amendments to this Agreement by forwarding a proposed amendment to the Depositary. Upon receiving such a proposal, the Depositary shall forward the proposal to the other Parties through diplomatic or other appropriate channels.

2. The Agreement may be amended in accordance with the following procedures:

    a. If agreed by at least a simple majority of all Parties as of the date of proposal of the amendment, negotiations shall be held to consider the proposal.

    b. Unless otherwise agreed, the Party proposing the amendment shall host the negotiations, which shall begin not more than 90 days after agreement is reached to hold such negotiations. All Parties shall have a right to participate in the negotiations.

    c. If adopted by at least a simple majority of the Parties attending such negotiations, the Depositary shall then prepare and transmit a certified copy of the amendment to the Parties for their acceptance.

    d. Any amendment shall enter into force, as between the Parties which have accepted it, 30 days following the date on which the Depositary has received written notification of acceptance from a simple majority of the Parties.

    e. Following entry into force of such an amendment, it shall enter into force for any other Party 30 days following the date the Depositary receives written notification of acceptance from that Party.

3. In lieu of the procedures set forth in paragraph 2, the Agreement may be amended in accordance with the following procedures:

    a. If all Parties as of the time of proposal of the amendment give written notice through diplomatic or other appropriate channels to the Party proposing the amendment of their consent to its adoption, the Party proposing the amendment shall so notify the Depositary, which shall then prepare and transmit a certified copy of such amendment to all of the Parties for their acceptance.

    b. An amendment so adopted shall enter into force for all Parties 30 days following the date on which the Depositary has received written notification of acceptance from all of the Parties.

Article 18—Withdrawal

A Party may withdraw from this agreement by giving written notice of withdrawal to the Depositary. The withdrawal shall be effective 12 months after receipt of the notice by the Depositary, unless the Party withdraws its notice by written communication to the Depositary prior to the end of the 12-month period.

Article 19—Responsibilities of the Depositary

1. The original of this Agreement shall be deposited with New Zealand, which is hereby designated as the Depositary of the Agreement.

2. The Depositary shall transmit certified copies of this Agreement and any amendments or protocols to all signatory and acceding States and all APEC member economies which have agreed to be bound by this Agreement in accordance with the Annex.

3. The Depositary shall notify all signatory and acceding States and all APEC member economies which have agreed to be bound by this Agreement in accordance with the Annex of:

    a. Expressions of consent to be bound by this Agreement and any amendments in accordance with Articles 20 and 17, and instruments of APEC member economies indicating their agreement to be bound by this Agreement in accordance with the Annex or their acceptance of any amendments in accordance with Article 17;

    b. The respective dates on which the Agreement enters into force in accordance with Article 20, paragraphs 2, 3, 4 and 6;

    c. Notifications regarding non-application of the Agreement received in accordance with Article 20, paragraph 5;

    d. Any notification of withdrawal received in accordance with Article 18;

    e. The convening of negotiations to consider amendments in accordance with Article 17, paragraph 2(a);

    f. The respective dates on which an amendment enters into force in accordance with Article 17, paragraphs 2(d), 2(e) and 3(b); and

    g. Notifications received pursuant to Article 4, paragraph 3 and Article 7, paragraph 7.

4. Following entry into force of this Agreement, the Depositary shall transmit a certified true copy of this Agreement to the Secretary General of the United Nations for registration and publication in accordance with Article 102 of the

Charter of the United Nations and to the Secretary General of the International Civil Aviation Organization in accordance with Article 83 of the Convention. The Depositary shall likewise transmit certified true copies of any amendments which enter into force.

5. The Depositary shall maintain a centralized register of airline designations and operating authorizations in accordance with Article 3, paragraphs 1 and 4 of this Agreement.

6. The Depositary shall make available to the Parties copies of any arbitral decision or award issued under Article 14 of this Agreement.

Article 20—Entry into Force

1. This Agreement shall be open for signature by Brunei Darussalam, Chile, New Zealand, Singapore, and the United States of America.

2. This Agreement shall enter into force on the date four of the States identified in paragraph 1 of this Article have signed not subject to ratification, acceptance or approval, or have deposited with the Depositary an instrument of ratification, acceptance or approval. The signatories to this Agreement may permit services consistent with the terms of the Agreement upon signature pending entry into force of the Agreement with respect to all of the States identified in paragraph 1 of this Article.

3. After this Agreement has entered into force in accordance with paragraph 2 of this Article, it shall enter into force for any other signatory on the date the Depositary receives the instrument of ratification, acceptance or approval of that signatory.

4. After this Agreement has entered into force in accordance with paragraph 2 of this Article, any State which is a party to the aviation security conventions listed in Article 7, paragraph 1 may accede to this Agreement by deposit of an instrument of accession with the Depositary.

5. This Agreement shall not apply between an acceding State or an APEC member economy which agrees to be bound by this Agreement in accordance with the Annex and any Party to this Agreement which, within 90 days of the date of the Depositary's notification to the Parties of the deposit of the instrument of accession or written instrument indicating agreement to be bound, notifies the Depositary in writing that it shall not apply between that Party and such acceding State or APEC member economy. Any signatory that expresses its consent to be bound after the Agreement has entered into force pursuant to paragraph 2 of this Article,

upon expressing its consent to be bound, may notify the Depositary in writing that the Agreement shall not apply between that signatory and any State that acceded to the Agreement, or any APEC member economy that agreed to be bound by the Agreement in accordance with the Annex, before the Agreement entered into force for that signatory.

6. This Agreement shall enter into force as between the acceding State and all Parties other than those which, pursuant to paragraph 5 of this Article, have notified the Depositary of the non-application of the Agreement, on the 30th day after the expiry of the 90-day period referred to in paragraph 5 of this Article.

Appendix

Australia; Brunei Darussalam; Canada; Chile; People's Republic of China; Hong Kong Special Administrative Region; Indonesia; Japan; Korea; Malaysia; Mexico; New Zealand; Papua New Guinea; Peru; Philippines; Russia; Singapore; Chinese Taipei; Thailand; United States; Vietnam

Convention on International Interests in Mobile Equipment ("Cape Town Convention")

THE STATES PARTIES TO THIS CONVENTION,

AWARE of the need to acquire and use mobile equipment of high value or particular economic significance and to facilitate the financing of the acquisition and use of such equipment in an efficient manner,

RECOGNISING the advantages of asset-based financing and leasing for this purpose and desiring to facilitate these types of transaction by establishing clear rules to govern them,

MINDFUL of the need to ensure that interests in such equipment are recognised and protected universally,

DESIRING to provide broad and mutual economic benefits for all interested parties,

BELIEVING that such rules must reflect the principles underlying asset-based financing and leasing and promote the autonomy of the parties necessary in these transactions,

CONSCIOUS of the need to establish a legal framework for international interests in such equipment and for that purpose to create an international registration system for their protection,

TAKING INTO CONSIDERATION the objectives and principles enunciated in existing Conventions relating to such equipment,

HAVE AGREED upon the following provisions:

Chapter I

Sphere of application and general provisions

Article 1—Definitions

In this Convention, except where the context otherwise requires, the following terms are employed with the meanings set out below:

(a) "agreement" means a security agreement, a title reservation agreement or a leasing agreement;

(b) "assignment" means a contract which, whether by way of security or otherwise, confers on the assignee associated rights with or without a transfer of the related international interest;

(c) "associated rights" means all rights to payment or other performance by a debtor under an agreement which are secured by or associated with the object;

(d) "commencement of the insolvency proceedings" means the time at which the insolvency proceedings are deemed to commence under the applicable insolvency law;

(e) "conditional buyer" means a buyer under a title reservation agreement;

(f) "conditional seller" means a seller under a title reservation agreement;

(g) "contract of sale" means a contract for the sale of an object by a seller to a buyer which is not an agreement as defined in (a) above;

(h) "court" means a court of law or an administrative or arbitral tribunal established by a Contracting State;

(i) "creditor" means a chargee under a security agreement, a conditional seller under a title reservation agreement or a lessor under a leasing agreement;

(j) "debtor" means a chargor under a security agreement, a conditional buyer under a title reservation agreement, a lessee under a leasing agreement or a person whose interest in an object is burdened by a registrable non-consensual right or interest;

(k) "insolvency administrator" means a person authorised to administer the reorganisation or liquidation, including one authorised on an interim basis, and includes a debtor in possession if permitted by the applicable insolvency law;

(*l*)   "insolvency proceedings" means bankruptcy, liquidation or other collective judicial or administrative proceedings, including interim proceedings, in which the assets and affairs of the debtor are subject to control or supervision by a court for the purposes of reorganisation or liquidation;

(m)   "interested persons" means:

(i)   the debtor;

(ii)   any person who, for the purpose of assuring performance of any of the obligations in favour of the creditor, gives or issues a suretyship or demand guarantee or a standby letter of credit or any other form of credit insurance;

(iii)   any other person having rights in or over the object;

(n)   "internal transaction" means a transaction of a type listed in Article 2(2)(a) to (c) where the centre of the main interests of all parties to such transaction is situated, and the relevant object located (as specified in the Protocol), in the same Contracting State at the time of the conclusion of the contract and where the interest created by the transaction has been registered in a national registry in that Contracting State which has made a declaration under Article 50(1);

(*o*)   "international interest" means an interest held by a creditor to which Article 2 applies;

(p)   "International Registry" means the international registration facilities established for the purposes of this Convention or the Protocol;

(q)   "leasing agreement" means an agreement by which one person (the lessor) grants a right to possession or control of an object (with or without an option to purchase) to another person (the lessee) in return for a rental or other payment;

(r)   "national interest" means an interest held by a creditor in an object and created by an internal transaction covered by a declaration under Article 50(1);

(s)   "non-consensual right or interest" means a right or interest conferred under the law of a Contracting State which has made a declaration under Article 39 to secure the performance of an obligation, including an obligation to a State, State entity or an intergovernmental or private organisation;

(t)   "notice of a national interest" means notice registered or to be registered in the International Registry that a national interest has been created;

(u)   "object" means an object of a category to which Article 2 applies;

(v)   "pre-existing right or interest" means a right or interest of any kind in or over an object created or arising before the effective date of this Convention as defined by Article 60(2)(a);

(w)   "proceeds" means money or non-money proceeds of an object arising from the total or partial loss or physical destruction of the object or its total or partial confiscation, condemnation or requisition;

(x)   "prospective assignment" means an assignment that is intended to be made in the future, upon the occurrence of a stated event, whether or not the occurrence of the event is certain;

(y)   "prospective international interest" means an interest that is intended to be created or provided for in an object as an international interest in the future, upon the occurrence of a stated event (which may include the debtor's acquisition of an interest in the object), whether or not the occurrence of the event is certain;

(z)   "prospective sale" means a sale which is intended to be made in the future, upon the occurrence of a stated event, whether or not the occurrence of the event is certain;

(aa) "Protocol" means, in respect of any category of object and associated rights to which this Convention applies, the Protocol in respect of that category of object and associated rights;

(bb) "registered" means registered in the International Registry pursuant to Chapter V;

(cc) "registered interest" means an international interest, a registrable non-consensual right or interest or a national interest specified in a notice of a national interest registered pursuant to Chapter V;

(dd) "registrable non-consensual right or interest" means a non-consensual right or interest registrable pursuant to a declaration deposited under Article 40;

(ee) "Registrar" means, in respect of the Protocol, the person or body designated by that Protocol or appointed under Article 17(2)(b);

(ff) "regulations" means regulations made or approved by the Supervisory Authority pursuant to the Protocol;

(gg) "sale" means a transfer of ownership of an object pursuant to a contract of sale;

(hh) "secured obligation" means an obligation secured by a security interest;

(ii) "security agreement" means an agreement by which a chargor grants or agrees to grant to a chargee an interest (including an ownership interest) in or over an object to secure the performance of any existing or future obligation of the chargor or a third person;

(jj) "security interest" means an interest created by a security agreement;

(kk) "Supervisory Authority" means, in respect of the Protocol, the Supervisory Authority referred to in Article 17(1);

(ll) "title reservation agreement" means an agreement for the sale of an object on terms that ownership does not pass until fulfilment of the condition or conditions stated in the agreement;

(mm) "unregistered interest" means a consensual interest or non-consensual right or interest (other than an interest to which Article 39 applies) which has not been registered, whether or not it is registrable under this Convention; and

(nn) "writing" means a record of information (including information communicated by teletransmission) which is in tangible or other form and is capable of being reproduced in tangible form on a subsequent occasion and which indicates by reasonable means a person's approval of the record.

Article 2—The international interest

1. This Convention provides for the constitution and effects of an international interest in certain categories of mobile equipment and associated rights.

2. For the purposes of this Convention, an international interest in mobile equipment is an interest, constituted under Article 7, in a uniquely identifiable object of a category of such objects listed in paragraph 3 and designated in the Protocol:

(a) granted by the chargor under a security agreement;

(b) vested in a person who is the conditional seller under a title reservation agreement; or

(c) vested in a person who is the lessor under a leasing agreement.

An interest falling within sub-paragraph (a) does not also fall within sub-paragraph (b) or (c).

3.   The categories referred to in the preceding paragraphs are:

(a)   airframes, aircraft engines and helicopters;

(b)   railway rolling stock; and

(c)   space assets.

4.   The applicable law determines whether an interest to which paragraph 2 applies falls within subparagraph (a), (b) or (c) of that paragraph.

5.   An international interest in an object extends to proceeds of that object.

Article 3—Sphere of application

1.   This Convention applies when, at the time of the conclusion of the agreement creating or providing for the international interest, the debtor is situated in a Contracting State.

2.   The fact that the creditor is situated in a non-Contracting State does not affect the applicability of this Convention.

Article 4—Where debtor is situated

1.   For the purposes of Article 3(1), the debtor is situated in any Contracting State:

(a)   under the law of which it is incorporated or formed;

(b)   where it has its registered office or statutory seat;

(c)   where it has its centre of administration; or

(d)   where it has its place of business.

2.   A reference in sub-paragraph (d) of the preceding paragraph to the debtor's place of business shall, if it has more than one place of business, mean its principal place of business or, if it has no place of business, its habitual residence.

Article 5—Interpretation and applicable law

1.   In the interpretation of this Convention, regard is to be had to its purposes as set forth in the preamble, to its international character and to the need to promote uniformity and predictability in its application.

2.   Questions concerning matters governed by this Convention which are not expressly settled in it are to be settled in conformity with the general principles on

which it is based or, in the absence of such principles, in conformity with the applicable law.

3. References to the applicable law are to the domestic rules of the law applicable by virtue of the rules of private international law of the forum State.

4. Where a State comprises several territorial units, each of which has its own rules of law in respect of the matter to be decided, and where there is no indication of the relevant territorial unit, the law of that State decides which is the territorial unit whose rules shall govern. In the absence of any such rule, the law of the territorial unit with which the case is most closely connected shall apply.

Article 6—Relationship between the Convention and the Protocol

1. This Convention and the Protocol shall be read and interpreted together as a single instrument.

2. To the extent of any inconsistency between this Convention and the Protocol, the Protocol shall prevail.

Chapter II

Constitution of an international interest

Article 7—Formal requirements

An interest is constituted as an international interest under this Convention where the agreement creating or providing for the interest:

(a) is in writing;

(b) relates to an object of which the chargor, conditional seller or lessor has power to dispose;

(c) enables the object to be identified in conformity with the Protocol; and

(d) in the case of a security agreement, enables the secured obligations to be determined, but without the need to state a sum or maximum sum secured.

Chapter III

Default remedies

Article 8—Remedies of chargee

1. In the event of default as provided in Article 11, the chargee may, to the extent that the chargor has at any time so agreed and subject to any declaration that may be made by a Contracting State under Article 54, exercise any one or more of the following remedies:

(a)   take possession or control of any object charged to it;

(b)   sell or grant a lease of any such object;

(c)   collect or receive any income or profits arising from the management or use of any such object.

2.   The chargee may alternatively apply for a court order authorising or directing any of the acts referred to in the preceding paragraph.

3.   Any remedy set out in sub-paragraph (a), (b) or (c) of paragraph 1 or by Article 13 shall be exercised in a commercially reasonable manner. A remedy shall be deemed to be exercised in a commercially reasonable manner where it is exercised in conformity with a provision of the security agreement except where such a provision is manifestly unreasonable.

4.   A chargee proposing to sell or grant a lease of an object under paragraph 1 shall give reasonable prior notice in writing of the proposed sale or lease to:

(a)   interested persons specified in Article 1(m)(i) and (ii); and

(b)   interested persons specified in Article 1(m)(iii) who have given notice of their rights to the chargee within a reasonable time prior to the sale or lease.

5.   Any sum collected or received by the chargee as a result of exercise of any of the remedies set out in paragraph 1 or 2 shall be applied towards discharge of the amount of the secured obligations.

6.   Where the sums collected or received by the chargee as a result of the exercise of any remedy set out in paragraph 1 or 2 exceed the amount secured by the security interest and any reasonable costs incurred in the exercise of any such remedy, then unless otherwise ordered by the court the chargee shall distribute the surplus among holders of subsequently ranking interests which have been registered or of which the chargee has been given notice, in order of priority, and pay any remaining balance to the chargor.

Article 9—Vesting of object in satisfaction; redemption

1.   At any time after default as provided in Article 11, the chargee and all the interested persons may agree that ownership of (or any other interest of the chargor in) any object covered by the security interest shall vest in the chargee in or towards satisfaction of the secured obligations.

2.   The court may on the application of the chargee order that ownership of (or any other interest of the chargor in) any object covered by the security interest shall vest in the chargee in or towards satisfaction of the secured obligations.

3.   The court shall grant an application under the preceding paragraph only if the amount of the secured obligations to be satisfied by such vesting is commensurate with the value of the object after taking account of any payment to be made by the chargee to any of the interested persons.

4.   At any time after default as provided in Article 11 and before sale of the charged object or the making of an order under paragraph 2, the chargor or any interested person may discharge the security interest by paying in full the amount secured, subject to any lease granted by the chargee under Article 8(1)(b) or ordered under Article 8(2). Where, after such default, the payment of the amount secured is made in full by an interested person other than the debtor, that person is subrogated to the rights of the chargee.

5.   Ownership or any other interest of the chargor passing on a sale under Article 8(1)(b) or passing under paragraph 1 or 2 of this Article is free from any other interest over which the chargee's security interest has priority under the provisions of Article 29.

Article 10—Remedies of conditional seller or lessor

In the event of default under a title reservation agreement or under a leasing agreement as provided in Article 11, the conditional seller or the lessor, as the case may be, may:

(a)   subject to any declaration that may be made by a Contracting State under Article 54, terminate the agreement and take possession or control of any object to which the agreement relates; or

(b)   apply for a court order authorising or directing either of these acts.

Article 11—Meaning of default

1.   The debtor and the creditor may at any time agree in writing as to the events that constitute a default or otherwise give rise to the rights and remedies specified in Articles 8 to 10 and 13.

2.   Where the debtor and the creditor have not so agreed, "default" for the purposes of Articles 8 to 10 and 13 means a default which substantially deprives the creditor of what it is entitled to expect under the agreement.

Article 12—Additional remedies

Any additional remedies permitted by the applicable law, including any remedies agreed upon by the parties, may be exercised to the extent that they are not inconsistent with the mandatory provisions of this Chapter as set out in Article 15.

Article 13—Relief pending final determination

1. Subject to any declaration that it may make under Article 55, a Contracting State shall ensure that a creditor who adduces evidence of default by the debtor may, pending final determination of its claim and to the extent that the debtor has at any time so agreed, obtain from a court speedy relief in the form of such one or more of the following orders as the creditor requests:

   (a) preservation of the object and its value;

   (b) possession, control or custody of the object;

   (c) immobilisation of the object; and

   (d) lease or, except where covered by sub-paragraphs (a) to (c), management of the object and the income therefrom.

2. In making any order under the preceding paragraph, the court may impose such terms as it considers necessary to protect the interested persons in the event that the creditor:

   (a) in implementing any order granting such relief, fails to perform any of its obligations to the debtor under this Convention or the Protocol; or

   (b) fails to establish its claim, wholly or in part, on the final determination of that claim.

3. Before making any order under paragraph 1, the court may require notice of the request to be given to any of the interested persons.

4. Nothing in this Article affects the application of Article 8(3) or limits the availability of forms of interim relief other than those set out in paragraph 1.

Article 14—Procedural requirements

Subject to Article 54(2), any remedy provided by this Chapter shall be exercised in conformity with the procedure prescribed by the law of the place where the remedy is to be exercised.

Article 15—Derogation

In their relations with each other, any two or more of the parties referred to in this Chapter may at any time, by agreement in writing, derogate from or vary the effect of any of the preceding provisions of this Chapter except Articles 8(3) to (6), 9(3) and (4), 13(2) and 14.

Chapter IV

The international registration system

Article 16—The International Registry

1. An International Registry shall be established for registrations of:

    (a) international interests, prospective international interests and registrable non-consensual rights and interests;

    (b) assignments and prospective assignments of international interests;

    (c) acquisitions of international interests by legal or contractual subrogations under the applicable law;

    (d) notices of national interests; and

    (e) subordinations of interests referred to in any of the preceding sub-paragraphs.

2. Different international registries may be established for different categories of object and associated rights.

3. For the purposes of this Chapter and Chapter V, the term "registration" includes, where appropriate, an amendment, extension or discharge of a registration.

Article 17—The Supervisory Authority and the Registrar

1. There shall be a Supervisory Authority as provided by the Protocol.

2. The Supervisory Authority shall:

    (a) establish or provide for the establishment of the International Registry;

    (b) except as otherwise provided by the Protocol, appoint and dismiss the Registrar;

    (c) ensure that any rights required for the continued effective operation of the International Registry in the event of a change of Registrar will vest in or be assignable to the new Registrar;

    (d) after consultation with the Contracting States, make or approve and ensure the publication of regulations pursuant to the Protocol dealing with the operation of the International Registry;

    (e) establish administrative procedures through which complaints concerning the operation of the International Registry can be made to the Supervisory Authority;

(f)   supervise the Registrar and the operation of the International Registry;

(g)   at the request of the Registrar, provide such guidance to the Registrar as the Supervisory Authority thinks fit;

(h)   set and periodically review the structure of fees to be charged for the services and facilities of the International Registry;

(i)   do all things necessary to ensure that an efficient notice-based electronic registration system exists to implement the objectives of this Convention and the Protocol; and

(j)   report periodically to Contracting States concerning the discharge of its obligations under this Convention and the Protocol.

3.   The Supervisory Authority may enter into any agreement requisite for the performance of its functions, including any agreement referred to in Article 27(3).

4.   The Supervisory Authority shall own all proprietary rights in the data bases and archives of the International Registry.

5.   The Registrar shall ensure the efficient operation of the International Registry and perform the functions assigned to it by this Convention, the Protocol and the regulations.

Chapter V

Other matters relating to registration

Article 18—Registration requirements

1.   The Protocol and regulations shall specify the requirements, including the criteria for the identification of the object:

(a)   for effecting a registration (which shall include provision for prior electronic transmission of any consent from any person whose consent is required under Article 20);

(b)   for making searches and issuing search certificates, and, subject thereto;

(c)   for ensuring the confidentiality of information and documents of the International Registry other than information and documents relating to a registration.

2.   The Registrar shall not be under a duty to enquire whether a consent to registration under Article 20 has in fact been given or is valid.

3.   Where an interest registered as a prospective international interest becomes an international interest, no further registration shall be required provided that the registration information is sufficient for a registration of an international interest.

4.   The Registrar shall arrange for registrations to be entered into the International Registry data base and made searchable in chronological order of receipt, and the file shall record the date and time of receipt.

5.   The Protocol may provide that a Contracting State may designate an entity or entities in its territory as the entry point or entry points through which the information required for registration shall or may be transmitted to the International Registry. A Contracting State making such a designation may specify the requirements, if any, to be satisfied before such information is transmitted to the International Registry.

Article 19—Validity and time of registration

1.   A registration shall be valid only if made in conformity with Article 20.

2.   A registration, if valid, shall be complete upon entry of the required information into the International Registry data base so as to be searchable.

3.   A registration shall be searchable for the purposes of the preceding paragraph at the time when:

  (a)   the International Registry has assigned to it a sequentially ordered file number; and

  (b)   the registration information, including the file number, is stored in durable form and may be accessed at the International Registry.

4.   If an interest first registered as a prospective international interest becomes an international interest, that international interest shall be treated as registered from the time of registration of the prospective international interest provided that the registration was still current immediately before the international interest was constituted as provided by Article 7.

5.   The preceding paragraph applies with necessary modifications to the registration of a prospective assignment of an international interest.

6.   A registration shall be searchable in the International Registry data base according to the criteria prescribed by the Protocol.

Article 20—Consent to registration

1.   An international interest, a prospective international interest or an assignment or prospective assignment of an international interest may be

registered, and any such registration amended or extended prior to its expiry, by either party with the consent in writing of the other.

2.   The subordination of an international interest to another international interest may be registered by or with the consent in writing at any time of the person whose interest has been subordinated.

3.   A registration may be discharged by or with the consent in writing of the party in whose favour it was made.

4.   The acquisition of an international interest by legal or contractual subrogation may be registered by the subrogee.

5.   A registrable non-consensual right or interest may be registered by the holder thereof.

6.   A notice of a national interest may be registered by the holder thereof.

Article 21—Duration of registration

Registration of an international interest remains effective until discharged or until expiry of the period specified in the registration.

Article 22—Searches

1.   Any person may, in the manner prescribed by the Protocol and regulations, make or request a search of the International Registry by electronic means concerning interests or prospective international interests registered therein.

2.   Upon receipt of a request therefor, the Registrar, in the manner prescribed by the Protocol and regulations, shall issue a registry search certificate by electronic means with respect to any object:

(a)   stating all registered information relating thereto, together with a statement indicating the date and time of registration of such information; or

(b)   stating that there is no information in the International Registry relating thereto.

3.   A search certificate issued under the preceding paragraph shall indicate that the creditor named in the registration information has acquired or intends to acquire an international interest in the object but shall not indicate whether what is registered is an international interest or a prospective international interest, even if this is ascertainable from the relevant registration information.

Article 23—List of declarations and declared
non-consensual rights or interests

The Registrar shall maintain a list of declarations, withdrawals of declaration and of the categories of nonconsensual right or interest communicated to the Registrar by the Depositary as having been declared by Contracting States in conformity with Articles 39 and 40 and the date of each such declaration or withdrawal of declaration. Such list shall be recorded and searchable in the name of the declaring State and shall be made available as provided in the Protocol and regulations to any person requesting it.

Article 24—Evidentiary value of certificates

A document in the form prescribed by the regulations which purports to be a certificate issued by the International Registry is prima facie proof:

(a) that it has been so issued; and

(b) of the facts recited in it, including the date and time of a registration.

Article 25—Discharge of registration

1. Where the obligations secured by a registered security interest or the obligations giving rise to a registered non-consensual right or interest have been discharged, or where the conditions of transfer of title under a registered title reservation agreement have been fulfilled, the holder of such interest shall, without undue delay, procure the discharge of the registration after written demand by the debtor delivered to or received at its address stated in the registration.

2. Where a prospective international interest or a prospective assignment of an international interest has been registered, the intending creditor or intending assignee shall, without undue delay, procure the discharge of the registration after written demand by the intending debtor or assignor which is delivered to or received at its address stated in the registration before the intending creditor or assignee has given value or incurred a commitment to give value.

3. Where the obligations secured by a national interest specified in a registered notice of a national interest have been discharged, the holder of such interest shall, without undue delay, procure the discharge of the registration after written demand by the debtor delivered to or received at its address stated in the registration.

4. Where a registration ought not to have been made or is incorrect, the person in whose favour the registration was made shall, without undue delay, procure its

discharge or amendment after written demand by the debtor delivered to or received at its address stated in the registration.

Article 26—Access to the international registration facilities

No person shall be denied access to the registration and search facilities of the International Registry on any ground other than its failure to comply with the procedures prescribed by this Chapter.

Chapter VI

Privileges and immunities of the Supervisory Authority and the Registrar

Article 27—Legal personality; immunity

1.   The Supervisory Authority shall have international legal personality where not already possessing such personality.

2.   The Supervisory Authority and its officers and employees shall enjoy such immunity from legal or administrative process as is specified in the Protocol.

3.   (a)   The Supervisory Authority shall enjoy exemption from taxes and such other privileges as may be provided by agreement with the host State.

(b)   For the purposes of this paragraph, "host State" means the State in which the Supervisory Authority is situated.

4.   The assets, documents, data bases and archives of the International Registry shall be inviolable and immune from seizure or other legal or administrative process.

5.   For the purposes of any claim against the Registrar under Article 28(1) or Article 44, the claimant shall be entitled to access to such information and documents as are necessary to enable the claimant to pursue its claim.

6.   The Supervisory Authority may waive the inviolability and immunity conferred by paragraph 4.

Chapter VII

Liability of the Registrar

Article 28—Liability and financial assurances

1.   The Registrar shall be liable for compensatory damages for loss suffered by a person directly resulting from an error or omission of the Registrar and its officers and employees or from a malfunction of the international registration system except where the malfunction is caused by an event of an inevitable and irresistible nature, which could not be prevented by using the best practices in

current use in the field of electronic registry design and operation, including those related to back-up and systems security and networking.

2.   The Registrar shall not be liable under the preceding paragraph for factual inaccuracy of registration information received by the Registrar or transmitted by the Registrar in the form in which it received that information nor for acts or circumstances for which the Registrar and its officers and employees are not responsible and arising prior to receipt of registration information at the International Registry.

3.   Compensation under paragraph 1 may be reduced to the extent that the person who suffered the damage caused or contributed to that damage.

4.   The Registrar shall procure insurance or a financial guarantee covering the liability referred to in this Article to the extent determined by the Supervisory Authority, in accordance with the Protocol.

Chapter VIII

Effects of an international interest as against third parties

Article 29—Priority of competing interests

1.   A registered interest has priority over any other interest subsequently registered and over an unregistered interest.

2.   The priority of the first-mentioned interest under the preceding paragraph applies:

 (a)   even if the first-mentioned interest was acquired or registered with actual knowledge of the other interest; and

 (b)   even as regards value given by the holder of the first-mentioned interest with such knowledge.

3.   The buyer of an object acquires its interest in it:

 (a)   subject to an interest registered at the time of its acquisition of that interest; and

 (b)   free from an unregistered interest even if it has actual knowledge of such an interest.

4.   The conditional buyer or lessee acquires its interest in or right over that object:

 (a)   subject to an interest registered prior to the registration of the international interest held by its conditional seller or lessor; and

(b) free from an interest not so registered at that time even if it has actual knowledge of that interest.

5.   The priority of competing interests or rights under this Article may be varied by agreement between the holders of those interests, but an assignee of a subordinated interest is not bound by an agreement to subordinate that interest unless at the time of the assignment a subordination had been registered relating to that agreement.

6.   Any priority given by this Article to an interest in an object extends to proceeds.

7.   This Convention:

(a) does not affect the rights of a person in an item, other than an object, held prior to its installation on an object if under the applicable law those rights continue to exist after the installation; and

(b) does not prevent the creation of rights in an item, other than an object, which has previously been installed on an object where under the applicable law those rights are created.

Article 30—Effects of insolvency

1.   In insolvency proceedings against the debtor an international interest is effective if prior to the commencement of the insolvency proceedings that interest was registered in conformity with this Convention.

2.   Nothing in this Article impairs the effectiveness of an international interest in the insolvency proceedings where that interest is effective under the applicable law.

3.   Nothing in this Article affects:

(a) any rules of law applicable in insolvency proceedings relating to the avoidance of a transaction as a preference or a transfer in fraud of creditors; or

(b) any rules of procedure relating to the enforcement of rights to property which is under the control or supervision of the insolvency administrator.

Chapter IX

Assignments of associated rights and international
interests; rights of subrogation

Article 31—Effects of assignment

1.   Except as otherwise agreed by the parties, an assignment of associated rights made in conformity with Article 32 also transfers to the assignee:

(a)   the related international interest; and

(b)   all the interests and priorities of the assignor under this Convention.

2.   Nothing in this Convention prevents a partial assignment of the assignor's associated rights. In the case of such a partial assignment the assignor and assignee may agree as to their respective rights concerning the related international interest assigned under the preceding paragraph but not so as adversely to affect the debtor without its consent.

3.   Subject to paragraph 4, the applicable law shall determine the defences and rights of set-off available to the debtor against the assignee.

4.   The debtor may at any time by agreement in writing waive all or any of the defences and rights of set-off referred to in the preceding paragraph other than defences arising from fraudulent acts on the part of the assignee.

5.   In the case of an assignment by way of security, the assigned associated rights revest in the assignor, to the extent that they are still subsisting, when the obligations secured by the assignment have been discharged.

Article 32—Formal requirements of assignment

1.   An assignment of associated rights transfers the related international interest only if it:

(a)   is in writing;

(b)   enables the associated rights to be identified under the contract from which they arise; and

(c)   in the case of an assignment by way of security, enables the obligations secured by the assignment to be determined in accordance with the Protocol but without the need to state a sum or maximum sum secured.

2.   An assignment of an international interest created or provided for by a security agreement is not valid unless some or all related associated rights also are assigned.

3.   This Convention does not apply to an assignment of associated rights which is not effective to transfer the related international interest.

Article 33—Debtor's duty to assignee

1.   To the extent that associated rights and the related international interest have been transferred in accordance with Articles 31 and 32, the debtor in relation to those rights and that interest is bound by the assignment and has a duty to make payment or give other performance to the assignee, if but only if:

(a)   the debtor has been given notice of the assignment in writing by or with the authority of the assignor; and

(b)   the notice identifies the associated rights.

2.   Irrespective of any other ground on which payment or performance by the debtor discharges the latter from liability, payment or performance shall be effective for this purpose if made in accordance with the preceding paragraph.

3.   Nothing in this Article shall affect the priority of competing assignments.

Article 34—Default remedies in respect of assignment by way of security

In the event of default by the assignor under the assignment of associated rights and the related international interest made by way of security, Articles 8, 9 and 11 to 14 apply in the relations between the assignor and the assignee (and, in relation to associated rights, apply in so far as those provisions are capable of application to intangible property) as if references:

(a)   to the secured obligation and the security interest were references to the obligation secured by the assignment of the associated rights and the related international interest and the security interest created by that assignment;

(b)   to the chargee or creditor and chargor or debtor were references to the assignee and assignor;

(c)   to the holder of the international interest were references to the assignee; and

(d)   to the object were references to the assigned associated rights and the related international interest.

Article 35—Priority of competing assignments

1.   Where there are competing assignments of associated rights and at least one of the assignments includes the related international interest and is registered, the provisions of Article 29 apply as if the references to a registered interest were

references to an assignment of the associated rights and the related registered interest and as if references to a registered or unregistered interest were references to a registered or unregistered assignment.

2.   Article 30 applies to an assignment of associated rights as if the references to an international interest were references to an assignment of the associated rights and the related international interest.

Article 36—Assignee's priority with respect to associated rights

1.   The assignee of associated rights and the related international interest whose assignment has been registered only has priority under Article 35(1) over another assignee of the associated rights:

(a)   if the contract under which the associated rights arise states that they are secured by or associated with the object; and

(b)   to the extent that the associated rights are related to an object.

2.   For the purposes of sub-paragraph (b) of the preceding paragraph, associated rights are related to an object only to the extent that they consist of rights to payment or performance that relate to:

(a)   a sum advanced and utilised for the purchase of the object;

(b)   a sum advanced and utilised for the purchase of another object in which the assignor held another international interest if the assignor transferred that interest to the assignee and the assignment has been registered;

(c)   the price payable for the object;

(d)   the rentals payable in respect of the object; or

(e)   other obligations arising from a transaction referred to in any of the preceding subparagraphs.

3.   In all other cases, the priority of the competing assignments of the associated rights shall be determined by the applicable law.

Article 37—Effects of assignor's insolvency

The provisions of Article 30 apply to insolvency proceedings against the assignor as if references to the debtor were references to the assignor.

Article 38—Subrogation

1.   Subject to paragraph 2, nothing in this Convention affects the acquisition of associated rights and the related international interest by legal or contractual subrogation under the applicable law.

2.   The priority between any interest within the preceding paragraph and a competing interest may be varied by agreement in writing between the holders of the respective interests but an assignee of a subordinated interest is not bound by an agreement to subordinate that interest unless at the time of the assignment a subordination had been registered relating to that agreement.

Chapter X

Rights or interests subject to declarations by Contracting States

Article 39—Rights having priority without registration

1.   A Contracting State may at any time, in a declaration deposited with the Depositary of the Protocol declare, generally or specifically:

(a)   those categories of non-consensual right or interest (other than a right or interest to which Article 40 applies) which under that State's law have priority over an interest in an object equivalent to that of the holder of a registered international interest and which shall have priority over a registered international interest, whether in or outside insolvency proceedings; and

(b)   that nothing in this Convention shall affect the right of a State or State entity, intergovernmental organisation or other private provider of public services to arrest or detain an object under the laws of that State for payment of amounts owed to such entity, organisation or provider directly relating to those services in respect of that object or another object.

2.   A declaration made under the preceding paragraph may be expressed to cover categories that are created after the deposit of that declaration.

3.   A non-consensual right or interest has priority over an international interest if and only if the former is of a category covered by a declaration deposited prior to the registration of the international interest.

4.   Notwithstanding the preceding paragraph, a Contracting State may, at the time of ratification, acceptance, approval of, or accession to the Protocol, declare that a right or interest of a category covered by a declaration made under sub-

paragraph (a) of paragraph 1 shall have priority over an international interest registered prior to the date of such ratification, acceptance, approval or accession.

Article 40—Registrable non-consensual rights or interests

A Contracting State may at any time in a declaration deposited with the Depositary of the Protocol list the categories of non-consensual right or interest which shall be registrable under this Convention as regards any category of object as if the right or interest were an international interest and shall be regulated accordingly. Such a declaration may be modified from time to time.

Chapter XI

Application of the Convention to sales

Article 41—Sale and prospective sale

This Convention shall apply to the sale or prospective sale of an object as provided for in the Protocol with any modifications therein.

Chapter XII

Jurisdiction

Article 42—Choice of forum

1.   Subject to Articles 43 and 44, the courts of a Contracting State chosen by the parties to a transaction have jurisdiction in respect of any claim brought under this Convention, whether or not the chosen forum has a connection with the parties or the transaction. Such jurisdiction shall be exclusive unless otherwise agreed between the parties.

2.   Any such agreement shall be in writing or otherwise concluded in accordance with the formal requirements of the law of the chosen forum.

Article 43—Jurisdiction under Article 13

1.   The courts of a Contracting State chosen by the parties and the courts of the Contracting State on the territory of which the object is situated have jurisdiction to grant relief under Article 13(1)(a), (b), (c) and Article 13(4) in respect of that object.

2.   Jurisdiction to grant relief under Article 13(1)(d) or other interim relief by virtue of Article 13(4) may be exercised either:

   (a)   by the courts chosen by the parties; or

(b)   by the courts of a Contracting State on the territory of which the debtor is situated, being relief which, by the terms of the order granting it, is enforceable only in the territory of that Contracting State.

3.   A court has jurisdiction under the preceding paragraphs even if the final determination of the claim referred to in Article 13(1) will or may take place in a court of another Contracting State or by arbitration.

Article 44—Jurisdiction to make orders against the Registrar

1.   The courts of the place in which the Registrar has its centre of administration shall have exclusive jurisdiction to award damages or make orders against the Registrar.

2.   Where a person fails to respond to a demand made under Article 25 and that person has ceased to exist or cannot be found for the purpose of enabling an order to be made against it requiring it to procure discharge of the registration, the courts referred to in the preceding paragraph shall have exclusive jurisdiction, on the application of the debtor or intending debtor, to make an order directed to the Registrar requiring the Registrar to discharge the registration.

3.   Where a person fails to comply with an order of a court having jurisdiction under this Convention or, in the case of a national interest, an order of a court of competent jurisdiction requiring that person to procure the amendment or discharge of a registration, the courts referred to in paragraph 1 may direct the Registrar to take such steps as will give effect to that order.

4.   Except as otherwise provided by the preceding paragraphs, no court may make orders or give judgments or rulings against or purporting to bind the Registrar.

Article 45—Jurisdiction in respect of insolvency proceedings

The provisions of this Chapter are not applicable to insolvency proceedings.

Chapter XIII

Relationship with other Conventions

Article 45 bis—Relationship with the *United Nations Convention on the Assignment of Receivables in International Trade*

This Convention shall prevail over the United Nations Convention on the Assignment of Receivables in International Trade, opened for signature in New York on 12 December 2001, as it relates to the assignment of receivables which are associated rights related to international interests in aircraft objects, railway rolling stock and space assets.

Article 46—Relationship with the *UNIDROIT Convention on International Financial Leasing*

The Protocol may determine the relationship between this Convention and the UNIDROIT Convention on International Financial Leasing, signed at Ottawa on 28 May 1988.

Chapter XIV

Final provisions

Article 47—Signature, ratification, acceptance, approval or accession

1.   This Convention shall be open for signature in Cape Town on 16 November 2001 by States participating in the Diplomatic Conference to Adopt a Mobile Equipment Convention and an Aircraft Protocol held at Cape Town from 29 October to 16 November 2001. After 16 November 2001, the Convention shall be open to all States for signature at the Headquarters of the International Institute for the Unification of Private Law (UNIDROIT) in Rome until it enters into force in accordance with Article 49.

2.   This Convention shall be subject to ratification, acceptance or approval by States which have signed it.

3.   Any State which does not sign this Convention may accede to it at any time.

4.   Ratification, acceptance, approval or accession is effected by the deposit of a formal instrument to that effect with the Depositary.

Article 48—Regional Economic Integration Organisations

1.   A Regional Economic Integration Organisation which is constituted by sovereign States and has competence over certain matters governed by this Convention may similarly sign, accept, approve or accede to this Convention. The Regional Economic Integration Organisation shall in that case have the rights and obligations of a Contracting State, to the extent that that Organisation has competence over matters governed by this Convention. Where the number of Contracting States is relevant in this Convention, the Regional Economic Integration Organisation shall not count as a Contracting State in addition to its Member States which are Contracting States.

2.   The Regional Economic Integration Organisation shall, at the time of signature, acceptance, approval or accession, make a declaration to the Depositary specifying the matters governed by this Convention in respect of which competence has been transferred to that Organisation by its Member States. The Regional Economic Integration Organisation shall promptly notify the Depositary

of any changes to the distribution of competence, including new transfers of competence, specified in the declaration under this paragraph.

3.   Any reference to a "Contracting State" or "Contracting States" or "State Party" or "States Parties" in this Convention applies equally to a Regional Economic Integration Organisation where the context so requires.

Article 49—Entry into force

1.   This Convention enters into force on the first day of the month following the expiration of three months after the date of the deposit of the third instrument of ratification, acceptance, approval or accession but only as regards a category of objects to which a Protocol applies:

(a)   as from the time of entry into force of that Protocol;

(b)   subject to the terms of that Protocol; and

(c)   as between States Parties to this Convention and that Protocol.

2.   For other States this Convention enters into force on the first day of the month following the expiration of three months after the date of the deposit of their instrument of ratification, acceptance, approval or accession but only as regards a category of objects to which a Protocol applies and subject, in relation to such Protocol, to the requirements of sub-paragraphs (a), (b) and (c) of the preceding paragraph.

Article 50—Internal transactions

1.   A Contracting State may, at the time of ratification, acceptance, approval of, or accession to the Protocol, declare that this Convention shall not apply to a transaction which is an internal transaction in relation to that State with regard to all types of objects or some of them.

2.   Notwithstanding the preceding paragraph, the provisions of Articles 8(4), 9(1), 16, Chapter V, Article 29, and any provisions of this Convention relating to registered interests shall apply to an internal transaction.

3.   Where notice of a national interest has been registered in the International Registry, the priority of the holder of that interest under Article 29 shall not be affected by the fact that such interest has become vested in another person by assignment or subrogation under the applicable law.

Article 51—Future Protocols

1.   The Depositary may create working groups, in co-operation with such relevant non-governmental organisations as the Depositary considers appropriate,

to assess the feasibility of extending the application of this Convention, through one or more Protocols, to objects of any category of high-value mobile equipment, other than a category referred to in Article 2(3), each member of which is uniquely identifiable, and associated rights relating to such objects.

2. The Depositary shall communicate the text of any preliminary draft Protocol relating to a category of objects prepared by such a working group to all States Parties to this Convention, all member States of the Depositary, member States of the United Nations which are not members of the Depositary and the relevant intergovernmental organisations, and shall invite such States and organisations to participate in intergovernmental negotiations for the completion of a draft Protocol on the basis of such a preliminary draft Protocol.

3. The Depositary shall also communicate the text of any preliminary draft Protocol prepared by such a working group to such relevant non-governmental organisations as the Depositary considers appropriate. Such non-governmental organisations shall be invited promptly to submit comments on the text of the preliminary draft Protocol to the Depositary and to participate as observers in the preparation of a draft Protocol.

4. When the competent bodies of the Depositary adjudge such a draft Protocol ripe for adoption, the Depositary shall convene a diplomatic conference for its adoption.

5. Once such a Protocol has been adopted, subject to paragraph 6, this Convention shall apply to the category of objects covered thereby.

6. Article 45 bis of this Convention applies to such a Protocol only if specifically provided for in that Protocol.

Article 52—Territorial units

1. If a Contracting State has territorial units in which different systems of law are applicable in relation to the matters dealt with in this Convention, it may, at the time of ratification, acceptance, approval or accession, declare that this Convention is to extend to all its territorial units or only to one or more of them and may modify its declaration by submitting another declaration at any time.

2. Any such declaration shall state expressly the territorial units to which this Convention applies.

3. If a Contracting State has not made any declaration under paragraph 1, this Convention shall apply to all territorial units of that State.

4.   Where a Contracting State extends this Convention to one or more of its territorial units, declarations permitted under this Convention may be made in respect of each such territorial unit, and the declarations made in respect of one territorial unit may be different from those made in respect of another territorial unit.

5.   If by virtue of a declaration under paragraph 1, this Convention extends to one or more territorial units of a Contracting State:

(a)   the debtor is considered to be situated in a Contracting State only if it is incorporated or formed under a law in force in a territorial unit to which this Convention applies or if it has its registered office or statutory seat, centre of administration, place of business or habitual residence in a territorial unit to which this Convention applies;

(b)   any reference to the location of the object in a Contracting State refers to the location of the object in a territorial unit to which this Convention applies; and

(c)   any reference to the administrative authorities in that Contracting State shall be construed as referring to the administrative authorities having jurisdiction in a territorial unit to which this Convention applies.

Article 53—Determination of courts

A Contracting State may, at the time of ratification, acceptance, approval of, or accession to the Protocol, declare the relevant "court" or "courts" for the purposes of Article 1 and Chapter XII of this Convention.

Article 54—Declarations regarding remedies

1.   A Contracting State may, at the time of ratification, acceptance, approval of, or accession to the Protocol, declare that while the charged object is situated within, or controlled from its territory the chargee shall not grant a lease of the object in that territory.

2.   A Contracting State shall, at the time of ratification, acceptance, approval of, or accession to the Protocol, declare whether or not any remedy available to the creditor under any provision of this Convention which is not there expressed to require application to the court may be exercised only with leave of the court.

Article 55—Declarations regarding relief pending final determination

A Contracting State may, at the time of ratification, acceptance, approval of, or accession to the Protocol, declare that it will not apply the provisions of Article 13 or Article 43, or both, wholly or in part. The declaration shall specify under which conditions the relevant Article will be applied, in case it will be applied partly, or otherwise which other forms of interim relief will be applied.

Article 56—Reservations and declarations

1.   No reservations may be made to this Convention but declarations authorised by Articles 39, 40, 50, 52, 53, 54, 55, 57, 58 and 60 may be made in accordance with these provisions.

2.   Any declaration or subsequent declaration or any withdrawal of a declaration made under this Convention shall be notified in writing to the Depositary.

Article 57—Subsequent declarations

1.   A State Party may make a subsequent declaration, other than a declaration authorised under Article 60, at any time after the date on which this Convention has entered into force for it, by notifying the Depositary to that effect.

2.   Any such subsequent declaration shall take effect on the first day of the month following the expiration of six months after the date of receipt of the notification by the Depositary. Where a longer period for that declaration to take effect is specified in the notification, it shall take effect upon the expiration of such longer period after receipt of the notification by the Depositary.

3.   Notwithstanding the previous paragraphs, this Convention shall continue to apply, as if no such subsequent declarations had been made, in respect of all rights and interests arising prior to the effective date of any such subsequent declaration.

Article 58—Withdrawal of declarations

1.   Any State Party having made a declaration under this Convention, other than a declaration authorised under Article 60, may withdraw it at any time by notifying the Depositary. Such withdrawal is to take effect on the first day of the month following the expiration of six months after the date of receipt of the notification by the Depositary.

2.   Notwithstanding the previous paragraph, this Convention shall continue to apply, as if no such withdrawal of declaration had been made, in respect of all rights and interests arising prior to the effective date of any such withdrawal.

Article 59—Denunciations

1.   Any State Party may denounce this Convention by notification in writing to the Depositary.

2.   Any such denunciation shall take effect on the first day of the month following the expiration of twelve months after the date on which notification is received by the Depositary.

3.   Notwithstanding the previous paragraphs, this Convention shall continue to apply, as if no such denunciation had been made, in respect of all rights and interests arising prior to the effective date of any such denunciation.

Article 60—Transitional provisions

1.   Unless otherwise declared by a Contracting State at any time, the Convention does not apply to a pre-existing right or interest, which retains the priority it enjoyed under the applicable law before the effective date of this Convention.

2.   For the purposes of Article 1(v) and of determining priority under this Convention:

(a)   "effective date of this Convention" means in relation to a debtor the time when this Convention enters into force or the time when the State in which the debtor is situated becomes a Contracting State, whichever is the later; and

(b)   the debtor is situated in a State where it has its centre of administration or, if it has no centre of administration, its place of business or, if it has more than one place of business, its principal place of business or, if it has no place of business, its habitual residence.

3.   A Contracting State may in its declaration under paragraph 1 specify a date, not earlier than three years after the date on which the declaration becomes effective, when this Convention and the Protocol will become applicable, for the purpose of determining priority, including the protection of any existing priority, to pre-existing rights or interests arising under an agreement made at a time when the debtor was situated in a State referred to in sub-paragraph (b) of the preceding paragraph but only to the extent and in the manner specified in its declaration.

Article 61—Review Conferences, amendments and related matters

1.   The Depositary shall prepare reports yearly or at such other time as the circumstances may require for the States Parties as to the manner in which the international regimen established in this Convention has operated in practice. In preparing such reports, the Depositary shall take into account the reports of the Supervisory Authority concerning the functioning of the international registration system.

2.   At the request of not less than twenty-five per cent of the States Parties, Review Conferences of States Parties shall be convened from time to time by the Depositary, in consultation with the Supervisory Authority, to consider:

(a)   the practical operation of this Convention and its effectiveness in facilitating the asset-based financing and leasing of the objects covered by its terms;

(b)   the judicial interpretation given to, and the application made of the terms of this Convention and the regulations;

(c)   the functioning of the international registration system, the performance of the Registrar and its oversight by the Supervisory Authority, taking into account the reports of the Supervisory Authority; and

(d)   whether any modifications to this Convention or the arrangements relating to the International Registry are desirable.

3.   Subject to paragraph 4, any amendment to this Convention shall be approved by at least a two-thirds majority of States Parties participating in the Conference referred to in the preceding paragraph and shall then enter into force in respect of States which have ratified, accepted or approved such amendment when ratified, accepted, or approved by three States in accordance with the provisions of Article 49 relating to its entry into force.

4.   Where the proposed amendment to this Convention is intended to apply to more than one category of equipment, such amendment shall also be approved by at least a two-thirds majority of States Parties to each Protocol that are participating in the Conference referred to in paragraph 2.

Article 62—Depositary and its functions

1.   Instruments of ratification, acceptance, approval or accession shall be deposited with the International Institute for the Unification of Private Law (UNIDROIT), which is hereby designated the Depositary.

2.   The Depositary shall:

(a)   inform all Contracting States of:

(i)   each new signature or deposit of an instrument of ratification, acceptance, approval or accession, together with the date thereof;

(ii)   the date of entry into force of this Convention;

(iii)   each declaration made in accordance with this Convention, together with the date thereof;

(iv) the withdrawal or amendment of any declaration, together with the date thereof; and

(v) the notification of any denunciation of this Convention together with the date thereof and the date on which it takes effect;

(b) transmit certified true copies of this Convention to all Contracting States;

(c) provide the Supervisory Authority and the Registrar with a copy of each instrument of ratification, acceptance, approval or accession, together with the date of deposit thereof, of each declaration or withdrawal or amendment of a declaration and of each notification of denunciation, together with the date of notification thereof, so that the information contained therein is easily and fully available; and

(d) perform such other functions customary for depositaries.

IN WITNESS WHEREOF the undersigned Plenipotentiaries, having been duly authorised, have signed this Convention.

DONE at Cape Town, this sixteenth day of November, two thousand and one, in a single original in the English, Arabic, Chinese, French, Russian and Spanish languages, all texts being equally authentic, such authenticity to take effect upon verification by the Joint Secretariat of the Conference under the authority of the President of the Conference within ninety days hereof as to the conformity of the texts with one another.

United States Model
Open Skies Agreement

January 12, 2012

AIR TRANSPORT AGREEMENT

BETWEEN

THE GOVERNMENT OF

THE UNITED STATES OF AMERICA

AND

THE GOVERNMENT OF

[country]

The Government of the United States of America and the Government of [country] (hereinafter, "the Parties");

Desiring to promote an international aviation system based on competition among airlines in the marketplace with minimum government interference and regulation;

Desiring to make it possible for airlines to offer the traveling and shipping public a variety of service options, and wishing to encourage individual airlines to develop and implement innovative and competitive prices;

Desiring to facilitate the expansion of international air transport opportunities;

Desiring to ensure the highest degree of safety and security in international air transport and reaffirming their grave concern about acts or threats against the security of aircraft, which jeopardize the safety of persons or property, adversely affect the operation of air transportation, and undermine public confidence in the safety of civil aviation; and

Being Parties to the Convention on International Civil Aviation, done at Chicago December 7, 1944;

Have agreed as follows:

2

Article 1

Definitions

For the purposes of this Agreement, unless otherwise stated, the term:

1.   "Aeronautical authorities" means, in the case of the United States, the Department of Transportation and in the case of [country], the [appropriate entity], and any person or agency authorized to perform functions exercised by the Department of Transportation or said [appropriate entity];

2.   "Agreement" means this Agreement and any amendments thereto;

3.   "Air transportation" means the public carriage by aircraft of passengers, baggage, cargo, and mail, separately or in combination, scheduled or charter, for remuneration or hire;

4.   "Airline of a Party" means an airline that has received its Air Operator's Certificate (AOC) from and has its principal place of business in the territory of that Party;

5.   "Convention" means the Convention on International Civil Aviation, done at Chicago December 7, 1944, and includes:

        a. any amendment that has entered into force under Article 94(a) of the Convention and has been ratified by both Parties, and

        b. any Annex or any amendment thereto adopted under Article 90 of the Convention, insofar as such Annex or amendment is at any given time effective for both Parties;

6.   "Full cost" means the cost of providing service plus a reasonable charge for administrative overhead;

7.   "International air transportation" means air transportation that passes through the airspace over the territory of more than one State;

8.   "Price" means any fare, rate, or charge for the carriage of passengers, baggage, or cargo (excluding mail) in air transportation, including surface transportation in connection with international air transportation, charged by airlines, including their agents, and the conditions governing the availability of such fare, rate, or charge;

9.   "Stop for non-traffic purposes" means a landing for any purpose other than taking on or discharging passengers, baggage, cargo, or mail in air transportation;

10.   "Territory" means the land areas, internal waters, and territorial sea under the sovereignty of a Party; and

3

11.   "User charge" means a charge imposed on airlines for the provision of airport, airport environmental, air navigation, or aviation security facilities or services including related services and facilities.

Article 2

Grant of Rights

1.   Each Party grants to the other Party the following rights for the conduct of international air transportation by the airlines of the other Party:

    a.   the right to fly across its territory without landing;

    b.   the right to make stops in its territory for non-traffic purposes;

    c.   the right to perform international air transportation between points on the following routes:

        (i)   for airlines of the United States, from points behind the United States via the United States and intermediate points to any point or points in [country] and beyond; [and for all-cargo service, between [country] and any point or points;]

        (ii)   for airlines of [country], from points behind [country] via [country] and intermediate points to any point or points in the United States and beyond; [and for all-cargo service, between the United States and any point or points;] and

    d.   the rights otherwise specified in this Agreement.

2.   Each airline of a Party may, on any or all flights and at its option:

    a.   operate flights in either or both directions;

    b.   combine different flight numbers within one aircraft operation;

    c.   serve behind, intermediate, and beyond points and points in the territories of the Parties in any combination and in any order;

    d.   omit stops at any point or points;

    e.   transfer traffic from any of its aircraft to any of its other aircraft at any point;

4

        f.   serve points behind any point in its territory with or without change of aircraft or flight number and hold out and advertise such services to the public as through services;

        g.   make stopovers at any points whether within or outside the territory of either Party;

        h.   carry transit traffic through the other Party's territory; and

        i.   combine traffic on the same aircraft regardless of where such traffic originates;

without directional or geographic limitation and without loss of any right to carry traffic otherwise permissible under this Agreement, provided that, [with the exception of all-cargo services,] the transportation is part of a service that serves a point in the homeland of the airline.

3.   On any segment or segments of the routes above, any airline of a Party may perform international air transportation without any limitation as to change, at any point on the route, in type or number of aircraft operated, provided that, [with the exception of all-cargo services,] in the outbound direction, the transportation beyond such point is a continuation of the transportation from the homeland of the airline and, in the inbound direction, the transportation to the homeland of the airline is a continuation of the transportation from beyond such point.

4.   Nothing in this Article shall be deemed to confer on the airline or airlines of one Party the rights to take on board, in the territory of the other Party, passengers, baggage, cargo, or mail carried for compensation and destined for another point in the territory of that other Party.

5.   Any airline of a Party performing charter international air transportation originating in the territory of either Party, whether on a one-way or round-trip basis, shall have the option of complying with the charter laws, regulations, and rules either of its homeland or of the other Party. If a Party applies different rules, regulations, terms, conditions, or limitations to one or more of its airlines, or to airlines of different countries, each airline of the other Party shall be subject to the least restrictive of such criteria. Nothing in this paragraph shall limit the rights of a Party to require airlines of both Parties to adhere to requirements relating to the protection of passenger funds and passenger cancellation and refund rights. Except with respect to the consumer protection rules referred to in this paragraph, neither Party shall require an airline of the other Party, in respect of the carriage of traffic from the territory of that other Party or of a third country on a one-way or round-trip basis, to submit more than a notice that it is complying with the applicable laws, regulations, and rules referred to in this paragraph or of a waiver of these laws, regulations, or rules granted by the applicable aeronautical authorities.

Article 3

Authorization

5

Each Party, on receipt of applications from an airline of the other Party, in the form and manner prescribed for operating authorizations and technical permissions, shall grant appropriate authorizations and permissions with minimum procedural delay, provided:

　　　a.　substantial ownership and effective control of that airline are vested in the other Party, nationals of that Party, or both;

　　　b.　the airline is qualified to meet the conditions prescribed under the laws and regulations normally applied to the operation of international air transportation by the Party considering the application or applications; and

　　　c.　the other Party is maintaining and administering the provisions set forth in Article 6 (Safety) and Article 7 (Aviation Security).

Article 4

Revocation of Authorization

1.　Either Party may revoke, suspend, limit, or impose conditions on the operating authorizations or technical permissions of an airline where:

　　　a.　that airline is not an airline of the other Party under Article 1(4);

　　　b.　substantial ownership and effective control of that airline are not vested in the other Party, the other Party's nationals, or both; or

　　　c.　that airline has failed to comply with the laws and regulations referred to in Article 5 (Application of Laws) of this Agreement.

2.　Unless immediate action is essential to prevent further noncompliance with subparagraph 1c of this Article, the rights established by this Article shall be exercised only after consultation with the other Party.

3.　This Article does not limit the rights of either Party to withhold, revoke, suspend, limit, or impose conditions on the operating authorization or technical permission of an airline or airlines of the other Party in accordance with the provisions of Article 6 (Safety) or Article 7 (Aviation Security).

Article 5

Application of Laws

6

1.   The laws and regulations of a Party relating to the admission to or departure from its territory of aircraft engaged in international air navigation, or to the operation and navigation of such aircraft while within its territory, shall be complied with by such aircraft upon entering, when departing from, or while within the territory of the first Party.

2.   While entering, within, or leaving the territory of one Party, its laws and regulations relating to the admission to or departure from its territory of passengers, crew or cargo on aircraft (including regulations relating to entry, clearance, aviation security, immigration, passports, customs and quarantine or, in the case of mail, postal regulations) shall be complied with by, or on behalf of, such passengers, crew or cargo of the other Party's airlines.

Article 6

Safety

1.   Each Party shall recognize as valid, for the purpose of operating the air transportation provided for in this Agreement, certificates of airworthiness, certificates of competency, and licenses issued or validated by the other Party and still in force, provided that the requirements for such certificates or licenses at least equal the minimum standards that may be established pursuant to the Convention. Each Party may, however, refuse to recognize as valid for the purpose of flight above its own territory, certificates of competency and licenses granted to or validated for its own nationals by the other Party.

2.   Either Party may request consultations concerning the safety standards maintained by the other Party relating to aeronautical facilities, aircrews, aircraft, and operation of airlines of that other Party. If, following such consultations, one Party finds that the other Party does not effectively maintain and administer safety standards and requirements in these areas that at least equal the minimum standards that may be established pursuant to the Convention, the other Party shall be notified of such findings and the steps considered necessary to conform with these minimum standards, and the other Party shall take appropriate corrective action. Each Party reserves the right to withhold, revoke, suspend, limit, or impose conditions on the operating authorization or technical permission of an airline or airlines of the other Party in the event the other Party does not take such appropriate corrective action within a reasonable time and to take immediate action, prior to consultations, as to such airline or airlines if the other Party is not maintaining and administering the aforementioned standards and immediate action is essential to prevent further noncompliance.

7

Article 7

Aviation Security

1.   The Parties affirm that their obligation to each other to protect the security of civil aviation against acts of unlawful interference forms an integral part of this Agreement. Without limiting the generality of their rights and obligations under international law, the Parties shall in particular act in conformity with the provisions of the Convention on Offenses and Certain Other Acts Committed on Board Aircraft, done at Tokyo September 14, 1963, the Convention for the Suppression of Unlawful Seizure of Aircraft, done at The Hague December 16, 1970, the Convention for the Suppression of Unlawful Acts against the Safety of Civil Aviation, done at Montreal September 23, 1971, and the Protocol for the Suppression of Unlawful Acts of Violence at Airports Serving International Civil Aviation, Supplementary to the Convention for the Suppression of Unlawful Acts against the Safety of Civil Aviation, done at Montreal February 24, 1988.

2.   The Parties shall provide upon request all necessary assistance to each other to prevent acts of unlawful seizure of civil aircraft and other unlawful acts against the safety of such aircraft, of their passengers and crew, and of airports and air navigation facilities, and to address any other threat to the security of civil air navigation.

3.   The Parties shall, in their mutual relations, act in conformity with the aviation security standards and appropriate recommended practices established by the International Civil Aviation Organization and designated as Annexes to the Convention; they shall require that operators of aircraft of their registry, operators of aircraft that have their principal place of business or permanent residence in their territory, and the operators of airports in their territory act in conformity with such aviation security provisions.

4.   Each Party agrees to observe the security provisions required by the other Party for entry into, for departure from, and while within the territory of that other Party and to take adequate measures to protect aircraft and to inspect passengers, crew, and their baggage and carry-on items, as well as cargo and aircraft stores, prior to and during boarding or loading. Each Party shall also give positive consideration to any request from the other Party for special security measures to meet a particular threat.

5.   When an incident or threat of an incident of unlawful seizure of aircraft or other unlawful acts against the safety of passengers, crew, aircraft, airports or air navigation facilities occurs, the Parties shall assist each other by facilitating communications and other appropriate measures intended to terminate rapidly and safely such incident or threat.

6.   When a Party has reasonable grounds to believe that the other Party has departed from the aviation security provisions of this Article, the aeronautical authorities of that Party may request immediate consultations with the aeronautical authorities of the other Party. Failure to reach a satisfactory agreement within 15 days from the date of such request shall constitute

8

grounds to withhold, revoke, suspend, limit, or impose conditions on the operating authorization and technical permissions of an airline or airlines of that Party. When required by an emergency, a Party may take interim action prior to the expiry of 15 days.

Article 8

Commercial Opportunities

1.   The airlines of each Party shall have the right to establish offices in the territory of the other Party for the promotion and sale of air transportation.

2.   The airlines of each Party shall be entitled, in accordance with the laws and regulations of the other Party relating to entry, residence, and employment, to bring in and maintain in the territory of the other Party managerial, sales, technical, operational, and other specialist staff required for the provision of air transportation.

3.   Each airline shall have the right to perform its own ground-handling in the territory of the other Party ("self-handling") or, at the airline's option, select among competing agents for such services in whole or in part. The rights shall be subject only to physical constraints resulting from considerations of airport safety. Where such considerations preclude self-handling, ground services shall be available on an equal basis to all airlines; charges shall be based on the costs of services provided; and such services shall be comparable to the kind and quality of services as if self-handling were possible.

4.   An airline of a Party may engage in the sale of air transportation in the territory of the other Party directly and, at the airline's discretion, through its agents, except as may be specifically provided by the charter regulations of the country in which the charter originates that relate to the protection of passenger funds, and passenger cancellation and refund rights. Each airline shall have the right to sell such transportation, and any person shall be free to purchase such transportation, in the currency of that territory or in freely convertible currencies.

5.   Each airline shall have the right to convert and remit to its country and, except where inconsistent with generally applicable law or regulation, any other country or countries of its choice, on demand, local revenues in excess of sums locally disbursed. Conversion and remittance shall be permitted promptly without restrictions or taxation in respect thereof at the rate of exchange applicable to current transactions and remittance on the date the carrier makes the initial application for remittance.

6.   The airlines of each Party shall be permitted to pay for local expenses, including purchases of fuel, in the territory of the other Party in local currency. At their discretion, the airlines of each Party may pay for such expenses in the territory of the other Party in freely convertible currencies according to local currency regulation.

9

7.   In operating or holding out the authorized services under this Agreement, any airline of one Party may enter into cooperative marketing arrangements such as blocked-space, code-sharing, or leasing arrangements, with

    a. an airline or airlines of either Party;

    b. an airline or airlines of a third country; [and

    c. a surface transportation provider of any country;]

provided that all participants in such arrangements (i) hold the appropriate authority and (ii) meet the requirements normally applied to such arrangements.

8.   Airlines and indirect providers of cargo transportation of both Parties shall be permitted, without restriction, to employ in connection with international air transportation any surface transportation for cargo to or from any points in the territories of the Parties or in third countries, including to and from all airports with customs facilities and to transport cargo in bond under applicable laws and regulations. Such cargo, whether moving by surface or by air, shall have access to airport customs processing and facilities. Airlines may elect to perform their own surface transportation or to provide it through arrangements with other surface carriers, including surface transportation operated by other airlines and indirect providers of cargo air transportation. Such intermodal cargo services may be offered at a single, through price for the air and surface transportation combined, provided that shippers are not misled as to the facts concerning such transportation.

Article 9

Customs Duties and Charges

1.   On arriving in the territory of one Party, aircraft operated in international air transportation by the airlines of the other Party, their regular equipment, ground equipment, fuel, lubricants, consumable technical supplies, spare parts (including engines), aircraft stores (including but not limited to such items of food, beverages and liquor, tobacco, and other products destined for sale to or use by passengers in limited quantities during flight), and other items intended for or used solely in connection with the operation or servicing of aircraft engaged in international air transportation shall be exempt, on the basis of reciprocity, from all import restrictions, property taxes and capital levies, customs duties, excise taxes, and similar fees and charges that are (a) imposed by the national authorities, and (b) not based on the cost of services provided, provided that such equipment and supplies remain on board the aircraft.

2.   There shall also be exempt, on the basis of reciprocity, from the taxes, levies, duties, fees, and charges referred to in paragraph 1 of this Article, with the exception of charges based on the cost of the service provided:

10

a. aircraft stores introduced into or supplied in the territory of a Party and taken on board, within reasonable limits, for use on outbound aircraft of an airline of the other Party engaged in international air transportation, even when these stores are to be used on a part of the journey performed over the territory of the Party in which they are taken on board;

b. ground equipment and spare parts (including engines) introduced into the territory of a Party for the servicing, maintenance, or repair of aircraft of an airline of the other Party used in international air transportation;

c. fuel, lubricants, and consumable technical supplies introduced into or supplied in the territory of a Party for use in an aircraft of an airline of the other Party engaged in international air transportation, even when these supplies are to be used on a part of the journey performed over the territory of the Party in which they are taken on board; and

d. promotional and advertising materials introduced into or supplied in the territory of one Party and taken on board, within reasonable limits, for use on outbound aircraft of an airline of the other Party engaged in international air transportation, even when these materials are to be used on a part of the journey performed over the territory of the Party in which they are taken on board.

3.   Equipment and supplies referred to in paragraphs 1 and 2 of this Article may be required to be kept under the supervision or control of the appropriate authorities.

4.   The exemptions provided by this Article shall also be available where the airlines of one Party have contracted with another airline, which similarly enjoys such exemptions from the other Party, for the loan or transfer in the territory of the other Party of the items specified in paragraphs 1 and 2 of this Article.

Article 10

User Charges

1.   User charges that may be imposed by the competent charging authorities or bodies of each Party on the airlines of the other Party shall be just, reasonable, not unjustly discriminatory, and equitably apportioned among categories of users. In any event, any such user charges shall be assessed on the airlines of the other Party on terms not less favorable than the most favorable terms available to any other airline at the time the charges are assessed.

2.   User charges imposed on the airlines of the other Party may reflect, but shall not exceed, the full cost to the competent charging authorities or bodies of providing the appropriate airport, airport environmental, air navigation, and aviation security facilities and services at the airport or within the airport system. Such charges may include a reasonable return on assets, after

11

depreciation. Facilities and services for which charges are made shall be provided on an efficient and economic basis.

3.   Each Party shall encourage consultations between the competent charging authorities or bodies in its territory and the airlines using the services and facilities, and shall encourage the competent charging authorities or bodies and the airlines to exchange such information as may be necessary to permit an accurate review of the reasonableness of the charges in accordance with the principles of paragraphs 1 and 2 of this Article. Each Party shall encourage the competent charging authorities to provide users with reasonable notice of any proposal for changes in user charges to enable users to express their views before changes are made.

4.   Neither Party shall be held, in dispute resolution procedures pursuant to Article 14, to be in breach of a provision of this Article, unless (a) it fails to undertake a review of the charge or practice that is the subject of complaint by the other Party within a reasonable amount of time; or (b) following such a review it fails to take all steps within its power to remedy any charge or practice that is inconsistent with this Article.

Article 11

Fair Competition

1.   Each Party shall allow a fair and equal opportunity for the airlines of both Parties to compete in providing the international air transportation governed by this Agreement.

2.   Each Party shall allow each airline to determine the frequency and capacity of the international air transportation it offers based upon commercial considerations in the marketplace. Consistent with this right, neither Party shall unilaterally limit the volume of traffic, frequency, or regularity of service, or the aircraft type or types operated by the airlines of the other Party, except as may be required for customs, technical, operational, or environmental reasons under uniform conditions consistent with Article 15 of the Convention.

3.   Neither Party shall impose on the other Party's airlines a first-refusal requirement, uplift ratio, no-objection fee, or any other requirement with respect to capacity, frequency, or traffic that would be inconsistent with the purposes of this Agreement.

4.   Neither Party shall require the filing of schedules, programs for charter flights, or operational plans by airlines of the other Party for approval, except as may be required on a non-discriminatory basis to enforce the uniform conditions foreseen by paragraph 2 of this Article or as may be specifically authorized in this Agreement. If a Party requires filings for information purposes, it shall minimize the administrative burdens of filing requirements and procedures on air transportation intermediaries and on airlines of the other Party.

12

Article 12

Pricing

1.   Each Party shall allow prices for air transportation to be established by airlines of both Parties based upon commercial considerations in the marketplace.

2.   Prices for international air transportation between the territories of the Parties shall not be required to be filed. Notwithstanding the foregoing, the airlines of the Parties shall provide immediate access, on request, to information on historical, existing, and proposed prices to the aeronautical authorities of the Parties in a manner and format acceptable to those aeronautical authorities.

Article 13

Consultations

Either Party may, at any time, request consultations relating to this Agreement. Such consultations shall begin at the earliest possible date, but not later than 60 days from the date the other Party receives the request unless otherwise agreed.

Article 14

Settlement of Disputes

1.   Any dispute arising under this Agreement, except those that may arise under Article 12 (Pricing), that is not resolved within 30 days of the date established for consultations pursuant to a request for consultations under Article 13 may be referred, by agreement of the Parties, for decision to some person or body. If the Parties do not so agree, either Party may give written notice to the other Party through diplomatic channels that it is requesting that the dispute be submitted to arbitration.

2.   Arbitration shall be by a tribunal of three arbitrators to be constituted as follows:

     a. Within 30 days after the receipt of a request for arbitration, each Party shall name one arbitrator. Within 60 days after these two arbitrators have been named, they shall by agreement appoint a third arbitrator, who shall act as President of the arbitral tribunal;

     b. If either Party fails to name an arbitrator, or if the third arbitrator is not appointed, in accordance with subparagraph a of this paragraph, either Party may request the President of the Council of the International Civil Aviation Organization to appoint the necessary arbitrator or arbitrators within 30 days. If the President of the Council is of the same nationality as one of the

13

Parties, the most senior Vice President who is not disqualified on that ground shall make the appointment.

3.   The arbitral tribunal shall be entitled to decide the extent of its jurisdiction under this Agreement and, except as otherwise agreed, shall establish its own procedural rules. The tribunal, once formed, may at the request of either Party recommend interim relief measures pending its final determination. If either of the Parties requests it or the tribunal deems it appropriate, a conference to determine the precise issues to be arbitrated and the specific procedures to be followed shall be held not later than 15 days after the tribunal is fully constituted.

4.   Except as otherwise agreed or as directed by the tribunal, the statement of claim shall be submitted within 45 days of the time the tribunal is fully constituted, and the statement of defense shall be submitted 60 days thereafter. Any reply by the claimant shall be submitted within 30 days of the submission of the statement of defense. Any reply by the respondent shall be submitted within 30 days thereafter. If either Party requests it or the tribunal deems it appropriate, the tribunal shall hold a hearing within 45 days after the last pleading is due.

5.   The tribunal shall attempt to render a written decision within 30 days after completion of the hearing or, if no hearing is held, after the last pleading is submitted. The decision of the majority of the tribunal shall prevail.

6.   The Parties may submit requests for interpretation of the decision within 15 days after it is rendered and any interpretation given shall be issued within 15 days of such request.

7.   Each Party shall, to the degree consistent with its national law, give full effect to any decision or award of the arbitral tribunal.

8.   The expenses of the arbitral tribunal, including the fees and expenses of the arbitrators, shall be shared equally by the Parties. Any expenses incurred by the President of the Council of the International Civil Aviation Organization in connection with the procedures of paragraph 2b of this Article shall be considered to be part of the expenses of the arbitral tribunal.

Article 15

Termination

Either Party may, at any time, give notice in writing to the other Party of its decision to terminate this Agreement. Such notice shall be sent simultaneously to the International Civil Aviation Organization. This Agreement shall terminate at midnight (at the place of receipt of the notice to the other Party) at the end of the International Air Transport Association (IATA) traffic season in effect one year following the date of written notification of termination, unless the notice is withdrawn by agreement of the Parties before the end of this period.

14

Article 16

Registration with ICAO

This Agreement and all amendments thereto shall be registered with the International Civil Aviation Organization.

Article 17

Entry into Force

This Agreement shall enter into force on the date of signature.

Upon entry into force, this Agreement shall supersede [specify].

IN WITNESS WHEREOF the undersigned, being duly authorized by their respective Governments, have signed this Agreement.

DONE at _____, this _____ day of _____, 20__, in two originals, in the English and _____ languages, both texts being equally authentic.

FOR THE GOVERNMENT OF THE   FOR THE GOVERNMENT OF [country]:
UNITED STATES OF AMERICA:

Regulation (EC) No. 261/2004 of the European Parliament and of the Council Official Journal L 046, 17/02/2004 P. 0001-0008

Official Journal L 046, 17/02/2004 P. 0001–0008

THE EUROPEAN PARLIAMENT AND THE COUNCIL OF THE EUROPEAN UNION, having regard to the Treaty establishing the European Community, and in particular Article 80(2) thereof; having regard to the proposal from the Commission(1); having regard to the opinion of the European Economic and Social Committee(2); after consulting the Committee of the Regions; acting in accordance with the procedure laid down in Article 251 of the Treaty(3), in the light of the joint text approved by the Conciliation Committee on 1 December 2003, Whereas:

(1)   Action by the Community in the field of air transport should aim, among other things, at ensuring a high level of protection for passengers. Moreover, full account should be taken of the requirements of consumer protection in general.

(2)   Denied boarding and cancellation or long delay of flights cause serious trouble and inconvenience to passengers.

(3)   While Council Regulation (EEC) No 295/91 of 4 February 1991 establishing common rules for a denied boarding compensation system in scheduled air transport(4) created basic protection for passengers, the number of passengers denied boarding against their will remains too high, as does that affected by cancellations without prior warning and that affected by long delays.

(4)   The Community should therefore raise the standards of protection set by that Regulation both to strengthen the rights of passengers and to ensure that air carriers operate under harmonised conditions in a liberalised market.

(5) Since the distinction between scheduled and non-scheduled air services is weakening, such protection should apply to passengers not only on scheduled but also on non-scheduled flights, including those forming part of package tours.

(6) The protection accorded to passengers departing from an airport located in a Member State should be extended to those leaving an airport located in a third country for one situated in a Member State, when a Community carrier operates the flight.

(7) In order to ensure the effective application of this Regulation, the obligations that it creates should rest with the operating air carrier who performs or intends to perform a flight, whether with owned aircraft, under dry or wet lease, or on any other basis.

(8) This Regulation should not restrict the rights of the operating air carrier to seek compensation from any person, including third parties, in accordance with the law applicable.

(9) The number of passengers denied boarding against their will should be reduced by requiring air carriers to call for volunteers to surrender their reservations, in exchange for benefits, instead of denying passengers boarding, and by fully compensating those finally denied boarding.

(10) Passengers denied boarding against their will should be able either to cancel their flights, with reimbursement of their tickets, or to continue them under satisfactory conditions, and should be adequately cared for while awaiting a later flight.

(11) Volunteers should also be able to cancel their flights, with reimbursement of their tickets, or continue them under satisfactory conditions, since they face difficulties of travel similar to those experienced by passengers denied boarding against their will.

(12) The trouble and inconvenience to passengers caused by cancellation of flights should also be reduced. This should be achieved by inducing carriers to inform passengers of cancellations before the scheduled time of departure and in addition to offer them reasonable re-routing, so that the passengers can make other arrangements. Air carriers should compensate passengers if they fail to do this, except when the cancellation occurs in extraordinary circumstances which could not have been avoided even if all reasonable measures had been taken.

(13) Passengers whose flights are cancelled should be able either to obtain reimbursement of their tickets or to obtain re-routing under satisfactory conditions, and should be adequately cared for while awaiting a later flight.

(14) As under the Montreal Convention, obligations on operating air carriers should be limited or excluded in cases where an event has been caused by extraordinary circumstances which could not have been avoided even if all reasonable measures had been taken. Such circumstances may, in particular, occur in cases of political instability, meteorological conditions incompatible with the operation of the flight concerned, security risks, unexpected flight safety shortcomings and strikes that affect the operation of an operating air carrier.

(15) Extraordinary circumstances should be deemed to exist where the impact of an air traffic management decision in relation to a particular aircraft on a particular day gives rise to a long delay, an overnight delay, or the cancellation of one or more flights by that aircraft, even though all reasonable measures had been taken by the air carrier concerned to avoid the delays or cancellations.

(16) In cases where a package tour is cancelled for reasons other than the flight being cancelled, this Regulation should not apply.

(17) Passengers whose flights are delayed for a specified time should be adequately cared for and should be able to cancel their flights with reimbursement of their tickets or to continue them under satisfactory conditions.

(18) Care for passengers awaiting an alternative or a delayed flight may be limited or declined if the provision of the care would itself cause further delay.

(19) Operating air carriers should meet the special needs of persons with reduced mobility and any persons accompanying them.

(20) Passengers should be fully informed of their rights in the event of denied boarding and of cancellation or long delay of flights, so that they can effectively exercise their rights.

(21) Member States should lay down rules on sanctions applicable to infringements of the provisions of this Regulation and ensure that these sanctions are applied. The sanctions should be effective, proportionate and dissuasive.

(22) Member States should ensure and supervise general compliance by their air carriers with this Regulation and designate an appropriate body to carry out such enforcement tasks. The supervision should not affect the rights of passengers and air carriers to seek legal redress from courts under procedures of national law.

(23) The Commission should analyse the application of this Regulation and should assess in particular the opportunity of extending its scope to all passengers having a contract with a tour operator or with a Community carrier, when departing from a third country airport to an airport in a Member State.

(24) Arrangements for greater cooperation over the use of Gibraltar airport were agreed in London on 2 December 1987 by the Kingdom of Spain and the United Kingdom in a joint declaration by the Ministers of Foreign Affairs of the two countries. Such arrangements have yet to enter into operation.

(25) Regulation (EEC) No 295/91 should accordingly be repealed,

HAVE ADOPTED THIS REGULATION:

ARTICLE 1: SUBJECT

1.   This Regulation establishes, under the conditions specified herein, minimum rights for passengers when: (a) they are denied boarding against their will; (b) their flight is cancelled; (c) their flight is delayed.

2.   Application of this Regulation to Gibraltar airport is understood to be without prejudice to the respective legal positions of the Kingdom of Spain and the United Kingdom with regard to the dispute over sovereignty over the territory in which the airport is situated.

3.   Application of this Regulation to Gibraltar airport shall be suspended until the arrangements in the Joint Declaration made by the Foreign Ministers of the Kingdom of Spain and the United Kingdom on 2 December 1987 enter into operation. The Governments of Spain and the United Kingdom will inform the Council of such date of entry into operation.

ARTICLE 2: DEFINITIONS

For the purposes of this Regulation:

(a)   "air carrier" means an air transport undertaking with a valid operating licence;

(b)   "operating air carrier" means an air carrier that performs or intends to perform a flight under a contract with a passenger or on behalf of another person, legal or natural, having a contract with that passenger;

(c)   "Community carrier" means an air carrier with a valid operating licence granted by a Member State in accordance with the provisions of Council Regulation (EEC) No 2407/92 of 23 July 1992 on licensing of air carriers;

(d)   "tour operator" means, with the exception of an air carrier, an organiser within the meaning of Article 2, point 2, of Council Directive 90/314/EEC of 13 June 1990 on package travel, package holidays and package tours(6);

(e)   "package" means those services defined in Article 2, point 1, of Directive 90/314/EEC;

(f) "ticket" means a valid document giving entitlement to transport, or something equivalent in paperless form, including electronic form, issued or authorised by the air carrier or its authorised agent;

(g) "reservation" means the fact that the passenger has a ticket, or other proof, which indicates that the reservation has been accepted and registered by the air carrier or tour operator;

(h) "final destination" means the destination on the ticket presented at the check-in counter or, in the case of directly connecting flights, the destination of the last flight; alternative connecting flights available shall not be taken into account if the original planned arrival time is respected;

(i) "person with reduced mobility" means any person whose mobility is reduced when using transport because of any physical disability (sensory or locomotory, permanent or temporary), intellectual impairment, age or any other cause of disability, and whose situation needs special attention and adaptation to the person's needs of the services made available to all passengers;

(j) "denied boarding" means a refusal to carry passengers on a flight, although they have presented themselves for boarding under the conditions laid down in Article 3(2), except where there are reasonable grounds to deny them boarding, such as reasons of health, safety or security, or inadequate travel documentation;

(k) "volunteer" means a person who has presented himself for boarding under the conditions laid down in Article 3(2) and responds positively to the air carrier's call for passengers prepared to surrender their reservation in exchange for benefits.

(l) "cancellation" means the non-operation of a flight which was previously planned and on which at least one place was reserved.

ARTICLE 3: SCOPE

1. This Regulation shall apply: (a) to passengers departing from an airport located in the territory of a Member State to which the Treaty applies; (b) to passengers departing from an airport located in a third country to an airport situated in the territory of a Member State to which the Treaty applies, unless they received benefits or compensation and were given assistance in that third country, if the operating air carrier of the flight concerned is a Community carrier.

2. Paragraph 1 shall apply on the condition that passengers: (a) have a confirmed reservation on the flight concerned and, except in the case of cancellation referred to in Article 5, present themselves for check-in: (i) as

stipulated and at the time indicated in advance and in writing (including by electronic means) by the air carrier, the tour operator or an authorised travel agent, (ii) or, if no time is indicated,—not later than 45 minutes before the published departure time; or (b) have been transferred by an air carrier or tour operator from the flight for which they held a reservation to another flight, irrespective of the reason.

3.   This Regulation shall not apply to passengers travelling free of charge or at a reduced fare not available directly or indirectly to the public. However, it shall apply to passengers having tickets issued under a frequent flyer programme or other commercial programme by an air carrier or tour operator.

4.   This Regulation shall only apply to passengers transported by motorised fixed wing aircraft.

5.   This Regulation shall apply to any operating air carrier providing transport to passengers covered by paragraphs 1 and 2. Where an operating air carrier which has no contract with the passenger performs obligations under this Regulation, it shall be regarded as doing so on behalf of the person having a contract with that passenger.

6.   This Regulation shall not affect the rights of passengers under Directive 90/314/EEC. This Regulation shall not apply in cases where a package tour is cancelled for reasons other than cancellation of the flight.

ARTICLE 4: DENIED BOARDING

1.   When an operating air carrier reasonably expects to deny boarding on a flight, it shall first call for volunteers to surrender their reservations in exchange for benefits under conditions to be agreed between the passenger concerned and the operating air carrier. Volunteers shall be assisted in accordance with Article 8, such assistance being additional to the benefits mentioned in this paragraph.

2.   If an insufficient number of volunteers comes forward to allow the remaining passengers with reservations to board the flight, the operating air carrier may then deny boarding to passengers against their will.

3.   If boarding is denied to passengers against their will, the operating air carrier shall immediately compensate them in accordance with Article 7 and assist them in accordance with Articles 8 and 9.

ARTICLE 5: CANCELLATION

1.   In case of cancellation of a flight, the passengers concerned shall: (a) be offered assistance by the operating air carrier in accordance with Article 8; and (b)

be offered assistance by the operating air carrier in accordance with Article 9(1)(a) and 9(2), as well as, in event of re-routing when the reasonably expected time of departure of the new flight is at least the day after the departure as it was planned for the cancelled flight, the assistance specified in Article 9(1)(b) and 9(1)(c); and (c) have the right to compensation by the operating air carrier in accordance with Article 7, unless:

(i)   they are informed of the cancellation at least two weeks before the scheduled time of departure; or

(ii)   they are informed of the cancellation between two weeks and seven days before the scheduled time of departure and are offered re-routing, allowing them to depart no more than two hours before the scheduled time of departure and to reach their final destination less than four hours after the scheduled time of arrival; or

(iii)   they are informed of the cancellation less than seven days before the scheduled time of departure and are offered re-routing, allowing them to depart no more than one hour before the scheduled time of departure and to reach their final destination less than two hours after the scheduled time of arrival.

2.   When passengers are informed of the cancellation, an explanation shall be given concerning possible alternative transport.

3.   An operating air carrier shall not be obliged to pay compensation in accordance with Article 7, if it can prove that the cancellation is caused by extraordinary circumstances which could not have been avoided even if all reasonable measures had been taken.

4.   The burden of proof concerning the questions as to whether and when the passenger has been informed of the cancellation of the flight shall rest with the operating air carrier.

ARTICLE 6: DELAY

1.   When an operating air carrier reasonably expects a flight to be delayed beyond its scheduled time of departure: (a) for two hours or more in the case of flights of 1500 kilometres or less; or (b) for three hours or more in the case of all intra-Community flights of more than 1500 kilometres and of all other flights between 1500 and 3500 kilometres; or (c) for four hours or more in the case of all flights not falling under (a) or (b), passengers shall be offered by the operating air carrier: (i) the assistance specified in Article 9(1)(a) and 9(2); and (ii) when the reasonably expected time of departure is at least the day after the time of departure

previously announced, the assistance specified in Article 9(1)(b) and 9(1)(c); and (iii) when the delay is at least five hours, the assistance specified in Article 8(1)(a).

2.   In any event, the assistance shall be offered within the time limits set out above with respect to each distance bracket.

ARTICLE 7: RIGHT TO COMPENSATION

1.   Where reference is made to this Article, passengers shall receive compensation amounting to: (a) EUR 250 for all flights of 1500 kilometres or less; (b) EUR 400 for all intra-Community flights of more than 1500 kilometres, and for all other flights between 1500 and 3500 kilometres; (c) EUR 600 for all flights not falling under (a) or (b).

In determining the distance, the basis shall be the last destination at which the denial of boarding or cancellation will delay the passenger's arrival after the scheduled time.

2.   When passengers are offered re-routing to their final destination on an alternative flight pursuant to Article 8, the arrival time of which does not exceed the scheduled arrival time of the flight originally booked (a) by two hours, in respect of all flights of 1500 kilometres or less; or (b) by three hours, in respect of all intra-Community flights of more than 1500 kilometres and for all other flights between 1500 and 3500 kilometres; or (c) by four hours, in respect of all flights not falling under (a) or (b), the operating air carrier may reduce the compensation provided for in paragraph 1 by 50%.

3.   The compensation referred to in paragraph 1 shall be paid in cash, by electronic bank transfer, bank orders or bank cheques or, with the signed agreement of the passenger, in travel vouchers and/or other services.

4.   The distances given in paragraphs 1 and 2 shall be measured by the great circle route method.

ARTICLE 8: RIGHT TO REIMBURSEMENT OR RE-ROUTING

1.   Where reference is made to this Article, passengers shall be offered the choice between: (a) reimbursement within seven days, by the means provided for in Article 7(3), of the full cost of the ticket at the price at which it was bought, for the part or parts of the journey not made, and for the part or parts already made if the flight is no longer serving any purpose in relation to the passenger's original travel plan, together with, when relevant, a return flight to the first point of departure, at the earliest opportunity; (b) re-routing, under comparable transport conditions, to their final destination at the earliest opportunity; or (c) re-routing,

under comparable transport conditions, to their final destination at a later date at the passenger's convenience, subject to availability of seats.

2.   Paragraph 1(a) shall also apply to passengers whose flights form part of a package, except for the right to reimbursement where such right arises under Directive 90/314/EEC.

3.   When, in the case where a town, city or region is served by several airports, an operating air carrier offers a passenger a flight to an airport alternative to that for which the booking was made, the operating air carrier shall bear the cost of transferring the passenger from that alternative airport either to that for which the booking was made, or to another close-by destination agreed with the passenger.

ARTICLE 9: RIGHT TO CARE

1.   Where reference is made to this Article, passengers shall be offered free of charge: (a) meals and refreshments in a reasonable relation to the waiting time; (b) hotel accommodation in cases where a stay of one or more nights becomes necessary, or where a stay additional to that intended by the passenger becomes necessary; (c) transport between the airport and place of accommodation (hotel or other).

2.   In addition, passengers shall be offered free of charge two telephone calls, telex or fax messages, or e-mails.

3.   In applying this Article, the operating air carrier shall pay particular attention to the needs of persons with reduced mobility and any persons accompanying them, as well as to the needs of unaccompanied children.

ARTICLE 10: UPGRADING AND DOWNGRADING

1.   If an operating air carrier places a passenger in a class higher than that for which the ticket was purchased, it may not request any supplementary payment.

2.   If an operating air carrier places a passenger in a class lower than that for which the ticket was purchased, it shall within seven days, by the means provided for in Article 7(3), reimburse (a) 30 % of the price of the ticket for all flights of 1500 kilometres or less, or (b) 50 % of the price of the ticket for all intra-Community flights of more than 1500 kilometres, except flights between the European territory of the Member States and the French overseas departments, and for all other flights between 1500 and 3500 kilometres, or (c) 75 % of the price of the ticket for all flights not falling under (a) or (b), including flights

between the European territory of the Member States and the French overseas departments.

ARTICLE 11: PERSONS WITH REDUCED MOBILITY OR SPECIAL NEEDS

1.   Operating air carriers shall give priority to carrying persons with reduced mobility and any persons or certified service dogs accompanying them, as well as unaccompanied children.

2.   In cases of denied boarding, cancellation and delays of any length, persons with reduced mobility and any persons accompanying them, as well as unaccompanied children, shall have the right to care in accordance with Article 9 as soon as possible.

ARTICLE 12: FURTHER COMPENSATION

1.   This Regulation shall apply without prejudice to a passenger's rights to further compensation. The compensation granted under this Regulation may be deducted from such compensation.

2.   Without prejudice to relevant principles and rules of national law, including case-law, paragraph 1 shall not apply to passengers who have voluntarily surrendered a reservation under Article 4(1).

ARTICLE 13: RIGHT OF REDRESS

In cases where an operating air carrier pays compensation or meets the other obligations incumbent on it under this Regulation, no provision of this Regulation may be interpreted as restricting its right to seek compensation from any person, including third parties, in accordance with the law applicable. In particular, this Regulation shall in no way restrict the operating air carrier's right to seek reimbursement from a tour operator or another person with whom the operating air carrier has a contract. Similarly, no provision of this Regulation may be interpreted as restricting the right of a tour operator or a third party, other than a passenger, with whom an operating air carrier has a contract, to seek reimbursement or compensation from the operating air carrier in accordance with applicable relevant laws.

ARTICLE 14: OBLIGATION TO INFORM PASSENGERS OF THEIR RIGHTS

1.   The operating air carrier shall ensure that at check-in a clearly legible notice containing the following text is displayed in a manner clearly visible to passengers: "If you are denied boarding or if your flight is cancelled or delayed for at least two hours, ask at the check-in counter or boarding gate for the text stating your rights, particularly with regard to compensation and assistance".

2.   An operating air carrier denying boarding or cancelling a flight shall provide each passenger affected with a written notice setting out the rules for compensation and assistance in line with this Regulation. It shall also provide each passenger affected by a delay of at least two hours with an equivalent notice. The contact details of the national designated body referred to in Article 16 shall also be given to the passenger in written form.

3.   In respect of blind and visually impaired persons, the provisions of this Article shall be applied using appropriate alternative means.

ARTICLE 15: EXCLUSION OF WAIVER

1.   Obligations vis-à-vis passengers pursuant to this Regulation may not be limited or waived, notably by a derogation or restrictive clause in the contract of carriage.

2.   If, nevertheless, such a derogation or restrictive clause is applied in respect of a passenger, or if the passenger is not correctly informed of his rights and for that reason has accepted compensation which is inferior to that provided for in this Regulation, the passenger shall still be entitled to take the necessary proceedings before the competent courts or bodies in order to obtain additional compensation.

ARTICLE 16: INFRINGEMENTS

1.   Each Member State shall designate a body responsible for the enforcement of this Regulation as regards flights from airports situated on its territory and flights from a third country to such airports. Where appropriate, this body shall take the measures necessary to ensure that the rights of passengers are respected. The Member States shall inform the Commission of the body that has been designated in accordance with this paragraph.

2.   Without prejudice to Article 12, each passenger may complain to any body designated under paragraph 1, or to any other competent body designated by a Member State, about an alleged infringement of this Regulation at any airport situated on the territory of a Member State or concerning any flight from a third country to an airport situated on that territory.

3.   The sanctions laid down by Member States for infringements of this Regulation shall be effective, proportionate and dissuasive.

ARTICLE 17: REPORT

The Commission shall report to the European Parliament and the Council by 1 January 2007 on the operation and the results of this Regulation, in particular regarding: the incidence of denied boarding and of cancellation of flights; the possible extension of the scope of this Regulation to passengers having a contract with a Community carrier or holding a flight reservation which forms part of a "package tour" to which Directive 90/314/EEC applies and who depart from a third-country airport to an airport in a Member State, on flights not operated by Community air carriers; the possible revision of the amounts of compensation referred to in Article 7(1). The report shall be accompanied where necessary by legislative proposals.

This Regulation shall enter into force on 17 February 2005. This Regulation shall be binding in its entirety and directly applicable in all Member States. Done at Strasbourg, 11 February 2004.

Index